Criminal Procedure

FOURTH EDITION

Joel Samaha

University of Minnesota

West/Wadsworth

I(T)P® An International Thomson Publishing Company

Belmont, CA • Albany, NY • Boston • Cincinnati • Johannesburg • London
Madrid • Melbourne • Mexico City • New York • Pacific Grove, CA • Scottsdale, AZ
Singapore • Tokyo • Toronto

Criminal Justice Editor: Sabra Horne
Development Editor: Dan Alpert
Project Development Editor: Claire Masson
Editorial Assistant: Cherie Hackelberg
Marketing Manager: Mike Dew
Production Services Manager: Debby Kramer
Print Buyer: Karen Hunt
Permissions Editor: Susan Walters

Production: Ruth Cottrell Books
Designer: Andrew Ogus
Copy Editor: Donald Pharr
Illustrator: Rogondino Associates
Cover Design: Joan Greenfield
Compositor: R&S Book Composition
Printer: R.R. Donnelley/Crawfordsville
Cover Printer: Phoenix Color Corp.

Printed in the United States of America
1 2 3 4 5 6 7 8 9 10

For more information, contact Wadsworth Publishing Company, 10 Davis Drive, Belmont, CA 94002, or
electronically at http://www.wadsworth.com

International Thomson Publishing Europe
Berkshire House
168-173 High Holborn
London, WC1V 7AA, United Kingdom

International Thomson Editores
Seneca, 53
Colonia Polanco
11560 México D.F. México

Nelson ITP, Australia
102 Dodds Street
South Melbourne
Victoria 3205 Australia

International Thomson Publishing Asia
60 Albert Street
#15-01 Albert Complex
Singapore 189969

Nelson Canada
1120 Birchmount Road
Scarborough, Ontario
Canada M1K 5G4

International Thomson Publishing Japan
Hirakawa-cho Kyowa Building, 3F
2-2-1 Hirakawa-cho, Chiyoda-ku
Tokyo 102 Japan

International Thomson Publishing Southern Africa
Building 18, Constantia Square
138 Sixteenth Road, P.O. Box 2459
Halfway House, 1685 South Africa

Library of Congress Cataloging-in-Publication Data
Samaha, Joel.
    Criminal procedure/Joel Samaha.—4th ed.
    p.   cm.
    Includes index.
    ISBN 0-534-54711-7
    1. Criminal procedure—United States—Cases. I. Title.
KF9619.S26   1998
345.73'05—dc21   98-11856

 This book is printed on acid-free recycled paper.

About the Author

Professor Joel Samaha teaches Criminal Law, Criminal Procedure, Introduction to Criminal Justice, and the History of Criminal Justice at the University of Minnesota. He is both a lawyer and a historian whose primary research interest is the history of criminal justice. He received his B.A., J.D., and Ph.D. from Northwestern University. Professor Samaha also studied at Cambridge University, England, while doing research for his first book, *Law and Order in Historical Perspective*, a quantitative and qualitative analysis of law enforcement in pre-industrial society.

Professor Samaha was admitted to the Illinois Bar. He taught at UCLA before coming to the University of Minnesota. At the University of Minnesota, he served as Chairman of the Department of Criminal Justice Studies from 1974 to 1978. Since then he has returned to teaching, research, and writing full-time. He has taught both television and radio courses in criminal justice, and has co-taught a National Endowment for the Humanities seminar in legal and constitutional history. He was named Distinguished Teacher at the University of Minnesota in 1974, a coveted award.

Professor Samaha is an active scholar. In addition to his monograph on pre-industrial law enforcement and a transcription with scholarly introduction of English criminal justice records during the reign of Elizabeth I, he has written numerous articles on the history of criminal justice, published in such scholarly journals as *Historical Journal, American Journal of Legal History, Minnesota Law Review, William Mitchell Law Review,* and *Journal of Social History*. In addition to his best-seller, *Criminal Law*, he has written two other successful textbooks, *Criminal Procedure*, now in its fourth edition, and *Criminal Justice*, now being revised for its fifth edition.

For Doug and my students

Contents

Table of Cases

Note: Principle cases are in italic type. Non-principal cases are in roman type.

Preface

Balancing the power of government to enforce the criminal law against the rights of individuals to life, liberty, privacy, and property is the central problem in the law of criminal procedure and in *Criminal Procedure*. It is a problem that fascinates my students, stimulates them to think, and provokes them to discuss it not only in class but also with their friends and family outside class. I am not surprised at my students' interest in criminal procedure. It has fascinated me for more than forty years, beginning in 1958 when I was fortunate enough to study criminal procedure at Northwestern University Law School under two distinguished professors, Claude R. Sowle and Fred E. Inbau. Professor Sowle, a brilliant advocate and a distinguished teacher, emphasized the philosophical underpinnings of the law of criminal procedure. Professor Inbau, a famous interrogator and highly respected student of the law of interrogation, spoke (and still speaks) with the authority of one who has actually applied abstract principles to everyday police practices. In 1968, I began work on what would eventually become my *Law and Order in Historical Perspective*, a reconstruction of the criminal process in sixteenth-century England. In 1971, I taught criminal procedure for the first time. I have done so ever since—during the regular terms, during the summers, and in the evenings. My students have included undergraduates, graduate students, and law students. That many of these students are now police officers, corrections officers, prison wardens, criminal defense attorneys, prosecutors, and judges testifies to their enduring interest in the law of criminal procedure and to their commitment to the application of formal law to informal real-life decision making.

Criminal Procedure, Fourth Edition, like its predecessors, reflects my conviction that the best way to learn the law of criminal procedure is to understand general principles and *critically* examine the application of these principles to real problems. By critically I don't mean *negatively*. *Criminal Procedure* does not aim at "bashing the system." Rather, it examines and weighs the principles that govern the balance between government power and individual life, liberty, privacy, and property. It tests the strong, honest, heartfelt feelings, wishes, and beliefs held about this balance in the light of reason, logic, and facts. *Criminal Procedure* proceeds on the assumptions that the general principles governing the balance between government and individuals have real meaning only in the context of a specific reality, and that reality makes sense only when seen in the light of general principles applied to facts.

Balancing Conflicting Interests

Criminal Procedure is organized according to the central theme of balancing conflicting interests. First, the law of criminal procedure balances the interest in obtaining the correct result in particular cases against the interest in fair process in all cases. This balancing of result and process is an example of the timeless puzzle of the ends justifying the means. In criminal procedure, the end is the correct result in the case at hand; the means is the process by which the result is obtained. The law of criminal procedure recognizes the importance of obtaining the correct result—that is, the ends both of freeing the innocent and convicting the guilty. But the law of criminal procedure also promotes the value of enforcing the law according to fair procedures. In other words, in the law of criminal procedure the end does not always justify the means. In fact, when forced to choose, our constitutional system requires that the means of fair procedures must trump the end of correct results. Or, to put it another way, fair proceedings for *all* people is more important than convicting even *one* guilty person by unfair means.

Facts Not Hunches

Hunches or whims are not enough to back up government invasions of liberty, privacy, and property. The U.S. Constitution and the constitutions of the states demand that the government back up all invasions of liberty, privacy, and property with facts. No police officer can justify detaining a person by claiming that she had a "hunch" that something was wrong. The greater the invasion, the more facts that government officers must produce to back up their invasions. Hence, to detain a person briefly on the street, police officers need only a few facts that arouse a "reasonable suspicion" that crime *may* be afoot. On the other hand, in order to convict defendants and send them to prison, the government has to prove that defendants are guilty "beyond a reasonable doubt." This reliance on facts to back up government action lies at the heart of our constitutional democracy.

Hearing before Condemnation

"A law that hears before it condemns" is the foundation of our constitutional system, said the great nineteenth-century lawyer Daniel Webster. A law that "hears before it condemns" is a law that deprives persons of life, liberty, privacy, and property only according to fair procedures. In the case of invasions prior to conviction, courts review street stops and frisks, arrest, searches, interrogation, and the conduct of identification procedures. In the case of conviction, courts are required to "hear" cases, either by trials or by approving guilty pleas, *before* defendants are "condemned" by conviction. This review by courts, known as judicial review, is an essential element of our legal system.

Organization of the Text and Cases

Criminal Procedure is a text-casebook. It contains text that explains, analyzes, and critically assesses the general principles, constitutional provisions, and court rules that govern the law of criminal procedure. Figures and tables depict graphically the main concepts and themes in the book. *Criminal Procedure* also relies heavily on cases carefully selected and edited for nonspecialists—those that apply these principles, provisions, and rules to actual events. The combination of text and cases presents a balanced but critical discussion of constitutional provisions as law enforcement officers, prosecutors, defense attorneys, judges, and juries actually apply them in three real-life settings—on the street, at the police station, and in court.

Overview of Chapters

Chapters 1 and 2 give an overview of the structure, process, and the constitutional provisions governing both the law and practice of criminal procedure. The book is based on the assumption that thinking critically about criminal procedure requires an understanding of our constitutional system. Therefore, Chapter 1 describes the steps in the formal criminal process from its inception on the street to final appeals in the courts. It also invites students to think critically about the role of discretion in decision making throughout the criminal process. Chapter 2 describes the major components of the constitutional framework of federalism, the separation of powers, and checks and balances. Then the chapter examines and critically analyzes the underpinnings of due process of law.

Chapters 3 through 9 arrange the constitutional provisions of criminal procedure chronologically as they occur in real life. Chapters 3 through 7 describe and critically examine searches and seizures. Five chapters on the subject of searches and seizures may seem heavy. However, government searches and seizures affect far more people than any other criminal procedure. Probably as a result of both this disproportionate effect and the complicated business of applying it in real life, there are more search and seizure cases than any other subject in the law of criminal procedure.

Chapter 3 describes and analyzes the search and seizure clause of the Fourth Amendment. It requires students not only to understand but also to think critically about the answer to two questions: When is a government action a search? When is a government action a seizure?

Chapter 4 describes and critically examines the myriad of brief encounters between police and individuals that take place on the street. It requires students to think critically about when brief detentions and patdowns on the street are "reasonable searches and seizures."

Chapter 5 describes and critically examines arrest, the Fourth Amendment seizure that means taking suspects into custody, usually by taking them to the police station. It requires students to think critically about three questions: When is a detention an arrest? What amounts to probable cause? What is the proper manner of arrest?

Chapter 6 describes and critically examines searches for evidence. It examines both searches with and without warrants. It requires students to think critically about when warrants are required, the exceptions to the warrant requirement, and the manner in which searches are conducted.

Chapter 7 describes and critically examines searches whose purpose is not obtaining evidence. These are searches that go beyond ordinary law enforcement inventory searches that take place after arrest but are not specifically for the purpose of gathering evidence. Chapter 7 also examines school searches, employee drug testing, and searches of prison visitors. It requires students think critically about the application of the Fourth Amendment to subjects not directly related to criminal law enforcement.

Chapters 8 and 9 describe and critically examine two highly publicized and widely known procedures—(1) police interrogation and confessions; and (2) police identification procedures, including lineups, "mug shots," and DNA testing. These chapters require students to think critically about the right to remain silent and the use of physical evidence to convict criminal defendants. The chapters also require students to think critically about the need for, the fairness of, and the reliability of interrogation and identifications procedures in obtaining the truth.

Chapter 10 describes and critically examines the remedies that suspects have when the government violates the constitutional rights discussed in Chapters 3 through 9. The chapter concentrates on a description and critical evaluation of the exclusionary rule and private lawsuits against the government under the

Civil Rights Act. But it also evaluates the defense of entrapment, reversible error, and expungement of criminal records. The chapter requires students to think critically about the nature, value, and purposes of the various remedies against mistakes and misconduct by government officials in the enforcement, prosecution, and disposition of criminal laws.

Chapter 11 critically examines judicial proceedings before trial; Chapter 12 describes and assesses the determination of guilt, both by formal trial and by guilty pleas. Chapter 13 describes and evaluates proceedings following conviction. The major proceedings include sentencing, appeal, and *habeas corpus*. Chapter 12 requires students to think critically about sentencing guidelines and mandatory minimum sentencing; about judicial review after conviction, mainly by means of appeals and review by means of *habeas corpus*.

Flexibility of Criminal Procedure

Some criminal procedure courses and many criminal procedure texts—particularly those designed for undergraduates—cover only the law of arrest, search, and seizure, interrogation, and identification procedures. In other words, these courses and texts focus on police practices—the contacts between individuals and the police on the street and at the police station. They usually cover the constitutional framework of criminal procedure, and they sometimes include discussions of the exclusionary rule. *Criminal Procedure* lends itself to this type of course because instructors can use either Chapters 3 through 9, which can stand alone, without covering either Chapters 1 and 2 on the general principles and constitutional provisions or Chapter 10 on remedies for illegal official conduct. Instructors who wish to teach the exclusionary rule and the constitutional provisions can add Chapter 2 and the first section of Chapter 10, which covers the exclusionary rule. The section on the exclusionary rule stands enough apart from the remainder of the chapter that students need not read the whole chapter to understand the material on the exclusionary rule.

Criminal Procedure is also suitable for courses that cover the entire criminal process, from the early encounters between individuals and the police on the street to procedures following conviction. And, for students in courses covering only police practices, Chapters 1, 2, and 10 through 13 should fill the gap should they wish to read about the subjects not covered in courses limited to police practices in the law of criminal procedure.

Text and Cases

The text and the edited cases complement each other. The text enriches the understanding of the cases, while the cases enhance the understanding of the text. The cases are not merely examples, illustrations, or attention grabbers, although surely they are all of these. The cases explain, clarify, elaborate upon, and most of all, apply the general principles, constitutional provisions, and rules to real-life situations. Moreover, the cases are excellent tools for introducing and developing the critical thinking skills of students of all levels.

The cases and the text are independent enough of each other that they can stand alone. They are set off clearly from each other in design—the text appears in a one-column format, while edited cases appear in two columns. The separation of text from cases allows instructors who favor the case analysis approach to emphasize cases over text, leaving the text for students to read if they need to do so in order to understand the cases. Instructors who favor the text approach can focus on the text, allowing the students to read the cases as enrichment or as examples of the principles, constitutional provisions, and rules discussed in the text.

The edited cases—edited carefully for non lawyers—present students with

- A full statement of the facts of the case.
- The application of the law to the facts of the case.
- Key portions of the reasoning of the court.

- The decision of the court.
- Key portions of the dissenting opinions, and when appropriate, parts of the concurring opinions.

Case questions at the beginning of the case focus on the main point in the edited cases. The **case background** gives a brief procedural history of the case. And the **Case Discussion** at the end of the case excerpts test whether students know the facts of the case, whether they understand the law of the case, and whether they comprehend the application of the law to the facts of the case. The Case Discussion also provides the basis for developing critical thinking skills, not to mention provoking exciting class discussions on the legal, ethical, and policy issues raised by the edited case.

Other Pedagogical Aids

However organized and presented, the law of criminal procedure is a complicated subject that embraces a host of technical concepts. I have tried to help students work through these complexities, primarily by writing clear, direct prose. In addition, each chapter contains a **Chapter Outline** and a list of the **Chapter Main Points.** I have also bold faced key terms in the text, which appear in a list of **Key Terms** at the end of each chapter. The key terms also appear in the Glossary at the end of the book. **Review Questions** at the end of each chapter provide a good test of whether students have identified and understood the main points in the chapter. Students frequently comment that the combination of the Chapter Outline and Chapter Main Points at the beginning of the chapter tell them what they should look for as they read and that the Key Terms and Review Questions at the end of each chapter tell them whether they have found and understood what they looked for. **Decision Points,** consisting of brief excerpts of both actual cases and hypothetical cases, focus on the practical application of principles discussed in the text and in the full excerpts. The Decision Points not only reinforce students' understanding of the law but provide them with the opportunity to think critically about a variety of problems in the practical applications of the law to real life.

Acknowledgments

Writing a book always accumulates many debts. Acknowledging these debts hardly repays them, but the past (and hopefully the future) success of *Criminal Procedure* requires that I acknowledge the people to whom I am indebted even if I can't repay them.

The thousands of University of Minnesota students—including police officers, corrections officers, probation and parole officers, prison wardens, prosecutors, defense attorneys, and judges who have taken my courses in the last twenty-six years—contributed more than they can ever know or than I can ever put into words. They asked stimulating questions, participated in lively discussions, and told me bluntly—sometimes even irreverently—what they *really* thought about *Criminal Procedure*. The book is much better because of their candor. I am also grateful for the guidance of the following pre-revision reviewers, whose excellent suggestions are reflected in this edition of *Criminal Procedure:* Frances Coles, California State University—San Bernadino; Janet Foster Goodwin, Yakima Valley Community College; Gregory Petrakis, University of Missouri—Kansas City; and Gene Straughan, Lewis and Clark State College.

Past teachers, without even knowing it, have also influenced *Criminal Procedure.* Professors Claude Sowle and Fred Inbau who taught me the law of criminal procedure at Northwestern University Law School sparked an interest that became a lifelong fascination with the subject. Sir Geoffrey Elton, Clare College, Cambridge, guided and stimulated my curiosity about the history of criminal procedure and taught me how to conduct disciplined research in the primary sources of sixteenth-century criminal justice administration. Finally, Professor Lacey Baldwin Smith, Northwestern University, the best teacher I ever had (and I've had many!), provided me with an outstanding example of how to transfer my own excitement about a subject I love to my students. He also taught me how to transform my convoluted English into readable prose.

Ruth Cottrell, probably the smoothest production editor in the history of the world, made the production of the book seem easy when I know better. The application of Donald Pharr's deft, painstaking editing skills saved the book from many errors and improved its clarity. Two people at Wadsworth deserve special mention. Dan Alpert seems to know how to both organize and synthesize complicated subjects. These enviably rare and invaluable skills applied to this edition will definitely make it easier for students to understand both *Criminal Procedure* and "criminal procedure." Sabra Horne gave me unqualified encouragement throughout the revision of *Criminal Procedure*, Fourth Edition. She has no idea how much her warmth, encouragement, and support have meant to me. Thanks for far more than I deserve to my loyal friend Sally. She continues to praise me and to put up with me even though I don't deserve either that much praise or support. Without Doug, my personal assistant, I acknowledge a simple, indisputable fact: I couldn't physically do my work. But there is more. Without his sharp critical skills, I couldn't have written the book I did. (As one who should know said, "I think you've met your match in Doug's critical thinking.") Without his companionship to fill the void created when my sons grew up, my inspiration would surely have flagged. I happily credit my students, my teachers, my editors, and Sally and Doug with making this a better book. For the book's shortcomings, I accept all the responsibility.

Joel Samaha
Professor and Attorney-at-Law
Minneapolis, Minnesota
May 2, 1998

Criminal Procedure

C H A P T E R   O N E

Overview of Criminal Procedure: A Question of Balance

C H A P T E R   O U T L I N E

CHAPTER MAIN POINTS

1. The fundamental feature of the law of criminal procedure in a constitutional democracy is balancing conflicting interests.

2. The major balances include society and individual; ends and means; law and discretion; federal, state, and local government; and executive, legislative, and judicial branches.

3. The law of criminal procedure balances the interest in obtaining the correct result in individual cases and the interest in ensuring fairness by means of procedural regularity in all cases.

4. The law of criminal procedure recognizes the central place of the individual and individual dignity in society.

5. All government invasions of liberty, privacy, and property require an objective basis.

6. The law of criminal procedure is organized such that the greater the invasions against private individuals, the greater the objective basis that is required to authorize the invasions.

7. The history of the law of criminal procedure in English and American law is largely the history of a pendulum swing between an emphasis on process and an emphasis on result.

8. In addition to the formal legal interest of balancing process and result, a number of informal organizational, ideological, and democratic interests also influence the law of criminal procedure.

9. The structure of criminal procedure exists within the broader structure of our federal, state, and local governments and within the constitutional system of checks and balances and the separation of powers.

10. The criminal process consists of a series of steps from the lesser invasions associated with investigation on the street to the greatest invasions that follow conviction.

11. Decisions in the criminal process result not only from legal rules but also from individual discretion.

Did the Ends Justify the Means?

After receiving permission to search Anthony Tognaci's person, Officer Cutcliffe noticed a bulge "a little bit higher than where his male organs would be, normally." She touched the bulge, and her partner removed the object from Tognaci's pants, which turned out to be a package containing narcotics taped between Tognaci's belt and the top of his zipper.

BALANCE—THE ESSENCE OF CRIMINAL PROCEDURE

If men were angels, no government would be necessary. If angels were to govern men, neither external nor internal controuls on government would be necessary. In framing a government which is to be administered by men over men, the great difficulty lies in this: You must first enable the government to controul the governed; and in the next place, oblige it to control itself.[1]

In this famous passage from *The Federalist*, the principal drafter of the Bill of Rights and future president, James Madison, clearly identifies the fundamental feature of the law of criminal procedure in a constitutional democracy—balance. Madison refers to the balance between government power and individual privacy, liberty, and property. But the law of criminal procedure consists of maintaining all of the following balances:

- Society and individual
- Ends and means
- Law, society, and ideology
- Federal, state, and local governments
- Executive, legislative, and judicial branches of government
- Formal rules and informal discretion

Maintaining these balances is difficult. According to United States Supreme Court Chief Justice William Rehnquist,

> Throughout the long history of political theory and the development of constitutional law in our country, the most difficult cases to decide have those in which two competing values, each able to marshall respectable claims on its behalf, meet in a contest in which one must prevail over the other.[2]

All the balances in the preceding list include competing values "able to marshall respectable claims" on their behalf.

SOCIETY AND INDIVIDUAL

Maintaining the balance between society and the individual or, to use Madison's terms, the balance between controlling the governed and controlling the government requires that government officials have enough power to discover, apprehend, prosecute, convict, and punish criminals on one side of the balance. On the other side, a constitutional democracy limits official power in order to provide the maximum amount of individual liberty, privacy, and property. James Madison, good eighteenth-century person that he was, accepted human nature for what it is. He knew that people are not angels. Left to do as they please, private persons will misbehave, and government officials will abuse power. In short, Madison expected excesses from both ordinary people and government officials who live in a real world inhabited by imperfect people.

ENDS AND MEANS

Crime control in a constitutional democracy depends on a second balance — the balance between ends and means. In criminal procedure, the "ends" side of the balance consists of the search for the truth in order to obtain the correct result. The correct result means *both* convicting the guilty *and* freeing the innocent. More than half a century ago, the widely respected professor of criminal law Jerome Hall summarized this side of the balance:

> [C]riminal procedure is a method of discovery, not one of demonstration of accepted truths. To comprehend the rational function of procedure it is essential to keep in mind that we start not with answers but with questions, that the entire apparatus is defensible and intelligible only on the premise that we seek answers which we initially do not possess, and that we seek the best answers possible.[3]

The commitment to use only fair means in order to convict the guilty and free the innocent lies at the means end of the ends/means balance. In a constitutional democracy, we do not believe in finding the truth at any price; we insist on procedural regularity as a means of finding and using the truth. The Bill of Rights to the U.S. Constitution and parallel provisions in every state constitution spell out a list of rules that public officials must follow in their search for — and their use of — the truth. The requirement of following the rules is familiar to anyone who participates in, or merely watches, a sporting event. Government officials, like football players, have to play by the rules. Some have called our system of criminal procedure the "sporting theory of justice" because of this similarity between sports and criminal justice.

Playing by the rules — what we might call the **principle of procedural regularity** — requires reaching beyond, and sometimes even overriding, the correct result in individ-

TABLE 1.1 OBJECTIVE BASES FOR INVASIONS OF PRIVACY AND LIBERTY

Objective Basis	Invasion of Privacy and Liberty
Reasonable suspicion. A few identifiable (articulable) facts or circumstances to support *suspicion* that crime *may* be afoot.	Investigatory stops.
Reasonable suspicion. A few identifiable (articulable) facts support a *suspicion* that a suspect *may* be armed.	Pat-down or frisk of outer clothing.
Probable cause. Enough articulable facts to support a *belief* that a crime *was* committed and that the suspect committed the crime.	Arrests and other detentions prior to trial.
Probable cause. Enough facts to support a *belief* a person or evidence *will* be found in the place or persons searched.	Searches of persons, houses, papers, and effects.
Proof beyond a reasonable doubt. Enough facts to withstand a *reasonable doubt* of guilt.	Convictions.

ual cases. On occasion this means that the reasonably suspect—and even the clearly guilty—may go free in order to serve the greater interest in procedural regularity. According to the principle of procedural regularity, it is better to free the guilty in individual cases than for the government to break the rules in order to find the truth.

The remaining chapters of this book examine the rules of procedural regularity that apply to each step in the criminal process. Here, it is enough to briefly touch on the general elements of procedural regularity required by our constitutional democracy.

Burden of Proof

"Facts, just the facts, ma'am," the police officer on the old television drama *Dragnet* used to say at least once in every episode. It is difficult to overstate the importance of facts in the law of criminal procedure. Gathering facts and presenting them as evidence lie at the heart of our law of criminal procedure. Public officials cannot know what actions to take without facts to inform them, even though their "hunches" may tell them where they might look. But hunch, whim, and mere suspicion count for nothing in supporting government invasions of individual privacy, liberty, and property. The Constitution requires that officials have enough facts, what we will call an **objective basis,** to back up every invasion of the privacy, liberty, and property of individuals.

Nearly everybody knows that convictions for crime require enough facts to add up to **proof beyond a reasonable doubt.** Many people also know that the police cannot arrest suspects or search them without enough facts to add up to "probable cause." What most people do not know is that the Constitution also requires an objective basis to back up lesser invasions of privacy, liberty, and property (see Table 1.1). To stop and detain people on the street without their consent, police cannot act on hunches, whims, or mere suspicion; they must have the factual basis known as reasonable suspicion, fewer facts than amount to probable cause but more than a hunch (see Chapter 4). To take suspicious individuals to the police station for further investigation, police need a still higher level of factual basis—probable cause, more facts than reasonable suspicion but fewer facts than proof beyond a reasonable doubt (see Chapter 5). Prosecutors need still more facts to charge suspects with crimes. Juries, or judges in trials without juries, cannot convict—the prerequisite to punishment—without proof beyond a reasonable doubt, the highest level of proof in the criminal process.

The basic idea behind these objective bases is that the greater the government intrusion or deprivation, the greater the quantity of facts required to authorize it. Chapters 3, 4, 5, 6, 9, and 11 fully discuss all the following levels of the objective bases:

1. Reasonable suspicion to stop suspicious persons on the street and other public places

2. Reasonable suspicion to frisk persons for weapons during stops

3. Probable cause to arrest suspects

4. Probable cause to search suspects

5. Probable cause to detain defendants for trial

6. Proof beyond a reasonable doubt to convict offenders

For now, it is enough to recognize the fundamental importance of these general ideas:

■ Facts—not hunch, whim, or mere suspicion—must support all government actions against citizens.

■ The greater the intrusion or deprivation, the higher the level of objective basis required to support it.

■ Facts are power in criminal procedure; they determine the course and outcome of all actions in criminal procedure.[4]

Based on enough facts and proper procedure, government actions to control crime are justified. But *justified* does not mean that only the guilty are stopped, frisked, arrested, searched, detained for trial, and convicted. Do not forget that not all suspects and defendants are guilty. Reasonable suspicion is not the equivalent of guilt; probable cause is not tantamount to guilt either; even proof beyond a reasonable doubt does not mean absolutely guilty. In order to protect the life, liberty, privacy, and property of some individuals, the government itself infringes on the life, liberty, privacy, and property of other people. The following hypothetical pairs demonstrate the parallel losses that citizens suffer both from offenders and from government:

1a. Allen wants Elaine's new stereo. When he knows she is out, he enters her apartment and takes the stereo.

1b. Officer McKenzie gets a search warrant to search Marty's apartment for a stolen stereo. He breaks into Marty's apartment, enters, finds the stereo, and takes it to the police station.

2a. Knowing that Michelle's father is very rich, Doug takes Michelle to a cabin in the woods against her will. He holds her there until her father pays him a million-dollar ransom.

2b. Officer Shapiro sees Ann grab Steve and forcibly take his wallet. The police officer chases Ann and catches her. She arrests Ann, takes her to the police station, books her, and then takes her to the jail, where she is locked up against her will. The court sets bail for Ann at $50,000.

3a. Michael approaches Kristen in a singles bar. He feels very attracted to her and makes advances to her. Kristen tells him to "get lost," but Michael persists and, against her will, feels her breasts.

3b. Corrections Officer Gonzales sees Brent hold up a bank. The officer arrests Brent and conducts a full body search.

4a. Katrina was jealous of Sandy for always getting better grades. Enraged because Sandy received an A in a criminal procedure class, whereas Katrina received only a C, Katrina stabbed Sandy to death. The state in which Katrina killed Sandy has a statute authorizing the death penalty. Katrina was tried, convicted, and sentenced to death for murdering Sandy. After waiting on death row for two years, Katrina was electrocuted. She screamed as the electric currents spread through her body; it took about five minutes to kill her.

4b. Tony has just shot Lisa. As he is running away with the gun in his hand, the police arrive. They order Tony to "halt." Tony stops, turns toward the officers, lifts the gun, and begins to squeeze the trigger. The officers shoot and kill him.

These simple examples illustrate the difference between the invasions arising out of the actions of criminals in the commission of crimes and the invasions brought about by government officials enforcing the criminal law. The criminal law prohibits private individuals from hurting other individuals. It defines specific harms as crimes and prescribes punishments for those who are convicted of committing them. The law of criminal procedure, on the other hand, empowers public officials to invade the rights of private persons in order to enforce the criminal law. However, notice what is often overlooked: individuals suffer invasions by *both* private criminals *and* public officials. But there is a critical difference between the two invasions. The Constitution *authorizes* government invasions when an objective basis—enough facts—justifies the invasions. The criminal law *prohibits* private individuals from inflicting such invasions. We can accept, and most of us support, government invasions when an objective basis and fairness ensured by procedural regularity stand behind them.

Adversary Process

The **adversary process** prescribes what evidence the government may present, how the government may present its evidence, how the defense may respond to the government's case, and how the defense may present its own evidence. In other words, both the government and the defense are allowed to tell their sides of the story, but only according to prescribed rules.[5] (See Chapter 12.)

The adversary process assumes that the truth will triumph in the end because both prosecutors and defense attorneys will present their cases in the strongest possible terms. Confidence in the ultimate accuracy of the adversary system stems from a deep belief in the value of the competitive spirit—the "sporting theory of justice" referred to above. Everyone wants to "win," according to the sporting theory. Hence, prosecutors will do their best to marshall all of the admissible facts to prove the guilt of **defendants.** Defendants do not want to be punished, and defense attorneys do not want to lose cases. Hence, both do their best to make sure that prosecutors follow the rules and to make sure that they do not prove defendants guilty according to the rules. Since the criminal trial—and the criminal process in general—operates on proof based on facts, the truth triumphs in the vigorous search for facts according to the rules.[6]

In reality, the competitive spirit can and does lead to excesses—namely, the desire to win at any cost. In order to control these excesses, judges act as umpires or neutral decision makers who make sure that both prosecution and defense play by the rules and do not gain an unfair advantage. Even with the safeguard of judicial supervision, truth is not always the victor in the adversary process. Superior persuasive ability, emotional appeals, and greater resources might put truth in jeopardy and allow lies, half-truths, and distortions to triumph.

Furthermore, the adversary system does not operate in pure form; it shares its importance in the criminal justice system with other goals. For example, prosecutors are not only supposed to win cases for the government but are also responsible for "doing justice." Doing justice can include *not* charging defendants. Instead, prosecutors might divert them into social service agencies for treatment or other help. Prosecutors might even supply defense counsel with evidence helpful to defendants' cases (a procedure called **discovery**). In addition, organizational interests may dictate that prosecutors' offices distribute resources more economically, efficiently, and effectively. That may mean prosecuting "major" crimes and not prosecuting "minor" crimes.

Accusatory System

The **accusatory system** is a basic part of the criminal side of the adversary process. The accusatory system places the burden of proof on the government in criminal cases. Summed up in the phrase "innocent until proven guilty," defendants do not have to prove their innocence; the government must prove their guilt. From police detection and investigation through conviction and punishment, the accusatory system requires the government to secure facts according to the law in order to authorize its actions.

The accusatory system is based on the ideal of the supremacy of the individual in a free society, on a suspicion of the corruptibility of government power and the abuses to which it can be put, and on the reality that in criminal prosecutions the government possesses enormous resources that individuals cannot match. Even wealthy and powerful defendants—and most are neither—can never acquire even a fraction of the investigative power that prosecutors have at their disposal. The best-known characteristics of the accusatory system are as follows:

- The **presumption of innocence** (the principle that defendants are presumed innocent unless and until they are proven guilty)
- The right of criminal defendants to remain silent and not to answer questions that might incriminate them
- The right to a lawyer to aid in the defense against criminal charges

All these characteristics further demonstrate the importance of the individual in the law—if not always in the practice—of criminal procedure.

Due Process

Another element of procedural regularity lies in the requirements of the Fifth and Fourteenth Amendments that criminal proceedings take place according to the two dimensions of due process of law:

1. Limiting the power of government
2. Promoting order, timeliness, and finality in decision making

The limited government dimension of due process focuses on controlling the means that police, prosecutors, and other agents of the government use to enforce the criminal law. The orderly, timely, finality dimension focuses on the interest in moving decision making in an orderly way, meeting deadlines, and reaching closure—settling matters without having to unduly reopen proceedings for continued reevaluation. Former United States Supreme Court justice John Marshall Harlan wrote of what he called "the principle that there must be some end to litigation." According to Justice Harlan,

> Both the individual criminal defendant and society have an interest in insuring that there will at some point be the certainty that comes with an end to litigation, and that attention will ultimately be focused not on whether a conviction was free from error but rather on whether the prisoner can be restored to a useful place in the community.[7]

The commitment to fair means in the search for truth, despite the discomfort it causes (particularly in times like ours, when public fear of violence and drugs runs high), has always had its staunch defenders. As an example from history, during the darkest days of World War II the threat of attack from Germany and Japan outside the country and the fear of subversion from inside the country ran high. When the government of the United States restricted civil liberties from within as a means of public safety, a New York lawyer defended the new federal rules of criminal procedure that limited the power of government in enforcing the criminal law:

> Whoever sets out to formulate rules for the administration of the criminal law is confronted with the limitations on the power of the Government embodied in the Bill of Rights. It is a commonplace that these provisions result in some impairment of the efficiency of law enforcement agencies. But it is part of our fundamental belief that this price is worth paying, since it safeguards the freedom of the whole population. . . . For at every step . . . the police and prosecutors are restricted by constitutional guarantees which sometimes thwart their desires.[8]

Human Dignity

Procedural regularity clearly demonstrates the central importance of the individual in our society. The supremacy of the individual means that criminal procedure respects every individual's dignity, autonomy, and equality with others vis-à-vis the government. The laudable end of criminal law enforcement can never justify excessive, false, cruel, or abusive means that invade individual autonomy and dignity. Nor can it tolerate different treatment and outcomes based on race, ethnicity, gender, or class. "Justice is blind," goes the old saying. Born in a revolution that glorified individual rights, committed itself to the ideal of equality, and suspected government power of all kinds and at all levels, the American criminal justice system reflects the concerns that brought our law of criminal procedure into being.

Protecting the supremacy of the individual creates an uncomfortable tension in our society. The very rules that protect everybody against government abuse of power also inhibit the search for the truth in individual cases. This inhibition can and probably does reduce to some degree the public safety of all people. Some guilty individuals will go free in order to ensure that the government will play by the rules! Professor Jerome Hall captured the dilemma caused by balancing result and process in these words, which bear remembering as you study criminal procedure:

[Criminal law's] ultimate ends are dual and conflicting. It must be designed from inception to end, to acquit the innocent as readily at least, as to convict the guilty. This presents the inescapable dilemma of criminal procedure . . . that the easier it is made to prove guilt, the more difficult it becomes to establish innocence.[9]

The balance between result and process never rests at a point that satisfies everyone; it is, in fact, a tension that has led to great dissatisfaction. Throughout history, those who fear criminals more than they fear government abuse of power stress the importance of correct result in particular cases. They complain of rules or "technicalities" that "handcuff the police" and allow criminals to go free. Those who fear government abuse of power more than they fear criminals complain that we have not sufficiently obliged the government to control itself, as Madison admonished us to do. The famous federal judge Learned Hand clearly took the side of government power. He argued that the inhibitions built into the criminal process stood in the way of obtaining the correct result, meaning, in Judge Hand's opinion, convicting the guilty. According to Judge Hand,

Under our criminal procedure the accused has every advantage. While the prosecution is held rigidly to the charge, he need not disclose the barest outline of his defense. He is immune from question or comment on his silence; he cannot be convicted when there is the least fair doubt in the minds of any one of the twelve. . . . Our dangers do not lie in too little tenderness to the accused. Our procedure has been always haunted by the ghost of the innocent man convicted. It is an unreal dream. What we need to fear is the archaic formalism and the watery sentiment that obstructs, delays, and defeats the prosecution of crime.[10]

Professor Joseph Goldstein, weighing in on the side of controlling government, takes sharp exception to Judge Hand's position. Goldstein believes that the process favors the government, not criminal suspects and defendants:

[T]he fact is that . . . [Judge Hand's] view does not accurately represent the process. Both doctrinally and practically, criminal procedure . . . does not give the accused "every advantage" but, instead, gives overwhelming advantage to the prosecution. The real effect of the "modern" approach has been to aggravate this condition by loosening standards of . . . proof without introducing compensatory safeguards earlier in the process. Underlying this development has been an inarticulate, albeit clearly operative, rejection of the presumption of innocence in favor of a presumption of guilt.[11]

HISTORY OF
CRIMINAL PROCEDURE

The tension between result and process displayed in James Madison's famous passage from *The Federalist* and in the disagreement between Judge Hand and Professor Goldstein is as old as Western law. The early twentieth-century legal scholar Roscoe Pound maintained that the history of criminal procedure is a pendulum swing between the two extremes of this tension. According to Pound, no system has perfectly balanced the power of the government to enforce the criminal law and the process to attain that end. Throughout Western history, societies have swung back and forth between first a predominant concern for the interest of society in criminal law enforcement and then, in reaction, a predominant concern for the interest of society in other values that transcend the obvious one of convicting the guilty.[12]

The early Roman republic established strong safeguards for individuals against government power in its law of criminal procedure. As a result, according to Professor Strachan-Davidson, the Romans created a criminal law "that in spite of abundant threats of capital punishment, became in practice the mildest ever known in the history of mankind." Strachan-Davidson refers to a case from the middle of the first century that brings into relief the Roman law's "mildness" and its respect for individual rights. The Roman praetor seized a notorious violent criminal. Tribune Novius, upon releasing the criminal, said this:

> Although I have been wounded by this hanger-on of Clodius and driven from my official duties by armed men distributed in garrisons, and General Pompeius has been besieged by them, yet when appeal is made to me, I will not follow the example of him with whom I find fault, and I will quash this sentence.[13]

In reaction to this mildness and its attendant emphasis on process, the government of the Roman Empire went to the other extreme. In the era of Imperial Rome, the provincial governors acted as both public prosecutors and judges. The emperor Hadrian noted that full-fledged trials were not necessary; merely sending an accused to trial conclusively proved his or her guilt.[14]

Several centuries later, in thirteenth-century England, the same conflict between result and process arose. In the Magna Carta, King John's barons successfully placed a number of checks on royal power. These checks emphasized process at the expense of result. As in Imperial Rome, the excess of process led to a reaction expressed in the aggrandizement of royal power during the sixteenth and seventeenth centuries. By the reign of King Charles I in the early 1600s, the royal Court of the Star Chamber had abandoned the common-law procedural safeguards for the accused in favor of royal power to convict the guilty. The expansion of royal power did not stop with creating new royal courts; it extended to the kings' political domination of the common-law judges. Through intimidation, favor, and other influence, the seventeenth-century English kings brought about decisions favorable to their own and the aristocracy's interests.

Although interference in the business of the courts was by no means new, a middle class increasingly eager for greater political influence regarded royal interference in judicial proceedings as intolerable. The English revolution—and the founding of the American colonies—was, at least in part, a reaction by the middle classes to this expansion of royal power and its emphasis on result at the expense of the interest in process.

The Articles of Confederation, written in response to what Americans perceived as British tyranny, went to the other extreme, creating a government too weak to govern. The United States Constitution represented an effort to balance government power—particularly, national government power—and individual liberty. As Alexander Hamilton wrote of this balance,

> In the commencement of a revolution which received its birth from the usurpations of tyranny, nothing was more natural than that the public mind should be influenced by an extreme spirit of jealousy. To resist these encroachments, and to nourish this spirit, was the great object of all our public and private institutions.

The zeal for liberty became predominant and excessive. In forming our Confederation, this passion alone seemed to actuate us, and we appear to have had no other view than to secure ourselves from despotism. The object certainly was a valuable one, and deserves our utmost attention; but, sir, there is another object, equally important, and which our enthusiasm rendered us little capable of regarding: I mean a principle of strength and stability in the organization of our government, and vigor in its operations.[15]

Even this balance did not satisfy Anti-Federalists. They feared government power too much to rely on such a general protection. The Bill of Rights, added as amendments to the Constitution, reflects the deep suspicion, even hostility, to government power among some of the middle classes who had experienced firsthand both a royal executive and an appointed judiciary impatient with individual rights. The Bill of Rights demonstrates the determination of the Anti-Federalists to protect individual interests against government intrusions and deprivations. Throughout the nineteenth century, concern for individual rights dominated the law of criminal procedure, if not its practice. A largely rural, widely scattered, sparse population that lived in villages and on farms and shared common values controlled political life. A weak government that allowed individual autonomy to flourish worked in that society.[16]

By the early twentieth century, however, America had changed. The country was increasingly urban, densely populated, industrial, and inhabited by peoples with values different from those of the dominant nineteenth-century Anglo-Saxon Protestant culture. Many people called upon the government to solve the problems that arose in transportation, health, business regulation, employment conditions, consumer protection, and the maintenance of public order. Deficiencies in criminal justice led to calls for both an expanded criminal law to regulate behavior and greater government power to enforce the law. These events took place during one of the recurring "crime waves," as the public perceived them. This wave, contemporaries imagined, had brought the incidence of crime to epidemic proportions.

Complaints spread that "technicalities" set criminals free and that constitutional safeguards made it difficult to convict known criminals. The newspapers, the new middle-class magazines, national conventions of criminal justice officials, professors, and lawyers loudly complained about how the criminal justice system favored criminals over innocent citizens. In other words, result was being sacrificed to process.

In the early years of the twentieth century, these complaints provoked open demands to amend the Constitution, sometimes drastically. At the 1910 annual meeting of the American Academy of Political and Social Science, a prestigious New York criminal lawyer, Samuel Untermeyer, told the conference that the Fourth Amendment protection against unreasonable searches and seizures and the Fifth Amendment protection against self-incrimination gave too much protection to criminals. He recommended, in his own words, a "shocking" solution: abolish the Fourth and Fifth Amendments. Others demanded similar treatment for the jury trial. This "palladium of liberty" and democracy ought to be abolished because sentimental jurors set wanton criminals free to prey on innocent people.[17]

Complaints about the ideal balance between result and process have not subsided appreciably since the turn of the twentieth century. The complaints of the early twentieth century fostered a tough law-and-order atmosphere and an accompanying enhanced police power that continued from the 1920s through the 1950s. During the 1960s, this enhanced police power spawned a reaction: the "due process revolution." Led by the United States Supreme Court, which was called the Warren Court after its chief justice, Earl Warren, this revolution tilted the balance of power toward process—so much so, said its critics, that it favored criminal defendants too much.[18]

The due process revolution produced another pendulum swing that led to calls for more attention to result—specifically, the result of convicting criminals. Much of the law of criminal procedure in this book reflects the fruits of that revolution and the subsequent reaction to it. From the 1970s to the early 1990s, the United States Supreme Court—first the Burger Court and then the Rehnquist Court, named after their respective chief justices, Warren Burger and William Rehnquist—and federal legislatures and all criminal justice agencies adopted sterner measures to protect society against crime and criminals. Beginning in the 1980s and increasingly in the early 1990s, federal judges especially upheld the exercise of government power to enforce the criminal law against the challenges of defendants.

The present, as the past, continues the history of efforts to balance process and result, both social interests basic to the quality of life in a free society. Individual freedom is worth little without safety and security from criminal attacks. On the other hand, a government that regularly practices unwarranted intrusions and deprivations does not provide individuals with the quality of life associated with free societies. In the words of Chief Justice Rehnquist, "Unregulated freedom is anarchy, and absolute order is despotism." Hence, society has an interest in protecting citizens both from attacks by private criminals who prey upon law-abiding citizens, their property, and their privacy and from government excesses that threaten the autonomy associated with life in a free society. The law of criminal procedure attempts to provide the government with enough power to enforce the criminal law, but not with so much power that the government itself threatens individual autonomy and privacy.[19]

Our first edited case, *Bostick v. State*, deals with the problem of balancing result and process. Before you read the case, make sure that you have studied carefully the section titled "How to Read, Analyze, and Find Cases."

 # HOW TO READ, ANALYZE, AND FIND CASES

Throughout this book, you will read excerpts of cases from four levels of courts: the United States Supreme Court, the United States Courts of Appeals, state supreme courts, and intermediate appellate state courts (see Figure 1.1). Most excerpted cases are United States Supreme Court cases. The United States Supreme Court has the final word in interpreting the United States Constitution. The United States Constitution, particularly its Bill of Rights, has much

to say about criminal procedure, as you will see throughout this book.

Sometimes, you will read United States courts of appeals cases. These intermediate federal appellate courts sometimes deal with issues not yet decided by the Supreme Court, and they apply the rules set by the Supreme Court to other cases.

Occasionally, you will also read cases from state courts. State cases are important for two reasons. First,

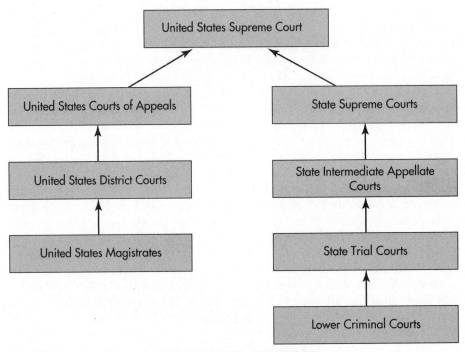

FIGURE 1.1 FEDERAL AND STATE COURT STRUCTURE

virtually every state has a bill of rights similar to and often identical to the United States Bill of Rights. States interpret and apply their constitutional provisions for themselves. Second, many criminal procedure cases originate, and frequently terminate, in state courts. In other words, the day-to-day judicial administration of criminal justice takes place in state courts, not the United States Supreme Court, or even the federal district courts (the federal trial courts) and courts of appeals (the intermediate federal appellate courts). The Supreme Court reviews only a few of the tens of thousands of decisions made by police officers, prosecutors, trial judges, and state appellate courts.

Keep the following points in mind when you read the case excerpts:

1. *The title.* The title in criminal cases always contains at least two names. The first name refers to the party that brought the action. It is always the government at the trial stage because the government initiates all criminal cases in the United States. The *v.* is an abbreviation of the Latin *ver-*

sus, meaning "against." The second name refers to the party against which the action was brought. In *Bostick v. State,* for example, the title tells us that a person named Bostick appealed a decision by the state, in this case the state of Florida.

2. *The citation.* The **citation** consists of the letters and numbers following the case title. The citation tells what court heard the case, when the court decided the case, and where you can find the case reported. The case citation, like a footnote, endnote, or other reference in articles and books, reveals the source of the material quoted or relied upon. In *Bostick v. State,* the citation 554 So.2d 1153 (Fla. 1989) means that you can find the case published in volume 554 of the *Southern Reporter,* second series, beginning on page 1153, and that the Florida Supreme Court decided the case in 1989. In legal citations, the number that appears before the title refers to a specific volume in a set of reports; the number following the title refers to the page on which the report of the case

begins. The abbreviation and words between the volume and the page numbers refer to the title of the publication reporting the case, in this case the *Southern Reporter.* If the case appears in more than one publication, references to these other publications also appear. For example, Supreme Court cases appear in three major publications: *United States Reports,* abbreviated to simply *U.S.; Supreme Court Reporter,* abbreviated *S.Ct.;* and *Lawyer's Edition,* abbreviated *L.Ed.*

3. *Appellate cases.* Most cases in this textbook are **appellate court cases.** This means that a lower court has already taken some action in the case and that one of the parties has asked a higher court to review the lower court's action. Parties seek appellate review of what they claim were errors by the trial court or unlawful conduct by police, judges, prosecutors, or defense lawyers. Sometimes, a convicted defendant **appeals.** Only defendants can appeal convictions; moreover, the government cannot appeal acquittals. However, many appellate reviews arise out of proceedings prior to trial. Both the government and the defendant can appeal pretrial proceedings.

4. *Suppression hearings.* Many cases involving alleged police misconduct arise out of what defendants maintain were erroneous rulings on pretrial motions to exclude evidence at proceedings called suppression hearings. *Bostick v. State* is a review of a ruling at a pretrial suppression hearing. According to Bostick, the police obtained drugs from a search that violated the Fourth Amendment. In a suppression hearing held before his trial, Bostick's lawyer moved to suppress, or exclude, the drugs from being used as evidence at the trial. The trial judge ruled that the evidence was admissible. Bostick appealed to the Florida Supreme Court, which reversed the trial court's ruling because, the Florida Supreme Court held, the seizure of the evidence violated the Fourth Amendment. Florida appealed to the United States Supreme Court. That case, *Florida v. Bostick* (note that the order of parties changes), you will read in Chapter 4.

5. *Appealing parties.* The cases refer variously to parties that seek review of lower-court decisions.

Most commonly, the appellate courts refer to the party who appeals as the **appellant** and to the party appealed against as the **appellee.** Both of these terms originate from the word *appeal.* A **petitioner** is a defendant whose case has come to the higher courts by petition. The principal petitions are *certiorari,* Latin for "to be certified," and *habeas corpus,* Latin for "you should have the body." *Habeas corpus,* a **collateral attack,** or separate proceeding from the criminal case itself, requires jailers, prison administrators, and others who hold defendants in custody to justify the detention of defendants who have petitioned the higher court to hear their cases. You can tell these proceedings by their title. Instead of a government name and a person's name in the title, you will find two persons' names, such as *Adams v. Williams* (Adams was the warden of the prison holding Williams; Williams was the prisoner).

Certiorari is discretionary; it does not require appellate courts to hear appeals. The Supreme Court grants only a small percentage of petitions for *certiorari.* It grants *certiorari* not because of the individual litigants, but because a case raises an important constitutional issue affecting large numbers of individuals. Most appeals to the United States Supreme Court are based on writs of *certiorari,* which are orders to lower courts to send up their proceedings for review. Four of the nine Supreme Court justices must vote to review a case—a requirement known as the **rule of four**—for the Court to hear the appeal on *certiorari.* The Court turns down most of these petitions, but those it accepts often make important law.

In the excerpts of older cases, you will find yet another name for the party that appeals. The older cases refer to the **plaintiff in error,** the party that claims the lower courts erred in their rulings.

6. *The opinions.* Most of the cases, particularly those of the United States Supreme Court, have at least two types of opinions, and sometimes three. The **majority opinion,** if one exists, is the law in the case. The United States Supreme Court has nine members; each has a vote and the right to submit an opinion. If all justices participate, five, a majority, can make the law. If the five agree to both

the reasoning and the judgment or decision, the opinion is called a majority opinion. Sometimes, justices agree with the decision, or result, in the case, but they do not agree with the reasons for the decision. They write separate, **concurring opinions,** giving their own reasons for the decision.

If a majority of the justices agree with a result in a case but they cannot agree on the reasons for the result, the opinion with the reasoning agreed to by the largest number of justices is called a **plurality opinion.** For example, suppose that seven justices agree with the result and four give one set of reasons, three give another set of reasons, and two dissent. The opinion to which the four subscribe is the plurality opinion. If justices do not agree with the court's decision, whether plurality or majority, they can vote against the decision and write their own **dissenting opinions** explaining why they do not agree with either the reasoning, the result, or both. Often, the dissenting opinions point to the future; many majority opinions of today are based on dissents from the past. The late Chief Justice Charles Evans Hughes once said a dissent should be "an appeal to the brooding spirit of the law, to the intelligence of a future day."[20]

The conflicting arguments and reasoning in the majority, plurality, concurring, and dissenting opinions will challenge you to think about the issues in the cases because, most of the time, all of the justices convincingly argue their views of the case. First, the majority's and the concurring justices' arguments will convince you; then the dissent will lead you to the opposite conclusion. This interplay teaches you an important point: plausible arguments support both the government's position and the defendant's position in most cases. Reasonable people do disagree!

You will notice that all the arguments in the majority, concurring, and dissenting opinions refer frequently to other cases that the court in this case or some other court has decided in the past. The prior cases are called **precedent.** The judges draw upon precedent to support their decisions because of the doctrine of *stare decisis.* The

doctrine requires that once courts have decided cases, these prior decisions (precedent) bind later courts to follow them. The doctrine applies only to the prior decisions of their own court or courts superior to them in their own **jurisdiction** (the geographical area or the subject matter over which the court has the authority to make decisions).

Supreme Court Justice and respected judicial philosopher Benjamin Cardozo once said this about precedent and the doctrine of *stare decisis:*

> It is easier to follow the beaten track than it is to clear another. In doing this, I shall be treading in the footsteps of my predecessors, and illustrating the process that I am seeking to describe, since the power of precedent, when analyzed, is the power of the beaten path.[21]

The idea of precedent is not peculiar to the law of criminal procedure, nor is it the basis only of legal reasoning. We are accustomed to the basic notion of precedent in ordinary life. We like to do things the way we have done them in the past. For example, if a professor asks multiple-choice questions covering only material in the text on three exams, you expect that the fourth examination will resemble the three prior exams. If on the fourth exam the professor gives you an essay examination covering material you heard in class but that did not appear in the text, you may not like it.

Not only may you not like it; you will probably think it is "unfair." Why? Precedent—the way we have done things before—makes life stable and predictable. Knowing what to expect, and counting on it, guides our actions in the future so that we can plan for and respond to challenges and solve problems. Changing this without warning seems unfair. In ordinary life, then, as in criminal procedure, following past practice gives stability, predictability, and a sense of fairness and justice to decisions.

Of course, doing things as we have done them, although comfortable, is not always right or good. Sometimes it also becomes uncomfortable. When that happens, we change (often reluctantly) and do things differently; these changes themselves become guides to future action. So, too, with legal precedent. Courts may change precedent, although they do so reluctantly. Courts, like individuals in ordinary life, do not like to change, particularly when it requires that they admit they were wrong. That is why, as you read the cases in this book, you will find few that overrule prior decisions. Instead, when courts wish to change, they will do so by **distinguishing cases.** This means that a court decides that a prior decision does not apply to the current case because the facts are different. For example, the rule governing the right to counsel in cases punishable by death need not be the same as the rule governing the right to counsel in a case involving a petty misdemeanor punishable by a fine.[22]

Throughout the book, as you read the case excerpts and even the discussion in the text, you should keep in mind the importance of precedent and the doctrine of *stare decisis* in the law of criminal procedure. You should notice whether the decisions are following past cases or breaking new ground.

7. *Questions.* To guide your reading and get the most out of the case excerpts, answer these questions about each case:

   a. *What are the specific facts demonstrating government action?* In other words, list specifically the government actions that led defendants to claim errors or misconduct.

   b. *What was the quantum of proof for the government action?* In other words, list specifically the facts that provided the objective basis for the government action. Technically, 7a and 7b refer to the facts of the case.

   c. *What constitutional provision, statute, or rule did the police, prosecutor, judge, defense counsel, or other official violate?* Technically, 7c refers to the issue in the case.

   d. *What did the court decide with respect to the questions or issues raised?* What legal principle can be drawn from the court's opinion? Technically, 7d refers to the decision or holding in the case.

   e. *What arguments and reasons did the court give to support its decision?* What arguments and reasons did the dissent give for not agreeing with the majority? Technically, 7e refers to the court's opinion, or another term, its *reasoning.*

   f. *What was the disposition in the case?* Common dispositions in criminal cases include (1) **affirmed,** meaning the appellate court upheld a lower court's action; (2) **reversed,** meaning the appellate court set aside, or nullified, the lower court's judgment; and (3) **remanded,** meaning the appellate court sent the case back to the court from which it came for further action. Notice that remanding a case does not necessarily mean the defendant will win the case. Fewer than half the parties that win Supreme Court cases ultimately triumph when the cases go back to lower courts, particularly to state courts. For example, in the famous *Miranda v. Arizona,* the prison gates did not open for Ernesto Miranda; he returned to prison. Technically, the disposition is called the decision in the case.

Do not expect to answer all these questions fully, at least not at first. The remaining chapters elaborate upon the answers to these questions.

Annotated Unedited Case

Reproduced here is a full case with no editing. I have annotated it so that you can understand all of the parts of the case. The annotations appear inside brackets [ ]. The annotations should help you read and understand the edited cases that appear in the excerpts throughout the book. Furthermore, they should aid you in reading and understanding cases that you may wish to look up for yourself or that your instructor assigns you.

Anthony L. TOGNACI, *Appellant, v. STATE of Florida, Appellee.*

[This is the full title of the case. Ordinarily, when cited in other works, you will only see the part of the title in capital letters, in this case *Tognaci v. State.*]

No. 89-1097.

[This is the docket, or file number, given to the case by the clerk of the court.]

District Court of Appeal of Florida, Fourth District. Dec. 12, 1990.

[This is the name of the court that heard the case and the date the court decided it.]

571 So.2d 76

[This is the citation of the case, telling you that you can find it reported in volume 571 of the *Southern Reporter,* second series (So.2d), at page 76.]

In a narcotics prosecution, the Circuit Court, Broward County, Mel Grossman, J., found that the consensual search of the defendant did not intrude into impermissible areas, and defendant appealed. The District Court of Appeal, Warner, J., held that trial court's determination that search did not exceed its scope when female officer searched male defendant's crotch area was not clearly erroneous where it was not clear from the evidence that the officer actually touched the defendant's genitals.

Affirmed.

Walden, J., concurred in result only.

[This is the syllabus of the court, a summary that is not part of the official record but that helps readers get a brief and quick view of the case.]

[1] SEARCHES AND SEIZURES k197

349k197

Trial court's determination that consensual search of narcotics defendant did not exceed its scope when the female officer searched the male defendant's crotch area was not clearly erroneous; it was not clear from the evidence that the officer actually touched the defendant's genitals.

[These are the famous headnotes in the West Key notes system established by West Publishing Company. The headnotes provide brief summaries of the main points of law in the case. Furthermore, they direct lawyers and students to other cases and discussions dealing with any topic in the key system. Notice here that the topic is Search and Seizures; the key number is 197. Many subheadings occur under searches and seizures, as you will see below. Each headnote is numbered in brackets (here [1]) so that you can match it to the paragraph or paragraphs in the court's opinion that discusses this point. See below the [1] bracketed paragraph number in the opinion.]

[2] SEARCHES AND SEIZURES k186

349k186

Persons encountered by law enforcement personnel in the public area of airport terminals, bus stations or train stations do not reasonably expect that their consent to the officer's search of their "person," without more, would include intimate contact with the genital area.

Harry Gulkin of Harry Gulkin, P.A., Fort Lauderdale, for appellant.

Robert A. Butterworth, Atty. General, Tallahassee, and Sylvia H. Alonso, Asst. Atty. Gen., West Palm Beach, for appellee.

[These are the names of the prosecutors and the lawyers who argued the case for the defendant on appeal.]

WARNER, Judge.

We affirm on the authority of *U.S. v. Blake*, 888 F.2d 795 (11th Cir. 1989), in that we cannot conclude that based on the totality of the circumstances before the court that the trial court's factual determinations were clearly erroneous.

[This is the decision of the court. Notice that the court relies on another case, *U.S. v. Blake*, to support its decision. This is the most common form of what is called legal reasoning, that is, comparing and contrasting cases already decided to back up what the court decides in this case.]

[1] [This bracketed number tells you that the paragraph refers to the first headnote at the beginning of the opinion.] The issue in this case [the issue is the legal question in the case] is whether the consensual search of the defendant exceeded its scope when the female officer searched the male appellant's crotch area. From the totality of the circumstances an affirmance is warranted mainly because it is not clear from the evidence that the officer actually touched appellant's genitals. [Here the court is applying the law of consent searches to the facts of this case. See Chapter 7 for a discussion of searches.] The testimony indicated that after receiving permission to search appellant's person, Officer Cutcliffe noticed a bulge "a little bit higher than where his male organs would be, normally." She pointed out for the court where she saw and touched the bulge, and her part-

ner who actually removed the object from the appellant's pants testified that the narcotics package was taped between his belt and the top of his zipper. Therefore, the court could reasonably conclude that this search did not intrude into impermissible areas. [These are the facts of the case; that is, the section tells us what happened in the case, the critical events as found by the trial court that raised the legal issue in the case.]

[2] [Here begins the opinion of the case, that is, the part of the case in which the court states the law and then applies the law to the facts of the case, using legal reasoning and argument.] However, we feel compelled to comment on what appears to be a routine investigative procedure used in the Broward County Sheriff's Office as revealed by the testimony in this case. The deputies are trained to make random encounters of the traveling public in airport terminals, bus stations, and train stations. They secure the person's "voluntary" consent to search the "person" and then proceed to search the crotch and genital area of the person without notifying them of the fact that they intend to search this most private area of the body in a public place. Officer Cutcliffe testified that she has searched hundreds of men's crotches without discovering any contraband. She has also searched women in the same fashion. We emphasize that these encounters are random, not generated by any articulable suspicion of wrongdoing, nor by a drug courier profile, nor by a fear for the officer's safety. And at least based upon the hundreds of searches which do not produce any drugs, we conclude from the testimony that the genital search is not a very effective investigative tool in stopping the drug trade. [In this paragraph the court is going beyond the law and giving its opinion on the police practices used here. This is not law, and lawyers cannot use it as such.]

If the Fourth Amendment means anything, it means that we citizens should be free from unreasonable searches of the most private areas of our bodies. We would agree with Federal District Judge Roettger in *U.S. v. Blake and Eason*, 718 F.Supp. 925 (S.D.Fla., 1988), that a person encountered by law enforcement in the public areas of an airport terminal could not reasonably expect that a consent to search their "person," without more, would include intimate contact with the genital area. [Here again, you see the common form of legal reasoning and argument—that is, to rely on the words, decisions, opinions, and facts of other cases to support the position taken in the present case.] That would be even more true under the facts of this case where a female officer is searching a man. Cf., e.g., *Sterling v. Cupp*, 44 Or. App. 755, 607 P.2d 206 (1980), as modified, 290 Or. 611, 625 P.2d 123 (1981); *Madyun v. Franzen*, 704 F.2d 954 (7th Cir. 1983), cert. denied, 464 U.S. 996, 104 S.Ct. 493, 78 L.Ed.2d 687 (1983); *Smith v. Fairman*, 678 F.2d 52 (7th Cir. 1982), cert. denied, 461 U.S. 907, 103 S.Ct. 1879, 76 L.Ed.2d 810 (1983) (all of which recognize that even a male prison inmate has a right of privacy against a frisk of the genital area by a female guard.) [Notice here the use of a number of cases that supposedly support the court's conclusion that it is a greater invasion of privacy for a female to touch the genitals of a man, and presumably vice versa. You could look up these cases in order to determine if they do or do not support the court's conclusion.]

Thus, this decision should not be read as a stamp of approval to the search procedure employed in this case. It just so happens that the search conducted revealed drugs in an area which could be within the legitimate scope of the consent before it extended to more private areas of the defendant's anatomy.

POLEN, J., concurs.

[Judge Polen concurs but did not write a concurring opinion. In the U.S. Supreme Court, many of whose opinions you will read in this book, judges who concur almost always write special concurring opinions either emphasizing something the majority did not or even disagreeing with the arguments and reasoning of the majority, but agreeing with the majority's final conclusions in the case.]

WALDEN, J., concurs in result only.

[Judge Walden obviously does not agree with the reasoning of the court, but he does concur in the decision that the search was lawful. We do not know why because no concurring opinion was filed in this case.]

CASE

Is Process More Important Than Result?

Bostick v. State,
554 So.2d 1153 (Fla. 1989), cert. granted
498 U.S. 894, 111 S.Ct. 241, 112 L.Ed.2d
201 (1990)
Barkett, Justice

FACTS

Two [Broward County sheriff's] officers, complete with badges, insignia and one of them holding a recognizable zipper pouch, containing a pistol, boarded a bus bound from Miami to Atlanta during a stopover in Fort Lauderdale. Eyeing the passengers, the officer, admittedly without articulable suspicion, picked out the defendant passenger and asked to inspect his ticket and identification.

The ticket, from Miami to Atlanta, matched the defendant's identification and both were immediately returned to him as unremarkable. However, the two police officers persisted and explained their presence as narcotic agents on the lookout for illegal drugs. In pursuit of that aim, they then requested the defendant's consent to search his luggage. Needless to say, there is conflict in the evidence about whether the defendant consented to the search of the second bag in which the contraband was found and as to whether he was informed of his right to refuse consent. However, any conflict must be resolved in favor of the state, it being a question of fact decided by the trial judge.

OPINION

The issue in this case arises out of the perpetual conflict between, on one hand, the right of an individual to be free from governmental interference and, on the other hand, the need of government to ensure the safety of its citizens. We start with the premise that every natural person has the inalienable right to live his or her life unimpeded by others. Each individual has the right to choose whether and with whom he or she will share personal information, conversation, or any other interaction personal to oneself.

This right of personal autonomy or privacy, however, is forfeited when an individual acts to harm another. Thus, when the state has reason to believe that an individual has committed a crime, the state has the power to interfere with that individual's autonomy through a seizure or a search. However, this power must be exercised within certain constitutional constraints.

One such constraint is article I, § 12, of the Florida Constitution, and its counterpart, the fourth amendment of the United States Constitution. Both guarantee the right to be free from unreasonable searches and seizures, and both apply to all "seizures" of the person, including arrests and brief detentions. . . . [T]hey apply to those situations when an "officer, by means of physical force or show of authority, has in some way restrained the liberty of a citizen." . . . [A] person has been "seized" within the meaning of the Fourth Amendment only if, in view of all the circumstances surrounding the incident, a reasonable person would have believed that he was not free to leave. . . .

We have no doubt that the Sheriff's Department's standard procedure of "working the buses" is an investigative practice implicating the protections against unreasonable seizures of the person. There is no doubt that these protections extend to the traveling public, including those who travel in vehicles, or vehicles for hire. The passenger . . . "shares with the driver a privacy interest in continuing his travels without governmental intrusion." Moreover, there is a well-established privacy interest in the luggage one carries during travels. . . .

We find that under the circumstances presented here, the government has exceeded its power to interfere with the privacy of an individual citizen who is not even suspected of any criminal wrongdoing. Indeed, the unlawful intrusion upon privacy that occurred here is eloquently described by Judge

Andrews, as quoted in *State v. Kerwick* (Fla. 4th DCA 1987), when he confronted the same Broward County Sheriff's policy in dispute in this case:

> [T]he evidence in this case has evoked images of other days, under other flags, when no man traveled his nation's roads or railways without fear of unwarranted interruption, by individuals who held temporary power in the Government. The spectre of American citizens being asked, by badge wielding police, for identification, travel papers—in short, a raison d'etre—is foreign to any fair reading of the Constitution, and its guarantee of human liberties. This is not Hitler's Berlin, nor Stalin's Moscow, nor is it white supremacist South Africa. Yet in Broward County, Florida, these police officers approach every person on board buses and trains ("that time permits") and check identification, tickets, ask to search luggage—all in the name of "voluntary cooperation" with law enforcement—to the shocking extent that just one officer, Damiano, admitted that during the previous nine months, he, himself, had searched in excess of three thousand bags! In the Court's opinion, the founders of the Republic would be thunderstruck.

We agree. The intrusion upon privacy rights caused by the Broward County policy is too great for a democracy to sustain. Without doubt the inherently transient nature of drug courier activity presents difficult law enforcement problems. Roving patrols, random sweeps, and arbitrary searches or seizures would go far to eliminate such crime in this state. Nazi Germany, Soviet Russia, and Communist Cuba have demonstrated all too tellingly the effectiveness of such methods. Yet we are not a state that subscribes to the notion that ends justify means. History demonstrates that the adoption of repressive measures, even to eliminate a clear evil, usually results only in repression more mindless and terrifying than the evil that prompted them. Means have a disturbing tendency to become the end result. And as

Judge Glickstein noted in his dissent in *Snider v. State* (Fla. 4th DCA 1986):

> Occasionally the price we must pay to make innocent persons secure from unreasonable search and seizure of their persons or property is to let an offender go. Those who suffered harassment from King George III's forces would say that is not a great price to pay. So would residents of the numerous totalitarian and authoritarian states of our day.

For the foregoing reasons . . . [t]he opinion below is quashed, and we remand for further proceedings consistent with this opinion. It is so ordered.

Chief Justice Ehrlich, and Justices Shaw and Kogan concur.

DISSENT

McDonald, Justice, dissenting.

. . . To many the practice of police boarding a bus seeking evidence of transportation of drugs is distasteful. I can accept that, but find nothing illegal about it so long as there are no overt acts of threat or intimidation in the procurement of a consent to search. The entire war on drugs is distasteful and society should accept some minimal inconvenience and minimal incursion on their rights of privacy in that fight. I would affirm Bostick's conviction. . . .

[NOTE: The state of Florida appealed the ruling that bus sweeps violate the Constitution to the United States Supreme Court. The Supreme Court reversed the Florida Supreme Court's decision for reasons discussed in Chapter 4.]

CASE DISCUSSION

Identify all the intrusions and deprivations against Bostick. What was their purpose? What facts did the officers have to justify these intrusions and deprivations? Did they need any? Why or why not? Why did the majority conclude that process was more important than result? Do you agree with the majority or the dissent in the case? Defend your answer.

DISCRETION AND
THE CRIMINAL PROCESS

The criminal process represents a balance between the formal rules embodied in the law of criminal procedure and informal discretionary decision making. The formal steps in criminal procedure outlined later on in the section describing the criminal process provide a framework within which formal rules function. But these formal steps allow wide latitude for informal decision making—discretion—to operate. The major steps in the criminal process are decision points. Each decision presents a criminal justice professional with the opportunity to decide whether or not to initiate, continue further, or terminate the criminal process. The police can investigate suspects or not, and arrest them or not, hence initiating the formal criminal process or stopping it. Prosecutors can charge suspects and continue the criminal process, divert suspects to some social service agency, or take no further action, effectively terminating the criminal process. Defendants can plead guilty (usually on their lawyers' advice) and avoid trial. Judges can suspend sentences or sentence convicted offenders to the maximum allowable penalty, hence either minimizing or maximizing the punishment the criminal law prescribes.

Formally, these decisions depend upon the law. Informally—that is, in daily practice—other influences determine whether the criminal process will continue or terminate. Less-visible **discretion,** the power to act without written rules, governs the informal side of criminal procedure. The public knows the informal side of criminal procedure mainly through criticisms of its agents: police who could have arrested a suspect but did not, or did arrest when they should not have; prosecutors who do not charge suspects or who participate in plea bargaining with them; and judges who release defendants on bail or impose "lenient" sentences. Some criticize discretion as "soft on crime"; others call it discriminatory law enforcement unfairly aimed at minorities.

Justice, fairness, efficiency, effectiveness, and economy all require both the certainty and the protection against abuses that written rules provide. The same goals also require discretion to soften the rigidity of written rules. The tension between formal law and informal discretion—a recurring theme in criminal procedure—is as old as law; arguments raged over it in Western civilization as early as the Middle Ages. The expense of full enforcement—maximum arrests, charges, sentences, and punishments—exceeds what the public will willingly pay.[23]

D e c i s i o n   P o i n t

The following incidents represent actions that the Chicago police took. Consider whether or not the officers should have made arrests.

1. A nineteen-year-old man standing in the street fired three shots at a woman standing in the doorway of her home, but missed. The police apprehended him and knew that neighbors witnessed the shooting, but they released him when the woman asked them to. The police explained that they do not ordinarily arrest when a victim is able to sign a complaint but does not do so.

2. More than a hundred officers at various levels were asked what they would do in the case discussed in Point 1, and about two-thirds said

they would release. One patrolman volunteered that he had witnessed an armed robbery but that he released the robber because the victim so requested.

3. Even when a police officer witnesses shoplifting, the uniform policy is to release the shoplifter if the merchant so requests.

4. Police often require a juvenile to make restitution for vandalism or a minor theft, but they usually release the juvenile when the owner is satisfied.

5. A police officer who finds a juvenile drinking something alcoholic is likely to pour out the beverage but is unlikely to take the juvenile into custody.

6. An ordinance makes it a crime to smoke in an elevator, but at least one citizen who has often ridden in an elevator in the police headquarters building with smokers and police has never witnessed a gesture toward enforcement.

7. A man who patronizes a prostitute is guilty of a crime under an Illinois statute, and he is also guilty under the more easily enforced ordinance regarding loitering for purposes of prostitution. Even when the evidence is clear and even when officers arrest the woman who is with the man, however, the officers never arrest the man unless he gives the officers a hard time. In most such cases, the police policy probably cannot be explained in terms of limited police resources.

8. Many officers say they never arrest for attempted bribery, even if witnesses see the attempt and are willing to testify. Some officers believe that a conviction is too improbable; others say the law is too harsh, given the expectations that citizens have developed on the basis of past police practices.

9. Patterns of systematically permitting parking in no-parking areas are common.

10. Almost all motorists know that the police are often lenient about some types of traffic violations.

11. The Chicago police found that jaywalking does not cause accidents and announced that nothing will be done to enforce the ordinance against jay-

walking, even though the ordinance remains on the books.

12. Spitting on the sidewalks is punishable by a fine of not less than $1 or more than $5, but officers unanimously say they do not enforce the ordinance.

13. Officers who find a couple having intercourse in a parked car generally do not arrest, even though the fornication statute has recently been re-enacted.

14. More than nine out of ten officers refuse to arrest for smoking marijuana in public, even though the possession of even a tiny quantity of marijuana is a crime. Supervising officers have generally asserted in interviews that the arrest should be made, but they generally acknowledge that they do not require their subordinates to comply with their views.

15. All patrol officers refrain from full enforcement of curfew laws, but the variations in nonarrest patterns from one officer to another are wide; some are fairly strict, and some are quite liberal.

16. Possession of unlabeled pills is a crime, but most officers say they do not arrest for a small number of such pills. Each officer follows her or his own idea of what the minimum should be for an arrest, with no guidance from superiors.

17. Even an individual caught in the act of burglary may be released by some officers if the burglar is an informer about narcotics dealers. The more usual reward to an informer is nonprosecution instead of nonarrest. No statute or ordinance authorizes special deals between police and informers, but such deals are a mainstay of enforcement of the narcotics laws.

Illinois law, Chicago ordinances, and police department rules formally require the police to arrest in all the above instances. Do you agree with the law? In which cases would you arrest? In which ones would you not arrest? What reasons can you give for not following the formal law, which requires arrest in all the cases?[24]

Police have several reasons for not arresting even when the law requires them to do so. One is economics. Budgets simply do not allow enough money to effect total enforcement; hence, the police must manage scarce resources wisely. Another reason for nonarrest is victims' preference. Mainly in misdemeanors, although to a considerable extent in felonies as well, police do not arrest if victims oppose arrest. Police are also less likely to arrest if the victim and suspect are related. Moreover, officers, or their departments, set priorities that informally rank offenses for arrest or discretionary disposition.

Sometimes, legislatures did not intend to cover conduct that technically violates a criminal statute. It is impossible for legislators to foresee all the ramifications of the statutes they enact. For example, it is a misdemeanor to drink in public parks in many cities. In Minneapolis, a gourmet group had a brunch in a city park because they thought the park provided the proper ambience in which to enjoy to the fullest their salmon mousse and imported French white wine. Not only did the police not arrest the group for drinking in the park, but the brunch also received press coverage as a social event of the highest respectability.

A public defender felt some consternation over the nonarrest. He pointed out that the police arrested, and the prosecutor was prepared to prosecute, a Native American caught washing down a tuna fish sandwich with cheap red wine in another Minneapolis park. The public defender—a bit of a wag—noted that both the gourmet club and the Native American were consuming items from the same food groups. These incidents display both the strengths and weaknesses of discretion. The legislature obviously did not intend the statute to cover drinking of the type in which the gourmet club engaged. Arresting them would have been foolish and contrary to the legislature's intent. On the other hand, arresting and prosecuting the Native American might well have been discriminatory, a wholly unintended and unacceptable result of law enforcement that is discretionary and selective.

Similar reasons of efficiency, fairness, legislative intent, and tempering of the rigidity of the law with the flexibility of discretion, as well as less acceptable and sometimes offensive motivations, affect the exercise of discretion that underlies prosecutors' decisions to charge, defense attorneys' advice to their clients to plead guilty, and judges' decisions in sentencing. The law does not require that laws be inflexibly enforced against everybody in exactly the same way. It does prohibit differential treatment based on unacceptable criteria, such as race, gender, social status, religion, and age. Differences based on acceptable criteria constitute justified disparities; differences based on unacceptable criteria constitute illegal discrimination. Hence, it is proper not to prosecute three white suburban youths caught throwing eggs at cars, because they have never been in trouble with the law before, apologized for what they did, and cleaned up the cars they hit with the eggs. It is illegal, discriminatory law enforcement to prosecute three urban African-American youths to "teach them a lesson" for insulting whites.

The implementation of United States Supreme Court decisions on the local level provides an excellent example of how informal discretion shapes formal decisions in criminal procedure. The Supreme Court's criminal procedure decisions are closely followed and receive wide publicity. However, rules pronounced from the highest court in the land do not automatically translate into conduct at the state and local levels. In other words, the Supreme Court's standards are not necessarily equivalent to actual practice. The extent to which those standards are turned into daily practice in state courts, local prosecutors' offices, and police departments is extremely limited.

The restrictions on the Supreme Court's power to supervise criminal justice administration and to infuse local behavior with constitutional norms stem from several sources. The Supreme Court—or any court, for that matter—does not enjoy the kind of power over practice that criminal justice administrators possess. The Court can review procedures only when defendants complain formally and then fight their cases through the prosecutors' offices, lower courts, state appellate courts, and finally up through the federal courts to the United States Supreme Court. Therefore, the cases that ultimately reach the Court are not representative of most, or even the most important, problems facing local agencies of criminal justice. Hence, the Court is left to issue decrees concerning defendants in only a very few, selected cases. In short, courts cannot initiate action; they can only decide cases that the government brings before them.

Virtually all cases that reach the Supreme Court are search-and-seizure cases and other cases that involve obtaining evidence. Defendants hope to avoid conviction owing to some illegal police action. Some of them, if they have the means to do so, pursue their objections all the way to the Supreme Court. Other cases never come to judicial attention at any level. For example, the station house indignities associated with booking and "mugging" suspects—taking their belts and shoelaces, and so on—practically never come to judicial attention because these actions do not result in seizing evidence that later becomes a search-and-seizure issue. Most people who believe that police mistreat them are "marginal types" who are happy enough to leave well enough alone once they are released from custody. Hence, most criminal suspects never bring their complaints to judicial attention for judicial supervision. This selection process badly skews the representation of cases.

In cases in which the Supreme Court establishes a constitutional standard, the decision must filter down through lower courts, magistrates, and police officials before it finally reaches suspects and defendants. By that time, informal practice has altered the formal rule announced by the Court. Discretion allows the democratic interest in local values, the organizational interest in distributing scarce resources, and personalities and prejudices to modify—sometimes dramatically—the rules in practice from the rules in Supreme Court opinions.

For example, police almost always measure their success by arrest clearances, not by convictions. Whether or not evidence will be legally admitted in court, or if so will convict defendants, is not of primary importance to most police. Of greater weight is whether they clear the case from their books, either by dropping the case or by having the prosecutor take it over. The police will exercise their discretion to arrest in line with these clearance requirements. According to Professor Anthony Amsterdam,

Police work is hard work; it is righteous work; it is combative work, and competitive. Policemen [and policewomen] are undereducated, they are scandalously underpaid, and their personal advancement lies in producing results according to the standards of the police ethic. When they go to the commander's office or to

court, their conformity to this ethic is almost always vindicated. Neither their superiors nor the judges whom they know nor the public find it necessary to impede
the performance of their duties with fettering rules respecting rights of suspects.
If the Supreme Court finds this necessary, it must be that the Court is out of step.
So its decisions—which are difficult to understand anyway—cannot really be
taken seriously.[25]

Similarly, prosecutors, judges, and defense attorneys are committed to the harmonious relationships within their courtroom work group, and that commitment affects
the way they fulfill their constitutional responsibilities. Supreme Court rulings about
defense attorneys' vigorous defense of their clients' interests, prosecutors' duty to do justice, and the speedy trial requirements imposed on the whole adjudicatory phase of the
criminal process are all tempered by the courtroom work group's values and relationships. Discretion permits prosecutors' decisions to charge, defense attorneys' advice to
their clients to plead guilty, and judges' accessions to plea bargains to conform to these
work group values.

The courtroom work group may emphasize getting along with one another and furthering individual ambitions more than doing justice and enabling the adversary system
to function. Negotiation, harmony, and accommodation conflict with, and often take
precedence over, the conflict, competition, and rivalry that formal adjudication specifies. The following description of a Chicago courtroom is typical of many work group
relationships in criminal courts:

> In many courtrooms daily sessions were frequently preceded (as well as followed)
> by "coffee klatches" held in the judge's chambers. The coffee klatches were usu-
> ally attended by the judge, public defender, the two assistant attorneys and a
> handful of private defense attorneys, who may or may not have had a case in that
> courtroom on the day in question. Conversations ranged from the fate of the
> Blackhawks or the Bulls the night before, the potential impact of some changes
> in criminal law or procedure, the cases scheduled for that day, to what happened
> in the annual football game between the state's attorney's office and the public
> defender's office. . . . In short, these sessions were not unlike those that might take
> place in any office or shop.[26]

In the final analysis, the formal constitutional rules of criminal procedure are modified, tempered, and ultimately translated into actual practice in the criminal process by
informal goals that must be reconciled with formal goals. The informal goals of getting
along with others in the work group, desires for career advancement, satisfying community pressures, and working within the constraints imposed by limited budgets com-
pete with the formal goals of controlling crime and ensuring due process. Discretion
allows these informal goals to shape decision making throughout the criminal process.

The Supreme Court's decisions—and all formal rules—filter through these discretionary informal influences. Discretion in the filtering modifies, and ultimately dilutes,
the rules. Hence, the criminal process in practice is an amalgam of the formal law of
criminal procedure and informal influences that enter the process by way of discretion.
Discretion and law complement each other in promoting and balancing the interests in
criminal procedure.

LAW, SOCIETY, AND IDEOLOGY

Perhaps the most controversial aspect of criminal procedure is the degree to which both its formal and informal aspects promote broad social and ideological interests. The determination of innocence or guilt in individual cases often gets subordinated to these interests. During the 1960s, the Warren Court emphasized such "liberal" societal interests as racial justice, equal treatment under the law, the control of government power, and the rights of individuals against the state. In the 1970s and 1980s, under the Burger and Rehnquist Courts, the Supreme Court has emphasized such "conservative" societal interests as the rights of victims, control of crime, and support for law enforcement.

Some support the role of criminal process in promoting the Warren Court's social agenda for instrumentalist reasons: a humane, dignified, nondiscriminatory, compassionate system of criminal justice builds public confidence and support for criminal law enforcement. Others argue that the integrity of the criminal process itself requires commitment to these broad social interests. Decisions ought to demonstrate commitment to the American values of equality, impartiality, and humaneness for their own sake because they are right and because they transcend the narrow interest of punishing criminals. Supporters of the social agenda of the Burger and Rehnquist Courts point to the serious crime problem across the nation, the value of "sending a message to criminals," and the need both to respond to victims and to support law enforcement officers upon whom crime control depends. Whether the social interests that are promoted emphasize crime control and victims' rights or the control of government and defendants' rights, they subordinate guilt or innocence in individual cases. An emphasis on the former allows some guilty individuals to go free to serve the larger social interest of limited government; an emphasis on the latter catches up some innocent persons in order to serve the larger social interest of supporting law enforcement.[27]

The criminal process also promotes the public interest in democracy by enlisting community participation in law enforcement. Determining law enforcement policies—community influence on priorities in police arrest, prosecution charging, and judicial sentencing—is one dimension of community participation. Citizens participate most actively in the criminal process by serving on grand and petty juries. Grand juries screen cases prior to trial; trial juries can acquit, even if their acquittals fly in the face of the law. Not even the Supreme Court can reverse not guilty verdicts; they stand final against all attack (see Chapter 11).

FEDERAL, STATE, AND LOCAL GOVERNMENTS

Federalism is a powerful political doctrine in the United States. According to federalist doctrine,

> the United States is a unique kind of republic composed of individual states and a single, overarching national government. Although the states are "constituent parts" of the United States, they are not in any essential way subordinate to the national government. Rather, the state and national governments together comprise a system of dual sovereignty in which each government is deemed to be an independent

sovereign, but in distinct spheres of action. Madison, for example, conceived that the national government would have primary responsibility for "external objects, as war, peace, negotiation, and foreign commerce"; the states, on the other hand would exercise sovereignty principally over, "the lives, liberties, and properties of the people."[28]

Criminal law and criminal procedure have traditionally been regarded as the "quintessential" local problem. Therefore, most criminal law enforcement has historically taken place at state and local levels. However, federal law enforcement is rapidly growing, mainly due to demands for a greater criminal justice response to drugs and violence. (Ironically, the greatest demands for an enhanced federal role in law enforcement comes from conservatives whose "quintessential" philosophical position is less government, and especially less federal government.) The principal criminal justice agencies are as follows:

- Police departments
- Prosecutors' offices
- **Lower criminal courts,** or courts of limited jurisdiction — alternatively called municipal, justice of the peace, or magistrate's courts — where most pretrial proceedings take place
- **Trial courts** — sometimes called superior or district courts — where criminal trials take place
- Probation departments, often associated with trial courts
- Jails
- Appellate courts that hear criminal appeals and collateral attacks from criminal trial proceedings
- Prisons
- Parole departments

Police departments are city and town agencies; trial courts and jails are district and county institutions; and appellate courts, prisons, and parole departments are statewide agencies. Local agencies employ more than three-fifths of all justice personnel, most of them police.[29]

The federal criminal justice system resembles the state and local systems (see Figure 1.1). The federal police agencies include the Federal Bureau of Investigation (FBI), the Drug Enforcement Agency (DEA), and others. Every region in the country has federal prosecutors — United States attorneys and their assistants. Federal magistrates issue warrants and conduct pretrial court proceedings. The United States district courts try cases and hear challenges to local and state jurisdictions, such as *habeas corpus* petitions. The courts of appeals, which constitute the intermediate federal court of appeals, hear appeals both from federal district courts and often from state courts involving constitutional questions. The United States Supreme Court, the court of last resort in the nation, finally resolves constitutional questions; no appeals remain from its interpretations. The United States is divided into thirteen circuits, with one court of appeals for each circuit, and each circuit is divided into several districts (see Figure 1.2).

District of Columbia Circuit
District of Columbia
First Circuit
Maine, Massachusetts, New Hampshire, Puerto Rico, Rhode Island
Second Circuit
Connecticut, Eastern District New York, Southern District New York, Western District New York, Vermont
Third Circuit
Delaware, New Jersey, Eastern District Pennsylvania, Middle District Pennsylvania, Western District Pennsylvania, Virgin Islands
Fourth Circuit
Maryland, Eastern District North Carolina, Middle District North Carolina, Western District North Carolina, South Carolina, Eastern District Virginia, Western District Virginia, Southern District West Virginia
Fifth Circuit
Eastern District Louisiana, Middle District Louisiana, Western District Louisiana, Northern District Mississippi, Southern District Mississippi, Eastern District Texas, Northern District Texas, Southern District Texas, Western District Texas
Sixth Circuit
Eastern District Kentucky, Western District Kentucky, Eastern District Michigan, Western District Michigan, Northern District Ohio, Southern District Ohio, Eastern District Tennessee, Middle District Tennessee, Western District Tennessee
Seventh Circuit
Central District Illinois, Northern District Illinois, Southern District Illinois, Northern District Indiana, Southern District Indiana, Eastern District Wisconsin, Western District Wisconsin
Eighth Circuit
Eastern District Arkansas, Western District Arkansas, Northern District Iowa, Southern District Iowa, Minnesota, Eastern District Missouri, Western District Missouri, Nebraska, North Dakota, South Dakota
Ninth Circuit
Alaska, Arizona, Central District California, Eastern District California, Northern District California, Southern District California, Guam, Hawaii, Idaho, Montana, Nevada, Oregon, Eastern District Washington, Western District Washington
Tenth Circuit
Colorado, Kansas, Eastern District Oklahoma, Western District Oklahoma, Utah, Wyoming
Eleventh Circuit
Middle District Alabama, Northern District Alabama, Southern District Alabama, Middle District Florida, Northern District Florida, Southern District Florida, Middle District Georgia, Northern District Georgia, Southern District Georgia
Federal Circuit
Washington, D.C.

FIGURE 1.2 FEDERAL CIRCUITS AND DISTRICTS

SEPARATION OF POWERS

Criminal procedure must operate according to the principles of federalism and the separation of powers. Federalism allocates power among three levels of government—federal, state, and local. The **separation of powers** requires that only legislatures make the laws, that only the executive enforce the laws, and that only the courts interpret the laws (see Chapter 2).[30]

As we have seen, criminal justice is of central concern in the United States, and has been throughout the twentieth century. The crisis of freedom created by the rise of totalitarian regimes during the 1930s, the renewed concern over inequality and inequity during the 1960s, and the fear of crime and drugs since the 1960s have all played their part in the concern over criminal justice. It is not surprising that the government reflects this concern. What is surprising is that the courts—particularly the United States Supreme Court—have played the predominant role in regulating and supervising criminal justice since the 1960s (see Chapter 2).

Judicial predominance is not the norm in most other countries, nor is it the ideal mechanism to control criminal justice in the United States. First, courts can decide only the cases that the prosecution decides to initiate and either the prosecution or defendants appeal. Therefore, the judiciary cannot orchestrate a planned and systematic supervision and regulation of criminal justice. Second, the judiciary has limited means to affect the day-to-day behavior of police, prosecutors, and court and corrections officers. According to the distinguished professor of criminal law Francis Allen,

> How can a court, however exalted, that stands at the apex of a complex judicial structure exercise its powers so as to achieve a genuine impact on the day-to-day behavior of police, prosecutory, judicial, and corrections officials throughout a nation of two hundred million inhabitants?[31]

THE CRIMINAL PROCESS

Criminal cases follow a chronological path through the criminal justice system. They begin with the lesser deprivations and intrusions during early encounters on the street between police and individuals and end in proceedings following conviction. Of course, many cases terminate prior to the last step on the path. Chapters 4 through 9, and 11 through 13 analyze in detail these steps along this path and the reasons that some cases terminate prior to the end of the path. The brief outline in this section is an overview designed to capture the sense of process that the detailed analyses in the remaining chapters may impede.

The principal steps through the criminal justice system include the following (see Figure 1.3):

1. Detection and investigation, largely a police responsibility
2. Charging and prosecuting, the duty of prosecutors
3. Adjudication, presided over by judges, with prosecutors and defense attorneys participating
4. Sentencing, the responsibility of trial court judges
5. Appeal and collateral attack, an appellate court function
6. Punishment, an administrative duty of corrections administrators and officers, with supervisory powers in the judiciary

These stages vary from state to state between states and the federal government, and sometimes between districts in the same state. In addition, the procedure differs for **felony** cases (serious crimes with penalties usually of more than one year in prison) and

A GENERAL VIEW OF THE CRIMINAL JUSTICE SYSTEM

This chart seeks to present a simple yet comprehensive view of the movement of cases through the criminal justice system. Procedures in individual jurisdictions may vary from the pattern shown here. The differing weights of the line indicate the relative volumes of cases disposed of at various points in the system, but this is only suggestive since no nationwide data of this sort exists.

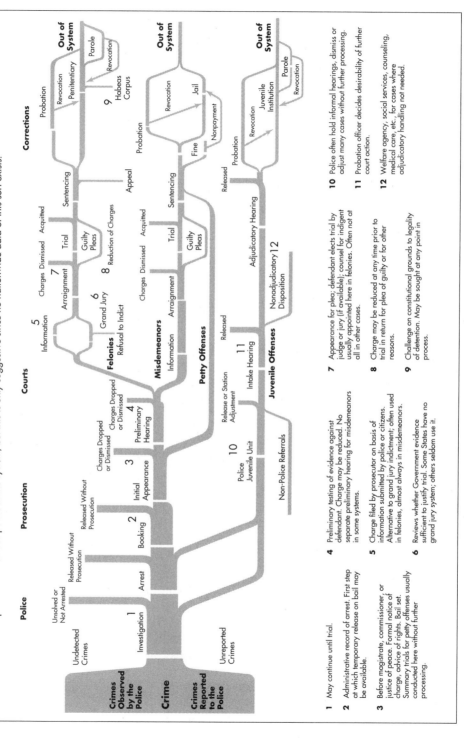

1 May continue until trial.

2 Administrative record of arrest. First step at which temporary release on bail may be available.

3 Before magistrate, commissioner, or justice of peace. Formal notice of charge, advice of rights. Bail set. Summary trials for petty offenses usually conducted here without further processing.

4 Preliminary testing of evidence against defendant. Charge may be reduced. No separate preliminary hearing for misdemeanors in some systems.

5 Charge filed by prosecutor on basis of information submitted by police or citizens. Alternative to grand jury indictment; often used in felonies, almost always in misdemeanors.

6 Reviews whether Government evidence sufficient to justify trial. Some States have no grand jury system; others seldom use it.

7 Appearance for plea; defendant elects trial by judge or jury (if available); counsel for indigent usually appointed in felonies. Often not at all in other cases.

8 Charge may be reduced at any time prior to trial in return for plea of guilty or for other reasons.

9 Challenge on constitutional grounds to legality of detention. May be sought at any point in process.

10 Police often hold informal hearings, dismiss or adjust many cases without further processing.

11 Probation officer decides desirability of further court action.

12 Welfare agency, social services, counseling, medical care, etc., for cases where adjudicatory handling not needed.

FIGURE 1.3 A GENERAL VIEW OF THE CRIMINAL JUSTICE SYSTEM

misdemeanor cases (less serious crimes with penalties of fines and less than one year in prison). Trial courts hear felony cases, for which the procedures are usually more elaborate and the punishment more severe. Lower criminal courts hear misdemeanors, for which the proceedings are less formal and the penalties lighter. Least formal of all, the justice of the peace courts are not courts of formal record. Sometimes, procedural differences depend solely upon whether offenders can be sentenced to prison or jail. Finally, informal practice does not always conform to formal rule. You must modify the following steps in the criminal process according to the rules and practice of your own and other specific jurisdictions.[32]

Detection and Investigation

Private individuals and police officers control the detection and investigative stage of the criminal process. Crimes come to official attention—and therefore criminal cases enter the criminal justice system—only if either police officers discover them or private individuals report them. The police discover some crimes on their own, either by witnessing them in progress or by questioning people who are behaving in suspicious ways under suspicious circumstances. However, most crimes come to official attention because private individuals report them to the police. Hence, the investigation process begins, in the vast majority of instances, when the police respond to the calls of private individuals. If it appears to the police that a crime has occurred, they file a report, and the crime becomes officially an offense "known to the police."[33]

Investigation can begin either before the police have a specific suspect in mind or after someone has identified an alleged offender. In the former case, investigation begins with the search for information about whether a crime was committed and who might have committed it. When the investigation focuses on a specific suspect, the process enters the **accusatory stage.** During the accusatory stage, the police collect information against the specific suspect.

Where officers observe a crime in progress, the investigation consists of gathering and securing the information that they and others directly observed at the scene and the physical evidence left there. The police arrest the suspect immediately, and the accusatory stage begins. Quite different is investigation prior to arrest, where the police do not witness crimes, as when they either observe merely suspicious behavior or learn of citizens' reports of crimes. In these cases, the police attempt to collect more information. They question suspicious people, commonly asking, "Do you have identification?" or "Why are you here?"; they interview possible witnesses; and they examine the crime scene for possible physical evidence (see Chapter 4).

The police rarely use other techniques for gathering information, although less obvious methods may prove important in some cases. For example, electronic surveillance occurs in a tiny proportion of cases; courts authorized it in only 1,154 cases nationwide in 1994, the latest figures available. Occasionally, police "sweep" high-crime areas, a highly visible investigative tactic. One dramatic example followed the shooting of a four-year-old boy hit in a spray of automatic rifle fire during a gang shoot-out in Los Angeles. Police Chief Daryl Gates "vowed to make 'war' on 'rotten little cowards' who shoot down little children." He dispatched one thousand officers into "gang-ridden" neighborhoods to investigate and apprehend the shooters and prevent further gang violence (see Chapter 4).[34]

Arrest. Once the police believe, based on information, that a crime was committed and that a specific suspect committed it, they can arrest the suspect. Sometimes, police arrest pursuant to warrants that magistrates approve in advance of the arrest. However, most arrests take place on officers' own initiative without prior judicial approval (see Chapter 5).

Crimes that officers observe firsthand lead to arrests more often than those that come to police attention either through police observing mere suspicious behavior or citizens reporting crimes. Most arrests involve public drunkenness, other disorderly conduct misdemeanors, and property offenses. Less than 10 percent are for serious felonies: 2 percent are for aggravated assault and robbery; less than 0.005 percent are for forcible rape and murder; and the remainder are spread among arson, nonviolent sex offenses, possession of weapons, and others. Between one-fifth and one-third of arrested persons are juveniles. Most go no further in the adult criminal process; instead, they enter the juvenile justice system.

Searches. Most searches immediately follow arrest, but searches can occur prior to arrest in some instances. They also accompany detention before, and incarceration after, conviction. The Constitution allows, under restrictions discussed in Chapter 6, a range of searches including pat-downs; body, strip, and body cavity searches; X-rays, extractions of bodily fluids, and surgical removal of evidence; and searches of papers, houses, and personal effects.

Booking. Shortly following arrest and the search incident to it, the police take suspects to the police station, the jail, or some other short-term holding facility. Here, the police usher suspects through the step in the criminal process called booking. An officer records in the police log or blotter the suspects' names, the time of their arrival at the facility, and the offenses for which they were arrested. Next, suspects are fingerprinted and photographed, told what they were booked for, and given permission to make a phone call.

If arrested for a minor offense, suspects might obtain immediate release on station house bail—either a small case security or a promise to appear before a magistrate at an appointed time. If subjects were arrested for a serious crime or are unable to post adequate security for a minor offense arrest, they are put in a lockup until they appear before a magistrate. Before entering the lockup, suspects undergo a more extensive search than the search incident to the arrest. This is called an inventory search, and it includes a full body search and occasionally a strip and body cavity search. The inventory search is conducted so that police can list suspects' personal belongings and take any contraband, weapons, and evidence not found at the time of the arrest (see Chapter 6).

Follow-up Investigation. After booking, a special police investigative unit, the detective unit, investigates many cases that patrol officers initially investigated. If patrol officers caught suspects red-handed, detectives may not follow up. Most follow-up investigation uses the basic techniques that patrol officers use: interviewing witnesses, including victims and suspects; searching suspects' homes; and examining crime scenes. Follow-up also includes tactics not available to arresting officers. Detectives conduct lineups or "show-ups" where witnesses identify suspects. The detectives may arrange for handwriting samples, take hair samples, and interrogate suspects. Police rarely use these intrusive techniques for misdemeanors, reserving them instead for serious felonies (see Chapters 7 and 8).[35]

The police department reviews the results of most police investigations. If the review discloses insufficient evidence to forward a case for further processing, the department closes the case. If the review leads to the conclusion that investigators have gathered sufficient evidence to take the criminal process another step, the department will transfer the case to the prosecutor's office. Police may also make alternative dispositions if they believe a noncriminal justice response is more appropriate. For example, most police departments do not process fights among acquaintances further; they "settle" the disputes within the police department by means of a warning, counseling, or a referral to social service agencies. Recently, at least in domestic assault cases, arrest and referral to prosecutors have replaced "settling" in a growing number of departments.[36]

Prosecution

If the police decide to take cases to prosecutors, they do so shortly after booking. At that point, the criminal process enters the stage called prosecution, or the initiation of formal judicial proceedings against suspects. The major responsibility for the judicial part of the criminal process lies with the lawyers in the criminal justice system — the prosecutors, defense counsel, and judges. The police transfer the results of their investigation — including incident reports written by patrol officers at the time of arrest, rap sheets, and other materials gathered by detectives — to the prosecutors.

Prosecutors review the case. In an initial screening, they decide whether to charge suspects with any crime at all and, if so, what crime; to dismiss cases outright; or to "divert" cases to some noncriminal justice agency, such as drug and alcohol treatment, family counseling, or juvenile court. In some jurisdictions, prosecutors review cases thoroughly before they charge suspects; in other jurisdictions, they do so superficially. Some prosecutors only glance at the police reports before charging; others review the written record extensively, as well as interview police officers and victims. Local practice varies, but, in general, prosecutors reject between 30 and 60 percent of all felony arrests in the initial screening. Most decisions to prosecute, divert, or dismiss depend on the facts of the case. To charge, prosecutors need more than probable cause to detain, but not proof beyond a reasonable doubt. In practice, however, most prosecutors do not charge unless they believe they can convict, which requires proof beyond a reasonable doubt.[37]

If prosecutors decide to charge suspects, they file the **complaint** (the charging document) in a magistrate's court. At the point where charges are filed, suspects officially become defendants (legally innocent citizens formally charged with crimes). In misdemeanor cases, the complaint serves as the only charging document; it is used throughout the criminal proceedings to the final disposition in the case. In felony cases, the complaint is only the first charging document. If the criminal process continues, informations or indictments eventually replace complaints after further review by judges, grand juries, or both.

Adjudication

Following the decision to charge, the criminal process enters the stage that requires judicial and defense counsels' participation. **Adjudication** means formal proceedings in court. As soon as prosecutors file charges, every step in the formal process of criminal justice demands judicial approval. Adjudication includes all the steps from defendants' first appearance in court through final disposition by guilty plea, jury verdict, appeal, or collateral attack.

First Appearance. At the **first appearance,** which takes only a few minutes, magistrates determine whether there is probable cause to detain suspects in custody without warrants. Most states require that officials holding defendants in custody bring them before magistrates without unnecessary delay—usually within hours, but sometimes within a longer period if they were taken into custody at night or on weekends. For defendants not in custody, several days or weeks may lapse between charge and first appearance (see Chapter 9).[38]

Magistrates perform several other functions at first appearances. They, or their clerks, read the charges against defendants and advise defendants of their rights to remain silent, to have an attorney, and to be assigned counsel if they cannot afford to hire one. Magistrates also determine if defendants are too poor to hire their own lawyers, and appoint counsel for these indigent defendants. They inform felony defendants that the next step in the process will be either the preliminary hearing or the grand jury review and set dates for preliminary hearings. In misdemeanor cases, where defendants do not have a right to a preliminary hearing, magistrates explain available pleas and ask defendants to plead. Most defendants—about 90 percent—eventually plead guilty.

Finally, magistrates set bail. If defendants have already posted station house bail, magistrates review that decision. They make initial bail decisions for felony defendants, most of whom remain in custody from arrest to first appearance. Magistrates then set the conditions under which defendants can obtain their release from custody. Sometimes, the condition is a mere promise to appear (release on recognizance, or ROR); sometimes, it is a money bond; occasionally, it restricts movement and associations and requires released persons to report their whereabouts periodically.[39]

Testing the Government's Case. The law requires prosecutors to test their decision to charge before the government can require defendants to answer criminal charges. Prosecutors, on behalf of the government, must satisfy a disinterested third party that they have probable cause to proceed to trial. Do not confuse the preliminary hearing with the first appearance. The first appearance determines probable cause to detain suspects without warrants following arrest; the **preliminary hearing** determines probable cause to try defendants. The probable cause at this point is more than that required to detain but considerably short of the proof beyond a reasonable doubt required for conviction. Two major mechanisms test the probable cause needed to require defendants to answer criminal charges:

1. Grand jury review
2. Preliminary hearing

If the government satisfies the grand jury, it issues the formal charging instrument, the **indictment.** If the government satisfies the judge presiding at the preliminary hearing, the judge issues an order to bind the defendant over for trial. Both actions require defendants to answer the criminal charges against them; until this point, they need not answer. *Answer* in this case does not mean that defendants must speak out of their own mouths; this would violate the right against self-incrimination (see Chapter 8). To answer here means to plead to the charges.

Preliminary hearings test the government's case in a public adversary forum. They follow the first appearance, usually within a few weeks. Prosecutors dispose of many cases by plea bargaining before the scheduled preliminary hearing. In thirty states, defendants have a right to preliminary hearings. In states where grand juries have the power to indict, the preliminary hearing status varies. In most of these jurisdictions, prosecutors can bypass the preliminary hearing and take cases directly to the grand jury. Several jurisdictions require grand jury indictment in capital cases or cases punishable by life imprisonment (see Chapter 11).

Preliminary hearings permit neutral magistrates to screen prosecutors' decisions to charge in order to avoid when possible, or justify if necessary, further intrusions against defendants and expenditures of government resources. Preliminary hearings test the government's case in an adversary setting. They are public proceedings; some call them minitrials. Prosecutors present a part of their case against defendants; defense attorneys sometimes cross-examine witnesses. Magistrates dismiss charges lacking probable cause in felony cases, usually permitting prosecutors to substitute misdemeanor charges. If magistrates find probable cause, they **bind over** defendants; that is, they send the case forward for trial.[40]

Grand jury review is the alternative to testing the government's case by preliminary hearing. About half the states require grand jury review, a secret proceeding to determine probable cause to go to trial. Grand juries indict, or formally charge, defendants for at least some felonies. The grand jury ranges from about nine to twenty-three members, depending on the jurisdiction. A unanimous decision is not necessary; a majority of the grand jury can indict.

If a majority of the grand jury agrees that the prosecution has the required quantum of proof, it issues the indictment. Indictments list the offense and approve the prosecutor's charge by marking it with the ancient notation **true bill.** If the grand jury rejects the prosecutor's case, charges are dismissed. Grand jury rejections are rare; they occur in only about 3 to 8 percent of the cases. Most prosecutors avoid presenting cases to grand juries unless they believe they have sufficient evidence to convict. Former United States attorney general Elliot Richardson said that as a prosecutor he never asked for an indictment unless he believed he had proof beyond a reasonable doubt to convict the defendant. Hence, the standard in practice is much higher than the legal requirement for a *prima facie* case—enough evidence to convict, if the evidence the defense presents does not later rebut it.[41]

Filing the Indictment or Information. When prosecutors file indictments in the trial courts after the grand jury issues them, indictments replace complaints as the principal charging documents. In jurisdictions not requiring grand jury review, prosecutors file a document called the **information,** a substitute for the grand jury indictment. Although grand juries do not screen informations, preliminary hearing bind-overs must support them.

Arraignment. Once the government has passed the evidentiary test, and assuming that prosecutors file the indictments or informations, courts arraign defendants. **Arraignment** means the process of bringing defendants before trial courts, informing them of the specific charges against them, and requiring them to plead to, or answer, those charges. They can plead guilty, not guilty, or **nolo contendere** ("no contest"), which means they do not admit guilt but agree not to fight the case. *Nolo contendere* allows defendants in civil actions arising out of the criminal case to defend the civil actions more effectively. If a victim sues the defendant, for example, the guilty plea acts as an admission of facts against the defendant; the *nolo contendere* plea requires the victim to prove the facts in the civil action. The court enters pleas of not guilty for defendants who refuse to plead. Up to 90 percent of all felony defendants plead guilty, either because they have already negotiated a plea with the government in return for reduced charges or lesser sentences, or because they believe the case against them is so strong that it is futile to contest it.[42]

Pretrial Motions. After arraignment but before trial, both prosecutors and defense counsel file motions asking the court to act on a range of questions. Most motions either challenge the court's jurisdiction—that is, its authority to hear the case—or request discovery—that is, order the government and defendants to reveal information in their possession to the other side. Motions to suppress illegally seized physical evidence and coerced confessions generate the most litigation; less frequently, defendants claim double jeopardy and speedy-trial violations. Despite the wide publicity given to excluding evidence and attempts to "get off on technicalities," defendants file pretrial motions in fewer than 10 percent of all cases.

Trial

The trial is the high point of the formal criminal process, even though trials dispose of only about 2 percent of all criminal cases. Most trials are brief affairs; misdemeanor trials frequently consume less than a day. Although some felony cases take longer, most are decided in only a few days. Complicated cases might last three weeks or longer. Such cases attract public attention, but they are rare.

Defendants have the right to a jury in all felony cases and in misdemeanors punishable by more than six months' incarceration. Juries traditionally had twelve members, but the size of juries is decreasing; some jurisdictions now require only six jurors. Although defendants can waive jury trial, most do not. In nearly all cases, jury verdicts, either for acquittal or for conviction, must be unanimous.

The basic ingredients in criminal trials are as follows:

1. Presumption of innocence, which means that defendants are deemed innocent until the government proves them guilty
2. Burden on the government to prove guilt beyond a reasonable doubt
3. Right of defendants not to help the government make its case
4. Presentation of evidence
5. Oral arguments
6. Opening and closing statements
7. Instructions to the jury
8. Jury deliberations
9. Verdicts

Most trials end in conviction (as many as 90 percent in some jurisdictions), probably because prosecutors go to trial only when they believe they can secure convictions. Rape and robbery cases are exceptions.[43]

Sentencing

Following guilty verdicts or guilty pleas, judges enter a judgment of conviction and schedule a time for sentencing convicted defendants, now officially offenders. Statutes prescribe sentences, but, to varying degrees, judges have discretion (the power to decide) to set alternative sentences. In misdemeanor cases, judges can choose among probation, suspended sentences, fines, and short jail terms. In felonies, judges have less discretion, particularly under recent statutes that prescribe mandatory sentences and narrow the maximum and minimum limits.

Review Proceedings

Two review proceedings can follow sentencing:

1. Appeal

2. Collateral attack

Appeals directly attack the conviction and must always follow it. Convicted offenders have no constitutional right to appeal, but every jurisdiction provides for automatic appeals in most cases. State felony appeals go to an intermediate appeals court first, if one exists, then to the state supreme court, and if a federal constitutional question arises, ultimately to the United States Supreme Court. In states without intermediate appeals courts, felony appeals go directly to supreme courts. Although all criminal cases can be appealed, in practice most appeals are limited to cases in which defendants have been sentenced to prison.

The American Bar Association Project on Standards for Criminal Justice, produced by some of the nation's leading authorities on criminal procedure, provides the following standard for appellate review:

> § 5.3 Appellate court disposition; scope of appellate review. (a) Appellate courts should exercise a broad scope of a review on matters of fact and law consistent with the fundamental rights subject to litigation in post conviction proceedings.
> (b) A statement of the basis or bases for decision in a reasoned opinion ought to accompany dispositions of appeals.[44]

Most courts comply with subsection (b). Appellate court opinions form the basis of much legal thinking and decision making, as well as instructional materials for law students, students of constitutional law, and students of criminal justice.

The government can appeal adverse rulings in criminal cases only when statutes authorize such appeals and the Constitution does not bar it. Perhaps the most important constitutional limitation on state appeals is the Fifth Amendment bar to double jeopardy. For example, the double jeopardy clause prohibits the state from appealing an acquittal. The clause does not bar appeals of guilty verdicts because reversal would result simply in reinstating the guilty verdict. Prosecutors may also appeal sentences without violating the double jeopardy clause.

Contrary to popular belief, most appeals do not result in reversal and freedom for defendants. Particularly in serious crimes where the evidence clearly indicates guilt, appellate courts rarely reverse. Most reversals occur in misdemeanors, in less serious felonies, or in cases where doubts exist about the proof of guilt. Although they make sensational journalism, clearly guilty violent criminals rarely go free in the real world. In fact, one researcher who studied a major appellate court in the San Francisco area concluded that the problem is at the other end—that courts do not afford enough protection to defendants in criminal cases.[45]

Collateral attack, or *habeas corpus*-type proceedings, differ from direct appeals. They are civil proceedings, distinct from the criminal case. The question in these separate proceedings is not guilt or errors in determining guilt. Collateral attack challenges the lawfulness of detention, either prior to or after conviction. Therefore, collateral attack need not await conviction; its basis is either detention in jail prior to conviction or imprisonment following conviction. All states have special collateral review proceedings. In addition, convicted defendants can challenge state or federal detention in federal courts through *habeas corpus*. Unlike appeals that can challenge any error in the trial proceedings, collateral attack can challenge only detention or imprisonment on constitutional grounds (see Chapter 13).

SUMMARY

The fundamental feature of the law of criminal procedure in our constitutional democracy is balance—between society and individual; between ends and means; among law, society, and ideology; among federal, state, and local governments; among executive, legislative, and judicial branches of government; between formal rules and informal discretionary decision making. The history of criminal procedure demonstrates a tension between ends and means. The search for truth or the correct result—apprehending, convicting, and punishing the guilty and freeing and vindicating the innocent—is the end. The interest in means emphasizes the process by which the government enforces the criminal law. Process interests include protecting the rights of the individual, timeliness, and finality—due process of law. The importance of procedural regularity in order to ensure the privacy, liberty, and property of persons demonstrates the central place of the individual and the value placed on individual dignity and autonomy in our society. It is difficult to stress too much the importance of facts in satisfying the requirement of procedural regularity.

The whole law of criminal procedure rests on the notion that an objective basis—that is, enough facts—backs up the actions of public officials. The law of criminal procedure also promotes the balancing of other interests, including the structural interests in separation of powers and checks and balances; the societal interests in fairness, equality, and human dignity; the organizational interests in economy, efficiency, harmony, and effectiveness; and the democratic interest in community participation in law enforcement. Because criminal procedure balances these interests, it is both focused on result and directed by means. American criminal procedure does not permit the search for truth at any price; means sometimes take precedence over ends.

The criminal process consists of a series of government invasions beginning with brief street contacts to investigate crime prior to formal criminal proceedings and extending to life imprisonment and capital punishment after conviction. These invasions require sufficient objective bases (reasonable suspicion, probable cause, proof beyond a reasonable doubt). The greater the intrusion or deprivation, the greater the objective basis that is required to back it up — as in reasonable suspicion to stop, probable cause to arrest, proof beyond a reasonable doubt to convict.

The structure of the American criminal justice system consists of both federal, state, and local agencies and executive, judicial, and legislative branches. The United States and state constitutions, statutes, and administrative rules allocate the power to enforce the criminal law among the agencies and branches that manage each step in the criminal process. The principal steps include investigation managed mainly by police; institution of formal charges managed by prosecutors; adjudication or formal court proceedings; sentencing; and review proceedings, including appeals and collateral attack.

Criminal procedure has another side, for a long time hidden from public view. Alongside the formal rules and structure, an informal decision-making process takes place. Citizens do not report all crimes to the police, police do not arrest all citizens they have probable cause to arrest, prosecutors do not prosecute every arrested suspect, juries do not convict all "guilty" defendants, and judges sentence offenders differently. It is in this informal side of criminal procedure that organizational and ideological interests play a large part. Both formal criminal procedure governed by written rules and informal discretion shaped by extralegal influence play their part in the administration of justice in the United States.

REVIEW QUESTIONS

1. Summarize and explain the significance of the dilemma posed by the quotation from James Madison at the opening of the chapter.

2. Identify and explain the significance of "balances" in the law of criminal procedure.

3. Identify all the major interests that the law of criminal procedure balances.

4. What is the ultimate mission of criminal procedure?

5. Describe the tension between ends and means in the law of criminal procedure.

6. Define what we mean by the balance between process and result in the law of criminal procedure.

7. Explain the adversary process as it operates in the law of criminal procedure.

8. Identify some of the goals of "doing justice" that prosecutors might try to accomplish.

9. What is the basic idea behind the accusatory system?

10. What are the best-known characteristics of the accusatory system?

11. Identify, define, and explain the main elements in the concept of procedural regularity.

12. Why does the balance between result and process cause discomfort in our society?

13. Describe the importance of facts in the law of criminal procedure and in the practice of criminal law enforcement.

14. Identify the main government invasions of individuals that criminal law enforcement causes.

15. What is the relation between the degree of government invasion and the objective basis to justify the invasion?

16. Explain the phrase "facts are power" in criminal procedure.

17. Explain the similarities between and the fundamental difference between the commission of crimes and the enforcement of criminal law.

18. Identify the basic tension in the history of criminal procedure, and briefly describe how this tension has affected the history of criminal procedure.

19. Identify and briefly describe the policy interests in the law of criminal procedure that go beyond the balancing of legal interests.
20. Identify and explain the major elements in the structure of criminal procedure in the United States.
21. Identify and explain the major steps in the criminal process.
22. Explain the importance of discretion in the criminal process.

KEY TERMS

accusatory stage when general investigation shifts to building a case against a specific suspect.

accusatory system the government bears the burden of proof.

adjudication decisions made in court.

adversary process the defense and the government are opponents, and impartial judges monitor proceedings.

affirmed an appellate court upholding the decision of a lower court.

appeals reviewing the proceedings of a lower court.

appellant the party appealing a lower court ruling or decision to a higher court.

appellate court case a case appealed from a trial or other lower court.

appellee the party appealed against.

arraignment the process of bringing a defendant to court to hear and plead to charges.

bind over to decide to send a case to trial.

certiorari a discretionary order of the Supreme Court to review a lower court decision.

citation identifies the source of a case.

collateral attack a proceeding to review the constitutionality of detention or imprisonment.

complaint a formal charging document to initiate a criminal proceeding.

concurring opinion statements in which justices agree with the decision, not the reasoning of a court's opinion.

defendant the person formally charged with a crime.

discovery the process in which information is obtained from the other side.

discretion informal, unwritten decision making in criminal procedure.

dissenting opinion part of an appellate court case in which justices write opinions disagreeing with the decision and reasoning of a court.

distinguishing cases recognizing that the rule in a prior decision does not apply to current facts.

federalism a political doctrine in which states are primarily responsible for laws regarding their people and the national government is responsible for larger and/or international issues.

felony a crime punishable by one year or more in prison.

first appearance a proceeding to determine probable cause, appoint an attorney, and set bail.

grand jury review a secret proceeding to test a government case.

habeas corpus an action that asks those who hold defendants to justify their detention.

indictment a formal criminal charge issued by a grand jury.

information a charging document filed by a prosecutor.

jurisdiction the authority of a court to hear and decide cases.

lower criminal courts courts conducting pretrial felony proceedings and misdemeanor trials.

majority opinion the law of a case in an appellate court.

misdemeanor an offense punishable by a fine or jail term of less than a year or both.

nolo contendere a plea by which a defendant accepts but does not admit charges.

objective basis the factual justification for government invasions of individual privacy, liberty, and property.

petitioner a party whose case has come to court by judicial writ.

plaintiff in error another term for appellant.

plurality opinion a statement in which the greatest number, but not a majority, of the justices favor a court's decision.

precedent a prior decision that is binding on a similar present case.

preliminary hearing the adversary proceeding that tests the government's case.

presumption of innocence the principle that defendants are presumed innocent until the government proves guilt beyond a reasonable doubt.

***prima facie* case** a case with enough facts to convict unless they are contradicted.

principle of procedural regularity "playing by the rules."

proof beyond a reasonable doubt the objective basis required for conviction.

remanded sent back to a lower court for further proceedings.

reversed overturned by an appellate court.

rule of four the requirement that four Supreme Court justices must vote to review a case for its appeal to be heard by the Supreme Court.

separation of powers a federalist doctrine in which power is divided among the legislative, executive, and judicial branches of government.

stare decisis the doctrine in which a prior decision binds a present case with similar facts.

trial courts courts that conduct trials.

true bill a bill of indictment stating that a grand jury finds sufficient evidence to prosecute.

Notes

1. James Madison, "The Federalist No. 51," Jacob E. Cooke, ed., *The Federalist* (Middletown, CT: Wesleyan University Press, 1961), 349.

2. William H. Rehnquist, "Is an Expanded Right of Privacy Consistent with Fair and Effective Law Enforcement? Or: Privacy, You've Come a Long Way Baby," *Kansas Law Review*, 23 (1974): 1, 2.

3. Jerome Hall, "Objectives of Federal Criminal Rules Revision," *Yale Law Journal* 51 (1942): 725.

4. Louis Michael Seidman, "Factual Guilt and the Burger Court: An Examination of Continuity and Change in Criminal Procedure," *Columbia Law Review* 80 (1980): 436–503.

5. Joseph Goldstein, "Reflections on Two Models: Inquisitorial Themes in American Criminal Procedure," *Stanford Law Review* 26 (1974): 1099.

6. The writings on the adversary system are legion. For a sample, see Joseph Goldstein, "Reflections on Two Models: Inquisitorial Themes in American Criminal Procedure," *Stanford Law Review* 26 (1974): 1009; Neef and Nagel, "The Adversary Nature of the American Legal System from a Historical Perspective," *New York Law Forum* 20 (1974): 123; Thurman Arnold, *Symbols of Government* (New Haven: Yale University Press, 1935); Herbert Packer, *The Limits of the Criminal Sanction* (Palo Alto, CA: Stanford University Press, 1968).

7. *Sanders v. United States*, 373 U.S. 1, 24–25, 83 S.Ct. 1068, 1081–1082, 10 L.Ed. 148 (1963).

8. Osmond K. Fraenkel, "From Suspicion to Accusation," *Yale Law Journal* 51 (1942): 748.

9. Hall, "Objectives of Federal Criminal Procedural Revision," 728.

10. Judge Learned Hand, *United States v. Garsson*, 291 Fed. 646, 659 (S.D.N.Y. 1922), denying a defense motion to inspect grand jury minutes.

11. Joseph Goldstein, "The State and the Accused: Balance and Advantage in Criminal Procedure," *Yale Law Journal* 69 (1960): 1149–99, 1152.

12. Roscoe Pound, "The Future of the Criminal Law," *Columbia Law Review* 21 (1921): 1–16.

13. James L. Strachan-Davidson, *Problems of the Roman Criminal Law* (1912), 114, 168.

14. Pound, "The Future of the Criminal Law," 9.

15. Quoted in Herbert J. Storing, *The Complete Anti-Federalist* (Chicago: University of Chicago Press, 1981), 71.

16. Robert Allen Rutland, *The Birth of the Bill of Rights* (Boston: Northeastern University Press, 1955); for a somewhat different view, see Forrest McDonald, *Novus Ordo Seclorum* (Lawrence, KS: University of Kansas Press, 1985).

17. American Academy of Political and Social Science, *Annals* 46 (1910).

18. Samuel Walker, *Popular Justice* (New York: Oxford University Press, 1980), 161–221, for the period 1920–1960; Thomas E. Cronin et al., *U.S. v. Crime*

in the Streets (Bloomington: Indiana University Press, 1981), for the 1960s and 1970s.

19. The classic modern work that discusses balancing the social interest in crime control and individual autonomy is Herbert Packer, *The Limits of the Criminal Sanction* (Stanford: Stanford University Press, 1968); Chief Justice Rehnquist's quotation is from "Is an Expanded Right of Privacy . . . ," 2.

20. Anthony Lewis, "The Blackmun Legacy," *New York Times*, 8 April 1994, A13.

21. Benjamin Cardozo, *The Nature of the Judicial Process* (New Haven, CT: Yale University Press, 1921), 62.

22. Frederick Schauer, "Precedent," *Stanford Law Review* 39 (1987): 571, contains a useful modern discussion of precedent.

23. Joel Samaha, "Discretion and Law in the Early Penitential Books," *Social Psychology and Discretionary Law* (New York: W. W. Norton, 1978).

24. Kenneth Culp Davis, *Police Discretion* (St. Paul: West Publishing Company, 1975).

25. Anthony Amsterdam, "The Supreme Court and the Rights of Suspects in Criminal Cases," *New York University Law Review* 45 (1970): 785–94.

26. Peter F. Nardulli, *The Courtroom Elite* (Cambridge, MA: Ballinger, 1978), 179. These observations are confirmed in a national survey reported in Paul B. Wice, *Chaos in the Courthouse* (New York: Praeger, 1985).

27. Seidman, "Factual Guilt and the Burger Court," 437–503.

28. James A. Gardner, "The Failed Discourse of State Constitutionalism," *Michigan Law Review*, 90 (1991): 761, 812–13.

29. *Report to the Nation on Crime and Justice* (Washington, DC: National Institute of Justice, 1983), 45.

30. Peter Aranella, "Rethinking the Functions of Criminal Procedure: The Warren and Burger Courts' Competing Ideologies," *Georgetown Law Journal* 72 (1983): 185–248.

31. Frances A. Allen, "The Judicial Quest for Justice: The Warren Court and the Criminal Cases," *University of Michigan Law Forum* (1975): 526.

32. Wayne R. LaFave and Jerold H. Israel, *Criminal Procedure* (St. Paul: West Publishing Company, 1984), 1: 11–32.

33. The vast social science literature on policing confirms this conclusion. See John A. Webster, "Police Task and Time Study," *Journal of Criminal Law, Criminology, and Police Science* 61 (1970): 94–100; Donald J. Black, *The Manners and Customs of the Police* (New York: Academic Press, 1980); Eric J. Scott, *Calls for Service: Citizen Demand and Initial Police Response* (Washington, DC: National Institute of Justice, July 1981); James Q. Wilson, *Thinking About Crime*, second edition (New York: Vintage Press, 1985), chap. 4; Jerome H. Skolnick and David H. Bayley, *The New Blue Line* (New York: Free Press, 1986).

34. Kathleen Maguire and Anne L. Pastore, *Sourcebook of Criminal Justice Statistics 1995* (Washington, DC: Bureau of Justice Statistics, 1996), Table 5.6, 448; "Police Deployed to Curb Gangs in Los Angeles," *New York Times*, 9 April 1988, 7.

35. Peter W. Greenwood and Joan Petersilia, *The Criminal Investigation Process* (Santa Monica, CA: Rand Corporation, 1975), discusses the follow-up step thoroughly. Using empirical data, the authors conclude that the follow-up investigation rarely yields significant evidence beyond what patrol officers have already obtained.

36. Lawrence W. Sherman and Richard A. Berk, "The Specific Deterrent Effects of Arrest for Domestic Assault," *American Sociological Review* 49 (1984): 261–72; *Police Report on Domestic Violence: A National Survey* (Washington, DC: Crime Control Institute, 1986).

37. Bureau of Justice Statistics, *The Prosecution of Felony Arrests, 1988* (Washington, DC: Bureau of Justice Statistics, February, 1992); Brian Forst, Judith Lucianovic, and Sarah J. Cox, *What Happens After Arrest* (Washington, DC: National Institute of Law Enforcement and Criminal Justice, 1977); Vera Institute of Justice, *Felony Arrests: Their Prosecution and Disposition in New York City's Courts* (New York: Vera Institute of Justice, 1977).

38. LaFave and Israel, *Criminal Procedure*, 1: 21.

39. Andy Hall et al., *Pretrial Release Program Options* (Washington, DC: National Institute of Justice, 1984).

40. LaFave and Israel, *Criminal Procedure*, 1: 23–25.

41. Elliot Richardson's comments were heard via television and radio several times during the week when the special prosecutor announced that he would not seek to indict former president Ronald Reagan's attorney general Edwin Meese; reporters wanted to know the significance of the special prosecutor's decision.

42. Arthur Rossett and Donald Cressey, *Justice by Consent: Plea Bargains in American Courthouses* (Philadelphia: J. B. Lippincott, 1976); William F. McDonald and James A. Cramer, eds., *Plea Bargaining* (Cambridge,

MA: Lexington Books, 1980); Albert Alschuler, "Plea Bargaining and Its History," *Columbia Law Review* 79 (1979): 1–43.

43. Barbara Boland et al., *The Prosecution of Felony Arrests, 1987* (Washington, DC: Bureau of Justice Statistics, 1990), 3.

44. American Bar Association Project on Standards for Criminal Justice, *Standards Relating to Postconviction Remedies* (Chicago: American Bar Association, 1967), 19.

45. Thomas Y. Davies, "Affirmed: A Study of Criminal Appeals and Decisionmaking Norms in a California Court of Appeal," *American Bar Foundation Research Journal* (1982): 548–52.

C H A P T E R   T W O

The Constitution and Criminal Procedure

CHAPTER MAIN POINTS

1. Criminal procedure is a method for enforcing the criminal law.

2. The ultimate source of the law of criminal procedure is the United States Constitution, particularly the Bill of Rights.

3. The main interpreter of the Constitution is the U.S. Supreme Court.

4. Day-to-day criminal procedure is mainly the business of state and local governments.

5. States can expand but not reduce rights guaranteed by the U.S. Constitution.

6. Federal and state statutes and rules are major sources of criminal procedure.

7. The Model Code of Pre-arraignment Procedure is a major advisory source of procedures from detection to arrest.

8. According to the U.S. Supreme Court, the Fourteenth Amendment due process clause requires the states to guarantee criminal suspects, defendants, and offenders in state proceedings most of the rights in the U.S. Bill of Rights.

9. The U.S. Supreme Court recognizes the need to allow not only for individual differences among states and between state and federal law enforcement, but also for local experimentation in criminal procedure.

"Did the Officers' Behavior 'Shock Your Conscience' "?

Having "some information that (the petitioner here) was selling narcotics," three deputy sheriffs of the County of Los Angeles, on the morning of July 1, 1949, made for the two-story dwelling house in which Rochin lived with his mother, common-law wife, brothers and sisters. Finding the outside door open, they entered and then forced open the door to Rochin's room on the second floor. Inside they found petitioner sitting partly dressed on the side of his bed, upon which his wife was lying. On a "night stand" beside the bed the deputies spied two capsules. When asked "Whose stuff is this?" Rochin seized the capsules and put them in his mouth. A struggle ensued, in the course of which the three officers "jumped upon him" and attempted to extract the capsules. The force they applied proved unavailing against Rochin's resistance.

He was handcuffed and taken to a hospital. At the direction of one of the officers a doctor forced an emetic solution through a tube into Rochin's stomach against his will. This "stomach pumping" produced vomiting. In the vomited matter were found two capsules which proved to contain morphine.

CONSTITUTIONALISM

Constitutionalism — "the idea that a constitution is a unique document of political foundation" — is "close to the heart of American political theory," according to constitutional scholar and professor of law James A. Gardner. Chief Justice John Marshall captured the essence of American constitutionalism in these words from the great case of *McCulloch v. Maryland:* "We must never forget that it is a *constitution* we are expounding" (emphasis added). The Chief Justice was referring to the idea that a constitution is different from other documents that courts have to interpret and that judges have to approach constitutional interpretation with these differences in mind. The differences include the following:

1. The Constitution is a higher form of law that speaks with a political authority that no ordinary law or other government action can ever match.
2. The Constitution is the expression of the whole people.
3. The Constitution always binds the government.
4. The Constitution cannot be changed by the government.
5. Only the direct action of the whole people themselves can change the Constitution.
6. The Constitution embodies the fundamental values of the American people.[1]

THE SOURCES
OF CRIMINAL PROCEDURE

Criminal procedure refers to the methods that the government uses to detect, investigate, apprehend, prosecute, convict, and punish criminals. Controlling the methods of criminal law enforcement stems from a variety of sources, including the following:

1. The United States and state constitutions
2. Federal and state court decisions
3. Federal and state statutes
4. Administrative rules. (See Table 2.1 for a detailed summary of these sources.)

The ultimate source of criminal procedure is the United States Constitution. The body of the Constitution includes some regulations of criminal procedure. Article I, § 9, prohibits bills of attainder (laws that name specific individuals as criminals) and *ex post facto* laws (retroactive criminal statutes) and recognizes *habeas corpus* (the right to challenge any government detention; see Chapter 12). Article III, § 2, guarantees trial by jury in all criminal cases and guarantees that trials shall take place in the jurisdiction where they were committed.

The first eight amendments to the Constitution, popularly known as the Bill of Rights, contain most of the regulations of criminal procedure. In fact, of the twenty-three rights guaranteed in the Bill of Rights, twelve guarantee rights to persons suspected of, charged with, and convicted of crimes. The Fourth, Fifth, Sixth, and Eighth Amendments regulate the power of police and courts to enforce the criminal law. Table 2.2 summarizes the rights guaranteed by the Bill of Rights. The guarantees set forth in both the body of the Constitution and in the Bill of Rights were initially intended to give suspects, defendants, and offenders rights only against the United States government. According to the doctrine of incorporation, discussed below in the section on incorporation, most of the rights guaranteed to individuals against the federal government also apply to state and local governments.

The U.S. Constitution and Federal Courts

The ultimate authority in criminal procedure may be the U.S. Constitution, but the Constitution is not self-explanatory. It requires—and receives—a lot of interpretation.

TABLE 2.1 SOURCES OF CRIMINAL PROCEDURE LAW

1. *United States Constitution.* The supreme law of the land, the ultimate source of authority in criminal procedure.
2. *State Constitutions.* Instruments with provisions that are parallel to those of the United States Constitution.
3. *United States Supreme Court Decisions.* Decisions that interpret, amplify, and apply federal constitutional standards to specific cases. These decisions are the law of the land.
4. *United States Court of Appeals and District Court Opinions.* Decisions that are the law only in the territory covered by their jurisdiction and only unless and until the United States Supreme Court rules on the question, at which point the Supreme Court decision takes precedence. Although not law beyond their own jurisdiction, these decisions address important issues and suggest results that other jurisdictions may follow.
5. *State Court Opinions.* Decisions that are the law only within a state. States can raise standards under provisions in state constitutions that are parallel to provisions in the federal Constitution, but they cannot reduce those standards below the minimum set by the United States Constitution as interpreted by the United States Supreme Court.
6. *Federal Rules of Criminal Procedure.* The rules established by the United States Supreme Court that govern practice in all federal courts from the filing of a criminal complaint to appeals from, and other challenges to, convictions in federal courts. Most states have adopted rules similar to the Federal Rules of Criminal Procedure.
7. *State Rules of Criminal Procedure.* Rules similar to the Federal Rules that govern procedure in state courts.
8. *Model Code of Pre-arraignment Procedure.* The American Law Institute's Model Code to govern practice in police–citizen encounters on the street not covered by the Federal Rules but sometimes found in state "stop-and-frisk" statutes. The code and commentary embody the arguments and recommendations of distinguished professionals and scholars of criminal justice. The code is not law, but courts often cite both its model provisions and the authoritative commentary accompanying the provisions.

The U.S. District Courts, U.S. Courts of Appeals, and the United States Supreme Court are the main interpreters of the Constitution. Figure 1.1 (page 14) depicts the court structure of the United States. The U.S. Supreme Court has the last word in interpreting the Constitution; its decisions bind all other courts, legislatures, executives, and criminal justice officials. However, the U.S. Constitution and Supreme Court are at the top of a pyramid of criminal justice administration that has a very wide state and local base. The Supreme Court depends on local courts and police to apply its decisions to day-to-day operations. Furthermore, U.S. court of appeals and district courts and state courts resolve constitutional questions of interpretation that the Supreme Court has not yet addressed and perhaps never will.[2]

State Constitutions and State Courts

State constitutions and state court decisions are another source of the law of criminal procedure. Every state guarantees its citizens **parallel rights**—rights similar to those in the United States Constitution and Bill of Rights. For example, virtually every state constitution guarantees parallel rights against unreasonable searches and seizures and self-incrimination, and the right to counsel and to jury trial. Some state constitutions provide additional rights to the parallel rights, such as the right to privacy.

TABLE 2.2 THE PROTECTIONS OF THE BILL OF RIGHTS

Fourth Amendment
Guarantee against
  1. unreasonable searches and seizures. The right of the people to be secure in their persons, houses, papers, and effects, against unreasonable searches and seizures, shall not be violated, and no warrants shall issue, but upon probable cause, supported by oath or affirmation, and particularly describing the place to be searched, and the persons or things to be seized.

Fifth Amendment
Guarantees of
  2. grand jury indictment
  3. double jeopardy
  4. due process
  5. self-incrimination. No person shall be held to answer for a capital, or otherwise infamous crime, unless on a presentment or indictment of a Grand Jury, except in cases arising in the land or naval forces, or in the militia, when in actual service in time of war or public danger; nor shall any person be subject for the same offence to be twice put in jeopardy of life or limb; nor shall be compelled in any criminal case to be a witness against himself, nor be deprived of life, liberty, or property, without due process of law. . . .

Sixth Amendment
Rights to
  6. public and speedy trial
  7. impartial jury
  8. notice of the nature and cause of accusation
  9. confrontation of opposing witnesses
  10. compulsory process
  11. assistance counsel. In all criminal prosecutions, the accused shall enjoy the right to a speedy and public trial, by an impartial jury of the State and district wherein the crime shall have been committed, which district shall have been previously ascertained by law, and to be informed of the nature and cause of the accusation; to be confronted with the witnesses against him; to have compulsory process for obtaining witnesses in his favor; and to have the assistance of counsel for his defense.

Eighth Amendment
Prohibitions against
  12. excessive bail
  13. cruel and unusual punishment. Excessive bail shall not be required, nor excessive fines imposed, nor cruel and unusual punishment inflicted.

State courts are a source of criminal procedure law in two types of cases:

1. State courts decide cases involving the U.S. Constitution.

2. State courts decide cases involving their own state constitutions.

In cases involving the United States Constitution, state court decisions are not final. They can always be appealed to the federal courts, and ultimately to the United States Supreme Court. Many, if not most, of the leading cases in this book started in state courts and were appealed to the United States Supreme Court. Practically speaking, however, the vast majority of criminal cases do not go beyond the state courts.

State courts are the final authority in cases decided on the basis of the provisions in their own state constitutions. The federal courts — even the United States Supreme Court — have no authority to interpret state constitutions as long as state constitutional provisions and the decisions interpreting them meet the standards set by the United

States Constitution. The United States Constitution sets only minimum standards or a floor. In other words, it defines the narrowest scope of a right. Someone once said that it does not pay a law much of a compliment to declare it constitutional. What the commentator meant was that the United States Constitution sets a *minimum* standard. States may not reduce the scope of a parallel right below the floor established by the federal minimum standard. However, they may raise the floor, and sometimes they do. Throughout this book, you will encounter instances where states have raised the constitutional minimum regarding certain rights, including these:

1. Right against unreasonable searches and seizures

2. Right against self-incrimination

3. Double jeopardy

4. Right to counsel

5. Trial by jury

6. Right against excessive bail

7. Right against cruel and unusual punishment[3]

The two cases excerpted here, *United States v. Robinson* and *People v. Brisendine*, are examples drawn from search and seizure law to demonstrate the idea of the federal constitutional minimum that states can raise. (We will thoroughly consider arrests and searches accompanying arrests in Chapters 5 and 6.) You should reconsider these cases, then, for the purpose of understanding arrests and searches incident to lawful arrests. Here, consider the importance and effects of differing standards between federal and state procedures.[4]

C A S E

Can Police Search Arrested Traffic Violators?

The Federal Standard: United States v. Robinson, 414 U.S. 218, 94 S.Ct. 467, 38 L.Ed.2d 427 (1973)

Robinson was convicted in the United States District Court for the District of Columbia of possession and facilitation of concealing heroin. The court of appeals reversed the conviction. The United States Supreme Court reversed the decision of the court of appeals. Justice Rehnquist wrote the opinion for the Court.

FACTS

On April 23, 1968, at approximately 11 P.M., Officer Richard Jenks, a 15-year veteran of the District of Columbia Metropolitan Police Department, observed the respondent driving a 1965 Cadillac near the intersection of 8th and C Streets, N.E., in the District of Columbia. Jenks, as a result of previous investigation following a check of respondent's operator's permit four days earlier, determined there was reason to believe that respondent was operating a motor vehicle after the revocation of his operator's permit. This is an offense defined by statute in the District of Columbia which carries a mandatory minimum jail term, a mandatory minimum fine, or both.

Jenks signaled respondent to stop the automobile, which respondent did, and all three of the occupants emerged from the car. At that point Jenks informed respondent that he was under arrest for "operating after revocation and obtaining a permit by misrepresentation." It was assumed by the Court of Appeals, and is conceded by the respondent here, that Jenks had probable cause to arrest respondent, and that he effected a full-custody arrest.

In accordance with procedure prescribed in police department instructions, Jenks then began to search respondent. He explained at a subsequent hearing that he was "face-to-face" with the respondent, and "placed [his] hands on [the respondent], [his] right hand to [the respondent's] left breast like this (demonstrating) and proceeded to pat him down thus [with the right hand]." During this patdown, Jenks felt an object in the left breast pocket of the heavy coat respondent was wearing, but testified that he "couldn't tell what it was" and also that he "couldn't actually tell the size of it." Jenks then reached into the pocket and pulled out the object, which turned out to be a "crumpled cigarette package." Jenks testified that at this point he still did not know what was in the package: "As I felt the package I could feel objects in the package but I couldn't tell what they were. . . . I knew they weren't cigarettes."

The officer then opened the cigarette pack and found 14 gelatin capsules of white powder which he thought to be, and which later analysis proved to be, heroin. Jenks then continued his search of respondent to completion, feeling around his waist and trouser legs, and examining the remaining pockets. The heroin seized from the respondent was admitted into evidence at the trial which resulted in his conviction in the District Court. . . .

OPINION

. . . A police officer's determination as to how and where to search the person of a suspect whom he has arrested is necessarily a quick ad hoc judgment which the Fourth Amendment does not require to be broken down in each instance into an analysis of each step in the search. . . . A custodial arrest of a person based on probable cause is a reasonable intrusion under the Fourth Amendment; that intrusion being lawful, a search incident to the arrest requires no additional justification. It is the fact of the lawful arrest which establishes the authority to search, and we hold that in the case of a lawful custodial arrest a full search of the person is not only an exception to the warrant re-

quirement of the Fourth Amendment, but is also a "reasonable" search under that Amendment. . . .

. . . Since it is the fact of custodial arrest which gives rise to the authority to search, it is of no moment that Jenks did not indicate any subjective fear of the respondent or that he did not himself suspect that respondent was armed. Having in the course of a lawful search come upon the crumpled package of cigarettes, he was entitled to inspect it; and when his inspection revealed the heroin capsules, he was entitled to seize them as "fruits, instrumentalities, or contraband" probative of criminal conduct. . . .

DISSENT

Justice Marshall, with whom Justice Douglas and Justice Brennan join, dissenting.

. . . "There is no formula for the determination of reasonableness. Each case is to be decided on its own facts and circumstances." . . . "The constitutional validity of a warrantless search is preeminently the sort of question which can only be decided in the concrete factual context of the individual case." And the intensive, at times painstaking, case-by-case analysis characteristic of our Fourth Amendment decisions bespeaks our "jealous regard for maintaining the integrity of individual rights."

In the present case, however, the majority turns its back on these principles, holding that "the fact of the lawful arrest" always established the authority to conduct a full search of the arrestee's person, regardless of whether in a particular case "there was present one of the reasons supporting the authority for a search of the person incident to a lawful arrest."

. . . The majority's attempt to avoid case-by-case adjudication of Fourth Amendment issues is not only misguided as a matter of principle, but is also doomed to fail as a practical application. . . . Although, in this particular case Officer Jenks was required by police department regulations to make an in-custody rather than to issue a citation, in most jurisdictions and for most traffic offenses the determination of whether to issue a citation or effect a full arrest is discretionary with the officer. There is always the possibility that a police officer, lacking probable cause to obtain a search warrant, will use a traffic arrest as a pretext to conduct a search. . . . I suggest this possibility not to impugn the integrity of our police, but merely to point out that case-by-case adjudication will always be necessary to determine whether a full arrest was effected for purely legitimate reasons or, rather, as a pretext for searching the arrestee. "An arrest may not be used as a pretext to search for evidence." . . .

The California Standard: People v. Brisendine, 13 Cal.3d 528, 119 Cal.Rptr. 315, 531 P.2d 1099 (1975)

Brisendine was convicted in the Superior Court of San Bernardino County of possession of marijuana and possession of a restricted dangerous drug, and was placed on probation. Brisendine appealed. The California Supreme Court reversed. Justice Mosk wrote the opinion for the court.

FACTS

On the night of June 3, 1970, two deputy sheriffs . . . were inspecting for county code violations in the Deep Creek area of the San Bernardino National Forest. The locale had been designated a "high fire hazard area" in which both open campfires and overnight camping were prohibited.

Upon finding two vehicles parked on the road the deputies proceeded into the forest on foot, where they came upon . . . Marlow Bartels, a lone camper whom they arrested for possession of marijuana. Bartels informed the officers there were other campers downstream who were also in possession of marijuana. . . .

Approximately half a mile from the place where they left Bartels the officers observed another campfire. Nearby were four young men in sleeping bags, one of whom was this defendant. Officer Norman placed the four under arrest for having an open campfire. . . . Prior to starting back, the officers conducted a thorough search of the persons and effects of all four youths. Denney picked up defendant's knapsack, squeezed it, determined that the outer layer was too solid to ascertain whether it contained weapons, and began a search of its compartments. The contraband was found in a side pocket of the pack: the marijuana was contained in a frosted plastic bottle with a cap on

it, and the tablets of restricted dangerous drugs were wrapped in tinfoil and enclosed in envelopes.

OPINION

Defendant contends that the search of his knapsack exceeded the legitimate purpose for which a search was authorized. . . . [W]e see no difference between traffic cases and the instant matter in terms of requiring the officer to point to the specific reasons why he believes weapons may be present. Defendant was arrested for one of the most minor of non traffic violations—a mere citation offense. In such a case the fact of the arrest does not justify a search of the belongings of the person cited: there can be no instrumentalities and there can be no fruits, and absent some showing on the part of the officer that he has good cause to fear for his safety, there can be no weapons search. . . .

Since the contraband was illegally seized in violation of Article I, § 13, of the California Constitution [which is identical to the search-and-seizure clause in the Fourth Amendment], we hold that it was erroneously received in evidence. . . .

The People . . . contend that notwithstanding the invalidity of the search under California law, the recent United States Supreme Court case of *United States v. Robinson* [1973] "should be dispositive of any question regarding the permissible scope of the search herein." We disagree. [That] case [was] decided under Supreme Court's view of the minimum standards required in order to satisfy the Fourth Amendment's proscription of unreasonable searches. Our holding today is based exclusively on Article I, § 13, of the California Constitution, which requires a more exacting standard for cases arising in this state. . . .

CASE DISCUSSION

Compare the federal and California interpretations of searches incident to arrests for minor offenses. Do you agree with the reasoning of the United States Supreme Court? With that of the California court? Why or why not? Do you agree with the federal or California standard in these cases? Do you think it is a good idea, in general, to permit states to raise constitutional standards, or should all the states in the nation operate according to one standard? Defend your answer. Does Justice Marshall have a point that these searches are "pretextual"—in other words, that the traffic arrest provided a pretext to search for drugs? If so, does it matter what the officers' motive for the search was? Should the Supreme Court—or any reviewing court—look at these cases individually or prescribe a "bright line" rule granting the police blanket authority to conduct searches incident to traffic arrests? Would such a bright line further the organizational interests of efficiency and predictability? The legal interest in result? Would it help to catch criminals?[5]

Federal and State Statutes and Rules

The U.S. and state constitutions are not complete codes of criminal procedure. Both federal and state legislatures can enact statutes and rules that set out in detail the procedures for the administration of criminal justice. Both the federal government and most states have adopted rules of criminal procedure. Written by judges but authorized and approved by legislatures, these rules govern specific procedures from arrest through appeal. The federal rules, which most states follow, grew out of a deep dissatisfaction with the administration of justice during the early decades of the twentieth century. In 1940, Congress authorized the Supreme Court to adopt rules of criminal procedure for the federal courts. Pursuant to this authorization, the Court appointed "a group of eminent practitioners and scholars" to research and draft rules that would effectively put the ideals of the Constitution into daily practice. According to criminal law scholar Professor Gerhard O. Mueller, "In three and one half years of hard labor the group produced the Federal Rules of Criminal Procedure. For the first time in history the premises of procedure had been assembled in a body, neatly organized, expressed tersely and concisely."[6]

Model Codes and Rules

The federal rules—and the state rules fashioned after them—do not address the period prior to arrest, specifically encounters between citizens and the police on the street (see Chapter 4). The American Law Institute, a group of distinguished practitioners and scholars, drafted the *Model Code of Pre-arraignment Procedure*, which fills this gap in existing rules. Although it is not law, courts frequently cite both the code and the authoritative commentary that accompanies it in decisions interpreting Fourth Amendment stop-and-frisk law. In addition, the code and its commentaries address the basic issues in the criminal process that arise in the interval between citizens' first contacts with police and arraignment (formal charge in court—see Chapters 4–9). The Model Code provisions provide possible resolutions to issues that arise during this critical period as well as stimulating arguments to support the proposals for resolving those issues. This textbook emphasizes Supreme Court decisions. However, it also recognizes the continuing legal and public policy issues in criminal procedure, the way the courts resolve them, and the arguments that underlie the resolution.

The focus on continuing legal and public policy problems and on the reasoning that underlies decisions will help you to understand better—and, hopefully, develop a method of resolving—general issues as they arise in specific cases. Table 2.1 (p. 49) sets out the major formal sources found in criminal procedure and in this text that address these issues. These sources—the Supreme Court, lower federal court, and state court opinions; the federal and state rules; and the model rules—address both the current rule in particular cases and the manner of resolving continuing constitutional and policy questions.

THE SUPREMACY CLAUSE AND JUDICIAL REVIEW

According to the United States Constitution, Article VI (the **supremacy clause**), ultimate authority rests in the United States Constitution:

> This constitution, and the laws of the United States which shall be made in pursuance thereof . . . shall be the supreme law of the land; and the judges in every state shall be bound thereby, anything in the constitution or laws of any state to the contrary notwithstanding.

In the great landmark case *Marbury v. Madison*, Chief Justice John Marshall established what later courts would call the principle of **judicial review.** The principle established that the United States Supreme Court had the power to review statutes and determine whether they violated the Constitution. In other words, the Supreme Court, not the legislative branch and not the executive branch, has the final say in what the Constitution means.[7]

Alexander Hamilton defended judicial review in the *Federalist Papers*:

> The interpretation of laws is the proper and peculiar province of the courts. A constitution is, in fact, and must be regarded by the judges as, a fundamental law. It therefore belongs to them to ascertain its meaning, as well as the meaning of any particular act proceeding from the legislative body. If there should happen to be an irreconcilable variance between the two, that which has the superior obligation and validity ought, of course, to be preferred; or, in other words, the Constitution ought to be preferred to the statute, the intention of the people to the intention of their agents.[8]

The supremacy clause and judicial review taken together establish that criminal procedure ultimately must answer to the United States Constitution, as the courts interpret the Constitution's relevant provisions.

DUE PROCESS OF LAW

Higher courts can review and overturn the decisions of courts beneath them by means of their **supervisory powers.** The power of judicial review and the supervisory power of courts give them enormous potential influence over the constitutionality and legality of criminal procedures. They have used this power not only to interpret specific rights guaranteed to criminal suspects, defendants, and convicted offenders but also to extend the power of the federal government into state and local criminal proceedings by means of the **due process clause** and the equal protection clause of the Fourteenth Amendment, which provide in part:

> No state shall . . . deprive any citizen of life, liberty, or property without due process of law; nor deny to any person within its jurisdiction the equal protection of the laws.

The Supreme Court has interpreted the Fourteenth Amendment due process clause to require states to grant most of the rights included in the Bill of Rights to persons in state proceedings.

History of the Due Process Clause

In view of the predominantly local focus of criminal justice, it is not surprising that the Bill of Rights does not apply directly to the states. As early as 1833, Supreme Court Chief Justice John Marshall noted that the question of whether the Bill of Rights extended to the states was "of great importance, but not of much difficulty." Speaking for the Court in *Barron v. Baltimore*, Marshall wrote the following:

> Had Congress [which proposed the Bill of Rights] engaged in the extraordinary occupation of improving the constitutions of the several states by affording the people additional protection from the exercise of power by their own governments in matters which concerned themselves alone, they would have declared this purpose in plain and intelligible language.[9]

The Fourteenth Amendment, adopted following the Civil War as part of the "Civil War amendments," extended the due process requirement to state action. However, due process does not define itself. It is a fluid term that lends itself to many varying interpretations. Some emphasize the word *process*, maintaining that due process guarantees a specific procedure for deciding cases. But what procedure? The Bill of Rights lists several. Are these the ones guaranteed? Yes, say some experts. The framers of the Bill of Rights were codifying a specific list of hard-fought and proudly won procedures to protect private persons against government excesses. No, say others. If due process were mere shorthand for the Bill of Rights, then the due process clause was superfluous. The Founders had no reason to list these rights, since the Fifth Amendment already included their shorthand term. The Fifth Amendment provides in part that "no person shall be denied life, liberty, or property without due process of law" (see Appendix). Therefore, either the Bill of Rights or the due process clause is superfluous. Besides, they say, the framers would not have frozen criminal procedure at a particular eighteenth-century moment in history. The authors of the Constitution looked forward; they hoped that the meaning of due process would evolve and expand to meet the needs and wants of an ever-advancing society.[10]

Others have emphasized the "life, liberty, or property" part of the clause, maintaining that due process is a substantive concept. The framers intended to prohibit government deprivations of life, liberty, and property, no matter what the particular process. The United States Supreme Court, under its power of judicial review, has defined Fourteenth Amendment due process differently over time. Until 1932, the Supreme Court repeatedly refused to apply the Fourteenth Amendment due process clause to state criminal proceedings.

Hurtado v. California, decided in 1884, began a line of cases in which the Supreme Court rejected the idea that due process was shorthand for the application of the specific provisions in the Bill of Rights to state criminal proceedings. The case involved Joseph Hurtado and José Estuardo, who had been close friends for several years. Then Hurtado discovered Estuardo was having an affair with Hurtado's wife. When Hurtado confronted Estuardo, Estuardo admitted it and said, "I am the meat and you are the knife; kill me if you like." Hurtado demanded instead that Estuardo leave Sacramento. Estuardo promised to leave but then reneged and renewed his pursuit of Hurtado's wife. The case began with a brawl in a Sacramento tavern. Hurtado assaulted Estuardo. A few days later, Hurtado shot Estuardo in the chest. Estuardo turned to flee; Hurtado shot him in the back. Estuardo fell to the ground; Hurtado shot him again, then bludgeoned him with the pistol.[11]

In the federal courts, and in most state courts of the time, a grand jury would have decided whether to indict Hurtado. But California did not follow the practice of indictment by grand jury review. Prosecutors charged defendants directly by a procedure called *information*. The Fifth Amendment requires grand jury indictment in capital or otherwise "infamous" crimes (see Appendix and Chapters 1 and 10). Following Hurtado's conviction, the judge sentenced him to "be hung by the neck until he is dead." After losing an appeal based on trial errors, Hurtado appealed on the ground that failure to indict by grand jury review violated his Fifth Amendment right to grand jury indictment in a capital case. Hurtado's lawyer advanced, for the first time, the argument that the Fourteenth Amendment provision for due process of law required states to provide grand jury indictment in capital cases.

The Supreme Court in an earlier case had decided that due process required "a fair trial in a court of justice, according to the modes of proceeding applicable to such case." Hurtado's lawyer argued that due process meant more, that it included all the ancient common-law rights inherited from England and recognized as fundamental to free people. Grand jury indictment, he maintained, was one of these fundamental rights. The Court rejected this argument, affirming Hurtado's conviction. According to Justice Stanley Matthews, including only procedures adopted in the past

> would be to deny every quality of the law but its age, and to render it incapable of progress or improvement. It would be to stamp on our jurisprudence the unchangeableness attributed to the laws of the Meades and Persians. [The Constitution and due process were made] for an undefined and expanding future, and for a people gathered from many nations and of many tongues. . . . [Since the common law drew] its inspiration from every fountain of justice, we are not to assume that the sources of its supply have been exhausted. On the contrary, we should expect that the new and various experiences of our own situation and system will mold and shape it into new and not less useful forms.[12]

Justice John Marshall Harlan, the lone dissenter, argued that the Fourteenth Amendment due process clause "impose[d] upon the states the same restrictions, in respect of proceedings involving life, liberty, and property, which had been imposed upon the general government." Despite the valiant efforts of his grandson Justice John Marshall Harlan II to prevent it from doing so, the Court later adopted much of the elder Harlan's view. Changing time and changing justices altered the meaning of due process; the dissent of that earlier time became the law of a later day.[13]

In the meantime, the Court continued to reject arguments that the due process clause of the Fourteenth Amendment incorporated the specific provisions of the Bill of Rights. In 1900, in *Maxwell v. Dow*, the Court held that due process does not require twelve-member juries. In 1908, the Court held that due process does not impose the Fifth Amendment self-incrimination clause on the states.

The German war machine of the First World War, and the rise of fascism in its aftermath, revived the historical suspicions that Americans had of arbitrary government. The constitutional history of criminal procedure reflects this suspicion. Perhaps, as Professor Francis Allen suggests, it is no coincidence that the Supreme Court decided the first case applying the Fourteenth Amendment due process clause to state criminal procedure at the time that Hitler was rising to power in Nazi Germany. Perhaps it was the glaring lack of respect for fair trial procedures. Perhaps it was the changed personnel of the Court. Whatever the reasons, the Supreme Court took its first step in nationalizing criminal procedure when it decided the landmark "Scottsboro case," *Powell v. Alabama*, in 1932.[14]

C A S E

Did the Trial Court Deny Them "Due Process" of Law?

Powell v. Alabama,
287 U.S. 45, 53 S.Ct. 55,
77 L.Ed. 158 (1932)

Defendants were convicted of rape in a state court. They appealed on the ground that the state court denied them due process of law. On writ of *certiorari*, the United States Supreme Court reversed the judgment of conviction and remanded the case for further proceedings. Justice Sutherland wrote the opinion of the Court. Justice Butler dissented.

FACTS

. . . [O]n the day when the offense is said to have been committed, these defendants, together with a number of other negroes, were upon a freight train on its way through Alabama. On the same train were seven white boys and two white girls. A fight took place between the negroes and the white boys, in the course of which the white boys, with the exception of one named Gilley, were thrown off the train. A message was sent ahead, reporting the fight and asking that every negro be gotten off the train. The participants in the fight, and the two girls, were in an open gon-

dola car. The two girls testified that each of them was assaulted by six different negroes in turn, and they identified the seven defendants as having been among the number. None of the white boys was called to testify, with the exception of Gilley, who was called in rebuttal.

Before the train reached Scottsboro, Alabama, a sheriff's posse seized the defendants and two other negroes. Both girls and the negroes then were taken to Scottsboro, the county seat. Word of their coming and of the alleged assault had preceded them, and they were met in Scottsboro by a large crowd. It does not sufficiently appear that the defendants were seriously threatened with, or that they were actually in danger of, mob violence; but it does appear that the attitude of the community was one of great hostility. The sheriff thought it necessary to call for the militia to assist in safeguarding the prisoners. Chief Justice Anderson [of the Alabama Supreme Court] pointed out in his opinion that every step that was taken from the arrest and arraignment to the sentence was accompanied by the military. Soldiers took the defendants to Gadsden for safekeeping, brought them back to Scottsboro for arraignment, returned them to Gadsden for safekeeping while awaiting trial, escorted them to Scottsboro for trial a few days later, and guarded the court house and grounds at every stage of the proceedings.

It is perfectly apparent that the proceedings, from beginning to end, took place in an atmosphere of tense, hostile and excited public sentiment. During the entire time, the defendants were closely confined or were under military guard. The record does not disclose their ages, except that one of them was nineteen; but the record clearly indicates that most, if not all, of them were youthful, and they are constantly referred to as "the boys." They were ignorant and illiterate. All of them were residents of other states, where alone members of their families or friends resided.

. . . [I]mmediately upon the return of the indictment, defendants were arraigned and pleaded not guilty. Apparently they were not asked whether they had, or were able to employ, counsel, or wished to have counsel appointed; or whether they had friends or relatives who might assist in that regard if communicated with. That it would not have been an idle ceremony to have given the defendants reasonable opportunity to communicate with their families and endeavor to obtain counsel is demonstrated by the fact that, very soon after conviction, able counsel appeared in their behalf. . . .

. . . [U]ntil the very morning of the trial no lawyer had been named or definitely designated to represent the defendants. Prior to that time, the judge had "appointed all the members of the bar" for the limited "purpose of arraigning the defendants."

OPINION

However guilty defendants, upon due inquiry, might prove to have been, they were, until convicted, presumed to be innocent. It was the duty of the court having their cases in charge to see that they were denied no necessary incident of a fair trial. With any error of the state court involving alleged contravention of the state statutes or constitution we, of course, have nothing to do. The sole inquiry which we are permitted to make is whether the federal Constitution was contravened. . . . [A]s to that, we confine ourselves . . . to the inquiry whether the defendants were in substance denied the right of counsel, and if so, whether such denial infringes the due process clause of the Fourteenth Amendment.

[The casual appointment of counsel,] in our opinion, [falls] far short of meeting, in any proper sense, a requirement for the appointment of counsel. How many lawyers were members of the bar does not appear; but, in the very nature of things, whether many or few, they would not, thus collectively named, have been given that clear appreciation of responsibility or impressed with that individual sense of duty which should and naturally would accompany the appointment of a selected member of the bar, specifically named and assigned.

Nor do we think the situation was helped by what occurred on the morning of the trial. At that time . . . Mr. Roddy stated to the court that he did not appear as counsel, but that he would like to appear along with counsel that the court might appoint; that he had not been given an opportunity to prepare the case; that he was not familiar with the procedure in Alabama, but merely came down [from Tennessee] as a friend of the people who were interested; that he thought the boys would be better off if he should step entirely out of the case. Mr. Moody, a member of the local bar, expressed a willingness to help Mr. Roddy in anything he could do under the circumstances. To this the court responded, "All right, all the lawyers that will; of course I would not require a lawyer to appear if—." And Mr. Moody continued, "I am willing to do that for him as a member of the bar; I will go ahead and help him do anything I can do." With this dubious understanding, the trials immediately proceeded. The defendants, young, ignorant, illiterate, surrounded by hostile sentiment, haled back and forth under guard of soldiers, charged with an atrocious crime regarded with especial horror in the community where they were to be tried, were thus put in peril of their lives [rape was a capital offense] within a few moments after counsel for the first time charged with any degree of responsibility began to represent them.

It is not enough to assume that counsel thus precipitated into the case thought there was no defense, and exercised their best judgment in proceeding to trial without preparation. Neither they nor the court could say what a prompt and thorough-going investigation might disclose as to the facts. No attempt was made to investigate. No opportunity to do so was given. Defendants were immediately hurried to trial. . . . Under the circumstances disclosed, we hold that defendants were not accorded the right of counsel in any substantial sense. To decide otherwise, would simply be to ignore actualities. . . .

It is true that great and inexcusable delay in the enforcement of our criminal law is one of the grave evils of our time. Continuances are frequently granted for unnecessarily long periods of time, and delays incident to the disposition of motions for new trial and hearings upon appeal have come in many cases to be a distinct reproach to the administration of justice. The prompt disposition of criminal cases is to be commended and encouraged. But in reaching that result a defendant, charged with a serious crime, must not be stripped of his right to have sufficient time to advise with counsel and prepare his defense. To do that is not to proceed promptly in the calm spirit of regulated justice but to go forward with the haste of the mob. . . .

The Constitution of Alabama (Cont. 1901, § 6) provides that in all criminal prosecutions the accused shall enjoy the right to have the assistance of counsel; and a state statute (Code 1923, § 5567) requires the court in a capital case, where the defendant is unable to employ counsel, to appoint counsel for him. The state Supreme Court held that these provisions had not been infringed, and with that holding we are powerless to interfere. The question, however, which it is our duty, and within our power, to decide, is whether the denial of the assistance of counsel contravenes the due process clause of the Fourteenth Amendment to the Federal Constitution. . . .

We do not overlook the case of *Hurtado v. California*, where this court determined that due process of law does not require an indictment by a grand jury as a prerequisite to prosecution by a state for murder. . . . But the *Hurtado* Case does not stand alone. In the later case of *Chicago, Burlington & Q. R. Co. v. Chicago*, this court held that a judgment of a state court, even though authorized by statute, by which private property was taken for public use without just compensation, was in violation of the due process of law required by the Fourteenth Amendment. . . .

Likewise, this court has considered that freedom of speech and of the press are rights protected by the due process clause of the Fourteenth Amendment, [a]lthough in the First Amendment, Congress is pro-

hibited in specific terms from abridging the right. . . . These later cases establish that notwithstanding the sweeping character of the language in the *Hurtado* Case, the rule laid down is not without exceptions. . . . The fact that the right involved is of such a character that it cannot be denied without violating those "fundamental principles of liberty and justice which lie at the base of all our civil and political institutions" (*Herbert v. State of Louisiana*) is obviously one of those compelling considerations which must prevail in determining whether it is embraced within the due process clause of the Fourteenth Amendment, although it be specifically dealt with in another part of the Federal Constitution.

Evidently this court, in the later cases enumerated, regarded the rights there under the consideration as of this fundamental character. That some such distinction must be observed is foreshadowed in *Twining v. New Jersey*, where Mr. Justice Moody, speaking for the court, said that " . . . It is possible that some of the personal rights safeguarded by the first eight Amendments against national action may also be safeguarded against state action, because a denial of them would be a denial of due process of law. If this is so, it is not because those rights are enumerated in the first eight Amendments, but because they are of such a nature that they are included in the conception of due process of law." While the question has never been categorically determined by this court, a consideration of the nature of the right and a review of the expressions of this and other courts makes it clear that the right to the aid of counsel is of this fundamental character.

It never has been doubted by this court, or any other so far as we know, that notice and hearing are preliminary steps essential to the passing of an enforceable judgment, and that they, together with a legally competent tribunal having jurisdiction of the case, constitute basic elements of the constitutional requirement of due process of law. The words of Webster, so often quoted, that by "the law of the land" is intended "a law which hears before it condemns," have been repeated in various forms of expression in a multitude of decisions. In *Holden v. Hardy*, the necessity of due notice and an opportunity of being heard is described as among the "immutable principles of justice which inhere the very idea of free government which no member of the Union may disregard." And Mr. Justice Field, in an earlier case, *Galpin v. Page,* said that the rule that no one shall be personally bound until he has had his day in court was as old as the law, and it meant that he must be cited to appear and afforded an opportunity to be heard. "Judgment without such citation and opportunity wants all the attributes of a judicial determination; it is judicial usurpation and oppression, and never can be upheld where justice is justly administered." . . .

What, then, does a hearing include? Historically and in practice, in our own country at least, it has always included the right to aid of counsel. . . . The right to be heard would be, in many cases, of little avail if it did not comprehend the right to be heard by counsel. Even the intelligent and educated layman has small and sometimes no skill in the science of law. If charged with crime, he is incapable, generally, of determining for himself whether the indictment is good or bad. He is unfamiliar with the rules of evidence. Left without the aid of counsel he may be put on trial without a proper charge, and convicted upon incompetent evidence, or evidence irrelevant to the issue or otherwise inadmissible. He lacks both the skill and knowledge adequately to prepare his defense, even though he has a perfect one. He requires the guiding hand of counsel at every step in the proceedings against him. Without it, though he be not guilty, he faces the danger of conviction because he does not know how to establish his innocence. If that be true of men of intelligence, how much more true is it of the ignorant and illiterate, or those of feeble intellect. If in any case, civil or criminal, a state or federal court were arbitrarily to refuse to hear a party by counsel, employed by and appearing for him, it reasonably may not be doubted that such a refusal would be a denial of a hearing, and, therefore, of due process in the constitutional sense. . . .

In the light of the facts outlined in the forepart of this opinion—the ignorance and illiteracy of the defendants, their youth, the circumstances of public hostility, the imprisonment and the close surveillance of the defendants by the military forces, the fact that their friends and family were all in other states and communication with them necessarily difficult, and above all that they stood in deadly peril of their lives—we think the failure of the trial court to give them reasonable time and opportunity to secure counsel was a clear denial of due process. . . .

[T]he necessity of counsel was so vital and imperative that the failure of the trial court to make an effective appointment of counsel was likewise a denial of due process within the meaning of the Fourteenth Amendment. Whether this would be so in other criminal prosecutions, or under other circumstances, we need not determine. All that is necessary now to decide, as we do decide, is that in a capital case, where the defendant is unable to employ counsel, and is incapable adequately of making his own defense because of ignorance, feeble-mindedness, illiteracy, or the like, it is the duty of the court, whether requested or not, to assign counsel for him as a necessary requisite of due process of law; and that duty is not discharged by an assignment at such a time or under such circumstances as to preclude the giving of effective aid in the preparation and trial of the case. To hold otherwise would be to ignore the fundamental postulate, already adverted to, "that there are certain immutable principles of justice which inhere in the very idea of free government which no member of the Union may disregard." . . .

The judgments must be reversed and the causes remanded for further proceedings not inconsistent with this opinion. Judgments reversed.

[NOTE: Justice Butler's dissent is omitted.]

CASE DISCUSSION

In precisely what way did the trial court deny Powell due process of law? How did the court formulate the fundamental fairness doctrine? What were the precise circumstances of this case that required the advice of counsel? Does this decision promote procedural regularity over obtaining the correct result, or does it attempt to do both? Explain how the right to counsel may not only ensure procedural regularity but also aid in obtaining the correct result in this case.

In 1936 the Supreme Court applied the due process clause to a state proceeding involving a forced confession. In *Brown v. Mississippi,* a sheriff hung Brown from a tree and brutally beat and whipped him until he confessed to murdering a white man. The trial court convicted Brown; the confession was the only evidence against him. Both the trial court and the Mississippi Supreme Court acknowledged that the confession was forced but let the conviction stand. Brown appealed to the United States Supreme Court. Mississippi argued that the United States Constitution did not prohibit the states from practicing compulsory self-incrimination. However, as Chief Justice Charles Evans Hughes wrote for the Court,

> The freedom of the State in establishing its policy is the freedom of constitutional government and is limited by the requirement of due process of law. . . . The rack and the torture chamber may not be substituted for the witness stand. . . . It would be difficult to conceive of methods more revolting to the sense of justice than those taken to procure the confession of [Brown], and the use of the confessions thus obtained as the basis for conviction and sentence was a clear denial of due process.[15]

Powell and *Brown* established the **fundamental fairness doctrine,** or the natural law theory of due process implied in *Hurtado v. California.* According to the fundamental fairness doctrine, due process is a general command, requiring states to provide the rudiments of a fair trial—that is, states must hear the facts before they condemn criminal defendants. The Constitution leaves the specific manner in which states choose to hear facts to the individual states and to developing notions of natural law.

During the 1930s, 1940s, and 1950s, excepting cases such as *Brown,* which involved extreme physical brutality, and *Powell,* where the states provided virtually no hearing, the Court continued to leave criminal procedure to the states, rejecting the idea that the specific provisions of the Bill of Rights applied to state criminal procedure. In *Palko v. Connecticut,* the Court ruled that the double jeopardy clause of the Fifth Amendment did not apply to state proceedings. Later, the Supreme Court held that the double jeopardy clause *did* apply to the states. Nevertheless, Justice Benjamin Cardozo's opinion became "one of the most influential in the history of the court." He rejected the argument that the Bill of Rights applied to the states. However, Justice Cardozo did concede that some rights are "implicit in the concept of ordered liberty and thus, through the Fourteenth Amendment, became valid as against the states." The Fourteenth Amendment imposed on the states only the rights that are "of the very essence of a scheme of ordered liberty." Some of these rights the Bill of Rights might include; others it may not. The question is this: Did the proceeding denying Palko double jeopardy subject him to "a hardship so shocking that our polity will not endure it? Does it violate those 'fundamental principles of liberty and justice which lie at the base of all our civil and political institutions?'" No, said Cardozo: ". . . The edifice of justice stands, in its symmetry, to many, greater than before."[16]

Justice Felix Frankfurter, a staunch supporter of fundamental fairness, used a variety of phrases to capture the doctrine's essential meaning. They included "[procedures that] offend the community's sense of fair play and decency" and "[conduct that] shocks the conscience." Writing for the Court, Justice Frankfurter applied the fundamental fairness doctrine in *Rochin v. California.*

CASE

Do the Police Actions "Shock the Conscience"?

Rochin v. California,
342 U.S. 165, 72 S.Ct. 205,
96 L.Ed. 183 (1952)

Rochin was convicted of the illegal possession of drugs. Rochin challenged the use of illegally seized drugs. The trial court admitted the evidence. Rochin appealed. The California appellate courts, including the California Supreme Court, upheld the conviction. The U.S. Supreme Court reversed. Justice Frankfurter wrote the opinion of the Court.

FACTS

Having "some information that (the petitioner here) was selling narcotics," three deputy sheriffs of the County of Los Angeles, on the morning of July 1, 1949, made for the two-story dwelling house in which Rochin lived with his mother, common-law wife, brothers and sisters. Finding the outside door open, they entered and then forced open the door to Rochin's room on the second floor. Inside they found petitioner sitting partly dressed on the side of his bed, upon which his wife was lying. On a "night stand" beside the bed the deputies spied two capsules. When asked "Whose stuff is this?" Rochin seized the capsules and put them in his mouth. A struggle ensued, in the course of which the three officers "jumped upon him" and attempted to extract the capsules. The force they applied proved unavailing against Rochin's resistance.

He was handcuffed and taken to a hospital. At the direction of one of the officers a doctor forced an emetic solution through a tube into Rochin's stomach against his will. This "stomach pumping" produced vomiting. In the vomited matter were found two capsules which proved to contain morphine.

Rochin was brought to trial before a California Superior Court, sitting without a jury, on the charge of possessing "a preparation of morphine" in violation of the California Health and Safety Code 1947, § 11500. Rochin was convicted and sentenced to sixty days' im-

prisonment. The chief evidence against him was the two capsules. They were admitted over petitioner's objection, although the means of obtaining them was frankly set forth in the testimony by one of the deputies, substantially as here narrated.

On appeal, the District Court of Appeal affirmed the conviction, despite the finding that the officer[s] "were guilty of unlawfully breaking into and entering defendant's room and were guilty of unlawfully assaulting and battering defendant while in the room," and "were guilty of unlawfully assaulting, battering, torturing and falsely imprisoning the defendant at the alleged hospital." One of the three judges, while finding that "the record in this case reveals a shocking series of violations of constitutional rights," concurred only because he felt bound by decisions of his Supreme Court. These, he asserted, "have been looked upon by law enforcement officers as an encouragement, if not an invitation, to the commission of such lawless acts." The Supreme Court of California denied without opinion Rochin's petition for a hearing. Two justice[s] dissented from this denial, and in doing so expressed themselves thus:

> . . . [A] conviction which rests upon evidence of incriminating objects obtained from the body of the accused by physical abuse is as invalid as a conviction which rests upon a verbal confession extracted from him by such abuse. . . . Had the evidence forced from defendant's lips consisted of an oral confession that he illegally possessed a drug . . . he would have the protection of the rule of law which excludes coerced confessions from evidence. But because the evidence forced from his lips consisted of real objects the People of this state are permitted to base a conviction upon it. (We) find no valid ground of distinction between a verbal confession extracted by physical abuse and a confession wrested from defendant's body by physical abuse.

This Court granted certiorari, because a serious question is raised as to the limitations which the Due Process Clause of the Fourteenth Amendment imposes on the conduct of criminal proceedings by the States.

OPINION

In our federal system the administration of criminal justice is predominantly committed to the care of the States. The power to define crimes belongs to Congress only as an appropriate means of carrying into execution its limited grant of legislative powers. U.S. Const. art. I, § 8, cl. 18. Broadly speaking, crimes in the United States are what the laws of the individual States make them. . . .

Accordingly, in reviewing a State criminal conviction under a claim of right guaranteed by the Due Process Clause of the Fourteenth Amendment, from which is derived the most far reaching and most frequent federal basis of challenging State criminal justice, "we must be deeply mindful of the responsibilities of the States for the enforcement of criminal laws, and exercise with due humility our merely negative function in subjecting convictions from state courts to the very narrow scrutiny which the Due Process Clause of the Fourteenth Amendment authorizes." Due process of law, "itself a historical product," is not to be turned into a destructive dogma against the States in the administration of their systems of criminal justice.

However, this Court too has its responsibility. Regard for the requirements of the Due Process Clause

> inescapably imposes upon this court an exercise of judgment upon the whole course of the proceedings (resulting in a conviction) in order to ascertain whether they offend those canons of decency and fairness which express the notions of justice of English-speaking peoples even toward those charged with the most heinous offenses.

These standards of justice are not authoritatively formulated anywhere as though they were specifics. Due process of law is a summarized constitutional guarantee of respect for those personal immunities which, as Mr. Justice Cardozo twice wrote for the

Court, are "so rooted in the traditions and conscience of our people as to be ranked as fundamental," or are "implicit in the concept of ordered liberty."

The Court's function in the observance of this settled conception of the Due Process Clause does not leave us without adequate guides in subjecting State criminal procedures to constitutional judgment. In dealing not with the machinery of government but with human rights, the absence of formal exactitude, or want of fixity of meaning, is not an unusual or even regrettable attribute of constitutional provisions. Words being symbols do not speak without a gloss. On the one hand the gloss may be the deposit of history, whereby a term gains technical content. Thus the requirements of the Sixth and Seventh Amendments for trial by jury in the federal courts have a rigid meaning. No changes or chances can alter the consent of the verbal symbol of "jury"—a body of twelve men who must reach a unanimous conclusion if the verdict is to go against the defendant. On the other hand, the gloss of some of the verbal symbols of the Constitution does not give them a fixed technical content, It exacts a continuing process of application.

When the gloss has thus not been fixed but is a function of the process of judgment, the judgment is bound to fall differently at different times and differently at the same time through different judges. Even more specific provisions, such as the guaranty of freedom of speech and the detailed protection against unreasonable searches and seizures, have inevitably evoked as sharp divisions in this Court as the least specific and most comprehensive protection of liberties, the Due Process Clause.

The vague contours of the Due Process Clause do not leave judges at large. We may not draw on our merely personal and private notions and disregard the limits that bind judges in their judicial function. Even though the concept of due process of law is not final and fixed, these limits are derived from considerations that are fused in the whole nature of our judicial process. These are considerations deeply rooted in reason and in the compelling traditions of the legal profession. The Due Process Clause places upon this Court the duty of exercising a judgment, within the narrow confines of judicial power in reviewing State convictions, upon interests of society pushing in opposite directions.

[COURT NOTE: "Burke's observations on the method of ascertaining law by judges are pertinent: 'Your committee do not find any positive law which binds the judges of the courts in Westminster-hall publicly to give a reasoned opinion from the bench, in support of their judgment upon matters that are stated before them. But the course hath prevailed from the oldest times. It hath been so general and so uniform, that it must be considered as the law of the land.' And Burke had an answer for those who argue that the liberty of the citizen cannot be adequately protected by the flexible conception of due process of law: ' . . . the English jurisprudence has not any other sure foundation, nor consequently the lives and properties of the subject any sure hold, but in the maxims, rules, and principles, and juridical traditionary line of decisions. . . .' "]

Due process of law thus conceived is not to be derided as resort to a revival of "natural law." To believe that this judicial exercise of judgment could be avoided by freezing "due process of law" at some fixed stage of time or thought is to suggest that the most important aspect of constitutional adjudication is a function for inanimate machines and not for judges, for whom the independence safeguarded by Article III of the Constitution was designed and who are presumably guided by established standards of judicial behavior. Even cybernetics has not yet made that haughty claim. To practice the requisite detachment and to achieve sufficient objectivity no doubt demands of judges the habit of self-discipline and self-criticism, incertitude that one's own views are incontestable and alert tolerance toward views not shared. But these are precisely the presuppositions of our judicial process. They are precisely the qualities society has a right to expect from those entrusted with ultimate judicial power.

Restraints on our jurisdiction are self-imposed only in the sense that there is from our decisions no immediate appeal short of impeachment or constitutional amendment. But that does not make due process of law a matter of judicial caprice. The faculties of the Due Process Clause may be indefinite and vague, but the mode of their ascertainment is not self-willed. In each case "due process of law" requires an evaluation based on a disinterested inquiry pursued in the spirit of science, on a balanced order of facts exactly and fairly stated, on the detached consideration of conflicting claims, on a judgment not ad hoc and episodic but duly mindful of reconciling the needs both of continuity and of change in a progressive society.

Applying these general considerations to the circumstances of the present case, we are compelled to conclude that the proceedings by which this conviction was obtained do more than offend some fastidious squeamishness or private sentimentalism about combatting crime too energetically. This is conduct that shocks the conscience. Illegally breaking into the privacy of the petitioner, the struggle to open his mouth and remove what was there, the forcible extraction of his stomach's contents—this course of proceeding by agents of government to obtain evidence is bound to offend even hardened sensibilities. They are methods too close to the rack and the screw to permit of constitutional differentiation.

It has long since ceased to be true that due process of law is heedless of the means by which otherwise relevant and credible evidence is obtained. This was not true even before the series of recent cases enforced the constitutional principle that the States may not base convictions upon confessions, however much verified, obtained by coercion. These decisions are not arbitrary exceptions to the comprehensive right of States to fashion their own rules of evidence for criminal trials. They are not sports in our constitutional law but applications of a general principle. They are only instances of the general requirement that States in their prosecutions respect certain decencies of civilized conduct. Due process of law, as a historic and generative principle, precludes defining, and thereby confining, these standards of conduct more precisely than to say that convictions cannot be brought about by methods that offend "a sense of justice" [*Brown v. Mississippi* (1936)]. It would be a stultification of the responsibility which the course of constitutional history has cast upon this Court to hold that in order to convict a man the police cannot extract by force what is in his mind but can extract what is in his stomach.

To attempt in this case to distinguish what lawyers call "real evidence" from verbal evidence is to ignore the reasons for excluding coerced confessions. Use of involuntary verbal confessions in State criminal trials is constitutionally obnoxious not only because of their unreliability. They are inadmissible under the Due Process Clause even though statements contained in them may be independently established as true. Coerced confessions offend the community's sense of fair play and decency. So here, to sanction the brutal conduct which naturally enough was condemned by the court whose judgment is before us, would be to afford brutality the cloak of law. Nothing would be more calculated to discredit law and thereby to brutalize the temper of a society.

In deciding this case we do not heedlessly bring into question decisions in many States dealing with essentially different, even if related, problems. We therefore put to one side cases which have arisen in the State courts through use of modern methods and devices for discovering wrongdoers and bringing them to book. It does not fairly represent these decisions to suggest that they legalize force so brutal and so offensive to human dignity in securing evidence from a suspect as is revealed by this record. Indeed the California Supreme Court has not sanctioned this mode of securing a conviction. It merely exercised its discretion to decline a review of the conviction. All the California judges who have expressed themselves in this case have condemned the conduct in the strongest language.

We are not unmindful that hypothetical situations can be conjured up, standing imperceptibly from the circumstances of this case and by gradations producing practical differences despite seemingly logical extensions. But the Constitution is "intended to preserve practical and substantial rights, not to maintain theories." On the facts of this case the conviction of the petitioner has been obtained by methods that offend the Due Process Clause. The judgment below must be reversed.

Reversed.

CONCURRING OPINION

Mr. Justice Black, concurring.

. . . In the view of a majority of the Court . . . the Fifth Amendment imposes no restraint of any kind on the states. They nevertheless hold that California's use of his evidence violated the Due Process Clause of the Fourteenth Amendment. Since they hold as I do in this case, I regret my inability to accept their interpretation without protest. But I believe that faithful adherence to the specific guarantees in the Bill of Rights insures a more permanent protection of individual liberty than that which can be afforded by the nebulous standards stated by the majority.

What the majority hold is that the Due Process Clause empowers this Court to nullify any state law if its application "shocks the conscience," offends "a sense of justice" or runs counter to the "decencies of civilized conduct." The majority emphasize that these statements do not refer to their own consciences or to their senses of justice and decency. For we are told that "we may not draw on our merely personal and private notions"; our judgment must be grounded on "considerations deeply rooted in reason and in the compelling traditions of the legal profession." We are further admonished to measure the validity of state practices, not by our reason, or by the traditions of the legal profession, but by "the community's sense of fair play and decency"; by the "traditions and conscience of our people"; or by "those canons of decency and fairness which express the notions of justice of English-speaking peoples." These canons are made necessary, it is said, because of "interests of society pushing in opposite directions."

If the Due Process Clause does vest this Court with such unlimited power to invalidate laws, I am still in doubt as to why we should consider only the notions of English-speaking peoples to determine what are immutable and fundamental principles of justice. Moreover, one may well ask what avenues of investigation are open to discover "canons" of conduct so universally favored that this Court should write them into the Constitution? All we are told is that the discovery must be made by an "evaluation based on a disinterested inquiry pursued in the spirit of science, on a balanced order of facts." . . .

Of even graver concern, however, is the use of philosophy to nullify the Bill of Rights. I long ago concluded that the accordion-like qualities of this philosophy must inevitably imperil all the individual liberty safeguards specifically enumerated in the Bill of Rights. . . .

CASE DISCUSSION

Why did the Court apply the Fourteenth Amendment to *Rochin v. California* and not to *Palko v. Connecticut*? What is different about the cases? Does the police conduct in this case "shock your conscience"? Is this a purely subjective test, or does it have an objective basis? Explain. Does the test mean that only physical brutality brings the due process clause to bear on state criminal procedure? Is this a good rule? Defend your answer. This is an excellent case to see the importance of concurring opinions. Notice that Justice Hugo L. Black agreed with the decision of the court but disagreed strongly with the majority's reasons for the decision. Justice Black and Justice Felix Frankfurter were the major protagonists in the debate over incorporation. Their opinions reveal their differences as well as indicate their commitment to individual rights. Which of the two views do you support? Explain your answer.

The Incorporation Doctrine

During the 1940s and 1950s, all the justices came to accept the idea that the Constitution limited state proceedings. However, they disagreed over how to define those limits. The fundamental fairness doctrine, or the idea that some higher natural law defined due process, fueled a great debate on and off the Court. A growing minority on the Court rejected the fundamental fairness doctrine. In its place, they more or less accepted the elder Justice John Marshall Harlan's **incorporation doctrine,** which held that the due process clause incorporated the specific provisions of the Bill of Rights.

By the 1960s, incorporation claimed a majority of the Court, which it still does. Justice Felix Frankfurter suffered a stroke in 1962 and retired. Justice Charles Whittaker retired the same year. President John F. Kennedy replaced them with two incorporationists, Justices Byron R. White and Arthur J. Goldberg. Led by Chief Justice Earl Warren, a former California prosecutor, the Court actively pursued the "constitutionalization" of state criminal procedure by means of the incorporation doctrine. The Court "policed" state criminal procedure by applying the due process clause to progressively earlier stages in the criminal process.[17]

First, the Court intervened between suspects and the police in the police station—extending the right to counsel and demanding that the police give the now famous Miranda warnings to arrested suspects in police custody (see Chapter 8 and the section on the right to counsel in Chapter 11). Then the court extended its policing powers to encounters between citizens and the police on the street before citizens were arrested or taken into custody. The Supreme Court also scrutinized brief detentions and weapons pat-down practices traditionally left to police discretion. As a result, the Supreme Court specifically reviewed the day-to-day activities of local police departments.[18]

Both the fundamental fairness doctrine and the incorporation doctrine promoted process interests in controlling government and the societal interest in equality for all races and classes, even if it meant sacrificing conviction in specific cases. However, the two doctrines differed in several respects. First, they defined due process differently. According to the fundamental fairness doctrine, the substantive concept of due process embodied the development of Anglo-American law from the time of the Magna Carta. According to Professor Jerold Israel,

The concept of due process dated back to the Magna Carta, and English and American commentators had discussed it at length. The proponents of fundamental fairness viewed those authorities as having established a flexible standard of justice that focused on the essence of fairness rather than the familiarity of form. Due process, under this view, was "a concept less rigid and more fluid than those envisaged in other specific and particular provisions of the Bill of Rights." Indeed, Justice Frankfurter described it as "perhaps, the least frozen concept of our law — the least confined to history and the most absorptive of powerful social standards of a progressive society." Its basic objective was to provide "respect enforced by law" for that feeling of just treatment which has evolved through centuries of Anglo [A]merican constitutional history and civilization. Thus, it had a "natural law" background, which extended beyond procedural fairness and imposed limits as well on the substance of state regulation.[19]

Under the fundamental fairness doctrine, due process might include some rights in the Bill of Rights totally, some partially, and some not at all. According to the incorporation doctrine, due process is simply a procedural guarantee; it ensures procedural regularity, namely, that guaranteed in the Bill of Rights. Justice Hugo L. Black, the incorporation doctrine's staunchest proponent, maintained that due process grants only a "right to be tried by an independent and unprejudiced court using established procedures and applying valid preexisting laws." According to Justice Black, due process absorbs all rights under the Bill of Rights; others maintain that it encompasses only some of those rights.[20]

The fundamental fairness doctrine derives its meaning independent of the Bill of Rights. In other words, the due process clause is not the equivalent of the rights guaranteed in the Fourth, Fifth, Sixth, and Eighth Amendments. The fundamental fairness doctrine applies the due process clause on a case-by-case basis. It does not restrict its inquiry to the Bill of Rights. Under it, the Supreme Court weighs all the circumstances and decides whether they violate the fundamental norms of American civilized society at a particular time and place. Not all the rights guaranteed in the Bill of Rights violate these fundamental norms; on the other hand, some actions not included in the Bill of Rights may do so. According to Professor Israel,

> If a defendant contended that a state had denied him due process of law by failing to recognize a right protected by the Bill of Rights, the issue presented was not whether that right, viewed in the abstract, was "implicit in the concept of ordered liberty." Rather, the issue was whether the state's action had resulted in a denial of fundamental fairness in the context of the particular case. . . . Due process under this approach was to be defined on a case-by-case basis, with its "full meaning . . . gradually ascertained by the process of inclusion and exclusion in the course of the decisions of cases as they arise."[21]

Fundamental fairness and incorporation also differ over the extent and specificity to which they require uniform treatment. Under the fundamental fairness doctrine, state and local systems of criminal justice could define most of their own criminal procedure law. The more-specific incorporation doctrine leaves the states less free to determine their own criminal procedure than does the fundamental fairness doctrine; they must accept the procedures outlined in the Bill of Rights.

TABLE 2.3 CASES INCORPORATING THE BILL OF RIGHTS

Unreasonable searches and seizures	*Wolf v. Colorado* (1949)
Exclusionary rule applied to state searches and seizures	*Mapp v. Ohio* (1961)
Self-incrimination	*Malloy v. Hogan* (1964)
Assistance of counsel	*Gideon v. Wainwright* (1963)
Confrontation of witnesses against the accused	*Pointer v. Texas* (1965)
Compulsory process to obtain witnesses	*Washington v. Texas* (1967)
Speedy trial	*Klopfer v. North Carolina* (1967)
Cruel and unusual punishment	*Robinson v. California* (1962)

When the Court finally adopted the incorporation doctrine, justices continued to disagree strongly over which provisions the Fourteenth Amendment incorporated. Some justices called for **total incorporation,** meaning that all the provisions were incorporated under the due process clause. Others called for **selective incorporation,** meaning that some rights were incorporated and others were not.

During the 1960s, the Supreme Court opted for the selective incorporation doctrine in applying the United States Constitution to state criminal proceedings. By the end of that decade, the selective incorporation doctrine had changed the "face of the law," according to Supreme Court Justice William Brennan. The decisions of that decade incorporated all but four of the Bill of Rights guarantees relating to criminal justice: public trial, notice of charges, prohibition of excessive bail, and prosecution by indictment. Table 2.3 presents a list of cases that brought about the incorporation of specific rights. In cases decided since the 1960s, the Court has suggested that Fourteenth Amendment due process incorporates all but indictment by grand jury.

Incorporated rights apply to the states exactly as in federal proceedings, according to the Supreme Court—"jot-for-jot and case for case," as one of the doctrine's severest critics, Justice John Harlan, put it. Justice Brennan defended the "jot for jot" approach this way:

> [O]nly impermissible subjective judgments can explain stopping short of the incorporation of the full sweep of the specific being absorbed.[22]

The critics of the incorporation doctrine—it had and still has many—charged that incorporation destroys federalism, interferes with local criminal justice, and eviscerates the need for both local variety and experiments with different solutions to problems in criminal justice administration. They maintain that the great differences among the states and among federal, state, and local systems of criminal justice demand local control and variation.

Critics rightly observe that federal criminal justice consists mainly of cases involving fraud, tax evasion, and other complex crimes. Investigation takes place largely in offices, not in the field. Hence, federal law enforcement differs markedly from the hurly-burly street crimes that bring local police in contact with violent individuals or strangers who are difficult to identify, apprehend, and bring to trial. Furthermore, most local police are not highly trained college graduates, as are the federal police, particularly FBI agents. Therefore, the Bill of Rights works well for federal criminal justice, these critics maintain, but not in local law enforcement, where, if anything, it impedes the effective administration of criminal justice. The incorporation doctrine imposes a federal practice that works effectively for only the 0.6 percent of criminal cases that are federal cases but not for the remaining 99.4 percent that are state cases, where it is ineffective.

The criticisms target all criminal justice agencies, but perhaps nothing generates more controversy than whether or not uniform standards ought to apply to local police departments. Cries that the United States Supreme Court was "running local police departments" from Washington and "handcuffing" local police by doing so were common during the late 1960s, following the decision in the famous *Miranda* case (see Chapter 7). Contrary to its opponents' fears, the incorporation doctrine has not imposed a straitjacket on state and local criminal justice. The Supreme Court's flexible interpretations of the constitutional protections permit local diversity and experimentation. The Court paid deference to local variation and experiment in *Chandler v. Florida*. Chandler argued that Florida's practice of televising trials violated his right to a fair trial. In rejecting the claim, Chief Justice Warren Burger, personally no fan of television in the courts, supported the right of local jurisdictions to follow their own practices:

> Dangers lurk in this, as in most experiments, but unless we were to conclude that television coverage under all conditions is prohibited by the Constitution, the state must be free to experiment. We are not empowered by the Constitution to oversee or harness state procedural experimentation; only when the state action infringes fundamental guarantees are we authorized to intervene. We must assume state courts will be alert to any factors that impair the fundamental rights of the accused. Absent a showing of prejudice of constitutional dimensions to these defendants, there is no reason for this Court either to endorse or to invalidate Florida's experiment.[23]

EQUAL PROTECTION OF THE LAW

The value of equality is deeply embedded in the concept of United States constitutionalism. In the years just prior to the Revolution, one commentator wrote the following:

> The least considerable man among us has an interest equal to the proudest nobleman, in the laws and constitution of his country.[24]

The Fourteenth Amendment to the United States Constitution commands that

> [N]o state shall . . . deny to any person within its jurisdiction the equal protection of the laws.

Equal protection of the law does not mean that the states must treat everybody alike. It means that states cannot arrest, prosecute, convict, sentence, and punish people according to unacceptable criteria. Therefore, courts will look suspiciously at certain classifications, particularly those based on race and ethnicity. The United States Supreme Court examined the requirements of equal protection in the decision to prosecute two African-American men for drug and firearm offenses in *United States v. Armstrong*.

C A S E

Did the Prosecution Violate Equal Protection?

United States v. Armstrong and others, 116 S.Ct. 1480 (1996)

Christopher Lee Armstrong, Aaron Hampton, Freddie Mack, Shelton Martin, and Robert Rozelle were indicted for selling crack and using a firearm in connection with drug trafficking. They moved for discovery on a claim of selective prosecution. The United States District Court for the Central District of California granted the motion. The government appealed. The court of appeals reversed. A rehearing *en banc* was granted. The court of appeals affirmed the district court. The government petitioned for a writ of *certiorari*, and the United States Supreme Court issued the writ. The Supreme Court reversed and remanded the case.

Rehnquist, C.J., delivered the opinion of the Court, in which O'Connor, Scalia, Kennedy, Souter, Thomas, and Ginsburg, JJ., joined and in which Breyer, J., joined in part. Souter, J., and Ginsburg, J., filed concurring opinions. Breyer, J., filed an opinion concurring in part and concurring in the judgment. Stevens, J., filed a dissenting opinion.

FACTS

In April 1992, respondents were indicted in the United States District Court for the Central District of California on charges of conspiring to possess with intent to distribute more than 50 grams of cocaine base (crack) and conspiring to distribute the same, in violation of 21 U.S.C. §§ 841 and 846 (1988 ed. and Supp. IV), and federal firearms offenses. For three months prior to the indictment, agents of the Federal Bureau of Alcohol, Tobacco, and Firearms and the Narcotics Division of the Inglewood, California, Police Department had infiltrated a suspected crack distribution ring by using three confidential informants. On seven separate occasions during this period, the informants had bought a total of 124.3 grams of crack from respondents and witnessed respondents carrying

firearms during the sales. The agents searched the hotel room in which the sales were transacted, arrested respondents Armstrong and Hampton in the room, and found more crack and a loaded gun. The agents later arrested the other respondents as part of the ring.

In response to the indictment, respondents filed a motion for discovery or for dismissal of the indictment, alleging that they were selected for federal prosecution because they are black. In support of their motion, they offered only an affidavit by a "Paralegal Specialist," employed by the Office of the Federal Public Defender representing one of the respondents. The only allegation in the affidavit was that, in every one of the 24 §§ 841 or 846 cases closed by the office during 1991, the defendant was black. Accompanying the affidavit was a "study" listing the 24 defendants, their race, whether they were prosecuted for dealing cocaine as well as crack, and the status of each case.

The Government opposed the discovery motion, arguing, among other things, that there was no evidence or allegation "that the Government has acted unfairly or has prosecuted non-black defendants or failed to prosecute them." The District Court granted the motion. It ordered the Government (1) to provide a list of all cases from the last three years in which the Government charged both cocaine and firearms offenses, (2) to identify the race of the defendants in those cases, (3) to identify what levels of law enforcement were involved in the investigations of those cases, and (4) to explain its criteria for deciding to prosecute those defendants for federal cocaine offenses.

The Government moved for reconsideration of the District Court's discovery order. With this motion it submitted affidavits and other evidence to explain why it had chosen to prosecute respondents and why respondents' study did not support the inference that the Government was singling out blacks for cocaine prosecution. The federal and local agents participating in the case alleged in affidavits that race played no role in their investigation. An Assistant United States

Attorney explained in an affidavit that the decision to prosecute met the general criteria for prosecution, because

> there was over 100 grams of cocaine base involved, over twice the threshold necessary for a ten year mandatory minimum sentence; there were multiple sales involving multiple defendants, thereby indicating a fairly substantial crack cocaine ring; . . . there were multiple federal firearms violations intertwined with the narcotics trafficking; the overall evidence in the case was extremely strong, including audio and videotapes of defendants; . . . and several of the defendants had criminal histories including narcotics and firearms violations.

The Government also submitted sections of a published 1989 Drug Enforcement Administration report which concluded that "[l]arge-scale, interstate trafficking networks controlled by Jamaicans, Haitians and Black street gangs dominate the manufacture and distribution of crack." J. Featherly & E. Hill, *Crack Cocaine Overview 1989*; App. 103.

In response, one of respondents' attorneys submitted an affidavit alleging that an intake coordinator at a drug treatment center had told her that there are "an equal number of caucasian users and dealers to minority users and dealers." Id., at 138. Respondents also submitted an affidavit from a criminal defense attorney alleging that in his experience many non-blacks are prosecuted in state court for crack offenses, id., at 141, and a newspaper article reporting that Federal "crack criminals . . . are being punished far more severely than if they had been caught with powder cocaine, and almost every single one of them is black." Newton, "Harsher Crack Sentences Criticized as Racial Inequity," *Los Angeles Times*, Nov. 23, 1992, p. 1.

The District Court denied the motion for reconsideration. When the Government indicated it would not comply with the court's discovery order, the court dismissed the case. [NOTE: We have never determined whether dismissal of the indictment, or some other sanction, is the proper remedy if a court determines that a defendant has been the victim of prosecution on the basis of his race. Here, "it was the government itself that suggested dismissal of the in-

dictments to the district court so that an appeal might lie." 48 F.3d 1508, 1510 (C.A.9 1995).]

A divided three-judge panel of the Court of Appeals for the Ninth Circuit reversed, holding that, because of the proof requirements for a selective-prosecution claim, defendants must "provide a colorable basis for believing that 'others similarly situated have not been prosecuted'" to obtain discovery. 21 F.3d 1431, 1436 (1994) (quoting *United States v. Wayte*, 710 F.2d 1385, 1387 (C.A.9 1983), aff'd, 470 U.S. 598, 105 S.Ct. 1524, 84 L.Ed.2d 547 (1985)). The Court of Appeals voted to rehear the case en banc, and the en banc panel affirmed the District Court's order of dismissal, holding that "a defendant is not required to demonstrate that the government has failed to prosecute others who are similarly situated." We granted certiorari to determine the appropriate standard for discovery for a selective-prosecution claim.

Neither the District Court nor the Court of Appeals mentioned Federal Rule of Criminal Procedure 16, which by its terms governs discovery in criminal cases. Both parties now discuss the Rule in their briefs, and respondents contend that it supports the result reached by the Court of Appeals. Rule 16 provides, in pertinent part:

> Upon request of the defendant the government shall permit the defendant to inspect and copy or photograph books, papers, documents, photographs, tangible objects, buildings or places, or copies or portions thereof, which are within the possession, custody or control of the government, and which are material to the preparation of the defendant's defense or are intended for use by the government as evidence in chief at the trial, or were obtained from or belong to the defendant. Fed. Rule Crim. Proc. 16(a)(1)(C).

OPINION

. . .

A selective-prosecution claim asks a court to exercise judicial power over a "special province" of the Executive. The Attorney General and United States Attorneys retain "broad discretion" to enforce the Nation's criminal laws. They have this latitude because they are designated by statute as the President's delegates to help him discharge his constitutional responsibility to "take Care that the Laws be faithfully executed." U.S. Const., Art. II, § 3; see 28 U.S.C. §§ 516, 547. As a result, "[t]he presumption of regularity supports" their prosecutorial decisions and "in the absence of clear evidence to the contrary, courts presume that they have properly discharged their official duties." In the ordinary case, "so long as the prosecutor has probable cause to believe that the accused committed an offense defined by statute, the decision whether or not to prosecute, and what charge to file or bring before a grand jury, generally rests entirely in his discretion."

Of course, a prosecutor's discretion is "subject to constitutional constraints." One of these constraints, imposed by the equal protection component of the Due Process Clause of the Fifth Amendment, is that the decision whether to prosecute may not be based on "an unjustifiable standard such as race, religion, or other arbitrary classification." A defendant may demonstrate that the administration of a criminal law is "directed so exclusively against a particular class of persons . . . with a mind so unequal and oppressive" that the system of prosecution amounts to "a practical denial" of equal protection of the law. *Yick Wo v. Hopkins*, 118 U.S. 356, 373, 6 S.Ct. 1064, 1073, 30 L.Ed. 220 (1886).

In order to dispel the presumption that a prosecutor has not violated equal protection, a criminal defendant must present "clear evidence to the contrary." . . . Judicial deference to the decisions of these executive officers rests in part on an assessment of the relative competence of prosecutors and courts. "Such factors as the strength of the case, the prosecution's general deterrence value, the Government's enforcement priorities, and the case's relationship to the Government's overall enforcement plan are not readily susceptible to the kind of analysis the courts are competent to undertake." It also stems from a concern not to unnecessarily impair the performance of a core executive constitutional function. "Examining the basis of a prosecution delays the criminal proceeding, threatens to chill law enforcement by subjecting the prosecutor's motives and decisionmaking to outside inquiry, and may undermine prosecutorial effective-

ness by revealing the Government's enforcement policy."

The requirements for a selective-prosecution claim draw on "ordinary equal protection standards." The claimant must demonstrate that the federal prosecutorial policy "had a discriminatory effect and that it was motivated by a discriminatory purpose." To establish a discriminatory effect in a race case, the claimant must show that similarly situated individuals of a different race were not prosecuted. . . .

The similarly situated requirement does not make a selective-prosecution claim impossible to prove. . . . [W]e invalidated an ordinance . . . adopted by San Francisco, that prohibited the operation of laundries in wooden buildings. *Yick Wo*, 118 U.S., at 374, 6 S.Ct., at 1073. . . . [*Yick Wo*] successfully demonstrated that the ordinance was applied against Chinese nationals but not against other laundry-shop operators. The authorities had denied the applications of 200 Chinese subjects for permits to operate shops in wooden buildings, but granted the applications of 80 individuals who were not Chinese subjects to operate laundries in wooden buildings "under similar conditions." We explained . . . why the similarly situated requirement is necessary:

> No latitude of intention should be indulged in a case like this. There should be certainty to every intent. Plaintiff in error seeks to set aside a criminal law of the State, not on the ground that it is unconstitutional on its face, not that it is discriminatory in tendency and ultimate actual operation as the ordinance was which was passed on in the *Yick Wo* case, but that it was made so by the manner of its administration. This is a matter of proof, and no fact should be omitted to make it out completely, when the power of a Federal court is invoked to interfere with the course of criminal justice of a State. 198 U.S., at 508, 25 S.Ct., at 759.

. . .

. . . [W]e turn to the showing necessary to obtain discovery in support of such a claim. If discovery is ordered, the Government must assemble from its own files documents which might corroborate or refute the defendant's claim. Discovery thus imposes many of the costs present when the Government must respond to a prima facie case of selective prosecution. It will divert prosecutors' resources and may disclose the Government's prosecutorial strategy. The justifications for a rigorous standard for the elements of a selective-prosecution claim thus require a correspondingly rigorous standard for discovery in aid of such a claim.

The parties, and the Courts of Appeals which have considered the requisite showing to establish entitlement to discovery, describe this showing with a variety of phrases, like "colorable basis," "substantial threshold showing," "substantial and concrete basis," or "reasonable likelihood." However, the many labels for this showing conceal the degree of consensus about the evidence necessary to meet it. The Courts of Appeals "require some evidence tending to show the existence of the essential elements of the defense," discriminatory effect and discriminatory intent.

In this case we consider what evidence constitutes "some evidence tending to show the existence" of the discriminatory effect element.... We think the required threshold—a credible showing of different treatment of similarly situated persons—adequately balances the Government's interest in vigorous prosecution and the defendant's interest in avoiding selective prosecution.

In the case before us, respondents' "study" did not constitute "some evidence tending to show the existence of the essential elements of" a selective-prosecution claim. The study failed to identify individuals who were not black, could have been prosecuted for the offenses for which respondents were charged, but were not so prosecuted. This omission was not remedied by respondents' evidence in opposition to the Government's motion for reconsideration. The newspaper article, which discussed the discriminatory effect of federal drug sentencing laws, was not relevant to an allegation of discrimination in decisions to prosecute. Respondents' affidavits, which recounted one attorney's conversation with a drug treatment center employee and the experience of another attorney defending drug prosecutions in state court, recounted hearsay and reported personal conclusions based on anecdotal evidence. The judgment of the Court of Appeals is therefore reversed, and the case is remanded for proceedings consistent with this opinion.

It is so ordered.

DISSENT

Justice Stevens, dissenting.

Federal prosecutors are respected members of a respected profession. Despite an occasional misstep, the excellence of their work abundantly justifies the presumption that "they have properly discharged their official duties." Nevertheless, the possibility that political or racial animosity may infect a decision to institute criminal proceedings cannot be ignored. For that reason, it has long been settled that the prosecutor's broad discretion to determine when criminal charges should be filed is not completely unbridled. As the Court notes, however, the scope of judicial review of particular exercises of that discretion is not fully defined. . . . Like Chief Judge Wallace of the Court of Appeals, however, I am persuaded that the District Judge did not abuse her discretion when she concluded that the factual showing was sufficiently disturbing to require some response from the United States Attorney's Office. Perhaps the discovery order was broader than necessary, but I cannot agree with the Court's apparent conclusion that no inquiry was permissible.

The District Judge's order should be evaluated in light of three circumstances that underscore the need for judicial vigilance over certain types of drug prosecutions. First, the Anti-Drug Abuse Act of 1986 and subsequent legislation established a regime of extremely high penalties for the possession and distribution of so-called "crack" cocaine. Those provisions treat one gram of crack as the equivalent of 100 grams of powder cocaine. The distribution of 50 grams of crack is thus punishable by the same mandatory minimum sentence of 10 years in prison that applies to the distribution of 5,000 grams of powder cocaine. The Sentencing Guidelines extend this ratio to penalty levels above the mandatory minimums: for any given quantity of crack, the guideline range is the same as if the offense had involved 100 times that amount in powder cocaine. These penalties result in sentences for crack offenders that average three to eight times longer than sentences for comparable powder offenders.

Second, the disparity between the treatment of crack cocaine and powder cocaine is matched by the disparity between the severity of the punishment imposed by federal law and that imposed by state law for the same conduct. For a variety of reasons, often including the absence of mandatory minimums, the existence of parole, and lower baseline penalties, terms of imprisonment for drug offenses tend to be substantially lower in state systems than in the federal system. The difference is especially marked in the case of crack offenses. The majority of States draw no distinction between types of cocaine in their penalty schemes; of those that do, none has established as stark a differential as the Federal Government. For example, if respondent Hampton is found guilty, his federal sentence might be as long as a mandatory life term. Had he been tried in state court, his sentence could have been as short as 12 years, less worktime credits of half that amount.

Finally, it is undisputed that the brunt of the elevated federal penalties falls heavily on blacks. While 65% of the persons who have used crack are white, in 1993 they represented only 4% of the federal offenders convicted of trafficking in crack. Eighty-eight percent of such defendants were black. During the first 18 months of full guideline implementation, the sentencing disparity between black and white defendants grew from preguideline levels: blacks on average received sentences over 40% longer than whites. See Bureau of Justice Statistics, *Sentencing in the Federal Courts: Does Race Matter?* 6–7 (Dec. 1993). Those figures represent a major threat to the integrity of federal sentencing reform, whose main purpose was the elimination of disparity (especially racial) in sentencing. The Sentencing Commission acknowledges that the heightened crack penalties are a "primary cause of the growing disparity between sentences for Black and White federal defendants."

. . .

In sum, I agree with the Sentencing Commission that "[w]hile the exercise of discretion by prosecutors and investigators has an impact on sentences in almost all cases to some extent, because of the 100-to-1 quantity ratio and federal mandatory minimum penalties, discretionary decisions in cocaine cases often have dramatic effects." The severity of the penalty heightens both the danger of arbitrary enforcement and the need for careful scrutiny of any colorable claim of discriminatory enforcement. In this case, the evidence was sufficiently disturbing to persuade the District Judge to order discovery that might help explain the conspicuous racial pattern of cases before her Court. I cannot accept the majority's conclusion that the District Judge either exceeded her power or abused her discretion when she did so. I therefore respectfully dissent.

SUMMARY

Criminal procedure is a method of criminal law enforcement that governs the detection, investigation, apprehension, prosecution, conviction, and sentencing of criminals. The United States Constitution, state constitutions, federal and state court decisions, statutes, and sets of rules are the primary sources that regulate criminal procedure. Criminal justice agencies exist at the federal, state, and local levels. The United States Constitution—the supreme law of the land—is the ultimate source of authority in criminal procedure. United States Supreme Court decisions interpreting the United States Constitution are also part of the supreme law of the land; their authority extends throughout the nation. The United States Constitution and decisions interpreting it set a minimum standard that states are free to raise; states sometimes do so. Individual state constitutions give criminal defendants parallel protections against unreasonable searches and seizures, self-incrimination, unfair jury trials, double jeopardy, cruel and unusual punishment, and other infringements on constitutional rights. In all these protections, individual states have established higher standards under their constitutions than what the United States Supreme Court has defined as federal standards.

The authority of the United States Constitution and Supreme Court over state and local criminal procedure stems generally from the supremacy clause and specifically from the Fourteenth Amendment's due process clause. Under the selective incorporation doctrine, most of the Bill of Rights has been extended to the states. The incorporation doctrine permits considerable diversity among the states.

Day-to-day law enforcement in America is primarily local. Minimum federal standards permit local variety in criminal justice administration. The U.S. Supreme Court recognizes the need to allow not only for individual differences among states and between state and federal law enforcement, but also for local experimentation in criminal procedure. The Court gives considerable deference to local criminal justice despite the incorporation doctrine. Finally, the Supreme Court has only limited capacity to enforce its decisions on day-to-day local practice. Community norms, organizational values, and individual personalities contribute to a gap between Supreme Court decisions handed down in Washington, D.C., and police, prosecution, and judicial behavior at the local level. Discretion allows these local, organizational, and personal norms to operate within the framework of the formal law of criminal procedure.

REVIEW QUESTIONS

1. Define *criminal procedure.*

2. Identify and describe the sources of the law of criminal procedure. What is the ultimate source of the law of criminal procedure?

3. What is the main interpreter of the Constitution in the United States?

4. What level of government conducts the main day-to-day business of criminal procedure?

5. Explain the role of states in defining the rights guaranteed by the U.S. Constitution.

6. Identify and explain the significance of the Model Code of Pre-arraignment Procedure.

7. According to the U.S. Supreme Court, what is the relationship of the Fourteenth Amendment due process clause to state criminal procedure?

8. Identify and explain the significance of the incorporation doctrine. Distinguish between total and selective incorporation.

9. What is the position of the U.S. Supreme Court with respect to individual differences among the states in criminal procedure?

KEY TERMS

criminal procedure the methods that the government uses to detect, investigate, apprehend, prosecute, convict, and punish criminals.

due process clause the Fifth and Fourteenth Amendment provisions prohibiting the federal government and the states, respectively, from depriving citizens of life, liberty, or property without due process of law.

fundamental fairness doctrine the principle that state procedures cannot violate basic standards of ordered liberty.

incorporation doctrine the principle that the Fourteenth Amendment due process clause incorporates the provisions of the Bill of Rights and applies them to state criminal procedure.

judicial review the power of courts to review legislation.

parallel rights state-granted rights similar to those in the U.S. Constitution and Bill of Rights.

selective incorporation the concept that only some federal rights are incorporated by the due process clause.

supervisory power the ability of the United States Supreme Court to oversee lower federal court and state court proceedings.

supremacy clause the principle that the United States Constitution and laws are supreme over state law.

total incorporation the principle that all federal rights are incorporated by the due process clause.

Notes

1. James A. Gardner, "The Failed Discourse of State Constitutionalism," *Michigan Law Review*, 90 (1991): 761, 814.

2. Anthony Amsterdam, "The Supreme Court and the Rights of Suspects in Criminal Cases," *New York University Law Review* 45 (1970): 785.

3. Shirley S. Abrahamson, "Criminal Law and State Constitutions: The Emergence of State Constitutional Law," *Texas Law Review* 63 (1985): 141; William J. Brennan, Jr., "The Bill of Rights and the States: The Revival of State Constitutions as Guardians of Individual Rights," *New York University Law Review* 61 (1986): 535; Peter J. Galie, "The Other Supreme Courts: Judicial Activism Among State Supreme Courts," *Syracuse Law Review* 33 (1982): 731–32; Barry Latzer, "Toward the Decentralization of Criminal Procedure: State Constitutional Law and Selective Incorporation," *Journal of Criminal Law and Criminology*, 87 (1996): 63.

4. "Developments in the Law: The Interpretation of State Constitutional Rights," *Harvard Law Review* 95 (1982): 1324, 1370–84; Donald E. Wilkes, Jr., "The New Federalism in Criminal Procedure: State Court Evasion of the Burger Court," *Kentucky Law Journal* 62 (1974): 420–51.

5. John M. Burkoff, "The Pretext Search Doctrine: Now You See It, Now You Don't," *University of Michigan Journal of Law Reform* 17 (1984): 523.

6. Gerhard O. W. Mueller, Foreword to Lester B. Orfield, *Criminal Procedure Under the Federal Rules* (Rochester, NY: Lawyers Co-operative Publishing Company, 1966), 1: xiv.

7. 5 U.S. (1 Cranch) 137, 2 L.Ed. 60 (1803).

8. *The Federalist* (Middletown, CT: Wesleyan University Press, 1961), 485–86.

9. *Barron v. Baltimore*, 32 U.S. (7 Pet.) 243 at 250, 8 L.Ed. 672 (1833).

10. The opinions in *Adamson v. California*, 332 U.S. 46, 67 S.Ct. 1672, 91 L.Ed. 1903 (1947), particularly Justice Felix Frankfurter's concurring opinion and Justice Hugo L. Black's dissenting opinion, articulate these views forcefully.

11. Richard C. Cortner, *The Supreme Court and the Second Bill of Rights* (Madison, WI: University of Wisconsin Press, 1981), 12–13.

12. *Hurtado v. California*, 110 U.S. 516, 530, 4 S.Ct. 111, 118, 28 L.Ed. 232 (1884); Cortner, *Supreme Court*, 18–19.

13. Ibid.

14. Francis A. Allen, "The Law as a Path to the World," *Michigan Law Review* 77 (1978): 157–58.

15. 297 U.S. 278, 56 S.Ct. 461, 80 L.Ed. 682 (1936).

16. *Palko v. Connecticut*, 302 U.S. 319, 328 58 S.Ct. 149, 153, 82 L.Ed. 288 (1937).

17. Fred Graham, *The Self-Inflicted Wound* (New York: Macmillan, 1970); Francis Allen, "The Judicial Quest for Penal Justice: The Warren Court and the Criminal Cases," *Illinois Law Forum* (1975): 518.

18. *Escobedo v. Illinois*, 378 U.S. 478, 84 S.Ct. 1758, 12 L.Ed.2d 977 (1964), on the right to counsel in police custody; *Miranda v. Arizona*, 384 U.S. 436, 86 S.Ct. 1602, 16 L.Ed.2d 694 (1966), on the warnings to suspects in custody.

19. Jerold H. Israel, "Selective Incorporation: Revisited," *Georgetown Law Journal* 71 (1982): 274.

20. *Duncan v. Louisiana*, 391 U.S. 145, 169, 88 S.Ct. 1444, 1457, 20 L.Ed.2d 491 (1968).

21. Israel, "Selective Incorporation," 278–79.

22. Justice John Marshall Harlan, concurring in *Duncan v. Louisiana*, 391 U.S. 145, 88 S.Ct. 1444, 20 L.Ed.2d 491 (1968) (incorporating the right to jury trial); Wayne R. LaFave and Jerold H. Israel, *Criminal Procedure* (St. Paul: West Publishing Company, 1984), 1: 97–98; Justice Brennan quoted in Henry J. Friendly, "The Bill of Rights as a Code of Criminal Procedure," *California Law Review* 53 (1965): 929, 936.

23. *Chandler v. Florida*, 449 U.S. 560, 101 S.Ct. 802, 66 L.Ed. 2d 740 (1981).

24. Quoted in Fred E. Inbau and others, *Criminal Law and Its Administration*, fourth edition, (Mineola, NY: Foundation Press, 1980), 209.

CHAPTER THREE

Searches, Seizures, and the Fourth Amendment

CHAPTER OUTLINE

1. Crime control depends on the gathering and use of information.

2. The police are mainly responsible for gathering information as well as for using it in crime prevention and in the investigation and apprehension of suspects.

3. The Fourth Amendment requires that an objective basis support Fourth Amendment searches and seizures.

4. In practice, searches and seizures not only aid in criminal law enforcement, but they also protect police officers, enhance prison and jail safety and security, protect the property of prisoners, and aid in the furtherance of noncriminal public policies.

5. The purpose of the Fourth Amendment is to prevent the government from conducting "unreasonable searches and seizures" in order to enforce the law and other public interests.

6. The Fourth Amendment protects privacy, liberty, and property.

7. The Fourth Amendment protects only invasions of liberty, privacy, and property that amount to "unreasonable searches and seizures" by government officials or their agents.

8. Fourth Amendment seizures require that a reasonable person encountering a show of authority by a government official would not feel free either to walk away or to otherwise terminate the encounter.

9. Fourth Amendment searches require that a government action invade a reasonable expectation of privacy.

10. Invasions of privacy, liberty, and property increase as encounters between citizens and officers move from the street and other public places to police stations and jails.

11. Information gathered by police officers through the use of their ordinary senses of sight, hearing, smell, and touch are not Fourth Amendment searches or seizures.

12. The Fourth Amendment does not prevent the gathering, seizure, and use of information found in open fields.

13. The Fourth Amendment does not prevent police officers from gathering and using information found in public places through the use of the officers' ordinary senses.

14. The Fourth Amendment does not protect abandoned property.

15. It is not a Fourth Amendment seizure to approach individuals on the street or in other public places and ask them questions.

16. Individuals may feel a moral obligation or psychological pressure to cooperate with police officers who approach them and question them, but the law does not require them to do so until they are "seized" within the meaning of the Fourth Amendment.

Did She "Search" the Trash?

Investigator Jenny Stracner of the Laguna Beach Police Department conducted a surveillance of Greenwood's home. She observed several vehicles make brief stops at the house during the late-night and early-morning hours, and she followed a truck from the house to a residence that had previously been under investigation as a narcotics trafficking location.

On April 6, 1984, Stracner asked the neighborhood's regular trash collector to pick up the plastic garbage bags that Greenwood had left on the curb in front of his house and to turn the bags over to her without mixing their contents with garbage from other houses. The trash collector cleaned his truck bin of other refuse, collected the garbage bags from the street in front of Greenwood's house, and turned the bags over to Stracner. The officer searched through the rubbish and found items indicative of narcotics use. On May 4, Investigator Robert Rahaeuser obtained Greenwood's garbage from the regular trash collector in the same manner as had Stracner. The garbage again contained evidence of narcotics use.

PURPOSES OF SEARCHES
AND SEIZURES

Crime control in a constitutional democracy depends on information (see Chapter 2). The chief information gatherers are the police. However, the police are not the only criminal justice officials who need and use the information. Prosecutors, defense counsel, judges, and juries all rely on information in the prosecution, conviction, sentencing, and punishment of offenders and in freeing the innocent from further involvement in the criminal justice system. The likely sources of information—criminals, potential criminals, victims, and witnesses—do not provide it willingly. Criminals do not readily divulge information that might incriminate them. Potential criminals usually do not announce their criminal schemes. Victims and other witnesses talk only reluctantly about what they know. This makes the job of the police more difficult, but it does not compel them to give up their pursuit of information.[1]

The police use three major methods to gather information:

1. *Searches and seizures* of persons, places, papers, and personal effects, analyzed in this chapter and in Chapters 4–7
2. *Interrogation* of suspects and witnesses, analyzed in Chapter 8
3. *Identification procedures,* such as lineups, showups, "mug shots," and DNA profiling, analyzed in Chapter 9

Searches and seizures serve all of the following purposes. Notice that gathering criminal evidence is only one of those purposes:

1. Gathering criminal evidence
2. Protecting police officers (frisks, Chapter 4, searches incident to arrest, Chapter 6)
3. Protecting jail and prison security (custodial searches, Chapter 7)
4. Protecting the property of detained suspects from loss or damage and jail administrators from lawsuits (inventory searches, Chapter 7)
5. Satisfying special needs (such as school searches and employee drug testing beyond criminal law enforcement—Chapter 7)

PURPOSE OF THE FOURTH AMENDMENT

The purpose of the Fourth Amendment is to make sure that the government does not pursue its legitimate interest in gathering and using information by means of "unreasonable searches and seizures." The reliance upon searches and seizures to further government interests has a long history. For example, the birth of search and seizure law in England goes back to the invention of the printing press. The fear of seditious libels against English monarchs led to the use of the power to search in order to discover and destroy these written attacks. The low respect that the English people had for their imported German kings (the four Georges of the House of Hanover) led to a barrage of seditious libels. **General warrants,** or **writs of assistance,** granted royal officers blanket authority to break into shops and homes in order to search for and seize seditious libels. The practice was to issue the writs at the beginning of a new monarch's reign; they were valid until the monarch died. Hence, the writs of assistance were akin to a blank check. Instead of leaving it to the holder to fill in the amount, the writ permitted the officer for as long as a reigning monarch lived to fill in the persons, homes, shops, offices, papers, and other personal effects that the officer wished to search. In the case of George III, that meant the authority was good for sixty years!

The general warrants were also used in combating smuggling in order to evade the customs duties on a growing list of goods imported into England from its rapidly expanding empire around the world. Writs of assistance to search houses and shops for smuggled goods were common in the American colonies. But the writs generated considerable controversy both in Britain and in the American colonies. In England, William Pitt spoke the most famous words ever uttered against the power of government to search in a speech to the House of Commons:

> The poorest man may in his cottage bid defiance to all the forces of the Crown. It may be frail—its roof may shake—the wind may blow through it—the storm may enter—but the King of England cannot enter—all his force dares not cross the threshold of the ruined tenement.

And, in America, the young lawyer and future president John Adams watched the great colonial trial lawyer James Otis argue the widely publicized writs of assistance case in Boston. Otis argued that writs of assistance were illegal, maintaining that only searches with specific dates, naming the places or persons to be searched and seized and based on probable cause, were lawful where free people lived. The arguments of the great lawyer Otis moved John Adams to write years later: "There was the Child Independence born." Despite the superb oratory hurled against the writs of assistance, both the Crown in the mother country and the governors in the colonies continued to use them widely. But the authors of the Bill of Rights did not forget their hostility to general warrants, and they wrote their opposition to them into the Fourth Amendment to the United States Constitution.

The Fourth Amendment is supposed to ensure that the government can gather the information it needs to control crime, protect officers, and meet special needs beyond criminal law enforcement. But it is also supposed to guarantee that the government does not gather information by means of "unreasonable searches and seizures." In the language of the amendment,

> The right of the people to be secure in their persons, houses, papers, and effects, against unreasonable searches and seizures shall not be violated, and no warrants shall issue but upon probable cause supported by oath or affirmation, and particularly describing the place to be searched, and the persons or things to be seized.

The Fourth Amendment protects three values essential to the quality of life in a free society:

1. **Privacy,** the right to be let alone from government invasions, is governed by the prohibition against unreasonable searches.
2. **Liberty,** the right of locomotion—that is, the right of individuals to come and go as they please, without government interference—is protected by the prohibition against unreasonable seizures.
3. **Property,** the right to acquire, own, possess, use, and dispose of property, is protected by the prohibitions against both unreasonable searches and seizures.

FOURTH AMENDMENT ANALYSIS

The determination of whether the government has complied with the Fourth Amendment involves the courts in a three-step analysis:

1. Was the government action a *search* or a *seizure*?
2. Assuming that the action was a search or a seizure, was it an *unreasonable* search or seizure?
3. If the search was unreasonable, should the evidence obtained be *excluded*?

TABLE 3.1 INTRUSIONS NOT AMOUNTING TO FOURTH AMENDMENT SEARCHES

Searches where suspect has no expectation of privacy
Private searches
Searches for items open to plain view, hearing, smell, and touch
Searches of open fields
Searches of areas open to the public
Searches of abandoned property
Searches of mere evidence

Government encounters with individuals range across a broad spectrum of activity that covers everything from trivial to severe invasions of liberty, privacy, and property. The Fourth Amendment refers only to government actions that are searches or seizures. (See Table 3.1 for a list of encounters that are not searches.) To determine whether a government action is a Fourth Amendment search requires a negative answer to this question:

Does the individual expect privacy, and, if so, is the expectation one that society is prepared to recognize as reasonable?

To determine whether a government action is a seizure requires an affirmative answer to this question:

Would a reasonable person encountering a show of authority by a government official feel free either to walk away or to otherwise terminate the encounter?

This and the following chapters examine government actions that may or may not involve the Fourth Amendment. These actions are arranged in a rough chronological order:

- Actions involving encounters between individuals and police officers on the street and in other public places (in this chapter and in Chapters 4–6)

- Actions involving encounters between individuals and officers at the police station (Chapters 8–9)

- Actions involving encounters between prisoners and officers in jails and prisons (Chapter 7)

As the encounters between individuals and the government move from the street to the police station and to jails and prisons, they not only change locations, but they also invade more deeply the privacy, liberty, and property of those who are subject to them. As the invasions deepen, the **objective basis**—the quantity of facts required to back up the invasions—also increases. (See Chapter 1 on the importance of facts.) It takes no facts at all to justify voluntary encounters that are neither Fourth Amendment searches nor seizures, some of which encounters are analyzed in this chapter. It takes only a few facts—*reasonable suspicion*—to justify the least-invasive searches and seizures, the stops and frisks analyzed in Chapter 4. It takes more facts—*probable cause*—to justify full-blown arrests, the searches and seizures that are the subjects of Chapters 5 and 6. It takes varying degrees of objective bases to support the invasions for the special needs searches discussed in Chapter 7.

In summary, the Fourth Amendment protects only against invasions of privacy, liberty, and property that meet the following criteria:

Privacy

1. The invasion of privacy must be by *government agents*, not private persons.
2. The invasion of privacy must involve "persons, houses, papers, and effects."
3. The invasion of privacy must be made for the purpose of obtaining, distributing, and using information about individuals.
4. The invasion of privacy must be "unreasonable."

Liberty

1. The invasion of liberty must be by government agents, not private persons.
2. The invasion of liberty deprives individuals of their freedom to come and go as they please.
3. The invasion of liberty must be "unreasonable."

Property. The property interests that the unreasonable search and seizure clause protect are the possession, use, and disposition of personal property, real property, and financial instruments.

FOURTH AMENDMENT "SEARCHES"

Until 1967, the United States Supreme Court defined searches according to what was called the **trespass doctrine.** This doctrine required physical intrusions into a "constitutionally protected area." Constitutionally protected areas included the places named in the Fourth Amendment itself—persons, houses, papers, and effects—as interpreted by the Supreme Court. According to the Court, searching persons includes touching their bodies, rummaging through their pockets, taking blood tests, and performing surgery to remove bullets. On the other hand, it is not a search to observe physical circumstances, such as handwriting samples or voice exemplars, to which courts have ordered suspects to submit. Houses include apartments, hotel rooms, garages, business offices, stores, and even warehouses. Papers include a broad range of personal writings, including diaries and letters. Effects include many items of personal property: cars, purses, briefcases, and packages.[2]

The privacy doctrine originated in a famous dissent written by Justice Louis Brandeis in the 1928 case of *Olmstead v. U.S.* In *Olmstead,* defendants' telephones were tapped without a warrant in order to find evidence of violations of the Prohibition laws. The government collected more than 775 pages of notes from the wiretaps and indicted more than 70 people. The Supreme Court applied the trespass doctrine to the case, holding that the government wiretaps were not Fourth Amendment searches of the defendants' houses, papers, or effects because there was no physical intrusion on their premises. Justice Brandeis dissented, arguing that although the wiretapping was not a physical trespass, it nevertheless amounted to a government invasion of the privacy that the Fourth Amendment protected. Justice Brandeis had this to say about the right to privacy:

> The makers of the Constitution . . . recognized the significance of man's spiritual nature, of his feelings and of his intellect. They knew that only a part of the pain, pleasure and satisfactions of life are to be found in material things. They sought

to protect Americans in their beliefs, their thoughts, their emotions and their sensations. They conferred, as against the Government, the right to be let alone — the most comprehensive of rights and the right most valued by civilized men.[3]

The late senator and constitutional scholar Sam Ervin reaffirmed the Brandeis notion of the right to privacy in 1983. According to Senator Ervin,

> The oldest and deepest hunger in the human heart is for a place where one may dwell in peace and security and keep inviolate from public scrutiny one's innermost aspirations and thoughts, one's most intimate associations and communications, and one's most private activities. This truth was documented by Micah, the prophet, 2,700 years ago when he described the Mountain of the Lord as a place where "they shall sit every man under his own vine and fig tree and none shall make them afraid."[4]

In 1967 the privacy doctrine elaborated in Justice Brandeis's dissent became the law of the land. In the landmark case *Katz v. U.S.*, the Supreme Court replaced the trespass doctrine with the privacy doctrine. According to the **privacy doctrine,** the Fourth Amendment protects persons, not places, when they have an expectation of privacy that society is prepared to recognize. The privacy doctrine balances the interest in obtaining the correct result in individual cases and the interest in fair process in all cases. Some Fourth Amendment cases concentrate on the process interest in limiting police power, such as where the courts exclude evidence that the police have illegally seized even though the evidence proves the defendant's guilt. Others focus on the process interest in individual privacy rights, such as where agents may not rummage through private papers without specific authorization. Still other cases focus on the interest in obtaining the correct result in specific cases, such as permitting officers to search suspects without warrants when they make an arrest so that suspects cannot destroy evidence. But in the end they all involve balancing the interest in obtaining the correct result in individual cases with the interest in guaranteeing fair process in all cases.

According to Professor Anthony Amsterdam, defense attorney and Fourth Amendment scholar,

> In the final analysis, the privacy test is a value judgment that rests upon whether, if the particular form of surveillance practiced by the police is permitted to go unregulated by constitutional restraints, the amount of privacy and freedom remaining to citizens would be diminished to a compass inconsistent with the aims of a free and open society.[5]

In other words, the privacy doctrine, and incidentally the Fourth Amendment generally, balances the interest in protecting society from criminals and the interest in protecting individuals from government invasions into their lives. In demonstrating that a government action is a search, defendants carry the burden of proving

- *Subjective privacy* — that is, the defendant personally expected to be left alone from government intrusion.
- *Objective privacy* — that is, the personal expectation of privacy is one that society is prepared to recognize.

The balance between the privacy of individuals and the security of society tends in practice to weigh most often in favor of the government need to provide security against criminals. According to former prosecutor and Fourth Amendment specialist John Wesley Hall, Jr.,

> When [society's need for security and the individual's need for privacy] are balanced, the former usually weighs heavily. . . . While this is perhaps a valid purpose in the administration of criminal justice, we must not lose sight of the fundamental precepts of the Fourth Amendment that the individual is to be free from arbitrary and oppressive governmental intrusions.[6]

Search and seizure court decisions reflect this balance in favor of the security of society. In practice, courts tread reluctantly on the power of the government to provide for security (see Chapter 2). For example, courts only infrequently question the actions of police in street encounters with citizens, such as those discussed in this and the following chapters. When courts do question the activities of the police, they concede great deference to police discretion. Dean Erwin Griswold, former solicitor general of the United States, adopted this "working rule" in deciding whether to appeal rulings by lower courts declaring searches illegal: "If the police officer acted decently, and if he did what you would expect a good, careful, conscientious police officer to do under the circumstances, then he should be supported."[7]

"Expectation of Privacy"

Justice John Marshall Harlan's concurring opinion in *Katz v. United States* stated a two-pronged test to determine whether government action amounts to a search:

1. The first prong, the subjective prong, asks whether a "person exhibited an actual [subjective] expectation of privacy."

2. The second prong, the objective prong, asks whether the actual or subjective expectation of privacy is "one that society is prepared to recognize as 'reasonable.'"

The Supreme Court adopted and applied the privacy doctrine as the primary means to determine whether government actions are searches in *Katz v. United States*. In that case, the Court defined *expectation of privacy*.

C A S E

Did He Have a Right to Privacy That Society Recognizes?

Katz v. United States
389 U.S. 347, 88 S.Ct. 507,
19 L.Ed.2d 576 (1967)

Katz was convicted under a federal statute of transmitting wagering information by telephone across state lines. The court of appeals affirmed the conviction. The Supreme Court granted certiorari *and reversed. Justice*

Stewart wrote the opinion of the Court. Justice Marshall did not participate. Justices Douglas and Brennan concurred. Justice Harlan concurred. Justice Black dissented.

FACTS

[The facts portion of this excerpt are taken from *Katz v. U.S.*, 369 F.2d 130 (9th Cir. 1966).]

In February of 1965 the appellant was seen placing calls from a bank of three public telephone booths during certain hours and on an almost daily basis. He was never observed in any other telephone booth. In the period of February 19 to February 25, 1965, at set hours, Special Agents of the Federal Bureau of Investigation placed microphones on the tops of two of the public telephone booths normally used by the appellant. The other phone was placed out of order by the telephone company. The microphones were attached to the outside of the telephone booths with tape. There was no physical penetration inside of the booths. The microphones were activated only while appellant was approaching and actually in the booth. Wires led from microphones to a wire recorder on top of one of the booths. Thus the F.B.I. obtained a record of appellant's end of a series of telephone calls.

A study of the transcripts of the recordings made of the appellant's end of the conversations revealed that the conversations had to do with the placing of bets and the obtaining of gambling information by the appellant.

On February 23, 1965, F.B.I. Agent Allen Frei rented a room next to the appellant's apartment residence. He listened to conversations through the common wall without the aid of any electronic device. He overheard the appellant's end of a series of telephone conversations and took notes on them. These notes and the tapes made from the telephone booth recordings were the basis of a search warrant which was obtained to search appellant's apartment. The search warrant called for "* * * bookmaking records, wagering paraphernalia, including but not limited to, bet slips, betting markers, run-down sheets, schedule sheets indicating the lines, adding machines, money, telephones, telephone address listings * * *." The articles seized are described in the return. They are all related to the categories described in the warrant.

During the conversations overheard by Agent Frei, the appellant made numerous comments to the effect that "I have Northwestern minus 7," and "Oregon plus 3." Also, there was a statement by the appellant such as, "Don't worry about the line. I have phoned Boston three times about it today."

At the trial evidence was introduced to show that from February 19 to February 25, 1965, inclusive, the appellant placed calls from two telephone booths located in the 8200 block of Sunset Boulevard in Los Angeles. The conversations were overheard and recorded every day except February 22. The transcripts of the recordings and the normal business records of the telephone company were used to determine that the calls went to Boston, Massachusetts, and Miami, Florida.

The testimony of Joseph Gunn of the Administrative Vice Division of the Los Angeles Police Department, who was the expert called by the government in the area of bookmaking, was that the transcripts of the conversations showed that bets were made and information assisting in the placing of bets was transmitted on the dates and at the times alleged in the indictment. Bets were recorded like "Give me Duquesne minus 7 for a nickel." Information relating to the line and the acquiring of credit was also transmitted.

In correlating the transcript of the telephone conversations and line sheets and markers found in appellant's residence during the search pursuant to the warrant, Officer Gunn concluded that appellant was placing wagers with a bookmaker for another person for a consideration.

On February 25, 1965, the appellant was arrested. He was advised by a Special Agent of the F.B.I., Emmett Doherty, that he had a right to remain silent, he had a right to consult counsel, and that any statements he made could be used against him in a court of law. The appellant was arrested on the street. He was later present in his apartment where another agent of the F.B.I. was involved in the search authorized by the search warrant. Appellant asked when he could have his records back. He stated that without them he was out of business and that he knew no other trade. During this exchange, in response to a question about interstate betting, the appellant said that he could not bet locally because the bookmakers would not pay off.

The next day, which was February 26, 1965, Agent Donovan of the F.B.I. met appellant in the lobby of his apartment building to return two personal items which had been taken at the time of the search. Donovan had been with Agent Doherty the day before when Doherty advised the appellant of his rights with respect to statements made to the Federal Agents. Appellant again asked why he could not have his records back. He stated without them he was out of business and that he had been a handicapper and a bettor most of his life. He suggested that if he got his records back he would continue to bet.

From all of the evidence in the case the court found the volume of business being done by the appellant indicated that it was not a casual incidental occupation of the appellant. The court found that he was engaged in the business of betting or wagering at the time of the telephone conversations which were transmitted and recorded.

. . . The petitioner was convicted of transmitting wagering information by telephone from Los Angeles to Miami and Boston, in violation of a federal statute. We granted certiorari to consider the constitutional questions thus presented.

OPINION

The petitioner has phrased those questions as follows:

A. Whether a public telephone booth is a constitutionally protected area so that evidence obtained by attaching an electronic listening recording device to the top of such a booth is obtained in violation of the right to privacy of the user of the booth.
B. Whether physical penetration of a constitutionally protected area is necessary before a search and seizure can be said to be violative of the Fourth Amendment to the United States Constitution.

We decline to adopt this formulation of the issues. In the first place, the correct solution of Fourth Amendment problems is not necessarily promoted by incantation of the phrase "constitutionally protected area." Secondly, the Fourth Amendment cannot be translated into a general constitutional "right to privacy." That Amendment protects individual privacy against certain kinds of governmental intrusion, but its protections go further, and often have nothing to do with privacy at all. Other provisions of the Constitution protect personal privacy from other forms of governmental invasion. But the protection of a person's general right to privacy—his right to be let alone by other people—is, like the protection of his prop-

erty and of his very life, left largely to the law of the individual states.

Because of the misleading way the issues have been formulated, the parties have attached great significance to the characterization of the telephone booth from which the petitioner placed his calls. The petitioner has strenuously argued that the booth was a "constitutionally protected area." The Government has maintained with equal vigor that it was not. But this effort to decide whether or not a given "area," viewed in the abstract, is "constitutionally protected" deflects attention from the problem presented by this case. For the Fourth Amendment protects people, not places. What a person knowingly exposes to the public, even in his own home or office, is not a subject of Fourth Amendment protection. But what he seeks to preserve as private, even in an area accessible to the public, may be constitutionally protected.

The Government stresses the fact that the telephone booth from which the petitioner made his calls was constructed partly of glass, so that he was visible after he entered it as he would have been if he had remained outside. But what he sought to exclude when he entered the booth was not the intruding eye—it was the uninvited ear. He did not shed his right to do so simply because he made calls from a place where he might be seen. No less than an individual in a business office, in a friend's apartment, or in a taxicab, a person in a telephone booth may rely upon the protection of the Fourth Amendment. One who occupies it, shuts the door behind him, and pays the toll that permits him to place a call is surely entitled to assume that the words he utters into the mouthpiece will not be broadcast to the world. To read the Constitution more narrowly is to ignore the vital role that the public telephone booth has come to play in private conversation.

The Government contends, however, that the activities of its agents in this case should not be tested by the Fourth Amendment requirements, for the surveillance technique they employed involved no physical penetration of the telephone booth from which the petitioner placed his calls. It is true that the absence of such penetration was at one time thought to foreclose further Fourth Amendment inquiry, for that Amendment was thought to limit only searches and seizures of tangible property. But "the premise that property interests control the right of the Government to search and seize has been discredited." *Warden v. Hayden*, 387 U.S. 294. Thus, although a closely divided Court supposed in *Olmstead [v. U.S.]* that surveillance without any trespass and without the seizure of any material object fell outside the ambit of the Constitution, we have since departed from the narrow view on which that decision rested.... Once this much is acknowledged, and once it is recognized that the Fourth Amendment protects people—and not simple "areas"—against unreasonable searches and seizures it becomes clear that the reach of that Amendment cannot turn upon the physical presence or absence of a physical intrusion into any given enclosure.

We conclude ... that the "trespass" doctrine ... can no longer be regarded as controlling. The Government's activities in electronically listening to and recording the petitioner's words violated the privacy upon which he justifiably relied while using the telephone booth and thus constituted a "search and seizure" within the meaning of the Fourth Amendment. The fact that the electronic device employed to achieve that end did not happen to penetrate the wall of the booth can have no constitutional significance.

[NOTE: The Court reversed the conviction because the FBI agents, although they had probable cause, did not get a warrant. (See the discussion on search warrants in Chapter 6.)]

CONCURRING OPINION

[The concurring opinions of Justices White, Douglas, and Brennan discussing exceptions to the warrant requirement are omitted.]

Justice Harlan, concurring.

... As the Court's opinion states, "the Fourth Amendment protects people, not places." The question, however, is what protection it affords to those people. Generally, as here, the answer to that question requires reference to a "place." My understanding of the rule that has emerged from prior decisions is that there is a twofold requirement, first that a person exhibited an actual (subjective) expectation of privacy and, second, that the expectation be one that society is prepared to recognize as "reasonable." Thus a man's home is, for most purposes, a place where he expects

privacy, but objects, activities, or statements that he exposes to "plain view" of outsiders are not "protected" because no intention to keep them to himself has been exhibited. On the other hand, conversations in the open would not be protected against being overheard, for the expectation of privacy under the circumstances would be unreasonable.

The critical fact in the case is that "[o]ne who occupies it [a telephone booth], shuts the door behind him, and pays the toll that permits him to place a call is surely entitled to assume" that his conversation is not being intercepted. The point is not that the booth is "accessible to the public at other times," but that it is a temporarily private place whose momentary occupants' expectations of freedom from intrusion are recognized as reasonable.

DISSENT

Mr. Justice Black, dissenting.

If I could agree with the Court that eavesdropping carried on by electronic means (equivalent to wiretapping) constitutes a "search" or "seizure," I would be happy to join the Court's opinion.... My basic objection is twofold: (1) I do not believe that the words of the Amendment will bear the meaning given them by today's decision, and (2) I do not believe that it is the proper role of this Court to rewrite the Amendment in order "to bring it into harmony with the times" and thus reach a result that many people believe to be desirable....

Tapping telephone wires, of course, was an unknown possibility at the time the Fourth Amendment was adopted. But eavesdropping (and wiretapping is nothing more than eavesdropping by telephone) was ... "an ancient practice which at common law was condemned as a nuisance. In those days the eavesdropper listened by naked ear under the eaves of houses or their windows, or beyond their walls seeking out private discourse." There can be no doubt that the Framers were aware of this practice, and if they had desired to outlaw or restrict the use of evidence obtained by eavesdropping, I believe that they would have used the appropriate language to do so in the Fourth Amendment. They certainly would not have left such a task to the ingenuity of language-stretching judges. No one, it seems to me, can read the debates on the Bill of Rights without reaching the conclusion that its Framers and critics well knew the meaning of the words they used, what they would be understood to mean by others, their scope and their limitations. Under these circumstances it strikes me as a charge against their scholarship, their common sense and their candor to give to the Fourth Amendment's language the eavesdropping meaning the Court imputes to it today.... The Fourth Amendment was aimed directly at the abhorred practice of breaking in, ransacking and searching homes and other buildings and seizing people's personal belongings without warrants issued by magistrates....

In interpreting the Bill of Rights, I willingly go as far as a liberal construction of the language takes me, but I simply cannot in good conscience give a meaning to words which they have never before been thought to have and which they certainly do not have in common ordinary usage. I will not distort the words of the Amendment in order to "keep the Constitution up to date" or "bring it into harmony with the times." It was never meant that this Court have such power, which in effect would make us a continuously functioning constitutional convention.

With this decision the Court has completed, I hope, its rewriting of the Fourth Amendment, which started only recently when the Court began referring incessantly to the Fourth Amendment not so much as a law against unreasonable searches and seizures as one to protect an individual's privacy. By clever word juggling the Court finds it plausible to argue that language aimed specifically at searches and seizures of things that can be searched and seized may, to protect privacy, be applied to eavesdropped evidence of conversations that can neither be searched nor seized. Few things happen to an individual that do not affect his privacy in one way or another. Thus, by arbitrarily substituting the Court's language, designed to protect privacy, for the Constitution's language, designed to protect against unreasonable searches and seizures, the Court has made the Fourth Amendment its vehicle for holding all laws violative of the Constitution which offend the Court's broadest concept of privacy.

As I said in *Griswold v. Connecticut,* (1965), "The Court talks about a constitutional 'right of privacy' as though there is some constitutional provision or provisions forbidding any law ever to be passed which might abridge the 'privacy' of individuals. But there is not." I made clear in that dissent my fear of the dangers involved when this Court uses the "broad, abstract and ambiguous concept" of "privacy" as a "comprehensive substitute" for the Fourth Amendment's guarantee against "unreasonable searches and seizures."

The Fourth Amendment protects privacy only to the extent that it prohibits unreasonable searches and seizures of "persons, houses, papers, and effects." No general right is created by the Amendment so as to give this Court the unlimited power to hold unconstitutional everything which affects privacy. Certainly the Framers, well acquainted as they were with the excesses of governmental power, did not intend to grant this Court such omnipotent lawmaking authority as that. The history of governments proves that it is dangerous to freedom to repose such powers in courts.

For these reasons I respectfully dissent.

CASE DISCUSSION

List the specific government invasions in the case. State the privacy and trespass doctrines. Why did the Court reject the trespass doctrine? Was it a good idea for it to do so? What interests does the privacy doctrine promote? How do the two tests differ in the interests they protect? Which test would you adopt? Should Katz go free because FBI agents acted unlawfully, even when they believed they could have gotten a warrant and believed they were acting according to the Constitution? (Refer to *United States v. Leon* in Chapter 10.) Explain your answer. Is Justice Black right in his dissent that there is no right to privacy in the Fourth Amendment? Is he right that the framers of the Bill of Rights did not intend to protect against eavesdropping in the Fourth Amendment? And do you agree that the Supreme Court does not have the authority to keep the Constitution "up to date"? Explain your answer.

Decision Point

1. *United States v. Billings.* While in a public bathroom, an officer noticed a man briefly pull up his pant leg and expose a bandage wrapped around his ankle. A white packet was clearly visible through the bandage. The officer arrested the man. Did the man have a reasonable expectation of privacy that society is prepared to recognize? A federal circuit court held that he did not. When the officer looked on the floor of the stall where the man was located and noticed the bandage in the gap between the stall's walls and the floor, the man had no reasonable expectation of privacy. Any patron could have noticed the bandage taped to the man's ankle if he had looked in the direction of the stall.[8]

2. *State v. Casconi.* The Oregon State Police conducted clandestine surveillance of a restroom in a freeway rest area. A hidden camera was directed at two doorless toilet stalls that were separated by a metal partition. The camera was located at a hole in an outside concrete wall. Urinals in the facility were partitioned from the toilets. The toilet interiors could not be seen from the building entrance or from the urinals. The officer operating the camera knew when persons entered or left the restroom by the sound of the door opening and by radio communication from an officer stationed outside in a van. The operator activated the camera whenever he thought illegal activity might occur. There was no warrant authorizing the surveillance. The defendant entered the restroom alone. He was filmed writing on the wall inside stall number one, exposing his genitals and masturbating. The officer saw the defendant only through the camera. When one person entered the restroom, he stopped masturbating and covered himself until the person left. When a second person entered to use a urinal, he continued to masturbate. Neither person could see the defendant. The officer did not see anyone look over, under, or into the defendant's stall. No one in the restroom saw the defendant expose his genitals or masturbate. The defendant contacted no one in the restroom. He was arrested outside. Casconi moved to suppress the evidence because, he ar-

gued, the surveillance was an unreasonable Fourth Amendment search.

Was surveillance of the restroom a Fourth Amendment "search"? The state argued that

> ... defendant's conduct in an open toilet in a public restroom was not protected, because acts open to public view are not protected. The state argues, in essence, that police conduct is not a search if the object of the search could have been discovered by conduct that would not be a search. It relies on *State v. Louis*, 296 Or. 57, 672 P.2d 708 (1981), for the proposition that acts that are open to public view are not protected from police observation. In *Louis*, the Supreme Court held that the use of a telephoto lens to photograph the defendant standing in view through his living room window was not a search, because the camera merely recorded what could already be seen by the general public through his window. The court went on to say: "[S]uch a case may not be made out, however, if objects or conduct in protected premises can be seen or overheard only by technologically enhanced efforts. A determined official effort to see or hear what is not plain to a less determined observer may become an official 'search.'"

The Court of Appeals of Oregon disagreed. According to the court,

> That information may be legally obtained does not mean that every method that can be used to obtain the same information does not invade an individual's privacy interest or constitute a search. . . . [I]f the officers had entered the defendant's living room without a warrant or exigent circumstances to observe what could be seen from the street, the result would have been an unlawful search. The question is not whether the acts recorded by the camera were "exposed to public view"; they were not. The question is whether using the concealed camera was a search.
>
> We must look to the nature of the act alleged to be a search. No one has a constitutional

privacy interest that shields him from all forms of scrutiny. To determine whether government use of technology and enhanced surveillance techniques violates a privacy interest, the court must decide whether it will "significantly impair 'the people's' freedom from scrutiny." Anyone who used the toilet involved here would expose himself (so to speak) to the camera. Simply because an individual chooses to use a public restroom or a stall without doors does not mean that he is automatically deprived of all privacy when he enters. "The final bastion of privacy is to be found in the area of human procreation and excretion" and "[if] a person is entitled to any shred of privacy, then it is to privacy as to these matters." Allowing the police to conduct hidden surveillance of a doorless toilet stall significantly impairs freedom from scrutiny.

A similar problem was posed in *State v. Holt*, 291 Or. 343, 630 P.2d 854 (1981). Although that case was decided when the Fourth Amendment and Article I, section 9, were generally regarded in Oregon caselaw as coextensive, the rationale is still helpful. In that case,

the court dealt with clandestine surveillance of the same public restroom as here. After an officer, from a hole above the toilet, noticed Holt's suspicious acts in the restroom, he entered the restroom and sat in the neighboring toilet stall. Although the officer had seen no illegal activity through the hole, while seated in the restroom he observed Holt masturbating and attempting to lure another person into some sort of participation. The court held that the defendant had no reasonable expectation of privacy under the Fourth Amendment, because he committed his acts so that other restroom users could see him. His conviction was affirmed. Here, the police observed defendant only by the hidden camera.

The use of the concealed camera unlawfully invaded defendant's privacy and, therefore, constituted a search. Or. Const. Art. I, § 9. Because the police had no warrant and the state offers no other support for the search, defendant's motion to suppress should have been granted.

The court reversed the trial court's decision and remanded the case for a new trial.[9]

Plain View, Hearing, Smell, and Touch

The discovery of weapons, contraband, and evidence by means of the ordinary senses of law enforcement officers — sight, touch, smell, and hearing — in any place where the officers have a lawful right to be are commonly called "plain view searches." But these discoveries are not really Fourth Amendment "searches" at all. The **plain view doctrine** associated with these misnamed "searches" is about the *seizure* of weapons, contraband, and evidence discovered by the ordinary senses of sight, smell, touch, and hearing. The discovery and subsequent seizure of items discovered by means of plain view, touch, hearing, and smell fall outside the Fourth Amendment only if they satisfy all three of the following conditions:

1. Officers are lawfully present when — and in the place where — the discovery of the evidence occurs.

2. Detection occurs without enhancing the ordinary senses by advanced technology.

3. The detection is inadvertent; that is, it requires no further action such as moving or opening items.

Lawful presence can refer to a number of situations. Officers may have a warrant to search some place for specific items related to one crime and discover in plain view evidence of another unrelated crime. Or they may be conducting a lawful search without a warrant and see contraband in plain view. These examples are true searches and will be discussed in Chapter 6. Officers are also lawfully present when they are conducting noncriminal business and inadvertently discover incriminating evidence. These are the cases that raise the question whether the discovery and subsequent seizure of weapons, contraband, or evidence are Fourth Amendment searches and seizures.

For example, suppose that police officers approach a car to check a motor vehicle registration. While talking to the driver, the officers see marijuana lying on the passenger seat. They can seize the marijuana without implicating the Fourth Amendment. The officers have a lawful right to approach drivers. They can look at what is plainly there for them to see. Therefore, they have not searched for the marijuana, and they have not seized it in the Fourth Amendment sense. If, however, the marijuana was hidden from view under some newspapers, and the officers reached inside the car and moved the papers, they would have conducted a search by moving the newspapers. The detection required further action than the use of the ordinary sense of sight.[10]

The plain view doctrine applies only to detection by the *ordinary* senses, not to discovery enhanced by technology. However, courts have distinguished between ordinary technological enhancements—flashlights, bifocals, and magnifying glasses—the use of which the courts say are not searches, and more high-powered technological enhancements, which the courts hold are searches. For example, in *United States v. Kim*, FBI agents used an 800-millimeter telescope with a 60-millimeter opening to observe activities in Kim's apartment. The surveillance took place nearly a quarter of a mile from the apartment. So powerful was the telescope that the agents could even see what Kim was reading. According to the federal district court that heard the case,

> It is inconceivable that the government can intrude so far into an individual's home that it can detect the material he is reading and still not be considered to have engaged in a search. . . . If government agents have probable cause to suspect criminal activity and feel the need for telescopic surveillance, they may apply for a warrant; otherwise, they have no right to peer into people's windows with special equipment not generally in use. The quest for evidence directed at Kim's apartment is not exempted from Fourth Amendment regulation by the plain view doctrine.[11]

The Supreme Court applied the plain view doctrine in *California v. Ciraolo*, where the police saw marijuana growing in a yard below from a plane from one thousand feet in the air. The police hired the plane because two privacy fences blocked their view from the ground. According to the Court, the use of the plane did not enhance the sense of sight, in this case the naked eye, such that it turned the observation into a Fourth Amendment search. A similar case involved Dow Chemical Corporation. Dow maintains elaborate security around a two-thousand-acre chemical plant that bars ground-level observation. When Dow refused the Environmental Protection Agency's (EPA's) request for an on-site inspection, the EPA employed a commercial air photographer to fly over the plant and take photographs to determine whether Dow was complying with EPA standards. The Supreme Court ruled that such aerial observation and photography were not Fourth Amendment searches.[12]

Because the doctrine covers smelling, tasting, touching, and hearing as well as seeing, *plain view* is too narrow a term to capture the full scope of the plain view doctrine. Consistent with the plain view doctrine, law enforcement officers may listen, touch, sniff, and look without implicating the Fourth Amendment.

Decision Point

"PLAIN HEARING"

United States v. Jackson, 588 F.2d 1046 (5th Cir. 1979)
For several years prior to Jackson's arrest, agents of the Drug Enforcement Administration had suspected him of narcotics laws violations. Despite their suspicions and a three-year investigation involving periodic surveillance of his conduct and activities, DEA agents had never observed Jackson passing heroin or uncovered any hard evidence that he was trafficking in narcotics. On July 4, 1977, Jackson and a Miss Beverly Pertilla checked into room 312 of the Kahler Plaza Hotel in Birmingham, Alabama. An off-duty Birmingham police officer working security at the hotel spotted Jackson on July 5 and notified the DEA of his presence. On July 6, Agent Hahn of the DEA and Sergeant Trucks of the Birmingham Police Department rented room 314 at the hotel for the purpose of monitoring Jackson's activities. Rooms 312 and 314 adjoin and are connected by a set of double doors. After entering room 314, officers determined that they could hear conversations in room 312 by lying on the motel room floor and pressing their ears to the ¾-inch crack at the bottom of their connecting door. Although at times their aural surveillance was impeded by the sounds of television, plumbing, and air conditioning in room 312, the officers had no difficulty in overhearing much of the conversation in the adjoining room. At no time did the officers use any electronic or mechanical device to assist them in their aural surveillance.

Using this eavesdropping technique, the officers on July 6 overheard Jackson make two telephone calls to Buffalo, New York. During these calls Jackson stated, "No, I haven't been able to contact my man yet. (Pause.) It is like gold." and "The stuff is coming from L.A. (Pause.) No problem with my man." On the morning of July 7, Jackson told his room guest, Beverly Pertilla, to call an airline and make flight reservations to Buffalo, New York. Sgt. Trucks immediately dispatched two undercover officers to the airport to set up surveillance. Shortly after Pertilla made the reservations, Jackson received a brief telephone call. He then cursed, seemed excited for several minutes, and told Pertilla that "the stuff may be in trouble" and "the stuff is worth $40,000."

Within twenty minutes, Jackson received another telephone call in which he stated, "Is the stuff all right? Is the suitcase still at the airport?" Following this conversation, Jackson told Pertilla, "I don't know what went wrong. The police followed him to the airport. The suitcase is still at the airport. The flight came in at 9:08 and I don't know what went wrong."

[NOTE: Jackson and Pertilla were later arrested, convicted, and sentenced to twelve years in prison and fines of $35,000 and $25,000, respectively, for possession and conspiracy to distribute heroin and cocaine. They claim that the eavesdropping violated their right to privacy and that the court should suppress the seized heroin and cocaine as evidence against them.]

Applying the privacy doctrine of *Katz v. United States* (excerpted earlier in this chapter), the court held that

> these appellants had not justifiable expectations of privacy with respect to their motel room conversations which were audible to the unaided ears of the government agents lawfully occupying an adjoining room. "It has long been settled that objects falling in the plain view of an officer who has a right to be in the position to have that view are subject to seizure and may be introduced into evidence." *Harris v. United States*, 390 U.S. 234, 236, 88 S.Ct. 992, 993, 19 L.Ed.2d 1067 (1968) (per curiam). The plain view doctrine defines certain sensory observations as being outside the scope of the Fourth Amendment's protections. This doctrine is entirely consistent with the *Katz* expectations standard since an individual can have no justifiable expectation of privacy as to activities he exposes to the plain view of others. We think that conversations in a motel room which are audible to one in an adjoining room constitute words exposed to the "plain view" of others. . . .

"PLAIN FEEL"

Minnesota v. Dickerson, 113 S.Ct. 2130, 124 L.Ed.2d 334 (1993)
Two police officers saw Dickerson leave a "crack house." They suspected that he had bought "crack"

while he was inside. During a frisk for weapons, one of the officers felt a small, hard object inside one of the pockets of Dickerson's nylon jacket. According to the officer, "I felt a lump, a small lump, in the front pocket. I examined it with my fingers and it slid and it felt to be a lump of crack cocaine in cellophane." The officer reached into the pocket and removed what turned out to be a small plastic bag containing one-fifth of one gram of cocaine. Was the feeling of the lump a search? Yes, according to the Supreme Court. The Court found that

> Although the officer was lawfully in a position to feel the lump in respondent's pocket . . . the incriminating character of the object was not immediately apparent to him. Rather, the officer determined that the item was contraband only after conducting a further search . . . [by "squeezing, sliding and otherwise manipulating the contents of the defendant's pocket"] — a pocket which the officer already knew contained no weapon. The "further search" of manipulating the lump exceeded the scope of the "plain feel" doctrine and, therefore, was an unreasonable search, according to the Court.

"PLAIN SMELL"

Agents from the DEA stopped a man who had just landed in a small private plane from South America. He had placed packages taken from the plane in a car parked a short distance away. He opened the trunk where he had put the packages at the request of the agents. When he did, the agents testified that the packages "reeked of marijuana." The agents seized the marijuana and arrested the man. He moved to suppress the marijuana on the grounds that the officers seized it illegally. The court denied the motion because the contents of the packages were inferable from their odor, a conclusion based on an extension of the plain view doctrine that includes evidence "that can be perceived by the sense of smell."[13]

According to the Supreme Court, the rationale of the plain view doctrine is that

> if contraband is left in open view and is observed by a police officer from a lawful vantage point, there has been no invasion of a legitimate expectation of privacy and thus no "search" within the meaning of the Fourth Amendment.[14]

Electronic surveillance often includes the use of highly sophisticated devices that can transform detections by the ordinary senses into Fourth Amendment searches. The Supreme Court dealt with the application of the Fourth Amendment to electronic eavesdropping in *United States v. White*.

C A S E

Is Electronic Eavesdropping a "Search"?

United States v. White
401 U.S. 745, 91 S.Ct. 1122,
28 L.Ed.2d 453 (1971)

White was tried and convicted for narcotics law violations on the basis of evidence overheard by means of

electronic eavesdropping by government agents. The U.S. Court of Appeals reversed the conviction. The U.S. Supreme Court granted certiorari *and reversed the Court of Appeals. Justice White announced the judgment of the Court, which Chief Justice Burger and Justices Stewart and Blackmun joined. Justice Black filed a statement concurring in the judgment. Justice Brennan concurred in the judgment. Justices Douglas, Harlan, and Marshall dissented.*

FACTS

. . . James A. White was tried and convicted under two consolidated indictments charging various illegal transactions in narcotics. He was fined and sentenced as a second offender to 25-year concurrent sentences. The issue before us is whether the Fourth Amendment bars from evidence the testimony of governmental agents who related certain conversations which had occurred between defendant White and a government informant, Harvey Jackson, and which the agents overheard by monitoring the frequency of a radio transmitter carried by Jackson and concealed on his person. On four occasions the conversations took place in Jackson's home; each of these conversations was overheard by an agent concealed in a kitchen closet with Jackson's consent and by a second agent outside the house using a radio receiver. Four other conversations—one in respondent's home, one in a restaurant, and two in Jackson's car—were overheard by the use of radio equipment. The prosecution was unable to locate and produce Jackson at the trial and the trial court over-ruled objections to the testimony of the agents who conducted the electronic surveillance. The jury returned a guilty verdict and defendant appealed.

The Court of Appeals . . . interpreted the Fourth Amendment to forbid the introduction of the agents' testimony in the circumstances of this case. Accordingly, the court reversed. . . . In our view, the Court of Appeals misinterpreted . . . the Fourth Amendment. . . .

OPINION

. . . The Court of Appeals understood *Katz* [*v. United States*, excerpted above] to render inadmissible against White the agents' testimony concerning conversations that Jackson broadcast to them. We cannot agree. *Katz* involved no revelation to the Government by a party to conversations with the defendant nor did the Court indicate in any way that a defendant has a justifiable and constitutionally protected expectation that a person with whom he is convers-

ing will not then or later reveal the conversation to the police. . . .

Our problem is not what the privacy expectations of particular defendants in particular situations may be or the extent to which they may in fact have relied on the discretion of their companions. Very probably, individual defendants neither know nor suspect that their colleagues have gone or will go to the police or are carrying recorders or transmitters. Otherwise, conversation would cease and our problem with these encounters would be nonexistent or far different from those now before us. Our problem, in terms of the principles announced in *Katz*, is what expectations of privacy are constitutionally "justifiable"—what expectations the Fourth Amendment will protect in the absence of a warrant. So far, the law permits the frustration of actual expectations of privacy by permitting authorities to use the testimony of those associates who for one reason or another have determined to turn to the police, as well as by authorizing the use of informants. If the law gives no protection to the wrongdoer whose trusted accomplice is or becomes a police agent, neither should it protect him when that same agent has recorded or transmitted the conversations which are later offered in evidence to prove the State's case.

Inescapably, one contemplating illegal activities must realize and risk that his companions may be reporting to the police. If he sufficiently doubts their trustworthiness, the association will very probably end or never materialize. But if he has no doubts, or allays them, or risks what doubt he has, the risk is his. In terms of what his course will be, what he will or will not do or say, we are unpersuaded that he would distinguish between probable informers with transmitters [and] the other. Given the possibility or probability that one of his colleagues is cooperating with the police, it is only speculation to assert that the defendant's utterances would be substantially different or his sense of security any less if he also thought it possible that the suspected colleague is wired for sound. At least there is no persuasive evidence that the difference in this respect between the electronically equipped and the unequipped agent is substantial enough to require discrete constitutional recognition, particularly under the Fourth Amendment, which is ruled by fluid concepts of "reasonableness."

Nor should we be too ready to erect constitutional barriers to relevant and probative evidence which is also accurate and reliable. An electronic recording will many times produce a more reliable rendition of what a defendant has said than will the unaided memory of a police agent. It may also be that with the recording in existence it is less likely that the informant will change his mind, less chance that threat of injury will suppress unfavorable evidence and less chance that cross-examination will confound the testimony. Considerations like these obviously do not favor the defendant, but we are not prepared to hold that a defendant who has no constitutional right to exclude the informer's unaided testimony nevertheless has a Fourth Amendment privilege against a more accurate version of the events in question. . . .

DISSENT

Justice Douglas, dissenting.

. . . The issue in this case is clouded and concealed by the very discussion of it in legalistic terms. What the ancients knew as "eavesdropping," we now call "electronic surveillance"; but to equate the two is to treat man's first gunpowder on the same level as the nuclear bomb. Electronic surveillance is the greatest leveler of human privacy ever known. How most forms of it can be held "reasonable" within the meaning of the Fourth Amendment is a mystery. To be sure, the Constitution and Bill of Rights are not to be read as covering only the technology known in the 18th century. Otherwise its concept of "commerce" would be hopeless when it comes to the management of modern affairs. At the same time, the concepts of privacy which the Founders enshrined in the Fourth Amendment vanish completely when we slavishly allow an all-powerful government, proclaiming law and order, efficiency, and other benign purposes, to penetrate all the walls and doors which men need to shield them from the pressures of a turbulent life around them and give them the health and strength to carry on. . . .

[According to the Court's decision,] must everyone live in fear that every word he speaks may be transmitted or recorded and later repeated to the entire world? I can imagine nothing that has a more chilling effect on people speaking their minds and expressing their views on important matters. The advocates of the regime should spend some time in totalitarian countries and learn first-hand the kind of regime they are creating here.

[Justice Harlan, dissenting.]

Since it is the task of the law to form and project, as well as mirror and reflect, we should not, as judges, merely recite the expectations and risks without examining the desirability of saddling them upon society. The critical question, therefore, is whether under our system of government, as reflected in the Constitution, we should impose on our citizens the risks of the electronic listener or observer without at least the protection of a warrant requirement. This question must, in my view, be answered by assessing the nature of a particular practice and the likely extent of its impact on the individual's sense of security balanced against the utility of the conduct as a technique of law enforcement. For those more extensive intrusions that significantly jeopardize the sense of security which is the paramount concern of Fourth Amendment liberties, I am of the view that more than self-restraint by law enforcement officials is required and at the least warrants should be necessary.

The impact of the practice of third-party bugging, must, I think be considered such as to undermine that confidence and sense of security in dealing with one another that is characteristic of individual relationships between citizens in a free society. It goes beyond the impact on privacy occasioned by the ordinary type of "informer" investigation. . . . The argument of the plurality opinion, to the effect that it is irrelevant whether secrets are revealed by the mere tattletale or the transistor, ignores the differences occasioned by third-party monitoring and recording which insures full and accurate disclosure of all that is said, free of the possibility of error and oversight that inheres in human reporting.

Authority is hardly required to support the proposition that words would be measured a good deal more carefully and communication inhibited if one suspected his conversations were being transmitted and transcribed. Were third-party bugging a prevalent practice, it might well smother that spontaneity—reflected in frivolous, impetuous, sacrilegious, and defiant discourse—that liberates daily life. Much offhand exchange is easily forgotten and one may count on the obscurity of his remarks, protected by the very fact of a limited audience, and the likelihood that the listener will either overlook or forget what is said, as well as the listener's inability to reformulate a conversation without having to contend with a documented record. All these values are sacrificed by a rule of law that permits official monitoring of private discourse limited only by the need to locate a willing assistant.

CASE DISCUSSION

Is the court saying that it is reasonable to expect that those in whom we confide may be wired for sound by the police? What interests is the Court balancing in this case? Which is most intrusive: listening to James A. White in his home, in Harvey Jackson's home, in a restaurant, on the street, or in a car? Or are they all about the same? Why? Why not? Does the dissent have a point that everyone will live in fear that what she or he says will be reported, or transmitted by radio, to the police? Should the police have been required to get a warrant here?

D e c i s i o n   P o i n t

1. Acting on reports that marijuana was being raised on Oliver's farm, two narcotics agents of the Kentucky State Police went to the farm to investigate. Arriving at the farm, they drove past Oliver's house to a locked gate with a "No Trespassing" sign. A footpath led around one side of the gate. The agents walked around the gate and along the road for several hundred yards, passing a barn and a parked camper. At that point, someone standing in front of the camper shouted, "No hunting is allowed; come back up here." The officers shouted back that they were Kentucky State Police officers, but found no one when they returned to the camper. The officers resumed their investigation of the farm and found a field of marijuana over a mile from Oliver's home. On the basis of the evidence, they arrested Oliver for manufacturing a controlled substance.

2. After receiving an anonymous tip that marijuana was being grown in the woods behind Thornton's residence, two police officers entered the woods by a path between Thornton's residence and a neighboring house. They followed a footpath through the woods until they reached two marijuana patches fenced with chicken wire. Later, after the officers determined that the patches were on Thornton's property, they obtained a warrant to search and seize the marijuana. On the basis of the evidence, the police arrested Thornton.

Were these two searches lawful? According to the United States Supreme Court, they were: "We conclude, from the text of the Fourth Amendment and from the historical and contemporary understanding of its purposes, that an individual has no legitimate expectation that open fields will remain free from warrantless intrusion by government officers." In Oliver's case, the trial court had suppressed the evidence, holding that the "No Trespassing" sign and the secluded location of the marijuana patches "evinced a reasonable expectation of privacy," but the Maine Supreme Judicial Court affirmed in Thornton's case. Which court holding, in your opinion, is the better rule?[15]

The Supreme Court has not decided whether the use of drug-sniffing dogs is a plain smell search. Clearly, dogs have a much keener sense of smell than humans, so their use compares to that of electronic devices to enhance the senses of sight and hearing. The lower courts are divided over whether dog sniffing is a Fourth Amendment search. The Fifth Circuit Court of Appeals addressed the issue in *Horton v. Goose Creek Independent School District*.

C A S E

Is a "Drug Sniff" by a Dog a Search?

Horton v. Goose Creek Independent School District
690 F.2d 470 (5th Cir. 1982)

Robert Horton, as next friend of Robby Horton, Heather Horton, and Sandra Sanchez, on their own behalf and on behalf of all others similarly situated, challenged the school district's use of a canine contraband detection program. The United States District Court for the Southern District of Texas entered summary judgment in favor of the school district. The students appealed. The Fifth Circuit U.S. Court of appeals affirmed in part, reversed in part, and remanded the case. Before Circuit Judges Wisdom, Randall and Tate. Per Curiam.

FACTS

The defendant, GCISD [Goose Creek Independent School District], adopted the challenged program in response to a growing drug and alcohol abuse problem in the schools. It contracted with a security services firm, Securities Associates International, Inc. (SAI), that provides dogs (generally Doberman pinschers and German shepherds) trained to alert their handlers to the presence of any one of approximately sixty different substances, including alcohol and drugs, both over-the-counter and controlled. The defendant conducted assemblies in the elementary schools to acquaint the children with the dogs and informed students in the junior and senior high schools of the program. On a random and unannounced basis, the dogs are taken to the various schools in the district, where they sniff students' lockers and automobiles. They also go into the classrooms, on leashes, to sniff the students themselves. During their "playtime" at the schools, the dogs are sometimes taken off their leashes. When a dog alerts the handler to the odor of an illicit substance on a student's person, after the sweep of the class is completed and the dog and handler have departed, a school official discreetly asks the student to leave the class and go to the administrator's office, where he is subjected to a search of pockets, purse, and outer garments. When a dog alerts his handler to an automobile, the student driver is asked to open the doors and the trunk. If he refuses, the school notifies the parents. When a dog alerts his handler to a locker, the school searches the locker without the consent of the student to whom it is assigned. If the student is found to possess substances that violate school policy, he may agree to seek outside counseling; otherwise the administrator may recommend to the superintendent that the student be suspended. Second-time violators do not have the option of counseling.

The named plaintiffs were all subjected to the sniffing of the canine drug detectors. Two of them, Robby Horton and Sandra Sanchez, triggered alerts. School officials questioned Sandra, took her purse, and searched it without her consent. They found a small bottle of perfume, which they returned to her. Robby was asked to empty his pockets, which he did. When nothing incriminating was found, the school officials searched his socks and lower pants legs but again found no contraband.

The plaintiffs brought this action, alleging a violation of the fourth amendment prohibition of unreasonable searches and seizures and a violation of the fourteenth amendment prohibition of deprivations of liberty and property without due process. . . . [T]he district court . . . held that the sniffing, although it is a search, is not unreasonable. Further, it held that reasonable cause is the standard for searches of students and their property by school officials acting in loco parentis [in the place of a parent], and the alert of the dogs provides reasonable cause for searches of lockers and cars as well as for searches of the pockets, purses, and outer garments of students. Finally, the district court held that the program does not violate the due process clause, because it subjects the students to minimal intrusion, humiliation, and fear. The plaintiffs appeal. . . .

OPINION

[The court reviewed a split of authority among the circuit courts, some holding that dog sniffing is a search and others holding that it is not.]

The problem presented in this case is the convergence of two troubling questions. First, is the sniff of a drug-detecting dog a "search" within the purview of the fourth amendment? Second, to what extent does the fourth amendment protect students against searches by school administrators seeking to maintain a safe environment conducive to education? On each question, we find an abundance of precedent but scant guidance.

Frequent use of drug-detecting dogs by law enforcement officials has led to a great number of cases challenging the admissibility of the fruits of a canine sniff. From these cases, one proposition is clear and universally accepted: if the police have some basis for suspecting an individual of possessing contraband, they may, consonant with the fourth amendment, use a drug-detecting dog to sniff checked luggage, shipped packages, storage lockers, trailers, or cars. While the rationales of these cases are not the same, the majority view is that the sniffing of objects by a dog is not a search. Only the Ninth Circuit has held that the sniffing of objects is a search, though it may at times be reasonable.

The decision to characterize an action as a search is in essence a conclusion about whether the fourth amendment applies at all. If an activity is not a search or seizure (assuming the activity does not violate some other constitutional or statutory provision), then the government enjoys a virtual carte blanche to do as it pleases. The activity is "excluded from judicial control and the command of reasonableness." We must analyze the question of whether dog sniffing is a search in terms of whether the sniffing offends reasonable expectations of privacy, *Katz v. United States* (1967) [excerpted earlier in this chapter], and must look at the degree of intrusiveness of the challenged action to determine whether it is the type of activity that can be tolerated in a free society. *Terry v. Ohio* (1968) [excerpted in Chapter 4].

We have already held that the sniffing by dogs of luggage checked in an airport, *Goldstein v. U.S.* (5th Cir. 1981), and luggage checked in a bus terminal, *United States v. Viera* (5th Cir. 1981), is not a search,

reasoning that "the passenger's reasonable expectation of privacy does not extend to the airspace surrounding that luggage." We noted that the appellants had released their bags to the custody of the airlines, thereby relinquishing—at least temporarily—all control over them. Other circuits have emphasized the minimal humiliation entailed in dogs sniffing unattended luggage.

The courts have in effect adopted a doctrine of "public smell" analogous to the exclusion from fourth amendment coverage of things exposed to the public "view." The courts have reasoned that if a police officer, positioned in a place where he has a right to be, is conscious of an odor, say, of marijuana, no search has occurred; the aroma emanating from the property or person is considered exposed to the public "view" and, therefore, unprotected. From this proposition the courts have concluded that the sniffing of a dog is "no different," or that the dog's olfactory sense merely "enhances" that of the police officer in the same way that a flashlight enhances the officer's sight.

. . . On the question of whether the dogs' sniffing of student lockers in public hallways and automobiles parked on public parking lots was a search, the sniffs occurred while the objects were unattended and positioned in public view. Had the principal of the school wandered past the lockers and smelled the pungent aroma of marijuana wafting through the corridors, it would be difficult to contend that a search had occurred. . . . The use of the dogs' nose to ferret out the scent from inanimate objects in public places is not treated any differently. We hold accordingly that the sniffs of the lockers and cars did not constitute a search and therefore we need make no inquiry into the reasonableness of the sniffing of the lockers and automobiles.

The use of the dogs to sniff the students, however, presents an entirely different problem. After all, the fourth amendment "protects people, not places." . . . The Second and Ninth Circuits specifically noted that people had not been sniffed when they upheld the constitutionality of dogs sniffing objects. The Seventh Circuit is the only circuit to have held that sniffs of school children do not constitute a search [*Doe v. Renfrow* (N.D.Ind. 1979)]. We note that there was apparently no evidence in *Renfrow* that the dogs actually touched the students, while the dogs in the GCISD program put their noses right up against the children's bodies. Furthermore, as was noted above, the *Renfrow* decision has been universally criticized by the commentators.

The students' persons certainly are not the subject of lowered expectations of privacy. On the contrary, society recognizes the interest in the integrity of one's person, and the fourth amendment applies with its fullest vigor against any intrusion on the human body. . . .

The circuit courts have unanimously assumed that the use of magnetometers in airport terminals to detect concealed weapons, an activity far less intrusive than the use of large dogs to sniff the bodies of children, is a search. The Fourth Circuit originally held that the magnetometer walk-through [was] still a search. Indeed, that is the very purpose of the magnetometer: to search for metal and disclose its presence in areas where there is a normal expectation of privacy.

The commentators agree that "the intensive smelling of people, even if done by dogs, (is) indecent and demeaning." 74 *Nw.U.L.Rev.* at 850; see also 71 *J. Crim.L. & Criminology* at 44. Most persons in our society deliberately attempt not to expose the odors emanating from their bodies to public smell. In contrast, where the Supreme Court has upheld limited investigations of body characteristics not justified by individualized suspicion, it has done so on the grounds that the particular characteristic was routinely exhibited to the public. *United States v. Dionisio* (1973) (voice exemplars); *United States v. Mara* (1973) (handwriting exemplars); *Davis v. Mississippi* (1969) (fingerprints). Intentional close proximity sniffing of the person is offensive whether the sniffer be canine or human. One can imagine the embarrassment which a young adolescent, already self-conscious about his or her body, might experience when a dog, being handled by a representative of the school administration, enters the classroom specifically for the purpose of sniffing the air around his or her person. . . .

Plaintiff, Heather Horton, described what happened when the dog entered the classrooms: "Well, we were in the middle of a major French exam and the dog came in and walked up and down the aisles and stopped at every desk and sniffed on each side all around the people, the feet, the parts where you keep your books under the desk." Ms. Horton went on to express her fear of the large dogs. The SAI representative testified that the dogs put their noses "up against" the persons they are investigating.

On the basis of our examination of the record which indicates the degree of personal intrusiveness involved in this type of activity, we hold that sniffing by dogs of the students' persons in the manner involved in this case is a search within the purview of the fourth amendment. We need not decide today whether the use of dogs to sniff people in some other manner, e.g., at some distance, is a search.

Our decision that the sniffing is a search does not, however, compel the conclusion that it is constitutionally impermissible. The fourth amendment does not prohibit all searches; it only restricts the government to "reasonable" searches. . . . [NOTE: The court referred to the reasonableness of administrative searches in schools. See *New Jersey v. T.L.O.* (1985), discussed in Chapter 7.]

We conclude that the use of dogs in dragnet sniff-searches of the students of GCISD is unconstitutional, but that the use of the dogs in similar dragnet sniffing of lockers and cars is not, and we direct the district court to grant relief by appropriate declaration and injunction. Although the use of the dogs in dragnet sniffing of lockers and cars is permissible, we must remand to the district court for the case to proceed to trial on the reliability of the dogs' reactions as the basis for further searches. . . .

Affirmed in part, reversed in part, and remanded.

CASE DISCUSSION

Why does the court distinguish among sniffing lockers, cars, and students? Do you agree that sniffing lockers and cars is not searching, but that sniffing students is? Defend your answer. What interests did the court balance in deciding the case? Do you think that the government need to enforce the drug laws outweighs the privacy interest of students? Does it matter in this case that the students bringing the action were "innocent"? What, if any, remedy would you give these students?

Open Fields

The Fourth Amendment does not prevent government officials from gathering and using against defendants information that they discover in open fields, even if the officers trespassed on privately owned property in order to find the information. According to the **open fields doctrine,** the U.S. Supreme Court has decided that "the special protection accorded by the Fourth Amendment to the people in their 'persons, houses, papers, and effects,' is not extended to the open fields." Society, said the Court, is not prepared to recognize any reasonable expectation of privacy in open fields:

> Open fields do not provide the setting for those intimate activities that the Amendment is intended to shelter from government interference or surveillance. There is no societal interest in protecting the privacy of those activities, such as the cultivation of crops, that occur in open fields.[16]

Some commentators maintain that if owners give notice that they expect privacy — such as by building fences or putting up "No Trespassing" signs — the open fields doctrine should not apply. Despite such suggestions, the Supreme Court has declined to limit the doctrine because of the practical difficulties that officers would face in administering it: "[P]olice officers would have to guess before every search whether landowners had erected fences sufficiently high, posted a sufficient number of warning signs, or located contraband in an area sufficiently secluded to establish a right of privacy."[17]

The open fields doctrine does not extend to the **curtilage,** that is, the area immediately surrounding a house. The curtilage refers to that area where family and other private activities take place, including the yard near the house, a pool and patio area, and an attached garage. Intrusions into the curtilage by government agents are Fourth Amendment searches. The Supreme Court has identified the following criteria to determine whether an area falls within the curtilage:

- Distance from the house
- Presence or absence of a fence around the area
- Use or purpose of the area
- Measures taken to prevent public view

In applying these criteria in *United States v. Dunn,* the Court concluded that Dunn's barn was not part of the curtilage because it was sixty yards from the house, it was fifty yards beyond a fence surrounding the house, it was not used for family purposes, and Dunn took no measures to hide it from public view.[18]

Public Places

The Fourth Amendment does not protect what the senses perceive in public places, including streets, parks, and other publicly owned areas. Public places also include privately owned businesses that are open to the public. The Fourth Amendment does protect the areas reserved for employees only, such as offices, restrooms, basements, and other places not open to the public. The Fourth Amendment does not protect the open areas of public restrooms. It does protect enclosed stalls, but not what government agents can see over and under partitions or through cracks or other gaps in partitions.[19]

Abandoned Effects

The Fourth Amendment does not protect abandoned property, the U.S. Supreme Court having ruled that a person retains no "reasonable expectation of privacy" in it. According to the law of property, **abandonment** consists of two elements:

1. The intent to throw away property

2. Acts that prove that intent

The mere act of giving up physical possession is not abandonment; abandonment requires an intent to relinquish control over the property. Furthermore, abandonment for purposes of the Fourth Amendment requires proof that the person abandoning the property has no reasonable expectation of privacy in it. The Supreme Court has adopted a totality-of-circumstances test to determine whether intentionally throwing away property has eliminated the reasonable expectation of privacy protected by the Fourth Amendment. The Court looks at the facts in each case to determine the intent to abandon, the actions indicating abandonment, and therefore the termination of a reasonable expectation of privacy in the items seized by the government. In the leading abandonment case decided during Prohibition, *Hester v. United States*, revenue agents chased Hester through open fields. When the agents fired a shot, Hester dropped the illegal liquor he was carrying. The Supreme Court held that the facts indicated that Hester intended to abandon the alcohol. And in *Abel v. United States*, decided during the Cold War, immigration officials arrested Abel in his hotel room. After Abel was arrested and checked out of the hotel, FBI agents who suspected Abel of being a Communist spy searched his hotel room. They seized several items that Abel had left behind in a wastepaper basket. The Court held that Abel had abandoned the room and, therefore, his reasonable expectation of privacy in what he left behind in the wastepaper basket.[20] Using this totality-of-circumstances approach to deciding abandonment, the Court has held that none of the following actions amounted to abandonment:

- Dropping drugs to the floor of a cab when the police approached[21]
- Putting down a bag of groceries and refusing to answer questions about it when the police approached, and then reaching for the bag when the police reached for it[22]
- Setting down a package several feet away from a telephone[23]

The question of whether items placed in the trash for collection by trash collectors are abandoned for purposes of the Fourth Amendment protection has caused a considerable amount of difficulty for the courts. Most have adopted the totality-of-circumstances test to determine whether owners have abandoned the trash and therefore relinquished their reasonable expectation of privacy. But they differ on what circumstances they consider important. The two that weigh most heavily are the following:

1. Whether actions showing that intentionally exposing trash to the possible exposure of its contents to trash collectors or members of the public means that the owners have assumed the risk that police officers or other government agents will also rummage through the trash looking for incriminating evidence with which to arrest, prosecute, and convict the owners of the trash with crimes

2. Whether private persons must take extraordinary action to demonstrate that they have retained an expectation of privacy in the property exposed to the risk of discovery by others

In *California v. Greenwood*, the U.S. Supreme Court applied the totality-of-circumstances test to determine whether trash left at the curb side for collection was abandoned.

C A S E

Was the Trash "Abandoned"?

California v. Greenwood
486 U.S. 35, 108 S.Ct. 1625,
100 L.Ed.2d 30 (1988)

Greenwood was arrested and charged with felony narcotics possession on the basis of contraband seized under two search warrants. Greenwood moved to set aside the warrants on the ground that they violated the Fourth Amendment. A California superior court granted the motion, and a California intermediate appellate court affirmed the superior court's decision. The California Supreme Court denied the state's petition for review. The U.S. Supreme Court granted certiorari and reversed the California Court of Appeals. Justice White wrote the opinion of the Court, in which Chief Justice Rehnquist and Justices Blackmun, Stevens, O'Connor, and Scalia joined. Justice Brennan filed a dissenting opinion, in which Justice Marshall joined. Justice Kennedy took no part in the consideration or decision of the case.

FACTS

In early 1984, Investigator Jenny Stracner of the Laguna Beach Police Department received information indicating that respondent Greenwood might be engaged in narcotics trafficking. Stracner learned that a criminal suspect had informed a federal drug-enforcement agent in February 1984 that a truck filled with illegal drugs was en route to the Laguna Beach address at which Greenwood resided. In addition, a neighbor complained of heavy vehicular traffic late at night in front of Greenwood's single-family home. The neighbor reported that the vehicles remained at Greenwood's house for only a few minutes.

Stracner sought to investigate this information by conducting a surveillance of Greenwood's home. She observed several vehicles make brief stops at the house during the late-night and early-morning hours, and she followed a truck from the house to a residence that had previously been under investigation as a narcotics trafficking location.

On April 6, 1984, Stracner asked the neighborhood's regular trash collector to pick up the plastic garbage bags that Greenwood had left on the curb in front of his house and to turn the bags over to her without mixing their contents with garbage from other houses. The trash collector cleaned his truck bin of other refuse, collected the garbage bags from the street in front of Greenwood's house, and turned the bags over to Stracner. The officer searched through the rubbish and found items indicative of narcotics use. She recited the information that she had gleaned from the trash search in an affidavit in support of a warrant to search Greenwood's home.

Police officers encountered both respondents at the house later that day when they arrived to execute the warrant. The police discovered quantities of cocaine and hashish during their search of the house. Respondents were arrested on felony narcotics charges. They subsequently posted bail. The police continued to receive reports of many late-night visitors to the Greenwood house. On May 4, Investigator Robert Rahaeuser obtained Greenwood's garbage from the regular trash collector in the same manner as had Stracner. The garbage again contained evidence of narcotics use.

Rahaeuser secured another search warrant for Greenwood's home based on the information from the second trash search. The police found more narcotics and evidence of narcotic trafficking when they executed the warrant. Greenwood was again arrested.

The Superior Court dismissed the charges against respondents on the authority of *People v. Krivda* (1971), which held that warrantless trash searches violate the Fourth Amendment and the California Constitution. The court found that the police would not have had probable cause to search the Greenwood home without the evidence obtained from the trash searches. The Court of Appeal affirmed. The court noted at the outset that the fruits of warrantless trash searches could no longer be suppressed if *Krivda* were based only on the California Constitution, because since 1982 the State has barred the suppression of evidence seized in violation of California law but not federal law. But *Krivda*, a decision binding on the Court of Appeal, also held that the fruits of warrantless trash searches were to be excluded under federal law. Hence, the Superior Court was correct in dismissing the charges against respondents. The California Supreme Court denied the State's petition for review of the Court of Appeal's decision. We granted certiorari, and now reverse.

OPINION

The warrantless search and seizure of the garbage bags left at the curb outside the Greenwood house would violate the Fourth Amendment only if respondents manifested a subjective expectation of privacy in their garbage that society accepts as objectively reasonable. Respondents do not disagree with this standard. They assert, however, that they had, and exhibited, an expectation of privacy with respect to the trash that was searched by the police: The trash, which was placed on the street for collection at a fixed time, was contained in opaque plastic bags, which the garbage collector was expected to pick up, mingle with the trash of others, and deposit at the garbage dump. The trash was only temporarily on the street, and there was little likelihood that it would be inspected by anyone.

It may well be that respondents did not expect that the contents of their garbage bags would become known to the police or other members of the public. An expectation of privacy does not give rise to Fourth Amendment protection, however, unless society is prepared to accept that expectation as objectively reasonable. Here, we conclude that respondents exposed

their garbage to the public sufficiently to defeat their claim to Fourth Amendment protection. It is common knowledge that plastic garbage bags left on or at the side of a public street are readily accessible to animals, children, scavengers, snoops, and other members of the public. Moreover, respondents placed their refuse at the curb for the express purpose of conveying it to a third party, the trash collector, who might himself have sorted through respondents' trash or permitted others, such as the police, to do so. Accordingly, having deposited their garbage "in an area particularly suited for public inspection and, in a manner of speaking, public consumption, for the express purpose of having strangers take it," respondents could have had no reasonable expectation of privacy in the inculpatory items that they discarded.

Furthermore, as we have held, the police cannot reasonably be expected to avert their eyes from evidence of criminal activity that could have been observed by any member of the public. Hence, "[w]hat a person knowingly exposes to the public, even in his own home or office, is not a subject of Fourth Amendment protection." We held in *Smith v. Maryland* [1979], for example, that the police did not violate the Fourth Amendment by causing a pen register to be installed at the telephone company's offices to record the telephone numbers dialed by a criminal suspect. An individual has no legitimate expectation of privacy in the numbers dialed on his telephone, we reasoned, because he voluntarily conveys those numbers to the telephone company when he uses the telephone. Again, we observed that "a person has no legitimate expectation of privacy in information he voluntarily turns over to third parties."

Similarly, we held in *California v. Ciraolo* [1986], that the police were not required by the Fourth Amendment to obtain a warrant before conducting surveillance of the respondent's fenced backyard from a private plane flying at an altitude of 1,000 feet. We concluded that the respondent's expectation that his yard was protected from such surveillance was unreasonable because "[a]ny member of the public flying in this airspace who glanced down could have seen everything that these officers observed."

Our conclusion that society would not accept as reasonable respondents' claim to an expectation of privacy in trash left for collection in an area accessible to the public is reinforced by the unanimous rejection of similar claims by the Federal Courts of Appeals. In *United States v. Thornton* (1984), the court observed that "the overwhelming weight of authority rejects the proposition that a reasonable expectation of privacy exists with respect to trash discarded outside the home and the curtilage thereof." In addition, of those state appellate courts that have considered the issue, the vast majority have held that the police may conduct warrantless searches and seizures of garbage discarded in public areas. [COURT NOTE: "Given that the dissenters are among the tiny minority of judges whose views are contrary to ours, we are distinctly unimpressed with the dissent's prediction that 'society will be shocked' to learn of today's decision."]

We reject respondent Greenwood's alternative argument for affirmance: that his expectation of privacy in his garbage should be deemed reasonable as a matter of federal constitutional law because the warrantless search and seizure of his garbage was impermissible as a matter of California law. He urges that the state-law right of Californians to privacy in their garbage, announced by the California Supreme Court in *Krivda*, survived the subsequent state constitutional amendment eliminating the suppression remedy as a means of enforcing that right. Hence, he argues that the Fourth Amendment should itself vindicate that right.

Individual states may surely construe their own constitutions as imposing more stringent constraints on police conduct than does the Federal Constitution. We have never intimated, however, that whether or not a search is reasonable within the meaning of the Fourth Amendment depends on the law of the particular state in which the search occurs. We have emphasized instead that the Fourth Amendment analysis must turn on such factors as "our societal understanding that certain areas deserve the most scrupulous protection from government invasion." We have already concluded that society as whole possesses no such understanding with regard to garbage left for collection at the side of a public street. Respondent's argument is no less than a suggestion that concepts of privacy under the laws of each state are to determine the reach of the Fourth Amendment. We do not accept this submission. . . .

The judgment of the California Court of Appeal is therefore reversed, and this case is remanded for further proceedings not inconsistent with this opinion. It is so ordered.

DISSENT

Justice Brennan, with whom Justice Marshall joins, dissenting.

Every week for two months, and at least once more a month later, the Laguna Beach police clawed through the trash that respondent Greenwood left in opaque, sealed bags on the curb outside his home. Complete strangers minutely scrutinized their bounty, undoubtedly dredging up intimate details of Greenwood's private life and habits. The intrusions proceeded without a warrant, and no court before or since has concluded that the police acted on probable cause to believe Greenwood was engaged in any criminal activity.

Scrutiny of another's trash is contrary to commonly accepted notions of civilized behavior. I suspect, therefore, that members of our society will be shocked to learn that the Court, the ultimate guarantor of liberty, deems unreasonable our expectation that the aspects of our private lives that are concealed safely in a trash bag will not become public.

A container which can support a reasonable expectation of privacy may not be searched, even on probable cause, without a warrant. Thus, as the Court observes, if Greenwood had a reasonable expectation that the contents of the bags that he placed on the curb would remain private, the warrantless search of those bags violated the Fourth Amendment.

The Framers of the Fourth Amendment understood that "unreasonable searches" of "paper[s] and effects" — no less than "unreasonable searches" of "person[s] and houses" — infringe privacy. . . . [S]o long as a package is "closed against inspection," the Fourth Amendment protects its contents, "wherever they may be," and the police must obtain a warrant to search it just "as is required when papers are subjected to search in one's own household." . . . In *Robbins v. California* [1981], for example, Justice Stewart, writing for a plurality of four, pronounced that "unless the container is such that its contents may be said to be in plain view, those contents are fully protected by the Fourth Amendment," and soundly rejected any distinction for Fourth Amendment purposes among various opaque, sealed containers. . . .

More recently, in *United States v. Ross* (1982), the Court, relying on the "virtually unanimous" agreement in *Robbins* . . . that a constitutional distinction between "worthy" and "unworthy" containers would be improper, held that a distinction among "paper bags, locked trunks, lunch buckets, and orange crates" would be inconsistent with "the central purpose of the Fourth Amendment. . . . [A] traveler who carries a toothbrush and a few articles of clothing in a paper bag or knotted scarf [may] claim an equal right to conceal his possessions from official inspection as the sophisticated executive with the locked attaché case." . . .

Our precedent, therefore, leaves no room to doubt that had respondents been carrying their personal effects in opaque, sealed plastic bags — identical to the ones they placed on the curb — their privacy would have been protected from warrantless police intrusion. So far as Fourth Amendment protection is concerned, opaque plastic bags are every bit as worthy as "packages wrapped in green opaque plastic" and "double-locked footlocker[s]."

Respondents deserve no less protection just because Greenwood used the bags to discard rather than to transport his personal effects. Their contents are not inherently any less private, and Greenwood's decision to discard them, at least in the manner in which he did, does not diminish his expectation of privacy.

A trash bag, like any of the above-mentioned containers, "is a common repository for one's personal effects" and, even more than many of them, is "therefore . . . inevitably associated with the expectation of privacy." " . . . [A]lmost every human activity ultimately manifests itself in waste products. . . ." . . . "If you want to know what is really going on in a community, look at its garbage." A single bag of trash testifies eloquently to the eating, reading, and recreational habits of the person who produced it. A search of trash, like a search of the bedroom, can relate intimate details about sexual practices, health, and personal hygiene. Like rifling through desk drawers or

intercepting phone calls, rummaging through trash can divulge the target's financial and professional status, political affiliations and inclinations, private thoughts, personal relationships, and romantic interests. It cannot be doubted that a sealed trash bag harbors telling evidence of the "intimate activity associated with the 'sanctity of a man's home and the privacies of life,'" which the Fourth Amendment is designed to protect.

. . . In evaluating the reasonableness of Greenwood's expectation that his sealed trash bags would not be invaded, the Court has held that we must look to "understandings that are recognized and permitted by society." Most of us, I believe, would be incensed to discover a meddler — whether a neighbor, a reporter, or a detective — scrutinizing our sealed trash containers to discover some detail of our personal lives. That was, quite naturally, the reaction to the sole incident on which the Court bases its conclusions that "snoops" and the like defeat the expectation of privacy in trash. When a tabloid reporter examined then-Secretary of State Henry Kissinger's trash and published his findings, Kissinger was "really revolted" by the intrusion and his wife suffered "grave anguish," N.Y. *Times*, July 9, 1975, p. A1, col. 8. The public response roundly condemning the reporter demonstrates that society not only recognized those reactions as reasonable, but shared them as well. Commentators variously characterized his conduct as "a disgusting invasion of personal privacy," "indefensible . . . as civilized behavior," and contrary to "the way decent people behave in relation to each other."

Beyond a generalized expectation of privacy, many municipalities, whether for reasons of privacy, sanitation, or both, reinforce confidence in the integrity of sealed trash containers by "prohibit[ing] anyone, except authorized employees of the Town . . . to rummage into, pick up, collect, move or otherwise interfere with articles or materials placed on . . . any public street for collection." . . .

That is not to deny that isolated intrusions into opaque, sealed trash containers occur. When, acting on their own, "animals, children, scavengers, snoops, [or] other members of the general public," actually rummage through a bag of trash and expose its contents to plain view, "police cannot reasonably be expected to avert their eyes from evidence of criminal activity that could have been observed by any member of the public." That much follows from cases like *Jacobsen*, which held that police may constitutionally inspect a package whose "integrity" a private carrier has already "compromised," because "[t]he Fourth Amendment is implicated only if the authorities use information with respect to which the expectation of privacy has not already been frustrated"; and *California v. Ciraolo*, which held that the Fourth Amendment does not prohibit police from observing what "[a]ny member of the public flying in this airspace who glanced down could have seen."

Had Greenwood flaunted his intimate activity by strewing his trash all over the curb for all to see, or had some non governmental intruder invaded his privacy and done the same, I could accept the Court's conclusion that an expectation of privacy would have been unreasonable. Similarly, had police searching the city dump run across incriminating evidence that, despite commingling with the trash of others, still retained its identity as Greenwood's, we would have a different case. But all that Greenwood "exposed . . . to the public," were the exteriors of several opaque, sealed containers. Until the bags were opened by police, they hid their contents from the public's view every bit as much as did *Chadwick's* double-locked footlocker and *Robbins'* green, plastic wrapping. Faithful application of the warrant requirement does not require police to "avert their eyes from evidence of criminal activity that could have been observed by any member of the public." Rather, it only requires them to adhere to norms of privacy that members of the public plainly acknowledge.

The mere possibility that unwelcome meddlers might open and rummage through the containers does not negate the expectation of privacy in its contents any more than the possibility of a burglary negates an expectation of privacy in the home; or the possibility of a private intrusion negates an expectation of privacy in an unopened package; or the possibility that an operator will listen in on a telephone conversation negates an expectation of privacy in the words spoken on the telephone. "What a person . . . seeks to preserve as private, even in an area accessible to the public, may be constitutionally protected." We have therefore repeatedly rejected attempts to justify a

State's invasion of privacy on the ground that the privacy is not absolute. See *Chapman v. United States* (1961) (search of a house invaded tenant's Fourth Amendment rights even though landlord had authority to enter house for some purposes); *Stoner v. California* (1964) (implicit consent to janitorial personnel to enter motel room does not amount to consent to police search of room); *O'Connor v. Ortega* (1987) (a government employee has a reasonable expectation of privacy in his office, even though "it is the nature of government offices that others—such as fellow employees, supervisors, consensual visitors, and the general public—may have frequent access to an individual's office"). . . .

Nor is it dispositive that "respondents placed their refuse at the curb for the express purpose of conveying it to a third party . . . who might himself have sorted through respondents' trash or permitted others, such as police, to do so." In the first place, Greenwood can hardly be faulted for leaving trash on his curb when a county ordinance commanded him to do so, and prohibited him from disposing of it in any other way. Unlike in other circumstances where privacy is compromised, Greenwood could not "avoid exposing personal belongings . . . by simply leaving them at home." More importantly, even the voluntary relinquishment of possession or control over an effect does not necessarily amount to a relinquishment of a privacy expectation in it. Were it otherwise, a letter or package would lose all Fourth Amendment protection when placed in a mail box or other depository with the "express purpose" of entrusting it to the postal officer or a private carrier; those bailees are just as likely as trash collectors (and certainly have greater incentive) to "sor[t] through" the personal effects entrusted to them, "or permi[t] others, such as police to do so." Yet, it has been clear for at least 110 years that the possibility of such an intrusion does not justify a warrantless search by police in the first instance.

In holding that the warrantless search of Greenwood's trash was consistent with the Fourth Amendment, the Court paints a grim picture of our society. It depicts a society in which local authorities may command their citizens to dispose of their personal effects in the manner least protective of the "sanctity of [the] home and the privacies of life," and then monitor them arbitrarily and without judicial oversight—a society that is not prepared to recognize as reasonable an individual's expectation of privacy in the most private of personal effects sealed in an opaque container and disposed of in a manner designed to commingle it imminently and inextricably with the trash of others. The American society with which I am familiar "chooses to dwell in reasonable security and freedom from surveillance," and is more dedicated to individuals' liberty and more sensitive to intrusions on the sanctity of the home than the Court is willing to acknowledge.

I dissent.

CASE DISCUSSION

What facts were relevant in determining whether Billy Greenwood intended to abandon his trash and thereby lose a reasonable expectation of privacy in it? What interests did the Court balance in this case? When you throw your trash away, do you abandon it totally or only for the purpose of having it destroyed? What does the dissent mean when it says that the Court "paints a grim picture of our society"? Do you agree? Explain your answer. Do you think that this case is important enough to get to the Supreme Court? Explain your answer.[24]

A number of states have declined to adopt the rule of abandoned trash formulated and applied in *California v. Greenwood*. They follow a rule similar to that adopted by the Vermont Supreme Court in the following Decision Point.

D e c i s i o n   P o i n t

State v. Morris, 680 A.2d Vt., 1996
A confidential informant told an officer of the Brattleboro Police Department that the defendant was selling marijuana from his apartment and from the parking lot of a certain grocery store. On March 1, 1993, a regularly scheduled trash collection day, two police officers went to the apartment building where the defendant resided and seized the five or six opaque trash bags that had been set out for collection near the curb about five or six feet from the building. From the exterior of the bags, there was no way to identify which tenant had deposited which bags. All the bags were transported to the police station and searched without a warrant. Inside the defendant's bags, which were identified through discarded pieces of mail, the police found marijuana seeds and stems and baggies containing flakes of marijuana.

Based on the items found in the trash, the information supplied by the confidential informant, and an unidentified neighbor's report that the defendant had received many different visitors during the past month, the police sought and obtained a warrant to search the defendant's residence. Approximately four

ounces of marijuana were found, and the defendant was charged with possession of marijuana. The defendant moved to suppress all evidence seized from his apartment on the ground that the search warrant was defective because it was based primarily on evidence discovered during an illegal, warrantless search of his garbage. The district court denied the defendant's motion to suppress, ruling that he had no expectation of privacy in his discarded garbage.

On appeal, following his conviction based upon a conditional plea of no contest, the defendant argued that the Vermont Constitution prohibits the warrantless search of opaque trash bags placed at curbside for collection on a regularly scheduled trash pick-up day. In response, the State contended that the Vermont Constitution does not prohibit the warrantless search of curbside trash. According to the Vermont Supreme Court,

> Given the facts of this case, we believe that defendant manifested a privacy interest recognized by society, and we conclude that unconstrained government inspection of people's trash is not

consistent with a free and open society. As Justice Brennan stated in his dissent in *California v. Greenwood*, 486 U.S. 35, 108 S.Ct. 1625, 100 L.Ed.2d 30 (1988), "Scrutiny of another's trash is contrary to commonly accepted notions of civilized behavior." Id. at 45, 108 S.Ct. at 1632 (Brennan, J., dissenting). While at first blush there may be a tendency to accept the notion that a person has no reasonable privacy interest in discarded trash, that attraction vanishes when one contemplates the "prospect of police officers, without any cause whatever, opening a securely tied and opaque trash bag, the contents of which are hidden from public view, and then searching the bag to determine the activities, behavior, habits, and lifestyles of persons who deposited the trash in front of their home for disposition by a trash collector." *People v. Hillman*, 834 P.2d 1271, 1278 (Colo. 1992) (Quinn, J., dissenting).

Because "almost every human activity ultimately manifests itself in waste products," it is understandable that persons would want to maintain privacy in the contents of their refuse. *Smith v. State*, 510 P.2d 793, 798 (Alaska 1973). An individual's trash will often reveal intimate details of that person's financial obligations, medical concerns, personal relationships, political associations, religious beliefs, and numerous other confidential matters. See *State v. Tanaka*, 67 Haw. 658, 701 P.2d 1274, 1276–77 (1985) ("Business records, bills, correspondence, magazines, tax records, and other telltale refuse can reveal much about a person's activities, associations, and beliefs."); see also *People v. Edwards*, 71 Cal.2d 1096, 80 Cal. Rptr. 633, 638, 458 P.2d 713, 718 (1969) (half truths leading to rumor and gossip may readily flow from attempt to "read" contents of another's trash). As Justice Brennan so cogently stated in his *Greenwood* dissent:

A search of trash, like a search of the bedroom, can relate intimate details about sexual practices, health, and personal hygiene. Like rifling through desk drawers or intercepting phone calls, rummaging through trash can divulge the target's financial and professional status,

political affiliations and inclinations, private thoughts, personal relationships, and romantic interests. It cannot be doubted that a sealed trash bag harbors telling evidence of the "intimate activity associated with the 'sanctity of a man's home and the privacies of life,'" which the Fourth Amendment is designed to protect.

Given the intimate details of people's lives that may be revealed by searching through their refuse, we conclude that persons have a reasonable interest in keeping private the contents of their sealed trash containers. See *State v. Hempele*, 120 N.J. 182, 576 A.2d 793, 803 (1990) (undoubtedly, most people would be upset to see another person sifting through their garbage, perusing their discarded mail, reading their bank statements, looking at their empty pharmaceutical bottles, and checking receipts to see what videotapes they rent).

We acknowledge that today's decision limits, to some extent, tactics that police may use in investigating reports of criminal activity. But improving the efficiency of law enforcement cannot come at the expense of the protection provided by Article 11 against unconstrained governmental intrusion into our private lives. See id. at 92, 616 A.2d at 783 ("Article 11 is the balance struck between liberty for the individual (privacy and a sense of security) and the convenience of unchecked crime detection."). We will not countenance under Article 11 a society in which authorities require citizens to dispose of their personal effects in a manner that is then deemed unworthy of protection from arbitrary governmental monitoring without judicial oversight.

In this case, defendant exposed to public view only the exterior of opaque trash bags, and in doing so, he sought to dispose of his personal possessions in the accepted manner that normally would result in commingling them inextricably with the trash of others. Nevertheless, without probable cause or judicial oversight, police searched through defendant's trash, as well as the trash of other apartment dwellers who had the misfortune of placing their garbage bags alongside those of someone suspected of having committed a crime. Such unconstrained governmental intrusion into people's private lives is inconsistent with Article 11 and a free and open society. Because the warrantless search of defendant's trash violated Article 11, the evidence obtained from that search, which was used to obtain a warrant to search defendant's home, must be suppressed and expunged from the affidavit supporting the search warrant.

Reversed and remanded.

FOURTH AMENDMENT "SEIZURES"

Officers who merely approach individuals without a show of force or other display of their authority have not seized them. They can ask questions, observe, or otherwise communicate with individuals without calling into action the Fourth Amendment seizure protection. According to Justice White, writing for a plurality of the Supreme Court in *Florida v. Royer* (excerpted in Chapter 5),

> [L]aw enforcement officers do not violate the Fourth Amendment by merely approaching an individual on the street or in another public place, by asking him if he is willing to answer some questions, [or] by putting questions to him if the person is willing to listen. . . . Nor would the fact that the officer identifies himself as a police officer without more, convert the encounter into a seizure.

By the same token, since officers have not "seized" them, people approached can walk away from or refuse to respond to officers' requests. This refusal or walking away is not by itself an objective basis to "seize" persons. Again in Justice White's words,

> The person approached, however, need not answer any question put to him; indeed, he may decline to listen to the questions at all and may go on his way. He may not be detained, even momentarily without reasonable, objective grounds for doing so; and his refusal to listen or answer does not, without more, furnish such grounds.[25]

Individuals may feel a psychological pressure, and as good citizens perhaps they should also feel a moral duty, to cooperate with police officers. In fact, the police and Supreme Court decisions urge cooperation. However, neither the feeling of psychological pressure nor the sense of moral duty by themselves can turn an encounter with the police into a Fourth Amendment seizure. Either an actual grabbing or a show of authority plus a submission to that authority must take place in order to turn the encounter into a Fourth Amendment seizure (see Chapter 4). For example, in *INS v. Delgado*, Immigration and Naturalization Services (INS) officers surrounded factories suspected of employing illegal aliens. The presence of INS agents was used to ensure that no employees "escaped" while other INS agents questioned them and asked them to display their "papers." The Supreme Court held that the questionings were not seizures even if INS agents surrounded the factories during the questioning. (See Table 4.1 in Chapter 4 for other examples of what is and what is not a show of force.)[26]

The American Law Institute takes the position that mere questioning by law enforcement officers is not a seizure. Its Model Code of Pre-arraignment Procedure provides as follows:

§110.1 Requests for Cooperation by Law Enforcement Officers (1) Authority to Request Cooperation. A law enforcement officer may . . . request any person to furnish information or otherwise cooperate in the investigation or prevention of crime. The officer may request the person to respond to questions, to appear at a police station, or to comply with any other reasonable request. In making requests . . . no officer shall indicate that a person is legally obliged to furnish information or otherwise to cooperate if no such legal obligation exists. Compliance with a request for information or other cooperation . . . shall not be regarded as involuntary or coerced solely on the ground that such request was made by one known to be a law enforcement officer.[27]

The Supreme Court defined and applied the definition of *seizure* in *California v. Hodari D.*

C A S E

When Did the Police "Seize" Him?

California v. Hodari D.
499 U.S. 621, 111 S.Ct. 1547,
113 L.Ed.2d 690 (1991)

Juvenile Hodari D. appealed from an order of the Superior Court, Alameda County, denying his motion to suppress and finding that he was in possession of cocaine. The California Court of Appeal reversed. The California Supreme Court denied the state's application for review. Certiorari was granted. The Supreme Court reversed and remanded. Justice Scalia wrote the opinion of the Court, in which Chief Justice Rehnquist and Justices White, Blackmun, O'Connor, Kennedy, and Souter joined. Justice Stevens, with whom Justice Marshall joined, filed a dissenting opinion.

FACTS

Late one evening in April 1988, Officers Brian McColgin and Jerry Pertoso were on patrol in a high-crime area of Oakland, California. They were dressed in street clothes but wearing jackets with "Police" embossed on both front and back. Their unmarked car proceeded west on Foothill Boulevard, and turned south onto 63rd Avenue. As they rounded the corner, they saw four or five youths huddled around a small red car parked at the curb. When the youths saw the officers' car approaching they apparently panicked, and took flight. The respondent here, Hodari D., and one companion ran west through an alley; the others fled south. The red car also headed south, at a high rate of speed. The officers were suspicious and gave chase. McColgin remained in the car and continued south on 63rd Avenue; Pertoso left the car, ran back north along 63rd, then west on Foothill Boulevard, and turned south on 62nd Avenue. Hodari, meanwhile, emerged from the alley onto 62nd and ran north. Looking behind as he ran, he did not turn and see Pertoso until the officer was almost upon him, whereupon he tossed away what appeared to be a small rock. A moment later, Pertoso tackled Hodari, handcuffed him, and radioed for assistance. Hodari was found to be carrying $130 in cash and a pager; and the rock he had discarded was found to be crack cocaine. In the juvenile proceeding brought against him, Hodari moved to suppress the evidence relating to the cocaine. The court denied the motion without opinion. The California Court of Appeal reversed, holding that Hodari had been "seized" when he saw Officer Pertoso running toward him, that this seizure was unreasonable under the Fourth Amendment, and that the evidence of cocaine had to be suppressed as the fruit of that illegal seizure. The California Supreme Court denied the state's application for review. We granted certiorari.

OPINION

As this case comes to us, the only issue presented is whether, at the time he dropped the drugs, Hodari had been "seized" within the meaning of the Fourth Amendment. [COURT FOOTNOTE: "California conceded below that Officer Pertoso did not have the 'reasonable suspicion' required to justify stopping Hodari, see *Terry v. Ohio* (1968). That it would be unreasonable to stop, for brief inquiry, young men who scatter in panic upon the mere sighting of the police is not self-evident, and arguably contradicts proverbial common sense. See Proverbs 28:1 ('The wicked flee when no man pursueth'). We do not decide that point here, but rely entirely upon the state's concession."]

If so, respondent argues, the drugs were the fruit of that seizure and the evidence concerning them was properly excluded. If not, the drugs were abandoned by Hodari and lawfully recovered by the police, and the evidence should have been admitted. (In addition, of course, Pertoso's seeing the rock of cocaine, at least if he recognized it as such, would provide reasonable suspicion for the unquestioned seizure that occurred when he tackled Hodari.)

We have long understood that the Fourth Amendment's protection against "unreasonable . . . seizures" includes seizure of the person. From the time of the founding to the present, the word "seizure" has meant a "taking possession." . . .

. . . Hodari contends (and we accept as true for purposes of this decision) that Pertoso's pursuit qualified as a "show of authority" calling upon Hodari to halt. The narrow question before us is whether, with respect to a show of authority as with respect to application of physical force, a seizure occurs even though the subject does not yield. We hold that it does not. . . .

Respondent contends that his position is sustained by the so-called *Mendenhall* test, formulated by Justice Stewart's opinion in *United States v. Mendenhall* (1980):

> A person has been "seized" within the meaning of the Fourth Amendment only if, in view of all the circumstances surrounding the incident, a reasonable person would have believed that he was not free to leave.

In seeking to rely upon that test here, respondent fails to read it carefully. It says that a person has been seized "only if," not that he has been seized "whenever"; it states a necessary, but not a sufficient condition for seizure — or, more precisely, for seizure effected through a "show of authority." *Mendenhall* establishes that the test for existence of a "show of authority" is an objective one: not whether the citizen perceived that he was being ordered to restrict his movement, but whether the officer's words and actions would have conveyed that to a reasonable person. Application of this objective test was the basis for our decision in the other case principally relied upon by respondent, where we concluded that the police cruiser's slow following of the defendant did not convey the message that he was not free to disregard the police and go about his business. We did not address in *[Michigan v.] Chesternut*, however, the question whether, if the *Mendenhall* test was met — if the message that the defendant was not free to leave had been conveyed — a Fourth Amendment seizure would have occurred.

Quite relevant to the present case, however, was our decision in *Brower v. Inyo County* (1989). In that case, police cars with flashing lights had chased the decedent for 20 miles — surely an adequate "show of authority" — but he did not stop until his fatal crash into a police-erected blockade. The issue was whether his death could be held to be the consequence of an unreasonable seizure in violation of the Fourth Amendment. We did not even consider the possibility that a seizure could have occurred during the course of the chase because, as we explained, that "show of authority" did not produce his stop. . . .

In sum, assuming that Pertoso's pursuit in the present case constituted a "show of authority" enjoining Hodari to halt, since Hodari did not comply with that injunction he was not seized until he was tackled. The cocaine abandoned while he was running was in this case not the fruit of a seizure, and his motion to exclude evidence of it was properly denied. We reverse the decision of the California Court of Appeal, and remand for further proceedings not inconsistent with his opinion.

It is so ordered.

DISSENT

Justice Stevens, with whom Justice Marshall joins, dissenting.

The court's narrow construction of the word "seizure" represents a significant, and in my view, unfortunate, departure from prior case law construing the Fourth Amendment. Almost a quarter of a century ago, in two landmark cases — one broadening the protection of individual privacy [*Katz v. United States*] and the other broadening the powers of law enforcement officers [*Terry v. Ohio*] — we rejected the method of Fourth Amendment analysis that today's majority endorses. In particular, the Court now adopts a definition of "seizure" that is unfaithful to a long line of Fourth Amendment cases. Even if the Court were defining seizure for the first time, which it is not, the definition that it chooses today is profoundly unwise. In its decision, the Court assumes, without acknowledging, that a police officer may now fire his weapon at an innocent citizen and not implicate the Fourth Amendment — as long as he misses his target. . . .

[DISSENT NOTE: "The Court's gratuitous quotation from Proverbs 28:1, mistakenly assumes that innocent residents have no reason to fear the sudden approach of strangers. We have previously considered, and rejected, this ivory-towered analysis of the real world for it fails to describe the experience of many residents, particularly if they are members of a minority. It has long been 'a matter of common knowledge' that men who are entirely innocent do sometimes fly from the scene of a crime through fear of being apprehended as the guilty parties, or from an unwillingness to appear as witnesses. Nor is it true as an accepted axiom of criminal law that 'the wicked flee when no man pursueth, but the righteous are as bold as a lion.'"] . . .

Whatever else one may think of today's decision, it unquestionably represents a departure from earlier Fourth Amendment case law. The notion that our prior cases contemplated a distinction between seizures effected by a touching on the one hand, and those effected by a show of force on the other hand, and that all of our repeated descriptions of the *Mendenhall* test stated only a necessary, but not a sufficient, condition for finding seizures in the latter category, is nothing if not creative lawmaking. Moreover, by narrowing the definition of the term seizure, instead of enlarging the scope of reasonable justifications for seizures, the Court has significantly limited the protection provided to the ordinary citizen by the Fourth Amendment. . . .

In this case the officer's show of force — taking the form of a head-on chase — adequately conveyed the message that respondent was not free to leave. . . . There was an interval of time between the moment that respondent saw the officer fast approaching and the moment when he was tackled, and thus brought under the control of the officer. The question is whether the Fourth Amendment was implicated at the earlier or the later moment.

Because the facts of this case are somewhat unusual, it is appropriate to note that the same issue would arise if the show of force took the form of a command to "freeze," a warning shot, or the sound of sirens accompanied by a patrol car's flashing lights. In any of these situations, there may be a significant time interval between the initiation of the officer's show of force and the complete submission by the citizen. At least on the facts of this case, the Court concludes that the timing of the seizure is governed by the citizen's reaction, rather than by the officer's conduct. One consequence of this conclusion is that the point at which the interaction between citizen and police officer becomes a seizure occurs, not when a reasonable citizen believes he or she is no longer free to go, but rather, only after the officer exercises control over the citizen. . . .

It is too early to know the consequences of the Court's holding. If carried to its logical conclusion, it will encourage unlawful displays of force that will frighten countless innocent citizens into surrendering whatever privacy rights they may still have. . . . The Court today defines a seizure as commencing, not with egregious police conduct, but rather, with submission by the citizen. Thus, it both delays the point at which "the Fourth Amendment becomes relevant" to an encounter and limits the range of encounters that will come under the heading of "seizure." Today's qualification of the Fourth Amendment means that innocent citizens may remain "secure in their persons . . . against unreasonable searches and seizures" only at the discretion of the police.

Some sacrifice of freedom always accompanies an expansion in the executive's unreviewable law enforcement powers. A court more sensitive to the purposes of the Fourth Amendment would insist on greater rewards to society before decreeing the sacrifice it makes today. Alexander Bickel presciently wrote that "many actions of government have two aspects: their immediate, necessarily intended, practical effects, and their perhaps unintended or unappreciated bearing on values we hold to have more general and permanent interest." The Court's immediate concern with containing criminal activity poses a substantial, though unintended, threat to values that are fundamental and enduring.

I respectfully dissent.

CASE DISCUSSION

What are the relevant facts in determining when the officer seized Hodari D.? What criteria does the Court use in determining when seizures occur? Why does the dissent see a danger in distinguishing between show-of-force stops and actual seizures? Do you agree

that this poses a danger? When do you think the officer stopped Hodari? Why is it important in this case? Why is it important generally? Consider the following remarks of Professor Richard Uviller, who observed the police in New York City for a period of a year:

> [the m]anifest confidence [exuded by the police] begets submission. And the cops learn the firm tone and hand that informs even the normally aggressive customer of the futility of resistance. It's effective. In virtually every encounter I have witnessed, the response of the person approached was docile, compliant, and respectful.[28]

Do you think Professor Uviller's observations support the argument that no reasonable person feels free to leave the presence of a police officer? Do you believe that it supports the argument that a request by a police officer is really a command that citizens are not free to deny? Defend your answer.

Not all the states have interpreted "seizure" in their state constitutions the way the United States Supreme Court interpreted it in *Hodari*. For example, Minnesota has a search and seizure provision identical to that of the Fourth Amendment. Nevertheless, the Minnesota Supreme Court chose not to follow *Hodari* in *In the Matter of the WELFARE of E.D.J.*

C A S E

Was He "Seized"?

In the Matter of the WELFARE of E.D.J.
502 N.W.2d 779 (1993)

After determining that a juvenile, E.D.J., abandoned drugs before he was seized, the District Court entered a judgment finding that E.D.J. had committed a delinquent act, and E.D.J. appealed. The Court of Appeals affirmed, and further review was sought. The Supreme Court reversed, and the adjudication of delinquency was vacated.

KEITH, Chief Justice.

FACTS

At 6:45 P.M. on February 22, 1992, two Minneapolis police officers on routine patrol saw three men—two were adults, one was a juvenile—standing on the southeast corner of 38th Street and Fourth Avenue South. The officers knew this corner to be an area of heavy trafficking in crack cocaine. When the three men saw the police car approaching from the west, they turned and began walking in an easterly direction on 38th, looking back again as they did so. The officers pulled up behind the men and ordered them to stop. The two older men stopped instantly. However, E.D.J., the juvenile, continued walking for approximately five steps, dropped something, took two more steps, then stopped and turned around.

E.D.J. was arrested and subsequently charged in juvenile court with having committed a delinquent act, specifically, fifth-degree possession of a controlled substance, namely crack cocaine. Minn.Stat. § 152.025, subd. 2(1) (1992). The trial court denied E.D.J.'s motion to suppress. Relying on *[California v.] Hodari [D.]*, it reasoned that E.D.J. abandoned the cocaine before he was seized and that therefore the abandonment was not the suppressible fruit of any illegal conduct.

At the trial on the merits, the trial court found that E.D.J. had committed a delinquent act. The trial court then placed E.D.J. on probation and ordered him to perform 40 hours of community service.

The court of appeals, also relying on *Hodari*, affirmed. We granted E.D.J.'s petition for review.

OPINION

In a series of decisions, we have articulated and reiterated the standard to be used by a trial court in determining at a suppression hearing in a criminal case whether an investigatory "seizure" of the person of the defendant by the police occurred. We have made it clear that the trial court should determine objectively, on the basis of the totality of the circumstances, whether a reasonable person in the defendant's shoes would have concluded that he or she was not free to leave.

Recently, the United States Supreme Court, in a sharp departure from this approach, concluded that, under the Fourth Amendment, a "seizure" of the person occurs only when police use physical force to restrain a person or, absent that, when a person physically submits to a show of authority by the police. *California v. Hodari*, 499 U.S. 621, 111 S.Ct. 1547, 113 L.Ed.2d 690 (1991).

Exercising our independent authority to interpret our own state constitution, *Michigan v. Long*, 463 U.S. 1032, 1041, 103 S.Ct. 3469, 3476, 77 L.Ed.2d 1201 (1983), we have concluded that trial courts in Minnesota, in determining whether a "seizure" of the person of the defendant by police occurred, should

not follow the recently adopted *Hodari* approach but should continue to apply the familiar approach we have previously articulated and reiterated. Following this familiar approach, we conclude that an unlawful "seizure" of the person occurred in this case and that the trial court erred in denying the motion to suppress evidence abandoned by appellant in response to the unlawful conduct of the police. Accordingly, we reverse the decision of the court of appeals and vacate the district court's determination that appellant, a juvenile, committed a delinquent act.

In *State v. Fuller*, 374 N.W.2d 722 (Minn. 1985), in an opinion by Justice Peterson, we said:

> It is axiomatic that a state supreme court may interpret its own state constitution to offer greater protection of individual rights than does the federal constitution. Indeed, as the highest court of this state, we are "'independently responsible for safeguarding the rights of [our] citizens.'" State courts are, and should be, the first line of defense for individual liberties within the federalist system. This, of course, does not mean that we will or should cavalierly construe our constitution more expansively than the United States Supreme Court has construed the federal constitution. Indeed, a decision of the United States Supreme Court interpreting a comparable provision of the federal constitution that, as here, is textually identical to a provision of our constitution, is of inherently persuasive, although not necessarily compelling, force.

The language of Minn. Const. art. I, § 10, is identical to that of the Fourth Amendment of the United States Constitution. The decisions of the United States Supreme Court interpreting and applying the Fourth Amendment are therefore decisions to which we invariably turn in the first instance whenever we are asked in a criminal case whether the police conduct constitutes an unreasonable search and seizure.

In this case the issue is whether a "seizure" occurred when the police pulled up and ordered E.D.J. to stop or whether it occurred moments later when he actually submitted to the order. The answer to the question given by the United States Supreme Court in its recent decision in *Hodari* is that the "seizure" did not occur until E.D.J. actually submitted to the authority of the police by stopping.

We do not "cavalierly" reject the *Hodari* approach. Rather, we reject it because (a) we have had considerable experience in applying the standard which the Court in *Hodari* rejected, (b) we are not persuaded by the arguments favoring the *Hodari* approach, and (c) we are persuaded that there is no need to depart from the pre-*Hodari* approach.

In *Terry v. Ohio*, 392 U.S. 1, 19 n. 16, 88 S.Ct. 1868, 1879 n. 16, 20 L.Ed.2d 889 (1968), Chief Justice Warren, speaking for the United States Supreme Court, stated that "not all personal intercourse between policemen and citizens involves 'seizures' of persons" and that a "seizure" occurs only "when the officer, by means of physical force or show of authority, has in some way restrained the liberty of a citizen."

In *United States v. Mendenhall*, 446 U.S. 544, 100 S.Ct. 1870, 64 L.Ed.2d 497 (1980), the Court elaborated on this. Justice Stewart, announcing the judgment of the Court in an opinion joined by one other justice, said:

> We conclude that a person has been "seized" within the meaning of the Fourth Amendment only if, in view of all of the circumstances surrounding the incident, a reasonable person would have believed that he was not free to leave. Examples of circumstances that might indicate a seizure, even where the person did not attempt to leave, would be the threatening presence of several officers, the display of a weapon by an officer, some physical touching of the person of the citizen, or the use of language or tone of voice indicating that compliance with the officer's request might be compelled. In the absence of some such evidence, otherwise inoffensive contact between a member of the public and the police cannot, as a matter of law, amount to a seizure of that person.

> On the facts of this case, no "seizure" of the respondent occurred. The events took place in the public concourse. The agents wore no uniforms and displayed no weapons. They did not summon the respondent to their presence, but instead approached her and identified themselves as federal agents. They requested, but did not demand to see the respondent's identification and ticket. Such conduct, without more, did not amount to an intrusion upon any constitutionally protected interest. The respondent was not seized simply by reason of the fact that the agents approached her, asked if she would show them her ticket and identification, and posed to her a few questions. Nor was it enough to establish a seizure that the person asking the question was a law enforcement official.

Three concurring justices did not comment on the Stewart standard; four dissenters did not question the standard used by Stewart but said he had overlooked certain facts that would support a determination that a "seizure" occurred.

The standard articulated by Justice Stewart in *Mendenhall* was fully accepted by a majority of the Court in *Florida v. Royer*, 460 U.S. 491 (1984). Specifically, a majority of the Court agreed that it was not a "seizure" for the police to merely approach the defendant in the airport and ask to see his ticket and his driver's license. In *Royer* the "line was crossed" only when the police went beyond this and identified themselves as narcotics officers, told Royer that he was suspected of transporting narcotics, and asked him to accompany them to a police room without telling him that he was free to leave.

As stated by Professor LaFave, the *Mendenhall/Royer* standard:

> rests upon the proposition that police, without having later to justify their conduct by articulating a certain degree of suspicion, should be allowed "to seek cooperation, even where this may involve inconvenience or embarrassment for the citizen, and even though many citizens will defer to this authority of the police because they believe—in some vague way—that they should." If "the moral and instinctive pressures to cooperate are in general sound and may be relied on by the police," then a street encounter does not amount to a fourth amendment seizure merely because of those pressures—that is, merely because the other party to the encounter is known to be a policeman. Rather, the

confrontation is a seizure only if the officer adds to those inherent pressures by engaging in conduct significantly beyond that accepted in social intercourse. The critical inquiry is whether the policeman, even if making inquiries a private citizen would not, has otherwise conducted himself in a manner which would be perceived as a nonoffensive contact if it occurred between two ordinary citizens. Wayne R. LaFave, "'Seizures' Topology: Classifying Detentions of the Person to Resolve Warrant, Grounds, and Search Issues," 17 *U.Mich.J.L.Ref.* 417, 424–25 (1984) (footnotes omitted).

We have been applying the *Mendenhall/Royer* standard ever since it was first articulated by Justice Stewart. Applying that standard, we have held, for example, that generally the mere act of approaching a person who is standing on a public street or sitting in a car that is parked and asking questions is not a "seizure." On the other hand, our cases, too numerous to even need citation, also fully support the generalization that without question "the stopping of a vehicle and the detention of its occupants constitutes a 'seizure' within the meaning of the Fourth Amendment."

. . .

We believe that the *Hodari* decision represents a departure from the *Mendenhall/Royer* approach. This is a belief shared by some of the leading commentators on the law of search and seizure. See, e.g., Wayne R. LaFave, *Search and Seizure* § 9.2A(d) (2d ed. Supp. 1993) (criticizing *Hodari*). In our view, *Hodari* adds another level of analysis, allowing a trial court to conclude that a seizure occurs only if (a) the *Mendenhall/Royer* test is satisfied and (b) the police either used physical force or the defendant submitted to the assertion of authority.

Were we persuaded that the additional level of analysis is justified, we would not hesitate to follow the United States Supreme Court's lead and interpret the identical provision of our state constitution accordingly. However, as we said earlier, we are not persuaded by the majority opinion in *Hodari*, and we are persuaded that there is no need to depart from the pre-*Hodari* approach.

Accordingly, exercising our independent authority to interpret our own state constitution, we have decided to continue to adhere to the pre-*Hodari* approach of determining, objectively and on the basis of the totality of the circumstances, whether a reasonable person in the defendant's shoes would have concluded that he or she was not free to leave.

We emphasize that following this approach does not mean that police necessarily must possess articulable suspicion before they follow a person in public or before they approach a person in public. What it does mean is that if a trial court later determines that, under all the circumstances, a reasonable person would have believed that because of the conduct of the police he was not free to leave, then there was a "seizure," and the police must be able to articulate reasonable suspicion justifying the seizure, else any evidence that is the fruit of the seizure is suppressible.

Here, as we have said, there clearly was a "seizure" once the police directed E.D.J. to stop, and the question becomes whether the police articulated a sufficient basis for the stop. We conclude that they did not.

Since there was a "seizure" of the person of E.D.J. and since the police did not articulate a sufficient basis for the "seizure," the cocaine should have been suppressed if it was a fruit of the illegality. Since E.D.J. abandoned the cocaine after he was unlawfully directed to stop, the abandonment was the suppressible fruit of the illegality. Without the evidence seized there was an insufficient basis for the delinquency adjudication. We therefore reverse the court of appeals and vacate the trial court's determination that E.D.J. committed a delinquent act.

Reversed and adjudication of delinquency vacated.

CASE DISCUSSION

What exactly were the reasons why the Minnesota Supreme Court decided not to follow *Hodari*? What is the definition of *seizure* adopted by the Minnesota Supreme Court? Which definition, in your opinion, is better? Defend your answer. Which definition sets the proper balance between "controlling the governed" and "controlling the government"? Explain your answer.

During the same Supreme Court term of *California v. Hodari D.*, the Court dealt with another kind of encounter, the rapidly growing police tactic of "bus sweeps" to look for illegal drugs and apprehend those who deal in and use them. Police officers board buses traveling between cities known for high drug use and sales. They approach passengers—admittedly without any specific information pointing to the guilt of any individual—supposedly at random, and ask passengers if they mind answering some questions or letting officers "check" their luggage or other packages they are carrying with them. In *Florida v. Bostick*, the Supreme Court decided whether "bus sweeps" are Fourth Amendment seizures.

C A S E

Did the Police "Seize" Bostick?

Florida v. Bostick
501 U.S. 429, 111 S. Ct. 2382,
115 L.Ed.2d 389 (1991)

A question was certified by the Florida District Court of Appeal, on appeal from the Circuit Court, Broward County, as to whether police, without articulable suspicion, could board a bus and ask at random for and receive consent to search a passenger's luggage when they advised the passenger that he had the right to refuse consent to the search. After rephrasing the question, the Florida Supreme Court answered no. On petition for writ of certiorari, *the Supreme Court reversed and remanded. Justice O'Connor wrote the opinion of the Court, in which Chief Justice Rehnquist and Justices White, Scalia, Kennedy, and Souter joined. Justice Marshall filed a dissenting opinion, in which Justices Blackmun and Stevens joined.*

FACTS

Two officers, complete with badges, insignia and one of them holding a recognizable zipper pouch, containing a pistol, boarded a bus bound from Miami to Atlanta during a stopover in Fort Lauderdale. Eyeing the passengers, the officers admittedly without articulable suspicion, picked out the defendant passenger and asked to inspect his ticket and identification. The ticket, from Miami to Atlanta, matched the defendant's identification and both were immediately returned to him as unremarkable. However, the two

police officers persisted and explained their presence as narcotics agents on the lookout for illegal drugs. In pursuit of that aim, they then requested the defendant's consent to search his luggage. Needless to say, there is a conflict in the evidence about whether the defendant consented to the search of the second bag in which the contraband was found and as to whether he was informed of his right to refuse consent. However, any conflict must be resolved in favor of the state, it being a question of fact decided by the trial judge.

Two facts are particularly worth noting. First, the police specifically advised Bostick that he had the right to refuse consent. Bostick appears to have disputed the point, but, as the Florida Supreme Court noted explicitly, the trial court resolved this evidentiary conflict in the State's favor. Second, at no time did the officers threaten Bostick with a gun. The Florida Supreme Court indicated that one officer carried a zipper pouch containing a pistol—the equivalent of carrying a gun in a holster—but the court did not suggest that the gun was ever removed from its pouch, pointed at Bostick, or otherwise used in a threatening manner. The dissent's characterization of the officers as "gun-wielding inquisitor[s]," is colorful, but lacks any basis in fact.

Bostick was arrested and charged with trafficking in cocaine. He moved to suppress the cocaine on the grounds that it had been seized in violation of his Fourth Amendment rights. The trial court denied the motion but made no factual findings. Bostick subsequently entered a plea of guilty, but reserved the right to appeal the denial of the motion to suppress.

The Florida District Court of Appeal affirmed, but considered the issue sufficiently important that it certified a question to the Florida Supreme Court. The Supreme Court reasoned that Bostick had been seized because a reasonable passenger in his situation would not have felt free to leave the bus to avoid questioning by the police. It rephrased and answered the certified question so as to make the bus setting dispositive in every case. It ruled categorically that "an impermissible seizure result[s] when police mount a drug search on buses during scheduled stops and question boarded passengers without articulable reasons for doing so, thereby obtaining consent to search the passengers' luggage." The Florida Supreme Court thus adopted a per se rule that the Broward County Sheriff's practice of "working the buses" is unconstitutional. The result of this decision is that police in Florida, as elsewhere, may approach persons at random in most public places, ask them questions and seek consent to a search, but they may not engage in the same behavior on a bus. We granted certiorari, to determine whether the Florida Supreme court's per se rule is consistent with our Fourth Amendment jurisprudence.

OPINION

The sole issue presented for our review is whether a police encounter on a bus of the type described above necessarily constitutes a "seizure" within the meaning of the Fourth Amendment. The State concedes, and we accept for purposes of this decision, that the officers lacked the reasonable suspicion required to justify a seizure and that, if a seizure took place, the drugs found in Bostick's suitcase must be suppressed as tainted fruit.

Our cases make it clear that a seizure does not occur simply because a police officer approaches an individual and asks a few questions. So long as a reasonable person would feel free "to disregard the police and go about his business," the encounter is consensual and no reasonable suspicion is required. . . .

There is no doubt that if this same encounter had taken place before Bostick boarded the bus or in the lobby of the bus terminal, it would not rise to the level of a seizure. The Court has dealt with similar en-

counters in airports and has found them to be "the sort of consensual encounter[s] that implicat[e] no Fourth Amendment interest." We have stated that even when officers have no basis for suspecting a particular individual, they may generally ask questions of that individual, ask to examine the individual's identification, and request consent to search his or her luggage—as long as the police do not convey a message that compliance with their requests is required.

Bostick insists that this case is different because it took place in the cramped confines of a bus. A police encounter is much more intimidating in this setting, he argues, because police tower over a seated passenger and there is little room to move around. . . . Bostick maintains that a reasonable bus passenger would not have felt free to leave under the circumstances of this case because there is nowhere to go on a bus. Also, the bus was about to depart. Had Bostick disembarked, he would have risked being stranded and losing whatever baggage he had locked away in the luggage compartment.

The Florida Supreme Court found this argument persuasive, so much so that it adopted a per se rule prohibiting the police from randomly boarding buses as a means of drug interdiction. The state court erred, however, in focusing on whether Bostick was "free to leave" rather than on the principle that those words were intended to capture. When police attempt to question a person who is walking down the street or through an airport lobby, it makes sense to inquire whether a reasonable person would feel free to continue walking. But when the person is seated on a bus and has no desire to leave, the degree to which a reasonable person would feel that he or she could leave is not an accurate measure of the coercive effect of the encounter. Here, for example, the mere fact that Bostick did not feel free to leave the bus does not mean that the police seized him. Bostick was a passenger on a bus that was scheduled to depart. He would not have felt free to leave the bus even if the police had not been present. Bostick's movements were "confined" in a sense, but this was the natural result of his decision to take the bus; it says nothing about whether or not the police conduct at issue was coercive. . . .

Bostick's freedom of movement was restricted by a factor independent of police conduct—i.e., by his being a passenger on a bus. Accordingly, the "free to leave" analysis on which Bostick relies is inapplicable. In such a situation, the appropriate inquiry is whether a reasonable person would feel free to decline the Officers' requests or otherwise terminate the encounter. . . . [A]s the Solicitor General correctly observes, an individual may decline an officer's request without fearing prosecution. We have consistently held that a refusal to cooperate, without more, does not furnish the minimal level of objective justification needed for a detention or seizure.

The facts of this case, as described by the Florida Supreme Court, leave some doubt whether a seizure occurred. Two officers walked up to Bostick on the bus, asked him a few questions, and asked if they could search his bags. As we have explained, no seizure occurs when police ask questions of an individual, ask to examine the individual's identification, and request consent to search his or her luggage—so long as the officers do not convey a message that compliance with their requests is required. Here, the facts recited by the Florida Supreme Court indicate that the officers did not point guns at Bostick or otherwise threaten him and that they specifically advised Bostick that he could refuse consent.

Nevertheless, we refrain from deciding whether or not a seizure occurred in this case. The trial court made no express findings of fact, and the Florida Supreme Court rested its decision on a single fact—that the encounter took place on a bus—rather than on the totality of the circumstances. We remand so that the Florida courts may evaluate the seizure question under the correct legal standard. We do reject, however, Bostick's argument that he must have been seized because no reasonable person would freely consent to a search of luggage that he or she knows contains drugs. This argument cannot prevail because the "reasonable person" test presupposes an innocent person. . . .

This Court, as the dissent correctly observes, is not empowered to suspend constitutional guarantees so that the Government may more effectively wage a "war on drugs." If that war is to be fought, those who fight it must respect the rights of individuals, whether or not those individuals are suspected of having committed a crime. By the same token, this Court is not empowered to forbid law enforcement practices simply because it considers them distasteful. . . .

We adhere to the rule that, in order to determine whether a particular encounter constitutes a seizure, a court must consider all the circumstances surrounding the encounter to determine whether the police conduct would have communicated to a reasonable person that the person was not free to decline the Officers' requests or otherwise terminate the encounter. That rule applies to encounters that take place on a city street or in a airport lobby, and it applies equally to encounters on a bus. The Florida Supreme Court erred in adopting a per se rule. The judgment of the Florida Supreme Court is reversed, and the case remanded for further proceedings not inconsistent with this opinion.

It is so ordered.

DISSENT

Justice Marshall, with whom Justice Blackmun and Justice Stevens join, dissenting.

. . . At issue in this case is a "new and increasingly common tactic in the war on drugs": the suspicionless police sweep of buses in interstate or intrastate travel. . . . These sweeps are conducted in "dragnet" style. The police admittedly act without an "articulable suspicion" in deciding which buses to board and which passengers to approach for interviewing. [DISSENT NOTE: . . . "[T]he approach of passengers during a sweep is [not] completely random. Indeed, at least one officer who routinely confronts interstate travelers candidly admitted that race is a factor influencing his decision whom to approach. See *United States v. Williams* (N.D. Ohio, June 13, 1989) ('Detective Zaller testified that the factors initiating the focus upon the three young black males in this case included: that they were young and black. . . .' [916 F.2d 714]) (the officers 'knew that the couriers, more often than not, were young black males' [1991]). Thus, the basis of the decision to single out particular passengers during a suspicionless sweep is less likely to be inarticulable than unspeakable."]

By proceeding systematically in this fashion, the police are able to engage in a tremendously high volume of searches. See, e.g., *Florida v. Kerwick* (Fla.App. 1987) (single officer employing sweep technique able to search over 3,000 bags in nine-month period). The percentage of successful drug interdictions is low. See

United States v. Flowers (sweep of 100 buses resulted in seven arrests).

To put it mildly, these sweeps "are inconvenient, intrusive, and intimidating." They occur within cramped confines, with officers typically placing themselves in between the passenger selected for an interview and the exit of the bus. Because the bus is only temporarily stationed at a point short of its destination, the passengers are in no position to leave as a means of evading the Officers' questioning. Undoubtedly, such a sweep holds up the progress of the bus. Thus, this "new and increasingly common tactic," burdens the experience of traveling by bus with a degree of governmental interference to which, until now, our society has been proudly unaccustomed. See, e.g., *State ex rel. Ekstrom v. Justice Court* (1983) (Feldman, J., concurring): ("The thought that an American can be compelled to 'show his papers' before exercising his right to walk the streets, drive the highways or board the trains is repugnant to American institutions and ideals").

This aspect of the suspicionless sweep has not been lost on many of the lower courts called upon to review the constitutionality of this practice. Remarkably, the courts located at the heart of the "drug war" have been the most adamant in condemning this technique. As one Florida court put it:

> [T]he evidence in this cause has evoked images of other days, under other flags, when no man traveled his nation's roads or railways without fear of unwarranted interruption, by individuals who held temporary power in the Government. The spectre of American citizens being asked, by badge-wielding police, for identification, travel papers—in short a raison d'etre—is foreign to any fair reading of the Constitution, and its guarantee of human liberties. This is not Hitler's Berlin, nor Stalin's Moscow, nor is it white supremacist South Africa. Yet in Broward County, Florida, these police officers approach every person on board buses and trains ("that time permits") and check identification [and] tickets, [and] ask to search luggage—all in the name of "voluntary cooperation" with law enforcement. . . . [Q]uoting *State v. Kerwick* (quoting trial court order).

The District Court for the District of Columbia spoke in equally pointed words:

> It seems rather incongruous at this point in the world's history that we find totalitarian states becoming more like our free society while we in this nation are taking on their former trappings of suppressed liberties and freedoms.
>
> The random indiscriminate stopping and questioning of individuals on interstate buses seems to have gone too far. If this Court approves such "bus stops" and allows prosecutions to be based on evidence seized as a result of such "stops," then we will have stripped our citizens of basic Constitutional protections. Such action would be inconsistent with what this nation has stood for during its 200 years of existence. If passengers on a bus passing through the Capital of this great nation cannot be free from police interference where there is absolutely no basis for the police officers to stop and question them, then the police will be free to accost people on our streets without any reason or cause. In this "anything goes" war on drugs, random knocks on the doors of our citizens' homes seeking "consent" to search for drugs cannot be far away. This is not America. *United States v. Lewis* (1990).

The question for this Court, then, is whether the suspicionless, dragnet-style sweep of buses in intrastate and interstate travel is consistent with the Fourth Amendment. The majority suggests that this latest tactic in the drug war is perfectly compatible with the constitution. I disagree.

. . . [The facts of this case] exhibit all of the elements of coercion associated with a typical bus sweep. Two officers boarded the Greyhound bus on which respondent was a passenger while the bus, en route from Miami to Atlanta, was on a brief stop to pick up passengers in Fort Lauderdale. The officers made a visible display of their badges and wore bright green "raid" jackets bearing the insignia of the Broward County Sheriff's Department; one held a gun in a recognizable weapons pouch. . . . Once on board, the officers approached respondent, who was sitting in the back of the bus, identified themselves as narcotics officers and began to question him. One officer stood in front of respondent's seat, partially blocking the narrow aisle through which respondent would have been required to pass to reach the exit of the bus.

As far as is revealed by facts on which the Florida Supreme Court premised its decision, the officers did not advise respondent that he was free to break off this "interview." . . . [T]he issue is not whether a passenger in respondent's position would have felt free to deny consent to the search of his bag, but whether such a passenger—without being apprised of his rights—would have felt free to terminate the antecedent encounter with the police.

Unlike the majority, I have no doubt that the answer to this question is no. Apart from trying to accommodate the officers, respondent had only two options. First, he could have remained seated while obstinately refusing to respond to the Officers' questioning. But in light of the intimidating show of authority that the officers made upon boarding the bus, respondent reasonably could have believed that such behavior would only arouse the Officers' suspicions and intensify their interrogation. Indeed, officers who carry out bus sweeps like the one at issue here frequently admit that this is the effect of a passenger's refusal to cooperate. The majority's observation that a mere refusal to answer questions, "without more," does not give rise to a reasonable basis for seizing a passenger, is utterly beside the point, because a passenger unadvised of his rights and otherwise unversed in constitutional law has no reason to know that the police cannot hold his refusal to cooperate against him.

Second, respondent could have tried to escape the Officers' presence by leaving the bus altogether. But because doing so would have required respondent to squeeze past the gun-wielding inquisitor who was blocking the aisle of the bus, this hardly seems like a course that respondent reasonably would have viewed as available to him.

. . . Even if respondent had perceived that the officers would let him leave the bus, moreover, he could not reasonably have been expected to resort to this means of evading their intrusive questioning. For so far as respondent knew, the bus's departure from the terminal was imminent. Unlike a person approached by the police on the street, or at a bus or airport terminal after reaching his destination, a passenger approached by the police at an intermediate point in a long bus journey cannot simply leave the scene and repair to a safe haven to avoid unwanted probing by law-enforcement officials. The vulnerability that an intrastate or interstate traveler experiences when confronted by the police outside of his "own familiar territory" surely aggravates the coercive quality of such an encounter. . . .

Rather than requiring the police to justify the coercive tactics employed here, the majority blames respondent for his own sensation of constraint. The majority concedes that respondent "did not feel free to leave the bus" as a means of breaking off the interrogation by the Broward County officers. But this experience of confinement, the majority explains, "was the natural result of his decision to take the bus." Thus, in the majority's view, because respondent's "freedom of movement was restricted by a factor independent of police conduct—i.e., by his being a passenger on a bus," respondent was not seized for purposes of the Fourth Amendment.

. . . By consciously deciding to single out persons who have undertaken interstate or intrastate travel, officers who conduct suspicionless, dragnet-style sweeps put passengers to the choice of cooperating or of exiting their buses and possibly being stranded in unfamiliar locations. It is exactly because this "choice" is no "choice" at all that police engage this technique. In my view, the Fourth Amendment clearly condemns the suspicionless, dragnet-style sweep of intrastate or interstate buses. Withdrawing this particular weapon from the government's drug-war arsenal would hardly leave the police without any means of combating the use of buses as instrumentalities of the drug trade. The police would remain free, for example, to approach passengers whom they have a reasonable, articulable basis to suspect of criminal wrongdoing. Alternatively, they could continue to confront passengers without suspicion so long as they took simple steps, like advising the passengers confronted of their right to decline to be questioned, to dispel the aura of coercion and intimidation that pervades such encounters. There is no reason to expect that such requirements would render the Nation's buses law-enforcement-free zones.

The majority attempts to gloss over the violence that today's decision does to the Fourth Amendment with empty admonitions. "If th[e] [war on drugs] is to be fought," the majority intones, "those who fight it must respect the rights of individuals, whether or not those individuals are suspected of having committed a crime." The majority's actions, however, speak louder than its words.

I dissent.

CASE DISCUSSION

How does the Court define *seizure*? Has it changed the definition from that of *Terry v. Ohio*? What specific facts are relevant to deciding whether the officers "seized" Bostick? Do you agree with the majority or the dissent that Bostick was seized? Do you believe that Bostick was free to not cooperate with the officers? Explain your answer. Would you feel free to end this encounter without cooperating? Would a "reasonable person" feel free to end the encounter without cooperating? Can you define *reasonable person*? As the officers were escorting Bostick off the bus, one said to him, "Why don't you run?" Bostick replied, "Why, so you can shoot me in the back?" Is this exchange relevant to determining whether Bostick (or a reasonable person) would feel free to leave or terminate the encounter with the police? What is the standard of a reasonable person? A reasonable law-abiding citizen? A reasonable member of a minority group? A reasonable person with a past history of poor relations with the police?[29]

D e c i s i o n   P o i n t

Sylvia Mendenhall arrived at the Detroit Metropolitan Airport on a commercial airline flight from Los Angeles early in the morning on February 10, 1976. As she disembarked from the airplane, she was observed by two agents of the DEA, who were present at the airport for the purpose of detecting unlawful traffic of narcotics. After observing the respondent's conduct, which appeared to the agents to be characteristic of persons unlawfully carrying narcotics, the agents approached her as she was walking through the concourse, identified themselves as federal agents, and asked to see her identification and airline ticket. The respondent produced her driver's license, which was in the name of Sylvia Mendenhall, and, in answer to a question of one of the agents, stated that she resided at the address appearing on the license. The airline ticket was issued in the name of "Annette Ford." When asked why the ticket bore a name different from her own, the respondent stated that she "just felt like using that name." In response to a further question, the respondent indicated that she had been in California only two days. Agent Anderson then specifically identified himself as a federal narcotics agent and, according to his testimony, the respondent "became quite shaken, extremely nervous. She had a hard time speaking."

After returning the airline ticket and driver's license to her, Agent Anderson asked the respondent if she would accompany him to the airport DEA office for further questions. She did so, although the record does not indicate a verbal response to the request. The office, which was located up one flight of stairs about fifty feet from where the respondent had first been approached, consisted of a reception area adjoined by three other rooms. At the office the agent asked the respondent if she would allow a search of her person and handbag and told her she had the right to decline the search if she desired. She responded: "Go ahead." She then handed Agent Anderson her purse, which contained a receipt for an airline ticket that had been issued to "F. Bush" three days earlier for a flight from Pittsburgh through Chicago to Los Angeles. The agent asked whether this was the ticket she had used for her flight to California, and the respondent stated that it was. . . .

The policewoman explained that the search would require that the respondent remove her clothing. The respondent stated that she had a plane to catch and was assured by the policewoman that if she was carrying no narcotics, there would be no problem. The respondent then began to disrobe without further comment. As the respondent removed her clothing, she took from her undergarments two small packages, one of which appeared to contain heroin, and handed both to the policewoman. The agents then arrested the respondent for possessing heroin.

Was Mendenhall "seized"? No, according to the United States Supreme Court:

> . . . [A] person has been "seized" within the meaning of the Fourth Amendment only if, in view of all of the circumstances surrounding the incident, a reasonable person would have believed that he was not free to leave. Examples of circumstances that might indicate a seizure, even where the person did not attempt to leave, would be the threatening presence of several officers, the display of a weapon by an officer, some physical touching of the person of the citizen, or the use of language or tone of voice indicating the compliance with the officer's request might be compelled. . . . On the facts of this case, no "seizure" of the respondent occurred. The events took place in the public concourse. The agents wore no uniforms and displayed no weapons. They did not summon the respondent to their presence, but instead approached her and identified themselves as federal agents. They requested, but did not demand to see the respondent's identification and ticket. Such conduct, without more, did not amount to an intrusion upon any constitutionally protected interest. . . . [30]

SUMMARY

Crime prevention and criminal investigation, apprehension, prosecution, and conviction depend on the gathering and use of information. The police are mainly responsible for gathering most of the information used in crime prevention, investigation, and apprehension. The police rely on information not only to perform their duties, but they also need information to justify the requirement that an objective basis back up all Fourth Amendment searches and seizures. Searches and seizures are best known as tools of criminal investigation and apprehension. In practice, however, searches and seizures are used to implement a number of other public policies. Searches and seizures of weapons protect the safety of police officers. Custodial searches aid in the preservation of jail and prison safety and security. Inventory searches protect the property of prisoners and limit the liability of prisons and jails from lawsuits. Employee drug testing and DWI checkpoints prevent accidents.

The Fourth Amendment protects the fundamental values of privacy, liberty, and property. The "unreasonable search" part of the Amendment protects privacy; the "unreasonable seizure" part of the Amendment protects liberty; both the "unreasonable search" and the "unreasonable seizure" parts protect property. The history of the law of search and seizure begins long before the adoption of the Fourth Amendment. In England, the law protected subjects from invasions of their homes and the seizures of their persons and property as early as the sixteenth century. The purpose of the Fourth Amendment is to prevent the government from gathering and using information by means of "unreasonable searches and seizures" in order to enforce the criminal law and carry out other legitimate noncriminal government interests. The Fourth Amendment does not protect against all invasions of liberty, privacy, and property. It protects against only those invasions that amount to "unreasonable searches and seizures."

A Fourth Amendment search requires that a government action invade a reasonable expectation of privacy. Defining *expectation of privacy* for purposes of a search involves two parts: a subjective expectation of privacy and an expectation that society is prepared to recognize. This definition of a Fourth Amendment search leaves government officials free to carry out a range of actions without the limits of the Fourth Amendment. Information gathered by police officers through the use of their ordinary senses of sight, hearing, smell, and touch are not Fourth Amendment searches or seizures. Neither does the Fourth Amendment prevent the gathering, seizure, and use of information found in open fields. Nor does the Fourth Amendment prevent police officers from gathering and using information they find in public places through the use of their ordinary senses. Finally, the Fourth Amendment does not protect abandoned property, such as trash left by the curb side for collection, even if the law requires residents to put their trash outside for public collection.

Two kinds of actions amount to Fourth Amendment seizures. Actual physical seizure — that is, grabbing and holding onto a person or thing — is a Fourth Amendment seizure. So, too, is a nonphysical show of authority by a government official, if a reasonable person encountering the show of authority would not feel free either to walk away or to otherwise terminate the encounter. It is not a seizure for a police officer to approach individuals on the street or in other public places and ask them questions. Citizens may feel morally obligated or psychologically pressured to remain and answer the questions. However, the Constitution does not require them to do so. They may walk away or otherwise carry on their business so long as the encounter is not a Fourth Amendment seizure.

REVIEW QUESTIONS

1. What does crime control primarily depend upon?

2. Identify the main methods by which police obtain information.

3. Identify and describe the major purposes of searches and seizures.

4. Identify and describe the major purposes of the Fourth Amendment.

5. Briefly summarize the history of the law of search and seizure.

6. Identify and define the three main values that the Fourth Amendment protects.

7. Identify the main steps in the analysis of Fourth Amendment cases.

8. Define a Fourth Amendment *search*.

9. Define a Fourth Amendment *seizure*.

10. Describe and explain the significance of encounters between individuals and police officers on the street and in other public places and encounters between them in police stations.

11. Explain the difference between the trespass doctrine and the privacy doctrine in the law of searches.

12. Identify and explain the two prongs of the test for determining whether a government action is a Fourth Amendment search.

13. Briefly explain how search decisions reflect the balance between individual privacy and societal security.

14. Identify and explain all the government actions that the U.S. Supreme Court has ruled do not qualify as Fourth Amendment searches.

15. Identify and define the two major types of actions that qualify as Fourth Amendment "seizures."

16. What nonlegal pressures may individuals feel when police officers approach and ask them questions? What legal obligation does a citizen have in such encounters if they are not Fourth Amendment seizures?

KEY TERMS

abandonment the intentional throwing away of property that removes it from the protection of the Fourth Amendment.

curtilage the area immediately surrounding a house that is not part of the open fields doctrine.

liberty the right of locomotion—that is, the right of citizens to come and go as they please, without government interference.

objective basis the quantity of facts required to justify government invasions in individual liberty, privacy, and property.

open fields doctrine the rule that the Fourth Amendment does not prevent government officials from gathering and using information they see, hear, smell, or touch in open fields.

plain view doctrine the rule that detection by means of the ordinary senses is not a Fourth Amendment search.

privacy the value that is sometimes called the right to be let alone from government invasions.

privacy doctrine the doctrine that holds that the Fourth Amendment protects persons, not places, when persons have an expectation of privacy that society is prepared to recognize.

property the right to acquire, own, possess, use, and dispose of property.

trespass doctrine the Fourth Amendment doctrine that requires physical intrusions into a "constitutionally protected area" to qualify as a search.

writs of assistance or **general warrants** the official documents, good for the life of the monarch, that granted blanket authority to search and seize.

Notes

1. Stephen A. Saltzberg and Daniel J. Capra, *American Criminal Procedure* (St. Paul: West Publishing Company, 1992), 23.

2. *Silverman v. United States*, 365 U.S. 505, 81 S.Ct. 679, 5 L.Ed.2d 734 (1961); Wayne R. LaFave and Jerold H. Israel, *Criminal Procedure* (St. Paul: West Publishing Co., 1984), 1: 162; Anthony Amsterdam, "Perspectives on the Fourth Amendment," *Minnesota Law Review* 58 (1973–74): 356–57.

3. *Olmstead v. United States*, 277 U.S. 438, 478, 48 S.Ct. 564, 572, 72 L.Ed. 944 (1928).

4. Sam J. Ervin, "The Exclusionary Rule: An Essential Ingredient of the Fourth Amendment," *Supreme Court Review* (1983): 283.

5. Amsterdam, "Perspectives on the Fourth Amendment," 349–477.

6. John Wesley Hall, Jr., *Search and Seizure* (New York: Lawyer's Co-operative Publishing Co., 1983), 6.

7. Quoted in Craig M. Bradley, "Two Models of the Fourth Amendment," *Michigan Law Review* 83 (1985): 1468, 1481.

8. 858 F.2d 617 (10th Cir. 1988).

9. 94 Or.App. 457, 766 P.2d 397 (1988).

10. Wayne R. LaFave, *Search and Seizure*, 2d ed. (St. Paul: West Publishing Co., 1987), 1: 321.

11. 415 F.Supp. 1252 (D.Hawaii 1976).

12. *California v. Ciraolo*, 476 U.S. 207, 106 S.Ct. 1809, 90 L.Ed.2d 210 (1986); *Dow Chemical Co. v. United States*, 476 U.S. 227, 106 S.Ct. 1819, 90 L.Ed.2d 226 (1986).

13. For a useful discussion of the extension of plain view to other senses, see *United States v. Pace*, 709 F.Supp. 948 (C.D. Cal. March 3, 1989).

14. *Minnesota v. Dickerson*, 113 S.Ct. 2130, 2137, 124 L.Ed.2d 334 (1993).

15. *Oliver v. United States*, 466 U.S. 170, 104 S.Ct. 1735, 80 L.Ed.2d 214 (1984).

16. *Oliver v. United States*, 466 U.S. 170 (1984).

17. American Law Institute, *Model Code of Pre-arraignment Procedure* (Philadelphia: American Law Institute, 1975), 164; *Oliver v. United States*, 466 U.S. 170, 104 S.Ct. 1735, 80 L.Ed.2d 214 (1984).

18. *United States v. Dunn*, 480 U.S. 294, 107 S.Ct. 1134, 94 L.Ed.2d 326 (1987).

19. Hall, *Search and Seizure*, 543–48.

20. *Hester v. United States*, 265 U.S. 57, 44 S.Ct. 445, 68 L.Ed. 898 (1924); *Abel v. United States*, 362 U.S. 217, 80 S.Ct. 683, 4 L.Ed.2d 668 (1960).

21. *Rios v. United States*, 364 U.S. 253, 80 S.Ct. 1431, 4 L.Ed.2d 1688 (1960).

22. *Smith v. Ohio*, 494 U.S. 541, 110 S.Ct. 1288, 108 L.Ed.2d 464 (1990).

23. *United States v. Boswell*, 347 A.2d 270 (D.C.App. 1975).

24. See "Note: Fourth Amendment—Further Erosion of the Warrant Requirement for Unreasonable Searches and Seizures: The Warrantless Trash Exception," *Journal of Criminal Law and Criminology* 79 (1988): 623–46, which discusses *California v. Greenwood* in depth; *People v. Howard*, 50 N.Y.2d 583, 430 N.Y.S.2d 578, 408 N.E.2d 908 (1980); see also discussion in LaFave and Israel, *Criminal Procedure*, 176–77.

25. *Florida v. Royer*, 460 U.S. 491, 497–98, 103 S.Ct. 1319, 1323–24, 75 L.Ed.2d 229 (1983), 497–98.

26. *INS v. Delgado*, 466 U.S. 210, 104 S.Ct. 1758, 80 L.Ed.2d 247 (1984).

27. American Law Institute, *Model Code of Pre-arraignment Procedure.*

28. H. Richard Uviller, *Tempered Zeal* (Chicago: Contemporary Books, 1988).

29. Robert V. Ward, "Consenting to a Search and Seizure in Poor and Minority Neighborhoods: No Place for a 'Reasonable Person,'" *Howard University Law Review* 36 (1993): 239, 254.

30. *United States v. Mendenhall*, 446 U.S. 544, 100 S.Ct. 1870, 64 L.Ed.2d. 497 (1980).

CHAPTER FOUR

Stop and Frisk

CHAPTER OUTLINE

CHAPTER MAIN POINTS

1. Stops and frisks represent the beginning of a progression of police–citizen encounters from less intrusive, informal street contacts to more intrusive practices in police stations.

2. The purpose of a stop is to gather and use information in the investigation of suspicious circumstances and people.

3. The purpose of a frisk is to protect the safety of officers who investigate suspicious persons and circumstances.

4. The power to detain and question suspicious persons is an ancient practice.

5. The reasonableness of stops and frisks depends on balancing the needs of law enforcement and the privacy and liberty of individuals.

6. Police–citizen encounters fall into three categories: voluntary contacts, stops, and arrests.

7. Stops fall into two categories: actual seizures and show-of-authority stops.

8. The reasonableness of a stop depends on its objective basis and its scope.

9. Reasonable suspicion consists of facts that under the totality of circumstances arouse a suspicion that a specific individual may have committed, may be committing, or may be about to commit a crime.

10. The scope of a lawful stop depends on its duration, location, and intrusiveness.

11. The requirements of duration, location, and intensity are relaxed in stops at international borders because of the special government need to control who and what enters the country.

12. The requirement of reasonable suspicion is relaxed in DWI roadblocks because of the special government interest in controlling and punishing drunk driving.

13. Lawful frisks require both a prior lawful stop and reasonable suspicion that the suspect is armed.

Were the Passengers "Seized"?

A scheduled bus travels through Logansport, Louisiana, sometimes stopping there if passengers board or debark in Logansport, to a final destination. When the bus drove into Logansport about 5:40 A.M. on December 13, 1994, the police chief signaled the bus driver to stop in front of the Logansport police station. Once the bus was stopped, the armed and uniformed police would then surround and enter the bus with a trained dog that would "work" the bus by sniffing the luggage of the passengers on the bus. Officers outside the bus would watch for suspicious moves or contraband being discarded by passengers. The Logansport police chief explained that searches were sometimes made after Logansport police had been informed that one or more passengers might be transporting contraband aboard the bus. (State v. Vikesdal, 688 So.2d 685 [La.App. 1997])

HISTORY OF STOP AND FRISK

The power to stop and question suspicious persons is at least as old as the common law of England. Ancient statutes and court decisions empowered constables to detain "suspicious nightwalkers" and hold them until morning in order to investigate their suspicious behavior. That practice was brought to the American colonies and continued well into the nineteenth century. Until the mid-1960s, police-initiated contacts with people on the street and in other public places did not arouse controversy. They were left to the discretion of individual officers. During the 1960s, the police discretionary power to stop and frisk became a matter of national concern. The due process revolution discussed in Chapter 2 led reformers to call for extending constitutional protections to all official–private individual contacts and subjecting those encounters to review by the courts. This resulted in a formalization of the period of criminal investigation occurring before the arrest of suspects. This formalization caused—and still causes—bitter controversy. The police and their supporters argue that their expertise and professional independence require that discretion, not formal rules, ought to govern street encounters prior to arrest. Civil libertarians, on the other hand, maintain that individuals, especially those on the "fringes of society," need—and a free society requires—the Constitution to follow private individuals wherever they go.[1]

For complex reasons not yet sorted out, the courts, led by the United States Supreme Court, formalized stop and frisk during the 1960s. Despite strong opposition at the time, and some modification over the years since then, this formalization has remained intact (see *Terry v. Ohio*, excerpted and discussed below).[2]

BALANCING INTERESTS
IN STOPS AND FRISKS

Stops and frisks balance the need for the initial investigation of suspicious activity, people, and circumstances against the right of people to come and go as they please without interference by the government. Stops and frisks allow law enforcement officers to temporarily freeze suspicious situations so that the officers can check them out. Information discovered during this brief freeze may confirm the initial suspicions of officers and provide enough facts to amount to probable cause to arrest suspects, the subject of Chapter 5. If the street investigation does not confirm the officers' suspicions, then the Fourth Amendment allows no further detention. Compared to full arrests and searches, stops and frisks are less intrusive. And unlike arrests, most searches, identification of suspects, and police interrogation, stops and frisks take place in familiar surroundings, not in the intimidating and strange atmosphere of police stations. Still, stops and frisks amount to significant invasions of liberty and privacy. Moreover, they are the first—and most of the time—the only invasions of liberty and privacy experienced by most people.

Law enforcement officers possess considerable discretion to investigate possible criminal activity. But they are not free to do as they please in conducting street investigations. When individuals go out into public, they do not leave the protections of the United States and state constitutions at home. These protections follow individuals out of their homes onto the street, to other public places, and even into police stations. The Fourth, Fifth, and Sixth Amendments are among these protections. They provide as follows:

- *Amendment IV.* The right of the people to be secure in their persons, houses, papers, and effects, against unreasonable searches and seizures shall not be violated, and no warrants shall issue but upon probable cause, supported by oath or affirmation, and particularly describing the place to be searched, and the persons or things to be seized. . . .

- *Amendment V.* No person shall be . . . compelled in any criminal case to be a witness against himself. . . .

- *Amendment VI.* In all criminal prosecutions, the accused shall . . . have the assistance of counsel for his defence.

Fourth Amendment seizures of persons fall under a broad spectrum of activities, from brief street stops to detention in jail. Fourth Amendment searches of persons include everything from protective pat-downs to strip and body-cavity searches. Police questioning ranges from the intensive hours-long grillings that take place behind closed doors inside police stations, which the Fifth Amendment self-incrimination clause clearly protects, to brief encounters on the street in which police officers engage people in voluntary conversations that have no protection under the Fifth Amendment. Police investigation also encompasses electronic surveillance and eavesdropping; identification procedures such as lineups, blood alcohol tests, and DNA profiling; and surgical intrusions into the body in search of evidence that the Fourth, Fifth, and Sixth Amendments may all protect. At no other stage of the criminal process are gradations in the degree of invasions on the liberty, privacy, and property of citizens more refined than during the period from initial investigation to the turning over of cases by police to prosecutors. During this same period the **objective basis**—the facts and reasonable inferences drawn by officers from the facts—for official action against individuals is also refined.

This and the following three chapters discuss these gradations and the objective bases required to support them. This chapter examines the broad range of initial contacts between individuals and the police on the street known as stops and frisks. Chapter 5 analyzes the greater invasions that accompany arrest, when suspects are taken to the less familiar and isolated surroundings of police stations and jails. Chapter 6 and, to some extent, Chapter 7 analyze the full searches that accompany and follow arrest. Chapters 8 and 9 focus on identification and identification procedures.

Both chronology and public policy considerations require that the discussion of stops and frisks take place before the examination of full-blown arrests, searches, identification, and interrogation of suspects. Street encounters between individuals and law enforcement officers mark the earliest point of official investigation. That is why they are discussed in this chapter. Of course, arrests, searches, identification procedures, and interrogation do not always follow each other in neat chronological order. Some searches precede arrest; others follow it. Interrogation usually follows arrest but not always. Identification may well concur with arrest. Nevertheless, in the vast majority of cases, street encounters mark the beginning—or at least the decision of whether to begin—criminal investigation.

Stops and frisks are matters of important public policy because of their impact on the public. Far more people are stopped and frisked than will ever experience directly or indirectly an arrest and full body search. Moreover, since stops and frisks frequently take place in public, others see the display of police power even if they do not experience it directly. Hence, stops and frisks may shape the public view of police power more than the greater invasions of arrest and custodial searches, because they are more open to public view.

Even though stops and frisks affect more people and are more visible, they require fewer facts to back them up. The reason for this lesser objective basis is that they involve lesser invasions of liberty and privacy. In short, stops and frisks represent the beginning of a progression from more visible but less intrusive informal street contacts requiring a minimal objective basis to more intrusive but less visible police station practices demanding more facts to authorize them under the Fourth, Fifth, and Sixth Amendments. Figure 4.1 depicts this progression and its basic characteristics.[3]

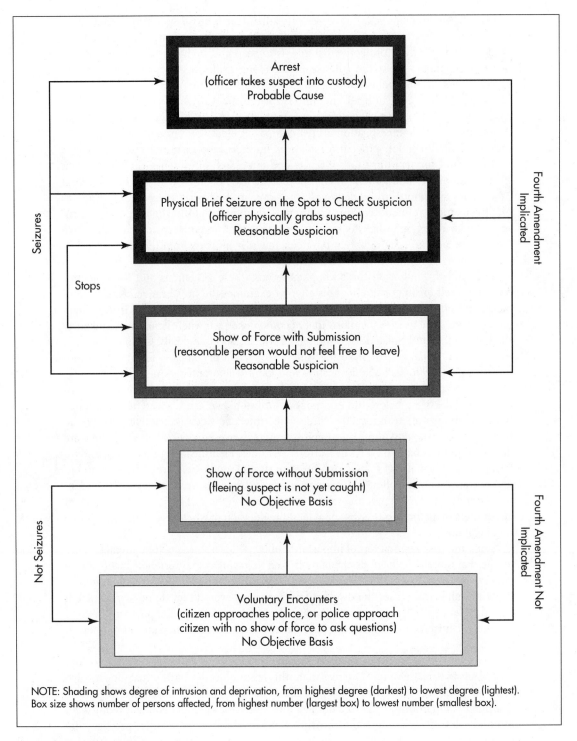

NOTE: Shading shows degree of intrusion and deprivation, from highest degree (darkest) to lowest degree (lightest). Box size shows number of persons affected, from highest number (largest box) to lowest number (smallest box).

FIGURE 4.1 SEIZURES

STOP-AND-FRISK LAW

Stop-and-frisk law focuses mainly on the application of the Fourth Amendment to law enforcement practices related to the investigation of suspicious people and circumstances. Stops and frisks take place mainly on the street, other public places, and in cars. **Stops** consist mainly of brief detentions that enable law enforcement officers to freeze a situation for the purpose of investigating suspicious persons. **Frisks** are patdowns of suspects to protect officers against the danger of concealed weapons.

Stop-and-frisk law, like all Fourth Amendment law, involves a three-step analysis. In the context of street investigation, the steps are as follows:

1. Were the government actions stops or frisks?

2. If the government action was a stop and/or a frisk, was it "unreasonable"?

3. If the stop or risk was "unreasonable," should evidence obtained be excluded from legal proceedings against defendants?

If the action of the government was not a search or a seizure, then the Fourth Amendment does not apply at all to the action (Chapter 3). If it was a reasonable search or seizure, then the exclusionary rule does not apply (see Chapter 10, on the exclusionary rule).

Two Approaches to Stop-and-Frisk Law

The Fourth Amendment consists of two clauses:

- *The Reasonableness clause:* "The right of the people to be secure in their persons, houses, papers, and effects, against unreasonable searches and seizures shall not be violated."

- *The Warrant clause:* ". . . and no warrants shall issue but upon probable cause, supported by oath or affirmation, and particularly describing the place to be searched, and the persons or things to be seized."

The United States Supreme Court has followed two approaches to interpreting the Fourth Amendment. Up to the 1960s, the Court used the **conventional Fourth Amendment approach.** According to the conventional approach, the warrant and reasonableness clauses are firmly connected. In fact, the warrant clause tells us what the general term *unreasonable* in the search and seizure clause means: all searches and seizures not based on both warrants and probable cause are unreasonable. Since the 1960s, the Court has shifted from the conventional to the **reasonableness Fourth Amendment approach.** According to the reasonableness approach, the two clauses of the amendment are distinct, and they address separate problems. The warrant clause prescribes what the Fourth Amendment requires when law enforcement officers want to obtain warrants. However, many cases do not require warrants or even probable cause, according to the Court. Therefore, the warrant clause cannot mean that searches and seizures without warrants are always "unreasonable." In other words, searches can be reasonable without either warrants or probable cause.

The Test of "Reasonableness"

Once the Supreme Court decided that there were more kinds of reasonable searches and seizures than those based on warrants and probable cause, the Court created a major problem of interpretation. In fact, the Fourth Amendment has generated more cases than any other subject in the law of criminal procedure. That problem is deciding which searches and seizures without warrants are unreasonable. The Court has formulated a method for determining the reasonableness of searches and seizures. One type of reasonable search and seizure is based on warrants and probable cause. The other type—which as a practical matter includes the vast majority of searches and seizures—must meet the **reasonableness test.**

The reasonableness of searches and seizures generally, and of stops and frisks specifically, depends on two elements:

1. The application of a balancing approach to the Fourth Amendment
2. The existence of an adequate objective basis for the search and seizure

The **balancing approach element** requires weighing these issues:

1. The government interest furthered by conducting the search or seizure
2. The invasions against individuals caused by the searches and seizures

According to the reasonableness test, a search or seizure is reasonable if it meets three conditions:

1. The search or seizure furthers a government interest.
2. The government interest outweighs the invasions of the privacy, liberty, and property of individuals.
3. The invasions of individual privacy, liberty, and property are supported by a sufficient objective basis.

The government interest most often furthered by searches and seizures is criminal law enforcement, but it also includes other interests, such as maintaining drug-free workplaces and schools, preserving safe and secure jails and prisons, and protecting police officers from injury and death (see Chapter 7 and the section on frisks below).

Balancing the need for searches and seizures against the invasion against individuals is a central feature of the law of stop and frisk, much of the law of arrest discussed in Chapter 5, and of the other searches and seizures discussed in Chapters 6 and 7. This balancing element of reasonableness is a broad—and some say too subjective—standard. According to Professor John M. Copacino, in balancing the interest of the government and the invasion of the individual

> the Supreme Court has been satisfied by broad characterization of the government's interest, usually unaccompanied by any hard evidence. Similarly, in assessing the harm caused to the individual by the intrusion, the Court does not cite any empirical evidence, expert testimony, or individual testimony from those who have been affected by the search or seizure. It simply proclaims its subjective judgment of the citizen's likely reactions.[4]

The Supreme Court has ruled that reasonableness depends on the **"totality of the circumstances"** surrounding specific searches and seizures in individual cases. This is called the **case-by-case method** of determining the reasonableness of searches. The case-by-case approach means also that no hard-and-fast rule—**bright line approach**—can guide the actions of law enforcement officers when they conduct searches and seizures. They must act on what all the facts surrounding their actions in light of their experience tell them is "reasonable." But their decision is not final. Later on, judges will review their actions and decide finally, again on a case-by-case basis considering all the circumstances, whether the actions viewed in light of the officers' experience were "reasonable."

Balancing the government and individual interests does not end the inquiry into the reasonableness of particular searches and seizures. The test of reasonableness also requires a case-by-case evaluation of whether the totality of circumstances demonstrates an adequate objective basis to back up the searches and seizures. The objective basis required to satisfy the reasonableness test ranges across a broad spectrum, from probable cause required to support full-blown searches and seizures to reasonable suspicion of a particular individual required to back up stops and frisks. DWI roadblocks, discussed later in this chapter, and some noncriminal law enforcement searches discussed in Chapter 7 do not require **individualized suspicion,** meaning facts and reasonable inferences from the facts that point to specific individuals. In these cases, other bases, such as random stops, satisfy the objective basis element of reasonableness under the Fourth Amendment.

Terry v. Ohio and Stop-and-Frisk Law

The law governing stops and frisks grew out of the practical problems that police officers face in preventing and investigating crime in large cities. Most police investigations of suspicious activity on the streets of large cities involve people whom the police do not know and will probably never see again. However, most suspicious behavior that police officers see does not provide enough facts to amount to probable cause, the objective basis for a lawful arrest (Chapter 5). For example, if officers observe two men peer in a shop window, turn as if to see if anyone is watching them, and continue this activity for about five minutes, the police do not have probable cause (the objective basis required) to arrest the two men. Should the police do nothing? Continue to watch the two men? Briefly detain them and pat them down for weapons? Arrest them, search them, and take them to the police station? The Fourth Amendment lends itself to at least three plausible interpretations concerning this and similar situations:

1. The Fourth Amendment applies only to full searches and arrests; hence, police discretion, not the Fourth Amendment, governs all brief street contacts.

2. Even brief street contacts and pat-downs are arrests and searches; therefore, to conduct them requires probable cause.

3. Stops and frisks are minimal Fourth Amendment searches and seizures that require reasonable suspicion (a lesser objective basis than probable cause) to back them up.[5]

If the police can take no action unless and until they have probable cause, as in alternative 2, criminal law enforcement suffers because the police will probably never see the suspects again. If the Constitution does not apply to these street encounters at all, as in alternative 1, then people on the street are subject to the will of the police alone. The Supreme Court resolved this trilemma by choosing the balancing approach of alternative 3. According to the Court, the police possess the authority to "freeze" suspicious episodes briefly in order to determine whether criminal activity "may be afoot." In addition to the power to freeze the situation, they must have the power to protect themselves. However, they cannot invade the privacy and freedom of movement of individuals on hunch, whim, or mere suspicion. They need some facts—not so many as would add up to probable cause, but enough—to permit a disinterested third party later to assess independently the foundation for the "freeze."[6]

Therefore, according to the Court, it is reasonable to freeze a suspicious situation briefly on the basis of a few **articulable facts** (specifically identifiable facts)—such as that a suspect is moving away at the sight of police, loitering, pacing up and down—in order to determine if a crime is really in the offing. It is also reasonable to pat down suspects on articulable facts in order to determine if they might be armed.[7]

Even in high-street-crime neighborhoods, most people obey the law and depend upon and want the police to protect them from crimes. Obviously, they need police protection more than the residents of "respectable" suburbs do. Law-abiding people in high-street-crime districts form lasting opinions about the police from these street encounters. The United States Supreme Court applied the reasonableness test to stops and frisks in its landmark decision *Terry v. Ohio.*

C A S E

Terry v. Ohio

392 U.S. 1, 88 S.Ct. 1868,
20 L.Ed.2d 889 (1968)

Terry was prosecuted for carrying a concealed weapon. An Ohio trial court overruled a pretrial motion to suppress the gun as evidence, and Terry and two cohorts were convicted. Terry appealed. An intermediate appellate court affirmed the conviction. The Ohio Supreme Court dismissed an appeal. The U.S. Supreme Court granted certiorari, and affirmed. Chief Justice Warren wrote the opinion of the Court. Justices Harlan, Black, and White wrote separate concurring opinions. Justice Douglas dissented.

FACTS

. . . Officer McFadden testified that while he was patrolling in plain clothes in downtown Cleveland at approximately 2:30 in the afternoon of October 31, 1963, his attention was attracted by two men, Chilton and Terry, standing on the corner of Huron Road and Euclid Avenue. He had never seen the two men before, and he was unable to say precisely what first drew his eye to them. However, he testified that he had been a policeman for 39 years and a detective for 35 and that he had been assigned to patrol this vicinity of downtown Cleveland for shoplifters and pickpockets for 30 years. He explained that he had developed routine habits of observation over the years and that he would "stand and watch people or walk and watch people at many intervals of the day." He added: "Now, in this case when I looked over they didn't look right to me at the time."

His interest aroused, Officer McFadden took up a post of observation in the entrance to a store 300 to 400 feet away from the two men. "I get more purpose to watch them when I seen their movements," he testified. He saw one of the men leave the other one and walk southwest on Huron Road, past some stores. The man paused for a moment and looked in a store window, then walked on a short distance, turned around and walked back toward the corner, pausing once again to look in the same store window. He rejoined his companion at the corner, and the two conferred briefly. Then the second man went through the same series of motions, strolling down Huron Road, looking in the same window, walking on a short distance, turning back, peering in the store window again, and returning to confer with the first man at the corner. The two men repeated this ritual alternately between five and six times apiece—in all, roughly a dozen trips. At one point, while the two were standing together on the corner, a third man approached them and engaged them briefly in conversation. This man then left the two others and walked west on Euclid Avenue. Chilton and Terry resumed their measured pacing, peering and conferring. After this had gone on for 10 to 12 minutes, the two men walked off together, heading west on Euclid Avenue, following the path taken earlier by the third man.

By this time Officer McFadden had become thoroughly suspicious. He testified that after observing their elaborately casual and oft-repeated reconnaissance of the store window on Huron Road, he suspected the two men of "casing a job, a stick-up," and that he considered it his duty as a police officer to investigate further. He added that he feared "they may have a gun." Thus, Officer McFadden followed Chilton and Terry and saw them stop in front of Zucker's store to talk to the same man who had conferred with them earlier on the street corner. Deciding that the situation was ripe for direct action, Officer McFadden approached the three men, identified himself as a police officer and asked for their names. At this point his knowledge was confined to what he had observed. He was not acquainted with any of the three men by name or by sight, and he had received no information concerning them from any other source. When the men "mumbled something" in response to his inquiries, Officer McFadden grabbed petitioner Terry, spun him around so that they were facing the other two, with Terry between McFadden and the others, and patted down the outside of his clothing. In the left breast pocket of Terry's overcoat Officer McFadden felt a pistol. He reached inside the overcoat pocket, but was unable to remove the gun. At this point, keeping Terry between himself and the others, the officer ordered all three men to enter Zucker's store. As they went in, he removed Terry's overcoat completely, removed a .38-caliber revolver from the pocket and ordered all three men to face the wall with their hands raised. Officer McFadden proceeded to pat down the outer clothing of Chilton and the third man, Katz. He discovered another revolver in the outer pocket of Chilton's overcoat, but no weapons were found on Katz. The officer testified that he only patted the men down to see whether they had weapons, and that he did not put his hands beneath the outer garments of either Terry or Chilton until he

felt their guns. So far as appears from the record, he never placed his hands beneath Katz' outer garments. Officer McFadden seized Chilton's gun, asked the proprietor of the store to call a police wagon, and took all three men to the station, where Chilton and Terry were formally charged with carrying concealed weapons.

[The trial court denied Terry's motion to suppress the gun as evidence] . . . on the ground that Officer McFadden, on the basis of his experience, "had reasonable cause to believe . . . that the defendants were conducting themselves suspiciously, and some interrogation should be made of their action." Purely for his own protection, the court held, the officer had the right to pat down the outer clothing of these men, who he had reasonable cause to believe might be armed. . . .

After the court denied their motion to suppress, Chilton and Terry waived jury trial and pleaded not guilty. The court adjudged them guilty, and the Court of Appeals for the Eighth Judicial District, Cuyahoga County, affirmed. The Supreme Court of Ohio dismissed their appeal. . . . We granted certiorari, to determine whether the admission of the revolvers in evidence violated petitioner's rights under the Fourth Amendment, made applicable to the States by the Fourteenth. We affirm the conviction.

OPINION

The Fourth Amendment provides that "the right of the people to be secure in their persons, houses, papers, and effects, against unreasonable searches and seizures, shall not be violated. . . ." This inestimable right of personal security belongs as much to the citizen on the streets of our cities as to the homeowner closeted in his study to dispose of his secret affairs. For, as this Court has always recognized, "No right is held more sacred, or is more carefully guarded, by the common law, than the right of every individual to the possession and control of his own person, free from all restraint or interference of others, unless by clear and unquestionable authority of law." . . . Unquestionably petitioner was entitled to the protection of the Fourth Amendment as he walked down the street in Cleveland. The question is whether in all the circumstances of this on-the-street encounter, his right to personal security was violated by an unreasonable search and seizure.

. . .

We would be less than candid if we did not acknowledge that this question thrusts to the fore difficult and troublesome issues regarding a sensitive area of police activity—issues which have never before been squarely presented to this Court. Reflective of the tensions involved are the practical and constitutional arguments pressed with great vigor on both sides of the public debate over the power of the police to "stop and frisk" . . . suspicious persons.

On the one hand, it is frequently argued that in dealing with the rapidly unfolding and often dangerous situations on city streets the police are in need of an escalating set of flexible responses, graduated in relation to the amount of information they possess. For this purpose it is urged that distinctions should be made between a "stop" and an "arrest" (or a "seizure" of a person), and between a "frisk" and a "search." Thus, it is argued, the police should be allowed to "stop" a person and detain him briefly for questioning upon suspicion that he may be connected with criminal activity. Upon suspicion that the person may be armed, the police should have the power to "frisk" him for weapons. If the "stop" and the "frisk" give rise to probable cause to believe that the suspect has committed a crime, then the police should be empowered to make a formal "arrest," and a full incident "search" of the person. This scheme is justified in part upon the notion that a "stop" and a "frisk" amount to a mere "minor inconvenience and petty indignity," which can properly be imposed upon the citizen in the interest of effective law enforcement on the basis of a police officer's suspicion.

On the other side the argument is made that the authority of the police must be strictly circumscribed by the law of arrest and search as it has developed to date in the traditional jurisprudence of the Fourth Amendment. It is contended with some force that there is not—and cannot be—a variety of police activity which does not depend solely upon the voluntary cooperation of the citizen and yet which stops short of an arrest based upon probable cause to make such an arrest. The heart of the Fourth Amendment, the argument runs, is a severe requirement of specific justification for any intrusion upon protected personal security, coupled with a highly developed system of judicial controls to enforce upon the agents of the State the commands of the Constitution. Acquiescence by the courts in the compulsion inherent in the field interrogation practices at issue here, it is urged, would constitute an abdication of judicial control over, and indeed an encouragement of, substantial interference with liberty and personal security by police officers whose judgment is necessarily colored by their primary involvement in "the often competitive enterprise of ferreting out crime." This, it is argued, can only serve to exacerbate police–community tensions in the crowded centers of our Nation's cities. . . .

Our first task is to establish at what point in this encounter the Fourth Amendment becomes relevant. That is, we must decide whether and when Officer McFadden "seized" Terry and whether and when he conducted a "search." There is some suggestion in the use of such terms as "stop" and "frisk" that such police conduct is outside the purview of the Fourth Amendment because neither action rises to the level of a "search" or "seizure" within the meaning of the Constitution. We emphatically reject this notion. It is quite plain that the Fourth Amendment governs "seizures" of the person which do not eventuate in a trip to the station house and prosecution for crime— "arrests" in traditional terminology. It must be recognized that whenever a police officer accosts an individual and restrains his freedom to walk away, he has "seized" that person. And it is nothing less than sheer torture of the English language to suggest that a careful exploration of the outer surfaces of a person's clothing all over his or her body in an attempt to find weapons is not a "search." Moreover, it is simply fantastic to urge that such a procedure performed in public by a policeman while the citizen stands helpless, perhaps facing a wall with his hands raised, is a "petty indignity." It is a serious intrusion upon the sanctity of the person, which may inflict great indignity and arouse strong resentment, and it is not to be undertaken lightly. [Court footnote: "Consider the following apt description: '(T)he officer must feel with sensitive fingers every portion of the prisoner's body. A thorough search must be made of the prisoner's arms and armpits, waistline and back, the groin and area about the testicles, and entire surface of the legs down to the feet.' Priar & Martin, *Searching and Disarming Criminals*, 45 J.Crim.L.C. & P.S. 481 (1954)."]

The danger in the logic which proceeds upon distinctions between a "stop" and an "arrest," or "seizure" of the person, and between a "frisk" and a "search" is twofold. It seeks to isolate from constitutional scrutiny the initial stages of the contact between the policeman and the citizen. And by suggesting a rigid all-or-nothing model of justification and regulation under the Amendment, it obscures the utility of limitations upon the scope, as well as the initiation, of police action as a means of constitutional regulation.

This Court has held in the past that a search which is reasonable at its inception may violate the Fourth Amendment by virtue of its intolerable intensity and scope. The scope of the search must be "strictly tied to and justified by" the circumstances which rendered its initiation permissible.

The distinctions of classical "stop-and-frisk" theory thus serve to divert attention from the central inquiry under the Fourth Amendment—the reasonableness in all the circumstances of the particular governmental invasion of a citizen's personal security. "Search" and "seizure" are not talismans. We therefore reject the notion that the Fourth Amendment does not come into play at all as a limitation upon police conduct if the officers stop short of something called a "technical arrest" or a "full-blown search."

In this case there can be no question, then, that Officer McFadden "seized" petitioner and subjected him to a "search" when he took hold of him and patted down the outer surfaces of his clothing. We must decide whether at that point it was reasonable for Officer McFadden to have interfered with petitioner's personal security as he did. And in determining whether the seizure and search were "unreasonable" our inquiry is a dual one—whether the officer's action was justified at its inception, and whether it was reasonably related in scope to the circumstances which justified the interference in the first place.

. . . [W]e deal here with an entire rubric of police conduct—necessarily swift action predicated upon the on-the-spot observations of the officer on the beat—which historically has not been, and as a practical matter could not be, subjected to the warrant procedure. Instead, the conduct involved in this case must be tested by the Fourth Amendment's general proscription against unreasonable searches and seizures. . . . In order to assess the reasonableness of Officer McFadden's conduct as a general proposition, it is necessary "first to focus upon the governmental interest which allegedly justifies official intrusion upon the constitutionally protected interests of the private citizen," for there is "no ready test for determining reasonableness other than by balancing the need to search (or seize) against the invasion which the search (or seizure) entails." And in justifying the particular intrusion the police officer must be able to point to specific and articulable facts which, taken together with rational inferences from those facts, reasonably warrant that intrusion. The scheme of the Fourth Amendment becomes meaningful only when it is assured that at some point the conduct of those charged with enforcing the laws can be subjected to the more detached, neutral scrutiny of a judge who must evaluate the reasonableness of a particular search or seizure in light of the particular circumstances. And in making that assessment it is imperative that the facts be judged against an objective standard: would the facts available to the officer at the moment of the seizure or the search "warrant a man of reasonable caution in the belief" that the action taken was appropriate? Anything less would invite intrusions upon constitutionally guaranteed rights based on nothing more substantial than inarticulate hunches, a result this Court has consistently refused to sanction. And simple "good faith on the part of the arresting officer is not enough." . . . If subjective good faith alone were the test, the protections of the Fourth Amendment would evaporate, and the people would be "secure in their persons, houses, papers, and effects," only in the discretion of the police. *Beck v. Ohio*, supra, at 97, 85 S.Ct. at 229.

Applying these principles to this case, we consider first the nature and extent of the governmental interests involved. One general interest is of course that of effective crime prevention and detection; it is this interest which underlies the recognition that a police officer may in appropriate circumstances and in an appropriate manner approach a person for purposes of investigating possibly criminal behavior even though there is no probable cause to make an arrest. It was this legitimate investigative function Officer McFadden was discharging when he decided to approach petitioner and his companions. He had observed Terry, Chilton, and Katz go through a series of acts, each of them perhaps innocent in itself, but which taken together warranted further investigation. There is nothing unusual in two men standing together on a street corner, perhaps waiting for someone. Nor is there anything suspicious about people in such circumstances strolling up and down the street, singly or in pairs. Store windows, moreover, are made to be looked in. But the story is quite different where, as here, two men hover about a street corner for an extended period of time, at the end of which it becomes apparent that they are not waiting for anyone or anything; where these men pace alternately along an identical route, pausing to stare in the same store window roughly 24 times; where each completion of this route is followed immediately by a conference between the two men on the corner; where they are joined in one of these conferences by a third man who leaves swiftly; and where the two men finally follow the third and rejoin him a couple of blocks away. It would have been poor police work indeed for an officer of 30 years' experience in the detection of thievery from stores in this same neighborhood to have failed to investigate this behavior further.

The crux of this case, however, is not the propriety of Officer McFadden's taking steps to investigate petitioner's suspicious behavior, but rather, whether there was justification for McFadden's invasion of Terry's personal security by searching him for weapons in the course of that investigation. We are now concerned with more than the governmental interest in investigating crime; in addition, there is the more immediate interest of the police officer in taking steps to assure himself that the person with whom he is dealing is not armed with a weapon that could unexpectedly and fatally be used against him. Certainly it would be unreasonable to require that police officers take unnecessary risks in the performance of their duties. American criminals have a long tradition of armed violence, and every year in this country many law enforcement officers are killed in the line of duty, and thousands more are wounded. Virtually all of these deaths and a substantial portion of the injuries are inflicted with guns and knives.

In view of these facts, we cannot blind ourselves to the need for law enforcement officers to protect themselves and other prospective victims of violence in situations where they may lack probable cause for an arrest. When an officer is justified in believing that the individual whose suspicious behavior he is investigating at close range is armed and presently dangerous to the officer or to others, it would appear to be clearly unreasonable to deny the officer the power to take necessary measures to determine whether the person is in fact carrying a weapon and to neutralize the threat of physical harm.

We must still consider, however, the nature and quality of the intrusion on individual rights which must be accepted if police officers are to be conceded the right to search for weapons in situations where probable cause to arrest for crime is lacking. Even a limited search of the outer clothing for weapons constitutes a severe, though brief, intrusion upon cherished personal security, and it must surely be an annoying, frightening, and perhaps humiliating experience. Petitioner contends that such an intrusion is permissible only incident to a lawful arrest, either for a crime involving the possession of weapons or for a crime the commission of which led the officer to investigate in the first place. . . .

Our evaluation of the proper balance that has to be struck in this type of case leads us to conclude that there must be a narrowly drawn authority to permit a reasonable search for weapons for the protection of the police officer, where he has reason to believe that he is dealing with an armed and dangerous individual, regardless of whether he has probable cause to arrest the individual for a crime. The officer need not be absolutely certain that the individual is armed; the issue is whether a reasonably prudent man in the circumstances would be warranted in the belief that his safety or that of others was in danger. And in determining whether the officer acted reasonably in such circumstances, due weight must be given, not to his inchoate and unparticularized suspicion or "hunch," but to the specific reasonable inferences which he is entitled to draw from the facts in light of his experience.

We must now examine the conduct of Officer McFadden in this case to determine whether his search and seizure of petitioner were reasonable, both at their inception and as conducted. He had observed Terry, together with Chilton and another man, acting in a manner he took to be preface to a "stick-up." We think on the facts and circumstances Officer McFadden detailed before the trial judge a reasonably prudent man would have been warranted in believing petitioner was armed and thus presented a threat to the officer's safety while he was investigating his suspicious behavior. The actions of Terry and Chilton were consistent with McFadden's hypothesis that these men were contemplating a daylight robbery—which, it is reasonable to assume, would be likely to involve the use of weapons—and nothing in their conduct from the time he first noticed them until the time he confronted them and identified himself as a police officer gave him sufficient reason to negate that hypothesis. Although the trio had departed the original scene, there was nothing to indicate abandonment of an intent to commit a robbery at some point. Thus, when Officer McFadden approached the three men gathered before the display window at Zucker's store he had observed enough to make it quite reasonable to fear that they were armed; and nothing in their response to his hailing them, identifying himself as a police officer, and asking their names served to dispel that reasonable belief. We cannot say his decision at that point to seize Terry and pat his clothing for weapons was the product of a volatile or inventive imagination, or was undertaken simply as an act of harassment; the record evidences the tempered act of a policeman who in the course of an investigation had to make a quick decision as to how to protect himself and others from possible danger, and took limited steps to do so.

The manner in which the seizure and search were conducted is, of course, as vital a part of the inquiry as whether they were warranted at all. The Fourth Amendment proceeds as much by limitations upon the scope of governmental action as by imposing preconditions upon its initiation. The entire deterrent purpose of the rule excluding evidence seized in violation of the Fourth Amendment rests on the assumption that "limitations upon the fruit to be gathered tend to limit the quest itself." Thus, evidence may not be introduced if it was discovered by means of a seizure and search which were not reasonably related in scope to the justification for their initiation.

We need not develop at length in this case, however, the limitations which the Fourth Amendment places upon a protective seizure and search for weapons. These limitations will have to be developed in the concrete factual circumstances of individual cases. Suffice it to note that such a search, unlike a search without a warrant incident to a lawful arrest, is not justified by any need to prevent the disappearance or destruction of evidence of crime. The sole justification of the search in the present situation is the protection of the police officer and others nearby, and it must therefore be confined in scope to an intrusion reasonably designed to discover guns, knives, clubs, or other hidden instruments for the assault of the police officer.

The scope of the search in this case presents no serious problem in light of these standards. Officer McFadden patted down the outer clothing of petitioner and his two companions. He did not place his hands in their pockets or under the outer surface of their garments until he had felt weapons, and then he merely reached for and removed the guns. He never did invade Katz' person beyond the outer surfaces of his clothes, since he discovered nothing in his patdown which might have been a weapon. Officer McFadden confined his search strictly to what was minimally necessary to learn whether the men were armed and to disarm them once he discovered the weapons. He did not conduct a general exploratory search for whatever evidence of criminal activity he might find.

We conclude that the revolver seized from Terry was properly admitted in evidence against him. At the time he seized petitioner and searched him for weapons, Officer McFadden had reasonable grounds to believe that petitioner was armed and dangerous, and it was necessary for the protection of himself and others to take swift measures to discover the true facts and neutralize the threat of harm if it materialized. The policeman carefully restricted his search to what was appropriate to the discovery of the particular items which he sought. Each case of this sort will, of course, have to be decided on its own facts. We merely hold today that where a police officer observes unusual conduct which leads him reasonably to conclude in light of his experience that criminal activity may be afoot and that the persons with whom he is dealing may be armed and presently dangerous, where in the course of investigating this behavior he identifies himself as a policeman and makes reasonable inquiries, and where nothing in the initial stages of the encounter serves to dispel his reasonable fear for his own or others' safety, he is entitled for the protection of himself and others in the area to conduct a carefully limited search of the outer clothing of such persons in an attempt to discover weapons which might be used to assault him. Such a search is a reasonable search under the Fourth Amendment, and any weapons seized may properly be introduced in evidence against the person from whom they were taken.

Affirmed.

CONCURRING OPINION

Justice Harlan, concurring.

. . . Where . . . a stop is reasonable . . . the right to frisk must be immediate and automatic if the reason for the stop is, as here, an articulable suspicion of a crime of violence. Just as a full search incident to a lawful arrest requires no additional justification, a limited frisk incident to a lawful stop must often be rapid and routine. There is no reason why an officer, rightfully but forcibly confronting a person suspected of a serious crime, should have to ask one question and take the risk that the answer might be a bullet. . . .

Justice White, concurring.

. . . I think an additional word is in order concerning the matter of interrogation during an investigative stop. There is nothing in the Constitution which prevents a policeman from addressing questions to anyone on the streets. Absent special circumstances, the person approached may not be detained or frisked but may refuse to cooperate and go on his way. However, given the proper circumstances, such as those in this case, it seems to me the person may be briefly detained against his will while pertinent questions are directed to him. Of course, the person stopped is not obliged to answer, answers may not be compelled, and refusal to answer furnishes no basis for an arrest, although it may alert the officer to the need for continued observation. In my view, it is temporary detention, warranted by the circumstances, which chiefly justifies the protective frisk for weapons. . . .

DISSENT

Justice Douglas, dissenting.

I agree that petitioner was "seized" within the meaning of the Fourth Amendment. I also agree that

frisking petitioner and his companions for guns was a "search." But it is a mystery how that "search" and that "seizure" can be constitutional by Fourth Amendment standards, unless there was "probable cause" to believe that (1) a crime had been committed or (2) a crime was in the process of being committed or (3) a crime was about to be committed.

. . . The requirement of probable cause has roots that are deep in our history. The general warrant, in which the name of the person to be arrested was left blank, and the writs of assistance, against which James Otis inveighed, both perpetuated the oppressive practice of allowing the police to arrest and search on suspicion. Police control took the place of judicial control, since no showing of "probable cause" before a magistrate was required. "That philosophy (rebelling against these practices) later was reflected in the Fourth Amendment. And as the early American decisions both before and immediately after its adoption show, common rumor or report, suspicion, or even 'strong reason to suspect' was not adequate to support a warrant for arrest. And that principle has survived to this day. . . ."

The infringement on personal liberty of any "seizure" of a person can only be "reasonable" under the Fourth Amendment if we require the police to possess "probable cause" before they seize him. Only that line draws a meaningful distinction between an officer's mere inkling and the presence of facts within the officer's personal knowledge which would convince a reasonable man that the person seized has committed, is committing, or is about to commit a particular crime. "In dealing with probable cause, . . . as the very name implies, we deal with probabilities. These are not technical; they are the factual and practical considerations of everyday life on which reasonable and prudent men, not legal technicians, act." *Brinegar v. United States*, 338 U.S. 160, 175, 69 S.Ct. 1302, 1310.

To give the police greater power than a magistrate is to take a long step down the totalitarian path. Perhaps such a step is desirable to cope with modern forms of lawlessness. But if it is taken, it should be the deliberate choice of the people through a constitutional amendment. Until the Fourth Amendment, which is closely allied with the Fifth, is rewritten, the person and the effects of the individual are beyond the reach of all government agencies until there are reasonable grounds to believe (probable cause) that a criminal venture has been launched or is about to be launched.

There have been powerful hydraulic pressures throughout our history that bear heavily on the Court to water down constitutional guarantees and give the police the upper hand. That hydraulic pressure has probably never been greater than it is today. Yet if the individual is no longer to be sovereign, if the police can pick him up whenever they do not like the cut of his jib, if they can "seize" and "search" him in their discretion, we enter a new regime. The decision to enter it should be made only after a full debate by the people of this country.

CASE DISCUSSION

Identify the specific invasions of liberty and privacy to which Officer McFadden subjected Terry and his cohorts. At what point did Officer McFadden "seize" Terry? What was the objective basis or the facts upon which Officer McFadden based his stop? His frisk? During the oral argument before the Supreme Court, it came out that in all of Officer McFadden's experience, he had never investigated a robbery; his experience was limited to shoplifting and pickpocketing. Is this important? It also came out during oral argument that Terry, Chilton, and Katz were much larger than Officer McFadden. Should that make a difference? What interests did the Court specifically refer to protecting in reaching its decision to formalize stops and frisks? Do you agree with the Court's evaluation of these interests? Which ones do you consider most important? Why?

Consider the following excerpt from the *amicus curiae* brief filed in *Terry v. Ohio*:

In the litigation now before the Court—as is usual in cases where police practices are challenged— two parties essentially are represented. Law enforcement officers, legal representatives of their respective States, ask the Court to broaden police powers, and thereby to sustain what has proved to

be a "good pinch." Criminal defendants caught with the goods through what in retrospect appears to be at least shrewd and successful (albeit constitutionally questionable) police work ask the Court to declare that work illegal and to reverse their convictions. Other parties intimately affected by the issues before the Court are not represented. The many thousands of our citizens who have been or may be stopped and frisked yearly, only to be released when the police find them innocent of any crime, are not represented. The records of their cases are not before the Court and cannot be brought here. Yet it is they, far more than those charged with crime, who will bear the consequences of the rules of constitutional law which this Court establishes. The determination of the quantum of "belief" or "suspicion" required to justify the exercise of intrusive police authority is precisely the determination of how far afield from instances of obvious guilt the authority stretches. To lower that quantum is to broaden the police net and, concomitantly, to increase the number (and probably the proportion) of innocent people caught up in it. The innocent are those this Court will never see.[8]

What interests does this brief consider most important? Law enforcement? Defendants' rights? Accurate results? Equality of treatment? Control of the police and procedural regularity? During oral argument of the case before the Supreme Court, Terry's lawyer revealed some of what happened at the suppression hearing. Terry's attorney said, among other things, that Officer McFadden testified that he did not know the men, that they walked normally, that they were standing in front of a store talking normally and were facing away from the store windows. When asked why he approached Terry, Chilton, and Katz, Officer McFadden replied, "Because . . . [I] didn't like them." Is this testimony important? Also, McFadden was white and Terry and Chilton were black. Is this important?

STOPS

Since *Terry v. Ohio*, the framework for analyzing police encounters with individuals can be divided into three categories:

1. *Voluntary encounters* that fall outside the Fourth Amendment—that is, "communication between police and individuals involving no coercion or detection"
2. *Stops*—brief "seizures" that require reasonable suspicion to support them
3. *Full-scale arrests*—detentions that require probable cause to justify them (see Figure 4.1 on p. 134)

Definition of *Stop*

The United States Supreme Court has ruled that two types of stops by law enforcement officers are Fourth Amendment "seizures":

1. **Actual seizure stops,** in which officers physically grab or lay hands on people, intending to seize them
2. **Show-of-authority stops,** in which officers draw weapons or otherwise display their authority to detain people and the detained people submit to the show of authority

Actual seizure stops require that the police not only physically lay hands on individuals but also that they do so with the intention of seizing the individuals. According to a majority of the Supreme Court, "Violation of the Fourth Amendment requires an intentional acquisition of physical control"—that is, "misuse of power, not the accidental effects of otherwise lawful government conduct." So, according to the Court,

> if a parked and unoccupied police car slips its brake and pins a passerby against a wall, it is likely that a tort has occurred, but not a violation of the Fourth Amendment. And the situation would not change if the passerby happened, by lucky chance, to be a serial murderer for whom there is an outstanding arrest warrant— even if, at the time he was pinned, he was in the process of running away from two pursuing constables. It is clear, in other words, that a Fourth Amendment seizure does not occur whenever there is a governmentally caused termination of an individual's freedom of movement (the innocent passerby), nor even whenever there is a govern[m]entally caused and governmentally desired termination of an individual's freedom of movement (the fleeing felon), but only when there is a governmental termination of freedom of movement through means intentionally applied.[9]

Show-of-authority stops require not only that the police show their authority but also that individuals submit to this showing. Whether individuals submit does not depend on subjective measurements, such as the intent of the officer to seize the person, or on the belief of individuals seized that the officer seized them. The Supreme Court applies an objective standard to show-of-authority stops called a **reasonable stop standard.** According to this standard, if a reasonable person would not feel free to leave or otherwise terminate the encounter following the show of authority, then the officer has seized the person. The belief is of a reasonable person, not the specific person the officer seized on this particular occasion. Professor Robert V. Ward of Howard University Law School argues that the reasonable person standard leads to unfair treatment of minorities. Pro-

TABLE 4.1 SHOW OF FORCE

Show of Force	Not a Show of Force
Setting up a roadblock	Approaching a citizen in public
Flashing an emergency light	Identifying oneself as a police officer
Ordering a person to leave a car	Merely asking questions
Surrounding a car	Requesting to search
Drawing a weapon	Following a pedestrian in a police car
Being in the presence of several officers	
Using a commanding tone of voice	

fessor Ward proposes an alternative that he maintains ought to ensure fair treatment. The alternative test "would encourage courts to consider all relevant factors," including the following:

- The race, ethnicity, and socioeconomic background of the suspect
- "Prior bad experiences of the defendant with the police"
- Any evidence of "police brutality and misconduct in the community where the search took place"[10]

Officers who approach individuals without a show of force in order to ask them questions have not seized them. Constitutionally speaking, individuals may simply walk away or refuse to answer any questions the officer asks. Naturally, individuals may feel a psychological pressure, or a moral duty as "good citizens," to cooperate. However, neither the feeling of pressure nor the sense of moral duty, in the absence of a show of force by the officer, will turn the encounter into a Fourth Amendment seizure. For example, Immigration and Naturalization Services (INS) officers surrounded factories suspected of employing illegal aliens. The presence of INS agents was used to ensure that no employees "escaped" while other INS agents questioned them and asked them to display their "papers." The Supreme Court held that the questionings were not seizures even if INS agents surrounded the factories during the questioning. See Table 4.1 for other examples of the Court's rulings and its comments on what is and is not a show of force.[11]

If officers accompany questioning with intimidating or coercive measures, they may convert a voluntary encounter into a seizure. Therefore, the courts view differently situations where police officers simply approach citizens and question them from those in which officers approach citizens and then forcibly detain them in order to question them. The forcible detention turns the voluntary encounter into a seizure. For example, in *Brown v. Texas*, two officers got out of their squad car in El Paso, Texas, approached Brown and his companion, and asked them to identify themselves and explain why they were in an alley. Brown not only refused to identify himself, but he also angrily asserted that the officers had no right to stop him. The officers then frisked Brown and arrested him for violating a Texas statute making it illegal for individuals to refuse to give their name and address to police officers. The Supreme Court held that the stop violated the Fourth Amendment because it turned the voluntary approach into a stop without factual foundation.[12]

Courts do not agree on exactly what circumstances in addition to brief questioning turn a contact into either a stop or an arrest. Some conclude that anything more than a brief detention at the scene for the purpose of asking a few questions turns a stop into an arrest. For example, in an instance where officers drew their guns, ordered a fleeing suspect to stop when they did not have probable cause to arrest him, forced him to the ground on his stomach, and handcuffed him, a Michigan court ruled that the police had arrested the suspect. An Illinois court held that an officer who blocked a suspect's car and drew his gun as he approached the suspect's car had lawfully stopped, but had not arrested, the suspect. A California court held that taking a suspect from the crime scene to a residence to check out a burglary was a lawful stop, not an arrest.

Reasonable Suspicion— Objective Basis for Stops

The reasonableness of stops depends not only on balancing the government need for stops and the invasion against individual suspects that stops entail. Reasonableness also depends on the objective basis—that is, the facts that officers rely on to back up their actions when they stop people. For example, when Officer McFadden stopped Terry and his companions in *Terry v. Ohio*, he relied on his direct observation of the three men pacing up and down and peering into a shop window in downtown Cleveland. This activity aroused his suspicion that the three men were "casing" the store and were about to rob it. The quantity of facts required to stop individuals is called **reasonable suspicion.** Reasonable suspicion contrasts with the standard for arrest, probable cause, solely on this quantitative basis. Probable cause requires more facts than reasonable suspicion because an arrest is a greater deprivation than a stop. Reasonable suspicion resembles probable cause "as the mist resembles the rain," to use Longfellow's metaphor.[13]

Probably the most cited attempt to explain reasonable suspicion appears in Chief Justice Warren Burger's opinion in *United States v. Cortez*. Chief Justice Burger's explanation is worth quoting at length:

> Courts have used a variety of terms to capture the elusive concept of what cause is sufficient to authorize police to stop a person. Terms like "articulable reasons" and "founded suspicion" are not self-defining; they fall short of the clear guidance dispositive of the myriad factual situations that arise. But the essence of all that has been written is that the totality of circumstances—the whole picture—must be taken into account. Based upon that whole picture the detaining officers must have a particularized and objective basis for suspecting the particular person stopped of criminal activity.
>
> The idea that an assessment of the whole picture must yield a particularized suspicion contains two elements, each of which must be present before a stop is permissible. First, the assessment must be based upon all the circumstances. The analysis proceeds with various objective observations, information from police reports, if such are available, and consideration of the modes of operation of certain kinds of lawbreakers. From these data, a trained officer draws inferences and makes deductions—inferences and deductions that may well elude an untrained person.
>
> The process does not deal with hard certainties, but with probabilities. Long before the law of probabilities was articulated as such, practical people formu-

lated certain common sense conclusions about human behavior; jurors as factfinders are permitted to do the same — and so are law enforcement officers. Finally, the evidence thus collected must be seen and weighed not in terms of library analysis by scholars, but as understood by those versed in the field of law enforcement.

The second element contained in the idea that an assessment of the whole picture must yield a particularized suspicion is the concept that the process just described must raise a suspicion that the particular individual being stopped is engaged in wrongdoing. Chief Justice Warren, speaking for the Court in *Terry v. Ohio*, said that "[t]his demand for specificity in the information upon which police action is predicated is the central teaching of this Court's jurisprudence."[14]

The Court has never stated the specific number of facts needed to add up to the two elements in reasonable suspicion referred to by Chief Justice Burger. Such an effort would be unwise even if it were possible. The quality and the quantity of facts required to raise reasonable suspicion that a specific individual may be involved in criminal activity must vary with the myriad of suspicious circumstances that the police encounter on the streets and in other public places. Officers can establish reasonable suspicion from a wide range of facts and circumstances derived from two primary sources:

1. **Direct information** — facts that officers acquire directly from their senses (what they see, hear, smell, and feel).

2. **Hearsay information** — facts that officers learn indirectly from what someone else tells them. This indirect information, called hearsay, might come from various sources, including victims, witnesses, other police officers, and anonymous, professional, or paid informants.

The First Circuit Court of Appeals applied the reasonable suspicion standard in *United States v. Trullo.*

C A S E

Did the Officers Have "Reasonable Suspicion"?

United States v. Trullo
809 F.2d 108 (1st Cir. 1987)

Trullo pled guilty to possession of cocaine with intent to distribute in a U.S. district court in the district of Massachusetts. He reserved his right to appeal his stop and arrest. The U.S. Court of Appeals affirmed the conviction before Judges Timbers, Coffin, and Bownes. Judge Timbers wrote the opinion of the court. Judge Bownes filed a dissenting opinion.

FACTS

. . . On May 2, 1985, at 1:00 P.M. two Boston police detectives and a DEA agent in an unmarked car were patrolling that portion of Boston known as the "Combat Zone" for drug activity. The Combat Zone is a high crime area known for prostitution and drug dealing. As the officers were stopped at a light, they noticed a gray Thunderbird automobile stopped on the curb of Washington Street with a man (whom we now know as appellant) at the wheel. Washington Street is the main street of this portion of the Combat Zone. As the officers watched, a second man approached the Thunderbird from the sidewalk and engaged appellant in a twenty second conversation through the open passenger-side window. The second man got into the car and had an additional five or ten second conversation with appellant. The car then pulled out and proceeded for two blocks until it made a right turn onto Hayward Place, a short street which connects Washington Street and Harrison Avenue. The officers followed the Thunderbird in their unmarked car.

While Hayward Place is trafficked during early morning and late afternoon rush hours, it was deserted at the time appellant entered it. The officers parked three car lengths behind appellant's car and had an unobstructed view of it. The officers observed appellant and the second man engaged in a thirty second discussion with their heads inclined toward each other. The second man then got out of the car and walked back toward Washington Street. One of the officers followed him on foot.

Appellant, with the other two officers following, drove his car out of Hayward Place onto Harrison Avenue where he stopped for a red light. The two officers, who were not in uniform, got out of their car and approached appellant's car on foot. The officer on the driver's side of appellant's car approached with his badge in his left hand and his drawn gun in his right hand. That officer identified himself as a police officer and asked appellant to get out of the car. As appellant opened the door and got out, the officer noticed a "bulge" in appellant's right-hand pants pocket. The officer asked appellant what it was and patted it with his hand. The officer testified that it felt hard and narrow like a knife. The officer reached into the pocket and found a knife with a spring-activated blade retracted in the handle. The officer then arrested appellant for carrying an illegal weapon in violation of state law. A subsequent search of appellant's person at the station house during booking disclosed two half-gram packets of cocaine in appellant's hat. An inventory search of appellant's car disclosed a fake oil can containing 22 half-gram packets of cocaine.

On May 17, 1985, appellant was indicted on one count of possession of cocaine with intent to distribute in violation of 21 U.S.C. s 841(a)(1) (1982). On June 10, 1985, appellant moved to suppress the cocaine seized from his person and car as products of an illegal search. Appellant claimed that the officers did not have either "articulable suspicion" to justify stopping appellant or probable cause to arrest him. . . .

In an opinion dated August 5, 1985, the district court granted the motion to suppress in part. The court held that the circumstances leading to the officers' stop of appellant provided sufficient articulable suspicion to permit a *Terry* stop. The court held that the officer's seizure of the knife also was justified under *Terry*. The court, therefore, refused to suppress the cocaine found on appellant's person as fruit of a lawful stop and arrest. [The court, however, held that an inventory search conducted at the same time] . . . was in bad faith and impermissible. It suppressed the cocaine found in the trunk. The government appealed that portion of the order suppressing the cocaine found in the trunk. We reversed the district court and held the inventory search to be permissible. 790 F.2d 205 (1st Cir. 1986). We did not address the court's *Terry* ruling.

On June 16, 1986, appellant entered a conditional plea of guilty, reserving his right to appeal the permissibility of his stop and arrest. See Fed.R.Crim.P. 11(a)(2). On July 18, 1986, the court sentenced appellant to two years in prison. He currently is serving the sentence. For the reasons stated below, we affirm the judgment of conviction and of course the propriety of the May 2, 1985, stop and arrest.

OPINION

. . . [T]he facts presented by this case . . . represent the outermost reaches of a permissible *Terry* stop; and it should be borne in mind that " . . . in law as in life, today's satisfactory explanation may very well be tomorrow's lame excuse." *United States v. Vazquez*, 605 F.2d 1269, 1280 (2d Cir. 1979). We wish to make clear at the outset that a determination of whether the stop was justified at its inception depends on the totality of the circumstances confronting the officer. "[T]he assessment must be based upon all of the circumstances." *United States v. Cortez*, 449 U.S. 411, 418 (1981). . . .

The initial factor which the officers considered was the nature of the Combat Zone, the area in which appellant's conduct took place. "Officers may consider the characteristics of the area in which they encounter a vehicle." . . . ("The reputation of an area for criminal activity is an articulable fact upon which a police officer may legitimately rely.";) *United States v. Gomez*, 633 F.2d 999, 1005 (2d Cir. 1980) . . . Here, appellant's activities took place in what is unquestionably a high crime area of Boston. The officers testified that narcotics transactions frequently take place there. The district court described the area as a "high crime area. It contains 'adult' movie theatres and bookstores and is a center of prostitution and the exchange of various forms of contraband. It has also been the scene of many stabbings and shootings, often fatal." Location alone, however, is insufficient to justify a *Terry* stop. . . . It would fly in the face of well-settled precedent were we to hold, as appellant invites us to do, that the location was of minimal consequence and should not serve as one appropriate factor in determining the reasonableness of a *Terry* stop. We decline the invitation.

A second articulable factor upon which we hold the officers justifiably could have relied was appellant's conduct. The initial conversation between appellant and the individual who approached his vehicle lasted only a few seconds, after which the second man entered appellant's vehicle. The two drove a very short distance, approximately a block and a half, and turned onto a deserted side street. After parking on that side street the two, with their heads inclined toward each other, engaged in a conversation of short duration. The second man then exited the vehicle and walked back in the direction from which the two had driven. The officers testified that such behavior was indicative of some sort of illegal transaction. In the officers' judgment a clandestine transaction had taken place, a judgment to which we give appropriate deference. . . .

The circumstances under which the officers acted "are to be viewed through the eyes of a reasonable and cautious police officer on the scene, guided by his experience and training." *United States v. McHugh*, 769 F.2d 860, 865 (1st Cir. 1985) ("[i]n assessing the import of the evidence, the expertise and experience of the law enforcement officers must also be taken into account."). The three officers who observed appellant's actions had collectively some twenty-eight years of experience in law enforcement.

The officers also had special expertise in the area of narcotics. Based on this experience and expertise, the officers unanimously determined that they were observing an illegal transaction.

We hold that the actions of the officers, based on the totality of the circumstances, were justified at their inception. . . . We affirm the judgment of conviction of appellant for possession of cocaine with intent to distribute. . . .

Affirmed.

DISSENT

Judge Bownes, dissenting.

. . .

The Supreme Court, interpreting *Terry*, has stressed that "[the] demand for specificity in the information upon which police action is predicated is the central teaching of this Court's Fourth Amendment jurisprudence." *United States v. Cortez*, 449 U.S. 411, 418, 101 S.Ct. 690, 695, 66 L.Ed.2d 621 (1981). The facts in *Terry* provide an example of reasonable suspicions based on specific observations and a graduated police response. General circumstances may be considered as factors in combination with specific facts but they do not suffice when they stand alone.

The Court has accordingly held that suspicions based solely on very general characteristics of a "drug courier profile" do not meet the specificity requirement. *Reid v. Georgia*, 448 U.S. 438, 440–41, 100 S.Ct. 2752, 2753–54, 65 L.Ed.2d 890 (1980). Similarly, the mere presence of an individual in a location known as a high crime area is not a "specific, objective" fact under *Terry*. *Brown v. Texas*, 443 U.S. 47, 51, 99 S.Ct. 2637, 2640, 61 L.Ed.2d 357 (1979). Finally, society's legitimate interest in encouraging trained police officers to use their judgment does not permit them to conduct searches and seizures at their "unfettered discretion."

The Court has upheld *Terry* stops where these general factors were combined with specific circumstances. Thus, in *United States v. Cortez*, 449 U.S. 411, 101 S.Ct. 690, 66 L.Ed.2d 621 (1981), the Supreme Court viewed the characteristics of the location of the stop to be of "critical importance." This general circumstance was combined in that case, involving the smuggling of aliens, with a police analysis of remarkable specificity, predicting the day, time, place, nature of the vehicle sought and other circumstances.

While I would not require that level of specificity in all cases, the specific facts here are sparse. A man let another man into his car after a brief conversation and drove about two and a half blocks, stopping on a deserted street. After they "appeared" to have another brief conversation, with heads inclined, the passenger exited the car and walked back where he came from. During the last conversation, the two men were in full view of the unmarked car containing the police officers and made no attempt to conceal what they were doing. The officers did not see any objects being exchanged.

The district judge apparently felt uneasy about simply deferring to the officers' judgment on these facts alone. After weighing the pros and cons of such deference, he stated:

> In my view the key to resolving the conflict in this case is the location. I agree with defense counsel that the same sequence of events occurring in the center of a suburban town would not have resulted in a stop by the police. . . . I have seen Hayward Place. It is a depressing and inhospitable location which one would hardly choose for a legitimate transaction.

For the district judge, then, the location was not only an important background element against which to interpret the specific facts, but the central "fact" itself. But this "fact," i.e., the Combat Zone, does not carry the dispositive weight attributed to it. . . . As the district judge noted:

> The case is complicated by the fact that the stop in this case occurred in the early afternoon, when there are legitimate businesses operating in the Combat Zone and Washington Street serves as a conduit for legitimate traffic to the downtown area. There are also many people in the Combat Zone for personal purposes that, while certainly not admirable, are not yet illegal. There is, moreover, a certain circularity to the reasoning concerning Hayward Place: that street is said to be an unlikely choice for a "legitimate transaction" but the main basis for concluding that there had been any transaction was that the car had stopped on Hayward Place.

The court cites appellant's conduct, as interpreted by trained police officers, as a second articulable basis for police suspicions. The paucity of the objectively suspicious elements of that conduct, however, means that the court is in fact according dispositive deference to the officers' discretion. . . .

Here . . . we are asked to find reasonable suspicion on the basis of quite general characteristics of a sizable area of the city, when the suspicion was not grounded in any specific information about date, time, or the particular individuals. Nor was there any finding that Hayward Place was a street known specifically for drug deals or other illegalities. The suspects did indeed commit the act of appearing to converse briefly on that street. Yet, although they are supposed to have gone to Hayward Place because it was deserted, they made no attempt to conceal themselves from a car that had followed them into the deserted street and that had parked behind them with an unobstructed view of their car. Their failure to conceal themselves is particularly striking because the second car, which we now know was an unmarked police car, contained three men who were observing them and discussing their observations. It would seem that, for the court, the Combat Zone is a per se region of lessened expectation of privacy, at all times of the day and at all periods of the year, where practically unlimited deference is granted to police officers' discretion. More particularly, the court, following the district judge's views about where one would "choose" to conduct one's affairs, has effectively eliminated any fourth amendment scrutiny of police suspicions concerning activity on Hayward Place. . . .

. . . The court's opinion provides no limiting criteria. Rather, it seems to allow armed stops of individuals who meet in the Combat Zone on the basis of unlimited deference to police discretion. I respectfully dissent.

CASE DISCUSSION

List the "articulable facts" that the court included in determining whether the police had reasonable suspicion to justify the stop of Trullo. What are the two parts of determining the lawfulness of the stop that the court applied here? Why does the court say that the facts of this case represent the "outermost reaches of a permissible *Terry* stop"? Why does the dissent say that the majority decision "seems to allow armed stops of individuals who meet in the Combat Zone on the basis of unlimited deference to police discretion"? Do you feel that you have a clearer—or foggier—idea of exactly what *reasonable suspicion* means after reading this case?

D e c i s i o n   P o i n t

U.S. v. Stanley, 915 F.2d 54 (1st Cir. 1990)

On Saturday, July 2, 1988, Officers Barry D. Souza and Mark A. Delaney, undercover agents with the Barnstable Police Department, were on patrol in an unmarked cruiser in the town of Hyannis, Massachusetts. At approximately 12:15 A.M., they proceeded to a parking lot abutting a free-standing bar. The parking lot is situated between the rear parking lot of a Sheraton Hotel and an auto parts store. Driving through the parking area, which was full of cars, Officer Souza noticed a grey Ford Thunderbird parked between two other cars. He observed the sole occupant, later identified as defendant Stanley, sitting in the driver's seat in a crouched position, "leaning towards the console, towards the passenger's seat, head down." Officer Souza also saw a faint light coming from the center console area of the vehicle. These observations, in addition to his knowledge that the area was a high-crime area, led Souza to suspect that the occupant of the car might be engaged in drug-related activity.

The detectives stopped their cruiser twenty feet behind and to the side of Stanley's car. As Officer Souza left the cruiser and approached the defendant's car, he saw the defendant turn his head towards the rear of the car and then lean towards the passenger seat. The officer suspected that Stanley had seen him approaching and was trying to hide narcotics. Officer Souza walked to the driver's side of the car and, while shining a flashlight on Stanley, shouted, "Police, freeze." The defendant recoiled from the officer and quickly reached back toward the passenger seat. Officer Souza testified later that he knew from experience that persons engaged in narcotics activities often carry firearms and that he feared that the defendant was attempting to reach one. When Stanley lunged to his right, Officer Souza opened the door on the driver's side and pulled the defendant from the vehicle. As he did so, he saw a shotgun lying across the passenger seat.

After Stanley was secured, the officers noticed a red plastic cup of water positioned on the car's center console, and the protective cap of a hypodermic syringe needle on the passenger seat. They also found a folded paper containing a small amount of cocaine.

Stanley was arrested for possession of a loaded sawed-off shotgun, drug paraphernalia, and cocaine. Stanley moved to suppress, as fruit of the allegedly unlawful search and seizure, the items seized from his person and motor vehicle by the arresting officers, as well as certain statements he made to them thereafter. The district court denied the motion.

Was the stop a reasonable seizure? Yes, according to the U.S. First Circuit Court of Appeals:

> We have recognized that a determination of whether the police action "was justified . . . depends on the totality of the circumstances confronting the officer." [*U.S. v.*] *Trullo*, 809 F.2d at 111. In evaluating these circumstances, "due weight must be given, not to his inchoate and unparticularized suspicion or 'hunch,' but to the specific reasonable inferences which he is entitled to draw from the facts in light of his experience."
>
> The district court found that Officer Souza's suspicion was reasonable, based on the location and the defendant's conduct both before and after the officers approached his car. Specifically, the court found that "the officer's observations of defendant's conduct and the faint light in the car did, in view of his experience in law enforcement in general and with drug investigation in particular, give credence to his

suspicion that defendant was engaged in a drug-related activity, warranting investigation." We now review each of these factors.

Location by itself is ordinarily insufficient to justify a stop; however, "officers may consider the characteristics of the area in which they encounter a vehicle." The district court found that Stanley was parked in an area known to the officers as one frequently used for illegal drug activities. Although the officers would not have been justified in stopping Stanley based merely on his presence in the parking lot, the reputation of the area for narcotics transactions was an appropriate factor in determining the reasonableness of an investigatory stop.

A second articulable factor is the conduct of defendant, considered in light of the officers' experience in law enforcement and in drug investigations in particular. The officers noticed defendant alone in his car, just after midnight, leaning over the center console which was slightly illuminated. He was apparently engaged in some purposeful activity which, under the circumstances, and given their experience, the officers suspected was drug-related. Their suspicions aroused, the officers approached the defendant's car. Stanley, upon seeing Souza, moved as though he were hiding something under the seat. This movement served to reinforce the officers' suspicion of drug-related activity. See *United States v. Gilliard*, 847 F.2d 21, 25 (1st Cir. 1988) (defendant's nervous behavior contributed to officer's legitimate concern for his safety); *United States v. Denney*, 771 F.2d 318, 322 (7th Cir. 1985) (furtive movement or leaning towards right side of vehicle was reasonably interpreted by officer as reaching for a weapon). Souza then shouted, "Police, freeze," thus imposing, for the first time, a restriction on defendant's freedom—the so-called *Terry* stop.

Although the defendant's actions might have seemed unremarkable to other passersby, "[c]onduct innocent in the eyes of the untrained may carry entirely different 'messages' to the experienced or trained observer." Thus, the circumstances "are to be viewed through the eyes of a reasonable and cautious police officer on the scene, guided by his experience and training." Officer Souza had been with the Barnstable Police Department for approximately nine years, and had participated in approximately twenty investigations and arrests in the Hyannis area involving narcotics and firearms violations. Considering the totality of the circumstances, we give weight to the officer's trained eye and judgment. We conclude on these facts that the district court had sufficient basis to determine that the investigatory stop, commencing with the shouting of "Police, freeze," was justified at its inception.

Appellant's argument that "[t]oo many alternative explanations, all of them innocent, exist which could explain [Stanley's behavior]," is misguided. We have noted that "'[i]t must be rare indeed that an officer observes behavior consistent only with guilt and incapable of innocent interpretation.'" Under *Terry*, the test is whether the circumstances give rise to a reasonable suspicion of criminal activity, not whether the defendant's actions are subject to no reasonable innocent explanation. . . .

Considering the totality of the circumstances and taking into account the experience of the police officers and their knowledge of the locale, we conclude that the district court did not err in determining that Officer Souza's investigatory stop of defendant Stanley was justified and that the scope of the actions taken by the officers was reasonably related to the circumstances that originally justified the stop. The judgment of the district court is therefore affirmed.

Table 4.2 suggests the kinds of information that officers can rely on as the building blocks of reasonable suspicion to back up stops. Taken together, some or all of the types of information in Table 4.2 amount to reasonable suspicion if they would lead an ex-

TABLE 4.2 DIRECT AND HEARSAY BASES FOR REASONABLE SUSPICION

Direct Information	Hearsay
Flight	Victim statement
Furtive movement	Eyewitness statement
Hiding	Fellow officer statement
Resisting an officer	Informant statement
Attempting to destroy evidence	Anonymous tip
Evasive answers	
Contradictory answers	
Weapons or contraband in plain view	

TABLE 4.3 REASONS INSUFFICIENT BY THEMSELVES TO AMOUNT TO REASONABLE SUSPICION

1. General suspicion that drug dealing went on in a tavern. *Ybarra v. Illinois*, 444 U.S. 85 (1979).
2. Driver double-parked within ten feet of a pedestrian in a drug trafficking location. *Rivera v. Murphy*, 979 F.2d 259 (1st Cir. 1992).
3. Other bar patrons, not the one detained, possessed weapons and contraband. *U.S. v. Jaramillo*, 25 F.3d 1146 (2d Cir. 1994).
4. Passenger leaving airplane appeared nervous in the presence of officers. *U.S. v. Caicedo*, 85 F.3d 1184 (6th Cir. 1996).
5. Driver of a car with out-of-state license plates and no noticeable luggage avoided eye contact with a patrol car. *U.S. v. Halls*, 40 F.3d 275 (8th Cir. 1995).
6. Hispanic-looking males in a heavy truck near the border who looked nervous, did not acknowledge police presence, and drove faster than the flow of traffic. *U.S. v. Garcia-Camacho*, 53 F.3d 244 (9th Cir. 1995).
7. Generalized suspicion of criminal activity in a high-crime neighborhood. *Brown v. Texas*, 443 U.S. 47 (1979).
8. Nervous man traveling alone who left an airline terminal quickly after picking up one suitcase and had a one-way ticket that he had bought with cash from a drug-source city. *U.S. v. Lambert*, 46 F.3d 1064 (10th Cir. 1995).
9. Driver failed to look at patrol car late at night. *U.S. v. Smith*, 799 F.2d 704 (11th Cir. 1986).
10. Mexican-appearing person, driving a car with out-of-state license plates and no suitcases, appeared nervous in talking with officers during discussion of a speeding ticket. *U.S. v. Tapia*, 912 F.2d 1367 (11th Cir. 1990).

perienced police officer to *suspect* that the person stopped *may* have committed, *may* be committing, or *may* be about to commit a crime or that his or her "curious or un-usual conduct would naturally trigger a police inquiry."[15]

Remember that it is the totality of circumstances, "the whole picture," that matters in determining reasonable suspicion. Each fact or circumstance is a building block in the construction of reasonable suspicion. Table 4.3 lists some kinds of information that, standing alone, courts have refused to accept as reasonable suspicion.

Anonymous Tips. In *Adams v. Williams,* excerpted later in this chapter in the section on frisks, the Supreme Court expanded the kinds of information that might support reasonable suspicion. Remember that in *Terry v. Ohio,* reasonable suspicion was based on

Officer McFadden's firsthand observations. At that time, it was widely believed that the watering down of the probable cause standard to reasonable suspicion for street stops was limited to reasonable suspicion based on the direct observations by the stopping officer. Secondhand or hearsay information such as that provided by informants, it was believed, did not amount to reasonable suspicion. In *Adams v. Williams*, the police officer stopped and frisked the occupant of a car on the basis of an informant's tip. The police officer knew the informant. The Court did not decide whether the tip of an anonymous informant could satisfy the reasonable suspicion standard. The Court settled the problem of anonymous tips in the drug possession case *Alabama v. White*.

C A S E

Is an Anonymous Tip Reasonable Suspicion?

Alabama v. White
496 U.S. 325, 110 S.Ct. 2412 (1990)

White, reserving her right to appeal the denial of her suppression motion, pled guilty to possession of marijuana and possession of cocaine. On her appeal, the Alabama Court of Criminal Appeals reversed. After granting the state's petition for certiorari, *the Supreme Court reversed and remanded the case. Justice White wrote the opinion of the Court, in which Chief Justice Rehnquist and Justices Blackmun, O'Connor, Scalia, and Kennedy joined. Justice Stevens filed a dissenting opinion, in which Justices Brennan and Marshall joined.*

FACTS

On April 22, 1987, at approximately 3 P.M., Corporal B. H. Davis of the Montgomery Police Department received a telephone call from an anonymous person, stating that Vanessa White would be leaving 235-C Lynwood Terrace Apartments at a particular time in a brown Plymouth station wagon with the right taillight lens broken, that she would be going to Dobey's Motel, and that she would be in possession of about an ounce of cocaine inside a brown attaché case. Corporal Davis and his partner Corporal P. A. Reynolds, proceeded to the Lynwood Terrace Apartments. The officers saw a brown Plymouth station wagon with a broken right taillight in the parking lot in front of the 235 building.

The officers observed respondent leave the 235 building, carrying nothing in her hands, and enter the station wagon. They followed the vehicle as it drove the most direct route to Dobey's Motel. When the vehicle reached the Mobile Highway, on which Dobey's Motel is located, Corporal Reynolds requested a patrol unit to stop the vehicle. The vehicle was stopped at approximately 4:18 P.M., just short of Dobey's Motel. Corporal Davis asked respondent to step to the rear of her car, where he informed her that she had been stopped because she was suspected of carrying cocaine in the vehicle. He asked if they could look for cocaine and respondent said they could look. The officers found a locked brown attaché case in the car and, upon request, respondent provided the combination to the lock. The officers found marijuana in the attaché case and placed respondent under arrest. During processing at the station, the officers found three milligrams of cocaine in respondent's purse.

Respondent was charged in Montgomery County court with possession of marijuana and possession of cocaine. The trial court denied respondent's motion to suppress and she pleaded guilty to the charges, reserving the right to appeal the denial of her suppression motion. The Court of Criminal Appeals of Alabama held that the officers did not have the reasonable suspicion necessary under *Terry v. Ohio* [1968] to justify the investigatory stop of respondent's car, and that the marijuana and cocaine were fruits of respondent's unconstitutional detention. The court concluded that respondent's motion to dismiss should have been granted and reversed her conviction. The Supreme Court of Alabama denied the State's petition for writ of certiorari, two justices dissenting. Because of differing views in the state and federal courts over whether an anonymous tip may furnish reasonable suspicion for a stop, we granted the State's petition for certiorari. We now reverse.

OPINION

Adams v. Williams [(1972), excerpted later in this chapter] sustained a *Terry* stop and frisk undertaken on the basis of a tip given in person by a known informant who had provided information in the past. We concluded that, while the unverified tip may have been insufficient to support an arrest or search warrant, the information carried sufficient "indicia of reliability" to justify a forcible stop. We did not address the issue of anonymous tips in Adams, except to say that "[t]his is a stronger case than obtains in the case of an anonymous telephone tip."

Illinois v. Gates (1983) [excerpted in Chapter 5] dealt with an anonymous tip in the probable cause context. The Court there [adopted] . . . a "totality of the circumstances" approach to determining whether an informant's tip establishes probable cause. *Gates* made clear, however, that . . . an informant's "veracity," "reliability," and "basis of knowledge" remain "highly relevant in determining the value of his report." These factors are also relevant in the reasonable suspicion context, although allowance must be made in applying them for the lesser showing required to meet that standard.

The opinion in *Gates* recognized that an anonymous tip alone seldom demonstrates the informant's basis of knowledge or veracity inasmuch as ordinary citizens generally do not provide extensive recitations of the basis of their everyday observations and given that the veracity of persons supplying anonymous tips is "by hypothesis largely unknown, and unknowable." . . . [We] said in *Adams*: "Some tips, completely lacking in indicia of reliability, would either warrant no police response or require further investigation before a forcible stop of a suspect would be authorized." Simply put, a tip such as this one, standing alone, would not "'warrant a man of reasonable caution in the belief' that [a stop] was appropriate."

. . . [I]n this case there is more than the tip itself. The tip was not as detailed, and the corroboration was not as complete, as in *Gates*, but the required degree of suspicion was likewise not as high. We discussed the difference in the two standards last Term in *United States v. Sokolow* (1989) [see the next case excerpt in this chapter]:

> The officer [making a *Terry* stop] . . . must be able to articulate something more than an "inchoate and unparticularized suspicion or 'hunch.'" The Fourth Amendment requires "some minimal level of objective justification" for making the stop. That level of suspicion is considerably less than proof of wrongdoing by a preponderance of the evidence. We have held that probable cause means "a fair probability that contraband or evidence of a crime will be found," and the level of suspicion required for a *Terry* stop is obviously less demanding than for probable cause.

Reasonable suspicion is a less demanding standard than probable cause not only in the sense that reasonable suspicion can be established with information that is different in quantity or content than that required to establish probable cause, but also in the sense that reasonable suspicion can arise from information that is less reliable than that required to show probable cause. *Adams v. Williams* demonstrates as much. We there assumed that the unverified tip from the known informant might not have been reliable enough to establish probable cause, but nevertheless found it sufficiently reliable to justify a *Terry* stop. Reasonable suspicion, like probable cause, is dependent upon both the content of information possessed by police and its degree of reliability. Both factors—quantity and quality—are considered in the "totality of the circumstances—the whole picture," that must be taken into account when evaluating whether there is reasonable suspicion. Thus, if a tip has a relatively low degree of reliability, more information will be required to establish the requisite quantum of suspicion than would be required if the tip were more reliable. . . .

Contrary to the court below, we conclude that when the officers stopped respondent, the anonymous tip had been sufficiently corroborated to furnish reasonable suspicion that respondent was engaged in criminal activity and that the investigative stop therefore did not violate the Fourth Amendment.

It is true that not every detail mentioned by the tipster was verified, such as the name of the woman leaving the building or the precise apartment from which she left; but the officers did corroborate that a woman left the 235 building and got into the particular vehicle that was described by the caller. With respect to the time of departure predicted by the informant, Corporal Davis testified that the caller gave a particular time when the woman would be leaving, but he did not state what that time was. He did testify that, after the call, he and his partner proceeded to the Lynwood Terrace Apartments to put the 235 building under surveillance. Given the fact that the officers proceeded to the indicated address immediately after the call and that respondent emerged not too long thereafter, it appears from the record before us that respondent's departure from the building was within the time frame predicted by the caller.

As for the caller's prediction of respondent's destination, it is true that the officers stopped her just short of Dobey's Motel and did not know whether she would have pulled in or continued past it. But given that the four-mile route driven by respondent was the most direct route possible to Dobey's Motel, but nevertheless involved several turns, we think respondent's destination was significantly corroborated. The Court's opinion in *Gates* gave credit to the proposition that because an informant is shown to be right about some things, he is probably right about other facts that he has alleged, including the claim that the object of the tip is engaged in criminal activity. Thus, it is not unreasonable to conclude in this case that the independent corroboration by the police of significant aspects of the informer's predictions imparted some degree of reliability to the other allegations made by the caller.

We think it also important that, as in *Gates*, "the anonymous [tip] contained a range of details relating not just to easily obtained facts and conditions existing at the time of the tip, but to future actions of third parties ordinarily not easily predicted." The fact that the officers found a car precisely matching the caller's description in front of the 235 building is an example of the former. Anyone could have "predicted" that

fact because it was a condition presumably existing at the time of the call. What was important was the caller's ability to predict respondent's future behavior, because it demonstrated inside information—a special familiarity with respondent's affairs.

The general public would have had no way of knowing that respondent would shortly leave the building, get in the described car, and drive the most direct route to Dobey's Motel. Because only a small number of people are generally privy to an individual's itinerary, it is reasonable for police to believe that a person with access to such information is likely to also have access to reliable information about that individual's illegal activities. When significant aspects of the caller's predictions were verified, there was reason to believe not only that the caller was honest but also that he was well informed, at least well enough to justify the stop.

Although it is a close case, we conclude that under the totality of the circumstances the anonymous tip, as corroborated, exhibited sufficient indicia of reliability to justify the investigatory stop of respondent's car. We therefore reverse the judgment of the Court of Criminal Appeals of Alabama and remand for further proceedings not inconsistent with this opinion.

So ordered.

DISSENT

Justice Stevens, with whom Justice Brennan and Justice Marshall join, dissenting.

Millions of people leave their apartments at about the same time every day carrying an attaché case and heading for a destination known to their neighbors. Usually, however, the neighbors do not know what the briefcase contains. An anonymous neighbor's prediction about somebody's time of departure and probable destination is anything but a reliable basis for assuming that the commuter is in possession of an illegal substance—particularly when the person is not even carrying the attaché case described by the tipster.

The record in this case does not tell us how often respondent drove from the Lynwood Terrace Apartments to Dobey's Motel; for all we know, she may have been a room clerk or telephone operator working the evening shift. It does not tell us whether Officer Davis made any effort to ascertain the informer's identity, his reason for calling, or the basis of his prediction about respondent's destination. Indeed, for all that this record tells us, the tipster may well have been another police officer who had a "hunch" that respondent might have cocaine in her attaché case.

Anybody with enough knowledge about a given person to make her the target of a prank, or to harbor a grudge against her, will certainly be able to formulate a tip about her like the one predicting Vanessa White's excursion. In addition, under the Court's holding, every citizen is subject to being seized and questioned by any officer who is prepared to testify that the warrantless stop was based on an anonymous tip predicting whatever conduct the officer just observed. Fortunately, the vast majority of those in our law enforcement community would not adopt such a practice. But the Fourth Amendment was intended to protect the citizen from the overzealous and unscrupulous officer as well as from those who are conscientious and truthful. This decision makes a mockery of that protection.

I respectfully dissent.

CASE DISCUSSION

What are the arguments the Court gives in favor of allowing an anonymous tip to establish reasonable suspicion? Does the Court say that all anonymous tips are enough to establish reasonable suspicion? What criteria does the Court use in allowing anonymous tips to establish reasonable suspicion? What arguments does the dissent give for not allowing the anonymous tip in this case to establish reasonable suspicion? What does the dissent mean that the decision makes a "mockery" of the Fourth Amendment? Do you agree? How would you decide this case? Does the use of the anonymous tip further the interest in correct result at the expense of due process, or the reverse? In an article criticizing the decision, Professor David S. Rudstein wrote the following:

> Under the Supreme Court's holding in *Alabama v. White*, any person with a bit of knowledge of another individual can make that individual the target of a prank, or if he harbors a grudge against the individual, can maliciously attempt to inconvenience and embarrass him, by formulating a tip about the individual similar to the one in *White* and then anonymously passing it on to the police.[16]

Is this likely? Explain your answer.

D e c i s i o n   P o i n t

State v. King, 499 N.W.2d 190 (Wis. 1993)
On April 27, 1992, Sergeant David Tianen of the Racine Police Department responded to a radio dispatch of shots fired in the 2000 block of Mead or Racine Street. On the way, Sergeant Tianen received an additional report over the radio describing the license plate number of a red and white Lincoln believed to be involved in the shooting. Approximately one block away from the location of the reported shooting, Sergeant Tianen observed a vehicle matching the type, color, and license plate number of the vehicle described in the report. After stopping the vehicle, Sergeant Tianen observed the driver, later identified as King, fidgeting and making repeated movements below the front seat. Concerned that King was concealing a weapon under the seat, Sergeant Tia-

nen ordered King out of the car and checked him for weapons. Finding none, Sergeant Tianen proceeded to check under the seat of the car, where he found a film canister and a plastic bag, both containing cocaine. King was then arrested and charged with possession with intent to deliver. The trial court denied King's motion to suppress the evidence of the cocaine seized after the stop and convicted him upon his plea of guilty. King appealed, seeking review of the denial of his motion to suppress.

Should the cocaine be excluded as evidence? The Wisconsin Court of Appeals said no:

> The validity of an investigatory stop is governed by *Terry v. Ohio*, 392 U.S. 1, 88 S.Ct. 1868, 20 L.Ed.2d 889 (1968), as codified by sec. 968.24,

Stats. *Terry* and its progeny require that a police officer reasonably suspect, in light of his or her experience, that some criminal activity has taken or is taking place before stopping an individual. The focus of an investigatory stop is on reasonableness, and the determination of reasonableness depends on the totality of the circumstances.

. . .

King relies on *Alabama v. White*, 496 U.S. 325, 110 S.Ct. 2412, 110 L.Ed.2d 301 (1990) . . . to assert that the anonymous tip information in this case was insufficient to supply police with a reasonable suspicion to justify an investigative stop. In *White*, an anonymous tipster informed police that the accused would be leaving a designated apartment at a particular time in a brown Plymouth station wagon with a broken taillight, that she would be going to a certain motel, and that she would be in possession of cocaine in a brown attaché case. The Supreme Court held that independent corroboration of significant aspects of the tip exhibited a sufficient degree of reliability to provide police with reasonable suspicion for the investigatory stop of the accused's vehicle.

. . .

King argues that, contrary to *White* . . . the police in this instance had no independent verification of the tip. For instance, the arresting officer never verified that there was a shooting, the tip did not include any predicted future activity or an explanation of the relationship between the described car and the shooting, no gun was visible to police before stopping the car, and no gun was found on King when police frisked him. Therefore, King asserts that the police had virtually no corroborating evidence linking the driver of the car with the reported shooting.

King's reliance on *White* . . . is misplaced. In . . . *White* . . . police received tips regarding future narcotics trafficking in which they were able to corroborate the anonymous tipster's information by observing the accused's behavior over a certain period of time. In contrast, police

in this case received a tip regarding gunshots in the street, a dangerous criminal activity already in progress.

King's argument contemplates a test where the evidence, in this case the seized cocaine, must establish some privity between the tip and the actual event. As King would argue, since the cocaine had no relationship to the reported shooting and the police did not observe or discover a gun on him, the police could not have reasonably associated King with the reported shooting, making the stop and subsequent search invalid. We expressly reject such a test. Rather, the focus of the test is on reasonableness.

The reasonableness of an investigatory stop such as occurred in this case depends on all the facts and circumstances that are present at the time of the stop. . . .

The facts and circumstances in this case . . . support a determination that the stop was reasonable. [First,] [t]he police were provided with a detailed description of the car reportedly involved in a shooting, including the model, color and license plate number. Shortly after receiving the report, Sergeant Tianen observed a car matching the description one block away from the reported shooting. Sergeant Tianen observed the driver suspiciously reaching under the car seat on numerous occasions.

Second, the circumstances also indicated a need for an investigative stop. . . . [T]here was no alternative means of further investigation available to Sergeant Tianen short of making the stop. The car was moving and if he did not react immediately the opportunity for further investigation would have been lost. Further, the fact that police were investigating a nighttime shooting incident in the streets must be considered an important factor.

We conclude that the trial court's findings of fact were not against the great weight and clear preponderance of the evidence. Therefore, . . . we conclude that the investigative stop was reasonable. Judgment affirmed.

Profiles. In addition to direct observation and hearsay, government agents also rely on profiles both as a reason for initially approaching people to check out possible criminal activity and as reasonable suspicion for stopping them. Profiles have been popular since the 1970s, when the government introduced an airline hijacker profile. Drug Enforcement Agent Paul Markonni developed the **drug courier profile** in 1974 while he was assigned to the Detroit DEA office. He also trained other agents in its use. Since then, it has become a "nationwide law enforcement tool." The use of the profile works this way. Officers stationed at airports observe travelers, looking for seven primary and four secondary characteristics.

Primary Characteristics:

1. Arrival or departure from "source" cities
2. Carrying little or no luggage, or empty suitcases
3. Traveling by an unusual itinerary
4. Use of an alias
5. Carrying unusually large amounts of cash
6. Purchasing tickets with large numbers of small bills
7. Unusual nervousness

Secondary Characteristics:

1. Use of public transportation when leaving airports
2. Immediately making telephone calls after getting off planes
3. Leaving false or fictitious callback numbers when leaving planes
4. Excessively frequent trips to source or distribution cities[17]

Their suspicions aroused, agents approach travelers, identify themselves, seek their consent to questioning, and ask to see their identification and ticket. If this does not remove their suspicion, they continue the questioning, asking travelers to accompany the agents to another location, usually a room used by law enforcement officers. Once inside the room, agents typically ask travelers to consent to searches of their persons and luggage. If travelers refuse, agents must either allow them to leave or "seize" them.[18]

Since the introduction of the airport drug courier profile, law enforcement has introduced a number of other profiles, including the following:

1. Illegal entry into the United States
2. International drug smugglers
3. Customers of suspected domestic drug dealers
4. Highway drug couriers[19]

Profiles are neither direct observation nor hearsay. Both direct observation and hearsay are based on individualized suspicion—that is, on facts specifically related to particular suspects. The drug courier profile, on the other hand, is based on suspicion derived from statistical data that place individuals into a suspect category. The Supreme Court dealt with the drug courier profile as a basis for reasonable suspicion in *United States v. Sokolow.*

◄ ▶ C A S E ◄ ▶

Is a "Drug Profile" Reasonable Suspicion?

United States v. Sokolow
490 U.S. 1, 109 S.Ct. 1581 (1989)

Sokolow was convicted in the United States District Court for the District of Hawaii of possessing cocaine with intent to distribute. He appealed. The Court of Appeals reversed and remanded. Certiorari was granted. The Supreme Court reversed. Justice Rehnquist delivered the opinion of the Court, in which Justices White, Blackmun, Stevens, O'Connor, Scalia, and Kennedy joined. Justice Marshall filed a dissenting opinion, in which Justice Brennan joined.

FACTS

This case involves a typical attempt to smuggle drugs through one of the Nation's airports. On a Sunday in July 1984, respondent went to the United Airlines ticket counter at Honolulu Airport, where he purchased two round-trip tickets for a flight to Miami leaving later that day. The tickets were purchased in the names of "Andrew Kray" and "Janet Norian," and had open return dates. Respondent paid $2,100 for the tickets from a large roll of $20 bills, which appeared to contain a total of $4,000. He also gave the ticket agent his home telephone number. The ticket agent noticed that respondent seemed nervous; he was about 25 years old; he was dressed in a black jumpsuit and wore gold jewelry; and he was accompanied by a woman, who turned out to be Janet Norian. Neither respondent nor his companion checked any of their four pieces of luggage.

After the couple left for their flight, the ticket agent informed Officer John McCarthy of the Honolulu Police Department of respondent's cash purchase of tickets to Miami. Officer McCarthy determined that the telephone number respondent gave to the ticket agent was subscribed to a "Karl Herman," who resided at 348-A Royal Hawaiian Avenue in Honolulu. Unbeknownst to McCarthy (and later to the DEA agents), respondent was Herman's roommate. The ticket agent identified respondent's voice on the answering

machine at Herman's number. Officer McCarthy was unable to find any listing under the name "Andrew Kray" in Hawaii. McCarthy subsequently learned that return reservations from Miami to Honolulu had been made in the names of Kray and Norian, with their arrival scheduled for July 25, three days after respondent and his companion had left. He also learned that Kray and Norian were scheduled to make stopovers in Denver and Los Angeles.

On July 25, during the stopover in Los Angeles, DEA agents identified respondent. He "appeared to be very nervous and was looking all around the waiting area." Later that day, at 6:30 P.M., respondent and Norian arrived at Honolulu. As before, they had not checked their luggage. Respondent was still wearing a black jumpsuit and gold jewelry. The couple proceeded directly to the street and tried to hail a cab, where Agent Richard Kempshall and three other DEA agents approached them. Kempshall displayed his credentials, grabbed respondent by the arm and moved him back onto the sidewalk. Kempshall asked respondent for his airline ticket and identification; respondent said that he had neither. He told the agents that his name was "Sokolow," but that he was traveling under his mother's maiden name, "Kray."

Respondent and Norian were escorted to the DEA office at the airport. There, the couple's luggage was examined by "Donker," a narcotics detector dog, which alerted to respondent's brown shoulder bag. The agents arrested respondent. He was advised of his constitutional rights and declined to make any statements. The agents obtained a warrant to search the shoulder bag. They found no illicit drugs, but the bag did contain several suspicious documents indicating respondent's involvement in drug trafficking. The agents had Donker reexamine the remaining luggage, and this time the dog alerted to a medium sized Louis Vuitton bag. By now, it was 9:30 P.M., too late for the agents to obtain a second warrant. They allowed respondent to leave for the night, but kept his luggage. The next morning, after a second dog confirmed Donker's alert, the agents obtained a warrant and found 1,063 grams of cocaine inside the bag.

Respondent was indicted for possession with the intent to distribute cocaine in violation of 21 U.S.C. § 841(a)(1). The United States District Court for Hawaii denied his motion to suppress the cocaine and other evidence seized from his luggage, finding that the DEA agents had a reasonable suspicion that he was involved in drug trafficking when they stopped him at the airport. Respondent then entered a conditional plea of guilty to the offense charged. The United States Court of Appeals for the Ninth Circuit reversed respondent's conviction by a divided vote, holding that the DEA agents did not have a reasonable suspicion to justify the stop. . . . We granted certiorari to review the decision of the Court of Appeals because of its serious implications for the enforcement of the federal narcotics laws. We now reverse.

OPINION

The Fourth Amendment requires "some minimal level of objective justification" for making the stop. That level of suspicion is considerably less than proof of wrongdoing by a preponderance of the evidence. . . . The concept of reasonable suspicion, like probable cause, is not "readily, or even usefully, reduced to a neat set of legal rules." . . .

Paying $2,100 in cash for two airplane tickets is out of the ordinary, and it is even more out of the ordinary to pay that sum from a roll of $20 bills containing nearly twice that amount of cash. Most business travelers, we feel confident, purchase airline tickets by credit card or check so as to have a record for tax or business purposes, and few vacationers carry with them thousands of dollars in $20 bills. We also think the agents had a reasonable ground to believe that respondent was traveling under an alias; the evidence was by no means conclusive, but it was sufficient to warrant consideration. While a trip from Honolulu to Miami, standing alone, is not a cause for any sort of suspicion, here there was more: surely, few residents of Honolulu travel from that city for 20 hours to spend 48 hours in Miami during the month of July.

Any one of these factors is not by itself proof of any illegal conduct and is quite consistent with innocent travel. But we think taken together they amount to reasonable suspicion. . . .

We do not agree with respondent that our analysis is somehow changed by the agents' belief that his behavior was consistent with one of the DEA's "drug courier profiles." [COURT NOTE: "Agent Kempshall testified that respondent's behavior 'had all the classic aspects of a drug courier.' Since 1974, the DEA has trained narcotics officers to identify drug smugglers on the basis of the sort of circumstantial evidence at issue here."] A court sitting to determine the existence of reasonable suspicion must require the agent to articulate the factors leading to that conclusion, but the fact that these factors may be set forth in a "profile" does not somehow detract from their evidentiary significance as seen by a trained agent.

Reversed and remanded. . . .

DISSENT

Justice Marshall, with whom Justice Brennan joins, dissenting.

Because the strongest advocates of Fourth Amendment rights are frequently criminals, it is easy to forget that our interpretations of such rights apply to the innocent and the guilty alike. In the present case, the chain of events set in motion when respondent Andrew Sokolow was stopped by Drug Enforcement Administration (DEA) agents at Honolulu International Airport led to the discovery of cocaine, and, ultimately, to Sokolow's conviction for drug trafficking. But in sustaining this conviction on the ground that the agents reasonably suspected Sokolow of ongoing criminal activity, the Court diminishes the rights of all citizens . . . "to be secure in their persons," as they traverse the Nation's airports. Finding this result constitutionally impermissible, I dissent.

The Fourth Amendment cabins government's authority to intrude on personal privacy and security by requiring that searches and seizures usually be supported by a showing of probable cause. The reasonable-suspicion standard is a derivation of the probable cause command, applicable only to those brief detentions which fall short of being full-scale searches and seizures and which are necessitated by law-enforcement exigencies such as the need to stop ongoing crimes, to prevent imminent crimes, and to protect law-enforcement officers in highly charged situations. *Terry v. Ohio* [1968]. By requiring reasonable suspicion as a prerequisite to such seizures, the Fourth Amendment protects innocent persons from being subjected to "overbearing or harassing" police conduct carried out solely on the basis of imprecise stereotypes of what criminals look like, or on the basis of irrelevant personal characteristics such as race.

To deter such egregious police behavior, we have held that a suspicion is not reasonable unless officers have based it on "specific and articulable facts." . . . [T]o detain, officers must "have a reasonable suspicion, based on objective facts, that the individual is involved in criminal activity." . . . The rationale for permitting brief, warrantless seizures is, after all, that it is impractical to demand strict compliance with the Fourth Amendment's ordinary probable-cause requirement in the face of ongoing or imminent criminal activity demanding "swift action predicated upon the on-the-spot observations of the officer on the beat." . . . Evaluated against this standard, the facts about Andrew Sokolow known to the DEA agents at the time they stopped him fall short of reasonably indicating that he was engaged at the time in criminal activity. It is highly significant that the DEA agents stopped Sokolow because he matched one of the DEA's "profiles" of a paradigmatic drug courier. In my view, a law enforcement officer's mechanistic ap-

plication of a formula of personal and behavioral traits in deciding who to detain can only dull the officer's ability and determination to make sensitive and fact-specific inferences "in light of his experience," particularly in ambiguous or borderline cases. Reflexive reliance on a profile of drug courier characteristics runs a far greater risk than does ordinary, case-by-case police work, of subjecting innocent individuals to unwarranted police harassment and detention. This risk is enhanced by the profile's "chameleon-like way of adapting to any particular set of observations."

CASE DISCUSSION

What were the facts upon which DEA agents based the "stop"? Should a drug profile alone add up to "reasonable suspicion that crime may be afoot"? Explain. Under what conditions, if any, should such "circumstantial" evidence as the drug profile provide the basis for stops? Does the Supreme Court's acceptance of the drug courier profile as part of reasonable suspicion promote the interest in obtaining the correct result? Procedural regularity? Crime control? Control of government? Explain. Should we have a rule that limits stops to investigating "serious crime"? If so, what crimes would you put on a list of serious crimes? Would you include suspected public drunkenness? Suspected prostitution? Suspected marijuana possession?

Race. The use of profiles and the use of anonymous tips are not the only problems that arise with respect to the kinds of facts that amount to reasonable suspicion based on the "totality of the circumstances." In *Buffkins v. City of Omaha*, the U.S. Eighth Circuit Court of Appeals considered whether race is a fact that can contribute to reasonable suspicion.

C A S E

Is Race a Fact Relevant to Reasonable Suspicion?

Buffkins v. City of Omaha
922 F.2d 465 (CA8, 1990)

Lu Ann Buffkins, a suspected drug courier, detainee at airport, brought action against police officers and the

city of Omaha to recover for a violation of § 1981, a violation of Fourth Amendment, false arrest, false imprisonment, malicious prosecution, and intentional infliction of emotional distress. The United States District Court for the District of Nebraska dismissed the city and § 1981 claim, directed a verdict in favor of the officers and the city on the Fourth Amendment claim, and entered judgment on the jury verdict in favor of officers. Buffkins appealed. The Court of Appeals affirmed in part, vacated in part, and remanded.

LAY, Chief Judge.

FACTS

On March 17, 1987, Omaha police received a tip that cocaine would be imported into the Omaha area before 5:00 P.M. by a black person or persons arriving on a flight from Denver. Officers Grigsby and Friend planned to meet at the Omaha airport to follow up on the tip. Both officers had a working knowledge of the "drug courier profile" and Grigsby had received special training from the Drug Enforcement Agency ("DEA") concerning interception of drug couriers in airports. Officer Grigsby expressed concern over the vagueness of the tip but decided to proceed to the airport to meet Friend.

The officers, dressed in plain clothes, met at the airport at approximately 2:30 P.M. The officers decided to monitor a flight that was scheduled to arrive from Denver at 3:40 P.M. The flight the officers watched was approximately one-half hour late. While surveying the deplaning passengers, the officers noticed Buffkins, the only black person exiting the plane. Buffkins was met by her sister, Hollis, at the gate. The officers later claimed that Hollis appeared nervous. Buffkins' other sister, Cheryl Nwachakwu, joined Buffkins and Hollis near the escalator leading down to the baggage carousel. The officers noticed that Buffkins carried a teddy bear with seams that appeared to have been resewn. Buffkins handed the teddy bear to Nwachakwu. Hollis left the airport without taking the teddy bear with her.

Grigsby approached Buffkins and Nwachakwu, identified himself as an officer conducting a narcotics investigation, and upon Buffkins' request presented identification. Grigsby and Friend then requested Buffkins to bring her luggage and come with them to answer questions. Nwachakwu was told she could leave. When Buffkins asked the officers who they were looking for, the officers told her about the tip. The officers picked up two of Buffkins' suitcases and escorted Buffkins and Nwachakwu to an office lo-

cated on the other side of the terminal. On the way to the office, Buffkins protested that the officers' conduct was racist and unconstitutional. Buffkins claims that she believed she had no choice but to cooperate with the officers' investigation and that neither officer told her she was free to go. Inside the security room, Buffkins gave the officers her driver's license and airline ticket, neither of which were suspicious. When Friend kneaded and felt the teddy bear, he did not detect any indication of contraband. Buffkins allegedly became increasingly loud during the interrogation. When the officers asked Buffkins if they could search her luggage, she refused, citing her rights under the Fourth Amendment. The officers eventually informed Buffkins that she was free to go and told her to "have a nice day," to which she replied "asshole system" or "I will have a nice day, asshole." The officers then decided to arrest Buffkins for disorderly conduct. When the officers told Buffkins they would have to confiscate her luggage and inventory it, Buffkins refused. The officers then allowed Nwachakwu to open and inspect Buffkins' luggage in their presence. It is undisputed that Buffkins was not carrying any drugs or contraband.

Both officers testified that Buffkins did not fit the drug courier profile and that they did not rely on the profile as a basis to stop Buffkins. Unlike many individuals who fit the "drug courier profile," Buffkins was neither the first nor the last passenger to deplane, she did not pay cash for her plane ticket, and she was not making a quick turn-around trip. Moreover, she had identification that was consistent with her airline ticket, she checked her luggage, and she did not arrive on an early flight when few police are present.

OPINION

Section 1983 provides as follows:

> Every person who, under color of [state law,] . . . subjects, or causes to be subjected, any citizen of the United States . . . to the deprivation of any rights, privileges, or immunities secured by the Constitution and laws, shall be liable to the party injured in an action at law . . . for redress. 42 U.S.C. § 1983 (1988).

Section 1981 states:

> All persons within the jurisdiction of the
> United States shall have the same right in every
> State and Territory to ... sue, be parties, give
> evidence, and to the full and equal benefit of
> all laws and proceedings for the security of per-
> sons and property as is enjoyed by white citi-
> zens. 42 U.S.C. § 1981 (1988).

I. Race Discrimination

Buffkins contends that the officers violated 42 U.S.C.
§ 1981 (1988) because they detained her solely on the
basis of her race. We disagree. Buffkins failed to show
that the officers' actions were racially motivated by
purposeful discrimination. The officers admittedly
identified Buffkins in part because of her race. We
conclude, however, that the officers' identification of
Buffkins was reasonable and nondiscriminatory in
light of the fact that her race matched the racial description of the person described in the tip. See *United
States v. Bautista*, 684 F.2d 1286, 1289 (9th Cir. 1982)
(police may detain a person for further investigation
when, together with other relevant facts, the person's
race matches the racial description of persons suspected of criminal activity), cert. denied, 459 U.S.
1211, 103 S.Ct. 1206, 75 L.Ed.2d 447 (1983).

II. Fourth Amendment Claim

Buffkins argues that the district court erred by directing a verdict in favor of the police officers on the
ground that they had a reasonable and articulable suspicion to detain her at the airport. We agree. We hold
as a matter of law that the seizure of Buffkins by the
police officers was illegal and violative of the plaintiff's constitutional right to be free from an unreasonable search and seizure. Thus, Buffkins is entitled to
redress under 42 U.S.C. § 1983.

    ... [The court ruled that the police made a Fourth
Amendment seizure of Buffkins; therefore, the court
went on to decide if the seizure was based on reasonable suspicion.]

    For the seizure of Buffkins to be constitutional
under the Fourth Amendment, the officers must have
had a reasonable articulable suspicion that she had
committed or was about to commit a crime. Reasonable suspicion must be formed before the seizure occurs. Although the officers did not need to have
probable cause before they seized Buffkins, they must

have had more than an unparticularized hunch or
suspicion that she was importing cocaine into the
Omaha area. To determine whether reasonable suspicion exists, it is necessary to consider the totality of
the circumstances. In *United States v. Sokolow*, 490
U.S. 1, 8, 109 S.Ct. 1581, 1586–87, 104 L.Ed.2d 1
(1989), the Supreme Court recognized that under
certain circumstances, "wholly lawful conduct might
justify the suspicion that criminal activity was afoot"
depending upon the "degree of suspicion that attaches to particular types of noncriminal acts."

    After viewing the totality of the circumstances in
the present case, we find the record totally devoid of
any facts or circumstances that would permit a finding
that the officers possessed a reasonable articulable suspicion that Buffkins was carrying drugs into the
Omaha area. Both officers testified that Buffkins did
not have any of the characteristics common to drug
couriers. The officers stopped Buffkins solely because
her race fit the racial description of the person described in the tip. Contrary to the district court's holding, Buffkins' race, apart from any other information
known to the officers, clearly could not create a reasonable and articulable suspicion of criminal activity.

    [In *United States v. Taylor*, 917 F.2d 1402 (6th Cir.
1990), Taylor, a black individual, was detained by
three plainclothes officers at the Memphis International Airport. At the time Taylor was stopped, he was
the only black person who had deplaned a flight arriving from Miami, Florida. At the evidentiary hearing, one of the officers who detained Taylor testified
that seventy-five percent of the people that the drug
task force follows are black. The Sixth Circuit held
that the detention was unlawful. The court noted that
"the agents were more apt to stop Taylor because of
his race" and that it could not "allow blacks and other
minorities to become subject to unreasonable stops
and governmental intrusions in airports because of
their race."]

    Innocent travellers cannot "be subject to virtually
random seizures" merely because of their race. The
officers could not have narrowed their suspicion to a
particular individual based on the tip alone. The tip
was very indefinite in that it did not state how many
individuals on the flight were involved in the illicit activity or give a physical description of the sex, height,
weight, clothing, or other characteristics of the per-

son[s] who would be carrying the drugs. In order to constitute a reasonable articulable suspicion the known facts must reasonably relate to the person about to be stopped and demonstrate a reasonable suspicion that the person has engaged or will engage in criminal activity. The officers also assert that prior to their approach of Buffkins, they noticed that Buffkins was carrying a teddy bear with seams that appeared to have been resewn. However, this additional fact cannot create a reasonable articulable suspicion. There is nothing suspicious about a passenger deplaning an airplane carrying a toy animal. Furthermore, Hollis left the airport without taking the bear with her. Officer Friend specifically testified at trial that a drug courier would have wanted to get the teddy bear out of the airport as soon as possible if it contained drugs.

[The defendants also argue that they believed that Hollis appeared nervous while waiting for the plane to land. However, nervousness alone would not have supplied the officers with the suspicion necessary for a *Terry*-type stop. See *United States v. Andrews*, 600 F.2d 563, 566 (6th Cir.) (nervousness is entitled to no weight because it is consistent with behavior of innocent airport travellers), cert. denied, 444 U.S. 878, 100 S.Ct. 166, 62 L.Ed.2d 108 (1979); *United States v. Gooding*, 695 F.2d 78, 84 (4th Cir. 1982).]

"Based upon the whole picture, [the officers could not have] . . . reasonably surmise[d] that . . . [Buffkins] was engaged in criminal activity." *Cortez*, 449 U.S. at 421–22, 101 S.Ct. at 696–97. Thus, we conclude that the officers did not, as a matter of law, possess any reasonable articulable suspicion to detain Buffkins in the manner described. We hold the district court erred in directing a verdict for the police officers on Buffkins' Fourth Amendment claim. [In a section 1983 action, the jury decides whether or not an individual has been seized within the meaning of the Fourth Amendment only if reasonable persons could differ on the conclusions to be drawn from the evidence. In the present case, however, no evidentiary facts exist that validate the officers' conduct in making the seizure and search.]

. . .

. . . [W]e affirm the district court's holding that the investigatory stop of Buffkins was not racially motivated. However, we hold the officers did not have a reasonable and articulable suspicion to effect a seizure of Buffkins as a matter of law. . . . Accordingly, the judgment of the district court is affirmed as to the dismissal of plaintiff's claim under section 1981 . . . and [we] remand all of plaintiff's other claims, both state and federal, to the district court for a new trial.

CASE DISCUSSION

List all the facts on which Officers Grigsby and Friend based their stop of Buffkins. How did the court arrive at the decision that the officers did not intentionally act on race discrimination? Do you think Grigsby and Friend's decision to stop Buffkins had to do with her race? Do you believe that the totality of circumstances, not including Buffkins' race, amount to reasonable suspicion as Chief Justice Burger defined it in *United States v. Cortez*, quoted on pages 148–149? Defend your answer, using the relevant facts from the case reported here.

Scope of Reasonable Stops

In 1968, when the United States Supreme Court established the constitutionality of street stops in *Terry v. Ohio*, the Court confined stops within narrow parameters. It gave officers the power to stop people without warrants and on less than probable cause only under the following specific circumstances:

1. A police officer directly observed suspicious behavior. In *Terry*, Officer McFadden himself had observed Terry and his companions walking up and down peering into a store window.

2. A police officer reasonably suspected a violent or other serious nonpossessory felony. In *Terry*, Officer McFadden suspected Terry of planning to commit armed robbery.

3. The detention was brief. Initially, Officer McFadden detained Terry for probably less than a minute; he grabbed him, spun him around, and frisked him.

4. The detention was on the spot; that is, the suspect was not moved from the immediate location of the stop. Terry was stopped on the street; he was moved after that into the nearest store only because Officer McFadden needed assistance.

5. The invasion of privacy and liberty was relatively mild. Officer McFadden made only a brief, on-the-spot stop and an outer clothing pat-down for weapons.

In other words, according to *Terry v. Ohio*, if law enforcement officers can point to specific facts arising out of their own direct observations that support their suspicion of violent crime, then it is reasonable to detain people briefly, on the spot, without their consent, in order to investigate the reasonable suspicions of the investigating officers. Four years after *Terry*, in *Adams v. Williams* (excerpted later in this chapter), the Court expanded the scope of lawful stops in two important ways. The suspected crime was the possession of illegal drugs, not a violent crime. The basis for reasonable suspicion was the word of an informant, not the officer's direct observation. Since *Adams v. Williams*, the number of street stops based on informant information conducted for the purpose of investigating possessory crimes has increased markedly.

Reasonableness requires that officers invade individual privacy and liberty only to the extent these invasions are required in order to gather enough information to decide among three alternatives:

1. Arrest suspects

2. Conduct further investigation

3. Release detained individuals

According to the Supreme Court, a court reviewing the reasonableness of stops must inquire "whether the officer's action was justified at its inception, and whether it was reasonably related in scope to the circumstances which justified the interference in the first place." Two actions "reasonably related in scope" are obtaining the stopped person's identity and "freezing" a suspicious situation for further investigation. Obtaining identification means getting a suspect's name and address. Police may also briefly question suspects about their presence and the circumstances at the scene that initiated the stop.

The Supreme Court has established that the proper scope of a lawful stop depends on four elements in the stop:

1. The *duration* of the stop—that is, how long officers detain suspects without their consent

2. The *location* of the stop, including both how public the place is where the stop takes place and whether officers move suspects before the officers have probable cause to arrest them

3. The *invasiveness* of the stop—that is, how intense the invasions were measured against the need to prevent and investigate the specific crime that prompted the stop

4. The *freedom* of suspects to walk away or to otherwise terminate the encounter and go about their business

The Supreme Court has refused to put a specific time limit on the duration of lawful stops. In *United States v. Sharpe*, the Court upheld a forty-five-minute stop as reasonable. According to the Court, "Much as a 'bright line' rule would be desirable, in evaluating whether an investigative detention is unreasonable, common sense and ordinary experience must govern over rigid criteria."[20]

Terry v. Ohio approved stops made for the purpose of preventing future crimes and intercepting crimes in progress. Both the prevention of crimes and the interruption of crimes in progress require immediate action that justifies watering down the probable cause and warrant requirements of the Fourth Amendment. The same urgency does not apply to the investigation of crimes already completed and "cold." Nevertheless, the Supreme Court has ruled that stops and frisks made for the purpose of investigating past crimes can be reasonable. In *United States v. Hensley*, the police stopped Hensley, who was named in a "wanted flier" distributed by a neighboring police department. The department suspected Hensley of driving the getaway car in a robbery that took place nearly two weeks before the police stopped him. The Sixth Circuit Court of Appeals ruled that *Terry* created only a narrow exception that strictly limits investigative stops to ongoing criminal activity. The Supreme Court overruled the Sixth Circuit. According to Justice O'Connor,

> . . . [T]he police are not shorn of authority to stop a suspect in the absence of probable cause merely because the criminal has completed his crime and escaped from the scene. The precise limits on investigatory stops to investigate past criminal activity are more difficult to define. The proper way to identify the limits is to apply the same test already used to identify the proper bounds of intrusions that further investigation of imminent or ongoing crimes. That test, which is grounded in the standard of reasonableness embodied in the Fourth Amendment, balances the nature and quality of the intrusion on personal security against the importance of the governmental interests alleged to justify the intrusion. When this balancing test is applied to stops to investigate past crimes, we think that probable cause to arrest need not always be applied.[21]

D e c i s i o n   P o i n t

The Supreme Court has held that a lawful stop can include the detention of all occupants in a house while police execute a search warrant for contraband.[22]

As Detroit police officers were about to execute a warrant to search a house for narcotics, they encountered Summers descending the front steps. They requested his assistance in gaining entry and detained him while they searched the premises. After finding narcotics in the basement and ascertaining that Summers owned the house, the police arrested him, searched his person, and found an envelope containing 8.5 grams of heroin in his coat pocket. In *Michigan v. Summers*, the United States Supreme Court held that "some seizures constitute such limited intrusions on the personal security of those detained and are justified by such substantial law enforcement interests that they may be made on less than probable cause, so long as police have an articulable basis for suspecting criminal activity." Since the police had a warrant to search Summers' house for contraband, that Summers owned the house constituted the facts necessary to justify the stop, "admittedly a significant restraint on his liberty."[23]

Officers who "freeze" suspicious situations to ask suspects "a few pertinent questions" ordinarily must restrict their activities to "on-the-spot" investigation. It is reasonable to ask suspects to step out of their cars or to sit in a patrol car while they are questioned. For example, in *United States v. Alvarez-Sanchez*, agents did not unlawfully stop Alvarez-Sanchez by asking him to accompany them to an administrative office fifteen feet from where they stopped him. However, it is not reasonable to transport suspects considerable distances from the place where the police stopped them.[24] According to the American Law Institute,

> The authority . . . is essentially an authority to immobilize a person, to keep contact with him, while a situation is sorted out, and a determination is made how further to proceed. This is expressed by the term [in the Model Code's provision] "remain in or near such place in the officer's presence." The concept is intended to be flexible.[25]

As for whether the scope of lawful stops of vehicles includes the authority to detain and move *passengers*, the United States Supreme Court decided that problem in *Maryland v. Wilson*.

C A S E

Were the Passengers Wrongfully Detained?

Maryland v. Wilson
117 S.Ct. 882 (1997)

Jerry Lee Wilson, a passenger in an automobile, moved to suppress crack cocaine obtained after a police officer ordered him to step out of the car during a traffic stop. The trial court granted the motion. The State appealed. The Maryland Court of Special Appeals affirmed. The State sought, and the Maryland Court of Appeals denied, certiorari. The State sought certiorari from the U.S. Supreme Court. After granting certiorari, the Supreme Court held that a police officer making a traffic stop may order passengers to get out of a car pending completion of the stop, and reversed and remanded the case. Justices Stevens and Kennedy dissented.

Rehnquist, C. J., delivered the opinion of the Court, in which O'Connor, Scalia, Souter, Thomas, Ginsburg, and Breyer, JJ., joined. Stevens, J., filed a dissenting opinion, in which Kennedy, J., joined. Kennedy, J., filed a dissenting opinion.

FACTS

At about 7:30 P.M. on a June evening, Maryland state trooper David Hughes observed a passenger car driving southbound on I-95 in Baltimore County at a speed of 64 miles per hour. The posted speed limit was 55 miles per hour, and the car had no regular license tag; there was a torn piece of paper reading "Enterprise Rent-A-Car" dangling from its rear. Hughes activated his lights and sirens, signaling the car to pull over, but it continued driving for another mile and a half until it finally did so.

During the pursuit, Hughes noticed that there were three occupants in the car and that the two passengers turned to look at him several times, repeatedly ducking below sight level and then reappearing. As Hughes approached the car on foot, the driver alighted and met him halfway. The driver was trembling and appeared extremely nervous, but nonetheless produced a valid Connecticut driver's license. Hughes instructed him to return to the car and retrieve the rental documents, and he complied. During this encounter, Hughes noticed that the front-seat passenger, respondent Jerry Lee Wilson, was sweating and also appeared extremely nervous. While the driver was sitting in the driver's seat looking for the rental papers, Hughes ordered Wilson out of the car.

When Wilson exited the car, a quantity of crack cocaine fell to the ground. Wilson was then arrested and charged with possession of cocaine with intent to distribute. Before trial, Wilson moved to suppress the evidence, arguing that Hughes' ordering him out of the car constituted an unreasonable seizure under the Fourth Amendment. The Circuit Court for Baltimore County agreed, and granted respondent's motion to suppress. On appeal, the Court of Special Appeals of Maryland affirmed, ruling that *Pennsylvania v. Mimms* does not apply to passengers. The Court of Appeals of Maryland denied certiorari. We granted certiorari, and now reverse.

OPINION

In *Mimms,* we considered a traffic stop much like the one before us today. There, Mimms had been stopped for driving with an expired license plate, and the officer asked him to step out of his car. When Mimms did so, the officer noticed a bulge in his jacket that proved to be a .38-caliber revolver, whereupon Mimms was arrested for carrying a concealed deadly weapon. Mimms, like Wilson, urged the suppression of the evidence on the ground that the officer's ordering him out of the car was an unreasonable seizure, and the Pennsylvania Supreme Court, like the Court of Special Appeals of Maryland, agreed.

We reversed, explaining that "[t]he touchstone of our analysis under the Fourth Amendment is always 'the reasonableness in all the circumstances of the particular governmental invasion of a citizen's personal security,'" and that reasonableness "depends 'on a balance between the public interest and the individual's right to personal security free from arbitrary interference by law officers.'" On the public interest side of the balance, we noted that the State "freely concede[d]" that there had been nothing unusual or suspicious to justify ordering Mimms out of the car, but that it was the officer's "practice to order all drivers [stopped in traffic stops] out of their vehicles as a matter of course" as a "precautionary measure" to protect the officer's safety. We thought it "too plain for argument" that this justification—officer safety—was "both legitimate and weighty." In addition, we observed that the danger to the officer of standing by the driver's door and in the path of oncoming traffic might also be "appreciable."

On the other side of the balance, we considered the intrusion into the driver's liberty occasioned by the officer's ordering him out of the car. Noting that the driver's car was already validly stopped for a traffic infraction, we deemed the additional intrusion of asking him to step outside his car "de minimis." Accordingly, we concluded that "once a motor vehicle has been lawfully detained for a traffic violation, the police officers may order the driver to get out of the vehicle without violating the Fourth Amendment's proscription of unreasonable seizures."

Respondent urges, and the lower courts agreed, that this per se rule does not apply to Wilson because he was a passenger, not the driver. . . . We must therefore now decide whether the rule of *Mimms* applies to passengers as well as to drivers. On the public interest side of the balance, the same weighty interest in officer safety is present regardless of whether the occupant of the stopped car is a driver or passenger. Regrettably, traffic stops may be dangerous encounters. In 1994 alone, there were 5,762 officer assaults and 11 officers killed during traffic pursuits and stops. Federal Bureau of Investigation, *Uniform Crime Reports: Law Enforcement Officers Killed and Assaulted* 71, 33 (1994). In the case of passengers, the danger of the officer's standing in the path of oncoming traffic would not be present except in the case of a passenger in the left rear seat, but the fact that there is more than one occupant of the vehicle increases the possible sources of harm to the officer.

On the personal liberty side of the balance, the case for the passengers is in one sense stronger than that for the driver. There is probable cause to believe that the driver has committed a minor vehicular offense, but there is no such reason to stop or detain the passengers. But as a practical matter, the passengers are already stopped by virtue of the stop of the vehicle. The only change in their circumstances which will result from ordering them out of the car is that they will be outside of, rather than inside of, the stopped car. Outside the car, the passengers will be denied access to any possible weapon that might be concealed in the interior of the passenger compartment. It would seem that the possibility of a violent encounter stems not from the ordinary reaction of a motorist stopped for a speeding violation, but from the fact that evidence of a more serious crime might be uncovered during the stop. And the motivation of a passenger to employ violence to prevent apprehension of such a crime is every bit as great as that of the driver.

. . .

In summary, danger to an officer from a traffic stop is likely to be greater when there are passengers in addition to the driver in the stopped car. While there is not the same basis for ordering the passengers out of the car as there is for ordering the driver out, the additional intrusion on the passenger is minimal. We therefore hold that an officer making a traffic stop may order passengers to get out of the car pending completion of the stop.

The judgment of the Court of Special Appeals of Maryland is reversed, and the case is remanded for proceedings not inconsistent with this opinion. It is so ordered.

DISSENT

Justice Stevens, joined by Justice Kennedy, dissented.

. . . My concern is not with the ultimate disposition of this particular case, but rather with the literally millions of other cases that will be affected by the rule the Court announces. Though the question is not before us, I am satisfied that—under the rationale of *Terry v. Ohio*, 392 U.S. 1, 88 S.Ct. 1868, 20 L.Ed.2d 889 (1968)—if a police officer conducting a traffic stop has an articulable suspicion of possible danger, the officer may order passengers to exit the vehicle as a defensive tactic without running afoul of the Fourth Amendment. Accordingly, I assume that the facts recited in the majority's opinion provided a valid justification for this officer's order commanding the passengers to get out of this vehicle. But the Court's ruling goes much farther. It applies equally to traffic stops in which there is not even a scintilla of evidence of any potential risk to the police officer. In those cases, I firmly believe that the Fourth Amendment prohibits routine and arbitrary seizures of obviously innocent citizens.

The majority suggests that the personal liberty interest at stake here . . . is outweighed by the need to ensure officer safety. The Court correctly observes that "traffic stops may be dangerous encounters." The magnitude of the danger to police officers is reflected

in the statistic that, in 1994 alone, "there were 5,762 officer assaults and 11 officers killed during traffic pursuits and stops." Ibid. There is, unquestionably, a strong public interest in minimizing the number of such assaults and fatalities. The Court's statistics, however, provide no support for the conclusion that its ruling will have any such effect.

Those statistics do not tell us how many of the incidents involved passengers. Assuming that many of the assaults were committed by passengers, we do not know how many occurred after the passenger got out of the vehicle, how many took place while the passenger remained in the vehicle, or indeed, whether any of them could have been prevented by an order commanding the passengers to exit. There is no indication that the number of assaults was smaller in jurisdictions where officers may order passengers to exit the vehicle without any suspicion than in jurisdictions where they were then prohibited from doing so. Indeed, there is no indication that any of the assaults occurred when there was a complete absence of any articulable basis for concern about the officer's safety—the only condition under which I would hold that the Fourth Amendment prohibits an order commanding passengers to exit a vehicle. In short, the statistics are as consistent with the hypothesis that ordering passengers to get out of a vehicle increases the danger of assault as with the hypothesis that it reduces that risk.

Furthermore, any limited additional risk to police officers must be weighed against the unnecessary invasion that will be imposed on innocent citizens under the majority's rule in the tremendous number of routine stops that occur each day. We have long recognized that "[b]ecause of the extensive regulation of motor vehicles and traffic . . . the extent of police–citizen contact involving automobiles will be substantially greater than police–citizen contact in a home or office." Most traffic stops involve otherwise law-abiding citizens who have committed minor traffic offenses. A strong interest in arriving at a destination—to deliver a patient to a hospital, to witness a kick-off, or to get to work on time—will often explain a traffic violation without justifying it. In the aggregate, these stops amount to significant law enforcement activity.

Indeed, the number of stops in which an officer is actually at risk is dwarfed by the far greater number of routine stops. If Maryland's share of the national total is about average, the State probably experiences about 100 officer assaults each year during traffic stops and pursuits. Making the unlikely assumption that passengers are responsible for one-fourth of the total assaults, it appears that the Court's new rule would provide a potential benefit to Maryland officers in only roughly 25 stops a year. These stops represent a minuscule portion of the total. In Maryland alone, there are something on the order of one million traffic stops each year. Assuming that there are passengers in about half of the cars stopped, the majority's rule is of some possible advantage to police in only about one out of every twenty thousand traffic stops in which there is a passenger in the car. And, any benefit is extremely marginal. In the overwhelming majority of cases posing a real threat, the officer would almost certainly have some ground to suspect danger that would justify ordering passengers out of the car.

In contrast, the potential daily burden on thousands of innocent citizens is obvious. That burden may well be "minimal" in individual cases. But countless citizens who cherish individual liberty and are offended, embarrassed, and sometimes provoked by arbitrary official commands may well consider the burden to be significant. In all events, the aggregation of thousands upon thousands of petty indignities has an impact on freedom that I would characterize as substantial, and which in my view clearly outweighs the evanescent safety concerns pressed by the majority.

The Court concludes today that the balance of convenience and danger that supported its holding in *Mimms* applies to passengers of lawfully stopped cars as well as drivers. In *Mimms* itself, however, the Court emphasized the fact that the intrusion into the driver's liberty at stake was "occasioned not by the initial stop of the vehicle, which was admittedly justified, but by the order to get out of the car." 434 U.S., at 111, 98 S.Ct., at 333. The conclusion that "this additional intrusion can only be described as de minimis" rested on the premise that the "police have already lawfully decided that the driver shall be briefly detained."

In this case as well, the intrusion on the passengers' liberty occasioned by the initial stop of the vehicle is not challenged. That intrusion was a necessary by-product of the lawful detention of the driver. But the passengers had not yet been seized at the time the car was pulled over, any more than a traffic jam

caused by construction or other state-imposed delay not directed at a particular individual constitutes a seizure of that person. The question is whether a passenger in a lawfully stopped car may be seized, by an order to get out of the vehicle, without any evidence whatsoever that he or she poses a threat to the officer or has committed an offense.

To order passengers about during the course of a traffic stop, insisting that they exit and remain outside the car, can hardly be classified as a de minimis intrusion. The traffic violation sufficiently justifies subjecting the driver to detention and some police control for the time necessary to conclude the business of the stop. The restraint on the liberty of blameless passengers that the majority permits is, in contrast, entirely arbitrary.

In my view, wholly innocent passengers in a taxi, bus, or private car have a constitutionally protected right to decide whether to remain comfortably seated within the vehicle rather than exposing themselves to the elements and the observation of curious bystanders. The Constitution should not be read to permit law enforcement officers to order innocent passengers about simply because they have the misfortune to be seated in a car whose driver has committed a minor traffic offense.

Unfortunately, the effect of the Court's new rule on the law may turn out to be far more significant than its immediate impact on individual liberty. Throughout most of our history the Fourth Amendment embodied a general rule requiring that official searches and seizures be authorized by a warrant, issued "upon probable cause, supported by Oath or affirmation, and particularly describing the place to be searched, and the persons or things to be seized." During the prohibition era, the exceptions for warrantless searches supported by probable cause started to replace the general rule. In 1968, in the landmark "stop and frisk" case *Terry v. Ohio*, the Court placed its stamp of approval on seizures supported by specific and articulable facts that did not establish probable cause. The Court crafted *Terry* as a narrow exception to the general rule that "the police must, whenever practicable, obtain advance judicial approval of searches and seizures through the warrant procedure." The intended scope of the Court's major departure from prior practice was reflected in its statement that the "demand for specificity in the information upon which police action is predicated is the central teaching of this Court's Fourth Amendment jurisprudence." In the 1970's, the Court twice rejected attempts to justify suspicionless seizures that caused only "modest" intrusions on the liberty of passengers in automobiles. Today, however, the Court takes the unprecedented step of authorizing seizures that are unsupported by any individualized suspicion whatsoever.

The Court's conclusion seems to rest on the assumption that the constitutional protection against "unreasonable" seizures requires nothing more than a hypothetically rational basis for intrusions on individual liberty. How far this ground-breaking decision will take us, I do not venture to predict. I fear, however, that it may pose a more serious threat to individual liberty than the Court realizes.

I respectfully dissent.

Justice Kennedy, dissenting.

I join in the dissent by Justice Stevens and add these few observations. The distinguishing feature of our criminal justice system is its insistence on principled, accountable decisionmaking in individual cases. If a person is to be seized, a satisfactory explanation for the invasive action ought to be established by an officer who exercises reasoned judgment under all the circumstances of the case. This principle can be accommodated even where officers must make immediate decisions to insure their own safety.

Traffic stops, even for minor violations, can take upwards of 30 minutes. When an officer commands passengers innocent of any violation to leave the vehicle and stand by the side of the road in full view of the public, the seizure is serious, not trivial. As Justice Stevens concludes, the command to exit ought not to be given unless there are objective circumstances making it reasonable for the officer to issue the order. (We do not have before us the separate question whether passengers, who, after all are in the car by choice, can be ordered to remain there for a reasonable time while the police conduct their business.)

The requisite showing for commanding passengers to exit need be no more than the existence of any circumstance justifying the order in the interests of the officer's safety or to facilitate a lawful search or investigation. As we have acknowledged for decades, special latitude is given to the police in effecting searches and seizures involving vehicles and their occupants. Just last Term we adhered to a rule permitting vehicle stops if there is some objective indication that a violation has been committed, regardless of the officer's real motives. We could discern no other, workable rule. Even so, we insisted on a reasoned explanation for the stop.

The practical effect of our holding in *Whren* [*v. U.S.*, excerpted and discussed in Chapter 6], of course, is to allow the police to stop vehicles in almost countless circumstances. When *Whren* is coupled with today's holding, the Court puts tens of millions of passengers at risk of arbitrary control by the police. If the command to exit were to become commonplace, the Constitution would be diminished in a most public way. As the standards suggested in dissent are adequate to protect the safety of the police, we ought not to suffer so great a loss.

Since a myriad of circumstances will give a cautious officer reasonable grounds for commanding passengers to leave the vehicle, it might be thought the rule the Court adopts today will be little different in its operation than the rule offered in dissent. It does no disservice to police officers, however, to insist upon exercise of reasoned judgment. Adherence to neutral principles is the very premise of the rule of law the police themselves defend with such courage and dedication.

Most officers, it might be said, will exercise their new power with discretion and restraint; and no doubt this often will be the case. It might also be said that if some jurisdictions use today's ruling to require passengers to exit as a matter of routine in every stop, citizen complaints and political intervention will call for an end to the practice. These arguments, however, would miss the point. Liberty comes not from officials by grace but from the Constitution by right.

For these reasons, and with all respect for the opinion of the Court, I dissent.

CASE DISCUSSION

List the specific invasions that the stop imposed on Jimmy Lee Wilson. Summarize the arguments of the majority for its decision that removing passengers is within the scope of lawful stops of vehicles. How do the dissenting justices answer these arguments? Which side has the better arguments? Defend your answer.

If officers detain suspects for an "unreasonably" long time or move them an "unreasonable" distance from the place they have stopped them or "unreasonably" interfere with suspects' freedom to depart or terminate the investigative detention, the stop becomes a full-blown arrest. For example, in *Florida v. Royer,* when police escorted Royer to a small room in an airport, took his airline ticket and identification, and retrieved his luggage, he was not free to leave and hence was arrested, not stopped.[26] (*Florida v. Royer* is excerpted in Chapter 5.)

In *Hayes v. Florida,* police were investigating a series of rape–burglaries. They went to Hayes's house, where they asked Hayes to accompany them to the police station for fingerprinting. At first he refused. When the officers threatened to arrest him if he did not accompany them voluntarily, he "blurted out" that he would rather go with them than face arrest. The fingerprints linked him to one of the crimes, and he was later convicted. Sustaining Hayes's claim that the seizure was unlawful, the Supreme Court held that

> [T]here was no probable cause to arrest, no consent to the journey to the police station, and no judicial authorization for such a detention for fingerprinting purposes. . . . [T]ransportation to and investigative detention at the station house without probable cause or judicial authorization together violate the Fourth Amendment. . . . There is no doubt that at some point in the investigative process, police procedures can qualitatively and quantitatively be so intrusive with respect to a suspect's freedom of movement and privacy interests as to trigger the full protection of the Fourth and Fourteenth Amendments. . . . [O]ur view [is] that the line is crossed when the police, without probable cause or warrant, forcibly remove a person from his home or other place in which he is entitled to be and transport him to the police station, where he is detained, although briefly, for investigative purposes. We adhere to the view that such seizures, at least where not under judicial supervision, are sufficiently like arrests to invoke the traditional rule that arrests may constitutionally be made only on probable cause.

Although several justices did not agree, the opinion went on to remark:

> None of the foregoing implies that a brief detention in the field for the purpose of fingerprinting, where there is only reasonable suspicion not amounting to probable cause, is necessarily impermissible under the Fourth Amendment. . . . There is support in our cases for the view that the Fourth Amendment would permit seizures for the purpose of fingerprinting, if there is reasonable suspicion that the suspect has committed a criminal act, if there is a reasonable basis for believing that fingerprinting will establish or negate the suspect's connection with that crime, and if the procedure is carried out with dispatch. . . .
>
> We also do not abandon the suggestion . . . that under circumscribed procedures, the Fourth Amendment might permit the judiciary to authorize the seizure of a person on less than probable cause and his removal to the police station for the purpose of fingerprinting. We do not, of course, have such a case before us. We do note, however, that some states . . . have enacted procedures for judicially authorized seizures for the purpose of fingerprinting. . . .[27]

D e c i s i o n   P o i n t

1. In *United States v. Sharpe*, 470 U.S. 675, 105 S.Ct. 1568, 84 L.Ed. 2d 605 (1985), agent Cooke of the DEA became suspicious of a pickup truck and a car traveling in tandem on a highway near a beach. He followed the two vehicles for twenty miles. He decided to make an "investigative stop" and radioed the state highway patrol for assistance. Officer Thrasher responded to the call. Cooke and Thrasher, each in his own vehicle, followed the truck and car for a time, then motioned them to pull off the side of the road. The car stopped, but the truck continued on the highway. Cooke approached the stopped car; Thrasher followed the truck. Cooke identified himself and asked for identification from the driver, Sharpe. Then Cooke attempted to radio Thrasher to find out if he had stopped the truck. Unable to reach Thrasher for several minutes, Cooke radioed local police for assistance. They arrived in about ten minutes. Cooke asked them to "maintain the situation" while he left to join Thrasher. In the meantime, Thrasher had stopped the truck about a half mile down the road. He approached the truck with his revolver drawn. He ordered the driver, Savage, to get out and assume a spread-eagle position against the side of the truck, then patted him down. Cooke arrived on the scene about fifteen minutes after Thrasher stopped the truck. Cooke put his nose to the truck and said he smelled marijuana. He then sought permission to look in the truck for marijuana. At this point, about twenty minutes had elapsed since the stop. Without Savage's permission, Cooke took the keys from the ignition, opened the rear of the truck, and discovered marijuana. Cooke returned to the car and arrested Sharpe. Approximately thirty to forty minutes had elapsed between the time Cooke stopped the car and the time he arrested Sharpe.

Were Sharpe's and Savage's stops lawful? The United States Supreme Court ruled that since the officers "diligently pursued a means of investigation that was likely to confirm or dispel their suspicions quickly, during which time it was necessary to detain" him, the stop of Savage was reasonable. Would you apply the Model Code twenty-minute limit to both stops?

2. In *Ebona v. State*, 577 P.2d 698 (Alaska 1978), two Juneau, Alaska, police officers observed Ebona sway as he walked down a Juneau street. Ebona got in his car. As he drove, his car swerved from the center lane to the right edge of the street. It did not at any time swerve into the oncoming traffic lane. The officers stopped the car and asked Ebona to get out. Ebona's eyes were bloodshot, his speech was slurred, an odor of alcohol was on his breath, and he was weaving back and forth. After performing sobriety checks, the officer arrested Ebona.

Was the stop lawful? Yes, according to the Alaska Supreme Court:

[A] police officer with a reasonable suspicion that imminent public danger exists or that serious harm that has recently occurred was caused by a particular person may stop that person.... [T]he Alaska rule, permitting a temporary stop when the officer has a reasonable suspicion that imminent public danger exists, or serious harm to persons or property has recently occurred, is ... more restrictive than the rule articulated by the Supreme Court in *Terry* [*v. Ohio*]. ... The significant dangers to persons or property that can possibly result when the operator's capacity to control a motor vehicle is impaired are apparent. A vehicle out of control, even on a relatively deserted street, poses a significant threat to property or individuals in proximity to the vehicle. Thus, we conclude that the record demonstrates that at the time in question Officer Smith had a suspicion that an imminent public danger existed by virtue of the manner in which the Ebona vehicle was being operated.

Remaining for resolution is the question whether Officer Smith's suspicion that an imminent public danger existed was reasonable in light of all the facts known to the officer prior to the investigatory stop of Ebona's vehicle. Here the test is an objective one: whether the facts known to the officer at the time of the stop would cause a reasonable person to have a suspicion that the manner in which the Ebona vehicle was being operated posed a threat of imminent public danger. We conclude that there is a sufficient evidentiary basis to sustain a holding that Officer Smith's suspicion of imminent public danger was reasonable in light of all the circumstances known to him prior to the making of the investigatory stop.

Stops at International Borders

Two kinds of Fourth Amendment stops—investigations at international borders to interdict drug traffic and roadblocks to prevent and detect drunk drivers—have aroused controversy. From the foundation of the government, United States Customs officers have had the power to search travelers who cross our borders without probable cause. According to the Supreme Court, the strong government need to control what and who enters the country lessens the privacy interests of international travelers, especially of aliens, and reduces the quantum of proof required to stop travelers who cross the borders into the United States. Opening suitcases for cursory inspection does not stir a great deal of controversy, but detentions for extensive questioning and searches of persons, particularly strip and body-cavity searches, have aroused major opposition. Border stops, and the controversy surrounding them, have taken on added significance as the government relies on them to intercept illegal drug smuggling and apprehend drug smugglers. The most controversial cases arise over "balloon swallowers," smugglers who bring drugs into the country in their alimentary canals, or couriers who hide drugs in their rectums or vaginas. The United States Supreme Court addressed the application of the Fourth Amendment to detentions at international borders for purposes of investigating "balloon swallowers" in *United States v. Montoya de Hernandez*.[28]

C A S E

Was the Detention Reasonable?

United States v. Montoya de Hernandez
473 U.S. 531, 105 S.Ct. 3304,
87 L.Ed.2d 381 (1985)

Montoya de Hernandez was charged with narcotics violations. She moved to suppress the narcotics; the district court denied the motion and admitted the cocaine in evidence. Montoya de Hernandez was convicted of possessing cocaine with intent to distribute and unlawful importation of cocaine. A divided court of appeals reversed the conviction. The government appealed to the United States Supreme Court. The Supreme Court reversed. *Justice Rehnquist wrote the opinion of the court, in which Chief Justice Burger and Justices White, Blackmun, Powell, and O'Connor joined. Justice Stevens filed an opinion concurring in the judgment. Justice Brennan filed a dissenting opinion, in which Justice Marshall joined.*

FACTS

Respondent arrived at Los Angeles International Airport shortly after midnight, March 5, 1983, on Avianca Flight 080, a direct 10-hour flight from

Bogota, Colombia. Her visa was in order so she was passed through Immigration and proceeded to the customs desk. At the customs desk she encountered Customs Inspector Talamantes, who reviewed her documents and noticed from her passport that she had made at least eight recent trips to either Miami or Los Angeles. Talamantes referred respondent to a secondary customs desk for further questioning. At this desk Talamantes and another inspector asked respondent general questions concerning herself and the purpose of her trip. Respondent revealed that she spoke no English and had no family or friends in the United States. She explained in Spanish that she had come to the United States to purchase goods for her husband's store in Bogota. The customs inspectors recognized Bogota as a "source city" for narcotics. Respondent possessed $5,000 in cash, mostly $50 bills, but had no billfold. She indicated to the inspectors that she had no appointments with merchandise vendors, but planned to ride around Los Angeles in taxicabs visiting retail stores such as J. C. Penney and K-Mart in order to buy goods for her husband's store with the $5,000.

Respondent admitted that she had no hotel reservations, but stated that she planned to stay at a Holiday Inn. Respondent could not recall how her airline ticket was purchased. When the inspectors opened respondent's one small valise they found about four changes of "cold weather" clothing. Respondent had no shoes other than the high-heeled pair she was wearing. Although respondent possessed no checks, waybills, credit cards, or letters of credit, she did produce a Colombian business card and a number of old receipts, waybills, and fabric swatches displayed in a photo album.

At this point Talamantes and the other inspector suspected that respondent was a "balloon swallower," one who attempts to smuggle narcotics into this country hidden in her alimentary canal. Over the years Inspector Talamantes had apprehended dozens of alimentary canal smugglers arriving on Avianca Flight 080. . . .

The inspectors requested a female customs inspector to take respondent to a private area and conduct a pat down and strip search. During the search the female inspector felt respondent's abdomen area and noticed a firm fullness, as if respondent were wearing a girdle. The search revealed no contraband, but the inspector noticed that respondent was wearing two pairs of elastic underpants with a paper towel lining the crotch area.

When respondent returned to the customs area and the female inspector reported her discoveries, the inspector in charge told respondent that he suspected she was smuggling drugs in her alimentary canal. . . . The inspector then gave respondent the option of returning to Colombia on the next available flight, agreeing to an x-ray, or remaining in detention until she produced a monitored bowel movement that would confirm or rebut the inspectors' suspicions. Respondent chose the first option and was placed in a customs office under observation. She was told that if she went to the toilet she would have to use a wastebasket in the women's restroom, in order that female inspectors could inspect her stool for balloons or capsules carrying narcotics. The inspectors refused respondent's request to place a telephone call. . . .

Respondent sat in the customs office, under observation, for the remainder of the night. . . . She remained detained in the customs office under observation, for most of the time curled up in a chair leaning to one side. She refused all offers of food and drink, and refused to use the toilet facilities. The Court of Appeals noted that she exhibited symptoms of discomfort with "heroic efforts to resist the usual calls of nature." . . .

At the shift change at 4:00 . . . the next afternoon, almost 16 hours after her flight had landed, respondent still had not defecated or urinated or partaken of food or drink. At that time customs officials sought a court order authorizing . . . [a]n x-ray, and a rectal examination. The Federal Magistrate issued an order just before midnight that evening, which authorized a rectal examination and involuntary x-ray. . . . A physician conducted a rectal examination and removed from respondent's rectum a balloon containing a foreign substance. Respondent was then placed formally under arrest. By 4:10 A.M. respondent had passed 6 similar balloons; over the next four days she passed 88 balloons containing a total of 528 grams of 80% pure cocaine hydrochloride.

After a suppression hearing the District Court admitted the cocaine in evidence against respondent. She was convicted of possession of cocaine with intent to distribute . . . [a]nd unlawful importation of cocaine. . . . A divided panel of the United States Court of Appeals for the Ninth Circuit reversed respondent's convictions. . . .

OPINION

The Fourth Amendment commands that searches and seizures be reasonable. What is reasonable depends upon all of the circumstances surrounding the search or seizure itself. . . . The permissibility of a particular law enforcement practice is judged by "balancing its intrusion on the individual's Fourth Amendment interest against its promotion of legitimate governmental interests." . . .

Here the seizure of respondent took place at the international border. Since the founding of our Republic, Congress has granted the Executive plenary authority to conduct routine searches and seizures at the border, without probable cause or a warrant, in order to regulate the collection of duties and to prevent the introduction of contraband into this - country. . . .

. . . [T]he Fourth Amendment's balance of reasonableness is qualitatively different at the international border than in the interior. Routine searches of the persons and effects of entrants are not subject to any requirement of reasonable suspicion, probable cause, or warrant, and first-class mail may be opened without a warrant on less than probable cause. . . .

These cases reflect longstanding concern for the protection of the integrity of the border. This concern is, if anything, heightened by the veritable national crisis in law enforcement caused by smuggling of illicit narcotics . . . [a]nd in particular by the increasing utilization of alimentary canal smuggling. This desperate practice appears to be a relatively recent addition to the smugglers' repertoire of deceptive practices, and it also appears to be exceedingly difficult to detect. . . .

Balanced against the sovereign's interests at the border are the Fourth Amendment rights of respondent. Having presented herself at the border for admission, and having subjected herself to the criminal enforcement powers of the Federal Government, . . . [r]espondent was entitled to be free from unreasonable search and seizure. But not only is this expectation of privacy less at the border than in the interior, . . . [t]he Fourth Amendment balance between the interests of the Government and the privacy right of the individual is also struck much more favorably to the Government at the border. . . .

We have not previously decided what level of suspicion would justify a seizure of an incoming traveler for purposes other than a routine border search. . . . The Court of Appeals viewed "clear indication" as an intermediate standard between "reasonable suspicion" and "probable cause." . . . No other court, including this one, has ever adopted . . . "[c]lear indication" language as a Fourth Amendment standard. . . . We do not think that the Fourth Amendment's emphasis upon reasonableness is consistent with the creation of a third verbal standard in addition to "reasonable suspicion" and "probable cause." . . .

We hold that detention of a traveler at the border, beyond the scope of a routine customs search and inspection, is justified at its inception if customs agents, considering all the facts surrounding the traveler and her trip, reasonably suspect that the traveler is smuggling contraband in her alimentary canal. . . . The facts, and their rational inferences, known to customs inspectors in this case clearly supported a reasonable suspicion that respondent was an alimentary canal smuggler. . . . The trained customs inspectors had encountered many alimentary canal smugglers and certainly had more than an "inchoate and unparticularized suspicion or 'hunch,'" . . . [t]hat respondent was smuggling narcotics in her alimentary canal. The inspectors' suspicion was a "'common-sense conclusio[n] about human behavior' upon which 'practical people,' . . . including government officials, are entitled to rely." . . .

The final issue in this case is whether the detention of respondent was reasonably related in scope to the circumstances which justified it initially. In this regard we have cautioned that courts should not indulge in "unrealistic second-guessing," . . . [a]nd we have noted that "creative judge[s], engaged in post hoc evaluations of police conduct can almost always imagine some alternative means by which the objectives of the police might have been accomplished." . . . The rudimentary knowledge of the human body which judges possess in common with the rest of humankind tells us that alimentary canal smuggling cannot be detected in the amount of time in which other illegal activity may be investigated through brief *Terry*-type stops. [*Terry v. Ohio* (1968).] It presents few, if any external signs; a quick frisk will not do, nor will even a strip search.

In the case of respondent the inspectors had available, as an alternative to simply awaiting her bowel movement, an x-ray. They offered her the alternative of submitting herself to that procedure. But when she refused that alternative, the customs inspectors were left with only two practical alternatives: detain her for such a time as necessary to confirm their suspicions, a detention which would last much longer than the typical *Terry* stop, or turn her loose into the interior carrying the reasonably suspected contraband drugs. . . . The inspectors in this case followed this former procedure. They no doubt expected that respondent, having recently disembarked from [a] 10-hour direct flight with a full and stiff abdomen, would produce a bowel movement without extended delay. But her visible efforts to resist the call of nature, which the court below labeled "heroic," disappointed this expectation and in turn caused her humiliation and discomfort.

Our prior cases have refused to charge police with delays in investigatory detention attributable to the suspect's evasive actions. . . . Respondent alone was responsible for much of the duration and discomfort of the seizure. Under these circumstances, we conclude that the detention was not unreasonably long. It occurred at the international border, where the Fourth Amendment balance of interests leans heavily to the Government. . . . Respondent's detention was long, uncomfortable indeed, humiliating; but both its length and its discomfort resulted solely from the method by which she chose to smuggle illicit drugs into this country. . . .

CONCURRING OPINION

Justice Stevens, concurring in the judgment.

If a seizure and search of the person of the kind disclosed by this record may be made on the basis of reasonable suspicion, we must assume that a significant number of innocent persons will be required to undergo similar procedures. The rule announced in this case cannot, therefore, be supported on the ground that respondent's prolonged and humiliating detention "resulted solely from the method by which she chose to smuggle illicit drugs into this country." . . . The prolonged detention of respondent was, however, justified by a different choice that respondent made; she withdrew her consent to an x-ray examination that would have easily determined whether the reasonable suspicion that she was concealing contraband was justified. . . .

DISSENT

Justice Brennan, with whom Justice Marshall joins, dissenting.

We confront a "disgusting and saddening episode" at our Nation's border. . . . "[T]hat the [respondent] so degraded herself as to offend the sensibilities of any decent citizen is not questioned." That is not what we face. For "[i]t is a fair summary of history to say that the safeguards of liberty have frequently been forged in controversies involving not very nice people." . . . The standards we fashion to govern the ferreting out of the guilty apply equally to the detention of the innocent, and "may be exercised by the most unfit and ruthless officers as well as by the fit and reasonable." . . . Nor is the issue whether there is a "veritable national crisis in law enforcement caused by smuggling illicit narcotics." . . . "[I]n our democracy such enforcement presupposes a moral atmosphere and a reliance upon intelligence whereby the effective administration of justice can be achieved with due regard for those civilized standards in the use of the criminal law which are formulated in our Bill of Rights."

The issue, instead, is simply this: Does the Fourth Amendment permit an international traveler, citizen or alien, to be subjected to the sort of treatment that occurred in this case without the sanction of a judicial officer and based on nothing more than the "reasonable suspicion" of low ranking investigative officers that something might be amiss? The Court today concludes that the Fourth Amendment grants such sweeping and unmonitored authority to customs officials. . . . I dissent.

Indefinite involuntary incommunicado detentions "for investigation" are the hallmark of a police state, not a free society. . . . In my opinion, Government officials may no more confine a person at the border under such circumstances for purposes of criminal investigation than they may within the interior of the country. The nature and duration of the detention here may well have been tolerable for spoiled meat or diseased animals, but not for human beings held on simple suspicion of criminal activity. . . . Finally, I believe that the warrant and probable cause safeguards equally govern Justice Stevens' proffered alternative of exposure to x-irradiation for criminal investigative purposes. . . .

. . . [T]he available evidence suggests that the number of highly intrusive border searches of suspicious-looking but ultimately innocent travelers may be very high. One physician who at the request of customs officials conducted many "internal searches" — rectal and vaginal examinations and stomach pumping — estimated that he had found contraband in 15 to 20 percent of the persons he had examined. It has similarly been estimated that only 16 percent of women subjected to body cavity searches at the border were in fact found to be carrying contraband. It is precisely to minimize the risk of harassing so many innocent people that the Fourth Amendment requires the intervention of a judicial officer. . . .

The Court argues, however, that the length and "discomfort" of de Hernandez' detention "resulted solely from the method by which she chose to smuggle illicit drugs into this country," and it speculates that only her "heroic" efforts prevented the detention from being brief and to the point. . . . Although we now know that de Hernandez was indeed guilty of smuggling drugs internally, such post hoc rationalizations have no place in our Fourth Amendment jurisprudence, which demands that we "prevent hindsight from coloring the evaluation of the reasonableness of a search or seizure." . . . At the time the authorities simply had, at most, a reasonable suspi-

cion that de Hernandez might be engaged in such smuggling.

Neither the law of the land nor the law of nature supports the notion that petty government officials can require people to excrete on command; indeed, the Court relies elsewhere on "[t]he rudimentary knowledge of the human body" in sanctioning the "much longer than . . . typical" duration of detentions such as this. And, with all respect to the Court, it is not "unreasonable second-guessing," to predict that an innocent traveler, locked away in incommunicado detention in unfamiliar surroundings in a foreign land, might well be frightened and exhausted as to be unable so to "cooperate" with the authorities. . . . It is tempting, of course, to look the other way in a case that so graphically illustrates the "veritable national crisis" caused by narcotics trafficking. But if there is one enduring lesson to be learned in the long struggle to balance individual rights against society's need to defend itself against lawlessness, it is that

> [i]t is easy to make light of insistence on scrupulous regard for the safeguards of civil liberties when invoked on behalf of the unworthy. It is too easy. History bears testimony that by such disregard are the rights of liberty extinguished, heedlessly at first, then stealthily, and brazenly in the end.

CASE DISCUSSION

What interests is the Court balancing in this case? Do you think that the majority or the dissent balanced them properly? Can a detention for this length of time ever constitute a lawful stop? Why? Why not? Could you write a rule that gives police and other law enforcement officers adequate guidance for how long they can detain suspects? Are the efforts to produce a bowel movement and the close observation to discover its contents an unwarranted invasion on human dignity? What, if anything, justifies such indignities?

Roadblocks

Are roadblocks—barricades set up for stopping vehicles and questioning their occupants—voluntary encounters or Fourth Amendment seizures? The government sets up vehicle roadblocks in order to question the occupants and/or inspect their vehicles for a wide range of purposes, including these:

- Driver's license and vehicle safety checks
- Weigh stations for trucks
- Game warden road checks
- Agricultural inspection stops
- Roadblocks established to solve a specific crime
- Border stops to check for smuggled goods, contraband, and/or illegal aliens
- Sobriety checkpoints
- Drug stops to check for the possession and transport of illegal drugs

Roadblocks to apprehend fleeing felons have a long history, and the courts have confirmed their legality. Roadblocks to check compliance with vehicle safety requirements also have a considerable history. Roadblocks to prevent illegal aliens from entering the country, or to apprehend them if they have entered, are also legal. More recently, and amid much more controversy, roadblocks to deter drunk driving and to apprehend drivers who are driving while intoxicated have become established law enforcement practice in some communities. The Supreme Court dealt with the application of the Fourth Amendment to random DWI roadblocks in *Michigan v. Sitz.*[29]

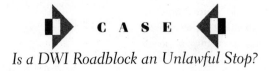

C A S E

Is a DWI Roadblock an Unlawful Stop?

Michigan v. Sitz
496 U.S. 444, 110 S.Ct. 2481 (1990)

Sitz and other drivers brought an action to challenge the constitutionality of a highway sobriety checkpoint program. The Circuit Court of Wayne County, Michigan, invalidated the program, and the Michigan Department of State Police appealed. The Court of Appeals of Michigan affirmed. The U.S. Supreme Court granted certiorari. The Supreme Court reversed and remanded the case. Chief Justice Rehnquist wrote the opinion of the Court, in which Justices White, O'Connor, Scalia, and Kennedy joined. Justice Blackmun filed an opinion concurring in the judgment. Justice Brennan filed a dissenting opinion, in which

Justice Marshall joined. Justice Stevens filed a dissenting opinion, in which Justices Brennan and Marshall joined in part.

FACTS

Petitioners, the Michigan Department of State Police and its Director, established a sobriety checkpoint pilot program in early 1986. The Director appointed a Sobriety Checkpoint Advisory Committee comprising representatives of the State Police force, local police forces, state prosecutors, and the University of Michigan Transportation Research Institute. Pursuant to its charge, the Advisory Committee created guidelines setting forth procedures governing checkpoint operations, site selection, and publicity. Under the guidelines, checkpoints would be set up at selected sites along state roads. All vehicles passing through a checkpoint would be stopped and their drivers briefly examined for signs of intoxication. In cases where a checkpoint officer detected signs of intoxication, the motorist would be directed to a location out of the traffic flow where an officer would check the motorist's driver's license and car registration and, if warranted, conduct further sobriety tests. Should the field tests and the officer's observations suggest that the driver was intoxicated, an arrest would be made. All other drivers would be permitted to resume their journey immediately.

The first—and to date the only—sobriety checkpoint operated under the program was conducted in Saginaw County with the assistance of the Saginaw County Sheriff's Department. During the hour-and-fifteen-minute duration of the checkpoint's operation, 126 vehicles passed through the checkpoint. The average delay for each vehicle was approximately 25 seconds. Two drivers were detained for field sobriety testing, and one of the two was arrested for driving under the influence of alcohol. A third driver who drove through without stopping was pulled over by an officer in an observation vehicle and arrested for driving under the influence.

On the day before the operation of the Saginaw County checkpoint, respondents filed a complaint in the Circuit Court of Wayne County seeking declaratory and injunctive relief from potential subjection to the checkpoints. Each of the respondents "is a licensed driver in the State of Michigan . . . who regularly travels throughout the State in his automobile." During pretrial proceedings, petitioners agreed to delay further implementation of the checkpoint program pending the outcome of this litigation.

After the trial, at which the court heard extensive testimony concerning, *inter alia*, the "effectiveness" of highway sobriety checkpoint programs, the court ruled that the Michigan program violated the Fourth Amendment and Art. 1, § 11, of the Michigan Constitution. On appeal, the Michigan Court of Appeals affirmed the holding that the program violated the Fourth Amendment and, for that reason, did not consider whether the program violated the Michigan

Constitution. After the Michigan Supreme Court denied petitioners' application for leave to appeal, we granted certiorari.

To decide this case the trial court performed a balancing test derived from our opinion in *Brown v. Texas* (1979). As described by the Court of Appeals, the test involved "balancing the state's interest in preventing accidents caused by drunk drivers, the effectiveness of sobriety checkpoints in achieving that goal, and the level of intrusion on an individual's privacy caused by the checkpoints." The Court of Appeals agreed that "the *Brown* three-prong balancing test was the correct test to be used to determine the constitutionality of the sobriety checkpoint plan." As characterized by the Court of Appeals, the trial court's findings with respect to the balancing factors were that the State has "a grave and legitimate" interest in curbing drunken driving; that sobriety checkpoint programs are generally "ineffective" and, therefore, do not significantly further that interest; and that the checkpoints' "subjective intrusion" on individual liberties is substantial. According to the court, the record disclosed no basis for disturbing the trial court's findings, which were made within the context of an analytical framework prescribed by this Court for determining the constitutionality of seizures less intrusive than traditional arrests.

OPINION

Petitioners concede, correctly in our view, that a Fourth Amendment "seizure" occurs when a vehicle is stopped at a checkpoint. . . . The question thus becomes whether such seizures are "reasonable" under the Fourth Amendment.

. . . We address only the initial stop of each motorist passing through a checkpoint and the associated preliminary questioning and observation by checkpoint officers. Detention of particular motorists for more extensive field sobriety testing may require satisfaction of an individualized suspicion standard. No one can seriously dispute the magnitude of the drunken driving problem or the States' interest in eradicating it. . . . "Drunk drivers cause an annual death toll of over 25,000 and in the same time span cause nearly one million personal injuries and more than five billion dollars in property damage." For decades, this Court has "repeatedly lamented the tragedy."

Conversely, the weight bearing on the other scale—the measure of the intrusion on motorists stopped briefly at sobriety checkpoints—is slight. . . . The trial court and the Court of Appeals, thus, accurately gauged the "objective" intrusion, measured by the duration of the seizure and the intensity of the investigation, as minimal.

With respect to what it perceived to be the "subjective" intrusion on motorists, however, the Court of Appeals found such intrusion substantial. The court first affirmed the trial court's finding that the guidelines governing checkpoint operation minimize the discretion of the officers on the scene. But the court also agreed with the trial court's conclusion that the checkpoints have the potential to generate fear and surprise in motorists. This was so because the record failed to demonstrate that approaching motorists would be aware of their option to make U-turns or turnoffs to avoid the checkpoints. On that basis, the court deemed the subjective intrusion from the checkpoints unreasonable.

We believe the Michigan courts misread our cases concerning the degree of "subjective intrusion" and the potential for generating fear and surprise. The "fear and surprise" to be considered are not the natural fear of one who has been drinking over the prospect of being stopped at a sobriety checkpoint but, rather, the fear and surprise engendered in law-abiding motorists by the nature of the stop. . . .

The Court of Appeals went on to consider as part of the balancing analysis the "effectiveness" of the proposed checkpoint program. Based on extensive testimony in the trial record, the court concluded that the checkpoint program failed the "effectiveness" part of the test, and that this failure materially discounted petitioners' strong interest in implementing the program. We think the Court of Appeals was wrong on this point as well. . . . Experts in police science might disagree over which of several methods of apprehending drunken drivers is preferable as an ideal. But for purposes of Fourth Amendment analysis, the choice among such reasonable alternatives remains with the governmental officials who have a unique understanding of, and a responsibility for, limited public resources, including a finite number of police officers.

. . . [T]his case involves neither a complete absence of empirical data nor a challenge of random highway stops. During the operation of the Saginaw County checkpoint, the detention of each of the 126 vehicles that entered the checkpoint resulted in the arrest of two drunken drivers. Stated as a percentage, approximately 1.5 percent of the drivers passing through the checkpoint were arrested for alcohol impairment. In addition, an expert witness testified at the trial that experience in other states demonstrated that, on the whole, sobriety checkpoints resulted in drunken driving arrests of around 1 percent of all motorists stopped. . . .

In sum, the balance of the state's interest in preventing drunken driving, the extent to which this system can reasonably be said to advance that interest, and the degree of intrusion upon individual motorists who are briefly stopped, weighs in favor of the state program. We therefore hold that it is consistent with the Fourth Amendment. The judgment of the Michigan Court of Appeals is accordingly reversed, and the case is remanded for further proceedings not inconsistent with this opinion.

Reversed.

DISSENT

Justice Brennan, with whom Justice Marshall joins, dissenting.

. . . The Court ignores the fact that in this class of minimally intrusive searches, we have generally required the Government to prove that it had reasonable suspicion for a minimally intrusive seizure to be considered reasonable. Some level of individualized suspicion is a core component of the protection the Fourth Amendment provides against arbitrary government action. By holding that no level of suspicion is necessary before the police may stop a car for the purpose of preventing drunken driving, the Court potentially subjects the general public to arbitrary or harassing conduct by the police. . . .

I do not dispute the immense social cost caused by drunken drivers, nor do I slight the government's efforts to prevent such tragic losses. Indeed, I would hazard a guess that today's opinion will be received favorably by a majority of our society, who would willingly suffer the minimal intrusion of a sobriety checkpoint stop in order to prevent drunken driving. But consensus that a particular law enforcement technique serves a laudable purpose has never been the touchstone of constitutional analysis.

The Fourth Amendment was designed not merely to protect against official intrusions whose social utility was less as measured by some "balancing test" than its intrusion on individual privacy; it was designed in addition to grant the individual a zone of privacy whose protections could be breached only where the "reasonable" requirements of the probable cause standard were met. Moved by whatever momentary evil has aroused their fears, officials—perhaps even supported by a majority of citizens—may be tempted to conduct searches that sacrifice the liberty of each citizen to assuage the perceived evil. But the Fourth Amendment rests on the principle that a true balance between the individual and society depends on the recognition of "the right to be let alone—the most comprehensive of rights and the right most valued by civilized men." *Olmstead v. United States* (1928) (Brandeis, J., dissenting).

In the face of the "momentary evil" of drunken driving, the Court today abdicates its role as the protector of that fundamental right. I respectfully dissent.

Justice Stevens, with whom Justice Brennan and Justice Marshall join . . . dissenting.

A sobriety checkpoint is usually operated at night at an unannounced location. Surprise is crucial to its method. The test operation conducted by the Michigan State Police and the Saginaw County Sheriff's Department began shortly after midnight and lasted until about 1 A.M.

. . . The record in this case makes clear that a decision holding these suspicionless seizures unconstitutional would not impede the law enforcement community's remarkable progress in reducing the death toll on our highways. Because the Michigan program was patterned after an older program in Maryland, the trial judge gave special attention to that state's experience. Over a period of several years, Maryland operated 125 checkpoints; of the 41,000 motorists passing through those checkpoints, only 143 persons (0.3%) were arrested. The number of man-

hours devoted to these operations is not in the record, but it seems inconceivable that a higher arrest rate could not have been achieved by more conventional means.

. . . Any relationship between sobriety checkpoints and an actual reduction in highway fatalities is even less substantial than the minimal impact on arrest rates. As the Michigan Court of Appeals pointed out,

> Maryland had conducted a study comparing traffic statistics between a county using checkpoints and a control county. The results of the study showed that alcohol-related accidents in the checkpoint county decreased by ten percent, whereas the control county saw an eleven percent decrease; and while fatal accidents in the control county fell from sixteen to three, fatal accidents in the checkpoint county actually doubled from the prior year.

In light of these considerations, it seems evident that the Court today misapplies the balancing test announced in *Brown v. Texas*. The Court overvalues the law enforcement interest in using sobriety checkpoints [and] undervalues the citizen's interest in freedom from random, unannounced investigatory seizures. . . .

. . . A Michigan officer who questions a motorist at a sobriety checkpoint has virtually unlimited discretion to detain the driver on the basis of the slightest suspicion. A ruddy complexion, an unbuttoned shirt, bloodshot eyes or a speech impediment may suffice to prolong the detention. Any driver who had just consumed a glass of beer, or even a sip of wine, would almost certainly have the burden of demonstrating to the officer that her driving ability was not impaired.

. . . These fears are not, as the Court would have it, solely the lot of the guilty. To be law abiding is not necessarily to be spotless, and even the most virtuous can be unlucky. Unwanted attention from the local police need not be less discomforting simply because one's secrets are not the stuff of criminal prosecutions. Moreover, those who have found—by reason of prejudice or misfortune—that encounters with the police may become adversarial or unpleasant without good cause will have grounds for worrying at any stop designed to elicit signs of suspicious behavior. Being stopped by the police is distressing even when it should not be terrifying, and what begins mildly may by happenstance turn severe. . . .

. . . In my opinion, unannounced investigatory seizures are, particularly when they take place at night, the hallmark of regimes far different from ours; the surprise intrusion upon individual liberty is not minimal. On that issue, my difference with the Court may amount to nothing less than a difference in our respective evaluations of the importance of individual liberty, a serious albeit inevitable source of constitutional disagreement. On the degree to which the sobriety checkpoint seizures advance the public interest, however, the Court's position is wholly indefensible.

It is well to recall the words of Mr. Justice Jackson, soon after his return from the Nuremberg Trials:

> These [Fourth Amendment rights], I protest, are not mere second-class rights but belong in the catalog of indispensable freedoms. Among deprivations of rights, none is so effective in cowing a population, crushing the spirit of the individual and putting terror in every heart. Uncontrolled search and seizure is one of the first and most effective weapons in the arsenal of every arbitrary government.

The Court's analysis of this issue resembles a business decision that measures profits by counting gross receipts and ignoring expenses. The evidence in this case indicates that sobriety checkpoints result in the arrest of a fraction of one percent of the drivers who are stopped, but there is absolutely no evidence that this figure represents an increase over the number of arrests that would have been made by using the same law enforcement resources in conventional patrols. Thus, although the gross number of arrests is more than zero, there is a complete failure of proof on the question whether the wholesale seizures have produced any net advance in the public interest in arresting intoxicated drivers. . . .

The most disturbing aspect of the Court's decision today is that it appears to give no weight to the citizen's interest in freedom from suspicionless unannounced investigatory seizures. . . . On the other hand, the Court places a heavy thumb on the law enforcement interest by looking only at gross receipts instead of net benefits. Perhaps this tampering with the scales of justice can be explained by the Court's obvious concern about the slaughter on our highways, and a resultant tolerance for policies designed to alleviate the problem by "setting an example" of a few motorists. . . .

This is a case that is driven by nothing more than symbolic state action—an insufficient justification for an otherwise unreasonable program of random seizures. Unfortunately, the Court is transfixed by the wrong symbol—the illusory prospect of punishing countless intoxicated motorists—when it should keep its eyes on the road plainly marked by the Constitution. I respectfully dissent.

CASE DISCUSSION

According to the Court, why are DWI checkpoints Fourth Amendment seizures? Why, according to the Court, are they reasonable seizures? What interests does the Court balance in reaching its result? What does Justice Stevens mean when he says that he and the majority disagree over the meaning of freedom? What does he have to say about the need and effectiveness of DWI checkpoints? What does Justice Brennan mean when he says that the degree of the intrusion begins, not ends, the inquiry about whether DWI checkpoints are reasonable seizures? How would you identify and balance the interests at stake in the DWI checkpoints? Are they effective? Explain. According to the American Civil Liberties Union (ACLU), "highly publicized local law enforcement efforts such as random roadblocks" are "Orwellian intrusions into individual privacy." What does the ACLU mean? Do you agree? Explain. After the United States Supreme Court decision, the *Sitz* case went back to Michigan, where the Michigan Supreme Court ruled that suspicionless stops are unreasonable seizures. See the "State Constitutional Law" box on *Sitz v. Michigan Department of State Police*.

STATE CONSTITUTIONAL LAW

Sitz v. Michigan
Department of State Police
506 N.W.2d 209, 218 (Mich. 1993)

FACTS

[The facts of this case appear in the case excerpt *Michigan v. Sitz*.]

OPINION

On August 1, 1988, the [Michigan] Court of Appeals unanimously affirmed the trial court's ruling that the sobriety checkpoints violated the Fourth Amendment, finding it unnecessary to decide if the state constitution offered greater protection. Following a denial of leave to appeal to this Court (1989), the defendants appealed to the United States Supreme Court, which granted certiorari. The United States Supreme Court reversed the decision of the Court of Appeals, finding that the Michigan sobriety checkpoint program did not violate the Fourth Amendment of the United States Constitution. The United States Supreme Court observed:

> In sum, the balance of the State's interest in preventing drunken driving, the extent to which this system can reasonably be said to advance that interest, and the degree of intrusion upon individual motorists who are briefly stopped, weighs in favor of the state program. We therefore hold that it is consistent with the Fourth Amendment. The judgment of the Michigan Court of Appeals is accordingly reversed, and the cause is remanded for further proceedings not inconsistent with this opinion. [*Sitz*, 496 U.S. at 455, 110 S.Ct. at 2488.]

On remand, the Court of Appeals held that "the indiscriminate suspicionless stopping of motor vehicles in the form of roving roadblocks violat[es] art. 1, § 11 of the Michigan Constitution." 193 Mich. App. 690, 699, 485 N.W.2d 135 (1992). This Court granted leave to appeal, 441 Mich. 869 (1992).

. . .

Because the United States Supreme Court established that Michigan's sobriety checkpoints do not violate the Fourth Amendment of the United States Constitution, the specific question presented in this case is whether sobriety checkpoints are unreasonable under art. 1, § 11 of the Michigan Constitution. . . .

. . .

The Michigan Declaration of Rights, like the federal Bill of Rights, is "drawn to restrict governmental conduct and to provide protection from governmental infringement and excesses. . . ." *Woodland v. Citizens Lobby*, 423 Mich. 188, 204, 378 N.W.2d 337 (1985). When there is a clash of competing rights under the state and federal constitutions, the Supremacy Clause, art. VI, cl. 2, dictates that the federal right prevails. Where a right is given to a citizen under federal law, it does not follow that the organic instrument of state government must be interpreted as conferring the identical right. Nor does it follow that where a right given by the federal constitution is not given by a state constitution, the state constitution offends the federal constitution. It is only where the organic instrument of government purports to deprive a citizen of a right granted by the federal constitution that the instrument can be said to violate the constitution.

. . .

. . . What is to be gleaned from our former cases is that the courts of this state should reject unprincipled creation of state constitutional rights that exceed their federal counterparts. On the other hand, our courts are not obligated to accept what we deem to be a major contraction of citizen protections under our constitution simply because the United States Supreme Court has chosen to do so.

We are obligated to interpret our own organic instrument of government.

. . .

No one will contend that an officer may promiscuously stop automobiles upon the public highway and demand the driver's license merely as a subterfuge to invade the constitutional right of the traveler to be secure against unreasonable search and seizure. Yet that is exactly what was done here. The officer cared nothing about seeing a driver's license, but he says he was suspicious that there was liquor in the car, and almost immediately after stopping the defendant he ordered him out of his car and proceeded to search it for liquor.

. . .

As long ago as 1889, the justices of this Court stated:

> Personal liberty, which is guaranteed to every citizen under our Constitution and laws, consists of the right of locomotion,— to go where one pleases, and when, and to do that which may lead to one's business or pleasure, only so far restrained as the rights of others may make it necessary for the welfare of all other citizens. One may travel along the public highways or in public places; and while conducting themselves in a decent and orderly manner, disturbing no other, and interfering with the rights of no other citizens, there, they will be protected under the law, not only in their persons, but in their safe conduct. The Constitution and the laws are framed for the public good, and the protection of all citizens, from the highest to the lowest; and no one may be restrained of his liberty, unless he has transgressed some law. [*Pinkerton v. Verberg*, 78 Mich. 573, 584, 44 N.W. 579 (1889).]

. . . [O]ur jurisprudence conclusively demonstrates that, in the context of automobile seizures, we have extended more expansive protection to our citizens than that extended in *Sitz*. This Court has never recognized the right of the state, without any level of suspicion whatsoever, to detain members of the population at large for criminal investigatory purposes. Nor has Michigan completely acquiesced to the judgment of "politically accountable officials" when determining reasonableness in such a context. *Sitz*, 496 U.S. at 453, 110 S.Ct. at 2487. In these circumstances, the Michigan Constitution offers more protection than the United States Supreme Court's interpretation of the Fourth Amendment.

. . .

The Michigan Constitution has historically treated searches and seizures for criminal investigatory purposes differently than those for regulatory or administrative purposes. These administrative or regulatory searches and seizures have traditionally been regarded as "reasonable" in a constitutional sense. However, seizures with the primary goal of enforcing the criminal law have generally required some level of suspicion, even if that level has fluctuated over the years.

We do not suggest that in a different context we might not reach a similar result under the balancing test of reasonableness employed in *Sitz*. Indeed, our precedent regarding automobiles implicitly incorporates a balancing test that is inherent in assessing the reasonableness of warrantless searches and seizures. We hold only that the protection afforded to the seizures of vehicles for criminal investigatory purposes has both an historical foundation and a contemporary justification that is not outweighed by the necessity advanced. Suspicionless criminal investigatory seizures, and extreme deference to the judgments of politically accountable officials is, in this context, contrary to Michigan constitutional precedent.

. . .

DISSENT

BRICKLEY, Justice (dissenting).

. . .

. . . [T]here are distinct advantages to uniformity in the interpretation of search and seizure constitutional provisions. The interstate flow of traffic on our intrastate and interstate highway system argues for uniformity in highway safety enforcement.... Technological advances in miniaturization and the concomitant development of easily concealed destructive devices (not to mention the lethal force of an automobile driven by an intoxicated person), coupled with increasing levels of violence and the threat of international terrorism, are going to continue to prompt the need for and the public acceptance of surveillance–inspection techniques that involve minimum inconveniences and intrusions as a necessary trade-off for the personal safety and security of the population at large. Such systematic and evenly enforced measures need not erode the traditional and accepted standards of probable cause and articulable suspi-

cion when employed in the customary criminal investigation context.

. . .

Accordingly, this is not, in my view, the time, nor does this case present the circumstances, to have the Michigan Constitution digress from the evolving Fourth Amendment standards as interpreted by the United States Supreme Court.

For the above-stated reasons, I believe that the Michigan Constitution is satisfied by the balancing analysis set forth in *Brown* and applied to this case by the United States Supreme Court, and not a determination of articulable suspicion or probable cause. I would hold that Michigan's sobriety checkpoint program withstands Michigan constitutional scrutiny. I would, therefore, reverse the decision of the Court of Appeals.

D e c i s i o n   P o i n t

1. *State v. Vikesdal*, 688 So.2d 685 (La.App. 1997). A scheduled bus travels through Logansport, Louisiana, sometimes stopping there if passengers board or debark in Logansport, to a final destination. When the bus drove into Logansport about 5:40 A.M. on December 13, 1994, the police chief signaled the bus driver to stop in front of the Logansport police station. The routing supervisor of the bus company (Kerrville Bus Lines) had earlier agreed to this procedure, according to the chief. Once the bus was stopped, the armed and uniformed police would then surround and enter the bus with a trained dog that would "work" the bus by sniffing the luggage of the passengers on the bus. Officers outside the bus would watch for suspicious moves or contraband being discarded by passengers. The Logansport police chief explained that searches were sometimes made after Logansport police had been informed that one or more passengers might be transporting contraband aboard the bus.

After the bus driver obeyed the chief's directions and stopped at the police station, the chief and the dog handler, in uniform and armed, with

the trained dog, approached the bus while other uniformed and armed officers (four to five) surrounded the outside of the bus. The chief entered the bus first, explaining to the passengers his purpose and telling them to remain in their seats while the dog "worked." Passengers were asked to remove their luggage from the upper luggage rack and place it in the center aisle of the bus; otherwise, the chief would do this. Passengers were also directed not to be afraid of the dog and not to move around or frighten the dog, which might "bite" if alarmed when "working."

Once these instructions were given and the luggage was on the floor, the dog was allowed to enter with his handler and "work" the bus. In one of the companion cases, Ammons, who had been seated near the rear of the bus, attempted to depart the bus while the dog was working. The chief stopped her, telling her to return to her seat for her own safety because of the dog's presence on the bus.

While "working" Vikesdal's bus under the described circumstances on the December early morning, the dog "alerted" on Vikesdal's luggage.

Police opened the luggage, finding the marijuana, after Vikesdal declined the police request that he consent to the search. This resulted in the seizure of the marijuana without a warrant and in Vikesdal's arrest.

The police chief explained how passengers were detained:

> Some of them get off to smoke, but . . . if someone got off the bus and didn't have a ticket to get off in Logansport I would . . . anybody would be suspicious why they got off the bus.
>
> Q. Would you prevent them from leaving?
> A. I probably would. . . . I would ask them for identification and I would ask them why were they getting off there and . . . I would tell them what we are doing and ask them where their baggage [was] and . . . why [they were] leaving [their bags on the bus]. . . . [I]f they [still] wanted to get off the bus then I would . . . check . . . and make sure [they were] not a burglar or something that is fixing to . . . get off the bus there and then go and rob something or kill somebody . . . [in] the town. . . . [If they] checked . . . out . . . okay, . . . then I would let them off the bus [without their bags]. We have had that to happen where a subject ran that had drugs on the bus. . . .

Was the bus sweep a reasonable search and the seizure of the marijuana a reasonable seizure? Perhaps according to the Fourth Amendment of the U.S. Constitution, but not according to the search and seizure provision of the Louisiana Constitution, ruled the Louisiana Court of Appeals:

> La. Const. art. I, § 5 (1974) affords even a passenger on a public bus the guarantee against "unreasonable searches, seizures or invasions of privacy [of his person and effects]," a guarantee that is broader for the citizen and more restrictive on the government than is provided in the Fourth Amendment to the U.S. Constitution.
>
> Under the circumstances above described—having the bus stop at the police station and being confronted with at least six uniformed police officers (Clark and the dog handler on the bus, and another four or five officers surrounding the bus)—we have no difficulty concluding that a reasonable bus passenger would not "feel free to decline" the police chief's "requests" or otherwise terminate the encounter. The chief explained that a passenger's attempt to leave the bus or terminate the encounter would provoke further questioning as to the reason for the passenger's desire to leave. Passengers who tried to end the encounter by exiting the bus after the dog boarded the bus did so at the risk of being physically harmed by the dog, according to Clark, who admitted that the dog's presence prevented one such passenger from exiting the bus, notwithstanding her desire and attempt to do so.
>
> The police conduct in this case was far more aggressive and obtrusive than the mere approaching of a citizen in a public place, such as an airport or a bus terminal, to "ask a few questions" or make other requests which the citizen may reasonably and freely choose to disregard. Vikesdal was clearly "seized" or detained in the constitutional sense, under either or both the federal and state constitutions, when police stopped and took charge of the bus, however briefly, to allow the drug-detecting dog to "work" the bus. The more critical issue is the second part of the constitutional analysis in the light of the case law, whether the seizure was "unreasonable."
>
> While vehicular travelers in general may have a reduced expectation of privacy while on the road than they have within the confines of their home, they do not abandon all constitutional protection by entering a vehicle, whether public or private. . . . [A]n automobile traveler's freedom from unreasonable seizure cannot be interfered with even for a limited time at the unbridled discretion of police officers, within the contexts of random and suspicionless stops of automobiles to check for driver's licenses and

vehicle registration, and additionally, for evidence of driver intoxication.

. . . Art. I, § 5 of the Louisiana Constitution explicitly protects an individual's right to be free from unreasonable "invasions of privacy," in addition to the protection against unreasonable searches and seizures. The state constitution thus affords greater protection of an individual's "right to be let alone" than does the Fourth Amendment. As a result of this expanded protection under the state constitution, the stopping of motorists at sobriety checkpoints or DWI roadblocks, even when the roadblocks are carefully regulated and governed by neutral criteria, rendering them "reasonable" under the Fourth Amendment, is considered "unreasonable" and therefore prohibited by Art. I, § 5 of the Louisiana Constitution. . . . [T]he seizure of the defendant's person here occurred without any reasonable suspicion or probable cause to believe that the defendant or anyone else on the bus had violated some law, in contravention of La. Const. art. I, § 5 and La.C.Cr.P. art. 215.1. The marijuana obtained from Vikesdal's luggage as a result of this unlawful seizure is not legally admissible.

2. *State v. Everson*, 474 N.W.2d 695 (N.D. 1991). During the summer of 1989, Larry Buck, a detective with the Stark County Sheriff's Office, Sgt. Don Glarum of the State Highway Patrol, and Stark County Deputy Sheriff Mike Adolph were assigned by their supervisors to establish a highway checkpoint in Stark County to coincide with the upcoming annual motorcycle rally in Sturgis, South Dakota. On June 26, 1989, District Eight Highway Patrol Captain David Messer issued Operation Order 2–89, which stated in part: "Due to the rally in Sturgis, South Dakota, and the large volume of drugs on our highways, the North Dakota Highway Patrol along with the Stark County Sheriff's Office and other agencies will conduct a driver's license and registration check. If probable cause presents its self [sic], for drugs and other contraband, a search will be con-

ducted. The check will be conducted on Highway 85 on 5–6 and 13–14 August, 1989. It will be the mission of the North Dakota Highway Patrol to attempt to alleviate the problem of drugs being transported by vehicle, on state highway's [sic] in North Dakota."

On July 17, 1989, Stark County Sheriff James Rice issued a memorandum in preparation for the operation that stated the following: "[C]heck points [sic] will be set up and operated as listed below: 1. All vehicles heading in an assigned direction will be stopped. 2. Vehicle registration will be checked for current status. 3. Driver of vehicle will be checked for current operator's driver's license. 4. A vehicle inspection will be conducted. Checkpoints will be located on #85, #22, #8 and #10 during assigned times."

On August 5–6 and 13–14, 1989, law enforcement officers conducted a checkpoint twelve miles south of Belfield on U.S. Highway 85. Personnel from the Stark, Billings, and Slope County Sheriff's Offices, the State Highway Patrol, the State Drug Enforcement Unit, the United States Border Patrol, and the Minot Police Department participated in the operation. On August 5 and 6, which coincided with the beginning of the motorcycle rally, all southbound traffic was stopped. On August 13 and 14, which coincided with the conclusion of the rally, all northbound traffic was stopped. The checkpoint was located in a small valley so that oncoming traffic could not see it from a long distance. A driver would first see a large sign that said "Please stop." The actual checkpoint was located approximately two-tenths of one mile from the sign. The checkpoint was conducted only during daylight hours.

Every vehicle was stopped at the checkpoint. The driver would first encounter three fluorescent orange traffic cones and an officer referred to as the "point man," who was located at an intersection of the highway and a gravel road. Parked on the gravel road on the driver's right were sheriffs' cars, a camper used as a command post, and Drug Enforcement Unit vehicles. Drug Enforcement Unit officers and sheriffs' deputies conducted searches of vehicles referred to this area if the driver consented to a search. Two Highway Patrol officers were stationed farther down the highway to conduct vehicle-safety inspections.

Was the checkpoint legal? A motorcyclist who was stopped and who had amphetamines and marijuana in his possession argued that the search and seizure violated the Fourth Amendment. The trial court ruled that the roadblock was "pretextual." According to the court,

> Although the State characterizes this roadblock as multi-purpose, the main purpose was to search for controlled substances. This is reflected by the lead person being a criminal investigator not a traffic officer, by the operation order for the Highway Patrol stating that the purpose was "to alleviate the problem of drugs being transported by the [sic] vehicle," by the point man having unconstrained discretion to send vehicles to the search area or the inspection area, and by the first and main area at the roadblock being the search area.

The North Dakota Supreme Court disagreed with the trial court:

> In analyzing the constitutionality of the checkpoint in this case, we begin by noting the trial court's apparent determination that the checkpoint was unconstitutional because it was conducted as a pretext or subterfuge to check for the presence of controlled substances. The State does not challenge the trial court's finding that the primary purpose of the checkpoint was to look for controlled substances, but asserts that this fact should not in itself invalidate the checkpoint. We agree.

Applying the reasoning and the holding of *Michigan v. Sitz* to the North Dakota roadblock, the court wrote the following:

> If a state may validly conduct a checkpoint for the purpose of apprehending drunk drivers, we think the state may validly conduct a checkpoint for the purpose of apprehending drug traffickers, a societal harm at least equal in magnitude to drunk driving. . . .

The North Dakota court used the following quotation from an Illinois Supreme Court opinion that upheld the constitutionality of a safety check roadblock as a pretext for finding drunk drivers:

> The official subterfuge with respect to the true purpose of the roadblock is not entitled to significant weight in the balancing process. The subjective reaction of drivers stopped at the roadblock would not have been substantially different had the participating officers been instructed that the primary purpose of the stop was to check on drunken drivers rather than on license violations. In this case the officers' observations of evidence of intoxication entailed slight, if any, additional intrusion on defendant. Contrary to the trial court's ruling, this checkpoint is not rendered unconstitutional merely because its true purpose was to apprehend narcotics traffickers.

In a strong dissent, the dissenting judge wrote this response:

> If we are to extend *Sitz* to condone a nonrandom roadblock whose purpose is to look for illegal drugs, then any nonrandom roadblock whose purpose is to look for evidence of any criminal conduct is permissible under the Fourth Amendment. But the war on drugs cannot suspend constitutional guarantees. . . . I assume, until the United States Supreme Court tells me otherwise, that the Fourth Amendment still has some application to vehicles. Drivers' expectations of privacy in those vehicles, so long as those drivers are obeying traffic laws, are not in the vicinity of or crossing a border, and are not drinking or otherwise using illegal substances, still find some protection under the Fourth Amendment and its requirement of reasonable suspicion in order to make a seizure reasonable. At least, I hope so.

The police officers here admitted using the safety inspection in order to achieve their purpose of "alleviating" the drug problem. In *State v. Kunkel*, 455 N.W.2d 208

N.D. 1990), police officers were equally candid. They admitted that their purpose in seizing a van and inventorying its contents was to search for drugs. But an inventory of property in police custody may not be used as a subterfuge for criminal investigation. Because the inventory search of the van was conducted to discover evidence of crime and not to fulfill the proper caretaking purpose of an inventory search, we held that the evidence was illegally obtained. We should achieve an analogous result here. I respectfully dissent.

3. *Galberth v. United States*, 590 A.2d 990 (D.C. App. 1991). Galberth was stopped at the roadblock at Montello Avenue and Queen Street, N.E., on December 5, 1989. Officer Cephas, a field officer assigned to the roadblock, testified that he received orders that all cars were to be stopped from 9:30 A.M. until 11:30 A.M. and the drivers asked for their licenses and registrations. Eight to ten officers were present, in uniform, and some were wearing visibility jackets; five to six marked police cars were also on the scene. Officer Cephas's instructions were that if any questions arose, then he was to run a Washington Area Law Enforcement Service (WALES) computer check to see if the driver had a valid license. No barriers, signs, or traffic cones were used to mark the roadblock, but Officer Cephas estimated that the police officers could be seen from about midway up the block. Officer Cephas testified that persons were stopped for approximately two to three minutes if there was no problem with their license.

The roadblock at Montello and Queen was part of a special operation in the Trinidad area of the city announced by the mayor to "cut down on the violence and homicides and narcotics trafficking in the Trinidad area, [by] attacking it from three different angles"—roadblocks, undercover operations, and high-visibility "saturation" patrols. Captain O'Donnell, the coordinator for Operation Clean Sweep for the Fifth District, testified that the roadblock program was designed to deal with "traffic problems such as speeding automobiles, vehicles frequenting the area committing traffic violations to purchase narcotics, stolen automobile traffic in the neighborhood, and things of that nature." As he explained, a high volume of narcotics trafficking brings with it a similarly heavy amount of automobile traffic, since many people come to the open air drug markets by car. Captain O'Donnell's commanding officer delegated to him the responsibility to select a site for the roadblocks, to notify his commanding officer of his selection, to assign a supervisor on the scene, and to periodically inspect the roadblock while it was in operation.

O'Donnell selected the Montello Avenue site because he knew from personal observation as well as citizen complaints that the area was plagued by heavy traffic created when individuals looking to buy drugs parked illegally for a brief period, and then sped away after making their purchase. However, the evidence he offered (in addition to his own observations) relating to traffic congestion was that in the past three years there had been over one hundred citizen complaints about drugs, traffic, abandoned cars, and trash in the area of Montello and Queen.

O'Donnell instructed Sergeant Bullock to operate the roadblock from 9:30 A.M. to 11:30 A.M., and then to conduct a high-visibility saturation patrol in the Trinidad area. Captain O'Donnell inspected the roadblock while it was in operation and explained that although the roadblock guidelines suggest using flares, flashing warning lights, or flashlights to increase the roadblock's visibility, he saw no need for them in this case because it was daytime and the police could be seen one hundred yards before a car entered the intersection. In addition, an escape route was available, allowing cars to turn down Holbrook Terrace and avoid passing through the roadblock.

Sergeant Bullock's report indicated that 226 cars, coming from three directions, were stopped, four arrests were made (three for no permit and one for operating after suspension), and seventeen traffic violation citations were issued.

Galberth was stopped at the roadblock and asked by Officer Cephas for his driver's license and registration. Galberth told the officer that he did not have his driver's license and that he must have forgotten to bring it. Cephas asked for Galberth's Social Security number, and the resulting computer check indicated that Galberth's license had expired in 1983. Cephas ordered Galberth out of the van and placed him under arrest for not having a valid operating permit. As Officer Cephas was patting Galberth down, he felt an object in Galberth's front coat that he thought might be a gun. Reaching into the pocket, Cephas found a .38 caliber revolver.

Galberth testified that he did not see the police until he reached the stop sign at the intersection and that there was no way that he could avoid being pulled over by the police. Mr. Lucas, a passenger in the van that Galberth was driving, testified that he too first noticed the police as the van approached the intersection about fifty to seventy-five feet before they came upon the police at the intersection. Lucas saw no visibility jackets, cones, or flares, although he did see police officers talking to people in other cars in the area.

Was the roadblock legal? No, according to the District of Columbia Circuit Court:

We agree with the government that there clearly were several purposes served by the roadblocks, and that the police may constitutionally benefit from the "spin-off" effect of an otherwise constitutional law enforcement program. . . . We must nonetheless consider the principal purpose underlying each of the roadblocks to determine their constitutionality. . . .

The trial judge . . . made the following finding about the government's purpose in establishing the roadblock: "Based on the evidence that the Court has received the Court is not really overwhelmed with the idea of traffic problems at Montello and Queen. That may have fit into the equation which caused the decision to set up the roadblock at that location, but the primary purpose, because the Court does not want

to taint the evidence which was really perceived, the primary purpose had to do with Operation Clean Sweep, violence, drugs and guns." . . . Galberth urges us to read the trial judge's statement as a finding that the police stopped his car in order to detect crimes related to "violence, drugs and guns." Under another plausible reading, the finding could mean that the police established the roadblock in order to disrupt the open air drug market. We conclude that under either reading of Judge Dixon's finding, the roadblock cannot survive.

. . . [T]he police may not use a roadblock in order to seek evidence of drug-related crimes. . . . If . . . the police established the Galberth roadblock in order to detect evidence of drugs or other crimes, the roadblock would be unconstitutional. . . . When the Supreme Court has upheld suspicionless roadblock seizures, the government's purpose in establishing the roadblock had some logical connection to the individuals likely to be in the vehicles that were stopped. Thus, the police set up permanent checkpoints because the flow of illegal aliens could not otherwise be effectively controlled and the checkpoints could reasonably be expected to lead to the arrest of "smugglers and illegal aliens who succumb to the lure of such highways" [*Martinez-Fuerte*]. Similarly, the government addressed the immense drunk driving problem by establishing sobriety checkpoints designed to prevent and apprehend impaired drivers [*Sitz*]. The purported deterrence rationale for the Galberth roadblock, by contrast, was addressed to problems of general law enforcement, namely deterring drug traffic and violence and preventing "violence, drugs and guns," not to problems predictably associated with persons who are stopped at the roadblock. Such a justification is antithetical to the Fourth Amendment.

FRISKS

Frisks and stops are intimately linked. Nonetheless, they are distinct law enforcement actions. Stops are seizures, referring to the deprivation-of-liberty dimension of the Fourth Amendment. Frisks are searches, referring to the intrusions-on-privacy dimension of the Fourth Amendment. (See also Chapters 5 and 6 for further discussion of these points.) Frisks require separate justification from that of stops; officers cannot automatically frisk all citizens whom they stop. The sole purpose for frisks is to protect officers from death or injury; the sole object is to disarm suspects. Officers may not stop citizens as a pretext to search for contraband. The justification for a frisk is always the need for and the lawfulness of a stop. A lawful stop is a prerequisite for any frisk. In other words, officers must first lawfully stop a citizen and second, contemporaneous with the stop, frisk the citizen.

Furthermore, facts sufficient to support a stop—reasonable suspicion that crime may be afoot—do not automatically add up to facts sufficient to support a frisk. Frisks require facts supporting a reasonable suspicion that the suspect is armed. Sometimes, the same facts may support both, as in *Terry v. Ohio*, where the suspected crime was armed robbery. In possessory crimes, this is not so.

Definition of *Frisk*

Frisks lie at the least intrusive end of a spectrum of Fourth Amendment searches. At the other end lie body cavity searches; between these ends of the spectrum lie full body and strip searches (see Chapter 6). According to the court in a leading stop-and-frisk case from New York, *People v. Rivera*, a frisk is a

> contact or patting of the outer clothing of a person to detect by the sense of touch, if a concealed weapon is being carried. . . . The sense of exterior touch here involved is not very far different from the sense of sight or hearing upon which police customarily act. . . . [It is] a minor inconvenience and petty indignity.[30]

Even the most superficial unwanted touchings significantly intrude on privacy. Physical touchings magnify the intrusiveness of police–citizen contacts. This is a primary reason why the Supreme Court has brought frisks within the scope of the Fourth Amendment. All the restrictions on the power to frisk relate to the importance placed upon the intrusive quality of unwanted body contacts by the police.

D e c i s i o n   P o i n t

Consider the following situations. Which are frisks? Searches? Neither?

1. Officers look for bulges that might be weapons, but do not touch the suspect.

2. An officer sees a bulge and asks a suspect to open his jacket; upon seeing a knife, the officer asks the suspect to hand over the weapon.

3. An officer asks a suspect to open her jacket so that the officer can see what is inside; the officer does not touch the suspect.

4. An officer reaches into an inside pocket of a suspect's open jacket and removes a knife; the officer does not touch the suspect's body.

5. An officer goes over a suspect's outer clothing lightly to detect weapons.

6. An officer reaches inside and under a suspect's heavy overcoat to feel for bulges.

7. An officer opens the handbag a suspect is carrying and looks inside.

8. An officer opens a suspect's handbag and empties its contents.

9. An officer pats down (goes over the outer clothing of) a suspect's companion.

10. An officer lightly feels a suspect's groin area.

11. An officer orders a suspect to raise his hands and lean up against a wall while the officer feels his outer clothing, including the groin area.

The reasonableness of frisks, like that of stops, depends on a balancing of the government need to enforce the criminal law and the rights of citizens—in the case of frisks, the right of citizens to the privacy of their persons. In a larger sense, both the right to privacy and the need to enforce the criminal law contribute to the same social interest: a sense of security based on the confidence that government will protect its citizens from both criminals and its own excesses.

No one can reasonably expect police officers to risk their lives unnecessarily in order to investigate suspicious persons and circumstances. Hence, the law permits police officers to conduct a superficial search in which they feel "once over the outer part of the body lightly," or pat-down for weapons, during a lawful stop. A lawful stop is a necessary condition of a lawful frisk. However, a lawful stop is not sufficient to make a frisk a reasonable search. The Fourth Amendment requires three conditions to make a frisk a lawful search:

1. A lawful stop

2. A pat-down of the outer clothing for the sole purpose of discovering weapons and disarming suspects

3. Reasonable suspicion that the suspect is armed

Hence, frisks cannot provide a pretext for the discovery and confiscation of contraband—usually in the form of illegal drugs.

Reasonable Suspicion for Frisks

Officers may frisk suspects whom they reasonably suspect are armed. No mechanistic formula determines the amount and quality of facts that add up to reasonable suspicion that a suspect is armed. However, some examples suggest the kind of objective basis that justifies particular frisks. In *Terry v. Ohio*, it was the nature of the crime. Officer McFadden reasonably suspected that Terry and his companions were about to commit armed robbery. If it was reasonable to suspect that they were going to commit armed robbery, it was, of course, also reasonable to suspect they would use weapons to do so. Hence, it was reasonable to frisk Terry and his companions for guns.

Other observations that may lead officers reasonably to suspect that individuals are armed include the following:

- Bulges in clothing[31]
- Sudden movement toward a pocket or other place that might contain a weapon[32]
- Knowledge that the suspect was armed on a previous occasion[33]

The objective basis for lawful frisks requires only that officers reasonably *suspect* that the person stopped *may* be armed; hence, if the frisk does not produce a weapon (which in four out of five cases it does not), the frisk remains lawful. In other words, that officers turn out to be wrong in their suspicions that suspects are armed does not turn the frisk into an unreasonable search. Furthermore, reasonable suspicion allows for taking into account the experience of police officers. That is to say, police officers, by their experience, can read more into facts surrounding complex criminal behavior than average citizens can. For example, the average person knows virtually nothing about factual patterns surrounding a drug operation, but experienced narcotics officers quickly grasp them. Taking the experience of the officer into account in determining reasonable suspicion allows for considerable latitude in order to benefit from that experience.[34]

Scope of Frisks

On the same day the United States Supreme Court decided *Terry v. Ohio*, it also decided whether frisks for evidence and contraband as well as weapons were lawful. In *Sibron v. New York*, the Court emphatically rejected this proposition on the ground that frisks are so intrusive that only saving officers from wounding and death can justify such an invasion of persons on less than probable cause.[35]

This does not mean that all evidence and contraband seized during frisks are unreasonable Fourth Amendment seizures. If officers reasonably suspect stopped persons are armed and in the course of a pat-down for weapons the officers come upon contraband or evidence, they may seize them. Critics maintain that officers abuse the frisk power in cases where the object of the stop is to discover contraband, particularly when the contraband is illegal drugs. They assert that the police are really looking for drugs and that they use the stop and pat-down as a pretext for discovering drugs. To avoid abuse, critics recommend limiting Fourth Amendment seizures on less than probable cause to crimes that directly threaten persons—that is, crimes of violence. Referring to the power to seize contraband found during frisks, the reporters for the American Law Institute's Model Pre-arraignment Code wrote the following:

> . . . [I]t is hard to ignore the fact that . . . any power will be abused. The courts have made it quite clear that in the name of police safety, they will always allow a frisk of extensive proportions, and it is difficult to see how this can be avoided. A corollary hard reality is that police will use this power not really to protect themselves but to seize and confiscate weapons and other contraband.[36]

The Supreme Court addressed both the pretext problem and reasonable suspicion in *Adams v. Williams*, the first major stop-and-frisk case decided after *Terry v. Ohio* and *Sibron v. New York*.

C A S E

Was the Stop a Pretext to Frisk for Drugs?

Adams v. Williams
407 U.S. 143, 92 S.Ct. 1921,
32 L.Ed.2d 612 (1972)

Williams's petition for federal habeas corpus *relief was denied by the district court. The court of appeals reversed, holding that the evidence used in the trial resulting in Williams's conviction had been obtained by an unlawful search. On writ of* certiorari, *the Supreme Court reversed, holding that the stop and frisk did not violate the Fourth Amendment. Justice Rehnquist wrote the opinion of the Court. Justice Brennan dissented.*

FACTS

Police Sgt. John Connolly was alone early in the morning on car patrol duty in a high-crime area of Bridgeport, Connecticut. At approximately 2:15 A.M. a person known to Sgt. Connolly approached his cruiser and informed him that an individual seated in a nearby vehicle was carrying narcotics and had a gun at his waist. After calling for assistance on his car radio, Sgt. Connolly approached the vehicle to investigate the informant's report. Connolly tapped on the car window and asked the occupant, Robert Williams, to open the door. When Williams rolled down the window instead, the sergeant reached into the car and removed a fully loaded revolver from Williams' waistband. The gun had not been visible to Connolly from outside the car, but it was in precisely the place indicated by the informant. Williams was then arrested by Connolly for unlawful possession of the pistol. A search incident to that arrest was conducted after other officers arrived. They found substantial quantities of heroin on Williams' person and in the car, and they found a machete and a second revolver hidden in the automobile.

OPINION

Respondent contends that the initial seizure of his pistol, upon which rested the later search and seizure of other weapons and narcotics, was not justified by the informant's tip to Sgt. Connolly. He claims that absent a more reliable informant, or some corroboration of the tip, the policeman's actions were unreasonable under the standards set forth in *Terry v. Ohio* [1968]. In *Terry,* this Court recognized that "a police officer may in appropriate circumstances and in an appropriate manner approach a person for purposes of investigating possibly criminal behavior even though there is no probable cause to make an arrest." The Fourth Amendment does not require a policeman who lacks the precise level of information necessary for probable cause to arrest to simply shrug his shoulders and allow a crime to occur or a criminal to escape. On the contrary, *Terry* recognizes that it may be the essence of good police work to adopt an intermediate response. A brief stop of a suspicious individual, in order to determine his identity or to maintain the status quo momentarily while obtaining more information, may be most reasonable in light of the facts known to the officer at the time.

The Court recognized in *Terry* that the policeman making a reasonable investigatory stop should not be denied the opportunity to protect himself from attack by a hostile suspect. "When an officer is justified in believing that the individual whose suspicious behavior he is investigating at close range is armed and presently dangerous to the officer or to others," he may conduct a limited protective search for concealed weapons. The purpose of this limited search is not to discover evidence of crime, but to allow the officer to pursue his investigation without fear of violence, and thus the frisk for weapons might be equally necessary and reasonable, whether or not carrying a concealed weapon violated any applicable state law. So long as the officer is entitled to make a forcible stop [COURT NOTE: "Petitioner does not contend that Williams acted voluntarily in rolling down the window in his car."] and has reason to believe that the suspect is armed and dangerous, he may conduct a weapons search limited in scope to this protective purpose.

Applying these principles to the present case, we believe that Sgt. Connolly acted justifiably in responding to his informant's tip. The informant was known to him personally and had provided him with information in the past. This is a stronger case than obtains in the case of an anonymous telephone tip. The informant here came forward personally to give information that was immediately verifiable at the scene. Indeed, under Connecticut law, the informant might have been subject to immediate arrest for making a false complaint had Sgt. Connolly's investigation proved the tip incorrect. Thus, while the Court's decisions indicate that this informant's unverified tip may have been insufficient for a narcotics arrest or search warrant, the information carried enough indicia of reliability to justify the officer's forcible stop of Williams.

In reaching this conclusion, we reject respondent's argument that reasonable cause for a stop and frisk can only be based on the officer's personal observation, rather than on information supplied by another person. Informants' tips, like all other clues and evidence coming to a policeman on the scene, may vary greatly in their value and reliability. One simple rule will not cover every situation. Some tips, completely lacking in indicia of reliability, would either warrant no police response or require further investigation before a forcible stop of a suspect would be authorized. But in some situations—for example, when the victim of a street crime seeks immediate police aid and gives a description of his assailant, or when a credible informant warns of a specific impending crime—the subtleties of the hearsay rule should not thwart an appropriate police response.

While properly investigating the activity of a person who was reported to be carrying narcotics and a concealed weapon and who was sitting alone in a car in a high-crime area at 2:15 in the morning, Sgt. Connolly had ample reason to fear for his safety. When Williams rolled down his window, rather than complying with the policeman's request to step out of the car so that his movements could more easily be seen, the revolver allegedly at Williams' waist became an even greater threat. Under these circumstances the policeman's action in reaching to the spot where the gun was thought to be hidden constituted a limited intrusion designed to insure his safety, and we con-

clude that it was reasonable. The loaded gun seized as a result of this intrusion was therefore admissible at Williams' trial.

Reversed.

DISSENT

Justice Brennan, dissenting.

The crucial question on which this case turns, as the court concedes, is whether, there being no contention that Williams acted voluntarily in rolling down the window of his car, the State had shown sufficient cause to justify Sgt. Connolly's "forcible" stop. I would affirm, believing, for the following reasons stated by Judge, now Chief Judge, Friendly, dissenting, that the State did not make that showing:

To begin, I have the greatest hesitancy in extending (*Terry v. Ohio*) to crimes like the possession of narcotics. . . . There is too much danger that, instead of the stop being the object and the protective frisk an incident thereto, the reverse will be true. Against that we have here the added fact of the report that Williams had a gun on his person. . . . (But) Connecticut allows its citizens to carry weapons, concealed or otherwise, at will, provided only they have a permit, and gives its police officers no special authority to stop for the purpose of determining whether the citizen has one. . . .

If I am wrong in thinking that *Terry* should not be applied at all to mere possessory offenses, . . . I would not find the combination of Officer Connolly's almost meaningless observation and the tip in this case to be sufficient justification for the intrusion. *Terry v. Ohio* was intended to free a police officer from the rigidity of a rule that would prevent his doing anything to a man reasonably suspected of being about to commit or having just committed a crime of violence, no matter how grave the problem or impelling the need for swift action, unless the officer had what a court would later determine to be probable cause for arrest. It was meant for the serious cases of imminent danger or of harm recently perpetrated to persons or property, not the conventional ones of possessory offenses. If it is to be extended to the latter at all, this should be only where observation by the officer himself or well authenticated information shows "that criminal activity may be afoot." I greatly fear that if the (contrary view) should be followed, *Terry* will have opened the sluice gates for serious and unintended erosion of the protection of the Fourth Amendment.

Justice Marshall, with whom Justice Douglas joins, dissenting.

Four years have passed since we decided *Terry v. Ohio*, . . . the first case in which this court explicitly recognized the concept of "stop and frisk" and squarely held that police officers may, under appropriate circumstances, stop and frisk persons suspected of criminal activity even though there is less than probable cause for an arrest. This case marks our first opportunity to give some flesh to the bones of *Terry et al.* Unfortunately, the flesh provided by today's decision cannot possibly be made to fit on *Terry*'s skeletal framework.

. . . (T)he most basic constitutional rule in this area is that "searches conducted outside the judicial process, without prior approval by judge o[r] magistrate, are per se unreasonable under the Fourth Amendment—subject only to a few specifically established and well-delineated exceptions." The exceptions are "jealously and carefully drawn." . . .

In today's decision, the Court ignores the fact that *Terry* begrudgingly accepted the necessity for creating an exception from the warrant requirement of the Fourth Amendment and treats this case as if warrantless searches were the rule rather than the "narrowly drawn" exception. This decision betrays the careful balance that *Terry* sought to strike between a citizen's right to privacy and his government's responsibility for effective law enforcement and expands the concept of warrantless searches far beyond anything heretofore recognized as legitimate. I dissent. . . .

The Court erroneously attempts to describe the search for the gun as a protective search incident to a reasonable investigatory stop. But, as in *Terry*, . . . there is no occasion in this case to determine whether or not police officers have a right to seize and to restrain a citizen in order to interrogate him. The facts are clear that the officer intended to make the search as soon as

he approached the respondent. He asked no questions; he made no investigation; he simply searched. There was nothing apart from the information supplied by the informant to cause the officer to search. Our inquiry must focus, therefore, as it did in *Terry*, on whether the officer had sufficient facts from which he could reasonably infer that respondent was not only engaging in illegal activity, but also that he was armed and dangerous. The focus falls on the informant.

The only information that the informant had previously given the officer involved homosexual conduct in the local railroad station. The following colloquy took place between respondent's counsel and the officer at the hearing on respondent's motion to suppress the evidence that had been seized from him.

Q: Now, with respect to the information that was given you about homosexuals in the Bridgeport Police Station (sic), did that lead to an arrest?

A: No.

Q: An arrest was not made.

A: No. There was no substantiating evidence.

Q: There was no substantiating evidence?

A: No.

Q: And what do you mean by that?

A: I didn't have occasion to witness these individuals committing any crime of any nature.

Q: In other words, after this person gave you the information, you checked for corroboration before you made an arrest. Is that right?

A: Well, I checked to determine the possibility of homosexual activity.

Q: And since an arrest was made, I take it you didn't find any substantiating information.

A: I'm sorry counselor, you say since an arrest was made.

Q: Was not made. Since an arrest was not made, I presume you didn't find any substantiating information.

A: No.

Q: So that you don't recall any other specific information given you about the commission of crimes by this informant.

A: No. . . .

Q: And you still thought this person was reliable.

A: Yes. . . .

We must decide whether or not the information possessed by this officer justified this interference with respondent's liberty. . . . *Terry* did not hold that whenever a policeman has a hunch that a citizen is engaging in criminal activity, he may engage in a stop and frisk. It held that if police officers want to stop and frisk, they must have specific facts from which they can reasonably infer that an individual is engaged in criminal activity and is armed and dangerous. It was central to our decision in *Terry* that the police officer acted on the basis of his own personal observations and that he carefully scrutinized the conduct of his suspects before interfering with them in any way. When we legitimated the conduct of the officer in *Terry* we did so because of the substantial reliability of the information on which the officer based his decision to act.

If the Court does not ignore the care with which we examined the knowledge possessed by the officer in *Terry* when he acted, then I cannot see how the actions of the officer in this case can be upheld. The Court explains what the officer knew about respondent before accosting him. But what is more significant is what he did not know. With respect to the scene generally, the officer had no idea how long respondent had been in the car, how long the car had been parked, or to whom the car belonged. With respect to the gun, the officer did not know if or when the informant had ever seen the gun, or whether the gun was carried legally, as Connecticut law permitted, or illegally. And with respect to the narcotics, the officer did not know what kind of narcotics respondent allegedly had, whether they were legally or illegally possessed, what the basis of the informant's knowledge was, or even whether the informant was capable of distinguishing narcotics from other substances.

Unable to answer any of these questions, the officer nevertheless determined that it was necessary to intrude on respondent's liberty. I believe that his determination was totally unreasonable. As I read *Terry*,

an officer may act on the basis of reliable information short of probable cause to make a stop, and ultimately a frisk, if necessary; but the officer may not use unreliable, unsubstantiated, conclusory hearsay to justify an invasion of liberty. *Terry* never meant to approve the kind of knee-jerk police reaction that we have before us in this case. . . .

Mr. Justice Douglas was the sole dissenter in *Terry*. He warned of the "powerful hydraulic pressures throughout our history that bear heavily on the Court to water down constitutional guarantees. . . ." While I took the position then that we were not watering down rights, but were hesitantly and cautiously striking a necessary balance between the rights of American citizens to be free from government intrusion into their privacy and their government's urgent need for a narrow exception to the warrant requirement of the Fourth Amendment, today's decision demonstrates just how prescient Mr. Justice Douglas was. It seems that the delicate balance that *Terry* struck was simply too delicate, too susceptible to the "hydraulic pressures" of the day. As a result of today's decision, the balance struck in *Terry* is now heavily weighted in favor of the government. And the Fourth Amendment, which was included in the Bill of Rights to prevent the kind of arbitrary and oppressive police action involved herein, is dealt a serious blow. Today's decision invokes the specter of a society in which innocent citizens may be stopped, searched, and arrested at the whim of police officers who have only the slightest suspicion of improper conduct.

CASE DISCUSSION

What fact was the foundation for the stop? For the frisk? Was the stop a pretext to find drugs? Did Officer John Connolly reasonably suspect that Robert Williams was armed? Explain. Should stop and frisk be limited to crimes threatening immediate violence? What interests would such a rule promote? Does it matter that the dissenters clearly believed that *Terry v. Ohio* involved a violent crime and that the Court intended to limit its holding to such crimes?

Terry v. Ohio, Sibron v. New York, and *Adams v. Williams* clarified two elements in the scope of lawful frisks:

1. They must accompany lawful stops.
2. Their sole purpose is to protect investigating officers.

In addition to these elements, courts have ruled that officers may use only the amount of bodily contact necessary to protect themselves. In most cases, this means that officers may lightly touch suspects' outer clothing in order to locate and seize concealed weapons. Courts are vague about how much further than these outer-clothing pat-downs that police officers may lawfully go.

The Model Code of Pre-arraignment Procedure includes the following circumstances that might justify more extensive contact than a pat-down of the outer clothing:

- Feeling a hard object inside a coat pocket that could be a weapon authorizes reaching inside the coat

- Encountering unusually bulky winter clothing may require feeling underneath the outer clothing

- Suspecting the contents of a closed handbag can justify opening the handbag

D e c i s i o n   P o i n t

In *Michigan v. Long*, two deputies saw a car swerve into a ditch and stopped to investigate. Long, the only occupant, met the deputies at the rear of the car, showed his driver's license, and started back toward the open door of the car when the deputies asked him for the car registration. The officers saw a large hunting knife on the floorboard, so one of the deputies frisked Long. The other then entered the vehicle and found an open pouch of marijuana under an arm rest.

Was the frisk lawful? The United States Supreme Court held that because

roadside encounters between police and suspects are especially hazardous, and . . . danger may arise from the possible presence of weapons in the area surrounding a suspect, [the] search of the passenger compartment of an automobile, limited to those areas in which a weapon may be placed or hidden, is permissible if the police officer possesses a reasonable belief based on "specific and articulable facts which, taken together with the rational inferences from those facts, reasonably warrant" the officer in believing that the suspect is dangerous and may gain immediate control of weapons.

The Court decided that these conditions were met.[37]

Conducting a protective search of an entire truck after finding weapons in a house that the driver just approached at high speed is also within the scope of a lawful frisk, according to the U.S. Seventh Circuit Court of Appeals.[38]

It is also within the scope of a lawful frisk to pat down all occupants of vehicles. How lawful is the "automatic companion" rule, adopted by several circuits, in which all companions in the immediate vicinity of a suspect are subject to pat-downs? For example, searching a suspect's companion's handbag has been ruled as lawful. However, the Sixth Circuit has rejected the automatic companion rule because, according to the court, the reasonable suspicion in *Terry v. Ohio* "has [not] been eroded to the point that an individual may be frisked based upon nothing more than an unfortunate choice of associates."[39]

SUMMARY

Police investigative activities range across a broad spectrum, including brief detentions, questioning, and weapons pat-downs in public as well as highly intrusive in-custody interrogation and strip and body cavity searches. According to the Supreme Court's interpretation of the Fourth Amendment, stops are seizures and frisks are searches. The Fourth Amendment does not encompass all the deprivations and intrusions associated with police investigation. It excludes voluntary encounters between citizens and police on the street, but it does cover brief detentions where police physically grab citizens, citizens submit to a police show of authority, or both.

The Fourth Amendment requires an objective basis for a stop; in other words, it requires facts that would lead a police officer to reasonably suspect that crime is afoot. Furthermore, the Fourth Amendment limits the duration, scope, and location of stops. Police may "freeze" a suspicious situation only long enough to conduct an on-the-spot check for ID and to investigate the reasons for suspicious persons' presence. Lawful stops authorize frisks for weapons. Officers who reasonably suspect that individuals are armed may pat them down—go over their outer clothing lightly—for weapons. The sole purpose of frisks is to protect officers; officers should not have to risk their lives unduly to investigate crime.

The Fourth Amendment applies less rigid standards to stops at international borders to intercept illegal drugs and apprehend drug smugglers. In these cases, officials may detain travelers longer and search them more extensively than in ordinary street stops. The Fourth Amendment also permits DWI checkpoints that detain citizens briefly for sobriety checks without the usually required reasonable suspicion. The special government need to prevent drunk driving and apprehend drunk drivers outweighs the privacy and liberty interest in brief highway stops, according to the Supreme Court.

Stop-and-frisk law balances a number of interests: (1) obtaining accurate and sufficient facts to support criminal investigation on the street; (2) protecting citizens against unwarranted or discriminatory invasions of privacy and other indignities in public places; (3) preserving and extending the rule of law to police encounters with citizens on the street; (4) satisfying organizational interests in efficient, economical, and harmonious police operations; and (5) reducing the police frustration with interference in their job that is sometimes called "handcuffing the police."

REVIEW QUESTIONS

1. Explain the purpose of stops and frisks.

2. Briefly describe the history of stop-and-frisk law.

3. What basic issues did the Supreme Court have to address when it decided *Terry v. Ohio*?

4. Define a *stop*.

5. What is the objective basis for a lawful stop? Give at least three examples of what such a basis might consist.

6. Explain the difference between actual seizure and show-of-authority stops. When is a person seized in a show-of-authority stop?

7. What three criteria measure the scope of a stop?

8. How and why does the Fourth Amendment apply more flexibly to stops and searches at international borders?

9. How and why does the Fourth Amendment apply more flexibly to DWI checkpoints?

10. Define a *frisk*.

11. What is the objective basis of a frisk? List three examples of what this basis might consist.

12. How extensive a search might a frisk include?

13. What are the major arguments in favor of allowing frisks? What are the major dangers?

KEY TERMS

actual seizure stops the physical grabbing of a suspect.

articulable facts the specific, identifiable facts that provide the objective basis for a stop.

balancing approach to the Fourth Amendment the element of reasonableness that balances government interest in law enforcement against individual interests in privacy and liberty.

bright line approach the determination of reasonableness according to a specific rule that applies to all cases.

case-by-case method the determination of reasonableness by considering the totality of circumstances in each individual case.

conventional Fourth Amendment approach wherein the warrant and reasonableness clauses are firmly connected.

direct information facts that police officers acquire directly from their physical senses.

drug courier profile a list of general characteristics that the government associates with illicit drug dealing.

frisks pat-downs of the outer clothing for weapons.

hearsay information derived from third persons, not known firsthand by the person providing it.

individualized suspicion facts that point to suspecting a particular individual of illegal activity.

objective basis the factual foundations required to back up official action against individuals.

reasonableness Fourth Amendment approach wherein the warrant and reasonableness clauses are distinct.

reasonableness test wherein the reasonableness of searches and seizures depends on balancing government and individual interests and the objective basis of the searches and seizures.

reasonable stop standard the rule under which a show-of-authority stop is determined by whether a reasonable person would believe that he or she was not free to leave or otherwise terminate an encounter with a police officer.

reasonable suspicion facts, apparent facts, or circumstances that would lead a reasonable person to suspect that a crime may have been, may be about to be, or may be in the process of being committed.

show-of-authority stops submissions to the display of official force.

stops brief, on-the-spot detentions that freeze suspicious situations so that law enforcement officers can determine whether to arrest, investigate further, or terminate further action.

"totality of circumstances" all the facts surrounding a government invasion of privacy, liberty, or property.

Notes

1. Loren G. Stern, "Stop and Frisk: An Historical Answer to a Modern Problem," *Journal of Criminal Law, Criminology, and Police Science* 58 (1967): 532; Frank Remington, "The Law Relating to 'On the Street' Detention, Questioning, and Frisking of Suspected Persons and Police Arrest Privileges in General," *Journal of Criminal Law, Criminology, and Police Science* 50 (1960): 390.

2. Leonard Levy, *The Origins of the Fifth Amendment* (New York: Oxford, 1968), discusses the history of these developments at great length. See also Wayne R. LaFave, "Street Encounters and the Constitution: Terry, Sibron, and Peters, and Beyond," *Michigan Law Review* 37 (1968): 39.

3. Wayland D. Pilcher, "The Law and Practice of Field Interrogation," *Journal of Criminal Law, Criminology,*

and *Police Science* 58 (1967): 465, 490 (between 3 and 4 percent of those stopped are arrested).

4. John M. Copacino, "Suspicionless Criminal Seizures After *Michigan Department of State Police v. Sitz*," *American Criminal Law Review* 31 (1994): 215.

5. George E. Dix, "Nonarrest Investigatory Detentions in Search and Seizure Law," *Duke Law Journal* (1985): 849, 853–54.

6. American Law Institute, *Model Code of Pre-arraignment Procedure: Proposed Official Draft, Complete Text, and Commentary* (Philadelphia: American Law Institute, 1975): 270–72.

7. *Adams v. Williams*, 407 U.S. 143, 92 S.Ct. 1921, 32 L.Ed.2d 612 (1972).

8. Philip B. Kurland and Gerhard Casper, eds., "Brief for the NAACP Legal Defense and Educational Fund, Inc., as Amicus Curiae" in the case of *Terry v. Ohio*, *Landmark Briefs and Arguments of the Supreme Court of the United States* (Washington, DC: University Publications of America, 1975).

9. *Brower v. Inyo*, 489 U.S. 593, 109 S.Ct. 1378, 103 L.Ed. 2d 628 (1989).

10. Robert V. Ward, "Consenting to a Search or Seizure in Poor and Minority Neighborhoods: No Place for a 'Reasonable Person,'" *Howard University Law Review* 36 (1993): 239, 254.

11. *INS v. Delgado*, 466 U.S. 210, 104 S.Ct. 1758, 80 L.Ed.2d 247 (1984).

12. *Brown v. Texas*, 443 U.S. 47, 99 S.Ct. 2637, 61 L.Ed.2d 357 (1979).

13. Quoted in J. Shane Craemer, *The Law of Arrest, Search and Seizure*, 3d ed. (New York: Holt, Rinehart and Winston, 1980), 37.

14. *United States v. Cortez*, 449 U.S. 411, 417–18, 101 S.Ct. 690, 694–95, 66 L.Ed. 2d 621 (1981).

15. *Adams v. Williams*, 407 U.S. 143, 92 S.Ct. 1921, 32 L.Ed. 2d 612 (1972).

16. David S. Rudstein, "White on White: Anonymous Tips, Reasonable Suspicion and the Constitution," *University of Kentucky Law Journal* 79 (1991): 679.

17. *U.S. v. Elmore*, 595 F.2d 1036, 1039, n. 3 (5th Cir. 1979), cert. denied, 447 U.S. 910 (1980).

18. Morgan Cloud, "Search and Seizure by the Numbers: The Drug Courier Profile and Judicial Review of Investigative Formulas," *Boston University Law Review* 65 (1985): 843, 848–49.

19. Ibid., 854.

20. *United States v. Sharpe*, 470 U.S. 675 (1985).

21. *United States v. Hensley*, 469 U.S. 221, 228, 105 S.Ct. 675, 679, 83 L.Ed. 2d 604 (1985).

22. 469 U.S. 221, 105 S.Ct. 675, 83 L.Ed.2d 604 (1985) (wanted flier).

23. *Michigan v. Summers*, 452 U.S. 692, 101 S.Ct. 2587, 69 L.Ed.2d 340 (1981).

24. *Hayes v. Florida*, 470 U.S. 811, 105 S.Ct. 1643, 84 L.Ed.2d 705 (1985); *United States v. Alvarez-Sanchez*, 774 F.2d. 1036 (11th Cir. 1985).

25. American Law Institute, "Commentary," *Model Code of Pre-arraignment Procedure*, 283.

26. *Florida v. Royer*, 460 U.S. 491, 103 S.Ct. 1319, 75 L.Ed.2d 229 (1983).

27. *Hayes v. Florida*, 470 U.S. 811, 105 S.Ct. 1643, 84 L.Ed.2d 705 (1985).

28. *United States v. Sharpe*, 470 U.S. 675, 682, 105 S.Ct. 1568, 1573, 84 L.Ed.2d 605 (1985); Rosemary Ryan Alexander, "Unwarranted Power at the Border: The Intrusive Body Search," *Southwestern Law Journal* 32 (1978): 1005–26; Gregory L. Waples, "From Bags to Body Cavities: The Law of Border Searches," *Columbia Law Review* 74 (1974): 53–87; Note, "Border Searches and the Fourth Amendment," *Yale Law Journal* 77 (1968): 1007–18; Note, "Intrusive Border Searches—Is Judicial Control Desirable," *University of Pennsylvania Law Review* 115 (1966): 276–87.

29. For extended discussions of *Michigan v. Sitz*, see Thomas Hickey and Michael Axline, "Drunk-Driving Roadblocks Under State Constitutions: A Reasonable Alternative to *Michigan v. Sitz*," *Criminal Law Bulletin* 28 (1992): 195; William P. Weiner and Larry S. Royster, "Sobriety Checkpoints in Michigan: The *Sitz* Case and Its Aftermath," *T. M. Cooley Law Review* 8 (1991): 243.

30. *People v. Rivera*, 14 N.Y.2d 441, 252 N.Y.S.2d 458, 462, 463, 201 N.E.2d 32 (1964).

31. *People v. McGowan*, 69 Ill.2d 73, 12 Ill. Dec. 733, 370 N.E.2d 537 (1977) (bulge in clothing).

32. *Commonwealth v. Hawkes*, 362 Mass. 786, 291 N.E.2d 411 (1973) (reaching toward pocket).

33. *State v. Giltner*, 56 Hawaii 374, 537 P.2d 14 (1975) (armed on previous occasion).

34. See Craemer, *Law of Arrest, Search, and Seizure*, for a discussion of the experienced police officer standard.

35. 392 U.S. 40, 88 S.Ct. 1889, 20 L.Ed.2d 917 (1968).

36. American Law Institute, "Stop and Frisk," *Model Code of Pre-arraignment Procedure*; Schwartz, 433, 461.

37. 463 U.S. 1032, 103 S.Ct. 3469, 77 L.Ed.2d 1201 (1983).

38. American Law Institute, *Model Code of Pre-arraignment Procedure*, 279; *Michigan v. Long*, 463 U.S. 1032, 103 S.Ct. 3469, 77 L.Ed.2d 1201 (1983); *United States v. Denney*, 771 F.2d 318 (7th Cir. 1985).

39. *United States v. Vigo*, 487 F.2d 295 (2d Cir. 1973).

CHAPTER FIVE

Seizures of Persons: Arrest

CHAPTER OUTLINE

CHAPTER MAIN POINTS

1. The purposes of arrest are to gather information in the investigation of criminals and to detain suspects during the investigation.

2. The law of arrest balances the interests of the need for information, procedural regularity, and individual liberty.

3. Arrests are greater invasions of liberty than stops and require a greater objective basis to back them up.

4. Like other seizures, whether arrests are seizures depends on their duration, location, and invasiveness.

5. The law of arrest governs when a seizure is an arrest, whether an arrest is an unreasonable seizure, and whether the court should exclude evidence obtained from unreasonable arrests.

6. Arrests are reasonable seizures if probable cause backs them up and they are made in the proper manner.

7. The probable cause requirement ensures an objective basis to back up arrests and permits magistrates to judge that basis independently.

8. Probable cause to arrest means facts or circumstances leading to the reasonable belief that a crime has been, is being, or is about to be committed and that the person arrested has committed it.

9. Both direct and hearsay information can establish probable cause.

10. The totality of circumstances determines the weight given to the information of informants.

11. In arrests with warrants, magistrates determine probable cause before arrest; in arrests without warrants, magistrates determine probable cause after arrest.

12. Arrests in homes require warrants, except in emergencies.

13. The rule that officers must witness misdemeanors in order to make an arrest without a warrant is relaxing, particularly in cases of domestic abuse.

14. Shooting suspects is a seizure; it is unreasonable unless suspects endanger police officers or others.

15. The standard of objective reasonableness based on the totality of circumstances determines whether the use of force in arresting suspects amounts to an unreasonable seizure.

Was He Arrested?

Royer was observed at Miami International Airport by two plainclothes detectives of the Dade County, Florida, Public Safety Department assigned to the county's Organized Crime Bureau, Narcotics Investigation Section. Detectives Johnson and Magdalena believed that Royer's appearance, mannerisms, luggage, and actions fit the so-called "drug courier profile."

Royer, apparently unaware of the attention he had attracted, purchased a one-way ticket to New York City and checked his two suitcases, placing on each suitcase an identification tag bearing the name "Holt" and the destination, "LaGuardia." As Royer made his way to the concourse that led to the airline boarding area, the two detectives approached him, identified themselves as police officers working out of the sheriff's office, and asked if Royer had a "moment" to speak with them; Royer said "Yes."

Upon request, but without oral consent, Royer produced for the detectives his airline ticket and his driver's license. The airline ticket, like the baggage identification tags, bore the name "Holt" whereas the driver's license carried respondent's correct name, "Royer." When the detectives asked about the discrepancy, Royer explained that a friend had made the reservation in the name of "Holt." Royer became noticeably more nervous during this conversation, whereupon the detectives informed him that they were in fact narcotics investigators and that they had reason to suspect him of transporting narcotics.

The detectives did not return the airline ticket and identification but asked Royer to accompany them to a room, approximately forty feet away, adjacent to the concourse. Royer said nothing in response but went with the officers as he had been asked to do. The room was later described by Detective Johnson as a "large storage closet" located in the stewardesses' lounge and containing a small desk and two chairs.

PURPOSES OF ARREST
AND ARREST LAW

Stops and arrests are both Fourth Amendment seizures. However, they differ in that arrests involve greater invasions of liberty than stops do. Stops briefly freeze street situations so that police officers can investigate suspicious persons and circumstances. Arrests are longer detentions in which officers ordinarily move suspects from open public places to police cars and stations. In addition to providing additional time for police officers to gather information, arrests provide prosecutors with time to decide whether to charge suspects with crimes. Hence, the decision to arrest—as does the decision to stop—allows the gathering of information in order to further the interest of punishing the guilty and setting the innocent free.

The law of arrest balances interests that extend beyond reaching the correct result in the case at hand. It also furthers the general interests in procedural regularity and individual autonomy in our constitutional democracy. Even where probable cause exists, arrests must still comport both with the human dignity valued in a free society and with the broad social interest in state impartiality regarding race, gender, status, and power. Restrictions on the manner and scope of arrest protect the integrity of the criminal process and control the natural excesses to which state power, like all power, is prone. These general interests in human dignity and impartiality can run counter to the interest in obtaining the correct result in individual cases. The law of arrest balances these general interests by defining *arrest* and establishing whether the scope, manner, duration, and conditions of arrests comply with the requirements of the Fourth Amendment.

THE DEFINITION OF *ARREST*

Whether Fourth Amendment seizures are stops or arrests depends on their duration, location, and invasiveness. As we saw in Chapter 4, stops are measured in minutes. Arrests, on the other hand, can last hours, sometimes even days. Stops ordinarily begin and end on the street or in other places familiar to people. Arrests, at least felony arrests, usually involve taking suspects to police stations, places where most people feel uncomfortable, isolated, and intimidated. Arrests produce written documents that become part of a person's record, or "rap sheet"; stops rarely get "written up." Interrogation (Chapter 8) and identification procedures (Chapter 9), such as participating in lineups,

TABLE 5.1 DEPRIVATIONS OF LIBERTY OF INDIVIDUALS

Deprivation	Objective Basis	Duration	Location	Degree of Invasion
Voluntary contact	None	Brief	On the spot	Moral and psychological pressure
Stop	Reasonable suspicion	Minutes	At or near the stop, on the street, or in another public place	Reveal identification and explain whereabouts
Arrest	Probable cause	Hours to a few days	Usually removal to a police station or other not-so-public place	Fingerprints, booking, photograph, interrogation, identification procedures
Detention	Probable cause promptly verified by magistrate	Days to months	Jail	Inventory, full body, strip, and body cavity searches; restricted contact with outside
Imprisonment	Proof beyond a reasonable doubt	Years to life	Prison	Same as detention, with heightened invasions of privacy, liberty, and property

frequently accompany felony arrests. Arrests can produce fear, anxiety, and loss of liberty that not only put an emotional strain on suspects but can also lead to at least a temporary loss of their income, and even to the loss of employment itself. These strains and losses extend beyond suspects themselves, embarrassing and causing economic hardship to the families of arrested people. These embarrassments and hardships rarely, if ever, accompany a Fourth Amendment stop.

On the continuum of encounters between private individuals and police officers, arrest lies between voluntary contacts and investigatory stops on one end of the continuum and detentions before conviction and imprisonment after conviction at the other end of the continuum. As with stops, the duration, location, and intrusiveness of a seizure determine whether the police have arrested an individual (see Table 5.1).

D e c i s i o n   P o i n t

Consider the following hypothetical situations. In which did an arrest take place? Review your answers after reading the rest of the chapter.

1. A police officer phones a woman and "requests" that she come down to the station to "discuss" an incident. The woman complies with the request.

2. Police officers stop a car. One officer stations herself at the driver's door; her partner stands at the passenger's door. The driver asks, "Are you arresting me?" One officer answers, "No, we're just detaining you until we get answers to some questions we have about your involvement in a burglary."

3. Police officers approach a man on the street, saying, "You're under arrest." They have made the approach from behind and cannot see the suspect's face. As soon as he turns to face the officers, they realize they have the wrong man. They release him immediately.

4. Police officers order a woman into their squad car and take her to the police station, where they question her. They write nothing down, nor do they book, fingerprint, or photograph her. She asks if she is under arrest. They answer, "No, we're just questioning you."

5. Police officers stop a man on the street. One officer says, "Come with us." The officers take the man first to a crime scene, then to his apartment, while they question him about a murder. They write a report and release him. The episode lasts two hours.

6. Police officers take a suspect to the station and book, fingerprint, and photograph her. They ask her questions, write a report, and release her. Neither they nor she mentions the word *arrest*.

How long must a seizure last to turn a stop into an arrest? How intrusive may a stop be until it becomes an arrest? How far must police officers move an individual in order to make a seizure an arrest? No bright line illuminates the distinction between stops and arrests. The Supreme Court dealt with these problems in *Florida v. Royer*.

C A S E

Was Royer Arrested?

Florida v. Royer
460 U.S. 491, 103 S.Ct. 1319,
75 L.Ed.2d 229 (1983)

Royer pleaded not guilty to felony possession of marijuana. Prior to trial, Royer moved to suppress the evidence obtained in the search of his suitcases. The trial court denied his motion to suppress. Royer changed his plea from not guilty to nolo contendere (no contest), reserving the right to appeal the denial of the suppression motion. Royer was convicted. The district court of appeal reversed Royer's conviction. The United States Supreme Court granted Florida's petition for writ of certiorari and affirmed the court of appeal's reversal of Royer's conviction. Justice White announced the judgment of the Court and delivered an opinion in which Justices Marshall, Powell, and Stevens joined. Justice Powell filed a concurring opinion. Justice Brennan filed an opinion concurring in the result. Justice Blackmun filed a dissenting opinion. Justice Rehnquist filed a dissenting opinion, in

which Chief Justice Burger and Justice O'Connor joined.

FACTS

On January 3, 1978, Royer was observed at Miami International Airport by two plainclothes detectives of the Dade County, Florida, Public Safety Department assigned to the County's Organized Crime Bureau, Narcotics Investigation Section. Detectives Johnson and Magdalena believed that Royer's appearance, mannerisms, luggage, and actions fit the so-called "drug courier profile."

[COURT NOTE: "The 'drug courier profile' is an abstract of characteristics found to be typical of persons transporting illegal drugs. In Royer's case, the detectives' attention was attracted by the following facts which were considered to be within the profile: a) Royer was carrying American Tourister luggage, which appeared to be heavy, b) he was young, apparently between 25–35, c) he was casually dressed, d) Royer appeared pale and nervous, looking around at other people, e) Royer paid for his ticket in cash with a large number of bills, and f) rather than completing the airline identification tag to be attached to checked luggage, which had space for a name, address, and telephone number, Royer wrote only a name and the destination."]

Royer, apparently unaware of the attention he had attracted, purchased a one-way ticket to New York City and checked his two suitcases, placing on each suitcase an identification tag bearing the name "Holt" and the destination, "LaGuardia." As Royer made his way to the concourse which led to the airline boarding area, the two detectives approached him, identified themselves as policemen working out of the sheriff's office, and asked if Royer had a "moment" to speak with them; Royer said "Yes."

Upon request, but without oral consent, Royer produced for the detectives his airline ticket and his driver's license. The airline ticket, like the baggage identification tags, bore the name "Holt," while the driver's license carried respondent's correct name, "Royer." When the detectives asked about the discrepancy, Royer explained that a friend had made the reservation in the name of "Holt." Royer became noticeably more nervous during this conversation, whereupon the detectives informed Royer that they were in fact narcotics investigators and that they had reason to suspect him of transporting narcotics.

The detectives did not return his airline ticket and identification but asked Royer to accompany them to a room, approximately forty feet away, adjacent to the concourse. Royer said nothing in response but went with the officers as he had been asked to do. The room was later described by Detective Johnson as a "large storage closet," located in the stewardesses' lounge and containing a small desk and two chairs. Without Royer's consent or agreement, Detective Johnson, using Royer's baggage check stubs, retrieved the "Holt" luggage from the airline and brought it to the room where respondent and Detective Magdalena were waiting. Royer was asked if he would consent to a search of the suitcases. Without orally responding to this request, Royer produced a key and unlocked one of the suitcases, which the detective then opened without seeking further assent from Royer. Drugs were found in that suitcase.

According to Detective Johnson, Royer stated that

he did not know the combination to the lock on the second suitcase. When asked if he objected to the detective opening the second suitcase, Royer said "no, go ahead," and did not object when the detective explained that the suitcase might have to be broken open. The suitcase was pried open by the officers and more marijuana was found. Royer was then told that he was under arrest. Approximately fifteen minutes had elapsed from the time the detectives initially approached respondent until his arrest upon the discovery of the contraband.

Prior to his trial for felony possession of marijuana, Royer made a motion to suppress the evidence obtained in the search of the suitcases. The trial court found that Royer's consent to the search was "freely and voluntarily given," and that, regardless of the consent, the warrantless search was reasonable because "the officer doesn't have the time to run out and get a search warrant because the plane is going to take off." . . . [See Chapter 6 on search warrants and on consent searches.] The District Court of Appeal reversed Royer's conviction. On appeal, a panel of the District Court of Appeal of Florida found that viewing the totality of the circumstances, the finding of consent by the trial court was supported by clear and convincing evidence. The panel decision was vacated and rehearing *en banc* granted. It is the decision of the *en banc* court that is reviewed here. . . . We granted the State's petition for certiorari, and now affirm. . . .

OPINION

The State proffers three reasons for holding that when Royer consented to the search of his luggage he was not being illegally detained. First, it is submitted that the entire encounter was consensual and hence Royer was not being held against his will at all. We find this submission untenable. Asking for and examining Royer's ticket and his driver'[s] license were no doubt permissible in themselves, but when the officers identified themselves as narcotics agents, told Royer that he was suspected of transporting narcotics, and asked him to accompany them to the police room, while retaining his ticket and driver's license and without indicating in any way that he was free to depart, Royer was effectively seized for the purposes of the Fourth Amendment. These circumstances surely amount to a show of official authority such that "a reasonable person would have believed he was not free to leave."

Second, the State submits that if Royer was seized, there existed reasonable, articulable suspicion to justify a temporary detention and that the limits of a *Terry*-type stop were never exceeded [*Terry v. Ohio* (1968)]. We agree with the State that when the officers discovered that Royer was traveling under an assumed name, this fact, and the facts already known to the officers—paying cash for a one-way ticket, the mode of checking the two bags, and Royer's appearance and conduct in general—were adequate grounds for suspecting Royer of carrying drugs and for temporarily detaining him and his luggage while they attempted to verify or dispel their suspicions in a manner that did not exceed the limits of an investigative detention. We also agree that had Royer voluntarily consented to the search of his luggage while he was justifiably being detained on reasonable suspicion, the products of the search would be admissible against him. We have concluded, however, that at the time Royer produced the key to his suitcase, the detention to which he was then subjected was a more serious intrusion on his personal liberty than is allowable on mere suspicion of criminal activity.

By the time Royer was informed that the officers wished to examine his luggage, he had identified himself when approached by the officers and had attempted to explain the discrepancy between the name shown on his identification and the name under which he had purchased his ticket and identified his luggage. The officers were not satisfied, for they informed him they were narcotics agents and had reason to believe that he was carrying illegal drugs. They requested him to accompany them to the police room. Royer went with them. He found himself in a small room—a large closet—equipped with a desk and two chairs. He was alone with two police officers who again told him that they thought he was carrying narcotics. He also found that the officers, without his consent, had retrieved his checked luggage from the airlines. What had begun as a consensual inquiry in a public place has escalated into an investigatory procedure in a police interrogation room, where the police, unsatisfied with previous explanations, sought to confirm their suspicions. The officers had Royer's ticket, they had his identification, and they had seized his luggage. Royer was never informed that he was free to

board his plane if he so chose, and he reasonably believed that he was being detained. At least as of that moment, any consensual aspects of the encounter had evaporated, and . . . *Terry v. Ohio* and the cases following it did not justify the restraint to which Royer was then subjected. As a practical matter, Royer was under arrest. Consistent with this conclusion, the State conceded . . . that Royer would not have been free to leave the interrogation room had he asked to do so. . . .

The case before us differs in important respects [from *United States v. Mendenhall* (1980); see Chapter 4]. Here, Royer's ticket and identification remained in the possession of the officers throughout the encounter; the officers also seized and had possession of his luggage. As a practical matter, Royer could not leave the airport without them. In *Mendenhall*, no luggage was involved, the ticket and identification were immediately returned, and the officers were careful to advise that the suspect could decline to be searched. Here, the officers had seized Royer's luggage and made no effort to advise him that he need not consent to the search. . . .

We do not suggest that there is a litmus-paper test for distinguishing a consensual encounter from a seizure for determining when a seizure exceeds the bounds of an investigative stop. Even in the discrete category of airport encounters, there will be endless variations in the facts and circumstances, so much variation that it is unlikely that the courts can reduce to a sentence or a paragraph a rule that will provide unarguable answers to the question whether there has been an unreasonable search or seizure in violation of the Fourth Amendment. . . .

The State's third and final argument is that Royer was not being illegally held when he gave his consent because there was probable cause to arrest him at that time. . . . The facts are that a nervous young man with two American Tourister bags paid cash for an airline ticket to a "target city." These facts led to inquiry, which in turn revealed that the ticket had been bought under an assumed name. The proffered explanation did not satisfy the officers. We cannot agree with the State, if this is its position, that every nervous young man paying cash for a ticket to New York City under an assumed name and carrying two heavy American Tourister bags may be arrested and held to answer for a serious felony charge. . . .

The judgment of the Florida Court of Appeal is accordingly Affirmed.

DISSENT

Justice Blackmun, dissenting.

The public has a compelling interest in detecting those who would traffic in deadly drugs for personal profit. Few problems affecting the health and welfare of our population, particularly our young, cause greater concern than the escalating use of controlled substances. Much of the drug traffic is highly organized and conducted by sophisticated criminal syndicates. The profits are enormous. And many drugs . . . may be easily concealed. As a result, the obstacles to detection of illegal conduct may be unmatched in any other area of law enforcement. In my view, the police conduct in this case was minimally intrusive. Given the strength of society's interest in overcoming the extraordinary obstacles to the detection of drug traffickers, such conduct should not be subjected to a requirement of probable cause. Because the Court holds otherwise, I dissent. . . .

Justice Rehnquist, with whom the Chief Justice and Justice O'Connor join, dissenting.

. . . The plurality focuses on the transfer of the place of the interview from the main concourse of the airport to the room off the concourse. . . . [Respondent] was alone with two officers who again told him that they thought he was carrying narcotics. He also found that the officers, without his consent, had retrieved his checked luggage from the airline. . . .

The question we must decide is what was unreasonable about the steps which these officers took with respect to this suspect in the Miami Airport on this particular day. . . . The plurality concludes that somewhere between the beginning of the 40-foot journey and the resumption of conversation in the room the investigation became so intrusive that [it left Royer] . . . "[a]s a practical matter . . . under arrest." But if Royer was legally approached in the first instance and consented to accompany the detectives to the room, it does not follow that his consent went up in smoke and he was "arrested" upon entering the room.

CASE DISCUSSION

What elements of Royer's detention are problematic—the duration, the intrusiveness, or the location of the detention? Why? Does Justice Rehnquist have a point in his dissent that all "thoughtful, serious" citizens would find this detention reasonable? Royer is guilty, so why set him free?

PROBABLE CAUSE

The reasonableness of an arrest depends on two critical elements:

1. The objective basis for the arrest
2. The manner in which officers arrest suspects

According to the Fourth Amendment, **probable cause** is the objective basis required for a reasonable arrest. Probable cause is a quantitative term, referring to both the number and the quality of facts and circumstances. It lies on a continuum between reasonable suspicion on one end and proof beyond a reasonable doubt on the other. Table 5.2 depicts roughly the primary objective basis requirements in criminal procedure. Probable cause to arrest means that there are enough facts and circumstances to lead police officers, in the light of their experience, to the reasonable *belief* that the person arrested *has* committed, *is* committing, or *is* about to commit a crime. (Contrast this definition with the reasonable-grounds-to-suspect standard for stops discussed in Chapter 4.) According to the United States Supreme Court, the determination of probable cause consists of two principal components:

TABLE 5.2 OBJECTIVE BASIS REQUIREMENTS

Encounter	Objective Basis	Duration	Location	Invasion
Voluntary contact	None required	Usually brief	On the spot	Voluntary compliance
Stop	Reasonable suspicion	Minutes	On or near the spot	Identification and brief explanation of presence and activity
Arrest	Probable cause	Hours to a few days	Jail	Photograph, booking, interrogation, lineup, showup, fingerprinting, full body search
Pretrial detention	Probable cause verified by magistrate	Days to months	Jail	Full body, strip, body cavity, inventory searches; limited access to outside world
Imprisonment	Proof beyond a reasonable doubt	Years	Prison	Highly restricted rights of liberty, privacy, and property

1. "The events which occurred leading up to the" arrest.
2. The "decision whether these historical facts, viewed from the standpoint of an objectively reasonable police officer, amount to . . . probable cause."[1]

Probable cause is an objective standard. The subjective belief of the police officer making an arrest is not probable cause, for the belief must be reasonable—that is, facts and circumstances must back it up. Hence, the relevant question in probable cause inquiries is not whether police officers in good faith honestly believe that those they arrest have committed, are committing, or are about to commit crimes. Rather, the question is whether their belief is *reasonable*. That is to say, do they have both the number and the quality of facts and circumstances required to back up their belief that the people they arrest have committed, are committing, or are about to commit crimes?

The probable cause requirement serves at least two purposes:

1. It ensures that the quality and quantity of facts and circumstances support the serious invasions of liberty that arrests entail.
2. It allows judges to decide for themselves whether probable cause exists.

The probable cause requirement balances the societal interest in law enforcement and the individual right of locomotion—the freedom to come and go as we please. According to the classic probable cause case, *Brinegar v. United States,*

> These long prevailing standards [of probable cause] seek to safeguard citizens from rash and unreasonable interferences with privacy and from unfounded charges of crime. They also seek to give fair leeway for enforcing the law in the community's protection. Because many situations which confront officers in the course of executing their duties are more or less ambiguous, room must be allowed for some mistakes on their part. But the mistakes must be those of

reasonable men, acting on facts leading sensibly to their conclusions of probability. The rule of probable cause is a practical, nontechnical conception affording the best compromise that has been found for accommodating these often opposing interests. Requiring more would unduly hamper law enforcement. To allow less would be to leave law-abiding citizens at the mercy of the officers' whim or caprice.[2]

Probable cause is a commonsense rule. Its day-to-day application rests mainly with officers on the street who need to make quick decisions without the benefit of the cool reflection that the leisurely atmosphere of a scholar's study, or even a courtroom, allows. According to the Court in *Brinegar*, "In dealing with probable cause . . . as the very name implies, we deal with probabilities. These are not technical; they are the factual and practical considerations of everyday life on which reasonable and prudent men, not legal technicians, act."[3] So, although officers may not arrest on hunch, whim, or mere suspicion, and albeit judges ultimately determine whether probable cause exists, courts tend to favor the facts as police see them. According to one judge,

> Police officers patrolling the streets do not prearrange the setting within which they operate. They do not schedule their steps in the calm reflective atmosphere of some remote law library. Events occur without warning and policemen are required as a matter of duty to act as a reasonably prudent policeman would under the circumstan[c]es as those circumstances unfold before him.[4]

One of the best discussions of probable cause and one of the clearest explanation of its application to the facts of a specific arrest appears in *Draper v. United States*.

C A S E

Did the Officers Have Probable Cause to Arrest?

Draper v. United States
358 U.S. 307, 79 S.Ct. 329,
3 L.Ed.2d 327 (1959)

Draper was prosecuted for knowingly concealing and transporting narcotic drugs in violation of federal narcotics laws. The United States District Court for the District of Colorado denied Draper's motion to suppress evidence, and Draper was convicted. Draper appealed. The court of appeals affirmed the conviction. The United States Supreme Court granted certiorari *and then affirmed the conviction. Justice Whittaker wrote the opinion of the Court. Chief Justice Warren and Justice Frankfurter took no part in this case.*

FACTS

The evidence offered at the hearing on the motion to suppress . . . established that . . . Marsh, a federal narcotic agent with 29 years' experience, was stationed at Denver; that . . . Hereford had been engaged as a "special employee" of the Bureau of Narcotics at Denver for about six months, and from time to time gave information to Marsh regarding violations of the narcotics laws, for which Hereford was paid small sums of money, and that Marsh had always found the information given by Hereford to be accurate and reliable. On September 3, 1956, Hereford told Marsh that James Draper (petitioner) recently had taken up abode at a stated address in Denver and "was peddling narcotics to several addicts" in that city. Four days later, on September 7, Hereford told Marsh "that Draper had gone to Chicago the day before (September 6) by train (and) that he was going to bring back three ounces of heroin (and) that he would return to Denver either on the morning of the 8th of September or the morning of the 9th of September also by train." Hereford also gave Marsh a detailed physical description of Draper and of the clothing he was wearing, and said that he would be carrying "a tan zipper bag," and that he habitually "walked real fast." [COURT NOTE: "Hereford told Marsh that Draper was a Negro of light brown complexion, 27 years of age, 5 feet 8 inches tall, weighed about 160 pounds, and that he was wearing a light colored raincoat, brown slacks, and black shoes."]

On the morning of September 8, Marsh and a Denver police officer went to the Denver Union Station and kept watch over all incoming trains from Chicago, but they did not see anyone fitting the description that Hereford had given. Repeating the process on the morning of September 9, they saw a person, having the exact physical attributes and wearing the precise clothing described by Hereford, alight from an incoming Chicago train and start walking "fast" toward the exit. He was carrying a tan zipper bag in his right hand and the left was thrust in his raincoat pocket. Marsh, accompanied by the police officer, overtook, stopped and arrested him. They then searched him and found the two "envelopes containing heroin" clutched in his left hand in his raincoat pocket, and found the syringe in the tan zipper bag. Marsh then took him (petitioner) into custody. Hereford died four days after the arrest and therefore did not testify at the hearing on the motion.

OPINION

The Narcotic Control Act of 1956, 70 Stat. 570, 26 U.S.C.A. 7607, provides, in pertinent part:

The Commissioner . . . and agents, of the Bureau of Narcotics . . . may—(2) make arrests without warrant for violations of any law of the United States relating to narcotic drugs . . . where the violation is committed in the presence of the person making the arrest or where

such person has reasonable grounds to believe that the person to be arrested has committed or is committing such violation.

The crucial question for us then is whether knowledge of the related facts and circumstances gave Marsh "probable cause" within the meaning of the Fourth Amendment, and "reasonable grounds" within the meaning of §104(a) to believe that petitioner had committed or was committing a violation of the narcotics laws. [COURT NOTE: "The terms 'probable cause' as used in the Fourth Amendment and 'reasonable grounds' as used in § 104 (a) of the Narcotic Control Act, 70 Stat. 570, are substantial equivalents of the same meaning."] If it did, the arrest, though without a warrant, was lawful and the subsequent search of petitioner's person and the seizure of the found heroin were validly made incident to a lawful arrest, and therefore the motion to suppress was properly overruled and the heroin was competently received in evidence at the trial.

Petitioner contends (1) that the information given by Hereford to Marsh was "hearsay" and, because hearsay is not legally competent evidence in a criminal trial, could not legally have been considered, but should have been put out of mind, by Marsh in assessing whether he had "probable cause" and "reasonable grounds" to arrest petitioner without a warrant, and (2) that, even if hearsay could lawfully have been considered, Marsh's information should be held insufficient to show "probable cause" and "reasonable grounds" to believe that petitioner had violated or was violating the narcotic laws and to justify his arrest without a warrant.

Considering the first contention, we find petitioner entirely in error. The criterion of admissibility in evidence, to prove the accused's guilt, of the facts relied upon to show probable cause goes much too far in confusing and disregarding the difference between what is required to prove guilt in a criminal case and what is required to show probable cause for arrest or search. It approaches requiring (if it does not in practical effect require) proof sufficient to establish guilt in order to substantiate the existence of probable cause. There is a large difference between the two things to be proved (guilt and probable cause), as well as between the tribunals which determine them, and therefore a like difference in the quanta and modes of proof required to establish them. . . .

Nor can we agree with petitioner's second contention that Marsh's information was insufficient to show probable cause and reasonable grounds to believe that petitioner had violated or was violating the narcotic laws and to justify his arrest without a warrant. The information given to narcotic agent Marsh by "special employee" Hereford may have been hearsay to Marsh, but coming from one employed for that purpose and whose information had always been found accurate and reliable, it is clear that Marsh would have been derelict in his duties had he not pursued it. And when, in pursuing that information, he saw a man, having the exact physical attributes and wearing the precise clothing and carrying the tan zipper bag that Hereford had described, alight from one of the very trains from the very place stated by Hereford and start to walk at a "fast" pace toward the station exit, Marsh had personally verified every facet of the information given him by Hereford except whether petitioner had accomplished his mission and had the three ounces of heroin on his person or in his bag. And surely, with every other bit of Hereford's information being thus personally verified, Marsh had "reasonable grounds" to believe that the remaining unverified bit of Hereford's information — that Draper would have the heroin with him — was likewise true.

"In dealing with probable cause . . . as the very name implies, we deal with probabilities. These are not technical; they are the factual and practical considerations of everyday life on which reasonable and prudent men, not legal technicians, act." Probable cause exists where "the facts and circumstances within their (the arresting officers') knowledge and of which they had reasonably trustworthy information (are) sufficient in themselves to warrant a man of reasonable caution in the belief that" an offense has been or is being committed.

We believe that, under the facts and circumstances here, Marsh had probable cause and reasonable grounds to believe that petitioner was committing a violation of the laws of the United States relating to narcotic drugs at the time he arrested him. The arrest was therefore lawful, and the subsequent search and seizure, having been made incident to that lawful arrest, were likewise valid. It follows that petitioner's motion to suppress was properly denied and that the seized heroin was competent evidence lawfully received at the trial. Affirmed.

DISSENT

Mr. Justice Douglas, dissenting.

Decisions under the Fourth Amendment, taken in the long view, have not given the protection to the citizen which the letter and spirit of the Amendment would seem to require. One reason, I think, is that wherever a culprit is caught red-handed, as in leading Fourth Amendment cases, it is difficult to adopt and enforce a rule that would turn him loose. A rule protective of law-abiding citizens is not apt to flourish where its advocates are usually criminals. Yet the rule we fashion is for the innocent and guilty alike. If the word of the informer on which the present arrest was made is sufficient to make the arrest legal, his word would also protect the police who, acting on it, hauled the innocent citizen off to jail.

Of course, the education we receive from mystery stories and television shows teaches that what happened in this case is efficient police work. The police are tipped off that a man carrying narcotics will step off the morning train. A man meeting the precise description does alight from the train. No warrant for his arrest has been — or, as I see it, could then be — obtained. Yet he is arrested; and narcotics are found in his pocket and a syringe in the bag he carried. This is the familiar pattern of crime detection which has been dinned into public consciousness as the correct and efficient one. It is, however, a distorted reflection of the constitutional system under which we are supposed to live. . . .

The Court is quite correct in saying that proof of "reasonable grounds" for believing a crime was being committed need not be proof admissible at the trial. It could be inferences from suspicious acts, e.g., consort with known peddlers, the surreptitious passing of a package, an intercepted message suggesting criminal activities, or any number of such events coming to the knowledge of the officer. But, if he takes the law into his own hands and does not seek the protection of a warrant, he must act on some evidence known to him. The law goes far to protect the citizen. Even suspicious acts observed by the officers may be as consistent with innocence as with guilt. That is not enough, for even the guilty may not be implicated on suspicion alone. The reason is, as I have said, that the standard set by the Constitution and by the statute is one that will protect both the officer and the citizen. For if the officer acts with "probable cause" or on "reasonable grounds," he is protected even though the citizen is innocent. This important requirement should be strictly enforced, lest the whole process of arrest revert once more to whispered accusations by people. When we lower the guards as we do today, we risk making the role of the informer—odious in our history—once more supreme. I think the correct rule was stated in *Poldo v. United States.* "Mere suspicion is not enough; there must be circumstances represented to the officers through the testimony of their senses sufficient to justify them in a good-faith belief that the defendant had violated the law."

Here the officers had no evidence—apart from the mere word of an informer—that petitioner was committing a crime. The fact that petitioner walked fast and carried a tan zipper bag was not evidence of any crime. The officers knew nothing except what they had been told by the informer. If they went to a magistrate to get a warrant of arrest and relied solely on the report of the informer, it is not conceivable to me that one would be granted. For they could not present to the magistrate any of the facts which the informer may have had. They could swear only to the fact that the informer had made the accusation. They could swear to no evidence that lay in their own knowledge. They could present, on information and belief, no

facts which the informer disclosed. No magistrate could issue a warrant on the mere word of an officer, without more. We are not justified in lowering the standard when an arrest is made without a warrant and allowing the officers more leeway than we grant the magistrate.

With all deference I think we break with tradition when we sustain this arrest. We said in *United States v. Di Re,* ". . . [A] search is not to be made legal by what it turns up. In law it is good or bad when it starts and does not change character from its success." In this case it was only after the arrest and search were made that there was a shred of evidence known to the officers that a crime was in the process of being committed.

CASE DISCUSSION

What were the facts that constituted probable cause in this case? Were they firsthand, hearsay, or a combination of the two? Why does the majority opinion seem to disturb Justice William O. Douglas? Do you think Justice Douglas is overreacting to the decision in this case? Or does he have a point that the hearsay provided by the informant constitutes nothing of substance that would lead a reasonable person to conclude that a crime was committed or in progress, and that James Draper committed it? Does the majority ruling favor crime control at the expense of procedural regularity and controlling of government? Does the Court give clear guidelines in regard to what constitutes probable cause to arrest? Explain.

D e c i s i o n   P o i n t

1. Des Moines police officers were patrolling the vicinity of the Another World Lounge at about 11:00 P.M. They noticed three men in the parking lot of the lounge crouching behind a car. The officers observed that the men were exchanging something, but they could not see what it was. The Another World Lounge was a notorious site for drug transactions. Based on their past experience with the location, the nature and furtiveness of the three men's actions, the notoriety of the location, and the lateness of the hour, the officers pulled their patrol car into the parking lot. Bumpus ran away from them into the bar. Once inside, Bumpus tried to conceal a black pouch from the officer who pursued him. Officer Bryan grabbed Bumpus's arm and asked Bumpus to step outside. Once outside, Bumpus threw the pouch over a fence and tried to flee. After a brief struggle, Bryan seized and arrested Bumpus. The court later decided that the arrest took place not when Officer

Bryan announced that Bumpus was under arrest, but at the moment Bryan seized Bumpus's arm inside the bar and escorted him outside.

Did Bryan have probable cause to arrest? The Iowa courts said yes: "While flight alone does not give rise to probable cause . . . in this case not only did Bump[us] flee from officers [who reasonably suspected he was involved in a drug deal], he attempted to . . . conceal [a] pouch." Therefore, at the moment he grabbed Bumpus's arm, Bryan had probable cause to arrest Bumpus.[5]

2. Detective Odesto, the arresting officer, testified at a suppression hearing that at 11:45 P.M., in a high-crime area in Manhattan, he observed the defendant, Brown, in the "company of someone [he] suspected of being a narcotics addict." The suspected addict walked away from Brown and entered a building, shortly returning to Brown. The two came "close together," Detective Odesto said, adding: "I observed what appeared to be a movement of hand. At that time I started to go across the street and intercepted the two persons when Mr. Brown walked in my direction (with a 'fast shuffling gait') and the other person walked in the opposite direction." Detective Odesto arrested Brown for possession of a narcotic drug. At the suppression hearing, Detective Odesto explained that this was typical behavior for drug transactions in that neighborhood:

> . . . Most of its persons engaged in the selling of narcotics do not carry narcotics on them. They usually have a place where it is stored in or carried by someone else. . . . [U]sually the person would have a conversation with the potential seller, give him his money . . . and then . . . the potential seller will go to his place where he stores the narcotics and bring it back, give it to that person, and they'll go in opposite directions.

Did Detective Odesto have probable cause to arrest Brown? The trial judge said yes; the appellate court reversed:

> Although the observed acts of the defendant and the suspected narcotic addict were not inconsistent with a culpable narcotics transaction, they were also susceptible of many innocent interpretations, even between persons with a narcotics background. The behavior, at most "equivocal and suspicious," was not supplemented by any additional behavior ra[i]sing "the level of inference from suspicion to probable cause." Thus, for example only, there was no recurring pattern of conduct sufficient to negate inferences of innocent activity, no overheard conversat[i]on between the suspects that might clarify the acts observed, no flight at the approach of the officer, and no misstatements when questioned about observed activity.
>
> The logical and practical problem is that even accepting ungrudgingly, as one should, the police officer's expertness in detec[t]ing a pattern of conduct characteristic of a particular criminal activity, the detected pattern, being only the superficial part of a sequence, does not provide probable cause for arrest if some sketchy pattern occurs just as fre[q]uently or even more frequently in innocent transactions. The point is that the pattern is equivocal and is neither uniquely nor generally associated with criminal conduct, and unless it is there is no probable cause. Thus, for example, the observation of a known or obvious prostitute talking to a man she meets (or accosts) on the street does not establish probable cause. More of a pattern must be shown, either by proof of the conversation or ensuing culpable conduct.[6]

3. Officers Lewis and Griffin were in the vicinity of 1232 Buchanan Street. They observed the defendant along with four other individuals in a courtyard area between 1133 Laguna and 1232 Buchanan. The defendant and the others were observed talking in a "huddle" formation with "a lot of hand movement" inside the huddle, but the officers could not see what was in the hands of any member of the group. The officers then walked toward the group, at which point everyone looked in the officers' direction, whispered, and quickly

dispersed. When the defendant saw the officers, he immediately turned around and started walking at a fast pace through the lobby of 1232 Buchanan. The officers followed him for a quarter of a block when Officer Griffin called out to the defendant. The defendant replied, "Who, me?" Officer Griffin answered, "Yes," and the defendant immediately ran away. The officers gave chase. Two minutes later, while still chasing the defendant, Officer Lewis saw him discard a plastic bag containing five white bundles. Officer Lewis scooped up the bag as he continued to give chase. Shortly thereafter, the officers apprehended the defendant.

Officer Lewis testified that during the four years he had been a patrolman he had made at least one hundred arrests concerning cocaine in the area frequented by the defendant that night. On cross-examination, Officer Lewis answered in the affirmative when asked if most of the black men he saw in the area usually had something to hide if they ran from police. The officer stated that prior to the chase he saw no contraband, nor was anything about the group's dispersal significant. Nor did the officer explain why they singled out the defendant to follow. The trial court denied the defendant's motion to suppress.

Did officers Lewis and Griffin have probable cause to arrest Washington? The court held that they did not:

> Prior to defendant's abandonment of the cocaine, the police lacked the "articulable suspicion that a person has committed or is about to commit a crime." The officers spotted the group of men in an open courtyard at 6:15 P.M.; the men made no attempt to conceal themselves and did not exhibit any furtive behavior. The hand gestures were, on the police officer's own testimony, inconclusive and unrevealing. Furthermore, the time at which the detention occurred is not the "late or unusual hour . . . from which any inference of criminality may be drawn." The fact that defendant was seen in what was a high crime area also does not elevate the facts into a reasonable suspicion of criminality. Courts have been "reluctant to conclude that a location's crime rate transforms otherwise innocent-appearing circumstances into circumstances justifying the seizure of an individual."

> Once the officers made their approach visible, they gave no justification for their decision to follow defendant apart from the others in the group. Neither officer knew defendant or knew of defendant's past criminal record, nor did Officer Lewis testify that defendant appeared to be a principal or a leader in the group. Further, the defendant had the right to walk away from the officers. He had no legal duty to submit to the attention of the officers; he had the freedom to "go on his way," free of stopping even momentarily for the officers. By walking at a brisk rate away from the officers, defendant could have been exercising his right to avoid the officers or avoid any other person, or could have simply walked rapidly through sheer nervousness at the sight of a police officer.

> We see no change in the analysis when defendant decided to run from the officers. Flight alone does not trigger an investigative detention; rather, it must be combined with other objective factors that give rise to an articulable suspicion of criminal activity. No such factors existed, nor does Officer Lewis's assertion that the "black men [they] see in the project usually have something to hide when they run" justify a detention. "[M]ere subjective speculation as to the [person's] purported motives . . . carries no weight." Thus, prior to defendant's abandonment of the contraband, the circumstances of defendant's actions were not reasonably consistent with criminal activity.

> Here, the officers conceded they had no objective factors upon which to base any suspicions that the group was involved in illegal activity, and the officers offered no explanation why they singled out defendant to

follow. Indeed, the only justification for engaging in pursuit was that defendant was a Black male, and that it was the officer's subjective belief that Black men run from police when they have something to hide. Thus, a single factor—the defendant's race—triggered the detention. . . . [7]

Quantity of Facts

The quantity of facts required to support probable cause may vary depending on the kind of crime involved and the degree of danger in the circumstances under which police arrest suspects. The United States Supreme Court has not set a rule for the exact quantity of facts required to add up to probable cause for particular offenses or categories of offenses. According to the Court, probable cause is not

> a finely-tuned standard, comparable to the standards of proof beyond a reasonable doubt or of proof by a preponderance of the evidence. . . . [I]t . . . [is a] fluid concept that takes [its] substantive content from the particular context in which the standard [is] being assessed.[8]

The lower federal courts and state courts have adopted different approaches. Some have adopted a sliding scale approach to probable cause, requiring fewer facts under dangerous circumstances than probable cause might otherwise compel. The Seventh Circuit Court of Appeals *en banc* addressed this question in *Llaguno v. Mingey.*

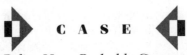

C A S E

Did the Police Have Probable Cause to Arrest?

Llaguno v. Mingey
763 F.2d 1560 (7th Cir. 1985)

Llaguno and others sued the Chicago police for violating their civil rights by entering and searching their home and arresting them in violation of the Fourth Amendment. The United States District Court rendered judgment for the defendant police. Llaguno appealed. A panel of the Seventh Circuit U.S. Court of Appeals held that the district court should have directed a verdict for the plaintiffs. On rehearing, the full Seventh Circuit Court held that sufficient evidence existed to constitute probable cause, that detaining Llaguno for forty-two hours was too long, and that Llaguno was entitled to a new trial due to serious errors at his trial. Judge Posner wrote the opinion of the court. Judge Wood, with whom Chief Judge Cummings and Judges Cudahy and Flaum join, dissented in part and concurred in part.

FACTS

On a night in Chicago in 1980, two young Hispanic men committed two robberies, killed four people and wounded three others (including a policeman), and abducted a young girl. When the getaway car crashed, the police were able to shoot and capture one of the killers (Garcia, who has since been sentenced to death) and recover the girl unharmed, but the other killer escaped on foot. A check of the license-plate number showed that the car was registered to Vilma Llaguno at an address two miles from the crash site and that it had not been reported stolen. The crash occurred at North and Oakley; Vilma Llaguno's address was Wabansia, near North Avenue, but farther west than Oakley. One of the robberies had taken place between the crash site and the Llaguno residence.

Several policemen, led by Sergeant Mingey, drove to their headquarters, picked up a shotgun and a sledgehammer there, and then drove to the Llaguno home, believing that the killer who had fled from the car when it crashed may have been living at Vilma Llaguno's address, and that fleeing felons often go home. (Mingey and several other policemen in the entry party are one group of defendants; the other consists of policemen involved in the protracted detention of David Llaguno, of which more shortly.) Upon arrival Mingey banged on the front door and ordered the woman who came to the door, Gloria Llaguno, to open it. She did so, and the police rushed in with drawn guns, searched the house, rounded up the occupants (the plaintiffs in this action), and herded them into the living room. Those seized included Gloria and her husband, several of their children (including David Llaguno), and several grandchildren—a total of 10 people. (Vilma Llaguno, who is Gloria Llaguno's daughter-in-law, was not at home.) In response to questions from the police, David revealed that it was his car that had crashed, and said he had loaned it to a friend.

When the police asked him who the friend was, he gave Garcia's name, according to David's testimony; according to the police, he refused to answer. They arrested him. Some of the plaintiffs testified at trial that the police threatened to shoot them, which the police denied; that the police had later come back to the house to speak to David; and that on these occasions they had entered the house without anyone's consent, which they also denied—while acknowledging having held David in custody for 42 hours after his arrest, during which time they neither charged him with a crime nor brought him before a magistrate.

While the police were at the Llaguno residence, the killer who had fled from the crash at North and Oakley was shot and killed by other policemen. He turned out to be Roger Llaguno, a son of Gloria and brother of David but not a resident of the house that police had entered. No charges were ever lodged against any of the occupants, including David.

OPINION

. . . In determining whether police are reasonable in entering a house without a warrant the trier of fact ought to consider not only how great the risk of delay was—that is, the probability of injury, escape, or destruction of evidence—but also how great the harm would have been had the risk materialized. The greater that harm would be, the less need be the probability that it would actually have occurred to justify the police in invading the interest (great though it is) in the privacy of the home. . . .

Even so, the police could enter the Llaguno house without a warrant or the homeowner's consent only if there was probable cause to believe the killer was in the house. Although the words "probable cause" appear only in the second clause of the Fourth Amendment, which deals with warrants . . . the words are also used to describe an essential ingredient of reasonableness; and all searches and seizures must be reasonable to comply with the Fourth Amendment. . . .

Probable cause means, in fact, a reasonable basis—"more than bare suspicion, but less than virtual certainty"—for believing that a search or seizure will be fruitful—will turn up evidence, or leads to evidence, or contraband, or the perpetrator of the crime. Emergency is not enough. An emergency, at least the kind of emergency, great but not apocalyptic in its menace, involved in this case, would not allow the police to search every house in Chicago or even every house on the Llaguno's block. . . . Even the fact that a multiple murderer is on the loose does not give the police a license to search and seize without a reasonable basis, though it may affect the judgment of what is reasonable. But although the present case is close to the line that separates arguably reasonable from unarguably unreasonable police behavior, it does not cross it. Probable cause—the area between bare suspicion and virtual certainty—describes not a point but a zone, within which the graver the crime the more latitude the police must be allowed. The shooting of seven persons (four fatally) by a team of criminals in the space of two hours is about as grave a crisis as a local police department will encounter.

The police must be allowed more leeway in resolving it than when they are investigating the theft of a bicycle. Especially when a multiple murderer is at large in circumstances suggesting that he may be about to kill again, the interest in public safety is paramount. . . .

The amount of information that prudent police will collect before deciding to make a search or an arrest, and hence the amount of probable cause they will have, is a function of the gravity of the crime, and especially the danger of its imminent repetition. If a multiple murderer is at large, the police must compress their investigation and make the decision to search or arrest on less information than if they could investigate at their leisure.

The police in this case had strong reason to believe that the killer who had fled on foot was Hispanic; and since the car had not been reported stolen and the registered owner had a Hispanic name, they had some reason to think the killer was either the owner or had been driving with the owner's permission. Although the car was registered to "Vilma" Llaguno, a woman's name—we now know—the police may not have known that Vilma is always a woman's first name (a matter on which the record is unclear); readers of Chekhov know that "Vanya" is a man's first name. Anyway, Vilma might have been the wife or sister or mother of the killer, in which event her address might have been his. And he might have sought refuge at her address (if she was a close relative) even if it was not also his, because the crash occurred on the major thoroughfare leading to the house (North Avenue), though not within easy walking distance (two miles).

Of course the killer who fled on foot might not have been Vilma's relative; the record does not reveal whether the police who entered the Llaguno home knew by then the name of the killer, Garcia, who had been seized at the crash. And if the fleeing killer was not a relative it was much less likely that he would flee to the home of the car's owner. And yet we think a reasonable jury could have found that the police had a reasonable probability, based on real if inconclusive information rather than inspired hunch or a dragnet mentality, of finding the killer in (or en route to or from) the Llaguno home. As it turned out, he was not there; but that just shows that the probability he would be there was not 100 percent. The police were not completely off base. The killer was, after all, a son

of the people who lived there, and he might well have fled there after the shooting spree, though in fact he did not.

Even so, it would not have been reasonable for the police to act on such limited information if they could have gotten better information first without incurring, or subjecting others to, great danger. There are several things they could have done. They could have tried to interview the occupants of the Llaguno home with the occupants' consent. They could have sealed off the house and questioned the occupants as they emerged. They could have questioned neighbors. They could have waited till Garcia had recovered enough from his wound to be questioned. But each of these alternatives was dangerous. If the killer had actually been in the house, the policemen's efforts to obtain the occupants' consent to a search could have alerted him to the presence of the police and allowed him to shoot before they could disarm him. Sealing off the house may have been difficult, because it was nighttime and the house was a detached house which would have had to be surrounded. If the killer had been there, as the police had some reason to think he was, sealing off the house might have led him to barricade it or take some of its occupants as hostages (people sometimes take their relatives hostage). Questioning Garcia, or the neighbors, could have caused a long delay in discovering whether the suspect was inside the house.

Given the gravity of the crimes they were investigating, the possibility that there would be more shootings unless the killer was seized immediately, and the information (limited as it was) that made it seem that he might well have fled to the Llaguno home, we cannot say, as a matter of law, that the police did not have probable cause to enter and search the house as they did. And if this is right, we do not think it makes a critical difference that they had no definite suspect in mind. . . . [T]here was a sufficient chain linking the house to the killer whom the police were pursuing to allow a reasonable jury to conclude that the police had probable cause to enter the house.

DISSENT

Harlington Wood, Jr., Circuit Judge, with whom Cummings, Chief Judge, and Cudahy and Flaum,

Circuit Judges, join, dissenting in part and concurring in part.

The essence of Judge Posner's opinion, as I read it, is simply that when you are short in probable cause you can make up that shortage by adding exigent circumstances. I cannot accept that dangerous, unnecessary, and undefinable blending of two separate and useful traditional concepts in order to justify a warrantless search of a private home at night. The bad factual circumstances in this case are leading us to a bad law for future cases. . . .

If, as the opinion holds, exigencies can substitute for probable cause, we are in effect sanctioning warrantless nighttime home entries for which no warrant would have been issued if one had been sought from a judicial officer. This is clearly an anomalous and untoward result. It seems to me that you have to concede that probable cause in the traditional sense is lacking in this case, and that a magistrate would not have authorized the search warrant. This is why the majority needs to invent this new blended warrantless search concept.

. . . [T]he jury will now have to be instructed with this new "mix-it-all-up-together" rule invented in this case. We will be headed into trackless legal underbrush. A person should be more secure in his home than that.

CASE DISCUSSION

What specific facts did the police have on which to base their arrest? Why did the court require fewer facts in this case? Would you have reduced the requirements for probable cause owing to the seriousness of the offenses in question—the committing of two robberies, the killing of four people, the wounding of three others, and the abducting of a young girl? Should "reasonableness" under the Fourth Amendment take into account that these suspects may have done terrible harm had the police not acted on the information they possessed? In other words, as the dissent says, "when you are short in probable cause you can make up that shortage by adding exigent circumstances." Do you agree? Why? Why not?

Direct and Hearsay Information

At the moment of arrest, police officers might have **direct information**—that is, facts known to them through their own senses, including what they see, hear, feel, taste, and even smell (such as marijuana or opium smoke). These facts need not point directly to guilt; they may include circumstances that reasonably lead to the belief that criminal activity has taken place, is in progress, or is about to occur. Probable cause may arise from a roster of firsthand facts and circumstances such as flight, furtive movements, hiding, attempts to destroy evidence, resisting of officers, evasive answers, contradictory explanations, fingerprints, hair samples, blood samples, and DNA information. (See also Table 4.2 on page 155 for a list of the kinds of information police may rely on both to stop and to arrest.)

Police officers need not rely solely on direct information. They may also rely on **hearsay**—that is, information they receive from third persons. These third persons include victims, witnesses, other police officers, and professional informants. According to the **hearsay rule,** courts cannot ordinarily admit hearsay as evidence at trial to prove guilt. However, the hearsay rule does not bar the use of hearsay in probable cause determinations. Hearsay evidence, if it is reliable and truthful, satisfies the probable cause requirement to arrest. One purpose of arrest—perhaps its main purpose—is to allow officials time to determine whether the criminal process should continue or terminate. Arrests are not trials. Rather, they are deprivations of liberty for the purpose of allowing the government time to decide whether to proceed to trial.

The technical nature of evidentiary rules applicable at trials does not suit actions either on the street or at the police station. The courtroom has not only experts in the law on hand to testify, but also the time to weigh the evidence. Police officers on the street and at the precinct station are not lawyers and are not expected to be. Nor do they have the leisure to sort out the evidence they have acquired. They must often either act immediately or forever lose their chance to make arrests. Allowing hearsay as a basis for probable cause reflects the deference that courts accord these realities. The Federal Rules of Criminal Procedure illustrate this deference; they allow a finding of probable cause based "upon hearsay evidence in whole or in part" (Rule 4). Not all hearsay carries equal weight; some informants are more trustworthy than others. In determining probable cause, magistrates weigh both the trustworthiness and the source of the information.[9]

It is easy to test the veracity and reliability of the direct information of officers. They submit **affidavits**—sworn statements—to what they observe. Courts also accept with little or no question information derived from victims and witnesses about an incident they directly observe and report to law enforcement officers. According to the court in *Allison v. State*, "[I]f the citizen or victim informant is an eyewitness this will be enough to support probable cause even without specific corroboration of reliability." This trustworthiness may not be assumed, however, if victims or witnesses refuse to identify themselves. Hence, courts rarely accept anonymous tips alone as sufficient to establish probable cause to arrest a citizen, although an anonymous tip may support reasonable suspicion to stop (see Chapter 4).[10]

Victims and witnesses are not the source of most hearsay information that the police obtain. Professional informants, most often individuals who derive their information from being part of the "criminal milieu," establish probable cause in most arrests that rely on hearsay. This is especially true of crimes without complaining witnesses, such as drug-related crimes. This type of informant poses greater problems of trustworthiness than do victims and witnesses. In *Jones v. United States*, the United States Court of Appeals for the District of Columbia wrote the following:

> It is notorious that the narcotics informer is often himself involved in the narcotics traffic and is often paid for his information in cash, narcotics, immunity from prosecution, or lenient punishment. . . . The reliability of such persons is obviously suspect. . . . [T]he present informer practice amounts to condoning felonies on condition that the confessed or suspected felon brings about the conviction of others. Under such stimulation it is to be expected that the informer will not infrequently reach for shadowy leads, or even seek to incriminate the innocent. The practice of paying fees to the informer for the cases he makes may also be expected from time to time, to induce him to lure no-users into the drug habit and then entrap them into law violations.[11]

Until 1983, courts tested the worth of the information provided by informants according to a **two-pronged test of reliability**, called the *Spinelli–Aguilar* **test** after the two cases that established the test. The first prong, called the **veracity prong**, assesses whether informants are basically honest people. One way to satisfy the veracity prong is to show that the informant has a "good track record." For example, an affidavit stating that the informant has given the police truthful information in the past demonstrates the informant's veracity. The information that Hereford had given Marsh accurate and reliable information for six months in *Draper v. U.S.* (excerpted above) is a good example of satisfying the veracity prong of the test. The information need not lead to conviction; the test requires only that the information be true and accurate. Also, if informants reveal information directly against their interest, it satisfies the veracity prong. For example, if an informant tells the police that she has bought crack cocaine from the suspect for two years, this satisfies the veracity test because "people do not lightly admit a crime and place critical evidence in the hands of the police in the form of their own admission."[12]

That an honest person supplies information does not guarantee its accuracy. The second prong of the *Spinelli–Aguilar* test, the **basis-of-knowledge prong,** focuses on the information itself, particularly the manner in which the informant acquired it. This prong asks questions such as these: How do informants know what they know? In a suspected drug arrest, for example, do they know the suspect has cocaine in his pocket because the informant saw him put it there? Or did the informant believe cocaine was in the suspect's pocket because of suspicious behavior—because the suspect repeatedly checked his pocket while looking around "furtively"? Or did the informant hear from a "friend" (hearsay on hearsay) that the suspect had cocaine in his pocket?

If the officer establishes the veracity of the informant but does not reveal the source of the informant's information, then the amount of detail in the information may satisfy the basis-of-knowledge prong. A good example of information sufficiently detailed to satisfy this prong is found in *Draper v. U.S.,* where Hereford described James Draper precisely, what he would wear, what time he would appear at the train station, how he would walk, and what he would carry. This amount of detail led the Court to conclude that Hereford gave so many details that the officers could "reasonably infer that the informant had gained his information in a reliable way."[13]

What if informants satisfy neither the veracity nor the basis-of-knowledge prong? According to the two-pronged *Spinelli–Aguilar* test, the informants' information does not satisfy the requirements of probable cause. The two-pronged test is what is often referred to as a **bright line rule;** that is, it sends clear directions to police and other officers about what they can and cannot do. It has the advantage of reducing discretion and uncertainty; it has the disadvantage of enforcing rigidity. To increase flexibility, and to make it easier to establish probable cause, the Supreme Court has created the **totality-of-circumstances test** of informant reliability. According to this test, veracity and basis of knowledge remain important, but they are only two of many circumstances that can enter into the probable cause determination. The Court discussed the totality-of-circumstances test in the case that established it, *Illinois v. Gates.*

C A S E

Did the Total Circumstances Add Up to Probable Cause?

Illinois v. Gates
462 U.S. 213, 103 S.Ct. 2317,
76 L.Ed.2d 527 (1983)

Petition for certiorari *was filed seeking review of a decision of the Illinois Supreme Court, which affirmed the* decision of the lower state court, which upheld an order granting a motion suppressing evidence seized pursuant to a search warrant. The Supreme Court reversed. Chief Justice Rehnquist wrote the opinion of the Court. Justice White filed a separate opinion concurring in the judgment. Justice Brennan filed a dissenting *opinion, in which Justice Marshall joined. Justice Stevens filed a dissenting opinion, in which Justice Brennan joined.*

FACTS

. . . Bloomingdale, Ill., is a suburb of Chicago located in DuPage County. On May 3, 1978, the Bloomingdale Police Department received by mail an anonymous handwritten letter which read as follows:

This letter is to inform you that you have a couple in your town who strictly make their living on selling drugs. They are Sue and Lance Gates, they live on Greenway, off Bloomingdale Rd. in the condominiums. Most of their buys are done in Florida. Sue, his wife, drives their car to Florida, where she leaves it to be loaded up with drugs, then Lance flys down and drives it back. Sue flys back after she drops the car off in Florida. May 3 she is driving down there again and Lance will be flying down in a few days to drive it back. At the time Lance drives the car back he has the trunk loaded with over $100,000.00 in drugs. Presently they have over $100,000.00 worth of drugs in their basement. They brag about the fact they never have to work, and make their entire living on pushers. I guarantee if you watch them carefully you will make a big catch. They are friends with some big drug dealers, who visit their house often.

Lance & Susan Gates, Greenway in Condominiums

The letter was referred by the Chief of Police of the Bloomingdale Police Department to Detective Mader, who decided to pursue the tip. Mader learned, from the office of the Illinois Secretary of State, that an Illinois driver's license had been issued to one Lance Gates, residing at a stated address in Bloomingdale. He contacted a confidential informant, whose examination of certain financial records revealed a more recent address for the Gates, and he also learned from a police officer assigned to O'Hare Airport that "L. Gates" had made a reservation on Eastern Airlines flight 245 to West Palm Beach, Fla., scheduled to depart from Chicago on May 5 at 4:15 P.M.

Mader then made arrangements with an agent of the Drug Enforcement Administration for surveillance of the May 5 Eastern Airlines flight. The agent later reported to Mader that Gates had boarded the flight, and that federal agents in Florida had observed him arrive in West Palm Beach and take a taxi to the nearby Holiday Inn. They also reported that Gates went to a room registered to one Susan Gates and that, at 7:00 A.M. the next morning, Gates and an unidentified woman left the motel in a Mercury bearing Illinois license plates and drove northbound on an interstate frequently used by travelers to the Chicago area. In addition, the DEA agent informed Mader that the license plate number of the Mercury [was] registered to a Hornet station wagon owned by Gates. The agent also advised Mader that the driving time between West Palm Beach and Bloomingdale was approximately 22 to 24 hours.

Mader signed an affidavit setting forth the foregoing facts, and submitted it to a judge of the Circuit Court of DuPage County, together with a copy of the anonymous letter. The judge of that court thereupon issued a search warrant for the Gates' residence and for their automobile. The judge, in deciding to issue the warrant, could have determined that the modus operandi of the Gates had been substantially corroborated. As the anonymous letter predicted, Lance Gates had flown from Chicago to West Palm Beach late in the afternoon of May 5th, had checked into a hotel room registered in the name of his wife, and, at 7:00 A.M. the following morning, had headed north, accompanied by an unidentified woman, out of West Palm Beach on an interstate highway used by travelers from South Florida to Chicago in an automobile bearing a license plate issued to him.

At 5:15 A.M. on March 7th, only 36 hours after he had flown out of Chicago, Lance Gates, and his wife, returned to their home in Bloomingdale, driving the car in which they had left West Palm Beach some 22 hours earlier. The Bloomingdale police were awaiting them, searched the trunk of the Mercury, and uncovered approximately 350 pounds of marijuana. A search of the Gates' home revealed marijuana, weapons, and other contraband. The Illinois Circuit Court ordered suppression of all these items, on the ground that the affidavit submitted to the Circuit Judge failed to support the necessary determination of probable cause to believe that the Gates' automobile and home contained the contraband in question. This decision was affirmed in turn by the Illinois Appellate Court and by a divided vote of the Supreme Court of Illinois.

OPINION

The Illinois Supreme Court concluded—and we are inclined to agree—that, standing alone, the anonymous letter sent to the Bloomingdale Police Department would not provide the basis for a magistrate's determination that there was probable cause to believe contraband would be found in the Gates' car and home. The letter provides virtually nothing from which one might conclude that its author is either honest or his information reliable; likewise, the letter gives absolutely no indication of the basis for the writer's predictions regarding the Gates' criminal activities. Something more was required, then, before a magistrate could conclude that there was probable cause to believe that contraband would be found in the Gates' home and car.

The Illinois Supreme Court also properly recognized that Detective Mader's affidavit might be capable of supplementing the anonymous letter with information sufficient to permit a determination of probable cause. In holding that the affidavit in fact did not contain sufficient additional information to sustain a determination of probable cause, the Illinois court applied a "two-pronged test," derived from our decision in *Spinelli v. United States.* The Illinois Supreme Court, like some others, apparently understood *Spinelli* as requiring that the anonymous letter satisfy each of the two independent requirements before it could be relied on. According to this view, the letter, as supplemented by Mader's affidavit, first had to adequately reveal the "basis of knowledge" of the letter writer— the particular means by which he came by the information given in his report. Second, it had to provide facts sufficiently establishing either the "veracity" of the affiant's informant, or, alternatively, the "reliability" of the informant's report in this particular case.

We agree with the Illinois Supreme Court that an informant's "veracity," "reliability" and "basis of knowledge" are all highly relevant in determining the value of his report. We do not agree, however, that these elements should be understood as entirely separate and independent requirements to be rigidly exacted in every case, which the opinion of the Supreme Court of Illinois would imply. Rather, as detailed below, they should be understood simply as closely intertwined issues that may usefully illuminate the commonsense, practical question whether there is "probable cause" to believe that contraband or evidence is located in a particular place. . . . The process does not deal with hard certainties, but with probabilities. Long before the law of probabilities was articulated as such, practical people formulated certain common-sense conclusions about human behavior, jurors as factfinders are permitted to do the same— and so are law enforcement officers. Finally, the evidence thus collected must be seen and weighed not in terms of library analysis by scholars, but as understood by those versed in the field of law enforcement.

. . . [P]robable cause is a fluid concept—turning on the assessment of probabilities in particular factual contexts—not readily, or even usefully, reduced to a neat set of legal rules. Informants' tips doubtless come in many shapes and sizes from many different types of persons. As we said in *Adams v. Williams* (1972) [excerpted in Chapter 4], "Informants' tips, like all other clues and evidence coming to a policeman on the scene may vary greatly in their value and reliability." Rigid legal rules are ill-suited to an area of such diversity. "One simple rule will not cover every situation." . . .

Moreover, the "two-pronged test" directs analysis into two largely independent channels—the informant's "veracity" or "reliability" and his "basis of knowledge." There are persuasive arguments against according these two elements such independent status. Instead, they are better understood as relevant considerations in the totality of circumstances analysis that traditionally has guided probable cause determinations: a deficiency in one may be compensated for, in determining the overall reliability of a tip, by a strong showing as to the other, or by some other indicia of reliability. . . .

The rigorous inquiry into the *Spinelli* prongs and the complex superstructure of evidentiary and analytical rules that some have seen implicit in our *Spinelli* decision, cannot be reconciled with the fact that many warrants are—quite properly—issued on the basis of nontechnical, common-sense judgments of laymen applying a standard less demanding than those used in more formal legal proceedings. Likewise, given the informal, often hurried context in which it must be applied, the "built-in subtleties," of the "two-pronged test" are particularly unlikely to assist magistrates in determining probable cause. . . .

If the affidavits submitted by police officers are subjected to the type of scrutiny some courts have deemed appropriate, police might well resort to warrantless searches, with the hope of relying on consent or some other exception to the warrant clause that might develop at the time of the search. . . .

Finally, the direction taken by decisions following *Spinelli* poorly serves "the most basic function of any government": "to provide for the security of the individual and of his property." *Miranda v. Arizona* (1966) (White, J., dissenting). The strictures that inevitably accompany the "two-pronged test" cannot avoid seriously impeding the task of law enforcement. If, as the Illinois Supreme Court apparently thought, that test must be rigorously applied in every case, anonymous tips seldom would be of greatly diminished value in police work.

Ordinary citizens, like ordinary witnesses, generally do not provide extensive recitations of the basis of their everyday observations. Likewise, as the Illinois Supreme Court observed in this case, the veracity of persons supplying anonymous tips is by hypothesis largely unknown, and unknowable. As a result, anonymous tips seldom could survive a rigorous application of either of the *Spinelli* prongs. Yet, such tips, particularly when supplemented by independent police investigation, frequently contribute to the solution of otherwise "perfect crimes." While a conscientious assessment of the basis for crediting such tips is required by the Fourth Amendment, a standard that leaves virtually no place for anonymous citizen informants is not.

For all these reasons, we conclude that it is wiser to abandon the "two-pronged test" established by our decisions in *Aguilar* and *Spinelli*. In its place we reaffirm the totality of the circumstances analysis that traditionally has informed probable cause determinations. The task of the issuing magistrate is simply to make a practical, common-sense decision whether, given all the circumstances set forth in the affidavit before

him, including the "veracity" and "basis of knowledge" of persons supplying hearsay information, there is a fair probability that contraband or evidence of a crime will be found in a particular place. . . .

Justice Brennan's dissent . . . suggests that "words such as 'practical,' 'nontechnical,' and 'common sense,' as used in the Court's opinion, are but code words for an overly-permissive attitude towards police practices in derogation of the right secured by the Fourth Amendment." . . . [N]o one doubts that "under our Constitution only measures consistent with the Fourth Amendment may be employed by government to cure [the horrors of drug trafficking]," but this agreement does not advance the inquiry as to which measures are, and which measures are not, consistent with the Fourth Amendment. "Fidelity" to the commands of the Constitution suggests balanced judgment rather than exhortation. The highest "fidelity" is achieved neither by the judge who instinctively goes furthest in upholding even the most bizarre claim of individual constitutional rights, any more than it is achieved by a judge who instinctively goes furthest in accepting the most restrictive claims of governmental authorities. The task of this Court, as of other courts, is to "hold the balance true," and we think we have done that in this case.

Our decisions applying the totality of circumstances analysis outlined above have consistently recognized the value of corroboration of details of an informant's tip by independent police work. . . .

The showing of probable cause in the present case was fully as compelling as that in *Draper* [*v. United States* (1959—excerpted earlier in this chapter)]. Even standing alone, the facts obtained through the independent investigation of Mader and the DEA at least suggested that the Gates were involved in drug trafficking. In addition to being a popular vacation site, Florida is well-known as a source of narcotics and other illegal drugs. Lance Gates' flight to Palm Beach, his brief, overnight stay in a motel, and apparent immediate return north to Chicago in the family car, conveniently awaiting him in West Palm Beach, is as suggestive of a pre-arranged drug run, as it is of an ordinary vacation trip.

In addition, the magistrate could rely on the anonymous letter, which had been corroborated in major part by Mader's efforts—just as had occurred in

Draper. The Supreme Court of Illinois reasoned that *Draper* involved an informant who had given reliable information on previous occasions, while the honesty and reliability of the anonymous informant in this case were unknown to the Bloomingdale police. While this distinction might be an apt one at the time the police department received the anonymous letter, it became far less significant after Mader's independent investigative work occurred. The corroboration of the letter's predictions that the Gates' car would be in Florida, that Lance Gates would fly to Florida in the next day or so, and that he would drive the car north toward Bloomingdale all indicated, albeit not with certainty, that the informant's other assertions also were true. "Because an informant is right about some things, he is more probably right about other facts," — including the claim regarding the Gates' illegal activity. . . .

Finally, the anonymous letter contained a range of details relating not just to easily obtained facts and conditions existing at the time of the tip, but to future actions of third parties ordinarily not easily predicted. The letter writer's accurate information as to the travel plans of each of the Gates was of a character likely obtained only from the Gates themselves, or from someone familiar with their not entirely ordinary travel plans. If the informant had access to accurate information of this type a magistrate could properly conclude that it was not unlikely that he also had access to reliable information of the Gates' alleged illegal activities.

Of course, the Gates' travel plans might have been learned from a talkative neighbor or travel agent; under the "two-pronged test" developed from *Spinelli,* the character of the details in the anonymous letter might well not permit a sufficiently clear inference regarding the letter writer's "basis of knowledge." But . . . probable cause does not demand the certainty we associate with formal trials. It is enough that there was a fair probability that the writer of the anonymous letter had obtained his entire story either from the Gates or someone they trusted. And corroboration of major portions of the letter's predictions provides just this probability. It is apparent, therefore, that the judge issuing the warrant had a "substantial basis for . . . conclud[ing]" that probable cause to search the Gates' home and car existed.

The judgment of the Supreme Court of Illinois therefore must be Reversed.

CONCURRING OPINION

Justice White, concurring in the judgment.

. . . Abandoning the "two-pronged test" of *Aguilar v. Texas,* the Court upholds the validity of the warrant under a new "totality of the circumstances" approach. Although I agree that the warrant should be upheld, I reach this conclusion in accordance with the *Aguilar–Spinelli* framework. . . . The question is whether those portions of the affidavit describing the results of the police investigation of the respondents, when considered in light of the tip, "would permit the suspicions engendered by the informant's report to ripen into a judgment that a crime was probably being committed." . . .

Gates' activity here . . . was quite suspicious. I agree with the Court that Lance Gates' flight to Palm Beach, an area known to be a source of narcotics, the brief overnight stay in a motel, and apparent immediate return North, suggest a pattern that trained law-enforcement officers have recognized as indicative of illicit drug-dealing activity. Even, however, had the corroboration related only to completely innocuous activities, this fact alone would not preclude the issuance of a valid warrant. The critical issue is not whether the activities observed by the police are innocent or suspicious. Instead, the proper focus should be on whether the actions of the suspects, whatever their nature, give rise to an inference that the informant is credible and that he obtained his information in a reliable manner. . . .

. . . [B]ecause I am inclined to believe that, when applied properly, the *Aguilar–Spinelli* rules play an appropriate role in probable cause determinations, and because the Court's holding may foretell an evisceration of the probable cause standard, I do not join the Court's holding. . . .

DISSENT

Justice Stevens, with whom Justice Brennan joins, dissenting.

The fact that Lance and Sue Gates made a 22-hour nonstop drive from West Palm Beach, Florida, to Bloomingdale, Illinois, only a few hours after Lance had flown to Florida provided persuasive evidence that they were engaged in illicit activity. That fact, however, was not known to the magistrate when he issued the warrant to search their home. What the magistrate did know at that time was that the anonymous informant had not been completely accurate in his or her predictions. The informant had indicated that "Sue drives their car to Florida where she leaves it to be loaded up with drugs. . . . Sue flies back after she drops the car off in Florida." Yet Detective Mader's affidavit reported that she "left the West Palm Beach area driving the Mercury northbound."

The discrepancy between the informant's predictions and the facts known to Detective Mader is significant for three reasons. First, it casts doubt on the informant's hypothesis that the Gates already had "over $100,000[.00] worth of drugs in their basement." The informant had predicted an itinerary that always kept one spouse in Bloomingdale, suggesting that the Gates did not want to leave their home unguarded because something valuable was hidden within. That inference obviously could not be drawn when it was known that the pair was actually together over a thousand miles from home.

Second, the discrepancy made the Gates' conduct seem substantially less unusual than the informant had predicted it would be. It would have been odd if, as predicted, Sue had driven down to Florida on Wednesday, left the car, and flown right back to Illinois. But the mere facts that Sue was in West Palm Beach with the car, that she was joined by her husband at the Holiday Inn on Friday, and that the couple drove north together the next morning are neither unusual nor probative of criminal activity.

Third, the fact that the anonymous letter contained a material mistake undermines the reasonableness of relying on it as a basis for making a forcible entry into a private home.

Of course, the activities in this case did not stop when the magistrate issued the warrant. The Gates drove all night to Bloomingdale, the officers searched the car and found 400 pounds of marijuana, and then they searched the house. However, none of these subsequent events may be considered in evaluating the warrant, and the search of the house was legal only if the warrant was valid. I cannot accept the Court's casual conclusion that, before the Gates arrived in Bloomingdale, there was probable cause to justify a valid entry and search of a private home. No one knows who the informant in this case was, or what motivated him or her to write the note. Given that the note's predictions were faulty in one significant respect, and were corroborated by nothing except ordinary innocent activity, I must surmise that the Court's evaluation of the warrant's validity has been colored by subsequent events. The officers did not enter the unoccupied house as soon as the warrant issued; instead, they waited until the Gates returned. It is unclear whether they waited because they wanted to execute the warrant without unnecessary property damage or because they had doubts about whether the informant's tips were really valid. In either event their judgment is to be commended.

Although the foregoing analysis is determinative as to the house search, the car search raises additional issues because "there is a constitutional difference between houses and cars." An officer who has probable cause to suspect that a highly movable automobile contains contraband does not need a valid warrant in order to search it. . . .

. . . [T]he Court . . . attaches no weight to the conclusions of the Circuit Judge of DuPage County, Illinois, of the three judges of the Second District of the Illinois Appellate Court, or of the five justices of the Illinois Supreme Court, all of whom concluded that the warrant was not based on probable cause. In a factbound inquiry of this sort, the judgment of three levels of state courts, all of whom are better able to evaluate the probable reliability of anonymous informants in Bloomingdale, Illinois, than we are, should be entitled to at least a presumption of accuracy. I would simply vacate the judgment of the Illinois Supreme Court and remand the case for reconsideration. . . .

CASE DISCUSSION

Define the totality-of-circumstances test that the Court adopts. What circumstances constituted probable cause in this case? Does Justice Byron R. White have a point when he says that the totality-of-circumstances test may "eviscerate" (remove the vital content of) the probable cause standard? Why do you think he makes such a strong statement?

THE MANNER OF ARREST

Probable cause alone is not enough to make an arrest a reasonable Fourth Amendment seizure. The manner in which officers execute the arrest is also reviewed. The probable cause requirement focuses on achieving a correct result in a particular case, but the manner of arrest focuses on the more general public interest in controlling the police. The law of arrest demonstrates that achieving the correct result is necessary yet not sufficient to satisfy the Fourth Amendment requirement of reasonableness. The manner of arrest must be reasonable during both the time prior to arrest in apprehending suspects and after arrest in subduing them.

The Warrant Requirement

According to the Fourth Amendment,

> The right of the people to be secure in their persons, houses, papers, and effects shall not be violated and no warrants shall issue but upon probable cause, supported by Oath or affirmation, and particularly describing the place to be searched, and the persons or things to be seized.

The Fourth Amendment consists of two clauses whose meaning and relationship to each other have puzzled both historians and judges. The **reasonableness clause** refers generally to the people's right to be free of unreasonable searches and seizures. The **warrant clause** refers specifically to the issuance of warrants. A dispute exists over what the framers of the Fourth Amendment intended by separating the reasonableness clause from the warrant clause. Some have argued that the framers in their haste inadvertently separated the two. According to this interpretation, the reasonableness clause depends on the warrant clause. In other words, all searches and seizures without warrants and probable cause are unreasonable.

Others maintain that the framers separated the clauses by design. According to this interpretation, the Founding Fathers intended to direct the warrant requirement only at the hated general warrants of their time. General warrants authorized customs officials and other Crown officers to enter and search all homes in a colony for an extended period of time on the blanket authority of a single warrant. As if filling in the amount on a signed blank check, the officers could fill in the name and address of any house they chose to search. Searches and seizures for ordinary crimes—what we call "street crimes" today—did not require prior judicial approval because local constables rarely abused the search authority.[14]

According to the Supreme Court's interpretation of the Fourth Amendment, arrests both with and without warrants can be reasonable seizures. Since the 1980s, the Court has emphasized the reasonableness clause and, therefore, the constitutionality of arrests without warrants. Practically speaking, the vast majority of arrests are made without warrants. In both kinds of arrests, however, it is left to magistrates to determine ultimately whether probable cause supports the arrests. In arrests with warrants, the judicial determination of probable cause takes place before arrests occur. In arrests without warrants, police officers initially decide probable cause, and magistrates review the probable cause decision after the officers make the arrest.

Arrest warrants must satisfy three requirements:

1. A neutral magistrate must determine probable cause prior to arrest.
2. Someone (nearly always a law enforcement officer) must swear to the facts supporting probable cause.
3. The warrant must specifically identify the arrested person.

Obtaining a warrant requires considerable prior investigation. Most arrest warrants involve white-collar suspects such as tax evaders, price fixers, and bribers. On the other hand, most arrests without warrants pertain to street crimes: robbery, burglary, narcotics violations, and larceny. This has led some to complain that middle-class criminals get prior judicial determination, whereas street criminals are at the mercy of "cops on the beat." However, it would be wrong to conclude that the system intentionally discriminates according to class. The consequences are due mainly to the types of crime, not the social status of the criminals involved. Street crimes rarely permit long-term investigations, whereas tax evasion and other white-collar crimes nearly always require detailed, extensive investigation.[15]

The requirement of prior determination of probable cause assumes that magistrates carefully review the information that law enforcement officers supply them. However, the cases and social science research indicate that

> there is little reason to be reassured by what we know about magistrates in operation. The magistrate can know there are factual issues to be explored only if he looks behind the particulars presented. Yet it is rare for such initiatives to be taken. Most magistrates devote very little time to appraising the affidavit's sufficiency. They assume that the affiant is being honest. . . . They tend to ask no questions and to issue warrants in routine fashion. Over the years the police have adapted their practice not only to the law's requirements but also to the opportunities presented by the manner in which the law is administered. They have often relied on the magistrate's passivity to insulate from review affidavits that are only apparently sufficient—sometimes purposely presenting them through officers who are "ignorant of the circumstances" and, therefore, less likely to provide awkward details in the unlikely event that questions are asked. . . .[16]

Summarizing the results of a study of probable cause determination, Professor Abraham S. Goldstein wrote the following:

> Proceedings before magistrates generally lasted only two to three minutes and the magistrate rarely asked any questions to penetrate the boilerplate language or the hearsay in the warrant. Witnesses other than the police applicant were never called. And the police often engaged in "magistrate shopping" for judges who would give only minimal scrutiny to the application.[17]

D e c i s i o n   P o i n t

1. In *Barnes v. State*, at the hearing held by the trial court (challenging the issuance of a warrant) in the absence of the jury, Justice of the Peace Matthews testified that, while he did not read all of the three-page, single-spaced affidavit presented him by Officers Blaisdale and Bridges but only "touched the high parts," he did question the officers in detail about its contents and about the ne-

cessity of the issuance of the warrant, he was acquainted with the requirements for showing probable cause, and it was only after satisfying himself that probable cause existed for the search of the premises described that he issued the warrant. Appellant's contention that Judge Matthews was not a "neutral and detached magistrate" is without merit.[18]

2. In *Clodfelter v. Commonwealth*, the court considered the defendant's threshold claim of invalidity of a search warrant which resulted in the June 16, 1975, search for and the seizure of contraband drugs from a hotel room rented by Clodfelter. While not challenging the sufficiency of the affidavit to state probable cause for the issuance of a search warrant, Clodfelter argues that the search warrant, and the search made pursuant thereto, were illegal and invalid. This is so, he says, because the affidavit shows that it was subscribed and sworn to before the issuing magistrate at 1:05 A.M. and the search warrant was issued two minutes later, at 1:07 A.M. While citing no authority for his position, Clodfelter argues "it is clear that two minutes is not sufficient time for a magistrate to exercise his constitutional and statutory duties to properly analyze the affidavit, and his failure to do so

makes the warrant invalid." In effect, Clodfelter argues for a per se rule that would invalidate any search warrant issued within a few minutes after the supporting affidavit is filed with the issuing magistrate.

We decline to adopt such a rule. The affidavit in question was on a one page printed form. Detective T. A. Collins, who signed the affidavit, testified that he filled in the relevant information showing the place to be searched, the contraband for which the search was to be conducted, and material facts establishing probable cause for issuance of the warrant and the offense in relation to which the search was to be made. He then presented the affidavit to the magistrate and made oath to its contents. Our review of the affidavit convinces us that a finding of probable cause by an experienced magistrate, who is by law presumed to have fully discharged his duties, within two minutes after receiving the affidavit would be neither unreasonable nor unusual. Moreover, the law looks with disfavor upon inflexible mechanical rules as tending to defeat rather than attain the ends of justice.[19]

The Fourth Amendment requires that magistrates base their probable cause determination on information sworn to under oath. The pain of perjury (the crime of lying under oath) encourages trustworthy facts. A sworn written statement (affidavit) submitted to an officer qualified to administer oaths and attached to the warrant satisfies the Fourth Amendment oath requirement. If the affidavit establishes probable cause, the magistrate issues the warrant.

The written statement is not always enough; sometimes it is purposely vague. For example, police officers who want to preserve the anonymity of undercover agents make only vague references to the circumstances surrounding the information. In these cases, supplemental oral information satisfies the requirement in some jurisdictions. However, other courts require that all information be in writing.[20]

Officers usually appear before magistrates with the written affidavit, but not all jurisdictions require that officers appear in person. For example, the Federal Rules of Criminal Procedure authorize officers to phone or radio their information to a federal magistrate. The magistrate records the information verbatim. If the information satisfies the probable cause requirement, the magistrate authorizes the officer to sign the magistrate's name to a warrant.

Rule 41. (c)(2) Warrant Upon Oral Testimony.

(A) General Rule. — If the circumstances make it reasonable to dispense with a written affidavit, a Federal magistrate may issue a warrant based upon sworn oral testimony communicated by telephone or other appropriate means.

(B) Application. — The person who is requesting the warrant shall prepare a document to be known as a duplicate original warrant and shall read such duplicate original warrant, verbatim, to the Federal magistrate. The Federal magistrate shall enter, verbatim, what is so read to such magistrate on a document to be known as the original warrant. The Federal magistrate may direct that the warrant be modified.

(C) Issuance. — If the Federal magistrate is satisfied that the circumstances are such as to make it reasonable to dispense with a written affidavit and that grounds for the application exist or that there is probable cause to believe that they exist, the Federal magistrate shall order the issuance of a warrant by directing the person requesting the warrant to sign the Federal magistrate's name on the duplicate original warrant. The Federal magistrate shall immediately sign the original warrant and enter on the face of the original warrant the exact time when the warrant was ordered to be issued. The finding of probable cause for a warrant upon oral testimony may be based on the same kind of evidence as is sufficient for a warrant upon affidavit.

(D) Recording and Certification of Testimony. — When a caller informs the Federal magistrate that the purpose of the call is to request a warrant, the Federal magistrate shall immediately place under oath each person whose testimony forms a basis of the application and each person applying for that warrant. If a voice recording device is available, the Federal magistrate shall record by means of such device all of the call after the caller informs the Federal magistrate that the purpose of the call is to request a warrant. Otherwise a stenographic or longhand verbatim record shall be made. If a voice recording devi[c]e is used or a stenographic record made, the Federal magistrate shall have the record transcribed, shall certify the accuracy of the transcription, and shall file a copy of the original record and the transcription with the court. If a longhand verbatim record is made, the Federal magistrate shall file a signed copy with the court.

(E) Contents. — The contents of a warrant upon oral testimony shall be the same as the contents of a warrant upon affidavit.

(F) Additional Rule for Execution. — The person who executes the warrant shall enter the exact time of execution on the face of the duplicate original warrant.

(G) Motion to Suppress Precluded. — Absent a finding of bad faith, evidence obtained pursuant to a warrant issued under this paragraph is not subject to a motion to suppress on the ground that the circumstances were not such as to make it reasonable to dispense with a written affidavit. The officer can execute the warrant pursuant to this electronic communication.[21]

Some argue that modern electronic advances should eliminate the need for most warrantless arrests. According to this argument, officers can obtain advance judicial approval for arrests, except in emergencies, without hindering effective law enforcement. If courts adopted this practice,

The Supreme Court [c]ould actually enforce the warrant doctrine to which it has paid lip service for so many years. That is, a warrant is always required for every search and seizure when it is practicable to obtain one. However, in order that this requirement be workable and not be swallowed by its exception, the warrant need not be in writing but rather may be phoned or radioed into a magistrate (where it will be tape recorded and the recording preserved) who will authorize or forbid the search orally. By making the procedure for obtaining a warrant less difficult (while only marginally reducing the safeguards it provides), the number of cases where "emergencies" justify an exception to the warrant requirement should be very small.[22]

The Fourth Amendment requires specific identification of the person to be arrested. To satisfy this **particularity requirement,** the Federal Rules of Criminal Procedure provide that an arrest warrant "shall contain the name of the defendant or, if his name is unknown, any name or description by which he can be identified with reasonable certainty." In one early case, the Supreme Court mandated that the description be sufficiently specific that it leave "nothing . . . to the discretion of the officer issuing the warrant." Although that ruling has never been challenged specifically, most cases in practice demand only that the executing officer identify the person with "reasonable certainty."[23]

The Fourth Amendment requires that neutral magistrates issue warrants. A personal interest either in issuing warrants in general or in issuing warrants against specific individuals destroys their neutrality. Therefore, one court declared a warrant illegally issued because the magistrate received a five-dollar fee for issuing warrants but no fee for declining to do so. The financial interest in issuing the warrants destroyed the magistrate's neutrality. Also, a state attorney general who had taken over a case in which he had issued a warrant pursuant to a state statute authorizing him to do so was not neutral, according to the reviewing court. As the prosecutor in the case, the attorney general benefited from the suspect's arrest.[24]

The desirability of having a magistrate determine probable cause before arrest has led some to argue that officers must always secure a warrant except in emergencies. In a leading case, *United States v. Watson,* the Supreme Court declined to make warrants a part of the reasonableness requirement of Fourth Amendment arrests. (See the Decision Point below.) Hence, as long as officers have probable cause, they do not need to obtain prior judicial approval to make the arrest. There is one major exception to this rule—arrests in homes (see the following section of this chapter).[25]

D e c i s i o n   P o i n t

On August 17, an informant of proven reliability delivered a stolen credit card to a federal postal inspector, alleging that he had received the card from Henry Watson, who had instructed the informant to purchase airline tickets with it. Although authorities had probable cause to arrest Watson, they neither arrested him immediately nor applied for an arrest warrant. Instead, they arranged for a meeting between the informant and Watson on August 22. The meeting was postponed until August 23, at which time the informant signaled to postal inspectors that Watson had indicated that he presently had additional stolen credit cards in his possession. The inspectors entered the restaurant where the meeting had taken place, arrested Watson without a warrant, and searched his person, finding nothing. Watson, however, consented to a search of his nearby car; that search yielded the stolen credit cards.

Was the arrest illegal because the officers had time to get a warrant but did not do so? The Court of Appeals for the Ninth Circuit ruled that when they have time, police must secure a warrant to make an arrest, even in a public place. The United States Supreme Court held that the warrantless arrest did not violate the Fourth Amendment:

Law enforcement officers may find it wise to seek arrest warrant[s] where practicable to do so, and their judgments about probable cause may be more readily accepted where backed by a warrant issued by a magistrate. But we decline to transform this judicial preference into a constitutional rule when the judgment of the Nation . . . has for so long been to authorize warrantless public arrests on probable cause rather than to encumber criminal prosecutions with endless litigation with respect to the existence of exigent circumstances, whether it was practicable to get a warrant, whether the suspect was about to flee, and the like.

In a dissenting opinion, Justice Marshall observed the following:

The Government's assertion that a warrant requirement would impose an intolerable burden stems, in large part, from the specious supposition that procurement of an arrest warrant would be necessary as soon as probable cause ripens. There is no requirement that a search warrant be obtained the moment police have probable cause to search. The same rule should obtain for arrest warrants, where it may even make more sense. . . .

This approach obviates most of the difficulties that have been suggested with an arrest warrant rule. Police would not have to cut their investigation short the moment they obtain probable cause to arrest, nor would undercover agents be forced suddenly to terminate their work and forfeit their covers. Moreover, if in the course of continued police investigation exigent circumstances develop that demand an immediate arrest, the arrest may be made without fear of unconstitutionality, so long as the exigency was unanticipated and not used to avoid the arrest warrant requirement. . . . [T]he requirement that officers about to arrest a suspect ordinarily obtain a warrant before they do so does not seem unduly burdensome. . . .[26]

Arrests in Homes

Because of the high privacy interest in homes, the United States Supreme Court has held that the Fourth Amendment requires a warrant to enter a private home to make arrests. There is an emergency exception to this warrant requirement. For example, when officers are in hot pursuit of a suspect who runs into a home, the Fourth Amendment does not require the foolish step of breaking off the chase at the door while officers obtain a warrant from a magistrate. The Court addressed the warrant requirement regarding entries into homes to arrest suspects in *Payton v. New York*.

C A S E

Did They Need a Warrant to Enter the Homes?

Payton v. New York
445 U.S. 573, 100 S.Ct. 1371,
63 L.Ed.2d 639 (1980)

Payton and another were convicted on felony charges. The New York trial judge held that the warrantless

entry into homes was authorized by New York statutes and refused to suppress evidence that was seized upon the entry. The New York Court of Appeals affirmed the convictions. The Supreme Court reversed, holding that the Fourth Amendment, applicable to the states through the Fourteenth Amendment, prohibits police from making warrantless and nonconsensual entries into suspects' homes in order to make routine felony arrests. Justice Stevens wrote the opinion of the Court, in which Justice Brennan, Stewart, Marshall, Blackmun, and Powell joined. Justice Blackmun filed a concurring opinion. Justice White filed a dissenting opinion, in which Chief Justice Burger and Justice Rehnquist joined. Justice Rehnquist filed a dissenting opinion.

FACTS

. . . On January 14, 1970, after two days of intensive investigation, New York detectives had assembled evidence sufficient to establish probable cause to believe that· Theodore Payton had murdered the manager of a gas station two days earlier. At about 7:30 A.M. on January 15, six officers went to Payton's apartment in the Bronx, intending to arrest him. They had not obtained a warrant. Although light and music emanated from the apartment, there was no response to their knock on the metal door. They summoned emergency assistance and, about 30 minutes later, used crowbars to break open the door and enter the apartment. No one was there. In plain view, however, was a .30-caliber shell casing that was seized and later admitted into evidence at Payton's murder trial.

In due course Payton surrendered to the police, was indicted for murder, and moved to suppress the evidence taken from his apartment. The trial judge held that the warrantless and forcible entry was authorized by the New York Code of Criminal Procedure, and that the evidence in plain view was properly seized. He found that exigent circumstances justified the officers' failure to announce their purpose before entering the apartment as required by the statute. He had no occasion, however, to decide whether those circumstances also would have justified the failure to obtain a warrant, because he concluded that the warrantless entry was adequately supported by the statute without regard to the circumstances. The Appellate Division, First Department, summarily affirmed.

On March 14, 1974, Obie Riddick was arrested for the commission of two armed robberies that had occurred in 1971. He had been identified by the victims in June 1973, and in January 1974 the police had learned his address. They did not obtain a warrant for his arrest. At about noon on March 14, a detective, accompanied by three other officers, knocked on the door of the Queens house where Riddick was living. When his young son opened the door, they could see Riddick sitting in bed covered by a sheet. They entered the house and placed him under arrest. Before permitting him to dress, they opened a chest of drawers two feet from the bed in search of weapons and found narcotics and related paraphernalia. Riddick was subsequently indicted on narcotics charges. At a suppression hearing, the judge held that the warrantless entry into his home was authorized by the revised New York Statute. . . .

The New York Court of [A]ppeals affirmed the convictions.

OPINION

. . . The Fourth Amendment protects the individual's privacy in a variety of settings. In none is the zone of privacy more clearly defined than when bounded by the unambiguous physical dimensions of an individual's home—a zone that finds its roots in clear and specific constitutional terms: "The right of the people to be secure in their . . . houses . . . shall not be violated." That language unequivocally establishes the proposition that "[a]t the very core [of the Fourth Amendment] stands the right of a man to retreat into his own home and there be free from unreasonable governmental intrusion." In terms that apply equally to seizures of property and to seizures of persons, the Fourth Amendment has drawn a firm line at the entrance to the house. Absent exigent circumstances, that threshold may not reasonably be crossed without a warrant. . . .

A majority of the States that have taken a position on the question permit warrantless entry into the home to arrest even in the absence of exigent circumstances. . . . But these current figures reflect a significant decline during the last decade in the number of States permitting warrantless entries for arrest. . . . A longstanding, widespread practice is not immune from constitutional scrutiny. But neither is it to be lightly brushed aside. . . . Seven state courts have recently held that warrantless home arrests violate their respective State constitutions. . . . That is significant because by invoking a state constitutional provision, a state court immunizes its decision from review by this Court. . . .

The parties have argued at some length about the practical consequences of a warrant requirement as a precondition to a felony arrest in the home. In the absence of any evidence that effective law enforcement has suffered in those States that already have such a requirement . . . we are inclined to view such argument with skepticism. More fundamentally, however, such arguments of policy must give way to a constitutional command that we consider to be unequivocal. . . .

Thus, for Fourth Amendment purposes, an arrest warrant founded on probable cause implicitly carries with it the limited authority to enter a dwelling in which the suspect lives when there is reason to believe the suspect is within.

Because no arrest warrant was obtained in either of these cases, the judgments must be reversed and the cases remanded to the New York Court of Appeals for further proceedings not inconsistent with this opinion.

It is so ordered.

DISSENT

Justice White, with whom the Chief Justice and Justice Rehnquist join, dissenting. . . .

These four restrictions on home arrests—felony, knock and announce, daytime, and stringent probable cause—constitute powerful and complementary protections for the privacy of interests associated with the home. The felony requirement guards against abusive or arbitrary enforcement and ensures that invasions of the home occur only in case of the most serious crimes. The knock-and-announce and daytime requirements protect individuals against fear, humiliation, and embarrassment of being roused from the beds in states of partial or complete undress. And these requirements allow the arrestee to surrender at his front door, thereby maintaining his dignity and preventing the officers from entering other rooms of the dwelling. The stringent probable-cause requirement would help ensure against the possibility that the police would enter when the suspect was not home, and, in searching for him, frighten members of the family or ransack parts of the house, seizing items

in plain view. In short, these requirements, taken together, permit an individual suspected of a serious crime to surrender at the front door of his dwelling and thereby avoid most of the humiliation and indignity that the Court seems to believe necessarily accompany a house entry. . . .

All of these limitations on warrantless arrest entries are satisfied on the facts of the present cases. The arrests here were for serious felonies—murder and armed robbery—and both occurred during daylight hours. The authorizing statutes required that the police announce their business and demand entry; neither Payton nor Riddick makes any contention that these statutory requirements were not fulfilled. And it is not argued that the police had no probable cause to believe that both Payton and Riddick were in their dwellings at the time of the entries. . . .

While exaggerating the invasion of personal privacy involved in home arrests, the Court fails to account for the danger that its rule will "severely hamper effective law enforcement." . . . The policeman on his beat must now make subtle discriminations that perplex even judges in their chambers.

. . . [P]olice will sometimes delay making an arrest, even after probable cause is established, in order to be sure that they have enough evidence to convict. Then, if they suddenly have to arrest, they run the risk that the subsequent exigency will not excuse their prior failure to obtain a warrant. This problem cannot effectively be cured by obtaining a warrant as soon as probable cause is established because of the chance that the warrant will go stale before the arrest is made.

Further, police officers will often face the difficult task of deciding whether the circumstances are sufficiently exigent to justify their entry to arrest without a warrant. This is a decision that must be made quickly in the most trying of circumstances. If the officers mistakenly decide that the exigent circumstances are lacking, they may refrain from making the arrest, thus creating the possibility that a dangerous criminal will escape into the community. The police could reduce the likelihood of escape by staking out all possible exits until the circumstances become clearly exigent or a warrant is obtained. But the costs of such a stakeout seem excessive in an era of risking crime and scarce police resources.

CASE DISCUSSION

Should there be a bright line rule that officers may never enter a home to arrest without a warrant? What exigent circumstances (emergencies) justify putting aside the warrant requirement, in your opinion? Is the dissent right in its contention that the four restrictions already imposed on warrantless arrests in homes satisfy the Fourth Amendment reasonableness standard? Explain.

Misdemeanor Arrests

The **common law**—the judge-made law deriving from medieval English custom and incorporated in American law when the English colonists first settled here—required warrants for misdemeanor arrests unless the misdemeanor was committed in the officer's presence. According to the United States Supreme Court, the Fourth Amendment does not require officers to secure a warrant if they do not witness a misdemeanor, despite the common-law "in-presence" requirement.[27]

Some states have relaxed the in-presence requirement for misdemeanor arrests. For example, Nebraska has enacted a statute permitting officers to arrest a suspect without a warrant if they have

> reasonable cause to believe that such person has committed . . . [a] misdemeanor, and the officer has reasonable cause to believe that such person either
> (a) will not be apprehended unless immediately arrested;
> (b) may cause injury to himself or others or damage to property unless immediately arrested;
> (c) may destroy or conceal evidence of the commission of such misdemeanor; or
> (d) has committed a misdemeanor in the presence of the officer.[28]

The Nebraska statute removes the in-presence requirement generally. However, most states have relaxed the requirement in domestic assault cases specifically. Several states have revised their laws to allow—even require—police officers to arrest for misdemeanor assaults in domestic cases.

Many domestic assaults are not felonies. Therefore, under the old rule, officers could not arrest a suspect in a typical domestic assault case unless the victim accompanied the officer to a police station to sign a complaint. Many victims were not willing to sign complaints, and many officers were unwilling to take them to the police station. Under the new legislation—or, in some cases, police department policy changes—this situation has improved. Hence, if one spouse with obvious bruises or welts tells an officer that the other spouse caused the injury, police officers can arrest without a warrant or a signed complaint, even if they did not witness the alleged assault.[29]

Deadly Force

For centuries, the common law permitted the use of deadly force to apprehend fleeing felons. Most American jurisdictions historically authorized the use of deadly force to make felony arrests. However, many individual police departments adopted rules that severely restricted the use of deadly force to make arrests. The gist of most of these rules is that officers may use deadly force only when it does not endanger innocent citizens and when it is required for apprehending "dangerous" suspects. Deadly force raises two Fourth Amendment questions:

1. Is shooting a suspect a seizure?

2. Assuming it is, was deadly force reasonably necessary to effect the arrest under the particular circumstances of the specific case where officers used it?

The Supreme Court addressed these questions in the landmark case *Tennessee v. Garner.*

C A S E

Did Hymon Violate the Constitution When He Shot Garner?

Tennessee v. Garner
471 U.S. 1, 105 S.Ct. 1694,
85 L.Ed.2d 1 (1985)

Garner's father sued under U.S.C.A. § 1983 (see Chapter 10), the "constitutional tort" statute. The district court held that the officer's actions were constitutional. The court of appeals reversed. The Supreme Court affirmed. Justice White wrote the opinion of the Court, in which Justices Brennan, Marshall, Blackmun, Powell, and Stevens joined. Justice O'Connor filed a dissenting opinion, in which Chief Justice Burger and Justice Rehnquist joined.

FACTS

At about 10:45 P.M. on October 3, 1974, Memphis Police Officers Elton Hymon and Leslie Wright were dispatched to answer a "prowler inside call." Upon arriving at the scene they saw a woman standing on her porch gesturing toward the adjacent house. She told them she had heard glass breaking and that "they" or "someone" was breaking in next door. While Wright radioed the dispatcher to say that they were on the scene, Hymon went behind the house. He heard a door slam and saw someone run across the back yard. The fleeing suspect, who was appellee–respondent's descendent, Edward Garner, stopped at a 6-feet-high chain link fence at the edge of the yard. With the aid of a flashlight, Hymon was able to see Garner's face and hands. He saw no sign of a weapon, and though

not certain, was "reasonably sure" and "figured" that Garner was unarmed. He thought Garner was 17 or 18 years old and about 5′5″ or 5′7″ tall. While Garner was crouched at the base of the fence, Hymon called out "police, halt" and took a few steps toward him. Garner began to climb over the fence. Convinced that if Garner made it over the fence he would elude capture, Hymon shot him. The bullet hit Garner in the back of the head. Garner was taken by ambulance to a hospital, where he died on the operating table. Ten dollars and a purse taken from the house were found on his body.

In using deadly force to prevent escape, Hymon was acting under the authority of a Tennessee statute and pursuant to Police Department policy. The statute provides that "[i]f, after notice of the intention to arrest the defendant, he either flee or forcibly resist, the officer may use all the necessary means to effect the arrest." Tenn. Code Ann. § 40-7-108 (1982). The Department policy was slightly more restrictive than the statute, but still allowed the use of deadly force in cases of burglary. The incident was reviewed by the Memphis Police Firearm's Review Board and presented to a grand jury. Neither took any action.

Garner's father then brought this action in the Federal District Court for the Western District of Tennessee, seeking damages under 42 U.S.C. § 1983 for asserted violations of Garner's constitutional rights. The complaint alleged that the shooting violated the Fourth, Fifth, Sixth, Eighth, and Fourteenth Amendments of the United States Constitution. It named as defendants Officer Hymon, the Police Department, its Director, and the Mayor and City of Memphis. After a 3-day bench trial, the District Court entered judgment for all defendants. It dismissed the claims against the Mayor and the Director for lack of evidence. It then concluded that Hymon's actions were authorized by the Tennessee statute, which in turn was constitutional. Hymon had employed the only reasonable and practicable means of preventing Garner's escape. Garner had "recklessly and heedlessly attempted to vault over the fence to escape, thereby assuming the risk of being fired upon."

The District Court . . . found that the statute, and Hymon's actions, were constitutional. The Court of Appeals reversed and remanded. . . .

OPINION

. . . Whenever an officer restrains the freedom of a person to walk away, he has seized that person. . . . [T]here can be no question that apprehension by the use of deadly force is a seizure subject to the reasonableness requirement of the Fourth Amendment.

A police officer may arrest a person if he has probable cause to believe that person committed a crime. Petitioners and appellant argue that if this requirement is satisfied the Fourth Amendment has nothing to say about how that seizure is made. The submission ignores the many cases in which this Court, by balancing the extent of the intrusion against the need for it, has examined the reasonableness of the manner in which a search or seizure is conducted. . . .

The use of deadly force to prevent the escape of all felony suspects, whatever the circumstances, is constitutionally unreasonable. It is not better that all felony suspects die than that they escape. Where the suspect poses no immediate threat to the officer and no threat to others, the harm resulting from failing to apprehend him does not justify the use of deadly force to do so. It is no doubt unfortunate when a suspect who is in sight escapes, but the fact the police arrive a little late or are a little slower afoot does not always justify killing the suspect. A police officer may not seize an unarmed, nondangerous suspect by shooting him dead. The Tennessee statute is unconstitutional insofar as it authorizes the use of deadly force against such fleeing suspects. . . .

Officer Hymon could not reasonably have believed that Garner—young, slight, and unarmed—posed any threat. Indeed, Hymon never attempted to justify his actions on any basis other than the need to prevent escape. . . . [T]he fact that Garner was a suspected burglar could not, without regard to the other circumstances, automatically justify the use of deadly force. Hymon did not have probable cause to believe that Garner, whom he correctly believed to be unarmed, posed any physical danger to himself or to others.

DISSENT

Justice O'Connor, with whom the Chief Justice and Justice Rehnquist join, dissenting.

For purposes of Fourth Amendment analysis, I agree with the Court that Officer Hymon "seized" Garner by shooting him. Whether that seizure was reasonable and therefore permitted by the Fourth Amendment requires a careful balancing of the important public interest in crime prevention and detection and the nature and quality of the intrusion upon legitimate interests of the individual. In striking this balance here, it is crucial to acknowledge that police use of deadly force to apprehend a fleeing criminal suspect falls within the "rubric of police conduct . . . necessarily [invoking] swift action predicated upon the on-the-spot observations of the officer on the beat." . . .

The public interest involved in the use of deadly force as a last resort to apprehend a fleeing burglary suspect relates primarily to the serious nature of the crime. Household burglaries represent not only the illegal entry into a person's home, but also "pos[e] a real risk of serious harm to others." According to recent Department of Justice statistics, "Three-fifths of all rapes in the home, three-fifths of all home robberies, and about a third of home aggravated and simple assaults are committed by burglars." . . .

Against the strong public interests justifying the conduct at issue here must be weighed the individual interests implicated in the use of deadly force by police officers. The majority declares that "[t]he suspect's fundamental interest in his own life need not be elaborated upon." This blithe assertion hardly provides an adequate substitute for the majority's failure to acknowledge the distinctive manner in which the suspect's interest in his life is even exposed to risk. For purposes of this case, we must recall that the police officer, in the course of . . . investigating a nighttime burglary, had reasonable cause to arrest the suspect and ordered him to halt. The officer's use of force resulted because the suspected burglar refused to heed this command and the office[r] reasonably believed that there was no means short of firing his weapon to apprehend the suspect. . . . "[T]he policeman's hands should not be tied merely because of the possibility that the suspect will fail to cooperate with legitimate actions by law enforcement personnel." . . .

CASE DISCUSSION

Should the Fourth Amendment apply to the manner of arrest? Is shooting a suspect a "seizure"? Professor H. Richard Uviller, a longtime student of police power and the Constitution, commented on the decision in *Tennessee v. Garner:*

> It is embarrassing for a law professor to be blindsided in his own territory. But the truth is, I didn't see it coming. It had never occurred to me that a police office[r] shooting to kill a fleeing felon might be engaging in an unconstitutional search and seizure. Of course, I can see the connection now that it has been explained to me, but I did not spontaneously equate a

deadly shot with an arrest. And I have had some prior acquaintance not only with the fourth amendment, but specifically with the issue of the bullet aimed at the back of a retreating felon.[30]

Would the rule in this case permit an officer to shoot a drunk driver swerving erratically down the road headed toward a town? A person wanted for a series of violent crimes but not presently armed who flees from the police? Will this rule embolden criminals? Has the Court tilted the balance too far toward process and societal interests and too far away from the interest in results? Defend your answer.

Tennessee is a civil action brought under United States Code Annotated § 1983 (see Chapter 10). Edward Garner's father sued because Officer Elton Hymon used deadly force with deadly effect. If Officer Hymon had only wounded Garner, the shooting would have had a different effect in a criminal case. For example, if the prosecutors had prosecuted Garner, he may not have been able to challenge the jurisdiction of the court. If the use of force was unlawful, courts might exclude the physical evidence seized from his person or incriminating statements made in the absence of the *Miranda* warnings. The Garner case makes none of this clear. The new doctrine that encompasses deadly force within the Fourth Amendment search-and-seizure clause awaits clarification through applications in criminal cases.[31]

Nondeadly Force

Although shooting is the most widely known and discussed means used to arrest suspects forcibly, it is not the most common means. In practice, police use nondeadly force and other mechanisms more frequently than shooting to arrest suspects unwilling to submit to authority. The alternatives to deadly force have come under close constitutional scrutiny since *Tennessee v. Garner.* As we saw, a divided Court ruled that deadly force was a Fourth Amendment seizure. The Supreme Court examined but did not specifically rule that chokeholds are seizures in *City of Los Angeles v. Lyons* (excerpted in Chapter 10). The Court has decided that chasing a suspect is not a seizure until the officer physically lays hands on the suspect (see Chapter 3, *California v. Hodari D.*). The Supreme Court addressed the use of force to subdue persons following a Fourth Amendment seizure in *Graham v. Connor.*

C A S E

Did the Officers Use Excessive Force?

Graham v. Connor
490 U.S. 386, 109 S.Ct. 1865,
104 L.Ed.2d 443 (1989)

Graham, a diabetic, brought a § 1983 action to recover damages for injuries allegedly sustained when law enforcement officers used physical force against him during an investigatory stop. The U.S. District Court directed a verdict for the defendant police officers. The court of appeals affirmed. The U.S. Supreme Court granted certiorari *and reversed. Chief Justice Rehnquist wrote the opinion of the Court, in which Justices White, Stevens, O'Connor, Scalia, and Kennedy joined. Justice Blackmun filed an opinion concurring in part and concurring in the judgment, in which Justices Brennan and Marshall joined.*

FACTS

On November 12, 1984, Graham, a diabetic, felt the onset of an insulin reaction. He asked a friend, William Berry, to drive him to a nearby convenience store so he could purchase some orange juice to counteract the reaction. Berry agreed, but when Graham entered the store, he saw a number of people ahead of him in the checkout line. Concerned about the delay, he hurried out of the store and asked Berry to drive him to a friend's house instead. Respondent Connor, an officer of the Charlotte, North Carolina, Police Department, saw Graham hastily enter and leave the store. The officer became suspicious that something was amiss and followed Berry's car. About one-half mile from the store, he made an investigative stop. Although Berry told Connor that Graham was simply suffering from a "sugar reaction," the officer ordered Berry and Graham to wait while he found out what, if anything, had happened at the convenience store. When Officer Connor returned to his patrol car to call for backup assistance, Graham got out of the car, ran around it twice, and finally sat down on the curb, where he passed out briefly.

In the ensuing confusion, a number of other Char-

lotte police officers arrived on the scene in response to Officer Connor's request for backup. One of the officers rolled Graham over on the sidewalk and cuffed his hands tightly behind his back, ignoring Berry's pleas to get him some sugar. Another officer said: "I've seen a lot of people with sugar diabetes that never acted like this. Ain't nothing wrong with the M. F. but drunk. Lock the S. B. up." Several officers then lifted Graham up from behind, carried him over to Berry's car, and placed him face down on its hood. Regaining consciousness, Graham asked the officers to check in his wallet for a diabetic decal that he carried. In response, one of the officers told him to "shut up" and shoved his face down against the hood of the car. Four officers grabbed Graham and threw him headfirst into the police car. A friend of Graham's brought some orange juice to the car, but the officers refused to let him have it. Finally, Officer Connor received a report that Graham had done nothing wrong at the convenience store, and the officers drove him home and released him.

At some point during his encounter with the police, Graham sustained a broken foot, cuts on his wrists, a bruised forehead, and an injured shoulder; he also claims to have developed a loud ringing in his right ear that continues to this day. He commenced this action under 42 U.S.C. § 1983 against the individual officers involved in the incident, all of whom are respondents here, alleging that they had used excessive force in making the investigatory stop, in violation of "rights secured to him under the Fourteenth Amendment to the United States Constitution and 42 U.S.C. § 1983." The case was tried before a jury. At the close of petitioner's evidence, respondents moved for a directed verdict. In ruling on that motion, the District Court considered the following four factors, which it identified as "[t]he factors to be considered in determining when the excessive use of force gives rise to a cause of action under § 1983";

1. the need for the application of force;
2. the relationship between that need and the amount of force that was used;

3. the extent of the injury inflicted; and

4. "[w]hether the force was applied in a good faith effort to maintain and restore discipline or maliciously and sadistically for the very purpose of causing harm."

Finding that the amount of force used by the officers was "appropriate under the circumstances," that "[t]here was no discernable injury inflicted," and that the force used "was not applied maliciously or sadistically for the very purpose of causing harm," but in "a good faith effort to maintain or restore order in the face of a potentially explosive situation," the District Court granted respondents' motion for a directed verdict.

A divided panel of the Court of Appeals for the Fourth Circuit affirmed.... We granted certiorari, and now reverse.

OPINION

Fifteen years ago, in *Johnson v. Glick* [1974], the Court of Appeals for the Second Circuit addressed a § 1983 damages claim filed by a pretrial detainee who claimed that a guard had assaulted him without justification. In evaluating the detainee's claim, Judge Friendly applied neither the Fourth Amendment nor the Eighth, the two most textually obvious sources of constitutional protection against physically abusive governmental conduct. Instead, he looked to "substantive due process," holding that "quite apart from any 'specific' of the Bill of Rights, application of undue force by law enforcement officers deprives a suspect of liberty without due process of law." As support for this proposition, he relied upon our decision in *Rochin v. California* (1952) [see Chapter 2], which used the Due Process Clause to void a state criminal conviction based on evidence obtained by pumping the defendant's stomach. If a police officer's use of force which "shocks the conscience" could justify setting aside a criminal conviction, Judge Friendly reasoned, a correctional officer's use of similarly excessive force must give rise to a due process violation actionable under § 1983. Judge Friendly went on to set forth four factors to guide courts in determining "whether the constitutional line has been crossed" by a particular use of force—the same four factors relied upon by the courts below in this case.

In the years following *Johnson v. Glick*, the vast majority of lower federal courts have applied its four-part "substantive due process" test indiscriminately to all excessive force claims lodged against law enforcement and prison officials under § 1983, without considering whether the particular application of force might implicate a more specific constitutional right governed by a different standard. Indeed, many courts have seemed to assume, as did the courts . . . in this case, that there is a generic "right" to be free from excessive force, grounded not in any particular constitutional provision but rather in "basic principles of § 1983 jurisprudence."

We reject this notion that all excessive force claims brought under § 1983 are governed by a single generic standard. As we have said many times, § 1983 "is not itself a source of substantive rights," but merely provides "a method for vindicating federal rights elsewhere conferred." *Baker v. McCollan* (1979). In addressing an excessive force claim brought under § 1983, analysis begins by identifying the specific constitutional right allegedly infringed by the challenged application of force.... In most instances, that will be either the Fourth Amendment's prohibition against unreasonable seizures of the person, or the Eighth Amendment's ban on cruel and unusual punishments, which are the two primary sources of constitutional protection against physically abusive governmental conduct. The validity of the claim must then be judged by reference to the specific constitutional standard which governs that right, rather than to some generalized "excessive force" standard. See *Tennessee v. Garner* (claim of excessive force to effect arrest analyzed under a Fourth Amendment standard); *Whitley v. Albers* (1986) (claim of excessive force to subdue convicted prisoner analyzed under an Eighth Amendment standard).

Where, as here, the excessive force claim arises in the context of an arrest or investigatory stop of a free citizen, it is most properly characterized as one invoking the protections of the Fourth Amendment, which guarantees citizens the right "to be secure in their persons . . . against unreasonable . . . seizures" of the person. . . . Today we . . . hold that all claims that law enforcement officers have used excessive force—deadly or not—in the course of an arrest, investigatory stop, or other "seizure" of a free citizen should be analyzed under the Fourth Amendment and its "reasonableness" standard, rather than under a "substantive due process" approach. Because the Fourth Amendment provides an explicit textual source of constitutional protection against this sort of physically intrusive governmental conduct, that Amendment, not the more generalized notion of "substantive due process," must be the guide for analyzing these claims. . . .

Determining whether the force used to effect a particular seizure is "reasonable" under the Fourth Amendment requires a careful balancing of "the nature and quality of the intrusion on the individual's Fourth Amendment interests" against the countervailing governmental interests at stake. Our Fourth Amendment jurisprudence has long recognized that the right to make an arrest or investigatory stop necessarily carries with it the right to use some degree of physical coercion or threat thereof to effect it. . . . With respect to a claim of excessive force, the . . . standard of reasonableness at the moment applies: "Not every push or shove, even if it may later seem unnecessary in the peace of a judge's chambers," *Johnson v. Glick*[,] violates the Fourth Amendment. The calculus of reasonableness must embody allowance for the fact that police officers are often forced to make split-second judgments—in circumstances that are tense, uncertain, and rapidly evolving—about the amount of force that is necessary in a particular situation.

As in other Fourth Amendment contexts, however, the "reasonableness" inquiry in an excessive force case is an objective one: the question is whether the officers' actions are "objectively reasonable" in light of the facts and circumstances confronting them, without regard to their underlying intent or motivation. See *Terry v. Ohio* (in analyzing the reasonableness of a particular search or seizure, "it is imperative that the facts be judged against an objective standard"). An officer's evil intentions will not make a Fourth Amendment violation out of an objectively reasonable use of force; nor will an officer's good intentions make an objectively unreasonable use of force constitutional.

Because petitioner's excessive force claim is one arising under the Fourth Amendment, the Court of Appeals erred in analyzing it under the four-part *Johnson v. Glick* test. That test, which requires consideration of whether the individual officers acted in "good faith" or "maliciously and sadistically for the very purpose of causing harm," is incompatible with a proper Fourth Amendment analysis. We do not agree with the Court of Appeals' suggestion, that the "malicious and sadistic" inquiry is merely another way of describing conduct that is objectively unreasonable under the circumstances. Whatever the empirical correlations between "malicious and sadistic" behavior and objective unreasonableness may be, the fact remains that the "malicious and sadistic" factor puts in issue the subjective motivations of the individual officers, which our prior cases make clear has no bearing on whether a particular seizure is "unreasonable" under the Fourth Amendment.

Nor do we agree with the Court of Appeals' conclusion, that because the subjective motivations of the individual officers are of central importance in deciding whether force used against a convicted prisoner violates the Eighth Amendment, it cannot be reversible error to inquire into them in deciding whether force used against a suspect or arrestee violates the Fourth Amendment. Differing standards under the Fourth and Eighth Amendments are hardly surprising: the terms "cruel" and "punishment" clearly suggest some inquiry into subjective state of mind, whereas the term "unreasonable" does not. Moreover, the less protective Eighth Amendment standard applies "only after the State has complied with the constitutional guarantees traditionally associated with criminal prosecutions." *Ingraham v. Wright* (1977). The Fourth Amendment inquiry is one of "objective reasonableness" under the circumstances, and subjective concepts like "malice" and "sadism" have no proper place in that inquiry.

Because the Court of Appeals reviewed the District Court's ruling on the motion for directed verdict under an erroneous view of the governing substantive law, its judgment must be vacated and the case remanded to that court for reconsideration of that issue under the proper Fourth Amendment standard.

It is so ordered.

CONCURRING OPINION

Justice Blackmun, with whom Justice Brennan and Justice Marshall join, concurring in part and concurring in the judgment.

I join the Court's opinion insofar as it rules that the Fourth Amendment is the primary tool for analyzing claims of excessive force in the prearrest context, and I concur in the judgment remanding the case to the Court of Appeals for reconsideration of the evidence under a reasonableness standard. In light of respondents' concession, however, that the pleadings in this case properly may be construed as raising a Fourth Amendment claim, I see no reason for the Court to find it necessary further to reach out to decide that prearrest excessive force claims are to be analyzed under the Fourth Amendment rather than under a substantive due process standard. I also see no basis for the Court's suggestion, that our decision in *Tennessee v. Garner* implicitly so held. Nowhere in *Garner* is a substantive due process standard for eval-

uating the use of excessive force in a particular case discussed; there is no suggestion that such a standard was offered as an alternative and rejected. . . .

CASE DISCUSSION

Define the standard that the Court adopted for determining whether force violates the Fourth Amendment. How does it differ from the test that the court of appeals applied in the case? Which test do you favor? Why did Justice Harry A. Blackmun write a concurring opinion? If you were applying the tests to the facts of this case, what decision would you reach? Defend your answer.

THE PERIOD AFTER ARREST

What happens after arrest depends on the seriousness of the crime and the circumstances surrounding the crime and the arrest. Immediately after arrest, as we have just seen, police officers may use force to subdue unruly suspects, to prevent escape, and to protect suspects themselves, officers, other citizens, or property. Once citizens have submitted to the arresting officer's authority, the officer may release them in misdemeanor cases. In felonies, the officer may take some or all of the following actions, depending on the circumstances of the case:

1. Search suspects (see Chapter 6).

2. Take suspects into custody; book suspects by putting their name and address, the time the crime was committed, and other information in the police blotter (see Chapter 1).

3. Conduct an inventory search and perhaps strip and body cavity searches of the prisoner (see Chapter 7).

4. Interrogate suspects (see Chapter 8).

5. Conduct lineups or other identification procedures (see Chapter 9).

6. Turn the results of the initial investigations over to prosecutors (see Chapter 11).

7. Present prisoners to a magistrate (see Chapter 11).

SUMMARY

Arrests are Fourth Amendment seizures. They are more intrusive than stops (discussed in Chapter 4). Arrested persons go to police stations, where the police may interrogate them intensively; then jail officials search them extensively, and law enforcement personnel make written records of their contact with the criminal justice system. The major elements in an arrest are (1) duration, (2) intensity, and (3) location. The decision to arrest balances the interest in reaching the correct result in the case at hand, and the interests in procedural regularity and individual autonomy in all cases.

The foundation for arrests is probable cause: facts or apparent facts that would lead a reasonable person to believe that a suspect has committed, is committing, or is about to commit a crime. Officers may acquire these facts firsthand by what they directly see, hear, feel, taste, or smell or learn them indirectly through hearsay—what victims, witnesses, other officers, or professional informants tell them. The probable cause standard is not rigid; although it is a quantitative measure, no set number of facts or apparent facts add up to probable cause. It is a commonsense notion, not a legal technicality, and the law permits individual police officers considerable leeway. Police meet the standard as long as they have enough specific information consistent with accuracy and later judicial assessment to determine its sufficiency.

Not only the foundation but also the manner of an arrest bears on its reasonableness. Arrests without warrants are reasonable seizures as long as probable cause supports them. However, entering houses to make arrests requires a warrant except in emergencies, such as the "hot pursuit" of a fleeing felon. The manner of arrest encompasses the time prior to, during, and following arrest. Hence, force (deadly and other) to effect arrests and means to subdue persons already arrested (such as chokeholds, stun guns, and mace) fall within the meaning of the term *seizure* under the Fourth Amendment.

REVIEW QUESTIONS

1. What interests does the law of arrest balance?

2. What determines the reasonableness of an arrest?

3. Compare an arrest with a stop.

4. Define *probable cause* and give an example of it.

5. What is the difference between hearsay and direct information? Which is more reliable? Why?

6. Identify the major kinds of informants, and briefly describe the reliability of each.

7. Explain the two-pronged and totality-of-circumstances tests to determine the trustworthiness of informants' evidence.

8. Why do police officers need a warrant to enter a private home to arrest a suspect? In what circumstances may police enter homes without warrants to arrest citizens?

9. Do you think spraying mace or using chokeholds to subdue arrested suspects is protected by the Fourth Amendment? By any other amendments? Explain.

10. When can police officers use deadly force to make arrests? If you were writing the law, what provision would you make covering deadly force?

11. Identify and explain the test for determining whether the use of force in executing an arrest is a reasonable seizure.

KEY TERMS

affidavits written statements sworn to before a person is officially authorized to administer oaths.

basis-of-knowledge prong the part of the two-pronged test of reliability that considers the source of an informant's information.

bright line rule a rule prescribing specific behavior.

common law the ancient, judge-made English law brought to America by the English colonists.

direct information information that officers know firsthand.

hearsay information that officers learn through third persons.

hearsay rule the principle under which indirect information is not admissible in court.

particularity requirement the requirement that a warrant must identify the person or place to be searched and the items or persons to be seized.

probable cause to arrest facts that would lead a reasonable person to believe that a crime has been, is being, or is about to be committed and that the person arrested is the perpetrator.

reasonableness clause the "unreasonable searches and seizures" section of the Fourth Amendment.

totality-of-circumstances test the test that considers all relevant issues to measure the trustworthiness of informants' information.

two-pronged test of reliability (*Spinelli–Aguilar* test) the test used to establish the veracity and basis of knowledge of an informant.

veracity prong the part of the two-pronged test of reliability that considers the honesty and reliability of an informant.

warrant clause the Fourth Amendment section relating to requirements of warrants.

Notes

1. *Ornelas v. U.S.*, 116 S.Ct. 1657 (1996), 1661–62.

2. Charles E. Moylan, Jr., "Hearsay and Probable Cause: An *Aguilar* and *Spinelli* Primer," *Mercer Law Review* 25 (1974): 742, 744; *Brinegar v. United States*, 338 U.S. 160, 176, 69 S.Ct. 1302, 1311, 93 L.Ed. 1879 (1949).

3. 338 U.S. 160, 69 S.Ct. 1302, 93 L.Ed. 1879 (1949).

4. *People v. Brown*, 24 N.Y.2d 421, 301 N.Y.S.2d 18, 248 N.E.2d 867, 869 (1969) (Jasen, J., dissenting); see also Craig M. Bradley, "Two Models of the Fourth Amendment," *Michigan Law Review* 83 (1985): 1470.

5. *State v. Bumpus*, 459 N.W.2d 619 (Iowa 1990).

6. *People v. Brown*, 24 N.Y.2d 421, 301 N.Y.S.2d 18, 248 N.E.2d 867 (1969).

7. *People v. Washington*, 192 Cal.App.3d 1120, 236 Cal.Rptr. 840 (1987).

8. *Ornelas v. U.S.*, 116 S.Ct. 1657 (1996), 1661.

9. *Federal Criminal Code and Rules*, 1987 ed. (St. Paul: West Publishing Company, 1987), 14.

10. The quotation is from *Allison v. State*, 62 Wis.2d 14, 214 N.W.2d 437 (1974); see also *Illinois v. Gates*, 462 U.S. 213, 103 S.Ct. 2317, 76 L.Ed.2d 527 (1983) (excerpted later in this chapter).

11. *Jones v. United States*, 266 F.2d 924, 928 (D.C. Cir. 1959).

12. *McCray v. Illinois*, 386 U.S. 300, 87 S.Ct. 1056, 18 L.Ed.2d 62 (1967) (past truthful information); *United States v. Harris*, 403 U.S. 573, 91 S.Ct. 2075, 29 L.Ed.2d 723 (1971) (admission against penal interest).

13. *Spinelli v. United States*, 393 U.S. 410, 89 S.Ct. 584, 21 L.Ed.2d 637 (1969).

14. Telford Taylor, *Two Studies in Constitutional Interpretation* (Columbus, OH: Ohio State University Press, 1968), 27–44.

15. Kenneth Mann, *Defending White Collar Crime* (New Haven, CT: Yale University Press, 1985).

16. Abraham S. Goldstein, "The Search Warrant, the Magistrate, and Judicial Review," *New York University Law Review* 62 (1987): 1173.

17. Ibid.

18. *Barnes v. State*, 520 S.W.2d 401 (Tex.Crim.App. 1975).

19. *Clodfelter v. Commonwealth*, 218 Va. 98, 235 S.E.2d 340 (1977).

20. *Fraizer v. Roberts*, 441 F.2d 1224 (8th Cir. 1971) (permitting supplementary oral information); *Orr v. State*, 382 So.2d 860 (Fla.App. 1980) (requiring all information in writing).

21. *Federal Rules of Criminal Procedure*, 41(c)(2).

22. Craig M. Bradley, "Two Models of the Fourth Amendment," *Michigan Law Review* 83 (1985): 1471.

23. *Federal Rules of Criminal Procedure*, 4(c)(1); *Marron v. United States*, 275 U.S. 192, 48 S.Ct. 74, 72 L.Ed. 231 (1927).

24. *Connally v. Georgia*, 429 U.S. 245, 97 S.Ct. 546, 50 L.Ed.2d 444 (1977) (fees for issuing warrants impaired neutrality); *Coolidge v. New Hampshire*, 403 U.S. 443, 91 S.Ct. 2022, 29 L.Ed.2d 564 (1971) (attorney general issuing warrants).

25. *United States v. Watson*, 423 U.S. 411, 96 S.Ct. 820, 46 L.Ed.2d 598 (1976).

26. Ibid.

27. *Price v. Tehan*, 84 Conn. 164, 79 A. 68 (1911); 76 A.L.R.2d 1444 (1961).

28. *Street v. Surdyka*, 492 F.2d 368 (4th Cir. 1974) (warrantless misdemeanor arrests do not violate Fourth Amendment); Neb. Rev. Stat. §29–404.02.

29. *Crime File: Domestic Violence* (Washington, DC: National Institute of Justice, 1985).

30. H. Richard Uviller, "Seizure by Gunshot: The Riddle of the Fleeing Felon," *New York University Review of Law of Social Change* 14 (1986): 705.

31. Ibid.

CHAPTER SIX

Searches for Evidence

CHAPTER OUTLINE

CHAPTER MAIN POINTS

1. The power of the government to search is both a powerful investigative tool and a deep invasion into the privacy of individuals.

2. The Fourth Amendment is a fundamental right against government invasions of privacy and property.

3. The Fourth Amendment prohibits only government invasions that violate an expectation of privacy that society recognizes.

4. Searches with warrants require prior approval by a magistrate.

5. Warrants require probable cause supported by an affidavit under oath or affirmation, a specific description of the place to be searched and the persons or things to be seized, timely execution, and timely return.

6. Courts allow wide interpretation of the scope of a search pursuant to warrant.

7. Officers must announce their presence before entering a home to search, but they may enter forcibly if they do not receive a prompt response.

8. The vast majority of searches are made without warrants.

9. Exigent circumstances justify searches without warrants.

10. Officers without warrants or probable cause can search lawfully arrested suspects and the area within the suspects' immediate control for the purpose of disarming the suspects and preserving evidence.

11. The Supreme Court has ruled that some pretext searches are reasonable under the Fourth Amendment.

12. Voluntary and knowing consent searches require neither a warrant nor probable cause.

13. In some circumstances, one person can consent to a search for a third person.

14. Officers who have probable cause can search vehicles without warrants because of the mobility of vehicles and reduced expectations of privacy in vehicles.

15. Police can seize containers on reasonable suspicion, and they can search containers in vehicles on probable cause without warrants.

Did He Consent to the Search?

This case arose on a stretch of Interstate 70 north of Dayton, Ohio, where the posted speed limit was 45 miles per hour because of construction. Robert D. Robinette was clocked at 69 miles per hour as he drove his car along this stretch of road, and he was stopped by Deputy Roger Newsome of the Montgomery County Sheriff's office. Newsome asked for and was handed Robinette's driver's license, and he ran a computer check which indicated that Robinette had no previous violations. Newsome then asked Robinette to step out of his car, turned on his mounted video camera, issued a verbal warning to Robinette, and returned his license.

At this point, Newsome asked, "One question before you get gone: [A]re you carrying any illegal contraband in your car? Any weapons of any kind, drugs, anything like that?" Robinette answered "no" to these questions, after which Deputy Newsome asked if he could search the car. Robinette consented. In the car, Deputy Newsome discovered a small amount of marijuana and, in a film container, a pill that was later determined to be methylenedioxymethamphetamine (MDMA).

THE IMPORTANCE OF THE SEARCH POWER

The authority to search is both a powerful investigative tool in the gathering of information and a potential instrument for carrying out severe invasions of the persons, privacy, and property of individuals. Perhaps no one more appreciated this twofold importance of the power to search than Supreme Court Justice Robert H. Jackson. **253**

President Truman appointed Justice Jackson to act as the chief prosecutor at the Nuremberg trials of Nazi war criminals following World War II. In the course of his work in presenting the case against the war criminals and in cross-examining Goering and other Nazi leaders, Justice Jackson learned in great detail of the Nazis' heinous invasions of the German people's persons, homes, property, and most private papers. What Justice Jackson learned in Nuremberg made a deep and lasting impression on the tough former prosecutor turned Supreme Court justice. When he returned to the Supreme Court, Justice Jackson spoke eloquently of the right against unreasonable searches and seizures in light of what he had learned in Germany. Justice Jackson worried that Americans did not appreciate the importance of the Fourth Amendment protection, and he opposed what he perceived as the Supreme Court's placing the Fourth Amendment in a "deferred" instead of the "preferred" position in which the Court had put First Amendment rights:[1]

> [The rights against unreasonable searches and seizures,] I protest, are not mere second-class rights but belong in the catalog of indispensable freedoms. Among deprivations of rights, none is so effective in cowing a population, crushing the spirit of the individual and putting terror in every heart. Uncontrolled search and seizure is one of the first and most effective weapons in the arsenal of every arbitrary government. And one need only briefly to have dwelt and worked among a people possessed of many admirable qualities but deprived of these rights to know that the human personality deteriorates and dignity and self-reliance disappear where homes, persons and possessions are subject at any hour to unheralded search and seizure by the police. But the right against searches and seizures is one of the most difficult to protect. Since the officers are themselves the chief invaders, there is no enforcement outside of court.[2]

Justice Jackson, as a former prosecutor, of course recognized the need for the power to search. That is why he pointedly referred to "uncontrolled" searches and seizures. He also realized that the power to search, however necessary, goes to bad officers as well as good officers and that the power to search affects both innocent and guilty people. Hence, Justice Jackson recognized that the Supreme Court has to balance the need for searches against the strong interest in individual privacy that they invade.

The law of searches, like that of arrests, stops, and frisks, involves a three-step analysis:

1. Was the government action a search? (See Chapter 3.)

2. If it was a search, was it reasonable? (See Chapters 4, 7, and following sections of this chapter.)

3. If it was not reasonable, then should the court bar fruits of the search as evidence against the defendant, prescribe other remedies, or both? (See Chapter 10.)

We divide the discussion of searches into two parts—searches for criminal evidence and other searches. The Fourth Amendment protects individuals against all unreasonable searches whether or not the purpose of the search is to obtain criminal evidence. This chapter discusses searches for criminal evidence. Chapter 7 discusses searches for purposes that go beyond law enforcement. These searches, usually referred to as *special needs searches*, include the following:

- *Inventory searches* of detained suspects and defendants
- *Custodial searches* of people detained in jails and prisons
- *Jail and prison searches* of employees in and visitors to jails and prisons for contraband and weapons
- *School searches* of students for drugs and weapons in schools
- *Employee drug testing*

Special needs searches are important in the law of criminal procedure even if their object is not to gather criminal evidence. In the first place, criminal justice personnel frequently conduct these searches. Moreover, whether or not for the purpose of gathering evidence, criminal justice officials frequently use the fruits of these searches in criminal proceedings. Officers who find evidence, contraband, or weapons while they conduct inventory searches or other searches not directly related to criminal law enforcement can seize the evidence, contraband, and weapons and use them in criminal proceedings.

SEARCHES WITH WARRANTS

The Fourth Amendment warrant clause provides that "no warrants shall issue, but upon probable cause, supported by oath or affirmation, and particularly describing the place to be searched, and the persons or things to be seized." (See Chapter 5 for a discussion of neutral magistrates and probable cause.)

The Particularity Requirement

The Fourth Amendment calls for search warrants "particularly describing the place to be searched, and the persons or things to be seized." Usually, a single dwelling address is sufficient to meet this requirement, such as a warrant to search "125 Willow Street" or "apartment 8-B in Colonial Terrace Apartments." However, a warrant to search "1135 Stone Street," where the address is a large apartment complex and only one apartment is the object of the search, authorizes a general search of all apartments in the building; this clearly violates the particularity requirement.[3]

The warrant must also specifically identify "the things to be seized" and may specify an entire class of items. So a search warrant that specified "address books, diaries, business records, documents, receipts, warranty books, guns, stereo equipment [and a] color television" as evidence in a theft case met the particularity requirement. Catchall categories are also acceptable if the context limits the seizure sufficiently. For example, a search warrant that authorized searching for and seizing "records, notes, [and] documents indicating involvement in and control of prostitution activity" was particular enough because officers were directed to seize only items related to prostitution. The United States Supreme Court analyzed the history and the importance of the particularity requirement in the landmark case on particularity, *Stanford v. Texas.*[4]

C A S E

Were the Books and Papers "Particularly Described"?

Stanford v. Texas
379 U.S. 476, 85 S.Ct. 506,
13 L.Ed.2d 431 (1965)

A Texas county judge denied Stanford's motion to annul a search warrant and return property seized under the authority of the warrant. The United States Supreme Court granted certiorari and set aside the county court's denial of Stanford's motion and remanded the case for further proceedings consistent with the Supreme Court's decision. Justice Stewart wrote the opinion for the Court.

FACTS

On December 27, 1963, several Texas law-enforcement officers presented themselves at the petitioner's San Antonio home for the purpose of searching it under authority of a warrant issued by a local magistrate. By the time they had finished, five hours later, they had seized some 2,000 of the petitioner's books, pamphlets, and papers. The question presented by this case is whether the search and seizure were constitutionally valid.

The warrant was issued under § 9 of Art. 6889–3A of the Revised Civil Statutes of Texas. The Article, enacted in 1955 and known as the Suppression Act, is a sweeping and many-faceted law which, among other things, outlaws the Communist Party and creates various individual criminal offenses, each punishable by imprisonment for up to 20 years. Section 9 authorizes the issuance of a warrant "for the purpose of searching for and seizing any books, records, pamphlets, cards, receipts, lists, memoranda, pictures, recordings, or any written instruments showing that a person or organization is violating or has violated any provision of this Act." The section sets forth various procedural requirements, among them that "if the premises to be searched constitute a private residence, such application for a search warrant shall be accompanied by the affidavits of two credible citizens."

The application for the warrant was filed in a Bexar County court by the Criminal District Attorney of that County. It recited that the applicant "* * * has good reason to believe and does believe that a certain place and premises in Bexar County, Texas, described as two white frame houses and one garage, located at the address of 1118 West Rosewood, in the City of San Antonio, Bexar County, Texas, and being the premises under the control and in charge of Hohn William Stanford, Jr., is a place where books, records, pamphlets, cards, receipts, lists, memoranda, pictures, recordings and other written instruments concerning the Communist Party of Texas, and the operations of the Communist Party in Texas are unlawfully possessed and used in violation of Articles 6889–3 [NOTE: Article 6889–3 of the Revised Civil Statutes of Texas, enacted in 1951 and known as the Texas Communist Control Law, provides, among other things, that various people and organizations defined by the law who fail to register with the Texas Department of Public Safety are guilty of criminal offenses punishable by imprisonment of up to 10 years.] and 6889–3A, Revised Civil Statutes of the State of Texas, and that such belief of this officer is founded upon the following information:"

> That this officer has received information from two credible persons that the party named above has such books and records in his possession which are books and records of the Communist Party including party lists and dues payments, and in addition other items listed above. That such information is of recent origin and has been confirmed by recent mailings by Stanford on the 12th of December, 1963, of pro-Communist material.

Attached to the application was an affidavit signed by two Assistant Attorneys General of Texas. The affidavit repeated the words of the application, except that the basis for the affiants' belief was stated to be as follows: "Recent mailings by Stanford on the 12th of December, 1963, of material from his home address, such material being identified as pro-Communist material and other information received in the course of investigation that Stanford has in his possession the books and records of the Texas Communist Party."

The district judge issued a warrant which specifically described the premises to be searched, recited the allegations of the applicant's and affiants' belief that the premises were "a place where books, records, pamphlets, cards, receipts, lists, memoranda, pictures, recordings and other written instruments concerning the Communist Party of Texas, and the operations of the Communist Party in Texas, are unlawfully possessed and used in violation of Article 6889–3 and Article 6889–3A, Revised Civil Statutes of the State of Texas," and ordered the executing officers "to enter immediately and search the above described premises for such items listed above unlawfully possessed in violation of Article 6889–3 and Article 6889–3A, Revised Civil Statutes, State of Texas, and to take possession of same."

The warrant was executed by the two Assistant Attorneys General who had signed the affidavit, accompanied by a number of county officers. They went to the place described in the warrant, which was where the petitioner resided and carried on a mail order book business under the trade name "All Points of View." The petitioner was not at home when the officers arrived, but his wife was, and she let the officers in after one of them had read the warrant to her.

After some delay occasioned by an unsuccessful effort to locate the petitioner in another part of town, the search began. Under the general supervision of one of the Assistant Attorneys General the officers spent more than four hours in gathering up about half the books they found in the house. Most of the material they took came from the stock in trade of the petitioner's business, but they took a number of books from his personal library as well. The books and pamphlets taken comprised approximately 300 separate titles, in addition to numerous issues of several different periodicals. Among the books taken were works by such diverse writers as Karl Marx, Jean Paul Sartre, Theodore Draper, Fidel Castro, Earl Browder, Pope John XXIII, and MR. JUSTICE HUGO L. BLACK. The officers also took possession of many of the petitioner's private documents and papers, including his marriage certificate, his insurance policies, his household bills and receipts, and files of his personal corre-

spondence. All this material was packed into 14 cartons and hauled off to an investigator's office in the county courthouse. The officers did not find any "records of the Communist Party" or any "party lists and dues payments."

The petitioner filed a motion with the magistrate who had issued the warrant, asking him to annul the warrant and order the return of all the property which had been seized under it. The motion asserted several federal constitutional claims. After a hearing the motion was denied without opinion. This order of denial was, as the parties agree, final and not appealable or otherwise reviewable under Texas law. The petitioner has attacked the constitutional validity of this search and seizure upon several grounds. We rest our decision upon just one, without pausing to assess the substantiality of the others. For we think it is clear that this warrant was of a kind which it was the purpose of the Fourth Amendment to forbid—a general warrant. Therefore, even accepting the premise that some or even all of the substantive provisions of Articles 6889–3 and 6889–3A of the Revised Civil Statutes of Texas are constitutional and have not been preempted by federal law, even accepting the premise that the warrant sufficiently specified the offense believed to have been committed and was issued upon probable cause, the magistrate's order denying the motion to annul the warrant and return the property must nonetheless be set aside.

OPINION

. . . The Fourth Amendment provides that "no Warrants shall issue, but upon probable cause, supported by Oath or affirmation, and particularly describing the place to be searched, and the persons or things to be seized." These words are precise and clear. They reflect the determination of those who wrote the Bill of Rights that the people of this new Nation should forever "be secure in their persons, houses, papers, and effects" from intrusion and seizure by officers acting under the unbridled authority of a general warrant. Vivid in the memory of the newly independent Americans were those general warrants known as writs of assistance under which officers of the Crown had so bedeviled the colonists. The hated writs of assistance had given customs officials blanket authority to search where they pleased for goods imported in violation of the British tax laws. They were denounced by James Otis as "the worst instrument of arbitrary power, the most destructive of English liberty, and the fundamental principles of law, that ever was found in an English law book," because they placed "the liberty of every man in the hands of every petty officer." The historic occasion of that denunciation, in 1761 at Boston, has been characterized as "perhaps the most prominent event which inaugurated the resistance of the colonies to the oppressions of the mother country." "Then and there," said John Adams, "then and there was the first scene of the first act of opposition to the arbitrary aims of Great Britain. Then and there the child Independence was born."

But while the Fourth Amendment was most immediately the product of contemporary revulsion against a regime of writs of assistance, its roots go far deeper. Its adoption in the Constitution of this new Nation reflected the culmination in England a few years earlier of a struggle against oppression which had endured for centuries. The story of that struggle has been fully chronicled in the pages of this Court's reports, and it would be a needless exercise in pedantry to review again the detailed history of the use of general warrants as instruments of oppression from the time of the Tudors, through the Star Chamber, the Long Parliament, the Restoration, and beyond.

What is significant to note is that this history is largely a history of conflict between the Crown and the press. It was in enforcing the laws licensing the publication of literature and, later, in prosecutions for seditious libel that general warrants were systematically used in the sixteenth, seventeenth, and eighteenth centuries. In Tudor England, officers of the Crown were given roving commissions to search where they pleased in order to suppress and destroy the literature of dissent, both Catholic and Puritan. In later years, warrants were sometimes more specific in content, but they typically authorized . . . the arrest and seizure of all the papers of a named person thought to be connected with a libel.

It was in the context of the latter kinds of general warrants that the battle for individual liberty and privacy was finally won — in the landmark cases of *Wilkes v. Wood* and *Entick v. Carrington.* The *Wilkes*

case arose out of the Crown's attempt to stifle a publication called *The North Briton,* anonymously published by John Wilkes, then a member of Parliament — particularly issue No. 45 of that journal. Lord Halifax, as Secretary of State, issued a warrant ordering four of the King's messengers "to make strict and diligent search for the authors, printers, and publishers of a seditious and treasonable paper, entitled, The North Briton, No. 45, * * * and them, or any of them, having found, to apprehend and seize, together with their papers." "Armed with their roving commission, they set forth in quest of unknown offenders; and unable to take evidence, listened to rumors, idle tales, and curious guesses. They held in their hands the liberty of every man whom they were pleased to suspect." Holding that this was "a ridiculous warrant against the whole English nation," the Court of Common Pleas awarded Wilkes damages against the Secretary of State. John Entick was the author of a publication called *Monitor* or *British Freeholder.* A warrant was issued specifically naming him and that publication, and authorizing his arrest for seditious libel and the seizure of his "books and papers." The King's messengers executing the warrant ransacked Entick's home for four hours and carted away quantities of his books and papers. In an opinion which this Court has characterized as a wellspring of the rights now protected by the Fourth Amendment, Lord Camden declared the warrant to be unlawful. "This power," he said, "so assumed by the secretary of state is an execution upon all the party's papers, in the first instance. His house is rifled; his most valuable secrets are taken out of his possession, before the paper for which he is charged is found to be criminal by any competent jurisdiction, and before he is convicted either of writing, publishing, or being concerned in the paper." *Entick v. Carrington.* Thereafter, the House of Commons passed two resolutions condemning general warrants, the first limiting its condemnation to their use in cases of libel, and the second condemning their use generally.

. . . [W]hat this history indispensably teaches is that the constitutional requirement that warrants must particularly describe the "things to be seized" is to be accorded the most scrupulous exactitude when the "things" are books, and the basis for their seizure is the ideas which they contain. No less a standard could be faithful to First Amendment freedoms. The constitutional impossibility of leaving the protection of those freedoms to the whim of the officers charged with executing the warrant is dramatically underscored by what the officers saw fit to seize under the warrant in this case.

The requirement that warrants shall particularly describe the things to be seized makes general searches under them impossible and prevents the seizure of one thing under a warrant describing another. As to what is to be taken, "nothing is left to the discretion of the officer executing the warrant." We need not decide in the present case whether the description of the things to be seized would have been too generalized to pass constitutional muster, had the things been weapons, narcotics or "cases of whiskey." The point is that it was not any contraband of that kind which was ordered to be seized, but literary material—"books, records, pamphlets, cards, receipts, lists, memoranda, pictures, recordings and other written instruments concerning the Communist Party of Texas, and the operations of the Communist Party in Texas." The indiscriminate sweep of that language is constitutionally intolerable. To hold otherwise would be false to the terms of the Fourth Amendment, false to its meaning, and false to its history.

Two centuries have passed since the historic decision in *Entick v. Carrington*, almost to the very day.

The world has greatly changed, and the voice of nonconformity now sometimes speaks a tongue which Lord Camden might find hard to understand. But the Fourth and Fourteenth Amendments guarantee to John Stanford that no official of the State shall ransack his home and seize his books and papers under the unbridled authority of a general warrant—no less than the law 200 years ago shielded John Entick from the messengers of the King.

The order is vacated and the cause remanded for further proceedings not inconsistent with this opinion. It is so ordered. Order vacated and cause remanded.

CASE DISCUSSION

According to Justice Stewart, what is the importance of all of the English cases that he surveys in the opinion? If you were the government in this case, what arguments could you make in favor of the warrant's satisfying the particularity requirement? If you were the defense, what arguments would you make in opposition to the warrant's satisfying the particularity requirement? Is the history that the Court surveys (and, in fact, the topic of the case) relevant in the 1990s? Explain your answer. Do you agree with the Court that there is a difference between books, weapons, and drugs for purposes of the particularity requirement? Explain your answer.

Electronic Search Warrants

Preparing an application for a search warrant, the affidavit to support it, and the warrant itself takes time. According to a study by the National Center for State Courts, the process takes an average of between three and four hours. Owing to the cumbersome traditional warrant process, the United States Supreme Court approved an electronic warrant process, which the Congress adopted in 1977. The Federal Rules of Criminal Procedure, Rule 41(d)2, authorize the issuance of a warrant upon sworn oral testimony given over the telephone or other electronic media "if the circumstances make it reasonable to dispense with a written affidavit."[5]

The electronic warrant process "has changed the equation" used to determine the need for a search warrant. Many of the exceptions to the warrant requirement are based on the circumstances that make it impractical to get a warrant. The electronic warrant process reduces the number of cases in which police officers can claim that circumstances required them to search without a warrant.

Execution of Search Warrants

Time. In most jurisdictions, statutes, court rules, or both require that officers execute search warrants within a specified time. For example, the Federal Rules of Criminal Procedure provide that the warrant "shall command the officer to search, within a specified period of time not to exceed 10 days, the person or place named for the property or person specified." The ten-day limit is common in jurisdictions that provide for specific execution times for warrants.[6]

In addition to the length of time given to serve warrants, about half the states require that officers execute search warrants during the daytime hours unless the warrant specifically authorizes otherwise. The Federal Rules of Criminal Procedure include such a limitation. Rule 41(c)(1) provides as follows: "The warrant shall be served in the daytime, unless the issuing authority, by appropriate provision in the warrant, and for reasonable cause shown, authorizes its execution at times other than daytime [daytime means between the hours 6:00 A.M. and 10:00 P.M.]."[7]

Occupants need not be present when officers enter premises in order to execute warrants. Despite the objection of one federal district court that a search warrant executed in the absence of the occupant constitutes an unreasonable search because a general search and "pilferage by officers of the law" may occur, the Fifth Circuit Court wrote that

> forcible entry pursuant to a search warrant of unoccupied premises is not per se a violation of the Fourth Amendment. . . . The statutory requirements of judicial supervision based on probable cause, the requisites of specificity in describing the premises and the items to be seized, and the delivery of a written inventory of the items taken to the occupant or other competent person provide adequate safeguards against potential abuse and sufficiently limit police discretion.[8]

Scope of Search. The Supreme Court has not ruled on how extensively officers can search pursuant to warrants. However, a number of lower courts have upheld searches of the entire premises of places named in a warrant. For example, it was reasonable for officers to search a briefcase found under a desk and seize incriminating evidence inside the case pursuant to a warrant to search "the premises of Hillside Press." But in upholding the search's validity, the First Circuit Court of Appeals noted that

> . . . we do not mean to suggest anything found on the premises would necessarily fall within the scope of a warrant to search premises. Nor would we imply that the result would be different if, when the officers entered, appellant was physically holding the briefcase. To allow our decision to be interpreted as giving carte blanche to seize any objects reposing within premises covered by a warrant would be a disservice to law enforcement officials, individuals who may find their personal privacy invaded by a premises search warrant, and courts which must rule on suppression motions.[9]

A search warrant to search "the premises" does not automatically authorize searching—or even frisking—persons who are on the premises during the search. For example, a warrant to search a tavern for evidence of narcotics did not authorize frisking the dozen patrons who were present during the search:

There is no reason to suppose that when the search warrant was issued . . . the authorities had probable cause to believe that any person found on the premises of the Aurora Tap Tavern, aside from "Greg" [the bartender,] would be violating the law. [The police had not probable cause to search Ybarra, a patron, either before or after they entered the tavern.] . . . It is true that the police possessed a warrant based on probable cause to search the tavern in which Ybarra happened to be at the time the warrant was executed. But, a person's mere propinquity to others independently suspected of criminality does not, without more, give rise to probable cause to search that person.[10]

The extent of the search depends on the nature of the items for which the warrant authorizes the search. If the warrant specifies searching for stolen refrigerators, officers would go beyond the warrant's scope by searching in the drawers of a dresser, to give an obvious example. According to the Supreme Court, "[T]he same meticulous investigation which would be appropriate in a search for two small canceled checks could not be considered reasonable where agents are seeking a stolen automobile."[11]

The seizure part of the search and seizure clause of the Fourth Amendment raises a question: What may the government seize in the course of a search? Clearly, the government may seize persons. So may it seize weapons, contraband, and the fruits of crime, such as stolen property. However, mere evidence — evidence that is not weaponry, contraband, or stolen goods — creates problems, particularly when it includes private papers such as diaries and letters. Seizing such items may not only invade privacy but also tread upon First Amendment rights to free speech.

Ever since the eighteenth century, the issue of seizing private papers has been controversial. In those days, the law of seditious libel declared a broad range of criticisms of the British royal family to be a crime. The unpopularity of the Hanoverian kings exposed them to considerable public ridicule and those who criticized them to criminal prosecution. In the famous case *Entick v. Carrington*, the English court ruled that purely private papers were protected against seizure even by the Crown. American constitutional doctrine followed this case. In *Gouled v. United States*, for example, the Supreme Court ruled that search warrants do not authorize entering houses and seizing private papers for the sole purpose of securing evidence. Hence, the **mere evidence rule** provided that officers could seize papers only if they were the fruits or instrumentalities of crime.[12]

In 1967, the Court rejected the mere evidence rule in *Warden v. Hayden*. While searching the house into which Hayden had fled following a robbery, police seized not only weapons and stolen money, but also clothing that was later used to convict Hayden. Obviously, the clothing was not contraband, a weapon, or a fruit of the robbery; it was mere evidence. The Court ruled that Hayden's clothing was admissible:

[N]othing in the nature of property seized as evidence renders it more private than property seized, for example, as an instrumentality; quite the opposite may be true. Indeed, the distinction is wholly irrational, since, depending on the circumstances, the same "papers and effects" may be "mere evidence" in one case and "instrumentalities" in another.[13]

The drafters of the American Law Institute's Model Code of Pre-arraignment Procedure maintain that private papers such as diaries and personal letters deserve special Fourth Amendment protection. According to the commentary accompanying the code,

> Seizure and disclosure of private letters and diaries is a particularly abrasive infringement of privacy. An area of complete freedom for personal conversation and writing . . . preserves important First Amendment values. The forced protection of private diaries and letters, to obtain admissions or other statements against interest runs perilously close to the ban on self-incrimination.[14]

The Supreme Court has not answered the question of whether the Fourth Amendment protects diaries and other highly personal papers.[15]

The "Knock and Announce" Rule. For seven centuries of English and United States history, law enforcement officers have followed a **knock and announce rule**— the practice of knocking and announcing their presence before they enter homes in order to search them. In *Wilson v. Arkansas* (1995), the Supreme Court unanimously decided that the Fourth Amendment *ordinarily* requires that officers knock and announce. According to the Court, the reasonableness of "no-knock" entries depends on the "totality of the circumstances" surrounding the entry. In other words, the Fourth Amendment does not prohibit all "no-knock" entries. Courts have to determine the reasonableness of unannounced entries on a "case-by-case" basis.[16]

In *Wilson v. Arkansas*, Sharlene Wilson sold marijuana to an Arkansas State Police informant. On one occasion, Wilson waved a semiautomatic pistol "in the informant's face, threatening to kill her if she turned out to be working for the police." Then Wilson sold the informant a bag of marijuana. The next day police officers obtained a warrant to search Wilson's home and to arrest her. Affidavits to support the warrant said that Wilson was previously convicted of arson and firebombing. Finding the door open when they went to Wilson's home to execute the warrant, they walked in, identified themselves, and told Wilson that they had a warrant. They seized "marijuana, methamphetamine, valium, narcotics paraphernalia, a gun, and ammunition." They found Wilson in the bathroom, flushing marijuana down the toilet. They arrested Wilson, who was charged with "delivery of marijuana, delivery of methamphetamine, possession of drug paraphernalia, and possession of marijuana." In a pretrial motion, Wilson argued that the search violated the Fourth Amendment because "the officers had failed to 'knock and announce' before entering her home." The trial court dismissed the motion, a jury convicted Wilson, and the Arkansas Supreme Court affirmed the conviction. Wilson appealed to the U.S. Supreme Court.[17]

In the opinion, Justice Clarence Thomas wrote that throughout English and United States history, the reasonableness of searches of homes depends "*in part* on whether law enforcement officers announced their presence and authority prior to entering" (emphasis added). Justice Thomas quoted the great eighteenth-century commentator William Blackstone on this point:

> "[W]hen the King is party, the sheriff (if the doors be not open) may break the party's house, either to arrest him, or to do other execution of the K[ing]'s process, if otherwise he cannot enter." To this rule, however, common-law courts appended an important qualification: "But before he breaks it, he ought to signify the cause of his coming, and to make request to open doors . . . , for the law with-

out a default in the owner abhors the destruction of breaking of any house (which is for the habitation and safety of man) by which great damage and inconvenience might ensue to the party, when no default is in him; for perhaps he did not know of the process, of which, if he had notice, it is to be presumed that he would obey it. . . ." ("[N]o precise form of words is required in a case of this kind. It is sufficient that the party hath notice, that the officer cometh not as a mere trespasser, but claiming to act under a proper authority. . . .")[18]

In *Wilson v. Arkansas*, the U.S. Supreme Court held that the "principle of announcement . . . is an element of the reasonableness inquiry under the Fourth Amendment." However, Justice Thomas wrote further that the Fourth Amendment does not "mandate a rigid rule of announcement that ignores countervailing law enforcement interests. . . ." Justice Thomas identified three possible countervailing law enforcement interests:

1. The safety of officers
2. The escape of a prisoner
3. The destruction of evidence[19]

Following the decision in *Wilson v. Arkansas*, the Wisconsin Supreme Court adopted a blanket exception to the knock and announce rule. In *State v. Richards*, the police had a warrant but did not "knock and announce their presence" before they entered and searched Steiney Richards's motel room looking for cocaine. On appeal of his conviction, the Wisconsin Supreme Court decided that "the police are never required to adhere to the rule of announcement when executing [a] search warrant involving felonious drug delivery." According to the court,

> Police officers face an unquantifiable risk of violence every time they go into a house to execute a search warrant. The Court has recognized the unique danger police officers face in suspects' houses because the officers are coming onto their adversaries' "turf" which has a configuration unknown to the officers. . . . These risks are only heightened when drugs are involved. The connection between drugs and weapons has been well documented by appellate courts. . . .[20]

In deciding that the public interest outweighed the privacy interests of Richards, the court wrote the following:

> . . . Although we acknowledge that privacy interests in the home are fundamental, we also conclude that these interests are not sufficient to elevate Richards' privacy interests over the public's interest in having police officers safely and effectively execute a search warrant for evidence of felonious drug delivery. Richards' privacy interests are only slightly advanced by a knock and announce rule. Although Richards correctly notes that people normally have the highest expectation of privacy in their homes, this argument is largely irrelevant in this case. There is no dispute that within a matter of seconds after the police arrived with a search warrant, they were entitled to enter Richards' dwelling, with or without permission, and conduct as thorough a search as was reasonably necessary. The search had been authorized by a neutral magistrate, and would have occurred regardless of whether the police knocked and announced their presence.

It is difficult to see, however, what actual protection is given to any right of privacy by the announcement rule. Once identity and purpose are stated, entry must always be permitted; if permission is denied, or even delayed for an inordinate amount of time, entry may be forced, provided the officer has a valid purpose in gaining admission. Since no discretion is vested in the occupant, in what manner does notice protect his privacy? . . . Thus balanced, the protections to privacy seem to be somewhat tenuous when compared to the potential for public harm. This is particularly true with respect to potential destruction of evidence, especially when one considers that the probable cause requirement would have to be met in any event. . . .

When we compare these limited privacy interests to the substantial interest the public has in allowing the police to safely and effectively execute a search warrant, the balance overwhelmingly favors the public interest. Police have widely regarded narcotics enforcement as a particularly dangerous area of police work for some time. However, beginning in the early 1980's, the hazards to police officers escalated. Street gangs, spawned by decay in America's cities, and already known for their propensity for irrational violence, entered the drug business on a major scale. In the 1960's and 1970's, the police confronted and adjusted to a higher level of violence.

When the risks of law enforcement change radically, the rules by which courts regulate the police should reflect those changes. Therefore, we conclude that exigent circumstances are always present in the execution of search warrants involving felonious drug delivery. The public interests in these circumstances far outweigh the minimal privacy interests of the occupants of the dwelling for which a search warrant has already been issued. Accordingly . . . we conclude that police are not required to adhere to the rule of announcement when executing a search warrant involving felonious drug delivery.[21]

Justice Shirley Abrahamson concurred in the judgment of the court, but she cautioned that

> . . . the crime statistics cited by the majority do not support the contention that "drug related violence is a growing contributor to police mortality." . . . [T]he total number of officers killed on duty declined from 1978 to 1991, as did the number of officers killed in arrest situations involving drug-related matters. Fewer officers (9 officers/4.3 percent) were murdered as a consequence of drug-related violence from 1992–94 than in the periods from 1978–81, 1982–86, or 1987–91. From 1978–94 about twice as many officers were killed in traffic pursuits or stops as were killed in arrest situations involving drug-related matters. During the same years, more officers were killed while answering disturbance calls for family quarrels than were killed in arrest situations involving drug-related matters. The one officer killed in Wisconsin in 1995 was answering a domestic disturbance call.
>   . . . [W]hile the death or injury of even one law enforcement officer is one too many, the empirical evidence cited does not support the majority's rationale that executing search warrants in drug cases is more dangerous to officers than other activities. If anything, those statistics argue that if law enforcement officers may dispense with the knock-and-announce rule in drug-related cases, they should be able to dispense with it altogether. . . .[22]

Therefore, according to Justice Abrahamson,

> Rather than . . . the sweeping blanket exception to the knock-and-announce rule . . . I would heed the instructions of *Wilson [v. Arizona]* . . . and assess the reasonableness of the no-knock entry in this case on the basis of the facts presented. The court's decision today ignores *Wilson*, dispenses with longstanding Fourth Amendment jurisprudence requiring the assessment of reasonableness in each particular case, and may place the very law enforcement officers it purports to protect in greater peril. . . .[23]

Inventory. In addition to prescribing the time, scope, and manner of entry in executing search warrants, most jurisdictions also require that officers compile an inventory of property seized during the execution of search warrants. According to the Federal Rules of Criminal Procedure, officers who seize property during the execution of a search warrant have to "give to the person from whom or from whose premises the property was taken a copy of the warrant and a receipt for the property taken." If the person is not at home, the officers must "leave the copy and receipt at the place from which the property was taken." Officers must also make a prompt **return of warrant** to the court that issued it, accompanied by a "written inventory of any property taken." Furthermore, the Federal Rules of Criminal Procedure require that

> the inventory shall be made in the presence of the applicant for the warrant and the person from whose possession or premises the property was taken, if they are present, or in the presence of at least one credible person other than the applicant for the warrant or the person from whose possession or premises the property was taken, and shall be verified by the officer. The federal magistrate shall upon request deliver a copy of the inventory to the person from whom or from whose premises the property was taken and to the applicant for the warrant.[24]

SEARCHES WITHOUT WARRANTS

The United States Supreme Court has repeatedly ruled that the Fourth Amendment mandates that officers obtain search warrants, with a few well-defined exceptions. Informally, however, these exceptions are numerous and broad enough to satisfy the strong preference of law enforcement officers for searches without warrants. Searches without warrants far outnumber searches with warrants. Hence, day-to-day practice reflects the informal preference of law enforcement officers more than it does the formal preference of the rulings of courts.[25]

One former Washington, D.C., assistant United States attorney wrote the following: "As anyone who has worked in the criminal justice system knows, searches conducted pursuant to these exceptions, particularly searches incident to arrest, automobile and 'stop and frisk' searches, far exceed searches performed pursuant to warrants." According to this attorney, the reason for so many exceptions "is simple: the clear rule that warrants are required is unworkable and to enforce it would lead to exclusion of evidence in many cases where the police activity was essentially reasonable."[26]

Law enforcement officers frequently express frustration with the delay that complying with the Fourth Amendment involves. One police officer said that it typically takes

TABLE 6.1 EXCEPTIONS TO THE SEARCH WARRANT REQUIREMENT

Incident to Arrest	Possible Danger to Officer or Others
Exigent Circumstances	Disappearance of Suspect
Frisks	Vehicle Searches
Hot Pursuit	Searches of Containers
Imminent Danger of Destruction of Evidence	Consent Searches

four hours from the time he decides he wants a warrant until the time he has one in his hand:

> [A]nd that's if everything goes right. You find people and girls get 'em typed and you can find the judges when they are sitting at the bench—because a lot of judges won't see people in their offices. [If you miss them there,] they leave and go to lunch and you have to wait until they come back for the afternoon dockets, and if they are already into the afternoon dockets, they are not going to interrupt the procedures [for a warrant]. So you sit and wait through three or four docket sessions. . . . It can take all day.[27]

This frustration leads officers to "get . . . around the Fourth Amendment." One detective explained how he gets around the warrant requirement by "shamming" consent:

> [You] tell the guy, "Let me come in and take a look at your house." And he says, "No, I don't want to." And then you tell him, "Then I'm going to leave Sam here, and he's going to live with you until we come back. Now we can do it either way." And very rarely do the people say, "Go get your search warrant, then. . . ."[28]

In this chapter we discuss four major exceptions to the warrant requirement in the search for criminal evidence:

1. Searches incident to arrest

2. **Exigent circumstance searches,** sometimes called emergency searches, where prompt action precludes the time it takes to get a warrant

3. Reduced expectation of privacy searches

4. Consent searches

"Special needs" beyond ordinary law enforcement searches, including inventory, inspection, and regulation searches, are discussed in Chapter 7. (See Table 6.1.)

Searches Incident to Arrest

The most frequently conducted searches are **searches incident to arrest**—that is, searches made at the time police arrest suspects. Police can lawfully search arrested suspects without either warrants or probable cause. For a time the courts debated whether officers could search suspects automatically when they arrested them or whether, as the Court had held in *Terry v. Ohio* with respect to frisks, they needed specific facts to support the search. However, the Supreme Court has ruled that searches incident to arrest need no independent justification other than the arrest itself. Searches incident to arrest are reasonable searches because they

1. Protect the officers making the arrest, whom suspects may injure or kill

2. Prevent the escape of arrested suspects who may possess the means of escape

3. Preserve evidence that suspects may destroy, damage, or abandon

Convenience is the main reason that police rely more heavily on searches incident to arrest than on other types of searches. Since the searches incident to arrest are warrantless searches, officers do not need to fill out forms, they do not have to appear before magistrates or prosecutors to show that they have probable cause to search, and they can search immediately without the delay that getting warrants causes. They prefer these searches to consent searches (next to searches incident to arrest the most frequently conducted type) because the officers do not need to prove later that the persons searched consented to the search (see the section below on consent searches). In fact, the convenience of searches incident to arrest is one reason that police officers decide to arrest in the first place: arrests provide officers with a justification for searching suspects.[29]

The rule that searches incident to arrest without either warrants or probable cause are reasonable reflects the balancing element in the reasonableness of searches. The government interests in protecting law enforcement officers, preserving evidence, preventing escapes of suspects, and detaining suspects are all at stake. Balanced against these interests is ensuring the privacy of individuals. Officers may search people whom they arrest without warrants in order to disarm them and to prevent them from escaping and destroying evidence. To protect the privacy of citizens, the Court has restricted the extent of these searches; police may search only to the extent necessary to protect officers, prevent escape, and preserve evidence. Until the late 1960s, the Supreme Court had authorized broad search authority contemporaneous with arrests. For example, if suspects were arrested while driving, the arresting officers could search not only the arrested person but also the entire vehicle, including the trunk. And if suspects were arrested in their homes, the officers could search the entire house where the arrest took place. In 1969, in *Chimel v. California*, the Supreme Court reconsidered the rule that police officers could search an entire house incident to an arrest without either a search warrant or probable cause to search.

C A S E

Was the Search "Incident" to the Arrest?

Chimel v. California
395 U.S. 752, 89 S.Ct. 2034,
23 L.Ed.2d 685 (1969)

Chimel was prosecuted for burglary. The Superior Court, Orange County, California, rendered judgment, and the defendant appealed. The California Supreme Court, vacating an opinion of the Court of Appeal, af-

firmed, and the defendant obtained certiorari. *The Supreme Court held that warrantless search of the defendant's entire house, incident to his proper arrest in the house on a burglary charge, was unreasonable because it extended beyond the defendant's person and the area from which he might have obtained either a weapon or something that could have been used as evidence against him. Justice Stewart wrote the opinion of the Court.*

FACTS

... Late in the afternoon of September 13, 1965, three police officers arrived at the Santa Ana, California, home of the petitioner with a warrant authorizing his arrest for the burglary of a coin shop. The officers knocked on the door, identified themselves to the petitioner's wife, and asked if they might come inside. She ushered them into the house, where they waited 10 or 15 minutes until the petitioner returned home from work. When the petitioner entered the house, one of the officers handed him the arrest warrant and asked for permission to "look around." The petitioner objected, but was advised that "on the basis of the lawful arrest," the officers would nonetheless conduct a search. No search warrant had been issued.

Accompanied by the petitioner's wife, the officers then looked through the entire three-bedroom house, including the attic, the garage, and a small workshop. In some rooms the search was relatively cursory. In the master bedroom and sewing room, however, the officers directed the petitioner's wife to open drawers and "to physically move contents of the drawers from side to side so that (they) might view any items that would have come from (the) burglary." After completing the search, they seized numerous items—primarily coins, but also several medals, tokens, and a few other objects. The entire search took between 45 minutes and an hour.

At the petitioner's subsequent state trial on two charges of burglary, the items taken from his house were admitted into evidence against him, over his objection that they had been unconstitutionally seized. He was convicted, and the judgments of conviction were affirmed by both the California Court of Appeal, and the California Supreme Court. . . . We granted certiorari in order to consider the petitioner's substantial constitutional claims.

OPINION

Without deciding the question, we proceed on the hypothesis that the California courts were correct in holding that the arrest of the petitioner was valid under the Constitution. This brings us directly to the question whether the warrantless search of the petitioner's entire house can be constitutionally justified as incident to that arrest. . . .

When an arrest is made, it is reasonable for the arresting officer to search the person arrested in order to remove any weapons that the latter might seek to use in order to resist arrest or effect his escape. Otherwise, the officer's safety might well be endangered, and the arrest itself frustrated. In addition, it is entirely reasonable for the arresting officer to search for and seize any evidence on the arrestee's person in order to prevent its concealment or destruction. And the area into which an arrestee might reach in order to grab a weapon or evidentiary items must, of course, be governed by a like rule. A gun on a table or in a drawer in front of one who is arrested can be as dangerous to the arresting officer as one concealed in the clothing of the person arrested. There is ample justification, therefore, for a search of the arrestee's person and the area "within his immediate control"—construing that phrase to mean the area from within which he might gain possession of a weapon or destructible evidence. There is no comparable justification, however, for routinely searching any room other than that in which an arrest occurs—or, for that matter, for searching through all the desk drawers or other closed or concealed areas in that room itself. Such searches, in the absence of well-recognized exceptions, may be made only under the authority of a search warrant. The "adherence to judicial processes" mandated by the Fourth Amendment requires no less. . . .

It is argued in the present case that it is "reasonable" to search a man's house when he is arrested in it. But that argument is founded on little more than a subjective view regarding the acceptability of certain sorts of police conduct, and not on consideration relevant to Fourth Amendment interests. Under such an unconfined analysis, Fourth Amendment protection in this area would approach the evaporation point. . . .

After arresting a man in his house, to rummage at will among his papers in search of whatever will convict him, appears to us to be indistinguishable from what might be done under a general warrant; indeed, the warrant would give more protection, for presumably it must be issued by a magistrate. . . . Application of sound Fourth Amendment principles to the facts of this case produces a clear result. The search here went far beyond the petitioner's person and the area from within which he might have obtained either a weapon or something that could have been used as evidence against him. There was no constitutional justification, in the absence of a search warrant, for extending the search beyond that area. The scope of the search was, therefore, "unreasonable" under the Fourth and Fourteenth Amendments and the petitioner's conviction cannot stand. . . .

Reversed. . . .

CASE DISCUSSION

What is the Court's definition of the area "within [a suspect's] immediate control"? Does the Court's definition promote the interest in individual liberty over crime control? Does it impede the search for truth? What, if anything, does it have to do with promoting the interest in procedural regularity? If you were defining the phrase, would you have included the whole house within the scope of the rule? Explain your answer, including what interests that you consider paramount in formulating your definition.

Three major issues arise in the cases involving searches incident to arrest:

1. How extensively can officers search incident to arrest?
2. What is the meaning of "incident" to arrest?
3. Does incident to arrest apply to arrests for minor crimes?

"Grabbable Area." *Chimel v. California* seemed to have stated a clear-cut rule. Contemporaneous with arrests, the police could search only the area under the immediate control of the arrested person, the so-called "grabbable area," in order to preserve evidence, protect the officers, and prevent escape. However, a considerable amount of confusion arose over the meaning of "immediate control" when it came to arresting suspects in vehicles. Immediately following the decision in *Chimel v. California*, it became clear that courts were divided over whether the immediate control rule applied to vehicles. Some courts extended the rule to searches of vehicles incident to arrests; others were reluctant to do so. A number of courts upheld searches of vehicles even when the arrested person was outside the vehicle, under the control of the police, and therefore highly unlikely to escape or obtain weapons or destroy evidence inside the vehicle. In *New York v. Belton*, the Supreme Court finally resolved what "immediate control" means in searches incident to arrests in vehicles.

C A S E

Was the Search "Incident to Arrest"?

New York v. Belton
453 U.S. 454, 101 S.Ct. 2860, 69 L.Ed2d
768 (1981)

Belton was indicted for possession of a controlled substance found in, and seized from, his car. After the trial court denied Belton's motion to suppress the cocaine

seized, Belton pleaded guilty to a lesser included offense, preserving his claim that the police seized the cocaine in violation of the Fourth and Fourteenth Amendments. The intermediate appeals court upheld the seizure, but the New York Court of Appeals reversed. The United States Supreme Court granted certiorari to the state and reversed on the ground that the seizure did not violate the Fourth Amendment. Justice Stewart wrote the opinion of the Court, which Chief Justice Burger and Justices Blackmun, Powell, and Rehnquist joined. Justice Rehnquist filed a concurring statement. Justice Stevens filed a statement concurring in the judgment. Justices Brennan and White filed dissenting opinions, in which Justice Marshall joined.

FACTS

On April 9, 1978, Trooper Douglas Nicot, a New York State policeman driving an unmarked car on the New York Thruway, was passed by another automobile traveling at an excessive rate of speed. Nicot gave chase, overtook the speeding vehicle, and ordered its driver to pull it over to the side of the road and stop. There were four men in the car, one of whom was Roger Belton, the respondent in this case. The policeman asked to see the driver's license and automobile registration, and discovered that none of the men owned the vehicle or was related to its owner. Meanwhile, the policeman had smelt burnt marihuana and had seen on the floor of the car an envelope marked "Supergold" that he associated with marihuana. He therefore directed the men to get out of the car, and placed them under arrest for unlawful possession of marihuana. He patted down each of the men and "split them up into four different areas of the Thruway at the time so they would not be in physical touching area of each other." He then picked up the envelope marked "Supergold" and found that it contained marihuana. After giving the arrestees the warnings required by *Miranda v. Arizona* [1966], the state policeman searched each one of them. He then searched the passenger compartment of the car. On the back seat he found a black leather jacket belonging to Belton. He unzipped one of the pockets of the jacket and discovered cocaine. Placing the jacket in his automobile, he drove the four arrestees to a nearby police station.

Belton was subsequently indicted for criminal possession of a controlled substance. In the trial court he moved that the cocaine the trooper had seized from the jacket pocket be suppressed. The court denied the motion. Belton then pleaded guilty to a lesser included offense.... The Appellate Division of the New York Supreme Court upheld the constitutionality of the search and seizure.... The New York Court of Appeals reversed....

OPINION

It is a first principle of Fourth Amendment jurisprudence that the police may not conduct a search unless they first convince a neutral magistrate that there is probable cause to do so. This Court has recognized, however, that "the exigencies of the situation" may sometimes make exemption from the warrant requirement "imperative." Specifically, the Court held in *Chimel v. California* [1969] that a lawful custodial arrest creates a situation which justifies the contemporaneous search without a warrant of the person arrested and of the immediately surrounding area. Such searches have long been considered valid because of the need "to remove any weapons that [the arrestee] might seek to use in order to resist arrest or effect his escape" and the need to prevent the concealment or destruction of evidence....

But no straightforward rule has emerged from the litigated cases respecting the question involved here—the question of the proper scope of a search of the interior of an automobile incident to a lawful custodial arrest of its occupants....

When a person cannot know how a court will apply a settled principle to a recurring factual situation, that person cannot know the scope of his constitutional protection, nor can a policeman know the scope of his authority. While the *Chimel* case established that a search incident to an arrest may not stray beyond the area within the immediate control of the arrestee, courts have found no workable definition of "the area within the immediate control of the arrestee" when that area arguably includes the interior of an automobile and the arrestee is its recent occupant. Our reading of the cases suggests the generalization that articles inside the relatively narrow compass of the passenger compartment of an automobile are in fact generally, even if not inevitably, within "the area into which an arrestee might reach in order to grab a weapon or evidentiary ite[m]." ... Accordingly, we hold that when a policeman has made a lawful custodial arrest of the occupant of an automobile, he may, as a contemporaneous incident of that arrest, search the passenger compartment of that automobile....

It follows from this conclusion that the police may also examine the contents of any containers found within the passenger compartment, for if the passenger compartment is within reach of the arrestee, so also will containers in it be within his reach.... The search of the jacket, therefore, was a search incident to a lawful custodial arrest, and it did not violate the Fourth and Fourteenth Amendments. Accordingly, the judgment is reversed. It is so ordered.

DISSENT

Justice Brennan, with whom Justice Marshall joins, dissenting....

It has long been a fundamental principle of Fourth Amendment analysis that exceptions to the warrant requirement are to be narrowly construed. Predicated on the Fourth Amendment's essential purpose of "shield[ing] the citizen from unwarranted intrusions into his privacy," this principle carries with it two corollaries. First, for a search to be valid under the Fourth Amendment, it must be "strictly tied to and justified by the circumstances which rend[er] its initiation permissible." Second, in determining whether to grant an exemption to the warrant requirement, courts should carefully consider the facts and circumstances of each search and seizure, focusing on the reasons supporting the exception rather than on any bright-line rule of general application....

In its attempt to formulate a "single, familiar standard ... to guide police officers, who have only limited time and expertise to reflect on and balance the social and individual interests involved in the specific circumstances they confront," the Court today disregards these principles, and instead adopts a fiction—that the interior of a car is always within the immediate control of an arrestee who has recently been in the car....

The Court seeks to justify its departure from the principles underlying *Chimel* [*v. California*, excerpted previously] by proclaiming the need for a new "bright-line" rule to guide the officer in the field. However, "the mere fact that law enforcement may be made more efficient can never by itself justify disregard of the Fourth Amendment." Moreover, the Court's attempt to forge a "bright-line" rule fails on its own terms. While the "interior/trunk" distinction may provide a workable guide in certain cases—for ex-

ample, where the officer arrests the driver of a car and then immediately searches the seats and the floor—in the long run, I suspect it will create far more problems than it solves. The Court's new approach leaves open too many questions and, more important, it provides the police and the courts with too few tools with which to find the answers.

CASE DISCUSSION

Does this case extend the concept of "grabbable area" too far? Explain. Do you prefer the bright line rule that the Court adopted or the case-by-case approach that the dissent favors? Why? Should the officer be permitted to search not only the interior of the car, but also the trunk? And under the hood? Should the officer be restricted to patting down the outer part of the jacket? Is the Court's expansion of the grabbable area applicable only to vehicle cases, or should it be a general rule? As one commentator on the case noted,

> Ten years ago most state court judges might have welcomed the Supreme Court's ... decision. The new automobile search rule for arrested motorists [that deems the interior of an automobile always to be within the "grabbing area"] ... certainly makes it easier for courts to apply the law of searches incident to arrest in such cases.... This new rule not only allows police to be more certain about the precise scope of their search powers, it also frees lower courts from the burden of case-by-case adjudication of the frequently disputed factual issue of actual grabbing area.[30]

Do you agree? Do you favor the per se rule for that reason? Why or why not?

Consider the concerns expressed by Professor Wayne LaFave, an expert on the law of search and seizure:

> There is good reason to be ... concerned with the Court's ... holding in *New York v. Belton* that in every instance in which "a policeman has made a lawful custodial arrest of the occupant of an automobile, he may, as a contemporaneous incident of that arrest, search the passenger compartment of that automobile." In all such

instance . . . "there is always the possibility that a police officer, lacking probable cause to obtain a search warrant, will use a traffic arrest as a pretext to conduct a search." Given that very few drivers can traverse any appreciable distance without violating some traffic regulation, this is indeed a frightening possibility. It is apparent that virtually anyone who ventures out onto the public streets and highways may then, with little effort by the police, be placed in a position where his or her person and vehicle are subject to search.[31]

Do you agree with Professor LaFave's contention that the ruling in *New York v. Belton* has created a "frightening possibility"?

The Meaning of *Incident*. "Incident to arrest" includes the time before and after arrest. For example, in *Cupp v. Murphy*, Portland, Oregon, police scraped Daniel Murphy's fingernails for blood residue that might have been that of his strangled wife. Police searched Murphy before they arrested him. The Court held that since the police had probable cause to arrest Murphy (even though they had not done so), the search was still incident to, or contemporaneous with, the arrest. In *United States v. Edwards*, Edwards was lawfully arrested shortly after 11:00 P.M. and put in jail. The next morning, the police took his clothing and searched it for paint chips that would link Edwards to a burglary. Despite the lapse of ten hours, and over a strong dissent arguing that the police had plenty of time to present their evidence to a neutral magistrate to obtain a search warrant, the Court ruled that the search was incident to the arrest.[32]

D e c i s i o n   P o i n t

1. A California police officer discovered a pistol and drugs on a hitchhiker during a lawful pat-down, arrested and handcuffed him, and put him in a police vehicle. Only then did a second officer open an unlocked suitcase that had been sitting on the road next to the suspect at the time of the arrest; inside the suitcase were more drugs.

    Was the search of the suitcase incident to the arrest? The California Court of Appeals said it was, holding that if a container is close enough that the arrested suspect could have reached it at the moment of arrest,

    > a search does not become unlawful because the police first separate the arrestee from the reach of the article, or handcuff or otherwise restrain the arrestee, so long as the search is made immediately thereafter, while the arrestee is still nearby at the scene of the arrest and before the arresting officers have turned their attention to tasks unrelated to

securing the safety of persons and property involved in the arrest.

2. Alaska police officers entered a tavern and arrested the bartender for selling drugs moments earlier to an informer. Fifteen minutes later, while the suspect was being held at the other end of the room, an officer searched the jacket from which the suspect had gotten the drugs, which had been hanging on a coat rack some ten to fifteen feet from the bar all along.

    Was the search of the jacket incident to the arrest? The Alaska Supreme Court ruled that it was not because the jacket was not accessible to the suspect at the moment of the arrest: "[P]hysical proximity at the time of the arrest—with the consequent threat to safety and risk of destruction—is the basic requirement upon which the search incident to arrest exception is predicated." The majority held that the exigencies of the situation at the point of the suspect's arrest did not call for a search of the jacket.[33]

Searches Incident to Arrest for Minor Crimes. The United States Supreme Court answered the question of whether officers may search incident to minor crimes in *United States v. Robinson* (excerpted in Chapter 2). Robinson was stopped and arrested for driving without a license. The arresting officer frisked Robinson. When he felt a lump in Robinson's coat pocket, he reached inside and found a crumpled-up cigarette package. He opened it and found heroin inside. Robinson was charged with illegally possessing narcotics. He moved to suppress the evidence, but the court denied his motion and admitted it over his objection. The heroin was the principal evidence that convicted Robinson. The Supreme Court upheld the conviction and, in so doing, ruled that full searches incident to traffic offenses—and presumably all other offenses that authorize taking suspects into custody—are reasonable. The Court first held that officers are not restricted to frisks incident to traffic arrests. The Court then went on:

> Nor are we inclined, on the basis of what seems to us to be a rather speculative judgment, to qualify the breadth of the general authority to search incident to a lawful custodial arrest on the assumption that persons arrested for the offense of driving while their license has been revoked are less likely to be possessed of dangerous weapons than are those arrested for other crimes. It is scarcely open to doubt that the danger to an officer is far greater in the case of extended exposure which follows the taking of a suspect into custody and transporting him to the police station than in the case of the fleeting contact resulting from a typical *Terry*-type stop. This is an adequate basis for treating all custodial arrests alike for purposes of search justification.

The Court rejected what it considered a call to review all cases in which police encounter citizens. Instead, as Justice William Rehnquist, writing for the Court, concluded,

> A police officer's determination as to how and where to search the person of a suspect whom he has arrested is necessarily a quick ad hoc judgment which the Fourth Amendment does not require to be broken down in each instance into an analysis of each step in the search. The authority to search the person incident to a lawful custodial arrest, while based upon the need to disarm and to discover evidence, does not depend upon what a court may later decide was the probability in a particular arrest situation that weapons or evidence would in fact be found upon the person of the suspect. A custodial arrest of a suspect based on probable cause is a reasonable intrusion under the Fourth Amendment; that intrusion being lawful, a search incident to the arrest requires no additional justification. It is the fact of the lawful arrest which establishes the authority to search, and we hold that in the case of a lawful custodial arrest a full search of the person is not only an exception to the warrant requirement of the Fourth Amendment, but is also a "reasonable" search under that Amendment.[34]

The majority decided that two interests justified the search:

1. The possible danger to police officers taking suspects into custody
2. The logical impossibility of the Court's reviewing every police decision

Hence, the Court decided to leave to police discretion whether suspects ought to be searched incident to their arrest. The combined decisions in *Murphy, Edwards,* and *Robinson* establish broad police power to search incident to arrest. These decisions again illustrate the U.S. Supreme Court's reluctance to second-guess the judgments of law enforcement officers, particularly early in the criminal process.

Some state courts have not been so reticent to "police the police" in terms of their power to search incident to arrest. Five states—Illinois, Michigan, Montana, New Hampshire, and Texas—adopted the *Robinson* rule. Six—Alaska, California, Hawaii, New York, Oregon, and West Virginia—rejected it.[35]

The Alaska Supreme Court, for example, ruled that the Alaska Constitution's search-and-seizure clause does not permit such broad power to search incident to traffic arrests. According to the court,

> Absent specific articulable facts justifying the intrusion . . . a warrantless search incident to an arrest, other than for weapons, is unreasonable and therefore violative of the Alaska Constitution if the charge on which the arrest is made is not one, evidence of which could be concealed on the person.[36]

The Alaska decision and others to the same effect in states such as California make clear that the federal Constitution sets a minimum standard that states may freely raise by interpreting provisions in their own constitutions more strictly than the United States Supreme Court interprets parallel federal provisions. (See Chapter 1 for a discussion of the relationship between state and federal constitutions.)

Searches Incident to Pretext Arrests. Searches incident to pretext arrests are searches in which police officers look for probable cause to arrest people for minor crimes, usually traffic offenses, when they have little or no evidence to arrest them for what the officers really want to investigate—drug-related offenses. **Pretext searches** are powerful investigative tools. Officers have clear probable cause to make arrests for traffic offenses because so many people violate some traffic laws. In the pretext search cases, officers have a hunch that a person is involved in some felony, usually a drug offense, but they lack probable cause to arrest for the drug offense. Useful and powerful as the pretext traffic arrest searches are in the investigation of drug law violations, critics present two arguments against them:

1. Pretext traffic arrests grant too much discretion to law enforcement officers because every driver is bound to violate at least one of the many traffic code provisions. (See the Case Discussion following the next excerpted case, *Whren v. U.S.*)

2. Officers will use this discretion to arrest disproportionately African Americans and Hispanics. (See the note following *Whren v. U.S.*)[37]

The validation of the pretext traffic arrest searches tilts the balance between government power to enforce the criminal law and the privacy rights of individuals too far in favor of the government, according to Professor Daniel S. Jonas:

> The conflict between liberty and law enforcement is particularly sharp in the area of pretextual police conduct. Police would have a powerful investigative tool if it were constitutional, for example, to arrest a felony suspect on the basis of a parking ticket that had not been paid, when the facts relating to the felony did not provide probable cause. Precisely because its investigative potential is so great, pretextual police conduct poses an alarming threat to individual freedom from government intrusion.[38]

The United States Supreme Court decided the reasonableness of searches incident to pretext traffic arrests in *Whren v. United States.*[39]

C A S E

Was the Pretext Search Reasonable?

Whren v. U.S.
1996 WL 305735 (1996)

Michael Whren and James Brown were convicted of drug offenses in the United States District Court for the District of Columbia, and they appealed. The Court of Appeals affirmed. The U.S. Supreme Court granted certiorari, and affirmed. Justice Scalia delivered the opinion of a unanimous Court.

FACTS

On the evening of June 10, 1993, plainclothes vice-squad officers of the District of Columbia Metropolitan Police Department were patrolling a "high drug area" of the city in an unmarked car. Their suspicions were aroused when they passed a dark Pathfinder truck with temporary license plates and youthful occupants waiting at a stop sign, the driver looking down into the lap of the passenger at his right. The truck remained stopped at the intersection for what seemed an unusually long time — more than 20 seconds. When the police car executed a U-turn in order to head back toward the truck, the Pathfinder turned suddenly to its right, without signalling, and sped off at an "unreasonable" speed. The policemen followed, and in a short while overtook the Pathfinder when it stopped behind other traffic at a red light. They pulled up alongside, and Officer Ephraim Soto stepped out and approached the driver's door, identifying himself as a police officer and directing the driver, petitioner Brown, to put the vehicle in park. When Soto drew up to the driver's window, he immediately observed two large plastic bags of what appeared to be crack cocaine in petitioner Whren's hands. Petitioners were arrested, and quantities of several types of illegal drugs were retrieved from the vehicle.

Petitioners were charged in a four-count indictment with violating various federal drug laws, including 21 U.S.C. §§ 844(a) and 860(a). At a pretrial suppression hearing, they challenged the legality of the stop and the resulting seizure of the drugs. They argued that the stop had not been justified by probable cause to believe, or even reasonable suspicion, that petitioners were engaged in illegal drug-dealing activity; and that Officer Soto's asserted ground for approaching the vehicle — to give the driver a warning concerning traffic violations — was pretextual. The District Court denied the suppression motion, concluding that "the facts of the stop were not controverted," and "[t]here was nothing to really demonstrate that the actions of the officers were contrary to a normal traffic stop." Petitioners were convicted of the counts at issue here. The Court of Appeals affirmed the convictions, holding with respect to the suppression issue that, "regardless of whether a police officer subjectively believes that the occupants of an automobile may be engaging in some other illegal behavior, a traffic stop is permissible as long as a reasonable officer in the same circumstances could have stopped the car for the suspected traffic violation." We granted certiorari.

OPINION

The Fourth Amendment guarantees "[t]he right of the people to be secure in their persons, houses, papers, and effects, against unreasonable searches and seizures." Temporary detention of individuals during the stop of an automobile by the police, even if only for a brief period and for a limited purpose, constitutes a "seizure" of "persons" within the meaning of this provision. See *Delaware v. Prouse,* 440 U.S. 648, 653, 99 S.Ct. 1391, 1395, 59 L.Ed.2d 660 (1979);

United States v. Martinez-Fuerte, 428 U.S. 543, 556, 96 S.Ct. 3074, 3082, 49 L.Ed.2d 1116 (1976); *United States v. Brignoni-Ponce*, 422 U.S. 873, 878, 95 S.Ct. 2574, 2578, 45 L.Ed.2d 607 (1975). An automobile stop is thus subject to the constitutional imperative that it not be "unreasonable" under the circumstances. As a general matter, the decision to stop an automobile is reasonable where the police have probable cause to believe that a traffic violation has occurred. See *Prouse, Pennsylvania v. Mimms*, 434 U.S. 106, 109, 98 S.Ct. 330, 332, 54 L.Ed.2d 331 (1977) (per curiam).

Petitioners accept that Officer Soto had probable cause to believe that various provisions of the District of Columbia traffic code had been violated. See 18 D.C. Mun. Regs. §§ 2213.4 (1995) ("An operator shall . . . give full time and attention to the operation of the vehicle"); 2204.3 ("No person shall turn any vehicle . . . without giving an appropriate signal"); 2200.3 ("No person shall drive a vehicle . . . at a speed greater than is reasonable and prudent under the conditions"). They argue, however, that "in the unique context of civil traffic regulations" probable cause is not enough. Since, they contend, the use of automobiles is so heavily and minutely regulated that total compliance with traffic and safety rules is nearly impossible, a police officer will almost invariably be able to catch any given motorist in a technical violation. This creates the temptation to use traffic stops as a means of investigating other law violations, as to which no probable cause or even articulable suspicion exists. Petitioners, who are both black, further contend that police officers might decide which motorists to stop based on decidedly impermissible factors, such as the race of the car's occupants. To avoid this danger, they say, the Fourth Amendment test for traffic stops should be, not the normal one (applied by the Court of Appeals) of whether probable cause existed to justify the stop; but rather, whether a police officer, acting reasonably, would have made the stop for the reason given.

. . .

[P]etitioners argue that the balancing inherent in any Fourth Amendment inquiry requires us to weigh the governmental and individual interests implicated in a traffic stop such as we have here. That balancing, petitioners claim, does not support investigation of minor traffic infractions by plainclothes police in unmarked vehicles; such investigation only minimally advances the government's interest in traffic safety, and may indeed retard it by producing motorist confusion and alarm — a view said to be supported by the Metropolitan Police Department's own regulations generally prohibiting this practice. And as for the Fourth Amendment interests of the individuals concerned, petitioners point out that our cases acknowledge that even ordinary traffic stops entail "a possibly unsettling show of authority"; that they at best "interfere with freedom of movement, are inconvenient, and consume time" and at worst "may create substantial anxiety," *Prouse*, 440 U.S., at 657, 99 S.Ct., at 1398. That anxiety is likely to be even more pronounced when the stop is conducted by plainclothes officers in unmarked cars.

It is of course true that in principle every Fourth Amendment case, since it turns upon a "reasonableness" determination, involves a balancing of all relevant factors. With rare exceptions not applicable here, however, the result of that balancing is not in doubt where the search or seizure is based upon probable cause. That is why petitioners must rely upon cases like *Prouse* to provide examples of actual "balancing" analysis. There, the police action in question was a random traffic stop for the purpose of checking a motorist's license and vehicle registration, a practice that — like the practices at issue in the inventory search and administrative inspection cases upon which petitioners rely in making their "pretext" claim — involves police intrusion without the probable cause that is its traditional justification. Our opinion in *Prouse* expressly distinguished the case from a stop based on precisely what is at issue here: "probable cause to believe that a driver is violating any one of the multitude of applicable traffic and equipment regulations." It noted approvingly that "[t]he foremost method of enforcing traffic and vehicle safety regulations . . . is acting upon observed violations," which afford the "'quantum of individualized suspicion'" necessary to ensure that police discretion is sufficiently constrained. What is true of *Prouse* is also true of other cases that engaged in detailed "balancing" to decide the constitutionality of automobile stops, such as *Martinez-Fuerte*, supra, which upheld checkpoint stops, see 428 U.S., at 556–562, 96 S.Ct., at 3082–

3085, and *Brignoni-Ponce*, supra, which disallowed so-called "roving patrol" stops: the detailed "balancing" analysis was necessary because they involved seizures without probable cause.

Where probable cause has existed, the only cases in which we have found it necessary actually to perform the "balancing" analysis involved searches or seizures conducted in an extraordinary manner, unusually harmful to an individual's privacy or even physical interests—such as, for example, seizure by means of deadly force, see *Tennessee v. Garner*, 471 U.S. 1, 105 S.Ct. 1694, 85 L.Ed.2d 1 (1985), unannounced entry into a home, see *Wilson v. Arkansas*, 514 U.S. —, 115 S.Ct. 1914, 131 L.Ed.2d 976 (1995), entry into a home without a warrant, see *Welsh v. Wisconsin*, 466 U.S. 740, 104 S.Ct. 2091, 80 L.Ed.2d 732 (1984), or physical penetration of the body, see *Winston v. Lee*, 470 U.S. 753, 105 S.Ct. 1611, 84 L.Ed.2d 662 (1985). The making of a traffic stop out-of-uniform does not remotely qualify as such an extreme practice, and so is governed by the usual rule that probable cause to believe the law has been broken "outbalances" private interest in avoiding police contact.

Petitioners urge as an extraordinary factor in this case that the "multitude of applicable traffic and equipment regulations" is so large and so difficult to obey perfectly that virtually everyone is guilty of violation, permitting the police to single out almost whomever they wish for a stop. But we are aware of no principle that would allow us to decide at what point a code of law becomes so expansive and so commonly violated that infraction itself can no longer be the ordinary measure of the lawfulness of enforcement. And even if we could identify such exorbitant codes, we do not know by what standard (or what right) we would decide, as petitioners would have us do, which particular provisions are sufficiently important to merit enforcement.

For the run-of-the-mine case, which this surely is, we think there is no realistic alternative to the traditional common-law rule that probable cause justifies a search and seizure. Here the District Court found that the officers had probable cause to believe that petitioners had violated the traffic code. That rendered the stop reasonable under the Fourth Amendment, the evidence thereby discovered admissible, and the upholding of the convictions by the Court of Appeals for the District of Columbia Circuit correct.

Judgment affirmed.

CASE DISCUSSION

Explain how the search in this case was a pretext. For what "crimes" did the officers have probable cause to arrest Brown and Whren? Of what was the probable cause? Explain the "could have" and "would have" tests to determine the reasonableness of the pretext search. What test did the Court adopt? Why? Do you agree with Professor Jonas in the quotation at the opening of this section that pretext searches threaten individual rights too much? That they give the government too much power? Or do you believe that the government needs this power to fight the "war on drugs"? Consider the following excerpt from the Petitioners' Brief in *Whren v. U.S.*:

> Justice Jackson's observation nearly a half-century ago is no less true today: "I am convinced that there are . . . many unlawful searches of homes and automobiles of innocent people which turn up nothing incriminating, in which no arrest is made, about which courts do nothing, and about which we never hear." *Brinegar v. United States*, 338 U.S. 160, 181 (1949) (Jackson, J., dissenting).
>
> Because police do not generally keep records of traffic stops that turn up nothing and in which no one is ticketed, it is no simple matter to substantiate Justice Jackson's suspicions. However, reporters from the *Orlando Sentinel* had the unique opportunity to document this phenomenon when they obtained 148 hours of video-taped "traffic" stops of 1,084 motorists along Interstate 95 in Florida. Brazil and Berry, "Color of Driver is Key to Stops in I-95 Videos," *Orlando Sentinel*, Aug. 23, 1992, at A1. Although all of the stops were purportedly based on traffic violations, only nine drivers (less than one percent) were issued citations. Searches were made in almost half the stops, but only five percent of all stops resulted in an arrest. Most shocking is how racially disproportionate the stops were. Although blacks and Hispanics

made up only five percent of the drivers on that stretch of I-95 and only fifteen percent of traffic convictions statewide, approximately seventy percent of those stopped were black or Hispanic. On average, stops of minority drivers lasted more than twice as long as stops of white drivers. For some, the tapes showed it was not the first time they had been singled out: "There is the bewildered black man who stands on the roadside trying to explain to the deputies that it is the seventh time he has been stopped. And the black man who shakes his head in frustration as his car is searched; it is the second time in minutes he has been stopped." This kind of baseless "checking out" of racial minorities generally gets public attention only when someone well-known speaks out.

Discovery materials in a class action involving pre-textual traffic stops along Interstate 95 near Philadelphia show a similar pattern. The class representatives alleged that, while returning from a church celebration in 1991, they were stopped and subjected to a sniff by a police dog before being told, "[i]n order to make this a legitimate stop, I'm going to give you a warning for obstruction of your car's rear-view mirror." The only object hanging from the mirror was a thin piece of string on which an air freshener had once been attached. When the driver pointed out that the officer could not have seen the string, the officer stated that they were stopped "because you are young, black and in a high drug-trafficking area, driving a nice car." Discovery materials and follow-up interviews in the Tinicum Township case showed:

First, the interdiction program is based on the power to make a pretextual traffic stop. Numerous vehicles have been stopped, for example, for having small items tied to their rearview mirrors, for outdated inspection stickers, or for other minor violations, all supposedly observed as the car passed the police at sixty miles per hour. Second, the stops are racially disproportionate. Third, claims of consent are rebutted by numerous innocent individuals who give consistent accounts of being told that they would have to wait for a police dog, have their car towed, or suffer other types of roadside detention unless they consented to a search.[40]

Consider the following remarks made by a police officer to researchers:

You can always get a guy legitimately on a traffic violation if you tail him for a while, and then a search can be made. You don't have to follow a driver very long before he will move to the other side of the yellow line and then you can arrest and search him for driving on the wrong side of the highway. In the event that we see a suspicious automobile or occupant and wish to search the person or the car, or both, we will usually follow the vehicle until the driver makes a technical violation of a traffic law. Then we have a means of making a legitimate search.[41]

First, present arguments that both defense lawyers and prosecutors might make to support the reasonableness of searches incident to pretext traffic arrests. Then assume the role of judge and decide the reasonableness of pretext traffic arrest searches in light of Fourth Amendment reasonableness.

Decision Point

On August 11, 1993, a reserve officer worked the 1 to 7 A.M. shift for the East Millinocket Police Department. At 1:20 A.M., when the bars were closing, he drove along Route 157 near a local nightclub. In the vicinity of the club, he clocked the defendant driving 59 m.p.h. in a 55 m.p.h. zone and stopped him. When he approached the car, he noticed that the de-

fendant's eyes were glassy and that he smelled of alcohol. The officer conducted field sobriety tests and arrested the defendant for OUI. No speeding ticket was issued.

The officer testified that at night he stops all drivers for any motor vehicle infractions, including a defective plate light or driving one mile over the speed limit. He testified that he makes these stops because "[t]here are several local bars in the area. That time of night, the bars are usually letting out. It weighs in your decision, but it's not totally part of your decision." When asked whether he would have stopped the defendant in the afternoon for driving four miles over the posted limit, the officer stated that he could not answer that "hypothetical."

Was the stop for speeding a pretext to "search" for evidence of drunk driving? The district court said yes. According to the district court,

> "[I]f the practice is to stop at 59 in a 55, that better be the practice all the time, not just at night when you use it as an excuse to find a drunk driver;" the officer was looking for any reason to stop a vehicle driving late at night, "[a]nd he would not have done that at another time of day." In response to the State's motion for further findings of fact and conclusions of law, the court found "that the officer's practice

during the daytime is to not stop speeders in the 1–4 m.p.h. over range. Late at night he stops for any violation, no matter how petty. The court finds that those stops are actually 'fishing expeditions' for OUI's."

The Maine Supreme Court affirmed:

> A pretextual stop occurs when an officer uses a legal justification to stop a vehicle to search for evidence of an unrelated serious crime for which he did not have the reasonable articulable suspicion necessary to support a stop. The test is not whether the officer lawfully could have stopped defendant, but whether a reasonable officer would have made the stop absent the invalid purpose. This test recognizes that it is the departure from routine practice that makes the officer's conduct arbitrary, and it is the arbitrariness which violates the Fourth Amendment. *State v. Haskell*, 645 A.2d 619 (Me. 1994)

Consent Searches

Police rely on consent searches in a substantial number of cases as a means to investigate crime. Consent searches definitely lighten the burden of law enforcement because consent searches require neither warrants nor probable cause. Police officers ordinarily seek consent for two reasons: convenience and necessity. Lawrence P. Tiffany, Donald M. McIntyre, Jr., and Daniel L. Rotenberg studied consent searches as part of the distinguished American Bar Foundation's massive research into the day-to-day operations of criminal justice in America. They found that officers prefer to search by consent even when they have the probable cause to obtain warrants because consent searches are convenient. Officers believe "that the search warrant procedure is overly technical and time-consuming, and that it has no corresponding advantages for them or meaningful protections for the individual." Furthermore, since suspects will plead guilty in most cases, and therefore judges will not exclude the evidence anyway, the officers will have wasted their time and effort in obtaining a warrant.[42]

Tiffany and his colleagues also found that police officers rely on consent searches out of necessity. In these cases, consent is their only avenue to looking for criminal evidence. For example, the police know that drug users and couriers travel by bus or plane from one city to another. They do not have probable cause to search most passengers or even reasonable suspicion to stop and question them. So they approach these passengers, explain the seriousness of the "drug problem," and ask their cooperation in helping to do something to help them. According to the anecdotal evidence supplied by officers who conduct bus and airport sweeps, consent to search usually follows these

WAIVER AND CONSENT TO SEARCH

The undersigned _____

residing at _____

_____ hereby authorizes

the following named St. Paul Police Officers _____

to search the _____

_____

(insert description of place or auto, lic. number, etc.)

owned by/or in possession of the undersigned.
I do hereby waive any and all objections that may be made by me to said
search and declare that this waiver and consent is freely and voluntarily given
of my own free will and accord.

Signed _____ day of _____ 19___ at _____ PM   AM

Signed _____

Witnessed _____

FIGURE 6.1 A SAMPLE WAIVER AND CONSENT TO SEARCH FORM

requests, especially when the officers are polite and explain why they want the cooperation of passengers. For example, Detective Perry Kendrick, who worked the Fort Lauderdale Airport, testified in one case that people willingly consent even to searches of
their crotches in the public part of airports. On one particular day, he said that he

> talked with 16 to 20 people and most consented, but one or two did not. He tes-
> tified further that initially some complain after the search, but that after the
> deputies explain their mission in interdicting narcotics moving from airport to air-
> port within the United States, that the persons understand and many "thank us
> for the job we're doing."[43]

Tests of Consent. Courts justify consent searches by two separate theories. Some
courts use a **voluntariness test,** based on the idea that a search following consent obtained without coercion or promises to secure it does not violate the Fourth Amendment. Others adopt a **waiver test,** based on the theory that individuals may waive their
Fourth Amendment rights but only if they do so voluntarily and intentionally (see Figure 6.1). The voluntariness test assumes that citizens do not have a right against all
searches, just against *unreasonable* ones. Hence, according to the voluntariness theory,
consent requires only that individuals do not agree to searches under coercion, promise,
or deception. According to the waiver test, however, consent is valid only if citizens
know they have the right against unreasonable government searches; know that they

have a right to refuse to consent to unreasonable government searches; and, knowing both, intentionally and voluntarily give up these rights.

The waiver test is stricter than the voluntariness test—that is to say, it makes it harder for the government to satisfy the requirements of the Fourth Amendment. To satisfy it, officers ordinarily must inform individuals that they have a right to refuse their consent and to warn them that if officers find incriminating evidence, officers will seize it and use it against the person consenting to the search. The voluntariness test, on the other hand, looks to the totality of circumstances surrounding the consent to determine if the suspect consented freely and voluntarily. These circumstances can include all of the following:

- Knowledge of constitutional rights in general
- Knowledge of the right to refuse consent
- Sufficient age and maturity to make an independent decision
- Intelligence to understand significance of consent
- Education of or experience with the workings of the criminal justice system
- Cooperation with officers, such as saying, "Sure, go ahead and search."
- Attitude toward the likelihood that officers will discover contraband
- Length of detention and nature of questioning regarding consent
- Coercive police behavior surrounding the consent

In the leading case of *Schneckloth v. Bustamonte*, the United States Supreme Court decided whether the voluntariness test satisfies the requirements of the Fourth Amendment or whether the Amendment requires the stricter waiver test.

C A S E

Did Bustamonte Voluntarily Consent?

Schneckloth v. Bustamonte
412 U.S. 218, 93 S.Ct. 2041,
36 L.Ed.2d 854 (1973)

In a habeas corpus *proceeding, the court of appeals, reversing the district court, held that the prosecution had failed to prove that Bustamonte consented to the search with the understanding that he could withhold his consent. The Supreme Court reversed, holding that the government need only show that Bustamonte consented voluntarily, which, according to the Court, he did. Justice Stewart wrote the opinion of the Court, in which Chief Justice Burger and Justices White, Blackmun, Powell, and Rehnquist joined. Justice Blackmun*

filed a concurring opinion. Justice Powell filed a concurring opinion, in which Chief Justice Burger and Justice Rehnquist joined. Justices Douglas, Brennan, and Marshall filed dissenting opinions.

FACTS

The respondent was brought to trial in California court upon a charge of possessing a check with intent to defraud. He moved to suppress the introduction of certain material as evidence against him on the ground that the material had been acquired through an unconstitutional search and seizure. In response to the motion, the trial judge conducted an evidentiary hearing where it was established that the material in question had been acquired by the State under the following circumstances:

While on routine patrol in Sunnyvale, California, at approximately 2:40 in the morning, Police Officer James Rand stopped an automobile when he observed that one headlight and its license plate light were burned out. Six men were in the vehicle. Joe Alcala and the respondent, Robert Bustamonte, were in the front seat with Joe Gonzales, the driver. Three older men were seated in the rear. When, in response to the policeman's question, Gonzales could not produce a driver's license, Officer Rand asked if any of the other five had any evidence of identification. Only Alcala produced a license, and he explained that the car was his brother's. After the six occupants had stepped out of the car at the officer's request and after two additional policemen had arrived, Officer Rand asked Alcala if he could search the car. Alcala replied, "Sure, go ahead." Prior to the search no one was threatened with arrest and, according to Officer Rand's uncontradicted testimony, it "was all very congenial at this time." Gonzales testified that Alcala actually helped in the search of the car, by opening the trunk and glove compartment. In Gonzales' words "[T]he police officer asked Joe [Alcala], he goes 'Does this trunk open?' and Joe said, 'Yes.' He went to the car and got the keys and opened up the trunk." Wadded up under the left rear seat, the police officers found three checks that had previously been stolen from a car wash.

. . . Consent could not be found, the court held, solely from the absence of coercion and a verbal expression of assent. Since the District Court had not determined that Alcala had known that his consent could have been withheld and that he could have refused to have his vehicle searched, the Court of Appeals vacated the order denying the writ and remanded the case for further proceedings. We granted certiorari to determine whether the Fourth and Fourteenth Amendments require the showing thought necessary by the Court of Appeals. . . .

OPINION

. . . The question whether a consent to a search was in fact "voluntary" or was the product of duress or co-

ercion, express or implied, is a question of fact to be determined from the totality of all the circumstances. While knowledge of the right to refuse consent is one factor to be taken into account, the government need not establish such knowledge as the sine qua non of an effective consent. As with police questioning, two competing concerns must be accommodated in determining the meaning of a "voluntary" consent—the legitimate need for such searches and the equally important requirement of assuring the absence of coercion. . . .

The problem of reconciling the recognized legitimacy of consent searches with the requirement that they be free from any aspect of official coercion cannot be resolved by any infallible touchstone. To approve such searches without the most careful scrutiny would sanction the possibility of official coercion; to place artificial restrictions upon such searches would jeopardize their basic validity. Just as was true with confessions, the requirement of a "voluntary" consent reflects a fair accommodation of the constitutional requirements involved. In examining all the surrounding circumstances to determine if in fact the consent to search was coerced, account must be taken of subtly coerced police questions, as well as the possibly vulnerable subjective state of the person who consents. Those searches that are the product of police coercion can thus be filtered out without undermining the continuing validity of consent searches. In sum, there is no reason for us to depart in the area of consent searches, from the traditional definition of "voluntariness." . . .

In this case, there is no evidence of any inherently coercive tactics—either from the nature of the police questioning or the environment in which it took place. Indeed, since consent searches will normally occur on a person's own familiar territory, the specter of incommunicado police interrogation in some remote station house is simply inapposite. There is no reason to believe, under circumstances such as are present here, that the response to a policeman's question is presumptively coerced; and there is, therefore, no reason to eject the traditional test for determining the voluntariness of a person's response. . . .

Our decision today is a narrow one. We hold only that when the subject of a search is not in custody and the State attempts to justify a search on the basis of his consent, the Fourth and Fourteenth Amendments require that it demonstrate that the consent was in fact voluntarily given, and not the result of duress or coercion, express or implied. Voluntariness is a question of fact to be determined from all the circumstances, and while the subject's knowledge of a right to refuse is a factor to be taken into account, the prosecution is not required to demonstrate such knowledge as a prerequisite to establishing a voluntary consent. Because the California court followed these principles in affirming the respondent's conviction, and because the Court of Appeals for the Ninth Circuit in remanding for an evidentiary hearing required more, its judgment must be reversed. It is so ordered.

DISSENT

Justice Marshall, dissenting.

Several years ago, Mr. Justice Stewart reminded us that "[t]he Constitution guarantees . . . a society of free choice. Such a society presupposes the capacity of its members to choose." I would have thought that the capacity to choose necessarily depends upon knowledge that there is a choice to be made. But today the Court reaches the curious result that one can choose to relinquish a constitutional right—the right to be free of unreasonable searches—without knowing that he has the alternative of refusing to accede to a police request to search. I cannot agree, and therefore dissent. . . .

The Court contends that if an officer paused to inform the subject of his rights, the informality of the exchange would be destroyed. I doubt that a simple statement by an officer of an individual's right to refuse consent would do much to alter the informality of the exchange, except to alert the subject to a fact that he surely is entitled to know. It is not without significance that for many years the agents of the Federal Bureau of Investigation have routinely informed subjects of their right to refuse consent when they request consent to search. . . . The reported cases in which the police have informed subjects of their right to refuse consent show, also, that the information can be given without disrupting the casual flow of events. What evidence there is, then, rather strongly suggests that nothing disastrous would happen if the police, before requesting consent, informed the subject that he had a right to refuse consent and that his refusal would be respected.

I must conclude, with some reluctance, that when the Court speaks of practicality, what it really is talking of is the continued ability of the police to capitalize on the ignorance of citizens so as to accomplish by subterfuge what they could not achieve by relying only on the knowing relinquishment of constitutional rights. Of course it would be "practical" for the police to ignore the commands of the Fourth Amendment, if by practicality we mean that more criminals will be apprehended, even though the constitutional rights of innocent people also go by the board. But such a practical advantage is achieved only at the cost of permitting the police to disregard the limitations that the Constitution places on their behavior, a cost that a constitutional democracy cannot long absorb.

I find nothing in the opinion of the Court to dispel my belief that, in such a case, "[u]nder many circumstances a reasonable person might read an officer's 'May I' as the courteous expression of a demand backed by force of law." [In] [m]ost cases . . . consent is ordinarily given as acquiescence in an implicit claim of authority to search. . . .

CASE DISCUSSION

Did Robert Bustamonte voluntarily consent? What specific facts demonstrate whether or not he consented? Do citizens ever consent to police, or are all police requests orders? Would you favor a waiver test? How would this case be decided using a waiver test? Consider the consent form used by the St. Paul, Minnesota, Police Department in Figure 6.1 (p. 280). If Bustamonte had signed this form, would his consent have been more creditable? Why or why not?

D e c i s i o n   P o i n t

This case arose on a stretch of Interstate 70 north of Dayton, Ohio, where the posted speed limit was 45 miles per hour because of construction. Respondent Robert D. Robinette was clocked at 69 miles per hour as he drove his car along this stretch of road, and he was stopped by Deputy Roger Newsome of the Montgomery County Sheriff's office. Newsome asked for and was handed Robinette's driver's license, and he ran a computer check which indicated that Robinette had no previous violations. Newsome then asked Robinette to step out of his car, turned on his mounted video camera, issued a verbal warning to Robinette, and returned his license.

At this point, Newsome asked, "One question before you get gone: [A]re you carrying any illegal contraband in your car? Any weapons of any kind, drugs, anything like that?" Robinette answered "no" to these questions, after which Deputy Newsome asked if he could search the car. Robinette consented. In the car, Deputy Newsome discovered a small amount of marijuana and, in a film container, a pill that was later determined to be methylenedioxymethamphetamine (MDMA). Robinette was then arrested and charged with knowing possession of a controlled substance, MDMA, in violation of Ohio Rev.Code Ann. § 2925.11(A) (1993).

Was the search the result of a valid consent? The Ohio Supreme Court ruled that the search resulted from an unlawful detention. The United States Supreme Court reversed. Writing for the majority was Chief Justice Rehnquist:

> We have long held that the "touchstone of the Fourth Amendment is reasonableness." Reasonableness, in turn, is measured in objective terms by examining the totality of the circumstances. In applying this test we have consistently eschewed bright-line rules, instead emphasizing the fact-specific nature of the reasonableness inquiry. . . . We have previously rejected a per se rule very similar to that adopted by the Supreme Court of Ohio in determining the validity of a consent to search. In *Schneckloth v. Bustamonte*, 412 U.S. 218, 93 S.Ct. 2041, 36 L.Ed.2d 854 (1973), it was argued that such a consent could not be valid unless the de-

fendant knew that he had a right to refuse the request. We rejected this argument: "While knowledge of the right to refuse consent is one factor to be taken into account, the government need not establish such knowledge as the sine qua non of an effective consent." And just as it "would be thoroughly impractical to impose on the normal consent search the detailed requirements of an effective warning," so too would it be unrealistic to require police officers to always inform detainees that they are free to go before a consent to search may be deemed voluntary.

> The Fourth Amendment test for a valid consent to search is that the consent be voluntary, and "[v]oluntariness is a question of fact to be determined from all the circumstances." The Supreme Court of Ohio having held otherwise, its judgment is reversed, and the case is remanded for further proceedings not inconsistent with this opinion.

In a lone dissent, Associate Justice John P. Stevens wrote the following:

> Several circumstances support the Ohio courts' conclusion that a reasonable motorist in respondent's shoes would have believed that he had an obligation to answer the "one question" and that he could not simply walk away from the officer, get back in his car, and drive away. The question itself sought an answer "before you get gone." In addition, the facts that respondent had been detained, had received no advice that he was free to leave, and was then standing in front of a television camera in response to an official command, are all inconsistent with an assumption that he could reasonably believe that he had no duty to respond. The Ohio Supreme Court was surely correct in stating: "Most people believe that they are validly in a police officer's custody as long as the officer continues to interrogate them. The police officer retains the upper hand and the accouterments of authority. That the officer lacks legal license to continue to de-

tain them is unknown to most citizens, and a reasonable person would not feel free to walk away as the officer continues to address him."

Moreover, as an objective matter it is fair to presume that most drivers who have been stopped for speeding are in a hurry to get to their destinations; such drivers have no interest in prolonging the delay occasioned by the stop just to engage in idle conversation with an officer, much less to allow a potentially lengthy search. I also assume that motorists—even those who are not carrying contraband—have an interest in preserving the privacy of their vehicles and possessions from the prying eyes of a curious stranger. The fact that this particular officer successfully used a similar method of obtaining consent to search roughly 786 times in one year, *State v. Retherford*, 93 Ohio App.3d 586, 591–592, 639 N.E.2d 498, 502, dism'd, 69 Ohio St.3d 1488, 635 N.E.2d 43 (1994), indicates that motorists generally respond in a manner that is contrary to their self-interest.

Repeated decisions by ordinary citizens to surrender that interest cannot satisfactorily be explained on any hypothesis other than an assumption that they believed they had a legal duty to do so.

The Ohio Supreme Court was therefore entirely correct to presume in the first syllabus preceding its opinion that a "continued detention" was at issue here. The Ohio Court of Appeals reached a similar conclusion. In response to the State's contention that Robinette "was free to go" at the time consent was sought, that court held—after reviewing the record—that "a reasonable person in Robinette's position would not believe that the investigative stop had been concluded, and that he or she was free to go, so long as the police officer was continuing to ask investigative questions." As I read the Ohio opinions, these determinations were independent of the bright-line rule criticized by the majority. I see no reason to disturb them. *Ohio v. Robinette*, 117 S.Ct. 417 (1996)

Scope of Consent. The reasonableness of consent searches depends on exactly how broad the scope of the consent those who have the authority to consent have actually given to those who conduct the searches. Consent searches are unreasonable if they exceed the scope of the consent. However, this does not mean that all searches that go beyond the consent actually given are unreasonable. The test is whether the officers who conduct the search, based on the totality of the circumstances, reasonably believe that the searches are within the scope of the consent they obtained. In *Florida v. Jimeno*, police asked for permission to search Jimeno's car. He agreed. The police searched not only the car itself but also a brown paper bag found in the trunk of the car. The officer found drugs in the paper bag. The Supreme Court upheld the reasonableness of the search. According to the Court, "The Fourth Amendment is satisfied when, under the circumstances, it is objectively reasonable for the officer to believe that the scope of the suspect's consent permitted him to open a particular container within the automobile."[44]

The scope of consent searches has become a major issue in the so-called consent crotch searches, one of the methods of drug law enforcement in major cities. Specially trained police officers patrol bus stations, airports, and railway stations. They approach people whom they have no reasonable suspicion to stop and ask for permission to search them. If the people agree, the officers immediately pat down their crotch area. The Supreme Court has not decided whether consent to search a person includes the consent to search the extremely private genital area of the body, especially if the search takes place in the public areas of busy airports, bus stations, and railway stations. The circuit courts are divided. Some have held that consent to search a person includes consent to search the groin area. Others have ruled that officers must ask specifically if they may search the groin area. The District of Columbia Circuit in an opinion written by Supreme Court Justice Clarence Thomas (sitting as a circuit judge) analyzed the reasonableness of consent crotch searches in *United States v. Rodney.*

C A S E

Did He Consent to a Search of His Crotch?

United States v. Rodney
956 F.2d 295 (C.A.D.C. 1992)

Rodney pleaded guilty to possession with intent to distribute crack cocaine. After the court denied his motion to suppress, Rodney appealed. The court of appeals affirmed before Judges Wald, Bader-Ginsberg, and Thomas. Justice Thomas wrote the opinion of the court. (Justice Thomas was a member of the U.S. Court of Appeals for the District of Columbia Circuit when the case was briefed and argued, and was designated Circuit Justice for this court.)

FACTS

. . . On February 17, 1990, Dylan Rodney stepped off a bus that had arrived in Washington, D.C., from New York City. As Rodney left the bus station, Detective Vance Beard, dressed in plain clothes and carrying a concealed weapon, approached him from behind. A second officer waited nearby. Beard displayed identification and asked if Rodney would talk to him. Rodney agreed. Beard asked Rodney whether he lived in either Washington or New York. Rodney replied that he lived in Florida, but had come to Washington to try to find his wife. She lived on Georgia Avenue, Rodney said, although he was unable to identify any more precise location. Beard asked Rodney whether he was carrying drugs in his travel bag. After Rodney said no, Beard obtained permission to search the bag. As he did so, the other officer advanced to within about five feet of Rodney. The search failed to turn up any contraband.

Beard then asked Rodney whether he was carrying drugs on his person. After Rodney again said no,

Beard requested permission to conduct a body search. Rodney said "Sure" and raised his arms above his head. Beard placed his hands on Rodney's ankles and, in one sweeping motion, ran them up the inside of Rodney's legs. As he passed over the crotch area, Beard felt small, rock-like objects. Rodney exclaimed: "That's me!" Detecting otherwise, Beard placed Rodney under arrest. At the police station, Beard unzipped Rodney's pants and retrieved a plastic bag containing a rock-like substance that was identified as cocaine base. Rodney was charged with possession and intent to distribute.

On April 10, 1990, Rodney moved to suppress the crack. Rodney argued (1) that he had not consented voluntarily to the body search; (2) that even if he had done so, the consent did not include a search of his crotch area; and (3) that his arrest was unsupported by probable cause. The district court held a hearing and denied the motion, finding that Rodney had "[given] his consent voluntarily to [the] search [of] his person and belongings." Rodney entered a conditional guilty plea, reserving the right to withdraw it if this court reversed the denial of his suppression motion.

OPINION

Rodney first contends that the district court erred in finding that his consent to the body search was voluntary, and therefore not prohibited by the Fourth Amendment. In determining the voluntariness of a consent, a district court must examine "the totality of all the surrounding circumstances—both the characteristics of the accused and the details of the interrogation." *Schneckloth v. Bustamonte,* 412 U.S. 218, 226, 93 S.Ct. 2041, 2047, 36 L.Ed.2d 854 (1973). Relevant factors include: the youth of the accused; his lack of education; or his low intelligence; the lack of any advice to the accused of his constitutional rights; the length of detention; the repeated and prolonged nature of the questioning; and the use of physical punishment such as the deprivation of food or sleep. We review only for clear error.

On this record, we find no clear error. On the one hand, some evidence suggests an involuntary consent. Rodney testified that he thought three, rather than two, officers were covering him; that the officers were much bigger than he; and that he was young (twenty-four) and relatively uneducated (to the tenth grade) at the time. He also testified that before the events leading to his arrest, he had had four unpleasant encounters with the police: each time he had refused their request to search him, but each time they had searched him anyway. On the other hand, Beard's testimony indicates that the police conduct here bore no resemblance to the sort of "aggressive questioning, intimidating actions, or prolonged police presence," *United States v. Brady*, 842 F.2d 1313, 1315 (D.C. Cir. 1988), that might invalidate a consent. During the encounter, according to Beard, his gun was concealed; he wore plain clothes and spoke in a conversational tone; and no other officer came within five feet of Rodney. The district court could have weighed Beard's evidence more heavily than Rodney's. Thus, even assuming that the court credited Rodney's testimony in addition to Beard's, the court committed no clear error in finding the consent voluntary.

Rodney next argues that even if he consented voluntarily to the body search, he did not consent to the search of his crotch area. A consensual search cannot exceed the scope of the consent. The scope of the consent is measured by a test of "'objective' reasonableness": it depends on how broadly a reasonable observer would have interpreted the consent under the circumstances. See *Florida v. Jimeno*, — U.S. —, 111 S.Ct. 1801, 1803–04, 114 L.Ed.2d 297 (1991). Here, Rodney clearly consented to a search of his body for drugs. We conclude that a reasonable person would have understood that consent to encompass the search undertaken here.

Under *Jimeno*, "[t]he scope of a search is generally defined by its expressed object." Id. 111 S.Ct. at 1804. In this case, Rodney authorized a search for drugs.

Dealers frequently hide drugs near their genitals. Indeed, Beard testified that his colleagues make up to 75 percent of their drug recoveries from around the crotch area. For these reasons, we conclude that a request to conduct a body search for drugs reasonably includes a request to conduct some search of that area.

Although *Jimeno* states the test "generally" used to determine the scope of a consent to search, we doubt that the Supreme Court would have us apply that test unflinchingly in the context of body searches. At some point, we suspect, a body search would become so intrusive that we would not infer consent to it from a generalized consent, regardless of the stated object of the search. For example, although drugs can be hidden virtually anywhere on or in one's person, a generalized consent to a body search for drugs surely does not validate everything up to and including a search of body cavities.

The search undertaken here, however, was not unusually intrusive, at least relative to body searches generally. It involved a continuous sweeping motion over Rodney's outer garments, including the trousers covering the crotch area. [COURT NOTE: At the suppression hearing, Rodney mimicked the search. Without objection, the prosecutor asked for the record to reflect that Rodney "ran both his hands from the base of his feet or ankle area up through the interior of his legs and including the crotch area with one motion."] In this respect, the search was no more invasive than the typical pat-down frisk for weapons described by the Supreme Court over two decades ago:

> [T]he officer must feel with sensitive fingers every portion of the [defendant's] body. A thorough search must be made of the [defendant's] arms and armpits, waistline and back, the groin and area about the testicles, and entire surface of the legs down to the feet. *Terry v. Ohio*, 392 U.S. 1, 17 n. 13, 88 S.Ct. 1868, 1877 n. 13, 20 L.Ed.2d 889 (1968)

We conclude that the frisk of Rodney's fully-clothed body involved nothing so intrusive, relative to body searches generally, as to require a separate consent above and beyond the consent to a body search that Rodney had given voluntarily.

Our conclusion is consistent with the Eleventh Circuit's decision in *United States v. Blake*, 888 F.2d

795 (11th Cir. 1989), on which Rodney relies heavily. In *Blake*, the officer performed a direct "'frontal touching'" of the defendant's private parts. The Eleventh Circuit found no clear error in the district court's invalidation of that search. In so doing, however, it expressly left open the question whether "the traditional frisk search, described in *Terry*" would have been encompassed within the scope of the consent given there. We hold only that Rodney's generalized consent authorized the kind of "traditional frisk search" undertaken here, and we express no view on questions involving putatively consensual searches of a more intrusive nature. . . .

We conclude that Rodney voluntarily consented to a search of his body for drugs, which encompassed the frisk undertaken here. . . . Accordingly, the judgment of conviction is Affirmed.

DISSENT

Wald, Circuit Judge, dissenting . . .

I disagree with the panel ruling that a citizen's consent to a search of his "person" on a public thoroughfare, given in response to a police request made in the absence of probable cause or even "reasonable suspicion" to believe that he has committed a crime, encompasses authority to conduct a palpation of the person's genital area in an effort to detect drugs. Because I believe that in this case such an intimate and intrusive search exceeded the scope of any general permission to search granted, I would find the search nonconsensual and the drugs seized inadmissible. . . .

. . . The issue before us is whether a person against whom there is no articulable suspicion of wrongdoing who is asked to submit to a body search on a public street expects that search to include manual touching of the genital area. I do not believe any such expectation exists at the time a cooperative citizen consents to an on-the-street search. Rather, that citizen anticipates only those kinds of searches that unfortunately have become a part of our urban living, searches ranging from airport security personnel passing a hand-held magnometer over a person's body, to having a person empty his pockets, and subject himself to a patting-down of sides, shoulders, and back. Any search that includes touching genital areas or breasts would not normally be expected to occur in public.

In all aspects of our society, different parts of the body are subject to very different levels of privacy and expectations about intrusions. We readily bare our heads, arms, legs, backs, even midriffs, in public, but, except in the most unusual circumstances, certainly not our breasts or genitals. On the streets, in elevators, and on public transportation, we often touch, inadvertently or even casually, each others' hands, arms, shoulders, and backs, but it is a serious affront, and sometimes even a crime, to intentionally touch another's intimate body parts without explicit permission; and while we feel free to discuss other people's hair, facial features, weight, height, noses or ears, similar discussions about genitals or breasts are not acceptable. Thus in any consensual encounter, it is not "objectively reasonable" for a citizen desiring to cooperate with the police in a public place to expect that permission to search her body includes feeling, even "fully clothed," the most private areas of her body. Under our social norms that requires "special permission," given with notice of the areas to be searched.

The majority dismisses the search here as not intolerable, however, because similar searches occur, even in public, pursuant to *Terry v. Ohio*, 392 U.S. 1, 88 S.Ct. 1868. First of all, *Terry* itself conceded that the search it authorized constituted "a serious intrusion upon the sanctity of the person, which may inflict great indignity and arouse strong resentment, and it is not to be undertaken lightly." 392 U.S. at 17, 88 S.Ct. at 1877; accord *United States v. Blake*, 888 F.2d at 801 (Shoob, J., concurring) (describing search of genital area without explicit consent as "outrageous conduct" by police officers, likely to lead to "fists thrown by indignant [persons] subjected to these searches"). Second, it is well to remember why the Court found such an intrusive public search to be permissible in certain circumstances: it was to protect the officer from ambush by hidden weapons in the custody of a person reasonably suspected of a crime. As the Supreme Court put it:

> The crux of this case . . . is . . . whether there was justification for [the officer's] invasion of Terry's personal security by searching him for weapons. We are now concerned with more than the governmental interest in investigating crime; . . . there is the more immediate interest

of the police officer in taking steps to assure himself that the person with whom he is dealing is not armed with a weapon that could unexpectedly and fatally be used against him. *Terry*, 392 U.S. at 23, 88 S.Ct. at 1881.

In consensual searches of citizens against whom there is no suspicion of crime, there is correlatively no comparable need for the officer to protect himself by doing a weapons pat-down. And even the kind of weapons search described in *Terry* must by its very nature be less intimate and intrusive than the manual search of a person's genital area for any small bump which might turn out to be a glassine envelope or a small rock of crack. In sum, *Terry* does not purport to define the limits of a cooperating citizen's right to privacy; it defines the balance between a suspect's right to privacy and the need of the police to protect themselves from ambush. The *Terry* authorization cannot, therefore, provide the safe haven for the police search of the intimate body parts of an ordinary citizen against whom there is no suspicion of crime.

Nor can the mere fact that drug couriers often hide their stash in the crotch area justify the search of such area without some elementary form of notice to the citizen that such an offensive procedure is about to take place. The ordinary citizen's expectation of privacy in intimate parts of her body is certainly well enough established to merit a particularized request for consent to such an intimate search in public. The Eleventh Circuit so found, and I do not find my colleagues' attempt to distinguish that case persuasive.

Whether the "touching" begins in the genital area, or ends up there after an initial "sweep" along the legs hardly seems material to the intensity of the intrusion; and indeed we cannot be sure at all from the record here that this search was really the equivalent of a *Terry* pat-down, which the *Blake* court did not reach; or something more intrusive. In any case, I agree with Judge Shoob's concurring opinion in *Blake* that "intimate searches may not occur as part of random stops absent explicit and voluntary consent." 888 F.2d at 801 (Shoob, J., concurring). . . .

A general consent to a search of a citizen's "person" in a public place does not include consent to touch the genital or breast areas. The majority today upholds a practice that allows police under the rubric of a general consent to conduct intimate body searches, and in so doing defeats the legitimate expectations of privacy that ordinary citizens should retain during cooperative exchanges with the police on the street. I believe the search was impermissible.

CASE DISCUSSION

Assume that you are Rodney's lawyer. Relying on the facts, argue that Rodney did not consent to a search at all. Now assume that you are the prosecutor and argue that Rodney voluntarily consented to the search. Then, assuming that Rodney agreed to a search of his person, take the same roles of defense and prosecuting attorneys and argue that Rodney did (did not) consent to a search of his crotch. Now assume you are the judge. Rule on the consent and its scope.

D e c i s i o n   P o i n t

1. The police arrested a man who had delivered a large quantity of drugs to an undercover police officer. The police then conducted a warrantless search of the man's car, in which they found several items. They asked the man if they could search his apartment. The police drew no weapons, informed the man that he could refuse to allow them to search, and asked the man if he realized what he was saying when he consented to the search. He replied, "Yes." Did he consent? A circuit court held that the totality of circumstances showed he consented.[45]

2. Rambo, while under the influence of narcotics, rationally and coherently answered officers' questions about his identification. He voluntarily directed the officers to his luggage, and no evidence of coercion by the officers existed. The Eighth Circuit Court of Appeals held that the consent was free and voluntary.[46]

3. Ceballos was forcibly arrested, given *Miranda* warnings, questioned for a few hours, threatened with a search warrant, offered low bail, and offered help in finding a job before he gave consent to search. The Second Circuit Court of Appeals held that Ceballos consented freely and voluntarily.[47]

4. Police stopped Jimeno's car for a traffic violation. Officer Trujillo had been following Jimeno's car after overhearing Jimeno arranging what Trujillo suspected was a drug deal. Officer Trujillo asked Jimeno for permission to search his car. Jimeno

consented. Officer Trujillo found cocaine inside a "folded paper bag" on the floorboard. Jimeno argued that consent to search his car did not include consent to open containers inside the car. The Supreme Court held that the consent to search the car included the consent to open and search the bag because Jimeno did not specifically place a restriction on the consent. That is, he should have said something like, "You can search the car, but you can't open any containers you find in the car."[48]

Third-Party Consent. One person can consent for another under some circumstances. Common relationships, such as the following, give authority to one member of the relationship to consent for the other: spouse–spouse, parent–child, roommate–roommate, employer–employee, landlord–tenant, and school administrator–student. Ordinarily, spouses can consent for each other. However, if spite motivates the consent, some courts have ruled that this consent is not effective. Parents can always consent for their minor children and for adult children who live at home.[49]

Employers cannot consent to searches of their employees' desks where employees have a reasonable expectation of privacy. For example, a school administrator could not consent to searching a guidance counselor's desk that was locked, was located in the counselor's office, and contained psychological profiles and other confidential student records. However, a factory owner could consent to searching items on top of an employee's workbench. Janitors, clerks, and drivers cannot consent to searches of their employers' premises, but managers can.[50]

C A S E

Was the Search a Valid Consent Search?

Illinois v. Rodriguez
497 U.S. 177, 110 S.Ct. 2793,
111 L.Ed.2d 148 (1990)

Rodriguez, who was charged with possession of a controlled substance with intent to deliver, moved to suppress seized evidence. The Circuit Court, Cook County, Illinois, granted the motion, and the People appealed. The Appellate Court affirmed without a published opinion. The People petitioned for a leave to appeal. The Illinois Supreme Court denied the petition

without a published opinion. The People petitioned for a writ of certiorari. The Supreme Court reversed and remanded. Justice Scalia wrote the opinion of the Court. Justice Marshall filed a dissenting opinion, in which Justices Brennan and Stevens joined.

FACTS

. . . On July 26, 1985, police were summoned to the residence of Dorothy Jackson on South Wolcott in Chicago. They were met by Ms. Jackson's daughter,

Gail Fischer, who showed signs of a severe beating. She told the officers that she had been assaulted by respondent Edward Rodriguez earlier that day in an apartment on South California. Fischer stated that Rodriguez was then asleep in the apartment, and she consented to travel there with the police in order to unlock the door with her key so that the officers could enter and arrest him. During this conversation, Fischer several times referred to the apartment on South California as "our" apartment, and said that she had clothes and furniture there. It is unclear whether she indicated that she currently lived at the apartment, or only that she used to live there.

The police officers drove to the apartment on South California, accompanied by Fischer. They did not obtain an arrest warrant for Rodriguez, nor did they seek a search warrant for the apartment. At the apartment, Fischer unlocked the door with her key and gave the officers permission to enter. They moved through the door into the living room, where they observed in plain view drug paraphernalia and containers filled with white powder that they believed (correctly, as later analysis showed) to be cocaine. They proceeded to the bedroom, where they found Rodriguez asleep and discovered additional containers of white powder in two open attaché cases. The officers arrested Rodriguez and seized the drugs and related paraphernalia.

Rodriguez was charged with possession of a controlled substance with intent to deliver. He moved to suppress all evidence seized at the time of his arrest, claiming that Fischer had vacated the apartment several weeks earlier and had no authority to consent to the entry. The Cook County Circuit Court granted the motion, holding that at the time she consented to the entry Fischer did not have common authority over the apartment. The Court concluded that Fischer was not a "usual resident" but rather an "infrequent visitor" at the apartment on South California, based upon its findings that Fischer's name was not on the lease, that she did not contribute to the rent, that she was not allowed to invite others to the apartment on her own, that she did not have access to the apartment when respondent was away, and that she had moved some of her possessions from the apartment. The Circuit Court also rejected the State's contention that, even if Fischer did not possess common author-

ity over the premises, there was no Fourth Amendment violation if the police reasonably believed at the time of their entry that Fischer possessed the authority to consent.

The Appellate Court of Illinois affirmed the Circuit Court in all respects. The Illinois Supreme Court denied the State's Petition for Leave to Appeal, and we granted certiorari.

OPINION

The Fourth Amendment generally prohibits the warrantless entry of a person's home, whether to make an arrest or to search for specific objects. *Payton v. New York* [excerpted in Chapter 5]. The prohibition does not apply, however, to situations in which voluntary consent has been obtained, either from the individual whose property is searched, see *Schneckloth v. Bustamonte* [excerpted above], or from a third party who possesses common authority over the premises [*United States v. Matlock*, 415 U.S., at 171, 94 S.Ct., at 993]. The State of Illinois contends that that exception applies in the present case.

As we stated in *Matlock*, "[c]ommon authority" rests "on mutual use of the property by persons generally having joint access or control for most purposes. . . ." The burden of establishing that common authority rests upon the State. On the basis of this record, it is clear that burden was not sustained. The evidence showed that although Fischer, with her two small children, had lived with Rodriguez beginning in December 1984, she had moved out on July 1, 1985, almost a month before the search at issue here, and had gone to live with her mother. She took her and her children's clothing with her, though leaving behind some furniture and household effects. During the period after July 1 she sometimes spent the night at Rodriguez' apartment, but never invited her friends there, and never went there herself when he was not home. Her name was not on the lease nor did she contribute to the rent. She had a key to the apartment, which she said at trial she had taken without Rodriguez' knowledge (though she testified at the preliminary hearing that Rodriguez had given her the key). On these facts the State has not established that, with respect to the South California apartment, Fischer had joint access or control for most purposes. To the contrary, the Appellate Court's determination of no common authority over the apartment was obviously correct.

The State contends that, even if Fischer did not in fact have authority to give consent, it suffices to validate the entry that the law enforcement officers reasonably believed she did. . . . [R]espondent asserts that permitting a reasonable belief of common authority to validate an entry would cause a defendant's Fourth Amendment rights to be "vicariously waived."

. . . What Rodriguez is assured by the trial right of the exclusionary rule, where it applies, is that no evidence seized in violation of the Fourth Amendment will be introduced at his trial unless he consents. What he is assured by the Fourth Amendment itself, however, is not that no government search of his house will occur unless he consents; but that no such search will occur that is "unreasonable." U.S. Const., Amdt. 4. There are various elements, of course, that can make a search of a person's house "reasonable"—one of which is the consent of the person or his cotenant. The essence of respondent's argument is that we should impose upon this element a requirement that we have not imposed upon other elements that regularly compel government officers to exercise judgment regarding the facts: namely, the requirement that their judgment be not only responsible but correct.

The fundamental objective that alone validates all unconsented government searches is, of course, the seizure of persons who have committed or are about to commit crimes, or of evidence related to crimes. But "reasonableness," with respect to this necessary element, does not demand that the government be factually correct in its assessment that that is what a search will produce. Warrants need only be supported by "probable cause," which demands no more than a proper "assessment of probabilities in particular factual contexts. . . ." *Illinois v. Gates* [excerpted in Chapter 5]. . . .

. . . [I]n order to satisfy the "reasonableness" requirement of the Fourth Amendment, what is generally demanded of the many factual determinations that must regularly be made by agents of the government—whether the magistrate issuing a warrant, the police officer executing a warrant, or the police officer conducting a search or seizure under one of the exceptions to the warrant requirement—is not that

they always be correct, but that they always be reasonable. As we put it in *Brinegar v. United States*, 338 U.S. 160, 176, 69 S.Ct. 1302, 1311, 93 L.Ed. 1879 (1949): "Because many situations which confront officers in the course of executing their duties are more or less ambiguous, room must be allowed for some mistakes on their part. But the mistakes must be those of reasonable men, acting on facts leading sensibly to their conclusions of probability."

We see no reason to depart from this general rule with respect to facts bearing upon the authority to consent to a search. Whether the basis for such authority exists is the sort of recurring factual question to which law enforcement officials must be expected to apply their judgment; and all the Fourth Amendment requires is that they answer it reasonably. The Constitution is no more violated when officers enter without a warrant because they reasonably (though erroneously) believe that the person who has consented to their entry is a resident of the premises, than it is violated when they enter without a warrant because they reasonably (though erroneously) believe they are in pursuit of a violent felon who is about to escape.

In the present case, the Appellate Court found it unnecessary to determine whether the officers reasonably believed that Fischer had the authority to consent, because it ruled as a matter of law that a reasonable belief could not validate the entry. Since we find that ruling to be in error, we remand for consideration of that question. The judgment of the Illinois Appellate Court is reversed, and the case is remanded for further proceedings not inconsistent with this opinion. So ordered.

DISSENT

Justice Marshall, with whom Justice Brennan and Justice Stevens join, dissenting.

. . . The majority agrees with the Illinois Appellate Court's determination that Fischer did not have authority to consent to the officer's entry of Rodriguez' apartment. The Court holds that the warrantless entry into Rodriguez' home was nonetheless valid if the officers reasonably believed that Fischer had authority to consent. The majority's defense of this position rests on a misconception of the basis for third-party consent searches. That such searches do not give rise to claims of constitutional violations rests not on the premise that they are "reasonable" under the Fourth Amendment, but on the premise that a person may voluntarily limit his expectation of privacy by allowing others to exercise authority over his possessions. Thus, an individual's decision to permit another "joint access [to] or control [over the property] for most purposes," *United States v. Matlock*, limits that individual's reasonable expectation of privacy and to that extent limits his Fourth Amendment protections. If an individual has not so limited his expectation of privacy, the police may not dispense with the safeguards established by the Fourth Amendment. . . .

Our prior cases discussing searches based on third-party consent have never suggested that such searches are "reasonable." In *United States v. Matlock*, this Court upheld a warrantless search conducted pursuant to the consent of a third party who was living with the defendant. The Court rejected the defendant's challenge to the search, stating that a person who permits others to have "joint access or control for most purposes . . . assume[s] that the risk that [such persons] might permit the common area to be searched." [S]ee also *Frazier v. Cupp*, 394 U.S. 731, 740, 89 S.Ct. 1420, 1425, 22 L.Ed.2d 684 (1969) (holding that defendant who left a duffel bag at another's house and allowed joint use of the bag "assumed the risk that [the person] would allow someone else to look inside"). As the Court's assumption-of-risk analysis makes clear, third-party consent limits a person's ability to challenge the reasonableness of the search only because that person voluntarily has relinquished some of his expectation of privacy by sharing access or control over his property with another person.

A search conducted pursuant to an officer's reasonable but mistaken belief that a third party had authority to consent is thus on an entirely different constitutional footing from one based on the consent of a third party who in fact has such authority. Even if the officers reasonably believed that Fischer had authority to consent, she did not, and Rodriguez' expectation of privacy was therefore undiminished. Rodriguez accordingly can challenge the warrantless intrusion into his home as a violation of the Fourth Amendment. This conclusion flows directly from *Stoner v. California*, 376 U.S. 483, 84 S.Ct. 889, 11 L.Ed.2d 856 (1964). There, the Court required the

suppression of evidence seized in reliance on a hotel clerk's consent to a warrantless search of a guest's room. The Court reasoned that the guest's right to be free of unwarranted intrusion "was a right . . . which only [he] could waive by word or deed, either directly or through an agent." Accordingly, the Court rejected resort to "unrealistic doctrines of 'apparent authority'" as a means of upholding the search to which the guest had not consented. . . .

Our cases demonstrate that third-party consent searches are free from constitutional challenge only to the extent that they rest on consent by a party empowered to do so. The majority's conclusion to the contrary ignores the legitimate expectations of privacy on which individuals are entitled to rely. That a person who allows another joint access to his property thereby limits his expectation of privacy does not justify trampling the rights of a person who has not similarly relinquished any of his privacy expectation.

Instead of judging the validity of consent searches, as we have in the past, based on whether a defendant has in fact limited his expectation of privacy, the Court today carves out an additional exception to the warrant requirement for third-party consent searches without pausing to consider whether "'the exigencies of the situation' make the needs of law enforcement so compelling that the warrantless search is objectively reasonable under the Fourth Amendment," *Mincey*, 437 U.S., at 394, 98 S.Ct., at 2414. Where this free-floating creation of "reasonable" exceptions to the warrant requirement will end, now that the Court has departed from the balancing approach that has long been part of our Fourth Amendment jurisprudence, is unclear. But by allowing a person to be subjected to a warrantless search in his home without his consent and without exigency, the majority has taken away some of the liberty that the Fourth Amendment was designed to protect.

CASE DISCUSSION

What are the relevant facts in determining whether the search in this case was a lawful search? How does the majority define *third-party consent*? How does the dissent define it? Why did the Supreme Court hold that the consent of Fischer made the search of Rodriguez's apartment a lawful search? Do you agree that someone can consent for another even when the person giving consent does not have the authority to do so? Do you agree that if you share your property with someone else that you "assume the risk" that the other person may give the police permission to search the property?

What arguments does the dissent make to reject the validity of Fischer's consent to search Rodriguez's apartment? What interests does the majority favor? How would the dissent balance the interests differently? How would you balance the interests in the case?

D e c i s i o n   P o i n t

Which of the following third-party consents are valid?

1. One lover consents to a search of the room shared with the other lover.

2. One roommate consents to a search of an entire apartment, including the other roommate's separate bedroom.

3. A homeowner consents to a search of the room that a houseguest occupies.

4. One joint user of a duffel bag consents to a search of the shared duffel bag.

5. A high school principal consents to a search of high school students' lockers.

6. A college dean permits a search of students' rooms for marijuana.

Courts have upheld all of the above searches on grounds that the consenting party's consent was valid against the other person.[51]

Withdrawing Consent. What if I consent to a search of my house, but when the police come close to finding contraband, I say: "Stop the search. I have changed my mind"? A compelling argument holds that guilty persons will use consent to a search merely to throw police off the track by consenting and will then withdraw the consent if it looks as if the search will produce incriminating evidence, contraband, or weapons. Despite this argument, the Model Code of Pre-arraignment Procedure provides as follows:

> Section 24.3(3) Withdrawal or Limitation of Consent. A consent . . . may be withdrawn or limited at any time prior to the completion of the search, and if so withdrawn or limited, the search . . . shall cease, or be restricted to the new limits, as the case may be. Things discovered and subject to seizure prior to such withdrawal or limitation of consent shall remain subject to seizure despite such change or termination of the consent.[52]

Case authority on this point is limited and divided. In an old Kentucky case, the court ruled that consent once given could not be withdrawn. In a more recent California case, the court ruled that persons authorized to consent may withdraw the consent at any time.[53]

Exigent Circumstance Searches

Exigent circumstance searches, sometimes called emergency searches, are based on the idea that it would be impractical or even dangerous to require officers to obtain warrants before conducting searches. The danger might be to officers or other individuals, as we have seen in the frisk cases justifying pat-downs for weapons incident to lawful stops. Or the danger could be to evidence that suspects or others might destroy during the time it takes to obtain a search warrant. Or the danger might be to the community if fleeing felons escape while officers are trying to obtain search warrants.

Frisks. We have already examined the frisk, in which the reasonable suspicion that a lawfully stopped suspect is armed justifies a pat-down for weapons (see Chapter 4).

Hot Pursuit. Hot pursuit is a second exigent circumstances exception to the warrant requirement, created by the need to apprehend a fleeing suspect. If officers are chasing a suspect whom they have probable cause to arrest, they can follow the suspect into a house to search for the suspect. The scope of the search is only as broad as required to prevent the suspect from escaping or resisting. Therefore, officers cannot search every nook and cranny of a house simply because they entered lawfully in hot pursuit. For example, they cannot search dresser drawers for contraband. Nor can they search every room of a hotel because a robber entered the hotel.[54]

Destruction of Evidence. If police officers have probable cause to search and they reasonably believe that evidence is in imminent danger of destruction, they can search without a warrant. For example, in *Cupp v. Murphy* the Supreme Court held that the police who had probable cause to believe that Murphy had strangled his wife could, without a warrant, take scrapings of what looked like blood under Murphy's fingernails because Murphy knew the police suspected him and he had a motive to destroy the "evanescent" bloodstain evidence. In *Schmerber v. California*, the Supreme Court held that the exigent circumstance of rapidly declining blood alcohol levels justified taking a blood alcohol test without a warrant. And in *Ker v. California*, the Court held that a warrantless entry into a home was justified by the reasonable fear that Ker was about to destroy or hide marijuana.[55]

Danger to Officer. Police officers may also dispense with a warrant if they have probable cause to believe that a suspect has committed a violent crime or that the suspect or others might endanger officers and other citizens. Therefore, police officers could enter a private home to search for an armed robbery suspect and weapons because these could endanger the lives of officers and the general public. Police could enter and search a house in a highly residential area because they reasonably believed that guns and bombs were in the house. A warrantless search for drug dealers was reasonable because by closing the garage doors and dimming the lights, the drug dealers indicated that they knew the police were coming, thereby leading to the reasonable belief that the officers were in danger. It was also reasonable to enter a house without a warrant to search for a weapon when police found a dead body on the front porch.[56]

Other dangers to the public include fires and explosions. Police officers at the scene of a fire do not need a warrant to remain in a burned building long enough to look for possible injured victims and to investigate the cause of the fire or explosion. Once officers determine the cause of the fire, however, they must get a warrant to search for evidence of crime. Furthermore, they cannot enter simply because a possible fire or explosion might occur. For example, it was not reasonable for officers to enter a house where a suspect stored inherently dangerous chemicals because the officers knew that the suspect was not at home and that the chemicals had been stored in the house for at least two weeks.[57]

Disappearance of Suspect. Police officers can also dispense with a search warrant if they have reason to believe a suspect will flee the jurisdiction. However, officers may search only to the extent necessary to prevent the escape or the resistance of suspects. For example, an officer was not justified in searching when the officer knew the suspect was in custody and could not flee.

Vehicle Searches

The Supreme Court created the vehicle exception to the search warrant requirement during Prohibition in the 1920s, when cars were increasingly used in alcohol-related crimes. The landmark case, *Carroll v. United States* (1925), reflected a fear of alcohol-related crimes during the 1920s comparable to the fear of crack cocaine in the 1990s. In *Carroll*, federal agents stopped a car they had probable cause to believe contained illegal liquor. The officers had no warrant to search the car, but they thoroughly ransacked it. After ripping out the upholstery, they found illegal alcohol under the seat upholstery. Carroll moved to suppress the alcohol because the officers had searched the car without a warrant. Referring to the scourge of bootlegging and violent crime stemming from it, the Court upheld the search of the car without a warrant.[58]

The Court held that the mobility of automobiles made warrantless searches of cars reasonable as long as probable cause supported the searches. Later, the Court added a second rationale for making warrantless vehicle searches reasonable: individuals have a lesser expectation of privacy in vehicles. The mobility and reasonable-expectation-of-privacy rationales work well for ordinary cars, trucks, and vans. They become more difficult to sustain when applied to motor homes or hybrid vehicles like recreational vehicles (RVs), which are used for both transportation and temporary living. The Court addressed the question of searching these hybrid vehicles in *California v. Carney*.

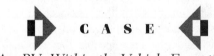

C A S E

Are RVs Within the Vehicle Exception?

California v. Carney
471 U.S. 386, 105 S.Ct. 2066,
85 L.Ed.2d 406 (1985)

After his motion to suppress evidence discovered in his motor home was denied, Charles Carney was convicted in a California superior court on a plea of nolo contendere. The California Court of Appeal affirmed. The

California Supreme Court reversed, holding that the search of the motor home was unreasonable because expectations of privacy in a motor home are more like those of a dwelling. On writ of certiorari, the United States Supreme Court reversed and remanded the case for further proceedings consistent with the Court's holding. The Supreme Court held that the warrantless search of Carney's motor home did not violate the

Fourth Amendment. Chief Justice Burger wrote the opinion of the Court, in which Justices White, Blackmun, Powell, Rehnquist, and O'Connor joined. Justice Stevens filed a dissenting opinion, in which Justices Brennan and Marshall joined.

FACTS

On May 31, 1979, Drug Enforcement Agency Agent Robert Williams watched respondent, Charles Carney, approach a youth in downtown San Diego. The youth accompanied Carney to a Dodge Mini Motor Home parked in a nearby lot. Carney and the youth closed the window shades in the motor home, including one across the front window. Agent Williams had previously received uncorroborated information that the same motor home was used by another person who was exchanging marihuana for sex. Williams, with assistance from other agents, kept the motor home under surveillance for the entire one and one-quarter hours that Carney and the youth remained inside. When the youth left the motor home, the agents followed and stopped him. The youth told the agents that he had received marihuana in return for allowing Carney sexual contacts.

At the officer's requests, the youth returned to the motor home and knocked on its door; Carney stepped out. The agents identified themselves as law enforcement officers. Without a warrant or consent, one agent entered the motor home and observed marihuana, plastic bags, and a scale of the kind used in weighing drugs on a table. Agent Williams took Carney into custody and took possession of the motor home. A subsequent search of the motor home at the police station revealed additional marihuana in the cupboards and refrigerator.

Respondent was charged with possession of marihuana for sale. At a preliminary hearing, he moved to suppress the evidence discovered in the motor home. The magistrate denied the motion. . . . Respondent renewed his suppression motion in the Superior Court. The Superior Court also rejected the claim. . . . Respondent then pleaded nolo contendere to the charges against him, and was placed on probation for three years. Respondent appealed from the order placing him on probation. The California Court of Appeal af-

firmed. . . . The California Supreme Court reversed the conviction. . . .

We granted certiorari. We reverse.

OPINION

. . . When a vehicle is being used on the highways, or if it is readily capable of such use and is found stationary in a place not regularly used for residential purposes — temporary or otherwise — the two justifications for the vehicle exception come into play. First, the vehicle is obviously readily mobile by the turn of the ignition key, if not actually moving. Second, there is a reduced expectation of privacy stemming from its use as a licensed motor vehicle subject to a range of police regulation inapplicable to a fixed dwelling. At least in these circumstances, the overriding societal interests in effective law enforcement justify an immediate search before the vehicle and its occupants become unavailable.

While it is true that respondent's vehicle possessed some, if not many of the attributes of a home, it is equally clear that the vehicle falls clearly within the scope of the exception . . . [R]espondent's motor home was readily mobile. Absent the prompt search and seizure, it could have readily been moved beyond the reach of the police. Furthermore, the vehicle was licensed to "operate on public streets; [was] serviced in public places; . . . and [was] subject to extensive regulation and inspection." And the vehicle was so situated that an objective observer would conclude that it was being used not as a residence but as a vehicle.

Respondent urges us to distinguish his vehicle from other vehicles within the exception because it was capable of functioning as a home. In our increasingly mobile society, many vehicles used for transportation can be and are being used not only for transportation but for shelter, i.e., as a "home" or "residence." To distinguish between respondent's motor home and an ordinary sedan for purposes of the vehicle exception would require that we apply the exception depending upon the size of the vehicle and the quality of its appointments. Moreover, to fail to apply the exception to vehicles such as a motor home ignores the fact that a motor home lends itself easily to use as an instrument of illegal drug traffic and other illegal activity. . . .

DISSENT

Justice Stevens, with whom Justice Brennan and Justice Marshall join, dissenting.

The character of "the place to be searched" plays an important role in Fourth Amendment analysis. In this case, police officers searched a Dodge/Midas Mini Motor Home. The California Supreme Court correctly characterized this vehicle as a "hybrid" which combines "the mobility attribute of an automobile . . . with most of the privacy characteristics of a house." . . .

When a motor home is parked in a location that is removed from the public highway, I believe that society is prepared to recognize that the expectations of privacy within it are not unlike the expectations one has in a fixed dwelling. . . .

Unlike a brick bungalow or a frame Victorian, a motor home seldom serves as a permanent lifetime abode. The motor home in this case, however, was designed to accommodate a breadth of ordinary living. Photographs in the record indicate that its height, length, and beam provided substantial living space inside: stuffed chairs surround a table; cupboards provide room for storage of personal effects; bunk beds provide sleeping space; and a refrigerator provides ample storage for food and beverages. Moreover, curtains and large opaque walls inhibit viewing the activities inside from the exterior of the vehicle. The interior configuration of the motor home establishes that the vehicle's size, shape, and mode of construction should have indicated to the officers that it was a vehicle containing mobile living quarters.

The State contends that officers in the field will have an impossible task determining whether or not other vehicles contain mobile living quarters. It is not necessary for the Court to resolve every unanswered question in this area in a single case, but common English usage suggests that we already distinguish between a "motor home" which is "equipped as a self-contained traveling home," a "camper" which is only equipped for "casual traveling and camping," and an automobile which is "designed for passenger transportation." Surely the exteriors of these vehicles contain clues about their different functions which could alert officers in the field to the necessity of a warrant.

CASE DISCUSSION

Why did the Court hold that Charles Carney had no more expectation of privacy in his motor home than he would have in an ordinary car? Do you agree? What facts does the dissent stress to demonstrate Carney's expectation of privacy that society should recognize? Do you agree? Reconsider *Carroll v. United States.* Do you think that the Court's reasoning in that case applies here? What interest does the majority promote in *California v. Carney?* What interests does the dissent promote? Which would you promote? And how would you decide the case?

The authority to search vehicles without warrants does not include the power to search drivers and passengers inside vehicles. The reporters for the Model Code of Prearraignment Procedure disputed this rule, arguing that it was "absurd to say that [before police begin to search the vehicle,] the occupants can take the narcotics out of the glove compartment and stuff them in their pockets, and drive happily away after the vehicle has been fruitlessly searched."[59] To avoid this "absurdity," the Model Code provides as follows:

> Section 260.3 (2) Searches of the Occupants. If the officer does not find the things subject to seizure by his search of the vehicle, and if
> (a) the things subject to seizure are of such a size and nature that they could be concealed on the person, and

(b) the officer has reason to suspect that one or more of the occupants of the vehicle may have the things subject to seizure so concealed, the officer may search the suspected occupants. . . .[60]

Container Searches

People have a reasonable expectation of privacy in their briefcases, purses, luggage, and other containers where they store personal papers that they wish to keep from public scrutiny. The expectation of privacy in personal containers is less than that in homes but more than that in vehicles. Therefore, in ordinary circumstances the police need a warrant and probable cause to search containers. In special circumstances the police may seize and search containers without warrants. When police have reasonable suspicion that containers contain evidence of crime, they can briefly detain the containers to prevent their loss or destruction, but they cannot search them without a warrant supported by probable cause. Consequently, it was reasonable for police officers to detain luggage on reasonable suspicion of drug trafficking where the detention lasted only twenty-five minutes, the suspect was free to go, and the luggage was subjected only to a dog sniff.[61]

The police may not only seize but they may also search containers when they have probable cause to believe that containers in vehicles contain evidence of crime. Until 1990, the Supreme Court had held that the police could search containers in vehicles only if they had probable cause to search the vehicle itself. If they had probable cause only to search the container, the Fourth Amendment required a warrant. In *California v. Acevedo*, the Court resolved this anomaly. The police observed Acevedo leave an apartment known to contain marijuana. He was carrying a brown paper bag the size of bags containing marijuana that the police had seen earlier. Acevedo put the bag in the trunk of his car. As he drove away, the police stopped his car, opened the trunk, and opened the bag. The bag contained marijuana. Overruling its earlier holdings, the Court held that when the police have probable cause to believe a container holds evidence of crime and that container is in a vehicle, they can search the container without a warrant. The Court reasoned that the recognized and important privacy interest in luggage must give way to the "broad scope of the automobile search." The risk that the mobility of the car might result in the loss of the marijuana and Acevedo's conviction outweighed Acevedo's expectation of privacy in the brown paper bag.[62]

SUMMARY

The Fourth Amendment protects the "people" against "unreasonable searches." Not all intrusions on privacy are searches, and many searches are reasonable. Therefore, analyzing government intrusions for purposes of the Fourth Amendment requires the answer to two questions:

1. Is the intrusion a search at all?

2. If it is a search, is it unreasonable?

Although it is nowhere mentioned in the Constitution, the Supreme Court has ruled that the Fourth Amendment protects privacy, specifically a person's reasonable expectation of privacy that society is prepared to recognize. Analysis of Fourth Amendment searches requires answering a third question: If the search is unreasonable, what is the remedy against the government for conducting illegal searches? The answer to this question is postponed until Chapter 10.

The Supreme Court relies on the reasonableness clause of the Fourth Amendment in balancing people's reasonable expectation of privacy against legitimate government needs, such as ensuring effective law enforcement, protecting the police, controlling the police, protecting public health and safety, and regulating public institutions such as schools, jails, and prisons. The outcome of the balance is that some invasions on privacy, such as searches of what the unaided senses perceive or of open fields or public places or abandoned property, are not searches at all. According to the Supreme Court, society is not prepared to recognize Fourth Amendment protection in these circumstances. The Fourth Amendment prohibits only unreasonable searches. The elements in determining reasonableness include the following:

1. Whether agents obtained a warrant that was based on probable cause and specifically identified the persons or places to be searched or both and the persons or things to be seized
2. Whether a recognized exception justifies a search without a warrant
3. Whether a search without a warrant requires probable cause, a lesser quantum of proof, or no individualized suspicion at all to support it

The principal recognized exceptions to the warrant requirement include these:

1. Searches incident to lawful arrests
2. Exigent circumstances, such as hot pursuit, possible destruction of evidence, possible danger to officers and others, and suspects who may flee the jurisdiction
3. Reduced expectation of privacy searches, such as searches of vehicles and searches of containers
4. Consent searches
5. Inventory searches
6. Inspections and regulatory searches

The administrative searches, directed mainly at persons not suspected of crime, offer less protection against government intrusion under the Fourth Amendment than that amendment affords criminal suspects in criminal law enforcement.

REVIEW QUESTIONS

1. What is the particularity requirement?
2. Under what circumstances may officers execute a search warrant without announcing their entry?
3. What are the two major purposes of warrantless searches incident to lawful arrests?
4. What are pretext searches, and what are the arguments for and against them?
5. Explain the "would" and "could" tests regarding pretext searches.

6. Explain the voluntariness and waiver tests for consent searches. Which test do you think is better? Give reasons for your answer.
7. Under what circumstances should third-party consent be permitted? Explain your answer.
8. What two major reasons justify warrantless searches of vehicles?
9. Under what circumstances should motor homes be considered vehicles? Why?

KEY TERMS

exigent circumstances circumstances requiring prompt action that eliminates the warrant requirement.

hot pursuit the exigent circumstance constituting the need to apprehend a fleeing suspect.

knock and announce rule the practice of law enforcement officers knocking and announcing their presence before entering a home to search it.

mere evidence rule the precept that the seizure of evidence that is not stolen property or contraband does not violate the Fourth Amendment.

pretext search a search that is made subsequent to an arrest for one crime but is motivated by the desire to search for evidence of another.

return of warrant the act of filing a search warrant with the court that issued it.

search incident to arrest a search made of a lawfully arrested suspect without probable cause or warrant.

voluntariness test a test in which the totality of circumstances is used to determine whether a consent to search was obtained without coercion, deception, or promises.

waiver test a test in which consent is based only on a knowing, specific, and intelligent waiver of a specific right.

Notes

1. Jeffrey D. Hockett, "Justice Robert H. Jackson, the Supreme Court, and the Nuremberg Trial," *The Supreme Court Review, 1990* (Chicago: University of Chicago Press, 1991), 257–99.

2. *Brinegar v. United States*, 338 U.S. 160, 69 S.Ct. 1302, 93 L.Ed. 1879 (1949), 180; for a more recent statement to the same effect, see John Wesley Hall, Jr., *Search and Seizure*, 2d ed. (Deerfield, IL: Clark Boardman, 1991), ix.

3. *Tomblin v. State*, 128 Ga.App. 823, 198 S.E.2d 366 (1973) (apartment 8-B); *United States v. Busk*, 693 F.2d 28 (3rd Cir. 1982); for many more examples of particularity of place, see *Georgetown Law Journal Project: Criminal Procedure* 75 (1997): 836, nn. 75–76.

4. *United States v. Fawole*, 785 F.2d 1141 (4th Cir. 1986) (address books, etc.); *United States v. Washington*, 782 F.2d 807 (9th Cir. 1986) (items related to prostitution); for more examples, see *Georgetown Law Journal Project: Criminal Procedure* 75 (1987): 735, nn. 137–40.

5. *State v. Lindsey*, 473 N.W.2d 857 (Minn. 1991).

6. For example, Rule 41 (c) (1), tit. U.S.C.A. (May 1, 1987).

7. Ibid.; definition of *daytime* is in Rule 41 (h).

8. *United States v. Gervato*, 474 F.2d 40 (3rd Cir. 1973); *Payne v. United States*, 508 F.2d 1391 (5th Cir. 1975).

9. *United States v. Micheli*, 487 F.2d 429 (1st Cir. 1973).

10. Ibid.

11. *Harris v. United States*, 331 U.S. 145, 67 S.Ct. 1098, 91 L.Ed. 1399 (1947).

12. 255 U.S. 298, 41 S.Ct. 261, 65 L.Ed. 647 (1920); Galloway, "The Intruding Eye: A Status Report on the Constitutional Ban Against Paper Searches," *Howard Law Journal* 25 (1982): 367.

13. 387 U.S. 294, 87 S.Ct. 1642, 18 L.Ed.2d 782 (1967).

14. American Law Institute, *Model Code of Pre-arraignment Procedure* (Philadelphia: American Law Institute, 1975), 505.

15. Wayne R. LaFave and Jerold H. Israel, *Criminal Procedure* (St. Paul: West Publishing Co., 1984), 1: 178–79.

16. *Wilson v. Arkansas*, 115 S.Ct. 1914 (1995).

17. *Wilson v. Arkansas*, 115 S.Ct. 1914 (U.S. 1995).

18. Ibid.

19. Ibid.

20. 1997 WL 202007 (U.S.).

21. Ibid.

22. Ibid.

23. Ibid.

24. *Federal Rules of Criminal Procedure*, Rule 41.

25. James B. Haddad, "Well-Delineated Exceptions, Claims of Sham, and Fourfold Probable Cause," *Journal of Criminal Law and Criminology* 68 (1977): 198–225; Paul Sutton, "The Fourth Amendment in Action: An Empirical View of the Search Warrant Process," *Criminal Law Bulletin* 22 (1986): 405–29.

26. Craig M. Bradley, "Two Models of the Fourth Amendment," *Michigan Law Review* 83 (1985): 1468, 1475.

27. Sutton, "The Fourth Amendment in Action," 411.

28. Ibid., 415.

29. Lawrence P. Tiffany, Donald McIntyre, Jr., and Daniel L. Rotenberg, *Detection of Crime: Stopping and Questioning, Search and Seizure, Encouragement, and Entrapment* (Boston: Little, Brown, 1967), 122–23.

30. Catherine Hancock, "State Court Activism and Searches Incident to Arrest," *Virginia Law Review* 68 (1982): 1085.

31. Wayne R. LaFave, "Police Rule Making and the Fourth Amendment," in Lloyd E. Ohlin and Frank J. Remington, eds., *Discretion in Criminal Justice* (Albany: State University of New York Press, 1993), 243.

32. *Cupp v. Murphy*, 412 U.S. 291, 93 S.Ct. 2000, 36 L.Ed.2d 900 (1973) (fingernail scraping); *United States v. Edwards*, 415 U.S. 800, 94 S.Ct. 1234, 39 L.Ed.2d 771 (1974).

33. Both reported in the *Criminal Law Reporter* 45 (May 3, 1989): 1017.

34. *United States v. Robinson*, 414 U.S. 218, 234–35, 94 S.Ct. 467, 476–77, 38 L.Ed.2d 427 (1973) (excerpted in Chapter 2).

35. Barry Latzer, *State Constitutions and Criminal Justice* (Westport, CT: Greenwood, 1991), 64.

36. *Zehrung v. State*, 569 P.2d 189 (Alaska 1977).

37. David A. Harriss, "'Driving While Black' and All other Traffic Offenses: The Supreme Court and Pretextual Traffic Stops," *Journal of Criminal Law and Criminology* 87 (1997): 544, 559–60.

38. Daniel S. Jonas, "Comment, Pretextual Searches and the Fourth Amendment: Unconstitutional Abuses of Power," *University of Pennsylvania Law Review* 137 (1989): 1792.

39. For another example of a pretext search, see *United States v. Trigg*, 925 F.2d 1064 (7th Cir. 1991), cert. denied, 502 U.S. 962, 112 S.Ct. 428, 116 L.Ed.2d 449 (1991).

40. *Petitioner's Brief*, U.S.S.Ct., February 16, 1996, 24–27, 1996 WL 75758.

41. Tiffany and others, *Detection of Crime*, 131.

42. Lloyd Weinreb, "Generalities of the Fourth Amendment," *University of Chicago Law Review* 47 (1974): 57–58; Tiffany and others, *Detection of Crime*, 157–61; John Wesley Hall, Jr., *Search and Seizure*, 382; Wayne R. LaFave, *Search and Seizure*, 2d ed. (St. Paul: West Publishing Company, 1987, 1993), 3: 147–49.

43. *United States v. Blake*, 718 F.Supp. 925, 927 (S.D.Fla. 1988).

44. *Florida v. Jimeno*, 500 U.S. 248, 248–49, 111 S.Ct 1801, 1802, 114 L.Ed.2d 297 (1991), 1802.

45. *United States v. Vasquez*, 858 F.2d 1387 (9th Cir. 1988).

46. *United States v. Rambo*, 789 F.2d 1289 (8th Cir. 1986).

47. *United States v. Ceballos*, 812 F.2d 42 (2d Cir. 1987).

48. *Florida v. Jimeno*, 500 U.S. 248, 111 S.Ct. 1801, 114 L.Ed.2d 297 (1991).

49. *State v. Gonzalez-Valle*, 385 So.2d 681 (Fla.App. 1980) (motive of spite vitiated consent); *Commonwealth v. Martin*, 358 Mass. 282, 264 N.E.2d 366 (1970) (amicable relations not relevant if people are living together); *United States v. DiPrima*, 472 F.2d 550 (1st Cir. 1973) (parent consent for child); also *State v. Kinderman*, 271 Minn. 405, 136 N.W. 577 (1965) (father consented to searching twenty-two-year-old son's room who lived at home in house father owned).

50. *Gillard v. Schmidt*, 579 F.2d 825 (3rd Cir. 1978) (psychological profiles in locked desk); *Commonwealth v. Glover*, 266 Pa.Super. 531, 405 A.2d 945 (1979) (search of workbench top).

51. *United States v. Matlock*, 415 U.S. 164, 94 S.Ct. 988, 39 L.Ed.2d 242 (1974) (lover's consent to search of shared bedroom); *United States v. Cataldo*, 433 F.2d 38 (2d Cir. 1970) (roommate's consent to search of separate bedroom); *Frazier v. Cupp*, 394 U.S. 731, 89 S. Ct. 1420, 22 L.Ed.2d 684 (1969) (shared duffel bag); *New Jersey v. T.L.O.*, 469 U.S. 325, 105 S.Ct. 733, 83 L.Ed.2d 720 (1985) (high school); *Piazzola v. Watkins*, 442 F.2d 284 (5th Cir. 1971) (dormitory rooms in college).

52. American Law Institute, *Model Code of Pre-arraignment Procedure*, 151; for discussion of arguments for and against allowing withdrawal of consent, ibid., 538.

53. *Smith v. Commonwealth*, 197 Ky. 192, 246 S.W. 449 (1923); *People v. Martinez*, 259 Cal.App.2d Supp. 943, 65 Cal.Rptr. 920 (1968).

54. *United States v. Santana*, 427 U.S. 38, 96 S.Ct, 2406, 49 L.Ed.2d 300 (1976); *Warden v. Hayden*, 387 U.S. 294, 87 S.Ct. 1642, 18 L.Ed.2d 782 (1967); *United States v. Winsor*, 846 F.2d 1569 (9th Cir. 1988) *(en banc)*.

55. *Cupp v. Murphy*, 412 U.S. 291, 93 S.Ct. 2000, 36 L.Ed.2d 900 (1973); *Schmerber v. California*, 384 U.S. 757, 86 S.Ct. 1826, 16 L.Ed.2d 908 (1966); *Ker v. California*, 374 U.S. 23, 83 S.Ct. 1623, 10 L.Ed.2d 726 (1963).

56. *Warden v. Hayden*, 387 U.S. 294, 87 S.Ct. 1642, 18 L.Ed.2d 782 (1967); *United States v. Lindsey*, 877 F.2d 777 (9th Cir. 1989); *United States v. Chavez*, 812 F.2d 1295 (10th Cir. 1987); *United States v. Doe*, 819 F.2d 206 (9th Cir. 1985).

57. *Michigan v. Clifford*, 464 U.S. 287, 104 S.Ct. 641, 78 L.Ed.2d 477 (1984) (plurality opinion); *United States v. Warner*, 843 F.2d 401 (9th Cir. 1988).

58. 267 U.S. 132, 45 S.Ct. 280, 69 L.Ed. 543 (1925).

59. *United States v. Di Re*, 332 U.S. 581, 68 S.Ct. 222, 92 L.Ed. 210 (1948); American Law Institute, *Model Code of Pre-arraignment Procedure*, 552.

60. American Law Institute, *Model Code of Pre-arraignment Procedure*, 163.

61. *United States v. Teslim*, 869 F.2d 316 (7th Cir. 1989).

62. *California v. Acevedo*, 500 U.S. 565, 111 S.Ct. 1982, 114 L.Ed.2d 619 (1991).

CHAPTER SEVEN

Special Needs Searches

CHAPTER OUTLINE

1. The Fourth Amendment protects the "people" generally, not just those in criminal cases, against "unreasonable searches and seizures."

2. The Supreme Court has adopted the balancing approach to determine the reasonableness of "special needs searches."

3. The balancing approach to reasonableness depends on weighing the totality of the circumstances on a case-by-case basis.

4. Special needs searches can be reasonable without either warrants or probable cause.

5. Inventory searches are reasonable without either warrants or probable cause if they follow established procedures.

6. Border searches are reasonable without either warrants or probable cause if the special need to protect the integrity of international borders outweighs the invasion of privacy of individuals.

7. Airport electronic searches are reasonable without either warrants or probable cause because the special need to prevent terrorism outweighs the minimal invasion of privacy in passing through the electronic metal-detecting devices.

8. Prisoners retain only a minimal right to privacy against searches made without either warrants or probable cause for the purposes of discipline, safety, and security.

9. Probationers and parolees retain a minimal interest in privacy against searches.

10. Employees of and visitors to prisons and jails have a reduced expectation of privacy weighed against the special needs of correctional facilities to maintain safety and security.

11. Students retain their Fourth Amendment rights, but if the special need of school administrators to conduct searches for the purposes of promoting learning and maintaining discipline and order outweighs the individual invasions of privacy, then searches of students are reasonable without either warrants or probable cause.

12. Random drug testing of employees constitutes a reasonable search because the special need of government to protect public safety outweighs the minimal invasion of privacy caused by collecting and analyzing urine samples.

13. In inspections and regulatory searches, the constitutionality of the intrusion depends on balancing the special government need to further a legitimate government interest against the privacy interests of innocent citizens who are not suspected of crimes.

Were the Searches "Reasonable"?

Mary Beth G. and Sharon N. were stopped for traffic violations; they were arrested and taken to detention centers because there were outstanding parking tickets against their cars. They were subjected to the strip search policy of the city of Chicago. That policy, as described by the city, required each woman placed in detention facilities of the Chicago Police Department and searched by female personnel to lift her blouse or sweater and unhook and lift her brassiere to allow a visual inspection of the breast area, to replace these articles of clothing and then pull up her skirt or dress or lower her pants and pull down any undergarments, to squat two or three times facing the detention aide, and to bend over at the waist to permit visual inspection of the vaginal and anal area. The city claimed that all searches were conducted in a closed room away from the view of all persons except the person conducting the search. The strip search policy was not applied to males. Men were searched thoroughly by hand. The male detainee would place his hands against the wall and stand normally while the searching officer, with his fingers, would go through the hair, into the ears, down the back, under the armpits, down both arms, down the legs, into the groin area, and up the front. The officer would also search the waistband and require the detainee to remove his shoes and sometimes his socks.

"SPECIAL NEEDS" SEARCHES

The Fourth Amendment refers to the right of the *people* against unreasonable searches. That is, the right against unreasonable searches and seizures is not limited to criminal suspects but extends to all people, even those who are completely beyond suspicion of criminal behavior. The other rights affecting the law of criminal procedure are more specific. They direct their protection to criminal cases, suspects, and defendants. For example, the Fifth Amendment right against self-incrimination refers to "criminal case[s]"; the Sixth Amendment right to counsel refers to "criminal prosecution[s]."

The Supreme Court has applied the Fourth Amendment to a wide range of **"special needs" searches**—government inspections and other regulatory measures. Although these searches may incidentally relate to criminal law enforcement, their primary purpose extends beyond the gathering and use of evidence in criminal cases. Special needs searches include the following types of government actions:

- Inspections and regulations at international borders
- Building inspections for health and safety
- Safety checks of vehicles on public highways
- Airport searches of passengers
- Searches of prisoners, probationers, and parolees
- Searches of employees and visitors to jails and prisons
- Searches of students and their lockers
- Drug testing of employees

The public needs for these searches go beyond criminal law enforcement. They are directed at public health and safety, and at the smooth and efficient administration of public agencies. The great variety of activities covered by special needs searches and the various purposes for them should not obscure the following elements that they have in common:

- They are directed primarily at people generally, not specific individuals suspected of crime.
- Although their primary purpose is regulation and administration, they can and do result in criminal prosecution and conviction.
- They do not require warrants.
- They do not require probable cause.
- Their reasonableness depends on balancing special government needs beyond criminal law enforcement against the privacy of individuals not suspected of crime.

Inspection and regulatory searches ordinarily require a lower standard of reasonableness than do searches for evidence of crime. Except for searches incident to arrest and consent searches, all searches for criminal evidence require at least probable cause and (according to the strong preference in the rhetoric of the Supreme Court) warrants. Inspections and regulatory searches, on the other hand, are reasonable without either probable cause or warrants. The Supreme Court has adopted the balancing approach to special needs searches. The public interest in regulation, health, safety, efficiency, and order rests on one side of the balance. On the other side is the invasion of individual privacy caused by the searches. If the totality of the circumstances of a specific case shows that the special needs of the government outweigh the invasions of individual privacy, then the search is reasonable. Ironically, the removal of the warrant and probable cause requirements from the determination of the reasonableness of inspection and regulatory searches ensures that innocent people get less protection from government invasions of privacy and property than the Fourth Amendment guarantees to criminal suspects in searches for evidence of crimes.

INVENTORY SEARCHES

Inventory searches consist of compiling lists of property in government custody. Impounded vehicles are the most common subject of inventory searches. Ordinarily, inventory searches of vehicles extend to inventories of the contents of closed containers inside of vehicles. Inventory searches also include inventories of purses, backpacks, and other containers that detained people bring with them into jails and other detention facilities. The United States Supreme Court has ruled that inventory searches are Fourth Amendment searches. However, the Court has also decided that inventory searches require neither probable cause nor warrants because they are not conducted for the purpose of criminal investigation. Inventory searches are conducted for three purposes:

1. To protect the property of the owners while it is in police custody

2. To protect law enforcement officers against lawsuits claiming the loss, destruction, or theft of property

3. To protect law enforcement officers, detained suspects, and offenders from danger[1]

The objective basis for inventory searches consists of following routine procedures in compiling the inventory. Therefore, inventory searches are reasonable only if they are conducted according to procedures established, approved, and put in writing by the appropriate law enforcement agency. This requirement reduces the chances that inventory searches will be used as pretexts for rummaging through the private belongings of individuals without search warrants. Despite the established written procedure requirement, law enforcement officers retain considerable discretion in conducting inventory searches. For example, in *Colorado v. Bertine*, one of the few United States Supreme Court cases involving inventory searches, a police officer decided to impound a van instead of allowing the owner, arrested for drunk driving, to have the van picked up. The police department did not prescribe rules to guide officers' discretion in such situations. During an inventory of the contents of a backpack found in the impounded vehicle, the police discovered cocaine. The United States Supreme Court held that the discretion left to the officer did not violate the requirement of established procedures for inventory searches, because the purpose of the inventory was not to conduct a criminal investigation.[2]

Discretion in conducting inventory searches is allowed. However, in the absence of probable cause, law enforcement officers cannot use inventory searches as pretexts for searches for incriminating evidence. The United States Supreme Court sharply distinguished searches incident to pretext arrests where probable cause exists from inventory searches in which there is no probable cause. Without probable cause, inventory searches must not be a ruse for a general rummaging in order to discover incriminating evidence. The policy or practice governing inventory searches should be designed to produce an inventory. The individual police officer must not be allowed so much latitude that inventory searches are turned into "a purposeful and general means of discovering evidence of crime."[3]

The United States Supreme Court determined the reasonableness of inventory searches in *South Dakota v. Opperman.*

C A S E

Was the Inventory Search Reasonable?

South Dakota v. Opperman
428 U.S. 364, 96 S.Ct. 3092,
49 L.Ed.2d 1000 (1976)

Opperman was convicted in a South Dakota court of possession of less than one ounce of marijuana, and he appealed. The South Dakota Supreme Court reversed, and certiorari *was granted. The Supreme Court reversed and remanded. Chief Justice Burger wrote the opinion of the Court. Justice Powell filed a concurring opinion. Justice Marshall, with whom Justices Brennan, White, and Stewart joined, dissented. Justice White filed a dissenting statement.*

FACTS

Local ordinances prohibit parking in certain areas of downtown Vermillion, S.D., between the hours of 2 A.M. and 6 A.M. During the early morning hours of December 10, 1973, a Vermillion police officer observed respondent's unoccupied vehicle illegally parked in the restricted zone. At approximately 3 A.M., the officer issued an overtime parking ticket and placed it on the car's windshield. The citation warned: "Vehicles in violation of any parking ordinance may be towed from the area."

At approximately 10 o'clock on the same morning, another officer issued a second ticket for an overtime parking violation. These circumstances were routinely reported to police headquarters, and after the vehicle was inspected, the car was towed to the city impound lot.

From outside the car at the impound lot, a police officer observed a watch on the dashboard and other items of personal property located on the back seat and back floorboard. At the officer's direction, the car door was then unlocked and, using a standard inventory form pursuant to standard police procedures, the officer inventoried the contents of the car, including the contents of the glove compartment which was unlocked. There he found marihuana contained in a plastic bag. All items, including the contraband, were removed to the police department for safekeeping.

[COURT NOTE: At respondent's trial, the officer who conducted the inventory testified as follows: Q. "And why did you inventory this car?" A. "Mainly for safekeeping, because we have had a lot of trouble in the past of people getting into the impound lot and breaking into cars and stealing stuff out of them." Q. "Do you know whether the vehicles that were broken into . . . were locked or unlocked?" A. "Both of them were locked, they would be locked." In describing the impound lot, the officer stated: A. "It's the old county highway yard. It has a wooden fence partially around part of it, and kind of a dilapidated wire fence, a makeshift fence."]

During the late afternoon of December 10, respondent appeared at the police department to claim his property. The marihuana was retained by police.

Respondent was subsequently arrested on charges of possession of marihuana. His motion to suppress the evidence yielded by the inventory search was denied; he was convicted after a jury trial and sentenced to a fine of $100 and 14 days incarceration in the county jail. On appeal, the Supreme Court of South Dakota reversed the conviction. The court concluded that the evidence had been obtained in violation of the Fourth Amendment prohibition against unreasonable searches and seizures. We granted certiorari, and we reverse.

OPINION

This Court has traditionally drawn a distinction between automobiles and homes or offices in relation to the Fourth Amendment. . . . [W]arrantless examinations of automobiles have been upheld in circumstances in which a search of a home or office would not. The reason for this well-settled distinction is twofold. First, the inherent mobility of automobiles creates circumstances of such exigency that, as a practical necessity, rigorous enforcement of the warrant requirement is impossible. But the Court has also upheld warrantless searches where no immediate danger was presented that the car would be removed from the jurisdiction.

Besides the element of mobility, less rigorous warrant requirements govern because the expectation of privacy with respect to one's automobile is significantly less than that relating to one's home or office. In discharging their varied responsibilities for ensuring the public safety, law enforcement officials are necessarily brought into frequent contact with automobiles. Most of this contact is distinctly non criminal in nature. Automobiles, unlike homes, are subjected to pervasive and continuing governmental regulation and controls, including periodic inspection and licensing requirements. . . .

The expectation of privacy as to automobiles is further diminished by the obviously public nature of automobile travel. Only two Terms ago, the Court noted: "One has a lesser expectation of privacy in a motor vehicle because its function is transportation and it seldom serves as one's residence or as the repository of personal effects. . . . A car has little capacity for escaping public scrutiny. It travels public thoroughfares where both its occupants and its contents are in plain view." *Cardwell v. Lewis*, 417 U.S., at 590, 94 S.Ct. at 2469.

In the interests of public safety and as part of what the Court has called "community caretaking func-

tions," *Cady v. Dombrowski*, 413 U.S. at 441, 93 S.Ct at 2528, automobiles are frequently taken into police custody. Vehicle accidents present one such occasion. To permit the uninterrupted flow of traffic and in some circumstances to preserve evidence, disabled or damaged vehicles will often be removed from the highways or streets at the behest of police engaged solely in caretaking and traffic-control activities. Police will also frequently remove and impound automobiles which violate parking ordinances and which thereby jeopardize both the public safety and the efficient movement of vehicular traffic. The authority of police to seize and remove from the streets vehicles impeding traffic or threatening public safety and convenience is beyond challenge.

When vehicles are impounded, local police departments generally follow a routine practice of securing and inventorying the automobiles' contents. These procedures developed in response to three distinct needs: the protection of the owner's property while it remains in police custody, the protection of the police against claims or disputes over lost or stolen property, and the protection of the police from potential danger. The practice has been viewed as essential to respond to incidents of theft or vandalism. In addition, police frequently attempt to determine whether a vehicle has been stolen and thereafter abandoned.

These caretaking procedures have almost uniformly been upheld by the state courts, which by virtue of the localized nature of traffic regulation have had considerable occasion to deal with the issue. . . . The majority of the Federal Courts of Appeals have likewise sustained inventory procedures as reasonable police intrusions. As Judge Wisdom has observed: "(W)hen the police take custody of any sort of container (such as) an automobile . . . it is reasonable to search the container to itemize the property to be held by the police. (This reflects) the underlying principle that the fourth amendment proscribes only unreasonable searches." *United States v. Gravitt*, 484 F.2d 375, 378 (CA5 1973), cert. denied, 414 U.S. 1135, 94 S.Ct. 879, 38 L.Ed.2d 761 (1974). These cases have recognized that standard inventories often include an examination of the glove compartment, since it is a customary place for documents of ownership and registration, as well as a place for the temporary storage of valuables. . . . In applying the reasonableness standard adopted by the Framers, this Court has consistently sustained police intrusions into automobiles impounded or otherwise in lawful police custody where the process is aimed at securing or protecting the car and its contents. . . . "It would be unreasonable to hold that the police, having to retain the car in their custody for such a length of time, had no right, even for their own protection, to search it." 386 U.S., at 61–62, 87 S.Ct. at 791.

. . .

The Vermillion police were indisputably engaged in a caretaking search of a lawfully impounded automobile. The inventory was conducted only after the car had been impounded for multiple parking violations. The owner, having left his car illegally parked for an extended period, and thus subject to impoundment, was not present to make other arrangements for the safekeeping of his belongings. The inventory itself was prompted by the presence in plain view of a number of valuables inside the car. As in *Cady*, there is no suggestion whatever that this standard procedure, essentially like that followed throughout the country, was a pretext concealing an investigatory police motive.

[COURT NOTE: The inventory was not unreasonable in scope. Respondent's motion to suppress in state court challenged the inventory only as to items inside the car not in plain view. But once the policeman was lawfully inside the car to secure the personal property in plain view, it was not unreasonable to open the unlocked glove compartment, to which vandals would have had ready and unobstructed access once inside the car. The "consent" theory advanced by the dissent rests on the assumption that the inventory is exclusively for the protection of the car owner. It is not. The protection of the municipality and public officers from claims of lost or stolen property and the protection of the public from vandals who might find a firearm, or as here, contraband drugs, are also crucial.]

On this record we conclude that in following standard police procedures, prevailing throughout the country and approved by the overwhelming majority of courts, the conduct of the police was not "unreasonable" under the Fourth Amendment.

The judgment of the South Dakota Supreme Court is therefore reversed, and the case is remanded for further proceedings not inconsistent with this opinion. Reversed and remanded.

DISSENT

Justice Marshall, joined by Justices Brennan and Stewart, dissenting.

. . .

. . . [T]he Court appears to suggest by reference to a "diminished" expectation of privacy, that a person's constitutional interest in protecting the integrity of closed compartments of his locked automobile may routinely be sacrificed to governmental interests requiring interference with that privacy that are less compelling than would be necessary to justify a search of similar scope of the person's home or office. This has never been the law. . . . While it may be that privacy expectations associated with automobile travel are in some regard less than those associated with a home or office, it is equally clear that "(t)he word 'automobile' is not a talisman in whose presence the Fourth Amendment fades away . . . ," *Coolidge v. New Hampshire*, 403 U.S. 443, 461, 91 S.Ct. 2022, 2035, 29 L.Ed.2d 564 (1971).

[COURT NOTE: It would be wholly unrealistic to say that there is no reasonable and actual expectation in maintaining the privacy of closed compartments of a locked automobile, when it is customary for people in this day to carry their most personal and private papers and effects in their automobiles from time to time.]

The Court's opinion appears to suggest that its result may in any event be justified because the inventory search procedure is a "reasonable" response to "three distinct needs: the protection of the owner's property while it remains in police custody . . . ; the protection of the police against claims or disputes over lost or stolen property . . . ; and the protection of the police from potential danger."

This suggestion is flagrantly misleading, however, because the record of this case explicitly belies any relevance of the last two concerns. In any event it is my view that none of these "needs," separately or together, can suffice to justify the inventory search procedure approved by the Court.

First, this search cannot be justified in any way as a safety measure, for though the Court ignores it the sole purpose given by the State for the Vermillion police's inventory procedure was to secure valuables. . . . Even aside from the actual basis for the police practice in this case, however, I do not believe that any blanket safety argument could justify a program of routine searches of the scope permitted here. . . .

Second, the Court suggests that the search for valuables in the closed glove compartment might be justified as a measure to protect the police against lost property claims. Again, this suggestion is belied by the record, since although the Court declines to discuss it the South Dakota Supreme Court's interpretation of state law explicitly absolves the police, as "gratuitous depositors," from any obligation beyond inventorying objects in plain view and locking the car. . . .

Finally, the Court suggests that the public interest in protecting valuables that may be found inside a closed compartment of an impounded car may justify the inventory procedure. I recognize the genuineness of this governmental interest in protecting property from pilferage. But even if I assume that the posting of a guard would be fiscally impossible as an alternative means to the same protective end, I cannot agree with the Court's conclusion. The Court's result authorizes, indeed it appears to require, the routine search of nearly every car impounded. In my view, the Constitution does not permit such searches as a matter of routine; absent specific consent, such a search is permissible only in exceptional circumstances of particular necessity. . . .

Because the record in this case shows that the procedures followed by the Vermillion police in searching respondent's car fall far short of these standards, in my view the search was impermissible and its fruits must be suppressed. First, so far as the record shows, the police in this case had no reason to believe that the glove compartment of the impounded car contained particular property of any substantial value. Moreover, the owner had apparently thought it adequate to protect whatever he left in the car overnight on the street in a business area simply to lock the car, and there is nothing in the record to show that the impoundment lot would prove a less secure location against pilferage, particularly when it would seem likely that the owner would claim his car and its contents promptly, at least if it contained valuables worth

protecting. Even if the police had cause to believe that the impounded car's glove compartment contained particular valuables, however, they made no effort to secure the owner's consent to the search. Although the Court relies, as it must, upon the fact that respondent was not present to make other arrangements for the care of his belongings, in my view that is not the end of the inquiry. Here the police readily ascertained the ownership of the vehicle, yet they searched it immediately without taking any steps to locate respondent and procure his consent to the inventory or advise him to make alternative arrangements to safeguard his property. Such a failure is inconsistent with the rationale that the inventory procedure is carried out for the benefit of the owner.

The Court's result in this case elevates the conservation of property interests indeed mere possibilities of property interests above the privacy and security interests protected by the Fourth Amendment. For this reason I dissent. On the remand it should be clear in any event that this Court's holding does not preclude a contrary resolution of this case or others involving the same issues under any applicable state law.

CASE DISCUSSION

What are the justifications for allowing inventory searches without either warrants or probable cause? Why should the evidence of crime obtained in an inventory search be admitted to convict a person when the purpose of the search was for noncriminal law enforcement purposes? Do you agree with the dissent that the expectation of privacy in the contents of a glove compartment should be recognized as reasonable by society? Assume that you are the lawyer for the government in this case. Answer the dissent's arguments that the inventory search of Opperman's car did not serve any of the purposes for inventory searches that the Court says justifies setting aside the warrant and probable cause requirements.

On remand to the South Dakota Supreme Court, this court held that the inventory search may satisfy the standard of reasonableness in the Fourth Amendment to the U.S. Constitution but that it did not pass constitutional muster regarding the search and seizure clause of the South Dakota Constitution, a provision that mirrors the Fourth Amendment in the U.S. Constitution. According to the court,

> . . . [F]or an inventory search to be reasonable, absent a warrant or circumstances constituting an exception to the warrant requirement, there must be a "minimal interference" with the individual's protected rights. We now conclude that as a matter of protection under [the South Dakota search and seizure clause] "minimal interference" with a citizen's constitutional rights means that noninvestigative police inventory searches of automobiles without a warrant must be restricted to safeguarding those articles which are within plain view of the officer's vision. We therefore affirm the rationale of our original decision as a matter of state constitutional law.[4]

The court ruled that the evidence should be excluded. Do you agree? Defend your answer.

BORDER SEARCHES

According to the United States Supreme Court in *United States v. Ramsey*, searches made at the border are reasonable without either warrants or probable cause. The special need of **border searches** is the long-standing right of the sovereign to protect itself by stopping and examining persons and property crossing into the country. Hence, searches for purposes of protecting the integrity of our international borders are reasonable just because they take place at or near the borders between the United States and Mexico or Canada, or adjacent to international waters.[5]

The Supreme Court declared border searches reasonable because the national interest in preventing illegal entry and smuggling weighs more heavily in the balance between the government interest in criminal law enforcement than the invasions of individual privacy. Therefore, superficial border checks require neither warrants nor an objective basis. If, however, the searches go beyond superficial invasions, then the courts require an objective basis, usually reasonable suspicion, to support them. For example, only articulable facts sufficient to support the reasonable suspicion that individuals are concealing contraband on their persons—illegal substances on their bodies—was held to justify a strip search in which individuals were "forced to disrobe to a state which would be offensive to the average person." Searches that go beyond disrobing to the highly invasive body cavity searches, such as examinations of the vagina or rectum, or the administration of laxatives to determine what is in the stomach, require a still higher objective basis—probable cause.[6]

D e c i s i o n   P o i n t

Based on the facts that certain incoming, letter-sized airmail envelopes were from Thailand—a known source of narcotics—and were bulky and much heavier than normal airmail letters, a customs inspector opened the envelopes for inspection at the General Post Office in New York City, considered a "border" for border search purposes. The envelopes contained heroin, which was seized and later used to convict the intended receiver. The customs inspector did not obtain a warrant to search the envelopes, even though the inspector had time to do so.

Was this an illegal search and seizure? The United

States Supreme Court held that the Fourth Amendment does not include customs inspectors opening envelopes because border searches without warrants are not "unreasonable." The border search exception rests on the need to control who and what may enter the country. Anything crossing the border falls within the border search exception.[7]

AIRPORT SEARCHES

Owing to the problems arising from airline hijacking and terrorist bombing, travelers pass through metal detectors before they can board airplanes. If the signal sounds, the travelers remove items from their person until the signal no longer sounds. They also pass their luggage through X-ray machines for examination, or sometimes inspectors open and search baggage without the X-ray machine. If inspectors discover suspicious items, they investigate further. The courts have declared these inspections to be searches and therefore protected by the Fourth Amendment. Applying the balancing approach, the Supreme Court held that airport searches are reasonable. Because the regulatory scheme entails minimal intrusions that apply equally to all passengers, it is neither arbitrary nor discriminatory. Furthermore, all passengers have advance notice that they must pass through the inspection. They are free not to board the airplane if they do not want to subject their person and luggage to these intrusions.[8]

D e c i s i o n   P o i n t

On the basis of four prior investigations, federal narcotics officers had reasonable grounds to suspect—but not probable cause to believe—that the luggage of a man named Place contained cocaine. After Place refused to consent to a search of his luggage at La-Guardia Airport, the officers took the suitcases to Kennedy Airport. About ninety minutes after the seizure, the luggage was subjected to a "sniff test" by a trained narcotics detection dog. The dog reacted positively to one suitcase. The officers kept the luggage over the weekend because it was late on Friday afternoon. On the following Monday, they obtained a warrant for the suitcase, which they searched and in which they found cocaine. Place was convicted of possession of cocaine with intent to distribute.

Did the police lawfully seize the luggage? The Supreme Court reversed Place's conviction, holding that the ninety-minute retention of the suitcases without probable cause violated the Fourth Amendment. At the same time, however, the Court held that

> when an officer's observations lead him to reasonably believe that a traveler is carrying narcotics, the principles of *Terry v. Ohio* [excerpted in Chapter 4] and its progeny would permit the officer to detain the luggage briefly to investigate the circumstances that aroused his suspicion, provided that the investigative detention is properly limited in scope.[9]

SEARCHES OF PRISONERS

Historically, prisoners had no Fourth Amendment rights. In fact, it was commonly held that the Constitution stopped at the prison gate. In frequently cited *Lanza v. New York*, for example, the United States Supreme Court ruled that "a jail shares none of the attributes of privacy of a home, automobile, an office or hotel room, . . . [and] official surveillance has traditionally been the order of the day in prisons."[10]

In the 1980s, the Court conceded that prisoners have an expectation of privacy that society recognizes but that it is "of a diminished scope." This privacy of diminished scope does not protect prisoners from "shakedowns"—routine, unannounced, thorough cell searches for weapons and contraband. These are reasonable because they maintain safety, order, and discipline in prisons, according to the Court. In *Hudson v. Palmer*, a guard maliciously conducted a shakedown and seized personal items such as photographs and other items that a prisoner possessed. A majority of the Supreme Court agreed that the shakedown did not violate the Fourth Amendment. In a strong dissent, however, Justice John Paul Stevens wrote the following:

> Personal letters, snapshots of family members, a souvenir, a deck of cards, a hobby kit, perhaps a diary or a training manual for an apprentice in a new trade, or even a Bible—a variety of inexpensive items may enable a prisoner to maintain contact with some part of his past and an eye to the possibility of a better future. Are all these items subject to unrestrained perusal, confiscation or mutilation at the hands of a possibly hostile guard? Is the Court correct in its perception that "society" is not prepared to recognize any privacy or possessory interest of the person inmate—no matter how remote the threat to prison security might be? . . . By telling prisoners that no aspect of their individuality, from a photo of a child to a letter from a wife, is entitled to constitutional protection, the Court breaks with the ethical tradition that I had thought was enshrined forever in our jurisprudence.[11]

In addition to cell searches, subjecting prisoners to full body searches, strip searches, and even body cavity searches without probable cause does not violate the Fourth Amendment if these searches follow contact with visitors or others who might transfer weapons or contraband to prisoners. In *Bell v. Wolfish* (excerpted in Chapter 11), for example, pretrial detainees had to expose their body cavities for visual inspection as part of a body search conducted after every visit with a person from outside the jail. The Supreme Court held that these practices are reasonable Fourth Amendment searches. However, the Fourth Amendment does not leave prisoners totally without protection from searches. The courts balance the interest in security, safety, and discipline against the privacy right of prisoners. Highly intrusive custodial searches when security, safety, and discipline do not require them can violate the rights of prisoners. The Seventh Circuit Court of Appeals addressed this question in *Mary Beth G. v. City of Chicago*.[12]

C A S E

Was the Strip Search Reasonable?

Mary Beth G. v. City of Chicago
723 F.2d 1263 (7th Cir. 1983)

Four women were arrested for misdemeanor traffic violations. While they were awaiting bail in lockups, ma-

trons strip-searched them. The four women challenged the constitutionality of Chicago's strip search policy. The district court entered judgment in favor of the women. The U.S. Seventh Circuit Court of Appeals held that the strip search policy violated the Fourth

Amendment, that the jury awards were not excessive, and that plaintiffs were entitled to attorney's fees. Judge Wood wrote the opinion of the court.

FACTS

Although the circumstances surrounding the arrests and detentions of each of the plaintiffs–appellees in these consolidated cases are not identical, the situations involve the following common elements: Each woman was arrested for a misdemeanor offense. Mary Beth G. and Sharon N. were stopped for traffic violations; they were arrested and taken to detention centers because there were outstanding parking tickets on their cars. Hinda Hoffman was stopped for making an improper left turn and was arrested and taken to the police station when she failed to produce her driver's license. And each was subjected to the strip search policy of the City of Chicago. That policy, as described by the City, required each woman placed in detention facilities of the Chicago Police Department and searched by female personnel to:

1. lift her blouse or sweater and unhook and lift her brassiere to allow a visual inspection of the breast area, to replace these articles of clothing and then

2. to pull up her skirt or dress or to lower her pants and pull down any undergarments, to squat two or three times facing the detention aide and to bend over at the waist to permit visual inspection of the vaginal and anal area.

In the description of the policy given by the City, the City claims that all searches were conducted in a closed room away from the view of all persons except the person conducting the search. This portion of the description was variously contradicted by the testimony of plaintiffs–appellees. We need not consider these additional allegations, however, because we believe the policy even as described is unconstitutional for the reasons we explain.

The strip search policy was not applied to males. Male detainees were subject to a strip search only if the arresting officers or detention aides had reason to believe that the detainee was concealing weapons or contraband. Otherwise, men were searched thoroughly by hand. The male detainee would place his hands against the wall and stand normally while the searching officer, with his fingers, would go through the hair, into the ears, down the back, under the armpits, down both arms, down the legs, into the groin area, and up the front. The officer would also search the waistband and require the detainee to remove his shoes and sometimes his socks. Originally, women detainees were also searched in this manner, but in 1952 the City changed its policy and began conducting the strip searches.

OPINION

. . . The City argues that its strip search policy is valid under two recognized exceptions to the warrant requirement. One exception allows warrantless searches incident to custodial arrests. A second exception permits warrantless searches incident to the detention of persons lawfully arrested. . . .

Our starting point is the balancing test announced in *[Bell v.] Wolfish* (1979), beginning with the magnitude of the invasion of personal rights. Strip searches involving the visual inspection of the anal and genital areas [are] "demeaning, dehumanizing, undignified, humiliating, terrifying, unpleasant, embarrassing, [and] repulsive, signifying degradation and submission. . . ."

Balanced against this invasion of personal privacy is the governmental interest in conducting the particular searches in question. In these cases, the governmental interest alleged by the City to justify these particular strip searches was the need to maintain the security of the City lockups by preventing misdemeanor offenders from bringing in weapons or contraband; the need was apparently felt to be so great that women misdemeanants were strip searched even when there was no reason to believe they were hiding weapons or contraband on their persons.

The evidence the City offered to demonstrate the need for requiring strip searches of women minor offenders to maintain jail security, however, belies its purported concerns. The affidavits of the lockup personnel, which lack specificity, suggests that only a few items have been recovered from the body cavities of women arrested on minor charges over the years. In the only analytical survey submitted by the City, conducted over a thirty-five day period in June and July of 1965, all of the items found in the body orifices of the

1,800 women searched during that period were taken from women charged with either prostitution (7 items), assault (1 item), or a narcotics violation (1 item). These are the kinds of crimes, unlike traffic or other offenses, that might give rise to a reasonable belief that the woman arrestee was concealing an item in a body cavity. Although a detention center may be a place "fraught with serious security dangers," *Bell v. Wolfish*, the evidence does not support the view that those dangers are created by women minor offenders entering the lockups for short periods while awaiting bail. Here, the "need for the particular search," a strip search, is hardly substantial enough, in light of the evidence regarding the incidence of weapons and contraband found in the body cavities of women minor offenders, to justify the severity of the governmental intrusion.

Balancing the citizen's right to be free from substantial government intrusions against the mission of law enforcement personnel to ensure a safer society is often a difficult task. While the need to assure jail security is a legitimate and substantial concern, we believe that, on the facts here, the strip searches bore an insubstantial relationship to security needs so that, when balanced against plaintiffs–appellees' privacy interests, the searches cannot be considered "reasonable." The reasonableness standard usually requires, "at a minimum, that the facts upon which an intrusion is based be capable of measurement against 'an objective standard,' whether this be probable cause or a less stringent test." The more intrusive the search, the closer governmental authorities must come to demonstrating probable cause for believing that the search will uncover the objects for which the search is being conducted. *Terry v. Ohio* (1968). Based on these principles, we agree with the district court that insuring the security needs of the City by strip searching plaintiffs–appellees was unreasonable without a reasonable suspicion by the authorities that either of the twin dangers of concealing weapons or contraband existed. . . .

Accordingly, because the court and jury . . . could reasonably conclude that the strip search policy of the City as applied in these cases was unreasonable under the fourth amendment, we uphold their determinations on this issue.

[Affirmed.]

CASE DISCUSSION

How did the court balance the special government need to maintain jails and the privacy interests of the individuals who sued the city? How did it arrive at the requirement of reasonable suspicion to justify strip searches? How would you balance these interests? Is a categorization of "prisoner" ever sufficient to justify custodial strip searches? Or must such searches always require individualized suspicion? Would you say that these searches require probable cause to believe that the person searched possesses weapons or contraband? Why or why not? The jury awarded the plaintiffs $25,000 each, except for Hinda Hoffman, who received $60,000 because male officers had watched and uttered rude remarks during her search. The city of Chicago claimed that the awards were excessive. Do you agree? How do you assess how much money these intrusions are worth? Why do you suppose the Chicago policy remained unchallenged for so many years?

SEARCHES OF PROBATIONERS AND PAROLEES

Probationers and parolees have diminished Fourth Amendment rights. Parolees can be arrested and their houses and vehicles searched without either warrants or probable cause. It is not evident whether the Fourth Amendment rights of probationers are as diluted as those of parolees, but, clearly, probationers may be searched without either probable cause or warrants. Courts adopt several theories to justify these reduced Fourth Amendment protections. Some maintain that parolees are in constructive custody—that is, still under state control even though they are released. Others contend that probation and parole are "acts of grace," meaning the state may impose any conditions that it wishes on the status of parole or probation. Still other courts have decided that consent searches and seizures are part of the "contract" of release. Still other courts adopt a balancing approach to the searches of probationers and parolees. Probation and parole are risks taken to help rehabilitate convicted offenders. To protect society from further crimes, reduced Fourth Amendment protections for probationers and parolees are reasonable.[13]

SEARCHES OF JAIL AND PRISON VISITORS AND EMPLOYEES

Prison and jail security permits not only shakedowns and searches of prisoners and pretrial detainees, but also searches of employees of and visitors to prisons. The Supreme Court has not decided whether these searches are unreasonable under the Fourth Amendment. In *Kennedy v. Hardiman*, three investigators surrounded Kennedy in the locker room of the Cook County Department of Corrections and subjected him to strip and body cavity searches. The United States District Court for the Northern District of Illinois ruled that such searches are reasonable if they are based on "reasonable suspicion." The Fifth Circuit Court of Appeals also addressed the question of strip-searching visitors (in the Louisiana prisons) in *Thorne v. Maggio*.[14]

C A S E

Was the Strip Search of the Prisoner's Family Reasonable?

**Thorne v. Maggio
765 F.2d 1270 (5th Cir. 1985)**

Prison inmates and visitors brought a civil rights action challenging the effected and attempted strip searches of their persons. The United States District Court for the Middle District of Louisiana entered a judgment in favor of the plaintiffs, and the defendants appealed. The court of appeals reversed and remanded the case to the district court, before Circuit Judges Gee, Tate, and Higginbotham. Judge Gee wrote the opinion of the court.

FACTS

In these consolidated cases, visitors to and inmates of the Louisiana State Penitentiary at Angola challenge effected and attempted strip searches of their persons.

[COURT NOTE: "In a strip search, the naked body of the subject is very thoroughly inspected, but not touched, by prison personnel of the same sex; the search is conducted in private."]

Peggy and Richard E. Thorne are the parents of Richard J. and Scott Thorne. The younger Thornes are inmates at Louisiana State Penitentiary (LSP), a maximum security facility for prisoners who pose severe security risks. Both brothers have been disciplined while in prison for possession of contraband drugs. LSP permits "contact" visits between inmates and approved friends and family. Mr. and Mrs. Thorne visited their sons at LSP. Before being allowed to do so, each was required to sign a form that stated, among other things, "I hereby agree to a personal search by security personnel of the [LSP] while on prison grounds." A large sign prominently posted just outside the front gate of LSP warned, "Beware Notice

If you enter the gates of Angola, you consent to a search of your person and property. . . ."

In November 1981, an LSP inmate told Captain Whistine, an LSP shift commander, that another inmate was receiving contraband in his legal mail and that Scott Thorne was regularly receiving narcotics through the visiting room, probably from his mother. Captain Whistine reported this information to Warden Byargeon. On the Warden's instructions, Captain Whistine ordered a mail watch on the first inmate's legal mail and notified all shifts that Mrs. Thorne was to be asked to submit to a strip search before being allowed to visit Scott Thorne.

Contraband was found in the first inmate's legal mail, lending credence to the informant. When Mrs. Thorne next arrived to visit Scott Thorne, Captain Whistine told her that she would have to be strip searched before seeing him. Mrs. Thorne refused, with some heat, to be searched. Escorted back to the front gates of the prison, she departed. The Warden had her name removed from the list of approved visitors to the prison. Mrs. Thorne was thus unable to visit either of her inmate sons. Mr. Thorne came to visit Scott Thorne the next day. He, too, was told that a strip search would be required before he could visit his son. Mr. Thorne consented to the search. No contraband was found and the visit took place. All four Thornes, sensitive to their rights as citizens, obtained counsel and brought actions under 42 U.S.C. §1983 against the Louisiana Department of Corrections and sundry LSP officials alleging that these doings infringed upon rights secured to them by the Constitution of the United States. Mrs. Thorne and her inmate sons asserted violations of alleged first amendment associational rights; Mr. Thorne alleged violation of his fourth amendment right to be free from unreasonable searches. The actions were consolidated and tried to a jury, which found for all of the Thornes as against some (but not all) of the defendants, awarding damages to each.

[COURT NOTE: "Richard and Scott were awarded damages of $5,000 each. Mr. Thorne was awarded damages of $10,000. Mrs. Thorne was originally awarded damages of $15,000. The trial court found this award to be excessive; it granted LSP's motion for a new trial, limited to Mrs. Thorne's damages, when she refused to consent to a remittitur of $10,000. At this second trial, Mrs. Thorne was awarded damages of $5,000. Although Mrs. Thorne made the district court's grant of a new trial on damages the subject of a cross appeal, we need not . . . reach this issue. . . ."]

Defendants (referred to collectively as "LSP") moved for judgment notwithstanding the verdict; the trial court denied their motion. From this denial, defendant appeal. We reverse.

OPINION

. . . The preeminence of prison security concerns was . . . emphasized in *Hudson v. Palmer* (1984). The *Hudson* Court held that "prisoners have no legitimate expectation of privacy and that the Fourth Amendment's prohibition on unreasonable searches does not apply in prison cells. . . ." The Court's reasoning is relevant here:

> The two interests here are the interest of society in the security of its penal institutions and the interest of the prisoner in privacy within his cell. The latter interest, of course, is already limited by the exigencies of the circumstances. A prison "shares none of the attributes of privacy of a home, an automobile, an office, or a hotel room." . . . We strike the balance in favor of institutional security, which we have noted is "central to all other corrections goals." A right of privacy in traditional Fourth Amendment terms is fundamentally incompatible with the close and continual surveillance of inmates and their cells required to ensure institutional security and internal order. We are satisfied that society would insist that the prisoner's expectation of privacy always yield to what must be considered the paramount interest in institutional security.

. . . *Hudson [v. Palmer]* indicate[s] unmistakably that security-related decisions of prison officials are to be reviewed only for reasonableness; if the decisions are rational (an exceedingly undemanding standard), courts are to look no further. The trial court here looked further; in so doing, it failed to accord LSP security-related decisions the deference demanded by the Supreme Court.

Mr. Thorne's Fourth Amendment Claim

As the other Thornes were not searched, they have no fourth amendment claims; as Mr. Thorne's visit does not implicate his freedom to associate in order to express ideas, he possesses no colorable first amendment ones. We turn to his fourth amendment claim.

As to it, LSP advances several arguments for reversal. In the first of these, LSP seems to argue that the trial court erred in finding the search of Mr. Thorne unreasonable because the finding was grounded on a theory different from LSP's: that a strip search of any prison visitor is reasonable as a matter of law, so long as the visitor has prior notice that he is subject to search and is given the option of leaving the prison rather than submitting to the search. LSP's contention thus appears to be that it was error for the trial court to consider the particular circumstances of Mr. Thorne's search. If this is in fact the contention, it is meritless. . . .

Although few searches are more intrusive than a body cavity search, we do not hold that such searches are per se unreasonable. . . . They not only help stem the flow of contraband into, within, and out of prisons, but they also have a beneficial deterrent effect. To prove the legal validity of a particular body cavity search, however, the government still must show that the search and seizure in question was reasonable under all the facts and circumstances. The relevant facts and circumstances will vary from case to case. In the prison context, however, the government always must show that a legitimate penological need necessitated the search, that the need could not have been satisfied by a more narrow means, and that the search and any consequent seizure were conducted in a reasonable manner. Depending on the facts of a particular case, proof of certain other factors may be necessary to prove reasonableness. Although *[United States v.] Lilly* [5th Cir. 1978] dealt with prison inmates rather than prison visitors, it would be anomalous indeed to accord the former class greater protection from unreasonable searches than the latter. Under *Lilly,* inquiry must be made into the reasonableness of a particular inmate search; the reasonableness of particular visitor searches must be determined in the same manner. See *Hunter v. Auger* (8th Cir. 1982) ("To justify the strip search of a particular visitor under the reasonable suspicion stan-

dard, prison officials must point to specific objective facts and rational inferences that they are entitled to draw from those facts. . . ."); *Security and Law Enforcement Employees, District Council 82 v. Carey* (2d Cir. 1984) (adopting *Hunter* reasonable suspicion standard for strip searches of prison employees); *Giles v. Akerman* (9th Cir. 1984), U.S. appeal pending (adopting reasonable suspicion standard for strip searches of arrestees charged with minor offenses).

There being no authority for the proposition that strip searches of prison visitors are per se reasonable, LSP's assignment of error must be rejected. It was not error for the trial court to look to the particular facts of Mr. Thorne's search to determine its reasonableness.

LSP next argues that the trial court erred in finding Mr. Thorne's search unreasonable under the fourth amendment, either because Mr. Thorne consented to his search or because he waived his fourth amendment rights when he entered the prison. LSP locates this consent or waiver in the visitor form signed by Mr. Thorne and in the warning notices posted at the prison gates. If accepted, this argument would render reasonable a strip search of any such prison visitor; as discussed above, such at-will, random searches are not reasonable under the Fourth Amendment. The argument must therefore fail. *United States v. Sihler* (5th Cir. 1977), the sole authority cited by LSP, does not compel a different result. In *Sihler,* we upheld the search of a prison employee's brown paper lunch bag on the ground of consent, both explicitly given by the employee and inferred from a sign at the prison gates warning that all persons entering would be subject to routine searches. Strip searches are not "routine;" they cannot be equated with the lunch bag search in *Sihler,* which thus provides no support for LSP's contention. There being no support for the contention, it is clearly meritless. The trial court did not err in rejecting LSP's "consent" defense.

Finally, LSP argues that the search of Mr. Thorne was justified by "reasonable suspicion," and that the trial court erred by holding the search unreasonable under this standard. The argument is untenable. "'[R]easonable suspicion' must be specifically directed to the person to be searched. . . . [T]he fourth amendment does not permit any automatic or casual transference of 'suspicion.'" *United States v. Afanador* (5th Cir. 1978).

To justify the strip search of a particular visitor under the reasonable suspicion standard, prison officials must point to specific objective facts and rational inferences that they are entitled to draw from those facts in light of their experience. Inchoate, unspecified suspicions fall short of providing reasonable grounds to suspect that a visitor will attempt to smuggle drugs or other contraband into the prison.

Here, no objective fact pointed to Mr. Thorne as a probable smuggler of drugs into LSP. That an informant pointed to Mrs. Thorne as a likely source of Scott Thorne's contraband does not suffice, under *Afanador*, to justify search of her husband. It is common knowledge that husbands and wives do not concur in all things. LSP offers no other facts on which reasonable suspicion of Mr. Thorne could have been grounded; it is thus clear that the trial court correctly found Mr. Thorne's search to have been without reasonable suspicion, and therefore in violation of the fourth amendment.

. . . LSP contends that the trial court erred in rejecting the individual defendants' defenses of qualified, or "good faith," immunity from liability for money damages. Under *Harlow v. Fitzgerald* (1982), officials "are shielded from liability for civil damages insofar as their conduct does not violate clearly established statutory or constitutional rights of which a reasonable person would have known." Whether an official may prevail in his qualified immunity defense depends upon the "objective reasonableness of [his] conduct as measured by reference to clearly established law." No other "circumstances" are relevant to the issue of qualified immunity.

LSP must prevail on this issue if it was not clearly established in December 1981 that strip searches of prison visitors conducted without "reasonable suspicion" violated the fourth amendment. We conclude that it was not.

First, at that time only one district court had yet ruled on the issue, *Black v. Amico* (W.D.N.Y. 1974) (applying "real suspicion" test to visitor strip search); and in 1979, in *Wolfish*, the Supreme Court had upheld routine strip searches of inmates. Second, in *Carey*—a 1984 decision on 1979–80 events—the Second Circuit affirmed prison officials' qualified immunity from damage liability for unconstitutional strip searches of prison employees on the ground that "[t]hese officials operated in an area in which the law was not charted clearly." We agree. The authorities cited in the foregoing section of our opinion make plain that at the time of the search of Mr. Thorne the law in this area was in a state of uncertainty. Indeed, in our Circuit portions of it become "clearly established" only today.

For the foregoing reasons, we reverse the judgments favorable to the Thornes and remand with instructions to enter judgment for the defendants.

CASE DISCUSSION

Should visitors to prisons have the right not to be searched? Explain. Did Richard E. Thorne waive his right, assuming that he had one? Are strip searches of visitors ever "reasonable"? What interests do they balance? How would you balance the interests involved? Why is LSP entitled to limited immunity? Do you agree with the "good faith" standard used to determine qualified immunity? Explain.

SEARCHES OF STUDENTS

Searches of students on the premises of educational institutions are reasonable even without probable cause and warrants. Based on a modified *in loco parentis doctrine*—that is, the principle under which a school stands in the place of parents while students are in school—school administrators may search students' lockers and personal belongings, as well as students themselves, on reasonable suspicion. This doctrine does not apply to college and university students who are not minors. Courts have used the balancing approach to support student searches.

D e c i s i o n   P o i n t

In *New Jersey v. T.L.O.*, a teacher at a New Jersey high school, upon discovering T.L.O., then a fourteen-year-old freshman, and her companion smoking cigarettes in a school lavatory in violation of a school rule, took them to the principal's office, where they met with the assistant vice-principal. When T.L.O., in response to the assistant vice-principal's questioning, denied that she had been smoking and claimed that she did not smoke at all, the assistant vice-principal demanded to see her purse. Upon opening the purse, he found a pack of cigarettes and also noticed a package of cigarette rolling papers that are commonly associated with the use of marijuana. He then proceeded to search the purse thoroughly and found some marijuana, a pipe, plastic bags, a fairly substantial amount of money, and two letters that implicated T.L.O. in marijuana dealing. Thereafter, the state brought delinquency charges against T.L.O. in juvenile court, which, after denying T.L.O.'s motion to suppress the evidence found in her purse, held that the Fourth Amendment applied to searches by school officials but that the search in question was reasonable and adjudged T.L.O. delinquent.

Does the Fourth Amendment apply to school searches? Was this search reasonable? According to the United States Supreme Court, the answer to both questions is yes. The Court held that the Fourth Amendment's prohibition on unreasonable searches

and seizures applies to searches conducted by public school officials and is not limited to searches conducted by law enforcement officers. Nor are school officials exempt from the amendment's dictates by virtue of the special nature of their authority over schoolchildren. In carrying out searches and other functions pursuant to disciplinary policies, school officials cannot claim immunity from the Fourth Amendment. For these purposes, they are not *in loco parentis*.

Children, while in school, possess a reasonable expectation of privacy. But striking a balance between schoolchildren's legitimate expectations of privacy and the school's equally legitimate need to maintain an environment in which learning can take place requires some easing of the restrictions to which searches by public authorities are ordinarily subject. Thus, school officials need not obtain a warrant before searching a student who is under their authority. Moreover, school officials need not be held subject to the requirement that searches be based on probable cause to believe that the subject of the search has violated or is violating the law. Rather, the legality of the search of a student should depend simply on the reasonableness of the search, under all the circumstances. Using this standard, the Supreme Court decided that the search of T.L.O. was reasonable.[15]

The Supreme Court has not addressed the problem of the extent to which the Fourth Amendment protects university students in administrative searches. However, the Fifth Circuit Court of Appeals addressed the privacy rights of college students in their dormitory rooms in *Piazzola v. Watkins*.

C A S E

Was the Room Search Reasonable?

Piazzola v. Watkins
442 F.2d 284 (5th Cir. 1971)

The defendants were convicted in jury trials of illegal possession of marijuana and sentenced to five years in

prison. The defendants appealed to the Court of Appeals of Alabama. The court affirmed the convictions. The Supreme Court of Alabama granted a motion to strike their petitions of certiorari. They submitted a petition for a writ of habeas corpus to the federal district court. The district court granted habeas corpus *and ordered their release. The U.S. Circuit Court affirmed before Rives, Thornberry, and Clark, circuit judges. Judge Rives wrote the opinion of the court.*

FACTS

On the morning of February 28, 1968, the Dean of Men of Troy State University was called to the office of the Chief of Police of Troy, Alabama, to discuss "the drug problem" at the University. Two State narcotic agents and two student informers from Troy State University were also present. Later on that same day, the Dean of Men was called to the city police station for another meeting; at this time he was informed by the officers that they had sufficient evidence that marijuana was in the dormitory rooms of certain Troy State students and that they desired the cooperation of University officials in searching these rooms. The police officers were advised by the Dean of Men that they would receive the full cooperation of the University officials in searching for the marijuana.

The informers, whose identities have not yet been disclosed, provided the police officers with names of students whose rooms were to be searched. Still later on that same day (which was during the week of final examinations at the University and was to be followed by a weeklong holiday) the law enforcement officers, accompanied by some of the University officials, searched six or seven dormitory rooms located in two separate residence halls. The rooms of both Piazzola and Marinshaw were searched without search warrants and without their consent. Present during the search of the room occupied by Marinshaw were two State narcotic agents, the University security officer, and a counselor of the residence hall where Marinshaw's room was located. Piazzola's room was searched twice. Present during the first search were two State narcotic agents and a University official; no evidence was found at this time. The second search of Piazzola's room, which disclosed the incriminating evidence, was conducted solely by the State and City police officials.

At the time of the seizure the University had in effect the following regulation:

The college reserves the right to enter rooms for inspection purposes. If the administration

deems it necessary, the room may be searched and the occupant required to open his personal baggage and any other personal material which is sealed.

Each of the petitioners was familiar with this regulation. After the search of the petitioners' rooms and the discovery of the marijuana, they were arrested, and the State criminal prosecutions and convictions ensued. . . .

OPINION

The Fourth Amendment protects "the right of the people to be secure in their persons, houses, papers, and effects, against unreasonable searches and seizures." The question is whether in the light of all of the facts and circumstances, including the University regulation, the search which disclosed the marijuana was an unreasonable search. The district judge made reasonableness the touchstone of his opinion as to the validity of the search. We find ourselves in agreement with his view that this search was unreasonable. In a case where the facts were similar, *People v. Cohen,* Judge Burstein said:

The police and the Hofstra University officials admitted that they entered the room in order to make an arrest, if an arrest was warranted. This was, in essence, a fishing expedition calculated to discover narcotics. It offends reason and logic to suppose that a student will consent to an entry into his room designed to establish grounds upon which to arrest him. Certainly, there can be no rational claim that a student will self-consciously waive his Constitutional right to a lawful search and seizure. Finally, even if the doctrine of implied consent were imported into this case, the consent is given, not to police officials, but to the University and the latter cannot fragmentize, share or delegate it.

Another case somewhat in point on the facts is *Commonwealth v. McCloskey.* There the court reversed a student's marijuana conviction because the policemen who entered his dormitory room to execute a search warrant did not knock or announce their presence and purpose before entering. In part, Judge Cercone speaking for the majority of the court said:

It was the Commonwealth's position that the Fourth Amendment protections do not apply to a search of a college dormitory room. The test to be used in determining the applicability of the Fourth Amendment protections is whether or not the particular locale is one . . . in which there was a reasonable expectation of freedom from governmental intrusion. *Mancusi v. De-Forte* (1968) (large office room shared by the defendant and other union officials). See also *Sabbath v. United States* (apartment); *Stoner v. California* (1964) (hotel room); and *Katz v. United States* (1967) (telephone booth).

A dormitory room is analogous to an apartment or a hotel room. It certainly offers its occupant a more reasonable expectation of freedom from governmental intrusion than does a public telephone booth. The defendant rented the dormitory room for a certain period of time, agreeing to abide by the rules established by his lessor, the University. As in most rental situations, the lessor, Bucknell University, reserved the right to check the room for damages, wear and unauthorized appliances. Such right of the lessor, however, does not mean McCloskey was not entitled to have a "reasonable expectation of freedom from governmental intrusion" or that he gave consent to the police search. Waiver of Fourth Amendment rights through consent to a search cannot be lightly inferred. Every reasonable presumption is against one's waiver of his constitutional rights. *Weed v. United States* (10 Cir. 1965) (university authority to consent to such search). In *Stoner v. California*, a hotel clerk allowed the police to search a guest's room, and the Supreme Court there stated: "It is important to bear in mind that it was the petitioner's constitutional right which was at stake here, and not the night clerk's nor the hotel's. It was a right, therefore, which only the petitioner could waive by word or deed, either directly or through an agent." Many other cases have held

that one in the position of a lessor cannot consent to a police search of a tenant's premises, even though the lessor, himself has a right to enter the room or apartment. See *United States v. Jeffers* (1951) and *Commonwealth v. Ellsworth* (1966) (hotel proprietor let police into a guest's room); *Chapman v. United States* (1961) and *Cunningham v. Heinze* (9th Cir. 1965), cert. denied (1966) (landlord allowed police search of tenant's room). . . .

. . . [W]e must conclude that a student who occupies a college dormitory room enjoys the protection of the Fourth amendment. True the University retains broad supervisory powers which permit it to adopt the regulation heretofore quoted, provided that regulation is reasonably construed and is limited in its application to further the University's function as an educational institution. The regulation cannot be construed or applied so as to give consent to a search for evidence for the primary purpose of a criminal prosecution. Otherwise, the regulation itself would constitute an unconstitutional attempt to require a student to waive his protection from unreasonable searches and seizures as a condition to his occupancy of a college dormitory room.

[COURT NOTE: "One of the 'Residence Hall Policies' of this University provides that 'College men are assumed to be mature adults with acceptable and established habits.' Another adjures students, 'Keep rooms locked at all times.' The University thus recognized that it cannot exercise that strict control of its students which might be permitted in a boys' school where an 'in loco parentis' standard would be more appropriate."]

Clearly the University had no authority to consent to or join in a police search for evidence of crime. The right to privacy is "no less important than any other right carefully and particularly reserved to the people." The results of the search do not prove its reasonableness. This search was an unconstitutional invasion of the privacy both of these appellees and of the students in whose rooms no evidence of marijuana was found. The warrantless search of these students' dormitory rooms cannot be justified. The judgment is therefore Affirmed.

DISSENT

Clark, Circuit Judge (concurring in part and dissenting in part).

I respectfully dissent from part 2 of the Court's opinion as to the defendant, Marinshaw. The college had a direct interest in keeping its dormitories free of the specific criminal activity here involved — the possession of the drug, marihuana. The regulation was a reasonable means of embodying this interest. Marinshaw was found to be familiar with the regulation. When he chose to place the evidence of this criminal conduct in his dormitory room he knowingly exposed this material to inspections by officials of the University. He cannot now reinstate as private an area he had agreed was thus accessible. A publicly owned dormitory room is not in my mind the equivalent of a private rooming house. I concur in the result as to the defendant, Piazzolo, because I do not believe the regulation can be validly construed to authorize the college to consent to an independent police search.

In all other respects I concur in the opinion of the majority.

CASE DISCUSSION

Did the students consent to this search? Was it reasonable to regulate the rooms? To search them? What if the university officials were inspecting for fire hazards, such as hot plates for cooking that violated regulations, and they found drugs? Could they seize the drugs? Use them against the students? What arguments can you give to support — or reject — the seizure of drugs and their use in evidence? Their seizure but not their use in evidence? Neither their seizure nor their use in evidence? What interests does each of these alternatives serve?

EMPLOYEE DRUG TESTING

Testing employees for the use of illicit drugs began in earnest during the 1980s. The purpose of the search is not criminal law enforcement. It is directed mainly at employees who may endanger public safety by flying airplanes, driving buses, or engineering trains while under the influence of illegal drugs. Drug testing reflects public concern about drug use in general and the deaths, injuries, and environmental damage stemming from transportation employees' abuse of alcohol. The Supreme Court dealt with the problem of balancing the government's interest in interdicting the importation of illegal drugs and government employees' right to privacy in *National Treasury Employees Union v. Von Raab.*

C A S E

Was the Urine Test a Reasonable Search?

**National Treasury Employees
Union v. Von Raab
489 U.S. 656, 109 S.Ct. 1384,
103 L.Ed.2d 685 (1989)**

The union and union president brought an action against United States Customs Service to obtain an in- *junction and to challenge the constitutionality of a drug-testing program that analyzed urine specimens of employees who applied for promotion to positions involving the interdiction of illegal drugs, the required carrying of firearms, or the handling of classified materials. Customs Service moved to dismiss. The United States District Court denied a motion to dismiss and granted injunctive and declaratory relief. The Customs Service appealed. The Court of Appeals for the Fifth Circuit vacated the injunction, and the Supreme Court granted* certiorari *to decide whether it violates the Fourth Amendment for the United States Customs Service to require a urinalysis test from employees who seek transfer or promotion to certain positions. Justice Kennedy wrote the opinion of the Court, in which Chief Justice Rehnquist and Justices White, Blackmun, and O'Connor joined. Justice Marshall filed a dissenting opinion, in which Justice Brennan joined. Justice Scalia filed a dissenting opinion, in which Justice Stevens joined.*

FACTS

The United States Customs Service, a bureau of the Department of the Treasury, is the federal agency responsible for processing persons, carriers, cargo, and mail into the United States, collecting revenue from imports, and enforcing customs and related laws. An important responsibility of the Service is the interdiction and seizure of contraband, including illegal drugs. In 1987 alone, Customs agents seized drugs with a retail value of nearly 9 billion dollars. In the routine discharge of their duties, many Customs employees have direct contact with those who traffic in drugs for profit. Drug import operations, often directed by sophisticated criminal syndicates, *United States v. Mendenhall* [1980 — see Chapter 3], may be effected by violence or its threat. As a necessary response, many Customs operatives carry and use firearms in connection with their official duties. In December 1985, respondent, the Commissioner of Customs, established a Drug Screening Task Force to explore the possibility of implementing a drug screening program within the Service. After extensive research and consultation with experts in the field, the Task Force concluded "that drug screening through urinalysis is technologically reliable, valid and accurate." Citing this conclusion, the Commissioner announced his intention to require drug tests of employees who applied for, or occupied, certain positions within the Service. The Commissioner stated his belief that "Customs is largely drug-free," but noted also that "unfortunately no segment of society is immune from the threat of illegal drug use." Interdic-

tion has become the agency's primary enforcement mission, and the Commissioner stressed that "there is no room in the Customs Service for those who break the laws prohibiting the possession and use of illegal drugs."

In May 1986, the Commissioner announced implementation of the drug-testing program. Drug tests were made a condition of placement or employment for positions that meet one or more of three criteria. The first is direct involvement in drug interdiction or enforcement of related laws, an activity the Commissioner deemed fraught with obvious dangers to the mission of the agency and the lives of customs agents. The second criterion is a requirement that the incumbent carry firearms, as the Commissioner concluded that "(p)ublic safety demands that employees who carry deadly arms and are prepared to make instant life or death decisions be drug free." The third criterion is a requirement for the incumbent to handle "classified" material, which the Commissioner determined might fall into the hands of smugglers if accessible to employees who, by reason of their own illegal drug use, are susceptible to bribery or blackmail. After an employee qualifies for a position covered by the Customs testing program, the Service advises him by letter that his final selection is contingent upon successful completion of drug screening. An independent contractor contacts the employee to fix the time and place for collecting the sample. On reporting for the test, the employee must produce photographic identification and remove any outer garments, such as a coat or a jacket, and personal belongings. The employee may produce the sample behind a partition, or in the privacy of a bathroom stall if he so chooses. To ensure against adulteration of the specimen, or substitution of a sample from another person, a monitor of the same sex as the employee remains close at hand to listen for the normal sounds of urination. Dye is added to the toilet water to prevent the employee from using the water to adulterate the sample.

Upon receiving the specimen, the monitor inspects it to ensure its proper temperature and color, places a tamper-proof custody seal over the container, and affixes an identification label indicating the date and the individual's specimen number. The employee signs a chain-of-custody form, which is initialed by the monitor, and the urine sample is placed in a plastic bag, sealed, and submitted to a laboratory. . . . The laboratory tests the sample for the presence of marijuana, cocaine, opiates, amphetamines, and phencyclidine. . . .

Petitioners, a union of federal employees and a union official, commenced this suit in the United States District Court for the Eastern District of Louisiana on behalf of current Customs Service employees who seek covered positions. Petitioners alleged that the Custom Service drug-testing program violated the Fourth Amendment. The District Court agreed. The court acknowledged "the legitimate governmental interest in a drug-free work place and work force," but concluded that "the drug testing plan constitutes an overly intrusive policy of searches and seizures without probable cause or reasonable suspicion, in violation of legitimate expectations of privacy." The court enjoined the drug testing program, and ordered the Customs Service not to require drug tests of any applicants for covered positions.

A divided panel of the United States Court of Appeals for the Fifth Circuit vacated the injunction. . . . We granted certiorari. We now affirm so much of the judgment of the court of appeals as upheld the testing of employees directly involved in drug interdiction or required to carry firearms. We vacate the judgment to the extent it upheld the testing of applicants for positions requiring the incumbent to handle classified materials, and remand for further proceedings.

OPINION

In *Skinner v. Railway Labor Executives [Association]*, decided today, we hold that federal regulations requiring employees of private railroads to produce urine samples for chemical testing implicate the Fourth Amendment, as those tests invade reasonable expectations of privacy. Our earlier cases have settled that the Fourth Amendment protects individuals from unreasonable searches conducted by the Government, . . . and, in view of our holding in [*Skinner*] that urine tests are searches, it follows that the Custom Service's drug testing program must meet the reasonableness requirement of the Fourth Amendment.

While we have often emphasized, and reiterate today, that a search must be supported, as a general matter, by a warrant issued upon probable cause, . . . neither a warrant nor probable cause, nor, indeed, any measure of individualized suspicion, is an indispensable component of reasonableness in every circumstance. . . . [O]ur cases establish that where a Fourth Amendment intrusion serves special governmental needs, beyond the normal need for law enforcement, it is necessary to balance the individual's privacy expectations against the Government's interests to determine whether it is impractical to require a warrant or some level of individualized suspicion in the particular context.

It is clear that the Customs Service's drug testing program is not designed to serve the ordinary needs of law enforcement. Test results may not be used in a criminal prosecution of the employee without the employee's consent. The purposes of the program are to deter drug use among those eligible for promotion to sensitive positions within the Service and to prevent the promotion of drug users to those positions. These substantial interests, no less than the Government's concern for safe rail transportation at issue in [*Skinner*], present a special need that may justify departure from the ordinary warrant and probable cause requirements. . . .

The Customs Service is our Nation's first line of defense against one of the greatest problems affecting the health and welfare of our population. We have adverted before to "the veritable national crisis in law enforcement caused by smuggling of illicit narcotics." *United States v. Montoya de Hernandez* [1985 — excerpted in Chapter 4]. See also *Florida v. Royer* [1983 — excerpted in Chapter 5]. Our cases also reflect the traffickers' seemingly inexhaustible repertoire of deceptive practices and elaborate schemes for importing narcotics, e.g., *United States v. Montoya de Hernandez*. . . . The record in this case confirms that, through the adroit selection of source locations, smuggling routes, and increasingly elaborate methods of concealment, drug traffickers have managed to bring into this country increasingly large quantities of illegal drugs. The record also indicates, and it is well known, that drug smugglers do not hesitate to use violence to protect their lucrative trade and avoid apprehension. Many of the Service's employees are often exposed to this criminal element and to the controlled substances they seek to smuggle into the country. . . .

Where the Government requires its employees to produce urine samples to be analyzed for evidence of illegal drug use, the collection and subsequent chemical analysis of such samples are searches that must meet the reasonableness requirement of the Fourth Amendment. Because the testing program adopted by the Customs Service is not designed to serve the ordinary needs of law enforcement, we have balanced the public interest in the Service's testing program against the privacy concerns implicated by the tests, without reference to our usual presumption in favor of the procedures specified in the Warrant Clause, to assess whether the tests required by Customs are reasonable. We hold that the suspicionless testing of employees who apply for promotion to positions directly involving the interdiction of illegal drugs, or to positions which require the incumbent to carry a firearm, is reasonable. The Government's compelling interests in preventing the promotion of drug users to positions where they might endanger the integrity of our Nation's borders or the life of the citizenry outweigh the privacy interests of those who seek promotion to these positions, who enjoy a diminished expectation of privacy by virtue of the special, and obvious, physical and ethical demands of those positions. We do not decide whether testing those who apply for promotion to positions where they would handle "classified" information is reasonable because we find the record inadequate for this purpose. The judgment of the Court of Appeals for the Fifth Circuit is affirmed in part and vacated in part, and the case is remanded for further proceedings consistent with this opinion. It is so ordered.

DISSENT

Justice Scalia, with whom Justice Stevens joins, dissenting.

The issue in this case is not whether Customs Service employees can constitutionally be denied promotion, or even dismissed, for a single instance of unlawful drug use, at home or at work. They assuredly can. The issue here is what steps can constitutionally be taken to detect such drug use. The Government asserts it can demand that employees perform "an excretory function traditionally shielded by great privacy," [while] "a monitor of the same sex . . . remains

close at hand to listen for the normal sounds," and that the excretion thus produced be turned over to the Government for chemical analysis. The Court agrees that this constitutes a search for purposes of the Fourth Amendment—and I think it obvious that it is a type of search particularly destructive of privacy and offensive to personal dignity. Until today this court had upheld a bodily search separate from arrest and without individualized suspicion of wrongdoing only with respect to prison inmates, relying upon the uniquely dangerous nature of that environment. See *Bell v. Wolfish* [1979—excerpted in Chapter 11]. Today, in *Skinner*, we allow a less intrusive bodily search of railroad employees involved in train accidents. I joined the Court's opinion there because the demonstrated frequency of drug and alcohol use by the targeted class of employees, and the demonstrated connection between such use and grave harm, rendered the search a reasonable means of protecting society. I decline to join the Court's opinion in the present case because neither frequency of use nor connection to harm is demonstrated or even likely. In my view the Customs Service rules are a kind of immolation of privacy and human dignity in symbolic opposition to drug use. . . .

The Court's opinion in the present case will be searched in vain for real evidence of a real problem that will be solved by urine testing of Customs Service employees. . . . The only pertinent points, it seems to me, are supported by nothing but speculation, and not very plausible speculation at that. . . . What is absent in the Government's justifications— notably absent, revealingly absent, and as far as I am concerned dispositively absent—is the recitation of even a single instance in which any of the speculated horribles actually occurred: an instance, that is, in which the cause of bribe-taking, or of poor aim, or of unsympathetic law enforcement, or of compromise of classified information, was drug use. Although the Court points out that several employees have in the past been removed from the Service for accepting bribes and other integrity violations, and that at least nine officers have died in the line of duty since 1974, there is no indication whatever that these incidents were related to drug use by Service employees.

The Court's response to this lack of evidence is that "(t)here is little reason to believe that American workplaces are immune from (the) pervasive social problem" of drug abuse. Perhaps such a generalization would suffice if the workplace at issue could produce such catastrophic social harm that no risk whatever is tolerable—the secured areas of a nuclear power plant. But if such a generalization suffices to justify demeaning bodily searches, without particularized suspicion, to guard against the bribing or blackmailing of a law enforcement agent, or the careless use of a firearm, then the Fourth Amendment has become frail protection indeed. In *Skinner*, we took pains to establish the existence of special need for the search or seizure—a need based not upon the existence of a "pervasive social problem" combined with speculation as to the effect of that problem in the field at issue, but rather upon well known or well demonstrated evils in that field, with well known or well demonstrated consequences. In *Skinner*, for example, we pointed to a long history of alcohol abuse in the railroad industry, and noted that in an 8-year period 45 train accidents and incidents had occurred because of alcohol- and drug-impaired railroad employees, killing 34 people, injuring 66, and causing more than $28 million in property damage. In the present case, by contrast, not only is the Customs Service thought to be "largely drug-free," but the connection between whatever drug use may exist and serious social harm is entirely speculative. Except for the fact that the search of a person is much more intrusive than the stop of a car, the present case resembles *Delaware v. Prouse* (1979), where we held that the Fourth Amendment prohibited random stops to check drivers' licenses and motor vehicle registration. The contribution of this practice to highway safety, we concluded, was "marginal at best" since the number of licensed drivers that must be stopped in order to find one unlicensed one "will be large indeed." . . .

There is only one apparent basis that sets the testing at issue here apart from all these other situations—but it is not a basis upon which the Court is willing to rely. I do not believe for a minute that the driving force behind these drug-testing rules was any of the feeble justifications put forward by counsel here and accepted by the Court. The only plausible explanation, in my view, is what the Commissioner himself offered in the concluding sentence of his memorandum to Customs Service employees an-

nouncing the program: "Implementation of the drug screening program would set an important example in our country's struggle with this most serious threat to our national health and security." Or as respondent's brief to this Court asserted: "if a law enforcement agency and its employees do not take the law seriously, neither will the public on which the agency's effectiveness depends." What better way to show that the Government is serious about its "war on drugs" than to subject its employees on the front line of that war to this invasion of their privacy and affront to their dignity? To be sure, there is only a slight chance that it will prevent some serious public harm resulting from Service employee drug use, but it will show to the world that the Service is "clean," and—most important of all—will demonstrate the determination of the Government to eliminate this scourge of our society! I think it obvious that this justification is unacceptable; that the impairment of individual liberties cannot be the means of making a point; that symbolism, even symbolism for so worthy a cause as the abolition of unlawful drugs, cannot validate an otherwise unreasonable search. There is irony in the Government's citation, in support of its position, of Justice Brandeis's statement in *Olmstead v. United States* (1928) that "(f)or good or for ill, (our Government) teaches the whole people by its example." Brandeis was there dissenting from the Court's admission of evidence obtained through an unlawful Government wiretap. He was not praising the Government's example of vigor and enthusiasm in combating crime, but condemning its example that "the end justifies the means." An even more apt quotation from that famous Brandeis dissent would have been the following:

> (I)t is . . . immaterial that the intrusion was in aid of law enforcement. Experience should teach us to be most on our guard to protect liberty when the Government's purposes are beneficent. Men born to freedom are naturally alert to repel invasion of their liberty by evil-minded rulers. The greatest dangers to liberty lurk in insidious encroachment by men of zeal, well-meaning but without understanding.

Those who lose because of the lack of understanding that begot the present exercise in symbolism are not just the Custom Service employees, whose dignity is thus offended, but all of us—who suffer a coarsening of our national manners that ultimately give the Fourth Amendment its content, and who become subject to the administration of federal officials whose respect for our privacy can hardly be greater than the small respect they have been taught to have for their own.

CASE DISCUSSION

What compelling government interest and what privacy interests did the Court balance in reaching its result in this case? What precise intrusions and deprivations do employees suffer in the Customs Service's drug-testing program? Does Justice Antonin Scalia have a point that no evidence established a link between the interest the government seeks to protect in the drug testing and the method used to protect the interest? Should the Court require empirical proof before it accepts plans to further governmental interests? Does the Court promote the interests of drug control at too high a cost to individual privacy? Or does it balance them properly? Explain your answer.

SUMMARY

The Fourth Amendment refers to the right of the "people" generally against "unreasonable searches and seizures." The other major rights related to the law of criminal procedure refer more specifically to individuals in criminal cases, such as the right against self-incrimination and the right to counsel. The broad scope of the language of the Fourth Amendment has led the Supreme Court to apply it to a wide range of cases not directly related to criminal law. These cases involve "special needs" for searches and seizures that extend beyond criminal law enforcement. These "special needs" include inspections and regulations at international borders; building inspections; safety checks of vehicles on public highways; airport searches of passengers; searches of prisoners, probationers, and parolees; searches of employees and visitors to jails and prisons; searches of students and their lockers; and, recently, drug testing of employees.

Special needs searches and seizures are reasonable without either warrants or probable cause. The Supreme Court has, instead of the warrant and probable cause requirements, adopted the balancing approach to determine the reasonableness of special needs searches and seizures. The Court has balanced the "special need" of the government to conduct the searches and seizures against the invasion of individual privacy caused by the searches. If the special need of the government outweighs the individual privacy interests of individuals, then the search is reasonable. The balancing approach to reasonableness depends on weighing the totality of the circumstances on a case-by-case basis.

The balancing approach has resulted in broadening the government's authority to regulate and inspect in a range of areas. Inventories of impounded vehicles and containers are reasonable without either warrants or probable cause if they follow established procedures to compile a list of items for the protection of the property detained and to prevent public liability for loss or damage of private property. Border searches are reasonable without either warrants or probable cause if the special need to protect the integrity of international borders outweighs the invasion of privacy of individual citizens in individual cases. Requiring passengers to pass through metal detectors and X-raying their luggage are reasonable searches without either warrants or probable cause because the special need to prevent terrorism outweighs the minimal invasion of privacy in passing through the electronic metal-detecting devices. Prisoners retain only a minimal right to privacy against searches made without either warrants or probable cause for the purposes of maintaining prison discipline, safety, and security. Probationers and parolees retain a minimal interest in privacy against searches because of the special need of the government to supervise those who have committed crimes. Employees of and visitors to prisons and jails have a reduced expectation of privacy weighed against the special needs of correctional facilities to maintain safety and security. Students retain their Fourth Amendment rights, but if the special needs of school administrators to conduct searches for the purposes of promoting learning and maintaining discipline and order outweigh the individual invasions of privacy, then searches of students are reasonable without either warrants or probable cause. Random drug testing of employees constitutes a reasonable search because the special need of government to protect public safety outweighs the minimal invasion of privacy caused by collecting and analyzing urine samples.

REVIEW QUESTIONS

1. What is the significance of the reference in the Fourth Amendment to the "people" generally?

2. Compare and contrast the "special needs" searches with the searches discussed in Chapter 6.

3. Explain how the balancing approach works in determining the reasonableness of special needs searches.

4. Define inventory searches, and explain and identify the main elements in determining their reasonableness.

5. Explain why border searches are reasonable without either warrants or probable cause.

6. What are the special needs in conducting airport searches?

7. What special needs do searches of prisoners, probationers, and parolees serve, and what is the expectation of privacy for people convicted of crimes?

8. When and for what purposes is it reasonable to search employees of and visitors to prisons without either warrants or probable cause?

9. When and for what purposes is it reasonable to search students without either warrants or probable cause?

10. What is the special need and what is the invasion of privacy involved in employee drug testing?

KEY TERMS

border searches searches of persons and property at or near the borders of the United States in order to protect the integrity of international borders.

in loco parentis **doctrine** the principle by which the government stands in place of parents.

inventory searches searches conducted without probable cause or warrants in order to protect property and the safety of police and to prevent claims against police.

"special needs" searches government inspections and other regulatory measures not conducted to gather criminal evidence.

Notes

1. *Colorado v. Bertine*, 479 U.S. 367, 107 S.Ct. 738, 93 L.Ed.2d 739 (1987).

2. Ibid.

3. *Whren v. U.S.*, 1996 WL 305735 (1996) (distinguishes between inventory searches without probable cause and pretext arrests based on probable cause); *Colorado v. Bertine*, 479 U.S., at 376, 107 S.Ct., at 743.

4. *State v. Opperman*, 247 N.W.2d 673, 675 (S.D. 1976).

5. 431 U.S. 606, 97 S.Ct. 1972, 52 L.Ed.2d 617 (1977).

6. Wayne R. LaFave and Jerold H. Israel, *Criminal Procedure* (St. Paul: West Publishing Co., 1984), 1: 327–28.

7. *United States v. Ramsey*, 431 U.S. 606, 97 S.Ct. 1972, 52 L.Ed.2d 617 (1977).

8. LaFave and Israel, *Criminal Procedure*, 332–33.

9. *United States v. Place*, 462 U.S. 696, 103 S.Ct. 2637, 77 L.Ed.2d 110 (1983).

10. 370 U.S. 139, 82 S.Ct. 1218, 8 L.Ed.2d 384 (1962).

11. *Hudson v. Palmer*, 468 U.S. 517, 104 S.Ct. 3194, 82 L.Ed.2d 393 (1984).

12. *Bell v. Wolfish*, 441 U.S. 520, 99 S.Ct. 1861, 60 L.Ed.2d 447 (1979) (strip search of detainees following visits); *Mary Beth G. v. City of Chicago*, 723 F.2d 1263 (7th Cir. 1983) (strip search of all women arrested for misdemeanors).

13. LaFave and Israel, *Criminal Procedure*, 336–38.

14. *Kennedy v. Hardiman*, 684 F.Supp. 540 (N.D.Ill. 1988).

15. *New Jersey v. T.L.O.*, 469 U.S. 325, 105 S.Ct. 733, 83 L.Ed.2d 720 (1985).

CHAPTER EIGHT

Interrogation and Confessions

CHAPTER OUTLINE

CHAPTER MAIN POINTS

1. It is difficult to determine the degree of abuse of police interrogation because of the secrecy that surrounds it.

2. Disagreement exists over the importance of confessions in the conviction of guilty defendants, and no reliable evidence is available to settle the dispute.

3. The Supreme Court has relied on the due process clause, the right to counsel, and the self-incrimination clause to review state confessions.

4. The due process approach to the review of confessions weighs the totality of circumstances in order to determine whether police coercion caused a defendant to confess.

5. The right to counsel approach to self-incrimination applies only after the start of formal proceedings.

6. The self-incrimination clause applies to custodial interrogation by the police.

7. General questioning at crime scenes, questioning during investigative stops, and questioning during booking are not considered custodial interrogation.

8. According to *Miranda v. Arizona*, custodial interrogation is inherently coercive if suspects are not warned of their rights.

9. The *Miranda* warnings are not a right and are not required if to do so would endanger public safety.

10. Defendants can waive their right to remain silent as long as the waiver is knowing and voluntary.

11. Confessions following waivers must be voluntary according to the totality of the circumstances.

12. Confessions are compelled if police conduct overbears the will of suspects and causes them to confess.

13. Coerced confessions are harmless errors if convictions are based on substantial evidence of guilt other than the confessions.

Was the Confession Voluntary?

In April 1977, Marshall Carruth was found murdered in Baker, Louisiana. The murder remained unsolved until 1982. In the summer of 1982, Kerry Van Welch told his estranged wife, Barbara, that he had killed a man. He had told her this once before, in 1980, but she had dismissed it at the time as just "talking big." After the second conversation, however, she became worried and told her father about the claimed murder. Her father relayed the information to a probation officer, who in turn talked to the Baker City Police Department.

In September 1982, officers Bourgoyne and Funderburk asked Welch to come to the police station for questioning. They advised him of his Miranda rights and left him with another officer, Stan Easley, a professed born-again Christian. Upon entering the room, he immediately identified himself as a police officer. Easley and Welch discussed forgiveness and salvation and prayed together for about three hours. During this time, Welch made incriminating statements.

THE SELF-INCRIMINATION SETTING

Perhaps no single procedure is more widely known, for good or ill, than police officers administering the *Miranda* warnings to criminal suspects. In her widely read *Miranda*, Liva Baker wrote the following in 1983:

> The word *Miranda* ha[s] become a staple of the law enforcement community's vocabulary, and prosecutors and judges alike re[fer] to the station house ritual of giving *Miranda* warnings as "mirandizing." The Hill Street blues read them over national television, and in a nationally syndicated comic strip, Peppermint Patty, on her first assignment at a school safety patrol, read them to a kindergartner who had crossed the street improperly. *Miranda* ha[s] become part of the popular culture.[1]

Change *Hill Street Blues* to any of the many current television "cop shows" and the statement is as true today as it was in 1983. Not only is *Miranda* well-known, but also perhaps no other police procedure has generated more hostility among the public. Television shows have not overlooked the strong public feelings about the *Miranda* warnings. In an episode of the popular *L.A. Law* of the 1980s, after the mythical state supreme court orders a new trial for a convicted murderer, the prosecutor complains, "It's a very sad day when a murderer's conviction is overturned on a technicality. But I assure the People this Office is committed to keeping that man in prison." On the currently popular *NYPD Blue*, the good cops Andy Sipowitz and his partner wage an unrelenting "war on *Miranda*." First, a "scumbag" murderer—or his lawyer—makes a "mockery of the system" by taunting the cops with his rights. Then Sipowitz and his partner threaten, shove, and often beat a confession out of the "worthless animal" called a suspect. We all know he's guilty, and we are invited to hate the system that provides such scumbags with rights. Even the comic strip *Spiderman* joined the "war on *Miranda*" waged by the instruments of popular culture. In one episode, Spiderman crashes through a window, rescues a robbery hostage from a gunman in view of officers and television cameras, and turns the robber over to the police. However, the police fail to administer the culprit the *Miranda* warnings. According to Spiderman, the robber goes free on a "technicality" that is supposed to protect society but instead "protects the criminal and endangers society."[2]

The popular portrayal of good cops and evil criminals does not match the complexity of the real picture of police work in police stations. Following arrest, most encounters between the police and criminal suspects take place in the police station. The atmosphere in police stations is strange, intimidating, and even hostile to suspects compared to the familiar and comfortable feeling of homes, bars, restaurants, and other places where many of the encounters discussed in Chapters 3–6 take place. Furthermore, the encounters between criminal suspects and officers in the police station are much more intrusive than those taking place on the street and other public places. Custodial searches, eyewitness identification (Chapter 9), and interrogation of suspects take longer, probe deeper, and generate more discomfort than the brief stops, questioning, and frisks on the street.

Investigation has focused on specific suspects by the time the police have made arrests. This period when the police have shifted their attention from a general investigation of a crime to building a case against a specific individual is called the **accusatory stage** of the criminal process. Invasions intensify during the accusatory stage. Police interrogation in surroundings unfriendly to suspects and lineups, showups, and other identification procedures intrude more deeply into citizens' privacy and subject them to greater deprivations than do stops, frisks, arrests, or other seizures and searches (discussed in Chapters 3–6). Hence, balancing the needs of law enforcement against the interests of privacy and liberty carries higher stakes for both private individuals and law enforcement during this stage. Defining the proper balance between these competing social interests during the period when the police hold suspects in custody but before prosecutors have formally charged them with crimes has generated tremendous controversy over the years. The controversy is seen mainly as an argument over the extent to which the Constitution protects citizens in police custody.

D e c i s i o n   P o i n t

In which of the following hypothetical situations are persons compelled to be witnesses against themselves?

1. A police officer asks a man he has stopped on the street, "What are you doing out at 1:30 A.M.?" The man replies, "I'm trying to buy some crack, as if it's any of your business."

2. An officer hears screams coming from an apartment. He enters without knocking and asks, "What's going on here?" A woman answers, "I just beat up my baby."

3. An elderly woman was beaten when she would not relinquish her purse to three muggers. She was left on the street and died of exposure. Officers in relays question an eighteen-year-old suspect for six hours without a break. Some officers take a belligerent tone, bullying the suspect and telling him he is in "big trouble." They never touch him. One officer befriends him, telling him the officer knows whoever took the purse didn't mean to kill the woman and that, anyway, it was really her fault for resisting. The suspect finally weakens and confesses.

4. A police officer, while interrogating a suspect in the police station, promises the suspect, "If you'll just tell me the truth about raping the college student, I'll see to it that the prosecutor only charges you with misdemeanor assault." The suspect asks, "You can do that?" The officer replies, "Sure, I wouldn't tell you something I couldn't do." The suspect says, "O.K., I did it." He later puts the confession in writing.

5. An officer tells a suspect brought to the police station for questioning, "You might as well admit you killed your husband, because your neighbor already told us he saw the whole thing." The officer is lying. The suspect replies, "My God, I knew I should have pulled the shades; that nosy bastard is always spying on me."

THE IMPORTANCE OF INTERROGATION

Nearly forty years ago, Supreme Court Justice Felix Frankfurter noted the importance of police interrogation:

> Despite modern advances in the technology of crime detection, offenses frequently occur about which things cannot be made to speak. And where there cannot be found innocent human witnesses to such offenses, nothing remains — if police investigation is not to be balked before it has fairly begun — but to seek out possible guilty witnesses and ask them questions, witnesses, that is, who are suspected of knowing something about the offense precisely because they are suspected of implication in it.[3]

Fred Inbau — law professor emeritus at Northwestern University, author of a leading manual on police interrogation, and celebrated interrogator[4] — has spelled out three reasons in support of Justice Frankfurter's position:

1. Police can solve many cases, even when the best-qualified police departments investigate them, only if guilty persons confess or other suspects provide information that forms the basis of convicting others.

2. Criminals will not admit they committed crimes unless police catch them in the act or question them in private for perhaps a period of hours.

3. "In dealing with criminal offenders, and consequently with criminal suspects who may actually be innocent, the interrogator must employ less refined methods than are considered appropriate for the transaction of ordinary, every-day affairs by and between law-abiding citizens."[5]

Interrogation—the questioning of suspects and criminal defendants—and incriminating admissions and confessions occur at four times:

1. Prior to arrest

2. Immediately following arrest but prior to formal charges

3. Following charges but prior to trial

4. During the trial

The second point—police interrogation during the period immediately following arrest but before formal charges—has provoked more debate since the early 1970s than perhaps any other subject in the law of criminal procedure. The controversy arises over three issues:

1. The importance of confessions in solving crimes and convicting criminals

2. The kinds and amount of pressure used in police interrogation

3. The extent of the abuse of interrogation

Empirical data will probably never fully resolve these issues. In *Miranda v. Arizona,* Chief Justice Earl Warren—himself an experienced former prosecutor—acknowledged the problems of getting information about what really happens in interrogation rooms:

> Interrogation still takes place in privacy. Privacy results in secrecy and this in turn results in a gap in our knowledge as to what in fact goes on in the interrogation room.[6]

Some recent empirical research is closing this gap. Sociologist Richard Leo spent more than 500 hours inside the interrogation rooms of a major urban police department and also viewed videotaped custodial interrogations from two other departments. He found the following:

1. That very few interrogations are coercive

2. That one in five suspects invokes one or more of his or her *Miranda* rights in order to avoid cooperating with the police

3. That interrogators use tactics advocated in police training manuals (fabricated evidence, "good guy–bad guy") in order to undermine the confidence of suspects and overbear their rational decision making

4. That detectives have become increasingly skilled in eliciting incriminating evidence during custodial interrogation

5. That the overwhelming number of custodial interrogations last less than one hour

6. That suspects who provide incriminating information are likely to be treated differently at every stage of the criminal process than suspects who do not provide incriminating information[7]

**TABLE 8.1 APPLICATION OF THE U.S. CONSTITUTION
TO INTERROGATIONS AND CONFESSIONS**

Amendment	Stage of Criminal Process
Fifth and Fourteenth Amendment due process	All stages
Sixth Amendment right to counsel	All stages after the initiation of formal proceedings
Fifth Amendment self-incrimination	Accusatory stage and all stages following

THE ABUSE OF INTERROGATION

Another difficulty in evaluating interrogation is defining what amounts to its abuse. At one extreme is the belief that secret interrogation is always an abuse of police questioning. At the other extreme is the belief that only beating, whipping, or threats of violence are abuses of police interrogation. In the middle is the notion that secret interrogation is proper as long as interrogators do not use trickery, cajolery, lies, and false promises. Commentators, courts, and advocates differ sharply over where to draw the line. Varying emphases on what interests criminal procedure ought to promote account for these differences. Those opposed to police interrogation emphasize the potential for wrong decisions, particularly the conviction of the innocent; the primacy of the individual; and the need for controlling police behavior. Those who favor broad police interrogation stress the need to get the facts and convict the guilty and the need for efficient, speedy administration of criminal justice. In other words, the disagreement over defining interrogation reflects differing emphases on the interests in obtaining the correct result in individual cases and ensuring fair processes in all cases.[8]

THE CONSTITUTION
AND SELF-INCRIMINATION

The right to remain silent is ancient. One of the most famous examples of remaining silent occurred nearly two thousand years ago in Judea. Jesus stood before Pontius Pilate, the Roman governor. The governor demanded to know, "Art thou King of the Jews?" Jesus answered artfully, "Thou sayest." Then chief priests and elders accused Jesus of many crimes. Jesus stood and "answered them nothing." Surprised, Pilate asked, "Hearest thou not how many things they witness against thee?" And still Jesus "answered him to never a word, insomuch that the governor marvelled greatly." The ancient Talmudic law embodied the oral teachings represented by the laws of Moses. One of its provisions was an absolute prohibition against self-incrimination. The right was not even waivable. The right to remain silent—bound up with the rule of voluntariness in the ancient common law—followed a controversial and complicated history until it finally appeared as the Fifth Amendment to the United States Constitution.[9]

The United States Supreme Court has relied on three provisions in the Constitution in developing doctrines related to the law of police interrogation and confessions (see Table 8.1):

■ Fourteenth Amendment due process clause—"No state shall . . . deprive any person of life, liberty, or property without due process of law."

- Sixth Amendment right to counsel clause — "In all criminal prosecutions, the accused shall . . . have the assistance of counsel for his defense."

- Fifth Amendment self-incrimination clause — "No person . . . shall be compelled in any criminal case to be a witness against himself."

The Due Process Approach

The due process, right to counsel, and self-incrimination doctrines overlap, but they follow a roughly chronological line. In *Brown v. Mississippi* (1936), the Supreme Court held that the Fourteenth Amendment due process clause prohibits the admission of forced confessions as evidence in criminal trials. In *Brown*, the police were investigating the murder of a white farmer, Raymond Stewart, who was found unconscious in his home in Kemper County, Mississippi, by neighbors. Many of the bones in his body were brutally broken, much of his skull was crushed into small pieces, and someone had split his shoulder with an ax. Stewart died, never regaining consciousness. An outraged citizenry conducted their own investigation. They believed that three blacks — Ed Brown (one of Stewart's tenant farmers), Yank Ellington, and Henry Shields — had committed the ghoulish crime. A mob gathered, rope in hand, and went to Yank Ellington's house. A deputy sheriff, Dial, went with them. The white men accused Ellington of murdering Stewart. When he denied that he had committed the crime,

> they seized him, and with the participation of the deputy they hanged him by a rope to the limb of a tree, having let him down, they hung him again, and when he was let down the second time, and he still protested his innocence, he was tied to a tree and whipped, and, still declining to accede to the demands that he confess, he was finally released, and he returned with some difficulty to his home, suffering intense pain and agony.[10]

Deputy Dial returned later with another man and arrested Ellington. On the way to the jail, the two stopped by the roadside and beat Ellington again. Dial told Ellington that he would continue to beat him until he confessed. Ellington agreed to confess to anything Dial dictated. Brown and Shields were then arrested and taken to the same jail. There, Dial, the jailer, and a number of other white men ordered the prisoners to strip, bent them over chairs, and beat them. After a period of severe beating, Brown and Shields also confessed. According to Chief Justice Charles Evans Hughes, who wrote the opinion for the Supreme Court reviewing this case:

> Further details of the brutal treatment to which these helpless prisoners were subjected need not be pursued. It is sufficient to say that in pertinent respects the transcript reads more like pages torn from some medieval account than a record made within the confines of a modern civilization which aspires to an enlightened constitutional government.[11]

The suspects were tried the next day, with the rope burns still showing on Ellington's neck. The judge admitted the confessions into evidence. The defendants testified to the beatings. The state's witnesses did not deny that they beat the defendants. In fact, Deputy Dial testified that Ellington's whipping was "not too much for a negro; not as much as I would have done if it were left to me." Defense counsel did not move to exclude the confessions. Brown, Ellington, and Shields were convicted later the same day and sentenced to death. The Mississippi Supreme Court affirmed the convictions, and the defendants appealed to the U.S. Supreme Court. Up to the time the Court agreed to review the confession in *Brown,* it had never agreed to review a confessions case from a state court. And in *Brown,* the Court did not rely specifically on the Fifth Amendment self-incrimination clause. Instead, the Court relied on the Fourteenth Amendment due process clause, which prohibits states from denying citizens "life, liberty, or property without due process of law."

The Supreme Court adopted a **reliability rationale** to exclude coerced confessions from judicial proceedings. According to this rationale, forced confessions are not admissible as evidence because they are not trustworthy—that is, they are not good proof. To admit unreliable evidence as proof of guilt would deny defendants of their lives (remember, these three were sentenced to death) without due process of law. The confessions were the only evidence introduced at the trial. As Chief Justice Hughes wrote for the Court,

> The state is free to regulate the procedure of its courts in accordance with its own conceptions of policy, unless in so doing it "offends some principle of justice so rooted in the traditions and conscience of our people as to be ranked as fundamental." . . . But the freedom of the state in establishing its policy is the freedom of constitutional government and is limited by the requirement of due process of law. . . . The rack and torture chamber may not be substituted for the witness stand. The state may not permit an accused to be hurried to conviction under mob domination—where the whole proceeding is but a mask—without supplying corrective process. . . . And the trial equally is a mere pretense where the state authorities have contrived a conviction resting solely on the confessions obtained by violence. The due process clause requires that "state action . . . shall be consistent with the fundamental principles of liberty and justice which lie at the base of all our civil and political institutions." It would be difficult to conceive of methods more revolting to the sense of justice than those taken to procure the confessions of these petitioners, and the use of the confessions thus obtained as the basis for conviction and sentence was a clear denial of due process.[12]

The unreliability of coerced confessions provided the rationale for the review of early state confessions cases. In *Ashcraft v. Tennessee,* the Court added the **accusatorial system rationale** to the reliability rationale for reviewing state confessions. In applying the accusatorial system rationale in *Rogers v. Richmond,* the Court excluded a confession secured after the police had threatened to bring Rogers's arthritic wife in for questioning. The confession was excluded not only to eliminate untrustworthy evidence from the particular case but also to uphold the accusatorial system of justice in the United States.[13] According to Justice Felix Frankfurter,

> Our decisions under [the Fourteenth Amendment] have made clear that convictions following the admission . . . of confessions which are involuntary, i.e., the product of coercion, either physical or psychological, cannot stand. This is so not because such confessions are unlikely to be true but because the methods used to extract them offend an underlying principle in the enforcement of our criminal law: that ours is an accusatorial and not an inquisitorial system—a system in which the State must establish guilt by evidence independently and freely secured and

may not by coercion prove its charge against an accused out of his own mouth. To be sure, confessions cruelly extorted may be and have been . . . found to be untrustworthy. But the constitutional principle of excluding confessions that are involuntary does not rest on this consideration. Indeed, in many of the cases in which the command of the Due Process clause has compelled us to reverse . . . convictions involving the use of confessions obtained by impermissible methods, independent corroborating evidence left little doubt of the truth of what the defendant had confessed.[14]

The Court added yet a third rationale for reviewing state confessions, the **fundamental fairness rationale.** According to the Court, coerced confessions are not only untrustworthy and contrary to the accusatorial system of justice; they also offend the fundamental fairness required by the due process clause. According to Chief Justice Warren, writing for a unanimous Court in *Spano v. New York,*

> The abhorrence of society to the use of involuntary confessions does not turn alone on their inherent untrustworthiness. It also turns on the deep-rooted feeling that the police must obey the law while enforcing the law; that in the end life and liberty can be as much endangered from illegal methods used to convict those thought to be criminals as from the actual criminals themselves. Accordingly, the actions of police in obtaining confessions have come under scrutiny in a long series of cases.[15]

During the thirty years from *Brown v. Mississippi* until *Miranda v. Arizona,* the Supreme Court overturned forty state confessions on the basis of the due process clause. Most of the early cases following *Brown* involved cases in which Southern white mobs rounded up poor blacks and tortured them until at least one of the blacks confessed. The Court was much more reluctant to overturn the convictions of less "sympathetic criminals" from other parts of the country. In *Lisenba v. California,* for example, Lisenba (an intelligent white business executive from California) confessed that he had "tied his wife to a chair, subjected her to rattlesnake bites, and then drowned her in a pond." The interrogation took place in several all-night sessions over a two-week period. His demands for a lawyer and to remain silent were ignored by the police. The Court refused to overturn the conviction. His admissions, in light of his intelligence and business experience, were "a calculated attempt to minimize his culpability after carefully considering statements by the accomplice."[16] According to Justice Jackson, in another case of "unsympathetic criminals" who "were convinced their dance was over and the time had come to pay the fiddler,"

> The limits in any case depend upon a weighing of the circumstances of pressure against the power of resistance of the person confessing. What would be overpowering to the weak of will or mind might be utterly ineffective against an experienced criminal.[17]

The Right to Counsel Approach

Even as the Supreme Court was developing the due process approach to the review of state confessions cases, a growing minority of the Court, led by Justices Hugo Black and William Douglas, was turning to stronger measures to control police interrogation. By 1958, a minority of four justices, including Chief Justice Earl Warren and Associate Justices Black, Douglas, and William Brennan, was prepared to call police custodial interrogation a critical stage in the prosecution of criminals and therefore protected by the Sixth Amendment, guaranteeing the right to counsel "in all criminal prosecutions." In *Crooker v. California*, Crooker, a former law student, was a houseboy to a woman with whom he was having an affair. She broke off the affair because she had found another boyfriend. After fourteen hours in police custody, Crooker confessed that he had stabbed and strangled his victim. No evidence appeared to show that the police had used force on Crooker. He was allowed to eat, drink, and smoke, and interrogation sessions lasted only about an hour at a time. However, the police did refuse Crooker's request to call his lawyer. The Supreme Court affirmed Crooker's conviction, but the four justices named above dissented. According to Justice Douglas's dissenting opinion, joined by Chief Justice Warren and Associate Justices Black and Brennan,

> The mischief and abuse of the third degree will continue as long as an accused can be denied the right to counsel at the most critical period of his ordeal. For what takes place in the secret confines of the police station may be more critical than what takes place at trial.[18]

By 1964, the membership of the Court had changed. The change in membership brought to a slim majority of five to four the right to counsel approach to police interrogation. In *Escobedo v. Illinois*, decided in 1964, the Supreme Court turned briefly to the Sixth Amendment right to counsel clause as a basis for reviewing state confessions cases. The Chicago police refused to allow Danny Escobedo to see his lawyer even though the attorney had come to the station at the request of Escobedo's mother and despite the lawyer's repeated requests to see his client. Escobedo confessed, but the Supreme Court ruled that the government could not introduce the confession into evidence because Escobedo had given it without the advice of counsel. Once police investigation focuses on a particular suspect, according to the Court, the prosecution has begun, and the right to counsel attaches. If defendants have confessed before trial and they have a right to counsel at trial, then trials are "no more than an appeal from the interrogation." Illinois argued, and four dissenting justices on the Supreme Court agreed, that bringing the Sixth Amendment right to counsel into interrogation rooms would end the use of confessions in law enforcement. Any lawyer present who is "worth her salt" is, of course, going to tell her clients not to say anything to the police. According to Justice White's dissenting opinion,

> I do not suggest for a moment that law enforcement will be destroyed by the rule announced today. The need for peace and order is too insistent for that. But it will be crippled and its task made a great deal more difficult. . . .[19]

The Self-Incrimination Approach

Just two years later, in 1966, the Court abruptly dropped the Sixth Amendment right to counsel basis for reviewing state confessions cases. In the landmark *Miranda v. Arizona*, the Court focused squarely on the Fifth Amendment self-incrimination clause as the primary constitutional provision that governs both federal and police interrogation and confessions.[20]

**TABLE 8.2 INCRIMINATING EVIDENCE
NOT PROTECTED BY THE FIFTH AMENDMENT**

Weapons	Photographs
Contraband	Appearance in lineup
Stolen property	Bullets removed from the body
Handwriting samples	Products of consent searches
Hair samples	Books, papers, documents
Voice samples	Records required by law to be kept
Fingerprints	

The due process, right to counsel, and self-incrimination doctrines do not mutually exclude one another; all are relevant in specific circumstances. The Court relies on the due process clause to review all government activity at any stage in the criminal process in order to determine whether government actions deny criminal defendants the fundamental elements of a fair trial. The Court relies on the right to counsel provision to govern interrogation and confessions after the government has initiated formal proceedings in the form of indictment, information, or arraignment (see Chapters 1 and 11). The Court relies on the Fifth Amendment self-incrimination clause to decide the voluntariness of police interrogation and confessions cases before indictment, information, or arraignment. And, of course, the Fifth Amendment always applies during formal proceedings, particularly the trial of criminal defendants.

THE DEFINITION
OF *SELF-INCRIMINATION*

The Fifth Amendment prohibits the government from compelling criminal suspects and defendants to be witnesses against themselves. It does not prohibit the government from gathering other kinds of incriminating evidence, particularly physical evidence (Chapters 4–6) and evidence derived from identification and examination procedures (Chapter 9). Supreme Court decisions have limited the protection of the Fifth Amendment self-incrimination clause to the gathering of testimonial evidence — that is, the content of some of the spoken words of criminal suspects. For example, the government can compel a suspect to speak in order to help a witness identify the suspect by means of the suspect's voice. According to the Supreme Court, the Fifth Amendment protects the content of speech, not the voice that utters the words. Nor, according to the Court, is it self-incrimination to require drivers in accidents to supply their names and addresses or in fact to reveal any information that statutes require individuals to disclose or to turn over to the government, including the words, figures, and other information contained in books, papers, and other records (see Table 8.2). Finally, the Court has ruled that the self-incrimination clause does not bar prosecutors from telling juries that defendants exercised their right to remain silent when police questioned them. Hence, juries can infer guilt from the refusal to answer police questions.[21]

STATE CONSTITUTIONAL LAW

Commonwealth v. Turner
499 Pa. 579, 454 A.2d 537 (1982)

FACTS

Following Turner's conviction in a shooting death in a bar, he was sentenced to a term of five to ten years imprisonment. Turner appealed, contending that a reference by the prosecutor, in his cross-examination of Turner, to Turner's silence before trial was a reversible error warranting the grant of a new trial. After Turner stated, on cross-examination, that he saw a drug dealer shooting at him, the prosecutor asked: "Did you ever tell the police that somebody was shooting at you?" Turner had not, at any time, given a statement to the police. This in-court testimony was the first occasion on which Turner offered an exculpatory version of the shooting. Before Turner answered, defense counsel objected to the question and, at sidebar, moved for a mistrial. The trial judge sustained the objection but denied the motion for mistrial, giving instead cautionary instructions to the jury voluntarily. These instructions were:

> Ladies and gentlemen of the jury, I told you at the beginning of this trial, when I gave preliminary instructions, the only evidence you are to consider when you deliberate as to your verdict is what you hear from this witness stand. I told you specifically, as I recall, and I reiterate it now, that questions asked by either of the lawyers or even the court are not evidence. A question was just asked before we went to sidebar by the Assistant District Attorney for this witness, the defendant. It has not been answered. It was objected to, I sustained the objection, and that means you are to disregard that question, or I say to you now you are to disregard that question entirely, as though it had never been asked during the course of the trial,

there were no further prosecutorial references to appellant's silence.

OPINION

The United States Supreme Court has recently established the constitutional permissibility of references at trial to post-arrest silence where the silence in question occurred prior to the giving of *Miranda* warnings. *Fletcher v. Weir*, 455 U.S. 603, 102 S.Ct. 1309, 71 L.Ed.2d 490 (1982). This holding is grounded upon the view that the giving of warnings mandated by the Court's decision in *Miranda v. Arizona*, 384 U.S. 436, 86 S.Ct. 1602, 16 L.Ed.2d 694 (1966), implicitly induces the accused to remain silent, and absent the giving of the warnings, there is no governmental inducement to remain silent. Accordingly, as a matter of federal constitutional law, the use of pre-*Miranda* silence is permissible to impeach the defendant's trial testimony of exculpatory events. In this Commonwealth, however, we have traditionally viewed such references to the accused's silence as impermissible. . . .

The view of this Court that there exists a strong disposition on the part of lay jurors to view the exercise of the Fifth Amendment privilege as an admission of guilt is well established. In *Commonwealth v. Haideman*, 449 Pa. 367, 371, 296 A.2d 765, 767 (1972), we stated:

> "We would be naive if we failed to recognize that most laymen view an assertion of the Fifth Amendment privilege as a badge of guilt." It is clear that "[t]he privilege against self-incrimination would be reduced to a hollow mockery if its exercise could be taken as equivalent either to a confession of guilt or a conclusive presumption of perjury."

. . .

Article 1, § 9 of the Pennsylvania Constitution provides that the accused "cannot be compelled to give evidence against himself . . . ," a right which is parallel to the federal constitutional right under the Fifth Amendment. We do not think that the accused should be protected only where there is governmental inducement of the exercise of the right. We acknowledge that this position is more restrictive than that taken by the United States Supreme Court in *Fletcher v. Weir.* However, we decline to hold, under the Pennsylvania Constitution, that the existence of *Miranda* warnings, or their absence, affects a person's legitimate expectation not to be penalized for exercising the right to remain silent. In *Commonwealth v. Easley,* 483 Pa. 337, 396 A.2d 1198 (1979), this Court in a footnote stated:

> [W]e do not believe any reason exists to differentiate between situations where the right to remain silent is exercised following warnings and where it is exercised without warnings being given. Whether or not the exercise of the right to remain silent is induced by being advised of it at the time of arrest or is self-motivated by prior knowledge of it by the accused should not limit or extend the effect of exercising the right.

McDermott, Justice, dissenting.

The common law, based on common experience, recognized, as does the Supreme Court, that silence has its risks. That facts and circumstances may indeed have natural, human inconsistency with silence. Moreover, and more important, "silence" is not the subject of the constitutional provision. The Fifth Amendment is not an exhortation to silence or a celebration of its golden qualities. It protects it when exercised, but it does not enforce or encourage silence. Hence, despite its enigmatic twist that *Miranda* "warnings" are an inducement to silence, the Supreme Court is at pains to say that the federal Constitution does not prohibit mention of the natural inconsistency that may exist between silence and the facts and circumstances of a case.

The Supreme Court therefore left the matter to the states in instances where no warnings or inducements to silence exist. Given this opportunity, the majority in this case continues its adventures in uncharted puddles. The majority explicitly acknowledges that the rule in Pennsylvania is more restrictive than the position taken by the Supreme Court. In doing so, I believe the Court has turned a cloak into a dagger. . . . Silence to save oneself or one's friends is not always invoked to thwart oppressors; it can be a greedy, self-centered thing of terrible consequence. The Constitution should not be distorted into a manual for escape artists to ward off every possible threat.

Decision Point

Police took Muniz to a booking center after arresting him for driving while intoxicated. According to a department policy of videotaping suspected drunk drivers in order to preserve a record of their condition, Officer Jerry Hosterman told Muniz that they would videotape his voice and actions. Officer Hosterman did not administer *Miranda* warnings. In the first segment of the video, Hosterman asked Muniz his height, weight, eye color, date of birth, and current age. Muniz answered that he was born on April 19, 1947, but said he was currently forty-nine. He then laughed, hit his head with his hand, and said, "I mean thirty-nine." Officer Hosterman asked Muniz the date of his sixth birthday. Muniz first uttered an inaudible sound, then admitted he could not calculate the date.

In the second segment of the video, Officer Hosterman administered three sobriety tests. Muniz's eyes jerked noticeably during the gaze test, he could not walk in a straight line, and he could not balance himself on one leg for more than a few seconds. Moreover, during the one-leg stance, when Muniz was supposed to count aloud from one to thirty, he managed to count only from one to six, missing number two. During the walk-the-line test, he did not count at all. Throughout the tests, he requested clarification of the instructions for the tests and attempted to explain his difficulties in performing the tests by referring to his advanced state of intoxication.

Did his actions and words violate the Fifth Amendment self-incrimination clause? According to the United States Supreme Court, all the bodily movements and Muniz's generally slurred speech during the tests were physical, not testimonial, evidence. However, the answer to the question about the date of his sixth birthday was incriminating testimonial evidence, acquired without the protection of the *Miranda* warnings.[22]

THE IMPORTANCE
OF *MIRANDA V. ARIZONA*

The due process approach to self-incrimination led the Supreme Court to adopt a voluntariness test to review confessions in state cases from 1936 until 1966. According to the voluntariness test, if the totality of circumstances surrounding incriminating statements and confessions obtained during interrogation indicated that suspects did not confess or make incriminating admissions voluntarily, the interrogations violated due process. By the 1960s, a combination of concern about police tactics used against suspects in the strange, secret, and intimidating surroundings of the police station, dissatisfaction with the vagueness of the totality-of-circumstances approach, and the need under it to decide every case on its own facts led to one of the most famous, most debated, and perhaps most hated decisions in the constitutional history of the United States.

In *Miranda v. Arizona*, a bare five to four majority of the United States Supreme Court established a rule to govern **custodial interrogation**—that is, interrogation occurring after the police take suspects into custody. The Court held that custodial interrogation is inherently coercive. Suspects are in strange surroundings and are not free to go home or call upon relatives and friends for support. Furthermore, skilled police officers, using trickery and psychological pressure, engage in rounds of incommunicado, secret missions calculated to "crack" the will of suspects. In these circumstances, guaranteeing voluntary confessions requires strong protection.

C A S E

Does the Fifth Amendment Apply to Custodial Interrogation?

Miranda v. Arizona
384 U.S. 436, 86 S.Ct. 1602 (1966)

The Supreme Court held that statements obtained from Miranda and others during incommunicado interrogation in a police-dominated atmosphere, without full warning of their constitutional rights, were inadmissible as having been obtained in violation of the Fifth Amendment privilege against self-incrimination.

Justice Harlan, Justice Stewart, Justice White, and Justice Clark dissented. Chief Justice Warren delivered the opinion of the Court.

FACTS

[NOTE: The Court decided four interrogation cases on the same day. Only the facts and discussion of *Miranda v. Arizona* (1966) are included in this excerpt.]

On March 13, 1963, petitioner, Ernesto Miranda, was arrested at his home and taken into custody to a Phoenix police station. He was there identified by the complaining witness. The police then took him to "Interrogation Room No. 2" of the detective bureau. There he was questioned by two police officers. The officers admitted at trial that Miranda was not advised that he had a right to have an attorney present. Two hours later, the officers emerged from the interrogation room with a written confession signed by Miranda. At the top of the statement was a typed paragraph stating that the confession was made voluntarily, without threats or promises of immunity and "with full knowledge of my legal rights, understanding any statement I make may be used against me."

At this trial before a jury, the written confession was admitted into evidence over the objection of defense counsel, and the officers testified to the prior oral confession made by Miranda during the interrogation. Miranda was found guilty of kidnapping and rape. He was sentenced to 20 to 30 years' imprisonment on each count, the sentences to run concurrently. On appeal, the Supreme Court of Arizona held that Miranda's constitutional rights were not violated in obtaining the confession and affirmed the conviction. In reaching its decision, the court emphasized heavily the fact that Miranda did not specifically request counsel. We reverse.

OPINION

From the testimony of the officers and by the admission of respondent, it is clear that Miranda was not in any way apprised of his right to consult with an attorney and to have one present during the interrogation, nor was his right not to be compelled to incriminate himself effectively protected in any other manner. Without these warnings the statements were inadmissible. The mere fact that he signed a statement which contained a typed-in clause stating that he had "full knowledge" of his "legal rights" does not approach the knowing and intelligent waiver required to relinquish constitutional rights. . . .

. . . The constitutional issue we decide in each of [the four related cases considered today] is the admissibility of statements obtained from a defendant questioned while in custody or otherwise deprived of his freedom of action in any significant way. In each [case], the defendant was questioned by police officers, detectives, or a prosecuting attorney in a room in which he was cut off from the outside world. In none of these cases was the defendant given a full and effective warning of his rights at the outset of the interrogation process. In all the cases, the questioning elicited oral admissions, and in three of them, signed statements as well which were admitted at their trials. They all thus share salient features — incommunicado interrogation of individuals in a police-dominated atmosphere, resulting in self-incriminating statements without full warnings of constitutional rights.

An understanding of the nature and setting of this in-custody interrogation is essential to our decisions today. The difficulty in depicting what transpires at such interrogations stems from the fact that in this country they have largely taken place incommunicado. From extensive factual studies undertaken in the early 1930s, including the famous Wickersham Report to Congress by a Presidential Commission, it is clear that police violence and the "third degree" flourished at that time. In a series of cases decided by this court long after these studies, the police resorted to physical brutality — beatings, hanging, whipping — and to sustained and protracted questioning incommunicado in order to extort confessions. . . .

Even without employing brutality, the "third degree" or the specific stratagems described above, the very fact of custodial interrogation exacts a heavy toll on individual liberty and trades on the weakness of individuals. . . .

In the cases before us today . . . we concern ourselves primarily with this interrogation atmosphere and the evils it can bring. . . . In these cases, we might not find the defendants' statements to have been involuntary in traditional terms. Our concern for adequate safeguards to protect precious Fifth Amendment rights is, of course, not lessened in the slightest. In each of these cases, the defendant was thrust into an unfamiliar atmosphere and run through menacing police interrogation procedures. The potentiality for compulsion is forcefully apparent, for example, in *Miranda*, where the indigent Mexican defendant was a seriously disturbed individual with pronounced sexual fantasies, and in *Stewart*, in which the defendant was an indigent Los Angeles Negro who had dropped out of school in the sixth grade. To be sure, the records do not evince overt physical coercion or patent psychological ploys. The fact remains that in none of these cases did the officer undertake to afford appropriate safeguards at the outset of the interrogation to insure that the statements were truly the product of free choice.

It is obvious that such an interrogation environment is created for no purpose other than to subjugate the individual to the will of his examiner. This atmosphere carries its own badge of intimidation. To be sure, this is not physical intimidation, but it is equally destructive of human dignity. The current practice of incommunicado interrogation is at odds with one of our Nation's most cherished principles — that the individual may not be compelled to incriminate himself. Unless adequate protective devices are employed to dispel the compulsion inherent in custodial surroundings, no statement obtained from the defendant can truly be the product of his free choice. . . .

We sometimes forget how long it has taken to establish the privilege against self-incrimination, the sources from which it came and the fervor with which it was defended. Its roots go back into ancient times. . . . [W]e may view the historical development of the privilege as one which groped for the proper scope of governmental power over the citizen. As a "noble principle often transcends its origins," the privilege has come rightfully to be recognized in part as an individual's substantive right, a "right to a private enclave where he may lead a private life. That right is the hallmark of our democracy." We have recently noted that the privilege against self-incrimination — the essential mainstay of our adversary system — is founded on a complex of values. All these policies point to one overriding thought: the constitutional foundation underlying the privilege is the respect a government — state or federal — must accord to the dignity and integrity of its citizens. To maintain a "fair state–individual balance," to require the government "to shoulder the entire load," to respect the inviolability of the human personality, our accusatory system of criminal justice demands that the government seeking to punish an individual produce the evidence against him by its own independent labors, rather than by the cruel, simple expedient of compelling it from his own mouth. . . .

It is impossible for us to foresee the potential alternatives for protecting the privilege which might be devised by Congress or the States in the exercise of their creative rule-making capacities. Therefore we cannot say that the Constitution necessarily requires adherence to any particular solution for the inherent compulsions of the interrogation process as it is presently conducted. Our decision in no way creates a constitutional straitjacket which will handicap sound efforts at reform, nor is it intended to have this effect. We encourage Congress and the States to continue their laudable search for increasingly effective ways of protecting the rights of the individual while promoting efficient enforcement of our criminal laws. However, unless we are shown other procedures which are at least as effective in apprising accused person of their right of silence and in assuring a continuous opportunity to exercise it . . . [the police must give the warnings outlined above and summarized below].

The principles announced today deal with the protection which must be given to the privilege against self-incrimination when the individual is first subjected to police interrogation while in custody at the station or otherwise deprived of his freedom of action in any significant way. It is at this point that our adversary system of criminal proceedings commences, distinguishing itself at the outset from the inquisitorial system recognized in some countries. Under the system of warnings we delineate today or under any other system which may be devised and found effective, the safeguards to be erected about the privilege must come into play at this point. . . . .

To summarize, we hold that when an individual is taken into custody or otherwise deprived of his freedom by the authorities in any significant way and is subjected to questioning, the privilege against self-incrimination is jeopardized. Procedural safeguards must be employed to protect the privilege and unless other fully effective means are adopted to notify the person of his right of silence and to assure that the exercise of the right will be scrupulously honored, the following measures are required. He must be warned prior to any questioning that he has the right to remain silent, that anything he says can be used against him in a court of law, that he has the right to the presence of an attorney, and that if he cannot afford an attorney one will be appointed for him prior to any questioning if he so desires. Opportunity to exercise these rights must be afforded him throughout the interrogation. After such warnings have been given, and such opportunity afforded him, the individual may knowingly and intelligently waive these rights and agree to answer questions or make a statement. But unless and until such warnings and waiver are demonstrated by the prosecution at trial, no evidence obtained as a result of interrogation can be used against him.

A recurrent argument made in these cases is that society's need for interrogation outweighs the privilege. This argument is not unfamiliar to this Court. The whole thrust of our foregoing discussions demonstrates that the Constitution has prescribed the rights of the individual when confronted with the power of government when it provided in the Fifth Amendment that an individual cannot be compelled to be a witness against himself. That right cannot be abridged. . . . In this connection, one of our country's distinguished jurists has pointed out: "The quality of a nation's civilization can be largely measured by the methods it uses in the enforcement of its criminal law."

If the individual desires to exercise his privilege, he has the right to do so. This is not for the authorities to decide. An attorney may advise his client not to talk to police until he has had an opportunity to investigate the case, or he may wish to be present with his client during any police questioning. In doing so an attorney is merely exercising the good professional judgment he has been taught. This is not cause for considering the attorney a menace to law enforcement. He is merely carrying out what he is sworn to do under his oath — to protect to the extent of his ability the rights of his client. In fulfilling this responsibility the attorney plays a vital role in the administration of criminal justice under our Constitution. In announcing these principles, we are not unmindful of the burdens which law enforcement officials must bear, often under trying circumstances. . . .

[Reversed.]

DISSENT

[Justice Clark's dissent is omitted.]

Justice Harlan, whom Justice Stewart and Justice White join, dissenting.

. . . The new rules are not designed to guard against police brutality or other unmistakably banned forms of coercion. Those who use third-degree tactics and deny them in court are equally able and destined to lie as skillfully about warnings and waivers. Rather, the thrust of the new rules is to negate all pressures, to reinforce the nervous or ignorant suspect, and ultimately to discourage any confession at all. The aim in short is toward "voluntariness" in a utopian sense, or to view it from a different angle, voluntariness with a vengeance.

. . . The Fifth Amendment . . . has never been thought to forbid all pressure to incriminate one's self in the situations covered by it. . . . This is not to say that short of jail or torture any sanction is permissible in any case; policy and history alike may impose sharp limits. However, the Court's unspoken assumption that any pressure violates the privilege is not supported by the precedents and it has failed to show why the Fifth Amendment prohibits that relatively mild pressure the Due Process Clause permits. The Court appears similarly wrong in thinking that precise knowledge of one's rights is settled prerequisite under the Fifth Amendment to the loss of its protections. . . . No Fifth Amendment precedent is cited for the Court's contrary view. . . .

. . . Legal history has been stretched before to satisfy deep needs of society. In this instance, however, the Court has not and cannot make the powerful showing that its new rules are plainly desirable in the context of our society, something which is surely demanded before those rules are engrafted onto the Constitution and imposed on every State and country in the land. Without at all subscribing to the generally black picture of police conduct painted by the Court, I think it must be frankly recognized at the outset that police questioning allowable under due process precedents may inherently entail some pressure on the suspect and may seek advantage in his ignorance or weaknesses. The atmosphere and questioning techniques, proper and fair though they be, can in themselves exert a tug on the suspect to confess, and in this light "(t)o speak of any confessions of crime made after arrest as being 'voluntary' or 'uncoerced' is somewhat inaccurate, although traditional. A confession is wholly and incontestably voluntary only if a guilty person gives himself up to the law and becomes his own accuser." Until today, the role of the Constitution has been only to sift out undue pressure, not to assure spontaneous confessions. . . .

What the Court largely ignores is that its rules impair, if they will not eventually serve wholly to frustrate, an instrument of law enforcement that has long and quite reasonably been thought worth the price paid for it. There can be little doubt that the Court's new code would markedly decrease the number of confessions. To warn the suspect that he may remain silent and remind him that his confession may be used in court are minor obstructions. To require also an express waiver by the suspect and an end to questioning whenever he demurs must heavily handicap questioning. And to suggest or provide counsel for the suspect simply invites the end of the interrogation. . . .

Justice White, whom Justice Harlan and Justice Stewart join, dissenting.

. . . The Court's duty to assess the consequences of its action is not satisfied by the utterance of the truth that a value of our system of criminal justice is "to respect the inviolability of the human personality" and to require government to produce the evidence against the accused by its own independent labors. More than the human dignity of the accused is involved; the human personality of others in the society must also be preserved. Thus the values reflected by the privilege are not the sole desideratum; society's interest in the general security is of equal weight.

The obvious underpinning of the Court's decision is a deep-seated distrust of all confessions. As the Court declares that the accused may not be interrogated without counsel present, absent a waiver of the right to counsel, and as the Court all but admonishes the lawyer to advise the accused to remain silent, the results add up to a judicial judgment that evidence from the accused should not be used against him in any way, whether compelled or not. This is the not so subtle overtone of the opinion—that it is inherently wrong for the police to gather evidence from the accused himself. And this is precisely the nub of this dissent. I see nothing wrong or immoral, and certainly nothing unconstitutional, in the police's asking a suspect whom they have reasonable cause to arrest whether or not he killed his wife or in confronting him with the evidence on which the arrest was based,

at least where he has been plainly advised that he may remain completely silent. . . .

. . . [I]t is by no means certain that the process of confessing is injurious to the accused. To the contrary it may provide psychological relief and enhance the prospects for rehabilitation. This is not to say that the value of respect for the inviolability of the accused's individual personality should be accorded no weight or that all confessions should be indiscriminately admitted. This Court has long read the Constitution to proscribe compelled confessions, a salutary rule from which there should be no retreat. But I see no sound basis, factual or otherwise, and the Court gives none, for concluding that the present rule against the receipt of coerced confessions is inadequate for the task of sorting out inadmissible evidence and must be replaced by the per se rule which is now imposed. Even if the new concept can be said to have advantages of some sort over the present law, they are far outweighed by its likely undesirable impact on other very relevant and important interests.

The most basic function of any government is to provide for the security of the individual and of his property. These ends of society are served by the criminal laws which for the most part are aimed at the prevention of crime. Without the reasonably effective performance of the task of preventing private violence and retaliation, it is idle to talk about human dignity and civilized values. . . .

In some unknown number of cases the Court's rule will return a killer, a rapist or other criminal to the streets and to the environment which produced him, to repeat his crime whenever it pleases him. As a consequence, there will not be a gain, but a loss, in human dignity. The real concern is not the unfortunate consequences of this new decision on the criminal law as an abstract, disembodied series of authoritative proscriptions, but the impact on those who rely on the public authority for protection and who without it can only engage in violent self-help with guns, knives, and the help of their neighbors similarly inclined. There is, of course, a saving factor: the next victims are uncertain, unnamed and underrepresented in this case. Nor can this decision do other than have a corrosive effect on the criminal laws as an effective device to prevent crime. A major component in its effectiveness in this regard is its swift and sure enforcement. The easier it is to get away with rape and murder, the less the deterrent effect on those who are inclined to attempt it. This is still good common sense. If it were not, we should posthaste liquidate the whole law enforcement establishment as a useless, misguided effort to control human conduct.

And what about the accused who has confessed or would confess in response to simple, non-coercive questioning and whose guilt could not otherwise be proved? Is it so clear that release is the best thing for him in every case? Has it so unquestionably been resolved that in each and every case it would be better for him not to confess and to return to his environment with no attempt whatsoever to help him? I think not. It may well be that in many cases it will be no less than a callous disregard for his own welfare as well as for the interests of his next victim.

There is another aspect to the effect of the Court's rule on the person whom the police have arrested on probable cause. The fact is that he may not be guilty at all and may be able to extricate himself quickly and simply if he were told the circumstances of his arrest and were asked to explain. This effort, and his release, must now await the hiring of a lawyer or his appointment by the court, consultation with counsel and then a session with the police or the prosecutor. Sim-ilarly, where probable cause exists to arrest several suspects, as where it will often be true that a suspect may be cleared only through the results of interrogation of other suspects. Here too the release of the innocent may be delayed by the Court's rule. . . .

CASE DISCUSSION

According to the Supreme Court, what do the words *custody* and *interrogation* mean? Why is custodial interrogation "inherently coercive," according to the majority? Does the Court outlaw all confessions and incriminating statements? What are the criteria for waiving the right against self-incrimination? On what grounds do the dissents disagree with the majority's decision? What interests are in conflict, according to the Court? How do the majority and the dissent explain the balance of interest established by the Constitution? How do they know what balance the Constitution precisely established among result, process, and the societal interests in dignity, crime control, and control of government? Which makes more sense regarding the law of police interrogation, the majority's bright line rule requiring warnings or the dissent's due process test weighing the totality of circumstances on a case-by-case basis?

The Supreme Court intended the *Miranda* warnings to provide a bright line—or *per se* **rule**—to guide the police in order to prevent coercion but still allow pressure. According to the Court, in order to avoid the inherently coercive nature of custodial interrogation, a coercive nature that will make confessions and other incriminating admissions involuntary, the police must provide suspects with the following warnings:

1. They "must . . . be informed in clear and unequivocal terms that [they have] the right to remain silent," to enlighten the ignorant and to relieve the pressures of the interrogation atmosphere for those who already know their rights.

2. They must be told that "anything said can and will be used against [them] in court," so suspects fully understand the consequences of talking to the police.

3. They "must be clearly informed that [they have] the right to consult with a lawyer and to have a lawyer with [them] during interrogation," because counsel is important to protecting the privilege against self-incrimination.

4. They must be told that if they cannot afford a lawyer, a lawyer will be appointed for them; otherwise, suspects may think they may have lawyers only if they can afford them.

The *Miranda* rules provide suspects with additional assurances that the police are not required to spell out specifically for suspects. These assurances include the following:

1. Suspects are free to exercise the privilege of remaining silent at any time, and if they "indicate in any manner, at any time prior to or during questioning," that they wish "to remain silent, the interrogation must cease." And if they state that they want an attorney, "the interrogation must cease until an attorney is present."

2. If the police obtain any statement without an attorney, a "heavy burden rests on the Government to demonstrate that [defendants] knowingly and intelligently waived [their] privilege against self-incrimination and [their] right to retained or appointed counsel." Waivers may not be presumed either by silence following warnings or from an eventual confession.

3. Statements obtained in violation of the rules may not be admitted into evidence.

4. Exercise of the privilege may not be penalized. Hence, prosecutors may not "use at trial the fact that [defendants] stood mute or claimed [their] privilege in the face of accusations."[23]

D e c i s i o n   P o i n t

During interrogation, a suspect asked the police officers questioning him if he could use the telephone to call his mother to see if she could get him an attorney. One officer asked him whether he was saying that he wanted them to stop questioning him until he had an attorney. They continued to question him, and he later confessed. In fact, he even cooperated with the police in the investigation. Did his request to call his mother constitute a request for an attorney that mandated the termination of questioning? According to the Pennsylvania Supreme Court, the officer's request for clarification of what the defendant meant and the defendant's cooperation did not validate the confession, because the defendant had made his wishes clear—he wanted a lawyer.[24]

The Effects of *Miranda v. Arizona*

Whenever police officers arrest anyone on television "cop shows," we hear the *Miranda* warnings, "Read him his rights," or both. From the day it was decided, *Miranda v. Arizona* has provoked intense controversy. Defense attorneys and civil libertarians hailed it as a new dawn in civilized society. Police, other law-enforcement-minded people, and wide segments of the public complained that the decision "handcuffed" the police, lamenting that law and order would soon break down. Neither the hopes nor the fears surrounding *Miranda* ever came to pass. According to most research, the *Miranda* decision has not significantly affected either law enforcement or crime levels.[25]

This is probably because the decision was not nearly so far reaching as both its supporters and detractors hoped. Television shows do not reflect the reality of *Miranda v. Arizona. Miranda* does not require that the police warn suspects whenever they arrest them. In fact, the decision requires the famous warnings only if officers intend to do both of the following:

1. Take the suspects into custody
2. Interrogate the suspects

These limits exclude a wide range of questioning by the police, including the following:

1. Questioning at the scene of the crime
2. Questioning of individuals in the fact-finding process
3. Volunteered statements of any kind
4. Questioning that is part of an investigatory stop (See Chapter 4.)[26]

Furthermore, the Supreme Court has ruled that the *Miranda* rules are not constitutional rights in themselves. Specifically, the warnings are not inherent in the self-incrimination clause of the Fifth Amendment. Rather, they are a mechanism by which to guarantee rights. In other words, they are **prophylactic rules,** rules intended to protect the real constitutional right—the right against self-incrimination. In the Supreme Court's words, *Miranda* "recognized that these procedural safeguards were not themselves rights protected by the Constitution but were instead measures to insure that the right against compulsory self-incrimination was protected." Presumably, therefore, other means to guard against the coercive nature of police interrogation can satisfy the requirements of the self-incrimination clause.[27]

Another effect of *Miranda* was to leave open for future decision the precise meaning of the key term *custodial interrogation* as it applies to police questioning and suspects' confessions.

The Meaning of *Interrogation*

The words *interrogation* and *confession* do not appear in the Fifth, Sixth, or Fourteenth Amendments. Their constitutional significance arises out of their relation to

1. The Fifth Amendment guarantee against compelling individuals to be witnesses against themselves
2. The Sixth Amendment right to counsel
3. The Fifth Amendment and Fourteenth Amendment guarantee against the denial of life, liberty, and property without due process of law

Interrogation means something different in each of these amendments. All three amendments prohibit physical coercion as a means to obtain confessions. Due process focuses almost exclusively on the element of coercion and its mirror image, voluntariness.

The Sixth Amendment says nothing about coercion; it guarantees the right to counsel in all "criminal prosecutions." Therefore, once the government starts formal proceedings against persons, the Sixth Amendment right to counsel guarantees that defendants have their lawyers present during interrogation without regard to coercion. Because the right to counsel arises after the government has begun the prosecution, when all the power of the government is devoted to prosecuting suspects, and because the right to counsel attaches irrespective of coercion, the Court has broadly interpreted interrogation that takes place after the initiation of formal proceedings. This broad interpretation has the effect of expanding the right to counsel during interrogations that occur after formal proceedings begin. In effect, it guarantees that defendants have a right to have their lawyers at all interrogations taking place after the initiation of formal proceedings.

Sixth Amendment interrogation includes more than direct questioning, such as, "Where were you Friday night?" In *Massiah v. United States*, for example, the police arranged for Massiah's codefendant to discuss with Massiah the pair's pending trial in a car while the codefendant was wired with a radio transmitter hooked up to police officers. The Court held that Massiah's right to counsel was violated even though officers never directly asked him anything. According to the Court, the incriminating words Massiah communicated to his codefendant resulted from interrogation because they "were deliberately elicited from him" by federal agents. Therefore, Sixth Amendment interrogation includes any statements "deliberately elicited" by law enforcement officers.[28]

The **deliberately-eliciting-a-response standard** probably excludes wholly passive actions that generate confessions. For example, planting an electronic listening device is not interrogation, because bugging does not "increase the defendant's predisposition toward making an incriminating response."[29]

The Fifth Amendment self-incrimination clause governs interrogation prior to the filing of formal charges against suspects. Fifth Amendment interrogation has a narrower definition than interrogation under the Sixth Amendment right to counsel. The Fifth Amendment self-incrimination clause requires more active questioning than deliberately eliciting a response. This is because, in the first place, the Fifth Amendment self-incrimination clause requires coercion; the Sixth Amendment right to counsel clause does not. Furthermore, the need for counsel, at least according to the United States Supreme Court, is much greater once technical judicial proceedings begin. A more practical—if not stated—reason for the narrower definition is the inhibiting influence on interrogation that the presence of lawyers would have.

Decision Point

BREWER V. WILLIAMS
430 U.S. 387 (1977)

On the afternoon of December 24, 1968, a ten-year-old girl named Pamela Powers went with her family to the YMCA (Young Men's Christian Association) in Des Moines, Iowa, to watch a wrestling tournament in which her brother was participating. When she failed to return from a trip to the washroom, a search for her began. The search was unsuccessful. Robert Williams, who had recently escaped from a mental hospital, was a resident of the YMCA. Soon after the girl's disappearance, Williams was seen in the YMCA lobby carrying some clothing and a large bundle wrapped in a blanket. He obtained help from a fourteen-year-old boy in opening the street door of the YMCA and the door to his automobile parked outside. When Williams placed the bundle in the front seat of his car, the boy "saw two legs in it and they

were skinny and white." Before anyone could see what was in the bundle, Williams drove away. His abandoned car was found the following day in Davenport, Iowa, roughly 160 miles east of Des Moines. A warrant was then issued in Des Moines for his arrest on a charge of abduction.

In the presence of the Des Moines chief of police and a police detective named Leaming, McKnight (one of Williams's attorneys) advised Williams that Des Moines police officers would be driving to Davenport to pick him up, that the officers would not interrogate him or mistreat him, and that Williams was not to talk to the officers about Pamela Powers until after consulting with McKnight upon his return to Des Moines. As a result of these conversations, it was agreed between McKnight and the Des Moines police officials that Detective Leaming and a fellow officer would drive to Davenport to pick up Williams, that they would bring him directly back to Des Moines, and that they would not question him during the trip.

Detective Leaming and his fellow officer arrived in Davenport at about noon to pick up Williams and return him to Des Moines. Soon after their arrival they met with Williams and Kelly, who, they understood, was acting as Williams's lawyer. Detective Leaming repeated the *Miranda* warnings and told Williams the following:

> [W]e both know that you're being represented here by Mr. Kelly and you're being represented by Mr. McKnight in Des Moines, and . . . I want you to remember this because we'll be visiting between here and Des Moines. . . .

The two detectives, with Williams in their charge, then set out on the 160-mile drive. At no time during the trip did Williams express a willingness to be interrogated in the absence of an attorney. Instead, he stated several times that "[w]hen I get to Des Moines and see Mr. McKnight, I am going to tell you the whole story." Detective Leaming knew that Williams was a former mental patient and knew also that he was deeply religious.

The detective and his prisoner soon embarked on a wide-ranging conversation covering a variety of topics, including the subject of religion. Then, not long after leaving Davenport and reaching the interstate highway, Detective Leaming delivered what has been referred to in the briefs and oral arguments as the "Christian burial speech." Addressing Williams as "Reverend," the detective said the following:

> I want to give you something to think about while we're traveling down the road. . . . Number one, I want you to observe the weather conditions, it's raining, it's sleeting, it's freezing, driving is very treacherous, visibility is poor, it's going to be dark early this evening. They are predicting several inches of snow for tonight, and I feel that you yourself are the only person that knows where this little girl's body is, that you yourself have only been there once, and if you got a snow on top of it you yourself may be unable to find it. And, since we'll be going right

past the area on the way into Des Moines, I feel that we could stop and locate the body, that the parents of this little girl should be entitled to a Christian burial for the little girl who was snatched away from them on Christmas [E]ve and murdered. And I feel we should stop and locate it rather than waiting until morning and trying to come back out after a snow storm and possibly not being able to find it at all.

Williams asked Detective Leaming why he thought their route to Des Moines would be taking them past the girl's body, and Leaming responded that he knew the body was in the area of Mitchellville—a town they would be passing on the way to Des Moines. Leaming then stated: "I do not want you to answer me. I don't want to discuss it any further. Just think about it as we're riding down the road."

As the car approached Grinnell, a town approximately one hundred miles west of Davenport, Williams asked whether the police had found the victim's shoes. When Detective Leaming replied that he was unsure, Williams directed the officers to a service station where he said he had left the shoes; a search proved unsuccessful. As they continued towards Des Moines, Williams asked whether the police had found the blanket, and directed police to the rest area where he said he had disposed of the blanket. Nothing was found. The car continued towards Des Moines, and as it approached Mitchellville, Williams said he would show the officers where the body was. He then directed the police to the body of Pamela Powers.

Was Williams interrogated? Yes, said the U.S. Supreme Court. According to the majority in a five-to-four decision:

> There can be no serious doubt . . . that Detective Leaming deliberately and designedly set out to elicit information from Williams just as surely as—and perhaps more effectively than—if he had formally interrogated him. Detective Leaming was fully aware before departing for Des Moines that Williams was being represented in Davenport by Kelly and in Des Moines by McKnight. Yet he purposely sought during William[s's] isolation from his lawyers to obtain as much incriminating information as

possible. Indeed, Detective Leaming conceded as much when he testified at William[s's] trial:

Q: In fact, Captain, whether he was a mental patient or not, you were trying to get all the information you could before he got his lawyer, weren't you?

A: I was sure hoping to find out where that little girl was, yes, sir.

Q: Well, I'll put it this way: You were hoping to get all the information you could before Williams got back to McKnight, weren't you.

A: Yes, sir.

In a dissenting opinion, Chief Justice Burger wrote the following:

The result in this case ought to be intolerable in any society which purports to call itself an organized society. It continues the Court — by the narrowest margin — on the much criticized course of punishing the public for the mistakes and misdeeds of law enforcement officers, instead of punishing the officer directly, if in fact he is guilty of wrongdoing. It mechanically and blindly keeps reliable evidence from juries whether the claimed constitutional violation involves gross police misconduct or honest human error.

Williams is guilty of the savage murder of a small child; no member of the Court contends he is not. While in custody, and after no fewer than five warnings of his rights to silence and to counsel, he led police to the concealed body of his victim. The Court concedes that Williams was not threatened or coerced and that he spoke and acted voluntarily and with full awareness of his constitutional rights. In the face of all this, the Court now holds that because Williams was prompted by the detective's statement — not interrogation but a statement — the jury must not be told how the police found the body.

Today's holding fulfills Judge (late Mr. Justice) Cardozo's grim prophecy that someday some court might carry the exclusionary rule to the absurd extent that its operative effect would exclude evidence relating to the body of a murder victim because of the means by which it was found. [Cardozo's prophecy: "The criminal is to go free because the constable has blundered. . . . A room is searched against the law, and the body of a murdered man is found. . . . The privacy of the home is infringed, and the murderer goes free." *People v. Defore* (1926).] In so ruling the Court regresses to playing a grisly game of "hide and seek," once more exalting the sporting theory of criminal justice which has been experiencing a decline in our jurisprudence. . . .

Custodial interrogation *before* the initiation of formal judicial proceedings means either direct questioning or its "functional equivalent." Under the **functional equivalent standard,** for example, confronting a reluctant suspect with an incriminating ballistics report was not interrogation because police did not "question" the suspect. In other words, the ballistics report elicited a response but was not the functional equivalent of direct questioning. However, Fifth Amendment interrogation does not require that officers ask a direct question, "punctuated by a question mark." The functional equivalent of interrogation includes any statement that the "average listener" understands to "call for a response." The Supreme Court established and applied the functional equivalent standard in *Rhode Island v. Innis*.[30]

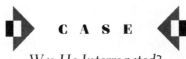

C A S E

Was He Interrogated?

Rhode Island v. Innis
446 U.S. 291, 100 S.Ct. 1682

A grand jury indicted Innis for kidnapping, robbery, and murder. Before trial, Innis moved to suppress as evidence incriminating statements made by him to the police, and a shotgun. The trial judge denied the motion. On appeal, the Rhode Island Supreme Court, in a three-to-two decision, set aside the conviction. On a writ of certiorari, the U.S. Supreme Court vacated the Rhode Island Supreme Court decision and remanded the case. Justice Stewart wrote the opinion for the Court, joined by Justices White, Blackmun, Powell, and Rehnquist. Justice White filed a concurring opinion. Chief Justice Burger concurred in the judgment of the Court. Justice Marshall dissented.

FACTS

On the night of January 12, 1975, John Mulvaney, a Providence, R.I., taxicab driver, disappeared after being dispatched to pick up a customer. His body was discovered four days later buried in a shallow grave in Coventry, R.I. He had died from a shotgun blast aimed at the back of his head.

On January 17, 1975, shortly after midnight, the Providence police received a telephone call from Gerald Aubin, also a taxicab driver, who reported that he had just been robbed by a man wielding a sawed-off shotgun. Aubin further reported that he had dropped off his assailant near Rhode Island College in a section of Providence known as Mount Pleasant. While at the Providence police station waiting to give a statement, Aubin noticed a picture of his assailant on a bulletin board. Aubin so informed one of the police officers present. The officer prepared a photo array, and again Aubin identified a picture of the same person. That person was the respondent. Shortly thereafter, the Providence police began a search of the Mount Pleasant area.

At approximately 4:30 A.M. on the same date, Patrolman Lovell, while cruising the streets of Mount Pleasant in a patrol car, spotted the respondent standing in the street facing him. When Patrolman Lovell stopped his car, the respondent walked towards it. Patrolman Lovell then arrested the respondent, who was unarmed, and advised him of his so-called *Miranda* rights. While the two men waited in the patrol car for other police officers to arrive, Patrolman Lovell did not converse with the respondent other than to respond to the latter's request for a cigarette.

Within minutes, Sergeant Sears arrived at the scene of the arrest, and he also gave the respondent the *Miranda* warnings. Immediately thereafter, Captain Leyden and other police officers arrived. Captain Leyden advised the respondent of his *Miranda* rights. The respondent stated that he understood those rights and wanted to speak with a lawyer. Captain Leyden then directed that the respondent be placed in a "caged wagon," a four-door police car with a wire screen mesh between the front and rear seats, and be driven to the central police station. Three officers, Patrolmen Gleckman, Williams, and McKenna, were assigned to accompany the respondent to the central station. They placed the respondent in the vehicle and shut the doors. Captain Leyden then instructed the officers not to question the respondent or intimidate or coerce him in any way. The three officers then entered the vehicle, and it departed.

While en route to the central station, Patrolman Gleckman initiated a conversation with Patrolman McKenna concerning the missing shotgun. As Patrolman Gleckman later testified:

> **A:** At this point, I was talking back and forth with Patrolman McKenna stating that I frequent this area while on patrol and [that because a school for handicapped children is located nearby,] there's a lot of handicapped children running around in this area, and God forbid one of them might find a weapon with shells and they might hurt themselves.

Patrolman McKenna apparently shared his fellow officer's concern:

A: I more or less concurred with him [Gleckman] that it was a safety factor and that we should, you know, continue to search for the weapon and try to find it.

While Patrolman Williams said nothing, he overheard the conversation between the two officers:

A: He [Gleckman] said it would be too bad if the little — I believe he said a girl — would pick up the gun, maybe kill herself.

The respondent then interrupted the conversation, stating that the officers should turn the car around so he could show them where the gun was located. At this point, Patrolman McKenna radioed back to Captain Leyden that they were returning to the scene of the arrest and that the respondent would inform them of the location of the gun. At the time the respondent indicated that the officers should turn back, they had traveled no more than a mile, a trip encompassing only a few minutes.

The police vehicle then returned to the scene of the arrest where a search for the shotgun was in progress. There, Captain Leyden again advised the respondent of his *Miranda* rights. The respondent replied that he understood those rights but that he "wanted to get the gun out of the way because of the kids in the area of the school." The respondent then led the police to a nearby field, where he pointed out the shotgun under some rocks by the side of the road.

On March 20, 1975, a grand jury returned an indictment charging the respondent with the kidnapping, robbery, and murder of John Mulvaney. Before trial, the respondent moved to suppress the shotgun and statements he had made to the police regarding it. After an evidentiary hearing [the trial court admitted the confession on the ground that Innis had waived his right to remain silent].

On appeal, the Rhode Island Supreme Court, in a 3–2 decision, set aside the respondent's conviction. . . . We granted certiorari to address for the first time the meaning of "interrogation" under *Miranda v. Arizona.*

OPINION

. . .

[T]he parties are in agreement that the respondent was fully informed of his *Miranda* rights and that he invoked his *Miranda* right to counsel when he told Captain Leyden that he wished to consult with a lawyer. It is also uncontested that the respondent was "in custody" while being transported to the police station. The issue, therefore, is whether the respondent was "interrogated" by the police officers in violation of the respondent's undisputed right under *Miranda* to remain silent until he had consulted with a lawyer. In resolving this issue, we first define the term "interrogation" under *Miranda* before turning to a consideration of the facts of this case.

The starting point for defining "interrogation" in this context is, of course, the Court's *Miranda* opinion. There the Court observed that "[b]y custodial interrogation, we mean questioning initiated by law enforcement officers after a person has been taken into custody or otherwise deprived of his freedom of action in any significant way." This passage and other references throughout the opinion to "questioning" might suggest that the *Miranda* rules were to apply only to those police interrogation practices that involve express questioning of a defendant while in custody.

We do not, however, construe the *Miranda* opinion so narrowly. The concern of the Court in *Miranda* was that the "interrogation environment" created by the interplay of interrogation and custody would "subjugate the individual to the will of his examiner" and thereby undermine the privilege against compulsory self-incrimination. The police practices that evoked this concern included several that did not involve express questioning. For example, one of the practices discussed in *Miranda* was the use of line-ups in which a coached witness would pick the defendant as the perpetrator. This was designed to establish that the defendant was in fact guilty as a predicate for further interrogation. A variation of this theme discussed in *Miranda* was the so-called "reverse line-up" in which a defendant would be identified by coached witnesses as the perpetrator of a fictitious crime, with the object of inducing him to confess to the actual crime of which he was suspected in order to escape the false prosecution. The Court in *Miranda* also included in its survey of interrogation practices the use of psychological ploys, such as to "posit" "the guilt of the subject," to "minimize the moral seriousness of the offense," and "to cast blame on the victim or on society." It is clear that these techniques of persuasion, no less than express questioning, were thought, in a custodial setting, to amount to interrogation. To limit the ambit of *Miranda* to express questioning would "place a premium on the ingenuity of the police to devise methods of indirect interrogation, rather than to implement the plain mandate of *Miranda*."

This is not to say, however, that all statements obtained by the police after a person has been taken into custody are to be considered the product of interrogation. As the Court in *Miranda* noted:

> Confessions remain a proper element in law enforcement. Any statement given freely and voluntarily without any compelling influences is, of course, admissible in evidence. The fundamental import of the privilege while an individual is in custody is not whether he is allowed to talk to the police without the benefit of warnings and counsel, but whether he can be interrogated. . . . Volunteered statements of any kind are not barred by the Fifth Amendment and their admissibility is not affected by our holding today.

> It is clear therefore that the special procedural safeguards outlined in *Miranda* are required not where a suspect is simply taken into custody, but rather where a suspect in custody is subjected to interrogation. "Interrogation," as conceptualized in the *Miranda* opinion, must reflect a measure of compulsion above and beyond that are inherent in custody itself.

. . .

We conclude that the *Miranda* safeguards come into play whenever a person in custody is subjected to either express questioning or its functional equivalent. That is to say, the term "interrogation" under *Miranda* refers not only to express questioning, but also to any words or actions on the part of the police (other than those normally attendant to arrest and custody) that the police should know are reasonably likely to elicit an incriminating response from the suspect.

The latter portion of this definition focuses primarily upon the perceptions of the suspect, rather than the intent of the police. This focus reflects the fact that the *Miranda* safeguards were designed to vest a suspect in custody with an added measure of protection against coercive police practices, without regard to objective proof of the underlying intent of the police. A practice that the police should know is reasonably likely to evoke an incriminating response from a suspect thus amounts to interrogation. But, since the police surely cannot be held accountable for the unforeseeable results of their words or actions, the definition of interrogation can extend only to words or actions on the part of police officers that they should have known were reasonably likely to elicit an incriminating response.

Turning to the facts of the present case, we conclude that the respondent was not "interrogated" within the meaning of *Miranda*. It is undisputed that the first prong of the definition of "interrogation" was not satisfied, for the conversation between Patrolmen Gleckman and McKenna included no express questioning of the respondent. Rather, that conversation was, at least in form, nothing more than a dialogue between the two officers to which no response from the respondent was invited.

Moreover, it cannot be fairly concluded that the respondent was subjected to the "functional equivalent" of questioning. It cannot be said, in short, that Patrolmen Gleckman and McKenna should have known that their conversation was reasonably likely to elicit an incriminating response from the respondent. There is nothing in the record to suggest that the officers were aware that the respondent was peculiarly susceptible to an appeal to his conscience concerning the safety of handicapped children. Nor is there anything in the record to suggest that the police knew that the respondent was unusually disoriented or upset at the time of his arrest.

The case thus boils down to whether, in the context of a brief conversation, the officers should have known that the respondent would suddenly be moved to make a self-incriminating response. Given the fact that the entire conversation appears to have consisted of no more than a few offhand remarks, we cannot say that the officers should have known that it was reasonably likely that Innis would so respond. This is not a case where the police carried on a lengthy harangue in the presence of the suspect. Nor does the record support the respondent's contention that, under the circumstances, the officers' comments were particularly "evocative." It is our view, therefore, that the respondent was not subjected by the police to words or actions that the police should have known were reasonably likely to elicit an incriminating response from him.

The Rhode Island Supreme Court erred, in short, in equating "subtle compulsion" with interrogation. That the officers' comments struck a responsive chord is readily apparent. Thus, it may be said, as the Rhode Island Supreme Court did say, that the respondent was subjected to "subtle compulsion." But that is not the end of the inquiry. It must also be established that a suspect's incriminating response was the product of words or actions on the part of the police that they should have known were reasonably likely to elicit an incriminating response. This was not established in the present case.

By way of example, if the police had done no more than to drive past the site of the concealed weapon while taking the most direct route to the police station, and if the respondent, upon noticing for the first time the proximity of the school for handicapped children, had blurted out that he would show the officers where the gun was located, it could not seriously be argued that this "subtle compulsion" would have constituted "interrogation" within the meaning of the *Miranda* opinion.

For the reasons stated, the judgment of the Supreme Court of Rhode Island is vacated, and the case is remanded to that court for further proceedings not inconsistent with this opinion.

It is so ordered.

DISSENT

Justice Marshall, with whom Justice Brennan joins, dissenting.

. . .

One can scarcely imagine a stronger appeal to the conscience of a suspect—any suspect—than the assertion that if the weapon is not found an innocent person will be hurt or killed. And not just any innocent person, but an innocent child—a little girl—a helpless, handicapped little girl on her way to school. The notion that such an appeal could not be expected to have any effect unless the suspect were known to have some special interest in handicapped children verges on the ludicrous. As a matter of fact, the appeal to a suspect to confess for the sake of others, to "display some evidence of decency and honor," is a classic interrogation technique. . . .

Justice Stevens, dissenting.

. . . In my view any statement that would normally be understood by the average listener as calling for a response is the functional equivalent of a direct question, whether or not it is punctuated by a question mark. The Court, however, takes a much narrower view. It holds that police conduct is not the "functional equivalent" of direct questioning unless the police should have known that what they were saying or doing was likely to elicit an incriminating response from the suspect. This holding represents a plain departure from the principles set forth in *Miranda*. . . .

In short, in order to give full protection to a suspect's right to be free from any interrogation at all, the definition of "interrogation" must include any police statement or conduct that has the same purpose or effect as a direct question. Statements that appear to call for a response from the suspect, as well as those that are designed to do so, should be considered interrogation. By prohibiting only those relatively few statements or actions that a police officer should know are likely to elicit an incriminating response, the Court today accords a suspect considerably less protection. Indeed, since I suppose most suspects are unlikely to incriminate themselves even when questioned directly, this new definition will almost certainly exclude every statement that is not punctuated with a question mark from the concept of "interrogation."

The difference between the approach required by a faithful adherence to *Miranda* and the stinted test applied by the Court today can be illustrated by comparing three different ways in which Officer Gleckman could have communicated his fears about the possible dangers posed by the shotgun to handicapped children. He could have: (1) directly asked Innis: Will you please tell me where the shotgun is so we can protect handicapped children from danger? (2) announced to the other officers in the wagon: If the man sitting in the back seat with me should decide to tell us where the gun is, we can protect handicapped children from danger, or (3) stated to the other officers: It would be too bad if a little handicapped girl would pick up the gun that this man left in the area and maybe kill herself.

In my opinion, all three of these statements should be considered interrogation because all three appear to be designed to elicit a response from anyone who in fact knew where the gun was located. Under the Court's test, on the other hand, the form of the statements would be critical. The third statement would not be interrogation because in the Court's view there was no reason for Officer Gleckman to believe that Innis was susceptible to this type of an implied appeal; therefore, the statement would not be reasonably likely to elicit an incriminating response. Assuming that this is true, then it seems to me that the first two statements, which would be just as unlikely to elicit such a response, should also not be considered interrogation. But, because the first statement is clearly an express question, it would be considered interrogation under the Court's test. The second statement, although just as clearly a deliberate appeal to Innis to reveal the location of the gun, would presumably not be interrogation because (a) it was not in form a direct

question and (b) it does not fit within the "reasonably likely to elicit an incriminating response" category that applies to indirect interrogation. . . .

CASE DISCUSSION

What relevant facts did the Court consider in determining whether the methods that the officers used violated the Fifth Amendment? What do you think the police officers' motives were in discussing the gun's location? Do you agree with the Court that their motives are irrelevant? Do you agree that there was no compulsion in this case? Should the police have known that their words or actions were "likely to elicit an incriminating response" from Innis? Is the majority more interested in result than in other interests? Or does it properly balance result and other interests? What other interests? Why does the dissent disagree with the majority's definition and application of the concept of interrogation? Should the police have more leeway in questioning suspects before the government initiates formal proceedings or after? Why? Why not?

The Meaning of *Custody*

Lower federal courts and state courts are mainly responsible for applying the definition of *custodial interrogation* to actual cases. The "totality of circumstances" by which they analyze interrogation on a case-by-case basis includes all of the following:

1. Whether officers had probable cause to arrest
2. Whether officers intended to hold suspects
3. Whether suspects believed that their freedom was significantly restricted
4. Whether the investigation had focused on the suspect at the time
5. The officers' language in summoning suspects
6. The physical surroundings of the interrogation
7. The amount of evidence of guilt that officers present to suspects
8. The duration of detention
9. The amount of pressure that officers use in detaining suspects
10. Whether it was reasonable for suspects to believe that they were either in custody or restrained to a degree comparable with arrest[31]

According to the United States Supreme Court, the inquiry ultimately boils down to "whether there was a formal arrest or restraint on freedom of movement of the degree associated with a formal arrest." The Court has decided that none of the following are in custody:

1. Suspects detained during routine traffic stops[32]
2. Probationers attending routine meetings with their probation officers[33]
3. Persons detained during the execution of search warrants[34]

Nevertheless, the question of when people are in custody has given the Court considerable difficulty over the years since *Miranda v. Arizona.* For example, in *Dunaway v. New York,* officers acted on instructions to "pick up Dunaway" and "bring him in." The officers did not tell Dunaway he was arrested, never touched him, and did not book him. Nevertheless, when the police questioned him without telling him he was free to go, the Court held that Dunaway was in custody.[35]

In *Miranda,* the Court included questioning outside police stations if suspects are "deprived of . . . [their] freedom of action in any significant way." The Court used this language in order to prevent police officers from circumventing the *Miranda* requirements by simply questioning suspects somewhere other than in a police station. *Miranda* aims at coercive atmospheres, not necessarily coercive physical locations. Police stations, according to the opinion, are inherently coercive settings. But circumstances outside police stations may also indicate a sufficiently coercive atmosphere to require warnings prior to interrogation. Hence, suspects questioned in squad cars are in custody.

Questioning suspects in familiar surroundings, such as their homes, is not custodial interrogation. It can be, however, if the totality of circumstances amounts to the coercive atmosphere envisioned in *Miranda.* In *Orozco v. Texas,* four police officers entered Orozco's bedroom at 4:00 A.M. to question him about a shooting. From the moment he gave them his name, the officers testified, Orozco was not free to go because he was under arrest. The Court held that the questioning that followed, in which Orozco made incriminating statements, took place while Orozco was "otherwise deprived of his liberty in [a] significant way."[36]

The Supreme Court addressed questioning outside police stations in *Oregon v. Mathiason.*

C A S E

Was He "in Custody"?

Oregon v. Mathiason
429 U.S. 492, 97 S.Ct. 711 (1977)

Carl Mathiason was convicted of first-degree burglary after a bench trial in which his confession was critical to the State's case. At trial he moved to suppress the confession. The trial court refused to exclude the confession because it found that Mathiason was not in custody at the time of his confession. The Oregon Court of Appeals affirmed the respondent's conviction, but on *his petition for review by the Supreme Court of Oregon, that court, by a divided vote, reversed the conviction. The State of Oregon petitioned for certiorari. The U.S. Supreme Court reversed. Per Curiam.*

FACTS

An officer of the State Police investigated a theft at a residence near Pendleton. He asked the lady of the house which had been burglarized if she suspected anyone. She replied that the defendant was the only one she could think of. The defendant was a parolee and a "close associate" of her son. The officer tried to contact defendant on three or four occasions with no success. Finally, about 25 days after the burglary, the officer left his card at defendant's apartment with a note asking him to call because "I'd like to discuss something with you." The next afternoon the defendant did call. The officer asked where it would be convenient to meet. The defendant had no preference; so the officer asked if the defendant could meet him at the state patrol office in about an hour and a half, about 5:00 P.M. The patrol office was about two blocks from defendant's apartment. The building housed several state agencies.

The officer met defendant in the hallway, shook hands and took him into an office. The defendant was told he was not under arrest. The door was closed. The two sat across a desk. The police radio in another room could be heard. The officer told defendant he wanted to talk to him about a burglary and that his truthfulness would possibly be considered by the district attorney or judge. The officer further advised that the police believed defendant was involved in the burglary and (falsely stated that) defendant's fingerprints were found at the scene. The defendant sat for a few minutes and then said he had taken the property. This occurred within five minutes after defendant had come to the office. The officer then advised defendant of his *Miranda* rights and took a taped confession.

At the end of the taped conversation the officer told defendant he was not arresting him at this time; he was released to go about his job and return to his family. The officer said he was referring the case to the district attorney for him to determine whether criminal charges would be brought. It was 5:30 P.M. when the defendant left the office.

The officer gave all the testimony relevant to this issue. The defendant did not take the stand either at the hearing on the motion to suppress or at the trial.

OPINION

. . .

Our decision in *Miranda* set forth rules of police procedure applicable to "custodial interrogation." "By custodial interrogation, we mean questioning initiated by law enforcement officers after a person has been taken into custody or otherwise deprived of his freedom of action in any significant way." Subsequently we have found the *Miranda* principle applicable to questioning which takes place in a prison setting during a suspect's term of imprisonment on a separate offense, and to questioning taking place in a suspect's home, after he has been arrested and is no longer free to go where he pleases.

In the present case, however, there is no indication that the questioning took place in a context where respondent's freedom to depart was restricted in any way. He came voluntarily to the police station, where he was immediately informed that he was not under arrest. At the close of a ½-hour interview respondent did in fact leave the police station without hindrance. It is clear from these facts that Mathiason was not in custody "or otherwise deprived of his freedom of action in any significant way."

Such a non custodial situation is not converted to one in which *Miranda* applies simply because a reviewing court concludes that, even in the absence of any formal arrest or restraint on freedom of movement, the questioning took place in a "coercive environment." Any interview of one suspected of a crime by a police officer will have coercive aspects to it, simply by virtue of the fact that the police officer is part of a law enforcement system which may ultimately cause the suspect to be charged with a crime.

But police officers are not required to administer *Miranda* warnings to everyone whom they question. Nor is the requirement of warnings to be imposed simply because the questioning takes place in the station house, or because the questioned person is one whom the police suspect. *Miranda* warnings are required only where there has been such a restriction on a person's freedom as to render him "in custody." It was that sort of coercive environment to which *Miranda* by its terms was made applicable, and to which it is limited. The officer's false statement about having discovered Mathiason's fingerprints at the scene was found by the Supreme Court of Oregon to be another circumstance contributing to the coercive environment which makes the *Miranda* rationale applicable. Whatever relevance this fact may have to other issues in the case, it has nothing to do with whether respondent was in custody for purposes of the *Miranda* rule.

The petition for certiorari is granted, the judgment of the Oregon Supreme Court is reversed, and the case is remanded for proceedings not inconsistent with this opinion.

So ordered.

DISSENT

. . . I cannot agree with the Court's conclusion that if respondent were not in custody no warnings were required. I recognize that *Miranda* is limited to custodial interrogation. . . . The rationale of *Miranda*, however, is not so easily cabined. *Miranda* requires warnings to "combat" a situation in which there are "inherently compelling pressures which work to undermine the individual's will to resist and to compel him to speak where he would not otherwise do so freely."

It is of course true, as the Court notes, that "(a)ny interview of one suspected of a crime by a police officer will have coercive aspects to it." But it does not follow that because police "are not required to administer *Miranda* warnings to everyone whom they question," that they need not administer warnings to anyone, unless the factual setting of the *Miranda* cases is replicated. Rather, faithfulness to *Miranda* requires us to distinguish situations that resemble the "coercive aspects" of custodial interrogation from those that more nearly resemble "(g)eneral on-the-scene questioning . . . or other general questioning of citizens in the fact-finding process" which *Miranda* states usually can take place without warnings.

In my view, even if respondent were not in custody, the coercive elements in the instant case were so pervasive as to require *Miranda*-type warnings. Respondent was interrogated in "privacy" and in "unfamiliar surroundings," factors on which *Miranda* places great stress. The investigation had focused on respondent. And respondent was subjected to some of the "deceptive stratagems," which called forth the *Miranda* decision. I therefore agree with the Oregon Supreme Court that to excuse the absence of warnings given these facts is "contrary to the rationale expressed in *Miranda*."

The privilege against self-incrimination "has always been 'as broad as the mischief against which it seeks to guard.'" Today's decision means, however, that the Fifth Amendment privilege does not provide full protection against mischiefs equivalent to, but different from, custodial interrogation. It is therefore important to note that the state courts remain free, in interpreting state constitutions, to guard against the evil clearly identified by this case.

I respectfully dissent.

CASE DISCUSSION

How did the Supreme Court define *custody* in this case? What are the facts relevant to determining whether the officers interrogated Mathiason while he was in custody? Do you agree that Mathiason was not in custody during the questioning? What facts do you rely on in order to answer the question? Does this decision favor the interest in arriving at the correct result, the interest in controlling the government, or both? Explain.

The Public Safety Exception
to *Miranda v. Arizona*

In at least one circumstance, incriminating statements made during custodial interrogation do not violate the Fifth Amendment, despite police failure to give the *Miranda* warnings and absent a suspect's effective waiver. If "a threat to the general public outweighs the need for the prophylactic rule protecting Fifth Amendment privilege against self-incrimination," the police need not give suspects the *Miranda* warnings. The Supreme Court formulated this **public safety exception** in *New York v. Quarles*.

▶ C A S E ◀

Did Public Safety Justify Not Giving the Miranda Warnings?

New York v. Quarles
467 U.S. 649 (1984)

Benjamin Quarles was charged in a New York trial court with criminal possession of a weapon. The trial court suppressed the gun in question and a statement made by Quarles because the statement was obtained by police before they read him his Miranda rights. That ruling was affirmed on appeal through the New York Court of Appeals. The U.S. Supreme Court granted certiorari, and reversed. Justice Rehnquist wrote the opinion of the Court, in which Chief Justice Burger and Justices White, Blackmun, and Powell joined. Justice O'Connor filed an opinion concurring in the judgment in part and dissenting in part. Justice Marshall filed a dissenting opinion, in which Justices Brennan and Stevens joined.

FACTS

On September 11, 1980, at approximately 12:30 A.M., Officer Frank Kraft and Officer Sal Scarring were on road patrol in Queens, N.Y., when a young woman approached their car. She told them that she had just been raped by a black male, approximately six feet tall, who was wearing a black jacket with the name "Big Ben" printed in yellow letters on the back. She told the officers that the man had just entered an A&P supermarket located nearby and that the man was carrying a gun.

The officers drove the woman to the supermarket, and Officer Kraft entered the store while Officer Scarring radioed for assistance. Officer Kraft quickly spotted respondent, who matched the description given by the woman, approaching a checkout counter. Apparently upon seeing the officer, respondent turned and ran toward the rear of the store, and Officer Kraft pursued him with a drawn gun. When respondent turned the corner at the end of the aisle, Officer Kraft lost sight of him for several seconds, and upon regaining sight of respondent, ordered him to stop and put his hands over his head.

Although more than three other officers had arrived on the scene by that time, Officer Kraft was the first to reach respondent. He frisked him and discovered that he was wearing a shoulder holster which was then empty. After handcuffing him, Officer Kraft asked him where the gun was. Respondent nodded in the direction of some empty cartons and responded, "[T]he gun is over there." Officer Kraft thereafter retrieved a loaded .38-caliber revolver from one of the cartons, formally placed respondent under arrest, and read him his Miranda rights from a printed card. Respondent indicated that he would be willing to answer questions without an attorney present. Officer Kraft then asked respondent if he owned the gun and where he had purchased it. Respondent answered that he did own it and that he had purchased it in Miami, Fla.

In the subsequent prosecution of respondent for criminal possession of a weapon, the judge excluded the statement, "the gun is over there," and the gun because the officer had not given respondent the warning required by our decision in *Miranda v. Arizona* before asking him where the gun was located. . . .

OPINION

We hold . . . that there is a "public safety" exception to the requirement that *Miranda* warning[s] be given before a suspect's answers may be admitted into evidence, and that the availability of that exception does not depend upon the motivation of the individual officers involved. In a kaleidoscopic situation such as the one confronting these officers, where spontaneity rather than adherence to a police manual is necessarily the order of the day, the application of the exception which we recognize today should not be made to depend on *post hoc* findings at a suppression hearing concerning the subjective motivation of the arresting officer. Undoubtedly most police officers, if placed in Officer Kraft's position, would act out of a host of different, instinctive, and largely unverifiable motives—their own safety, the safety of others, and perhaps as well the desire to obtain incriminating evidence from the suspect.

Whatever the motivation of individual officers in such a situation, we do not believe that the doctrinal underpinnings of *Miranda* require that it be applied in all its rigor to a situation in which police officers ask questions reasonably prompted by a concern for public safety. . . .

The police in this case, in the very act of apprehending a suspect, were confronted with the immediate necessity of ascertaining the whereabouts of a gun which they had every reason to believe the suspect had just removed from his empty holster and discarded in the supermarket. So long as the gun was concealed somewhere in the supermarket, with its actual whereabouts unknown, it obviously posed more than one danger to the public safety: an accomplice might make use of it, a customer or employee might later come upon it. In such a situation, if the police are required to recite the familiar *Miranda* warnings before asking the whereabouts of the gun, suspects in Quarles' position might well be deterred from responding. . . .

We conclude that the need for answers to questions in a situation posing a threat to the public safety outweighs the need for the prophylactic rule protecting the Fifth Amendment's privilege against self-incrimination. We decline to place officers such as Officer Kraft in the untenable position of having to consider, often in a matter of seconds, whether it best serves society for them to ask the necessary questions without the *Miranda* warnings and render whatever probative evidence they uncover inadmissible, or for them to give the warnings in order to preserve the admissibility of evidence they might uncover but possibly damage or destroy their ability to obtain that evidence and neutralize the volatile situation confronting them.

In recognizing a narrow exception to the *Miranda* rule in this case, we acknowledge that to some degree we lessen the desirable clarity of that rule. . . . The exception will not be difficult for police officers to apply because in each case it will be circumscribed by the exigency which justifies it. We think police officers can and will distinguish almost instinctively between questions necessary to secure their own safety or the safety of the public and questions designed solely to elicit testimonial evidence from a suspect. . . .

We hold that the Court of Appeals in this case erred in excluding the statement, "the gun is over there," and the gun because of the officer's failure to read respondent his *Miranda* rights before attempting to locate the weapon. . . .

DISSENT

Justice Marshall, with whom Justice Brennan and Justice Stevens join, dissenting. . . .

The majority's entire analysis rests on the factual assumption that the public was at risk during Quarles' interrogation. This assumption is completely in conflict with the facts as found by New York's highest court. Before the interrogation began, Quarles had been "reduced to a condition of physical powerlessness." Contrary to the majority's speculations, Quarles was not believed to have, nor did he in fact have an accomplice to come to his rescue. When the questioning began, the arresting officers were sufficiently confident of their own safety to put away their guns. As Officer Kraft acknowledged at the suppression hearing, "the situation was under control." Based on Officer Kraft's own testimony, the New York Court of Appeals found: "Nothing suggests that any of the officers was by that time concerned for his own physical safety." The Court of Appeals also determined that there was no evidence that the interrogation was prompted by the arresting officers' concern for public safety. . . .

. . . [N]o customers or employees were wandering about the store in danger of coming across Quarles' discarded weapon. Although the supermarket was open to the public, Quarles' arrest took place during the middle of the night when the store was apparently deserted except for the clerks at the check-out counter. The police could have easily cordoned off the store and searched for the missing gun. Had they done so, they would have found the gun forthwith. The police were well aware that Quarles had discarded the weapon somewhere near the scene of the arrest. As the State acknowledged before the New York Court of Appeals:

After Officer Kraft had handcuffed and frisked the defendant in the supermarket, he knew with a high degree of certainty that the defendant's gun was within the immediate vicinity of the encounter. He undoubtedly would have searched for it in the carton a few feet away without the defendant having looked in that direction and saying that it was there. . . .

If after plenary review two appellate courts so fundamentally differ over the threat to public safety presented by the simple and uncontested facts of this case, one must seriously question how law enforcement officers will respond to the majority's new rule in the confusion and haste of the real world.

CASE DISCUSSION

What exactly does the Court mean by a "public safety exception"? What facts in this case indicate that the danger to public safety justified foregoing the *Miranda* warnings? Justice Sandra Day O'Connor predicts that we will now see "a finespun new doctrine on public safety exigencies incident to custodial interrogation, complete with hairsplitting distinctions that currently plague our Fourth Amendment jurisprudence." Do you agree? Does this decision weaken the Fifth Amendment? If so, how? Does it weaken other interests? If so, which ones? If you favor a public safety exception, does it apply to the facts in this case? Consider the facts that the dissent stresses.

D e c i s i o n   P o i n t

STATE V. LOPEZ
652 A.2d 696 (N.H. 1994)

On March 23, 1991, at approximately 9:00 P.M., a young man approached Roscoe Powers on a Main Street sidewalk in Nashua. The man pointed a gun at Powers and asked him for money. Powers turned and ran, and the man chased after him, catching up with him as Powers slipped on the ice. The man shot Powers in the chest. Powers managed to keep moving, and his assailant continued to pursue him. Finally, when Powers drew a knife and turned to confront the man, he was gone. Powers survived the assault.

Less than an hour later, on nearby West Pearl Street, a young man approached Robbie Goyette and a friend as they sat in a car. The man pointed a gun and asked the two for money. Goyette refused and drove off. The man ran alongside the car and shot Goyette in the neck, killing him.

Thomas MacLeod, a Nashua police officer, was on duty that night and learned of the shootings. At around 10:00 P.M., a sergeant ordered him to search for possible suspects, giving him a description from witnesses to the shootings. MacLeod combed the neighborhood without success but then heard a loud scream coming from a building on Spring Street, approximately two blocks away from the shootings. As he neared the building's entrance, Eduardo Lopez emerged from the doorway and walked toward him.

Lopez fit the description MacLeod had been given and was carrying a three- or four-foot-long wooden hand rail. MacLeod told him to stop, but Lopez ignored him. Thinking Lopez might be the one who shot Powers and Goyette, MacLeod drew his gun and ordered him to drop the hand rail. Lopez refused, retorting, "F— you. I am not dropping the stick. You're going to have to shoot me." MacLeod replied that he did not want to shoot him and, holstering his gun, took some steps toward Lopez. Lopez swung the stick at MacLeod, striking his shoulder and breaking the hand rail in two. MacLeod grabbed Lopez, and the two fell to the ground, struggling.

MacLeod tried to handcuff Lopez but soon gave up. At the suppression hearing, MacLeod explained, "I felt that [Lopez] was very wir[y], he appeared to be very strong, at that time and I didn't want to have the Defendant escape. . . ." The two stood up, and MacLeod pushed Lopez against the side of the building. Lopez grabbed MacLeod's throat, making it difficult for the officer to breath. Lopez told him, "I'll f—ing kill you if you don't let me go." At this point, MacLeod noticed Lopez was wearing an empty shoulder holster. Not knowing whether the gun used in the shootings had been recovered yet, MacLeod asked him where it was. Lopez replied, "It's upstairs." MacLeod asked Lopez no further questions and eventually succeeded in handcuffing him with the help of another officer. The gun used in the shootings was found in a nearby parking lot, but the manufacturer's box for the gun, and Lopez's fingerprints on the gun manual inside the box, were found in the building in which Lopez was first seen. These items were obtained pursuant to a search warrant.

Should Lopez's response, "It's upstairs," have been suppressed? No, said the New Hampshire Supreme Court. According to the court,

> *Miranda v. Arizona* requires exclusion at trial of a defendant's responses to custodial interrogation if the questioning is not preceded by adequate safeguards, such as the familiar *Miranda* warnings, that protect the defendant's right against self-incrimination. *New York v. Quarles* created the public safety exception to the general *Miranda* rule. . . . Following *Quarles*, we have no difficulty in applying the federal public safety exception to this case. At the time Officer MacLeod asked Lopez where the gun was, MacLeod reasonably believed that Lopez had just committed two ruthless assaults. Based on this belief, and MacLeod's own perceptions of the man, it was objectively clear that Lopez was strong-willed, physically unmanageable, and a serious danger to the officer and the public. MacLeod could reasonably view Lopez as a violent and truly dangerous man.
>
> When MacLeod saw the empty shoulder holster, the peril to public safety was obvious. Mac-

Leod could barely restrain Lopez. Hence, there was an alarming risk that Lopez might regain control of the gun, harm the officer, escape, and commit other brutal crimes. MacLeod also did not know whether Lopez had been working alone or with an unseen accomplice who still had access to the weapon. Finally, as in *Quarles*, the missing gun posed a serious hazard to the general public. The crimes occurred on a Saturday night in downtown Nashua, and MacLeod encountered Lopez just two blocks away. MacLeod's question about the gun's location was necessary to secure the safety of the public. We note that MacLeod made no inquiries regarding the crimes or Lopez' role in them, instead asking only this one, essential question. Thus, we can say that it was not designed solely to elicit testimonial evidence.

> Lopez suggests that his response to MacLeod indicated that the gun was out of harm's way. While this may be true, the focus of our inquiry is on the objective necessity of an officer's interrogation at the time it is made. MacLeod could not know the answer Lopez would give him. Moreover, the gun's actual location in the middle of a nearby parking lot evidences the kind of danger MacLeod could reasonably have feared. Anyone, including teen-aged children out for the evening, could have stumbled upon it, with perilous consequences.
>
> Affirmed.

◆

Waiver of *Miranda* Rights

Despite fears that the requirements of *Miranda v. Arizona* "handcuffed the police," virtually all defendants waive their rights and confess after police read them their rights. Hence, what are a valid **waiver** and a voluntary confession become crucial in most cases involving incriminating statements. *Miranda* permits police officers to question suspects while in custody if they can prove that suspects waived their right to remain silent

1. Voluntarily

2. Knowingly

3. Intelligently

If, however, suspects "indicate in any manner, at any time prior to or during questioning, that [they] wish to remain silent . . . the interrogation must cease," because they have "shown that [they] intend to exercise [their] . . . Fifth Amendment privilege."

Express waivers, whether oral or written, are not required. However, neither is mere silence a voluntary, knowing, intelligent waiver. In *North Carolina v. Butler*, a six-to-three decision in which a vigorous dissent argued that the Supreme Court should adopt a "simple prophylactic rule requiring police to obtain an express waiver," the Court held as follows:

> An express written or oral statement of waiver of the right to remain silent or of the right to counsel is usually strong proof of the validity of that waiver, but is not inevitably either necessary or sufficient to establish waiver. The question is not one of form, but rather whether the defendant in fact knowingly and voluntarily waived the rights delineated in the *Miranda* case. As was unequivocally said in *Miranda*, mere silence is not enough. That does not mean that the defendant's silence, coupled with an understanding of his rights and a course of conduct indicating waiver, may never support a conclusion that a defendant did not waive his rights. The courts must presume that a defendant did not waive his rights; the prosecution's burden is great; but in at least some cases waiver can be clearly inferred from the actions and words of the person interrogated.

In determining whether suspects have voluntarily, knowingly, and intelligently waived their right against self-incrimination, courts are required to consider the **totality of circumstances** surrounding the alleged waiver. Factors commonly considered include the suspect's

- Intelligence
- Education
- Age
- Familiarity with the criminal justice system
- Physical condition
- Mental condition
- Ability to understand English

D e c i s i o n   P o i n t

Which of the following is a knowing and intelligent waiver of rights under *Miranda v. Arizona*?

1. Suspect never indicated that he wanted a lawyer.

2. No evidence shows that suspect was threatened, tricked, or cajoled.[37]

3. Suspect invoked right to counsel and then, after a five-hour ride in the back of a squad car, signed a waiver when police officers asked "if there was anything he would like to tell the[m]."[38]

4. Suspect asked for a lawyer, was not given one, and then signed a waiver after repeated warnings and "nagging" by police officers.[39]

5. After refusing to sign an express waiver, defendant talked to the police.[40]

6. Defendant stated that he had nothing more to say when he was presented with a waiver form, but then responded to questions during an interview that followed.[41]

7. Defendant called his family instead of an attorney, and then made incriminating statements.[42]

These were all considered voluntary, intelligent, and knowing waivers.

VOLUNTARY SELF-INCRIMINATION

Great fears and hopes — depending on whether those who voiced them were more afraid of street criminals or more afraid of government abuse of power — were expressed that *Miranda v. Arizona* would end the use of confessions as a tool in the gathering and use of criminal evidence. That has not happened, although as we have seen, Richard Leo found that 20 percent of suspects do invoke their right to silence and/or an attorney and refuse to talk. One experienced interrogator, Sergeant James DeConcini of the Minneapolis Police Department, suggests that the reason so many suspects waive their right to remain silent and agree to police interrogation is that knowledge is a two-way street. Not only do police officers want to know what suspects know about crimes, but suspects also want to know how much police officers know about them. Suspects believe that by cooperating with the police, they may find out if the police "have something on them."

That most suspects waive their right to remain silent and agree to custodial interrogation brings us back to the due process requirement of voluntariness. Police officers who interrogate suspects may not have satisfied the requirements of the Constitution even if they have properly warned suspects and have secured a knowing and voluntary waiver of their right to remain silent. The Fifth Amendment prohibits the police from *compelling* suspects to confess. Therefore, all admissions and confessions obtained during interrogation must be voluntary. Voluntariness, according to the Supreme Court, is a legal question that depends on the totality of the circumstances of each individual case. A confession is involuntary under the **voluntariness test** if all the circumstances in the case demonstrate the following:

1. Coercive actions by police officers or others who conduct the interrogation
2. A causal link between the coercive actions and the incriminating admissions and confessions

According to Chief Justice Rehnquist, writing for a majority of the Supreme Court in *Colorado v. Connelly,*

> . . . [T]he cases considered by this Court over the 50 years since *Brown v. Mississippi* have focused on the crucial element of police overreaching. While each confession case has turned on its own set of factors justifying the conclusion that police conduct was oppressive, all have contained a substantial element of coercive police conduct. Absent police conduct causally related to the confession, there is simply no basis for concluding that any state actor has deprived a criminal defendant of due process of law. . . . [A]s interrogators have turned to more subtle forms of psychological persuasion, courts have found the mental condition of the defendant a more significant factor in the "voluntariness" calculus. But this fact does not justify a conclusion that a defendant's mental condition, by itself apart from its relation to official coercion, should ever dispose of the inquiry into constitutional "voluntariness."[43]

The most common circumstances that courts consider in determining whether coercive action has caused people to confess include the following:

- Place of questioning
- Whether suspect initiated the contact with law enforcement
- Whether *Miranda* warnings were given

- Number of interrogators
- Length of the questioning
- Denial of food, water, and toilet facilities
- Threats, promises, lies, and tricks
- Denial of access to a lawyer
- Characteristics of the suspect, such as age, gender, race, physical and mental condition, education, drug problems, and experience with the criminal justice system

Courts have found the following circumstances insufficiently coercive to violate the Fifth Amendment:

- Promises of leniency
- Promises of treatment
- Confrontation of the accused with other evidence of guilt
- Interrogator's appeal to defendant's emotions
- Interrogator's false and misleading statements[44]

The United States Supreme Court applied the voluntariness test to the totality of circumstances surrounding a confession in *Colorado v. Connelly.*

C A S E

Did He Confess Voluntarily?

Colorado v. Connelly
479 U.S. 157, 107 S.Ct. 515 (1986)

The trial court suppressed statements made by Connelly. The state appealed the order of the trial court suppressing the statements. The Colorado Supreme Court affirmed. The U.S. Supreme Court granted cer-tiorari, reversed, and remanded the case. Chief Justice Rehnquist delivered the opinion of the Court, in which Justices White, Powell, O'Connor, and Scalia joined, and in all but Part III–A of which Justice Blackmun joined. Justice Blackmun filed an opinion concurring in part and concurring in the judgment. Justice Stevens filed an opinion concurring in part and dissenting in part. Justice Brennan filed a dissenting opinion, in which Justice Marshall joined.

FACTS

On August 18, 1983, Officer Patrick Anderson of the Denver Police Department was in uniform, working in an off-duty capacity in downtown Denver. Respondent Francis Connelly approached Officer Anderson and, without any prompting, stated that he had murdered someone and wanted to talk about it. Anderson immediately advised respondent that he had the right to remain silent, that anything he said could be used against him in court, and that he had the right to an attorney prior to any police questioning. Respondent stated that he understood these rights but he still wanted to talk about the murder. Understandably bewildered by this confession, Officer Anderson asked respondent several questions. Connelly denied that he had been drinking, denied that he had been taking any drugs, and stated that, in the past, he had been a patient in several mental hospitals. Officer Anderson again told Connelly that he was under no obligation to say anything. Connelly replied that it was "all right," and that he would talk to Officer Anderson because his conscience had been bothering him. To Officer Anderson, respondent appeared to understand fully the nature of his acts.

Shortly thereafter, Homicide Detective Stephen Antuna arrived. Respondent was again advised of his rights, and Detective Antuna asked him "what he had on his mind." Respondent answered that he had come all the way from Boston to confess to the murder of Mary Ann Junta, a young girl whom he had killed in Denver sometime during November 1982. Respondent was taken to police headquarters, and a search of police records revealed that the body of an unidentified female had been found in April 1983. Respondent openly detailed his story to Detective Antuna and Sergeant Thomas Haney, and readily agreed to take the officers to the scene of the killing. Under Connelly's sole direction, the two officers and respondent proceeded in a police vehicle to the location of the crime. Respondent pointed out the exact location of the murder. Throughout this episode, Detective Antuna perceived no indication whatsoever that respondent was suffering from any kind of mental illness.

Respondent was held overnight. During an interview with the public defender's office the following morning, he became visibly disoriented. He began giving confused answers to questions, and for the first time, stated that "voices" had told him to come to Denver and that he had followed the directions of these voices in confessing. Respondent was sent to a state hospital for evaluation. He was initially found incompetent to assist in his own defense. By March 1984, however, the doctors evaluating respondent determined that he was competent to proceed to trial.

At a preliminary hearing, respondent moved to suppress all of his statements. Dr. Jeffrey Metzner, a psychiatrist employed by the state hospital, testified that respondent was suffering from chronic schizophrenia and was in a psychotic state at least as of August 17, 1983, the day before he confessed. Metzner's interviews with respondent revealed that respondent was following the "voice of God." This voice instructed respondent to withdraw money from the bank, to buy an airplane ticket, and to fly from Boston to Denver. When respondent arrived from Boston, God's voice became stronger and told respondent either to confess to the killing or to commit suicide. Reluctantly following the command of the voices, respondent approached Officer Anderson and confessed.

Dr. Metzner testified that, in his expert opinion, respondent was experiencing "command hallucinations." This condition interfered with respondent's "volitional abilities; that is, his ability to make free and rational choices." Ibid. Dr. Metzner further testified that Connelly's illness did not significantly impair his cognitive abilities. Thus, respondent understood the rights he had when Officer Anderson and Detective Antuna advised him that he need not speak. Dr. Metzner admitted that the "voices" could in reality be Connelly's interpretation of his own guilt, but explained that in his opinion, Connelly's psychosis motivated his confession.

On the basis of this evidence the Colorado trial court decided that respondent's statements must be suppressed because they were "involuntary." Relying on our decisions in *Townsend v. Sain*, 372 U.S. 293, 83 S.Ct. 745, 9 L.Ed.2d 770 (1963), and *Culombe v. Connecticut*, 367 U.S. 568, 81 S.Ct. 1860, 6 L.Ed.2d 1037 (1961), the court ruled that a confession is admissible only if it is a product of the defendant's rational intellect and "free will." Although the court found that the police had done nothing wrong or coercive in securing respondent's confession, Connelly's illness destroyed his volition and compelled him to confess. The trial court also found that Connelly's mental state vitiated his attempted waiver of the right to counsel and the privilege against compulsory self-incrimination. Accordingly, respondent's initial statements and his custodial confession were suppressed.

. . . The Colorado Supreme Court affirmed the trial court's decision to suppress all of Connelly's statements.

OPINION

The Due Process Clause of the Fourteenth Amendment provides that no State shall "deprive any person of life, liberty, or property, without due process of law." Just last Term, in *Miller v. Fenton*, 474 U.S. 104, 109, 106 S.Ct. 445, 449, 88 L.Ed.2d 405 (1985), we held that by virtue of the Due Process Clause "certain interrogation techniques, either in isolation or as applied to the unique characteristics of a particular suspect, are so offensive to a civilized system of justice that they must be condemned." Indeed, coercive government misconduct was the catalyst for this Court's seminal confession case, *Brown v. Mississippi*, 297 U.S. 278, 56 S.Ct. 461, 80 L.Ed. 682 (1936). . . .

Thus the cases considered by this Court over the 50 years since *Brown v. Mississippi* have focused upon the crucial element of police overreaching. While each confession case has turned on its own set of factors justifying the conclusion that police conduct was oppressive, all have contained a substantial element of coercive police conduct. Absent police conduct causally related to the confession, there is simply no basis for concluding that any state actor has deprived a criminal defendant of due process of law. Respondent correctly notes that as interrogators have turned to more subtle forms of psychological persuasion, courts have found the mental condition of the defendant a more significant factor in the "voluntariness" calculus. But this fact does not justify a conclusion that a defendant's mental condition, by itself and apart from its relation to official coercion, should ever dispose of the inquiry into constitutional "voluntariness."

. . .

Our "involuntary confession" jurisprudence is entirely consistent with the settled law requiring some sort of "state action" to support a claim of violation of the Due Process Clause of the Fourteenth Amendment. The Colorado trial court, of course, found that the police committed no wrongful acts, and that finding has been neither challenged by respondent nor disturbed by the Supreme Court of Colorado. The latter court, however, concluded that sufficient state action was present by virtue of the admission of the confession into evidence in a court of the State.

The difficulty with the approach of the Supreme Court of Colorado is that it fails to recognize the essential link between coercive activity of the State, on the one hand, and a resulting confession by a defendant, on the other. The flaw in respondent's constitutional argument is that it would expand our previous line of "voluntariness" cases into a far-ranging requirement that courts must divine a defendant's motivation for speaking or acting as he did even though there be no claim that governmental conduct coerced his decision.

. . .

We have previously cautioned against expanding "currently applicable exclusionary rules by erecting additional barriers to placing truthful and probative evidence before state juries. . . . " *Lego v. Twomey*, 404 U.S. 477, 488–489, 92 S.Ct. 619, 626, 30 L.Ed.2d 618 (1972). We abide by that counsel now. "[T]he central purpose of a criminal trial is to decide the factual question of the defendant's guilt or innocence," and while we have previously held that exclusion of evidence may be necessary to protect constitutional guarantees, both the necessity for the collateral inquiry and the exclusion of evidence deflect a criminal trial from its basic purpose. Respondent would now have us require sweeping inquiries into the state of mind of a criminal defendant who has confessed, inquiries quite divorced from any coercion brought to bear on the defendant by the State. We think the Constitution rightly leaves this sort of inquiry to be resolved by state laws governing the admission of evidence and erects no standard of its own in this area. A statement rendered by one in the condition of respondent might be proved to be quite unreliable, but this is a matter to be governed by the evidentiary laws of the forum, and not by the Due Process Clause of the Fourteenth Amendment. . . .

We hold that coercive police activity is a necessary predicate to the finding that a confession is not "voluntary" within the meaning of the Due Process Clause of the Fourteenth Amendment. We also conclude that the taking of respondent's statements, and their admission into evidence, constitute no violation of that Clause.

. . .

We think that the Supreme Court of Colorado erred in importing into this area of constitutional law notions of "free will" that have no place there. There is obviously no reason to require more in the way of a "voluntariness" inquiry in the *Miranda* waiver context than in the Fourteenth Amendment confession context. The sole concern of the Fifth Amendment, on which *Miranda* was based, is governmental coercion. Indeed, the Fifth Amendment privilege is not concerned "with moral and psychological pressures to confess emanating from sources other than official coercion." The voluntariness of a waiver of this privilege has always depended on the absence of police overreaching, not on "free choice" in any broader sense of the word. See *Moran v. Burbine*, 475 U.S., at 421, 106 S.Ct., at 1141 ("[T]he relinquishment of the right must have been voluntary in the sense that it was the product of a free and deliberate choice rather than intimidation, coercion or deception. . . . [T]he record is devoid of any suggestion that police resorted to physical or psychological pressure to elicit the statements"); *Fare v. Michael C.*, 442 U.S. 707, 726–727, 99 S.Ct. 2560, 2572–2573, 61 L.Ed.2d 197 (1979) (The defendant was "not worn down by improper interrogation tactics or lengthy questioning or by trickery or deceit. . . . The officers did not intimidate or threaten respondent in any way. Their questioning was restrained and free from the abuses that so concerned the Court in *Miranda*").

Respondent urges this Court to adopt his "free will" rationale, and to find an attempted waiver invalid whenever the defendant feels compelled to waive his rights by reason of any compulsion, even if the compulsion does not flow from the police. But such a treatment of the waiver issue would "cut this Court's holding in [*Miranda*] completely loose from its own explicitly stated rationale." *Beckwith v. United States*, 425 U.S. 341, 345, 96 S.Ct. 1612, 1615, 48 L.Ed.2d 1 (1976). *Miranda* protects defendants against government coercion leading them to surrender rights protected by the Fifth Amendment; it goes no further than that. Respondent's perception of coercion flowing from the "voice of God," however important or significant such a perception may be in other disciplines, is a matter to which the United States Constitution does not speak.

The judgment of the Supreme Court of Colorado is accordingly reversed, and the cause is remanded for further proceedings not inconsistent with this opinion. . . .

It is so ordered.

. . .

DISSENT

Justice Brennan, with whom Justice Marshall joins, dissenting.

Today the Court denies Mr. Connelly his fundamental right to make a vital choice with a sane mind, involving a determination that could allow the State to deprive him of liberty or even life. This holding is unprecedented: "Surely in the present stage of our civilization a most basic sense of justice is affronted by the spectacle of incarcerating a human being upon

the basis of a statement he made while insane. . . ." *Blackburn v. Alabama*, 361 U.S. 199, 207, 80 S.Ct. 274, 280, 4 L.Ed.2d 242 (1960). Because I believe that the use of a mentally ill person's involuntary confession is antithetical to the notion of fundamental fairness embodied in the Due Process Clause, I dissent.

The respondent's seriously impaired mental condition is clear on the record of this case. At the time of his confession, Mr. Connelly suffered from a "long-standing severe mental disorder," diagnosed as chronic paranoid schizophrenia. He had been hospitalized for psychiatric reasons five times prior to his confession; his longest hospitalization lasted for seven months. Mr. Connelly heard imaginary voices and saw nonexistent objects. He believed that his father was God, and that he was a reincarnation of Jesus.

. . .

The state trial court found that the "overwhelming evidence presented by the Defense" indicated that the prosecution did not meet its burden of demonstrating by a preponderance of the evidence that the initial statement to Officer Anderson was voluntary. While the court found no police misconduct, it held:

> [T]here's no question that the Defendant did not exercise free will in choosing to talk to the police. He exercised a choice both [sic] of which were mandated by auditory hallucination, had no basis in reality, and were the product of a psychotic break with reality. The Defendant at the time of the confession had absolutely in the Court's estimation no volition or choice to make.

The trial court also held that the State had not shown by clear and convincing evidence that the defendant had waived his *Miranda* right to counsel and to self-incrimination "voluntarily, knowingly and intelligently."

The Supreme Court of Colorado affirmed after evaluating "the totality of circumstances" surrounding the unsolicited confession and the waiver of *Miranda* rights. 702 P.2d 722, 728 (1985).

The absence of police wrongdoing should not, by itself, determine the voluntariness of a confession by a mentally ill person. The requirement that a confession be voluntary reflects a recognition of the importance of free will and of reliability in determining the admissibility of a confession, and thus demands an inquiry into the totality of the circumstances surrounding the confession.

Today's decision restricts the application of the term "involuntary" to those confessions obtained by police coercion. Confessions by mentally ill individuals or by persons coerced by parties other than police officers are now considered "voluntary." The Court's failure to recognize all forms of involuntariness or coercion as antithetical to due process reflects a refusal to acknowledge free will as a value of constitutional consequence. But due process derives much of its meaning from a conception of fundamental fairness that emphasizes the right to make vital choices voluntarily: "The Fourteenth Amendment secures against state invasion . . . the right of a person to remain silent unless he chooses to speak in the unfettered exercise of his own will. . . ." *Malloy v. Hogan*, 378 U.S. 1, 8, 84 S.Ct. 1489, 1493, 12 L.Ed.2d 653 (1964). This right requires vigilant protection if we are to safeguard the values of private conscience and human dignity.

. . .

A true commitment to fundamental fairness requires that the inquiry be "not whether the conduct of state officers in obtaining the confession is shocking, but whether the confession was 'free and voluntary.' . . ." *Malloy v. Hogan*, supra, 378 U.S., at 7, 84 S.Ct., at 1493.

. . .

Since the Court redefines voluntary confessions to include confessions by mentally ill individuals, the reliability of these confessions becomes a central concern. A concern for reliability is inherent in our criminal justice system, which relies upon accusatorial rather than inquisitorial practices. While an inquisitorial system prefers obtaining confessions from criminal defendants, an accusatorial system must place its faith in determinations of "guilt by evidence independently and freely secured." *Rogers v. Richmond*, 365 U.S. 534, 541, 81 S.Ct. 735, 739, 5 L.Ed.2d 760 (1961). In *Escobedo v. Illinois*, 378 U.S. 478, 84 S.Ct. 1758, 12 L.Ed.2d 977 (1964), we justified our reliance upon accusatorial practices:

> "We have learned the lesson of history, ancient and modern, that a system of criminal law enforcement which comes to depend on the 'confession' will, in the long run, be less reliable and more subject to abuses than a system which depends on extrinsic evidence independently secured through skillful investigation."

. . .

I dissent.

CASE DISCUSSION

List all the facts relevant to deciding whether Connelly's confession was voluntary. What are the two parts of the test that the U.S. Supreme Court announced for determining whether confessions are voluntary? Do you agree with the majority that the confession was voluntary? If yes, what persuaded you? If no, do you agree with the dissent? Explain why.

D e c i s i o n   P o i n t

1. In April 1977, Marshall Carruth was found murdered in Baker, Louisiana. The murder remained unsolved until 1982. In the summer of 1982, Kerry Van Welch told his estranged wife, Barbara, that he had killed a man. He had told her this once before, in 1980, but she had dismissed it at the time as just "talking big." After the second conversation, however, she became worried and told her father about the claimed murder. Her father relayed the information to a probation officer, who in turn talked to the Baker City Police Department.

Baker Police Officers Bourgoyne and Funderburk asked Barbara Welch if she would tape her telephone conversations with her husband and, if possible, get him to talk about the murder. She consented, and in August 1982 the police recorded two conversations between the Welches. During the second conversation, Kerry Welch admitted killing Carruth.

In September 1982, Bourgoyne and Funderburk asked Welch to come to the police station for questioning. They advised him of his *Miranda* rights. He initially denied any involvement in the Carruth murder. After the police informed him of the existence of the tapes of his conversations, he said that they might as well shoot him because he wasn't going to spend the rest of his life in prison.

At this point the officers left Welch, and another officer, Stan Easley, went in. Easley, a professed born-again Christian, had listened to the tapes. In the course of his conversations with his wife, Welch had expressed fear that God would never forgive him for the murder. Easley apparently was concerned that Welch misunderstood the nature of divine forgiveness. Upon entering the room, he immediately identified himself as a police officer. Easley and Welch discussed forgiveness and salvation and prayed together for about three hours. During this time, Welch made incriminating statements.

After the prayer session, Bourgoyne asked Easley whether Welch had confessed. Easley said that he had not asked Welch anything like that. Bourgoyne then asked Welch whether he would make a statement, and Welch made an oral statement in which he admitted to the killing. Later, Welch apologized to his father-in-law and expressed a desire to apologize to the victim's family.

Was the confession the produce of police coercion? No, said the United States Fifth Circuit Court of Appeals. According to the court,

> There can be no doubt that Welch's confession was not the product of will overborne by the police. One does not have to be devout to accept the fact that Welch was concerned about his salvation and about divine forgiveness. However, this concern existed before his conversations with Easley. At most, the police set up a situation that allowed Welch to focus for some time on those concerns with a fellow Christian in

the hope that his desire to be saved would lead him to confess. What coercion that existed was sacred, not profane. *Welch v. Butler*, 835 F.2d 92 (5th Cir. 1988)

2. Cayward, a nineteen-year-old man, was suspected by the police of sexually assaulting and smothering his five-year-old niece. The police had focused their investigation on Cayward. They conducted an extensive interview of him in three stages. Although they suspected him, they did not think they had sufficient evidence with which to charge him. With the knowledge of the state attorney's office, the police fabricated two scientific reports that they intended to use as ploys in interrogating Cayward. One false report was prepared on stationery of the Florida Department of Criminal Law Enforcement; another was prepared on stationery of Life Codes, Inc., a testing organization. These false reports indicated that a scientific test established that the semen stains on the victim's underwear came from Cayward. The police showed the reports to Cayward as a device to induce a confession. The reports were presented as genuine, and their significance was explained to the defendant. After the interview concluded, Cayward asked, "What happens now?" The investigator told him, "We are going to the grand jury," and indicated that the state would seek the death penalty. Cayward then indicated his involvement and confessed, first unrecorded and later on tape.

Was Cayward's confession admissible? No, said the Florida Court of Appeals. According to the court,

> . . . [P]olice deception does not render a confession involuntary per se. While Florida courts have frequently condemned the articulation by the police of incorrect, misleading statements to suspects, they have upheld the resulting confessions. Police deception does not automatically invalidate a confession especially where there is no doubt that the defendant was read and understood his *Miranda* rights. A clear majority of state and federal courts have taken a stand similar to that advanced by Florida's appellate courts.

The instant case, however, presents a different question and one which appears to be one of first impression not only in Florida but in the United States. The reporters are filled with examples of the police making false verbal assertions to a suspect, but counsel has not indicated nor has our research revealed any case in which the police actually manufactured false documents and used them precisely as the police did in this case. Our inquiry then is whether there is a qualitative difference between the verbal artifices deemed acceptable and the presentation of the falsely contrived scientific documents challenged here. We think there is, and we agree with the trial judge that the police overstepped the line of permitted deception.

. . .

We think . . . that both the suspect's and the public's expectations concerning the built-in adversariness of police interrogations do not encompass the notion that the police will knowingly fabricate tangible documentation or physical evidence against an individual. Such an idea brings to mind the horrors of less advanced centuries in our civilization when magistrates at times schemed with sovereigns to frame political rivals. This is precisely one of the parade of horrors civics teachers have long taught their pupils that our modern judicial system was designed to correct. Thus we think the manufacturing of false documents by police officials offends our traditional notions of due process of law under both the federal and state constitutions.

In addition to our spontaneous distaste for the conduct we have reviewed in this matter, we have practical concerns regarding use of the false reports beyond the inducement of a confession. Unlike oral misrepresentations, manufactured documents have the potential of indefinite life and the facial appearance of authenticity. A report falsified for interrogation purposes might well be retained and filed in police paperwork. Such reports have the potential of finding their way into the courtroom.

. . .

We are further concerned that false documents retained in police or state attorney's files might be disclosed to the media as a result of the public records law. A suspect's reputation could be unwittingly yet unfairly and permanently marred and his right to a fair trial jeopardized by the media's innocent reporting of false documents.

We can also conceive of an unintended scenario where a manufactured document, initially designed only for use in interrogation, might be admitted as substantive evidence against a defendant. Although one hopes that such an error would be discovered in preparation for trial, the reality of our courts' heavy caseloads is that counsel and trial judges routinely accept as true documents which appear to be reliable reports from known government and private agencies. . . .

Additionally, were we to approve the conduct taken in this case, we might be opening the door for police to fabricate court documents, including warrants, orders, and judgments. We think that such a step would drastically erode and perhaps eliminate the public's recognition of the authority of court orders, and without the citizenry's respect, our judicial system cannot long survive.

A final factor, which weighs heavily in our decision, concerns the increased confidence the public generally feels toward the police. This feeling of assurance has been earned over the course of several decades by increased professionalism of law enforcement agencies, education, and community involvement. We recognize that law enforcement officers must be allowed a degree of latitude in interrogating suspects, and we acknowledge the role of confessions in the administration of the criminal justice system. We must, however, decline to undermine the rapport the police have developed with the public by approving participation of law enforcement officers in practices which most citizens would consider highly inappropriate. We think that for us to sanction the manufacturing of false documents by the police would greatly lessen the respect the public has for the criminal justice system and for those sworn to uphold and enforce the law. In a word, in administration of the criminal law, we simply cannot allow the end of securing a confession to justify the means employed in this case. *State v. Cayward* 552 So.2d 971 (Fla.App. 1989)

Voluntary does not mean "totally free of influence." The *Miranda* warnings were intended to remove *coercion* from police custodial interrogation. They were not meant to eliminate all *pressure* on criminal suspects. According to one commentator,

> At trial, after establishing probable cause of guilt and when the defendant enjoys the protection of a neutral bench, a personal advocate, and public scrutiny, the government may not so much as put a polite question to the defendant. But, between arrest and commitment, the police may badger, trick, and manipulate the suspect in an environment solely within their control and to which no other witness is admitted. With respect to confessions, society insists on enjoying "at one and the same time the pleasures of indulgence and the dignity of disapproval."[45]

"HARMLESS ERROR" AND COERCED CONFESSIONS

Until 1990, the United States Supreme Court had held that admitting incriminating statements made in violation of the due process clause is reversible error—that is, an error in the proceedings that requires the reviewing court to reverse the trial court's judgment in the case (see Chapter 10). In *Arizona v. Fulminante*, a majority of the Court held that the **harmless error rule** (reversal is not required if the error did not affect the outcome of the proceedings) should apply to coerced confessions. Oreste Fulminante raped, tortured, and left his stepdaughter to die in the Arizona desert. During Fulminante's imprisonment for another crime in another state, a police informant got Fulminante to confess to his stepdaughter's murder by promising him protection against prisoners hostile to child murderers. In a trial for the murder, Fulminante moved to exclude his confession from evidence. The Court held that although the confession was coerced, Fulminante's conviction could stand if sufficient evidence other than the confession existed to convict him. In other words, if he could be convicted on other evidence, the error in admitting a coerced confession was harmless.[46]

SUMMARY

Following arrest, the intrusions and deprivations to suspects and the costs of administering them significantly increase. Custodial identification procedures, searches, and interrogation all entail greater deprivations and intrusions than do searches and seizures conducted before suspects are taken into custody. The Fourteenth Amendment due process clause, the Fifth Amendment self-incriminating clause, and the Sixth Amendment right to counsel clause apply to custodial interrogation and to confessions and other incriminating statements made while suspects are in custody. The Fifth Amendment protects only communicative evidence—that is, words amounting to testimony against suspects who utter them. It protects the content of the words, however, not the words themselves. The self-incrimination clause does not protect the answers to general questions asked during investigation, questions during investigative stops, informational questions during booking, or answers on forms required by law. Nor does the self-incrimination clause apply to physical evidence—such as that produced during searches and seizures and that produced during identification procedures—including blood samples, fingerprints, hair samples, and voice exemplars.

Custodial interrogation and the incriminating statements resulting from it are secret proceedings. Therefore, it is not possible to know what actually goes on in the interrogation room. Recently, some empirical research has taken us inside interrogation rooms and enlightened us about what really happens during custodial interrogation. Interested parties—the police and the suspect—usually have widely different descriptions of what happens during interrogation.

According to *Miranda v. Arizona*, custodial interrogation is inherently coercive without adequate warnings of the right against self-incrimination and the right to a lawyer. *Custody* means not only interrogation at the police station but also interrogation in other places where a suspect's liberty has been deprived in any significant way. *Interrogation* means the deliberate eliciting of a response, according to the Sixth Amendment right to counsel. It means the more active direct questioning or its functional equivalent in Fifth Amendment self-incrimination. Interrogation without custody does not require *Miranda* warnings. Custody without interrogation does not require the warnings. The *Miranda* warnings are not themselves rights; they are a procedure to protect the right against self-incrimination and the right to counsel. If other procedures protect these rights, then the Constitution does not require administering the *Miranda* warnings to suspects.

Suspects can waive their rights against self-incrimination and to counsel, if they do so voluntarily and intelligently. That is, they must know they have the right, and they must give it up of their own free will. Mere silence is not a waiver. However, waiver does not require some affirmative police misconduct that overbears the will of suspects.

Incriminating statements made following a valid waiver do not violate the Fifth Amendment if suspects voluntarily make them. The Fifth Amendment prohibits only compelled self-incrimination. *Compelled* means something more than "pressure." According to the Supreme Court, confessions are compelled only if the totality of the circumstances in individual cases shows that police misconduct causes suspects to confess by overbearing their free will. The Court has made it clear that confessions obtained by force, the threat of force, or by false promises are compelled. It has regarded lies, tricks, plays on psychological weakness, and other kinds of police conduct used to convince suspects to confess or make incriminating statements as circumstances in the totality surrounding individual cases. Also part of the totality of the circumstances are characteristics of the suspect, including age, intelligence, education, mental stability, and familiarity with the criminal justice system.

Until 1990, involuntary confessions required automatic reversal of convictions. In *Arizona v. Fulminante*, a bare majority of the Supreme Court held that the harmless error rule now applies to the admission of compelled incriminating statements. Incriminating statements that affect the outcome of the trial require reversal; incriminating statements that do not affect the outcome of the trial do not require reversal.

REVIEW QUESTIONS

1. Compare the popular view of *Miranda v. Arizona* and the reality of police interrogation.

2. What is the heart of the controversy surrounding the decision in *Miranda v. Arizona*?

3. Explain the dispute about the importance of, and summarize the empirical evidence regarding, custodial interrogation and the resulting incriminating evidence.

4. Explain the cases for and against police interrogation.

5. Describe the state of our knowledge of the abuse of police interrogation.

6. What three constitutional provisions has the Supreme Court relied upon in reviewing confessions cases?

7. Explain how the Supreme Court has applied the provisions identified in question 6 to confessions cases.

8. Summarize the facts and explain the significance of *Brown v. Mississippi*.

9. What are the main rationales that the Supreme Court has used to prohibit the admission of involuntary confessions into evidence against the accused in criminal trials?

10. Summarize the facts and explain the significance of *Escobedo v. Illinois*.

11. To what kinds of self-incriminating evidence does the Fifth Amendment apply?

12. Identify the main types of self-incriminating evidence not protected by the Fifth Amendment.

13. What combination of developments led the Supreme Court to decide *Miranda v. Arizona*?

14. List the *Miranda* "warnings" that police are required to give suspects.

15. Identify and define the two conditions under which the police are required to give individuals the *Miranda* warnings.

16. What effects has the decision in *Miranda v. Arizona* had on the number of confessions?

17. Does the Constitution require the giving of the *Miranda* warnings? Explain.

18. Explain the difference between the meaning of interrogation according to the Sixth Amendment right to counsel clause and the meaning of interrogation according to the Fifth Amendment self-incrimination clause.

19. Describe and explain the significance of the "public safety exception" to the *Miranda* warning requirement.

20. Explain fully how suspects can waive their right against self-incrimination.

21. What two elements make a confession involuntary, according to the Supreme Court in *Colorado v. Connelly*?

22. What are the main kinds of circumstances that the courts take into account in the totality-of-circumstances test to determine the voluntariness of confessions?

23. Explain the significance of the Court's decision in *Arizona v. Fulminante*.

KEY TERMS

accusatorial system rationale the justification for reviewing state confessions cases based on the idea that confessions are typical of inquisitorial, not adversarial, systems of justice.

accusatory stage the point at which the criminal process focuses on a specific suspect.

custodial interrogation the questioning that occurs after the police have taken suspects into custody.

deliberately-eliciting-a-response standard the test that determines whether information has been prompted from suspects without their knowledge, effectively denying them the right of counsel.

functional equivalent standard the test for determining Fifth Amendment interrogation.

fundamental fairness rationale the justification for reviewing state confessions cases based on the idea that coerced confessions violate due process of law even if they are true.

harmless error rule a mistake in lower court proceedings that does not affect the outcome of the case and does not require reversal.

interrogation the questioning of suspects and criminal defendants by the police.

per se **rules** specific rules that apply with little or no discretion.

prophylactic rules mechanisms to guarantee rights, not themselves constitutional rights.

public safety exception the rule that *Miranda* warnings need not be administered if doing so endangers the public.

reliability rationale the justification for reviewing state confessions based on their untrustworthiness.

totality of circumstances the conditions used to determine both the voluntariness of a waiver of rights and of incriminating statements.

voluntariness test the standard that relies on the totality of circumstances to determine whether waivers and confessions are voluntary.

waiver the giving up or relinquishing of a right.

Notes

1. Liva Baker, *Miranda: Crime, Law, and Politics* (New York: Atheneum, 1983), 404.

2. Quoted in Daniel Yeager, "Rethinking Custodial Interrogation," *American Criminal Law Review* 28 (1990): n. 3.

3. *Culombe v. Connecticut*, 367 U.S. 568, 81 S.Ct. 1860, 6 L.Ed.2d 1037 (1961).

4. Yale Kamisar, "The Importance of Being Guilty," *Journal of Criminal Law and Criminology* 68 (1977): 190.

5. Fred E. Inbau, "Police Interrogation and Limitations," *Journal of Criminal Law, Criminology, and Police Science* 52 (1961): 19.

6. 384 U.S. 436 (1966), 448.

7. Richard Leo, "Inside the Interrogation Room," *Journal of Criminal Law and Criminology* 86 (1996): 266, 302.

8. For thorough discussions of these matters, see Kamisar, "Importance of Being Guilty," 182–97; Steven J. Schulhofer, "Reconsidering *Miranda*," *University of Chicago Law Review* 54 (1987): 435–61; Steven J. Schulhofer, "Confessions and the Court," *Michigan Law Review* 79 (1981): 865–93; Gerald M. Caplan, "Questioning *Miranda*," *Vanderbilt Law Review* 38 (1985): 1417–76; Welsh S. White, "Defending *Miranda*," *Vanderbilt Law Review* 39 (1986): 1–22.

9. Matthew 27:11–14; See Leonard Levy, *The Origins of the Fifth Amendment* (New York: Oxford University Press, 1968), for a detailed history of the right to remain silent.

10. *Brown v. Mississippi*, 297 U.S. 278, 281, 56 S.Ct. 461, 462, 80 L.Ed.682 (1936).

11. Ibid.

12. Ibid.

13. *Ashcraft v. Tennessee*, 322 U.S. 143, 64 S.Ct. 921, 88 L.Ed. 1192 (1944); Francis Allen, "The Supreme Court, Federalism, and State Systems of Criminal Justice," *DePaul Law Review* 8 (1959): 213, 235.

14. *Rogers v. Richmond*, 365 U.S. 534, 540, 81 S.Ct. 735, 738, 5 L.Ed.2d 760 (1961).

15. *Spano v. New York*, 360 U.S. 315, 319, 79 S.Ct. 1202, 1204, 3 L.Ed.2d 1265 (1959).

16. David M. Nissman and Ed Hagen, *Law of Confessions*, 2d ed. (Chicago: Clark, Boardman, and Callahan, 1994), 1–7, 9.

17. *Stein v. New York*, 346 U.S. 156, 184, 73 S.Ct. 1077, 1092, 97 L.Ed. 1522 (1953).

18. *Crooker v. California*, 357 U.S. 433, 444–445, 78 S.Ct. 1287, 1298–1295, 2 L.Ed.2d 1448 (1958).

19. *Escobedo v. Illinois*, 378 U.S. 478, 499, 84 S.Ct. 1758, 1769, 12 L.Ed.2d 977 (1964).

20. *Miranda v. Arizona*, 384 U.S. 436, 86 S.Ct. 1602, 16 L.Ed.2d 694 (1966).

21. *United States v. Dionisio*, 410 U.S. 1, 93 S.Ct. 764, 35 L.Ed.2d 67 (1973).

22. *Pennsylvania v. Muniz*, 496 U.S. 582, 110 S.Ct. 2638, 110 L.Ed.2d 528 (1990).

23. *Miranda v. Arizona*, 384 U.S. 436, 86 S.Ct. 1602, 16 L.Ed.2d 694 (1966); for complete discussions of *Miranda* and the controversy surrounding the case, see the references in notes 1 and 8 here.

24. *Commonwealth v. Zook,* 520 Pa. 210, 553 A.2d 920 (1989).

25. Schulhofer, "Reconsidering *Miranda,*" 463–61.

26. *Miranda v. Arizona,* 384 U.S. 436, 86 S.Ct. 1602, 16 L.Ed.2d 694 (1966).

27. *Michigan v. Tucker,* 417 U.S. 433, 94 S.Ct. 2357, 41 L.Ed.2d 182 (1974).

28. *Massiah v. United States,* 377 U.S. 201, 84 S.Ct. 1199, 12 L.Ed.2d 246 (1964).

29. *Massiah v. United States,* 377 U.S. 201, 84 S.Ct. 1199, 12 L.Ed.2d 246 (1964); *United States v. Henry,* 447 U.S. 264, 100 S.Ct. 2183, 65 L.Ed.2d 115 (1980) (passive listening device).

30. Quotations are from Justice John Paul Stevens's dissent in *Rhode Island v. Innis,* 446 U.S. 291, 100 S.Ct. 1682, 64 L.Ed.2d 297 (1980).

31. *Georgetown Law Journal* 75 (1997): 951–54.

32. *Berkemer v. McCarty,* 468 U.S. 420 (1984).

33. *Minnesota v. Murphy,* 465 U.S. 420 (1984).

34. *Michigan v. Summers,* 452 U.S. 692 (1981).

35. *Dunaway v. New York,* 442 U.S. 200, 99 S.Ct. 2248, 60 L.Ed.2d 824 (1979).

36. *United States v. Lee,* 699 F.2d 466 (9th Cir. 1982) (questioning in police car); *Beckwith v. United States,* 425 U.S. 341, 96 S.Ct. 1612, 48 L.Ed.2d 1 (1976) (questioning at home); *Orozco v. Texas,* 394 U.S. 324, 89 S.Ct. 1095, 22 L.Ed.2d 311 (1969) (questioning at 4:00 A.M.).

37. *Connecticut v. Barrett,* 479 U.S. 523 (1987).

38. *Henderson v. Florida,* 473 U.S. 916 (1985).

39. *Watkins v. Virginia,* 475 U.S. 1099 (1986).

40. *U.S. v. Barahona,* 990 F.2d 412 (8th Cir. 1993).

41. *U.S. v. Banks,* 78 F.3d 1190 (7th Cir. 1995).

42. *Watkins v. Callahan,* 724 F.2d (1st Cir. 1984).

43. *Colorado v. Connelly,* 479 U.S. 157, 163, 107 S.Ct. 515, 2786, 93 L.Ed.2d 473 (1986).

44. "Twenty-Sixth Annual Review of Criminal Procedure," *Georgetown Law Journal* 85 (1997): 967–68.

45. Donald A. Dripps, "Forward: Against Police Interrogation—And the Privilege Against Self-Incrimination," *Journal of Criminal Law and Criminology* 78 (1988): 701.

46. *Arizona v. Fulminante,* 499 U.S. 279, 111 S.Ct. 1246, 113 L.Ed.2d 302 (1991).

C H A P T E R   N I N E

Identification Procedures

C H A P T E R   O U T L I N E

CHAPTER MAIN POINTS

1. Proving that a crime was committed is easier than identifying the perpetrator.

2. Identification procedures are critical in many cases involving defendants who are strangers to witnesses.

3. The identification of strangers is fraught with the danger of unreliability.

4. Reliability of identification depends on perception at the event, memory following the event, and recall at the time of identification.

5. Lineups are more reliable than show-ups, and both are more reliable than photographic arrays.

6. Photographic arrays are the most frequently used identification procedure.

7. Suspects have a right to counsel at lineups and show-ups taking place after the state initiates formal proceedings.

8. No right to counsel exists either at identification procedures not involving confrontations between suspects and witnesses or confrontations before charges are filed.

9. Due process affords protection in all identification procedures.

10. Due process involves a two-pronged inquiry: (1) whether the procedure was unnecessarily suggestive and (2) whether the suggestive procedure created a very substantial likelihood of mistaken identification.

11. Courts rarely exclude evidence derived from identification procedures despite empirical proof of their unreliability.

12. Suspects who refuse to participate in identification procedures face comments on their refusal at trial, penalties, and even compulsory participation.

13. DNA (deoxyribonucleic acid) testing can either include individuals as possible suspects or exclude them.

14. Most courts accept the theory of DNA testing and the techniques for conducting the tests, but they question whether the administration of the test produces accurate results.

15. The correct identification of a criminal suspect by means of DNA testing depends on whether a reported match is true, whether the suspect is the source of the trace of DNA, and whether the suspect is the perpetrator of the crime.

Should the Court Grant the Motion?

Thomas was indicted for rape and sodomy in the first degree, sexual abuse in the first degree, and burglary in the second degree. The victim was worried that she might have contracted AIDS from the rape and sodomy. The prosecutor moved to have Thomas tested for the AIDS virus because the evidence presented to the grand jury "establishes that defendant forcibly and repeatedly engaged in acts of sexual intercourse and oral sodomy with the victim, and did thereby expose said victim to his body and sexual fluids."

IMPORTANCE AND DANGERS
OF EYEWITNESS IDENTIFICATION

Proving that a crime was committed, and how it was committed, is easier than identifying the perpetrator. In some cases, of course, identification is not a major problem. Some suspects are caught red-handed; victims and witnesses personally know others; others confess. Technological advances have led to the increasing use of novel scientific evidence to identify criminals. Bite-mark evidence helped to convict the notorious serial rapist Ted Bundy. Fiber evidence helped to convict Wayne Williams of the murder of two out of thirty young victims in Atlanta. This chapter examines the best-known "novel scientific evidence," DNA (deoxyribonucleic acid) testing. DNA lifts samples of body fluid, much like lifting fingerprints, and then matches these samples with the body fluids of the suspect. Heralded as the "single greatest advance in the 'search for truth' . . . since . . . cross-examination," many courts have found DNA evidence admissible. However, problems have come to light in the use of DNA, and now some courts are rethinking their initial enthusiasm for it.

The most common — and probably most problematic — cases are those in which the prosecution has to rely on the eyewitness identification of strangers. (Obviously, eyewitness identification is not a problem when witnesses know the suspect.) This chapter focuses on the three major procedures used by the police to help eyewitnesses identify suspects whom the witnesses do not know:

1. **Lineups**

2. **Show-ups**

3. **Photo arrays**

In a lineup, witnesses identify suspects standing in a line with other individuals. In a show-up, witnesses attempt to identify suspects without other possible suspects present. This may be in the police station, or it may be elsewhere. Police officers may take witnesses to observe suspects at work or in other likely places. In both lineups and show-ups, a **confrontation**—that is, an encounter—occurs between suspects and the witnesses who may incriminate them. Suspects may not actually see the witnesses, but witnesses look directly at suspects, perhaps through a one-way mirror. In photo identification, witnesses look at a picture or pictures—"mug shots"—in order to identify suspects. Eyewitness identification procedures are critical in many cases; in some, they are the only evidence available. They are also fraught with the danger of identifying the wrong person.

Eyewitness identification of strangers is notoriously low in reliability even in the most ideal settings. The most common identification procedures used in criminal procedure—lineups and photographic identification procedures—do not take place in ideal settings and, hence, render eyewitness identification of suspects and defendants still less reliable. According to one expert, faulty identifications present the "greatest single threat to the achievement of our ideal that no innocent man shall be punished." Best guesses (reliable exact figures are not available) are that about half of all wrongful convictions are due to eyewitness error. To take but one example, seven eyewitnesses swore that Bernard Pagano, a Roman Catholic priest, robbed them with a small, chrome-plated pistol. In the middle of Pagano's trial, Ronald Clouser admitted that he, not Father Pagano, had committed the robberies.[1]

Misidentification occurs because of three normal mental processes taking place at three points in time:

1. *Perception*—the information taken in by the brain at the time of the original event

2. *Memory*—the information retained from the original event in the interval between the original event and the lineup, show-up, or photographic array

3. *Recall*—the information retrieved at the time of the lineup, show-up, or photographic array

Improper suggestive measures used by law enforcement probably account for some errors in identification. However, according to the widely accepted findings of psychologists who have studied perception, memory, and recall, the great majority of instances of mistaken identity are probably attributable both to the inherent unreliability of human perception and memory and to human susceptibility to *un*intentional (and often quite subtle) suggestive influences.[2]

As to the witnessing of the original event, the brain does not record exactly what the eye sees. For about a century, psychologists have demonstrated that the eye is not a camera that records exact images on the brain. Cameras have no expectations. Human expectations and the higher thought processes associated with human mental activity definitely do influence people's perceptions. Like beauty, the physical characteristics of the perpetrators of crimes are in the eye of the beholder. The brain cannot process all that the eye sees because of natural limits on perception. Furthermore, observers—even trained observers—pay selective attention to the events they experience. They notice only certain features of events, leaving later gaps in memory. The accuracy of initial impressions depends on a variety of circumstances, including the

- Length of time the witness observed the stranger
- Distractions taking place during the observation
- Focus of the observation
- Stress to the witness during the observation
- Race of the witness and the stranger[3]

The longer the witness observes the stranger, the more reliable the perception. However, distractions such as other activity during the observation reduce reliability. Witnesses who gain a general impression, such as a whole face, are more reliable than those who focus on a single characteristic, such as a scar. But many witnesses focus on other details, such as in what experts call "weapon focus," where they may remember a gun but not the person who carried it. The perceptions of highly stressed witnesses are less reliable than those of witnesses under low stress. Distractions and stress play a particularly large role in criminal events—that is, in the events where accuracy is most important. According to C. Ronald Huff, an identification expert who conducted one study,

> Many of the cases we have identified involve errors by victims of robbery and rape, where the victim was close enough to the offender to get a look at him—but under conditions of extreme stress. . . . Such stress can significantly affect perception and memory and should give us cause to question the reliability of such eyewitness testimony.[4]

Identifying a stranger of the same race is more reliable than identifying someone of a different race. In one famous experiment, researchers showed observers a photo of a white man brandishing a razor blade in an altercation with a black man on a subway. When asked immediately afterward to describe what they saw, over half the subjects reported that the black man was carrying the weapon:

> . . . [C]onsiderable evidence indicates that people are poorer at identifying members of another race than of their own. Some studies have found that, in the United States at least, whites have greater difficulty recognizing blacks than vice versa. Moreover, counterintuitively, the ability to perceive the physical characteristics of a person from another racial group apparently does not improve significantly upon increased contact with other members of that race. Because many crimes are cross-racial, these factors may play an important part in reducing the accuracy of eyewitness perception.[5]

Another problem is fading memory. It fades most during the first few hours following the identification of a stranger, then remains stable for several months. However, what happens during the lapse of time can dramatically affect the reliability of memory. Curiously, witnesses' confidence about their recall grows as time passes, whereas memory is actually fading. The confidence of witnesses is highly unreliable, despite the heavy weight accorded this confidence by judges and juries. The dangers of suggestion are high following an event. The mind combines everything about the event, whether the witness learned it at the time of the original event or later, and stores all of the information in a single "bin." According to psychologist and respected eyewitnesses research expert Elizabeth Loftus, witnesses in her research add to their stories depending on how she describes an incident. Later, they draw this information out of the "bin" during the identification process.[6]

Steven Penrod, identification researcher at the University of Wisconsin, says that embellishment is natural to all of us: "A witness tells his story to the police, to the family, then to friends, then to the prosecutor." As the story gets retold, it becomes less reality and more legend: "[Witnesses] feel very confident about what they now think happened and that confidence is communicated to the jury."[7]

Witnesses tend to treat lineups and photographic arrays as multiple-choice tests without a "none of the above" choice. And they regard show-ups as true/false tests. They feel that they have to choose, as all students know, the "best" likeness in the lineups and the "true" or "false" likeness in the show-ups. They feel pressured by the possibility that they might look foolish if they "don't know the answer." So they respond easily to suggestion, particularly in uncomfortable or threatening situations. Suggestions—mostly not intended, it should be stressed—by authority figures, such as the police, aggravate these tendencies. For example, witnesses will feel pressure simply because the police have arranged an identification procedure. Witnesses believe that the police must have found the culprit or they would not have gone to the trouble of arranging the identification event. Hence, the witnesses believe that the culprit must be among the people in the lineup, show-up, or photo array.

Once witnesses have positively identified a stranger, it is difficult to shake their conclusion—even if it is wrong. This fact is extremely important for at least three reasons. First, a convincing amount of research runs counter to the commonsense idea that confidence bespeaks accuracy. Quite the contrary—according to the research, confidence says little if anything about accuracy; it might even show less accuracy. Second, the confidence of an eyewitness regarding his or her identification plays a major role in the decisions of jurors. Most jurors believe a confident identification. They readily dismiss other evidence in the face of confident eyewitness identification. Thus, the confident, but wrong, identification of a suspect is particularly damning.[8]

Finally, despite the dangers of faulty identification, the courts rarely reject eyewitness identification testimony. For example, during trials, prosecutors often ask victims or other witnesses if they see the person in the courtroom who committed the crime. If the witnesses answer yes, which they invariably do, then prosecutors ask them to point to that person, which they also invariably do. Moreover, courts also regularly admit evidence of prior identifications, such as those made during lineups. As one court said,

> We think it is evident that an identification of an accused by a witness for the first time in the courtroom may often be of little testimonial force, as the witness may have had opportunities to see the accused and to have heard him referred to by a certain name; whereas a prior identification, considered in connection with the circumstances surrounding its making, serves to aid the court in determining the trustworthiness of the identification made in the courtroom.[9]

THE CONSTITUTION AND
IDENTIFICATION PROCEDURES

The possibility of mistaken identification has led to efforts to reduce its likelihood. Of course, no legal rules or procedures can do anything to improve the inherent limits of human perception and memory. The only part of the identification process that law enforcement agencies and courts can affect is the recall of information during identification procedures. Sometimes, these efforts take the form of police department rules regarding the number of persons required to participate in lineups and the number of photographs required in arrays, the makeup of the people who participate in lineups and the characteristics and quality of photographs in arrays, and the conditions under which witnesses participate in lineups, show-ups, and photographic arrays. Sometimes, the effort involves the testimony of expert witnesses or instructions of judges to juries during trial regarding the problems of reliability in identification procedures.

The Supreme Court has relied on the Constitution to afford protection against mistaken identification. The Court relies on three provisions in the Constitution in its efforts to ensure accurate identification:

1. The Sixth Amendment right to counsel
2. The Fifth Amendment due process clause
3. The Fourteenth Amendment due process clause (See Table 9.1.)

The Court has ruled out both the Fifth Amendment self-incrimination clause, which dominates interrogations and confessions, and the Fourth Amendment, which governs searches and seizures of evidence, to improve the accuracy of eyewitness identification. Therefore, according to the Court, it does not violate defendants' right against self-incrimination to stand in a lineup, to speak words when asked to do so, or to put on items of clothing (see Chapter 8). Nor is it an unreasonable search and seizure to require suspects to produce blood samples, even when the government intrudes into the body, removes the blood, seizes it, and uses it against the suspect (see Chapter 3). According to the Supreme Court, the self-incrimination clause—which says that "no person shall be compelled to be a witness against himself"—refers to testimonial evidence. What does this mean? Clearly, it includes spoken and written words. But what about other incriminating evidence that suspects might provide, such as blood, hair, voice samples, or fingerprints? The Court has ruled that although such evidence may be incriminating, the Fifth Amendment does not apply. For example, in *Schmerber v. California*, Schmerber was convicted for driving while intoxicated. The evidence against him included a blood alcohol test ordered by a police officer without Schmerber's consent. According to the Court,

> . . . We . . . must . . . decide whether the withdrawal of the blood and admission in evidence of the analysis involved in this case violated petitioner's [Fifth Amendment] privilege [against self-incrimination]. We hold that the privilege protects an accused only from being compelled to testify against himself, or otherwise provide the State with evidence of a testimonial or communicative nature, and that the withdrawal of blood and use of the analysis in question in this case did not involve compulsion to these ends.

TABLE 9.1 THE CONSTITUTION AND IDENTIFICATION PROCEDURES

Identification Procedure	Before Formal Proceedings	After Formal Proceedings
Lineup	Due Process	Right to Counsel Due Process
Show-up	Due Process	Right to Counsel Due Process
Photographic Array	Due Process	Due Process

It could not be denied that in requiring petitioner to submit to the withdrawal and chemical analysis of his blood the State compelled him to submit to an attempt to discover evidence that might be used to prosecute him for a criminal offense. He submitted only after the police officer rejected his objection and directed the physician to proceed. The officer's direction to the physician to administer the test over petitioner's objection constituted compulsion for the purposes of privilege. The critical question, then, is whether petitioner was thus compelled "to be a witness against himself."

History and a long line of authorities in lower courts have consistently limited [the Fifth Amendment's] protection to situations in which the State seeks to submerge those values by obtaining the evidence against an accused through "the cruel, simple expedient of compelling it from his own mouth.... In sum, the privilege is fulfilled only when the person is guaranteed the right 'to remain silent unless he chooses to speak in the unfettered exercise of his own will.'" ... [I]t offers no protection against compulsion to submit to fingerprinting, photographing, or measurements, to write or speak for identification, to appear in court, to stand, to assume a stance, to walk, or to make a particular gesture.[10]

D e c i s i o n   P o i n t

1. Hudson was arrested and, following a preliminary hearing, was bound over to a grand jury for possible indictment for first-degree murder. While awaiting the hearing, he was detained in custody. Upon a report that Hudson suffered from acquired immunodeficiency syndrome (AIDS), the sheriff took Hudson to county health officials for an examination. Hudson objected on religious grounds to the blood test for the AIDS virus. After an evidentiary hearing, the court ordered that a blood sample be taken.

Was the test lawful? The Tennessee Supreme Court ruled that it was. As the court reasoned,

It is apparent that this is not a case of random blood sampling, and the testimony clearly shows that the sheriff and public health officials have reasonable cause to carry out the blood test. If the test is negative, the matter will be at an end. If it is positive, special care and treatment will be required for appellant either in the county jail or at a separate facility. The operation of the jail itself, the safety of the sheriff and his staff, and the safety and welfare of other persons incarcerated in the jail are involved, and any alleged religious belief or conviction of appellant must yield to concerns for the public safety and welfare which are clearly established by the evidence. Further, the appellant's own health, welfare and treatment, both as a prisoner and as a potential patient, justify the blood test which the public health officials propose to conduct. *Haywood County v. Hudson*, 740 S.W.2d 718 (Tenn. 1987).

2. Thomas was indicted for rape and sodomy in the first degree, sexual abuse in the first degree, and burglary in the second degree. The victim was worried that she might have contracted AIDS from the rape and sodomy. The prosecutor moved to have Thomas tested for the AIDS virus because the evidence presented to the grand jury "establishes that defendant forcibly and repeatedly engaged in acts of sexual intercourse and oral sodomy with the victim, and did thereby expose said victim to his body and sexual fluids."

Should the court grant the motion? A New York court ordered the test taken:

[T]his Court holds and determines that the victim has a right to know whether she may have been exposed to the AIDS virus by reason of having been exposed to the body and sexual fluids of the defendant. This Court finds and determines that it has inherent discretionary power to order the defendant to submit to such a blood test simply because it is the intelligent, humane, logical, and proper course of action under the circumstances. The mental anguish suffered by the victim knowing that she was forcibly raped and sodomized by a former inmate of the New York Department of Correctional Services is real and continuing, and the intrusion upon defendant of a routine drawing of a blood sample is very minimal and commonplace.

Hopefully, the result of such a blood test will be negative, thereby relieving the victim of her understandable anxiety. In the unlikely event that the AIDS test of defendant's blood were to prove positive, the defendant could indeed be eventually subjected to a prosecution for depraved indifference murder. However, if the defendant is afflicted with the AIDS virus, he may already be subject to a death sentence which could well claim his life long before he ever serves 7 years in state prison.

This Court holds and determines that the People's motion should be granted in all respects, and that the defendant will be required to permit the taking of samples of blood from his body in a manner not involving an unreasonable intrusion thereof, or a risk of serious physical injury thereto. The results of such AIDS Antibody Test shall be disclosed not only to the defendant, but also to the victim of the defendant's crimes. In the event that the test for AIDS were positive, the results will also be disclosed to the New York State Department of Correctional Services. *People v. Thomas*, 139 Misc.2d 1072, 529 N.Y.S.2d 429 (1988).

3. Brian Barlow was marching at the head of the San Francisco Gay Freedom Day Marching Band and Twirling Corps in a Gay Pride Parade in San Diego. He became involved in a scuffle with police monitoring the event. During the struggle, he bit one of the officers on the right shoulder, puncturing the skin and leaving a drop of blood. Barlow bit another officer on the right knuckle, breaking the skin and drawing blood. Barlow was arrested. To treat his injuries sustained in the struggle, he was taken to the hospital. There, before any *Miranda* warnings had been given, an officer, concerned for his colleagues' well-being, asked Barlow if he was a homosexual and if he had AIDS. Barlow replied that he was a homosexual and said, "You better take it that I do have AIDS for the officers' sake." Responsive to that statement, Barlow was taken to the central police station, where, without a warrant and over his objection, blood samples for AIDS analysis were taken.

Was the blood constitutionally taken? The California Court of Appeal ruled that extracting Barlow's blood violated his Fourth Amendment rights because police did not have probable cause to believe that the extraction would prove his intent to kill the officers—the crime with which Barlow was charged. *Barlow v. Superior Court*, 190 Cal.App.3d 1652, 236 Cal.Rptr. 134 (1987).

Identification procedures take place at three times:

1. Prior to formal charges
2. Between the initiation of formal adversary proceedings and the trial
3. At the trial

The Right to Counsel

The right to counsel attaches only after adversary proceedings against the accused begin. (See Chapter 11 for a discussion of when adversary proceedings begin.) And it applies only to identification procedures involving a confrontation between the accused and the witnesses. Witnesses face accused in lineups and show-ups, but not in photographic displays. The due process clause, on the other hand, applies to all identification procedures—lineups, show-ups, and photographic arrays—whenever they occur (see Table 9.1).

The Supreme Court addressed the requirement of the right to counsel during a lineup after indictment in *United States v. Wade.*[11]

C A S E

Did He Have a Right to Counsel at a Lineup?

United States v. Wade
388 U.S. 218, 87 S.Ct. 1926,
18 L.Ed.2d 1149 (1967)

Wade was convicted before the United States District Court of bank robbery. He appealed. The court of appeals reversed the conviction and ordered a new trial. The U.S. Supreme Court granted certiorari. *The Court vacated the judgment of the court of appeals and remanded the case with direction. Justice Brennan delivered the opinion for the Court. Chief Justice Warren and Justices Douglas, Fortas, Black, White, Harlan, and Stewart dissented in part.*

FACTS

The federally insured bank in Eustace, Texas, was robbed on September 21, 1964. A man with a small strip of tape on each side of his face entered the bank, pointed a pistol at the female cashier and the vice president, the only persons in the bank at the time, and forced them to fill a pillowcase with the bank's money. The man then drove away with an accom-

plice who had been waiting in a stolen car outside the bank. On March 23, 1965, an indictment was returned against respondent, Wade, and two others for conspiring to rob the bank, and against Wade and the accomplice for the robbery itself. Wade was arrested on April 2, and counsel was appointed to represent him on April 26. Fifteen days later an FBI agent, without notice to Wade's lawyer, arranged to have the two bank employees observe a line-up made up of Wade and five or six other prisoners and conducted in a courtroom of the local county courthouse. Each person in the line wore strips of tape such as allegedly worn by the robber and upon direction each said something like "put the money in the bag," the words allegedly uttered by the robber. Both bank employees identified Wade in the line-up as the bank robber.

At trial, the two employees, when asked on direct examination if the robber was in the courtroom, pointed to Wade. The prior line-up identification was then elicited from both employees on cross-examination. At the close of the testimony, Wade's counsel moved for a judgment of acquittal or, alternatively, to strike the officials' courtroom identifications on the ground that conduct of the line-up, without notice to and in the absence of his appointed counsel, violated his Fifth Amendment privilege against self-incrimination and his Sixth Amendment right to the assistance of counsel. The motion was denied, and Wade was convicted. The Court of Appeals for the Fifth Circuit reversed the conviction and ordered a new trial at which the in-court identification evidence was to be excluded, holding that, though the line-up did not violate Wade's Fifth Amendment rights, "the lineup, held as it was, in the absence of counsel, already chosen to represent appellant, was a violation of his Sixth Amendment rights. . . ." We granted certiorari. . . . We reverse the judgment of the Court of Appeals and remand to that court with direction to enter a new judgment vacating the conviction and remanding the case to the District Court for further proceedings consistent with this opinion. . . .

OPINION

. . . [T]oday's law enforcement machinery involves critical confrontations of the accused by the prosecution at pretrial proceedings where the results might well settle the accused's fate and reduce the trial itself to a mere formality. In recognition of these realities of modern criminal prosecution, our cases have construed the Sixth Amendment guarantee to apply to "critical" stages of the proceedings. . . .

. . . [T]he period from arraignment to trial was "perhaps the most critical period of the proceedings" . . . during which the accused "requires the guiding hand of counsel . . . ," if the guarantee is not to prove an empty right. . . .

. . . [W]e [must] scrutinize any pretrial confrontation of the accused to determine whether the presence of his counsel is necessary to preserve the defendant's basic right to a fair trial as affected by his right meaningfully to cross-examine the witnesses against him and to have effective assistance of counsel at the trial itself. It calls upon us to analyze whether potential substantial prejudice to defendant's rights inheres in the particular confrontation and the ability of counsel to help avoid that prejudice. . . .

The government characterizes the line-up as a mere preparatory step in the gathering of the prosecution's evidence, not different—for Sixth Amendment pur-

poses—from various other preparatory steps, such as systemized or scientific analyzing of the accused's fingerprints, blood sample, clothing, hair, and the like. . . .

But the confrontation compelled by the State between the accused and the victim or witnesses to a crime to elicit identification evidence is peculiarly riddled with innumerable dangers and variable facts which might seriously, even crucially, derogate from fair trial. The vagaries of eyewitness identification are well-known; the annals of criminal law are rife with instances of mistaken identification. . . .

Moreover, "[i]t is a matter of common experience that, once a witness has picked out the accused at the line-up, he is not likely to go back on his word later on, so that in practice the issue of identity may (in the absence of other relevant evidence) for all practical purposes be determined there and then, before the trial. . . ."

The impediments to an objective observation are increased when the victim is the witness. Line-ups are prevalent in rape and robbery prosecutions and present a particular hazard that a victim's understandable outrage may excite vengeful or spiteful motives. In any event, neither witnesses nor line-up participants are apt to be alert for conditions prejudicial to the suspect. . . . Improper influences may go undetected by a suspect, guilty or not, who experiences the emotional tension which we might expect in one being confronted with potential accusers. . . . In short, the accused's inability effectively to reconstruct at trial any unfairness that occurred at the line-up may deprive him of his only opportunity meaningfully to attack the credibility of the witness'[s] courtroom identification. . . .

Since it appears that there is grave potential for prejudice, intentional or not, in the pretrial line-up, which may not be capable of reconstruction at trial, and since presence of counsel itself can often avert prejudice and assure a meaningful confrontation at trial, there can be little doubt that for Wade the post indictment line-up was a critical stage of the prosecution at which he was "as much entitled to such aid [of counsel] . . . as at the trial itself." Thus both Wade and his counsel should have been notified of the impending line-up, and counsel's presence should have been a requisite to conduct of the line-up, absent an "intelligent waiver." . . .

The judgment of the Court of Appeals is vacated and the case is remanded to the court with direction to enter a new judgment vacating the conviction and remanding the case to the District Court for further proceedings consistent with this opinion.

It is so ordered.

DISSENT

Justice White, whom Justice Harlan and Justice Stewart join, dissenting in part and concurring in part.

The court has again propounded a broad constitutional rule barring use of a wide spectrum of relevant and probative evidence, solely because a step in its ascertainment or discovery occurs outside the presence of defense counsel. This was the approach of the Court in *Miranda v. Arizona* [1966]. I objected then to what I thought was an uncritical and doctrinaire approach without satisfactory factual foundation. I have much the same view of the present ruling and therefore dissent from the judgment. . . .

To all intents and purposes, courtroom identifications are barred if pretrial identifications have occurred without counsel being present. The rule applies to any line-up, to any other techniques employed to produce an identification and a fortiori to a face-to-face encounter between the witness and the suspect alone, regardless of when the identification occurs, in time or place, and whether before or after indictment or information. . . .

The premise for the Court's rule is not the general unreliability of eyewitness identifications nor the difficulties inherent in observation, recall, and recognition. The Court assumes a narrower evil as the basis for its rule—improper police suggestion which contributes to erroneous identifications. The Court apparently believes that improper police procedures are so widespread that a broad prophylactic rule must be laid down, requiring the presence of counsel at all pretrial identifications, in order to detect recurring instances of police misconduct. . . .

The Court goes beyond assuming that a great majority of the country's police departments are following improper practices at pretrial identifications. To find the line-up a "critical" stage of the proceeding and to exclude identifications made in the absence of counsel, the Court must also assume that police "suggestion," if it occurs at all, leads to erroneous rather than accurate identifications and that reprehensible police conduct will have an unavoidable and largely undiscoverable impact on the trial. . . .

. . . [R]equiring counsel at pretrial identifications as an invariable rule trenches on other valid state interests. One of them is its concern with the prompt and efficient enforcement of its criminal laws. Identifications frequently take place after arrest but before an indictment is returned or an information is filed. The police may have arrested a suspect on probable cause but may still have the wrong man. Both the suspect and the State have every interest in a prompt identification at that stage, the suspect in order to secure his immediate release and the State because prompt and early identification enhances accurate identification and because it must know whether it is on the right investigative track. Unavoidably, however, the absolute rule requiring the presence of counsel will cause significant delay and it may very well result in no pretrial identification at all. . . .

Nor do I think the witnesses themselves can be ignored. They will now be required to be present at the convenience of counsel rather than their own. Many may be much less willing to participate if the identification stage is transformed into an adversary proceeding not under the control of a judge. Others may fear for their own safety if their identity is known at an early date, especially when there is no way of knowing until the line-up occurs whether or not the police really have the right man. . . .

Law enforcement officers have the obligation to convict the guilty and to make sure they do not convict the innocent. They must be dedicated to making the criminal trial a procedure for the ascertainment of the true facts surrounding the commission of the crime. To this extent, our so-called adversary system is not adversary at all; nor should it be. But defense counsel has no comparable obligation to ascertain or present the truth. Our system assigns him a different mission. He must be and is interested in preventing the conviction of the innocent, but, absent a voluntary plea of guilty, we also insist that he defend his client whether he is innocent or guilty. . . . Whether today's judgment would be an acceptable exercise of supervisory power over federal courts is another question. But as a constitutional matter, the judgment in this case is erroneous. . . .

CASE DISCUSSION

What reasons did the Court give for holding that Wade had the right to a lawyer at his lineup? What interests does this holding promote? Does it promote process at the expense of result? Does it favor the guilty over the innocent? Why did Justice White dissent? Do you think that Justice White's solution improves the efficiency and effectiveness of criminal justice administration? If Wade's constitutional right to a lawyer was violated, what remedy should he get? Dismissal? Exclusion of the lineup identification? Others? Give reasons for your choice. Consider the following passage from an article by one researcher:

... [S]uggestive procedures used to facilitate identification of the accused are only a minor cause of the unreliability of eyewitness testimony. Problems of perception and memory can often play a far greater role in producing an inaccurate identification. Many subtle, and often imperceptible, social influences may operate at the retrieval stage, reducing the reliability of the resulting identification. Presence of counsel can do nothing to alleviate or even detect these factors. The witness may have erred long before an attorney is contacted to represent the defendant, and even well before the police have a particular suspect in mind.[12]

In view of this comment, does the right to counsel help to produce reliable eyewitness testimony?

In *Kirby v. Illinois*, the Supreme Court moved away from the control of police misconduct that provided at least one rationale for the decision in *United States v. Wade*. In *Kirby*, the Court relied solely on the interest in obtaining the correct result. Also, the Court declined to extend the right to counsel to lineups occurring before indictment. The Court held that only after "the institution of judicial proceedings" does the Sixth Amendment right to counsel apply to lineups. According to the Court, the due process clause provides adequate protection against unreliable eyewitness testimony derived from identification procedures that are unnecessarily and impermissibly suggestive:

In this case we are asked to import into routine police investigation an absolute constitutional guarantee historically and rationally applicable only after the onset of formal prosecutorial proceedings. We decline to do so. . . . What has been said does not suggest that there may not be occasions during the course of a criminal investigation when the police do abuse identification procedures. Such abuses are not beyond the reach of the Constitution. . . . The Due Process Clause of the Fifth and Fourteenth Amendments forbids a lineup that is unnecessarily suggestive and conducive to irreparable mistaken identification.[13]

The result of *Kirby v. Illinois* is the following:

1. The Sixth Amendment right to counsel and confrontation applies to lineups staged *after* "formal prosecutorial proceedings" commence.

2. The Fifth and Fourteenth Amendment due process clauses apply to identification procedures whenever they take place.

Although the United States Supreme Court has held that the Sixth Amendment right to counsel applies only to post-indictment lineups, some states have interpreted the parallel state right to counsel in state constitutions more broadly. In *Blue v. State*, for example, the Alaska Supreme Court held that the Alaska Constitution guaranteed the right to counsel before formal charges or indictment occurs.[14]

Due Process

The right to counsel applies only to lineups and show-ups conducted *after* the initiation of formal proceedings—the smallest number of cases. It does not apply to the greatest number of identification cases—lineups and show-ups before the commencement of formal proceedings and photo identification at any time. The reason is that they are not "confrontations," as the Supreme Court has interpreted the confrontation clause in the Sixth Amendment. Therefore, most identification procedures take place without the presence of defense counsel.

Defendants must rely on the due process clauses of the Fifth and Fourteenth Amendments to ensure correct identification at lineups and show-ups before trial, and photographic identification whenever it occurs. The Supreme Court has established a two-stage inquiry in order to determine whether identification procedures deny defendants life, liberty, or property without due process of law:[15]

1. Defendants have to prove that the lineup, show-up, or photographic array was "impermissibly suggestive."[16]

2. If the lineup, show-up, or photographic array was impermissibly and unnecessarily suggestive, the court determines whether the totality of the circumstances demonstrates that the suggestive procedure was "so corrupting as to lead to a very substantial likelihood of irreparable misidentification."[17]

To determine reliability under the totality of the circumstances, courts consider the following five factors:

1. The opportunity of witnesses to view defendants at the time of the crime
2. The degree of the attention of the witnesses at the time of the crime
3. The accuracy of the witnesses' description of defendants prior to the identification
4. The level of certainty of witnesses when identifying defendants at the time of the identification procedure
5. The length of time between the crime and the identification procedure[18]

Hence, if the totality of circumstances indicates that the identification was reliable, it is admissible as evidence, even if it was unnecessarily or impermissibly suggestive.[19]

D e c i s i o n   P o i n t

Dr. Paul Behrendt was stabbed to death in the kitchen of his home in Garden City, Long Island, at about midnight, August 23. Mrs. Behrendt, his wife, followed her husband to the kitchen and jumped the assailant. The assailant knocked her to the floor and stabbed her eleven times. The police found a shirt on the kitchen floor with keys in the pocket, which they traced to Theodore Stovall. The police arrested Stovall on the afternoon of August 24. Mrs. Behrendt was hospitalized to save her life. The police arranged with Mrs. Behrendt's surgeon to allow the police to bring Stovall to the hospital at noon on August 25. The police handcuffed Stovall to one of five officers who, with two members of the staff of the district attorney, brought him to the hospital room. Stovall was the only black person in the room. Mrs. Behrendt identified Stovall as her attacker after one of the officers asked her if Stovall "was the man" and after Stovall spoke a "few words for voice identification."

At Stovall's trial, Mrs. Behrendt testified about her hospital room identification, and she also identified Stovall in court. He was convicted and sentenced to death. After several appeals upholding his conviction, Stovall eventually arrived in the United States Supreme Court in a *habeas corpus* proceeding. The Supreme Court, Justice William Brennan, held that the identification procedure did not deny Stovall due process. The Court conceded that show-ups — that is, procedures showing suspects singly to witnesses — are highly suggestive and widely condemned:

> We turn . . . to the question of whether petitioner . . . is entitled to relief on his claim that . . . the confrontation conducted in this case was so unnecessarily suggestive and conducive to irreparable mistaken identification that he was denied due process of law. This is a recognized ground of attack upon a conviction independent of any right to counsel claim. The practice of showing suspects singly to persons for the purpose of identification, and not as part of a lineup, has been widely condemned. However, a claimed violation of due process of law in the conduct of a confrontation depends on the totality of the circumstances surrounding it, and the record in the present case reveals that the showing of Stovall to Mrs. Behrendt in an immediate hospital confrontation was imperative.

> Here was the only person in the world who could possibly exonerate Stovall. Her words, and only her words, "He is not the man" could have resulted in freedom for Stovall. The hospital was not far distant from the courthouse and jail. No one knew how long Mrs. Behrendt might live. Faced with the responsibility of identifying her attacker, with the need for immediate action and with the knowledge that Mrs. Behrendt could not visit the jail, the police followed the only feasible procedure and took Stovall to the hospital room. Under these circumstances, the usual police station line-up, which Stovall now argues he should have had, was out of the question. *Stovall v. Denno*, 388 U.S. 293, 87 S.Ct. 1967, 18 L.Ed.2d 1199 (1967).

LINEUPS

Lineups, more reliable than either show-ups or photographic displays, depend for their reliability on making sure that enough individuals participate in them and that the participants share similar characteristics. The International Association of Chiefs of Police recommends the following standards for establishing lineups that will produce accurate identification:

- Five or six participants
- The same gender, the same race, and nearly the same age
- Same or similar height, weight, skin and hair color, and body build
- Similar clothing

Despite these recommendations, in practice most lineups consist mainly of police officers and inmates of the local jail. Frequently, this is because police officers and jail inmates are the only people available. Courts rarely exclude evidence based on lineups that do not meet the requirements of the IACP. A typical example is *Martin v. United States.*

C A S E

Was the Lineup Impermissibly Suggestive?

Martin v. United States
462 F.2d 60 (5th Cir. 1972)

Martin was convicted of bank robbery and sentenced to twelve years in prison. He appealed the denial of a motion to vacate his conviction and sentence because the trial court allowed the introduction of evidence obtained by an improperly conducted lineup. The case was decided by Circuit Judges Tuttle, Morgan, and Roney. Judge Tuttle wrote the opinion for the court.

FACTS

. . . [Martin charged that the following errors were made in conducting the lineup:]

1. [T]he three other persons in the lineup with Martin were either FBI agents or local police officers.

2. There was a likelihood that the witness, St. Onge, had known one or more of them to be law enforcement officers before seeing them in the lineup.

3. St. Onge may have seen Martin in the custody of one or more of them.

4. More critically, although St. Onge had, on some occasion, referred to Martin and his brother as "boys" or "young men" or, possibly, even as "teenagers," the other persons in the lineup varied in age from twenty-eight to forty-one, whereas Martin was eighteen years old and his brother was twenty years old; the twenty-eight-year-old agent was seven inches taller than Martin, and the one nearest Martin's height was thirty-three years old.

5. Certain identifying articles of clothing worn by the other three men would clearly make Martin the "odd" man in the group.

The trial court . . . required the government to reply to this charge. [Responses were made by the government by the furnishing of affidavits dealing with all of these matters.] The Court then found that on these affidavits, there was nothing to "taint" the lineup. . . . On appeal . . . this court . . . remanded the case to the trial court to resolve the issue of the possible "taint" in the lineup.

OPINION

Upon remand, the trial court made it plain that there was no issue before it except the question whether the circumstances surrounding the lineup were such as would jeopardize the integrity of the proceeding in conflict with the principles implicit in the Supreme Court's decision in *United States v. Wade* (1967) and *Gilbert v. California* (1967). All of the persons involved in the prior confrontation were present in court and testified. The three persons who participated in the lineup all testified that they had not seen St. Onge prior to their appearing in the lineup with Martin, and they all testified that there were no clothing characteristics or indicia of official status on their persons and that they had even withdrawn pencils and other cards from their pockets and in some instances, at least, had opened the collars of their shirts. They testified that none of them wore jackets, because Martin was without one. St. Onge testified that he had not seen any of the three persons prior to their appearing in the lineup and that he did not know that any of them were law enforcement officers, nor did he know anything about them at all. He testified that he did not see Martin in the custody of any of them and that he, in fact, identified Martin because of the way he looked and because of the clothing he wore. He testified that he had been one of the two men who had sought to rent a boat from him earlier in the day.

Although it is quite difficult to understand how a person placed in the position of St. Onge, knowing the suspect to be either a "boy" or a "young man" or a "teenager," when he was in fact an 18 year old youth, would have a fair opportunity to compare him with the three men who stood in the line with him in the police station on the night of the lineup when the youngest of the three was 10 years older than Martin but was seven inches taller and the one nearest his height was 33 years of age and the third man was 41 years old, the trial court, nevertheless, had no hesitancy in finding as a fact that, "I find nothing else about the procedures in the preparation for or carrying out of the lineup and the identification that impugned its integrity. Accordingly, the lineup was not tainted."

This finding by the trial court is protected by the "clearly erroneous" rule; that is to say, we cannot interfere with it unless we determine that such a finding of fact was "clearly erroneous." We have no photographs; we are unable to see the persons involved and we are unable to compare the appearance of even the 41 year old participant in the lineup with the 18 year old, Martin. Nor are we able to determine whether a person like St. Onge would, by some alchemy, be able automatically to spot a law enforcement official as contrasted to the accused. In short, there is no basis on which we would be justified in setting aside this finding of fact by the trial court.

We recognize that much of the thrust of *Wade* and *Gilbert* has been blunted by the fact that the Supreme Court stated that it is peculiarly a problem for the trial court to ascertain whether a taint exists at the time of the lineup and whether a subsequent identification has in any way been purged of such taint. Nevertheless, all parties agree that essential requirements of fairness and absence of "suggestive influences" protect the potential accused in such lineups. However, here this trial court has made its fact determination and we cannot overrule it as a matter of law. . . .

We, therefore, affirm the judgment of the trial court . . . that the lineup was not improperly conducted.

The judgment is affirmed.

CASE DISCUSSION

Which of the recommendations for accuracy of lineups did the police use in the identification of Martin? What was suggestive about the makeup of the lineup? How could you improve it? Why did the court admit the identification based on the lineup? Do you think that the lineup was impermissibly suggestive? Do you think that the court should have admitted it? Defend your answer. Would the model instructions reproduced in Figure 9.1 help to reduce the chances of misidentification? Why?

Suggestive lineups do not lead automatically to the exclusion of identifications made at them. According to the U.S. Supreme Court, suggestive procedures do not violate the due process rights of defendants unless the totality of circumstances demonstrates that the suggestive procedures gave rise to a "substantial likelihood of misidentification." Consider the five circumstances that play the major role in determining whether there is a substantial likelihood of misidentification:

1. Opportunity of the witness to view the suspect at the time of the crime
2. Degree of attention the witness devoted to viewing the suspect
3. Accuracy of the description of the suspect given by the witness
4. Level of certainty of the witness in his or her identification
5. Length of time between the crime and the identification[20]

Behind each of these circumstances lies an assumption. The assumptions, in the order of the circumstances listed, are as follows:

1. The better the opportunity to view a person, the more accurate a later identification.
2. The greater the attention paid to a person, the more accurate a later identification.

One important issue in this case is the identification of the defendant as the perpetrator of the crime. The government has the burden of proving identity, beyond a reasonable doubt. It is not essential that the witness himself be free from doubt as to the correctness of his statement. You, the jury, however, must be satisfied beyond a reasonable doubt of the accuracy of the identification of the defendant before you may convict him. If you are not convinced beyond a reasonable doubt that the defendant was the person who committed the crime, you must find the defendant not guilty.

Identification testimony is an expression of belief or impression by the witness. Its value depends on the opportunity the witness had to observe the offender at the time of the offense and to make a reliable identification later. In appraising the identification testimony of a witness, you should consider the following:

1. *Are you convinced that the witness had the capacity and an adequate opportunity to observe the offender?* Whether the witness had an adequate opportunity to observe the offender at the time of the offense will be affected by matters such as how long or short a time was available, how far or close the witness was, how good the lighting conditions were, and whether the witness had had occasion to see or know the person in the past. [In general, a witness bases any identification he makes on his perception through the use of his senses. Usually, the witness identifies an offender by the sense of sight—but this is not necessarily so, and he may use other senses. (Sentences in brackets to be used only if appropriate. Instructions to be inserted or modified as appropriate to the proof and contentions.)]

2. *Are you satisfied that the identification made by the witness subsequent to the offense was the product of his own recollection?* You may take into account both the strength of the identification and the circumstances under which the identification was made. If the identification by the witness may have been influenced by the circumstances under which the defendant was presented to him for identification, you should scrutinize the identification with great care. [You may also consider the length of time that lapsed between the occurrence of the crime and the next opportunity of the witness to see the defendant, as bearing on the reliability of the identification. You may in addition take into account that an identification made by picking the defendant out of a group of similar individuals is generally more reliable than one which results from the presentation of the defendant alone to the witness.]

[3. *Are you sure that the witness is reliable?* You may take into account any occasions in which the witness failed to make an identification of the defendant or made an identification that was inconsistent with his identification at trial.]

4. *Finally, are you confident that the witness is credible?* You must consider the credibility of each identification witness in the same way as that of any other witness: consider whether he is truthful, and consider whether he had the capacity and opportunity to make a reliable observation on the matter covered in his testimony.

I again emphasize that the burden of proof on the prosecutor extends to every element of the crime charged, and this specifically includes the burden of proving beyond a reasonable doubt the identity of the defendant as the perpetrator of the crime with which he stands charged. If, after examining the testimony, you have a reasonable doubt as to the accuracy of the identification, you must find the defendant not guilty.

FIGURE 9.1 MODEL IDENTIFICATION INSTRUCTIONS

3. The more accurate the description of a person, the more accurate a later identification.

4. The greater the level of certainty of identification, the more accurate the description.

5. The shorter the interval between an observation and a later identification, the more accurate the identification.

Professor Gerald F. Uelman conducted an experiment to test these assumptions. He found some validity to the first assumption. However, none of the circumstances did much to improve the accuracy of identification. The experiment showed that between one-half and more than three-fourths of the identifications were wrong when witnesses had a good opportunity to observe, paid careful attention, gave an accurate description, had a high level of certainty, and were allowed a short interval between observation and identification.[21]

D e c i s i o n   P o i n t

1. On September 11, 1980, Alan McFadden was in jail in Choctaw County, Mississippi, on charges unrelated to the conviction from which he now seeks relief. Officers from nearby Neshoba County came and took him (he claims involuntarily, the State claims voluntarily) to a police lineup. The lineup consisted of four men, including McFadden, all of them black. McFadden claims, and the State does not dispute, that while he is only 5'6" and weighs 130 pounds, two of the other men in the lineup were 6'6" and 6'5" and weighed almost 200 pounds each; the fourth, McFadden's accomplice, was 5'10".

   McFadden was tried for the robbery of a jewelry store. At his trial, four eyewitnesses to the robbery, including two store employees and two customers, "positively and unequivocally" identified McFadden as one of the robbers. The robbery had taken place at about noon, the store had been well-lighted, and the robbers had been in the store for about fifteen minutes. McFadden's attorney cross-examined each eyewitness concerning her view of the robbers and her identification of them at the lineup. McFadden was convicted of armed robbery and sentenced to life imprisonment.

   Was the lineup unnecessarily suggestive and unreliable? According to the court,

   > Unnecessarily suggestive out-of-court identifications are not per se subject to exclusion . . . ; they are admissible if, under the totality of the circumstances, they are sufficiently reliable. To evaluate reliability, the court should consider (1) the opportunity of the witnesses to view the criminal at the crime; (2) their degree of attention; (3) the accuracy of their prior descriptions of the criminal; (4) the level of certainty they

   > demonstrated when confronted with the accused; and (5) the length of time between crime and confrontation. . . . While the height and weight disparities were serious and unnecessary, they are the only tainted aspects of the lineup to which McFadden refers, and alone they are insufficient to overcome the indicia of reliability. . . .[22]

2. Hugh Houston and Patricia Roseboro were working at a grocery store when two men came in with dark scarves covering their faces from just under the eyes to below the mouth. One of the men also wore a toboggan that covered the top of his head and forehead to about an inch above the eyebrows, and he had a sawed-off shotgun. Though Houston did not know this defendant, he had seen him several times before either in the neighborhood or in the store, and he recognized the toboggan wearer as being the defendant. Houston was so sure he recognized the defendant that when told that it was a holdup he thought it was a joke, but he changed his mind when the robber knocked him down with the sawed-off shotgun. Houston then gave the robbers the money in the cash register, and they left. Houston first described his assailant to the police as being twenty to twenty-five years old and 5'11", but his testimony at trial was that the defendant was only 5'4"; however, Houston readily chose the defendant's photograph from an array of six pictures shown to him by the police, and he picked the defendant out of a lineup as well. But Mrs. Roseboro, who told the officers shortly after the holdup that she would be able to identify the robbers if she saw them again, could not identify the defendant from either the photographs or the lineup, and though present during the trial she did not testify.

In this case the identification issue was not just a substantial feature of the State's case; it was the entire case. The only evidence linking the defendant to the crime was the testimony of one witness, Houston, who first described the culprit as being seven inches taller than the defendant, even though he claimed to have seen the defendant on previous occasions. The only other person present when the crime was committed had as good an opportunity to observe the criminals, but she could not identify the defendant as being one of them. And, of course, the identification problem, never entirely free of difficulty, even when the subject's face is clearly visible, was greatly compounded here, since most of the criminal's head and face was covered.

As many judges and psychologists have noted, "convictions based solely on 'one eyewitness' identifications represent 'conceivably the greatest single threat to the achievement of our ideal that no innocent man shall be punished.'" This, of course, is because the human mind often plays tricks on us. One of the tricks that it sometimes plays is that a person seen briefly before in one place and situation is thought, even by the keenest of us, to be another person, seen in a different context altogether. This common experience of mankind, known to social scientists as "unconscious transference," has been much discussed in their literature, and the likelihood of the experience being repeated under various circumstances has been confirmed by experiments of different kinds.

That in this case Houston, in good conscience, could have picked the defendant out of the lineup not because he recognized him from the robbery but because he looked familiar from being in the area earlier is certainly quite possible. In an effort to guard against the baleful effects of this possibility, the defendant submitted a requested jury instruction, which included the following:

> I instruct you that the State has the burden of proving the identify [sic] of the defendant as the perpetrator of the crime charged beyond a reasonable doubt. This means that you, the jury, must be satisfied beyond a reasonable doubt that the defendant was the perpetrator of the crime charged before you may return a verdict of guilty.
>
> The main aspect of identification is the observation of the defendant by the witness at the time of the events.
>
> Examining the testimony of the witness, Hugh Houston, as to his observation of the perpetrator at the time of the crime, you should consider that the perpetrator was wearing a mask. However, your consideration must go further. The identification of the defendant by the witness, Hugh Houston, as the perpetrator of the offense must be purely the product of his recollection of the offender and derived only from the observation made at the time of the offense. In making this determination, you should consider the manner in which the witness was confronted with the defendant after the offense, the conduct and comments of the persons in charge of the investigation and any circumstances or pressures which may have influenced the witness in making an identification, and which would cast out upon or reinforce the accuracy of the witness'[s] identification of the defendant.

Should the trial judge have given the instruction? Yes, according to the North Carolina Court of Appeal:

> Under the peculiar circumstances of the case, this was a proper instruction, and from defendant's viewpoint, a necessary one. It would have directed the jury's attention to the possibility that defendant had been identified because he looked familiar to the witness from being seen earlier in the area, rather than because the witness remembered him from the crime. Since this instruction was crucial to defendant's case, the circumstances supported it, and it had been timely and properly requested, defendant was entitled to have the substance of it presented to the jury. . . . Thus, a new trial is required. *State v. Smith*, 309 S.E.2d 695 (N.C. App., 1983)

SHOW-UPS

Show-ups—identifications of a single person—are considerably more suggestive and substantially less reliable than lineups. The main reason for their unreliability is that presenting a single person to identify is suggestive. Despite the unreliability of show-ups, courts usually admit testimony derived from them in several circumstances. For example, if show-ups take place within a few hours of a crime, two reasons justify admitting identifications from them:

1. The need to solve the crime quickly

2. The desire for fresh, accurate eyewitnesses

Situations in which courts admit show-up identifications include the following:

1. Witnesses accidentally confront suspects, such as when they run into each other in courthouse corridors.

2. Show-ups occur in emergencies, such as when witnesses are hospitalized.

3. Suspects are at large, such as when police cruise crime scenes with witnesses.

4. External circumstances "prove" the identification accurate, such as when the witness already knows the suspect.[23]

Despite criticism of show-ups, the United States Supreme Court has not automatically excluded their admission. Instead, the Court applies the same totality of circumstances test to show-ups that it applies to lineups. The Court applied the totality of circumstances test in *Neil v. Biggers*, a rape case in which the police used a show-up to identify the defendant.

C A S E

Was the Show-Up Reliable?

Neil v. Biggers
409 U.S. (1972)

Biggers was convicted of rape and sentenced to twenty years' imprisonment. The State's evidence consisted in part of testimony concerning a station-house identification of the respondent by the victim. The Tennessee Supreme Court affirmed. On certiorari, *the judgment of the Tennessee Supreme Court was affirmed by an equally divided U.S. Supreme Court. The respondent then brought a federal* habeas corpus *action. Justice Powell wrote the opinion of the Court.*

FACTS

The victim testified at trial that on the evening of January 22, 1965, a youth with a butcher knife grabbed her in the doorway to her kitchen:

A: (H)e grabbed me from behind, and grappled—twisted me on the floor. Threw me down on the floor.

Q: And there was no light in the kitchen?

A: Not in the kitchen.

Q: So you couldn't have seen him then?

A: Ye[s], I could see him, when I looked up in his face.

Q: In the dark?

A: He was right in the doorway—it was enough light from the bedroom shining through. Yes, I could see who he was.

Q: You could see? No light? And you could see him and know him then?

A: Yes.

When the victim screamed, her 12-year-old daughter came out of her bedroom and also began to scream. The assailant directed the victim to "tell her (the daughter) to shut up, or I'll kill you both." She did so, and was then walked at knife point about two blocks along a railroad track, taken into a woods, and raped there. She testified that "the moon was shining brightly, full moon." After the rape, the assailant ran off, and she returned home, the whole incident having taken between 15 minutes and half an hour.

She then gave the police what the Federal District Court characterized as "only a very general description," describing him as "being fat and flabby with smooth skin, bushy hair and a youthful voice." Additionally, though not mentioned by the District Court, she testified at the *habeas corpus* hearing that she had described her assailant as being between 16 and 18 years old and between five feet ten inches and six feet tall, as weighing between 180 and 200 pounds, and as having a dark brown complexion. This testimony was substantially corroborated by that of a police officer who was testifying from his notes.

On several occasions over the course of the next seven months, she viewed suspects in her home or at the police station, some in lineups and others in showups, and was shown between 30 and 40 photographs. She told the police that a man pictured in one of the photographs had features similar to those of her assailant, but identified none of the suspects. On August 17, the police called her to the station to view respondent, who was being detained on another charge. In an effort to construct a suitable lineup, the police checked the city jail and the city juvenile home. Finding no one at either place fitting respondent's unusual physical description, they conducted a showup instead.

The showup itself consisted of two detectives walking respondent past the victim. At the victim's request, the police directed respondent to say "shut up or I'll kill you." The testimony at trial was not altogether clear as to whether the victim first identified him and then asked that he repeat the words or made her identification after he had spoken. In any event, the victim testified that she had "no doubt" about her identification. At the *habeas corpus* hearing, she elaborated in response to questioning.

The victim testified:

Q: What physical characteristics, if any, caused you to be able to identify him?

A: First of all, — uh — his size, — next I could remember his voice.

Q: What about his voice? Describe his voice to the Jury.

A: Well, he has the voice of an immature youth — I call it an immature youth. I have teen-age boys. And that was the first thing that made me think it was the boy.

The colloquy continued, with the victim describing the voice and other physical characteristics. At the *habeas corpus* hearing, the victim and all of the police witnesses testified that a visual identification preceded the voice identification.

A: That I have no doubt, I mean that I am sure that when I — see, when I first laid eyes on him, I knew it was the individual, because his face — well, there was just something that I don't think I could ever forget. I believe —

Q: You say when you first laid eyes on him, which time are you referring to?

A: When I identified him — when I seen him in the courthouse when I was took up to view the suspect.

OPINION

We must decide whether, as the courts below held, this identification and the circumstances surrounding it failed to comport with due process requirements. We have considered on four occasions the scope of due process protection against the admission of evidence deriving from suggestive identification procedures. In *Stovall v. Denno* (1967), the Court held that the defendant could claim that "the confrontation conducted . . . was so unnecessarily suggestive and condu[cive] to irreparable mistaken identification that he was denied due process of law." This, we held, must be determined "on the totality of the circumstances." We went on to find that on the facts of the case then before us, due process was not violated, emphasizing that the critical condition of the injured witness justified a showup in her hospital room. At trial, the witness, whose view of the suspect at the time of the crime was brief, testified to the out-of-court identification, as did several police officers present in her hospital room, and also made an in-court identification.

Subsequently, in a case where the witnesses made in-court identifications arguably stemming from previous exposure to a suggestive photographic array, the Court restated the governing test:

> (W)e hold that each case must be considered on its own facts, and that convictions based on eye-witness identification at trial following a pretrial identification by photograph will be set aside on that ground only if the photographic identification procedure was so impermissibly suggestive as to give rise to a very substantial likelihood of irreparable misidentification. *Simmons v. United States* (1968).

Again we found the identification procedure to be supportable, relying both on the need for prompt utilization of other investigative leads and on the likelihood that the photographic identifications were reliable, the witnesses having viewed the bank robbers for periods of up to five minutes under good lighting conditions at the time of the robbery.

The only case to date in which this Court has found identification procedures to be violative of due process is *Foster v. California* (1969). There, the witness failed to identify Foster the first time he confronted him, despite a suggestive lineup. The police then arranged a showup, at which the witness could make only a tentative identification. Ultimately, at yet another confrontation, this time a lineup, the witness was able to muster a definite identification. We held all of the identifications inadmissible, observing that the identifications were "all but inevitable" under the circumstances.

In the most recent case of *Coleman v. Alabama* (1970), we held admissible an in-court identification by a witness who had a fleeting but "real good look" at his assailant in the headlights of a passing car. The witness testified at a pretrial suppression hearing that he identified one of the petitioners among the participants in the lineup before the police placed the participants in a formal line. Mr. Justice Brennan for four members of the Court stated that this evidence could support a finding that the in-court identification was "entirely based upon observations at the time of the

assault and not at all induced by the conduct of the lineup."

Some general guidelines emerge from these cases as to the relationship between suggestiveness and misidentification. It is, first of all, apparent that the primary evil to be avoided is "a very substantial likelihood of irreparable misidentification." . . . It is the likelihood of misidentification which violates a defendant's right to due process. . . . Suggestive confrontations are disapproved because they increase the likelihood of misidentification, and unnecessarily suggestive ones are condemned for the further reason that the increased chance of misidentification is gratuitous. But . . . the admission of evidence of a showup without more does not violate due process.

. . . [The Court then turned to deciding whether] unnecessary suggestiveness alone requires the exclusion of evidence. [COURT NOTE: "The District Court stated: 'In this case it appears to the Court that a line-up, which both sides admit is generally more reliable than a show-up, could have been arranged. The fact that this was not done tended needlessly to decrease the fairness of the identification process to which petitioner was subjected.'"] While we are inclined to agree with the courts below that the police did not exhaust all possibilities in seeking persons physically comparable to respondent, we do not think that the evidence must therefore be excluded. The purpose of a strict rule barring evidence of unnecessarily suggestive confrontations would be to deter the police from using a less reliable procedure when a more reliable one may be available, and would not be based on the assumption that in every instance the admission of evidence of such a confrontation offends due process. . . .

We turn, then, to the central question, whether under the "totality of the circumstances" the identification was reliable even though the confrontation procedure was suggestive. As indicated by our cases, the factors to be considered in evaluating the likelihood of misidentification include the opportunity of the witness to view the criminal at the time of the crime, the witness'[s] degree of attention, the accuracy of the witness'[s] prior description of the criminal, the level of certainty demonstrated by the witness at the confrontation, and the length of time between the crime and the confrontation.

Applying these factors, we disagree with the District Court's conclusion. In part, as discussed above, we think the District Court focused unduly on the relative reliability of a lineup as opposed to a showup, the issue on which expert testimony was taken at the evidentiary hearing. . . .

We find that the District Court's conclusions on the critical facts are unsupported by the record and clearly erroneous. The victim spent a considerable period of time with her assailant, up to half an hour. She was with him under adequate artificial light in her house and under a full moon outdoors, and at least twice, once in the house and later in the woods, faced him directly and intimately. She was no casual observer, but rather the victim of one of the most personally humiliating of all crimes. Her description to the police, which included the assailant's approximate age, height, weight, complexion, skin texture, build, and voice, might not have satisfied Proust but was more than ordinarily thorough. She had "no doubt" that respondent was the person who raped her. In the nature of the crime, there are rarely witnesses to a rape other than the victim, who often has a limited opportunity for observation. The victim here, a practical nurse by profession, had an unusual opportunity to observe and identify her assailant. She testified at the *habeas corpus* hearing that there was something about his face "I don't think I could ever forget."

There was, to be sure, a lapse of seven months between the rape and the confrontation. This would be a seriously negative factor in most cases. Here, however, the testimony is undisputed that the victim made no previous identification at any of the showups, lineups, or photographic showings. Her record for reliability was thus a good one, as she had previously resisted whatever suggestiveness inheres in a showup. Weighing all the factors, we find no substantial likelihood of misidentification. The evidence was properly allowed to go to the jury.

DISSENT

Justice Brennan, with whom Justices Douglas and Stewart concur, concurring in part and dissenting in part.

. . . Regrettably . . . the Court . . . addresses the merits and delves into the factual background of the case to reverse the District Court's finding, upheld by the Court of Appeals, that under the "totality of the circumstances," the pre-*Stovall* showup was so impermissibly suggestive as to give rise to a substantial likelihood of misidentification. This is an unjustified departure from our long-established practice not to reverse findings of fact concurred in by two lower courts unless shown to be clearly erroneous.

As the Court recognizes . . . [an] identification obtained as a result of an unnecessarily suggestive showup may still be introduced in evidence if, under the "totality of the circumstances," the identification retains strong indicia of reliability. After an extensive hearing and careful review of the state court record, however, the District Court found that, under the circumstances of this case, there existed an intolerable risk of misidentification. Moreover, in making this determination, the court specifically found that "the complaining witness did not get an opportunity to obtain a good view of the suspect during the commission of the crime," "the showup confrontation was not conducted near the time of the alleged crime, but rather, some seven months after its commission," and the complaining witness was unable to give "a good physical description of her assailant" to the police. . . .

CASE DISCUSSION

Why was the show-up "unnecessarily" and "impermissibly" suggestive? How could the police have improved this identification procedure? What specific circumstances did the Court consider in determining the reliability of the show-up? Why did the Court decide that the identification was reliable, despite its suggestiveness? Do you agree? Explain. Is the Court promoting the interest in correct result or perhaps satisfying the demand for crime control, particularly in a terrible crime like rape? If the latter, is this a proper interest for the Supreme Court to promote? Defend your answer. Does the dissent have a point in arguing that the Supreme Court should not interfere with the findings of the courts closest to the proceedings? Also, do the lower court findings regarding the likelihood of misidentification make sense? Explain your answer.

D e c i s i o n   P o i n t

1. Foster was convicted of robbing a Western Union office. The police put Foster, the only one wearing a leather jacket similar to the robber's, in a lineup with two other men who were considerably shorter than Foster. When the manager could not identify the robber, the police permitted a show-up. The witness–manager still made only a tentative identification. Ten days later, in a second lineup, the manager identified Foster, who was the only person from the first lineup to appear in the second. The Supreme Court decided that "the suggestive elements in this identification procedure made it all but inevitable" that the manager would identify Foster, "whether or not he was in fact the man. In effect, the police repeatedly said to the witness, 'This is the man.'"

   Did the second lineup deny Foster due process of law? The United States Supreme Court ruled that it did because it was unnecessarily and impermissibly suggestive. This is the only United States Supreme Court case to date in which the Court has held an identification procedure to violate due process, and four justices dissented. It is one of a very few cases in which any federal or state court has found an identification procedure a violation of due process. Can you account for this record? *Foster v. California*, 394 U.S. 440, 89 S.Ct. 1127, 22 L.Ed.2d 402 (1969).

2. The victims in this case had arranged to purchase marijuana from Ford's brother. Upon arriving at the apartment building where the transaction was to take place, Ford, his brother, and another man led the victims to a well-lighted basement storage room. There, the three men robbed the victims at gunpoint. The robbery took about four minutes. The victims identified Ford in a show-up conducted less than one-and-one-half hours after the crime. During the show-up, appellant was wearing handcuffs, but the handcuffs were not visible to the victims. Ford's motion to suppress the identification evidence was denied, and he was convicted of aiding and abetting aggravated robbery in the first degree.

   Did the show-up violate Ford's due process

rights? No, said the Minnesota Court of Appeals. Applying the five factors discussed in *Neil v. Biggers* (see above), the court wrote the following:

> Application of the five factors in this case satisfies us that there was no substantial likelihood of misidentification. Both victims had several minutes to view the robbers in good lighting, both before and during the robbery. One victim testified that he saw appellant's face several times and made a special effort to remember it. Appellant matched the general description both victims had initially given to police. Both victims were certain of their identifications; indeed, one victim clearly distinguished between the robbers, expressing more certainty about the identification of appellant than of another individual who was displayed to the victims, but then not charged. Finally, the show-up was conducted less than one and one-half hours after the crime, leaving little opportunity for the victims to have forgotten their assailants.
>
> Appellant argues that the fact he was handcuffed during the identification procedure makes it impermissibly suggestive. We disagree. The handcuffs were not visible to the victims during the identification and no other circumstances suggest that the identification was tainted by use of the handcuffs.
>
> Appellant implies that the victims' identifications were not accurate because, although they both identified a third individual as a perpetrator, police concluded that there was not enough evidence to refer that individual for prosecution. The failure to prosecute, though, does not mean that the victims were wrong in their identification of that person.
>
> Finally, appellant cites social science authority for the proposition that the stress of being robbed makes it difficult to retain an accurate identification memory. We believe that, despite this assertion and whatever the

merit that authority might have as applied in another circumstance, analysis of the *Biggers* factors indicates the identification procedure in this case did not create a substantial like- lihood of irreparable misidentification. Affirmed. *State v. Ford*, 1996 WL 278227 (Minn.App. 1996)

PHOTOGRAPHIC IDENTIFICATION

The least reliable form of eyewitness identification is a photographic array. A photograph is only two-dimensional, hence not entirely true to life. The fewer the photos used in the array, the less reliable the identifications. Also, photographs in which the suspect stands out are highly suggestive. In addition, police can make remarks — such as "Is this the one?" or "The suspect is in this group of photos" — that lead to the identification of particular people. Despite their recognized unreliability — and despite the urging of commentators that courts should exclude them if lineups and show-ups can be substituted — photographs are the most widely used means of identification. Courts regularly admit photographic identifications into evidence. They have the clear approval of the United States Supreme Court, which said, "[T]his procedure has been used widely and effectively in criminal law enforcement."[24]

The Court applies the same totality-of-circumstances test to photographic identification that it applies to lineups and show-ups. Courts have generally rejected defendants' claims that the totality of circumstances demonstrates that suggestive photographic identification — even the least reliable single-photograph identification — has created a substantial likelihood of unreliability. The Supreme Court reviewed a single-photograph identification in *Manson v. Brathwaite.*

C A S E

Was the Photographic Identification Reliable?

Manson v. Brathwaite
432 U.S. 98, 97 S.Ct. 2243,
53 L.Ed.2d 140 (1977)

Brathwaite was charged with and convicted of the possession and sale of heroin. At his trial, the prosecution introduced Brathwaite's photograph as identification. The Connecticut Supreme Court affirmed the conviction. Brathwaite filed a petition for habeas corpus *in the federal district court, alleging that the admission of identification testimony denied him due process. The district court dismissed the petition, but the court of appeals reversed. The United States Supreme Court granted* certiorari. *The Court held that the due process*

clause did not compel the exclusion of the identification evidence; its reliability depended on the totality of the circumstances that the jury should decide. Justice Blackmun wrote the opinion for the Court. Chief Justice Burger and Justices Stewart, White, Powell, Rehnquist, and Stevens joined. Justice Stevens filed a concurring opinion. Justice Marshall, whom Justice Brennan joined, dissented.

FACTS

Jimmy D. Glover, a full-time trooper of the Connecticut State Police, in 1970 was assigned to the Narcotics Division in an undercover capacity. On May 5 of that year, about 7:45 P.M. [Eastern Daylight Time], and while there was still daylight, Glover and Henry Alton Brown, an informant, went to an apartment building at 201 Westland, in Hartford, for the purpose of purchasing narcotics from "Dickie Boy" Cicero, a known narcotics dealer. Cicero, it was thought, lived on the third floor of that apartment building. Glover and Brown entered the building, observed by backup Officers D'Onofrio and Gaffey, and proceeded by stairs to the third floor. The area was illuminated by natural light from a window in the third floor hallway. The door was opened 12 to 18 inches in response to the knock. Glover observed a man standing at the door and, behind him, a woman. Brown identified himself. Glover then asked for "two things" of narcotics. The man at the door held out his hand, and Glover gave him two $10 bills. The door closed. Soon the man returned and handed Glover two glassine bags. While the door was open, Glover stood within two feet of the person from whom he made the purchase and observed his face. Five to seven minutes elapsed from the time the door first opened until it closed the second time.

Glover and Brown then left the building. This was about eight minutes after their arrival. Glover drove to headquarters where he described the seller to D'Onofrio and Gaffey. Glover at that time did not know the identity of the seller. He described him as being "a colored man, approximately five feet eleven inches tall, dark complexion, of heavy build. He was wearing at the time blue pants and a plaid shirt." D'Onofrio, suspecting from this description that respondent might be the seller, obtained a photograph of respondent from the Records Division of the Hartford Police Department. He left it at Glover's office. D'Onofrio was not acquainted with respondent personally, but did know him by sight and had seen him "[s]everal times" prior to May 5. Glover, when alone, viewed the photograph for the first time upon his return to headquarters on May 7; he identified the person shown as the one from whom he had purchased the narcotics. . . .

Respondent was arrested on July 27 while visiting at the apartment of a Mrs. Ramsey on the third floor of 201 Westland. This was the apartment at which the narcotics sale had taken place on May 5.

Respondent was charged, in a two-count information, with possession and sale of heroin. . . . At his trial in January 1971, the photograph from which Glover had identified respondent was received in evidence without objection on the part of the defense. Glover also testified that, although he had not seen respondent in the eight months that had elapsed since the sale, "there [was] no doubt whatsoever" in his mind that the person shown on the photograph was respondent. Glover also made a positive in-court identification without objection.

No explanation was offered by the prosecution for the failure to utilize a photographic array or to conduct a line-up.

Respondent, who took the stand in his own defense, testified that on May 5, the day in question, he had been ill at his Albany Avenue apartment ("a lot of back pains, muscle spasms . . . a bad heart . . . high blood pressure . . . neuralgia in my face, and sinus"), and that at no time on that particular day had he been at 201 Westland. His wife testified that she recalled, after her husband had refreshed her memory, that he was home all day on May 5. . . .

The jury found respondent guilty on both counts of the information. He received a sentence of not less than six nor more than nine years. His conviction was affirmed per curiam by the Supreme Court of Connecticut. . . .

Fourteen months later, respondent filed a petition for *habeas corpus* in the United States District Court for the District of Connecticut. He alleged that the admission of the identification testimony at his state trial deprived him of due process of law to which he was entitled under the Fourteenth Amendment. The District Court . . . dismissed respondent's petition. On appeal, the United States Court of Appeals for the Second Circuit reversed, with instructions to issue the writ unless the State gave notice of a desire to retry respondent and the new trial occurred within a reasonable time to be fixed by the District Judge. . . .

We granted certiorari. . . .

OPINION

[T]he District court observed that the "sole evidence tying Brathwaite to the possession and sale of heroin consisted in his identifications by the police undercover agent, Jimmy Glover." . . . Petitioner at the onset acknowledges that "the procedure in the instant case was suggestive (because only one photograph was used) and unnecessary" (because there was no emergency or exigent circumstance). . . . The respondent . . . proposes a *per se* rule of exclusion that he claims is dictated by the demands of the Fourteenth Amendment's guarantee of due process. . . . [T]he Courts of Appeals appear to have developed at least two approaches to such evidence. The first, or *per se* approach, employed by the Second Circuit in the present case, focuses on the procedures employed and requires exclusion of the out-of-court identification evidence, without regard to reliability, whenever it had been obtained through unnecessarily suggest[ive] confrontation procedures. The justifications advanced are the elimination of evidence of uncertain reliability, deterrence of the police and prosecutors, and the stated "fair assurance against the awful risks of misidentification."

The second, or more lenient, approach is one that continues to rely on the totality of the circumstances. It permits the admission of the confrontation evidence if, despite the suggestive aspect, the out-of-court identification possesses certain features of reliability. Its adherents feel that the *per se* approach is not mandated by the Due Process Clause of the Fourteenth Amendment. This second approach, in contrast to the other, is ad hoc and serves to limit the societal costs imposed by a sanction that excludes relevant evidence from consideration and evaluation by the trier of fact.

Mr. Justice Stevens . . . observed: "There is a surprising unanimity among scholars in regarding such a rule (the *per se* approach) as essential to avoid serious risk of miscarriage of justice." He pointed out that well-known federal judges have taken the position that

> evidence of, or derived from, a showup identification should be inadmissible unless the prosecutor can justify his failure to use a more reliable identification procedure. Indeed, the ALI (American Law Institute) Model Code of Pre-Arraignment Procedure . . . frowns upon the use of a showup or the display of only a single photograph.

The respondent here stresses the same theme and the need for deterrence of improper identification practice, a factor he regards as pre-eminent. Photographic identification, it is said, continues to be needlessly employed. . . . He argues that a totality rule cannot be expected to have a significant deterrent impact; only a strict rule of exclusion will have direct and immediate impact on law enforcement agents. Identification evidence is so convincing to the jury that sweeping exclusionary rules are required. Fairness of the trial is threatened by suggestive confrontation evidence, and thus, it is said, an exclusionary rule has an established constitutional predicate.

There are, of course, several interests to be considered and taken into account. The driving force behind *United States v. Wade* [1967], *Gilbert v. California* [1967], and *Stovall* [*v. Denno* (1967)], all decided on the same day, was the Court's concern with the problems of eyewitness identification. Usually, a witness must testify about an encounter with a total stranger under circumstances of emergency or emotional stress. The witness'[s] recollection of the stranger can be distorted easily by the circumstances or by later actions of the police. Thus *Wade* and its companion cases reflect the concern that the jury not hear eyewitness testimony unless that evidence has aspects of reliability. It must be observed that both approaches before us are responsive to this concern. The *per se* rule, however, goes too far since its application automatically and peremptorily, and without consideration of alleviating factors, keeps evidence from the jury that is reliable and relevant.

The second factor is deterrence. Although the *per se* approach has the more significant deterrent effect, the totality approach also has an influence on police behavior. The police will guard against unnecessarily suggestive procedures under the totality rule, as well as the *per se* one, for fear that their actions will lead to the exclusion of identifications as unreliable.

The third factor is the effect on the administration of justice. Here the *per se* approach suffers serious drawbacks since it denies the trier reliable evidence, [and] it may result, on occasion, in the guilty going free. Also, because of its rigidity, the *per se* approach may make error by the trial judge more likely than the totality approach. And in those cases in which the identification is reliable despite an unnecessarily suggestive identification procedures reversal is a Draconian sanction. Certainly, inflexible rules of exclusion that may frustrate rather than promote justice have not been viewed recently by this Court with unlimited enthusiasm. . . .

The standard, after all, is that of fairness as required by the Due Process Clause of the Fourteenth Amendment. *Stovall*, with its references to "the totality of the circumstances," and *Biggers*, with its continuing stress on the same totality, did not, singly or together, establish a strict exclusionary rule or new standard of due process. . . .

We therefore conclude that reliability is the linchpin in determining the admissibility of identification testimony. . . . The factors to be considered are set out in *Biggers*. These include the opportunity of the witness to view the criminal at the time of the crime, the witness'[s] degree of attention, the accuracy of his prior description of the criminal, the level of certainty demonstrated at the confrontation, and the time between the crime and the confrontation. Against these factors is to be weighed the corrupting effect of the suggestive identification itself.

We turn, then, to the facts of this case and apply the analysis:

1. *The opportunity to view.* Glover testified that for two to three minutes he stood at the apartment door, within two feet of the respondent. The door opened twice, and each time the man stood at the door. The moments passed, the conversation took place, and payment was made. Glover looked directly at his vendor. It was near sunset, to be sure, but the sun had not yet set, so it was not dark or even dusk or twilight. Natural light from outside entered the hallway through a window. There was natural light, as well, from inside the apartment.

2. *The degree of attention.* Glover was not a casual or passing observer, as is so often the case with eyewitness identification. Trooper Glover was a trained police officer on duty—and specialized and dangerous duty—when he called at the third floor of 201 Westland in Hartford on May 5, 1970. Glover himself was a Negro and unlikely to perceive only general features of "hundreds of Hartford black males," as the Court of Appeals stated.

It is true that Glover's duty was that of ferreting out narcotics offenders and that he would be expected in his work to produce results. But it is also true that, as a specially trained, assigned, and experienced officer, he could be expected to pay scrupulous attention to detail, for he knew that his claimed observations would be subject later to close scrutiny and examination at any trial.

3. *The accuracy of the description.* Glover's description was given to D'Onofrio within minutes after the transaction. It included the vendor's race, his height, his build, the color and style of his hair, and the high cheekbone facial feature. It also included clothing the vendor wore. No claim has been made that respondent did not possess the physical characteristics so described. D'Onofrio reacted positively at once. Two days later, when Glover was alone, he viewed the photograph D'Onofrio produced and identified its subject as the narcotics seller.

4. *The witness'[s] level of certainty.* There is no dispute that the photograph in question was that of respondent. Glover, in response to a question whether the photograph was that of the person from whom he made the purchase, testified: "There is no question whatsoever." This positive assurance was repeated.

5. *The time between the crime and the confrontation.* Glover's description of his vendor was given to D'Onofrio within minutes of the crime. The photographic identification took place only two days later. We do not have here the passage of weeks or months between the crime and the viewing of the photograph.

These indicators of Glover's ability to make an accurate identification are hardly outweighed by the corrupting effect of the challenged identification itself. Although identifications arising from single-photograph displays may be viewed in general with suspicion, we find in the instant case little pressure on the witness to acquiesce in the suggestion that such a display entails. D'Onofrio had left the photograph at Glover's office and was not present when Glover first viewed it two days after the event. There thus was little urgency and Glover could view the photograph at his leisure. And since Glover examined the photograph alone, there was no coercive pressure to make an identification arising from the presence of another. The identification was made in circumstances allowing care and reflection.

Although it plays no part in our analysis, all this assurance as to the reliability of the identification is hardly undermined by the facts that respondent was arrested in the very apartment where the sale had taken place, and that he acknowledged his frequent visits to the apartment.

Surely, we cannot say that under all circumstances of this case there is "a very substantial likelihood of irreparable misidentification." Short of that point, such evidence is for the jury to weigh. We are content to rely upon the good sense and judgment of American juries[,] for evidence with some element of untrustworthiness is customary grist for the jury mill. Juries are not so susceptible that they cannot measure intelligently the weight of identification testimony that has some questionable feature.

Of course, it would have been better had D'Onofrio presented Glover with a photographic array including "so far as practicable . . . a reasonable number of persons similar to any person then suspected whose likeness is included in the array." *Model Code*, § 160.2(2). The use of that procedure would have enhanced the force of the identification at trial and would have avoided the risk that the evidence would be excluded as unreliable. But we are not disposed to view D'Onofrio's failure as one of constitutional dimension to be enforced by a rigorous and unbending exclusionary rule. The defect, if there be one, goes to the weight and not to the substance.

We conclude that the criteria laid down in *Biggers* are to be applied in determining the admissibility of evidence offered by the prosecution concerning a post-*Stovall* identification, and that those criteria are satisfactorily met and complied with here.

The judgment of the Court of Appeals is reversed.

It is so ordered.

[NOTE: Justice Stevens's concurring opinion is omitted.]

DISSENT

Justice Marshall, with whom Justice Brennan joins, dissenting.

Today's decision can come as no surprise to those who have been watching the Court dismantle the protections against mistaken eyewitness testimony erected a decade ago in *United States v. Wade*. But it is still distressing to see the Court virtually ignore the teaching of experience embodied in those decisions and blindly uphold the conviction of a defendant who may well be innocent. . . .

. . . [I]n determining the admissibility of the identification in this case, the Court considers two alternatives, a *per se* exclusionary rule and a totality-of-the-circumstances approach. The Court weighs three factors in deciding . . . the totality approach. In my view, the Court wrongly evaluates the impact of these factors.

First, the Court acknowledges that one of the factors, deterrence of police use of unnecessarily suggestive identification procedures, favors the *per se* rule. Indeed, it does so heavily, for such a rule would make it unquestionably clear to the police they must never use a suggestive procedure when a fairer alternative is available. I have no doubt that conduct would quickly conform to the rule.

Second, the Court gives passing consideration to the dangers of eyewitness identification recognized in the *Wade* trilogy. It concludes, however, that the grave risk of error does not justify adoption of the *per se* approach because that would too often result in exclusion of relevant evidence. In my view this conclusion totally ignores the lessons of *Wade*. The dangers of mistaken identification are . . . simply too great to permit unnecessarily suggestive identifications. . . . While the Court is "content to rely on good sense and judgment of American juries," the impetus for . . . *Wade* was repeated miscarriages of justice resulting from juries' willingness to credit inaccurate eyewitness testimony.

First, the *per se* rule here is not "inflexible." Where evidence is suppressed, for example, as the fruit of an unlawful search, it may well be forever lost to the prosecution. Identification evidence, however, can by its very nature be readily and effectively reproduced. The in-court identification . . . if it has a source independent of an uncounseled or suggestive procedure, is one example. Similarly, when a prosecuting attorney learns that there has been a suggestive confrontation, he can easily arrange another lineup conducted under scrupulously fair conditions. . . . The evidence of an additional, properly conducted confrontation will be more persuasive to a jury, thereby increasing the chance of a justified conviction where a reliable identification was tainted by a suggestive confrontation. At the same time, however, the effect of an unnecessarily suggestive identification which has no value whatsoever in the law enforcement process will be completely eliminated.

Second, other exclusionary rules have been criticized for preventing jury consideration of relevant and usually reliable evidence in order to serve interests unrelated to guilt or innocence, such as discouraging illegal searches or denial of counsel. Suggestively obtained eyewitness testimony is excluded, in contrast, precisely because of its unreliability and concomitant irrelevance. Its exclusion both protects the integrity of the truth-seeking function of the trial and discourages police use of needlessly inaccurate and ineffective investigatory methods.

Indeed, impermissibly suggestive identifications are not merely worthless law enforcement tools. They pose a grave threat to society at large in a more direct way than most governmental disobedience of the law. For if the police and the public erroneously conclude, on the basis of an unnecessarily suggestive confrontation, that the right man has been caught and convicted, the real outlaw must still remain at large. Law enforcement has failed in its primary function and has left society unprotected from the depredations of an active criminal.

For these reasons, I conclude that adoption of the *per se* rule would enhance, rather than detract from, the effective administration of justice. In my view, the Court's totality test will allow seriously unreliable and misleading evidence to be put before juries. Equally important, it will allow dangerous criminals to remain on the streets while citizens assume that police actions [have] given them protection. According to my calculus, all three of the factors upon which the Court relies point to acceptance of the *per se* approach.

Even more disturbing than the Court's reliance on the totality test, however, is the analysis it uses, which suggests a reinterpretation of the concept of due process violations in identification procedures may not be measured by whether the government employed procedures violating standards of fundamental fairness. By relying on the probable accuracy of a challenged identification, instead of the necessity for its use, the Court seems to be ascertaining whether the defendant was probably guilty. Until today, I had thought that "[e]qual justice under law" meant that the existence of constitutional violations did not depend on the race, sex, religion, nationality, or likely guilt of the accused. The Due Process Clause requires adherence to the same high standard of fundamental fairness in dealing with every criminal defendant, whatever his personal characteristics and irrespective of the strength of the State's case against him. Strong evidence that the defendant is guilty should be relevant only to the determination [of] whether an error of constitutional magnitude was nevertheless harmless beyond a reasonable doubt. By importing the question of guilt into the initial determination of whether there was a constitutional violation, the apparent effect of the Court's decision is to undermine the protection afforded by the Due Process Clause. . . .

CASE DISCUSSION

What precisely was the totality of circumstances taken into account in this case? Do you think it demonstrates "a very substantial likelihood of irreparable misidentification"? Do you agree that Jimmy D. Glover had sufficient opportunity to observe Brathwaite? To describe him accurately? To identify the photograph positively? If not, was this harmless error? Is the dissent correct in saying that the Court is "dismantling the protections against mistaken eyewitness testimony erected . . . in *United States v. Wade*"? Is the dissent correct in arguing that the Court wrongfully evaluated the impact of the exclusionary rule and the totality of circumstances? Evaluate those arguments. Would you side with the dissent or the majority in this case? Has the majority sacrificed accuracy at the expense of finality? At the expense of law enforcement, as the dissent maintains? Is the majority fostering a false sense of security in that the public believes the government has caught the criminal in many cases in which the criminal remains at large?

D e c i s i o n   P o i n t

A government informer told authorities that he had discussed a bank robbery with Ash. Acting on this information, an FBI agent showed four witnesses five black-and-white mug shots of black males of generally the same age, height, and weight, one of which was Ash. All four witnesses made uncertain identifications of Ash's picture. Ash, along with a codefendant, Bailey, was indicted for robbery.

Trial was finally set, nearly three years after the crime. In preparing for trial, the prosecutor decided to use a photographic display to determine whether the witnesses he planned to call would be able to make in-court identifications. Shortly before the trial, an FBI agent and the prosecutor showed five color photographs to the four witnesses who had previously tentatively identified the black-and-white photograph of Ash. Three of the witnesses selected the picture of Ash, but one was unable to make any selection. None of the witnesses selected the picture of Bailey that was in the group.

Did this post-indictment identification deny Ash his right to counsel? The Supreme Court said no:

Pretrial photographic identifications . . . are hardly unique in offering the possibilities for the actions of the prosecutor to unfairly prejudice the accused. Evidence favorable to the accused may be withheld; testimony of witnesses may be manipulated; the results of laboratory tests may be contrived. In many ways the prosecutor, by accident or design, may improperly subvert the trial. The primary safeguard against abuses of this kind is the ethical responsibility of the prosecutor, who, as so often has been said, may "strike hard blows" but not "foul ones." If that safeguard fails, review remains available under due process standards. These same safeguards apply to misuse of photographs. . . . We are not persuaded that the risks inherent in the use of photographic displays are so pernicious that an extraordinary system of safeguards is required. We hold, then, that the Sixth Amendment does not grant the right to counsel at photographic displays conducted by the Government for the purpose of allowing a witness to attempt identification of the offender.

The dissent argued as follows:

The dangers of mistaken identification . . . are applicable in large measure to photographic as well as corporeal ([of] the body) identification. Indeed, in reality, preservation of the photographs affords little protection to the unrepresented accused. For although retention of the photographs may mitigate the dangers of misidentification due to the suggestiveness of the photographs themselves, it cannot in any sense reveal to the defense counsel the more subtle, and therefore more dangerous, suggestiveness that might derive from the manner in which photographs were displayed or any accompanying comments or gestures. Finally, and unlike the line-up situation, the accused himself is not even present at the photographic identification, thereby reducing the likelihood that irregularities in the procedures will ever come to light. *United States v. Ash*, 413 U.S. 300, 93 S.Ct. 2568, 37 L.Ed.2d 619 (1973).

REFUSAL TO COOPERATE
IN IDENTIFICATION PROCEDURES

Suspects' refusal to cooperate in identification procedures can have several consequences. Prosecutors can comment on such refusal at trial, urging jurors to read guilt into the refusal. Furthermore, courts sometimes put suspects who refuse to cooperate in civil or criminal contempt, subjecting them to fines and incarceration. Finally, police may conduct the procedures over suspects' objections, as they did in *Schmerber v. California* (discussed earlier in this chapter). Officers may even use force to secure compliance as long as they use only the force reasonably necessary to conduct the identification procedure.[25]

DNA PROFILE IDENTIFICATION

DNA (deoxyribonucleic acid) testing can potentially identify suspects or exclude them as suspects in cases where perpetrators have left DNA at the scene of a crime or where victims have left DNA on items traceable to perpetrators. This capacity to use DNA to identify criminal suspects has come about because of the rapid advances in molecular biology in the past fifteen years. DNA is a long, double-stranded molecule found in everyone's chromosomes. Chromosomes are carried in the nucleus of body cells that have nuclei. These include white blood cells, sperm cells, cells surrounding the hair roots, and saliva cells. DNA testing involves comparing the DNA samples in the nuclei of cells found at crime scenes with either similar DNA samples taken from the nuclei of cells of suspects or DNA samples left by victims on items traceable to perpetrators. The most widely used test is called **DNA fingerprinting** or **DNA profiling.** In this test, long sections of DNA are broken into fragments. Fragments that tend to vary from person to person are measured. If samples from crime scenes have different lengths from those of the suspect, that excludes the suspect. If the sample at the scene and that of the suspect have the same lengths, the samples might have a common source. However, they might also match by chance. In order to reduce the element of chance, laboratories measure six or more distinct fragments. Two commercial laboratories (Cellmark Diagnostics Corporation and Lifecodes Corporation) and the FBI are the major sites for DNA testing in the United States.[26]

DNA testing quickly entered the legal system, heralded by one court as "the greatest advance in crime fighting technology since fingerprinting." But then a serious scientific controversy broke out over DNA testing. Some challenged the theory of DNA itself. Others challenged the testing methods. Most, however, accepted the soundness of the theory and the testing technology. Instead, they attacked the admission of the tests. According to Professor Edward Imwinkelried of the University of California Davis Law School,

> My reading of the proficiency studies of forensic DNA testing laboratories is that the most common cause of error is not the inherent limitations of the technique, but the way in which the specific test was conducted. What the courts don't understand is that no matter how impressive studies are of the validity of a scientific technique, they are worthless as a guarantee of reliability unless you replicate the variables of the experiment.[27]

In 1989 defense counsels who were knowledgeable about DNA testing obtained the aid of disinterested scientists in order to successfully challenge DNA evidence in *People v. Castro*. Lifecodes, the laboratory that did the testing, violated its own rules and was charged with scientific fraud. In the face of a unanimity of scientific opinion, including even experts hired by the prosecution, Lifecodes admitted that the testing did not amount to a match. The wide coverage that the case received in both the popular and scientific press led to a full-scale debate. So heated did the controversy become, according to John Hicks, head of the FBI Laboratory Division, that "[t]his is no longer a search for the truth, it is a war."[28]

Most courts in which lawyers have submitted DNA testing have admitted the tests as evidence. But the courts are divided regarding the standards for admission of DNA evidence. Some courts have adopted the *Frye* **standard.** According to the *Frye* standard, named after *Frye v. United States*, DNA evidence is admissible if the technique is "sufficiently established to have gained general acceptance in the particular field in which it belongs." Other courts have adopted a *Frye* **plus standard.** According to *Frye* plus, in addition to gaining general acceptance, admissibility requires showing that "the testing laboratory in the particular case performed the accepted scientific techniques in analyzing forensic samples." A third group of courts has adopted the **Federal Rules of Evidence standard.** According to this standard, the test is whether the relevancy of the evidence outweighs the tendency of the evidence to unfairly prejudice the defendant. A fourth group of courts has adopted a **relevancy plus standard.** According to this hybrid standard, the *Frye* standard and other requirements are added to the Federal Rules of Evidence standard.[29]

The correct identification of criminal suspects by means of DNA testing, whatever the standard that courts adopt, depends on the answers to the following three questions and the inferences that jurors or other fact finders make about them:

1. Is a reported match between the sample at the scene of the crime and the sample from the suspect a true match?

2. Is the suspect the source of the trace of DNA left at the scene of the crime?

3. Is the suspect the perpetrator of the crime?

A *reported* match strongly suggests a *true* match. However, mistakes in DNA processing do occur. Technical errors, such as enzyme failures, salt concentrations, and dirt spots, can produce misleading patterns. Human errors, including contaminations, mislabelings, misrecordings, misrepresentations, case mix-ups, and errors of interpretation, also occur. Assuming that the match is true, it strongly suggests that the suspect is the source of the trace of DNA left at the scene of the crime. But the match might be coincidental. The coincidence depends on the frequency of matching traits among the population, usually the ethnic group of the suspect. However, the validity of this reference population depends on the correct identification of the suspect's ethnic group. Source probability errors also occur. Prosecutors, experts, and jurors often exaggerate the weight to give to the match between the trace and the suspect by speaking in terms of odds. According to one trial transcript, for example, after testifying that the blood of a victim matched a sample from a blanket, the following exchange took place:

Q: [Prosecutor]: And in your profession and in the scientific field when you say match what do you mean?

A: [Expert]: They are identical.

Q: [Prosecutor]: So the blood on the blanket can you say it came from [the victim]?

A: [Expert]: With great certainty I can say that those two DNA samples match and they are identical. And with population statistics we can derive a probability of it being anyone other than the victim.

Q: [Prosecutor]: What is the probability in this case?

A: [Expert]: In this case that probability is that it is one in 7 million chances that it could be anyone other than that victim.[30]

According to Professor Jonathan Koehler at the University of Texas at Austin, however, the expert's claim that population statistics can determine the probability that the victim was not the source is false.[31]

Finally, evidence that the suspect is the source of the trace is also evidence that the suspect committed the crime. But not necessarily—the suspect could have left the trace innocently either before or after the commission of the crime. So the use of the match to prove guilt depends on an inference, perhaps a fair inference, but not automatic or always correct.

Whatever the problems and criticisms of the use of DNA testing to identify suspects and link them to crimes, the impact of DNA (and other scientific evidence, too, for that matter) is substantial. According to one researcher, about 25 percent of jurors said they would have voted not guilty if it were not for the introduction of scientific evidence. In another survey, 75 percent of judges and lawyers throughout the United States said that they believed judges accorded scientific evidence more credibility than other kinds of evidence, and 70 percent said that they believed jurors did the same.[32] The Minnesota Supreme Court considered these problems in *State v. Bloom.*

C A S E

Is a DNA Profile Admissible?

State v. Bloom
516 N.W.2d 159 (Minn. 1994)

Bloom was charged with rape. The district court, in a hearing on a motion to suppress, excluded evidence of DNA testing. The state appealed directly to the Minnesota Supreme Court, which reversed. Chief Justice Keith wrote the opinion for the court. Justices Page, Tomljanovich, and Gardebring concurred. Justice Coyne dissented.

FACTS

Shortly after 1:00 A.M. on November 23, 1992, J.L.P., a 34-year-old woman, was entering her home in Brooklyn Park when she was grabbed from behind by a Caucasian man. The man, whom she did not see well enough to identify, forced her into her car, pulling a stocking cap over her face. He drove her to a different location, ordered her into the back seat, and told her if she did not comply with his demands he would penetrate her vagina with a screwdriver. He forced her to submit to fellatio, digital penetration and ordinary sexual penetration. He also bit the victim on her breasts. After assaulting her, he drove her home and dropped her off, then abandoned her car nearby.

After preserving semen samples taken from the victim in the sexual assault examination and other semen samples found in the car, the BCA prepared a DNA profile of the samples. This consisted of six separate probes and resulting autorads for comparison with autorads made from probes of known DNA. James Liberty, who does forensic work at the BCA and has attended an FBI course on forensic aspects of DNA technology, testified that using information from two of the six probes to make a computer search of the BCA's sex-offender DNA database, he came up with five potential suspects, including defendant, whose DNA matched at those two loci. Comparing the probe data of the five potential suspects found in this manner, he determined that one of them, defendant, "stood out." Then, by comparing the database pattern of all five loci available in defendant's prior database profile he determined that there was a match with the pattern at all five loci on the autorads made from the assailant's semen.

Liberty then did another complete DNA test on both the assailant's semen and on a new sample of defendant's blood, taken after his arrest, as well as on blood from the victim's boyfriend and from another individual, and he produced new autorads. The victim's boyfriend and the other individual were excluded as possible sources. The defendant's DNA profile matched the crime scene sample at all nine loci tested. After using five loci and finding a match at each, Liberty made some calculations and concluded that there was a 1 in 93,700 chance that a randomly selected person would match at all five points.

Professor Daniel Hartl, a Professor of Biology at Harvard and an earlier critic of some of the statistical computations that forensic scientists were making based on FBI databases, testified (by telephone) for the state at the suppression hearing that, using the "interim ceiling method" recommended by the National Research Council, there was a 1 in 634,687 chance of a random match across the five loci. He testified that Liberty had obtained the less-impressive 1 in 93,700 figure by making some "adjustments" that were not needed because the interim ceiling approach, which Liberty too had used, had those adjustments built into it. Dr. Hartl, if permitted, would further testify at trial that in fact there was a nine-loci match and that in his opinion the nine-loci match constituted "overwhelming evidence that, to a reasonable degree of scientific certainty, the DNA from the victim's vaginal swab came from [defendant], to the exclusion of all others."

The trial court . . . ruled (1) that the jury could be told (a) that defendant's DNA was consistent with crime scene samples on each of the nine bands tested, (b) the frequency of each individual band and (c) non-statistical opinion testimony that defendant's DNA profile is consistent with that of the assailant, but (2) the jury could not be told (a) that the frequency of the profile in the population based on five tests is 1 in 634,687 (or, for that matter, 1 in 93,700) or (b) that the opinion of Dr. Hartl is as just quoted. . . .

OPINION

Th[is] appeal give[s] this court an opportunity to revisit an issue that recently has been the focus of considerable controversy in the scientific community. The issue is not, as some have put it, the admissibility of DNA identification evidence in criminal prosecutions but the form that the presentation of that evidence takes.

DNA is a long, double-stranded molecule found in chromosomes carried in cell nuclei. William C. Thompson, Evaluating the Admissibility of New Genetic Identification Tests: Lessons from the "DNA War," 84 *J.Crim.L. & Criminology* 22, 26 n. 18 (1993). It occurs in all cells that have a nucleus, including white blood cells, sperm cells, cells surrounding hair roots, and cells in saliva. Committee on DNA Tech. in Forensic Science, Nat'l Research Council, DNA Technology in Forensic Science S–1 (Prepublication Copy 1992) [hereinafter NRC Report]. Most sections of DNA molecules vary little among individuals within a species. However, some sections are polymorphic, meaning they do vary. If two fragments do not match, they could not have a common source, but if they do match, they might have a common source. Researchers as yet have not developed DNA profiles that cannot be shared by two or more people. David T. Wasserman, The Morality of Statistical Proof and the Risk of Mistaken Liability, 13 *Cardozo L.Rev.* 935, 973 (1991). However, the theory underlying forensic use of DNA profiles is that "as the number and variability of the polymorphisms utilized in the typing procedure increases, the odds of two people having the same profile become vanishingly small."

The "vanishingly small" probability figure that experts come up with in case after case is the probability of a random match. Carefully stated, it is the probability that a randomly selected person, if tested, would have the same DNA profile as that of the sample left at the scene. Richard Lempert, Some Caveats Concerning DNA As Criminal Identification Evidence: With Thanks to the Reverend Bayes, 13 *Cardozo L.Rev.* 303, 305–06 (1991). Thus, when the figure given is 1 in 1 billion, the expert is saying (if the expert chooses words carefully) that there is a 1 in 1 billion chance that a randomly selected person would have the same DNA profile as that of the sample left at the scene.

The basic unmodified approach to obtaining the statistic is to estimate the percentage of people in the population with identical DNA at each particular locus and then, using the so-called product or multiplication rule, to combine the individual frequencies by multiplying them against each other and by the number 2. Underlying the use of the product rule is the assumption that the frequency of a match at a particular locus is independent of the frequency of each of the other individual matches against which it is multiplied.

There are a number of potential sources of error in computing the probability figure. These include:

(a) The databases which one uses may seriously underestimate the frequency in the population of a particular pattern of DNA at a particular locus.

(b) The databases may be unrepresentative, failing to take into account variations among population subgroups, or variations in particular geographical locales, in the frequency of certain DNA patterns at particular loci.

(c) The assumption of statistical independence may be invalid. . . . As stated by Lempert, "evidence of a DNA match is not nearly so probative as people have thought because suspect populations are not random agglomerations with respect to the likelihood of sharing the [traits] compared in DNA analysis."

(d) The laboratory's "false positive match rate" affects the reliability of the figure obtained using the product rule. False positive matches do occur, as the result of sloppy laboratory procedures, the poor quality of the materials used, the quality of the DNA sample obtained from the scene, the protocols calling for a match, and human error.

(e) If there was an error in concluding that there was a match at even one band in a particular case, then there is a very real chance that the jury will be told in that case that the chance of a random match is extremely small when in reality there is no match at all.

Because of these factors, the NRC in its 1992 report recommended the use of an extremely conserva-

tive "interim ceiling method" for estimating random match probabilities. (It is this method that the state's expert, Professor Hartl, used in this case to arrive at the 1 in 634,687 figure.)

One of the concerns expressed in our cases, which we discuss in detail later, has been that admission of the random match probability figure will confuse jurors. There is a chain of inferences that the jurors must make in order to get from the starting point, the testimony as to the probability of a random match, to the conclusion that the defendant is the perpetrator of the crime. Those inferential steps include: match report — true match — source — present at scene — perpetrator. See Jonathan J. Koehler, Error and Exaggeration in the Presentation of DNA Evidence at Trial, 34 *Jurimetrics* 21 (1993).

Errors may occur at each step:

(a) The inference that the reported match is a true match. Most expert witnesses are technicians. Andre A. Moenssens, Novel Scientific Evidence in Criminal Cases: Some Words of Caution, 84 *J.Crim.L. & Criminology* 1, 5 (1993). Forensic scientists typically do not know much about the underlying statistical theory and, even if they do, "are often reluctant to acknowledge [, for example,] that a reported match could be something other than a true match." This reluctance is not confined to forensic scientists: In courtroom testimony, forensic scientists and their academic supports often insist that the probability of a false positive is zero — that is, that false positives are impossible. Although the falsity of these claims has been demonstrated repeatedly, the claims still continue to be made. * * * Currently, juries often hear nothing about false positives, other than broad assurance that they never occur. * * * [J]urors hear impressive numbers that appear to quantify with precision the frequency of the DNA profile, accompanied (when the issue is raised at all) by a vague, non-quantitative discussion of the chances of a false positive.

(b) The inference that a true match means defendant is the source. There is nothing inherently wrong in a jury using its inference that the match is a true match as the basis for another inference, specifically, that the defendant is the source. What is important is that the jury know that it has to go through the process of making the inference. The probability that a randomly selected person would have the same profile as the sample found at the scene is not the probability that someone other than the defendant is the source. But it is commonly assumed that it is the probability that someone other than defendant is the source. This is what is often referred to as "source probability error." In order to give an opinion as to the probability that someone other than defendant is the source, one would first have to estimate the size of the potential source population. "Source probability errors are frequently committed in the popular press." See e.g., "DNA Data: Letting Jurors Know the Whole Score," *Minneapolis Star-Tribune*, Feb. 1, 1994, at 10A (stating that, as the result of a trial judge's ruling, "jurors will hear testimony on the odds * * * that the DNA evidence against [the defendant] actually belongs to someone else").

Unfortunately, source probability errors "are also committed by the courts and by experts who should know better." . . . Indeed, amicus briefs in this appeal make the same mistake. One can understand attorneys and judges, who are not trained in statistics, making this mistake. And one can understand forensic scientists, most of whom are technicians, making this mistake. But even the best of the scientists make it occasionally.

(c) The inference that defendant was the source means defendant was at the scene. There is nothing inherently wrong in using the inference that defendant was the source to infer defendant was at the scene as long as jurors know that the one does not necessarily follow from the other.

(d) The inferences that defendant was the source and that he was at the scene mean defendant committed the crime. An even more egregious kind of error than "source probability error" is that which has been dubbed "prosecutor's fallacy," the fallacious equation of random match probability with the probability that the defendant is the perpetrator of the crime. As Koehler says, it really should not be called "prosecutor's fallacy" because experts, defense attorneys, judges and reporters also sometimes make the mistake; he therefore refers to it as "ultimate issue error." One has no way of knowing how often jurors make the error but it is quite possible that such error by jurors is common. Koehler explains, "[A] suspect who actually is the source of the trace may not be the perpetrator of the crime. The suspect may have left

the trace innocently either before or after the crime was committed." Indeed, the use of a person's bodily fluids to frame that person is not beyond the realm of possibility.

Forensic use of DNA evidence is a very recent development. The first forensic use was in Great Britain less than 10 years ago. Kenneth R. Kreiling, DNA Technology in Forensic Science, 33 *Jurimetrics* 449, 456–57 (1993). Those who are not by nature skeptical "rushed" to admit the evidence in criminal cases. In the "first wave of cases, expert testimony for the prosecution rarely was countered, and courts readily admitted RFLP findings." D. H. Kaye, The Admissibility of DNA Testing, 13 *Cardozo L.Rev.* 353, 357 (1991).

Then law reviews began publishing critical articles dealing with a number of issues, including the standards used for determining individual matches, the adequacy of the studies estimating the frequency of individual traits in the population, the validity of the assumption of independence, the possibility of false matches, and the misleading presentation of things such as random match probability and the possibility of false matches. Unfortunately, the FBI and others advancing the "cause" of the easy admission of DNA evidence have not always behaved admirably.

[COURT NOTE: Harsh criticism of the FBI's alleged role in suppressing negative DNA research, in refusing scrutiny of its databases, in intimidating certain scientists, and in attempting to undermine the NRC Committee's independence appears in Thompson, as well as in Peter J. Neufeld, Have You No Sense of Decency, 84 *J.Crim.L. & Criminology* 189 (1993). Thompson states that at one point the FBI, in response to an NRC Prospectus that suggested the new committee would also "[a]ssess and describe the degree of certainty of DNA evidence in ways useful to the courts," threatened to withhold funding of the new study unless the NRC limited the scope of its inquiry to procedures for estimating frequency of DNA profiles in a reference population.]

Because of all the criticism, a Committee on DNA Technology in Forensic Sciences was formed by the National Research Council. The committee's report, which we referred to earlier, was released in 1992. . . . The NRC report has not put an end to the controversy. Indeed, it appears that the FBI is sufficiently concerned about the response of courts and critics to the NRC report that it has agreed to fund a new study by the NRC in the hope that that will help end what former-FBI Director Sessions called a "crisis."

While Minnesota was one of the first courts to admit DNA identification evidence in criminal trials, we took the cautious approach in doing so, insisting that the new forensic techniques receive adequate scrutiny and insisting that proper procedures be followed if the evidence is to be admitted. . . . As we said at the outset of this opinion, the issue in this case is not the admissibility of DNA evidence but the form that the presentation of the evidence takes. . . .

. . . [N]otwithstanding the fact that the intense debate continues concerning the most reliable, accurate way of estimating random match probability and the proper role of statistical evidence in criminal trials, we now conclude, based on all the circumstances, including the very conservative nature of the probability figures obtained using the NRC's approach, that a DNA exception to the rule against admission of quantitative, statistical probability evidence in criminal prosecutions to prove identity is justified. Accordingly, any properly qualified prosecution or defense expert may, if evidentiary foundation is sufficient, give an opinion as to random match probability using the NRC's approach to computing that statistic.

We also conclude that, in an appropriate case, where there is an underlying statistical foundation for such an opinion, a properly qualified expert should be allowed to say more than that the DNA test results merely are consistent with the defendant's being the source of the physical evidence left behind by the assailant. . . .

We have concluded that the DNA expert should be allowed to express the opinion that there is a "match" between the defendant's DNA profile and that left by the assailant at the scene or on the victim. The strength of the expert's opinion is something the jury should be told; it will depend in part on the degree of the expert's confidence in the opinion and in part on the underlying statistical foundation for the opinion. We also agree with Professor Kreiling that the expert should be allowed to phrase the opinion this way: that given a reliable multi-locus match, the probability that the match is random or coincidental is extremely low.

The expert should not, of course, be allowed to say that a particular profile is unique. Nor should the expert be allowed to say that defendant is the source to the exclusion of all others or to express an opinion as to the strength of the evidence. But should a properly qualified expert, assuming adequate foundation, be allowed to express an opinion that, to a reasonable scientific certainty, the defendant is (or is not) the source? We believe so. . . .

We believe that allowing this sort of verbal, qualitative, non-statistical presentation of the underlying statistical evidence will lead to more agreement among reputable experts at trials and may decrease the likelihood of there being a battle of experts (over the reliability of the random match probability figure), with one expert canceling out or discrediting the other.

Needless to say, any rule of evidence "cuts both ways." The defendant in a criminal case has the same right as the state to present both quantitative and/or qualitative DNA evidence under the rules we today articulate. Moreover, the trial court of necessity retains its historic power under Minn.R.Evid. 403 and of course has the responsibility of crafting appropriate cautionary instructions. Prosecutors and trial courts are cautioned that we will not hesitate to award a new trial to a defendant if our review of the trial record reveals that quantitative or qualitative DNA identification evidence was presented in a misleading or improper way.

Reserved in part and remanded for trial. . . .

DISSENT

Justice Coyne (dissenting).

I dissent. I agree, of course, as I did five years ago when we decided in *State v. Schwartz*, 447 N.W.2d 422 (Minn. 1989), that when a proper foundation has been laid—that is, when there has been a showing that the tests were performed in accordance with appropriate laboratory standards and controls—DNA test results are admissible into evidence. At that time we hedged DNA testing about with the same procedural safeguards applicable to other kinds of scientific evidence: to insure a fair trial, the test data and methodology must be available for independent review by or on behalf of the opposing party, and the admissibility of statistical probability evidence should be limited pursuant to Rule 403 of the Minnesota Rules of Evidence, which permits the exclusion of relevant evidence if its probative value is substantially outweighed by the danger of unfair prejudice.

Today the majority has bulldozed that hedge into oblivion, ostensibly in the interest of "scientific proof," with only a backward glance at the reason for excluding statistical probability evidence. Statistical probabilities are certainly useful tools for indicating the direction and utility of further scientific research and for supporting certain conclusions with respect to the validity and use of the results of the research. Statistics have, however, been known to lie — either inadvertently or purposefully. The debate surrounding the National Research Council's recommendation for the development of a conservative "interim ceiling method" and the Council's acknowledgment that the methods of calculating the probability of a random match, current at the time its 1992 report was issued, rest on inadequate data and unjustified assumptions about population substructure, both bear witness to the fallibility of statistical evidence. More germane to the present case, perhaps, is the wide divergence in the statistical probabilities proffered by the state's two experts, both professing to use the "interim ceiling method." The BCA's forensic technician is prepared to testify to a 1 in 93,700 chance that a randomly selected person's DNA would match at the five loci where he matched the defendant's record to the specimen found at the crime scene. The imported expert, however, is prepared to testify to a 1 in 634,687 chance of a random match.

The accuracy of a statistical probability may be of little moment to the scientific community because although discovery of the falsity of an assumption underlying a statistical probability may destroy the value of the statistic, that discovery may confirm the validity of the basic research. If, however, an erroneous statistical probability plays any significant role in the conviction of an innocent person, the error has not only destroyed the life of the innocent person but has in some sense dehumanized the community. . . .

In the light of the potential for invalidity of the assumptions about the frequency of a particular pattern of DNA at a given locus, about population substructure, and about statistical independence, I am not persuaded that there is any more justification for admitting statistical probabilities with respect to DNA than there was for admitting probabilities in *State v. Carlson*, 267 N.W.2d 170 (Minn. 1978), or in any of its progeny. If the underlying assumption is wrong, the statistics are worthless. Conversely, the price of error is too high.

More to the point, perhaps, than the potential for error in these statistics is their potential for misuse. The state's imported expert witness is prepared, as I have already noted, to testify that there is a 1 in 634,687 chance of a random match at the five loci in question. That figure is, in a sense, fictitious; the witness concedes that he used the "interim ceiling approach" with its built-in adjustments. Statistical probabilities are, of course, only probabilities — estimates, not certainties. As the witness undoubtedly recognizes, however, the mere recitation of the number 634,687 conveys an aura of mathematical precision, lending the probability a credibility it may not deserve and a weight to which it has no logical claim.

A quarter-of-a-century ago the California Supreme Court observed that "[m]athematics, a veritable sorcerer in our computerized society, while assisting the trier of fact in the search for the truth, must not [be allowed to] cast a spell over him." *People v. Collins*, 68 Cal.2d 319, 66 Cal.Rptr. 497, 438 P.2d 33, 33 (1968) (en banc). Surely, the almost universal acceptance of accuracy and precision in mathematical calculations has not diminished in the intervening years.

More inimical to our traditional system of legal proof in criminal trials than undeserved credibility is the danger that the fact finder will understand the statistic represents something which it does not — namely, that the probability refers to the odds that someone else than the defendant is the source of the specimen found at the scene of the crime. That mistake has so often found its way into the rhetoric of public figures and in erroneous reports in the public press that it may be impossible to erase it from the mind of the fact finder. Even the state's expert fell into that trap on cross-examination.

Moreover, it seems to me that the preoccupation with statistical evidence is very likely to divert attention away from those aspects of DNA evidence which are deserving of closer examination. Are the test results reliable? What is the laboratory's "false positive

424

match rate"? Does the laboratory which performed the tests observe rigorous, scientific standards and quality control? Did the technicians follow laboratory protocol in the tests in question? Does the laboratory have an objective and quantitative procedure for identifying patterns, and a clearly defined procedure for declaring a match, identifying potential artifacts and designing internal controls to determine the presence of the artifact in a particular test? In short, there are inherent limits to any particular technique, test results can be skewed by a medium which does not meet quality controls or by defective equipment, and there is always the possibility of human error. If the match reported in the present case is erroneous at any one of the five loci, there is no match at all and the statistical probabilities of a random match have no relevance whatever.

Despite my conviction that the admission of statistical probabilities is more likely to be misleading than helpful and that it introduces unfairness into a criminal trial, I do believe that DNA typing has now demonstrated sufficient reliability and particularity to justify some modification of the rule set out in the *Kim* case. It seems to me that it is more accurate to inform the jury that matches like those present in this case are "rare" or even "extremely rare" than to say only that the test is "consistent with" defendant being the source of the specimen found at the scene of the crime. In keeping with expert testimony in other contexts, I also consider admissible an expression, given an appropriate foundation for the opinion, that to a reasonable degree of scientific certainty the defendant is the source of the specimen. That information places the jury in a suitable position to assess the

DNA evidence and protect the right of the defendant to a fair trial while at the same time avoiding the pitfalls attendant upon the illusion of mathematical precision.

This court has heretofore adhered to the principle that conviction of the defendant in a criminal trial depends on the jury's determination that, based on all of the evidence before it, the state has proved the defendant's guilt beyond a reasonable doubt and that a criminal trial should not be resolved by a battle of experts. That a civil case should turn on the opinion of competing experts is considered by some as cause for alarm. That a criminal trial should be determined on the basis of probability estimates ought to give all of us pause.

That mine is the lone dissenting voice in this matter does not shake my conviction that the day will come when this court regrets today's decision.

CASE DISCUSSION

According to the court, what inferences must jurors make when using DNA evidence, and what are the problems with each? On the basis of this case, do you believe that DNA evidence should be admitted? If so, under what conditions? Assume that you are a judge. Would you admit the evidence? What would you allow the experts to say? Assume that you are the prosecutor. Argue for the admissibility of the evidence and for the expert to tell the jury the "odds" of a random person in the population having the same DNA. Now assume that you are the defense attorney. Argue that the evidence is not admissible or, if it is, that the experts should not be allowed to talk about the odds.

SUMMARY

Whatever the problems connected to proving that a crime was committed and how it was committed, identifying the perpetrator in many cases is more difficult. Identification procedures take on critical importance in identifying strangers. However, identifying strangers is fraught with the danger of misidentification. The reliability of identification depends on perception at the original event, memory in the interval between the original event, and recall of the initial observation during identification procedures. Initial eyewitness observations are unreliable because of the natural imperfection of human perception. Memory fades and gets distorted by time and outside influences. Suggestion — usually not intended — during identification procedures distorts the mental process of recalling.

Measures taken to improve the reliability of identification procedures include regulating the number and makeup of lineups and photographic displays, providing jury instructions, and supplying expert testimony on the reliability of various identification procedures.

The Supreme Court has sought to improve the reliability of eyewitness identification by applying to identification procedures the Sixth Amendment rights to counsel and to confront the witness and the Fifth Amendment and Fourteenth Amendment due process clauses. The right to counsel applies to all confrontations after the government initiates formal proceedings against defendants. Both lineups and show-ups are considered Sixth Amendment confrontations; photographic identifications are not confrontations. The due process clauses apply to all identification procedures. The Court uses a two-pronged test in applying due process to identification procedures. First, it inquires whether a procedure was unduly suggestive and raises a likelihood of unreliability. If the procedure was impermissibly suggestive, the identification is not automatically excluded. It may be admissible if under the totality of the circumstances it is still reliable. Courts rarely deem eyewitness identification inadmissible, leaving it to the jury to decide the procedure's reliability. The primary interest that the U.S. Supreme Court promotes in applying the Constitution to identification procedures is the interest in obtaining the correct result, despite some early suggestions that the Court's rules would help control government misconduct in administering unduly suggestive identification procedures. No constitutional provision can, of course, improve the reliability of either original perceptions or interim memory. Therefore, the Court can direct its efforts only at the accuracy and reliability of recall during identification procedures.

Lineups are the most reliable identification procedure, followed by show-ups. Photographic identification is the least reliable identification procedure. Lineups are the least frequently used procedure, photographic displays the most widely used. Refusal to cooperate in identification procedures can lead to comment on the refusal at trial, penalties such as fines or even incarceration, and compulsory participation in lineups or show-ups.

DNA, the long, double-stranded molecule found in everyone's chromosomes, has the potential to identify criminal suspects accurately. The theory and the techniques for DNA testing are widely, although not universally, accepted as sound. Initially, courts enthusiastically admitted DNA testing as an identification procedure. However, after knowledge of human error in the administration of the tests that led to misidentifications, and after criticisms of the use of statistical estimates involving the chances of random appearances of matches, some courts have drawn back from their initial enthusiasm. Courts have established a number of standards for determining both the admissibility and the credibility of DNA testing. The correct identification of criminal suspects by means of DNA testing depends on whether a reported match between the suspect and the sample is true, whether the suspect is the source of the trace of DNA left at the scene of the crime, and whether the suspect is the perpetrator of the crime. Although reported matches suggest true matches, mistakes do occur. Although true matches suggest that the suspect is the source of the sample, this could be coincidental.

And, although the sample is that of the perpetrator, someone else could be the perpetrator. These are all matters that call for inferences that jurors must draw, and these inferences are instrumental in linking DNA testing to both the identification and the conviction of defendants.

REVIEW QUESTIONS

1. Explain the importance and dangers of identification procedures.

2. Identify and describe the major kinds of eyewitness identification.

3. What are the major reasons for misidentification?

4. What does the reliability of identification mainly depend upon?

5. What is the most reliable identification procedure? What procedure is the most widely used?

6. When does the right to counsel apply to identification procedures, and why?

7. When does due process apply to identification procedures?

8. Explain the two-pronged test that the Supreme Court adopted to evaluate due process claims during identification procedures.

9. What are the circumstances that the Court relies on in evaluating the totality of circumstances surrounding an identification procedure?

10. What is the effect of an unduly suggestive but reliable identification procedure?

11. What are the consequences of refusing to participate in an identification procedure?

12. Explain DNA testing and its potential value as an identification procedure.

13. What was the initial response and later reaction of the courts to the admissibility of DNA testing? Explain the change.

14. Explain whether the problems of DNA evidence arise out of the theory, the techniques, or the administration of the tests.

15. Identify and fully explain the three steps upon which the correct identification of criminal suspects by means of DNA testing depends.

16. Identify and describe the four major standards that courts use to determine the admissibility of DNA testing as evidence.

KEY TERMS

confrontation a lineup or show-up in which the witness and the suspect are physically present in the same place.

DNA fingerprinting or **DNA profiling** measuring and comparing the lengths of selected strands of DNA in chromosomes.

Federal Rules of Evidence standard the test of admissibility of DNA testing by considering whether the relevancy of the evidence outweighs the tendency of the evidence to unfairly prejudice the defendant.

Frye **standard** the rule that DNA evidence is admissible if the technique is "sufficiently established to have gained general acceptance in the particular field in which it belongs."

Frye **plus standard** the test of admissibility that requires showing not only general acceptance of

DNA theory but also that "the testing laboratory in the particular case performed the accepted scientific techniques in analyzing forensic samples."

lineup an identification procedure in which the suspect stands in a line with other individuals.

photo array a procedure in which the witness observes pictures or "mug shots" in order to identify the suspect.

relevancy plus standard the test of the admissibility evidence that adds the *Frye* standard and other requirements to the Federal Rules of Evidence standard.

show-up a procedure in which the witness identifies the suspect without other possible suspects present.

Notes

1. "Pagano Case Points Finger at Lineups," *National Law Journal* (September 10, 1979): 1.

2. "Notes: Did Your Eyes Deceive You? Expert Psychological Testimony on the Unreliability of Eyewitness Identification," *Stanford Law Review* 29 (1977): 970.

3. Gary L. Wells, "Eyewitness Behavior," *Law and Human Behavior* 4 (1980): 238.

4. Quoted in Martin Yant, *Presumed Guilty: When Innocent People Are Wrongly Convicted* (Buffalo: Prometheus Books, 1991), 99.

5. Samuel R. Gross, "Loss of Innocence: Eyewitness Identification and Proof of Guilt," *Journal of Legal Studies* 16 (1987): 398–99; "Notes: Did Your Eyes Deceive You?" 982–83.

6. Cited in Yant, *Presumed Guilty,* 100.

7. Quoted in Yant, *Presumed Guilty,* 100.

8. "Notes: Did Your Eyes Deceive You?" 969; David Bazelon, "Eyewitness News," *Psychology Today* (March 1980): 102–04; Wayne R. LaFave and Jerold H. Israel, *Criminal Procedure* (St. Paul: West Publishing Company, 1984), 1: 551–53; Gross, "Loss of Innocence," 401.

9. *Basoff v. State,* 208 Md. 643, 119 A.2d 917 (1956).

10. *Schmerber v. California,* 384 U.S. 757, 86 S.Ct. 1826.

11. LaFave and Israel, *Criminal Procedure,* 556.

12. "Notes: Did Your Eyes Deceive You?" 994.

13. 406 U.S. 682, 92 S.Ct. 1877, 32 L.Ed.2d 411 (1972).

14. 558 P.2d 636.

15. *Manson v. Braithwaite,* 432 U.S. 98, 116, 97 S.Ct. 2243, 2254, 53 L.Ed.2d 140 (1977).

16. "Twenty-Sixth Annual Review of Criminal Procedure," *Georgetown Law Journal* 85 (1997): 944–45.

17. Ibid.

18. Ibid., 945–46.

19. *Rodriguez v. Young,* 906 F.2d 1153 (7th Cir. 1990).

20. *Manson v. Braithwaite,* 432 U.S. 98, 97 S.Ct. 2243, 53 L.Ed.2d 140 (1977).

21. Gerald F. Uelman, "Testing the Assumptions of *Neal v. Biggers:* An Experiment in Eyewitness Identification," *Criminal Law Bulletin* 16 (1980): 359–68.

22. *McFadden v. Cabana,* 851 F.2d 784 (5th Cir. 1988).

23. LaFave and Israel, *Criminal Procedure,* 590–91.

24. Ibid., 588–60.

25. Ibid., 557–58.

26. Kenneth R. Kreiling, "DNA Technology in Forensic Science," *Jurimetrics Journal* 33 (1993): 449; William C. Thompson, "Evaluating the Admissibility of New Genetic Identification Tests: Lessons From the 'DNA War,'" *Journal of Criminal Law and Criminology* 84 (1993): 26–27.

27. Quoted in Stephanie Goldberg, "A New Day for DNA?" *American Bar Association Journal* 78 (April, 1992): 85.

28. *People v. Wesley,* 140 Misc.2d 306, 533 N.Y.S.2d 643 (Cty.Ct. 1988), affirmed 183 A.D.2d 75, 589 N.Y.S.2d 197 (1992) ("greatest advance . . ." and "war" quoted in Thompson, "Evaluating the Admissibility . . . ," 23; *People v. Castro,* 144 Misc.2d 956, 545 N.Y.S.2d 985 (Bronx Cty. 1989); Kenneth R. Kreiling, "DNA Technology in Forensic Science," *Jurimetrics Journal* 33 (1993): 449.

29. Goldberg, "A New Day for DNA?" 84.

30. Quoted in Jonathan J. Koehler, "Error and Exaggeration in the Presentation of DNA Evidence at Trial," *Jurimetrics Journal* 34 (1994): 21.

31. Ibid.

32. Koehler, "Error and Exaggeration in the Presentation of DNA Evidence at Trial," 21; surveys of jurors, judges, and lawyers are reported in Paul C. Giannelli, "Criminal Discovery, Scientific Evidence, and DNA," *Vanderbilt Law Review* 44 (1991): 794.

CHAPTER TEN

Remedies for Constitutional Violations

CHAPTER OUTLINE

CHAPTER MAIN POINTS

1. Excluding illegally seized evidence is the most widely used remedy against police violations of the Fourth, Fifth, and Sixth Amendments.

2. "Process" remedies against improper and erroneous government actions include dismissal, the entrapment defense, reversal, and the expungement of records.

3. "Victims" of illegal state intrusions and deprivations can sue officials, their agencies, and the government for injuries suffered or secure court orders prohibiting further illegal state action.

4. Informal reward and sanction within criminal justice agencies is an administrative remedy against improper government action.

5. Exclusion, process, civil, criminal, and administrative remedies are not mutually exclusive; they may all be pursued to redress the same action.

6. None of the existing remedies is totally satisfactory to enforce constitutional standards.

Can He Sue the Government?

Early in the morning, as Doug Durbin returned home from a local tavern, Deputy Sheriff Ray Sowers followed him and waited outside of Durbin's home. Deputy Tom Furrer later arrived as a backup. Sowers, flicking an electric stun gun on and off, ordered Durbin out of his house. Durbin, who complied, was arrested for drunk driving. After taking one step toward his house, the two deputies tackled Durbin and threw him to the ground. Though Durbin never attempted to resist, Sowers began to beat him on the back of his head with his fist. In the patrol car on the way to the jail, Sowers slammed on the brakes, causing Durbin, who was handcuffed and thus defenseless, to smash into the screen with his face.

NATURE AND KINDS OF REMEDIES

Everyone knows what the consequences are — or at least what they should be — when private individuals commit crimes. They are arrested, prosecuted, and punished. Most people are not so clear about what happens — or should happen — when public officials break the laws they are charged with upholding. This chapter examines the various remedies available to private individuals against unconstitutional and other improper law enforcement. The mechanisms to enforce the constitutional standards and the values that underpin the law of criminal procedure include three types of actions:

1. *Legal and administrative actions against individual officers*, including criminal prosecution, civil lawsuits, and disciplinary action within the officer's agency or department

2. *Civil actions against the heads of criminal justice agencies, the agencies themselves, or the government unit responsible for the agency*, including suits for damages and court orders (injunctions) prohibiting specific conduct, issued against the heads of criminal justice agencies, the agencies themselves, or the government unit having jurisdiction over the agency

3. *Process remedies affecting the outcome of criminal cases,* including dismissing cases, reversing convictions, and excluding or suppressing evidence[1]

These remedies are not mutually exclusive. For example, the government can prosecute police officers who break into and enter a house and damage property while conducting an unlawful search. The victim can sue the same officers for damage to property and violation of constitutional rights occurring as a result of the illegal search. The department can dismiss or suspend the officers from duty for conducting the illegal search. Moreover, the victim might seek a court order restraining police from conducting further illegal searches; sue the chief of police, the police department, and the city with jurisdiction over the police department for the illegal searches; or do both. Finally, a court may exclude the evidence obtained from the illegal search and, in some instances, even dismiss the case against the victim of government lawbreaking—even if the defendant is clearly guilty! This rarely happens in practice, but it could; the law does not require that injured parties choose one action above others.

THE EXCLUSIONARY RULE

The best-known, most widely discussed, and most controversial consequence of illegal government action is the exclusionary rule. The **exclusionary rule** prohibits the government from using evidence obtained in violation of four constitutional rights:

1. The right against self-incrimination guaranteed by the Fifth Amendment

2. The right against unreasonable searches and seizures prohibited by the Fourth Amendment

3. The right to counsel guaranteed by the Sixth Amendment

4. The right to due process of law guaranteed by the Fifth and Fourteenth Amendments

The exclusionary rule prohibits not only the use of illegally obtained evidence itself but also the use of evidence obtained as the result of illegal methods. This **fruit of the poisonous tree doctrine** prohibits the government from using illegal methods to obtain information indirectly that it could not secure directly. For example, suppose that the police compel a suspect to tell them where she hid a murder weapon. They go to the location and get the weapon. The government cannot use this fruit (the gun) of the poisonous tree (the forced incriminating statement).

Occasionally, the U.S. Supreme Court has also extended the rule beyond constitutional rights to exclude evidence obtained in violation of specific statutes, such as those involving federal wiretapping legislation.[2]

The Supreme Court has relied on three rationales to justify the exclusionary rule:

1. The constitutional rationale

2. The judicial integrity rationale

3. The deterrence rationale

The **constitutional rationale** rests on the idea that the exclusionary rule is an essential part of the rights against unreasonable searches and seizures in the Fourth Amendment, the right against self-incrimination in the Fifth Amendment, the right to counsel in the Sixth Amendment, and the due process clauses of the Fifth and the Fourteenth

Amendments. The notion that the exclusionary rule is itself a right stems from the legal axiom that a right without a remedy is no right at all; it is like "one hand clapping." According to Justice William Rufus Day, in *Weeks v. United States*, the case that created the exclusionary rule for the federal system:

> If letters and private documents can . . . be seized and held and used in evidence against a citizen accused of an offense, the protection of the Fourth Amendment declaring his right to be secure against such searches and seizures is of no value, and, so far as those thus placed are concerned, may as well be stricken from the Constitution.[3]

The **judicial integrity rationale** is based on the idea that the honor and honesty of courts forbid them to participate, even indirectly, in unconstitutional conduct. The rule of law requires that the government obtain criminal convictions without violating fundamental rights. In *Olmstead v. United States*, Justice Oliver Wendell Holmes stated this rationale as the dilemma of having to choose between excluding reliable evidence in order to preserve the integrity of the courts:

> [W]e must consider two objects of desire, both of which we cannot have, and make up our minds which to choose. It is desirable that criminals should be detected, and to that end that all available evidence should be used. It also is desirable that the Government should not itself foster and pay for other crimes, when they are the means by which the evidence is to be obtained. . . . For my part, I think it is less evil that some criminals should escape than that the Government should play an ignoble part.[4]

The **deterrence rationale** is based on the notion that excluding evidence obtained in violation of the Constitution prevents illegal law enforcement. If courts exclude illegally obtained evidence in the conviction of criminals, then officers will stop using illegal methods to get the evidence in the first place. The rule is directed at general — not specific — deterrence. That is to say, it does not aim to punish the individual officer who acts illegally. Rather, the rule aims to send a message to law enforcement officials in general who may contemplate illegal actions in the future. Justice Potter Stewart, perhaps the Supreme Court justice most learned about the Fourth Amendment, put it succinctly:

> The rule is calculated to prevent, not to repair. Its purpose is to deter — to compel respect for the constitutional guaranty in the only effective available way — by removing the incentive to disregard it.[5]

Until the 1980s, a majority of the Supreme Court never agreed on one of these rationales exclusively, referring to one or more of them in various cases. Justice Stewart refers to the Court's inability to agree on a rationale in describing his efforts to reach consensus in writing the Court's opinion in *Elkins v. United States*, a major case on the Fourth Amendment exclusionary rule:

> In my first draft of the opinion, I expressly stated that the exclusionary rule was not constitutionally required . . . and was grounded in the Court's supervisory power. This position bothered both Justice [William O.] Douglas and Justice

[William] Brennan, each of whom separately wrote to me urging that the Court leave open the question. Justice [Hugo L.] Black, on the other hand, expressed agreement with what I had written. So, in later drafts of the opinion, the question as to the doctrinal basis for the exclusionary rule was left unresolved.[6]

By the 1980s, however, a majority of the Court came to rely exclusively on deterrence as the only justification for excluding valid evidence. The Court weighed the social cost of letting criminals go free by excluding evidence of guilt against the possible deterrent effect of exclusion on law enforcement officers. If the social costs outweighed the deterrent effect (and in virtually every case the Court found that it did), then the evidence was admissible.

In *United States v. Leon* (excerpted later in this section), the Supreme Court specifically rejected the rationale that the exclusionary rule is a constitutional right. Instead, the Court held, exclusion is merely a remedy, a prophylactic against the violation of constitutional rights. The debate over rationales for the exclusionary rule brings into bold relief the tension between ends and means—between the conflicting interests of result and process in the law of criminal procedure. The rule excludes good evidence because of bad practices. It puts the search for truth second to the rights of individuals, to the integrity of the courts, and to the deterrence of police misconduct. The rule stands for the proposition that the Constitution supports criminal law enforcement, but not at any price. Violating rights is simply too high a price to pay for obtaining convictions. If the government does not obey the law, the public loses confidence in the law. That lost confidence, in turn, breeds contempt for and hostility toward the law. In the end, both law and order suffer.[7]

No one has put the case for the exclusionary rule better than Associate Justice Louis D. Brandeis, in his much-quoted dissent in *Olmstead v. United States:*

> Decency, security, and liberty alike demand that government officials shall be subjected to the same rules of conduct that are commands to the citizen. In a government of laws, existence of the government will be imperiled if it fails to observe the law scrupulously. Our government is the potent, the omnipresent teacher. For good or for ill, it teaches the whole people by its example. Crime is contagious. If the government becomes a lawbreaker, it breeds contempt for law; it invites every man to become a law unto himself; it invites anarchy. To declare that in the administration of the criminal law the end justifies the means—to declare that the government may commit crimes in order to secure the conviction of a private criminal—would bring terrible retribution. Against that pernicious doctrine this court should resolutely set its face.[8]

Social Costs and Deterrent Effects

Both the question of the social cost in lost convictions and that of the effectiveness of the exclusionary rule in deterring unconstitutional police behavior have generated heated debate among scholars. Since the 1970s, a majority of the Supreme Court has routinely concluded that the social cost outweighs the deterrent effect of the rule. However, some empirical research questions the soundness of that conclusion. Research in the 1960s and 1970s was not conclusive, and in some cases not valid. Research conducted in the late 1980s and the early 1990s suggests that the social cost is not so high as the Supreme Court indicates and that the deterrent effects to police misconduct may be considerable.

In an extensive study of the effects of the exclusionary rule on the behavior of Chicago narcotics officers, Myron W. Orfield, Jr., then of the University of Chicago, reported several important findings. Orfield found that the rule has educated Chicago narcotics officers about its meaning and application. This is so for a number of reasons. Narcotics officers are nearly always in court when judges suppress the evidence the officers have obtained. Moreover, the officers nearly always understand the reasons that the court excluded the evidence. This firsthand learning about the meaning of the exclusionary rule has led Chicago narcotics officers to seek search warrants more often than before the adoption of the exclusionary rule by the Supreme Court. Furthermore, their learning experiences in court have led them to pay more attention to the law of search and seizure when they do not have warrants. Prior to the decision in *Mapp v. Ohio*, the case in which the United States Supreme Court ruled that the exclusionary rule applied to the states (see below), police officers rarely bothered to obtain warrants. By 1987 — at least in the narcotics division of the Chicago Police Department — "virtually all preplanned searches that are not 'buy busts' or airport-related searches occur with warrants." Orfield's study demonstrates that Chicago narcotics officers know what the exclusionary rule means. As a result of this knowledge, they try to get warrants whenever they can and they exercise more care when they search without warrants.[9]

Orfield's study also demonstrates that the exclusionary rule "punishes" officers who conduct illegal searches. The Chicago Police Department initiated an officer rating system in response to the exclusionary rule. The loss of evidence due to exclusion is a personal liability to police officers. Suppression of evidence can negatively affect both assignments and promotions. However, Orfield also found that police officers lie in court in order to avoid the suppression of illegally seized evidence. This in-court police perjury does limit the effectiveness of the exclusionary rule. But strong responses by both the police department and the courts have reduced the impact of police perjury on the practical application of the exclusionary rule. Finally, Orfield reported that every officer in his study believed that the courts should retain the rule. They saw the rule as a positive development that contained just about the right amount of a deterrent element, although they would like a "good faith" exception to warrantless searches. They believed that a tort remedy (discussed below) would "overdeter" the police in their search for and seizure of evidence.[10]

The social costs of letting guilty criminals go free by excluding credible evidence that would convict them is not nearly so high as is commonly thought. Researchers have found that the exclusionary rule affects only a minuscule number of cases in an extremely narrow range of crimes. The rule rarely, if ever, affects the outcome of murder, rape, robbery, and assault cases. It is primarily the prosecutions of illegal drug dealing, gambling, and pornography that suffer from it. In California, for example, the rule is overwhelmingly connected to the loss of nonviolent illegal drug offenses, not of violent felonies. In that state, illegally seized evidence led to dismissals in a mere 0.8 percent of all criminal cases and only 4.8 percent of felonies. Less than one-tenth of 1 percent of all criminal cases will be dismissed because the police seized evidence illegally. The rule leaves violent crimes and serious property offenses virtually unaffected.[11]

In view of its limited application, restrictions on the exclusionary rule hardly seem adequate cause for either critics to rejoice that these restrictions will make society safer or for supporters to lament that they will trammel individual liberties. Perhaps the strongest claim for the exclusionary rule as a policy instrument is that it helps to ensure judicial integrity. Courts, by excluding illegally obtained evidence, keep the criminal justice system pure. The exclusionary rule exacts the price of setting a few criminals free in order to maintain the rule of law for everybody. It sacrifices the correct result in an individual case for the general interest in the essential fairness of constitutional government for all people.[12]

The American Bar Association gathered information from police officers, prosecutors, defense attorneys, and judges in representative urban and geographically distributed locations regarding the problems that they face in their work. They also conducted a telephone survey of eight hundred police administrators, prosecutors, judges, and defense attorneys based on a stratified random selection technique in order to obtain a representative group of small to large cities and counties. The results showed the following:

> Although the prosecutors and police . . . interviewed believe that a few Fourth Amendment restrictions are ambiguous or complex, and thus, present training and field application problems, they do not believe that Fourth Amendment rights or their protection via the exclusionary rule are a significant impediment to crime control. . . . A number of . . . police officials also report that the demands of the exclusionary rule and resulting police training on Fourth Amendment requirements have promoted professionalism in police departments across the country. Thus, the exclusionary rule appears to be providing a significant safeguard of Fourth Amendment protections for individuals at modest cost in terms of either crime control or effective prosecution. This "cost," for the most part, reflects the values expressed in the Fourth Amendment itself, for the Amendment manifests a preference for privacy and freedom over that level of law enforcement efficiency which could be achieved if police were permitted to arrest and search without probable cause or judicial authorization.[13]

History of the Exclusionary Rule

James Madison, in an address to Congress in 1789, urged adoption of the Bill of Rights:

> If these rights are incorporated into the Constitution, independent tribunals of justice will consider themselves in a peculiar manner the guardians of those rights; they will be an impenetrable bulwark against every assumption of power in the Legislative or Executive; they will naturally be led to resist every encroachment upon rights expressly stipulated for in the Constitution by the declaration of rights.[14]

Perhaps this passage explains the Constitution's silence on remedies to enforce constitutional rights. Judges would devise remedies to enforce them. Whatever the reason, the Court left enforcement to civil lawsuits until the twentieth century. In the meantime, the criminal did not go free because the "constable blundered."[15]

All this dramatically changed in 1914, when the United States Supreme Court created the exclusionary rule to apply to federal cases in *Weeks v. United States*. While Fremont Weeks was at work in Union Station, Kansas City, Kansas, police officers unlawfully entered his house without a warrant. They searched the house and seized "all of his books, letters, money, papers, note[s], evidences of indebtedness, stock certificates, insurance policies, deeds, abstracts of title, bonds, candies, clothes, and other property." The police then arrested Weeks at work. He was charged with gambling in violation of federal statutes. The trial court refused Weeks's motion to return the seized evidence. Weeks was convicted and sentenced to a fine and imprisonment. On appeal, the United States Supreme Court reversed the conviction, holding that

> the letters . . . were taken from the house of the accused by an official of the United States, acting under color of his office, in direct violation of the constitutional rights of the defendant; that having made a seasonable application for their return, which was heard and passed upon by the court, there was involved in the order refusing the application a denial of the constitutional rights of the accused[;] and that the court should have restored these letters to the accused. In holding them and permitting their use upon the trial, we think prejudicial error was committed.[16]

The United States became unique among the nations of the world in excluding good evidence from court because law enforcement officers used illegal methods to obtain it. Of course, the rule of *Weeks v. United States* applied only to federal law enforcement; the states were left to enforce the rights as they saw fit. Furthermore, the rule applied only to the private papers, not the contraband, that Weeks had demanded the government return to him. Nevertheless, the case began an expansion of the exclusionary rule to enforce the Fourth Amendment.

In 1920, the Court broadened the rule in *Silverthorne Lumber Co. v. United States*. In that case, the government illegally raided the Silverthorne Lumber Company's offices, seized books and papers, copied and photographed those materials, and used what the evidence revealed to subpoena the original records. Justice Oliver Wendell Holmes, writing for the Court, held that the federal government could not illegally seize papers, study them, and then use what it had learned from them to order the papers produced. In sweeping language, Holmes wrote that the Fourth Amendment forbade "*any* advantages the Government can gain over the object of its pursuit by doing the forbidden act" (emphasis added).[17]

In 1925 the Court converted these limited rules "into a full-blown rule of exclusion at federal trials." In *Agnello v. United States*, the government had illegally seized cocaine from Frank Agnello's house. Agnello argued that the court should have suppressed the cocaine at his trial. The Supreme Court refused to recognize a distinction between papers and contraband. According to Justice Potter Stewart, by 1925, "the annexation of the exclusionary rule to the Fourth Amendment was complete."[18]

Two questions remained:

1. Does the due process clause of the Fourteenth Amendment include prohibitions against unreasonable searches and seizures?

2. If so, does it also annex the exclusionary rule as a remedy?

In 1949, thirty-five years after *Weeks* created the rule, the Court answered yes to the first question and no to the second. In *Wolf v. Colorado*, the Court declared that "scrutiny of one's privacy against arbitrary intrusion by the police" is a fundamental right enforceable against the states through the due process clause of the Fourteenth Amendment. However, the Court went on to hold that the exclusionary rule was not an essential part of the right; the states are free to adopt other means to enforce constitutional rights. Due process requires enforcement, not the specific method of enforcement.

In 1961, in *Mapp v. Ohio*, the Court reversed itself on the exclusionary rule, in somewhat unusual circumstances. Dollree Mapp was convicted of possession of pornography. The principal question the Supreme Court was asked to review was the constitutionality of Ohio's pornography statute. The only question regarding the police was whether their conduct violated the "shock-the-conscience" test of *Rochin v. California* (excerpted in Chapter 2). Until the first draft of the opinion circulated among the justices, the only mention of *Wolf* was the three sentences in the twenty-page **amicus curiae brief** of the American Civil Liberties Union. (An *amicus curiae* brief is an argument submitted by a party that has a strong interest in a case but is not a party to it.) In fact, when asked, during oral arguments, Mapp's attorney candidly admitted he had never heard of *Wolf*. As Justice Stewart later recalled,

> I was shocked when Justice [Tom C.] Clark's proposed Court opinion reached my desk. I immediately wrote him a note expressing my surprise and questioning the wisdom of overruling an important doctrine in a case in which the issue was not briefed, argued, or discussed by the state courts, by the parties' counsel, or at our conferences following the oral argument. After my shock subsided, I wrote a brief memorandum concurring in the judgment . . . and agreeing with Justice Harlan's dissent that the issue was not properly before the Court. The *Mapp* majority, however, stood its ground. . . . The case . . . provides significant insight into the judicial process and the evolution of law—a first amendment controversy was transformed into perhaps the most important search-and-seizure case in history.[19]

C A S E

Should the Court Exclude the Evidence?

Mapp v. Ohio
367 U.S. 643, 81 S.Ct. 1684,
6 L.Ed.2d 1081 (1961)

Cleveland police officers seized pornography from Mapp's home. She was tried and convicted of illegal possession of pornography. Over her objection, the trial court admitted the pornography in evidence against her. On appeal, the Ohio Supreme Court, although conceding that the police might have seized the evidence illegally, upheld the conviction. Mapp appealed to the United States Supreme Court. The Supreme Court reversed Mapp's conviction. Justice Clark delivered the opinion of the Court.

FACTS

On May 23, 1957, three Cleveland police officers arrived at appellant's residence in that city pursuant to in-

formation that "a person [was] hiding out in the home, who was wanted for questioning in connection with a recent bombing, and that there was a large amount of policy paraphernalia being hidden in the home." Miss Mapp and her daughter by a former marriage lived on the top floor of the two-family dwelling. Upon their arrival at that house, the officers knocked on the door and demanded entrance but appellant, after telephoning her attorney, refused to admit them without a search warrant. They advised their headquarters of the situation and undertook a surveillance of the house.

The officers again sought entrance some three hours later when four or more additional officers arrived on the scene. When Miss Mapp did not come to the door immediately, at least one of the several doors to the house was forcibly opened and the policemen gained admittance.

[COURT NOTE: "A police officer testified that 'we did pry the screen door to gain entrance'; the attorney on the scene testified that a policeman 'tried . . . to kick the door' and then 'broke the glass in the door and somebody reached in and opened the door and let them in'; the appellant testified that 'The back door was broken.' "]

Meanwhile Miss Mapp's attorney arrived, but the officers, having secured their own entry, and continuing in their defiance of the law, would permit him neither to see Miss Mapp nor to enter the house. It happens that Miss Mapp was halfway down the stairs from the upper floor to the front door when the officers, in this high-handed manner, broke into the hall. She demanded to see the search warrant. A paper, claimed to be a warrant, was held up by one of the officers. She grabbed the "warrant" and placed it in her bosom. A struggle ensued in which the officers recovered the piece of paper as a result of which they handcuffed appellant because she had been "belligerent" in resisting their official rescue of the "warrant" from her person.

Running roughshod over appellant, a policeman "grabbed" her, "twisted [her] hand," and she "yelled [and] pleaded with him" because "it was hurting." Appellant, in handcuffs, was then forcibly taken upstairs to her bedroom where the officers searched the dresser, a chest of drawers, a closet and some suitcases. They also looked in a photo album and through personal papers belonging to the appellant. The search spread to the rest of the second floor including the child's bedroom, the living room, the kitchen, and a dinette. The basement of the building and a trunk found therein were also searched. The obscene materials for possession of which she was ultimately convicted were discovered in the course of that widespread search.

At the trial no search warrant was produced by the prosecution, nor was the failure to produce one explained or accounted for. At best, "There is, in the record, considerable doubt as to whether there ever was any warrant for the search of defendant's home." The Ohio Supreme Court believed a "reasonable argument" could be made that the conviction should be reversed "because the 'methods' employed to obtain the [evidence] . . . were such as to 'offend a sense of justice,' " but the court found determinative the fact that the evidence had not been taken "from defen-

dant's person by the use of brutal or offensive physical force against defendant."

OPINION

The State says that even if the search were made without authority, or otherwise unreasonably, it is not prevented from using the unconstitutionally seized evidence at trial, citing *Wolf v. Colorado* (1949), in which the Court did indeed hold "that in a prosecution in a State court for a State crime the Fourteenth Amendment does not forbid the admission of evidence obtained by an unreasonable search and seizure." On this appeal, of which we have noted probable jurisdiction, it is urged once again that we review that holding.

. . . In 1949, 35 years after *Weeks* [*v. United States* (1914)] was announced, this Court, in *Wolf v. Colorado,* . . . for the first time, discussed the effect of the Fourth Amendment upon the States through the operation of the Due Process Clause of the Fourteenth Amendment. . . . [T]he Court decided that the *Weeks* exclusionary rule would not then be imposed upon the States as "an essential ingredient of the right." . . .

The Court in *Wolf* . . . stated that "[t]he contrariety of views of the States" on the adoption of the exclusionary rule of *Weeks* was "particularly impressive"; and . . . that it could not "brush aside the experience of the States which deem the incidence of such conduct by the police too slight to call for a deterrent remedy . . . by overriding the [States'] relevant rules of evidence." While in 1949, prior to the *Wolf* case, almost two-thirds of the States were opposed to the use of the exclusionary rule, now, despite the *Wolf* case, more than half of those since passing upon it, by their own legislative or judicial decision, have wholly or partly adopted or adhered to the *Weeks* rule. Significantly, among those now following the rule is California which, according to its highest court, was "compelled to reach that conclusion because other remedies have completely failed to secure compliance with the constitutional provisions. . . ."

. . . [T]he second basis elaborated in *Wolf* in support of its failure to enforce the exclusionary doctrine against the States was that "other means of protection" have been afforded "the right of privacy." The experience of California that such other remedies have been worthless and futile is buttressed by the experience of other States. The obvious futility of relegating the Fourth Amendment to the protection of other remedies has, moreover, been recognized by this Court since *Wolf.* . . .

Since the Fourth Amendment's right of privacy has been declared enforceable against the States through the Due Process Clause of the Fourteenth, it is enforceable against them by the same sanction of exclusion as is used against the Federal Government. Were it otherwise, then . . . the assurance against unreasonable federal searches and seizures would be "a form of words," valueless and undeserving of mention in a perpetual charter of inestimable human liberties, so too, without that rule the freedom from state invasions of privacy would be so ephemeral and so neatly severed from its conceptual nexus with the freedom from all brutish means of coercing evidence as not to merit this Court's high regard as a freedom "implicit in the concept of ordered liberty." . . .

There are those who say, as did Justice (then Judge) Cardozo, that under our constitutional exclusionary doctrine "[t]he criminal is to go free because the constable has blundered." In some cases this will undoubtedly be the result. But, "there is another consideration—the imperative of judicial integrity." "The criminal goes free, if he must, but it is the law that sets him free. Nothing can destroy a government more quickly than its failure to observe its own laws, or worse, its disregard of the charter of its own existence. . . ." [As Justice Brandeis, dissenting in *Olmstead v. United States*, 277 U.S. 438 (1928), 485, wrote,]

> Our Government is the potent, the omnipresent teacher. For good or for ill, it teaches the whole people by its example. . . . If the Government becomes a lawbreaker, it breeds contempt for law; it invites every man to become a law unto himself; it invites anarchy.

Nor can it lightly be assumed that, as a practical matter, adoption of the exclusionary rule fetters law enforcement. Only last year this Court expressly considered that contention and found that "pragmatic evidence of a sort" to the contrary was not wanting. The Court noted that

[t]he federal courts themselves have operated under the exclusionary rule of *Weeks* for almost half a century; yet it has not been suggested either that the Federal Bureau of Investigation has thereby been rendered ineffective, or that the administration of criminal justice in the federal courts has thereby been disrupted. Moreover, the experience of the states is impressive. . . . The movement towards the rule of exclusion has been halting but seemingly inexorable.

. . . Our decision, founded on reason and truth, gives to the individual no more than that which the Constitution guarantees him, to the police officer no less than that to which honest law enforcement is entitled, and, to the courts, that judicial integrity so necessary in the true administration of justice.

The judgment of the Supreme Court of Ohio is reversed and the cause remanded for further proceedings not inconsistent with this opinion. Reversed and remanded.

DISSENT

Mr. Justice Harlan, whom Mr. Justice Frankfurter and Mr. Justice Whittaker join, dissenting. . . .

At the heart of the majority's opinion in this case is the following syllogism: (1) the rule excluding in federal criminal trial evidence which is the product of an illegal search and seizure is "part and parcel" of the Fourth Amendment; (2) *Wolf* held that the "privacy" assured against federal action by the Fourth Amendment is also protected against state action by the Fourteenth Amendment; and (3) it is therefore "logically and constitutionally necessary" that the *Weeks* exclusionary rule should also be enforced against the States.

This reasoning ultimately rests on the unsound premise that because *Wolf* carried into the States, as part of "the concept of ordered liberty" embodied in the Fourteenth Amendment, the principle of "privacy" underlying the Fourth Amendment, it must follow that whatever configurations of the Fourth Amendment have been developed in the particularizing federal precedents are likewise to be deemed a part of "ordered liberty," and as such are enforceable against the States. For me, this does not follow at all. . . . Since there is not the slightest suggestion that Ohio's policy is "affirmatively to sanction . . . police incursion into privacy" what the Court is now doing is to impose upon the States not only federal substantive standards of "search and seizure" but also the basic federal remedy for violation of those standards. For I think it entirely clear that the *Weeks* exclusionary rule is but a remedy which, by penalizing past official misconduct, is aimed at deterring such conduct in the future.

I would not impose upon the States this federal exclusionary remedy. . . . [NOTE: The memorandum of Justice Stewart and the concurring opinions of Justices Black and Douglas are omitted.]

CASE DISCUSSION

Has the Court improperly overruled *Wolf v. Colorado*? What relevance does Justice Stewart's recollection have? Does the exclusionary rule invade the prerogative of states? Should states decide for themselves how best to enforce constitutional rights? Should citizens have a "right" to remedy of exclusion? Why or why not? Should the criminal Dollree Mapp go free because the Cleveland police blundered? Why or why not? Does Mapp have no remedy if the Court admits the illegal omitted evidence? What possible other remedies might she have? Which would you recommend? Should Mapp go free because the police violated her rights? Why or why not? What interests did the Court balance? Which should take precedence? Even if the Court excludes the evidence, is Mapp really set free? Explain.

Exceptions to the Exclusionary Rule

The exclusionary rule does not ban illegally obtained evidence from all criminal proceedings against all persons. The U.S. Supreme Court relies on a balancing approach in applying the rule. It weighs the cost of exclusion in hindering the obtaining of the correct result in individual cases against the benefits of exclusion in deterring illegal government actions. For that reason, the Court has limited the application of the rule to cases in which it has concluded that exclusion will deter police misconduct. Based on the deterrence rationale, the Court has created the following five exceptions to the exclusionary rule:

1. *Collateral use exception.* Exclusion does not apply to proceedings outside the prosecution's case-in-chief.

2. *Independent source exception.* The evidence was obtained from a source independent of the illegal conduct.

3. *Attenuation exception.* The connection between the illegal conduct and the acquisition of the evidence is so remote that it dissipates the taint of the illegal conduct.

4. *Inevitable discovery exception.* The evidence would have inevitably been discovered by lawful means.

5. *Good faith exception.* Law enforcement officers act in a good faith reliance on what appears to be a valid search warrant.

Collateral Use Exception. The United States Supreme Court has held that the exclusionary rule does not apply to proceedings other than to the prosecution's case-in-chief against defendants. In *United States v. Calandra*, for example, the Court refused to extend the rule to grand jury proceedings because "any incremental deterrent effect which might be achieved by extending the rule to grand jury proceedings is uncertain at best."[20]

For the same reason, the Court has held that the exclusionary rule does not prevent the use of some illegally seized evidence even in the criminal trial itself. For example, the government can use evidence illegally seized from codefendants and coconspirators because "the additional extension of the exclusionary rule would not outweigh its costs." Only the victims of the fruit of illegal searches can call for its suppression. In addition, prosecutors can use illegally seized evidence to **impeach** defendants' testimony—that is, show testimony to be untruthful. For example, in *Walder v. United States*, Walder was tried for purchasing and possessing heroin. During direct examination, Walder denied that he had ever bought or possessed heroin. The government then introduced heroin capsules seized during an illegal search to prove that Walder was lying. The Court admitted the capsules but cautioned the jury they could not consider the heroin capsules to prove Walder's guilt, only to impeach his testimony.[21]

Independent Source Exception. The **independent source doctrine** allows the admission of evidence initially discovered during an illegal search and later seized during activities not connected to the initial illegality. The independent source doctrine rests on the idea that "while the government should not profit from its misconduct, it also should not be placed in a worse position than it would have occupied had the misconduct not occurred." For example, in *Segura v. United States*, New York Drug Enforcement Task Force agents received permission from an Assistant U.S. Attorney at about 7:30 in the evening to arrest Segura and one of his drug-dealing cohorts. Although the agents had probable cause to support a search warrant, the Assistant U.S. Attorney advised the officers that they could not obtain a search warrant for Segura's apartment until the next day because of the lateness of the hour. The Assistant U.S. Attorney advised the agents to make the arrests anyway and to secure the apartment until the next day, when the agents could get the search warrant. The agents surveyed the apartment until Segura and another came home. The agents arrested Segura and entered his apartment, admittedly illegally. They secured the premises and saw drug paraphernalia in plain view. Two agents remained in the apartment for nineteen hours until other officers could obtain a search warrant. The Supreme Court held that cocaine and records of drug sales seized pursuant to the warrant were admissible as evidence. The search of the apartment and seizure of the drugs and transaction records obtained pursuant to the search warrant were independent of the initial illegal entry into the apartment. Therefore, the initial entry did not taint the later search and seizure pursuant to the search warrant. The later search was legal, and the evidence seized was admissible.[22]

Inevitable Discovery Exception. Closely related to the independent source doctrine, the **inevitable discovery exception** permits the use of illegally obtained evidence if the evidence would have come to light by another lawful means, independent of the illegal law enforcement action (see the Decision Point below).

Attenuation Exception. According to the attenuation exception, if the connection between the seizure of the evidence and the illegal conduct is remote enough, this distance dissipates the taint on the evidence and the evidence is admissible. To apply the **attenuation doctrine,** the Supreme Court requires that the prosecution demonstrate a break in the chain of events between the initial misconduct and the eventual acquisition of evidence (see the Decision Point below). The Court considers three factors in determining whether the chain has been broken:

1. Amount of time elapsed between the misconduct and the acquisition of the evidence

2. Intervening circumstances between the illegal conduct and obtaining the evidence

3. Purpose and the flagrancy of the misconduct

D e c i s i o n   P o i n t

1. In *Wong Sun v. United States,* six federal narcotics agents illegally broke into Toy's laundry, chased him into the living quarters at the back of his shop, where Toy's wife and child were sleeping, and handcuffed him. Toy told the agents that Yee had been selling narcotics. The agents immediately went to Yee, who surrendered heroin to the agents and implicated Wong Sun. The agents then arrested Wong Sun. After a lawful arraignment, the court released Wong Sun on his own recognizance. Several days later, he returned voluntarily to the police station and confessed to narcotics violations. Was the confession the fruit of a poisonous tree? The Supreme Court ruled that Wong Sun's confession was not the fruit of his illegal arrest because "the connection between this arrest and his statements had become so attenuated as to dissipate the taint."[23]

2. Shortly after a ten-year-old girl disappeared from a Young Men's Christian Association in Des Moines, Iowa, over two hundred volunteers began searching the area for the girl. Meanwhile, police arrested Williams in Davenport, Iowa, in connection with the girl's disappearance. The police in Davenport told Williams's attorney that they would not question Williams on the way from Davenport to Des Moines. During the trip, however, one of the officers initiated a conversation with Williams regarding the case. Ultimately, Williams told the police where he hid the body. Williams was charged with murder; he objected to the admission of the evidence, arguing that the discovery was causally linked to the illegal interrogation. Should the evidence be admitted?

   In *Nix v. Williams* (based on the same prosecution as *Brewer v. Williams,* excerpted in Chapter 8), the United States Supreme Court ruled that evidence was admissible even though the police violated the defendant's right to counsel in order to obtain the information. The Court concluded that the body would have been discovered during a thorough search conducted independent of the defendant's statements.[24]

The Good Faith Exception. A final exception to the exclusionary rule, the good faith exception is not related to the fruit of the poisonous tree doctrine. The **good faith exception** allows the admission of evidence if the police reasonably and honestly relied on a search warrant valid on its face but defective in fact. The good faith exception has generated tremendous controversy. Civil libertarians believe that a conservative majority on the Supreme Court has strangled the right to privacy secured by the Fourth Amendment. Law-and-order supporters claim that the Court has finally taken the handcuffs off the police in criminal law enforcement and that a safer society is in the offing. The Court's majority and dissenting opinions in *United States v. Leon* reflect that controversy.[25]

C A S E

Is There a "Good Faith" Exception to the Exclusionary Rule?

United States v. Leon
468 U.S. 897, 104 S.Ct. 3405,
82 L.Ed.2d 677 (1984)

Police officers obtained a search warrant that led to the seizure of large quantities of drugs and other evidence. Leon and others were indicted and moved to suppress the drugs and other evidence. The U.S. District Court granted the motion to suppress. The U.S. Court of Appeals affirmed the decision of the district court. The Supreme Court granted certiorari *and reversed the judgment of the court of appeals.*

Justice White delivered the opinion of the Court, in which Chief Justice Burger and Justices Blackmun, Powell, Rehnquist, and O'Connor joined. Justice Blackmun filed a concurring opinion. Justice Brennan filed a dissenting opinion, in which Justice Marshall joined. Justice Stevens filed a dissenting opinion.

FACTS

In August 1981, a confidential informant of unproven reliability informed an officer of the Burbank Police Department that two persons known to him as "Armando" and "Patsy" were selling large quantities of cocaine and methaqualone from their residence at 620 Price Drive in Burbank, Cal. The informant also indicated that he had witnessed a sale of methaqualone by "Patsy" at the residence approximately five months earlier and had observed at that time a shoe box containing a large amount of cash that belonged to "Patsy." He further declared that "Armando" and "Patsy" generally kept only small quantities of drugs at their residence and stored the remainder at another location in Burbank.

On the basis of this information, the Burbank police initiated an extensive investigation focusing first on the Price Drive residence and later on two other residences as well. Cars parked at the Price Drive residence were determined to belong to respondents Armando Sanchez, who had previously been arrested for possession of marihuana, and Patsy Stewart, who had

no criminal record. During the course of the investigation, officers observed an automobile belonging to respondent Ricardo Del Castillo, who had previously been arrested for possession of 50 pounds of marihuana, arrive at the Price Drive residence. The driver of that car entered the house, exited shortly thereafter carrying a small paper sack, and drove away. A check of Del Castillo's probation records led the officers to respondent Alberto Leon, whose telephone number Del Castillo had listed as his employer's. Leon had been arrested in 1980 on drug charges, and a companion had informed the police at that time that Leon was heavily involved in the importation of drugs into this country. Before the current investigation began, the Burbank officers had learned that an informant had told a Glendale police officer that Leon stored a large quantity of methaqualone at his residence in Glendale. During the course of the investigation, the Burbank officers learned that Leon was living at 716 South Sunset Canyon in Burbank.

Subsequently, the officers observed several persons, at least one of whom had prior drug involvement, arriving at the Price Drive residence and leaving with small packages; observed a variety of other material activity at the two residences as well as at a condominium at 7902 Via Magdalena; and witnessed a variety of relevant activity involving respondent's automobiles. The officers also observed respondents Sanchez and Stewart board separate flights for Miami. The pair later returned to Los Angeles together, consented to a search of their luggage that revealed only a small amount of marihuana, and left the airport.

Based on these and other observations summarized in the affidavit, officer Cyril Rombach of the Burbank Police Department, an experienced and well-trained narcotics investigator, prepared an application for a warrant to search 620 Price Drive, 716 South Sunset Canyon, 7902 Via Magdalena, and automobiles registered to each of the respondents for an extensive list of items believed to be related to respondents' drug-trafficking activities. Officer Rombach's extensive application was reviewed by several Deputy District Attorneys.

A facially valid search warrant was issued in September 1981 by a state Superior Court Judge. The ensuing searches produced large quantities of drugs at the Via Magdalena and Sunset Canyon addresses and a small quantity at the Price Drive residence. Other evidence was discovered at each of the residences and in Stewart's and Del Castillo's automobiles. Respondents were indicted by a grand jury in the District Court for the Central District of California and charged with conspiracy to possess and distribute cocaine and a variety of substantive counts.

The respondents then filed motions to suppress the evidence seized pursuant to the warrant. The District Court held an evidentiary hearing and . . . granted the motions to suppress. . . . The District Court denied the Government's motion for reconsideration and a divided panel of the Court of Appeals for the Ninth Circuit affirmed. . . . The Court of Appeals refused the Government's invitation to recognize a good-faith exception to the Fourth Amendment exclusionary rule. The Government's petition for certiorari . . . presented . . . the question "[w]hether the Fourth Amendment exclusionary rule should be modified so as not to bar the admission of evidence seized in reasonable, good-faith reliance on a search warrant that is subsequently held to be defective." We granted certiorari to consider the propriety of such a modification. . . .

OPINION

We have concluded that, in the Fourth Amendment context, the exclusionary rule can be modified somewhat without jeopardizing its ability to perform its intended functions. Accordingly, we reverse the judgment of the Court of Appeals. . . .

The Fourth Amendment contains no provision expressly precluding the use of evidence obtained in violation of its commands. . . . The rule thus operates as "a judicially operated remedy designed to safeguard Fourth Amendment rights generally through its deterrent effect, rather than a personal constitutional right of the party aggrieved."

Whether the exclusionary sanction is appropriately imposed in a particular case, our decisions make clear, is "an issue separate from the question whether the Fourth Amendment rights of the party seeking to involve the rule were violated by police conduct." Only the former question is currently before us, and it must be resolved by weighing the costs and benefits of preventing the use in the prosecution's case-in-chief of inherently trustworthy tangible evidence obtained in reliance on a search warrant issued by a detached and neutral magistrate that ultimately is found to be defective.

The substantial social costs exacted by the exclusionary rule for the vindication of Fourth Amendment rights have long been a source of concern. "Our cases have consistently recognized that unbending application of the exclusionary sanction to enforce ideals of governmental rectitude would impede unacceptably the truth-finding functions of judge and jury." An objectionable collateral consequence of this interference with the criminal justice system's truth-finding function is that some guilty defendants may go free or receive reduced sentences as a result of favorable plea bargains. Particularly when law enforcement officers have acted in objective good faith or their transgressions have been minor, the magnitude of the benefit conferred on such guilty defendants offends basic concepts of the criminal justice system. . . .

. . . [T]he balancing approach that has evolved in various contexts . . . "forcefully suggests that the exclusionary rule be more generally modified to permit the introduction of evidence obtained in the reasonable good-faith belief that a search or seizure was in accord with the Fourth Amendment. . . ." No empirical researcher, proponent or opponent of the rule, has yet been able to establish with any assurance whether the rule has a deterrent effect. . . .

[COURT NOTE: "Researchers have only recently begun to study extensively the effects of the exclusionary rule on the disposition of felony arrests. One study suggests that that rule results in the nonprosecution or nonconviction of between 0.6% and 2.35% of individuals arrested for felonies. Davies, A Hard Look at What We Know (and Still Need to Learn) About the 'Costs' of the Exclusionary Rule: The NIJ Study and Other Studies of 'Lost' Arrests, 1983 A.B.F. Res. J. 611, 621. The estimates are higher for particular crimes the prosecution of which depends heavily on physical evidence. Thus, the cumulative loss due to nonprosecution or nonconviction of individuals arrested on felony drug charges is probably in the range of 2.8% to 7.1%. Davies' analysis of California data suggests that screening by police and prosecutors results in the release because of illegal searches or seizures of as many as 1.4% of all felony arrestees, that 0.9% of felony arrestees are released, because of illegal searches or seizures, at the preliminary hearing or after trial, and that roughly 0.05% of all felony arrestees benefit from reversals on appeal because of illegal searches. See also K. Brosi, *A Cross-City Comparison of Felony Case Processing* 16, 18–19 (1979); U.S. General Accounting Office, *Report of the Comptroller General of the United States, Impact of the Exclusionary Rule on Federal Criminal Prosecutions* 10–11, 14 (1979); F. Feeny, F. Dill, & A. Weir, *Arrests Without Convictions: How Often They Occur and Why* 203–206 (National Institute of Justice 1983); National Institute of Justice, *The Effects of the Exclusionary Rule: A Study in California* 1–2 (1982); Nardulli, The Societal Cost of the Exclusionary Rule: An Empirical Assessment, 1983 *A.B.F. Res. J.* 585, 600. The exclusionary rule has also been found to affect the plea-bargaining process. S. Schlesinger, *Exclusionary Injustice: The Problem of Illegally Obtained Evidence* 63 (1977). Many of these researchers have concluded that the impact of the exclusionary rule is insubstantial, but the small percentages with which they deal mask a large absolute number of felons who are released because the cases against them were based in part on illegal searches or seizures. '[A]ny rule of evidence that denies the jury access to clearly probative and reliable evidence must bear a heavy burden of justification, and must be carefully limited to the circumstances in which it will pay its way by deterring official lawlessness.' *Illinois v. Gates*, 462 U.S., at 257–258, 103 S.Ct., at 2342 (White, J., concurring in judgment). Because we find that the rule can have no substantial deterrent effect in the sorts of situations under consideration in this case, we conclude that it cannot pay its way in those situations."]

But even assuming that the rule effectively deters some police misconduct and provides incentives for the law enforcement profession as a whole to conduct itself in accord with the Fourth Amendment, it cannot be expected, and should not be applied, to deter objectively reasonable law enforcement activity....

We conclude that the marginal or nonexistent benefits produced by suppressing evidence obtained in objectively reasonable reliance on a subsequently invalidated search warrant cannot justify the substantial costs of exclusion. We do not suggest, however, that exclusion is always inappropriate in cases where an officer has obtained a warrant and abided by its terms....

Suppression ... remains an appropriate remedy if the magistrate or judge in issuing a warrant was misled by information in an affidavit that the affiant knew was false or would have known was false except for his reckless disregard of the truth. The exception we recognize today will also not apply in cases where the issuing magistrate wholly abandoned his judicial role; in such circumstances, no reasonably trained officer should rely on the warrant. Nor would an officer manifest objective good faith in relying on a warrant based on an affidavit "so lacking in indicia of probable cause as to render official belief in its existence entirely unreasonable." Finally, depending on the circumstances of the particular case, a warrant may be so facially deficient—i.e., in failing to particularize the place to be searched or the things to be seized—that the executing officers cannot reasonably presume it to be valid....

When the principles we have enunciated today are applied to the facts of this case, it is apparent that the judgment of the Court of Appeals cannot stand.... In the absence of an allegation that the magistrate abandoned his detached and neutral role, suppression is appropriate only if the officers were dishonest or reckless in preparing their affidavit or could not have harbored an objectively reasonable belief in the existence of probable cause.... Officer Rombach's application for a warrant clearly was supported by much more than a "bare bones" affidavit. The affidavit related the results of an extensive investigation and, as the opinions of the divided panel of the Court of Appeals make clear, provided evidence sufficient to create disagreement among thoughtful and competent judges as to the existence of probable cause. Under these circumstances, the officers' reliance on the magistrate's determination of probable cause was objectively reasonable, and application of the extreme sanction of exclusion is inappropriate.

Accordingly, the judgment of the Court of Appeals is reversed.

CONCURRING OPINION

Justice Blackmun, concurring. . . .

I join the Court's opinion in the case, because I believe that the rule announced today advances the legitimate interests of the criminal justice system without sacrificing the individual rights protected by the Fourth Amendment. I write separately, however, to underscore what I regard as the unavoidably provisional nature of today's decisions.

As the Court's opinion in this case makes clear, the Court has narrowed the scope of the exclusionary rule because of an empirical judgment that the rule has little appreciable reliance on search warrants. . . . What must be stressed, however, is that any empirical judgment about the effect of the exclusionary rule in a particular class of cases necessarily is a provisional one. By their very nature, the assumptions on which we proceed today cannot be cast in stone. . . . If it should emerge from experience that, contrary to our expectations, the good-faith exception to the exclusionary rule results in a material change in police compliance with the Fourth Amendment, we shall have to reconsider what we have undertaken here. . . .

If a single principle may be drawn from this Court's exclusionary rule decisions, it is that the scope of the exclusionary rule is subject to change in light of changing judicial understanding about the effects of the rule outside the confines of the courtroom. It is incumbent on the Nation's law enforcement officers, who must continue to observe the Fourth Amendment in the wake of today's decision, to recognize the double-edged nature of that principle.

DISSENT

Justice Brennan, with whom Justice Marshall joins, dissenting.

Ten years ago, I expressed that the Court's decision "may signal that a majority of my colleagues have positioned themselves to reopen the door [to evidence secured by official lawlessness] still further and abandon altogether the exclusionary rule in search-and-seizure cases." Since then, in case after case, I have witnessed the Court's gradual but determined strangulation of the rule. It now appears that the Court's victory over the Fourth Amendment is complete. . . . [T]oday the Court sanctions the use in the prosecution's case in chief of illegally obtained evidence against the individual whose rights have been violated—a result that had previously been thought to be foreclosed.

The Court seeks to justify this result on the ground that the "costs" of adhering to the exclusionary rule in cases like those before us exceed the "benefits." But the language of deterrence and of cost/benefit analysis, if used indiscriminately, can have a narcotic effect. It creates an illusion of technical precision and ineluctability. It suggests that not only constitutional principle but also empirical data support the majority's result. When the Court's analysis is examined carefully, however, it is clear that we have not been treated to an honest assessment of the merits of the exclusionary rule, but have instead been drawn into a curious world where the "costs" of excluding illegally obtained evidence loom to exaggerated heights and where the "benefits" of such exclusion are made to disappear with a mere wave of the hand. . . .

. . . [S]ince the Fourth Amendment became part of the Nation's fundamental law in 1791, what the Framers understood then remains true today—that the task of combating crime and convicting the guilty will in every era seem of such critical and pressing concern that we may be lured by the temptations of expediency into forsaking our commitment to protecting individual liberty and privacy. It was for that very reason that the Framers of the Bill of Rights insisted that law enforcement efforts be permanently and unambiguously restricted in order to preserve personal freedoms. In the constitutional scheme they ordained, the sometimes unpopular task of ensuring that the government's enforcement efforts remain within the strict boundaries fixed by the Fourth Amendment was entrusted to the courts. . . .

The Court's decisions over the past decade have made plain that the entire enterprise of attempting to assess the benefits and costs of the exclusionary rule in various contexts is a virtually impossible task for the judiciary to perform honestly or accurately. Although the Court's language in those cases suggests that some specific empirical basis may support its analyses, the reality is that the Court's opinions represent inherently unstable compounds of intuition, hunches, and occasional pieces of partial and often inconclusive data. . . . To the extent empirical data is available regarding the general costs and benefits of the exclusionary rule, it has shown, on the one hand, as the Court acknowledges today, that the costs are not as substantial as critics have asserted in the past, and, on the other hand, that while the exclusionary rule may well have certain deterrent effects, it is extremely difficult to determine with any degree of precision whether the incident of unlawful conduct by police is now lower than it was prior to *Mapp* [*v. Ohio* (1961)]. The Court has sought to turn this uncertainty to its advantage by casting the burden of proof upon proponents of the rule. "Obviously," however, "the assignment of the burden of proof on an issue where evidence does not exist and cannot be obtained is outcome determinative. [The] assignment of the burden is merely a way of announcing a predetermined conclusion."

By remaining within its redoubt of empiricism and by basing the rule solely on the deterrence rationale, the Court has robbed the rule of legitimacy. A doctrine that is explained as if it were an empirical proposition but for which there is only limited empirical support is both inherently unstable and an easy mark for critics. The extent of this Court's fidelity to Fourth Amendment requirements, however, should not turn on such statistical uncertainties. . . . "[P]ersonal liberties are not rooted in the law of averages." Rather than seeking to give effort to the liberties secured by the Fourth Amendment through guesswork about deterrence, the Court should restore to its proper place the principle framed 70 years ago in *Weeks* [*v. United States* (1914)] that an individual whose privacy has been invaded in violation of the Fourth Amendment has a right grounded in that Amendment to prevent the government from subsequently making use of any evidence so obtained.

CASE DISCUSSION

What interests does the good faith exception promote? Should Alberto Leon go free because the government violated his rights? Why? Why not? Does he really go free if the evidence is excluded? Explain. What remedy, if any, would you provide for Leon in this case?

Consider the statistics cited in the *Leon* Court's note on empirical research. Do they indicate that the costs of the exclusionary rule are too high? Defend your answer. According to Thomas Y. Davies, who studied the exclusionary rule in California and whose research the Court cites, prosecutors almost never reject cases involving violent crimes because of the exclusionary rule. He found that prosecutors rejected for prosecution 0.06 percent of homicide, 0.09 percent of forcible rape, and 0.13 percent of assault cases because of illegal searches and seizures. They rejected less than .5 percent of theft cases and only 0.19 percent of burglary cases. The largest number of cases rejected for prosecution due to illegal searches and seizures involved the possession of small amounts of drugs. Other studies reached similar results—that is, the exclusionary rule affects only a small portion of cases, and of those small number most are not crimes against persons. Furthermore, all cases rejected or lost involving illegally obtained evidence are not lost because of the exclusionary rule. For example, Peter F. Nardulli found that in some cases of drug possession, the police were not interested in successful prosecution but rather in getting contraband off the street.[26]

A number of states have declined to adopt the good faith exception to their own constitutions. In *Stringer v. State*, the Mississippi Supreme Court reasoned that under the Mississippi Constitution, "the fundamental flaw in [*United States v.*] *Leon* is that its new 'insight' — that in the type of cases we are concerned with it is the issuing magistrate who violates the accused's Fourth Amendment rights, not the officer — suggests a *greater* need for the exclusionary rule, not a lesser one." The court concluded that the exclusionary rule is "our only practicable means of getting the attention of the issuing magistrates who disregard the rights of persons to be free of searches except under warrants issued on probable cause." Do you agree with the Mississippi Supreme Court? Explain.[27]

Standing

Not everyone has **standing**—the right to seek in court the exclusion of evidence or other remedies for the violation of constitutional rights. Defendants have standing to challenge only the violation of their own constitutional rights, not somebody else's. Standing is fairly easy to determine in cases involving violations of the Fifth Amendment right against self-incrimination and of the Sixth Amendment right to counsel. Only the person who makes an illegal confession or who acted without the advice of counsel can assert the claim. However, Fourth Amendment violations are not so straightforward, because one illegal search and seizure can affect the rights of several people. Prior to 1978, the Supreme Court followed a two-step procedure in standing cases. First, it determined whether those who asserted violations fit into three broad categories of people having standing to claim Fourth Amendment violations. They included anyone who

1. had a possessory interest in the premises searched

2. had a possessory interest in the items seized

3. was legitimately present at the scene of the search

If the person who asserted the right had standing to claim the right, the Court moved on to the second stage: it determined whether defendants had a "reasonable expectation of privacy" in the areas searched or in the items seized. For example, in *United States v. Jeffers*, Jeffers stashed his drugs in his aunts' hotel room, for which he had a key and permission to enter whenever he wished. The Supreme Court ruled that Jeffers had standing because he had a possessory interest in the premises searched and the items seized. Then the Court held that Jeffers had a reasonable expectation of privacy in this place for his stash and therefore standing to challenge its admissibility.[28]

In *Rakas v. Illinois* (1978), the Supreme Court abandoned the two-step process for deciding standing. In *Rakas*, the police stopped a car that they suspected of being the getaway car in a recent robbery. The three defendants were passengers. The police searched the car and found a sawed-off rifle under the front passenger seat and a box of shells in the locked glove compartment. The defendants asserted that any defendant at whom searches are directed has standing to contest the legality of the search, according to what they called a target theory, and that since they were legitimately in the car at the time of the search, they had standing to object to the search. The Supreme Court rejected the target theory, in part because it would unjustifiably extend the exclusionary rule. Then the Court announced the new **one-step rule** for the determination of standing: defendants can seek to exclude evidence from a search or seizure only if their "legitimate expectation of privacy" is violated. Finally, the Court overruled an earlier case holding that legitimate presence on the premises searched *automatically* gave rise to a legitimate expectation of privacy, hence conferring standing to challenge searches and seizures.[29]

OTHER PROCESS REMEDIES

In addition to the exclusionary rule, defendants can rely on the following process remedies to enforce their rights:

1. Motion to dismiss
2. Defense of entrapment
3. Reversible error
4. Expungement of criminal records

Dismissal

Historically, courts did not consider how defendants got to court. The duty of courts was to ensure that proceedings against defendants were properly conducted once defendants had appeared, however they got there. Although the exclusionary rule banned the use of illegally seized evidence to prove guilt, no parallel rule banned courts from asserting jurisdiction over illegally seized persons. The practice of proceeding against defendants who were in court because of illegal seizures generated controversy. Although the United States Supreme Court has not ruled on the point, the Second Circuit Court of Appeals relaxed the rule in the often-cited case *United States v. Toscanino.*

C A S E

Should the Charges Be Dismissed?

United States v. Toscanino
500 F.2d 267 (2d Cir. 1974)

Toscanino was convicted of a narcotics offense and sentenced to up to twenty years in prison and fined $20,000. He appealed. The U.S. Court of Appeals remanded the case to the U.S. District Court for further proceedings. Judge Mansfield wrote the opinion of the court.

FACTS

. . . Toscanino, who is a citizen of Italy, and four others were charged with conspiracy to import narcotics into the United States in violation of 21 U.S.C. §§ 173 and 174 in a one count indictment returned by a grand jury sitting in the Eastern District on February 22, 1973. Toscanino does not question the sufficiency of the evidence or claim any error with respect to the conduct of the trial itself. His principal argument, which he voiced prior to trial and again after the jury verdict was returned, is that the entire proceedings in the district court against him were void because his presence within the territorial jurisdiction of the court has been illegally obtained. He alleged that he had been kidnapped from his home in Montevideo, Uruguay, and brought into the Eastern District only after he had been detained for three weeks of interrogation accompanied by physical torture in Brazil. He offered to prove the following:

On or about January 6, 1973 Francisco Toscanino was lured from his home in Montevideo, Uruguay by a telephone call. This call had been placed by or at the direction of Hugo Campos Hermedia. Hermedia was at that time and still is [a] member of the police in Montevideo, Uruguay. In his effort [and others mentioned below], however, . . . Hermedia was acting ultra vires [beyond the scope of his authority] in that he was the paid agent of the United States government. . . .

. . . The telephone call ruse succeeded in bringing Toscanino and his wife, seven months pregnant at the time, to an area near a deserted bowling alley in the City of Montevideo. Upon their arrival there Hermedia together with six associates abducted Toscanino. This was accomplished in view of Toscanino's terrified wife by knocking him unconscious with a gun and throwing him into the rear seat of Hermedia's car. Thereupon Toscanino, bound and b[l]indfolded, was driven to [the] Uruguayan–Brazilian border by a circuitous route.

At one point during the long trip to the Brazilian border discussion was had among Toscanino's captors as to changing the license plates of the abductor's car in order to avoid detention by the Uruguayan authorities. At another point the abductor's car was abruptly brought to a halt, and Toscanino was ordered to get out. He was brought to an apparently secluded place and told to lie perfectly still or he would be shot then and there. Although his blindfold prevented him from seeing, Toscanino could feel the barrel of the gun against his head and could hear the rumbling noises of what appeared to be [a] Uruguayan military convoy. A short time after the noise of the convoy had died away, Toscanino was placed in another vehicle and whisked to the border. There by pre-arrangement and again at the connivance of the United States government, the car was met by a group of Brazilians who took custody of the body of Francisco Toscanino.

At no time had there been any formal or informal request on the part of the United States of the government of Uruguay for the extradition of Francisco Toscanino nor was there any legal basis to justify this rank criminal enterprise. In fact, the Uruguayan government claims that it had no prior knowledge of the kidnapping nor did it consent thereto and had indeed condemned this kind of apprehension as alien to its laws.

Once in the custody of Brazilians, Toscanino was brought to Porto Allegre where he was held incommunicado for eleven hours. His request to consult with counsel, the Italian Consulate, and his family were all denied. During this time he was denied food and water.

Later that same day Toscanino was brought to Brasilia. . . . For seventeen days Toscanino was incessantly tortured and interrogated. Throughout this entire period the United States government and the United States Attorney for the Eastern District of New York prosecuting this case were aware of the interrogation and did in fact receive reports as to its progress. Furthermore, during this period of torture and interrogation a member of the United States Department of Justice, Bureau of Narcotics and Dangerous Drugs was present at one or more intervals and actually participated in portions of the interrogation. . . . [Toscanino's] captors denied him sleep and all forms of nourishment for days at a time. Nourishment was provided intravenously in a manner precisely equal to an amount necessary to keep him alive. Reminiscent of the horror stories told by our military men who returned from Korea and China, Toscanino was forced to walk up and down a hallway for seven or eight hours at a time. When he could no longer stand he was kicked and beaten but all in a manner contrived to punish without scarring. When he would not answer, his fingers were pinched with metal pliers. Alcohol was flushed into his eyes and nose and other fluids . . . were forced up his anal passage. Incredibly, these agents of the United States government attached electrodes to Toscanino's earlobes, toes, and genitals. Jarring jolts of electricity were shot throughout his body, rendering him unconscious for indeterminate periods of time but again leaving no physical scars.

Finally on or about January 25, 1973 Toscanino was brought to Rio de Janeiro where he was drugged by Brazilian–American agents and placed on Pan American Airways Flight 202 destined for the waiting arms of the United States government. On or about January 26, 1973 he woke in the United States, was arrested on the aircraft, and was brought immediately to Thomas Puccio, Assistant United States Attorney.

At no time during the government's seizure of Toscanino did it ever attempt to accomplish its goal through any lawful channels whatsoever. From start to finish the government unlawfully, willingly and deliberately embarked upon a brazenly criminal scheme violating the laws of three separate countries.

Toscanino's motion for an order vacating the verdict, dismissing the indictment and ordering his return to Uruguay was denied by the district court on

November 2, 1973, without a hearing. Relying principally on the decision of the Supreme Court in *Ker v. Illinois* (1886), the court held that the manner in which Toscanino was brought into the territory of the United States was immaterial to the court's power to proceed, provided he was physically present at the time of trial.

OPINION

In an era marked by a sharp increase in kidnapping activities, both here and broad ... we face the question as we must in the state of the pleadings, of whether a federal court must assume jurisdiction over the person of a defendant who is illegally apprehended abroad and forcibly abducted by government agents to the United States for the purpose of facing criminal charges here. . . .

... [U]nder the so-called *"Ker-Frisbie"* rule, due process was limited to the guarantee of a constitutionally fair trial, regardless of the method by which jurisdiction was obtained over the defendant. Jurisdiction gained through an indisputably illegal act might still be exercised, even though the effect could be to reward police brutality and lawlessness in some cases.

Since *Frisbie* the Supreme Court, in [what] one distinguished legal luminary describes as a "constitutional revolution," has expanded the interpretation of "due process." No longer is it limited to the guarantee of "fair" procedure at trial. In an effort to deter police misconduct, the term has been extended to bar the government from realizing directly the fruits of its own deliberate and unnecessary lawlessness in bringing the accused to trial. . . .

Faced with a conflict between the two concepts of due process, the one being the restricted version found in *Ker-Frisbie* and the other the expanded and enlightened interpretation expressed in more recent decisions of the Supreme Court, we are persuaded that to the extent that the two are in conflict, the *Ker-Frisbie* version must yield. Accordingly, we view the due process as now requiring a court to divest itself of jurisdiction over the person of a defendant where it has been required as the result of the government's deliberate, unnecessary and unreasonable invasion of the accused's constitutional rights. This conclusion represents but an extension of the well-recognized power of federal courts in the civil context to decline to exercise jurisdiction over a defendant whose presence has been secured by force or fraud.

[This case is remanded for further proceedings.]

CASE DISCUSSION

Should it matter how the defendant got to court? Once there, if the proceedings are fair, should the defendant rely on other remedies? Which ones? Does this case demonstrate too much concern for the interest in fair proceedings and not enough for the conviction of the clearly guilty? Why or why not? In your judgment, just how offensive must the government's actions be to require dismissal? Explain.

The government need not permanently drop charges following the dismissal of charges by a court. If police or other enforcement agents secure defendants by lawful arrests, prosecutors can start over in new proceedings not tainted by original unlawful arrests. Of course, police cannot wait outside and arrest defendants as they walk out the courtroom door. Once the police remove the taint of the original arrest, however, proceedings may continue.

The Defense of Entrapment

Entrapment consists of government agents inducing individuals to commit crimes that they otherwise would not commit. Under limited circumstances, entrapment is a defense to crimes—that is, it results in the dismissal of the criminal prosecution generated by the entrapment. The defense of entrapment was not recognized in American courts until the twentieth century. In 1864 the New York Supreme Court explained why courts traditionally rejected the defense:

> Even if inducements to commit crime could be assumed to exist in this case, the allegation of the defendant would be but the repetition of the pleas as ancient as the world, and first interposed in Paradise: "The serpent beguiled me and I did eat." That defense was overruled by the great Lawgiver, and whatever estimate we may form, or whatever judgment pass upon the character or conduct of the tempter, this plea has never since availed to shield crime or give indemnity to the culprit, and it is safe to say that under any code of civilized, not say Christian ethics, it never will.[30]

In 1904 another court summed up this attitude toward entrapment:

> We are asked to protect the defendant, not because he is innocent, but because a zealous public officer exceeded his powers and held out a bait. The courts do not look to see who held out the bait, but to see who took it.[31]

The earlier attitude had its basis in an indifference to government inducements to commit crimes. After all, "once the crime is committed, why should it matter what particular incentives were involved and who offered them?" Attitudes have shifted from indifference to a "limited sympathy" toward entrapped defendants and a growing intolerance of government inducements to entrap otherwise law-abiding people.[32]

The present law of entrapment attempts to balance criminal predisposition and law enforcement practices. That is, it aims to catch the habitual criminal but not at the expense of the otherwise law-abiding person. The entrapment defense did not come about because of the difficulties in apprehending violent criminals or other crimes with complaining victims. Rather, it arose because the police find it particularly difficult to detect consensual crimes or crimes without complaining victims, mainly in cases of illicit drugs, gambling, pornography, prostitution, and official wrongdoing.

The use of government inducement as a law enforcement tool is neither new nor limited to United States. The practice is associated with some highly unsavory characters throughout history and the world. Ancient tyrants and modern dictators alike have relied on government agents to induce innocent people to commit crimes (the infamous *agents provocateurs*) so that these autocrats can silence and destroy their political opponents. From the days of Henry VIII to the era of Hitler, Mussolini, Franco, and Stalin to the dictators of our own time, most of the world's police states have employed government informers to encourage dissidents to admit their disloyalty. Unfortunately, inducement is not simply a tool of dictators in the oppression of their opponents. In all societies and political systems, the tactic creates the risk that law-abiding people will commit crimes that they would not commit in the absence of the inducement. Furthermore, government enticement flouts the essential purposes of government. The great Victorian British Prime Minister William Gladstone wisely admonished government to make it easy to do right and difficult to do wrong. Moreover, inducement to criminality flies in the face of the entreaty of the Lord's Prayer to "lead us not into temptation, but deliver us from evil."[33]

Law enforcement encouragement occurs when officers engage in the following activities:

1. Pretend they are victims

2. Intend to entice suspects to commit crimes

3. Communicate the enticement to suspects

4. Influence the decision to commit crimes[34]

Encouragement requires the simulation of reality. Officers present the opportunity to commit a crime when agents are available to gather evidence to prove the guilt of those who receive the encouragement. Usually, it is not enough for officers to simply present an opportunity, or even to request that targets commit crimes. Officers must *actively* encourage the commission of crimes because most individuals about to commit crimes are wary of strangers. Active encouragement includes such tactics as

- Making repeated requests to commit a crime

- Forming personal relationships with suspects

- Appealing to personal considerations

- Promising benefits from committing the crime

- Supplying contraband

- Helping to obtain contraband[35]

Encouragement becomes entrapment when the encouraging behavior crosses the line from acceptable to *un*acceptable encouragement. **Entrapment** is a *defense* to crime; it is not a constitutional *right*. The U.S. Supreme Court has held that Congress, in the enactment of criminal statutes, did not intend to permit government agents to lure innocent citizens into committing crimes so that government can punish them. However, entrapment is an **affirmative defense.** That means that in order to introduce the defense, defendants have to show some evidence of entrapment. Thereafter, the burden may shift to the prosecution to prove that defendants were not entrapped. The jury — or the judge in trials without juries — decides whether officers in fact entrapped defendants. Until recently in federal courts and in some state courts, defendants who denied that they had committed the crime with which they were charged could not use the entrapment defense.

Subjective and Objective Tests of Entrapment. The majority of state and the federal courts have adopted the **subjective test of entrapment.** The subjective test focuses on the predisposition of defendants to commit crimes. According to this view, only defendants who acted under the following conditions could claim the defense of entrapment:

1. Initially, defendants had no desire to commit crimes.

2. The government induced defendants into criminality.

The crucial question in the subjective test is where the criminal intent originated. If it originated with the defendant, then the government did not entrap the defendant. If it originated with the government, then the government did entrap the defendant. For example, in the leading case of *Sherman v. United States*, Kalchinian, a government informant and undercover agent, met Sherman in a drug treatment center. He struck up a friendship with Sherman and eventually asked Sherman to get him some heroin. Sherman, an addict, first refused. Following persistent begging and pleading that extended over several weeks, Sherman finally relented and supplied Kalchinian with the requested heroin. The police promptly arrested Sherman. The U.S. Supreme Court ruled that the intent originated with the government. Sherman was in treatment for his addiction—hence, hardly predisposed to commit a drug offense, according to the Court.[36]

Once defendants have shown some evidence that the government agent induced the defendant to commit the crime, the government can prove predisposition by indicating one of the following circumstances:

- Prior convictions for similar offenses
- Defendant's willingness to commit similar offenses
- Defendant's display of some criminal expertise in carrying out the offense
- Defendant's ready ability to commit the crime

As the list indicates, proving predisposition can depend on either the character of defendants or their past and present conduct. The United States Supreme Court applied the predisposition test of entrapment in *Jacobson v. United States*.

C A S E

Did the Government Entrap Jacobson?

Jacobson v. United States
503 U.S. 540, 112 S.Ct. 1535,
118 L.Ed.2d 174 (1992)

Keith Jacobson was indicted for violating a provision of the Child Protection Act of 1984 that criminalizes the knowing receipt through the mails of a "visual depiction [that] involves the use of a minor engaging in sexually explicit conduct...." Jacobson asserted the defense of entrapment. He was found guilty after a jury trial. The court of appeals affirmed his conviction. The Supreme Court reversed. Justice White wrote the opinion of the Court, in which Justices Blackmun, Stevens, Souter, and Thomas joined. Justice O'Connor filed a dissenting opinion, in which Chief Justice Rehnquist and Justices Kennedy and Scalia joined.

FACTS

In February 1984, petitioner, a 56-year-old veteran-turned-farmer who supported his elderly father in Nebraska, ordered two magazines and a brochure from a California adult bookstore. The magazines, entitled Bare Boys I and Bare Boys II, contained photographs of nude preteen and teenage boys. The contents of

the magazines startled petitioner, who testified that he had expected to receive photographs of "young men 18 years or older." On cross-examination, he explained his response to the magazines:

PROSECUTOR: ... [Y]ou were shocked and surprised that there were pictures of very young boys without clothes on, is that correct?

JACOBSON: Yes, I was.

PROSECUTOR: Were you offended? ...

JACOBSON: I was not offended because I thought these were a nudist type publication. Many of the pictures were out in a rural or outdoor setting. There was—I didn't draw any sexual connotation or connection with that.

The young men depicted in the magazines were not engaged in sexual activity, and petitioner's receipt of the magazines was legal under both federal and Nebraska law. Within three months, the law with respect to child pornography changed; Congress passed the Act illegalizing the receipt through the mails of sexually explicit depictions of children. In the very month that the new provision became law, postal inspectors found petitioner's name on the mailing list of the California bookstore that had mailed him Bare Boys I and II. There followed, over the next 2 1/2 years, repeated efforts by two Government agencies, through five fictitious organizations and a bogus pen pal, to explore petitioner's willingness to break the new law by ordering sexually explicit photographs of children through the mail.

The Government began its efforts in January 1985 when a postal inspector sent petitioner a letter supposedly from the American Hedonist Society, which in fact was a fictitious organization. The letter included a membership application and stated the Society's doctrine: that members had the "right to read what we desire, the right to discuss similar interests with those who share our philosophy, and finally that we have the right to seek pleasure without restrictions being placed on us by outdated puritan morality." Petitioner enrolled in the organization and returned a sexual attitude questionnaire that asked him to rank on a scale of one to four his enjoyment of various sexual materials, with one being "really enjoy," two being "enjoy," three being "somewhat enjoy," and four being "do not enjoy." Petitioner ranked the entry "[p]re-teen sex" as a two, but indicated that he was opposed to pedophilia.

For a time, the Government left petitioner alone. But then a new "prohibited mail specialist" in the Postal Service found petitioner's name in a file, and in May 1986, petitioner received a solicitation from a second fictitious consumer research company, "Midlands Data Research," seeking a response from those who "believe in the joys of sex and the complete awareness of those lusty and youthful lads and lasses of the neophite [sic] age." The letter never explained whether "neophite" referred to minors or young adults. Petitioner responded: "Please feel free to send me more information. I am interested in teenage sexuality. Please keep my name confidential."

Petitioner then heard from yet another Government creation, "Heartland Institute for a New Tomorrow" (HINT), which proclaimed that it was "an organization founded to protect and promote sexual freedom and freedom of choice. We believe that arbitrarily imposed legislative sanction restricting your sexual freedom should be rescinded through the legislative process." The letter also enclosed a second survey. Petitioner indicated that his interest in "[p]re-teen sex–homosexual" material was above average, but not high. In response to another question, peti-

tioner wrote: "Not only sexual expression but freedom of the press is under attack. We must be ever vigilant to counter attack right wing fundamentalists who are determined to curtail our freedoms."

HINT replied, portraying itself as a lobbying organization seeking to repeal "all statutes which regulate sexual activities, except those laws which deal with violent behavior, such as rape. HINT is also lobbying to eliminate any legal definition of 'the age of consent.'" These lobbying efforts were to be funded by sales from a catalog to be published in the future "offering the sale of various items which we believe you will find to be both interesting and stimulating." HINT also provided computer matching of group members with similar survey responses; and, although petitioner was supplied with a list of potential "pen pals," he did not initiate any correspondence.

Nevertheless, the Government's "prohibited mail specialist" began writing to petitioner, using the pseudonym "Carl Long." The letter employed a tactic known as "mirroring," which the inspector described as "reflect[ing] whatever the interests are of the person we are writing to." Petitioner responded at first, indicating that his interest was primarily in "male–male items." Inspector "Long" wrote back: "My interests too are primarily male–male items. Are you satisfied with the type of VCR tapes available? Personally, I like the amateur stuff better if its [sic] well produced as it can get more kinky and also seems more real. I think the actors enjoy it more."

Petitioner responded: "As far as my likes are concerned, I like good looking young guys (in their late teens and early 20's) doing their thing together." Petitioner's letters to "Long" made no reference to child pornography. After writing two letters, petitioner discontinued the correspondence. By March 1987, 34 months had passed since the Government obtained petitioner's name from the mailing list of the California bookstore, and 26 months had passed since the Postal Service had commenced its mailings to petitioner. Although petitioner had responded to surveys and letters, the Government had no evidence that petitioner had ever intentionally possessed or been exposed to child pornography. The Postal Service had not checked petitioner's mail to determine whether he was receiving questionable mailings from persons—other than the Government—involved in the child pornography industry. At this point, a second Government agency, the Customs Service, included petitioner in its own pornography sting, "Operation Borderline," after receiving his name on lists submitted by the Postal Service. Using the name of a fictitious Canadian company called "Produit Outaouais," the Customs Service mailed petitioner a brochure advertising photographs of young boys engaging in sex. Petitioner placed an order that was never filled. The Postal Service also continued its efforts in the Jacobson case, writing to petitioner as the "Far Eastern Trading Company Ltd." The letter began:

> As many of you know, much hysterical nonsense has appeared in the American media concerning "pornography" and what must be done to stop it from coming across the borders. This brief letter does not allow us to give much comment; however, why is your government spending millions of dollars to exercise international censorship while tons of drugs, which make yours the world's most crime ridden country, are passed through easily?

The letter went on to say:

> [W]e have devised a method of getting these to you without prying eyes of U.S. Customs seizing your mail. . . . After consultations with American solicitors, we have been advised that once we have posted our material through your system, it cannot be opened for any inspection without authorization of a judge.

The letter invited petitioner to send for more information. It also asked petitioner to sign an affirmation that he was "not a law enforcement officer or agent of the U.S. Government acting in an undercover capacity for the purpose of entrapping Far Eastern Trading Company, its agents or customers." Petitioner responded. A catalogue was sent, and petitioner ordered Boys Who Love Boys, a pornographic magazine depicting young boys engaged in various sexual activities. Petitioner was arrested after a controlled delivery of a photocopy of the magazine. When petitioner was asked at trial why he placed such an order, he explained that the Government had succeeded in piquing his curiosity:

> Well, the statement was made of all the trouble and the hysteria over pornography and I wanted to see what the material was. It didn't describe the—I didn't know for sure what kind of sexual action they were referring to in the Canadian letter. . . .

In petitioner's home, the Government found the Bare Boys magazines and materials that the Government had sent to him in the course of its protracted investigation, but no other materials that would indicate the petitioner collected or was actively interested in child pornography.

Petitioner was indicted for violating 18 U.S.C. §2552(a)(2)(A). The trial court instructed the jury on the petitioner's entrapment defense, petitioner was convicted, and a divided Court of Appeals for the Eighth Circuit, sitting en banc, affirmed, concluding that "Jacobson was not entrapped as a matter of law." We granted certiorari.

OPINION

There can be no dispute about the evils of child pornography or the difficulties that laws and law enforcement have encountered in eliminating it. Likewise, there can be no dispute that the Government may use undercover agents to enforce the law. "It is well settled that the fact that officers or employees of the Government merely afford opportunities or facilities for the commission of the offense does not defeat the prosecution. Artifice and stratagem may be employed to catch those engaged in criminal enterprises." *Sorrells v. United States* (1932); *Sherman v. United States* (1958), *United States v. Russell* (1973). In their zeal to enforce the law, however, Government agents may not originate a criminal design, implant in an innocent person's mind the disposition to commit a criminal act, and then induce commission of the crime so that the Government may prosecute. Where the Government has induced an individual to break the law and the defense of entrapment is at issue, as it was in this case, the prosecution must prove beyond reasonable doubt that the defendant was disposed to commit the criminal act prior to first being approached by Government agents. . . .

Had the agents in this case simply offered petitioner the opportunity to order child pornography through the mails, and petitioner—who must be presumed to know the law—had promptly availed himself of this criminal opportunity, it is unlikely that his entrapment defense would have warranted a jury instruction. But that is not what happened here. By the time petitioner finally placed his order, he had already been the target of 26 months of repeated mailings and communications from Government agents and fictitious organizations. Therefore, although he had become predisposed to break the law by May 1987, it is our view that the Government did not prove that this predisposition was independent and not the product of the attention that the Government had directed at petitioner since January 1985.

The prosecution's evidence of predisposition falls into two categories: evidence developed prior to the Postal Service's mail campaign, and that developed during the course of the investigation. The sole piece of preinvestigation evidence is petitioner's 1984 order and receipt of the Bare Boys magazines. But this is scant if any proof of petitioner's predisposition to commit an illegal act, the criminal character of which a defendant is presumed to know. It may indicate a predisposition to view sexually-oriented photographs that are responsive to his sexual tastes; but evidence that merely indicates a generic inclination to act within a broad range, not all of which is criminal, is of little probative value in establishing predisposition. Furthermore, petitioner was acting within the law at the time he received these magazines. Receipt through the mails of sexually explicit depictions of children for noncommercial use did not become illegal under federal law until May 1984, and Nebraska had no law that forbade petitioner's possession of such material until 1988. Neb.Rev.Stat. §28–813.01 (1989).

Evidence of predisposition to do what once was lawful is not, by itself, sufficient to show predisposition to do what is now illegal, for there is a common understanding that most people obey the law even when they disapprove of it. This obedience may reflect a generalized respect for legality or the fear of prosecution, but for whatever reason, the law's prohibitions are matters of consequence. Hence, the fact that petitioner legally ordered and received the Bare Boys

magazines does little to further the Government's burden of proving that petitioner was predisposed to commit a criminal act. This is particularly true given petitioner's unchallenged testimony that he did not know until they arrived that the magazines would depict minors.

The prosecution's evidence gathered during the investigation also fails to carry the Government's burden. Petitioner's responses to the many communications prior to the ultimate criminal act were at most indicative of certain personal inclinations, including a predisposition to view photographs of preteen sex and a willingness to promote a given agenda by supporting lobbying organizations. Even so, petitioner's responses hardly support an inference that he would commit the crime of receiving child pornography through the mails. Furthermore, a person's inclinations and "fantasies . . . are his own and beyond the reach of the government. . . ." On the other hand, the strong argument inference is that, by waving the banner of individual rights and disparaging the legitimacy and constitutionality of efforts to restrict the availability of sexually explicit materials, the Government not only excited petitioner's interest in sexually explicit materials banned by law but also exerted substantial pressure on petitioner to obtain and read such material as part of a fight against censorship and the infringement of individual rights. . . .

Petitioner's ready response to these solicitations cannot be enough to establish beyond reasonable doubt that he was predisposed, prior to the Government acts intended to create predisposition, to commit the crime of receiving child pornography through the mails. The evidence that petitioner was ready and willing to commit the offense came only after the Government had devoted 2 1/2 years to convincing him that he had or should have the right to engage in the very behavior proscribed by law. Rational jurors could not say beyond a reasonable doubt that petitioner possessed the requisite predisposition prior to the Government's investigation and that it existed independent of the Government's many and varied approaches to petitioner. As was explained in *Sherman*, where entrapment was found as a matter of law, "the Government [may not] pla[y] on the weaknesses of an innocent party and beguil[e] him into committing crimes which he otherwise would not have attempted."

Law enforcement officials go too far when they "implant in the mind of an innocent person the disposition to commit the alleged offense and induce its commission in order that they may prosecute." Like the *Sorrel[l]s* court, we are

> unable to conclude that it was the intention of the Congress in enacting this statute that its processes of detection and enforcement should be abused by the instigation by government officials of an act on the part of persons otherwise innocent in order to lure them to its commission and to punish them.

When the Government's quest for convictions leads to the apprehension of an otherwise law-abiding citizen who, if left to his own devices, likely would have never run afoul of the law, the courts should intervene.

Because we conclude that this is such a case and that the prosecution failed, as a matter of law, to adduce evidence to support the jury verdict that petitioner was predisposed, independent of the Government's acts and beyond a reasonable doubt, to violate the law by receiving child pornography through the mails, we reverse the Court of Appeals' judgment affirming the conviction of Keith Jacobson.

It is so ordered.

DISSENT

Justice O'Connor, with whom the Chief Justice and Justice Kennedy join, and with whom Justice Scalia joins except as to Part II, dissenting.

Keith Jacobson was offered only two opportunities to buy child pornography through the mail. Both times, he ordered. Both times, he asked for opportunities to buy more. He needed no Government agent to coax, threaten, or persuade him; no one played on his sympathies, friendship, or suggested that his committing the crime would further a greater good. In fact, no Government agent even contacted him face-to-face. The Government contends that from the enthusiasm with which Mr. Jacobson responded to the chance to commit a crime, a reasonable jury could

permissibly infer beyond a reasonable doubt that he was predisposed to commit the crime. I agree. . . .

Today, the Court holds that Government conduct may be considered to create a predisposition to commit a crime, even before any Government action to induce the commission of the crime. In my view, this holding changes entrapment doctrine. Generally, the inquiry is whether a suspect is predisposed before the government induces the commission of the crime, not before the Government makes initial contact with him. There is no dispute here that the Government's questionnaires and letters were not sufficient to establish inducement; they did not even suggest that Mr. Jacobson should engage in any illegal activity. . . . Yet the Court holds that the Government must prove not only that a suspect was predisposed to commit the crime before the opportunity to commit it arose, but also before the Government came on the scene.

The rule that preliminary Government contact can create a predisposition has the potential to be misread by lower courts as well as criminal investigators as requiring that the Government must have sufficient evidence of a defendant's predisposition before it ever seeks to contact him. Surely the Court cannot intend to impose such a requirement, for it would mean that the Government must have a reasonable suspicion of criminal activity before it begins an investigation, a condition that we have never before imposed.

The Court denies that its new rule will affect run-of-the-mill sting operations, and one hopes that it means what it says. Nonetheless, after this case, every defendant will claim that something the Government agent did before soliciting the crime "created" a predisposition that was not there before. For example, a bribe taker will claim the description of the amount of money available was so enticing that it implanted a disposition to accept the bribe later offered. A drug buyer will claim that the description of the drug's purity and effects was so tempting that it created the urge to try it for the first time. . . .

The crux of the Court's concern in this case is that the Government went too far and "abused" the "processes of detection and enforcement" by luring an innocent person to violate the law. Consequently, the Court holds that the Government failed to prove beyond a reasonable doubt that Mr. Jacobson was predisposed to commit the crime. It was, however, the jury's task, as the conscience of the community, to decide whether or not Mr. Jacobson was a willing participant in the criminal activity here or an innocent dupe. The jury is the traditional "defense against arbitrary law enforcement." . . . There is no dispute that the jury in this case was fully and accurately instructed on the law of entrapment, and nonetheless found Mr. Jacobson guilty. Because I believe there was sufficient evidence to uphold the jury's verdict, I respectfully dissent.

CASE DISCUSSION

What specific facts demonstrate that the government induced Keith Jacobson to order the child pornography? What evidence demonstrates that Jacobson was predisposed to commit the crime? Why did the Court reverse the conviction even though the jury convicted him? What does the dissent mean when it says that the majority has changed the law of entrapment? Do you agree with news stories following the Court's decision saying that the decision ties the hands of law enforcement officers? Defend your answer.

Decision Point

A man on trial in federal court for distributing cocaine claimed that he was entrapped by an old high school friend, who, unknown to the defendant, was a government informant. The informant repeatedly asked the defendant to get him some cocaine. The man finally agreed. The government offered proof that the man, now twenty-five, had been convicted of distributing a small amount of cocaine when he was nineteen, that he was able to obtain a quarter ounce of cocaine quickly and with no difficulty, and that when he transferred the cocaine to the informant he was cool, smooth, relaxed, and confident. The jury rejected the entrapment defense and convicted the defendant.

A minority of courts have adopted an **objective test of entrapment.** The objective test of entrapment focuses not on the predisposition of defendants but instead on the actions that government agents take to induce individuals to commit crimes. According to the objective government inducing test, if the government engages in conduct that would induce an "ordinar[ily] law-abiding" citizen to commit the crime, the court should dismiss the case. This test is a prophylactic rule aimed to deter "unsavory police methods."[37]

Due Process and Entrapment. Defendants do not have a constitutional right against entrapment, but government conduct in rooting out crime may be so outrageous that it violates due process. In those circumstances, according to Justice William Rehnquist, speaking for a plurality in *Hampton v. United States*, the remedy is not to release the defendant predisposed to commit a crime but to sanction the law enforcement officer's misconduct. However, a majority of the Court did not accept this view. Justice Lewis Powell, in a concurring opinion with which the dissenters agreed, argued that defendants should have available the defense of entrapment in cases of severe police "overreaching," despite defendants' predisposition to commit the crime. According to Justice Powell,

The plurality thus says that the concept of fundamental fairness inherent in the guarantee of due process would never prevent the conviction of a predisposed defendant, regardless of the outrageousness of police behavior in light of the surrounding circumstances. I do not understand *[United States v.] Russell* or earlier cases delineating the predisposition-focused defense of entrapment to have gone so far.[38]

D e c i s i o n   P o i n t

1. An undercover agent for the FBI, with the knowledge of other federal agents, developed a sexual relationship with a target. After developing the relationship, she asked the target to sell drugs to some "friends" who, unknown to the target, were also FBI agents. The Ninth Circuit Court of Appeals said that it saw "no principled way to identify a fixed point along the continuum from casual physical contact to intense physical bonding beyond which the relationship becomes 'shocking' when entertained by an informant." The court rejected the due process claim.[39]

2. Narcotics agents offered a five-year-old child $5 to tell where her mommy hid her heroin. The court rejected the due process claim.[40]

3. Defendant's friend and former brother-in-law, an informer, persuaded defendant over a period of time to go in on a drug deal. The informer claimed that he desperately needed money to care for himself and his family. The court denied the defense of entrapment.[41]

4. An undercover agent told defendant that he worked for a dentist whose son was an addict. Because of a change in the law, the dentist could no longer write prescriptions for narcotics to supply his son. The officer said his boss needed to get good heroin off the street because the son "was in pretty bad shape [and they] didn't think he would live very long." After twenty requests, defendant purchased narcotics and resold them to the undercover agent without a profit. A majority of the court upheld the conviction.[42]

5. Which of the following police activities violate due process?
   a. They arrange for sales of drugs to other agents.
   b. They assist in illegally importing drugs.
   c. They threaten buyers in their role as drug dealers.
   d. They assist the manufacture of illegal drugs.

None, according to various lower federal courts.

Federal law enforcement agencies usually limit encouragement tactics to consensual crimes. However, local law enforcement agencies have expanded their reliance on encouragement in order to combat street mugging. One ploy uses decoys who pretend to be drunk. They lie down with money visibly protruding from their pockets, hence inviting would-be muggers to take the money. This ploy was used in *Oliver v. State*. Disguised as a vagrant in an old Marine Corps jacket, the decoy officer slumped against a palm tree, pretending to be intoxicated and asleep. His associates concealed themselves nearby. The decoy prominently displayed a ten-dollar bill, positioning it to protrude from the left breast pocket of his jacket. This was done, the decoy later testified, "to provide an opportunity for a dishonest person to prove himself."

Oliver, who had the misfortune to come walking down the street, saw the decoy and evidently felt moved to assist him. Shaking and nudging the decoy with his foot, Oliver attempted to warn the decoy that the police would arrest him if he did not move on. The decoy did not respond, and Oliver stepped away. Up to this point, Oliver had shown no disposition whatever to commit any criminal act. Then Oliver saw the ten-dollar bill protruding from the decoy's pocket. He reached down and took it. "Thanks, home boy," he said. Thereupon, he was arrested by the decoy and two other officers.[43]

Reversible Error

The process remedies discussed above—the exclusionary rule, dismissal, and entrapment—are all directed and are available almost exclusively against police misconduct. But what about prosecutors', judges', and defense attorneys' misconduct? The remedy against them, apart from removing them by impeachment or denying them reelection, is generally restricted to reversing convictions based on their errors. Many appeals not based on the exclusionary rule charge errors by judges, prosecutors, and defense counsel. Sometimes, appellate courts reverse or overturn lower courts' decisions. Errors in proceedings that result in reversals are called **reversible errors.** Reversible errors affect the outcome of a case. If, for example, a judge makes a mistake and instructs the jury that murder does not require an intention to kill and the jury convicts a defendant of murder when the defendant was only negligent, the error is reversible because negligently killing another person does not constitute murder.

Harmless errors do not affect the outcome of a case; hence, they do not require reversal. For example, if the court admitted illegally seized evidence but sufficient additional evidence existed to convict the defendant, admitting the illegal evidence would not affect the outcome of the case; therefore, the resulting harmless error does not require reversal. The Supreme Court does not review many cases involving reversible error. The intermediate appellate courts review most of these cases.

Expungement of Arrest Records

A basic principle in American justice is that citizens are innocent until proven guilty. But how many people bother to sort out in their minds what *guilty* really means? Do they distinguish among conviction, indictment, arrest, and merely bringing in for questioning? People often suffer intrusions and deprivations after an arrest, even if no further actions follow. For example, employment applications frequently ask if applicants have ever been arrested, and police keep arrest records for use in future investigations.

Expungement—the removal of records from official files—offers one remedy for these injuries. The U.S. Supreme Court has not ruled on the constitutional requirements, if any, of expungement, although all nine justices joined in a decision that FBI "rap sheets" are never subject to disclosure under the Freedom of Information Act. However, the Pennsylvania Supreme Court reviewed an expungement order under the Pennsylvania expungement statute in *Commonwealth v. D.M.*

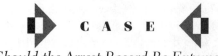

C A S E

Should the Arrest Record Be Expunged?

Commonwealth v. D.M.
695 A.2d 770 (Penn. 1997)

Appellee, a schoolteacher, was tried for indecent assault and corrupting the morals of a minor, and was acquitted in a bench trial in a Philadelphia municipal court. He petitioned for expunction of his arrest record, which was granted by the court of common pleas. The Commonwealth appealed. The Superior Court affirmed. The Commonwealth appealed. The Pennsylvania Supreme Court affirmed. Flaherty, Chief Justice.

FACTS

Appellee, D.M., was employed as a substitute music teacher at a middle school in the Philadelphia school district. On February, 21, 1992, an incident occurred between appellee and a student. During the first period of the day, appellee was assigned a class consisting of students with disciplinary, social, and academic problems. During the first period, four students volunteered to assist appellee in cleaning and straightening up the classroom and office during a later period. The complainant, an eleven-year-old girl, and three other students arrived in the classroom during the third period. When they arrived, appellee was seated in his office, which had a door to the classroom and a large window which formed part of the wall between the office and the classroom. Appellee assigned the complainant to straighten up papers in his office while the other girls were to straighten up the classroom. Seated at his desk, appellee could see the girls in the classroom behaving disruptively, so he got up, passed behind the complainant in the two feet of space between the desk and the wall, and entered the classroom to control the girls.

The complainant testified that appellee touched her breast area and pushed up against her buttocks with his erect penis for several seconds when he left the office. She also testified that he apologized at the end of the class period, asking her not to mention it to anyone because he needed his job. Appellee testified

categorically that he did not touch the girl inappropriately, and that he inadvertently bumped into her with his left hip on the way out of the office because the space was so confined. He testified that he thought nothing of it because his attention was focused on the girls misbehaving in the classroom. Only later in the period, when the complainant told him, "What you did was wrong," did he remember the incident and apologize. The defense called seven character witnesses who testified that appellee had a reputation for veracity and for being a law-abiding citizen.

After hearing closing arguments by counsel, the court delivered the following verdict:

> The court finds this case most difficult. Independently I find each witness to be credible. You can say how can he do that? Well, I'm impressed with both witnesses. Even though there is of course divergence in some of the story. The standard is beyond a reasonable doubt. I realize both witnesses are of a credible nature. The law is that character witnesses alone can create a reasonable doubt. And in this case a deciding factor [is] the character witnesses who have created a reasonable doubt in my mind. Therefore, I find you not guilty.

A month after this acquittal, appellee petitioned the court of common pleas to expunge his arrest record. Following a hearing, the court granted the petition. The court stated:

> I am going to grant it. He was found not guilty at trial. The defendant was found not guilty at trial after a full trial. We don't know the reason for this not guilty, presumably it's because the Commonwealth witnesses were not believed. The Commonwealth had an opportunity to fairly address the issue in the case, factual issue, present them and they had their day in court. A full day in court and there was a resolution by the finding of the not guilty. There is nothing

else remaining other than the fact that there is an allegation which has been proven—not been proven rather, not been proven which is what this country is all about.

In its written opinion in support of the expungement order, the court quoted the factors set forth in *Commonwealth v. Wexler*, 494 Pa. 325, 330, 431 A.2d 877, 879 (1981). The court held that the Commonwealth did not sustain its burden of overcoming appellee's interest in expungement following his acquittal. Part of its reasoning was: "The stigma of an arrest for indecent assault and corrupting the morals of a minor is uniquely disproportionate to the [ease] with which such an accusation can be made."

On appeal, the en banc Superior Court affirmed the expungement order. The Superior Court's application of *Wexler*, supra, is not entirely clear. In discussing *Wexler*, the court stated:

While it is true that *Wexler* espouses a balancing test that in some cases would include some reconsideration of the "strength of the Commonwealth's case" and other trial factors, several aspects of the decision deserve consideration. 1) *Wexler* was dealing with expunction of records of petitioners whose criminal liability was extinguished by *nol pros* and not, as here, by acquittal at trial. 2) The approved language by Judge Spaeth in *Iacino* was from a concurring opinion with one joinder and was also from a case where non-culpability was not established by verdict (*nolle prosse* after suppression of evidence).

. . . We must be mindful that the law offers no greater absolution to an accused than acquittal of the charges, and that expunction of an arrest record, after being found not guilty, is not a matter of judicial clemency. Under these circumstances, the courts should not undertake to carve out exceptions to the basic proposition that expunction should follow acquittal.

We reiterate the authority of *Wexler* and the balancing test approved therein as the means of deciding petitions to expunge the records of all arrests which are terminated without convictions except in cases of acquittals. *Wexler* set forth relevant factors, neither an exclusive nor an exhaustive catalogue, for an expungement court to consider:

These include the strength of the Commonwealth's case against the petitioner, the reasons the Commonwealth gives for wishing to retain the records, the petitioner's age, criminal record, and employment history, the length of time that has elapsed between the arrest and the petition to expunge, and the specific adverse consequences the petitioner may endure should expunction be denied.

The Superior Court opinion in this case distinguished the *Wexler* decision on the basis that *Wexler* involved the termination of a prosecution by *nol pros*, whereas this case involved an acquittal by the fact-finder following a trial. This court has never addressed an expungement in the context of an acquittal. We hold, in agreement with the reasoning of the Superior Court, that the *Wexler* balancing is unnecessary, indeed inappropriate, when a petitioner has been tried and acquitted.

The problem is in attempting to apply the first factor of *Wexler*—the strength of the Commonwealth's case against the petitioner—after a trial which resulted in a verdict of acquittal. We regard it as improper to go behind a verdict of acquittal and purport to assess the strength of the prosecution's case. A defendant enters a trial cloaked in the presumption of innocence and when the fact-finder reaches a verdict of acquittal, there is no justification to search for reasons to undermine the verdict. Such a defendant has achieved the strongest vindication possible under our criminal tradition, laws, and procedures; we hold that he is entitled to expunction of the arrest record.

All the factors listed in *Wexler*, and similar additional considerations, should be evaluated in expunction cases which are terminated without conviction for reasons such as *nolle prosequi* or ARD. The consequences of retention of an arrest record may be affected by the provisions of the Criminal History Record Information Act, 18 Pa.C.S. § 9101 et seq., effective January 1, 1980. This statute may affect the balancing of interests pertaining to expungement. The statute provides some, but not all, of the protection petitioners seek through expungement of arrest records.

For instance, 18 Pa.C.S. § 9121(b)(2) forbids criminal history record-keeping agencies from disseminating to an individual or noncriminal justice agency any record of an arrest which did not result in a conviction if it is more than three years old. Title 18 Pa.C.S. § 9124(b)(1) forbids licensing and certification boards from even considering arrests not resulting in convictions, regardless of their age, when acting on an application for a license, certificate, or permit. Title 18 Pa.C.S. § 9125 forbids any employer from denying employment on the basis of an arrest not resulting in conviction. Title 18 Pa.C.S. §§ 9181 and 9183 provide sanctions for violation of the statute, including administrative discipline, injunctive relief, actual damages, attorney's fees, costs of litigation, and punitive damages.

These protections in the criminal history record statute may reduce the adverse effect of retaining an arrest record in some cases. In cases of acquittal, however, we hold that a petitioner is automatically entitled to the expungement of his arrest record.

The order of the Superior Court is affirmed.

DISSENT

Newman, Justice, dissenting.

I respectfully disagree with the Majority Opinion that a petitioner is automatically entitled to the expungement of his or her arrest record following an acquittal. Instead, I would apply the balancing factors set forth in *Commonwealth v. Wexler*, 494 Pa. 325, 431 A.2d 877 (1981), even for an acquittal. Here, after weighing the Commonwealth's interest in preserving Appellee D.M.'s arrest record and his interest in expungement, I would deny his request for expungement. Therefore, I respectfully dissent.

With regard to expungement, the Criminal History Record Information Act (the Act), 18 Pa.C.S. § 9101 et seq., provides in part:

(a) Specific proceedings.—Criminal history record information shall be expunged in a specific criminal proceeding when:
(1) No disposition has been received or, upon request for criminal history record information, no disposition has been recorded in the reposi-

tory within 18 months after the date of arrest and the court of proper jurisdiction certifies to the director of the repository that no disposition is available and no action is pending. Expungement shall not occur until the certification from the court is received and the director of the repository authorizes such expungement; or
(2) A court order requires that such nonconviction data be expunged.
(b) Generally.—Criminal history record information may be expunged when:
(1) An individual who is the subject of the information reaches 70 years of age and has been free of arrest or prosecution for ten years following final release from confinement or supervision; or
(2) An individual who is the subject of the information has been dead for three years.
* * *
(f) District attorney's notice.—The court shall give ten days prior notice to the district attorney of the county where the original charge was filed of any applications for expungement under the provisions of (a)(2). 18 Pa.C.S. § 9122.

Thus, although the statute strictly limits expungement of records following a conviction, 18 Pa.C.S. § 9122(b)(1),(2), it provides no guidelines for expungement of nonconviction data. However, by permitting expungement of nonconviction data pursuant to a court order, 18 Pa.C.S. § 9122(a)(2), the legislature contemplated judicial review of expungement requests where the prosecution results in an acquittal. If, as the Majority proclaims, expungement is automatic upon acquittal, judicial review of expungement petitions, as expressly provided in the Act, is reduced to a mere formality in the case of an acquittal.

Also, a rule of automatic expungement following an acquittal is inconsistent with our decision in *Wexler*, in which this Court held that:

[i]n determining whether justice requires expungement, the Court in each particular case, must balance the individual's right to be free from the harm attendant to the maintenance of the record against the Commonwealth's interest in preserving such records. . . .

We clarified that if, in the underlying prosecution, "the Commonwealth does not bear its burden of proof beyond a reasonable doubt . . . or admits that it is unable to bear its burden of proof . . . the Commonwealth must bear the burden of justifying why the arrest record should not be expunged." *Wexler* thus anticipated that where, as here, a defendant was acquitted because the Commonwealth failed to establish the charges beyond a reasonable doubt, the Commonwealth may successfully defeat expungement by proffering compelling evidence justifying the retention of the arrest record. Expungement is not, therefore, automatic in the case of an acquittal pursuant to *Wexler*.

The factors, outlined in *Wexler,* that courts should consider in determining each party's respective interests include: (1) the strength of the Commonwealth's case against the petitioner; (2) the reasons given by the Commonwealth for retaining the records; (3) the petitioner's age, criminal record, and employment history; (4) the length of time that has elapsed between the arrest and the petition to expunge; and (5) the specific adverse consequences that the petitioner may endure should expungement be denied.

Applying these factors in *Wexler*, we ordered expungement of the petitioner's arrest record where, in the underlying action, the trial court granted the prosecution's petition to *nol pros* the informations against him. Specifically, in that case, Martin Wexler and his minor daughter were arrested following a search of his residence that disclosed the presence of marijuana and drug paraphernalia in his daughter's bedroom. After his daughter entered into a consent decree on the drug charges lodged against her, the Commonwealth filed a petition to *nol pros* the charge of corrupting a minor lodged against him. The Commonwealth averred in its petition that Wexler's activities "will not give rise" to the charge pending against him. The court granted the Commonwealth's petition. Wexler then filed a petition to expunge his arrest record. At the expungement hearing, the assistant district attorney stated that "we felt that we could not prove . . . [Wexler] at this time guilty beyond a reasonable doubt. . . ." We concluded that these circumstances placed a heavy burden on the Commonwealth to justify retention of his arrest record. The Com-

monwealth however, failed to advance any reason, beyond its suggestion that Wexler should have known of his daughter's drug dealing, in support of retaining his record. We emphasized that the Commonwealth failed to provide any analysis of Wexler's particular case or cite any special facts justifying retention of the record. Therefore, we held that the Commonwealth did not meet its burden of showing why retention of the arrest record was necessary.

In contrast, I believe that the Commonwealth met its burden of establishing a compelling law enforcement interest in retaining Appellee's arrest record here. Appellee is a substitute school teacher who was accused of indecent assault and corrupting the morals of an eleven-year-old female student. Although the charges remained unproven at trial, Appellee never challenged the validity of his arrest on those charges. Further, and more significantly, the trial court found the complainant to be credible. R.R. at 89a. She testified that Appellee pressed his penis up against her backside as she bent over arranging papers on his desk. This alleged sexual contact occurred while the complainant was alone with Appellee, cleaning his office, pursuant to his request. Persuaded, however, by the testimony of Appellee and his character witnesses, the trial court found that the Commonwealth had not established the charges beyond a reasonable doubt.

Although an acquittal is the strongest exoneration available to an accused pursuant to our criminal laws, I do not believe that it mandates expungement in this case. Because the trial court credited the complainant's testimony, it cannot be said that the Commonwealth lacked a strong case. Additionally, as of this appeal, the School District of Philadelphia still employs Appellee. As argued by the Commonwealth, Pennsylvania has a powerful interest as *parens patriae* in protecting the welfare of minors generally, and particularly when those children are in attendance at public schools. The general public places great trust in public school teachers, who like Appellee, exercise extraordinary control over their students during school hours. It is in society's best interest to make available to a school district any information that may indicate the propensity of an employee or potential employee to commit serious crimes against minor students. This interest is particularly strong in the case of alleged sexual abuse, which when unaccompanied by physical evidence, as here, is entirely dependent upon credibility determinations.

As previously stated, the trial court found the complainant's allegations of sexual abuse credible, but ultimately found the Commonwealth had not proven the charges beyond a reasonable doubt. However, with his arrest record expunged, Appellee is free to seek employment elsewhere in the Commonwealth without any additional scrutiny or oversight. Moreover, if he is ever again accused of sexual misconduct, law enforcement authorities will discover an unblemished record. Should a future charge of sexual misconduct allege similar behavior, the authorities will have no basis to evaluate a possible *modus operandi*.

Conversely, I can discern no real harm to Appellee attendant to the retention of his arrest record. Because Appellee filed his petition to expunge only one month after his acquittal, he severely inhibits review of his post-arrest history to determine whether expungement is warranted. However, the most salient feature of Appellee's post-arrest circumstances is his continued employment as a school teacher. Thus, despite the presumed stigma of a criminal arrest, the retention of Appellee's arrest record has not impeded his pursuit of a livelihood. Moreover, contrary to Appellee's assertion, a denial of expungement will not forever "shackle" him to unproven charges of indecent assault and corrupting the morals of a minor. The Criminal History Record Information Act provides ample protection against unwarranted dissemination of his arrest record to noncriminal justice agencies and individuals. Specifically, the Act precludes law enforcement authorities from disseminating to such parties information relating to criminal proceedings where three (3) years have elapsed from the date of arrest, no conviction has occurred, and no proceedings seeking a conviction are pending. 18 Pa.C.S. § 9121(b)(2). Further, when determining an application for licensing, certification, registration or permission to engage in a trade, profession or occupation, no Commonwealth board or department may consider records of an arrest that did not result in a conviction. 18 Pa.C.S. § 9124. Any person or agency who violates these strictures is subject to sanctions including administrative discipline and civil penalties. 18 Pa.C.S. §§ 9181, 9183.

Where Appellee continues in his employment as a public school teacher despite a credible accusation of indecent assault by a minor student, and the Criminal History Record Information Act severely limits the dissemination and use of his arrest record, I would deny his petition for expungement.

Castille, J., joins in this dissenting opinion.

CASE DISCUSSION

Identify and describe the standard for allowing expungement decided by the majority and the standard favored by the dissent. What reasons does the majority give for its decision? What objections does the dissent make to the majority decision? What reasons does the dissent give for its standard? Which do you favor? Why?

Decision Point

"Ennis C. Allen, Jr. was indicted and tried in a court of the State of North Carolina on charges relating to the possession and manufacture of heroin. The arrest information, including fingerprint samples, was entered in the North Carolina computerized criminal files and forwarded to the identification division of the Federal Bureau of Investigation. The FBI fed the information into the National Crime Information Center's interstate identification index. Thereafter, Allen was tried and acquitted. Information to that effect was entered into the North Carolina file and the FBI index. Allen had previously been a federal employee and, following his arrest and trial, made unsuccessful attempts to secure federal employment. In one instance, matters went so far that he received an indication that his application might well have procured him the job except for the delay occasioned by the presence on his record of the information relating to his arrest and trial.

"There is no assertion on Allen's behalf attacking the constitutional validity of the statutes under which Allen was tried. There was no assertion that in North Carolina a statute mandated destruction of an arrest record. There is no claim made of irregularity in the North Carolina proceedings. There was, indeed, not even a suggestion that the information on file was in any respect inaccurate. It was solely Allen's claim that the bringing of the information about his arrest, trial and acquittal before a prospective employer would have unjust adverse consequences. However, Allen has sought to proceed solely against the record keepers at the North Carolina and the federal level in an attempt to have the truthful information expunged. He received advice that he might seek administrative relief within the federal government by which he could insure himself that the 'derogatory' information was not considered in connection with reviewing his job application. Allen, however, declined to avail himself of that possible remedy. In such cir-cumstances the district court did not abuse its equitable discretion in denying the requested relief of expungement. It is a relief confined to 'exceptional circumstances.' . . .

"In considering . . . [expungement] courts must be cognizant that the power to expunge 'is a narrow one, and should not be routinely used whenever a criminal prosecution ends in an acquittal, but should be reversed for the unusual or extreme case.' Such extreme circumstances have been found and records ordered to be expunged where procedures of mass arrests rendered judicial determination of probable cause impossible, *Sullivan v. Murphy* (1973); where the court determined the sole purpose of the arrests was to harass civil rights workers, *United States v. McLeod* (5th Cir. 1967); where the police misused the police records to the detriment of the defendant, *Wheeler v. Goodman*, (W.D.N.C. 1969); or where the arrest was proper but was based on a statute later declared unconstitutional, *Kowall v. United States* (W.D.Mich. 1971)."[44]

CIVIL ACTIONS:
SUING THE GOVERNMENT

Individuals can sue the government, its agencies, and its agents for their wrongful actions. Individuals who bring these actions, called **plaintiffs,** usually seek one of two remedies:

1. Damages—money to compensate for the violation of their rights
2. Injunctions—court orders requiring government, its agencies, or its agents to do, or stop doing, something that the plaintiffs claim violates their rights.

Lawsuits brought by private plaintiffs against the government, agencies, and agents arise from both federal and state sources.

State Law Sources for Civil Actions

Most actions by public officials that violate the United States Constitution are also state **torts**—that is, they also violate duties imposed on all individuals, for which state law provides a monetary remedy called **damages.** For example, illegal searches and seizures may include all of the following torts, for which plaintiffs can sue for damages under the law of most states:

- wrongful death
- assault
- battery

- false arrest
- false imprisonment
- trespass
- breaking and entering
- burglary

Individual offices are liable for their own torts — that is, private individuals can sue individual police officers and other employees for damages. However, the **doctrine of official immunity** limits the liability of individual criminal justice personnel for their torts. According to this doctrine,

> a public official charged by law with duties which call for the exercise of his judgment or discretion is not personally liable to an individual unless he is guilty of a willful or malicious wrong.[45]

According to the Minnesota Supreme Court, for example, "[t]o encourage responsible law enforcement . . . police are afforded a wide degree of discretion precisely because a more stringent standard could inhibit action." By that reasoning, a police officer was not liable for the death of a small boy killed during a high-speed chase by an officer attempting to apprehend a fleeing shoplifter. The court held that official immunity protected the officer. Otherwise, said the court, officers in the future might hold back in their vigorous enforcement of the law.[46]

The **doctrine of *respondeat superior*** imposes liability on state and local governments and their agencies for the torts of their individual employees. That is, private persons can sue the departments or local governments responsible for the departments for torts committed by employees during the course of their employment. However, not all state courts have adopted the doctrine of *respondeat superior*. States that do not follow this rule grant government units **vicarious official immunity.** Vicarious official immunity allows the government unit to benefit from the official immunity of its employees. To determine whether government units are entitled to the defense of vicarious official immunity, courts apply a **balancing test of local government liability.** This test balances two elements:

1. The need for effective law enforcement
2. The need for protection against the public at risk created by criminal law enforcement

In the same high-speed chase referred to in the last paragraph, the Minnesota Supreme Court applied the balancing test. It found that the need to enforce the criminal law outweighed the risk to the public brought on by the high-speed chase. The municipality was not liable for the death of the boy caused by the high-speed chase because liability would too stringently hamper law enforcement.[47]

Federal Law Sources for Civil Actions

In addition to state tort law, there are two sources of civil actions against the government and its officers:

1. Federal constitutional tort actions
2. Section 1983 actions

According to the United States Supreme Court, officers who violate the constitutional rights of private individuals have committed a **federal constitutional tort.** This action, available only against federal officers, is rarely used. Most actions for violating rights are brought under the federal Civil Rights Act of 1871, also known as the Ku Klux Klan Act, passed following the Civil War. This act allows individuals to sue state and local governments, their agencies, and their agents for violations of the rights guaranteed by the United States Constitution. Suits under the Civil Rights Act are commonly called **Section 1983 actions,** because these actions arise under Chapter 42, §1983, of the United States Code, which provides the following:

> Every person who, under color of any statute, ordinance, regulation, custom, or usage, of any State or Territory, subjects, or causes to be subjected, any citizen of the United States or other person within the jurisdiction thereof to the deprivation of any rights, privileges, or immunities secured by the Constitution and laws, shall be liable to the party injured in an action at law, suit in equity, or other proper proceeding for redress.[48]

According to the United States Supreme Court, *under color* means the "misuse of power, possessed by virtue of state law and made possible only because the wrongdoer is clothed with the authority of state law." The courts have interpreted *under color of any statute, ordinance, regulation, custom, or usage* broadly. In the leading case of *Monroe v. Pape*, plaintiffs brought a §1983 action for damages against the City of Chicago and thirteen Chicago police officers who broke into the plaintiffs' home in the early morning, routed them from bed, and made them stand naked in the living room while the officers ransacked their entire house. On appeal to the United States Supreme Court, the Court held that §1983 not only provided a federal "remedy where state law was inadequate" but also provided "a federal remedy where the state remedy, though adequate in theory, was not available in practice." In the words of Justice Douglas,

> It is no answer that the State has a law which *if enforced* would give relief [emphasis added]. The federal remedy is supplementary to the state remedy, and the latter need not be first sought and refused before the federal one is invoked. Hence the fact that Illinois by its constitution and laws outlaws unreasonable searches and seizures is no barrier to the present suit in federal court.[49]

This does not mean that state and local officers and agencies are liable every time they violate the federal constitutional rights of private individuals. The Supreme Court has created a defense of **qualified immunity** for officers whose actions are "objectively reasonable." Qualified immunity shields officers from "liability for civil damages insofar as their conduct does not violate clearly established statutory or constitutional rights of which a reasonable person would have known." According to the Court,

> Reliance on the objective reasonableness of an official's conduct, as measured by reference to clearly established law, should avoid excessive disruption of government and permit the resolution of many insubstantial claims on summary judgment. On summary judgment, the judge appropriately may determine, not only the currently applicable law, but whether that law was clearly established at the time an action occurred. If the law at that time was not clearly established, an official could not reasonably be expected to anticipate subsequent legal developments, nor could he fairly be said to "know" that the law forbade conduct not previously identified as unlawful. . . . If the law was clearly established, the immunity defense ordinarily should fail, since a reasonably competent public official should know the

law governing his conduct. Nevertheless, if the official pleading the defense claims extraordinary circumstances and can prove that he neither knew nor should have known of the relevant legal standard, the defense should be sustained. . . . [50]

Qualified immunity, according to the Court, strikes a balance "between the interests in vindication of citizens' constitutional rights and in public officials' effective performance of their duties." In view of this balance, Justice Antonin Scalia wrote the following, speaking for the Court in the leading qualified immunity case of *Anderson v. Creighton*, a case in which FBI agents searched the Creightons' home without a warrant and without probable cause, looking for one of the Creightons' relatives:

> It should not be surprising, therefore, that our cases establish that the right the official is alleged to have violated must have been "clearly established:" . . . The contours of the right must be sufficiently clear that a reasonable official would understand that what he is doing violates the right. This is not to say that an official action is protected by qualified immunity unless the very action in question has previously been held unlawful; but it is to say that in the light of pre-existing law the unlawfulness must be apparent. [51]

According to the Court in *Anderson v. Creighton*, the test of "objective reasonableness" strikes the proper balance in §1983 actions by granting qualified immunity if "a reasonable officer *could* have believed" (emphasis added) the action was lawful. The Court conceded that Fourth Amendment law clearly requires both probable cause and a warrant to search homes, except in exigent circumstances (see Chapter 6). So FBI Agent Anderson had clearly conducted an "unreasonable search" of the Creightons' home. But, said the Court, violating the Fourth Amendment does not automatically translate into civil liability under §1983. If Anderson *could* have believed his unreasonable search was reasonable, the search was objectively reasonable for purposes of suing a government agent. Therefore, the Creightons could not prevail in their §1983 action against Anderson. The tongue-twisting and almost comical-sounding result of the objectively reasonable rule is this: a search clearly unreasonable in fact is still objectively reasonable if an officer could have believed the search was reasonable. [52]

The United States Supreme Court is the final interpreter of §1983. However, the vast majority of §1983 cases are decided by the lower federal courts or sometimes in state courts in actions that join individuals, departments, and government units in both §1983 actions and state tort law claims. Most plaintiffs lose their suits whether they sue individual officers, departments, or governments. *Hall v. St. Helena Parish Sheriff's Department and others* is typical of these cases in that it was decided by a lower federal court. Furthermore, the case illustrates how plaintiffs can sue individual officers, their supervisors, and their departments under both the federal Civil Rights Act and state tort law. The case is an exception, however, in that the plaintiff succeeded in his claims. Because he won, the case illustrates how types and amounts of damages are determined. **Compensatory damages** are the amount of money needed to compensate plaintiffs for injuries actually suffered, such as medical bills, wages lost, pain and suffering, and the cost of hiring a lawyer. **Punitive damages** are the amount of money intended to punish defendants for their malicious and intentional wrongdoing. *Hall v. St. Helena Parish Sheriff's Department and others* illustrates all of these complicated issues.

◗ C A S E ◖

Are the Sheriff, the Department, and the Deputies Liable?

Hall v. St. Helena Parish Sheriff's Department, Duncan Bridges, Sheriff, David Lea, and Alton Clark, Jr., and others 668 F.Supp. 535 (M.D.La. 1987)

Cleo Hall brought suit under §1983 against two deputy sheriffs and the sheriff for an unlawful post-arrest beating. The district court entered judgment for Hall and held that (1) the deputy was liable for the unlawful beating, (2) the sheriff was not liable under §1983 but was liable under Louisiana law in his official capacity, (3) punitive damages would be awarded against the deputy in the amount of $100,000, and (4) Hall was entitled to attorney fees in the amount of $5,625. John V. Parker, Chief Judge.

FACTS

On Saturday, February 20, 1982, plaintiff, Cleo Hall, and Fabian Scott, two nineteen year old Negro men who resided in or near Greensburg, Louisiana, were returning home from a job hunting trip to Houston, Texas. They were traveling in plaintiff's 1982 Ford automobile. Both had found employment on a construction job due to start in Houston in about a week. They left Houston fairly early in the morning and alternated driving. On the way, each drank "a couple of beers" and Hall, at least, also drank "some vodka."

Hall and Scott arrived safely in Greensburg in the early afternoon and made a stop at "the malt shop," where they returned a borrowed camera and visited with Mary McCoy and Linda Hurst, neither of whom smelled alcohol on them or noticed anything unusual about either of them.

Somewhere near the hour of 4:00 P.M., Hall and Scott drove north from Greensburg on Louisiana Highway 43 for the purpose of delivering Scott to his home. Hall was driving and as he attempted to make a left turn into a side road, the vehicle went into the roadside ditch. Neither occupant of the vehicle was

injured and the vehicle was not significantly damaged — it was still operable.

A passing motorist reported the accident to the St. Helena Parish sheriff's office. Hall and Scott, with the aid of passers-by, were attempting to get the vehicle out of the ditch when Deputy Alton D. Clark, Jr., Caucasian, arrived to investigate the accident.

Clark testified that he smelled alcohol on the breath of both Hall and Scott and that he, after viewing Hall's driver's license, ordered both to get into and stay in the rear seat of the sheriff's vehicle. Clark testified that he intended to obtain a blood alcohol reading on Hall in order to determine whether he would charge him with operating a vehicle while under the influence of alcoholic beverages. Clark was unsure as to his reason for arresting Scott. Neither Hall nor Scott was informed that he was under arrest or why he was being detained. The accident report indicates that Hall was issued a citation for reckless operation of a vehicle in violation of LSA–R.S. 14:99.

In ten or fifteen minutes, Deputy David Lea, Caucasian, arrived to assist Clark at the scene. Both deputies were acquainted with both young men, who were still seated in the rear of Clark's vehicle. Clark and Lea had both heard a report that a short time before the accident, a "white lady" had been almost run off the road by another vehicle on Highway 43. Lea ascertained from Clark that Hall was the driver of the Hall vehicle and then approached the Clark vehicle where approximately the following colloquy took place (all the words are not necessarily exact but I find as a fact that the tone is accurate):

Lea: "Boy, were you driving that car?"

Hall: "Yes, I was."

Lea: "Why did you run that white lady off the road back there?"

Hall: "I didn't run no white lady off the road."

Lea: "Boy, I ought to beat your ass."

Hall: "If you do, I'll take you to court."

Lea: "Get your black ass out of that car."

As Hall opened the door and put one foot on the ground prior to leaving the vehicle, Lea began hitting him with his fists. After several blows, Hall hit Lea back. Lea stumbled back and drew his pistol which he first pointed at Hall and then used to pistol whip him around the head. Lea hit Hall repeatedly with the barrel of the pistol and after a number of blows, Hall collapsed on the highway in a bloody heap. Lea then proceeded to kick Hall with his booted foot. Hall apparently lost consciousness and an ambulance was summoned. When it arrived, Lea would not permit the attendants to pick Hall up but insisted that Hall get up without assistance.

Hall was taken to the St. Helena Parish Hospital where five lacerations in the temple area on the left side of his head were noted. The lacerations were cleaned and debrided and three lacerations required sutures, a total of seven stitches. Hall was then taken to the parish jail where, shortly thereafter, he fainted and he was then returned to the hospital. Hall remained in the hospital until February 23, 1982, primarily for observation and testing. He was administered pain medication during his stay. Hall complained, in addition to the injuries to his head, of pain in the jaw and left ribs where Lea had kicked him. Skull x-rays disclosed that the skull was not fractured and other x-rays established that there were no bones broken. A brain scan established that there was no brain damage. Dr. J. W. Varnado testified that Hall suffered no permanent injury. Hall claims that he still has headaches and that there is a "knot" in his jaw. During Hall's stay in the hospital, several blood samples were taken from him and, according to the testimony of a forensic scientist at Hall's state court trial, laboratory testing produced results of ".15" and ".14." No explanation of these results were presented to this court.

Dr. Varnado's bill was $100. No evidence was offered as to any other medical expense incurred by Hall.

When Hall was returned to the parish jail from the hospital he found that he was facing a great many charges. Although the evidence offered to this court is sketchy as to precisely what charges were lodged, it seems to be undisputed that they included, simple battery (LSA–R.S. 14:35), reckless driving (LSA–R.S.

14:99), DWI (LSA–R.S. 14:98), resisting an officer (LSA–R.S. 14:108) and public intimidation (LSA–R.S. 14:122). Again, the evidence presented to this court is sketchy but it seems to be undisputed that Hall was placed on trial in state court and that he was convicted of at least public intimidation, although he was apparently found not guilty of DWI. Plaintiff testified that he was convicted of public intimidation "and something else" and that he was sentenced to one year in jail, a fine and to pay the costs of prosecution in the amount of $3,500. Hall further testified that he was later arrested for not paying the costs. No further evidence was offered on this point.

Made defendants in this action are deputies Clark and Lea and Sheriff Duncan Bridges.

This case was held open following the trial in order that plaintiff might obtain the deposition of Sheriff Duncan Bridges. That effort failed, apparently because of the sheriff's health, but the parties have stipulated that if Sheriff Bridges had testified, "he would admit to the following":

(a) Duncan Bridges and the St. Helena Parish Sheriff's Department failed to provide any training to Officer David Lea concerning when to use force and the amount of force to be used on a suspect.

(b) That Officer David Lea had no post recruit training in this area.

(c) After David Lea was found guilty in federal court in violating Mrs. Rena Day's civil rights, Sheriff Bridges failed to discipline, suspend or reprimand Officer Lea or to investigate his actions.

(d) Almost immediately after the plaintiff's arrest, a group of concerned black citizens came to Sheriff Bridges concerning complaints they had about the manner in which the plaintiff was arrested. Sheriff Bridges spoke to the group, but made no further inquiries or investigations concerning the incident.

(e) St. Helena Parish Sheriff's Department at the time of this incident, did not have a policy or did not convey a policy to the deputies of how to handle an arrestee if the arrestee resisted.

There is no evidence that Sheriff Bridges participated in or was even aware of the beating which Lea administered to Hall or that the beating was a result of Lea's implementation of any policy established by the sheriff. Deputies Clark and Lea were both acting under color of state law in the performance of their official duties at the time of Hall's beating on February 20, 1982.

OPINION

This court has jurisdiction under 28 U.S.C. §1343(a)(3), since this is an action brought under 42 U.S.C. §1983 to redress the deprivation, under color of state law, of rights and privileges secured by the Constitution of the United States. Plaintiff also asserts pendent state law claims under Louisiana law.

Plaintiff claims that his arrest by Clark was illegal because no probable cause existed. The ultimate outcome of the prosecution of state court charges against plaintiff is basically irrelevant to the existence of probable cause. It is well settled that in §1983 cases, if an arrest is effected for which the police officer had reasonable cause to arrest on any related statutory provision, an acquittal of the offense charged does not vitiate probable cause for the arrest. Accordingly, if Clark had probable cause to arrest Hall for any charge, prosecuted or not, the initial arrest was lawful.

Deputy Clark had before him a vehicle in the roadside ditch which had left the roadway while the driver was making a left turn in broad daylight in dry weather. Deputy Clark concluded in the accident report that the vehicle was traveling too fast to safely make the turn. The driver smelled of alcohol and there were beer cans and a vodka bottle in the vehicle. These facts are sufficient to justify the initial arrest of Hall for reckless driving, for operation of the vehicle while under the influence of alcohol, or for violation of LSA–R.S. 32:64 which generally prohibits operation of a vehicle at a speed "greater than is reasonable and prudent under the conditions and potential hazards then existing." Thus, Hall's initial arrest by Clark was based upon probable cause and was lawful.

Although the initial arrest be lawful, the Fourteenth Amendment shields the person arrested from post-arrest brutality, "inspired by malice rather than merely careless or unwise excess of zeal so that it amount(s) to an abuse of official power that shocks the conscience." [The Supreme Court has replaced this test with the "objective reasonableness" test outlined in *Graham v. Connor*, excerpted in Chapter 5.]

Here, Lea's deliberate, malicious beating of Hall was completely unwarranted. Hall was seated peacefully in the rear of the vehicle where Clark had instructed him to remain. He was unarmed; he posed no threat of harm to anyone; he posed no threat of imminent attempt to escape. To attack a peacefully secured arrested person is unconscionable. To repeatedly strike an unarmed man in the head with the barrel of a pistol is to invite a skull fracture or other serious injury. Lea clearly violated Hall's Fourteenth Amendment right to be secure in his person and Lea is liable to Hall under 42 U.S.C. §1983. Lea is also liable under general principles of Louisiana tort law for his conduct.

The civil rights claim against Clark is more difficult. Although Clark clearly falsely arrested Scott, the passenger, Scott is not a party to this action and this court has found that Clark's initial arrest of Hall was lawful. Clark has varied his testimony from time to time, both as to what he saw and heard as well as to what happened. There is no evidence, however, that Clark participated in the pistol whipping of Hall, that he was aware of Lea's intentions, or that Clark could have prevented or stopped the beating. Clark's actions (or inactions) simply do not rise to that excess of zeal which shocks the conscience and constitutes a violation of 42 U.S.C. §1983. Accordingly, there will be no recovery against Clark under §1983. Moreover, there is no evidence that would support a state law negligence recovery against Clark.

Plaintiff insists that the sheriff must be held liable under §1983 because of his failure to provide training to Deputy Lea "concerning when to use force and the amount of force to be used on a suspect" (see stipulation), and his failure to investigate the incident involving plaintiff's injury (see stipulation).

A state supervisory official cannot be held for the actions of a subordinate under §1983 solely on the basis of vicarious liability. *Monell v. Dept. of Social Services*, 436 U.S. 658, 98 S.Ct. 2018, 56 L.Ed.2d 611 (1978).

This is not a case where a law enforcement officer was guilty of using excessive force in the course of subduing a person that he was attempting to arrest. Here their arrest had already been effected before Lea arrived at the scene and the person arrested was peacefully seated in the rear of the police vehicle. No adult (and few children) ought to require training that it is wrong to attack without provocation a person already arrested. Lea's egregious conduct in this case was his and his alone. There is no evidence to support a finding that Sheriff Bridges is liable to Hall for failure to train Lea not to attack unarmed arrestees.

There is no evidence in this record that the sheriff ordered the beating of Hall or that it was administered pursuant to any custom, practice or policy instituted by the sheriff. There being no personal or policy involvement of the sheriff, his "failure to investigate" Lea following the beating cannot impose §1983 liability upon him. Liability under §1983 requires personal involvement of the defendant, either by action or preincident approval of a custom or policy. Thus, this record does not support §1983 liability of Sheriff Bridges.

The result is different, however, under the pendent state law claims. Under Louisiana law, a parish sheriff is liable in his official, but not personal, capacity as an employer of a deputy, for the deputy's torts in the course and scope of employment. Louisiana Civil Code art. 2320; *Jenkins v. Jefferson Parish Sheriff's Office*, 402 So.2d 669 (La. 1981). Although Sheriff Bridges is not liable under §1983, he is liable under general principles of Louisiana law, in his official capacity, for Lea's tort.

As noted earlier, the medical evidence is that Hall suffered no permanent injury or disability from Lea's beating. He was rendered unconscious and some blows with the pistol were severe. He was in the hospital for three days, he received medication for pain and he did suffer headaches and soreness for some time after his release from the hospital. Hall has proved $100 as the fee of the attending physician and, while the hospital records were received as evidence, no proof of the cost of his hospital stay was offered to the court. Consequently, Hall has proved special damages only in the amount of $100.

Hall is also entitled to an award of compensatory damages in the amount of $5,000 for his physical and mental pain and suffering and the physical injury inflicted upon him by Lea.

Accordingly, there will be judgment in favor of plaintiff in the amount of $5,100 against Lea under 42 U.S.C. §1983 and against Sheriff Bridges in his official capacity in solido with Lea under Louisiana law.

Punitive damages are allowed in appropriate cases under 42 U.S.C. §1983. Punitive damages, as distinct from compensatory damages, are awarded, "with the specific purpose of deterring or punishing violations of constitutional rights." *Carey v. Piphus*, 435 U.S. 247, 98 S.Ct. 1042, 1049 n. 11, 55 L.Ed.2d 252 (1978).

Lea's unwarranted, deliberate and malicious beating of an unarmed and peaceful arrestee demands both punishment and that an example be made so as to deter other law enforcement officers who might be tempted to deprive people of their constitutional protections.

This is not the first case in which this court has found Deputy Lea violated the constitutional rights of a citizen by an unprovoked and armed attack. See *Mrs. Rena Day v. David Lea, et al*, Civil Action 81–827 of the docket of this court.

Punitive damages will be awarded against Lea in the amount of $100,000. That amount has a sound ring to it and it is sufficient both to punish Lea for his transgression and to attract the attention of others who might be similarly tempted and perhaps to deter them from similar conduct.

Plaintiff is also entitled to an award for attorney's fees under 42 U.S.C. §1988 and counsel has submitted an itemization of time spent on the case totaling 115.75 hours, to which no exception has been taken by defendants. Counsel suggests that $85 per hour would be appropriate and that attorney's fees in the amount of $9,838.75 should be awarded in this case.

This case was neither complex nor difficult. The trial was one day. Counsel's post-trial brief was not very helpful to the court. . . . [A] reasonable fee for counsel in this case is $75 per hour and that a reasonable number of hours productively devoted to this case could not exceed 75. . . . [T]he court has noted particularly that counsel's time sheets reveal some 112 "telephone conferences" with co-counsel, or a total of 28 hours conferring with co-counsel about the case. The court considers that to be excessive discussion. This court concludes that the sum of $5,625 is an ample fee for services performed by counsel and that will be the amount awarded against Lea under 42 U.S.C. §1988. Attorney's fees are not allowed under Louisiana law in tort cases.

In post-trial brief, counsel for plaintiff has invited the court to award plaintiff damages because of the "false charges" lodged against him by Lea in an effort to punish and silence plaintiff as well as for the "additional punitive measures . . . taken in the sentence and fine aspect of plaintiff's criminal case," because a "simple one car accident . . . was escalated by Deputy Lea into a major tragedy in plaintiff's life, resulting in plaintiff being physically injured and humiliated to suffer incarceration, trial, conviction of a felony, economic hardship." Neither plaintiff's pleadings nor the pretrial order in this case contain any attack or challenge to plaintiff's state court conviction and there is no evidence as to what state court remedies, if any, plaintiff has pursued. While the line of jurisprudence exemplified by *Battieste v. City of Baton Rouge*, 732 F.2d 439 (5th Cir. 1984) might permit a challenge to plaintiff's state court conviction via a §1983 action, there is absolutely no evidence in this record upon which a federal challenge could be mounted. Ac-cordingly, this case is limited to the post arrest personal injuries inflicted upon plaintiff by Deputy Lea.

Judgment will be entered accordingly.

CASE DISCUSSION

Why were the sheriff and the sheriff's department not liable for damages to Hall? Why was insufficient training not a ground for liability? Why wasn't Deputy Sheriff Clark liable? What precisely were Cleo Hall's "damages"? What criteria would you use to attach a dollar amount to the injuries that Hall suffered? How do you think the court arrived at the figure of $5,000 for compensatory damages for "pain and suffering"? $100,000 for punitive damages? Do you think that punitive damages deter officers who have insurance or whose departments insure them? Explain. What interests do lawsuits against law enforcement officers promote?

Bringing and winning a §1983 action against a government, department, or head of a department for the torts of their employees is more complicated than suing the individual employees who committed the torts. In fact, until the case of *Monell v. New York City Department of Social Services*, the U.S. Supreme Court had ruled that Congress did not intend to include local governments within the scope of §1983. In *Monell*, the Court undertook "a fresh analysis of debate on the Civil Rights Act of 1871" and concluded that the legislative history of the Act "compels the conclusion that Congress *did* intend municipalities and other local government units to be included among those persons to whom §1983 applies." The Court established the following guidelines for suing local governing bodies for damages or injunctions:

1. Citizens can sue local government units for unconstitutional actions that "implement or execute a policy statement, ordinance, regulation, or decision officially adopted and promulgated by that body's officers."

2. Citizens can sue local government units for unconstitutional actions taken pursuant to "custom, even though such a custom has not received formal approval through the body's decisionmaking channels."

3. Government units are liable only if their unconstitutional actions under 1 or 2 "*caused* a constitutional tort."

This decision clearly imposes liability on local government units for the torts of their employees. However, just as clearly, government liability for the torts of individual employees is not a simple matter of applying the doctrine of *respondeat superior*. It takes more than an employer/employee relationship to impose §1983 liability. According to the Court in *Monell*, a local government cannot be sued for an injury inflicted solely by its employees or agents. Instead, it is when execution of a government's policy or custom, whether made by its lawmakers or by those whose edicts or acts may fairly be said to represent official policy, inflicts the injury that the government as an entity is responsible under §1983.[53]

In *Thurman v. City of Torrington*, the District Court of Connecticut dealt with the question of whether the failure of police officers to prevent injuries in a domestic violence case was caused by a policy of treating domestic assault cases as different from stranger assaults, thus violating the equal protection clause of the Fourteenth Amendment.

C A S E

Did the Police Department Violate Civil Rights?

Thurman v. City of Torrington
595 F.Supp. 1521 (D.Conn. 1984)

Thurman and her son brought a civil action against the city and the police officers thereof, alleging that plaintiffs' constitutional rights were violated by the nonperformance or malperformance of official duties by the officers in regard to threats and assaults by the wife's estranged husband. On the city's motion to dismiss the complaint or various claims therein, the District Court held that a violation of the Fourteenth Amendment's equal protection clause was stated by the wife's complaint, thus precluding the dismissal of her action against the city. The district court issued an order consistent with the opinion. Senior District Judge Blumenfeld wrote the court's opinion.

FACTS

. . . In October 1982, Charles Thurman attacked plaintiff Tracey Thurman at the home of Judy Bentley and Richard St. Hilaire in the City of Torrington. Mr. St. Hilaire and Ms. Bentley made a formal complaint of the attack to one of the unnamed defendant police officers and requested efforts to keep the plaintiff's husband, Charles Thurman, off their property.

On or about November 5, 1982, Charles Thurman returned to the St. Hilaire–Bentley residence and using physical force took the plaintiff Charles J. Thurman, Jr. from said residence. Plaintiff Tracey Thur-

man and Mr. St. Hilaire went to Torrington police headquarters to make a formal complaint. At that point, unnamed defendant police officers of the City of Torrington refused to accept a complaint from Mr. St. Hilaire even as to trespassing.

On or about November 9, 1982, Charles Thurman screamed threats to Tracey while she was sitting in her car. Defendant police officer Neil Gemelli stood on the street watching Charles Thurman scream threats at Tracey until Charles Thurman broke the windshield of plaintiff Tracey Thurman's car while she was inside the vehicle. Charles Thurman was arrested after he broke the windshield, and on the next day, November 10, 1982, he was convicted of breach of peace. He received a suspended sentence of six months and a two-year "conditional discharge," during which he was ordered to stay completely away from the plaintiff Tracey Thurman and the Bentley–St. Hilaire residence and to commit no further crimes. The court imposing probation informed the defendants of this sentence.

On December 31, 1982, while plaintiff Tracey Thurman was at the Bentley–St. Hilaire residence, Charles Thurman returned to said residence and once again threatened her. She called the Torrington Police Department. One of the unnamed police officer defendants took the call, and, although informed of the violation of the conditional discharge, made no attempt to ascertain Charles Thurman's whereabouts or to arrest him.

Between January 1, 1983 and May 4, 1983, numerous telephone complaints to the Torrington Police Department were taken by various unnamed police officers, in which repeated threats of violence to the plaintiffs by Charles Thurman were reported and his arrest on account of the threats and violation of the terms of his probation was requested.

On May 4 and 5, 1983, the plaintiff Tracey Thurman and Ms. Bentley reported to the Torrington Police Department that Charles Thurman had said that he would shoot the plaintiffs. Defendant police officer Storrs took the written complaint of plaintiff Tracey Thurman who was seeking an arrest warrant for her husband because of his death threat and violation of his "conditional discharge." Defendant Storrs refused to take the complaint of Ms. Bentley. Plaintiff Tracey Thurman was told to return three weeks later on June 1, 1983 when defendant Storrs or some other person connected with the police department of the defendant City would seek a warrant for the arrest of her husband.

On May 6, 1983, Tracey filed an application for a restraining order against Charles Thurman in the Litchfield Superior Court. That day, the court issued an ex parte restraining order forbidding Charles Thurman from assaulting, threatening, and harassing Tracey Thurman. The defendant City was informed of this order.

On May 27, 1983, Tracey Thurman requested police protection in order to get to the Torrington Police Department, and she requested a warrant for her husband's arrest upon her arrival at headquarters after being taken there by one of the unnamed defendant police officers. She was told that she would have to wait until after the Memorial Day holiday weekend and was advised to call on Tuesday, May 31, to pursue the warrant request.

On May 31, 1983, Tracey Thurman appeared once again at the Torrington Police Department to pursue the warrant request. She was then advised by one of the unnamed defendant police officers that defendant Schapp was the only policeman who could help her and that he was on vacation. She was told that she would have to wait until he returned. That same day, Tracey's brother-in-law, Joseph Kocsis, called the Torrington Police Department to protest the lack of action taken on Tracey's complaint. Although Mr. Kocsis was advised that Charles Thurman would be arrested on June 8, 1983, no such arrest took place.

On June 10, 1983, Charles Thurman appeared at the Bentley–St. Hilaire residence in the early afternoon and demanded to speak to Tracey. Tracey, remaining indoors, called the defendant police department asking that Charles be picked up for violation of his probation. After about 15 minutes, Tracey went outside to speak to her husband in an effort to persuade him not to take or hurt Charles Jr. Soon thereafter, Charles began to stab Tracey repeatedly in the chest, neck and throat.

Approximately 25 minutes after Tracey's call to the Torrington Police Department and after her stabbing, a single police officer, the defendant Petrovits, arrived on the scene. Upon the arrival of Officer Petrovits at the scene of the stabbing, Charles Thurman was holding a bloody knife. Charles then dropped the knife and, in the presence of Petrovits, kicked the plaintiff Tracey Thurman in the head and ran into the Bentley–St. Hilaire residence. Charles returned from within the residence holding the plaintiff Charles Thurman, Jr. and dropped the child on his wounded mother. Charles then kicked Tracey in the head a second time. Soon thereafter, defendants DeAngelo, Nukirk, and Columbia arrived on the scene but still permitted Charles Thurman to wander about the crowd and continue to threaten Tracey. Finally, upon approaching Tracey once again, this time while she was lying on a stretcher, Charles Thurman was arrested and taken into custody.

It is also alleged that at all times mentioned above, except for approximately two weeks following his conviction and sentencing on November 10, 1982, Charles Thurman resided in Torrington and worked there as a counterman and short order cook at Skie's Diner. There he served many members of the Torrington Police Department including some of the named and unnamed defendants in this case. In the course of his employment Charles Thurman boasted to the defendant police officer patrons that he intended to "get" his wife and that he intended to kill her.

OPINION

The defendant City now brings a motion to dismiss the claims against it. The City first argues that the plaintiff's complaint should be dismissed for failure to allege the deprivation of a constitutional right. Though the complaint alleges that the action of the defendants deprived the plaintiff Tracey Thurman of her constitutional right to equal protection of the laws, the defendant City argues that the equal protection clause of the fourteenth amendment "does not guarantee equal application of social services." Rather, the defendant City argues that the equal protection clause "only prohibits intentional discrimination that is racially motivated."

The defendant City's argument is clearly a misstatement of the law. The application of the equal protection clause is not limited to racial classifications or racially motivated discrimination. The equal protection clause will be applied to invalidate state laws which classify on the basis of alienage for the purpose of the distribution of economic benefits unless that law is necessary to promote a compelling or overriding state interest. The equal protection clause will be applied to strike down classifications based on legitimacy at birth if they are not related to an important governmental objective. And lastly, the equal protection clause will be applied to a legitimate state interest. Classifications on the basis of gender will be held invalid under the equal protection clause unless they are substantially related to strike down classifications which are not rationally related to a legitimate governmental purpose.

In the instant case, the plaintiffs allege that the defendants use an administrative classification that manifests itself in discriminatory treatment violative of the equal protection clause. Police protection in the City of Torrington, they argue, is fully provided to persons abused by someone with whom the victim has no domestic relationship. But the Torrington police have consistently afforded lesser protection, plaintiffs allege, when the victim is (1) a woman abused or assaulted by a spouse or boyfriend, or (2) a child abused by a father or stepfather. The issue to be decided, then, is whether the plaintiffs have properly alleged a violation of the equal protection clause of the fourteenth amendment.

Police action is subject to the equal protection clause and section 1983 whether in the form of commission of violative acts or omission to perform required acts pursuant to the police officer's duty to protect. City officials and police officers are under an affirmative duty to preserve law and order, and to protect the personal safety of persons in the community. This duty applies equally to women whose personal safety is threatened by individuals with whom they have or have had a domestic relationship as well as to all other persons whose personal safety is threatened, including women not involved in domestic relationships. If officials have notice of the possibility of attacks on women in domestic relationships or other persons, they are under an affirmative duty to take reasonable measures to protect the personal safety of such persons in the community. Failure to perform this duty would constitute a denial of equal protection of the laws.

Although the plaintiffs point to no law which on its face discriminates against victims abused by someone with whom they have a domestic relationship, the plaintiffs have alleged that there is an administrative classification used to implement the law in a discriminatory fashion. It is well settled that the equal protection clause is applicable not only to discriminatory legislative action, but also to discriminatory governmental action in administration and enforcement of the law. Here the plaintiffs were threatened with assault in violation of Connecticut law. Over the course of eight months the police failed to afford the plaintiffs protection against such assaults, and failed to take action to arrest the perpetrator of these assaults. The plaintiffs have alleged that this failure to act was pursuant to a pattern or practice of affording inadequate protection, or no protection at all, to women who have complained of having been abused by their husbands or others with whom they have had close relations. Such a practice is tantamount to an administrative classification used to implement the law in a discriminatory fashion.

If the City wishes to discriminate against women who are the victims of domestic violence, it must articulate an important governmental interest for doing so. In its memorandum and at oral argument the City has failed to put forward any justification for its disparate treatment of women. . . . Such a practice was at one time sanctioned by law:

> English common law during the eighteenth century recognized the right of husbands to physically discipline their wives. Subsequently,

American common law in the early nineteenth century permitted a man to chastise his wife "'without subjecting himself to vexatious prosecutions for assault and battery, resulting in the discredit and shame of all parties concerned.'" Some restrictions on the right of chastisement evolved through cases which defined the type, severity, and timing of permissible wife-beating. . . . B. Finesmith, "Police Response to Battered Women: Critique and Proposals for Reform," 14 *Seton Hall L.Rev.* 74, 79 (1983). In our own country a husband was permitted to beat his wife so long as he didn't use a switch any bigger around than his thumb. . . .

Today, however, any notion of a husband's prerogative to physically discipline his wife is an "increasingly outdated misconception." *Craig v. Boren*, 429 U.S. at 198–99, 97 S.Ct. at 457–58. As such it must join other "archaic and overbroad" premises which have been rejected as unconstitutional. . . .

A man is not allowed to physically abuse or endanger a woman merely because he is her husband. Concomitantly, a police officer may not knowingly refrain from interference in such violence, and may not "automatically decline to make an arrest simply because the assaulter and his victim are married to each other." *Bruno v. Codd*, 90 Misc.2d 1047, 1049, 396 N.Y.S.2d 974, 976 (1976), rev'd on other grounds, 64 App.Div.2d 502, 407 N.Y.S.2d 165 (1978), aff'd, 47 N.Y.2d 582, 419 N.Y.S.2d 901, 393 N.E.2d 976 (1979). Such inaction on the part of the officer is a denial of the equal protection of the laws.

In addition, any notion that defendants' practice can be justified as a means of promoting domestic harmony by refraining from interference in marital disputes, has no place in the case at hand. Rather than evidencing a desire to work out her problems with her husband privately, Tracey pleaded with the police to offer her at least some measure of protection. Further, she sought and received a restraining order to keep her husband at a distance. . . . Accordingly, the defendant City of Torrington's motion to dismiss the plaintiff Tracey Thurman's complaint on the basis of failure to allege violation of a constitutional right is denied.

Plaintiff Charles Thurman, Jr. also claims that the City of Torrington denied him the equal protection of the laws. He alleges that the defendants fail to protect children against the domestic violence of fathers and stepfathers. This claim fails on several grounds. Other than the June 10, 1983 assault, Charles Thurman, Jr. has alleged no attacks made against him. Unlike his mother Tracey Thurman, Charles was not alleged to be the victim of an attack in October of 1982 at the home of Judy Bentley and Richard St. Hilaire. It is also not alleged that Charles Thurman, Jr. was present on November 9, 1982, when his father broke the windshield of the vehicle carrying Tracey Thurman. There is no allegation that one of the conditions of Charles Thurman's discharge following his conviction for breach of peace on November 10, 1982 was to keep away from Charles Thurman, Jr., while it is alleged that one of the conditions was that he was to stay away from the plaintiff Tracey Thurman. Additionally, there is no allegation that the May 6, 1983 restraining order issued by the Litchfield Superior Court forbidding Charles Thurman from assaulting, threatening and harassing plaintiff Tracey Thurman, was issued in order to protect Charles Thurman, Jr. as well. Thus Charles Thurman Jr. did not suffer from a continuous failure of the police to provide him protection as did his mother, Tracey Thurman. The isolated failure of the defendants to prevent the June 10, 1983 assault on Charles Thurman, Jr. does not violate any constitutional rights. Charles Thurman, Jr.'s failure to adequately allege that the defendants denied him equal protection of the law requires that all claims of Charles Thurman, Jr. be dismissed for failure to state a claim upon which relief can be granted.

The plaintiffs have alleged in paragraph 13 of their complaint as follows:

During the period of time described herein, and for a long time prior thereto, the defendant City of Torrington acting through its Police Department, condoned a pattern or practice of affording inadequate protection, or no protection at all, to women who have complained of having been abused by their husbands or others with whom they have had close relations. Said pattern, custody or policy, well known to the individual defendants, was the basis on which they ignored said numerous complaints and reports of threats to the plaintiffs with impunity.

While a municipality is not liable for the constitutional torts of its employees on a *respondeat superior* theory, a municipality may be sued for damages under section 1983 when "the action that is alleged to be unconstitutional implements or executes a policy statement, ordinance, regulation, or decision officially adopted and promulgated by the body's officers" or is "visited pursuant to governmental 'custom' even though such a custom has not received formal approval through the body's official decision-making channels." *Monell v. New York City Department of Social Services*, 436 U.S. 658, 690, 98 S.Ct. 2018, 2035, 56 L.Ed.2d 611 (1978).

Some degree of specificity is required in the pleading of a custom or policy on the part of a municipality. Mere conclusory allegations devoid of factual content will not suffice. As this court has pointed out, a plaintiff must typically point to the facts outside his own case to support his allegation of a policy on the part of a municipality.

In the instant case, however, the plaintiff Tracey Thurman has specifically alleged in her statement of facts a series of acts and omissions on the part of the defendant police officers and police department that took place over the course of eight months. From this particularized pleading a pattern emerges that evidences deliberate indifference on the part of the police department to the complaints of the plaintiff Tracey Thurman and to its duty to protect her. Such an ongoing pattern of deliberate indifference raises an inference of "custom" or "policy" on the part of the municipality. Furthermore, this pattern of inaction climaxed on June 10, 1983 in an incident so brutal that under the law of the Second Circuit that "single brutal incident may be sufficient to suggest a link between a violation of constitutional rights and a pattern of police misconduct." *Owens v. Haas*, 601 F.2d 1242, 1246 (2d Cir.), cert. denied, 444 U.S. 980, 100 S.Ct.

483, 62 L.Ed.2d 407 (1979). Finally, a complaint of this sort will survive dismissal if it alleges a policy or custom of condoning police misconduct that violates constitutional rights and alleges "that the City's pattern of inaction caused the plaintiffs any compensable injury." *Batista v. Rodriguez*, 702 F.2d 393, 397–98 (2d Cir.1983); *Escalera v. New York City Housing Authority*, 425 F.2d 853, 857 (2d Cir.), cert. denied, 400 U.S. 853, 91 S.Ct. 54, 27 L.Ed.2d 91 (1970) ("an action, especially under the Civil Rights Act, should not be dismissed at the pleadings stage unless it appears to a certainty that plaintiffs are entitled to no relief under any state of the facts, which could be proved in support of their claims"). Accordingly, defendant City of Torrington's motion to dismiss the plaintiffs claims against it, on the ground that the plaintiffs failed to properly allege a custom or policy on the part of the municipality, is denied. . . .

For the reasons stated above, the City's motion to dismiss the complaint for failure to allege the deprivation of a constitutional right is denied; the City's motion to dismiss the claims of Charles Thurman, Jr. is granted; the City's motion to dismiss claims against it for failure to properly allege a "custom" or "policy" on the part of the City is denied. . . .

So ordered.

CASE DISCUSSION

What constitutional rights did the city allegedly violate? What facts did the plaintiff allege to demonstrate the unconstitutional acts? What facts demonstrate a "custom" or "policy"? Did these facts cause injury to Tracey Thurman? Explain. Why did the court grant the motion to dismiss the complaint alleging violations of the constitutional rights of Charles Thurman, Jr.? Was he not injured? Explain.

Wayne LaFave, Jr., an expert on criminal procedure and the author of many leading works on the subject, has commented that the rule requiring courts to determine whether an unconstitutional action was caused by the "execution of a government's policy or custom" raises difficult questions, such as

- Is a directive in a police department manual official policy?
- Is the lack of sufficient police training ever official policy?
- Is a pattern of nondiscipline for the actions of officers official policy?[54]

The Ninth Circuit Court of Appeals examined the question of whether the failure to train officers was a policy that could form the basis of a §1983 action in *Davis v. Mason County.*

C A S E

Can They Sue the County for the Sheriff's Failure to Train Deputies?

Davis v. Mason County
927 F.2d 1473 (9th Cir. 1991)

Mason County, its sheriff, and several deputies appeal from a jury verdict finding them liable under 42 U.S.C. §1983 for damages for excessive force used while arresting citizens in four separate incidents. We affirm the jury verdict and find municipal liability of Mason County and the Sheriff's Department.

Before Wallace, Chief Judge, Pregerson and Nelson, Circuit Judges. Judge Pregerson wrote the opinion of the court.

FACTS

Each of the plaintiffs–appellees' complaints arose out of traffic stops which resulted in arrests, beatings, and false charges that were later dropped. The incidents occurred within a nine-month period between June, 1985 and March, 1986.

A. The Durbin Incident

Early on the morning of June 29, 1985 as Doug Durbin returned home from a local tavern, Deputy Ray Sowers followed him and waited outside of Durbin's home. Deputy Tom Furrer later arrived as backups. Sowers, flicking an electric stun gun on and off, ordered Durbin out of his house. Durbin, who complied, was arrested for drunk driving. After taking one step toward his house, the two deputies tackled Durbin and threw him to the ground. Though Durbin never attempted to resist, Sowers began to beat him on

the back of his head with his fist. In the patrol car on the way to the jail Sowers slammed on the brakes, causing Durbin, who was handcuffed and thus defenseless, to smash into the screen with his face.

Durbin was charged with driving while intoxicated [Durbin's breathalyzer test, taken at the Mason County Jail, read .05, well below the legal definition of intoxication], resisting arrest and obstructing an officer. Yet after Durbin signed a "Release and Satisfaction" against Mason County, the charges against him were dismissed.

B. The Taylor Incident

Deputy Doug Quantz pulled over Don Taylor as he was driving through Shelton on the afternoon of July 20, 1985, allegedly for driving too fast. Quantz ordered Taylor to spread-eagle against the patrol vehicle and proceeded to conduct a pat-down search. Under the guise of this search, Quantz twisted the skin on Taylor's arms and legs, struck him on the sides, hit him in the testicles, and slammed him against the side of the patrol car. Later, in the jail elevator, Quantz hit Taylor in the kidneys with his fist.

After signing a "Partial Covenant Not to Sue," promising not to bring charges against Mason County, the charges against Taylor, including reckless driving, obstructing an officer, and resisting arrest, were dropped.

C. The Davis/Broughton Incident

John Davis and his fifteen year-old nephew, Wayne Broughton, were driving a loaded hay wagon drawn by a team of four horses on the afternoon of July 28, 1985. Because some cars were slowed behind the wagon, Deputy Jack Gardner came alongside the wagon in his patrol vehicle and, using his loud-speaker, ordered Davis to pull over. Davis lost control over the horses, who had been frightened by the noise of the loudspeaker. Gardner pulled in front of the wagon, took out his gun, pointed it at Davis and Broughton and threatened to shoot if they did not stop. As Davis got down from the wagon to attend to his horses, Gardner beat him on the legs with his nightstick and struck him on the head. He then knocked him down on the ground and continued to beat him. After Deputies Pete Cribben and Garry Ohlde arrived at the scene, all three hit him, kicked him, and shocked him with an electric stun gun. According to one witness, Davis "looked like he had been dipped in a bucket of blood" after the officers finished beating him.

Deputy Gardner's wife, who had been riding with him as a passenger and who was not an officer, ordered Broughton down from the wagon, and then took him by the arm and put him in the patrol car. After being questioned for an hour, Broughton was released.

Davis was arrested and charged with felony assault, resisting arrest and obstructing an officer. The misdemeanor charges were dismissed, and a jury, which found that Davis was acting in self-defense, acquitted him of the felony charge.

D. The Rodius Incident

When Deputy Ray Sowers observed four young people talking between a car and a truck on the evening of March 15, 1986, he pulled over both vehicles. Sowers ordered Ed Rodius, a passenger in the truck, into the patrol car after he asked why they had been stopped. When Rodius refused to comply, Sowers jumped on Rodius, choked him, pulled on his hair, and then threw him to the ground and rubbed his face on the gravel of the parking lot.

Rodius was arrested and charged with possession of alcohol as a minor, purchasing liquor, and resisting arrest. Rodius was tried twice on the resisting arrest charge. The first trial resulted in a hung jury, and the second was declared a mistrial after the prosecution violated a motion in limine by referring to the case at

bar in front of the jury. The Mason County Prosecutor's office eventually dismissed the charges.

In the present case, the jury returned verdicts against all the individual deputies and the County, awarding $528,000 in compensatory damages. Punitive damages were awarded only against the individual deputies, not the County. The jury awarded $225,000 in punitive damages and $150,000 compensatory to Davis; $10,000 in punitive and $5,000 compensatory to Broughton; $25,000 in punitive and $5,000 compensatory to Durbin; $25,000 in punitive and $0 compensatory to Rodius; and $35,000 in punitive and $1,500 compensatory to Taylor. The district court awarded attorneys' fees, expenses, and costs to plaintiffs in the amount of $323,559.65.

Defendants–appellants timely appeal. This court has jurisdiction over the appeal under 28 U.S.C. §1291.

OPINION

. . . Plaintiffs sued the individual deputies, Mason County, and the Sheriff's Department for violation of their federal constitutional rights protected by the Fourth Amendment. Municipalities may be held liable under 42 U.S.C. §1983 for actions which result in a deprivation of constitutional rights. However, a municipality cannot be held liable on a respondeat superior theory. . . . Municipal liability is incurred under section 1983 only when "execution of a government's policy or custom, whether made by its lawmakers or by those whose edicts or acts may fairly be said to represent official policy, inflicts the injury. . . ."

The Supreme Court recently addressed the issue whether the inadequacy of police training may result in municipal liability under section 1983 in *City of Canton v. Harris*, 489 U.S. 378, 109 S.Ct. 1197, 103 L.Ed.2d 412 (1989). In determining liability the Court said that the adequacy of the training program must be assessed in relation to the tasks the officers must perform. Further, the failure to train must "reflect a 'deliberate' or 'conscious' choice by a municipality — a 'policy.' . . ."

To establish municipal liability under section 1983, it must be shown that the decisionmaker possesses final authority to establish municipal policy with respect to the action ordered. . . . According to

Washington law . . . "[t]he sheriff is the chief executive officer and conservator of the peace of the county." As chief executive officers, sheriffs possess final authority with respect to the training of their deputies, and thus it may be fairly said that their actions constitute county policy on the subject. . . . Mason County is liable as a matter of law for failing to train its officers on the constitutional limits of force. . . . The training of peace officers on the use of force is a type of law enforcement practice that falls squarely within the policymaking authority of a County Sheriff.

The trial judge instructed the jury that failure to train could serve as the basis of County liability if the County exhibited a "reckless disregard for" or a "deliberate indifference to" the safety of its inhabitants. . . . The instructions given by the district court allowed the jury to find municipal liability only upon a showing of "reckless disregard" or "deliberate indifference." We do not find the court's instructions, taken as a whole, to be inconsistent with the "deliberate indifference" standard enunciated in *City of Canton.* In *City of Canton,* the Court stated that

> the need for more or different training [may be] so obvious, and the inadequacy so likely to result in the violation of constitutional rights, that the policymakers of the city can reasonably be said to have been deliberately indifferent.

Similarly, the district court in this case instructed that a person acts with reckless disregard when he "disregards a substantial risk that a wrongful act may occur of which he is aware, or which is so obvious that he must have been aware of it, and his disregard of that risk is a gross deviation from conduct that a reasonable person would exercise in the same situation." The district court's definition of reckless disregard is effectively the same as the language cited from *City of Canton;* both allow a jury to impose municipal liability in failure-to-train cases for acts that so clearly violate the rights of an individual that the policymakers can be said to be deliberately indifferent.

. . . The jury instructions on this issue were nevertheless harmless because Mason County's failure to adequately train its deputies constituted deliberate indifference as a matter of law. The training that the deputies received was woefully inadequate, if it can be said to have existed at all. Sheriff Stairs himself never attended the State Training Academy and Undersheriff Harry "Bud" Hays had neither training nor experience. Although Washington law requires all police officers to complete academy training within fifteen months of hire, Deputy Sowers did not complete the academy until sixteen months after he was hired.

Instead of academy training, the Sheriff's Department devised a "field training program" for the officers. While this program may have seemed adequate on paper, in practice it was never followed. Indeed, one of the Department's two original field training officers, both of whom quit, called the program "a joke." The field training program was supposed to include tests, reports, and reviews by the field training officer and supervising sergeant on a periodic basis, yet there is no evidence that this was ever done. Although the program was supposed to last twelve months, in actuality it lasted only for a small fraction of that time. [Sowers received only three or four weeks of field training before he was sent out on patrol alone.] One of plaintiffs' experts testified that as a result of the inadequacy of the field training program, the Department "sent officers out on the street to perform police services without any training whatsoever." The officers involved in these four incidents had received minimal or no training.

At the time of the Durbin incident (June 29, 1985), Sowers had not attended the State Academy. His only training besides minimal field training, which was cut short, consisted of the explorer cadets, a program in which teenagers with interest in law enforcement rode with officers. Deputy Quantz had received no training whatsoever prior to the Taylor incident (July 20, 1985). Although Deputies Gardner and Ohlde had attended the State Academy prior to the Davis incident (July 28, 1985), Deputy Cribben had not. He had only received minimal police-type training in other contexts, such as private security guard.

The issue is not whether the officers had received any training—most of the deputies involved had some training, even if it was minimal at best—rather the issue is the adequacy of that training. More importantly, while they may have had some training in the use of force, they received no training in the constitutional limits of the use of force. The Supreme Court in *City of Canton* declared: if "the need for more or different training is so obvious, and the inadequacy so likely to result in the violation of constitutional rights, . . . the policymakers of the city can reasonably be said to have been deliberately indifferent to the need." The Court went on to say in a footnote that "the need to train officers in the constitutional limitations on the use of deadly force can be said to be 'so obvious,' that failure to do so could properly be characterized as 'deliberate indifference' to constitutional rights."

In the case at bar, the deprivation of plaintiffs' Fourth Amendment rights was a direct consequence of the inadequacy of the training the deputies received. Mason County's failure to train its officers in the legal limits of the use of force constituted "deliberate indifference" to the safety of its inhabitants as a matter of law. Moreover, there was certainly more than enough evidence presented regarding the inadequacy of training in order to survive Mason County's motion for a directed verdict on the issue of municipal liability. . . .

The jury awarded punitive damages against the individual deputies totaling $320,000. A jury may award punitive damages under section 1983 either when a defendant's conduct was driven by evil motive or intent, or when it involved a reckless or callous indifference to the constitutional rights of others.

Unless the amount of damages is grossly excessive, unsupported by the evidence, or based solely on speculation, the reviewing court must uphold the jury's determination of the amount.

The deputies make four arguments regarding the amount of punitive damages awarded. First, they argue that the punitive damages award should be stricken because there was insufficient evidence of any evil intent or motive. Second, they contend that the jury should have been instructed that their net worth should be considered in assessing punitive damages. Third, the deputies assert that because remedial measures were taken, punitive damages were unnecessary. Finally, they argue that since the jury awarded Rodius $0 in compensatory damages, he should not have been awarded punitive damages.

The deputies' argument that the punitive damages award should be stricken because there was insufficient evidence of evil intent or motive is completely without merit because the alternative basis for assess-

ing punitive damages is "reckless or callous indifference to the federally protected rights of others." The jury could certainly infer that there was "reckless or callous indifference" based upon the evidence presented of the excessive force used.

Plaintiffs concede that evidence of the deputies' net worth would have been relevant in assessing punitive damages. However, the deputies did not offer this evidence before the jury, and they did not object when the jury was not instructed on this issue. In order to preserve the issue on appeal, objections to jury instructions must be specific.

The deputies believe that the remedial measures taken rendered punitive damages unnecessary. . . . [P]unitive damages were assessed only against individual defendants. The jury obviously felt that the punitive damages were necessary to deter future unlawful and egregious behavior by the deputies. The jury's decision on this issue should stand.

Rodius received $25,000 in punitive damages and $0 in compensatory damages. The deputies' argument that the jury erred in awarding punitive damages while not awarding compensatory damage fails. The Supreme Court has held that punitive damages may be available under Section 1983 where there has been a violation of constitutional rights even though the victim is unable to show compensable injury.

. . .

Although Mason County argues that Broughton cannot state a claim for emotional distress because he has not exhibited any objective symptoms of emotional distress, Washington law does not require physical manifestations in order to make an emotional distress claim.

Further, the jury had to evaluate defendants' behavior in this incident and determine whether it was so outrageous as to go beyond bounds of decency. After hearing testimony from Dr. Beaton that Broughton suffered from post-traumatic stress syndrome as a result of seeing his uncle bloodied by the deputies and having a gun pointed at him, the jury decided in the affirmative the fact question of whether the defendants' behavior was "so outrageous in character and so extreme in degree to go beyond all possible bounds of decency and be regarded as atrocious and utterly intolerable in a civilized community." Having so decided, the jury's verdict should stand. . . .

. . .

A district court has broad discretion to grant attorneys' fees and costs. . . . We review its decision only for an abuse of discretion. "Due to the trial judge's familiarity with the litigation, review of the trial court's exercise of discretion in awarding attorneys' fees is narrow."

Plaintiffs–appellees requested $575,658.13 in attorneys' fees and $99,201.63 in costs and expenses of litigation pursuant to the Attorney's Fees Awards Act of 1976, 42 U.S.C. § 1988. The district court awarded $4,348.57 in costs pursuant to 28 U.S.C. § 1920, and $249,588.00 in attorneys' fees and $69,623.08 in expenses of litigation under 42 U.S.C. § 1988. Mason County contests the award of expert witness fees, travel expenses, and attorneys' fees.

The district court granted $29,217.18 for plaintiffs' expert witnesses, the largest element of expenses awarded. Mason County argues that payment of expert witness fees as expenses is precluded by the Supreme Court's decision in *Crawford Fitting Co. v. J.T. Gibbons, Inc. Crawford Fitting* holds that "when a prevailing party seeks reimbursement for fees paid to its own expert witnesses, a federal court is bound by the limit of [28 U.S.C., § 1821(b), limits witness fees to $30.00 per day], absent contract or explicit statutory authority to the contrary." . . . In our opinion . . . a prevailing plaintiff [can] recover reasonable expert witness fees regardless of the limits of 28 U.S.C. §§ 1821 and 1920. But after the opinion was filed the Supreme Court in *West Virginia University Hospitals, Inc. v. Casey,* — U.S. —, 111 S.Ct. 1138, 113 L.Ed.2d 68 (March 19, 1991), reached the opposite conclusion. The Court held that "[42 U.S.C.] § 1988 conveys no authority to shift expert fees." — U.S. at —, 111 S.Ct. at 1148. . . . We remand to the district court with instructions to modify the award of expert witness fees consistent with *Casey.*

Mason County contends that costs other than expert witness fees should also be limited to those available under 28 U.S.C. § 1920. The only costs disputed below were travel expenses. Because this court will not consider issues not raised below, our review will be limited to travel expenses. Mason County fails to see that like the expert witness fees, the travel expenses were not granted as costs under section 1920, but rather as out-of-pocket expenses, compensable under section 1988. Courts have generally held that expenses incurred during the course of litigation which are normally billed to fee-paying clients should be taxed under section 1988. As the Eleventh Circuit said in *Dowdell:*

> Reasonable attorneys' fees under the [Attorney's Fees Awards] Act must include reasonable expenses because attorneys' fees and expenses are inseparably intertwined as equally vital components of the costs of litigation. The factually complex and protracted nature of civil rights litigation frequently makes it necessary to make sizeable out-of-pocket expenditures which may be as essential to success as the intellectual skills of the attorneys. If these costs are not taxable, and the client, as is often the case, cannot afford to pay for them, they must be borne by counsel, reducing the fees award correspondingly.

Thus, following the reasoning adopted in upholding the award of expert witness fees, we also affirm the district court's award of travel expenses pursuant to section 1988.

However, it is unclear why the district court granted $12,845.25 for travel expenses as part of the $249,588.00 attorneys' fees, and $4,135.83 for travel expenses as part of the $69,623.08 award for expenses of litigation. Because the award of travel expenses may have been double-counted, we remand on this issue.

Mason County disputes the amount awarded in attorneys' fees. Specifically, they question whether $135/hour accurately reflected the prevailing market rate in Western Washington. Further, they argue that the award should have been adjusted for billing judgment and reduced to the extent plaintiffs did not prevail on their claims for injunctive relief.

First, the hourly rate granted was reasonable for the Western District of Washington. Plaintiffs submitted affidavits from the relevant community in support of their hourly fee request. Generally, the relevant community is one in which the district court sits. Western Washington is the relevant community here, for it is where the court is located and where three of plaintiffs–appellees' attorneys practice. The court did not abuse its discretion in setting the hourly fees based on the prevailing rates there.

Second, the court did not abuse its discretion in determining the amount of the award. The trial court used the "lodestar" method of calculation in addition to the twelve-factor analysis. The "lodestar" figure is simply the multiplication of the number of hours reasonably expended by the reasonable hourly rate. The twelve factors . . . include such considerations as the novelty of the case, the experience, reputation and ability of the attorneys, and the skill required to perform the legal service properly. After careful consideration of the twelve factors, the district court granted $249,588.00 in fees. There was no abuse of discretion.

Third, attorneys' fees should not be reduced to the extent that plaintiffs–appellees did not prevail on their claims for injunctive relief. Plaintiffs submitted an affidavit which attested to the minute amount of time actually spent on the injunction claim. Mason County did not produce any evidence in support of their assertion that plaintiffs spent "much of their time" working on the issue of injunctive relief. Moreover, "[w]here a plaintiff has obtained excellent results, his attorney should recover a fully compensatory fee. . . . In these circumstances the fee award should not be reduced simply because the plaintiff failed to prevail on every contention raised in the lawsuit." There were excellent results in this case. The jury returned verdicts in favor of every plaintiff and against every defendant. Of the twenty basic verdicts in this case, plaintiffs prevailed on eighteen. We affirm the amount awarded in attorneys' fees.

A jury found Mason County, its sheriff and several deputies liable under 42 U.S.C. §1983, and awarded damages to five plaintiffs who were arrested without probable cause, beaten and then subjected to false criminal charges by Mason County deputies. We hold that Mason County's failure to adequately train its officers in the constitutional limits of the use of force constituted deliberate indifference to the safety of its inhabitants as a matter of law. The jury's verdict is sustained. In addition, we remand to the district court to determine the proper accounting of travel expenses for plaintiffs' attorneys and of expert witness fees.

Affirmed.

CASE DISCUSSION

Why was the county liable in this case? Why was inadequate training sufficient ground for liability? What interests do civil actions against law enforcement officers promote? Do they put process over result? What precisely were the plaintiffs' "damages"? How can you measure the dollar value of the injuries they suffered? How do you think the court arrived at the dollar amounts? Do the amounts seem proper? Explain. Do you agree with the court's conclusion regarding punitive damages? What standard could you apply to measure punitive damages? What interests would such a standard promote? (See Chapters 3–7 on unlawful searches and seizures.) How did the court assess and award costs?

Most lawsuits against criminal justice officials arise out of alleged police misconduct, usually the use of excessive force in conducting searches and seizures. A few defendants sue prosecutors for abuse of discretion in the decision to charge suspects with crimes. According to the leading case *Imbler v. Pachtman* (1976), the **absolute immunity** granted prosecutors extends to conduct "initiating a prosecution and in presenting the state's case, insofar as that conduct is intimately associated with [the] judicial phase of the criminal process." That case left open the question of whether absolute immunity extends to "those aspects of the prosecutor's responsibility that cast him in the role of an administrator or investigative officer rather than that of an advocate." In 1991 the Supreme Court reviewed the liability of prosecutors to civil lawsuits in *Burns v. Reed*.

▶ C A S E ◀

Did the Prosecutor Enjoy Absolute Immunity?

Burns v. Reed
500 U.S. 478, 111 S.Ct. 1934,
114 L.Ed.2d 547 (1991)

Burns brought a civil rights action against the state prosecutor. The United States District Court for the Southern District of Indiana granted the state prosecutor's motion for a directed verdict. Burns appealed. The Court of Appeals for the Seventh Circuit affirmed. The United States Supreme Court granted certiorari. The Supreme Court affirmed in part and reversed in part. Justice White wrote the opinion for the Court, which Chief Justice Rehnquist and Justices Stevens, O'-Connor, Kennedy, and Souter joined. Justice Scalia filed a concurring and dissenting opinion in which Justice Blackmun joined and Justice Marshall joined in part.

FACTS

The relevant facts are not in dispute. On the evening of September 2, 1982, petitioner Cathy Burns called the Muncie, Indiana, police and reported that an unknown assailant had entered her house, knocked her unconscious, and shot and wounded her two sons while they slept. Two police officers, Paul Cox and Donald Scroggins, were assigned to investigate the incident. The officers came to view petitioner as their primary suspect, even though she passed a polygraph examination and a voice stress test, submitted exculpatory handwritten samples, and repeatedly denied shooting her sons. Speculating that petitioner had multiple personalities, one of which was responsible for the shootings, the officers decided to interview petitioner under hypnosis. They became concerned, however, that hypnosis might be an unacceptable investigation technique, and therefore sought the advice of the Chief Deputy Prosecutor, respondent Richard Reed. Respondent told the officers that they could proceed with the hypnosis.

While under hypnosis, petitioner referred to the assailant as "Katie" and also referred to herself by that name. The officers interpreted that reference as supporting their multiple-personality theory. As a result, they detained petitioner at the police station and sought respondent's advice about whether there was probable cause to arrest petitioner. After hearing about the statements that petitioner had made while under hypnosis, respondent told the officers that they "probably had probable cause" to arrest petitioner. Based on that assurance, the officers placed petitioner under arrest.

[COURT NOTE: "Following her arrest, petitioner was placed in the psychiatric ward of a state hospital for four months. During that time, she was discharged from her employment, and the State obtained temporary custody of her sons. The medical experts at the hospital eventually concluded that petitioner did not have multiple personalities, and she was released."]

The next day, respondent and Officer Scroggins appeared before a county court judge in a probable cause hearing, seeking to obtain a warrant to search petitioner's house and car. During that hearing, Scroggins testified, in response to respondent's questioning, that petitioner had confessed to shooting her children. Neither the officer nor respondent informed the judge that the "confession" was obtained under hypnosis or that petitioner had otherwise consistently denied shooting her sons. On the basis of the misleading presentation, the judge issued a search warrant.

Petitioner was charged under Indiana law with attempted murder of her sons. Before trial, however, the trial judge granted petitioner's motion to suppress the statements given under hypnosis. As a result, the prosecutor dropped all charges against petitioner. On January 31, 1985, petitioner filed an action in the United States District Court for the Southern District of Indiana against respondent, Officers Cox and Scroggins, and others. She alleged that the defendants were liable under 42 U.S.C. §1983 for violating her rights under the Fourth, Fifth, and Fourteenth Amendments to the United States Constitution, and she sought compensatory and punitive damages. Petitioner reached a settlement with several of the defendants, and the case proceeded to trial against respondent. After petitioner presented her case, the District Court granted respondent a directed verdict, finding that respondent was absolutely immune from liability for his conduct.

Petitioner appealed to the United States Court of Appeals for the Seventh Circuit. That court affirmed. It held that "a prosecutor should be afforded absolute immunity for giving legal advice to police officers about the legality of their prospective investigative conduct." In a brief footnote, the court also held that respondent was absolutely immune from liability for his role in the probable cause hearing. Because the Courts of Appeals are divided regarding the scope of absolute prosecutorial immunity, we granted certiorari.

OPINION

Title 42 U.S.C. §1983 is written in broad terms. It purports to subject "[e]very person" acting under color of state law to liability for depriving any other person in the United States of "rights, privileges, or immunities secured by the Constitution and laws." The Court has consistently recognized, however, that §1983 was not meant "to abolish wholesale all common-law immunities." *Pierson v. Ray* (1967). The section is to be read "in harmony with general principles of tort immunities and defenses rather than in derogation of them." *Imbler v. Pachtman* (1976). In addition, we have acknowledged that for some "special functions," it is "better to leave unredressed the wrongs done by dishonest officers than to subject those who try to do their duty to the constant dread of retaliation."

Imbler was the first case in which the Court addressed the immunity of state prosecutors from suits under §1983. . . . The Court observed that at common law prosecutors were immune from suits for malicious prosecution and for defamation, and that this immunity extended to the knowing use of false testimony before the grand jury and at trial.

The interests supporting the common-law immunity were held to be equally applicable to suits under §1983. . . . [T]here was "concern that harassment by

unfounded litigation would cause a deflection of the prosecutor's energies from his public duties, and the possibility that he would shade his decisions instead of exercising the independence of judgment required by his public trust."

The Court in *Imbler* declined to accord prosecutors only qualified immunity because, among other things, suits against prosecutors for initiating and conducting prosecutions "could be expected with some frequency, for a defendant often will transform his resentment at being prosecuted into the ascription of improper and malicious actions to the State's advocate," lawsuits would divert prosecutors' attention and energy away from their important duty of enforcing the criminal law, prosecutors would have more difficulty than other officials in meeting the standards for qualified immunity, and potential liability "would prevent the vigorous and fearless performance of the prosecutor's duty that is essential to the proper functioning of the criminal justice system." The Court also noted that there are other checks on prosecutorial misconduct, including the criminal law and professional discipline.

The Court therefore held that prosecutors are absolutely immune from liability under §1983 for their conduct in "initiating a prosecution and in presenting the State's case," insofar as that conduct is "intimately associated with the judicial phase of the criminal process." Each of the charges against the prosecutor in *Imbler* involved conduct having that association, including the alleged knowing use of false testimony at trial and the alleged deliberate suppression of exculpatory evidence. *The Court expressly declined to decide whether absolute immunity extends to "those aspects of the prosecutor's responsibility that cast him in the role of an administrator or investigative officer rather than that of an advocate." It was recognized, though, that "the duties of the prosecutor in his role as advocate for the State involve actions preliminary to the initiation of a prosecution and actions apart from the courtroom"* . . . [emphasis added]. We have been "quite sparing" in our recognition of absolute immunity, and have refused to extend it any "further than its justification would warrant."

We now consider whether the absolute prosecutorial immunity recognized in *Imbler* is applicable to

(a) respondent's participation in a probable cause hearing, which led to the issuance of a search warrant, and

(b) respondent's legal advice to the police regarding the use of hypnosis and the existence of probable cause to arrest petitioner.

We address first respondent's appearance as a lawyer for the State in the probable cause hearing, where he examined a witness and successfully supported the application for a search warrant. The decision in *Imbler* leads to the conclusion that respondent is absolutely immune from liability in a §1983 suit for that conduct. . . .

Like witnesses, prosecutors and other lawyers were absolutely immune from damages liability at common law for making false or defamatory statements in judicial proceedings (at least so long as the statements were related to the proceeding), and also for eliciting false and defamatory testimony from witnesses. . . .

The prosecutor's actions at issue here — appearing before a judge and presenting evidence in support of a motion for a search warrant — clearly involve the prosecutor's "role as advocate for the State," rather than his role as "administrator or investigative officer," the protection for which we reserved judgment in *Imbler*. Moreover, since the issuance of a search warrant is unquestionably a judicial act, appearing at a probable cause hearing is "intimately associated with the judicial phase of the criminal process." It is also connected with the initiation and conduct of a prosecution, particularly where the hearing occurs after arrest, as was the case here.

. . . [P]retrial court appearances by the prosecutor in support of taking criminal action against a suspect present a substantial likelihood of vexatious litigation that might have an untoward effect on the independence of the prosecutor. Therefore, absolute immunity for this function serves the policy of protecting the judicial process, which underlies much of the Court's decision in *Imbler*. . . .

Accordingly, we hold that the respondent's appearance in court in support of an application for a search warrant and the presentation of evidence at that hearing are protected by absolute immunity.

Turning to respondent's acts of providing legal advice to the police, we note first that neither respondent nor the court below has identified any historical or common-law support for extending absolute immunity to such actions by prosecutors. . . .

The next factor to be considered — risk of vexatious litigation — also does not support absolute immunity for giving legal advice. The Court of Appeals asserted that absolute immunity was justified because "a prosecutor's risk of becoming entangled in litigation based on his or her role as a legal advisor is as likely as the risks associated with initiating and prosecuting a case." We disagree. In the first place, a suspect or defendant is not likely to be as aware of a prosecutor's role in giving advice as a prosecutor's role in initiating and conducting a prosecution. But even if a prosecutor's role in giving advice to the police does carry with it some risk of burdensome litigation, the concern with litigation in our immunity cases is not merely a generalized concern with interference with an official's duties, but rather is a concern with interference with the conduct closely related to the judicial process. Absolute immunity is designed to free the judicial process from the harassment and intimidation associated with litigation. That concern therefore justifies absolute prosecutorial immunity only for actions that are connected with the prosecutor's role in judicial proceedings, not for every litigation-inducing conduct.

The Court of Appeals speculated that anything short of absolute immunity would discourage prosecutors from performing their "vital obligation" of giving legal advice to the police. . . . Although the absence of absolute immunity for the act of giving legal advice may cause prosecutors to consider their advice more carefully, "[w]here an official could be expected to know that his conduct would violate statutory or constitutional rights, he should be made to hesitate." Indeed, it is incongruous to allow prosecutors to be absolutely immune from liability for giving advice to the police, but to allow police officers only qualified immunity for following the advice. Ironically, it would mean that the police, who do not ordinarily hold law degrees, would be required to know the clearly established law, but prosecutors would not. . . .

As a final basis for allowing absolute immunity for legal advice, the Court of Appeals observed that there are several checks other than civil litigation to prevent abuses of authority by prosecutors. Although we agree, we note that one of the most important checks, the judicial process, will not necessarily restrain out-of-court activities by a prosecutor that occur prior to the initiation of a prosecution, such as providing legal advice to the police. This is particularly true if a suspect is not eventually prosecuted. In those circumstances, the prosecutor's action is not subjected to the "crucible of the judicial process." In sum, we conclude that respondent has not met his burden of showing that the relevant factors justify an extension of absolute immunity to the prosecutorial function of giving legal advice to the police. [Parties claiming absolute immunity have to prove by a preponderance of the evidence that they should receive absolute immunity.]

For the foregoing reasons, we affirm in part and reverse in part the judgment of the Court of Appeals. It is so ordered.

CASE DISCUSSION

What reasons does the Court give for the absolute immunity of prosecutors? Why do police enjoy only qualified immunity whereas prosecutors enjoy absolute immunity? Why did the Court treat the prosecutor's appearance at the search warrant hearing differently from the prosecutor's provision of legal advice to the police? Should the immunity cover both, neither, or one but not the other? Why?

D e c i s i o n   P o i n t

Some important questions about recovering for damages are not as easily answered if the suit involves injuries less apparent than the clearly brutal treatment received by the plaintiffs in the case excerpts in this chapter. These cases are unusual, even if they are disturbing. Far more common are property damages caused by *lawful* searches and seizures or unlawful searches and seizures that are not so disturbing. Should "victims" recover for damages in the following cases?

1. A door worth $500 is irreparably damaged when police enter a house with the wrong address on a warrant to search an unoccupied house.

2. The same type of door is damaged when the correct house is entered pursuant to a lawful search warrant that produces evidence sufficient to convict the house's owner.

3. The same type of door is broken pursuant to a lawful entry that produces evidence against the house's owner and involves no further proceedings.

4. The same type of door is broken pursuant to an unlawful entry that the police honestly believe is lawful.

5. The same type of door is broken pursuant to an unlawful search, but the "victim" turns out to be

guilty of the crime that led the police to search for evidence.

If the victims are entitled to recover, who should pay? Individual officers who did the damage? Their superiors? The police department? The municipality under whose jurisdiction the department is located?

The Senate proposed legislation to answer some of these questions. It provided, in part, the following:

Section 2692. Tort Claims; Illegal Search and Seizure

(a) The United States shall be liable for any damages resulting from a search or seizure conducted by an investigative or law enforcement officer, acting within the scope of his office or employment, in violation of the United States Constitution.

(b) Any person aggrieved by such a violation may recover actual damages and such punitive damages as the court may award under subsection (c).

(c) Punitive damages may be awarded by the court, upon consideration of all the circumstances of the case, including—

(1) The extent of the investigation o[r] law enforcement officer's deviation from permissible conduct.

(2) The extent to which the violation was willful, reckless, or grossly negligent;

(3) The extent to which the aggrieved person's privacy was invaded;

(4) The extent of the aggrieved person's personal injury, both physical and mental;

(5) The extent of the property damage; and

(6) The effect such an award would have in preventing future violations of the United States Constitution.

(d) Notwithstanding subsections (b) and (c), the recovery of any person who is convicted of any offense for which evidence of such offense was seized in violation of the United States Constitution is limited to actual physical injury and to actual property damage sustained as a result of the unconstitutional search and seizure.

(e) No judgment, award, or compromise, or settlement of any action brought under this section shall exceed the amount of $25,000, including actual and punitive damages.[55]

---◆---

Those who sue the government rarely win their cases. Not often do the juries awarding damages look favorably on "criminals" who want to collect money from police officers who "were only doing their jobs." According to Anthony Amsterdam, prominent defense attorney and constitutional law professor,

> Where are the lawyers going to come from to handle these cases for the plaintiffs? . . . [W]hat on earth would possess a lawyer to file a claim for damages . . . in an ordinary search-and-seizure case? The prospect of a share in the substantial damages to be expected? The chance to earn a reputation as a police-hating lawyer, so that he can no longer count on straight testimony concerning the length of skid marks in his personal injury cases? The gratitude of his client when his filing of the claim causes the prosecutor to refuse a lesser-included-offense plea or to charge priors or pile on "cover" charges? The opportunity to represent his client without fee in these resulting criminal matters?
>
> Police cases are an unadulterated investigative and litigate nightmare. Taking on the police in any tribunal involves a commitment to the most frustrating and thankless legal work I know. And the idea that an unrepresented, inarticulate, prosecution-vulnerable citizen can make a case against a team of professional investigators and testifiers in any tribunal beggars belief. Even in a tribunal having recognized responsibilities and some resources to conduct independent investigations, a plaintiff without assiduous counsel devoted to developing his side of the case would be utterly outmastered by the police. No, I think we shall have airings of police searches and seizures on suppression motions or not at all.[56]

Therefore, police officers enjoy two forms of protection against civil liability:

1. Qualified immunity (discussed above).
2. The practical advantage of the reluctance of juries and judges to award damages against them. (Incidentally, judges, defense attorneys, and, as we have seen, prosecutors for the most part enjoy even greater protection — absolute immunity from lawsuits arising out of their duties.)

Because of the obstacles to suing police officers, some have suggested that the following changes might improve the chances of recovery:

- Government liability for illegal acts of officers
- Minimum liquidated damages, meaning paid-up or settled amounts of money for particular wrongs
- Restrictions on defenses based on reputation, such as where damage to reputation is difficult to prove when the plaintiff is a "disreputable person"[57]

INJUNCTION

Injunctions are court orders directed to police departments and other criminal justice agencies ordering them to cease illegal conduct. Sometimes, injunctions order agencies to desist from actions against specific individuals or groups of individuals. For example, in *Lankford v. Gelston,* police engaged in a mass search-and-arrest action to apprehend two armed robbers who had shot a police officer. The officers broke into houses at all hours without probable cause, ransacked houses, and took residents to police stations in the middle of the night. Plaintiffs asked for an injunction against the particular searches involved on the specific occasion.

Sometimes, injunctions take aim at general police department policies that affect the plaintiff who seeks the injunction. For example, in *City of Los Angeles v. Lyons,* an injunction was sought against the Los Angeles Police Department's use of chokeholds.

CASE

Should the Court Order the Police to Stop Using Chokeholds?

City of Los Angeles v. Lyons
461 U.S. 95, 103 S.Ct. 1660, 75 L.Ed.2d 675 (1983)

Lyons brought a civil rights action against the city, seeking damages, injunctive relief, and declaratory relief. On remand after an appeal, the United States District Court for the Central District of California granted preliminary injunctive relief, and the Court of Appeals, Ninth Circuit, affirmed. On grant of certiorari, *the Supreme Court reversed. Justice Marshall dissented and filed an opinion in which Justice Brennan, Justice Blackmun, and Justice Stevens joined. Justice White wrote the opinion of the Court.*

FACTS

Adolph Lyons is a 24-year-old Negro male who resides in Los Angeles. . . . [A]t about 2 A.M. on October 6, 1976, Lyons was pulled over to the curb by two officers of the Los Angeles Police Department (LAPD) for a traffic infraction because one of his headlights was burned out. The officers greeted him with drawn revolvers as he exited from the car. Lyons was told to face his car and spread his legs. He did so. He was then ordered to clasp his hands and put them on top of his head. He again complied. After one of the officers completed a patdown search, Lyons dropped his hands, but was ordered to place them back above his head and slammed them onto his head. Lyons complained about the pain caused by the ring of keys he was holding in his hand. Within 5 to 10 seconds, the officer began to choke Lyons by applying a forearm against his throat. As Lyons struggled for air, the officer handcuffed him, but continued to apply the chokehold—either the "bar arm control" hold or the "carotid-artery control" hold or both—until he blacked out. When Lyons regained consciousness, he was lying face down on the ground, choking, gasping for air, and spitting up blood and dirt. He had urinated and defecated.

[COURT NOTE: "The police control procedures at issue in this case are referred to as 'control holds,' 'chokeholds,' 'strangleholds,' and 'neck restraints.' All these terms refer to two basic control procedures: the 'carotid' hold and the 'bar arm' hold. In the 'carotid' hold, an officer positioned behind a subject places one arm around the subject's neck and holds the wrist of that arm with his other hand. The officer, by using his lower forearm and bicep muscle, applies pressure concentrating on the carotid arteries located on the sides of the subject's neck. 'Bar arm' pressure causes pain, reduces the flow of oxygen to the lungs, and may render the subject unconscious."]

He was issued a traffic citation and released. . . . On February 7, 1977 . . . respondent, Adolph Lyons, filed a complaint for damages, injunction, and declaratory relief [under §1983 of the United States Code] in the United States District Court for the Central District of California. The defendants were the City of Los Angeles and four of its police officers. . . . Counts I through IV of the complaint sought damages against the officers and the City. Count V, with which we are principally concerned here, sought a preliminary and permanent injunction against the City barring the use of the control holds. The count alleged that the City's police officers, "pursuant to the authorization, instruction and encouragement of Defendant City of Los Angeles, regularly and routinely apply these chokeholds in innumerable situations where they are not threatened by the use of any deadly force whatsoever," that numerous persons have been injured as the result of the application of the chokeholds, that Lyons and others similarly situated are threatened with irreparable injury in the form of bodily injury and loss of life, and that Lyons "justifiably fears that any contact he has with Los Angeles Police officers may result in his being choked and strangled to death without provocation, justification or other legal excuse."

Lyons alleged the threatened impairment of rights protected by the First, Fourth, Eighth, and Fourteenth Amendments. Injunctive relief was sought against the use of the control holds "except in situations where the proposed victim of said control rea-

sonably appears to be threatening the immediate use of deadly force." Count VI sought declaratory relief against the City, i.e., a judgment that use of the chokeholds absent the threat of immediate use of deadly force is a per se violation of various constitutional rights. . . .

The District Court found that Lyons had been stopped for a traffic infringement and that without provocation or legal justification the officers involved had applied a "Department-authorized chokehold which resulted in injuries to the plaintiff." The court further found that the department authorizes the use of the holds in situations where no one is threatened by death or grievous bodily harm, that officers are insufficiently trained, that the use of the holds involves a high risk of injury or death as then employed, and that their continued use in situations where neither death nor serious injury is threatened "is unconscionable in a civilized society." The court concluded that such use violated Lyon's substantive due process rights under the Fourth Amendment. A preliminary injunction was entered enjoining "the use of both the carotid artery and arm bar holds under circumstances which do not threaten death or serious bodily injury." An improved training program and regular reporting and recordkeeping were also ordered. The Court of Appeals affirmed [and] in a brief per curiam opinion stated that the District Court had not abused its discretion in entering a preliminary injunction. We granted certiorari, and now reverse.

OPINION

Since our grant of certiorari, circumstances pertinent to the case have changed. Originally, Lyons' complaint alleged that at least two deaths had occurred as a result of the applications of chokeholds by the police. His first amended complaint alleged that 10 chokehold-related deaths had occurred. By May 1982, there had been five more such deaths. On May 6, 1982, the Chief of Police in Los Angeles prohibited the use of the bar-arm chokehold in any circumstances. A few days later, on May 12, 1982, the Board of Police Commissioners imposed a 6-month moratorium on the use of the carotid-artery chokehold except under circumstances where deadly force is authorized.

Based on these events, on June 3, 1982, the City filed in this Court a memorandum suggesting a question of mootness, reciting the facts but arguing that the case was not moot. [*Mootness* means that the issue raised in the case is "dead" or "merely academic."] Lyons in turn filed a motion to dismiss the writ of certiorari [as] improvidently granted. We denied that motion but reserved the question of mootness for later consideration.

In his brief and at oral argument, Lyons has reasserted his position [that] in light of changed conditions, an injunction decree is now unnecessary because he is no longer subject to a threat of injury. He urges that the preliminary injunction should be vacated. The City, on the other hand, while acknowledging that subsequent events have significantly changed the posture of this case, again asserts that the case is not moot because the moratorium is not permanent and may be lifted at any time.

We agree with the City that the case is not moot, since the moratorium by its terms is not permanent. Intervening events have not "irrevocably eradicated the effects of the alleged violation." We nevertheless hold, for another reason, that the federal courts are without jurisdiction to entertain Lyons' claims for injunctive relief.

It goes without saying that those who seek to invoke the jurisdiction of the federal courts must satisfy the threshold requirement imposed by Art. III of the Constitution by alleging an actual case or controversy. Plaintiffs must demonstrate a "personal stake in the outcome" in order to "assure that concrete adverseness which sharpens the presentation of issues" necessary for the proper resolution of constitution questions. Abstract injury i[s] not enough. The plaintiff must show that he "has sustained or is immediately in danger of sustaining some direct injury" as a result of the challenged official conduct and the injury or threat of injury must be both "real and immediate," not "conjectural" or "hypothetical." . . .

Lyons has failed to demonstrate a case or controversy with the City that would justify the equitable relief sought. Lyons' standing to seek the injunction requested depended on whether he was likely to suffer future injury from the use of the chokeholds by police officers. Count V of the complaint alleged the traffic stop and choking incident five months before. That

Lyons may have been illegally choked by the police on October 6, 1976, while presumably affording Lyons standing to claim damages against the individual officers and perhaps against the City, does nothing to establish a real and immediate threat that he would again be stopped for a traffic violation, or for any other offense, by an officer or officers who would illegally choke him into unconsciousness without any provocation or resistance on his part. The additional allegation in the complaint that the police in Los Angeles routinely apply chokeholds in situations where they are not threatened by the use of deadly force falls far short of the allegations that would be necessary to establish a case or controversy between these parties.

In order to establish an actual controversy in this case, Lyons would have had not only to allege that he would have another encounter with the police but also to make the incredible assertion either (1) that all police officers in Los Angeles always choke any citizen with whom they happen to have an encounter, whether for the purpose of arrest, issuing a citation, or for questioning, or (2) that the City ordered or authorized police officers to act in such a manner. Although Count V alleged that the City authorized the use of the control holds in situations where deadly force was not threatened, it did not indicate why Lyons might be realistically threatened by police officers who acted within the strictures of the City's policy. If, for example, chokeholds were authorized to be used only to counter resistance to an arrest by a suspect, or to thwart an effort to escape, any future threat to Lyons from the City's policy or from the conduct of the police officers would be no more real than the possibility that he would again have an encounter with the police and that either he would illegally resist arrest or detention or the officers would disobey their instructions and again render him unconscious without any provocation. . . .

Absent a sufficient likelihood that he will again be wronged in a similar way. Lyons is no more entitled to an injunction than any other citizen of Los Angeles; and a federal court may not entertain a claim by any or all citizens who no more than assert that certain practices of law enforcement officers are unconstitutional. This is not to suggest that such undifferentiated claims should not be taken seriously by local authorities. Indeed, the interest of an alert and interested citizen is an essential element of an effective and fair government, whether on the local, state, or national level. A federal court, however, is not the proper forum to press such claims unless the requirements for entry and the prerequisites for injunctive relief are satisfied.

We decline the invitation to slight the preconditions for equitable relief; for as we have held, recognition of the need for a proper balance between state and federal authority counsels restraint in the issuance of injunctions against state officers engaged in the administration of the State's criminal laws in the absence of irreparable injury which is both great and immediate. . . . [T]he normal principals [*sic*] of equity, comity, and federalism . . . should inform the judgment of federal courts when asked to oversee state law enforcement authorities. In exercising their equitable powers federal courts must recognize "[t]he special delicacy of the adjustment to be preserved between federal equitable power and State administration of its own law." . . .

. . . [W]ithholding injunctive relief does not mean that the "federal law will exercise no deterrent effect in these circumstances." If Lyons has suffered an injury barred by the Federal Constitution, he has a remedy for damages under §1983. Furthermore, those who deliberately deprive a citizen of his constitutional rights risk conviction under the federal criminal laws.

Beyond these considerations the state courts need not impose the same standing or remedial requirements that govern federal-court proceedings. The individual States may permit their courts to use injunctions to oversee the conduct of law enforcement authorities on a continuing basis. But this is not the role of a federal court, absent far more justification than Lyons has proffered in this case. The judgment of the Court of Appeals is accordingly reversed.

DISSENT

Justice Marshall, with whom Justice Brennan, Justice Blackmun, and Justice Stevens join, dissenting.

The District Court found that the City of Los Angeles authorizes its police officers to apply life-threatening chokeholds to citizens who pose no threat of violence, and that respondent, Adolph Lyons, was subjected to such a chokehold. The Court today holds that a federal court is without power to enjoin the enforcement of the city's policy, no matter how flagrantly unconstitutional it may be. Since no one can show that he will be choked in the future, no one—not even a person who, like Lyons, has almost been choked to death—has standing to challenge the continuation of the policy. The city is free to continue the policy indefinitely as long as it is willing to pay damages for the injuries and deaths that result. I dissent from this unprecedented and unwarranted approach to standing.

There is plainly a "case or controversy" concerning the constitutionality of the city's chokehold policy. The constitutionality of that policy is directly implicated by Lyons' claim for damages against the city. The complaint clearly alleges that the officer who choked Lyons was carrying out an official policy, and a municipality is liable under 42 U.S.C. §1983 for the conduct of its employees only if they acted pursuant to such a policy. Lyons therefore has standing to challenge the city's chokehold policy and to obtain whatever relief a court may ultimately deem appropriate. None of our prior decisions suggests that his requests for particular forms of relief raise any additional issues concerning his standing. Standing has always depended on whether a plaintiff has a "personal stake in the outcome of the controversy," not on the "precise nature of the relief sought." . . .

Although the city instructs its officers that use of a chokehold does not constitute deadly force, since 1975 no less than 16 persons have died following the use of a chokehold by an LAPD police officer. Twelve had been Negro males. [DISSENT NOTE: "Thus in a city where Negro males constitute 9% of the population, they have accounted for 75% of the deaths resulting from the use of chokeholds. In addition to his other allegations, Lyons alleged racial discrimination in violation of the Equal Protection Clause of the Fourteenth Amendment."]

The evidence submitted to the District Court established that for many years it has been the official policy of the city to permit officers to employ chokeholds in a variety of situations where they face no threat of violence. In reported "altercations" between LAPD officers and citizens the chokeholds are used more frequently than any other means of physical restraint. Between February 1975 and July 1980, LAPD officers applied chokeholds on at least 975 occasions, which represented more than three-quarters of the reported altercations.

It is undisputed that chokeholds pose a high and unpredictable risk of serious injury or death. Chokeholds are intended to bring a subject under control by causing pain and rendering him unconscious. Depending on the position of the officer's arm and the force applied, the victim's voluntary or involuntary reaction, and his state of health, an officer may inadvertently crush the victim's larynx, trachea, or hyoid. The result may be either cardiac arrest or asphyxiation. An LAPD officer described the reaction of a person to being choked as "do[ing] the chicken," in reference apparently to the reactions of a chicken when its neck is wrung. The victim experiences extreme pain. His face turns blue as he is deprived of oxygen, he goes into spasmodic convulsions, his eyes roll back, his body wiggles, his feet kick up and down, and his arms move about wildly. . . .

The Court errs in suggesting that Lyons' prayer for injunctive relief in Cou[n]t V of his first amended complaint concerns a policy that was not responsible for his injuries and that therefore could not support an award of damages. . . . There is no basis for the Court's assertion that Lyons has failed to allege "that the City either orders or authorizes application of the chokeholds where there is no resistance or other provocation. . . ."

CASE DISCUSSION

What interests did the Supreme Court balance in its decision? Does the Court favor law enforcement over individual rights? Result over process? What standards did the Court use to determine whether or not Adolph Lyons had a case against the Los Angeles Police Department? Do you think it is fair to require Lyons to show that he may suffer chokeholds again before he can ask for relief in court? What arguments does the dissent present to grant Lyons relief? Do you agree with the arguments? What, if any, remedies would you prescribe in this case? Explain.

INTERNAL AGENCY DISCIPLINE

The remedies for enforcing constitutional standards raise complicated issues. Formally, injured citizens can select from a broad range of means to protect themselves against injuries from government wrongdoing. Informally, however, the remedies are not so all-encompassing. Practically speaking, the exclusionary rule predominates as a remedy, but it protects only guilty persons. Obviously, innocent people have no need to challenge evidence against them. Plaintiffs have frequently sued the government and its agents for constitutional torts, but they rarely succeed in getting the damages or injunctions they seek. Prosecutors, judges, and defense attorneys are immune from civil suits. Prejudices against "unsavory" victims and for hardworking police officers tend to prevent jury awards in civil cases against law enforcement officers.

These shortcomings have led to heavier reliance on internal discipline. This remedy rests upon the confidence that the principles and practice of administrative rule making will reduce government misconduct. This complex concept relies on the following core ideas: police departments, prosecutors' offices, public defenders' offices, and even courts should state their policies and formulate written rules to implement those policies. The task of formulating rules should involve the broad participation of department or agency personnel, particularly those such as patrol officers, assistant attorneys, and others who are mainly responsible for carrying out the rules day-to-day.

Once rules have been formulated, policy makers should put them into writing. To enforce them requires review, rewards for compliance, and sanctions for violations. Rewards might include promotion and merit increases. Sanctions might include reprimand, counseling, suspension, and, in extreme cases, dismissal. Supporters of internal discipline believe that this combination of rewards for compliance and sanctions for violation can most effectively control government officials and, therefore, protect citizens against improper state intrusions and deprivations.

A Senate bill with respect to unlawful searches and seizures put this idea into legislative form, as follows:

> Section 2693. Sanctions Against Investigative or Law Enforcement Officers; Illegal Search and Seizure
>
> An investigative or law enforcement officer who conducts a search or seizure in violation of the United States Constitution shall be subject to appropriate discipline in the discretion of the Federal agency employing such officer, if that agency determines, after notice and hearing, that the officer conducted such search and seizure lacking a good faith belief that such search or seizure was constitutional.[58]

Despite the suits for damages and injunctions and the internal rule-making procedures in place in most criminal justice agencies, the exclusionary rule remains the principal, if less-than-satisfactory, remedy for government lawbreaking in criminal law enforcement. You have encountered it in Chapters 3 through 9 of this text, dealing with police practices. The other process remedies arise in Chapters 11 through 13, dealing with prosecutors, defense attorneys, and judges in judicial proceedings.

SUMMARY

Criminal law deals with private persons who violate the criminal code. However, one aspect of the law of criminal procedure answers this question: What shall be the recourse of the private individual when the government breaks the law? Several remedies are available to private individuals who suffer injury from official misconduct or even the honest mistakes of public officials. One group of remedies is directed at the criminal process. These include

1. Excluding illegally seized evidence
2. Dismissing criminal cases against the victims of official lawbreaking
3. Reversing convictions where the government has made reversible errors

Individuals injured by official lawbreaking can also sue the officer directly, the agency employing the officer, or the government unit with jurisdiction over the officer or agency. These suits might arise directly under the United States Constitution and state constitutions for violations of constitutional rights. They might also stem from state tort actions or state statutes. Most are brought under §1983 of the United States Code, or the Civil Rights Act, which gives private persons a right to sue for damages when states violate their constitutional rights. Plaintiffs in private lawsuits can obtain either monetary damages or court orders (injunctions) prohibiting specific government action.

The government might also prosecute officers whose illegal conduct constitutes a crime. Illegal searches constitute burglary, breaking and entering, and criminal trespass in some instances. Illegal arrests, depending on the circumstances, constitute kidnapping or assault. Finally, agencies can impose internal disciplinary action, including suspension and dismissal, against officers' misconduct.

REVIEW QUESTIONS

1. Define the *exclusionary rule* and describe its history.

2. Identify and explain the three rationales for the exclusionary rule. Which rationale does the present Supreme Court adopt, and why?

3. Identify the major social costs of the exclusionary rule. What does empirical research tell us about the social costs of the exclusionary rule?

4. Identify and describe the major exceptions to the exclusionary rule.

5. Define the *fruit of the poisonous tree doctrine*, and then identify the principal exceptions to it.

6. Define the *good faith exception* and explain its rationale.

7. Define and explain the significance of the doctrine of *standing*.

8. Explain how and under what circumstances the remedy of "dismissal" works.

9. Identify, define, and explain the three principal tests of entrapment. Give examples of each.

10. Explain the relationship between due process and the defense of entrapment.

11. Define and explain how *reversible error* works.

12. Define *expungement* and explain when it is available.

13. Identify and define the principal remedies that individuals seek when they sue the government or its agents.

14. Define *constitutional torts* and explain when they provide grounds for suing the government.

15. What are the principal state tort actions available to individuals against governments and their agents?

16. Explain "immunity." When is it available to local and state governments and their agents? When is it available to the federal government and its agents?

17. What did the Supreme Court decide in *Anderson v. Creighton*? What is the significance of the decision?

18. What are the requirements for suing the government under §1983? How do they differ from suing individual government agents?

19. What immunity do prosecutors have from lawsuits by individuals?

20. How successful are those who sue the government or their agents? Explain why.

21. What are the remedies available under internal agency discipline? Explain the strengths and the weaknesses of internal discipline.

KEY TERMS

absolute immunity the absence of liability for actions within the scope of duties.

affirmative defense a defense in which defendants must introduce evidence in their favor.

amicus curiae **brief** an argument submitted by a party that has a strong interest in a case but is not a party to it.

attenuation doctrine the principle that evidence remote from illegal conduct is admissible.

balancing test of local government liability the test that balances the need for effective law enforcement against avoiding putting members of the public at risk.

compensatory damages the amount of money needed to account for injuries actually suffered by a plaintiff.

constitutional rationale the idea that the exclusionary rule is an essential part of constitutional rights.

damages a remedy in private lawsuits in the form of money for injuries.

deterrence rationale the justification that excluding evidence obtained in violation of the Constitution prevents illegal law enforcement.

doctrine of official immunity the rule that limits the liability of individual criminal justice personnel if sued for willful or malicious wrongdoing.

doctrine of *respondeat superior* the rule that sees a superior as liable for a subordinate's torts within the scope of employment.

entrapment a defense to crime based on a law enforcement officer's illegal inducement to commit the crime.

exclusionary rule the rule that illegally seized evidence cannot be admitted in criminal trials.

expungement the removal of criminal records from official files.

federal constitutional tort the legal action based on the violation of constitutional rights by federal officers.

fruit of the poisonous tree doctrine the principle that evidence derived from illegally obtained sources is not admissible.

good faith exception the principle that evidence is not excluded when police reasonably rely on a defective search warrant.

harmless errors errors not affecting the outcome of a case.

impeach to show that a witness's credibility is suspect.

independent source doctrine the principle of admitting evidence obtained independently of illegal conduct.

inevitable discovery rule the principle of admitting illegally seized evidence that would eventually come to light by alternative legal means.

injunctions court orders to act or to refrain from acting.

judicial integrity rationale the idea that the honor and honesty of the courts justify the exclusionary rule.

objective test of entrapment the test of entrapment that focuses on the actions of government agents to induce defendants to commit crimes.

one-step rule the rule stating that defendants have standing to object to searches only if their expectation of privacy is violated.

plaintiffs parties who bring a civil action.

punitive damages the amount of money needed to punish defendants for malicious and intentional wrongdoing.

qualified immunity immunity from tort action that is granted if a party was acting reasonably within the scope of duties.

reversible errors errors that affect the outcome of a case.

Section 1983 action an action brought under the Civil Rights Act, U.S. Code §1983, for violation of federal civil rights under color of state law.

standing the right to challenge a government's constitutional violations.

subjective test of entrapment the test of entrapment that focuses on the predisposition of defendants to commit crimes.

torts civil lawsuits for damages.

vicarious official immunity the rule that allows government units to benefit from the official immunity of their employees.

Notes

1. Jon O. Newman, "Suing the Lawbreakers: Proposals to Strengthen the Section 1983 Damage Remedy for Law Enforcers' Misconduct," *Yale Law Journal* 87 (1978): 447–67.

2. *Mapp v. Ohio*, 367 U.S. 643, 81 S.Ct. 1684, 6 L.Ed.2d 1081 (1961); *Miranda v. Arizona*, 384 U.S. 436, 86 S.Ct. 1602, 16 L.Ed.2d 694 (1966); *United States v. Wade*, 388 U.S. 218, 87 S.Ct. 1926, 18 L.Ed.2d 1149

(1967); *Gelbard v. United States*, 408 U.S. 41, 92 S.Ct. 2357, 33 L.Ed.2d 179 (1972); *United States v. Caceres*, 440 U.S. 741, 99 S.Ct. 1465, 59 L.Ed.2d 733 (1979).

3. Potter Stewart, U.S. Supreme Court justice, retired, "The Road to *Mapp v. Ohio* and Beyond: The Origins, Development, and Future of the Exclusionary Rule in Search-and-Seizure Cases," *Columbia Law Review* 83 (1983): 1365, 1380–83; quotation from *Weeks v. United*

States, 232 U.S. 383, 393, 34 S.Ct. 341, 344, 58 L.Ed. 652 (1914); the "one hand clapping" quotation is Professor Richard Uviller's in his *Tempered Zeal* (Chicago: Contemporary Books, 1988).

4. 277 U.S. 438, 470, 48 S.Ct. 564, 575, 72 L.Ed.2d 944 (1928).

5. Milton A. Loewenthal, "Evaluating the Exclusionary Rule in Search and Seizure," *University of Missouri at Kansas City Law Review* 49 (1980): 24–40; Justice Stewart, writing for the Court in *Elkins v. United States,* 364 U.S. 206, 217, 80 S.Ct. 1437, 1444, 4 L.Ed.2d 1669 (1960).

6. Stewart, "Road to *Mapp v. Ohio,*" 1379.

7. William A. Schroeder, "Deterring Fourth Amendment Violations," *Georgetown Law Journal* 69 (1981): 1361, 1378–86.

8. 277 U.S. 438, 468.

9. Myron W. Orfield, Jr., "The Exclusionary Rule and Deterrence: An Empirical Study of Chicago Narcotics Officers," *University of Chicago Law Review* 54 (1987): 1017–18, 1029.

10. Ibid., 1027–28.

11. National Institute of Justice, *The Effects of the Exclusionary Rule: A Study of California* (Washington, DC: U.S. Government Printing Office, 1982), 12.

12. Yale Kamisar, "Does (Did) (Should) the Exclusionary Rule Rest on a 'Principled Basis' Rather Than on 'Empirical Propositions'?" *Creighton Law Review* 16 (1983): 565.

13. American Bar Association, *Criminal Justice in Crisis* (Chicago: American Bar Association, 1988), 11.

14. *Annals of Congress* 1 (1789): 439.

15. Justice Benjamin Cardozo in *People v. Defore,* 242 N.Y. 13, 150 N.E. 585 (1926).

16. 232 U.S. 383, 34 S.Ct. 341, 58 L.Ed. 652 (1914).

17. 251 U.S. 385, 391, 40 S.Ct. 182, 64 L.Ed. 319 (1920).

18. Stewart, "Road to *Mapp v. Ohio,*" 1376–77.

19. *Wolf v. Colorado,* 338 U.S. 25, 69 S.Ct. 1359, 93 L.Ed. 1782 (1949); *Mapp v. Ohio,* 367 U.S. 643, 81 S.Ct. 1684, 6 L.Ed.2d 1081 (1961); Justice Stewart explains the circumstances of the case's appeal in "Road to *Mapp v. Ohio,*" 1367.

20. *United States v. Calandra,* 414 U.S. 338, 94 S.Ct. 613, 38 L.Ed.2d 561 (1974).

21. *Alderman v. United States,* 394 U.S. 165, 174, 89 S.Ct. 961, 966, 22 L.Ed.2d 176 (1969); *Walder v. United States,* 347 U.S. 62, 74 S.Ct. 354, 98 L.Ed. 503 (1954); also to the same effect, *Harris v. New York,* 401 U.S.

222, 91 S.Ct. 643, 28 L.Ed.2d 1 (1971); but see *United States v. Hinckley,* 672 F.2d 115 (D.C.Cir. 1982).

22. "Twenty-Sixth Annual Review of Criminal Procedure," *Georgetown Law Journal* 79 (1997): 978; *Nardone v. United States,* 308 U.S. 338, 60 S.Ct. 266, 84 L.Ed. 307 (1939), and *Wong Sun v. United States,* 371 U.S. 471, 83 S.Ct. 407, 9 L.Ed.2d 441 (1963) (tainted fruit); *Segura v. United States,* 468 U.S. 796, 104 S.Ct. 3380, 82 L.Ed.2d 599 (1984).

23. 371 U.S. 471, 83 S.Ct. 407, 9 L.Ed.2d 441 (1963).

24. 467 U.S. 431, 104 S.Ct. 2501, 81 L.Ed.2d 377 (1984).

25. See also Ashdown, "Good Faith, the Exclusionary Remedy, and Rule-Oriented Adjudication in the Criminal Process," *William and Mary Law Review* 24 (1983): 335; Ball, "Good Faith and the Fourth Amendment: The 'Reasonable' Exception to the Exclusionary Rule," *Journal of Criminal Law and Criminology* 69 (1978): 635; Yale Kamisar, "Gates, 'Probable Cause,' 'Good Faith,' and Beyond," *Iowa Law Review* 69 (1984): 551; Schlag, "Assaults on the Exclusionary Rule: Good Faith, Limitations, and Damage Remedies," *Journal of Criminal Law and Criminology* 73 (1982): 875.

26. Thomas Y. Davies, "A Hard Look at What We Know (and Still Need to Learn) About the 'Social Costs' of the Exclusionary Rule: The NIJ Study and Other Studies of 'Lost' Arrests," *American Bar Foundation Research Journal* 1983: 640; Peter F. Nardulli, "The Societal Costs of the Exclusionary Rule Revisited," *University of Illinois Law Review* 1987: 235.

27. *Stringer v. State,* 477 So.2d 1335 (Miss. 1985).

28. *Federal Rules of Criminal Procedure,* 12(b)(3).

29. *Rakas v. Illinois,* 439 U.S. 128, 99 S.Ct. 421, 58 L.Ed.2d 387 (1978); *United States v. Jeffers,* 342 U.S. 48, 72 S.Ct. 93, 96 L.Ed. 59 (1951); *Rawlings v. Kentucky,* 448 U.S. 98, 100 S.Ct. 2556, 65 L.Ed.2d 633 (1980).

30. *Board of Commissioners v. Backus,* 29 How. Pr. 33, 42 (1864).

31. *People v. Mills,* 178 N.Y. 274, 70 N.E. 786, 791 (1904).

32. Paul Marcus, "The Development of Entrapment Law," *Wayne Law Review* 33 (1986): 5.

33. Jonathan C. Carlson, "The Act Requirement and the Foundations of the Entrapment Defense," *Virginia Law Review* 73 (1987): 1011.

34. *United States v. Jenrette,* 744 F.2d 817 (D.C.Cir. 1984) (one of the Abscam cases); "Gershman, Abscam, the Judiciary, and the Ethics of Entrapment," *Yale Law Journal* 91 (1982): 1565 (history of Abscam); L. Tiffany

and others, *Detection of Crime* (Boston: Little, Brown, 1967) (quotation defining *encouragement*).

35. Wayne R. LaFave and Jerold H. Israel, *Criminal Procedure* (St. Paul: West, 1984), 1: 412–13.

36. 356 U.S. 369, 78 S.Ct. 819, 2 L.Ed.2d 848 (1958).

37. American Law Institute, *Model Penal Code and Commentaries* (Philadelphia: American Law Institute, 1985), Part I, 1: 411–12, 406–7.

38. 425 U.S. 484, 96 S.Ct. 1646, 48 L.Ed.2d 113 (1976).

39. *United States v. Simpson*, 813 F.2d 1462 (9th Cir. 1987).

40. Noted in Ibid.

41. *United States v. Struyf*, 701 F.2d 875 (11th Cir. 1983).

42. *People v. Toler*, 26 Ill.2d 100, 185 N.E.2d 874 (1962).

43. *Cruz v. State*, 465 So.2d 516 (Fla. 1985); *Oliver v. State*, 101 Nev. 308, 703 P.2d 869 (1985).

44. *Allen v. Webster*, 742 F.2d 153 (4th Cir. 1984).

45. *Susla v. State*, 311 Minn. 166, 247 N.W.2d 907, 912 (1976).

46. *Pletan v. Gaines et al.*, 494 N.W.2d 38, 40 (Minn. 1992).

47. Ibid. at 42–43.

48. 42 U.S.C.A. §1983 (1976).

49. *Monroe v. Pape*, 365 U.S. 167, 81 S.Ct. 473, 5 L.Ed.2d 492 (1961).

50. *Harlow v. Fitzgerald*, 457 U.S. 800, 102 S.Ct. 2727, 73 L.Ed.2d 396 (1982).

51. *Anderson v. Creighton*, 483 U.S. 635, 107 S.Ct. 3034, 97 L.Ed.2d 523 (1987).

52. Ibid.

53. *Monell v. New York City Department of Social Services*, 436 U.S. 658, 98 S.Ct. 2018, 56 L.Ed.2d 611 (1978).

54. Wayne R. LaFave, *Search and Seizure*, 2d ed. (St. Paul: West, 1987), 1: 248–49.

55. §751, 97th Cong., 1st Sess. (1981).

56. Anthony Amsterdam, "Perspectives on the Fourth Amendment," *Minnesota Law Review* 58 (1974): 430. For a further discussion of the legal and practical difficulties arising out of suing police officers, see Project, "Suing the Police in Federal Court," *Yale Law Journal* 88 (1979): 781; Martin J. Jaron Jr., "The Threat of Personal Liability Under the Federal Civil Rights Act: Does It Interfere with the Performance of State and Local Government?" *The Urban Lawyer* 13 (1981): 1; and Theodore Eisenberg, "Section 1983: Doctrinal Foundations and an Empirical Study," *Cornell Law Quarterly* 67 (1982): 482.

57. Caleb Foote, "Tort Remedies for Police Violations of Individual Rights," *Minnesota Law Review* 39 (1955): 493; Newman, "Suing the Lawbreakers," 447–67.

58. §751, 97th Cong., 1st Sess. (1981).

CHAPTER ELEVEN

Initiating Formal Proceedings

CHAPTER OUTLINE

CHAPTER MAIN POINTS

1. Formal proceedings begin when prosecutors file complaints, information, or indictments in criminal courts.

2. Prosecutors have broad, and largely unreviewable, discretion to charge suspects with crimes.

3. The police must bring suspects arrested without warrants promptly before a magistrate to determine probable cause to detain suspects.

4. At the first appearance in court, the magistrate notifies defendants of their constitutional rights, sets bail, determines probable cause to detain, and assigns lawyers to indigent individuals.

5. Pretrial release and detention balance the needs of individual rights, community safety, and the expenditure of public resources.

6. All decisions following the filing of a complaint require formal judicial approval.

7. Defendants have a right to counsel in all criminal prosecutions.

8. Poor defendants have a right to effective counsel without charge.

Should the Charges Be Dropped?

The defendant was charged with the criminal sale and possession of cocaine. By the time he was indicted, the defendant was in an advanced stage of AIDS and related complicating illnesses. He had pneumocystis carinii pneumonia, the virus had invaded his brain and his stomach, and peripheral nerve damage caused pain and suffering to the extent that doctors ordered him to limit his physical exercise to sitting in a chair for one hour a day. Doctors' prognosis was death within three to four months.

THE INITIATION
OF FORMAL PROCEEDINGS

Following arrest, interrogation, and identification procedures, the action in the criminal process moves from the police station to the courts. In the interval between the end of police investigation and the first time that defendants appear in court, both the police and the prosecutor make critical decisions. The police decide if, on the basis of their investigation, the case deserves either formal judicial action or termination. The police release suspects outright if they believe suspects are not guilty. Or, if searches and seizures, interrogation, lineups, show-ups, and photographic identification have maintained a *suspicion* but not a *belief* that they have a strong case, the police may release suspects with the admonition that the police may "call them later." In misdemeanor cases, even if the police believe that suspects are guilty, police may release them on the informal condition that they get "help," such as drug and alcohol treatment or family counseling, or with the warning that they "stay out of trouble."

In most jurisdictions, the police take to the prosecutor's office the cases that they decide ought to result in criminal charges. Prosecutors then make an independent judgment concerning the disposition of cases that the police bring to them. They can release suspects outright by not charging them and releasing them. Or they may decide not to charge but, instead of releasing suspects outright, divert the case into a program for community service, restitution, substance abuse, or family violence treatment. If suspects participate in these programs, prosecutors agree to discontinue the criminal process before the initiation of formal judicial proceedings.

If prosecutors decide to charge, they start formal judicial proceedings by filing a complaint, information, or indictment. These proceedings test the objective basis for the decision to charge. In these proceedings, disinterested parties—either judges or grand juries—assess the facts that the government has to prove its case. If the government presents the required amount of proof, defendants must appear to answer the criminal charges against them.

D e c i s i o n   P o i n t

Suppose that a store detective catches the following three shoplifters at about the same time. The detective reports all the incidents to the prosecutor's office. Which ones should the prosecutor charge with crimes? Divert into a program? Dismiss?

1. A student took a cassette recorder to record his criminal procedure class because the professor talks too fast. He works part time to pay for school, and although he could have paid for the recorder, it would have been difficult. He has never been in trouble with the law before and says he will pay for the recorder.

2. A woman who works only occasionally took a cordless phone for a friend who agreed to pay $35, half the phone's value. The woman has taken compact disks, tape cassettes, and an answering machine from the same store within the past six months.

3. A fifty-year-old woman slipped a pair of stereo earphones in her purse. The woman is wealthy and indignantly denies that she intended to steal the earphones. She tells the detective she put the device in her bag because she wanted to pick up some film, batteries, and other small items and simply forgot she had put it there.

Once prosecutors decide to charge them with crimes, suspects make their **first appearance,** which takes place in the lower criminal courts. At the point of charging, suspects formally become criminal defendants.

The first appearance should not be confused with three other judicial proceedings that take place prior to trial. Grand jury review and preliminary hearings test the government's case against defendants to make sure that probable cause exists to require defendants to answer criminal charges (see Chapter 12). **Arraignment** brings defendants to court to hear the charges formally and requires defendants to plead to the charges. The first appearance, on the other hand, mainly serves to prepare defendants for possible further advances into the criminal process.

The decision to initiate judicial criminal proceedings has grave implications, as the Supreme Court has observed:

The initiation of judicial criminal proceedings is far from a mere formalism. It is the starting point of our whole system of adversary criminal justice. For it is only then that the Government has committed itself to prosecute, and only then that the adverse positions of Government and defendant have solidified. It is then that a defendant finds himself faced with the prosecutorial forces of organized society, and immersed in the intricacies of substantive and procedural criminal law. It is this point, therefore, that marks the commencement of the "criminal prosecutions."[1]

THE DECISION TO CHARGE

Once the police bring a case from the police station to the prosecutor, lawyers take over the management of the criminal process. The police recede into the background except as lawyers need them for clarification, further investigation, and witness accounts. The police may be in the background, but they are not without influence. They informally influence the charging decision. They control the cases that prosecutors receive. Finally, prosecutors are likely to take at face value the recommendations of officers with a reputation for establishing "good" cases. They are equally likely to discount cases from officers with a poor track record.

Prosecutors drop some cases without further action. They **"divert"** some suspects into drug or psychological treatment programs or into restitution plans. In these diversion cases, prosecutors agree not to charge suspects with crimes if the suspects pay back victims or perform community service. The number of cases that prosecutors decide not to pursue ranges from a few in some jurisdictions to nearly half of all cases in others. Several interests lie behind the decision to charge. In some cases, prosecutors have insufficient evidence — no witnesses, weak witnesses, or poor physical evidence, confessions, and other admissions of suspects — to support prosecution. Available witnesses may be neither reliable nor convincing. Witness problems predominate in violent crime where victims know their assailants. In over half of these cases, witnesses and victims do not cooperate because they are either afraid or have a change of heart over prosecuting people whom they know. Sometimes, prosecutors cannot use evidence because the police seized it illegally. Contrary to the popular belief that many guilty criminals go unpunished owing to excluded evidence, however, fewer than 2 percent of all cases are dismissed for this reason.[2]

Prosecutors transfer some cases to other courts or out of the criminal justice system. Matters of jurisdiction and the interests of justice affect the decision to transfer cases. Prosecutors may believe that restitution for petty theft serves justice better than criminal prosecutions, that wife battering belongs in family court, or that juvenile court better serves some juveniles old enough to face trial as adults.

D e c i s i o n   P o i n t

The defendant was charged with the criminal sale and possession of cocaine. By the time he was indicted, the defendant was in an advanced stage of AIDS and related complicating illnesses. He had pneumocystis carinii pneumonia, the virus had invaded his brain and his stomach, and peripheral nerve damage caused pain and suffering to the extent that doctors ordered him to limit his physical exercise to sitting in a chair for one hour a day. Doctors' prognosis was death within three to four months.

Should the government continue the case against the defendant? The government dropped the case because "it did not appear that the interest of justice would be substantially served by the defendant's continued prosecution under this indictment." The court noted that

the uncompromising rampage of the multiple disease processes have condemned this defendant to a painful, imminent death. When the rationale for incarceration becomes unjustifiable because of . . . a deadly disease, it becomes imperative to allow the sufferer to live his last days in the best circumstances possible and with dignity and compassion.[3]

Insufficient resources make it impossible to prosecute every case, even when prosecutors have convincing evidence. Prosecutors set priorities: petty thefts go to restitution to allow time for armed robbery; violent sex offenses take precedence over prostitution; and a few well-known tax evaders serve as examples to deter tax evasion. According to some experts, selective prosecution infringes on the legislature's prerogative to make laws. Others say that selectively prosecuting some individuals in a category—like "fat cats" or notorious tax evaders—undermines impartial law enforcement and violates the equal protection clause. Courts have not accepted these arguments.

According to former prosecutor and Supreme Court Justice Robert Jackson, the power to charge gives a prosecutor "more control over life, liberty, and reputation than any other person in America." In 1967, President Johnson's Crime Commission concluded that prosecutors are

> the key administrative officer[s] in the processing of cases. Yet this decision is largely hidden from view because discretion, not formal law, controls prosecutors' charging decisions. Unlike police discretion, which, formally anyway, is illegal, prosecutors are lawfully granted broad discretion in the charging process.[4]

Nothing has changed much since 1967. In one case, a Baltimore Oriole pitcher threw a ball from the bullpen in Fenway Park and hit a Boston Red Sox fan in the head. The fan obtained a complaint against the pitcher, but the district attorney decided not to charge. The fan sought an order compelling the district attorney to prosecute. In denying the request, the court said the following: "A district attorney has wide discretion over whether to prosecute an individual, just as he has wide discretion in determining whether to discontinue a prosecution once commenced. . . . The plaintiff has no constitutional right to direct the conduct of a public prosecutor."[5]

The power to prosecute is broad but not unlimited. Prosecutors cannot prosecute anyone they please. For example, they cannot prosecute out of vindictiveness. In *Thigpen v. Roberts*, Roberts lost control of his car, struck a truck, and killed a passenger. He paid fines in a justice of the peace court on a reckless driving citation. When Roberts asserted his right to trial *de novo* (a new trial in a lower criminal court), the prosecutor obtained a felony indictment, charging Roberts with manslaughter. After conviction, the judge sentenced Roberts to twenty years in prison. On appeal, the United States

Supreme Court ruled that the prosecutor acted vindictively by using his power to "up the ante" in order to discourage misdemeanants from appealing convictions on citations in justice of the peace courts. Cases in which the courts hold that prosecutors prosecuted vindictively are rare.[6] However, the United States Fourth Circuit Court of Appeals did decide a case of prosecutorial vindictiveness in *U.S. v. Williams.*

C A S E

Was the Prosecution Vindictive?

United States v. Williams
47 F.3d 658 (4th Cir. 1995)

The United States District Court for the Eastern District of Virginia dismissed an indictment alleging the distribution of crack cocaine. Williams appealed. The Court of Appeals reversed and remanded. Donald Russell, Circuit Judge.

FACTS

Nathaniel Williams was charged in the General District Court of the City of Virginia Beach, Virginia with two counts of distributing "crack" cocaine, a felony offense under Virginia law. On September 23, 1993, Williams and his defense attorney appeared for the preliminary hearing. The prosecutor, Michael Cummings, discussed the case with Williams's attorney and advised that he would refer Williams's case for federal prosecution unless Williams pled guilty to the two state charges and agreed to cooperate with the state. The prosecutor warned that federal prosecution would subject Williams to a much more severe mandatory minimum sentence.

Williams's attorney inquired as to the amount of cooperation the police would require of Williams. The prosecutor directed the attorney to Detective Robert Christian of the Virginia Beach Police Department, who explained that the state would expect Williams to make several undercover drug purchases, to testify before grand juries and in open court, and to disclose all information of any criminal activities known to him.

Williams's preliminary hearing was continued to October 7, 1993 to allow him time to consider the proposal. On that day, the prosecutor repeated that he would refer Williams's case for federal prosecution unless Williams agreed both to enter guilty pleas to the state charges and to cooperate with the Virginia Beach police. However, Williams's attorney advised the prosecutor that Williams would not cooperate with the police because he feared for his safety and life, and the safety of his family.

The preliminary hearing went forward, and Williams's case was certified for consideration by the grand jury on November 1, 1993. However, on October 22, 1993, before the state grand jury had a chance to consider the case, a federal grand jury indicted Williams on two counts of distributing crack cocaine in violation of 21 U.S.C. § 841(a)(1) for the same offenses that had been charged in state court. The state prosecutor, who was cross-designated as a Special Assistant United States Attorney, presented Williams's case to the federal grand jury.

Williams moved to dismiss the indictment on grounds of vindictive prosecution. On January 10, 1994, the district court filed an order dismissing the federal indictment. The district court reasoned that a criminal defendant has the right to enter an unconditional plea of guilty to charges in an indictment. The prosecutor, however, demanded that Williams plead guilty and cooperate with the police in order to avoid a more severe federal prosecution. According to the district court, Williams had the right to refuse to cooperate with the police and to enter an unconditional plea of guilty to the state charges. By referring Williams's case for federal prosecution, the prosecutor retaliated against Williams for exercising his lawful right to enter an unconditional plea to the state charges. According to the district court, the prosecutor's actions amounted to prosecutorial vindictiveness and violated Williams's Fifth Amendment due process rights.

After the district court denied the government's motion for reconsideration, the government appealed to this Court.

OPINION

The Supreme Court has clearly stated that, where a criminal defendant exercises a procedural right and successfully attacks a criminal conviction, the state cannot retaliate against the defendant by seeking a harsher punishment upon retrial. "To punish a person because he has done what the law plainly allows him to do is a due process violation of the most basic sort. . . ." *Bordenkircher v. Hayes*, 434 U.S. 357, 363, 98 S.Ct. 663, 668, 54 L.Ed.2d 604 (1978). It is thus a violation of due process to penalize a criminal defendant for exercising his constitutional rights, or for pursuing a statutory right of appeal or collateral remedy. Due process requires that "vindictiveness against a defendant for having successfully attacked his first conviction must play no part in the sentence he receives after a new trial."

For the same reason, a prosecutor cannot reindict a convicted defendant on more severe charges after the defendant has successfully invoked an appellate remedy. *Blackledge v. Perry*, 417 U.S. 21, 27, 94 S.Ct. 2098, 2102, 40 L.Ed.2d 628 (1974). Even if the prosecutor does not have any actual retaliatory motivation in seeking a harsher indictment, such an indictment nonetheless constitutes a due process violation because due process requires that the criminal defendant be freed of even the apprehension of a retaliatory motivation on the part of the state.

In the pretrial setting, however, the Supreme Court has allowed prosecutors to threaten criminal defendants with harsher prosecution during plea negotiations and to carry out those threats if the defendants refuse to accept the prosecution's plea offers. Although the state may not retaliate against a defendant for exercising his legal rights, "in the 'give-and-

take' of plea bargaining, there is no such element of punishment or retaliation so long as the accused is free to accept or reject the prosecution's offer." In *Bordenkircher*, the Supreme Court held that there was no prosecutorial vindictiveness where a prosecutor, after the defendant refused to plead guilty to the original charges carrying a sentence of two to ten years imprisonment, indicted a defendant under a recidivist statute carrying a mandatory life term.

A prosecutor's threats to seek a harsher indictment are constitutionally legitimate even though the prosecutor's goal in making those threats is to convince the defendant to waive his right to plead not guilty. "Plea bargaining flows from 'the mutuality of advantage' to defendants and prosecutors, each with his own reasons for wanting to avoid trial. [A]cceptance of the basic legitimacy of plea bargaining necessarily implies rejection of any notion that a guilty plea is involuntary in a constitutional sense simply because it is the end result of the bargaining process." The main purpose of plea bargaining is to encourage a criminal defendant to plead guilty and give up his right to trial by offering a more lenient sentence if he pleads guilty or threatening harsher punishment if he refuses to plead guilty. A criminal justice system that tolerates and encourages plea negotiations must allow prosecutors to impose difficult choices on defendants even though the risk of more severe punishment may discourage a defendant from asserting his trial rights.

If a prosecutor brings additional charges after a defendant refuses to accept a plea bargain, a court cannot presume that the additional charges are an impermissible penalty for the defendant's refusal. . . . In the pretrial situation, then, a defendant must show that a prosecutor's decision to bring more severe charges against him was motivated by actual vindictiveness.

Although . . . a prosecutor, in the context of plea negotiations, can threaten to bring a more severe indictment against a defendant to pressure him into pleading guilty, the prosecutor's action in the case before us differs because Cummings, the prosecutor, threatened to bring the more severe charges if Williams did not plead guilty and cooperate with the police. Requiring Williams's cooperation in addition to the guilty plea, in the context of plea negotiations, does not raise the prosecutor's conduct to the level of prosecutorial vindictiveness.

. . . [A] prosecutor, in the context of plea negotiations, may threaten a defendant with a more severe prosecution and carry out those threats if the defendant refuses to cooperate with the police in the criminal investigation of another person. A defendant's cooperation with the police is a legitimate concession for a prosecutor to seek during plea negotiations. Although the prosecutor may not retaliate against a defendant for exercising a legal right, in the give-and-take of plea bargaining, there is no element of retaliation as long as the defendant is free to refuse the government's demand of cooperation with the authorities. Although a defendant has the right not to cooperate, a prosecutor may pressure a defendant to waive that right by threatening a more severe indictment. The right not to cooperate is certainly no more important than the right of an accused to a trial, and yet the Supreme Court has allowed prosecutors, during plea negotiations, to use the threat of a harsher indictment to pressure a defendant to plead guilty and thus waive his right to trial. If it is constitutionally permissible to use the threat of more severe punishment to encourage a guilty plea, certainly it is legitimate to use the same tactics to encourage a defendant to cooperate with the authorities in the criminal investigation and prosecution of another.

A prosecutor's threat to bring a more severe indictment if the defendant refuses to cooperate does not amount to vindictiveness as long as the defendant, should he refuse to cooperate, is not treated worse than he would have been if no plea bargain had been offered. However, a prosecutor in the pretrial setting should not be locked into the charges in his initial indictment, which might not represent the extent to which an individual is subject to prosecution. Just as a prosecutor may forego legitimate charges in an effort to obtain the defendant's cooperation, a prosecutor may seek a more severe indictment if an initial expectation that the defendant would cooperate proves unfounded. Thus, a court should not presume vindictiveness where a prosecutor decides to bring more severe charges against a defendant who has refused to cooperate, even if the prosecutor is carrying out a threat made in plea negotiations.

We conclude that Williams has not made out a claim for prosecutorial vindictiveness. Although due process requires that a criminal defendant remain free from even the apprehension of a retaliatory motivation on the part of the state, Cummings's conduct did not rise to that level. Although Cummings threatened to refer Williams's case for a more severe federal prosecution if Williams did not agree to plead guilty to the state charges and to cooperate with the Virginia police, and carried out his threat when Williams refused to cooperate, the decision to seek a more severe indictment did not create the apprehension of a retaliatory motivation on the part of the State. In the context of plea bargaining, a prosecutor may legitimately threaten a more severe indictment in order to pressure a defendant to plead guilty and to cooperate with the police.

Cummings could have referred Williams's case for federal prosecution without entering into plea negotiations. Federal prosecution was appropriate based on the amount of cocaine with which the defendant was involved. In his affidavit in support of the government's motion for reconsideration (after the district court dismissed the case), Cummings explained that he was going to refer Williams's case for federal prosecution because of the quantity of cocaine involved, but he held off because Detective Christian wanted to first determine whether Williams would cooperate. Unless the state received a concession such as cooperation, the state would normally have referred Williams's case for federal prosecution. Furthermore, even though Cummings referred Williams's case to the federal authorities after Williams refused to accept his demand that he cooperate with the Virginia state police, a standing committee of three senior Assistant United States Attorneys reviewed Williams's case and determined that federal prosecution was appropriate. Williams was not entitled to a plea bargain, and Cummings could have referred the case to federal authorities without entering into plea negotiations. By offering Williams the option of pleading guilty to the state charges and cooperating with the police, Cummings gave Williams a chance to avoid federal prosecution. Although the plea offer took the form of a threat, Williams nonetheless gained an opportunity he would not have had if Cummings had referred the case to federal authorities without making the plea offer.

If the prosecutor had initially sought a federal indictment against Williams and then offered more lenient state charges if Williams pled guilty and agreed to cooperate, the prosecutor's actions would not have violated Williams's due process rights. [The prosecutor simply reversed his tactics by originally bringing charges under Virginia law and threatening more severe federal charges if Williams did not agree to cooperate.] If the prosecutor could initially bring more severe charges and negotiate down to more lenient charges if the defendant cooperates, we see no problem allowing the prosecutor to bring more lenient initial charges and threaten to bring more severe charges if the defendant refuses to cooperate.

For the foregoing reasons, we reverse the judgment of the district court. Because we hold that the prosecutor's actions did not amount to prosecutorial vindictiveness, we need not reach the issue of whether the district court's dismissal of the federal indictment was the appropriate remedy for the due process violation. We remand to the district court for further proceedings consistent with this opinion.

CASE DISCUSSION

List all the facts relevant to deciding whether the prosecutor prosecuted Williams vindictively. Exactly what test does the court apply to the facts in determining whether the prosecution was vindictive? How would you apply the test to these facts? Do you agree with the court's application of the test? Defend your answer. If the prosecution was not vindictive, was it fair? Explain your answer.

Even if prosecutions are not vindictive, prosecutors can select cases to prosecute only according to acceptable criteria. According to the *United States Attorney's Manual,*

> In determining whether to commence or recommend prosecution or take other actions, the attorney or the government should not be influenced by:
> 1. the person's race; religion; sex; national origin; or political association, activities, or beliefs;
> 2. his/her own personal feelings concerning the person, the person's associates, or the victim; or
> 3. the possible effect of his/her decision on his/her own professional or personal circumstances.[7]

Hence, prosecutors cannot prosecute only African Americans for murder, only poor people for stealing, or only young people for drug use. That would violate the equal protection clause of the Constitution. They cannot prosecute a personal enemy or fail to prosecute someone whom it may damage their professional advancement to charge. However, they need not treat everyone alike. For example, they may prosecute "big shots" in order to make examples of them. The Seventh Circuit Court of Appeals, in a case involving selecting a public official for prosecution, said the following:

> It makes good sense to prosecute those who will receive the media's attention. Publication of the proceedings may enhance the deterrent effect of the prosecution and maintain public faith in the precept that public officials are not above the law.[8]

Prosecutors may also selectively charge only some individuals within a large group of violators because the government does not have the resources to prosecute everyone who violates certain laws, such as the tax codes.

PROBABLE CAUSE DETERMINATION

Defendants held in custody without an arrest warrant—that is, without a judicial determination that probable cause supports their detention—present an urgent situation. Nearly all the suspects detained without a warrant and prior to the filing of formal charges against them are suspected of street crimes, such as robbery, burglary, and theft, or personal crimes of violence, such as rape, assault, and murder. All states have rules requiring that criminal justice officials promptly present before a judicial officer suspects held in custody without warrants.

The basic idea behind these rules is that independent magistrates must determine whether probable cause supports the detention following arrest. The interest in law enforcement allows the police in the first instance to arrest citizens without a prior judicial determination of probable cause. Otherwise, suspects might escape, commit further crimes, or destroy evidence. Once suspects are in custody, however, those dangers lessen and the interests in due process and the protection of innocent citizens from unwarranted detention take precedence. The judicial determination of probable cause at the first appearance, or a similar proceeding, should not be confused with the determination made at preliminary hearings and grand jury reviews. The probable cause to detain pending the filing of formal charges tests the quantum of proof required to arrest and detain a suspect. The preliminary hearing and grand jury review test the factual basis of the government's decision to take the case on to trial. These two determinations are confusing because the term for the objective basis required to support both is the same: *probable cause*. The best way to describe the difference is that it takes less probable cause to justify a detention pending charges than it takes to charge suspects with crimes and proceed to try them.

According to the Supreme Court in *Gerstein v. Pugh*, the Fourth Amendment requires that the police take suspects detained without arrest warrants promptly to a magistrate for a determination of probable cause. Lower federal courts and the state courts have long held that the Fourth Amendment allows the police only enough time to complete the "administrative steps incident to arrest." These steps vary among jurisdictions, but usually include the following:

- Completing paperwork
- Searching the suspect
- Conducting an inventory search
- Inventorying property
- Fingerprinting the suspect
- Photographing the suspect
- Checking for a possible prior criminal record of the suspect

- Testing laboratory samples
- Interrogating the suspect
- Checking an alibi
- Conducting a lineup
- Comparing the crime with similar crimes[9]

Some jurisdictions explicitly restrict the time allowed the police to complete these administrative details. Limits range from twenty-four to thirty-six hours.[10] The Supreme Court decided what *prompt* means in *County of Riverside v. McLaughlin.*

C A S E

Was Judicial Determination of Probable Cause "Prompt"?

County of Riverside v. McLaughlin
500 U.S. 44, 111 S.Ct. 1661,
114 L.Ed.2d 49 (1991)

McLaughlin and others brought a class action under 42 U.S.C. § 1983 challenging the manner in which the County of Riverside, California, provides probable cause determinations to persons arrested without a warrant. The district court granted a preliminary injunction. The Ninth Circuit Court of Appeals affirmed. The Supreme Court granted certiorari, *vacated the judgment of the court of appeals, and remanded the case. Justice O'Connor wrote the opinion of the Court. Justices Marshall, Stevens, and Scalia dissented.*

FACTS

In August 1987, Donald Lee McLaughlin filed a complaint in the United States District Court for the Central District of California, seeking injunctive and declaratory relief on behalf of himself and "all others similarly situated." The complaint alleged that McLaughlin was then currently incarcerated in the Riverside County Jail and had not received a probable cause determination. He requested "an order and judgment requiring that the defendants and the County of Riverside provide in-custody arrestees, arrested without warrants, prompt probable cause, bail and arraignment hearings." Shortly thereafter, McLaughlin moved for class certification. The County moved to dismiss the

complaint, asserting that McLaughlin lacked standing to bring the suit because he had failed to show, as required by *Los Angeles v. Lyons* (1983), that he would again be subject to the allegedly unconstitutional conduct—i.e., a warrantless detention without a probable cause determination....

... [A] second amended complaint named three additional plaintiffs—Johnny E. James, Diana Ray Simon, and Michael Scott Hyde—individually and as class representatives. The amended complaint alleged that each of the named plaintiffs had been arrested without a warrant, had received neither prompt probable cause nor bail hearings, and was still in custody.... In March 1989, plaintiffs asked the District Court to issue a preliminary injunction requiring the County to provide all persons arrested without a warrant a judicial determination of probable cause within 36 hours of arrest. The District Court issued the injunction, holding that the County's existing practice violated this Court's decision in *Gerstein.* Without discussion, the District Court adopted a rule that the County provide probable cause determinations within 36 hours of arrest, except in exigent circumstances. The court "retained jurisdiction indefinitely" to ensure that the County established new procedures that complied with the injunction.

The United States Court of Appeals for the Ninth Circuit consolidated this case with another challenging an identical preliminary injunction issued against the County of San Bernardino. On November 8,

1989, the Court of Appeals affirmed the order granting the preliminary injunction against Riverside County. . . . The Court of Appeals . . . determined that the County's policy of providing probable cause determinations at arraignment within 48 hours was "not in accord with *Gerstein's* requirement of a determination 'promptly after arrest'" because no more than 36 hours were needed "to complete the administrative steps incident to arrest." The Ninth Circuit thus joined the Fourth and Seventh Circuits in interpreting *Gerstein* as requiring a probable cause determination immediately following completion of the administrative procedures incident to arrest. By contrast, the Second Circuit understands *Gerstein* to "stress the need for flexibility" and to permit States to combine probable cause determinations with other pretrial proceedings. *Williams v. Ward* (1988), cert. denied (1989). We granted certiorari to resolve this conflict among the Circuits as to what constitutes a "prompt" probable cause determination under *Gerstein*.

OPINION

. . . In *Gerstein v. Pugh* (1975), this Court held unconstitutional Florida procedures under which persons arrested without a warrant could remain in police custody for 30 days or more without a judicial determination of probable cause. In reaching this conclusion we attempted to reconcile important competing interests. On the one hand, States have a strong interest in protecting public safety by taking into custody those persons who are reasonably suspected of having engaged in criminal activity, even where there has been no opportunity for a prior judicial determination of probable cause. On the other hand, prolonged detention based on incorrect or unfounded suspicion may unjustly "imperil [a] suspect's job, interrupt his source of income, and impair his family relationships." We sought to balance these competing concerns by holding that States "must provide a fair and reliable determination of probable cause as a condition for any significant pretrial restraint of liberty, and this determination must be made by a judicial officer either before or promptly after arrest."

The Court thus established a "practical compromise" between the rights of individuals and the reali-

ties of law enforcement. . . . We left it to the individual States to integrate prompt probable cause determinations into their differing systems of pretrial procedures. . . .

Inherent in *Gerstein's* invitation to the States to experiment and adapt was the recognition that the Fourth Amendment does not compel an immediate determination of probable cause upon completing the administrative steps incident to arrest. Plainly, if a probable cause hearing is constitutionally compelled the moment a suspect is finished being "booked," there is no room whatsoever for "flexibility and experimentation by the States." Incorporating probable cause determinations "into the procedure for setting bail or fixing other conditions of pretrial release"—which *Gerstein* explicitly contemplated—would be impossible. Waiting even a few hours so that a bail hearing or arraignment could take place at the same time as the probable cause determination would amount to a constitutional violation. Clearly, *Gerstein* is not that inflexible. . . .

But flexibility has its limits; *Gerstein* is not a blank check. A State has no legitimate interest in detaining for extended periods individuals who have been arrested without probable cause. The Court recognized in *Gerstein* that a person arrested without a warrant is entitled to a fair and reliable determination of probable cause and that this determination must be made promptly. Unfortunately, as lower court decisions applying *Gerstein* have demonstrated, it is not enough to say that probable cause determinations must be "prompt." This vague standard simply has not provided sufficient guidance. Instead, it has led to a flurry of systemic challenges to city and county practices, putting federal judges in the role of making legislative judgments and overseeing local jail house operations.

Our task in this case is to articulate more clearly the boundaries of what is permissible under the Fourth Amendment. Although we hesitate to announce that the Constitution compels a specific time limit, it is important to provide some degree of certainty so that States and counties may establish procedures with confidence that they fall within constitutional bounds. Taking into account the competing interests articulated in *Gerstein*, we believe that a jurisdiction that provides judicial determinations of probable cause within 48 hours of arrest will, as a general matter, comply with the promptness requirement of *Gerstein*. For this reason, such jurisdictions will be immune from systemic challenges.

This is not to say that the probable cause determination in a particular case passes constitutional muster simply because it is provided within 48 hours. Such a hearing may nonetheless violate *Gerstein* if the arrested individual can prove that his or her probable cause determination was delayed unreasonably. Examples of unreasonable delay are delays for the purpose of gathering additional evidence to justify the arrest, a delay motivated by ill will against the arrested individual, or delay for delay's sake. In evaluating whether the delay in a particular case is unreasonable, however, courts must allow a substantial degree of flexibility. Courts cannot ignore the often unavoidable delays in transporting arrested persons from one facility to another, handling late-night bookings where no magistrate is readily available, obtaining the presence of an arresting officer who may be busy processing other suspects or securing the premises of an arrest, and other practical realities.

Where an arrested individual does not receive a probable cause determination within 48 hours, the calculus changes. In such a case, the arrested individual does not bear the burden of proving an unreasonable delay. Rather, the burden shifts to the government to demonstrate the existence of a bona fide emergency or other extraordinary circumstance. The fact that in a particular case it may take longer than 48 hours to consolidate pretrial proceedings does not qualify as an extraordinary circumstance. Nor, for that matter, do intervening weekends. A jurisdiction that chooses to offer combined proceedings must do so as soon as is reasonably feasible, but in no event later than 48 hours after arrest. . . .

For the reasons we have articulated, we conclude that Riverside County is entitled to combine probable cause determinations with arraignments. The record indicates, however, that the County's current policy and practice do not comport fully with the principles we have outlined. The County's current policy is to offer combined proceedings within two days, exclusive of Saturdays, Sundays, or holidays. As a result, persons arrested on Thursdays may have to wait until the following Monday before they receive a probable cause determination. The delay is even longer if there

is an intervening holiday. Thus, the County's regular practice exceeds the 48-hour period we deem constitutionally permissible, meaning that the County is not immune from systemic challenges, such as this class action.

As to arrests that occur early in the week, the County's practice is that "arraignment[s] usually tak[e] place on the last day" possible. There may well be legitimate reasons for this practice; alternatively, this may constitute delay for delay's sake. We leave it to the Court of Appeals and the District Court, on remand, to make this determination. The judgment of the Court of Appeals is vacated and the case is remanded for further proceedings consistent with this opinion.

It is so ordered.

DISSENT

[NOTE: Justices Stevens's and Marshall's dissent is omitted.]

Justice Scalia, dissenting.

. . . The Court views the task before it as one of "balanc[ing] [the] competing concerns" of "protecting public safety," on the one hand, and avoiding "prolonged detention based on incorrect or unfounded suspicion," on the other hand. It purports to reaffirm the "practical compromise" between these concerns struck in *Gerstein v. Pugh*. There is assuredly room for such an approach in resolving novel questions of search and seizure under the "reasonableness" standard that the Fourth Amendment sets forth. But not, I think, in resolving those questions on which a clear answer already existed in 1791 and has been generally adhered to by the traditions of our society ever since. As to those matters, the "balance" has already been struck, the "practical compromise" reached — and it is the function of the Bill of Rights to preserve that judgment, not only against the changing views of Presidents and Members of Congress, but also against the changing views of Justices whom Presidents appoint and Members of Congress confirm to this Court. . . .

"The Fourth Amendment requires a judicial determination of probable cause as a prerequisite to extended restraint of liberty," "either before or promptly after arrest." Though how "promptly" we did not say, it was plain enough that the requirement left no room for intentional delay unrelated to the completion of "the administrative steps incident to arrest." Plain enough, at least, that all but one federal court considering the question understood *Gerstein* that way. Today, however, the Court discerns something quite different in *Gerstein*. It finds that the plain statements set forth above (not to mention the common-law tradition of liberty upon which they were based) were trumped by the implication of a later dictum in the case which, according to the Court, manifests a "recognition that the Fourth Amendment does not compel an immediate determination of probable cause upon completing the administrative steps incident to arrest."

. . . [D]etermining the outer boundary of reasonableness is a[n] . . . objective and . . . manageable task. We were asked to undertake it in *Gerstein*, but declined—wisely, I think, since we had before us little data to support any figure we might choose. As the Court notes, however, *Gerstein* has engendered a number of cases addressing not only the scope of the procedures "incident to arrest," but also their duration. The conclusions reached by the judges in those cases, and by others who have addressed the question, are surprisingly similar. I frankly would prefer even more information, and for that purpose would have supported reargument on the single question of an outer time limit. The data available are enough to convince me, however, that certainly no more than 24-hours is needed.

[DISSENT NOTE: "The Court claims that the Court of Appeals 'concluded that it takes 36 hours to process arrested persons in Riverside County.' The court concluded no such thing. It concluded that 36-hours (the time limit imposed by the District Court) was 'ample' time to complete the arrest, and that the county had provided no evidence to demonstrate the contrary. The District Court, in turn, had not made any evidentiary finding to the effect that 36-hours was necessary, but for unexplained reasons said that it 'declines to adopt the 24-hour standard [generally applied by other courts], but adopts a 36-hour limit, except in exigent circumstances.' Before this Court, moreover, the county has acknowledged that 'nearly 90 percent of all cases . . . can be completed in 24-hours or less,' and the examples given to explain the other 10 percent are entirely unpersuasive (heavy traffic on the Southern California freeways; the need to wait for arrestees who are properly detainable because they are visibly under the influence of drugs to come out of that influence before they can be questioned about other crimes; the need to take blood and urine samples promptly in drug cases) with one exception: awaiting completion of investigations and filing of investigation reports by various state and federal agencies. We have long held, of course, that delaying a probable-cause determination for the latter reason—effecting what Judge Posner has aptly called 'imprisonment on suspicion, while the police look for evidence to confirm their suspicion'—is improper."]

With one exception, no federal court considering the question has regarded 24 hours as an inadequate amount of time to complete arrest procedures, and with the same exception every court actually setting a limit for probable-cause determination based on those procedures has selected 24 hours. (The exception would not count Sunday within the 24-hour limit. . . .) And state courts have similarly applied a 24-hour limit under state statutes requiring presentment without "unreasonable delay." . . .

. . . A few weeks before issuance of today's opinion there appeared in the *Washington Post* the story of protracted litigation arising from the arrest of a student who entered a restaurant in Charlottesville, Virginia, one evening to look for some friends. Failing to find them, he tried to leave—but refused to pay a $5 fee (required by the restaurant's posted rules) for failing to return a red tab he had been issued to keep track of his orders. According to the story, he "was taken by police to the Charlottesville jail" at the restaurant's request. "There, a magistrate refused to issue an arrest warrant," and he was released. That is how it used to be; but not, according to today's decision, how it must be in the future. If the Fourth Amendment meant then what the Court says it does now, the student could lawfully have been held for as long as it would have taken to arrange for his arraignment, up to a maximum of 48 hours.

Justice Story wrote that the Fourth Amendment "is little more than the affirmance of a great constitutional doctrine of the common law." It should not become less than that. One hears the complaint, nowadays, that the Fourth Amendment has become constitutional law for the guilty; that it benefits the career criminal (through the exclusionary rule) often and directly, but the ordinary citizen remotely if at all. By failing to protect the innocent arrestee, today's opinion reinforces that view. The common-law rule of prompt hearing had as its primary beneficiaries the innocent—not those whose fully justified convictions must be overturned to scold the police; nor those who avoid conviction because the evidence, while convincing, does not establish guilt beyond a reasonable doubt; but those so blameless that there was not even good reason to arrest them. While in recent years we have invented novel applications of the Fourth Amendment to release the unquestionably guilty, we today repudiate one of its core applications so that the presumptively innocent may be left in jail. Hereafter, a law-abiding citizen wrongfully arrested may be compelled to await the grace of a Dickensian bureaucratic machine, as it churns its cycle for up to two days—never once given the opportunity to show a judge that there is absolutely no reason to hold him, that a mistake has been made. In my view, this is the image of a system of justice that has lost its ancient sense of priority, a system that few Americans would recognize as our own.

I respectfully dissent.

CASE DISCUSSION

What reasons does the Court give for deciding that under ordinary circumstances, forty-eight hours is a reasonable time to satisfy the Fourth Amendment interest in providing a prompt determination of probable cause? What interests did the Court balance in making its decision? What administrative steps and specific circumstances did the Court consider in balancing these interests? What reasons does the Court give for maintaining that the Fourth Amendment requires a probable cause hearing within twenty-four hours? What does the history of the common law have to do with decisions made in 1992? In interpreting the Fourth Amendment, should the Court look at the deadline that a majority of states prescribe for the probable cause hearing on detentions following arrests without warrants? What rule would you adopt? Why?

FIRST APPEARANCE

The **criminal complaint** (the formal charging document) grants magistrates the jurisdiction to preside over the first appearance. Although in a few jurisdictions police file complaints directly with courts, in most large urban districts, prosecutors must sign complaints *before* judges review them for probable cause. Ordinarily, complaints state the crime with which suspects are charged. Attached to the complaint are police incident reports, confessions, results of identification procedures, affidavits of witnesses and informants, and other products of police investigation.

Practice varies among jurisdictions, but typically the magistrate at the first appearance does the following:

1. Determines probable cause to detain defendants arrested without warrants

2. Informs defendants of the charges against them

3. Informs defendants of their constitutional rights

4. Appoints attorneys for indigent defendants

5. Sets bail

6. Accepts pleas of defendants charged with misdemeanors

Defendants charged with felonies do not plead at this time; they await arraignment following preliminary hearings and grand jury review. If charged with misdemeanors, particularly ones punishable by small fines, however, defendants usually plead — nearly always guilty — at the first appearance.

Informing Suspects of Their Rights

When suspects — now defendants — first appear in court, magistrates advise them of the nature of the charges against them, although in felonies and gross misdemeanors they are not called upon to plead since they have not had time to consult with lawyers. If defendants do not already have them, the court gives defendants copies of the complaint and supporting affidavits and other documents. Typically, court rules provide as those outlined here:

> The judge, judicial officer, or other duly appointed personnel shall advise the defendant substantially as follows:
> (a) That he is not required to say anything or submit to interrogation and that anything he says may be used against him in this or in any subsequent proceedings;
> (b) That he has a right to counsel in all subsequent proceedings, including police line-ups and interrogations, and if he appears without counsel and is financially unable to afford counsel, that counsel will forthwith be appointed without cost to him if he is charged with an offense punishable upon conviction by incarceration;
> (c) That he has a right to communicate with his counsel and that a continuance will be granted if necessary to enable defendant to obtain or speak to counsel;
> (d) That he has a right to a jury trial or a trial to the court;
> (e) That if the offense is a misdemeanor, he may either plead guilty or not guilty, or demand a complaint prior to entering a plea. The judge, judicial officer, or other duly authorized personnel may advise a number of defendants at once of these rights, but each defendant shall be asked individually before he is arraigned whether he heard and understood these rights as explained earlier.[11]

Detaining and Releasing Defendants

Most defendants are released on bail while they wait for trial or other disposition of their cases. In some jurisdictions, the quantity exceeds 90 percent. Nevertheless, pretrial detention remains a serious problem because detaining even 10 percent of defendants contributes to jail overcrowding. The principal reason for detention is that defendants cannot post bail. Detention can last for considerable time periods: 33 percent of defendants remain in detention for more than thirty days and 20 percent for more than ninety days. Finally, detention prior to trial places a heavy burden on local jurisdictions. Housing an individual detainee prior to trial costs about $30 a day, on the average.[12]

Courts rely on a variety of release mechanisms. About 20 percent of defendants secure release without appearing before judges. In minor cases, defendants obtain a **citation release,** or a summons to appear, similar to that used in traffic offenses. Or they post bond according to **bail schedules** that list amounts required for various offenses. Defendants can obtain release any time by posting the amount in the appropriate schedule.[13]

Judges can attach a variety of conditions to release. They release some defendants on their **own recognizance (O.R.)** — that is, on the promise of defendants to appear in court. Some judges release defendants on the relatively nonrestrictive condition that they either report periodically to a pretrial release program or promise to reside in the community until trial. Sometimes judges attach more restrictive conditions in a **supervised release,** in which defendants must report to the police department; a program for drug, alcohol, or mental illness treatment; employment programs; or third persons such as relatives.[14]

Money bonds, or releases made in return for the payment of money, take a variety of forms. The least-restrictive unsecured bond requires defendants to pay only if they fail to appear. The court-administered deposit bond requires defendants to post 10 percent of the bond's amount; if they appear, the court returns the deposit. Under privately administered bail bonds, bail bondsmen or bondswomen (most are men) charge 10 percent of the amount of the bond they advance. Defendants forfeit this 10 percent fee even if they appear.[15]

Courts frequently reconsider the initial decision to grant a pretrial release and the conditions attached to it. As many as half of all defendants who do not initially obtain release may do so as a result of this bail review after the initial appearance. Since up to thirty days may pass before bail review, however, the critical release decision occurs at the first appearance.[16]

A typical state provision to guide judges in making the bail decision reads as follows:

[T]he court, judge or judicial officer shall impose the first of the following conditions of release which will reasonably assure the appearance of the person for trial or hearing, or when otherwise required, or, if no single condition gives that assurance, any combination of the following conditions:
(a) Place the person in the care and supervision of a designated person or organization agreeing to supervise him;
(b) Place restrictions on travel, association, or place of abode during his period of release;
(c) Require the execution of an appearance bond in an amount set by the court with sufficient solvent sureties, or the deposit of cash or other sufficient security in lieu thereof; or
(d) Impose any other condition deemed reasonably necessary to assure appearance as required, including a condition requiring that the person return to custody after specified hours. In any event, the court shall also fix the amount of money bail without other conditions upon which the defendant may obtain his release.[17]

Pretrial detention imposes a severe deprivation on defendants. Incarceration, temporary loss of wages or even permanent loss of a job, separation from family and friends, restrictions on aiding in their defense, and loss of reputation may all result. Furthermore, these deprivations occur *before* conviction. Defendants may be incarcerated on probable cause before the state proves beyond a reasonable doubt that they have committed crimes. On the other hand, pretrial release incurs costs for society. Defendants may not appear for trial, released defendants may commit further crimes, and the community may experience anxiety over the threats to public safety that released defendants might pose. The decision of whether to release or detain defendants prior to trial, then, requires balancing the rights of individuals to be free until they are proved guilty and the need of the community to feel safe from crime and its interest in bringing criminals to justice.

Both bail and pretrial detention raise the same basic question: Do the purposes of bail and detention and the foundation upon which they rest warrant the deprivations that they produce? That question boils down into two specific questions:

1. What constitutional rights do defendants have in connection with bail and pretrial detention?

2. What proper purposes do bail and pretrial detention serve?

THE CONSTITUTION AND BAIL

The Constitution does not guarantee defendants an absolute right to bail, despite the severe deprivations that pretrial detention entails. However, it does place restrictions on the state's power to deny bail, and it imposes standards on the conditions of pretrial detention. The two amendments to the United States Constitution relevant to pretrial release and detention are these:

1. *Eighth Amendment.* Excessive bail shall not be required . . . nor cruel and unusual punishments inflicted.

2. *Fourteenth Amendment.* No state shall . . . deprive any person of life, liberty, or property, without due process of law; nor deny to any person within its jurisdiction equal protection of the laws.

In a leading Supreme Court bail case, *Stack v. Boyle*, Chief Justice Fred M. Vinson, writing for the Court, said this about bail:

> From the passage of the Judiciary Act of 1789, to the present . . . federal law has unequivocally provided that a person arrested for a non-capital offense *shall* be admitted to bail. This traditional right to freedom permits the unhampered preparation of a defense, and serves to prevent the infliction of punishment prior to conviction. . . . Unless this right to bail before trial is preserved, the presumption of innocence, secured only after centuries of struggle, would lose its meaning.[18]

In *Stack*, twelve people were charged with conspiring to violate the Smith Act, which made it a crime to advocate the violent overthrow of the government. The case arose at the height of the Cold War, when anticommunism and fear of radicalism gripped the nation. The trial court fixed bail at $50,000. The Supreme Court ruled that amounts exceeding those necessary to secure the petitioners' appearance at trial violated the Eighth Amendment. The Court held that magistrates must calculate how much money to attach to release to minimize the risk that defendants will not appear.

The amount necessary to secure defendants' appearance at trial, of course, varies according to a number of circumstances. Judges typically take the following conditions into account:

1. Seriousness of the offense charged

2. Weight of the evidence against the defendant

3. Defendant's family ties, employment, financial resources, character, and mental condition

4. Length of defendant's residence in the community

5. Defendant's prior criminal record

6. Defendant's prior record of appearing or "jumping" bail

Judges do not take a defendant's word for information about these conditions. Most large urban jurisdictions provide for prerelease investigations, administered by either the probation department or a special agency for pretrial release.

No amount of bail may be high enough to secure the appearance of wealthy defendants. In *United States v. Abrahams*, for example, Abrahams had three previous convictions, was an escaped prisoner from another state, had given false information at a prior bail hearing, had failed to appear on a former bail of $100,000, had failed to appear on a previous charge in California from which he was a fugitive, had several aliases, and had recently transferred $1.5 million to Bermuda! The First Circuit Court of Appeals upheld the district court's finding that no condition "or any combination . . . will reasonably assure the appearance of defendant for trial if admitted to bail." According to former Attorney General William French Smith, this problem is particularly acute among major drug dealers, who can post bail of as high as a million dollars with no difficulty: "Some of these people net $250,000 to $500,000 a month from their drug sales. Paying bail of $100,000 is like getting rid of pocket money to these people."[19]

At the other extreme—and much more commonly—any amount may be too much for poor individuals to pay. Professor Caleb Foote, a noted bail scholar, believes that our bail system violates the Constitution in several ways by denying poor defendants

1. Due process because detention adversely affects the outcome of their cases, owing to their inability to help with their defense

2. Equal protection of the law because they are detained solely owing to their poverty

3. The Eighth Amendment right against excessive bail because they cannot raise any amount that the court requires[20]

The Fifth Circuit Court of Appeals dealt with the problem of indigent defendants' bail in *Pugh v. Rainwater*. Florida's bail system provided for a range of conditions for release. However, the system did not establish a presumption in favor of release on recognizance, nor did it establish a priority for nonfinancial conditions. As the court ruled,

> Because it gives the judge essentially unreviewable discretion to impose money bail, the rule [is] . . . discriminatory . . . : When a judge decides to set money bail, the indigent will be forced to remain in jail. We hold that equal protection standards are not satisfied unless the judge is required to consider less financially onerous forms of release before he imposes money bail. Requiring a presumption in favor of non-money bail accommodates the State's interest in assuring the defendant's appearance at trial as well as the defendant's right to be free pending trial, regardless of his financial status.[21]

Hence, as the court put it later on rehearing, for "an indigent, whose appearance at trial could reasonably be assured by one of the alternative forms of release, pretrial confinement for inability to post money bail would constitute imposition of an excessive restraint."[22]

Pretrial detention clearly impedes defendants' ability to prepare their best defense. They cannot help locate either witnesses or physical evidence more accessible to them than to outside investigators. Cramped jail quarters and restricted visiting hours inhibit conferences with attorneys. Pretrial detention affects defendants' appearance and demeanor in the courtroom: rumpled clothes, a pallid complexion, and other results of confinement are difficult to conceal. Released defendants, on the other hand, can both help in their own defense and demonstrate to the court that they are working and maintaining their responsibilities to themselves and, if present, to their families.[23]

Preventive Detention

Commentators, lawyers, courts, and criminal justice personnel have hotly debated whether the only legitimate purpose for bail and pretrial detention is to secure defendants' appearance at trial. Might courts impose **preventive detention**? That is, they could detain "dangerous" defendants—those who pose a threat to community safety and specific individuals—to prevent them from doing or threatening further harm while they await trial. Troubling reports show that defendants released on bail commit crimes or intimidate, hurt, and terrorize victims and potential witnesses.

Congress enacted the Bail Reform Act of 1984, which authorizes federal courts to detain arrested individuals when a judge determines, after a hearing, that no condition of release would "reasonably" ensure the appearance of the individual and "safety of . . . the community." Defendants have a right to testify at the hearing, to present evidence, to be appointed to counsel, and to cross-examine witnesses. To detain defendants, the court must have "clear and convincing evidence": more than probable cause but less than proof beyond a reasonable doubt (see Chapter 12).

Several empirical—and constitutional—questions surround preventive detention. The major empirical question is whether probable cause to believe a person has committed a crime predicts future dangerous or criminal behavior. Most available research suggests this question is difficult to answer, both because *dangerous* is a vague term and because human behavior, particularly violent behavior, cannot easily be foreseen. The constitutional question is whether preventive detention violates the Eighth Amendment prohibition against cruel and unusual punishment and the due process clause requiring a fair trial, because detention presumes guilt and punishes prior to conviction beyond a reasonable doubt.[24]

The Supreme Court has addressed preventive detention, or the detention of "dangerous" defendants prior to trial, in *United States v. Salerno.*

C A S E

Were Their Pretrial Detentions "Punishment"?

United States v. Salerno
481 U.S. 739, 107 S.Ct. 2095,
95 L.Ed.2d 697 (1987)

Salerno and Cafaro were committed for pretrial detention pursuant to the Bail Reform Act by a United States district court. The court of appeals vacated the *commitment and remanded. On writ of* certiorari, *the United States Supreme Court reversed. Chief Justice Rehnquist wrote the opinion of the Court, which Justices White, Blackmun, Powell, O'Connor, and Scalia joined. Justice Marshall wrote a dissenting opinion, which Justice Brennan joined. Justice Stevens also wrote a dissenting opinion.*

FACTS

Respondents Anthony Salerno and Vincent Cafaro were arrested on March 21, 1986, after being charged in a 29-count indictment alleging various Racketeer Influenced and Corrupt Organizations Act (RICO) violations, mail and wire fraud offenses, extortion, and various criminal gambling violations. The RICO counts alleged 35 acts of racketeering activity, including fraud, extortion, gambling, and conspiracy to commit murder. At respondent[s'] arraignment, the Government moved to have Salerno and Cafaro detained pursuant to § 3142(e) [of the Bail Reform Act of 1984], on the ground that no condition of release would assure the safety of the community or any person. The District Court held a hearing at which the Government made a detailed proffer of evidence. The Government's case showed that Salerno was the "boss" of the Genovese Crime Family of La Cosa Nostra and that Cafaro was a "captain" in the Genovese Family. According to the Government's proffer, based in large part on conversations intercepted by a court-ordered wiretap, the two respondents had participated in wide-ranging conspiracies to aid their illegitimate enterprises through violent means. The Government also offered the testimony of two of its trial witnesses, who would assert that Salerno personally participated in two murder conspiracies. Salerno opposed the motion for detention, challenging the credibility of the Government's witnesses. He offered the testimony of several character witnesses as well as a letter from his doctor stating that he was suffering from a serious medical condition. Cafaro presented no evidence at the hearing, but instead characterized the wiretap conversations as merely "tough talk."

OPINION

The Bail Reform Act of 1984 allows a federal court to detain an arrestee pending trial if the government demonstrates by clear and convincing evidence after an adversary hearing that no release conditions "will reasonably assure . . . the safety of any other person and the community." The United States Court of Appeals for the Second Circuit struck down this provision of the Act as facially unconstitutional, because, in that court's words, this type of pretrial detention violates "substantive due process." We granted certiorari because of a conflict among the Courts of Appeals regarding the validity of the Act. We hold that, as against the facial attack mounted by these respondents, the Act fully comports with constitutional requirements. We therefore reverse.

Responding to "the alarming problems of crimes committed by persons on release," Congress formulated the Bail Reform Act of 1984. . . . To this end, § 3141(a) of the Act requires a judicial officer to determine whether an arrestee shall be detained. § 3142(e) provides that

> [i]f, after a hearing pursuant to the provisions of subsection (f), the judicial officer finds that no condition or combination of conditions will reasonably assure the appearance of the person as required and the safety of any other person and the community, he shall order the detention of the person prior to trial. . . .

The judicial officer is not given unbridled discretion in making the detention determination. Congress has specified the consideration relevant to that decision. These factors include the nature and seriousness of the charges, the substantiality of the government's evidence against the arrestee, the arrestee's background and characteristics, and the nature and seriousness of the danger posed by the suspect's release. Should a judicial officer order detention, the detainee is entitled to expedited appellate review of the detention order. . . .

Respondents present two grounds for invalidating the Bail Reform Act's provisions permitting pretrial detention on the basis of future dangerousness.

1. They rely upon the Court of Appeals' conclusion that the Act exceeds the limitations placed upon the Federal Government by the Due Process Clause of the Fifth Amendment.

2. They contend that the Act contravenes the Eighth Amendment's proscription against excessive bail.

We treat those contentions in turn. . . . Respondents first argue that the Act violates substantive due process because the pretrial detention it authorizes constitutes impermissible punishment before trial. The Government, however, has never argued that pretrial detention could be upheld if it were "punishment." . . . [P]retrial detention under the Bail Reform Act is regulatory, not penal. . . .

The government's interest in preventing crime by arrestees is both legitimate and compelling. . . . On the other side of the scale, of course, is the individual's strong interest in liberty. We do not minimize the importance and fundamental nature of this right. But, as our cases hold, this right may, in circumstances where the government's interest is sufficiently weighty, be subordinated to the greater needs of society. . . .

Respondents also contend that the Bail Reform Act violates the Excessive Bail Clause of the Eighth Amendment. . . . We think that the Act survives a challenge founded upon the Eighth Amendment. . . . While we agree that a primary function of bail is to safeguard the courts' role in adjudicating the guilt or innocence of defendants, we reject the proposition that the Eighth Amendment categorically prohibits the government from pursuing other admittedly compelling interests through regulation of pretrial release. . . . Nothing in the text of the Bail Clause limits permissible government considerations solely to questions of flight. . . .

We believe that when Congress has mandated detention on the basis of a compelling interest other than prevention of flight, as it has here, the Eighth Amendment does not require release on bail.

In our society liberty is the norm, and detention prior to trial or without trial is the carefully limited exception. We hold that the provisions for pretrial detention in the Bail Reform Act of 1984 fall within that carefully limited exception. The Act authorizes the detention prior to trial of arrestees charged with serious felonies who are found after an adversary hearing to pose a threat to the safety of individuals or to the community which no condition of release can dispel. . . . We are unwilling to say that this congressional determination, based as it is upon that primary concern of every government—a concern for the safety and indeed the lives of its citizens—on its face violates either the Due Process Clause of the Fifth Amendment or the Excessive Bail Clause of the Eighth Amendment.

The judgment of the Court of Appeals is therefore Reversed.

DISSENT

Justice Marshall, with whom Justice Brennan joins, dissenting.

This case brings before the Court for the first time a statute in which Congress declares that a person innocent of any crime may be jailed indefinitely, pending the trial of allegations which are legally presumed to be untrue, if the Government shows to the satisfaction of a judge that the accused is likely to commit crimes, unrelated to the pending charges, at any time in the future. Such statutes, consistent with the usages of tyranny and the excesses of what bitter experience teaches us to call the police state, have long been thought incompatible with the fundamental human rights protected by our Constitution. Today a majority of this Court holds otherwise. Its decision disregards basic principles of justice established centuries ago and enshrined beyond the reach of governmental interference in the Bill of Rights. . . .

The majority finds that "Congress did not formulate the pretrial detention provisions as punishment for dangerous individuals," but instead was pursuing the "legitimate regulatory goal" of "preventing danger to the community." Concluding that pretrial detention is not an excessive solution to the problem of preventing danger to the community, the majority thus finds that no substantive element of the guarantee of due process invalidates the statute. . . .

The absurdity of this conclusion arises, of course, from the majority's cramped concept of substantive due process. The majority proceeds as though the only substantive right protected by the Due Process Clause is a right to be free from punishment before conviction. The majority's technique for infringing this right is simple: merely redefine any measure which is claimed to be punishment as "regulation," and, magically, the Constitution no longer prohibits its imposition. . . .

"The principle that there is a presumption of innocence in favor of the accused is the undoubted law, axiomatic and elementary, and its enforcement lies at the foundation of the administration of our criminal law." Our society's belief, reinforced over the centuries, that all are innocent until the state has proved them to be guilty, like the companion principle that guilt must be proved beyond a reasonable doubt, is "implicit in the concept of ordered liberty."

The statute now before us declares that persons who have been indicted may be detained if a judicial officer finds clear and convincing evidence that they pose a danger to individuals or to the community. . . . The conclusion is inescapable that the indictment has been turned into evidence, if not that the defendant is guilty of the crime charged, then that left to his own devices he will soon be guilty of something else. "If it suffices to accuse, what will become of the innocent?" . . .

"It is a fair summary of history to say that the safeguards of liberty have frequently been forged in controversies involving not very nice people." *United States v. Rabinowitz* (1950) (Frankfurter, J., dissenting). Honoring the presumption of innocence is often difficult; sometimes we must pay substantial social costs as a result of our commitment to the values we espouse. But at the end of the day the presumption of innocence protects the innocent; the shortcuts we take with those whom we believe to be guilty injure only those wrongfully accused and, ultimately, ourselves.

Throughout the world today there are men, women, and children interned indefinitely, awaiting trials which may never come or which may be a mockery of the word, because their governments believe them to be "dangerous." Our Constitution, whose construction began two centuries ago, can shelter us forever from the evils of such unchecked power. Over two hundred years it has slowly, through our efforts, grown more durable, more expansive, and more just. But it cannot protect us if we lack the courage, and the self-restraint, to protect ourselves. Today, a majority of the Court applies itself to an ominous exercise in demolition. Theirs is truly a decision which will go forth without authority, and come back without respect.

I dissent.

CASE DISCUSSION

Is pretrial detention punishment or a "regulatory device"? What criteria do you use to answer this question? What did Chief Justice John Marshall mean when he said "If it suffices to accuse, what will become of the innocent?" Does pretrial detention undermine the presumption of innocence? What, in your opinion, is the proper purpose or purposes of bail? Defend your answer.

Conditions of Pretrial Confinement

Detention prior to trial, whether to secure defendants' appearance or to protect public safety, is nonetheless confinement. Jailed defendants are not free to leave; they lie in cells, subject to jail discipline and routine, and they must conform to rules intended to preserve safety and order within the detention facility. But jailed defendants are legally innocent; they do not forfeit their constitutional rights simply because of their incarceration. A number of years ago, someone asked one jail administrator if surveillance of jailed defendants in cells through two-way mirrors of which inmates were unaware violated defendants' right to privacy. The administrator replied, "They have no rights," but this is untrue. Jailed defendants *do* have rights, but they are "diminished" because of confinement. The United States Supreme Court addressed the questions—what rights? and how diminished?—in *Bell v. Wolfish*.

C A S E

Were They "Punished" Before Conviction?

Bell v. Wolfish
441 U.S. 520, 99 S.Ct. 1861,
60 L.Ed.2d 447 (1979)

Inmates brought a class action in federal district court challenging the constitutionality of numerous conditions of confinement and practices in the Metropolitan Correctional Center, a federally operated, short-term custodial facility for pretrial detainees in New York City. The district court, on several constitutional grounds, enjoined various practices in the facility. The court of appeals affirmed the district court's rulings. On writ of certiorari, the United States Supreme Court reversed. Justice Rehnquist wrote the opinion of the Court, which Chief Justice Burger and Justices Stewart, White, and Blackmun joined. Justice Powell filed an opinion concurring in part and dissenting in part. Justice Marshall filed a dissenting opinion. Justice Stevens filed a dissenting opinion, which Justice Brennan joined.

FACTS

The MCC (Metropolitan Correctional Center) differs markedly from the familiar image of a jail; there are no barred cells, dank, colorless corridors, or clanging steel gates. It was intended to include the most advanced and innovative features of modern design of detention facilities. "[I]t represented the architectural embodiment of the best and most progressive penological planning." The key design element of the 12-story structure is the "modular" or "unit" concept, whereby each floor designed to house inmates has one or two largely self-contained residential units that replace the traditional cellblock jail construction. Each unit in turn has several clusters or corridors of private rooms or dormitories radiating from a central 2-story "multipurpose" or common room, to which each inmate has free access approximately 16 hours a day. Because our analysis does not turn on the particulars of the MCC concept design, we need not discuss them further.

With the MCC opened in August 1975, the planned capacity was 449 inmates, an increase of 50% over the former West Street facility. Despite some dormitory accommodations, the MCC was designed primarily to house these inmates in 389 rooms, which originally were intended for single occupancy. While the MCC was under construction, however, the number of persons committed to pretrial detention began to rise at an "unprecedented" rate. The Bureau of Prisons took several steps to accommodate this unexpected flow of persons assigned to the facility, but despite these efforts, the inmate population at the MCC rose above its planned capacity within a short time after its opening. To provide sleeping space for this increased population, the MCC replaced the single bunks in many of the individual rooms and dormitories with double bunks. Also, each week some newly arrived inmates had to sleep on cots in the common areas until they could be transferred to residential rooms as space became available.

On November 28, 1975, less than four months after the MCC had opened, the named respondents initiated this action by filing in the District Court a petition for writ of habeas corpus. . . . The petition served up a variable potpourri of complaints that implicated virtually every facet of the institution's conditions and practices. Respondents charged, *inter alia*, that they had been deprived of their statutory and constitutional rights because of overcrowded conditions, undue length of confinement, improper searches, inadequate recreational, educational, and employment opportunities, insufficient staff, and objectionable restrictions on the purchase and receipt of personal items and books. The District Court, in the words of the Court of Appeals for the Second Circuit, "intervened broadly into almost every facet of the institution" and enjoined no fewer than 20 MCC practices on constitutional and statutory grounds. The Court of Appeals largely affirmed the District Court's constitutional rulings and in the process held that under the Due Process Clause of the Fifth Amendment, pretrial detainees may "be subjected to only those 'restrictions and privations' which 'inhere in their confinement itself or which are justified by compelling necessities of jail administration.'" We granted certiorari to consider the important constitutional questions raised by these decisions and to resolve an apparent conflict among the Circuits. We now reverse.

OPINION

. . . Not every disability imposed during pretrial detention amounts to "punishment" in the constitutional sense. . . . Once the Government has exercised its conceded authority to detain a person pending trial, it obviously is entitled to employ devices that are calculated to effectuate this detention. Traditionally, this has meant confinement in a facility which, no matter how modern or antiquated, results in restricting the movement of a detainee in a manner in which he would not be restricted if he simply were free to walk the streets pending trial. Whether it be called a jail, a prison, or a custodial center, the purpose of the facility is to detain. Loss of freedom of choice and privacy are inherent incidents of confinement in such a facility. And the fact that such detention interferes with the detainee's understandable desire to live as comfortably as possible and with as little restraint as possible during confinement does not convert the conditions or restrictions of detention into "punishment." . . .

Judged by this analysis, respondents' claim that "double-bunking" violated their due process rights fails. . . . On this record, we are convinced as a matter of law that "double-bunking" as practiced at the MCC did not amount to punishment and did not, therefore, violate respondents' rights under the Due Process Clause of the Fifth Amendment.

Each of the rooms at the MCC that house pretrial detainees has a total floor space of approximately 75 square feet. Each of them designated for "double-bunking" contains a double bunkbed, certain other items of furniture, a wash basin, and an uncovered toilet. Inmates are generally locked into their rooms from 11 P.M. to 6:30 A.M. and for brief periods during the afternoon and evening head counts. During the rest of the day, they may move about freely between their rooms and the common areas. . . .

We disagree with both the District Court and the Court of Appeals that there is some sort of "one man, one cell" principle lurking in the Due Process Clause of the Fifth Amendment. While confining a given number of people in a given amount of space in such a manner as to cause them to endure genuine privations and hardships over an extended period of time might raise serious questions under the Due Process Clause as to whether those conditions amounted to punishment, nothing even approaching such hardship is shown by this record.

Detainees are required to spend only seven or eight hours each day in their rooms, during most or all of which they presumably are sleeping. During the remainder of the time, the detainees are free to move between their rooms and the common area. While "double-bunking" may have taxed some of the equipment or particular facilities in certain of the common areas, this does not mean that the conditions at the MCC failed to meet the standards required by the Constitution. Our conclusion in this regard is further buttressed by the detainees' length of stay at the MCC. Nearly all of the detainees are released within 60 days. We simply do not believe that requiring a detainee to share toilet facilities and this admittedly small sleeping space with another person for generally a maximum period of 60 days violates the Constitution. . . .

. . . [M]aintaining institutional security and preserving internal order and discipline are essential goals that may require limitation or retraction of the retained constitutional rights of both convicted prisoners and pretrial detainees. "[C]entral to all other corrections goals is the institutional consideration of internal security within the corrections facilities themselves." . . .

Finally . . . the problems that arise in the day-to-day operations of the corrections facility are not susceptible of easy solutions. Prison administrators therefore should be accorded wide-ranging deference in the adoption and execution of policies and practices that in their judgment are needed to preserve internal order and discipline and to maintain institutional security. . . .

Inmates at all Bureau of Prison facilities, including the MCC, are required to expose their body cavities for visual inspection as part of a strip search conducted after every contact visit with a person from

528 INITIATING FORMAL PROCEEDINGS

outside the institution. Corrections officials testified that visual cavity searches were necessary not only to discover but also to deter the smuggling of weapons, drugs, and other contraband into the institution. The District Court upheld the strip-search procedure but prohibited the body-cavity searches, absent probable cause to believe that the inmate is concealing contraband. Because petitioners proved only one instance in the MCC's short history where contraband was found during a body-cavity search, the Court of Appeals affirmed. In its view, the "gross violation of personal privacy inherent in such a search cannot be outweighed by the government's security interest in maintaining a practice of so little actual utility."

Admittedly, this practice instinctively gives us the most pause. However, assuming for present purposes that inmates, both convicted prisoners and pretrial detainees, retain some Fourth Amendment rights upon commitment to a corrections facility, we nonetheless conclude that these searches do not violate that Amendment. The Fourth Amendment prohibits only unreasonable searches, and under the circumstances, we do not believe that these searches are unreasonable. . . .

A detention facility is a unique place fraught with serious security dangers. Smuggling of money, drugs, weapons, and other contraband is all too common an occurrence. And inmate attempts to secrete these items into the facility by concealing them in body cavities is documented in this record. That there has been only one instance where an MCC inmate was discovered attempting to smuggle contraband into the institution on his person may be more a testament to the effectiveness of this search technique as a deterrent than to any lack of interest on the part of the inmates to secrete and import such items when the opportunity arises. . . .

There was a time not too long ago when the federal judiciary took a completely "hands-off" approach to the problem of prison administration. In recent years, however, these courts largely have discarded this "hands-off" attitude and have waded into this complex arena. . . . But many of these same courts have, in the name of the Constitution, become increasingly enmeshed in the minutiae of prison operations. Judges, after all, are human. They, no less than others in our society, have a natural tendency to be-

lieve that their individual solutions to often intractable problems are better and more workable than those of the persons who are actually charged with and trained in the running of the particular institution under examination. But under the Constitution, the first question to be answered is not whose plan is best, but in what branch of the Government is lodged the authority to initially devise the plan. . . . The wide range of "judgment calls" that meet constitutional and statutory requirements are confided to officials outside of the Judicial Branch of Government.

DISSENT

Mr. Justice Stevens, with whom Mr. Justice Brennan joins, dissenting.

This is not an equal protection case. An empirical judgment that most persons formally accused of criminal conduct are probably guilty would provide a rational basis for a set of rules that treat them like convicts until they establish their innocence. No matter how rational such an approach might be—no matter how acceptable in a community where equality of status is the dominant goal—it is obnoxious to the concept of individual freedom protected by the Due Process Clause. If ever accepted in this country, it would work a fundamental change in the character of our free society.

Nor is this an Eighth Amendment case. That provision of the Constitution protects individuals convicted of crimes from punishment that is cruel and unusual. The pretrial detainees whose rights are at stake in this case, however, are innocent men and women who have been convicted of no crimes. Their claim is not that they have been subjected to cruel and unusual punishment in violation of the Eighth Amendment, but that to subject them to any form of punishment at all is an unconstitutional deprivation of their liberty.

This is a due process case. The most significant—and I venture to suggest the most enduring—part of the Court's opinion today is its recognition of this initial constitutional premise. The Court squarely holds that "under the Due Process Clause, a detainee may not be punished prior to an adjudication of guilt in accordance with due process of law." . . .

Prior to conviction every individual is entitled to

the benefit of a presumption both that he is innocent of prior criminal conduct and that he has no present intention to commit any offense in the immediate future. . . .

It is not always easy to determine whether a particular restraint serves the legitimate, regulatory goal of ensuring a detainee's presence at trial and his safety and security in the meantime, or the unlawful end of punishment. . . . [Discussion of double-bunking, searches of mail, and cells is omitted.]

The body-cavity search—clearly the greatest personal indignity—may be the least justifiable measure of all. After every contact visit a body-cavity search is mandated by the rule. The District Court's finding that searches have failed in practice to produce any demonstrable improvement in security is hardly surprising. Detainees and their visitors are in full view during all visits, and are fully clad. To insert contraband into one's private body cavities during such a visit would indeed be "an imposing challenge to nerves and agility." There is no reason to expect, and the petitioners have established none, that many pretrial detainees would attempt, let alone succeed, in surmounting this challenge absent the challenged rule. Moreover, as the District Court explicitly found, less severe alternatives are available to ensure that contraband is not transferred during visits. Weapons and other dangerous instruments, the items of greatest legitimate concern, may be discovered by the use of metal detecting devices or other equipment commonly used for airline security. In addition, inmates are required, even apart from the body-cavity searches, to disrobe, to have their clothing inspected, and to present open hands and arms to reveal the absence of any concealed objects. These alternative procedures "amply satisf[y]" the demands of security. In my judgment, there is no basis in this regard to disagree.

It may well be, as the Court finds, that the rules at issue here were not adopted by administrators eager to punish those detained at MCC. The rules can be explained as the easiest way for administrators to ensure security in the jail. But the easiest course for jail officials is not always one that our Constitution allows them to take. If fundamental rights are withdrawn and severe harms are indiscriminately inflicted on detainees merely to secure minimal savings in time and effort for administrators, the guarantee of due process is violated.

CASE DISCUSSION

How can you distinguish between detention and punishment? One critic said that it was all well and good for Supreme Court justices to say this case involved detention, not punishment, but it probably would be little comfort for the detainees to know that. Does it matter that most pretrial detainees are subject to confinement because they cannot afford bail? What interests are at stake in this case? How would you balance them?

THE RIGHT TO COUNSEL

Lawyers pervade the administration of criminal justice. Historically, they staffed only courts, prosecutors' offices, and defense attorneys' offices. Since the formalization of criminal procedure during the due process revolution discussed in Chapter 2, however, even police departments and corrections agencies now hire lawyers. The complex, technical rules of law and procedure require experts to advise personnel inside and outside the criminal justice system. Here, we concentrate on counsel for suspects, defendants, and appellants.

The Sixth Amendment to the United States Constitution establishes the constitutional basis for the right to a lawyer in criminal cases: "In all criminal prosecutions, the accused shall enjoy the right . . . to have the assistance of counsel for his defense." Throughout American history, courts have ruled that the Sixth Amendment guarantees the right to retained counsel—that is, a lawyer paid for by the client in criminal cases. In *Chandler v. Fretag*, the United States Supreme Court held that the right to retained counsel was an "unqualified" right under the Fifth and Fourteenth Amendments' due process clauses. The courts have not always held that the Constitution guarantees the right to appointed counsel—that is, a lawyer for people who cannot afford to hire their own. Until recently, **indigent defendants** (poor defendants) relied on counsel *pro bono* (for the good of doing so), a lawyer who volunteered to represent poor defendants without a fee. Even today, many jurisdictions rely on lawyers who donate their services to represent poor defendants. Large jurisdictions, including the federal government, have permanent defenders (called "public defenders") paid by the public to defend poor clients.

As we have seen in Chapter 2, in *Powell v. Alabama* (1932) the United States Supreme Court ruled that "fundamental fairness" requires that courts appoint lawyers for indigent defendants who cannot otherwise get a fair hearing. In *Johnson v. Zerbst* (1938) the Supreme Court elaborated the reasons for the right to counsel:

> [The right to counsel is] necessary to insure fundamental human rights of life and liberty. Omitted from the Constitution as originally adopted, provisions of this and other Amendments were submitted by the first Congress . . . as essential barriers against arbitrary or unjust deprivation of human rights. The Sixth Amendment stands as a constant admonition that if the constitutional safeguards it provides be lost, justice will not "still be done." It embodies a realistic recognition of the obvious truth that the average defendant does not have the professional legal skill to protect himself when brought before a tribunal with power to take his life or liberty, wherein the prosecution is represented by experienced and learned counsel. That which is simple, orderly, and necessary to the lawyer—to the untrained layman—may appear intricate, complex, and mysterious.[25]

Zerbst recognized only a limited right to counsel. It held that the Sixth Amendment guaranteed poor defendants in federal cases a right to a lawyer in court proceedings. It said nothing about the applicability of the Sixth Amendment right to counsel to state proceedings or to proceedings prior to trial. The right to counsel was tied to guaranteeing criminal defendants a fair trial, based on the fundamental fairness doctrine.

The Supreme Court took up the right to counsel in state proceedings in *Betts v. Brady* (1942). Betts was convicted of robbery and sentenced to prison. At his trial, he asked for a lawyer, claiming that he was too poor to afford one. The judge denied his request because Carroll County, Maryland, the site of the trial, provided counsel only in murder and rape cases. Hearings on Betts's petition for *habeas corpus* eventually reached the Supreme Court. The Court, adopting the fundamental fairness approach, decided that the due process clause did not incorporate the Sixth Amendment. The Court went further to hold that, except in special circumstances, denial of counsel does not deprive a defendant of a fair trial. In other words, the right to counsel was not "inherent in the concept of ordered liberty" (see Chapter 2).

The Court reviewed the history of representation by counsel, noting that English courts did not permit representation by counsel in felony cases until 1843. It concluded that the Sixth Amendment right to counsel "allowed" counsel but did not "compel the state to provide counsel for a defendant." The Court interpreted parallel state provisions of the right to counsel similarly:

This material demonstrates that, in the great majority of the states, it has been the considered judgment of the people, their representatives and their courts that appointment of counsel is not a fundamental right, essential to a fair trial. . . . In the light of this evidence we are unable to say that the concept of due process incorporated in the Fourteenth Amendment obligates the states, whatever may be their own views, to furnish counsel in every such case.[26]

In *Gideon v. Wainwright* (1963) the Court accepted Clarence Gideon's petition for *certiorari*. The Court agreed to review the Florida Supreme Court's dismissal of Gideon's petition for *habeas corpus* based on a claim similar to that of Betts. The Court ordered the parties to argue the question of whether the Court should overrule *Betts v. Brady*.

C A S E

Did He Have a Right to a Lawyer?

**Gideon v. Wainwright
372 U.S. 335, 83 S.Ct. 792,
9 L.Ed.2d 799 (1963)**

Gideon brought habeas corpus *proceedings against the director of the Division of Corrections. The Florida Supreme Court denied all relief. The U.S. Supreme Court granted* certiorari. *The Court reversed and remanded the case to the Florida Supreme Court for further action. Justice Black wrote the opinion of the Court.*

FACTS

Petitioner was charged in a Florida state court with having broken and entered a poolroom with intent to commit a misdemeanor. This offense is a felony under Florida law. Appearing in court without funds and without a lawyer, petitioner asked the court to appoint counsel for him, whereupon the following colloquy took place:

THE COURT: Mr. Gideon, I am sorry, but I cannot appoint Counsel to represent you in this case. Under the laws of the State of Florida, the only time the Court can appoint Counsel to represent a Defendant is when that person is charged with a capital offense. I am sorry, but I will have to deny your request to appoint Counsel to defend you in this case.

THE DEFENDANT: The United States Supreme Court says I am entitled to be represented by Counsel.

Put to trial before a jury, Gideon conducted his defense about as well as could be expected from a layman. He made an opening statement to the jury, cross-examined the State's witnesses, presented witnesses in his own defense, declined to testify himself, and made a short argument "emphasizing his innocence to the charge contained in the Information filed in this case." The jury returned a verdict of guilty, and petitioner was sentenced to serve five years in the state prison. Later, petitioner filed in the Florida Supreme Court this habeas corpus petition attacking his conviction and sentence on the ground that the trial court's refusal to appoint counsel for him denied him rights "guaranteed by the Constitution and the Bill of Rights by the United States Government." [COURT NOTE: "Later in the petition for habeas corpus, signed and apparently prepared by petitioner himself, he stated, 'I, Clarence Earl Gideon, claim that I was denied the rights of the 4th, 5th and 14th amendments of the Bill of Rights.'"]

Treating the petition for habeas corpus as properly before it, the State Supreme Court, "upon consideration thereof" but without an opinion, denied all relief. Since 1942, when *Betts v. Brady* was decided by a divided Court, the problem of a defendant's federal constitutional right to counsel in a state court has been a continuing source of controversy and litigation in both state and federal courts. To give this problem another review here, we granted certiorari. Since Gideon was proceeding in forma pauperis, we appointed counsel to represent him and requested both sides to discuss in their briefs and oral arguments the following: "Should this Court's holding in *Betts v. Brady* be overruled?"

OPINION

The facts upon which Betts claimed that he had been unconstitutionally denied the right to have counsel appointed to assist him are strikingly like the facts upon which Gideon here bases his federal constitutional claim. Betts was indicted for robbery in a Maryland state court. On arraignment, he told the trial judge of his lack of funds to hire a lawyer and asked the court to appoint one for him. Betts was advised that it was not the practice in that county to appoint counsel for indigent defendants except in murder and rape cases. He then pleaded not guilty, had witnesses summoned, cross-examined the State's witnesses, examined his own, and chose not to testify himself. He was found guilty by the judge, sitting without a jury, and sentenced to eight years in prison.

Like Gideon, Betts sought release by habeas corpus, alleging that he had been denied the right to assistance of counsel in violation of the Fourteenth Amendment. Betts was denied any relief, and on review this Court affirmed. It was held that a refusal to appoint counsel for an indigent defendant charged with a felony did not necessarily violate the Due Process Clause of the Fourteenth Amendment, which for reasons given the Court deemed to be the only applicable federal constitutional provision. The Court said:

> Asserted denial (of due process) is to be tested by an appraisal of the totality of facts in a given case. That which may, in one setting, constitute a denial of fundamental fairness, shocking to the universal sense of justice, may, in other circumstances, and in the light of other considerations, fall short of such denial.

Treating due process as "a concept less rigid and more fluid than those envisaged in other specific and particular provisions of the Bill of Rights," the Court held that refusal to appoint counsel under the particular facts and circumstances in the *Betts* case was not so "offensive to the common and fundamental ideas of fairness" as to amount to a denial of due process. Since the facts and circumstances of the two cases are so nearly indistinguishable, we think the *Betts v. Brady* holding if left standing would require us to reject Gideon's claim that the Constitution guarantees him the assistance of counsel.

Upon full consideration we conclude that *Betts v. Brady* should be overruled. The Sixth Amendment provides, "In all criminal prosecutions, the accused shall enjoy the right . . . to have the Assistance of Counsel for his defence." We have construed this to mean that in federal courts counsel must be provided for defendants unable to employ counsel unless the right is competently and intelligently waived [*Johnson v. Zerbst* (1938)]. Betts argued that this right is extended to indigent defendants in state courts by the Fourteenth Amendment. In response the Court stated that, while the Sixth Amendment laid down no rule for the conduct of the states, the question recurs whether the constraint laid by the amendment upon the national courts expresses a rule so fundamental and essential to a fair trial, and so, to due process of law, that it is made obligatory upon the states by the Fourteenth Amendment.

In order to decide whether the Sixth Amendment's guarantee of counsel is of this fundamental nature, the Court in *Betts* set out and considered "(r)elevant data on the subject . . . afforded by constitutional and statutory provisions subsisting in the colonies and the states prior to the inclusion of the Bill of Rights in the national Constitution, and in the constitutional, legislative, and judicial history of the states to the present date." On the basis of this historical data the Court concluded that "appointment of counsel is not a fundamental right, essential to a fair trial." It was for this reason the *Betts* Court refused to accept the contention that the Sixth Amendment's guarantee to counsel for indigent federal defendants was extended to, or, in the words of that Court, "made obligatory upon the states by the

Fourteenth Amendment." Plainly, had the Court concluded that appointment of counsel for an indigent criminal defendant was "a fundamental right, essential to a fair trial," it would have held that the Fourteenth Amendment requires appointment of counsel in a state court, just as the Sixth Amendment requires in a federal court.

We think the Court in *Betts* had ample precedent for acknowledging that those guarantees of the Bill of Rights which are fundamental safeguards of liberty immune from federal abridgment are equally protected against state invasion by the Due Process Clause of the Fourteenth Amendment. This same principle was recognized, explained, and applied in *Powell v. Alabama* (1932) [excerpted in Chapter 2], a case upholding the right of counsel, where the Court held that despite sweeping language to the contrary in *Hurtado v. California* (1884) [discussed in Chapter 2], the Fourteenth Amendment "embraced" those "fundamental principles of liberty and justice which lie at the base of our civil and political institutions," even though they had been "specifically dealt with in another part of the Federal Constitution." In many cases other than *Powell* and *Betts*, this Court has looked to the fundamental nature of original Bill of Rights guarantees to decide whether the Fourteenth Amendment makes them obligatory on the States. . . .

For the same reason, though not always in precisely the same terminology, the Court has made obligatory on the States the . . . Fourth Amendment's prohibition of unreasonable searches and seizures, and the Eighth's ban on cruel and unusual punishment. On the other hand, this Court in *Palko v. Connecticut* (1937) refused to hold that the Fourteenth Amendment made the double jeopardy provision of the Fifth Amendment obligatory on the States. In so refusing, however, the Court, speaking through Mr. Justice Cardozo, was careful to emphasize that "immunities that are valid as against the federal government by force of the specific pledges of particular amendments have been found to be implicit of ordered liberty, and thus, through the Fourteenth Amendment, become valid as against the states" and that guarantees "in their origin . . . effective against the federal government alone" had by prior cases "been taken over from the earlier articles of the Federal Bill of Rights and brought within the Fourteenth Amendment by a process of absorption."

We accept *Betts v. Brady's* assumption, based as it was on our prior cases, that a provision of the Bill of Rights which is "fundamental and essential to a fair trial" is made obligatory upon the States by the Fourteenth Amendment. We think the Court in *Betts* was wrong, however, in concluding that the Sixth Amendment's guarantee of counsel is not one of these fundamental rights. Ten years before *Betts v. Brady*, this Court, after full consideration of all the historical data examined in *Betts*, had unequivocally declared that "the right to the aid of counsel is of this fundamental character." *Powell v. Alabama*. While the Court at the close of its *Powell* opinion did by its language, as this Court frequently does, limit its holding to the particular facts and circumstances of that case, its conclusions about the fundamental nature of the right to counsel are unmistakable. . . .

. . .

. . . [I]n our adversary system of criminal justice, any person haled into court, who is too poor to hire a lawyer, cannot be assured a fair trial unless counsel is provided for him. This seems to us to be an obvious truth. Governments, both state and federal, quite properly spend vast sums of money to establish machinery to try defendants accused of crime. Lawyers to prosecute are everywhere deemed essential to protect the public's interest in an orderly society. Similarly, there are few defendants charged with crime, few indeed, who fail to hire the best lawyers they can get to prepare and present their defenses. That government hires lawyers to prosecute and defendants who have the money hire lawyers to defend are the strongest indications of the wide-spread belief that lawyers in criminal courts are necessities, not luxuries.

The right of one charged with crime to counsel may not be deemed fundamental and essential to fair trials in some countries, but it is in ours. From the very beginning, our state and national constitutions and laws have laid great emphasis on procedural and substantive safeguards designed to assure fair trials before impartial tribunals in which every defendant stands equal before the law. This noble ideal cannot be realized if the poor man charged with crime has to face his accusers without a lawyer to assist him. A defendant's need for a lawyer is nowhere better stated than in the moving words of Mr. Justice Sutherland in *Powell v. Alabama:*

> The right to be heard would be, in many cases, of little avail if it did not comprehend the right to be heard by counsel. Even the intelligent and educated layman . . . requires the guiding hand of counsel at every step in the proceedings against him. Without it, though he be not guilty, he faces the danger of conviction because he does not know how to establish his innocence.

The Court in *Betts v. Brady* departed from the sound wisdom upon which the Court's holding in *Powell v. Alabama* rested. Florida, supported by two other States, has asked that *Betts v. Brady* be left intact. Twenty-two States, as friends of the Court, argue that *Betts* was "an anachronism when handed down" and that it should now be overruled. We agree. The judgment is reversed and the cause is remanded to the Supreme Court of Florida for further action not inconsistent with this opinion. Reversed.

CONCURRING OPINION

Mr. Justice Harlan, concurring.

I agree that *Betts v. Brady* should be overruled. . . .

In agreeing with the Court that the right to counsel in a case such as this should now be expressly recognized as a fundamental right embraced in the Fourteenth Amendment, I wish to make a further observation. When we hold a right or immunity, valid against the Federal Government, to be "implicit in the concept of ordered liberty" and thus valid against the States, I do not read our past decisions to suggest that by so holding, we automatically carry over an entire body of federal law and apply it in full sweep to the States. Any such concept would disregard the frequently wide disparity between the legitimate interests of the States and of the Federal Government, the divergent problems that they face, and the significantly different consequences of their actions. In what is done today I do not understand the Court to depart from the principles laid down in *Palko v. Connecticut,* or to embrace the concept that the Fourteenth Amendment "incorporates" the Sixth Amendment as such.

On these premises I join in the judgment of the Court.

CASE DISCUSSION

What exactly did the Court decide that the right to counsel means? On what theory did it apply the right to counsel to state proceedings? Why did Justice John Marshall Harlan write a concurring opinion? Why did the Court take the unusual step of overruling its decision in *Betts v. Brady*? Do you agree that the right to counsel should apply to state proceedings, or should states decide for themselves whether poor criminal defendants in their jurisdictions have a right to a lawyer assigned by the court? Does the Court apply the right to counsel to state proceedings to further the interest in correct result? To further the interest in process? As a matter of efficiency? Explain.

Gideon left several Sixth Amendment questions unanswered, including the following:

1. When does the right to counsel attach; that is, at what proceedings does a citizen have a right to have a lawyer present? Or, more specifically, what does *prosecution* mean under the Sixth Amendment?

2. What is a "criminal prosecution," according to the Sixth Amendment? Do "all prosecutions" include even petty misdemeanors, such as disorderly conduct?

3. How poor is "indigent"?

4. Does *counsel* mean "effective counsel"?

TABLE 11.1 ATTACHMENT OF THE SIXTH AMENDMENT RIGHT TO COUNSEL

Stage of the Criminal Process	Sixth Amendment Right to Counsel?
Investigative stop	No
Frisk for weapons	No
Arrest	No
Search following arrest	No
Custodial interrogation	No
Photographic identification	No
Lineup before formal charge	No
First appearance	No
Lineup following formal charges	Yes
Arraignment	Yes
Preliminary hearing	Yes
Grand jury review	No
Pretrial motions and hearings	Yes
Trial	Yes
Appeals and collateral attacks	Yes

When the Right to Counsel Attaches

The Sixth Amendment guarantees the right to counsel in "prosecutions." What proceedings does prosecution include? Clearly, it includes the trial and appeal, when special legal expertise most applies. But what about the stages prior to trial? The Supreme Court has ruled that the right to counsel attaches to all "critical stages" in the proceedings. Table 11.1 shows all the major stages in the criminal process and designates which ones are critical for purposes of the right to counsel. (See Chapter 1 for a discussion of the major stages listed here.)

Critical stages in the criminal prosecution include all those that take place after the government files formal charges. Ordinarily, this means that defendants have a right to counsel at all proceedings that take place after the first appearance. More problematic are events taking place in police stations, particularly during interrogation and identification procedures. The Supreme Court first applied the right to a lawyer in police stations in 1964, in *Escobedo v. Illinois*. The Court held that the right to counsel attached at the accusatory stage of a criminal case—that is, at the point when general investigation focused on a specific suspect. The police in *Escobedo* had decided that Danny Escobedo had committed the crime. They refused to permit him to talk to his lawyer during interrogation, even though his attorney was in the police station. The Court did not follow *Escobedo* in later cases. Instead, it shifted to a different approach to interrogation cases. In the famous *Miranda v. Arizona*, decided in 1966, the Court held that the Fifth Amendment right against self-incrimination granted the right to a lawyer at custodial interrogations (see Chapter 8 for discussions of *Miranda* and *Escobedo*).

In pretrial identification procedures, such as lineups and show-ups, the Court held that the Sixth Amendment right to counsel attached to all critical stages in criminal proceedings. The Court ruled in *United States v. Wade* (1967) that a lineup conducted after a defendant was indicted was a critical stage. And in *Kirby v. Illinois* (1972) the Court decided that a lineup prior to the initiation of formal proceedings was not a critical stage in the prosecution of defendants.

The Meaning of "All Criminal Prosecutions"

In 1932, *Powell v. Alabama* established the rule that the right to appointed counsel applied to capital cases—that is, cases involving the death penalty. In *Gideon v. Wainwright* (1963) the Court extended the right to counsel to felonies against property. In 1972 the Court further extended the protection to misdemeanors punishable by jail terms. In *Argersinger v. Hamlin*, Argersinger, a Florida indigent, was convicted of carrying a concealed weapon, a misdemeanor punishable by up to six months' imprisonment, a $1,000 fine, or both. A Florida rule limited assigned counsel to "non-petty offenses punishable by more than six months imprisonment." The Court struck down the rule, holding that absent a knowing and intelligent waiver, offenses punishable by incarceration, whether classified as petty, misdemeanor, or felony, required the right to counsel.[27]

Argersinger did not decide if indigents had the right to assigned counsel in "all" criminal cases. In *Argersinger*, the Court noted a practical problem in applying the right to counsel: insufficient resources to provide everyone with a lawyer. Although budgetary considerations cannot determine constitutional rights in the abstract, available resources affect the implementation of those rights. This mix of practice and theory surfaced again in *Scott v. Illinois*. The Court specifically addressed the question of whether the right to assigned counsel extends to offenses that do not actually result in prison sentences.

C A S E

Do Indigents Have a Right to Assigned Counsel for Shoplifting?

Scott v. Illinois
440 U.S. 367, 99 S.Ct. 1158,
59 L.Ed.2d 383 (1979)

Scott was convicted of theft and fined $50 after a bench trial in the Circuit Court of Cook County, Ill. His conviction was affirmed by the state intermediate appellate court and then by the Supreme Court of Illinois, over Scott's contention that the Sixth and Fourteenth Amendments to the United States Constitution required that Illinois provide trial counsel to him at its expense. The Supreme Court granted certiorari *and affirmed. Justice Rehnquist wrote the opinion of the Court, which Chief Justice Burger and Justices Stewart, White, and Powell joined. Justice Powell filed a concurring opinion. Justice Brennan filed a dissenting opinion, which Justices Marshall and Stevens joined. Justice Blackmun filed a dissenting opinion.*

FACTS

Petitioner Scott was convicted of shoplifting merchandise valued at less than $150. The applicable Illinois statute set the maximum penalty for such an offense at a $500 fine or one year in jail, or both. The petitioner argues that a line of this Court's cases culminating in *Argersinger v. Hamlin* requires state provision of counsel whenever imprisonment is an authorized penalty.

The Supreme Court of Illinois rejected this contention, quoting the following language from *Argersinger*: "We hold, therefore, that absent a knowing and intelligent waiver, no person may be imprisoned for any offense, whether classified as petty, misdemeanor, or felony, unless he was represented by counsel at his trial."

Under the rule we announce today, every judge will know when the trial of a misdemeanor starts that no imprisonment may be imposed, even though local law permits it, unless the accused is represented by counsel. He will have a measure of the seriousness and gravity of the offense and therefore know when to name a lawyer to represent the accused before the trial starts. The Supreme Court of Illinois went on to state that it was "not inclined to extend *Argersinger*" to the case where a defendant is charged with a statutory offense for which imprisonment upon conviction is authorized but not actually imposed upon the defendant. We agree with the Supreme Court of Illinois that the Federal Constitution does not require a state trial court to appoint counsel for a criminal defendant such as petitioner, and we therefore affirm its judgment. . . .

There is considerable doubt that the Sixth Amendment itself, as originally drafted by the Framers of the Bill of Rights, contemplated any guarantee other than the right of an accused in a criminal prosecution in a federal court to employ a lawyer to assist in his defense. . . .

The Court held in *Duncan v. Louisiana* (1968) that the right to jury trial in federal court guaranteed by the Sixth Amendment was applicable to the States by virtue of the Fourteenth Amendment. The Court held, however:

> It is doubtless true that there is a category of petty crimes or offenses which is not subject to the Sixth Amendment jury trial provision and should not be subject to the Fourteenth Amendment jury trial requirement here applied to the States. Crimes carrying possible penalties up to six months do not require a jury trial if they otherwise qualify as petty offenses. . . .

In *Baldwin v. New York* (1970) the controlling opinion of Mr. Justice White concluded that "no offense can be deemed 'petty' for purposes of the right to trial by jury where imprisonment for more than six months is authorized."

In *Argersinger*, the State of Florida urged that a similar dichotomy be employed in the right-to-counsel area: Any offense punishable by less than six months in jail should not require appointment of counsel for an indigent defendant. The *Argersinger* Court rejected this analogy, however, observing that

"the right to trial by jury has a different genealogy and is brigaded with a system of trial to a judge alone."

The number of separate opinions in *Gideon, Duncan, Baldwin,* and *Argersinger* suggests that constitutional line drawing becomes more difficult as the reach of the Constitution is extended further, and as efforts are made to transpose lines from one area of Sixth Amendment jurisprudence to another. The process of incorporation creates special difficulties, for the state and federal contexts are often different and application of the same principle may have ramifications distinct in degree and kind. The range of human conduct regulated by state criminal laws is much broader than that of the federal criminal laws, particularly on the "petty" offense part of the spectrum. As a matter of constitutional adjudication, we are, therefore, less willing to extrapolate an already extended line when, although the general nature of the principle sought to be applied is clear, its precise limits and their ramifications become less so. We have now in our decided cases departed from the literal meaning of the Sixth Amendment. And we cannot fall back on the common law as it existed prior to the enactment of that Amendment, since it perversely gave less in the way of right to counsel to accused felons than to those accused of misdemeanors.

In *Argersinger*, the Court rejected arguments that social cost or lack of available lawyers militated against its holding, in some part because it thought these arguments were factually incorrect. But they were rejected in much larger part because of the Court's conclusion that incarceration was so severe a sanction that it should not be imposed as a result of a criminal trial unless an indigent defendant had been offered appointed counsel to assist in his defense, regardless of the cost to the States implicit in such a rule. The Court in its opinion repeatedly referred to trials "where an accused is deprived of his liberty," and to "a case that actually leads to imprisonment even for a brief period." The Chief Justice in his opinion concurring in the result also observed that "any deprivation of liberty is a serious matter."

Although the intentions of the *Argersinger* Court are not unmistakably clear from its opinion, we conclude today that *Argersinger* did indeed delimit the constitutional right to appointed counsel in state criminal proceedings.

Even were the matter res nova, we believe that the central premise of *Argersinger*—that actual imprisonment is a penalty different in kind from fines or the mere threat of imprisonment—is eminently sound and warrants adoption of actual imprisonment as the line defining the constitutional right to appointment of counsel. *Argersinger* has proved reasonably workable, whereas any extension would create confusion and impose unpredictable, but necessarily substantial, costs on 50 quite diverse States.

[COURT NOTE: "Unfortunately, extensive empirical work has not been done. That which exists suggests that the requirements of *Argersinger* have not proved to be unduly burdensome. See, e.g., Ingraham, The Impact of *Argersinger*—One Year Later, 8 *Law & Soc. Rev.* 615 (1974). That some jurisdictions have had difficulty implementing *Argersinger* is certainly not an argument for extending it. S. Krantz, C. Smith, D. Rossman, P. Froud & J. Hoffman, *Right to Counsel in Criminal Cases* 1–18 (1976)."]

We therefore hold that the Sixth and Fourteenth Amendments to the United States Constitution require only that no indigent criminal defendant be sentenced to a term of imprisonment unless the State has afforded him the right to assistance of appointed counsel in his defense. The judgment of the Supreme Court of Illinois is accordingly Affirmed. . . .

DISSENT

Justice Brennan, with whom Justice Marshall and Justice Stevens join, dissenting.

The Court, in an opinion that at best ignores the basic principles of prior decisions, affirms Scott's conviction without counsel because he was sentenced only to pay a fine. In my view, the plain wording of the Sixth Amendment and the Court's precedents compel the conclusion that Scott's uncounseled conviction violated the Sixth and Fourteenth Amendments and should be reversed. . . .

. . .

First, the "authorized imprisonment" standard more faithfully implements the principles of the Sixth Amendment identified in *Gideon*. The procedural rules established by state statutes are geared to the nature of the potential penalty for an offense, not to the actual penalty imposed in particular cases. The authorized penalty is also a better predictor of the stigma and other collateral consequences that attach to conviction of an offense. . . . By contrast, the "actual imprisonment" standard . . . denies the right to counsel in criminal prosecutions to accuseds who suffer the severe consequences of prosecution other than imprisonment.

Second, the "authorized imprisonment" test presents no problems of administration. It avoids the necessity for time-consuming consideration of the likely sentence in each individual case before trial and the attendant problems of inaccurate predictions, unequal treatment, and apparent and actual bias. . . .

Finally, the "authorized imprisonment" test ensures that courts will not abrogate legislative judgments concerning the appropriate range of penalties to be considered for each offense. Under the "actual imprisonment" standard

[t]he judge will . . . be forced to decide in advance of trial—and without hearing the evidence—whether he will forego entirely his judicial discretion to impose some sentence of imprisonment and abandon his responsibility to consider the full range of punishments established by the legislature. His alternatives, assuming the availability of counsel, will be to appoint counsel and retain the discretion vested in him by law, or to abandon this discretion in advance and proceed without counsel.

. . . The apparent reason for the Court's adoption of the "actual imprisonment" standard for all misdemeanors is concern for the economic burden that an "authorized imprisonment" standard might place on the States. But, with all respect, that concern is both irrelevant and speculative. This Court's role in enforcing constitutional guarantees for criminal defendants cannot be made dependent on the budgetary decisions of state governments. A unanimous Court made that clear in *Mayer v. Chicago* (1971), in rejecting a proposed fiscal justification for providing free transcripts for appeals only when the appellant was subject to imprisonment:

This argument misconceives the principle of *Griffin* [*v. Illinois* (1956)]. . . . *Griffin* does not represent a balance between the needs of the accused and the interests of society; its principle is a flat prohibition against pricing indigent defendants out of as effective an appeal as would be available to others able to pay their own way. The invidiousness of the discrimination that exists when criminal procedures are made available only to those who can pay is not erased by any differences in the sentences that may be imposed. The State's fiscal interest is, therefore, irrelevant.

In any event, the extent of the alleged burden on the States is, as the Court admits, speculative. Although more persons are charged with misdemeanors punishable by incarceration than are charged with felonies, a smaller percentage of persons charged with misdemeanors qualify as indigent, and misdemeanor cases as a rule require far less attorney time.

[COURT NOTE: "See Uniform Rules of Criminal Procedure, Rule 321(b), Comment, 10 U.L.A. 70 (1974) (estimates that only 10% of misdemeanor defendants, as opposed to 60%–65% of felony defendants, meet the necessary indigency standard); National Legal Aid and Defender Assn. The Other Face of Justice, Note I, (1973) (survey indicates national average is 65% indigency in felony cases and only 47% in misdemeanor cases). The National Advisory Commission on Criminal Justice Standards and Goals adopted a maximum caseload standard of 150 felony cases or 400 misdemeanor cases per attorney per year. National Advisory Commission on Criminal Justice Standards and Goals, *Courts*, Standard 13.12, (1973). See also The Other Face of Justice, supra, Table 109."]

Furthermore, public defender systems have proved economically feasible, and the establishment of such systems to replace appointment of private attorneys can keep costs at acceptable levels even when the number of cases requiring appointment of counsel increases dramatically. The public defender system alternative also answers the argument that an authorized imprisonment standard would clog the courts with inexperienced appointed counsel.

[COURT NOTE: "A study conducted in the State of Wisconsin, which introduced a State Public Defender System after the Wisconsin Supreme Court in *State ex rel. Winnie v. Harris* (1977) extended the right to counsel in the way urged by petitioner in this case, indicated that the average cost of providing counsel in a misdemeanor case was reduced from $150–$200 to $90 by using a public defender rather than appointing private counsel."]

Perhaps the strongest refutation of respondent's alarmist prophecies that an authorized imprisonment standard would wreak havoc on the States is that the standard has not produced that result in the substantial number of States that already provide counsel in all cases where imprisonment is authorized—States that include a large majority of the country's population and a great diversity of urban and rural environments. Moreover, of those States that do not yet provide counsel in all cases where any imprisonment is authorized, many provide counsel when periods of imprisonment longer than 30 days, 3 months, or 6 months are authorized. In fact, Scott would be entitled to appointed counsel under the current laws of at least 33 States. . . .

. . .

Mr. Justice Blackmun, dissenting.

. . . I would hold that the right to counsel secured by the Sixth and Fourteenth Amendments extends at least as far as the right to jury trial secured by those Amendments. Accordingly, I would hold that an indigent defendant in a state criminal case must be afforded appointed counsel whenever the defendant is prosecuted for a nonpetty criminal offense, that is, one punishable by more than six months' imprisonment, or whenever the defendant is convicted of an offense and is actually subjected to a term of imprisonment.

This resolution, I feel, would provide the "bright line" that defendants, prosecutors, and trial and appellate courts all deserve and, at the same time, would reconcile on a principled basis the important considerations that led to the decisions in *Duncan, Baldwin,* and *Argersinger.* On this approach, of course, the judgment of the Supreme Court of Illinois upholding petitioner Scott's conviction should be reversed, since he was convicted of an offense for which he was constitutionally entitled to a jury trial. I therefore, dissent.

CASE DISCUSSION

Should every defendant who cannot afford a lawyer have one in all criminal cases at state expense? Would such an interpretation of the right to counsel promote the public interest in result over process? Or would it promote both result and process? Would it serve the societal interest in aiding the poor and weak in our so-ciety? Should it do so? Should economic considera-tions be taken into account in deciding who should have constitutional rights? What interests does taking them into account promote? Sacrifice? Is Justice Harry A. Blackmun's recommendation for a "bright line" rule a good one?

The Standard of Indigence

The Supreme Court has never defined *indigence*. However, federal appellate courts have established some general guidelines:

1. Indigence does not mean total destitution.
2. Only defendants' earnings and assets can be considered, not the help their friends and relatives might provide.
3. Actual, not potential, earnings are the measure.
4. The state may tap future earnings, however, by establishing **recoupment programs,** programs designed to collect in the future the costs of counsel, transcripts, and other defense expenditures.

Some jurisdictions have established specific standards for determining indigence. Minnesota's rules for judges' assessment of indigence at defendants' first appearance are typical:

Rule 5.02 Appointment of Counsel
Subd. 1. Felonies and Gross Misdemeanors. If the defendant is not represented by counsel and is financially unable to afford counsel, the judge or judicial offi-cer shall appoint counsel for him.
Subd. 2. Misdemeanors. Unless the defendant charged with a misdemeanor pun-ishable upon conviction by incarceration voluntarily waives counsel in writing or on the record, the court shall appoint counsel for him if he appears without coun-sel and is financially unable to afford counsel. . . .
Subd. 3. Standard of Indigence. A defendant is financially unable to obtain coun-sel if he is financially unable to obtain adequate representation without substan-tial hardship for himself or his family.

1. A defendant will be presumed to be financially unable to afford counsel if:
a. his cash assets are less than $300.00 when entitled to only a court trial; or
b. his current weekly net income does not exceed $500.00 when entitled to a jury trial; and
c. his current weekly net income does not exceed forty times the federal mini-mum hourly wage . . . if he is unmarried and without dependents; or,
d. his current weekly net income and that of his spouse do not exceed sixty times the federal minimum hourly wage . . . if he is married and without dependents. In determining the amounts under either section (c) or section (d), for each de-pendent the amount shall be increased by $25.00 per week.

2. A defendant who has cash assets or income exceeding the amounts in paragraph (1) shall not be presumed to be financially able to obtain counsel. The determination shall be made by the court as a practical matter, taking into account such other factors as the defendant's length of employment or unemployment, prior income, the value and nature of his assets, number of children and other family responsibilities, number and nature of debts arising from any source, the amount customarily charged by members of the practicing bar for representation of the type in question, and any other relevant factor.

3. In determining whether a defendant is financially able to obtain adequate representation without substantial hardship to himself or his family:

a. cash assets include those assets which may be readily converted to cash . . . without jeopardizing the defendant's ability to maintain his home or employment. A single family automobile shall not be considered an asset.

b. the fact that defendant has posted or can [post] bail is irrelevant. . . .

c. the fact that the defendant is employable but unemployed shall not be in itself proof that he is financially able to obtain counsel without substantial hardship to himself or his family.

d. the fact that parents or other relatives of the defendant have the financial ability to obtain counsel for the defendant is irrelevant, except under the following circumstances:

    i. where the defendant is unemancipated, under the age of 21 years, living with his parent or other relatives, and such parents or other relatives have the clear ability to obtain counsel; or

    ii. where the parents or other relatives of the defendant have the financial ability to obtain counsel for the defendant but are unwilling to do so only because of the relatively minor nature of the charge.

Under part (1) . . . a defendant will be presumed financially unable to retain his own attorney and counsel shall be appointed for him. . . . Part (1) provides a presumption of indigence and is not to be taken as indicating that a defendant with a higher income and assets must obtain his own attorney. A defendant with a higher income or assets should still be appointed counsel if [he] is unable . . . to obtain adequate representations without substantial hardship to himself or his family. . . .

Subd. 4. Financial Inquiry. An inquiry to determine financial eligibility of a defendant for the appointment of counsel shall be made whenever possible prior to the court appearance and by such persons as the court may direct.

Subd. 5. Partial Eligibility and Reimbursement. The ability to pay part of the cost of adequate representation at any time while the charges are pending against a defendant shall not preclude the appointment of counsel for the defendant. The court may require a defendant, to the extent of his ability, to compensate the governmental unit charged with paying the expense of appointed counsel.[28]

The Right to Effective Counsel

The Sixth Amendment, according to *Powell v. Alabama*, requires effective representation, but until recently the Supreme Court did not clearly define what *effective* means. In the absence of Supreme Court guidance, both federal and state lower courts adopted the **mockery of justice standard.** Under this standard, only circumstances so shocking that they reduced the trial to a farce satisfied defendants' claims of ineffective representation by counsel. One judge put it this way: "[I]neffective assistance existed only when the trial was a farce, or mockery of justice, or was shocking to the conscience of the reviewing court, or the purported representation was only perfunctory, in bad faith, a sham, [or] a pretense." Even lawyers who appeared in court drunk did not violate this standard.[29]

Courts and commentators have criticized the mockery of justice standard as too subjective, vague, and narrow. The standard's focus on the trial excludes many serious errors that might occur in preparing for trial. Furthermore, in the overwhelming majority of cases that result in guilty pleas, the standard is totally irrelevant. Judge Bazelon, an experienced and respected federal judge, said that the test requires "such a minimal level of performance from counsel that it is itself a mockery of the Sixth Amendment." He continued, "I have often been told that if my court were to reverse in every case in which there was inadequate counsel, we would have to send back half the convictions in my jurisdiction."[30]

Courts hesitate to get involved in the ineffectiveness question. Close scrutiny by trial judges of defense attorneys' performance may well lead to a degree of interference intolerable both to the adversary system and to the professional independence of defense attorneys. Furthermore, judges who criticize lawyers' performance are, in a sense, criticizing themselves, since they are members of the same profession. Hence, trial judges hesitate to criticize too quickly the lawyers who practice before their courts.[31]

Most jurisdictions have abandoned the mockery of justice standard, replacing it with the **reasonably competent attorney standard.** According to this standard, judges measure lawyers' performance against the "customary skills and diligence that a reasonably competent attorney would perform under similar circumstances." Attorneys must be more diligent under the reasonably competent attorney standard than was required under the mockery of justice standard. However, both the mockery of justice and the reasonably competent attorney standards are "vague to some appreciable degree and . . . susceptible to greatly varying subjective impressions." The Supreme Court has declined to rule that the Constitution mandates either standard.[32]

In the 1980s and 1990s, the Court took a more active role in reviewing ineffective representation claims. In 1984 the Court examined the question in *Strickland v. Washington.*

C A S E

Did His Lawyer "Effectively" Represent Him?

Strickland v. Washington
466 U.S. 668, 104 S.Ct. 2052,
80 L.Ed.2d 674 (1984)

Strickland pleaded guilty to three capital murder charges. Finding numerous aggravating circumstances and no mitigating circumstance, the trial judge sen- *tenced respondent to death on each of the murder counts. The Florida Supreme Court affirmed, and respondent then sought collateral relief in state court on the ground,* inter alia, *that counsel had rendered ineffective assistance at the sentencing proceeding. The trial court denied relief, and the Florida Supreme Court affirmed. Respondent then filed a* habeas corpus *petition in federal district court advancing the claim of ineffective assistance of counsel. After an evidentiary hearing, the district court denied relief. The court of appeals ultimately reversed and remanded the case. The United States Supreme Court reversed, holding that Strickland was not denied the effective representation of counsel and that, assuming counsel's conduct was unreasonable, respondent suffered insufficient prejudice to warrant setting aside his death sentence. Justice O'Connor delivered the opinion of the Court, in which Chief Justice Burger and Justices White, Blackmun, Powell, Rehnquist, and Stevens joined. Justice Brennan filed an opinion concurring in part and dissenting in part. Justice Marshall filed a dissenting opinion.*

FACTS

During a 10-day period in September 1976, respondent planned and committed three groups of crimes, which included three brutal stabbing murders, torture, kidnapping, severe assaults, attempted murders, attempted extortion, and theft. After his two accomplices were arrested, respondent surrendered to police and voluntarily gave a lengthy statement confessing to the third of the criminal episodes. The State of Florida indicted respondent for kidnapping and murder and appointed an experienced criminal lawyer to represent him.

Counsel actively pursued pretrial motions and discovery. He cut his efforts short, however, and he experienced a sense of hopelessness about the case, when he learned that, against his specific advice, respondent had also confessed to the first two murders. By the date set for trial, respondent was subject to indictment for three counts of first-degree murder and multiple counts of robbery, kidnapping for ransom, breaking and entering and assault, attempted murder, and conspiracy to commit robbery. Respondent waived his right to a jury trial, again acting against counsel's advice, and pleaded guilty to all charges, including the three capital murder charges. In the plea colloquy, respondent told that trial judge that, although he had committed a string of burglaries, he had no significant prior criminal record and that at the time of his criminal spree he was under extreme stress caused by his inability to support his family. He

also stated, however, that he accepted responsibility for the crimes. The trial judge told respondent that he had "a great deal of respect for people who are willing to step forward and admit their responsibility" but that he was making no statement at all about his likely sentencing decision.

Counsel advised respondent to invoke his right under Florida law to an advisory jury at his capital sentencing hearing. Respondent rejected the advice and waived the right. He chose instead to be sentenced by the trial judge without a jury recommendation. In preparing for the sentencing hearing, counsel spoke to respondent about his background. He also spoke on the telephone with respondent's wife and mother, though he did not follow up on the one successful effort to meet with them. He did not otherwise seek out character witnesses for respondent. Nor did he request a psychiatric examination, since his conversations with his client gave no indication that respondent had psychological problems.

Counsel decided not to present and hence not to look further for evidence concerning respondent's character and emotional state. That decision reflected trial counsel's sense of hopelessness about overcoming the evidentiary effect of respondent's confessions to the gruesome crimes. It also reflected the judgment that it was advisable to rely on the plea of colloquy for evidence about respondent's background and about his claim of emotional stress: the plea colloquy communicated sufficient information about these subjects, and by foregoing the opportunity to present new evidence on these subjects, counsel prevented the State from cross-examining respondent on his claim and from putting on psychiatric evidence of his own.

Counsel also excluded from the sentencing hearing other evidence he thought was potentially damaging. He successfully moved to exclude respondent's "rap sheet." Because he judged that a presentence report might prove more detrimental than helpful, as it would have included respondent's criminal history and thereby would have undermined the claim of no significant history of criminal activity, he did not request that one be prepared.

At the sentencing hearing, counsel's strategy was based primarily on the trial judge's remarks at the plea colloquy as well as on his reputation as a sentencing judge who thought it important for a convicted defendant to own up to his crime. Counsel argued that respondent's remorse and acceptance of responsibility justified sparing him from the death penalty. Counsel also argued that respondent had no history of criminal activity and that respondent committed the crimes under extreme mental or emotional disturbance, thus coming within the statutory list of mitigating circumstances. He further argued that respondent should be spared death because he had surrendered, confessed, and offered to testify against a codefendant and because respondent was fundamentally a good person who had briefly gone badly wrong in extremely stressful circumstances. The State put on evidence and witnesses largely for the purpose of describing the details of the crimes. Counsel did not cross-examine the medical experts who testified about the manner of death of respondent's victims. . . .

In short, the trial judge found numerous aggravating circumstances and no (or a single comparatively significant) mitigating circumstance. With respect to each of the three convictions for capital murder, the trial judge concluded: "A careful consideration of all matters presented to the court impels the conclusion that there are insufficient mitigating circumstances . . . to outweigh the aggravating circumstances." He therefore sentenced respondent to death on each of the three counts of murder and to prison terms for other crimes. The Florida Supreme Court upheld the convictions and sentences on direct appeal.

Respondent subsequently sought collateral relief in state court on numerous grounds, among them that counsel had rendered ineffective assistance at the sentencing proceeding. Respondent challenged counsel's assistance in six respects. He asserted that counsel was ineffective because he failed to move for a continuance to prepare for sentencing, to request a psychiatric report, to investigate and present character witnesses, to seek a presentence investigation report, to present meaningful arguments to the sentencing judge, and to investigate the medical examiner's reports or cross-examine the medical experts. . . .

The trial court denied relief without an evidentiary hearing, finding that the record evidence conclusively showed that the ineffectiveness claim was meritless. . . . The court specifically found:

[As] a matter of law, the record affirmatively demonstrates beyond any doubt that even if [counsel] had done each of the . . . things [that respondent alleged counsel had failed to do] at the time of sentencing, there is not even the remotest chance that the outcome would have been any different. The plain fact is that the aggravating circumstances proved in this case were completely overwhelming. . . .

The Florida Supreme Court affirmed the denial of relief. [NOTE: Washington filed a *habeas corpus* petition in United States district court, and the district court denied the petition. He appealed to the United States Court of Appeals. Florida filed petition for writ of *certiorari* to the United States Supreme Court.]

OPINION

. . . [W]e granted certiorari to consider the standards by which to judge a contention that the Constitution required that a criminal judgment be overturned because of the actual ineffective assistance of counsel. . . . The same principle applies to a capital sentencing proceeding such as that provided by Florida law. . . . A capital sentencing proceeding, like the one involved in this case, is sufficiently like a trial in its adversarial format and in the existence of standards for decision, that counsel's role in the proceeding is comparable to counsel's role at trial—to ensure that the adversarial testing process works to produce a just result under the standards governing decision. For purposes of describing counsel's duties, therefore, Florida's capital sentencing proceeding need not be distinguished from an ordinary trial.

A convicted defendant's claim that counsel's assistance was so defective as to require reversal of a conviction of death sentence has two components. First, defendant must show that counsel's performance was deficient. This requires showing that counsel made errors so serious that counsel was not functioning as the "counsel" guaranteed the defendant by the Sixth Amendment. Second, the defendant must show that the deficient performance prejudiced the defense. This requires showing that counsel's errors were so serious as to deprive the defendant of a fair trial, a trial whose result is reliable. Unless a defendant makes both showings, it cannot be said that the conviction or death sentence resulted from a breakdown in the adversary process that renders the result unreliable.

As all the Federal Court of Appeals have now held, the proper standard for attorney performance is that of reasonably effective assistance. . . .

Application of the governing principle is not hard in this case. The facts as described above make clear that the conduct of respondent's counsel at and before respondent's sentencing proceeding cannot be found unreasonable. They also make clear that, even assuming the challenged conduct of counsel was unreasonable, respondent suffered insufficient prejudice to warrant setting aside his death sentence.

With respect to the performance component, the record shows that respondent's counsel made a strategic choice to argue for the extreme emotional distress mitigating circumstance and to rely as fully as possible on respondent's acceptance of responsibility for his crimes. Although counsel understandably felt hopeless about respondent's prospects, nothing in the record indicates that counsel's sense of hopelessness distorted his professional judgment. Counsel's strategy choice was well within the range of professionally reasonable judgments, and the decision not to seek more character or psychological evidence than was already in hand was likewise reasonable.

The trial judge's views on the importance of owning up to one's crimes were well known to counsel. The aggravating circumstances were utterly overwhelming. Trial counsel could reasonably surmise from his conversations with respondent that character and psychological evidence would be of little help. Respondent had already been able to mention at the plea colloquy the substance of what there was to know about his financial and emotional troubles. Restricting testimony on respondent's character to what had come in at the plea colloquy ensured that contrary character and psychological evidence and respondent's criminal history, which counsel had successfully moved to exclude, would not come in. On these facts, there can be little question, even without application of the presumption of adequate performance, that trial counsel's defense, though unsuccessful, was the result of reasonable professional judgment.

With respect to the prejudice component, the lack of merit of respondent's claim is even more stark. The evidence that respondent says his trial counsel should have offered at the sentencing hearing would barely have altered the sentencing profile offered to the sentencing judge. As the state courts and District Courts found, at most this evidence shows that numerous people who knew respondent thought he was generally a good person and that a psychiatrist and a psychologist believed he was under considerable emotional stress that did not rise to the level of extreme disturbance. Given the overwhelming aggravating factors, there is no reasonable probability that the omitted evidence would have changed the conclusion that the aggravating circumstances outweighed the mitigating circumstances and, hence, the sentence imposed. Indeed, the admission of the evidence respondent now offers might even have been harmful to his case: his "rap sheet" would probably have been admitted into evidence, and the psychological reports would have directly contradicted respondent's claim that the mitigating circumstance of extreme emotional disturbance applied to his case.

We conclude, therefore, that the District Court properly declined to issue a writ of habeas corpus. The judgment of the Court of Appeals is accordingly Reversed.

DISSENT

Justice Marshall, dissenting.

. . . My objection to the performance standard adopted by the Court is that it is so malleable that, in practice, it will either have no grip at all or will yield excessive variation in the manner in which the Sixth Amendment is interpreted and applied by different courts. To tell lawyers and the lower courts that counsel for a criminal defendant must behave "reasonably" and must act like "a reasonably competent attorney," is to tell them almost nothing. In essence, the majority has instructed judges called upon to assess claims of ineffective assistance of counsel to advert to their own intuitions regarding what constitutes "professional" representation, and has discouraged them from trying to develop more detailed standards governing the performance of defense counsel. In my view, the Court has thereby not only abdicated its own responsibility to interpret the Constitution, but also impaired the ability of the lower courts to exercise theirs.

The debilitating ambiguity of an "objective standard of reasonableness" in this context is illustrated by the majority's failure to address important issues concerning the quality of representation mandated by the Constitution. It is an unfortunate but undeniable fact that a person of means, by selecting a lawyer and paying him enough to ensure he prepares thoroughly, usually can obtain better representation than that available to an indigent defendant, who must rely on appointed counsel, who, in turn, has limited time and resources to devote to a given case. Is a "reasonably competent attorney" a reasonably competent adequately paid retained lawyer or a reasonably competent appointed attorney? It is also a fact that the quality of representation available to ordinary defendants in different parts of the country varies significantly. Should the standard of performance mandated by the Sixth Amendment vary by locale? The majority offers no clues as to the proper responses to these questions. . . .

Second and more fundamentally, the assumption on which the Court's holding rests is that the only purpose of the constitutional guarantee of effective assistance of counsel is to reduce the chance that innocent persons will be convicted. In my view, the guarantee also functions to ensure that convictions are obtained only through fundamentally fair procedures. The majority contends that the Sixth Amendment is not violated when a manifestly guilty defendant is convicted after a trial in which he was represented by a manifestly ineffective attorney. I cannot agree. Every defendant is entitled to a trial in which his interests are vigorously and conscientiously advocated by an able lawyer. A proceeding in which the defendant does not receive meaningful assistance in meeting the forces of the State does not, in my opinion, constitute due process. . . .

CASE DISCUSSION

What were the totality of circumstances that led the Court to conclude that Strickland received "reasonably effective" assistance of counsel? Why did the Court conclude that even if Strickland did not receive effective assistance, the sentence would have been the same anyway? What reasons did the dissent give for not joining the majority? Do you think the Court promoted the interest in finality at the expense of obtaining the correct result? Do you think the Court responded to the societal interest in crime control? If so, did it do so at the expense of procedural regularity? Explain.

SUMMARY

Shortly after arrest, the police forward some cases to prosecutors. Prosecutors decide whether to dismiss the cases, to divert those arrested into social and community service programs or civil courts, or to file formal charges against defendants. Prosecutors possess enormous discretion in deciding whether to charge and what specific charges to bring against criminal suspects. Although prosecutors wield wide power, they have limited discretion in charging criminal suspects. Constitutional rules against discriminatory prosecution, the formal rules of evidence, and the satisfaction of justice, organizational, and societal interests restrain prosecutors' decisions to charge.

The first appearance takes place shortly after the decision to charge, particularly for defendants detained without warrants or prior judicial determination of probable cause to detain them. The first appearance is a brief proceeding before magistrates or other judicial officers in the lower criminal courts. Judicial officers perform several functions at the first appearance, including

1. determining probable cause to detain if such determination has not already taken place,

2. reading the charges against defendants,

3. informing defendants of their constitutional rights,

4. determining indigence and assigning attorneys for defendants qualifying as indigent, and

5. setting bail.

The criminal complaint acts as the charging instrument at the first appearance. The Supreme Court has not ruled that the first appearance constitutes adversary proceedings for purposes of the Sixth Amendment right to counsel.

The right to counsel did exist in criminal cases at the common law. At the time of its adoption and for a considerable period following, the Sixth Amendment right to counsel meant only that defendants who could afford them had the right to have lawyers represent them at criminal trials. The Supreme Court and the state courts have expanded the scope of the right since the early years following the adoption of the United States Constitution. It now extends to pretrial proceedings, such as custodial interrogation, lineups after indictment, and all stages following the inception of judicial proceedings. Furthermore, defendants who cannot afford attorneys have a constitutional right to appointed counsel, except for petty offenses. Finally, indigent defendants have a right to *effective* counsel under the Sixth Amendment.

The Eighth Amendment prohibits excessive bail. Most defendants are released during determination of the charges against them. The Constitution permits setting bail by money, bond, or other conditions sufficient to secure defendants' appearance at trial. Furthermore, the Constitution allows preventive detention—that is, detention of defendants whose dangerousness (likelihood of committing other offenses or endangering the community or specific individuals such as victims and witnesses) justifies holding them in custody during the determination of the charges against them. The Supreme Court has ruled that preventive detention is a regulatory device; it does not constitute cruel and unusual punishment, nor does it deny defendants due process of law.

REVIEW QUESTIONS

1. Distinguish between the arrest, interrogation, and identification stage in the criminal process (discussed in Chapters 5 through 9) and the charging and first appearance stage (discussed in this chapter).

2. What are the acceptable and unacceptable criteria upon which prosecutors can decide to charge?

3. What decisions must prosecutors make when police bring them cases for further action?

4. Describe the major functions that magistrates perform at the initial appearance.

5. How does the initial appearance differ from arraignment? Preliminary hearings? Grand jury review?

6. Should an absolute right to bail exist? Explain.

7. In your opinion, what is a good definition of *indigent*?

8. What are the arguments in favor of and against preventive detention? Which do you think are most persuasive?

9. What are all the result, process, organization, and broad social interests that are balanced and

promoted in the decisions to charge defendants, assign counsel to indigent defendants, and release or detain defendants prior to trial? How would you balance these interests?

10. With respect to the Sixth Amendment right to counsel, when does the right attach, to what kinds of cases does it apply, and what does *effective counsel* mean?

KEY TERMS

arraignment the bringing of a defendant to court to hear and plead to criminal charges.

bail schedules lists of amounts of bail required for specific offenses.

citation release a summons to appear in court in lieu of being detained.

criminal complaint the formal charging document.

divert to transfer a case from the criminal justice system to a community service, restitution, or treatment program.

first appearance the appearance of a defendant in court for determination of probable cause, determination of bail, assignment of attorney, and notification of rights.

indigent defendants defendants who are too poor to afford a lawyer.

mockery of justice standard the standard under which counsel is deemed ineffective only if circumstances reduced the trial to a farce.

own recognizance (O.R.) a type of pretrial release made on the promise of the defendant to appear in court.

preventive detention pretrial detention based on the need to preserve community safety.

pro bono (for the good of doing so) when lawyers provide their services to defendants without a fee.

reasonably competent attorney standard performance measured by customary skills and diligence.

recoupment programs when states can recover from indigent defendants expenses for their defense.

supervised release pretrial release conditioned on the defendant's reporting to an agency or a third person.

Notes

1. *Kirby v. Illinois,* 406 U.S. 682, 92 S.Ct. 1877, 32 L.Ed.2d 411 (1972).

2. Barbara Boland et al., *The Prosecution of Felony Arrests, 1982* (Washington, DC: National Institute of Justice, May 1988); Thomas Y. Davies, "A Hard Look at What We Know (and Still Need to Learn) About the 'Costs' of the Exclusionary Rule: The NIJ Study and Other Studies of 'Lost' Arrests," *American Bar Foundation Research Journal* (Summer 1983): 611, n. 89; Peter F. Nardulli, "The Societal Cost of the Exclusionary Rule: An Empirical Assessment," *American Bar Foundation Research Journal* (Summer 1983): 585–609.

3. *People v. Camargo,* 135 Misc.2d 987, 516 N.Y.S.2d 1004 (1986).

4. *Journal of the American Judicature Society* 34 (1940): 18–19; President's Commission on Law Enforcement and the Administration of Justice, *The Challenge of Crime in a Free Society* (Washington, DC: Government Printing Office, 1967), 10; Wayne R. LaFave,

   "The Prosecutor's Discretion in the United States," *American Journal of Comparative Law* 18 (1970): 533–35.

5. *Manning v. Municipal Court,* 372 Mass. 315, 361 N.E.2d 1274 (1977).

6. *Thigpen v. Roberts,* 468 U.S. 27, 104 S.Ct. 2916, 82 L.Ed.2d 23 (1984).

7. § 9–27.260.

8. *United States v. Peskin,* 527 F.2d 71 (7th Cir. 1975).

9. *Sanders v. City of Houston,* 543 F.Supp. 694, 700 (S.D. Texas 1982).

10. "*Williams v. Ward:* Compromising the Constitutional Right to Prompt Determination of Probable Cause Following Arrest," *Minnesota Law Review* 74 (1989): 225; Wendy Brandes, "Post-Arrest Detention and the Fourth Amendment: Refining the Standard of *Gerstein v. Pugh,*" *Columbia Journal of Law and Contemporary Problems* 22 (1989): 445–88.

11. *Minnesota Rules of Court: State and Federal, Rules of Criminal Procedure* (St. Paul: West, 1987), Rule 5.01, 112.

12. Mary A. Toborg, *Pretrial Release: A National Evaluation of Practices and Outcomes* (Washington, DC: National Institute of Justice, 1981).

13. Ibid.

14. Ibid.

15. Malcolm M. Feeley, *The Process Is the Punishment: Handling Cases in a Lower Criminal Court* (New York: Russell Sage Foundation, 1979), especially Chap. 4.

16. Ibid.

17. *Minnesota Rules of Court*, Rule 6.02, Subd. 1, 118–19.

18. 342 U.S. 1, 72 S.Ct. 1, 96 L.Ed.3 (1951).

19. 575 F.2d 3 (1st Cir. 1978), cert. denied, 439 U.S. 821, 99 S.Ct. 85, 58 L.Ed.2d 112 (1978); quoted in *Pretrial Reporter* 5 (June 1981).

20. Caleb Foote, "The Coming Constitutional Crisis in Bail," *University of Pennsylvania Law Review* 113 (1965): 959–1185.

21. *Pugh v. Rainwater*, 557 F.2d 1189 (5th Cir. 1977).

22. Ibid.

23. "The Unconstitutional Administration of Bail: *Bellamy v. The Judges of New York City*," *Criminal Law Bulletin* 8 (1972): 459–506.

24. For the empirical dimension of the problem, see Mark H. Moore et al., *Dangerous Offenders: The Elusive Target of Justice* (Cambridge, MA: Harvard University Press, 1984).

25. 304 U.S. 458, 462, 58 S.Ct. 1019, 1022, 82 L.Ed. 1461 (1938).

26. *Betts v. Brady*, 316 U.S. 455, 471, 62 S.Ct. 1252, 1261, 86 L.Ed. 1595 (1942).

27. *Powell v. Alabama*, 287 U.S. 45, 53 S.Ct. 55, 77 L.Ed. 158 (1932); *Gideon v. Wainwright*, 372 U.S. 335, 83 S.Ct. 792, 9 L.Ed.2d 799 (1963); *Argersinger v. Hamlin*, 407 U.S. 25, 92 S.Ct. 2006, 32 L.Ed.2d 530 (1972).

28. *Minnesota Rules of Court: State and Federal*, Rule 5, 112, 114, 115.

29. *Williams v. Beto*, 354 F.2d 698 (5th Cir. 1965); Finer, "Ineffective Assistance of Counsel," *Cornell Law Review* 58 (1973): 1077.

30. Smithburn and Springman, "Effective Assistance of Counsel: In Quest of a Uniform Standard," *Wake Forest Law Review* 17 (1980): 497; Erickson, "Standards of Competency for Defense Counsel in a Criminal Case," *American Criminal Law Review* 17 (1979): 233; Bazelon, "The Detective Assistance of Counsel," *University of Cincinnati Law Review* 42 (1973): 22.

31. Waltz, "Inadequacy of Trial Defense Representation as a Ground for Postconviction Relief in Criminal Cases," *Northwestern University Law Review* 59 (1964): 289.

32. Wayne R. LaFave and Jerold H. Israel, *Criminal Procedure* (St. Paul: West, 1984), 2: 99–102.

CHAPTER TWELVE

Trial and Conviction

CHAPTER MAIN POINTS

1. The government tests the objective basis of its case either in a preliminary hearing before a judge or by grand jury review before a group of citizens.

2. Defendants are required to appear in court to hear and answer the charges against them if indicted by a grand jury or bound over by a preliminary hearing.

3. The objective basis for binding over for trial is a higher degree of probable cause than that required for arrest.

4. Preliminary hearings are public adversary proceedings; grand jury review involves secret, *ex-parte* proceedings.

5. Result, due process, and organizational interests predominate in pretrial motions and hearings.

6. Double jeopardy gives the state "one fair shot" at conviction.

7. A speedy trial promotes the due process interest of timeliness.

8. A change of venue promotes the interest in a fair trial.

9. Judicial bias does not deny defendants a fair trial; personal bias does.

10. The suppression hearing promotes the interest in controlling government.

11. Most convictions result from guilty pleas, not trials.

12. Conviction by trial promotes the interests in fact-finding by the adversary process and procedural regularity.

13. Conviction by guilty plea promotes the interests in fact-finding, efficiency, and predictability.

14. The right to jury trial does not include the rights to trial by jury in all criminal cases, to trial by a twelve-member jury, and to conviction by a unanimous guilty verdict.

15. The presentation of evidence is the high point in the adversary criminal process.

16. Trials promote the search for truth and procedural regularity.

17. Empirical evidence does not necessarily support the conclusion that conviction by guilty plea promotes organizational interests at the expense of obtaining the correct result.

18. Defendants forfeit their rights against self-incrimination, to trial by jury, and to confront their accusers and witnesses when they plead guilty.

19. Guilty pleas do not violate the U.S. Constitution if defendants plead guilty knowingly and voluntarily.

Did the Government Prove
"Guilt Beyond a Reasonable Doubt"?

At Werbrouck's trial for violating federal gambling laws, the government proved the

following: Werbrouck owned and operated the Holiday Inn Motel and the adjoin-

ing Lincoln Highway Inn Restaurant in South Bend, Indiana. Werbrouck moved

out of his personal room at the Holiday Inn to allow a gambling casino to move in.

He permitted certain motel rooms to be physically altered for gambling purposes,

including the building of partition walls and the installation of a steel door,

cameras, monitors, and electronically controlled door locks. Werbrouck charged no

rent for the motel casino rooms and regularly provided customers free food and

drinks from his adjoining restaurant. He held keys to the electronically controlled

doors and at times admitted persons to the rooms. Werbrouck was observed in the

gambling casino.

TESTING THE
GOVERNMENT'S CASE

Court proceedings following the decision to charge and the first appearance in court represent the most formal aspects of the law of criminal procedure. Rules, not discretion, govern the preliminary hearing and grand jury review to test the government's case, the pretrial motions, and the hearings on those motions. Still more intricate, complex, and highly technical rules govern the centerpiece of formal criminal justice, the criminal trial. Discretion plays only a minor role in the formal action taken during the period from charge to trial to conviction. However, discretion does not disappear; it only becomes less visible. Most cases charged out of the prosecutor's office never go to trial; guilty pleas dispose of most cases. These guilty pleas either arise out of the defendant's decision to admit to the crime and hope for the best or result from negotiations between the government and the defendant—the much-maligned and even-more-misunderstood plea bargain. These decisions take place outside of the courtroom itself, either in the corridors and other rooms inside the courthouse or at other places outside the courthouse. The courtroom proceedings only ratify these informal proceedings.

The decision to charge indicates the government's commitment to criminal prosecution. The first appearance readies defendants for the consequences of this decision (see Chapter 11). Before the government can require defendants to answer the charges against them, however, prosecutors must test the factual foundation of the government's case before disinterested parties. This test is conducted for a good reason. Pursuing the criminal process beyond arrest and charge subjects defendants to further intrusions and deprivations. These include continued confinement for detained defendants and the conditions imposed on bail for released defendants. For all defendants, further proceedings require additional appearances in court and time, money, and energy devoted to preparing a defense. Other intrusions and deprivations, although indirect, are no less consequential. These entail separation from family and friends, loss of wages and employment, and, in some instances, loss of reputation and emotional well-being. As one court observed, "[W]hile in theory a trial provides a defendant with a full opportunity to contest and disprove charges against him, in practice, the handing up of an indictment will often have a devastating personal and professional impact that a later dismissal or acquittal can never undo."[1]

Costs accrue to society as well as to defendants. Taxpayers pay prosecutors, judges, and public defenders. Indirectly, defendants and their families often become burdens on society for at least the period of the criminal proceedings and sometimes for a considerable period following. It cost more than $25 for each day the government detained one person in a local jail in 1983. The cost has more than doubled since then.[2]

Two mechanisms are used to test the government's case against defendants:

1. Grand jury review
2. Preliminary hearings

These proceedings satisfy six goals in addition to testing the government's case:

1. Procedural regularity
2. Preservation of individual dignity
3. Promotion of public confidence in criminal justice
4. Promotion of equality
5. Promotion of impartiality
6. Community participation in criminal proceedings

In short, testing the government's case balances society's interests in criminal law enforcement, accurate fact-finding, individual rights, the rule of law, and broad social goals in a free and democratic society.

When prosecutors seek an **indictment,** they test the government's case by presenting it to a grand jury. When they draw up an **information**—a formal accusation outlining the charges—they test the case at a preliminary hearing before a judge. If the government establishes the required objective basis in grand jury review, the grand jury returns the indictment as a **true bill,** which is a record of the number of grand jurors voting for indictment. If the government satisfies the evidentiary standard in the preliminary hearing, the judge will **bind over** the defendant, or send the case on for trial. In either case, the true bill and the bind-over require defendants to answer the criminal charges; that is, they constitute the formal charging instruments that can bring defendants before a court. The formal answer to these charges—the **plea**—takes place at the **arraignment,** a proceeding that brings a defendant to court to hear and to plead to, or formally answer, criminal charges.

Formally, the preliminary hearing and grand jury review determine the objective basis—that is, whether probable cause exists to try defendants and, hence, proceed further in the criminal process. Pretrial screening also aids organizational interests, particularly the informal negotiation that takes place outside the restrictions that adversary proceedings impose. For example, preliminary hearings affect both pleas and plea bargaining. If the prosecution has a strong case, these proceedings are "educational experiences" for defendants, persuading them to plead guilty or at least to plea bargain. (See the section below on plea bargaining.) This pressure to negotiate guilty pleas rather than determine guilt by adversary proceedings is always high. Moreover, the preliminary hearing helps the defense counsel prepare tactics and strategy by offering counsel the opportunity to learn more about the prosecution's case. Although not formally visible, these underlying considerations nonetheless have a potent effect on preliminary hearings.

The Fifth Amendment requires grand jury indictment for all serious crimes. The original states included similar provisions in their own constitutions. In the middle of the nineteenth century, some of the newer states adopted the information-and-preliminary-hearing alternative to grand jury indictment. In recent years, the older states have also adopted the use of information and preliminary hearing. The nineteen states that still require indictment permit defendants to waive the right to grand jury review and substitute information and preliminary hearing. The remaining states permit prosecutors to choose between indictment and information.

PRELIMINARY HEARINGS
AND GRAND JURY REVIEW

Both grand jury review and preliminary hearings test the government's case for the quantum of proof required to go to trial. However, they differ in several important respects (see Table 12.1). Preliminary hearings are public; grand jury proceedings are secret. Preliminary hearings are adversary proceedings in which the defense can challenge the prosecution's case; grand juries hear only the prosecution's case without the defense's participation. Judges preside over preliminary hearings; prosecutors manage grand jury proceedings without judicial participation. In preliminary hearings, magistrates determine the sufficiency of the evidence; grand jury review relies on lay determination of the facts—grand jurors are not lawyers, but citizens selected to serve a term as grand jurors. Finally, defendants and their lawyers attend preliminary hearings; grand jury proceedings are *ex parte* proceedings—that is, they take place outside the presence of defendants and their counsel.

TABLE 12.1 CONTRASTS BETWEEN PRELIMINARY HEARING AND GRAND JURY REVIEW

Preliminary Hearing	Grand Jury Review
Held in public	Secret proceeding
Adversary hearing	Only government's case presented
Judge presides	Prosecutor presides
Judge determines the facts	Grand jurors decide the facts
Defendant present and represented by counsel	*Ex parte*, that is, defendant not present and not represented by counsel

The differences between preliminary hearings and grand jury proceedings illustrate varying emphases on interests in the criminal process. The preliminary hearing stresses adversarial, open, accusatory values and represents control by experts. Grand jury review, on the other hand, underscores the value of the democratic dimension of the criminal process: lay participation in criminal proceedings. However, both determine whether sufficient evidence exists to proceed further into the criminal process.

PRELIMINARY HEARING

The preliminary hearing, sometimes called the preliminary examination, is a judicial hearing held sometime after the first appearance (discussed in Chapter 11). The time lapse between the first appearance and the preliminary hearing varies among jurisdictions, and even within jurisdictions, according to whether defendants are in custody or released on bail. For example, the Federal Rules of Criminal Procedure, which many states follow in rough outline, provide as follows:

> If the defendant does not waive the preliminary examination, the magistrate shall schedule a preliminary examination. Such examination shall be held within a reasonable time but in any event not later than 10 days following the initial appearance if the defendant is in custody and no later than 20 days if he is not in custody. . . .[3]

A magistrate, justice of the peace, municipal court judge, or other member of the lower-court judiciary usually presides over the preliminary hearing. However, statutes in most jurisdictions authorize all judges to conduct preliminary hearings.

The Right to a Preliminary Hearing

The United States Constitution does not grant defendants the right to a preliminary hearing. In *Lem Woon v. Oregon*, a unanimous Supreme Court held that the elimination of all pretrial screening does not violate the due process clause of the Fourteenth Amendment. If states do provide for preliminary hearings, however, the Sixth Amendment guarantees defendants a right to counsel at the hearing. Preliminary hearings, according to *Coleman v. Alabama*, are a critical stage in the criminal process. To have a fair trial, at the preliminary hearing defendants need the expertise of counsel "meaningfully to cross-examine the witness against" themselves.[4]

The Court listed the functions that counsel could perform at the preliminary hearing:

1. The lawyer's skilled examination and cross-examination of witnesses may expose fatal weaknesses in the State's case that may lead the magistrate to refuse to bind the accused over.

2. The skilled interrogation of witnesses by an experienced lawyer can fashion a vital impeachment tool for use in cross-examination of the State's witnesses at the trial, or to preserve testimony favorable to the accused of a witness who does not appear at the trial.

3. Trained counsel can more effectively discover the case of a proper defense to meet that case at the trial.

4. Counsel can also be influential at the preliminary hearing in making effective arguments for the accused on such matters as the necessity for an early psychiatric examination or bail.[5]

Rule 5(c) of the Federal Rules of Criminal Procedure provides for preliminary hearings in all cases, with three exceptions: (1) petty offenses, (2) waiver by defendants, and (3) indictment or information (charging defendants with crimes on the prosecutor's own authority) filed before the scheduled time for the preliminary hearing.[6]

Federal prosecutors commonly manipulate Rule 5(c) to suit their purposes. With judges' cooperation, prosecutors sometimes schedule indictments to avoid preliminary hearings. In some jurisdictions, for example, United States attorneys arrange for their districts to have no more than one preliminary hearing for every hundred felonies. They can even stop a preliminary hearing in progress. If a preliminary hearing is not proceeding well for the government, prosecutors may obtain a continuance, meanwhile obtaining an indictment that eliminates the need for the preliminary hearing.[7] Although one court acknowledged

> sympathy with the notion that the government ought not to be allowed to freely abandon its prosecution in a preliminary examination the moment that an unfavorable ruling is made or an adverse result is imminent, [the court nonetheless ruled that] consistent with the strong weight of authority . . . no substantive rights of the defendant have been lost.[8]

Thirty-one states provide for preliminary hearings. Prosecutors initiate prosecution in these states by means of an instrument called an *information*, which is a charge brought on the prosecutor's sole authority. The preliminary hearing provides the opportunity to review judicially the evidence supporting the information. Nineteen states have provisions that are similar to the Fifth Amendment to the United States Constitution and guarantee grand jury review in cases of serious crimes. Preliminary hearings are not ordinarily required in these jurisdictions. However, these states, called indictment states, allow prosecutors to choose between grand jury review and information followed by preliminary hearings as the means to test the quantum of proof and to compel defendants to answer the charges against them. In some jurisdictions, prosecutors routinely choose information for misdemeanors and indictment for felonies.

Prosecutors frequently choose information and preliminary hearing rather than grand jury review in indictment states. Unlike federal prosecutors, state prosecutors rarely seek prior indictments to avoid preliminary hearings for practical reasons. Grand juries, particularly in large cities, have heavy caseloads whose schedules prosecutors cannot easily control. In addition, prosecutors find preliminary hearings useful for the reasons mentioned later in this chapter in the section on the preliminary hearing's ancillary functions.[9]

In the rare instances when prosecutors avoid preliminary hearings, the reasons for doing so include the following:

1. Saving time where many witnesses and exhibits must be presented or where numerous defendants require separate hearings
2. Avoiding defense discovery (one party's providing evidence in its possession to the other party), particularly to protect informants who are key witnesses
3. Limiting the number of times that complainants, especially victims of sex offenses, will have to testify in public

Critics maintain that one reason not often mentioned for avoiding preliminary hearings is that it enables prosecutors to push weak cases through a "pliable" grand jury when they would fail to win a preliminary bind-over.[10]

A few states have interpreted their state constitutions to require preliminary hearings even where grand jury review has taken place. For example, the California Supreme Court ruled that the state's equal protection clause guaranteed preliminary hearings to criminal defendants, even though the Fourteenth Amendment to the United States Constitution does not require that states provide defendants with preliminary hearings.[11]

Differences Between Preliminary Hearing and Trial

Preliminary hearings are adversary proceedings. Hence, they are open, public proceedings. Prosecutors, defense counsel, and defendants are present. The prosecution presents evidence, and the defense can challenge the prosecution's evidence and present its own. But preliminary hearings are not full-blown trials. Ordinarily, the prosecution presents only sufficient evidence to satisfy the bind-over standard. Usually, this means that one or two prosecution witnesses appear, and perhaps the prosecutor introduces some physical evidence. Typically, the defense introduces no witnesses and often no evidence at all, restricting its role instead to challenging the prosecution's evidence by cross-examination.

Significantly, preliminary hearings do not follow the rigid rules of evidence adhered to at trial. Courts vary greatly in the degree to which they relax the rules of evidence in preliminary hearings. Some jurisdictions require that only evidence admissible at trial can be presented at preliminary hearings. Others apply the rules of evidence "generally" to preliminary hearings, permitting magistrates to consider some evidence that would be inadmissible at trial. In some jurisdictions, court rules or statutes make explicit what types of evidence that magistrates can accept in preliminary hearings. In others, appellate courts adopt general guidelines, such as that the rules at preliminary hearings need not be applied "as rigidly as in trials." In a few jurisdictions, magistrates have complete discretion to disregard the rules of evidence.[12]

The Objective Basis for Binding Over

The **objective basis**—amount and quality of evidence or facts needed to authorize binding over a defendant to answer formal charges—adopted by most courts is probable cause that a crime has been committed and that the defendant committed it. However, courts vary in interpreting probable cause in the context of the preliminary hearing. Some hold that probable cause to bind over is the same as probable cause to arrest. Others hold that probable cause to bind over requires a higher evidentiary standard than arrest because graver consequences follow binding over. Binding over leads to longer detention and can lead to the ordeals of criminal prosecution, conviction, and punishment. Furthermore, even if defendants are not convicted, they must pay attorney's fees, suffer stigma from the prosecution, and subject their family to hardships as well. The state must expend scarce resources to prove guilt, thereby draining such resources from other services. The bind-over standard reflects the idea that the greater the intrusion and deprivation, the higher the factual foundation required to authorize them.

Just how many facts satisfy the bind-over standard cannot be stated precisely. Some courts have adopted a *prima facie* **case** requirement. According to this standard, the judge can bind a defendant over if the prosecution presents evidence that could convict if the defense did not rebut it at trial. Others have adopted a directed verdict standard:

> Since the examining magistrate's determination of the minimum quantum of evidence required to find probable cause to bind over is somewhat analogous in function to the court's ruling on a motion for a directed verdict at trial as to whether there is sufficient evidence to warrant submission of the case to the jury, we have decided to adopt a "directed verdict" rule in defining the minimum quantum of credible evidence necessary to support a bind-over determination. The examining magistrate should view the case as if it were a trial and he were required to rule on whether there is enough credible evidence to send the case to the jury. Thus, the magistrate should dismiss the complaint when, on the evidence produced, a trial court would be bound to acquit as a matter of law. The minimum quantum of evidence required by this bind-over standard is more than that for probable cause for arrest but less than would "prove the defendant's guilt beyond a reasonable doubt."[13]

Determining whether prosecutors have established the quantum of evidence required to bind over falls mainly to trial courts. A challenge to the trial court's decision to bind over, when it occurs, ordinarily gets resolved in the intermediate appellate courts of the state, whose principal business is reviewing the sufficiency of evidence to support the findings of trial courts.[14]

Hearsay Testimony

The government can introduce neither hearsay nor illegally seized evidence at trial. Judges largely disregard these prohibitions in preliminary hearings. In federal courts, bind-over decisions may be based on hearsay in whole or in part. Many states follow the federal rule, but frequently with limitations. For example, Colorado prohibits hearsay evidence at preliminary hearings if better evidence is available, such as when the victim is in court and can testify.[15]

Arguments are made both for and against admitting hearsay evidence at preliminary hearings. Supporters of its admission argue that

1. Hearsay can often be reliable.

2. Magistrates, who are often not lawyers, cannot apply the hearsay rule competently.

3. It places too heavy a burden on witnesses to require them to appear at both preliminary hearings and trials.

4. Testimony is not in dispute and need not be given directly.

5. Grand juries can indict on hearsay.

6. Magistrates can issue warrants on hearsay, and the standard for preliminary hearings should be the same.[16]

The arguments against admitting hearsay include the following:

1. Prohibiting hearsay protects defendants from the ordeal of going to trial on insufficient evidence to convict.

2. Allowing hearsay conflicts with the right of the defense to challenge the prosecution's case and cross-examine witnesses.

3. Applying the hearsay rule should present no difficulties, since lawyers are there to interpret its provisions.

4. Appearing at preliminary hearings does not excessively burden witnesses.[17]

Illegally Obtained Evidence

The states are divided over admitting illegally seized evidence at preliminary hearings: most states admit it; several exclude it. Two arguments support admitting illegally obtained evidence at preliminary hearings. First, the function of the hearings is to determine probable cause; excluding relevant evidence hampers that determination. Second, to permit challenges to evidence at the preliminary hearing interferes with the efficient and economical administration of justice because the question of whether the police obtained evidence illegally then has to be answered twice: first at the preliminary hearing and then again later, at a special suppression hearing, other pretrial hearing, or during the trial itself.[18]

The Right to Cross-Examine

The Sixth Amendment confrontation clause does not guarantee the defense the right to cross-examine the prosecution's witnesses at the preliminary hearing. Nevertheless, all jurisdictions permit such cross-examination. But the right to cross-examine at the preliminary hearing is not as extensive as the right to cross-examine at trial. For example, most jurisdictions do not permit cross-examination for the sole purpose of discovering the prosecution's case.[19]

Courts are divided on whether to terminate cross-examination aimed at developing **affirmative defenses**—such as self-defense and entrapment—that acknowledge a crime was committed but rely on a justification that relieves the defendant of criminal responsibility for it. In *State v. Altman*, the Arizona Supreme Court upheld the magistrate's refusal to permit cross-examination on entrapment, on the ground that "full and complete exploration of all facts of the case is reserved for trial and is not the function of a preliminary examination."[20]

In *Jennings v. Superior Court*, on the other hand, the California Supreme Court stated the following:

> The purpose of the preliminary hearing is to weed out groundless or unsupported charges of grave offense, and to relieve the accused of the degradation and expense of a criminal trial. . . . To effectuate this constitutional and statutory purpose the defendant must be permitted, if he chooses, to elicit testimony or introduce evidence tending to overcome the prosecution's case or establish an affirmative defense.[21]

Ancillary Functions of the Preliminary Hearing

The preliminary hearing serves primarily to screen cases that the government has seriously committed itself to pursue. In addition to testing the government's case, the preliminary hearing performs several secondary but useful functions, which include providing an opportunity for discovery, obtaining information to be used in the future impeachment of witnesses, and the gathering of perpetuating testimony.

Preliminary hearings provide an opportunity for defense attorneys to learn more about the prosecution's case. Despite the prevailing view that the preliminary hearing is not a vehicle for discovery, "in practice this hearing may provide the defense with the most valuable technique available." **Discovery** is a process whereby one party to a legal action notifies the other party about evidence that it will introduce at trial. It modifies the pure adversary nature of proceedings in criminal cases by informing the accused in advance of the facts mustered against her or him, but it facilitates the adversary process by ensuring that the accused can prepare an adequate defense. It promotes a fair and equal fight between a powerful state and defendants with limited resources. In practice, discovery principally benefits defendants because at preliminary hearings, prosecutors, not the defense, must present evidence to justify sending defendants to trial.[22]

In addition to hearing, and occasionally seeing, the prosecution's evidence, defense counsel can cross-examine prosecution witnesses and subpoena potential trial witnesses. The extent of discovery depends on several circumstances. If the prosecution relies on hearsay, then, of course, the defense cannot cross-examine the source of this evidence. Furthermore, some states restrict cross-examination to direct rebuttal, thereby preventing the defense from broad inquiry into the prosecution's case. Moreover, prosecutors frequently call only the minimum number of witnesses, which also sharply limits discovery.[23]

Court-prescribed or statutory discovery rules provide opportunities for discovery outside the preliminary hearing. For example, such rules make arresting officers' reports available to defendants. If defendants can discover the prosecution's case in these other ways, they may choose not to use the preliminary hearing for that purpose because the tactical costs may be too high. The experienced defense lawyer Anthony Amsterdam writes about these tactical considerations:

> Frequently counsel may find that s/he is working at cross-purposes in seeking to discover and lay a foundation for impeachment simultaneously. S/he will obviously have to accommodate these objectives in particular situations with an eye to which objective is more important in dealing with an individual prosecution witness. If

counsel vigorously cross-examines a witness, in an effort to get a contradiction or concession on record, the witness will normally dig in and give a minimum of information in an effort to save his or her testimonial position; and, more than likely, s/he will be uncooperative if counsel thereafter attempts to interview the witness prior to trial. On the other hand, if counsel engages the witness in routine examination, amiable and ranging, counsel may be able to pick up many clues for investigation and for planning of the defense. Of course, some witnesses resent any form of cross-examination. If counsel thinks that this type of witness is lying or confused, counsel may wish to pin the witness down. Under no circumstances, however, should counsel educate the witness about the weakness of his or her testimony.[24]

These tactical considerations curtail the use of the preliminary hearing for discovery purposes. Professor Samuel Dash refers to this shortcoming in federal court preliminary hearings. According to Professor Dash, discovery is

> not the discovery to prepare [the accused's] defense for trial, but it is the kind of discovery in which he is confronted with his accuser and informed of what he is charged with, and given some indication as to the strength of the Government's case. This is the kind of discovery that allows him to make decisions as to his plea, not as to how he will present evidence, and how he will combat the Government's case.[25]

Cross-examining prosecution witnesses might aid the defense even if it produces little in the way of discovery. The Supreme Court recognized this advantage in *Coleman v. Alabama*, a leading case on the preliminary hearing. Justice William Brennan, writing for the Court, noted that "the skilled interrogation of witnesses by an experienced lawyer can fashion a vital impeachment tool for use in cross-examination of the State's witnesses at the trial. . . ."[26]

The preliminary hearing also provides several opportunities to **impeach** witnesses — that is, to destroy their credibility. For example, witnesses frequently make damaging statements at preliminary hearings because prosecutors have not prepared them as well as they would for trial. Furthermore, the more witnesses say at the preliminary hearing, the greater the chances they will contradict themselves at the trial. These contradictions are more damaging than those made to police because at preliminary hearings, witnesses make them under oath.

Too much cross-examination, however, has pitfalls for the defense. Professor Anthony Amsterdam's statement about tactical considerations indicates some of these (see above). Too much focus on witnesses' weaknesses educates them about those weaknesses and provides them with the opportunity to correct them. Witnesses may "rehabilitate" themselves "for the trial and state at the hearing [that they were] confused, but that everything is now clear in [their] mind." If witnesses might otherwise "soften" their view of the facts with passing time, lessening their "emotional involvement," extensive cross-examination might "harden" their position and make them less likely to "retreat to a more friendly position." Witnesses may also recant, or change their mind about, their testimony. Finally, if witnesses are not available later at the trial, defense counsel may discover that they have presented damaging testimony and prefer not to appear at trial.[27]

A frequent problem in criminal trials is that witnesses cannot testify; they die, fall ill, disappear, or are otherwise not available. If they have testified at the preliminary hearing, their testimony may be used at trial under certain conditions. Although an advantage technically accessible to both prosecution and defense, in practice, perpetuating testimony helps the prosecution most because the defense calls witnesses at preliminary hearings only infrequently. Despite the U.S. Supreme Court's statement that preliminary hearings provide the opportunity to "preserve testimony favorable to the accused of a witness who does not appear at the trial," defense attorneys generally consider perpetuation a *dis*advantage of preliminary hearings.[28]

The **hearsay rule** prohibits the introducing of a statement from someone not in court as evidence to prove the truth of the matter stated. For example, I cannot as a witness testify that Jeff murdered Colleen because Sharon told me that he did. I cannot give testimony to prove the truth of Sharon's out-of-court statement. However, if Sharon's statement was tested for its credibility prior to trial, then it falls under the prior testimony exception. The **prior testimony exception** admits testimony taken under oath prior to trial, if witnesses are not available to testify at the trial. Testimony at preliminary hearings, if competently tested, falls within the exception.

Despite the exception, prosecutors cannot introduce prior testimony unless they comply with the Sixth Amendment's **confrontation requirement,** which provides, "In all criminal prosecutions, the accused shall enjoy the right . . . to be confronted with the witnesses against him. . . ."

The Supreme Court addressed the confrontation question in relation to testimony from preliminary hearings introduced at trial in *California v. Green.* Green was charged with furnishing marijuana to Porter, a minor. Porter testified at the preliminary hearing, but when the prosecution called him to testify at Green's trial, he was evasive and uncooperative, claiming that he could not remember matters about which the prosecution examined him.

The prosecution introduced Porter's testimony from the preliminary hearing "to prove the truth of the matter asserted in his statements." The defense objected, claiming that mere lapse of memory did not render Porter "unavailable." The state court held the preliminary testimony inadmissible because it violated Green's Sixth Amendment right to confrontation; the Supreme Court reversed. The Court held that if the defense had the opportunity to fully cross-examine Porter at the preliminary hearing, then Green had "confronted" Porter, and the Sixth Amendment requirement was satisfied.[29]

D e c i s i o n   P o i n t

The defense cross-examined only one eyewitness to a murder at the preliminary hearing. The preliminary hearing was held on short notice, but the defense brought out numerous facts relating to the witness's morals and capacity for observation. The defense did not have access to the ballistic reports and autopsy reports because they were not available at the time of the preliminary hearing. The witness was not available at the trial. Should the witness's testimony be admitted at the trial?

The Fifth Circuit Court of Appeals held that the testimony was admissible because the cross-examination was extensive enough to bring out all the information the witness could supply. Furthermore, there was no suggestion that the ballistics and autopsy reports would have led to any pertinent facts not covered at the preliminary hearing.[30]

GRAND JURY REVIEW

The grand jury has an ancient heritage. Originating in medieval England as a council of local residents that helped the king look into matters of royal concern—crime, revenues, and official misconduct—the grand jury was an investigating body. By the time of the American Revolution, the grand jury assumed another fundamental function: it screened criminal cases to protect citizens from malicious and unfounded prosecution. Hence, the grand jury acquired dual functions: to act as a sword to root out crime and corruption and as a shield to protect innocent citizens from unwarranted state intrusion.

The shield function particularly attracted the colonists because it protected them from prosecution for antiroyalist sentiments. For that reason, the Fifth Amendment to the United States Constitution provides that "[n]o person shall be held to answer for a capital, or otherwise infamous crime, unless on a presentment or indictment by a Grand Jury. . . ." Most state constitutions have similar provisions.

In 1859, Michigan became the first state to provide for an alternative to grand jury screening by adopting the information, a formal charging instrument drawn by the prosecutor without the grand jury. Several states followed suit. In 1884, the United States Supreme Court ruled that grand jury screening is not essential to preserving "fundamental principles of liberty and justice" under the Fourteenth Amendment due process clause. Hence, the Fifth Amendment grand jury clause does not apply to the states.[31]

Today, thirty-one states permit prosecutors to choose between information (usually with a requirement that a preliminary hearing bind-over support it) and indictment. Since prosecutors nearly always select information and preliminary hearing, these states are called information states. Five of these states require indictments, but only in capital cases, including life imprisonment cases. The remaining nineteen states, called indictment states, require grand jury screening. The official charging instrument in these states must be an indictment. Prosecutors have absolute discretion to choose between information and indictment in information states. Reasons for choosing the grand jury include the following:

1. The desire of prosecutors to avoid a preliminary hearing
2. The efforts of prosecutors to erect a buffer against negative public opinion in politically sensitive cases
3. The desire of prosecutors to share responsibility in difficult cases

In most indictment jurisdictions, defendants can waive their right to such screening, although some of those jurisdictions prohibit waivers in capital cases. Most waivers occur as part of a plea bargaining arrangement in which defendants plead guilty.[32]

Grand Jury Composition and Selection

Grand juries in individual jurisdictions differ greatly in both composition and screening procedures. Hence, generalizations about grand jury operation do not describe any particular jurisdiction's grand jury operation. This section outlines the operation of the federal grand jury in the Southern District of New York, a jurisdiction that includes Manhattan, the Bronx, and several New York counties as far north as Albany.[33]

Federal grand juries consist of not fewer than sixteen or more than twenty-three jurors. To qualify, prospective grand jurors

1. Must be United States citizens

2. Must be over eighteen years old

3. Must reside in the jurisdiction

4. Must have no felony convictions

5. Must speak, write, and read English

6. Must suffer no physical impairments that might hamper their participation, such as insufficient hearing or vision

The jurisdiction sometimes summons nearly two hundred citizens for jury service — many more than are needed. The process of narrowing down the number of potential jurors and selecting the final sixteen to twenty-three is called **purging the grand jury.** The process eliminates prospective grand jurors with compelling reasons not to serve — business, family, and health obligations — but it often impairs the grand jury's representative nature. Federal grand juries overrepresent retired persons or those not burdened with other responsibilities.

Every grand jury has a foreperson who acts as an administrator for the grand jury. The principal duties of the foreperson include

1. Signing indictments

2. Swearing in witnesses who appear before the grand jury

3. Arranging grand juror absences

4. Giving directions to witnesses

5. Maintaining order and decorum in the grand jury room

Judges appoint forepersons, a position not often sought by members of grand juries. Some judges ask for volunteers; if no one offers to serve, judges turn to other election methods. Other judges simply pick the first juror they see. Some choose members who admit to previous jury experience.

In some jurisdictions, grand jury forepersons do not represent a fair cross section of the community. For example, in the Eastern District of North Carolina, between 1974 and 1981 not a single African American or woman was selected to serve as foreperson. This selection pattern led to claims that the jurisdiction's selection process violated the Constitution. The United States Supreme Court rejected these claims. The Court concluded that grand jury forepersons were just there to "mind the store." As Chief Justice Warren Burger wrote, "The responsibilities of the grand jury foreman are essentially clerical in nature. . . . Simply stated, the role of the foreman of a federal grand jury is not so significant to the administration of justice that discrimination in the appointment of that office impugns the fundamental fairness of the process itself so as to undermine the integrity of the indictment."[34]

Grand Jury Proceedings

After swearing in the grand jurors, judges **charge the grand jury,** giving a speech that varies somewhat according to individual judges' preference. Some charges constitute calls to action against specific dangers. Others resemble stump speeches for law and order or constitutional rights. Almost all include a history and outline of grand jury duties and responsibilities, warnings about the secrecy of grand jury proceedings, and admonitions to protect the innocent and condemn the guilty. Following the charge, judges turn grand jurors over to prosecutors to conduct grand jury proceedings. Unlike preliminary hearings, grand jury proceedings do not require a judge's participation.

Grand jury secrecy severely restricts those who may legally attend proceedings. In addition to the grand jurors themselves, only the prosecutor, witnesses called to testify, and stenographers appear in the grand jury room. Defendants do not appear, nor do witnesses' attorneys, even though these witnesses are often themselves **grand jury targets,** that is, people who are under suspicion and investigation. However, witnesses may, and frequently do, bring their lawyers to the courthouse for consultation outside the grand jury room.

Jurors may question witnesses. In some jurisdictions, they do so only through the prosecutor; in others, they do so directly. In some jurisdictions, prosecutors inform the grand jurors that if witnesses exercise their Fifth Amendment right to remain silent, jurors should not infer guilt from such silence. Prosecutors may also inform grand jurors that they can order witnesses to appear to support hearsay evidence. After some questioning, prosecutors may temporarily excuse witnesses so that grand jurors may question prosecutors. If jurors want to question witnesses or have prosecutors do so, recesses provide them with the opportunity to discuss questions with prosecutors. If prosecutors think it unwise to ask the questions, jurors rarely oppose them. Either stenographers or electronic devices record all testimony given before grand juries.

After all witnesses have testified and prosecutors have introduced any other evidence, prosecutors draw up an indictment and present it to the grand jury for consideration. Prosecutors then sum up the reasons that the evidence constitutes a crime and leave during grand jury deliberations, which ordinarily take only a few minutes. Grand juries rarely disagree with prosecutors' recommendations. Forepersons sign both the indictment and another document called a true bill, recording the number of jurors who voted to indict. Federal grand jury proceedings require twelve jurors' concurrence to indict.

The entire grand jury, accompanied by the prosecutor, then proceeds to a designated courtroom to **hand up the indictment,** an action that amounts to the formal filing of charges, requiring defendants to answer in court. After judges check to make sure all documents are in order, they accept the indictment, which becomes a matter of public record. They also accept the true bill, but it does not become a public record. The judges' acceptance initiates the criminal prosecution by indictment.

The Debate Over the Grand Jury

Since the sixteenth century, observers have found much to criticize about the grand jury. The Elizabethan justice of the peace William Lambarde's charges to the Kent grand juries have preserved these early criticisms. Justice Lambarde lauded the grand juries' capacity to aid in law enforcement but scorned their conduct in carrying out their responsibilities. Mainly, Lambarde attacked their sword function, maintaining that they were too timid in rooting out wrongdoing, but he also found them wanting in screening cases.[35]

In modern times, the debate has shifted to the grand jury's screening function. From the early twentieth century, the confidence that many reformers had in science and experts led them to call for eliminating lay participation in criminal justice. Nowhere was their condemnation more forceful than in their consideration of the jury. They wanted both grand and petty juries abolished. In their place, trained experts would more effectively weigh the evidence. Two prestigious presidential commissions, the Wickersham Commission, appointed by President Herbert Hoover, and the National Advisory Commission, appointed by President Richard Nixon, urged the abolition of mandatory grand jury review. Since the early 1980s, most legal commentary has condemned the grand jury.[36]

Critics make several arguments against grand jury screening. They maintain that grand juries are prosecutors' rubber stamp. As one former prosecutor said, "A [prosecutor] can indict anybody, at any time, for almost anything before a grand jury." Statistics bear these critics out, at least on the surface. In only a small percentage of cases do grand juries issue **no-bills** (refusals to indict). Even the no-bills do not necessarily demonstrate grand jury independence. In sensitive or controversial cases, prosecutors choose grand jury review over preliminary hearing to put the burden for deciding whether or not to charge on the grand jury.[37]

Critics also condemn the nonadversary nature of grand jury review, which prevents it from either effectively screening cases or adequately protecting citizens against unwarranted prosecutions. Moreover, the secrecy of grand jury proceedings creates doubts and suspicion. That defendants and their lawyers cannot attend grand jury sessions provides further ammunition for critics. This exclusion is both unfair and results in inadequate screening. In addition, critics maintain that grand jury review is inefficient, expensive, and time-consuming. Impaneling and servicing a grand jury is costly in terms of space, human resources, and money. The members must be selected, notified, sworn, housed, fed, and provided with a multitude of services.

Finally, grand juries screen cases more slowly than do magistrates. The law surrounding grand jury proceedings is complex and technical, giving rise to delay in proceedings and in later successful challenges to grand jury proceedings. Use of a grand jury may result in prosecutions' failing for reasons unrelated to innocence. In several jurisdictions, the intricacies and complexities of impaneling a grand jury guarantee attack by a skilled defense attorney and frequently result in dismissal of charges for minor discrepancies in the impaneling procedure.[38]

Supporters rely on a number of arguments to uphold grand jury review. First, they maintain, grand juries cost no more than preliminary hearings. Preliminary hearings have become elaborate affairs to which lawyers, judges, other court personnel, and witnesses devote a great deal of court time. Furthermore, the number of requests that defense attorneys make for continuances leads to a greater delay in, and a better chance of successful challenges to, preliminary hearings than grand jury proceedings.

Grand jury supporters also reject the contention that the grand jury does not effectively screen cases. They cite prosecutors who believe that grand juries constitute valuable sounding boards and that grand jurors definitely have minds of their own. The high percentage of indictments grand juries return is not the important figure, according to supporters. Rather, the percentage of convictions—as high as 98 percent—based on indictments demonstrates that grand juries effectively screen out cases that should not go to trial.[39]

Finally, perhaps grand jury review represents democracy at work. Supporters maintain that what grand jury review loses in its secret and nonadversary proceedings it more than recaptures in community participation in screening criminal cases. Citizen participation enhances public confidence in the criminal justice system. In a system where most cases do not go to trial, grand jury proceedings provide private citizens with their only opportunity to participate actively on the "front lines" of the criminal process. In fact, grand jurors are not nearly as representative of the community as trial jurors, who are not wholly representative either. Grand jury duty spans a long period of time, usually a year, and requires service at least two or three days a week. Only citizens with considerable free time can devote such extended—if valuable—service in the criminal process.[40]

Irregular Grand Jury Proceedings

Irregularities in grand jury proceedings and challenges to indictments stem from several sources. Grand jury composition that either discriminates or does not reflect a representative community cross section is one source. In addition, grand jurors' personal and individual biases might taint indictments. The evidence submitted—or withheld—also affects the review. For example, some jurisdictions allow prosecutors to present to grand juries only evidence admissible at trial. Some require that prosecutors provide grand jurors with **exculpatory evidence**—evidence that shows the defendant did not commit the crime. Finally, the defense might challenge indictments for prosecutorial misconduct.

The principal question that tainted indictments raise is what remedies should redress tainted grand jury proceedings. The remedy depends on the interests that jurisdictions choose to promote. Jurisdictions committed to accurate fact-finding may conclude that, despite irregular proceedings, if a proper trial produced a conviction, then the tainted indictment should not affect the conviction. According to one court, "[E]rrors before the grand jury, such as perjured testimony, normally can be corrected at trial, where evidentiary and procedural rules safeguard the accused's constitutional rights."[41]

Jurisdictions committed to broad social goals such as encouraging community participation in law enforcement or ending racial and gender discrimination might dismiss the indictment and reverse a conviction based upon it. The rationale behind these decisions is "that the court should strive to preserve societal values—deterrence of official misconduct and preservation of the appearance of fairness—regardless of whether the misconduct results in prejudice to the defendant."[42]

Before dismissing an indictment for prosecutorial misconduct, some courts require defendants to prove two things:

1. That "prosecutorial misconduct is a long-standing or common problem in grand jury proceedings. . . ."

2. That the grand jury was prejudiced by the prosecutor's actions. In other words, the defendant must prove that the misconduct affected the outcome of the case and was not simply **harmless error**—that is, an error that did not affect the outcome of the case.

The U.S. Supreme Court has largely left it to individual jurisdictions to fashion remedies for irregular grand jury proceedings.

SUMMARY OF PRELIMINARY
HEARING AND GRAND JURY REVIEW

Following the decision to prosecute and the initial appearance that prepares the defense for that prosecution, the government must test its decision to prosecute before disinterested parties. Preliminary hearings and grand jury review represent the two mechanisms to test the factual sufficiency of the government's case against defendants. To require defendants to answer criminal charges, the government must satisfy either a judge in a preliminary hearing or a grand jury in a grand jury review by presenting facts sufficient to demonstrate probable cause that a crime was committed and that the defendant committed it. Neither the U.S. Supreme Court nor any other body has ever prescribed the number of facts that satisfy this quantum of proof. However, probable cause to bring defendants to trial requires more facts than probable cause to arrest or to detain following arrest until preliminary hearing. In other words, it takes more facts to arraign defendants than to arrest them.

Important contrasts between preliminary hearing and grand jury review include these:

1. Preliminary hearings are public hearings; grand jury review takes place in secret.

2. Preliminary hearings are adversary proceedings in which the defense and the prosecution argue; only the government presents its case to the grand jury.

3. Judges preside over preliminary hearings; the prosecutor predominates in grand jury deliberations.

4. Judges determine the facts in preliminary hearings; grand jurors decide the facts in grand jury proceedings.

5. Defendants are present and are represented in preliminary hearings; grand jury review is *ex parte*.

The preliminary hearing and grand jury review proceedings vary among jurisdictions. However, both constitute a decision point that can result either in greater expenditures of public resources and greater deprivations to defendants and their families or in termination of the criminal process. In arriving at these decisions, balancing the legal interests in result and process weighs heavily but does not solely determine the decision. Informally, the interests in efficiency, economy, human dignity, and community participation in criminal justice also play their parts.

Specifically, the informal process of plea bargaining proceeds alongside and is intimately related to the formal decision-making process in preliminary hearings and grand jury review. The amount and quality of evidence against the defendant and the hardship of further criminal proceedings affect both formal testing of the government's case and informal plea negotiations. It is no coincidence that guilty pleas take place near in time to these formal proceedings. Frequently, the arraignment reflects the influence of informal plea bargaining more than it does that of formal fact-finding in preliminary hearings and grand jury review.

PRETRIAL MOTIONS

Following the grand jury proceeding or preliminary hearing, the criminal process enters a period when finality, timeliness, and other due process interests increasingly affect formal court decisions. The filing, hearing, and determination of pretrial motions focus on these interests. Organizational interests in negotiating the charges, settling disputes, and avoiding the conflict and uncertainty of adversary proceedings also become prominent. Most plea negotiations take place and plea bargains are struck sometime during the period between grand jury screening, preliminary hearings, hearings on pretrial motions, and trial. The time, energy, and resources devoted to filing, arguing, and resolving the issues raised by pretrial motions create anxiety and impose costs. If decisions go against defendants, pretrial motions lead to costly, time-consuming trials and, ultimately, to the great deprivation of criminal punishment.

The Origins of Pretrial Motions

Pretrial motions grew out of the ancient common-law pleadings, a highly stylized method of deciding cases in English law. The pleader for the Crown entered the first pleading—the indictment that initiated the criminal process. The indictment formed the legal basis for the arraignment that required defendants to appear in court to hear the charges and to plead to, or answer, them. Defendants could answer the indictment only according to rigidly prescribed rules. The most frequent pleas were either not guilty or guilty, but others were possible. The *plea to jurisdiction* challenged the court's authority to hear the case. The *plea in abatement* challenged the technical sufficiency of the indictment due to defects in the grand jury process. The *motion to quash* challenged the form and substance of the indictment; the *demurrer* claimed that the indictment failed to state an offense. The *plea in bar* raised claims prohibiting action, such as double jeopardy and statute of limitations.

The indictment, along with the information, remains the only pleading that initiates criminal proceedings. Except for the guilty, not guilty, *nolo contendere*, and insanity pleas, the pretrial motions have replaced the other common-law pleadings available to the defense to answer the state's charges. (**Nolo contendere** pleas are pleas not to contest the indictment.) The Federal Rules of Criminal Procedure, for example, provide the following:

Rule 12(a) *Pleadings and Motions.* Pleadings in criminal proceedings shall be the indictment and the information, and the pleas of not guilty, guilty, and nolo contendere. All other pleas, and demurrers and motions to quash are abolished, and defenses and objections raised before trial which heretofore could have been raised by one or more of them shall be raised only by motion to dismiss or grant appropriate relief, as provided in these rules.

Rule 12(b) *Pretrial Motions.* Any defense, objection, or request which is capable of determination without the trial of the general issue may be raised before trial by motion. Motions may be written or oral at the discretion of the judge. The following must be raised prior to trial:

(1) Defenses and objections based on defects in the institution of prosecution; or

(2) Defenses and objections based on defects in the indictment or information (other than that it fails to show jurisdiction in the court or to charge an offense which objections shall be noticed by the court at any time during the pendency of the proceedings); or

(3) Motion to suppress evidence. . . .

Subsequent sections of this chapter analyze and discuss issues surrounding the following pretrial motions:

1. Double jeopardy
2. Speedy trial
3. Change of venue
4. Change of judge
5. Suppression of evidence

Double Jeopardy Motions

The Fifth Amendment to the United States Constitution provides in part: "No person . . . shall . . . be subject for the same offence to be twice put in jeopardy of life or limb. . . ." Although the words *life or limb*, strictly defined, apply only to crimes punishable by death or corporal punishment, the courts interpret double jeopardy to include all crimes, including decisions in juvenile proceedings. In *Palko v. Connecticut* (1937), the U.S. Supreme Court held that the double jeopardy clause did not apply to the states through the due process clause of the Fourteenth Amendment (see Chapter 2). Connecticut tried Palko for first-degree murder; the jury convicted him of a lesser included offense, second-degree murder—that is, the less serious crime of second-degree murder, all of whose elements are included in the more serious crime of first-degree murder. The state retried Palko for first-degree murder over his objection that the second trial violated the double jeopardy clause. Justice Benjamin Cardozo, writing for a divided court, asked this question:

> Is that kind of double jeopardy to which the statute has subjected him a hardship so acute and shocking that our polity will not endure it? Does it violate those "fundamental principles of liberty and justice" which lie at the base of all our civil and political institutions? The answer surely must be "no."[43]

During the due process revolution of the 1960s, the Supreme Court reconsidered the double jeopardy clause and held that it *did* apply to the states through the Fourteenth Amendment.

The prohibition against double jeopardy protects several interests both of the state and of the individual defendants. It allows the government "one fair shot" to serve the public interest in convicting criminals. At the same time, it limits the government from using its disproportionate share of power and resources to subject citizens accused of crimes to repeated attempts to convict them. Furthermore, it protects individuals from the embarrassment, expense, and ordeal—and the anxiety and insecurity—that repeated prosecutions generate. Defendants also have an interest in completing their trials under one tribunal and jury. In addition, both the state and defendants have an interest in the finality and integrity of judgments not susceptible to repeated reconsideration. Finally, the prohibition against double jeopardy reduces costs both to defendants and to the state. Retrials consume time that impedes the efficient and economical disposition of other cases on crowded criminal court calendars.

The Fifth Amendment prohibition against double jeopardy attaches as soon as the state "put[s defendants] to trial." In jury trials, this occurs upon the impaneling and swearing in of the jury. In **bench trials**—that is, trials without juries, where judges find the facts—jeopardy attaches when the court begins to hear evidence. Jeopardy attaches at this point in the proceedings because until the court begins to hear evidence, the trial has not started. In trials without juries, defendants have a "valued right to have . . . [their] trial[s] completed by a particular tribunal." The Supreme Court referred to the history of this definition of jury trials when it struck down Montana's rule that despite swearing in of the jury, jeopardy did not attach until the first witness commenced testifying:

> The reason for holding that jeopardy attaches when the jury is empaneled and sworn lies in the need to protect the interest of an accused in retaining a chosen jury. . . . It is an interest with roots deep in the historic development of trial by jury in the Anglo-American system of criminal justice. Throughout that history there ran a strong tradition that once banded together a jury should not be discharged until it had completed its solemn task of announcing a verdict.[44]

The attachment of jeopardy has been called the linchpin of the double jeopardy inquiry. But the Fifth Amendment prohibits *double* jeopardy. Therefore, attachment of jeopardy is the first, but not the only, inquiry. Applying the double jeopardy clause also requires defining *double*. The double jeopardy clause prohibits three kinds of actions:

1. A second prosecution for the same offense after *conviction*

2. A second prosecution for the same offense after *acquittal*

3. Multiple *punishments* for the same offense

Where jeopardy has attached but proceedings terminate prior to conviction or acquittal, the double jeopardy clause does not prevent a second prosecution for the same offense in two types of cases. If the *defendant* moves to dismiss the case or asks for or acquiesces in a mistrial, and the judge rules in the defendant's favor, the prosecution may reprosecute after the dismissal without offending the double jeopardy clause. Furthermore, even where defendants object to dismissal or mistrial, the government may reprosecute for the same offense if the judge dismissed the case or ordered a mistrial owing to **manifest necessity**—that is, a circumstance that requires termination to serve the ends of justice. The classic example of manifest necessity is the **hung jury,** a jury unable to reach a verdict. The Supreme Court ruled that reprosecution following a hung jury did not violate the double jeopardy clause:

> We think, [wrote the Court,] that in cases of this nature, the law has invested Courts of justice with the authority to discharge a jury from giving any verdict, whenever, in their opinion, taking all the circumstances into consideration, there is a manifest necessity for the act, or the ends of public justice would otherwise be defeated. They are to exercise a sound discretion on the subject; and it is impossible to define all the circumstances, which would render it proper to interfere. To be sure, the power ought to be used with the greatest of caution, under urgent circumstances.[45]

The manifest necessity doctrine is not limited to hung juries. It also applies to a range of situations where the prosecution is in a no-win situation. For example, when a court declared a mistrial over the defendant's objection because of a defect in the indictment that would have provided a basis for overturning any conviction if the trial proceeded, the U.S. Supreme Court ruled that multiple prosecution did not violate the double jeopardy clause. The Court balanced two interests in reaching its decision, saying that "a defendant's valued right to have his trial completed by a particular tribunal must in some instances be subordinated to the public's interests in fair trials designed to end in just judgments." According to the Court,

> A trial judge properly exercises his discretion to declare a mistrial . . . if a verdict of conviction could be reached but would have to be reversed on appeal due to an obvious procedural error in the trial. If an error would make reversal on appeal a certainty, it would not serve "the ends of public justice" to require that the Government proceed with its proof, when, if it succeeded before the jury, it would automatically be stripped of that success by an appellate court.[46]

Defendants waive their right against double jeopardy if they move for mistrials or file a substantive appeal. Prosecution for the same offense following an acquittal always puts defendants in double jeopardy. The double jeopardy clause prohibits both multiple *punishments* and multiple *prosecutions*. The main purpose of the double jeopardy clause is to restrain prosecutors and judges. Legislatures remain free to define crimes and prescribe punishments. Once legislatures act, however, "courts may not impose more than one punishment for the same offense and prosecutors ordinarily may not attempt to secure that punishment in more than one trial."

The double jeopardy clause prohibits successive prosecutions or punishments for greater included offenses and **lesser included offenses** (crimes composed of some of, but not all, the elements of a more serious crime). For example, if a defendant is convicted or acquitted of first-degree murder, the government cannot then prosecute the defendant for the same conduct as second-degree murder. Nor could it prosecute for first-degree murder after acquittal or conviction of second-degree murder arising out of the same offense. The Supreme Court applied the double jeopardy clause to prosecutions for joyriding and theft in *Brown v. Ohio.*

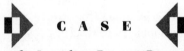

C A S E

Does Conviction for Joyriding Prevent Prosecution for Theft?

Brown v. Ohio
432 U.S. 161, 97 S.Ct. 2221,
53 L.Ed.2d 187 (1977)

The question in this case is whether the double jeopardy clause of the Fifth Amendment bars prosecution and punishment for the crime of stealing an automobile following prosecution and punishment for the lesser included offense of operating the same vehicle without the owner's consent. Justice Powell wrote the opinion of the Court.

FACTS

On November 29, 1973, the petitioner, Nathaniel Brown, stole a 1965 Chevrolet from a parking lot in East Cleveland, Ohio. Nine days later, on December 8, 1973, Brown was caught driving the car in Wickliffe, Ohio. The Wickliffe police charged him with "joyriding[,]" taking or operating the car without the owner's consent in violation of Ohio Rev. Code Ann. § 4549.04(D) (1973, App. 342). The complaint charged that "on or about December 8, 1973, . . . Nathaniel H. Brown did unlawfully and purposely take, drive or operate a certain motor vehicle to wit; a 1965 Chevrolet . . . without the consent of the owner[,] one Gloria Ingram. . . ."

[COURT NOTE: "§ 4549.04(D) provided at the time: 'No person shall purposely take, operate, or keep any motor vehicle without the consent of its owner.' A violation was punishable as a misdemeanor. § 4549.04 was repealed effective January 1, 1974."] Brown pleaded guilty to this charge and was sentenced to 30 days in jail and a $100 fine.

Upon his release from jail on January 8, 1974, Brown was returned to East Cleveland to face further charges, and on February 5 he was indicted by the Cuyahoga County grand jury. The indictment was in two counts, the first charging the theft of the car "on or about the 29th day of November 1973," in violation of Ohio Rev. Code Ann. § 4549.04(A) (1973, App. 342), and the second charging joyriding on the same date in violation of § 4549.04(D). A bill of particulars filed by the prosecuting attorney specified that "on or about the 29th day of November, 1973, . . . Nathaniel Brown unlawfully did steal a Chevrolet motor vehicle, and take, drive or operate such vehicle without the consent of the owner, Gloria Ingram. . . ." [COURT NOTE: "§ 4549.04(A) provided: 'No person shall steal any motor vehicle.' A violation was punishable as a felony."]

Brown objected to both counts of the indictment on the basis of former jeopardy. On March 18, 1974, at a pretrial hearing in the Cuyahoga County Court of Common Pleas, Brown pleaded guilty to the auto theft charge on the understanding that the court would consider his claim of former jeopardy on a motion to withdraw the plea. Upon submission of the motion, the court overruled Brown's double jeopardy objections. The court sentenced Brown to six months in jail but suspended the sentence and placed Brown on probation for one year.

The Ohio Court of Appeals affirmed. It held that under Ohio law the misdemeanor of joyriding was included in the felony of auto theft:

Every element of the crime of operating a motor vehicle without the consent of the owner is also an element of the crime of auto theft. "The difference between the crime of stealing a motor vehicle, and operating a motor vehicle

without the consent of the owner is that conviction for stealing requires proof of an intent on the part of the thief to permanently deprive the owner of possession." . . . (T)he crime of operating a motor vehicle without the consent of the owner is a lesser included offense of auto theft. . . .

Although this analysis led the court to agree with Brown that "for purposes of double jeopardy the two prosecutions involve the same statutory offense," it nonetheless held the second prosecution permissible:

The two prosecutions are based on two separate acts of the appellant, one which occurred on November 29th and one which occurred on December 8th. Since appellant has not shown that both prosecutions are based on the same act or transaction, the second prosecution is not barred by the double jeopardy clause.

The Ohio Supreme Court denied leave to appeal. We granted certiorari to consider Brown's double jeopardy claim, and we now reverse.

OPINION

The Double Jeopardy Clause of the Fifth Amendment, applicable to the States through the Fourteenth, provides that no person shall "be subject for the same offense to be twice put in jeopardy of life or limb." It has long been understood that separate statutory crimes need not be identical either in constituent elements or in actual proof in order to be the same within the meaning of the constitutional prohibition. The principal question in this case is whether auto theft and joyriding, a greater and lesser included offense under Ohio law, constitute the "same offense" under the Double Jeopardy Clause.

Because it was designed originally to embody the protection of the common-law pleas of former jeopardy, the Fifth Amendment double jeopardy guarantee serves principally as a restraint on courts and prosecutors. The legislature remains free under the Double Jeopardy Clause to define crimes and fix punishments; but once the legislature has acted courts may not impose more than one punishment for the same offense and prosecutors ordinarily may not attempt to secure that punishment in more than one trial.

The Double Jeopardy Clause "protects against a second prosecution for the same offense after acquittal. It protects against a second prosecution for the same offense after conviction. And it protects against multiple punishments for the same offense." Where consecutive sentences are imposed at a single criminal trial, the role of the constitutional guarantee is limited to assuring that the court does not exceed its legislative authorization by imposing multiple punishments for the same offense. Where successive prosecutions are at stake, the guarantee serves "a constitutional policy of finality for the defendant's benefit." That policy protects the accused from attempts to relitigate the facts underlying a prior acquittal, and from attempts to secure additional punishment after a prior conviction and sentence. The established test for determining whether two offenses are sufficiently distinguishable to permit the imposition of cumulative punishment was stated in *Blockburger v. United States* (1932): "The applicable rule is that where the same act or transaction constitutes a violation of two distinct statutory provisions, the test to be applied to determine whether there are two offenses or only one, is whether each provision requires proof of an additional fact which the other does not. . . ."

This test emphasizes the elements of the two crimes. "If each requires proof of a fact that the other does not, the *Blockburger* test is satisfied, notwithstanding a substantial overlap in the proof offered to establish the crimes. . . ."

If two offenses are the same under this test for purposes of barring consecutive sentences at a single trial, they necessarily will be the same for purposes of barring successive prosecutions. Where the judge is forbidden to impose cumulative punishment for two crimes at the end of a single proceeding, the prosecutor is forbidden to strive for the same result in successive proceedings. Unless "each statute requires proof of an additional fact which the other does not," the Double Jeopardy Clause prohibits successive prosecutions as well as cumulative punishment.

[COURT NOTE: "The *Blockburger* test is not the only standard for determining whether successive prosecutions impermissibly involve the same offense. Even if two offenses are sufficiently different to permit the imposition of consecutive sentences, successive prosecutions will be barred in some circumstances where the second prosecution requires the relitigation of factual issues already resolved by the first. Thus in *Ashe v. Swenson*, where an acquittal on a charge of robbing one of several participants in a poker game established that the accused was not present at the robbery, the Court held that principles of collateral estoppel embodied in the Double Jeopardy Clause barred prosecutions of the accused for robbing the other victims. And in *In re Nielsen* [1889], the Court held that a conviction of a Mormon on a charge of cohabiting with his two wives over a 2 1/2 year period barred a subsequent prosecution for adultery with one of them on the day following the end of that period. In both cases, strict application of the *Blockburger* test would have permitted imposition of consecutive sentences had the charges been consolidated in a single proceeding. In *Ashe*, separate convictions of the robbery of each victim would have required proof in each case that a different individual had been robbed. In *Nielsen*, conviction for adultery required proof that the defendant had sexual intercourse with one woman while married to another; conviction for cohabitation required proof that the defendant lived with more than one woman at the same time. Nonetheless, the Court in both cases held the separate offenses to be the 'same' for purposes of protecting the accused from having to '"run the gauntlet" a second time.' Because we conclude today that a lesser included and a greater offense are the same under *Blockburger*, we need not decide whether the repetition of proof required by the successive prosecutions against Brown would otherwise entitle him to the additional protection offered by *Ashe* and *Nielsen*."] We are mindful that the Ohio courts "have the final authority to interpret . . . that State's legislation." Here the Ohio Court of Appeals has authoritatively defined the elements of the two Ohio crimes: Joyriding consists of taking or operating a vehicle without the owner's consent, and auto theft consists of joyriding with the intent permanently to deprive the owner of possession. Joyriding is the lesser included offense. The prosecutor who has established joyriding need only prove the requisite intent in order to establish auto theft; the prosecutor who has established auto theft necessarily has established joyriding as well. Applying the *Blockburger* test, we agree with the Ohio Court of Appeals that joyriding and auto theft, as defined by the court, constitute "the same statutory offense" within the meaning of the Double Jeopardy Clause. For it is clearly not the case that "each (statute) requires proof of a fact which the other does not." As is invariably true of a greater and lesser included offense, the lesser offense[,] joyriding[,] requires no proof beyond that which is required for conviction of the greater auto theft. The greater offense is therefore by definition the "same" for purposes of double jeopardy as any lesser offense included in it.

This conclusion merely restates what has been this Court's understanding of the Double Jeopardy Clause at least since *In re Nielsen* was decided in 1889. In that case the Court endorsed the rule that "where . . . a person has been tried and convicted for a crime which has various incidents included in it, he cannot be a second time tried for one of those incidents without being twice put in jeopardy for the same offense."

Although in this formulation the conviction of the greater precedes the conviction of the lesser, the opinion makes it clear that the sequence is immaterial. Thus, the Court treated the formulation as just one application of the rule that two offenses are the same unless each requires proof that the other does not. And as another application of the same rule, the Court cited with approval the decision of *State v. Cooper,* where the New Jersey Supreme Court held that a conviction for arson barred a subsequent felony-murder indictment based on the death of a man killed in the fire. Whatever the sequence may be, the Fifth Amendment forbids successive prosecution and cumulative punishment for a greater and lesser included offense.

After correctly holding that joyriding and auto theft are the same offense under the Double Jeopardy Clause, the Ohio Court of Appeals nevertheless concluded that Nathaniel Brown could be convicted of both crimes because the charges against him focused on different parts of his 9-day joyride. We hold a different view. The Double Jeopardy Clause is not such a fragile guarantee that prosecutors can avoid its limitations by the simple expedient of dividing a single crime into a series of temporal or spatial units. The applicable Ohio statutes, as written and as construed

in this case, make the theft and operation of a single car a single offense. Although the Wickliffe and East Cleveland authorities may have had different perspectives on Brown's offense, it was still only one offense under Ohio law. Accordingly, the specification of different dates in the two charges on which Brown was convicted cannot alter the fact that he was placed twice in jeopardy for the same offense in violation of the Fifth and Fourteenth Amendments.

[COURT NOTE: "We would have a different case if the Ohio Legislature had provided that joyriding is a separate offense for each day in which a motor vehicle is operated without the owner's consent. We also would have a different case if in sustaining Brown's second conviction the Ohio courts had construed the joyriding statute to have that effect. We then would have to decide whether the state courts' construction, applied retroactively in this case, was such 'an unforeseeable judicial enlargement of a criminal statute' as to violate due process."]

Reversed.

DISSENT

Justice Blackmun, whom Chief Justice Burger and Justice Rehnquist join, dissenting.

The Court reverses the judgment of the Ohio Court of Appeals because the Court does not wish this case to slip by without taking advantage of the opportunity to pronounce some acceptable but hitherto unenunciated (at this level) double jeopardy law. I dissent because, in my view, this case does not deserve that treatment.

I, of course, have no quarrel with the Court's general double jeopardy analysis. I am unable to ignore as easily as the Court does, however, the specific finding of the Ohio Court of Appeals that the two prosecutions at issue here were based on petitioner's separate and distinct acts committed, respectively, on November 29 and on December 8, 1973.

Petitioner was convicted of operating a motor vehicle on December 8 without the owner's consent. He subsequently was convicted of taking and operating the same motor vehicle on November 29 without the owner's consent and with the intent permanently to deprive the owner of possession. It is possible, of course, that at some point the two acts would be so closely connected in time that the Double Jeopardy Clause would require treating them as one offense. This surely would be so with respect to the theft and any simultaneous unlawful operation. Furthermore, as a matter of statutory construction, the allowable unit of prosecution may be a course of conduct rather than the separate segments of such a course. I feel that neither of these approaches justifies the Court's result in the present case. Nine days elapsed between the two incidents that are the basis of petitioner's convictions. During that time the automobile moved from East Cleveland to Wickliffe. It strains credulity to believe that petitioner was operating the vehicle every minute of those nine days. A time must have come when he stopped driving the car. When he operated it again nine days later in a different community, the Ohio courts could properly find, consistently with the Double Jeopardy Clause, that the acts were sufficiently distinct to justify a second prosecution. Only if the Clause requires the Ohio courts to hold that the allowable unit of prosecution is the course of conduct

would the Court's result here be correct. On the facts of this case, no such requirement should be inferred, and the state courts should be free to construe Ohio's statute as they did. . . .

In my view, we should not so willingly circumvent an authoritative Ohio holding as to Ohio law. I would affirm the judgment of the Court of Appeals.

CASE DISCUSSION

What specific facts are relevant to determining whether Nathaniel Brown was put in double jeopardy? Why does the Court distinguish between and make a separate rule for successive prosecutions and successive punishments? Define the *Blockburger* rule. Does it make sense to have a stricter rule for successive prosecutions than for successive punishments? Or, as the dissent argues, should the *Blockburger* rule apply to all cases? Why or why not? Was this really one crime? Or does the dissent have the better argument that it was more than one crime? Defend your answer.

———————————————■□————————————————

Double jeopardy not only bars successive prosecutions and punishments for the same *offense*; it also bans successive determinations of fact. According to the doctrine of **collateral estoppel,** if one prosecution conclusively settles an issue of fact in favor of the defendant, then the government is barred from opening the issue in a subsequent prosecution. For example, if a robber robs six people, and a jury in the trial of one of the victims finds the defendant is not the robber, then the government is collaterally estopped from charging the defendant again for the robbery of one of the other victims.

It is not double jeopardy to prosecute and punish a defendant for the same acts in separate jurisdictions. According to the **dual sovereignty doctrine,** a crime arising out of the same facts in one state is not the same crime in another state. The Supreme Court's definition of *same offense* is not "identical." The dual sovereignty doctrine arises most often when the same conduct constitutes a crime under both *state* and *federal* law. In *Heath v. Alabama*, the Supreme Court addressed this unusual situation: if one state convicts a defendant under its laws, does the double jeopardy clause bar a *second state* from prosecuting the defendant again for a like offense under the second state's laws? Larry Heath hired Charles Owens and Gregory Lumpkin to kill his wife, who was then nine months' pregnant, for $2,000. The killers fulfilled their contract. Heath was sentenced to life imprisonment in a Georgia court after he pleaded guilty. Since part of the crime was committed in Alabama, Alabama then prosecuted Heath. He was also convicted in an Alabama court of murder committed during a kidnapping and was sentenced to death. He appealed the conviction on the grounds of double jeopardy. The Supreme Court affirmed the conviction, holding that successive prosecutions for the same crime in two different states did not constitute double jeopardy.[47] According to Justice O'Connor, writing for the majority of the Court,

> To deny a State its power to enforce its criminal laws because another State has won the race to the courthouse "would be a shocking and untoward deprivation of the historic right and obligation of the States to maintain peace and order within their confines." Such a deprivation of a State's sovereign powers cannot be justified by the assertion that under "interest analysis" the State's legitimate penal interests will be satisfied through a prosecution conducted by another State. A State's interest in vindicating its sovereign authority through enforcement of its laws by definition can never be satisfied by another State's enforcement of its own laws. The Court has always understood the words of the Double Jeopardy Clause to reflect this fundamental principle, and we see no reason why we should reconsider that understanding today.[48]

Prosecuting a defendant in a series of trials for separate offenses arising out of the same incident does not subject the defendant to double jeopardy, although it might violate the due process clause.[49]

Speedy Trial Motions

The Sixth Amendment provides that "[i]n all criminal trials, the accused shall enjoy the right to a speedy . . . trial." However, the notion that defendants are entitled to have their cases timely decided is much older than the Bill of Rights. In 1187, King Henry II provided for "speedy justice" in the Assizes of Clarendon. King John promised in the Magna Carta in 1215 that "every subject of this realme . . . may . . . have justice . . . speedily without delay." In his *Institutes*—according to Thomas Jefferson, "the universal elementary book of law students"—Sir Edward Coke wrote that the English itinerant justices in 1600 "have not suffered the prisoner to be long detained, but at their next coming have given the prisoner full and speedy justice . . . without detaining him long in prison." The Virginia Declaration of Rights in 1776 (the state's "bills of rights") and the speedy trial clause of the Sixth Amendment quoted at this paragraph's outset reflect this history. And even though the state constitutions guarantee speedy trial, the Supreme Court has extended the federal speedy trial protection of the Sixth Amendment to the states.[50]

The speedy trial clause promotes and balances several interests. For the accused, it prevents prolonged detention prior to trial, reduces the anxiety and uncertainty surrounding criminal prosecution, and guards against weakening the defense's case through loss of alibi witnesses and other evidence. Hence, the decision to quickly go to trial affects the intrusions and deprivations that defendants suffer in criminal prosecutions. The speedy trial provision also promotes the interest in arriving at the correct result in individual cases. Delay means lost evidence and lost witnesses—or at least the loss of their memory—not only for the defense, but also for the prosecution. The clause also promotes process goals, particularly that decisions should be made in a timely fashion. Organizational interests are at stake as well. Failure to provide prompt trials contributes to large case backlogs, particularly in urban areas. Furthermore, long pretrial detention is costly: maintaining prisoners in jails costs on average about $50 a day. In addition, of course, lost wages and greater welfare burdens result from incarceration.

Finally, since most detained defendants are poor, both the process interest in ensuring equal protection of the laws and the societal interest in protecting the poor and less powerful are at stake in speedy trial decisions.[51]

According to the U.S. Supreme Court, the Sixth Amendment does not protect against delay prior to formal accusation because the speedy trial clause specifically refers to the "accused." Therefore, time begins to measure as delay for purposes of the Sixth Amendment speedy trial clause as soon as citizens are arrested or otherwise formally charged. Defendants are not without relief from delays prior to charge. The **statutes of limitations**—laws specifying the length of time permitted between the commission of a crime and the initiation of prosecution—and the due process clause provide relief from precharge delays. Hence, when the Court rejected a speedy trial violation in a delay of three years between the commission of the crime and an indictment, the Court's opinion was as follows: "[T]he due process clause of the Fifth Amendment would require dismissal of the indictment if it were shown at trial that the pre-indictment delay . . . caused substantial prejudice to appellants' rights to a fair trial and that the delay was an intentional device to gain tactical advantage over the accused." Furthermore, some states have extended the speedy trial clauses of their constitution to the preaccusation stage. For example, the Alaska Supreme Court recognizes speedy trial rights even before the state initiates formal charges.[52]

The speedy trial clause bans only *undue* delays. Three possible approaches determine what constitutes undue delay:

1. A bright line rule prescribing a specific number of days until trial
2. A **demand-waiver rule** that measures delay only from the time defendants demand a speedy trial
3. A balancing test that weighs what courts determine are relevant considerations

According to the U.S. Supreme Court, flexibility governs the determination of whether delays violate the speedy trial clause; hence, the Court has adopted the balancing test. Here are the four elements that determine whether delay prejudices the defendant:

1. The length of the delay
2. The reason for the delay
3. The defendant's assertion of his or her right to a speedy trial
4. The prejudice that delay causes to the defendant's case

The Supreme Court has ruled that only two remedies are available for the violation of the speedy trial clause:

1. **Dismissal without prejudice,** which allows a new prosecution for the same offense
2. **Dismissal with prejudice,** the more drastic remedy that bars future prosecution for the same offense

According to a unanimous Supreme Court, even though there is enough evidence for conviction, undue delay subjects defendants to "emotional stress" that requires dismissal as "the only possible remedy." The Court's ruling has raised strong objections because dismissal will make courts "extremely hesitant" to find speedy trial violations.[53]

Although the Sixth Amendment does not require it, several states have enacted statutes or court rules that set time limits for bringing cases to trial. These limits vary widely among the states. The federal Speedy Trial Act provides definite time periods for bringing defendants to trial. The government must initiate prosecution within thirty days following arrest (sixty days if no grand jury is in session), arraign defendants within ten days after filing indictments or informations, and bring defendants to trial within sixty days following arraignment. According to the act, the following delays are not counted in computing days:

1. Delays needed to determine the defendant's competency to stand trial

2. Delays due to other trials of the defendant

3. Delays due to hearings on pretrial motions

4. Delays because of **interlocutory appeals**—provisional appeals that interrupt the proceedings, such as an appeal from a ruling on a pretrial motion

Change-of-Venue and Continuance Motions

The Sixth Amendment provides that "[i]n all criminal prosecutions, the accused shall enjoy the right to a . . . public trial, by an impartial jury of the State and district wherein the crime shall have been committed." A defendant's pretrial motion to change **venue**—the place where the trial is held—waives the Sixth Amendment right to have a trial in the state and district where the crime was committed. Only defendants, not the prosecution, may move to change venue, and changes of venue are not automatic. According to Rule 21(a) of the Federal Rules of Criminal Procedure,

> The court upon motion of the defendant shall transfer the proceeding as to that defendant to another district . . . if the court is satisfied that there exists in the district where the prosecution is pending so great a prejudice against the defendant that the defendant cannot obtain a fair and impartial trial at any place fixed for holding court in that district.[54]

Defendants waive their right to a trial in the place where the crime was committed because they believe they cannot get an impartial public trial in that location. When courts rule on the motion, they balance the right to a public trial in the place where the crime was committed against the right to an impartial trial. In that respect, changing venue reflects the interest in obtaining a proper result in the individual case—prejudiced jurors cannot find the truth. Process values are also at stake: the integrity of the judicial process requires a calm, dignified, reflective atmosphere; due process demands unbiased fact-finding; the equal protection clause prohibits trying defendants who are the object of public outrage differently from other defendants.

Change of venue impedes organizational interests. Moving proceedings to jurisdictions farther away, providing for witnesses to appear, and working in unfamiliar court surroundings prevent the smooth, efficient, economical resolution of criminal cases. Furthermore, society has a strong interest in maintaining public confidence in the criminal justice system and providing an outlet for community reaction to crime. Citizens resent moving trials both because they wish to follow the proceedings and because they feel affronted that their own jurisdiction cannot ensure a fair trial.

In *Sheppard v. Maxwell*, the United States Supreme Court held that "where there is a reasonable likelihood that the prejudicial news prior to trial will prevent a fair trial, the judge should continue the case until the threat abates, or transfer it to another county not so permeated with publicity." In this case, Ohio tried Dr. Sam Sheppard for the bludgeoning murder of his pregnant wife, Marilyn, a Cleveland socialite. The case attracted enormous press coverage both prior to and during the trial. Lurid headlines and long stories appeared regularly, detailing the brutality of the murder and Sheppard's failure to cooperate with authorities. The editorials accused Sheppard of the murder. One on the front page charged that "somebody is getting away with murder," alleging that Sheppard's wealth and prominent social position protected him from strong police investigation. Finally, the papers printed detailed analyses of evidence that came to light during the investigation, editorializing about its credibility, relevance, and materiality to the case.[55]

The trial itself attracted widespread publicity. The press, the public, and other observers filled the courtroom. One local radio station set up broadcasting facilities on the third floor of the courthouse. Television and newsreel cameras waiting outside on the courthouse steps filmed jurors, lawyers, witnesses, and other participants in the trial. All the jurors were exposed to the heavy publicity prior to the trial. Referring to the "carnival atmosphere" at the trial, the Supreme Court concluded that Sheppard was entitled to a new trial without showing actual prejudice—a reasonable likelihood of prejudice was sufficient.

The **reasonable-likelihood-of-prejudice test** requires courts to balance four elements:

1. The nature and extent of publicity that evidences community bias and poses a danger to a fair trial
2. The size of the community from which jury panels are selected
3. The nature and gravity of the offense
4. The status of the victim and the accused

These elements may vary in intensity, and, in fact, not all need to be present in each case; rather, they are guidelines by which judges measure the likelihood that the accused will receive a fair trial.

Most courts do not grant changes of venue even if defendants show that trial in the jurisdiction where the crime took place will meet the reasonable-likelihood-of-prejudice test or will produce a reasonable likelihood of prejudice. Instead, they adopt an **actual prejudice test** to determine whether to change the venue or take less drastic measures to eliminate prejudice due to pretrial publicity. Unless the government concedes prejudice, defendants must show that adverse publicity actually negatively affected—prejudiced—their case. Practically speaking, this means proving that the adverse publicity prior to trial reached prospective jurors. Hence, most pretrial motions for change of venue are not resolved until after the *voir dire*—examination of prospective trial jurors.

Under the actual prejudice test, the courts consider circumstances such as the number of jurors who have opinions that the defendant is guilty, the number of jurors exposed to pretrial publicity, the jurors' knowledge of the details of the crime, and the information introduced at *voir dire*. Courts seldom find that defendants have adequately shown that the jury is partial. For example, in *Swindler v. State*, Swindler showed that three jurors had both read and heard about the case, and over 80 percent of prospective jurors were excused for cause. Despite this showing, the Arkansas Supreme Court upheld Swindler's death sentence, rejecting Swindler's claim that the trial court's refusal to grant his motion for change of venue denied him a fair trial.[56]

Several reasons explain why so few defendants prevail in demonstrating actual prejudice. Trials at distant locations burden witnesses, communities have a substantial interest in the trial taking place where the crime was committed, and a change of prosecutors might disrupt the government's case. Perhaps equally important, under the actual prejudice test, the court cannot decide the partiality question until the jury has been impaneled. After the considerable resources courts invest in the *voir dire*, they transfer cases only reluctantly. For the most part, these decisions do not reach the United States Supreme Court. If they go beyond the trial court, ordinarily, intermediate state appellate courts resolve the issues.

In *Sheppard v. Maxwell*, the U.S. Supreme Court said, "[T]he trial court might well have proscribed extra-judicial statements by any lawyer, party, witness, or court official." The Court has never ruled on the constitutionality of orders to these persons; however, it has declared that "gag orders" directed at the press violate the First Amendment free press guarantee. In *Nebraska Press Association v. Stuart*, the Court ruled that barring the press from reporting what transpired at a public preliminary hearing constituted prior restraint. A fundamental First Amendment principle prohibits imposing a restraint on statements before they are published, except when such publications constitute a "clear and present danger" to the country, invade privacy, or are obscene.[57]

The right to a public trial is a personal right that only defendants may invoke. However, the press and the public have a right of access to criminal trials. The right of access promotes the public interest in "ensuring that the individual citizen can effectively participate in and contribute to our republican system of government." The keys to defining the right of access are the long tradition of openness and the contribution that public access makes to the criminal justice system's functioning. Under these guiding principles, the right of access extends not only to trials, but also to pretrial proceedings: first appearance, preliminary hearings, hearings on pretrial motions, and *voir dire* examinations. The press has no right of access either to the secret grand jury proceedings or to trial jury deliberations.[58]

The First Amendment right to free press, linked to the community's interest in law enforcement, and the defendant's right to a public trial, associated with the individual's interest in governmental accountability, must be balanced against the due process guarantee that defendants receive fair trials. Hence, the press's right of access to all public proceedings and its freedom to report those proceedings are not absolute; the defendant's right to a fair trial may restrict both access and reporting. Judges may close proceedings "necessitated by a compelling government interest, and . . . narrowly tailored to serve that interest." The Supreme Court held that a compelling government interest protected minor victims of sex crimes "from further" trauma that press coverage would generate.[59]

Change-of-Judge Motions

The right to a fair trial includes not only the rights to an impartial jury and an atmosphere not poisoned by prejudice, but also the right to an unbiased judge. According to the U.S. Supreme Court,

> [I]t certainly violates the Fourteenth Amendment and deprives a defendant in a criminal case of due process of law to subject his liberty or property to the judgment of a court, the judge of which has a direct, personal, substantial pecuniary interest in reaching a conclusion against him in his cases.[60]

Hence, when a mayor who also acted as a justice of the peace received fees and costs he levied on violators, the personal interest disqualified the judge from hearing such cases.

Personal prejudice is not limited to pecuniary interests. Judges cannot hear cases in which they have a personal interest. A relationship to any of the parties in a case or an involvement in any affairs related to a case might influence the judge and affect judicial impartiality. Judges cannot conduct contempt proceedings following trials over which they have presided and in which defendants have personally insulted or otherwise vilified judges; another judge must decide the contempt issue. However, judges can try cases in which they conducted preliminary proceedings, such as determining probable cause to issue warrants, presiding over preliminary hearings, and resolving pretrial motions.

Judges regularly issue arrest warrants on the basis that officers have probable cause to believe that a crime has been committed and that the person named in the warrant committed it. Judges also preside at preliminary hearings, where they must decide whether the evidence is sufficient to hold a defendant for trial. Neither of these pretrial involvements has been thought to raise any constitutional barrier against the judge presiding over the criminal trial and, if the trial is without a jury, against making the necessary determination of guilt or innocence.[61]

Personal bias denies defendants a fair trial; judicial bias does not. **Judicial bias** means the favoring of a particular legal principle. Hence, judges who oppose the death penalty have a judicial bias, but that does not disqualify them from presiding over capital murder trials. In other words, although judicial philosophy unquestionably leads to judicial bias, judges are assumed to be capable of putting their judicial biases aside and deciding cases fairly.

Jurisdictions have different grounds for disqualifying judges, depending upon the interests that disqualification promotes. Several interests govern disqualification standards:

1. The organizational interest in the cost of justice
2. The process interests in the fairness and timeliness of judicial proceedings
3. The result interest in correct decisions
4. The societal interest in the maintaining of public confidence in the judicial process
5. The professional and personal interests of judges in their own capacity to maintain neutrality

Motions to Suppress

The principal subjects of the motion to suppress are confessions and evidence seized during searches. Most jurisdictions follow the **orthodox rule** that courts, not juries, determine whether evidence is admissible. Many jurisdictions require that courts decide the question of admissibility before trial. Some states permit the jury to reconsider the admissibility question at trial. The motion to suppress primarily promotes the interest in controlling government misconduct. Controlling the government requires pretrial determination of the admissibility question. If the jury hears or sees the evidence, that may influence its decision. To effectively control government misconduct, convictions must not rest on evidence "tainted" by government misconduct. In suppression, therefore, the interest in ensuring that the police act lawfully in obtaining evidence outweighs the interest in obtaining the right result in particular cases. As Justice Byron R. White wrote in *Lego v. Twomey,*

... [T]here may be a relationship between the involuntariness of a confession and its unreliability. But our decision was not based in the slightest on the fear that juries might misjudge the accuracy of confessions and arrive at erroneous determinations of guilt or innocence. That case was not aimed at the possibility of convicting innocent men. Quite the contrary, we feared that the reliability and truthfulness of even coerced confessions could permissibly influence a jury's judgment as to voluntariness. The use of coerced confessions, whether true or false, is forbidden because the method used to extract them offends constitutional principles.[62]

Motions to suppress promote the process interests in timeliness and finality, as well as the organizational interests in efficiency and economy. Deciding the admissibility question prior to trial enables the trial to proceed smoothly, without the interruptions and delay caused when jurors must leave the room while judges decide whether to admit questionable evidence. The court in *State v. Broxton* considered the advantages and disadvantages of pretrial determination of admissibility:

There are obvious advantages and disadvantages in a separate hearing either before or at trial. . . . It may be well for the state and defense to know before trial whether the confessions will come in. . . . But on the other hand, when the issue is tried outside the presence of the jury, the issue must then be retried before the jury both under the orthodox and the Massachusetts rules. A replay is rarely as satisfactory, for there is absent the freshness of the first cross-examination. Moreover, the burden upon all concerned, principal and witnesses, is substantial, to say nothing of the burden on the judicial process which already moves at a snail's pace in criminal matters. . . .[63]

According to the United States Supreme Court, the Constitution does not require the state to prove beyond a reasonable doubt that confessions are voluntary—a preponderance of the evidence suffices. A majority of jurisdictions follow this rule; a minority have adopted the proof-beyond-a-reasonable-doubt standard. Most jurisdictions require defendants to bear the burden of proof in suppressing evidence seized pursuant to searches. In consent searches, however, the state must prove that defendants voluntarily consented. Defendants also bear the burden of proof in eyewitness identification cases. Defendants must prove that the state illegally denied counsel or conducted an unreasonably suggestive confrontation, such as those discussed in Chapter 9.[64]

Pretrial suppression hearings determine not only whether sufficient evidence supports the motion and who bears the burden of presenting it, but also how much weight to give the evidence.

CONVICTION

Conviction results in the greatest deprivations in the criminal process: loss of property, liberty, privacy, and perhaps even life itself. Hence, the factual foundation or quantum of proof required to convict is the highest—proof beyond a reasonable doubt—and the procedures to determine it are the most elaborate in the formal criminal process. Guilty pleas determine conviction in the vast majority of cases. Some of these guilty pleas result from negotiations, but many are **straight pleas,** or pleas of guilty without negotiation. Trials, on the other hand, result from pleas of not guilty and account for only about 10 to 15 percent of the convictions in criminal cases. The process of conviction promotes the same interests as decisions at other stages in the criminal process. The trial promotes fact-finding by the adversary process, procedural regularity, and public participation in criminal proceedings. The guilty plea promotes efficiency, economy, harmony, and speed. Plea negotiations also promote fact-finding, using the informal discussion and give-and-take that occur in reaching an agreement over the plea.

CONVICTION BY TRIAL

Article III, § 2, of the United States Constitution commands the following:

> The Trial of all Crimes, except in Cases of Impeachment, shall be by Jury; and such Trial shall be held in the State where the Crimes shall have been committed.

The Fifth Amendment guarantees that

> No person shall be . . . compelled in any criminal case to be a witness against himself. . . .

And the Sixth Amendment mandates that

> In all criminal prosecutions, the accused shall enjoy the right to a speedy and public trial, by an impartial jury of the State and District wherein the crime shall have been committed . . . to be confronted with the witnesses against him, . . . and to have the assistance of Counsel for his defense.

Conviction by trial operates within this constitutional framework. Of course, defendants can waive their right to conviction by trial, as they obviously do when they plead guilty.

Jury Trial

Jury trial has an ancient history, with roots in the societies of the Teutonic tribes in Germany and the Normans before their conquest of England. The Assizes of Clarendon in 1187 and, more directly, the Magna Carta in 1215 reveal traces of its origins. Jury trial appeared in the English Bill of Rights in 1689; it came to America with the English colonists. From the start, the colonists resented royal interference with the right to jury trial. Complaints regarding that interference appear in the Stamp Act Congress's resolutions, the First Continental Congress's resolves, and the Declaration of Independence. Article III, § 2, of the United States Constitution reflects that history, and the Sixth Amendment reveals that the drafters of the Bill of Rights believed that the right needed even stronger assurances. Every state has adopted a right-to-trial-by-jury provision in its constitution, and the U.S. Supreme Court has extended its protection to the states through the due process clause of the Fourteenth Amendment.[65]

Jury trial promotes several interests. It checks and balances government power by interposing an independent body between the state with all of its resources and a single individual. Furthermore, it balances official power with citizen participation in criminal law enforcement. In addition, it guarantees that accused citizens who prefer that other citizens decide their innocence or guilt shall have that preference honored. In extending the Sixth Amendment's jury trial right to the states, Justice Byron R. White wrote the following:

> The guarantees of jury trial . . . reflect a profound judgment about the way in which law should be enforced and justice administered. . . . Providing an accused with the right to be tried by a jury of his peers gave him an inestimable safeguard against the corrupt or overzealous prosecutor and against the compliant, biased, or eccentric judge. . . . Beyond this, the jury trial . . . reflect[s] a . . . reluctance to entrust plenary powers over the life and liberty of the citizen to one judge or to a group of judges. Fear of unchecked power, so typical of our State and Federal Governments in other respects, found expression in the criminal law in this insistence upon community participation in the determination of guilt or innocence.[66]

Despite this long history and the several clauses in the Constitution commanding trial by jury, the courts have not taken literally the words *all crimes* in Article III, § 2, and *all criminal prosecutions* in the Sixth Amendment. The U.S. Supreme Court has ruled that the right to jury trial excludes "petty offenses" from its scope. The Court based its conclusion on the historical reality of the common law that did not protect petty offenses by jury trial.[67]

In the absence of specific legislation drawing a line, the Court has used a potential six months' imprisonment to divide serious from petty crimes. However, the "moral quality" of some offenses might take them outside the petty offense category even if the penalty is less than six months' imprisonment. Under the **moral seriousness standard,** courts have held that defendants have a right to jury trial in conspiring to deceive immigration officials, driving while intoxicated, and shoplifting cases, despite the minor penalties ordinarily attached to them.[68]

The Supreme Court at one time ruled that the right to jury trial included the right to the historical twelve jurors; it has since retreated from that position. In upholding Florida's six-member jury, Justice Byron R. White concluded that the Court could "not pretend" to know the Framers' intent; that the number twelve was a historical accident, based on superstition about the number itself (twelve apostles, twelve tribes of Israel, twelve stones); and that history does not give sufficient reasons to maintain the twelve-member jury in the twentieth century. Rather, the Court ruled that numbers sufficient to achieve the goals of the jury—protecting the innocent from unfounded prosecution, providing checks and balances, arriving at the truth, enabling community representation in law enforcement—satisfied the right-to-jury-trial requirement. Furthermore, according to the Court, twelve-member juries give the defendant neither an advantage in finding individuals more likely to acquit nor a significant better chance of obtaining a whole jury representative of the whole community:

> . . . [T]hat the jury at common law was composed of precisely 12 is a historical accident, unnecessary to effect the purposes of the jury system and wholly without significance "except to mystics." To read the Sixth Amendment as forever codifying a feature so incidental to the real purpose of the Amendment is to ascribe a blind formalism to the Framers which would require considerably more evidence

than we have been able to discover in the history and language of the Constitution or in the reasoning of our past decisions.[69]

The twelve-member jury has strong supporters, despite the Court's dismissal of it as superstitious, supported only by mystics. Justice John Marshall Harlan called the Court's argument "much too thin." If the number twelve was merely an accident, it was one that "has recurred without interruption since the 14th century." Furthermore, Justice Harlan argued, if "12 jurors are not essential, why are six?" "Can it be doubted that a unanimous jury of 12 provides a greater safeguard than a majority vote of six? The uncertainty that will henceforth plague the meaning of trial by jury is itself a further reason for not hoisting the anchor of history." Finally, Justice Harlan contended, "The [Court's] circumvention of history is compounded by the cavalier disregard of numerous pronouncements of this Court that reflect the understanding of the jury as one of twelve members and have fixed expectations accordingly."[70]

Support for the twelve-member jury comes not only from judges but also from scholars. Social scientists have found that juries with twelve members both obtain more reliable verdicts and represent more of the community than do juries with fewer than twelve members. Hans Zeisel, a major authority on the jury, writes this about the twelve-member jury:

> Suppose that in a given community, 90 percent of the people share one viewpoint and the remaining 10 percent have a different viewpoint. Suppose further that we draw 100 twelve-member and 100 six-member juries. Using standard statistical methods, it can be predicted that approximately 72 of the twelve-member juries will contain a representative of the 10 percent minority, as compared to only 47 juries composed of six persons. This difference is by no means negligible.[71]

The Supreme Court addressed the requirement of a twelve-member jury in *Ballew v. Georgia*.

C A S E

Does a Five-Member Jury Guarantee a Jury Trial?

Ballew v. Georgia
435 U.S. 223, 98 S.Ct. 1029, 55 L.Ed.2d
234 (1978)

Ballew, charged with a misdemeanor, was tried before a five-member jury pursuant to Georgia law and convicted. On writ of certiorari, *the Supreme Court reversed the judgment, holding that the five-member jury violated Ballew's right to jury trial. The Court remanded the case for proceedings consistent with its decision. Justice Blackmun announced the Court's judgment and delivered an opinion, which Justice Stevens joined. Justice*

Stevens filed a concurring statement. Justice White filed a statement concurring in the judgment. Justice Powell filed an opinion concurring in the judgment, which Chief Justice Burger and Justice Rehnquist joined. Justice Brennan filed a separate opinion, which Justices Stewart and Marshall joined.

FACTS

In November 1973, petitioner Claude Davis Ballew was the manager of the Paris Adult Theatre at 320 Peachtree Street, Atlanta, Ga. On November 9, two investigators from the Fulton County Solicitor General's office viewed at the theater a motion picture film entitled "Behind the Green Door."

On September 14, 1974, petitioner was charged in a two-count misdemeanor accusation with "distributing obscene materials in violation of the Georgia Code in that the said accused did, knowing the obscene nature thereof, exhibit a motion picture film entitled 'Behind the Green Door' that contained obscene and indecent scenes."

Petitioner was brought to trial in the Criminal Court of Fulton County. After a jury of 5 persons had been selected and sworn, petitioner moved that the court impanel a jury of 12 persons. That court, however, tried its misdemeanor cases before juries of five persons pursuant to Ga. Const., Art. 6. paragraph 16, § 1. Petitioner contended that for an obscenity trial, a jury of only five was constitutionally inadequate to assess the contemporary standards of the community. He also argued that the Sixth and Fourteenth Amendments required a jury of at least six members in criminal cases.

The motion for a 12-person jury was overruled, and the trial went on to its conclusion before the 5-person jury that had been impaneled. At the conclusion of the trial, the jury deliberated for 38 minutes and returned a verdict of guilty on both counts of the accusation. The court imposed a sentence of one year and a $1,000 fine on each count, the periods of incarceration to run concurrently and to be suspended upon payment of the fines.

The Supreme Court of Georgia denied certiorari. We granted certiorari.

OPINION

The Fourteenth Amendment guarantees the right of trial by jury in all state nonpetty criminal cases. The purpose of the jury trial is to prevent oppression by the Government. This purpose is attained by the participation of the community in determinations of guilt and by the application of the common sense of laymen who, as jurors, consider the case. Rather than requiring 12 members, then, the Sixth Amendment mandated a jury only of sufficient size to promote group deliberation, to insulate members from outside intimidation, and to provide a representative cross-section of the community.

When the Court in *Williams v. Florida* (1970) permitted the reduction in jury size — or, to put it another way, when it held that a jury of six was not unconstitutional — it expressly reserved ruling on the issue whether a number smaller than six passed constitutional scrutiny. The Court refused to speculate when this so-called "slippery slope" would become too steep. We face now, however, the two-fold question whether a further reduction in the size of the state criminal trial jury does make the grade too dangerous, that is, whether it inhibits the functioning of the jury as an institution to a significant degree, and, if so, whether any state interest counterbalances and justifies the disruption so as to preserve its constitutionality.

First, recent empirical data suggest that progressively smaller juries are less likely to foster effective group deliberation. At some point, this decline leads to inaccurate fact-finding and incorrect application of the common sense of the community to the facts. The smaller the group, the less likely are members to make critical contributions necessary for the solution of a given problem. As juries decrease in size, then, they are less likely to have members who remember each of the important pieces of evidence or argument. Furthermore, the smaller the group, the less likely it is to overcome the biases of its members to obtain an accurate result. When individual and group decisionmaking were compared, it was seen that groups performed better because prejudices of individuals were frequently counterbalanced, and objectivity resulted.

Second, the data now raise doubts about the accuracy of the results achieved by smaller and smaller panels. Statistical studies suggest that the risk of convicting an innocent person rises as the size of the jury diminishes. Third, the data suggest that the verdicts of jury deliberation in criminal cases will vary as juries become smaller, and that the variance amounts to an imbalance to the detriment of one side, the defense. Fourth, [a jury's] decrease in size foretells problems not only for jury decisionmaking, but also for the representation of minority groups in the community. The Court repeatedly has held that meaningful community participation cannot be attained with the exclusion of minorities or other identifiable groups from jury service.

While we adhere to, and reaffirm our holding in *Williams v. Florida*, these studies, most of which have been made since *Williams* was decided in 1970, lead us to conclude that the purpose and functioning of the jury in a criminal trial is seriously impaired, and to a constitutional degree, by a reduction in size to below six members. With the reduction in the number of jurors below six creating a substantial threat to Sixth and Fourteenth Amendment guarantees, we must consider whether any interest of the State justifies the reduction. We find no significant state advantage in reducing the number of jurors from six to five.

. The States utilize juries of less than 12 primarily for administrative reasons. Savings in court time and in financial costs are claimed to justify the reductions. A reduction in size from six to five or four or even three would save the States little. They could reduce slightly the daily allowances, but with a reduction from six to five the saving would be minimal.

The judgment of the Court of Appeals is reversed, and the case is remanded for further proceedings not inconsistent with this opinion. It is so ordered.

CASE DISCUSSION

Why does a six-member jury satisfy the Constitution, but not a five-member jury, according to the Court? How does the Court arrive at its conclusion? Does social science research provide a better guide to how many jurors should constitute a jury than does history? Explain your answer.

The Supreme Court has followed a pattern in ruling on unanimity similar to that in its ruling on numbers of jurors. In 1900, the Court held that the Sixth Amendment guaranteed conviction by unanimous jury verdicts. In 1972, in *Apodaca v. Oregon*, the Court decided that verdicts of eleven to one and ten to two did not violate two convicted felons' right to jury trial:

> A requirement of unanimity . . . does not materially contribute to . . . [the jury's] commonsense judgment. . . . [A] jury will come to such a verdict as long as it consists of a group of laymen representative of a cross section of the community who have the duty and the opportunity to deliberate, free from outside attempts at intimidation, on the question of a defendant's guilt. In terms of this function we perceive no difference between juries required to act unanimously and those permitted to convict or acquit by votes of 10 to two or 11 to one. Requiring unanimity would obviously produce hung juries in some situations where nonunanimous juries will convict or acquit. But in either case, the interest of the defendant in having the judgment of his peers interposed between himself and the officers of the state who prosecute and judge him is equally well served.[72]

The Court also rejected the argument that proof beyond a reasonable doubt required unanimous verdicts. In a companion case to *Apodaca*, *Johnson v. Louisiana*, the Court upheld a nine-to-three majority jury verdict of guilty in a robbery case. Justice Byron R. White wrote for the Supreme Court five-to-four majority: "[N]ine jurors—a substantial majority of the jury—were convinced by the evidence. Disagreement of the three jurors does not alone establish reasonable doubt, particularly when such a heavy majority of the jury, after having considered the dissenters' views, remains convinced of guilt."[73]

The *Apodaca* and *Johnson* decisions have received harsh criticism from some quarters. Critics maintain that unanimous verdicts instill confidence in the criminal justice process, guarantee that the jury carefully reviews the evidence, ensure the hearing and consideration of minority viewpoints, prevent government oppression, support the principle that convicting innocent defendants is worse than freeing guilty ones, and fulfill the proof-beyond-a-reasonable-doubt requirement.[74]

The Court has not answered the question of how many votes short of unanimity satisfy the Sixth Amendment. However, it did address the problem of what happens when a case involves neither twelve members nor unanimity. A unanimous Court struck down a Louisiana provision that misdemeanors punishable by more than six months "shall be tried before a jury of six persons, five of whom must concur to render a verdict." The Court reasoned that to preserve the right to jury trial, it needed to draw a line at nonunanimous verdicts of six-member juries, noting that only two states permitted such verdicts; hence, the "near-uniform judgment of the nation" provided a useful guide to draw the line on the other side of the Louisiana provision.[75]

The jury's function — except in a few states — is to decide the facts and apply them to the law. Nevertheless, juries have the power to acquit even when the facts clearly point to conviction. Jury acquittals are final; the prosecution cannot appeal them. Juries usually acquit despite proof beyond a reasonable doubt when they sympathize with defendants or when the state prosecutes defendants for violating unpopular laws. Acquittals in mercy killings — technically, first-degree murder — represent one obvious example of **jury nullification,** the practice of acquitting in the face of sufficient proof to convict.

Jury nullification has an ancient lineage. The "pages of history shine on instances of the jury's exercise of its prerogative to disregard uncontradicted evidence and instructions of the judge." In the famous Peter Zenger case, the jury flouted the facts and the judge's instructions, and acquitted Zenger of the charge of sedition. The U.S. Supreme Court has not confronted the question directly, but its language supports the conclusion that the Sixth Amendment encompasses jury nullification. According to the Court in *Sparf & Hansen v. United States,*

> If a jury may rightfully disregard the direction of the court in matters of law and determine for themselves what the law is in the particular case before them, it is difficult to perceive any legal ground upon which a verdict of conviction can be set aside by the court as being against law.[76]

Nullification promotes, as perhaps no other doctrine in criminal procedure does, the interest in community participation in criminal law enforcement. Juries become safety valves for exceptional cases and act not only on the law strictly defined in judges' instructions, but also on "informal communication from the total culture."[77]

The equal protection clause of the Fourteenth Amendment prohibits juries that systematically exclude members of the defendant's racial, gender, ethnic, religious, or other group. The right to an impartial jury also requires that juries represent a fair cross section of the community. To meet these constitutional mandates, the Federal Jury Selection and Service Act requires that juries be "selected at random from a fair cross-section of the community in the district or division wherein the court convenes," and further that "[n]o citizen shall be excluded from service as a grand or petit juror in the district courts of the United States on account of race, color, religion, sex, national origin, or economic status."[78]

Most states have adopted similar provisions. To implement them, jurisdictions select jurors at random from the local census, tax rolls, city directories, telephone books, and driver's license lists. Some states, mainly in New England and the South, use the "key-man" system, in which civic and political leaders recommend people whom they know. Understandably, the "key-man" system undergoes repeated challenges that it does not represent a fair cross section of the community and that it discriminates against various segments in the community.[79]

Most prospective jurors ask to be excused. Courts rarely refuse their requests; they find "it easier, administratively and financially, to excuse unwilling people. . . ." Common excuses include economic hardship, advanced age, illness, the need to care for small children, and the distance between home and the courthouse. Jurisdictions frequently disqualify some groups from jury service: persons below voting age, convicted felons, and persons not able to write and read English. Some categories also receive exemptions because of their occupation: doctors, pharmacists, teachers, clergy, lawyers, judges, criminal justice professionals, and some other public employees.[80]

From the panel of prospective jurors, the attorneys for the government and the defendant select the jurors who will actually serve. The principal method for ensuring the trial jury's impartiality is the *voir dire*—literally, "to speak the truth"—in which defense and prosecution examine prospective jurors. Attorneys for both sides can have prospective jurors they find unacceptable removed by means of **jury challenges.** Attorneys for both sides have **peremptory challenges,** or the power to remove jurors without showing cause. The number of challenges depends on the jurisdiction. At common law, prosecutors had an unlimited number of peremptory challenges in felony cases, and the defendant had thirty-five. Today, the numbers vary depending on the jurisdiction. In the federal system, each side has twenty peremptories in capital offenses and three in misdemeanors. In felony cases, the defendant has ten, and the government has six. Lawyers use peremptory challenges to eliminate prospective jurors who appear either sympathetic to the other side or at least not sympathetic to their own side.

The government and defense also have an unlimited number of **challenges for cause,** which are challenges based on showing that particular prospective jurors would deny defendants an impartial jury trial. Attorneys use challenges for cause only in instances where they can demonstrate juror bias to the judge's satisfaction. Neither the government nor the defense exercises the challenge for cause frequently; ordinarily, from one to three of these challenges are used to assemble a jury of twelve.[81]

The *voir dire* provides the opportunity for lawyers to decide whether to accept prospective jurors; hence, their freedom to question prospective jurors bears heavily on their making sound decisions about jurors' impartiality. Trial judges have considerable discretion to determine the scope of *voir dire* questioning; appellate courts rarely reverse on the grounds that the trial judge refused to permit certain questions. *Ham v. South Carolina* was one of the few instances in which the defendant achieved reversal for a judge's refusal to permit his counsel to ask a question. Ham was a bearded, black civil rights activist convicted of marijuana possession. His counsel tried to elicit prospective jurors' opinions concerning their prejudice about either Ham's race or his beard. The trial court prohibited the questioning. The U.S. Supreme Court ruled in the defendant's favor regarding the trial judge's refusal to inquire about race prejudice, but not for his refusal to question the prospective jurors about Ham's beard:

While we cannot say that prejudice against people with beards might not have been harbored by one or more of the potential jurors in this case, this is the beginning and not the end of the inquiry as to whether the Fourteenth Amendment required the trial judge to interrogate the prospective jurors about such possible prejudice. Given the traditionally broad discretion accorded to the trial judge in conducting voir dire, and or inability to constitutionally distinguish possible prejudice against beards from a host of other possible similar prejudices, we do not believe the petitioners' constitutional rights were violated when the trial judge refused to put this question.[82]

The courts have applied the ruling on questioning race prejudice narrowly. In *Dukes v. Waitkevitch*, for example, the First Circuit Court of Appeals ruled that the trial court did not commit constitutional error when it refused to inquire into race prejudice in a case where the black defendant participated in a gang rape of white women. In capital cases, however, the U.S. Supreme Court has ruled otherwise:

> The risk of racial prejudice infecting capital sentencing proceedings is especially serious in light of the complete finality of the death sentence. . . . We hold that a capital defendant accused of an interracial crime is entitled to have prospective jurors informed of the race of the victim and questioned on the issue of racial bias.[83]

Balanced against the interest in obtaining impartial juries to ensure accurate results as well as promote the societal interests in community participation in law enforcement, prejudice-free proceedings, and public confidence in criminal justice are the organizational interests in efficiency, economy, and dispatch. According to the United States Supreme Court,

> It is of course true that any examination on the *voir dire* is a clumsy and imperfect way of detecting suppressed emotional commitments to which all of us are to some extent subject, unconsciously or subconsciously. It is of the nature of our deepest antipathies that often we do not admit them even to ourselves; but when that is so, nothing but an examination, utterly impracticable in a courtroom, will disclose them, an examination extending even at times for months, and even then unsuccessful. No such examination is required; indeed, it was exactly the purpose of Criminal Rule 24(a), which allows the judge to frame questions on the *voir dire* if he thinks best, to avoid interminable examinations sometimes extending for weeks on end that had frequently resulted from the former method. If trial by jury is not to break down by its own weight, it is not feasible to prove more than the upper levels of a juror's mind.[84]

The problem of the bias — if not outright prejudice — of so-called "death-qualified" jurors has troubled courts. Supporters of the death penalty believe that jurors who are opposed to the death penalty cannot act impartially. Opponents of the death penalty believe that jurors who support the death penalty are biased toward conviction. The United States Supreme Court dealt with the issue of "death-qualified" jury in *Lockhart v. McCree*.

◧ C A S E ◨

Are Death-Qualified Juries Impartial?

Lockhart v. McCree
476 U.S. 162, 106 S.Ct. 1758,
90 L.Ed.2d 137 (1986)

After his conviction for capital felony-murder was af-firmed on direct appeal, Lockhart filed a habeas cor-pus *petition. The United States District Court for the Eastern District of Arkansas granted relief, and the Cir-cuit Court for the Eighth Circuit affirmed. On writ of* certiorari, *the United States Supreme Court reversed. Justice Rehnquist delivered the opinion of the Court, which Chief Justice Burger and Justices White, Powell, and O'Connor joined. Justice Blackmun concurred in the result. Justice Marshall filed a dissenting opinion, which Justices Brennan and Stevens joined.*

FACTS

In the case we address the question, Does the Consti-tution prohibit the removal for cause, prior to the guilt phase of a bifurcated capital trial, of prospective jurors whose opposition to the death penalty is so strong that it would prevent or substantially impair the performance of their duties as jurors at the sentencing phase of the trial? We hold that it does not.

On the morning of February 14, 1978, a gift shop and service station in Camden, Arkansas, was robbed, and Evelyn Boughton, the owner, was shot and killed. That afternoon, Ardia McCree was arrested in Hot Springs, Arkansas, after a police officer saw him driv-ing a maroon and white Lincoln Continental match-ing an eye-witness' description of the getaway car used by Boughton's killer. The next evening, McCree ad-mitted to police that he had been at Boughton's shop at the time of the murder. He claimed, however, that a tall black stranger wearing an overcoat first asked him for a ride, then took McCree's rifle out of the back of the car and used it to kill Boughton. McCree also claimed that, after the murder, the stranger rode with McCree to a nearby dirt road, got out of the car, and walked away with the rifle. McCree's story was contradicted by two eyewitnesses who saw McCree's

car between the time of the murder and the time when McCree said the stranger got out and walked away, and who stated that they saw only one person in the car. The police found McCree's rifle and a bank bag from Boughton's shop alongside the dirt road. Based on ballistics tests, an F.B.I. officer testified that the bullet that killed Boughton had been fired from McCree's rifle.

McCree was charged with capital felony murder. In accordance with Arkansas law, the trial judge at voir dire removed for cause, over McCree's objec-tions, those prospective jurors who stated that they could not under any circumstances vote the imposi-tion of the death penalty. Eight prospective jurors were excluded for this reason. The jury convicted McCree of capital felony murder, but rejected the State's request for the death penalty, instead setting McCree's punishment at life imprisonment without parole.

The District Court held a hearing on the "death qualification" issue in July 1981, receiving in evidence numerous social science studies concerning the atti-tudes and beliefs of "*Witherspoon*-excludables" [jurors opposed to the death penalty], along with the poten-tial effects of excluding them from the jury prior to the guilt phase of a bifurcated capital trial. In August 1983, the court concluded, based on the social sci-ence evidence, that "death qualification" produced juries that "were more prone to convict" capital de-fendants than "non-death-qualified" juries.

The Eighth Circuit found "substantial evidentiary support" for the District Court's conclusion and af-firmed the grant of habeas relief on the ground that such removal for cause violated McCree's constitu-tional right to a jury selected from a fair cross-section of the community.

OPINION

Of the six studies introduced by McCree that at least purported to deal with the central issue in this case, namely, the potential effects on the determination of guilt or innocence of excluding "*Witherspoon*-excludables*" from the jury, three were also before this Court when it decided *Witherspoon*. There, this Court reviewed the studies and concluded:

> The data adduced by the petitioner . . . are too tentative and fragmentary to establish that jurors not opposed to the death penalty tend to favor the prosecution in the determination of guilt. We simply cannot conclude, either on the basis of the record now before us or as a matter of judicial notice, that the exclusion of jurors opposed to capital punishment results in an unrepresentative jury on the issue of guilt or substantially increases the risk of conviction. In the light of the presently available information, we are not prepared to announce a per se constitutional rule requiring the reversal of every conviction returned by a jury selected as this one was.

It goes almost without saying that if these studies were "too tentative and fragmentary" to make out a claim of constitutional error in 1968, the same studies, unchanged but for having aged some eighteen years, are still not sufficient to make out such a claim in this case.

Nor do the three post-*Witherspoon* studies introduced by McCree on the "death qualification" issue provide substantial support for the "per se constitutional rule" McCree asks this Court to adopt. All three of the "new" studies were based on the responses of individuals randomly selected from some segment of the population, but who were not actual jurors sworn under oath to apply the law to the facts of an actual case involving the fate of an actual capital defendant. We have serious doubts about the value of these studies in predicting the behavior of actual jurors. In addition, two of the three "new" studies did not even attempt to simulate the process of jury deliberation, and none of the "new" studies was able to predict to what extent, if any, the presence of one or more "*Witherspoon*-excludables" on a guilt-phase jury would have altered the outcome of the guilt determination.

Finally, and most importantly, only one of the six "death qualification" studies introduced by McCree even attempted to identify and account for the presence of so-called "nullifiers," or individuals who, because of their deep-seated opposition to the death penalty, would be unable to decide a capital defendant's guilt or innocence fairly and impartially.

Having identified some of the more serious problems with McCree's studies, however, we will assume for purposes of this opinion that the studies are both methodologically valid and adequate to establish that "death qualification" in fact produces juries somewhat more "conviction-prone" than "non-death-qualified" juries. We hold, nonetheless, that the Constitution does not prohibit the States from "death qualifying" juries in capital cases.

We have never invoked the fair cross-section principle to invalidate the use of either for-cause or peremptory challenges to prospective jurors, or to require petit juries, as opposed to jury panels or venires, to reflect the composition of the community at large. We remain convinced that an extension of the fair cross-section requirement to petit juries would be unworkable and unsound, and we decline McCree's invitation to adopt such an extension.

The essence of a "fair cross-section" claim is the systematic exclusion of "a 'distinctive' group in the community." In our view, groups defined solely in terms of shared attitudes that would prevent or substantially impair members of the group from performing one of their duties as jurors, such as the "*Witherspoon*-excludables" at issue here, are not "distinctive groups" for fair cross-section purposes.

Our prior jury-representativeness cases, have involved such groups as blacks, women, and Mexican-Americans. The wholesale exclusion of these large groups from jury service clearly contravened the fair cross-section requirement. The exclusion from jury service of large groups of individuals not on the basis of their inability to serve as jurors, but on the basis of some immutable characteristic such as race, gender, or ethnic background, undeniably gave rise to an "appearance of unfairness."

The group of "*Witherspoon*-excludables" involved in the case at bar differs significantly from the groups we have previously recognized as "distinctive." "Death qualification," unlike the wholesale exclusion of blacks, women, or Mexican-Americans from jury service, is carefully designed to serve the State's concededly legitimate interest in obtaining a single jury that can properly and impartially apply the law to the facts of the case at both the guilt and sentencing phases of a capital trial.

Furthermore, unlike blacks, women, and Mexican-Americans, *"Witherspoon-*excludables" are singled out for exclusion in capital cases on the basis of an attribute that is within the individual's control. It is important to remember that not all who oppose the death penalty are subject to removal for cause in capital cases; those who firmly believe that the death penalty is unjust may nevertheless serve as jurors in capital cases so long as they state clearly that they are willing to temporarily set aside their own beliefs in deference to the rule of law.

McCree argues that, even if we reject the Eighth Circuit's fair cross-section holding, we should affirm the judgment below on the alternative ground, adopted by the District Court, that "death qualification" violated his constitutional right to an impartial jury. We do not agree. According to McCree, when the State "tips the scales" by excluding prospective jurors with a particular viewpoint, an impermissibly partial jury results. We have consistently rejected this view of jury impartiality, including as recently as last Term when we squarely held that an impartial jury consists of nothing more than "jurors who will conscientiously apply the law and find the facts."

cally different from those of the excluded jurors. Death-qualified jurors are, for example, more likely to believe that a defendant's failure to testify is indicative of his guilt, more hostile to the insanity defense, more distrustful of defense attorneys, and less concerned about the danger of erroneous convictions. This pro-prosecution bias is reflected in the greater readiness of death-qualified jurors to convict or to convict on more serious charges. And, finally, the very process of death qualification—which focuses attention on the death penalty before the trial has even begun—has been found to predispose the jurors that survive it to believe that the defendant is guilty.

The evidence thus confirms, and is itself corroborated by, the more intuitive judgments of scholars and of so many of the participants in capital trials—judges, defense attorneys, and prosecutors. The chief strength of respondent's evidence lies in the essential unanimity of the results obtained by researchers using diverse subjects and varied methodologies. Even the Court's haphazard jabs cannot obscure the power of the array. Faced with the near unanimity of authority supporting respondent's claim that death qualification gives the prosecution a particular advantage in the guilt phase of capital trials, the majority here makes but a weak effort to contest that proposition.

DISSENT

Justice Marshall, with whom Justice Brennan and Justice Stevens join, dissenting.

The data strongly suggest that death qualification excludes a significantly large subset—at least 11% to 17%—of potential jurors who could be impartial during the guilt phase of trial. Among the members of this excludable class are a disproportionate number of blacks and women.

The perspectives on the criminal justice system of jurors who survive death qualification are systemati-

CASE DISCUSSION

Do death-qualified juries deny defendants fair trials? Is the majority or the dissent "right" in interpreting the statistics? Should juries represent a fair cross section of attitudes in the community? Why? Why not? Why are attitudes different from race, ethnicity, and gender, according to the Court? Should they be? Explain. How would you have decided this case? Defend your decision.

The Right to a Public Trial

Both the Sixth Amendment right to confrontation and the due process clauses of the Fifth and Fourteenth Amendments guarantee the defendant's right to a public trial. The right encompasses two dimensions:

1. Access of the public in general to attend proceedings
2. Right of defendants to attend

The right extends to "every stage of the trial," including jury selection, communications between judge and jury, **jury instructions** (judges' explanations of the law to the jury), and in-chamber conversations between judge and jurors. It does not include brief conferences at the bench outside the defendant's hearing or other brief conferences involving only questions of law.

Public trials support the defendants' interest in avoiding persecution through secret proceedings, enhance community participation in law enforcement, and aid in the search for truth by encouraging witnesses to come forth who otherwise might not. These interests are not absolute. Courtroom size limits public access. Furthermore, the need to protect threatened witnesses justifies closing the courtroom. Also, shy and introverted witnesses may not come forward in a public trial. Moreover, protecting undercover agents authorizes exclusion of the public during their testimony. Finally, judges might restrict access during sensitive proceedings.

For example, according to an opinion of the Seventh Circuit Court of Appeals,

> exclusion of spectators during the testimony of an alleged rape victim "is a frequent and accepted practice when the lurid details of such a crime must be related by a young lady." . . . Primary justification for this practice lies in protection of the personal feelings of the complaining witness. . . . Rape constitutes an intrusion upon areas of the victim's life, both physical and psychological, to which our society attaches the deepest sense of privacy. Shame and loss of dignity, however unjustified from a moral standpoint, are natural byproducts of an attempt to recount details of a rape before a curious . . . audience. The ordeal of describing an unwanted sexual encounter before persons with no more than a prurient interest in it aggravates the original injury. Mitigation of the ordeal is a justifiable concern of the public and of the trial court.[85]

Defendants do not possess an absolute right to attend their own trials; they forfeit their right to attend by disruptive behavior. For example, Allen, who was on trial for armed robbery, repeatedly interrupted the judge in a "most abusive and disrespectful manner" and threatened him: "When I go out for lunchtime, you're going to be a corpse here." When the judge warned Allen that he could attend only so long as he behaved himself, Allen answered: "There is going to be no proceeding. I'm going to start talking all through the trial. There's not going to be no trial like this." The judge, according to the U.S. Supreme Court, properly removed Allen from the courtroom:

> It is essential to the proper administration of criminal justice that dignity, order, and decorum be the hallmarks of all court proceedings in our country. The flagrant disregard in the courtroom of elementary standards of proper conduct should not and cannot be tolerated. We believe that trial judges confronted with disruptive, contumacious, stubbornly defiant defendants must be given sufficient discretion to meet the circumstances of each case. We think there are at least three constitutionally permissible ways for a trial judge to handle an obstreperous defendant like Allen: (1) bind and gag him, thereby keeping him present; (2) cite him for contempt; (3) take him out of the courtroom until he promises to conduct himself properly.[86]

Judges may also exclude defendants from some questioning of child witnesses in sex abuse cases. For example, Stincer was on trial for sodomizing two children, aged eight and seven. The trial court conducted an in-chambers hearing to determine whether the children could remember certain details and whether they understood the significance of telling the truth in court. The judge permitted Stincer's lawyer to attend but refused Stincer's request to do so. The Supreme Court upheld the judge's ruling because Stincer had an adequate opportunity to "confront" the children during the trial.

Courts can also require dangerous defendants to appear only under sufficient guard to protect the public, witnesses, and court officials from harm and to prevent defendants' escape. Under ordinary circumstances, however, defendants have the right to attend trial in a way that will not prejudice their cases. The government cannot bring defendants to court in jail dress, nor can it require that its witnesses appear in shackles. Such apparel prejudices the jury, furthers no state policy, and acts mainly against poor defendants.[87]

Presenting the Evidence

The adversary process reaches its high point in presenting evidence. Each side follows strict, technical rules in presenting its case to the fact-finders, whether they be jurors or the judge in a bench trial. Since the consequences are the most severe in the criminal process, the state must prove the defendant guilty beyond a reasonable doubt, the highest standard of proof in the law. The main stages in presenting the evidence include the following:

1. Opening statements, with the prosecution first, followed by the defense
2. The state's case, including cross-examination by defense counsel
3. The defendant's case, including cross-examination by the prosecution
4. Closing arguments
5. Instructions to the jury
6. Jury deliberations
7. Jury verdict
8. Judgment of the court

The defense need not present any evidence or, in fact, speak at all. The burden rests solely upon the government to prove defendants' guilt beyond a reasonable doubt. Defendants need not either prove their innocence or raise a reasonable doubt about the government's case. Furthermore, the right against self-incrimination permits defendants to remain silent throughout the trial. Hence, trials may proceed, and some do, in which neither defendants nor their lawyers present a case for the defense. Not only does the Constitution permit this, but strategy and tactics may dictate it. The presentation of evidence promotes and balances the interest in arriving at the truth against the process values of controlling government officials, the societal interest in community participation in criminal justice administration, and the interest in maintaining public confidence in a fair and just legal system and process. In the presentation of evidence, promoting organizational interests plays a lesser role; criminal trials are perhaps the least efficient and harmonious, as well as the most expensive, stage of the criminal process. Even in the trial, however, decorum and proper exchanges between defense and prosecution receive attention, if not paramount concern.

The Supreme Court ruled in *In re Winship* that due process requires both federal and state prosecutors to prove every element of a crime beyond a reasonable doubt:

> The **reasonable doubt standard** is bottomed on a fundamental value determination of our society that it is far worse to convict an innocent man than to let a guilty man go free. [Two propositions cannot be disputed:] First, in a judicial proceeding in which there is a dispute about the facts of some earlier event, the factfinder cannot acquire unassailably accurate knowledge of what happened. Instead, all the factfinder can acquire is a belief of what probably happened. The intensity of this belief—the degree to which a factfinder is convinced that a given act actually occurred—can, of course, vary. In this regard, a standard of proof represents an attempt to instruct the factfinder concerning the degree of confidence our society thinks he should have in the correctness of factual conclusions for a particular type of adjudication. Although the phrases "preponderance of the evidence" and "proof beyond a reasonable doubt" are quantitatively imprecise, they do communicate to the finder of fact different notions concerning the degree of confidence he is expected to have in the correctness of his factual conclusions.
>
> A second proposition, which is really nothing more than a corollary of the first, is that the trier of fact will sometimes, despite his best efforts, be wrong in his factual conclusions. [This can lead to one of two results. On the one hand] would be the conviction of an innocent man. On the other hand, an erroneous factual determination can result . . . in the acquittal of a guilty man.[88]

Despite the constitutional requirement of proof beyond a reasonable doubt, the U.S. Supreme Court has not decided that due process requires judges to define *proof beyond a reasonable doubt*. Nevertheless, courts have struggled to define the reasonable doubt standard for juries. Judges, in defining the standard, have more often confused than clarified the meaning of reasonable doubt. Here are some of the common definitions found in the cases:

- A doubt that would cause prudent people to hesitate before acting in a matter of importance to themselves
- A doubt based on reason and common sense
- A doubt that is neither frivolous or fanciful nor can be easily explained away
- Substantial doubt
- Persuasion to a reasonable or moral certainty

Two definitions by trial judges that brought about reversal on appeal are the following:

- Doubt beyond that which is reasonable is about "7½ on a scale of 10."
- The reasonable doubt standard is met when the "scales of justice are substantially out of equipoise."[89]

Some states prohibit trial judges from defining *reasonable doubt*, leaving juries to decide for themselves what it means. The U.S. Supreme Court dealt with the problem of jury instructions and this issue in *Victor v. Nebraska*.

C A S E

Did the Definition of Proof
Beyond a Reasonable Doubt Violate Due Process?

Victor v. Nebraska
114 S.Ct. 1239, 127 L.Ed.2d 583 (1994)

Sandoval was convicted of multiple murder and sentenced to death. The California Supreme Court affirmed the conviction and the sentences. The United States Supreme Court granted certiorari and affirmed. Justice O'Connor wrote the opinion of the Court. Justices Blackmun, Souter, and Ginsburg joined only part of this opinion.

FACTS

On October 14, 1984, petitioner Sandoval shot three men, two of them fatally, in a gang-related incident in Los Angeles. About two weeks later, he entered the home of a man who had given information to the police about the murders and shot him dead; Sandoval then killed the man's wife because she had seen him murder her husband. Sandoval was convicted on four counts of first-degree murder. The jury found that Sandoval personally used a firearm in the commission of each offense, and found the special circumstance of multiple murder. Cal. Penal Code Ann. § 12022.5 (West 1992) and Cal. Penal Code Ann. § 190.2(a)(3) (West 1988). He was sentenced to death for murdering the woman and to life in prison without possibility of parole for the other three murders. The California Supreme Court affirmed the convictions and sentences. 4 Cal. 4th 155 (1992), modified, 4 Cal. 4th 928a, 841 P.2d 862 (1993).

The jury in Sandoval's case was given the following instruction on the government's burden of proof: "A defendant in a criminal action is presumed to be innocent until the contrary is proved, and in case of a reasonable doubt whether his guilt is satisfactorily shown, he is entitled to a verdict of not guilty. This presumption places upon the State the burden of proving him guilty beyond a reasonable doubt.

"Reasonable doubt is defined as follows: It is not a mere possible doubt; because everything relating to human affairs, and depending on moral evidence, is open to some possible or imaginary doubt. It is that state of the case which, after the entire comparison and consideration of all the evidence, leaves the minds of the jurors in that condition that they cannot say they feel an abiding conviction, to a moral certainty, of the truth of the charge."

The California Supreme Court rejected Sandoval's claim that the instruction . . . violated the Due Process Clause.

OPINION

The instruction given in Sandoval's case has its genesis in a charge given by Chief Justice Shaw of the Massachusetts Supreme Judicial Court more than a century ago: "[W]hat is reasonable doubt? It is a term often used, probably pretty well understood, but not easily defined. It is not mere possible doubt; because every thing relating to human affairs, and depending on moral evidence, is open to some possible or imaginary doubt. It is that state of the case, which, after the entire comparison and consideration of all the evidence, leaves the minds of jurors in that condition that they cannot say they feel an abiding conviction, to a moral certainty, of the truth of the charge. The burden of proof is upon the prosecutor. All the presumptions of law independent of evidence are in favor of innocence; and every person is presumed to be innocent until he is proved guilty. If upon such proof there is reasonable doubt remaining, the accused is entitled to the benefit of it by an acquittal. For it is not sufficient to establish a probability, though a strong one arising from the doctrine of chances, that the fact charged is more likely to be true than the contrary; but the evidence must establish the truth of the fact to a reasonable and moral certainty; a certainty that convinces and directs the understanding, and satisfies the reason and judgment, of those who are bound to act conscientiously upon it. This we take to be proof beyond reasonable doubt." *Commonwealth v. Webster*, 59 Mass. 295, 320 (1850).

. . .

Sandoval's primary objection is to the use of the phrases "moral evidence" and "moral certainty" in the instruction. As noted, this part of the charge was lifted verbatim from Chief Justice Shaw's *Webster* decision. . . .

. . . [W]hen Chief Justice Shaw penned the *Webster* instruction in 1850, moral certainty meant a state of subjective certitude about some event or occurrence. As the Massachusetts Supreme Judicial Court subsequently explained: "Proof 'beyond a reasonable doubt' . . . is proof 'to a moral certainty,' as distinguished from an absolute certainty. As applied to a judicial trial for crime, the two phrases are synonymous and equivalent; each has been used by eminent judges to explain the other; and each signifies such proof as satisfies the judgment and consciences of the jury, as reasonable men, and applying their reason to the evidence before them, that the crime charged has been committed by the defendant, and so satisfies them as to leave no other reasonable conclusion possible." *Commonwealth v. Costley*, 118 Mass. 1, 24 (1875). Indeed, we have said that "[p]roof to a 'moral certainty' is an equivalent phrase with 'beyond a reasonable doubt.'"

We recognize that the phrase "moral evidence" is not a mainstay of the modern lexicon, though we do not think it means anything different today than it did in the 19th century. The few contemporary dictionaries that define moral evidence do so consistently with its original meaning. See, e.g., *Webster's New Twentieth Century Dictionary* 1168 (2d ed. 1979) ("based on general observation of people, etc. rather than on what is demonstrable"); *Collins English Dictionary* 1014 (3d ed. 1991) (similar); 9 *Oxford English Dictionary* 1070 (2d ed. 1989) (similar).

Moreover, the instruction itself gives a definition of the phrase. The jury was told that "everything relating to human affairs, and depending on moral evidence, is open to some possible or imaginary doubt"—in other words, that absolute certainty is unattainable in matters relating to human affairs. Moral evidence, in this sentence, can only mean empirical

evidence offered to prove such matters—the proof introduced at trial.

This conclusion is reinforced by other instructions given in Sandoval's case. The judge informed the jurors that their duty was "to determine the facts of the case from the evidence received in the trial and not from any other source." The judge continued: "Evidence consists of testimony of witnesses, writings, material objects, or anything presented to the senses and offered to prove the existence or non-existence of a fact." The judge also told the jurors that "you must not be influenced by pity for a defendant or by prejudice against him," and that "[y]ou must not be swayed by mere sentiment, conjecture, sympathy, passion, prejudice, public opinion or public feeling." These instructions correctly pointed the jurors' attention to the facts of the case before them, not (as Sandoval contends) the ethics or morality of Sandoval's criminal acts. Accordingly, we find the reference to moral evidence unproblematic.

We are somewhat more concerned with Sandoval's argument that the phrase "moral certainty" has lost its historical meaning, and that a modern jury would understand it to allow conviction on proof that does not meet the beyond a reasonable doubt standard. Words and phrases can change meaning over time: a passage generally understood in 1850 may be incomprehensible or confusing to a modern juror. And although some contemporary dictionaries contain definitions of moral certainty similar to the 19th century understanding of the phrase, see *Webster's Third New International Dictionary* 1468 (unabridged 1981) ("virtual rather than actual, immediate, or completely demonstrable"); 9 *Oxford English Dictionary*, supra, at 1070 ("a degree of probability so great as to admit of no reasonable doubt"), we are willing to accept Sandoval's premise that "moral certainty," standing alone, might not be recognized by modern jurors as a synonym for "proof beyond a reasonable doubt." But it does not necessarily follow that the California instruction is unconstitutional. . . .

. . . [T]he moral certainty language cannot be sequestered from its surroundings. In the *Cage* instruction, the jurors were simply told that they had to be morally certain of the defendant's guilt; there was nothing else in the instruction to lend meaning to the phrase. Not so here. The jury in Sandoval's case was told that a reasonable doubt is "that state of the case which, after the entire comparison and consideration of all the evidence, leaves the minds of the jurors in that condition that they cannot say they feel an abiding conviction, to a moral certainty, of the truth of the charge." The instruction thus explicitly told the jurors that their conclusion had to be based on the evidence in the case. Other instructions reinforced this message. The jury was told "to determine the facts of the case from the evidence received in the trial and not from any other source." The judge continued that "you must not be influenced by pity for a defendant or by prejudice against him. . . . You must not be swayed by mere sentiment, conjecture, sympathy, passion, prejudice, public opinion or public feeling." Accordingly, there is no reasonable likelihood that the jury would have understood moral certainty to be disassociated from the evidence in the case.

We do not think it reasonably likely that the jury understood the words moral certainty either as suggesting a standard of proof lower than due process requires or as allowing conviction on factors other than the government's proof. At the same time, however, we do not condone the use of the phrase. As modern dictionary definitions of moral certainty attest, the common meaning of the phrase has changed since it was used in the *Webster* instruction, and it may continue to do so to the point that it conflicts with the *Winship* standard. Indeed, the definitions of reasonable doubt most widely used in the federal courts do not contain any reference to moral certainty. See Federal Judicial Center, *Pattern Criminal Jury Instructions* 28 (1988); 1 E. Devitt & C. Blackmar, *Federal Jury Practice and Instructions* § 11.14 (3d ed. 1977). But we have no supervisory power over the state courts, and in the context of the instructions as a whole we cannot say that the use of the phrase rendered the instruction given in Sandoval's case unconstitutional.

Finally, Sandoval objects to the portion of the charge in which the judge instructed the jury that a reasonable doubt is "not a mere possible doubt." The *Cage* instruction included an almost identical reference to "not a mere possible doubt," but we did not intimate that there was anything wrong with that part of the charge. That is because "[a] 'reasonable doubt,'

at a minimum, is one based upon 'reason.' " *Jackson v. Virginia,* supra, at 317. A fanciful doubt is not a reasonable doubt. As Sandoval's defense attorney told the jury: "[A]nything can be possible. . . . [A] planet could be made out of blue cheese. But that's really not in the realm of what we're talking about." Sandoval (excerpt from closing argument). That this is the sense in which the instruction uses "possible" is made clear from the final phase of the sentence, which notes that everything "is open to some possible or imaginary doubt." We therefore reject Sandoval's challenge to this portion of the instruction as well.

[The opinion in *Victor v. Nebraska* that appears at this point is omitted from this excerpt.]

The Due Process Clause requires the government to prove a criminal defendant's guilt beyond a reasonable doubt, and trial courts must avoid defining reasonable doubt so as to lead the jury to convict on a lesser showing than due process requires. In these cases, however, we conclude that "taken as a whole, the instructions correctly conveyed the concept of reasonable doubt to the jury." *Holland v. United States,* 348 U.S., at 140. There is no reasonable likelihood that the jurors who determined petitioners' guilt applied the instructions in a way that violated the Constitution. The judgments in both cases are accordingly Affirmed.

CONCURRING OPINION

Justice Kennedy, concurring.

It was commendable for Chief Justice Shaw to pen an instruction that survived more than a century, but, as the Court makes clear, what once might have made sense to jurors has long since become archaic. In fact, some of the phrases here in question confuse far more than they clarify.

Though the reference to "moral certainty" is not much better, California's use of "moral evidence" is the most troubling, and to me seems quite indefensible. The derivation of the phrase is explained in the Court's opinion, but even with this help the term is a puzzle. And for jurors who have not had the benefit of the Court's research, the words will do nothing but baffle.

I agree that use of "moral evidence" in the California formulation is not fatal to the instruction here. I cannot understand, however, why such an unruly term should be used at all when jurors are asked to perform a task that can be of great difficulty even when instructions are altogether clear. The inclusion of words so malleable, because so obscure, might in other circumstances have put the whole instruction at risk.

With this observation, I concur in full in the opinion of the Court.

Justice Ginsburg, concurring in part and concurring in the judgment.

. . .

. . . While judges and lawyers are familiar with the reasonable doubt standard, the words "beyond a reasonable doubt" are not self-defining for jurors. Several studies of jury behavior have concluded that "jurors are often confused about the meaning of reasonable doubt," when that term is left undefined. See Note, Defining Reasonable Doubt, 90 *Colum. L. Rev.* 1716, 1723 (1990) (citing studies). Thus, even if definitions of reasonable doubt are necessarily imperfect, the alternative—refusing to define the concept at all—is not obviously preferable. Cf. Newman, supra, at ("I find it rather unsettling that we are using a formulation that we believe will become less clear the more we explain it.").

Fortunately, the choice need not be one between two kinds of potential juror confusion—on one hand, the confusion that may be caused by leaving "reasonable doubt" undefined, and on the other, the confusion that might be induced by the anachronism of "moral certainty," the misplaced analogy of "hesitation to act," or the circularity of "doubt that is reasonable." The Federal Judicial Center has proposed a definition of reasonable doubt that is clear, straightforward, and accurate. That instruction reads:

> "[T]he government has the burden of proving the defendant guilty beyond a reasonable doubt. Some of you may have served as jurors in civil cases, where you were told that it is only necessary to prove that a fact is more likely true than not true. In criminal cases, the government's proof must be more powerful than that. It must be beyond a reasonable doubt.
>
> "Proof beyond a reasonable doubt is proof that leaves you firmly convinced of the defendant's guilt. There are very few things in this

world that we know with absolute certainty, and in criminal cases the law does not require proof that overcomes every possible doubt. If, based on your consideration of the evidence, you are firmly convinced that the defendant is guilty of the crime charged, you must find him guilty. If on the other hand, you think there is a real possibility that he is not guilty, you must give him the benefit of the doubt and find him not guilty." Federal Judicial Center, *Pattern Criminal Jury Instructions* 17–18 (1987) (instruction 21).

This instruction plainly informs the jurors that the prosecution must prove its case by more than a mere preponderance of the evidence, yet not necessarily to an absolute certainty. The "firmly convinced" standard for conviction, repeated for emphasis, is further enhanced by the juxtaposed prescription that the jury must acquit if there is a "real possibility" that the defendant is innocent. This model instruction surpasses others I have seen in stating the reasonable doubt standard succinctly and comprehensibly.

. . .

CONCURRING
AND DISSENTING OPINION

Justice Blackmun, with whom Justice Souter joins, concurring in part and dissenting in part.

. . .

Our democracy rests in no small part on our faith in the ability of the criminal justice system to separate those who are guilty from those who are not. This is a faith which springs fundamentally from the requirement that unless guilt is established beyond all reasonable doubt, the accused shall go free. It was not until 1970, however, in *In re Winship*, 397 U.S. 358, that the Court finally and explicitly held that "the Due Process Clause protects the accused against conviction except upon proof beyond a reasonable doubt of every fact necessary to constitute the crime with which he is charged." In *Winship*, the Court recounted the long history of the reasonable doubt standard, noting that it "dates at least from our early years as a Nation." The Court explained that any "society that values the good name and freedom of every individual should not condemn a man for commission of a crime when there is a reasonable doubt about his guilt."

Despite the inherent appeal of the reasonable-doubt standard, it provides protection to the innocent only to the extent that the standard, in reality, is an enforceable rule of law. To be a meaningful safeguard, the reasonable-doubt standard must have a tangible meaning that is capable of being understood by those who are required to apply it. It must be stated accurately and with the precision owed to those whose liberty or life is at risk. Because of the extraordinarily high stakes in criminal trials, "[i]t is critical that the moral force of the criminal law not be diluted by a standard of proof that leaves people in doubt whether innocent men are being condemned."

. . .

CASE DISCUSSION

Consider the definitions of *reasonable doubt* given in the opinion. Do they clarify what it means for you? Do you agree with Justice Ginsburg that the committee of the Judicial Conference of the United States provides the best definition? Would you require courts to define the term? Or would you do as some courts do and allow (or require) juries to define the term for themselves? Defend your answer.

D e c i s i o n   P o i n t

At Werbrouck's trial for violating federal gambling laws, the government proved the following:

1. Werbrouck owned and operated the Holiday Inn Motel and the adjoining Lincoln Highway Inn Restaurant in South Bend, Indiana.

2. Werbrouck moved out of his personal room at the Holiday Inn to allow a gambling casino to move in.

3. He permitted certain motel rooms to be physically altered for gambling purposes, including the building of partition walls and the installation of a steel door, cameras, monitors, and electronically controlled door locks.

4. Werbrouck charged no rent for the motel casino rooms and regularly provided customers free food and drinks from his adjoining restaurant.

5. He held keys to the electronically controlled doors and at times admitted persons to the rooms.

6. Werbrouck was observed in the gambling casino.

Werbrouck claimed that this was insufficient evidence to prove beyond a reasonable doubt and establish his involvement with the gambling business either as a principal or as an aider and abettor. Did the preceding facts constitute proof beyond a reasonable doubt? The federal court of appeals held that the "jury and trial court could plainly have concluded that the defendant was guilty beyond a reasonable doubt."[90]

Prosecutors and defense counsel may make opening statements—that is, address the jury before they present their evidence. Prosecutors make their opening statements first; defense counsel address the jury either immediately after the prosecutor's opening statement or, in a few jurisdictions, following the presentation of the state's case. The opening statements have a narrow scope: to outline the case that the two sides hope to prove, not to prove the case. Proving the case falls to the presentation-of-evidence phase of the criminal trial. In fact, it is unprofessional for either side to refer to any evidence in which the attorneys do not have a good faith belief in both competency and admissibility in court. It is rare for them to do so, but appeals courts have occasionally reversed when prosecutors have referred to points they intend to prove with evidence they know is inadmissible, incompetent, or both.[91]

The prosecution carries the burden of proof in criminal prosecution; the defense need only raise a reasonable doubt about the proof in order to gain an acquittal. Hence, the prosecution presents its case-in-chief first. In presenting its case, the rules of evidence restrict what evidence the state may use, mainly excluding illegally obtained testimony and physical evidence and most hearsay. The prosecution must prove every element in the case, but the defense frequently **stipulates** (agrees not to contest) some material facts, particularly those which might prejudice the defendant's case — detailed photographs and descriptions of a brutally murdered victim, for example. The prosecution can decline a stipulation. Most courts do not compel the prosecution to accept stipulations because to do so might weaken the force, persuasiveness, and coherence of the prosecution's case.[92]

The state ordinarily presents all the available eyewitnesses to the crime — that is, the *res gestae* witnesses. In some instances, if the prosecution does not call a material witness, particularly a victim, the defense can ask for a **missing witness instruction,** an instruction to the effect that jurors can infer that the witness's testimony would have been unfavorable to the prosecution. The prosecution can ask the court to inform the jury that a key witness is unavailable and not to draw negative inferences from the failure to testify. Prosecutors may decide not to call witnesses such as spouses, priests, and doctors whom they know will claim a valid privilege; doing so may result in reversible error.[93]

The Sixth Amendment confrontation clause includes the right to cross-examine the prosecution's witnesses. In *Smith v. Illinois*, the prosecution's key witness, an informant, testified that he bought heroin from Smith; the trial court allowed the informant to conceal his real name and address and to use an alias. The U.S. Supreme Court ruled that this violated Smith's right to confrontation:

> [W]hen the credibility of a witness is at issue, the very starting point in "exposing falsehood and bringing out the truth" through cross-examination must necessarily be to ask the witness who he is and where he lives. The witness'[s] name and address open countless avenues of in-court examination and out-of-doors investigation. . . . It is of the essence of a fair trial that reasonable latitude be given to the cross-examiner, even though he is unable to state to the court what facts a reasonable cross-examination might develop. . . . To say that prejudice can be established only by showing that the cross-examination, if pursued, would necessarily have brought out facts tending to discredit testimony in chief, is to deny a substantial right and withdraw one of the safeguards essential to a fair trial.[94]

Only compelling reasons can limit the defendant's right to cross-examine witnesses.[95]

The confrontation clause also restricts the prosecution's use of **hearsay testimony** — out-of-court statements offered to prove the truth of the statements. Hearsay violates the confrontation clause because defendants cannot ferret out the truth through the adversary process unless the defense can cross-examine the witnesses against them. Therefore, the jury cannot have an adequate basis for fact-finding.

The confrontation clause does not absolutely bar hearsay testimony. The prosecution can introduce hearsay if it meets two tests:

1. It demonstrates the witness's unavailability and, hence, the necessity to use out-of-court statements.

2. It shows that the state obtained the evidence under circumstances that clearly establish its reliability.

In *Ohio v. Roberts*, the majority of the Supreme Court found that the state satisfied the tests under these circumstances:

1. The witness's mother said the witness, her daughter, left home, saying she was going to Tucson, two years earlier.
2. Shortly thereafter, a San Francisco social worker contacted the mother concerning a welfare claim her daughter filed there.
3. The mother was able to reach her daughter once, by phone.
4. When the daughter called a few months prior to the trial, she told her mother she was traveling but did not reveal her whereabouts.

The dissent argued that relying solely on the parents was not sufficient; the prosecution had the burden to go out and find the witness.[96]

The Sixth Amendment guarantees the defendant's right "to have compulsory process for obtaining witnesses in [his or her] . . . favor. . . ." This means that defendants can compel witnesses to come to court to testify for them. Most states provide indigent defendants with process without charge. Some states permit prescribed numbers of such process without showing cause. Others require that defendants demonstrate that witnesses have material, relevant, and useful evidence. Most states do not provide compulsory process without charge for evidence that merely corroborates or adds to evidence already available. Furthermore, most states require that defendants state in detail precisely why they need the evidence.

The Fifth Amendment provides that "no person . . . shall be compelled in any criminal case to be a witness against himself. . . ." This means that the state cannot call defendants to the witness stand in criminal trials. It also prohibits the prosecution from commenting on defendants' refusal to testify; it even entitles defendants to ask judges to instruct juries not to infer guilt from defendants' silence. However, if defendants decide to take the stand in order to tell their side of the story, the prosecution can cross-examine defendants as they would any other witness.

The defense need not present a case; cross-examining the prosecution's witnesses alone may raise a reasonable doubt about the proof against the defendant. Or defendants may call their own witnesses to rebut the prosecution's witnesses or to raise a reasonable doubt about their guilt—to establish alibis, for example. Defendants may also have affirmative defenses that negate their criminal liability: self-defense, insanity, duress, and entrapment. They may have evidence that reduces the grade of the offense, such as provocation to reduce murder to manslaughter or diminished capacity to reduce first-degree murder to second-degree murder. The prosecution, of course, has the right to cross-examine defense witnesses and otherwise to challenge the defenses that defendants raise.

At the end of the presentation of the evidence, both the state and the defense make their **closing arguments.** Prosecutors close first, the defense follows, and then prosecution rebuts. Prosecutors cannot waive their right to make a closing argument and save their remarks for rebuttal. Waiving the right to make a closing argument automatically bars prosecution rebuttal. Furthermore, prosecutors cannot raise "new" matters in rebuttal: they must restrict rebuttal to matters introduced in either their or the defense's closing argument. Fairness dictates this procedure; the defense should hear all the arguments in favor of conviction before responding to them.

Formally, prosecutors have the duty not only to convict criminals, but also to seek justice. The American Bar Association Standard for Criminal Justice includes the following guidelines for prosecutors. It is improper to

1. Misstate intentionally the evidence or mislead the jury

2. Refer to evidence excluded or not introduced at trial

3. Express personal belief or opinion about the truth or falsity of the evidence or the defendant's guilt

4. Engage in argument that diverts jurors' attention by injecting issues beyond the case or predicting consequences of the jury's verdict

5. Make arguments calculated to inflame jurors' passions and prejudices[97]

Violating these standards rarely results in reversal. "If every remark made by counsel outside of the testimony were grounds for a reversal, comparatively few verdicts would stand, since in the ardor of advocacy, and in the excitement of the trial, even the most experienced counsel are occasionally carried away by this temptation."[98]

When determining whether to reverse convictions based on improper closing arguments, appellate courts consider whether:

1. Defense counsel invited or provoked the remarks.

2. Defense counsel made timely objection to the remarks.

3. The trial judge took corrective action, such as instructing the jury to disregard the remarks.

4. The comments were brief and isolated in an otherwise proper argument.

5. Other errors occurred during the trial.

6. The evidence of guilt was overwhelming.[99]

Appellate courts, although rarely reversing convictions for them, frequently express their displeasure with prosecutors' improper remarks during closing arguments. In Minnesota, the state's intermediate appeals court warned that if prosecutors persisted in ignoring the standards for proper arguments, the court was prepared to reverse convictions to control their excesses.[100]

D e c i s i o n   P o i n t

Bowen was convicted of raping and murdering a twelve-year-old girl. The prosecutor, in the course of the closing statement, made several comments focusing on the accused: "And now we come up here with this idea that a man . . . is subject to be rehabilitated and released back into society. Yeah, I guess he can be rehabilitated. Hitler could have been. I believe in about six or eight months if I'd had him chained to a wall and talked to him and beat him on one side of the head for a while with a stick telling him you believe this don't you then beat him on the other side with a stick telling him you believe that don't you I believe I could have rehabilitated Hitler." The prosecutor went on to call Bowen "a product of the devil," a "liar," who was "no better than a beast." And, "You know for a criminal to go without proper punishment is a disgrace to the society we live in and it's shown to us every day by the fruits that we reap from day to day in our society when we have the bloody deeds such as this occur."

Were the prosecutor's remarks improper? Should Bowen's conviction be vacated? The circuit court of appeals affirmed the conviction. It conceded that the remarks were improper but found "no reasonable probability that, absent the improper statements of opinion, Bowen would not have been sentenced to death."[101]

———————————————■□———————————————

The American Bar Association places on defense counsel restraints similar to those imposed on prosecutors in closing arguments. However, defense closing statements do not raise concerns, because appellate review rarely occurs. If juries acquit defendants, the state cannot appeal because doing so would put defendants in double jeopardy under the Fifth and Fourteenth Amendments; if the defense appeals, then only prosecution errors are at issue. Of course, defense closing arguments may neutralize otherwise improper closing remarks made by the prosecution, if the defense invited or provoked the prosecution's remarks.

Jury Instructions

Before jurors begin their deliberations, judges "instruct" them about the law and how they should apply it. The principal matters in the jury instructions include the following:

1. The respective roles of the judge to decide the law and the jury to decide the facts
2. The principle that defendants are presumed innocent until proven guilty
3. The principle that the state bears the burden of proving guilt beyond a reasonable doubt
4. The definition of all the elements of the crime with which the defendant is charged
5. Jury room procedures

Both prosecution and defense submit requested instructions to the judge prior to jury instruction; they may object to the judge's refusal to give the requested instruction and frequently base appeals on such failure. A number of jurisdictions rely on **pattern instructions**—published standard instructions for matters relevant to most cases. Supporters praise pattern instructions' clarity, accuracy, impartiality, and efficiency; critics call them too abstract to aid jurors. Studies indicate that jurors understand only about half the contents of judges' instructions to them, whether pattern or individually crafted.[102]

The judge **sequesters the jury**—orders them to retire to a separate room under supervision and without interruption to deliberate together until they reach a verdict. The jurors take the instructions, any exhibits received in evidence, and a list of the charges against the defendant with them to the jury room. During the course of their deliberations, they may request the court for further instruction or information concerning the evidence or any other matter. The court can discharge hung juries—juries unable to reach a verdict after protracted deliberations.

In most cases, the jury returns one of three verdicts:

1. Guilty
2. Not guilty
3. Special, mainly related to insanity or capital punishment

If the jury acquits (issues the not guilty verdict), the defendants' ordeal with the criminal process ends immediately; they are free to go. If the jury convicts, the case continues to **judgment**—the only authentic decision that determines the final outcome of the case. Juries cannot pass judgment on defendants; only the court has the authority to render judgment. Following the court's judgment of guilt or acquittal, the criminal trial ends.

CONVICTION BY GUILTY PLEA

There are two types of guilty plea:

1. Straight pleas

2. Negotiated pleas

Straight guilty pleas are ordinarily made in clear-cut cases, in which proof of guilt is overwhelming. **Negotiated pleas,** or those in which the state makes concessions in return for a guilty plea, appear mainly in large urban courts. They arise when the state has problems with witnesses who are not reliable or the case is otherwise weak, and defendants have a strong defense or can gain the jury's sympathy. Until the 1970s, the negotiated plea, although common, did not receive formal recognition by the courts. Since *Brady v. United States*, decided in 1970, the Supreme Court has recognized and approved its legality.[103]

Defendants plead guilty in exchange for the government's taking one of three actions:

1. Dismissing other charges

2. Recommending a particular sentence or refraining from making a recommendation

3. Agreeing to a specific sentence

Conviction by guilty plea, whether negotiated or straight, promotes several interests, but according to the United States Supreme Court, "the chief virtues of the plea system [are] speed, economy, and finality."

Whatever might be the situation in an ideal world, the fact is that the guilty plea and the often concomitant plea bargain are important components of this country's criminal justice system. Properly administered, they can benefit all concerned. The defendant avoids extended pretrial incarceration and the anxieties and uncertainties of a trial; he gains a speedy disposition of his case, the chance to acknowledge his guilt, and a prompt start in realizing whatever potential there may be for rehabilitation. Judges and prosecutors conserve vital and scarce resources. The public is protected from the risks posed by those charged with criminal offense who are at large on bail while awaiting completion of criminal proceedings.[104]

The arguments for and against conviction by plea are heated, complex, and by no means empirically resolved. Some say that negotiation better serves the search for truth and factual accuracy; others argue that the adversary process best serves the ends of justice. Some maintain that guilty pleas save time; others contend that plea negotiations more than make up for time saved in trials. Some urge that the criminal justice system would collapse under its own weight if only a few of the now vast majority of defendants who plead guilty asserted their right to trial; others contend that jurisdictions that prohibit plea bargaining find it makes little difference. Some maintain that the guilty plea intimidates the innocent and emboldens the guilty; others say that the outcomes of convictions by plea and by trial do not materially differ. The public and police officers oppose plea bargaining because they believe that it "lets criminals off." The available empirical data do not resolve these questions. Nevertheless, most of the cases studied adopt the view outlined by the Supreme Court: conviction by plea serves the organizational interest in economy, speed, and finality.[105]

The Guilty Plea and the Constitution

The social scientists and the policy makers have not resolved the empirical and policy issues surrounding conviction by plea; the Supreme Court has settled the question of its legality and constitutionality. The guilty plea, whether or not negotiated, waives three constitutional rights. By pleading guilty, defendants stand as witnesses against themselves, hence putting aside the Fifth Amendment's protection against self-incrimination. Defendants who plead guilty also forego both the right to trial and the right to confront the witnesses against them that the Sixth Amendment guarantees. Hence, to satisfy the Constitution, defendants who plead guilty must waive their Fifth and Sixth Amendment rights—they must plead guilty voluntarily, knowingly, and intelligently. According to the U.S. Supreme Court,

> The criminal justice system enforces a minimum requirement that [a defendant's] plea be the voluntary expression of his own choice. But the plea is more than an admission of past conduct; it is the defendant's consent that judgment of conviction may be entered without a trial—a waiver of his right to trial before a jury or a judge. Waivers of constitutional rights not only must be voluntary but must be knowing, intelligent acts done with sufficient awareness of the relevant circumstances and likely consequences.[106]

Trial judges have a duty to ensure that defendants plead voluntarily, intelligently, and knowingly. The Supreme Court has established the following standard for trial judges' inquiries:

> A plea of guilty entered by one fully aware of the direct consequences, including the actual value of any commitments made to him by the court, prosecutor, or his own counsel, must stand unless induced by threats (or promises to discontinue improper harassment), misrepresentation (including unfulfilled or unfulfillable promises), or perhaps by promises that are by their nature improper as having no prior relationship to the prosecutor's business (e.g. bribes).[107]

The Supreme Court has held that a trial judge's failure to ask a defendant questions concerning his plea constituted reversible error because the trial court accepted the plea "without an affirmative showing that it was intelligent and voluntary." A court cannot presume that defendants waive the three fundamental rights by pleading guilty "from a silent record." All jurisdictions now require that judges inform defendants that by pleading guilty they waive their rights to trial, to confrontation, and not to incriminate themselves.[108]

Furthermore, the Court has ruled that to plead voluntarily, defendants must know "the true nature of the charge[s]" against them. Therefore, when one defendant pleaded guilty to second-degree murder without knowing the elements of the crime, and neither defense counsel nor the trial judge explained to him that second-degree murder required an intent to kill, that defendant's version of what he did negated intent, and the Court ruled that the record did not establish a knowing plea. Most jurisdictions now require that judges determine that guilty pleas rest upon a "factual basis." To determine the factual basis, judges might ask defendants to describe the conduct that led to the charges, ask prosecutor and defense attorneys similar questions, and consult presentence reports.[109]

Negotiated Pleas and the Constitution

Brady v. United States established that negotiated pleas were not *per se* involuntary, but it did not address the variety of situations in which plea negotiations occur and under which they may be voluntary. One problem arises when defendants plead guilty following threats, made during negotiations, that the prosecutor will seek indictment for more serious charges if defendants do not accept a bargain.

A second problem arises when prosecutors or defendants break the bargains they make. For example, after New York indicted Santobello on two felony counts, he pleaded guilty to one lesser included offense in exchange for the prosecutor's agreement not to make a sentence recommendation. At the sentencing hearing, the prosecutor broke his part of the bargain and asked for a maximum sentence. When defense counsel objected that the prosecutor had broken the state's bargain, the judge said the following:

> Mr. Aronstein [defense counsel], I am not at all influenced by what the District Attorney says. . . . It doesn't make a particle of difference what the District Attorney says he will do, or what he doesn't do.
>
> I have here . . . a probation report. I have here a history of a long, serious criminal record. I have a picture of the life history of this man. . . .
>
> He is unamenable to supervision in this community. He is a "professional criminal." . . . Just putting him away is the only means of halting his antisocial activities, and protecting you, your family, me, my family, protecting society. . . . Plain language, put him behind bars.
>
> Under this plea, I can only send him to the New York Correctional Institution for men for one year, which I am hereby doing.

Santobello appealed. Here is the U.S. Supreme Court's ruling:

> This phase of the process of criminal justice and the adjudicative element inherent in accepting a plea of guilty, must be attended by safeguards to insure the defendant what is reasonably due in the circumstances. Those circumstances will vary, but a constant factor is that when the plea rests in any significant degree on a promise or agreement of the prosecutor, so that it can be said to be part of the inducement or consideration, such promise must be fulfilled.[110]

The Supreme Court has also ruled that prosecutors can repudiate agreements if defendants do not keep the promises they make under the agreements. Therefore, when a defendant promised to testify against codefendants as part of a plea bargain and reneged on his promise, the Court held that the prosecutor acted legally in invalidating the agreement and initiating prosecution on the original charge. If courts reject bargains, defendants may withdraw their guilty pleas unless courts inform defendants before they plead that the court may not accept the plea.[111]

Sometimes defendants plead guilty but maintain that they are innocent. Usually, the reason for their plea is that the prosecution has a strong case against them. They have pleaded guilty in exchange for a lesser charge, a recommendation for a less severe sentence, or an agreed sentence because they believe going to trial will result in conviction and a more severe sentence even though they are innocent. In other words, they are what the law calls **factually innocent**—that is, they did not commit the crime—but they are **legally guilty** because enough evidence exists to convict them. The Supreme Court addressed this problem in *North Carolina v. Alford*.

C A S E

Was His Plea Voluntary?

North Carolina v. Alford
400 U.S. 25, 91 S.Ct. 160, 27 L.Ed.2d 162
(1970)

Alford was indicted for the capital offense of first-degree murder. North Carolina law provided for the penalty of life imprisonment when a plea of guilty was accepted to a first-degree murder charge; for the death penalty following a jury verdict of guilty, unless the jury recommended life imprisonment; and for a term of from two to thirty years' imprisonment for second-degree murder. Alford's attorney recommended that Alford plead guilty to second-degree murder, which the prosecutor accepted. Alford pleaded guilty and was sentenced to thirty years in prison. On writ of habeas corpus, the court of appeals found Alford's plea involuntary. On writ of certiorari, *the Supreme Court reversed, holding that the trial judge did not commit constitutional error by accepting the guilty plea. Justice White wrote the opinion of the Court, which Chief Justice Burger and Justices Harlan, Stewart, and Blackmun joined. Justice Black filed a statement concurring in the judgment. Justice Brennan filed a dissenting opinion, which Justices Douglas and Marshall joined.*

FACTS

On December 2, 1963, Alford was indicted for first-degree murder, a capital offense under North Carolina law. The court appointed an attorney to represent him, and this attorney questioned all but one of the various witnesses who appellee said would substantiate his claim of innocence. The witnesses, however, did not support Alford's story but gave statements that strongly indicated his guilt. Faced with strong evidence of guilt and no substantial evidentiary support for the claim of innocence, Alford's attorney recommended that he plead guilty, but left the ultimate decision to Alford himself. The prosecutor agreed to accept a plea of guilty to a charge of second-degree murder, and on December 10, 1963, Alford pleaded guilty to the reduced charge.

Before the plea was finally accepted by the trial court, the court heard the sworn testimony of a police officer who summarized the State's case. Two other witnesses besides Alford were also heard. Although there was no eyewitness to the crime, the testimony indicated that shortly before the killing Alford took his gun from his house, stated his intention to kill the victim and returned home with the declaration that he had carried out the killing. After the summary presentation of the State's case, Alford took the stand and testified that he had not committed the murder but that he was pleading guilty because he faced the threat of the death penalty if he did not do so. In response to the questions of his counsel, he acknowledged that his counsel had informed him of the difference between second- and first-degree murder and of his rights in case he chose to go to trial. The trial court then asked appellee if, in light of his denial of guilt, he still desired to plead guilty to second-degree murder and appellee answered, "Yes, sir. I plead guilty on—from the circumstances that he [Alford's attorney] told me." After eliciting information about Alford's prior criminal record, which was a long one, the trial court sentenced him to 30 years' imprisonment, the maximum penalty for second-degree murder.

After giving his version of the events of the night of the murder, Alford stated: "I pleaded guilty on second degree murder because they said there is too much evidence, but I ain't shot no man, but I take the fault for the other man. We never had an argument in our life and I just pleaded guilty because they said if I didn't they would gas me for it, and that is all."

In response to questions from his attorney, Alford affirmed that he had consulted several times with his attorney and with members of his family and had been informed of his rights if he chose to plead not guilty. Alford then reaffirmed his decision to plead guilty to second-degree murder:

Q: [by Alford's attorney] And you authorized me to tender a plea of guilty to second degree murder before the court?

A: Yes, sir.

Q: And in doing that, you have again affirmed your decision on that point?

A: Well, I'm still pleading that you all got me to plead guilty. I plead the other way, circumstantial evidence; that the jury will prosecute me on—on the second. You told me to plead guilty, right. I don't—I'm not guilty but I plead guilty.

On appeal, a divided panel of the Court of Appeals for the Fourth Circuit reversed on the ground that Alford's guilty plea was made involuntarily.

OPINION

The standard [for determining the validity of a quality plea is] whether the plea represents a voluntary and intelligent choice among the alternative courses of action open to the defendant. Ordinarily, a judgment of conviction resting on a plea of guilty is justified by the defendant's admission that he committed the crime charged against him and his consent that judgment be entered without a trial of any kind. The plea usually subsumes both elements, and justifiably so, even though there is no separate, express admission by the defendant that he committed the particular acts claimed to constitute the crime charged in the indictment. Here Alford entered his plea but accompanied it with the statement that he had not shot the victim.

State and lower federal courts are divided upon whether a guilty plea can be accepted when it is accompanied by protestations of innocence and hence contains only a waiver of trial but no admission of guilt. Some courts, giving expression to the principle that "[o]ur law only authorizes a conviction where guilt is shown," require that trial judges reject such pleas. But others have concluded that they should not "force any defense on a defendant in a criminal case," particularly when advancement of the defense might "end in disaster."

While most pleas of guilty consist of both a waiver of trial and an express admission of guilt, the latter element is not a constitutional requisite to the imposition of criminal penalty. An individual accused of crime may voluntarily, knowingly, and understandably consent to the imposition of a prison sentence even if he is unwilling or unable to admit his participation in the acts constituting the crime.

Nor can we perceive any material difference between a plea that refuses to admit commission of the criminal act and a plea containing a protestation of innocence when, as in the instant case, a defendant intelligently concludes that his interests require entry of a guilty plea and the record before the judge contains strong evidence of actual guilt. Here the State had a strong case of first-degree murder against Alford. Whether he realized or disbelieved his guilt, he insisted on his plea because in his view he had absolutely nothing to gain by a trial and much to gain by pleading. Because of the overwhelming evidence against him, a trial was precisely what neither Alford nor his attorney desired. Confronted with the choice between a trial for first-degree murder, on the one hand, and a plea of guilty to second-degree murder, on the other, Alford quite reasonably chose the latter and thereby limited the maximum penalty to a 30-year term. When his plea is viewed in light of the evidence against him, which substantially negated his claim of innocence and which further provided a means by which the judge could test whether the plea was being intelligently entered, its validity cannot be seriously questioned. In view of the strong factual basis for the plea demonstrated by the State and Alford's clearly expressed desire to enter it despite his professed belief in his innocence, we hold that the trial judge did not commit constitutional error in accepting it.

Alford now argues in effect that the State should not have allowed him this choice but should have insisted on proving him guilty of murder in the first degree. The States in their wisdom may take this course by statute or otherwise and may prohibit the practice of accepting pleas to lesser included offenses under any circumstances. But this is not the mandate of the Fourteenth Amendment and the Bill of Rights. The prohibitions against involuntary or unintelligent pleas should not be relaxed, but neither should an exercise in arid logic render those constitutional guarantees counterproductive and put in jeopardy the very human values they were meant to preserve.

The Court of Appeals judgment directing the issuance of the writ of habeas corpus is vacated and the case is remanded to the Court of Appeals for further proceedings consistent with this opinion. It is so ordered.

DISSENT

Justice Brennan, with whom Justice Douglas and Justice Marshall join, dissenting.

The facts set out in the majority opinion demonstrate that Alford was "so gripped by fear of the death penalty" that his decision to plead guilty was not voluntary but was "the product of duress as much so as choice reflecting physical constraint."

CASE DISCUSSION

Did Alford knowingly and voluntarily plead guilty? Consider the dissent's comment that Alford was "so gripped by fear of the death penalty" that his decision was "the product of duress." Can defendants ever plead guilty if they believe they are innocent? Why? Why not?

SUMMARY

Following the preliminary hearing or grand jury review, formal proceedings increasingly focus on procedural regularity and the search for truth through the adversarial process. At the same time, the informal negotiating process continues, furthering the organizational interests in efficiency, harmony, and predictability. Most felony defendants plead guilty or strike plea bargains during this stage in the criminal process. The decisions to proceed to trial, to file pretrial motions, and to enter into plea negotiations all draw upon public resources and result in greater expense to defendants of means, continued deprivations of liberty to poorer defendants, and increasing anxiety to all defendants and their families.

The pretrial motions grew out of the ancient common-law pleadings that severely restricted defendants to pleas of guilty or not guilty, to the court's jurisdiction, to the technical sufficiency of the indictment of double jeopardy and of the statute of limitations. Indictments and informations that form the legal basis for arraignment remain the only government pleadings. Defendants can plead guilty, not guilty, *nolo contendere,* or insanity. The pretrial motions have replaced other pleadings of criminal defendants.

The principal pretrial motions discussed in this chapter have mainly to do with (1) double jeopardy, (2) speedy trial, (3) change of venue, (4) change of judge, and (5) suppression of evidence. The essence of double jeopardy procedural law is that the government should have "one fair shot" at convicting defendants. To allow more threatens interests in finality and timeliness, causes defendants undue anxiety, and subjects both the government and individual defendants to unwarranted expense and other burdens. The right to a speedy trial has ancient roots: in 1187, King Henry II promised his subjects "speedy justice." A speedy trial promotes interests in timeliness and finality and prevents the government from subjecting individual defendants to undue anxiety, expense, and loss of liberty. The motions to change venue and judge mainly relate to balancing the interest in obtaining the correct result by reducing prejudice that might corrupt the truth-finding function against the community interest in trying defendants in the place where they committed their crimes. Finally, the motion to suppress balances the legal interests in obtaining the correct result and maintaining procedural regularity and the societal interests in sanctioning abuse of government power and controlling crime.

Once the parties have resolved the issues raised by pretrial motions, either in formal hearings or informally by plea bargaining, the decision to release defendants or to proceed to the final decision point—determining innocence or guilt—occurs. The determination of guilt can take place either formally in trial or by guilty pleas.

Conviction, particularly by trial, leads to the greatest expenditures of public money and time and to the greatest deprivations to criminal defendants—loss of property, liberty, and occasionally life. Even acquittal does not represent total vindication, and it certainly follows considerable deprivations. Conviction or acquittal may follow the formal public trial that emphasizes adversary fact-finding, procedural regularity, and community participation. Conviction may also ensue from informal plea negotiation or straight guilty pleas. Negotiated pleas can reflect the search for truth through informal fact-gathering, efficiency, predictability, and organizational harmony.

The trial adheres to formal and strictly prescribed procedures to present evidence, challenge it, and assess its truth. Judges preside over trials, and lawyers present the physical evidence and examine the witnesses. Judges decide the law in a case and also the facts in bench trials. Juries decide the facts in jury trials. A jury's guilty or not guilty verdict embodies its decision regarding the truth or falsity of the facts. Jury selection aims to impanel an impartial cross section of the community, although not necessarily a mirror reflection. Juries are biased in favor of older, established elements in the population.

Most convictions do not result from trials. Some defendants enter straight guilty pleas, either because they want to admit their guilt or because the government's case leaves them no alternative. Others plead guilty following plea negotiations. In negotiations, both the government and defendants concede something. Negotiations sometimes arise out of the desire to maintain harmonious relations within the courtroom work group. Sometimes, the weakness of the government's case encourages negotiated pleas. In addition, the pressures of heavy caseloads contribute to bypassing formal proceedings in the name of efficiency and managing scarce resources. Finally, negotiations are more predictable than trials.

The guilty plea depends on defendants' giving up their rights to trial, to confront the witnesses against them, and against self-incrimination. Nevertheless, the U.S. Supreme Court has held plea bargaining constitutional on the ground that defendants can waive their constitutional rights. The Court has also recognized it as a necessity in modern criminal justice in dealing with heavy caseloads.

The trial and guilty plea bring together all the major themes and represent the last decision point in criminal procedure. They constitute the greatest expenditures of public resources and the greatest deprivations to individual defendants. The highest quantum of proof—proof beyond a reasonable doubt—must support the decision to convict. Conviction proceeds along both formal and informal lines. The trial, the negotiated plea, and the straight guilty plea promote the legal interests in obtaining the correct result and procedural regularity and the organizational interests in harmony, efficiency, economy, and predictability. They also reflect the societal interests in controlling both government and crime. Finally, the criminal trial jury represents par excellence the democratic interest in community participation in criminal justice administration.

REVIEW QUESTIONS

1. What are the main differences between grand jury review and preliminary hearings?

2. Describe the principal functions of the preliminary hearing. Which one or ones are most important? Explain.

3. Distinguish between the quantum of proof required to arrest and that required to bind over or indict.

4. Do defendants have a right to a preliminary hearing? Explain.

5. What rules of evidence apply to preliminary hearings?

6. What is the root of the criticism that preliminary hearings are becoming "minitrials"?

7. What interests do preliminary hearings further? Which do they minimize?

8. What interests do grand jury reviews emphasize? Which do they reduce?

9. Should grand jury review be abolished? Give reasons for and against.

10. What are the remedies for improper grand jury proceedings?

11. What predominant interests do pretrial motions promote?

12. Define *double jeopardy* and explain its primary purpose.

13. When does time start to elapse for speedy trial purposes?

14. What elements are taken into account in determining whether to grant a motion to change venue?

15. What is the difference between personal and judicial bias? Which is used to determine whether to grant a change of judge?

16. What is the orthodox rule in deciding the admissibility of evidence?

17. What interest does suppression primarily promote?

18. Compare and contrast the interests promoted in conviction by plea and by trial.

19. What are the arguments against extending the right to jury trial to all criminal cases?

20. What are the arguments for and against twelve-member juries? Six-member juries? Fewer-than-six-member juries?

21. What are the arguments for and against unanimous jury verdicts?

22. Define *jury nullification*. What are the reasons for and against it?

23. Why is the presentation of evidence the high point in the criminal process?

24. What are the main advantages and disadvantages of guilty pleas?

25. Distinguish between straight and negotiated guilty pleas.

26. Why do defendants enter straight guilty pleas?

27. What rights do defendants forfeit when they plead guilty?

28. Can defendants voluntarily plead guilty if they believe they are innocent? Explain.

KEY TERMS

actual prejudice test proof that a defendant cannot get a fair trial.

affirmative defense a defense, such as self-defense or insanity, that requires defendants to present facts in addition to denying the charge.

arraignment the bringing of defendants to court to hear and to plead to criminal charges.

bench trial a trial without a jury.

bind over to send a criminal case on for trial.

challenges for cause removals of prospective jurors upon showing partiality.

charge the grand jury the address of the judge to the grand jury.

closing arguments the final arguments by the prosecution and the defense, given directly to the jury.

collateral estoppel the doctrine that an issue of fact determined in favor of the defendant prohibits the government from retrying the same issue in a later prosecution.

confrontation requirement the Sixth Amendment right of defendants to confront the accusers and witnesses against them.

demand-waiver rule when a delay in trial is measured from the point that a defendant demands a speedy trial.

discovery one party's providing evidence in its possession to the other party.

dismissal with prejudice the termination of a case with the provision that it cannot be prosecuted again.

dismissal without prejudice the termination of a case with the provision that it can be prosecuted again.

dual sovereignty doctrine the principle which holds that a crime arising out of the same facts in one state is not the same crime in another state.

ex parte **proceedings** proceedings in which the defendant is not present or represented.

exculpatory evidence evidence that tends to justify, exclude, or clear a criminal defendant from guilt.

factually innocent defendants who did not commit the crime.

grand jury targets grand jury witnesses who are themselves under investigation.

hand up the indictment to deliver an indictment to the judge.

harmless error an irregularity in proceedings that does not affect the outcome of the case.

hearsay rule the ban on introducing into evidence out-of-court statements to prove the truth of the matter stated.

hearsay testimony evidence not coming from the personal knowledge of witnesses, but from the repetition of what they have heard others say.

hung jury a jury that is unable to reach a verdict after protracted deliberations.

impeach to show that a witness's testimony is not credible.

indictment a formal charging instrument issued by the grand jury.

information a formal charging instrument drawn up by the prosecutor.

interlocutory appeals provisional appeals taken before judgment.

judgment the final outcome of a case.

judicial bias the favoring of a particular legal principle.

jury challenges removals of prospective jurors.

jury instructions a judge's explanation of law to a jury.

jury nullification the jury's authority to reach a not guilty verdict despite proof of guilt.

legally guilty the cases in which the government has proved beyond a reasonable doubt the guilt of defendants.

lesser included offenses crimes composed of some, but not all, of the elements of a more serious crime.

manifest necessity a circumstance that requires the termination of proceedings.

missing witness instruction the instruction that jurors can draw a negative inference from prosecution witnesses' failure to testify.

moral seriousness standard the principle that the Sixth Amendment right to a jury trial extends to morally serious misdemeanors.

negotiated pleas guilty pleas entered in return for concessions from the state.

no-bill grand jury finding of insufficient evidence.

nolo contendere a plea not to contest the indictment.

objective basis the amount and quality of evidence or facts needed to authorize a government invasion.

orthodox rule the principle that courts decide the admissibility of evidence.

pattern instructions published, standard jury instructions.

peremptory challenges removals of jurors without showing cause.

plea a defendant's answer to the government's criminal charge.

prima facie **case** a case with enough evidence to convict unless rebutted.

prior testimony exception the rule that testimony given under oath prior to trial is admissible at trial.

purging the grand jury eliminating prospective grand jurors who have compelling reasons not to serve.

reasonable doubt standard doubt based on facts that would cause a reasonable person to hesitate before making a decision of importance to himself or herself.

reasonable-likelihood-of-prejudice test the determination that circumstances may prevent a fair trial.

res gestae **witness** eyewitness.

sequester the jury put the jury in a room to deliberate without outside interference.

statutes of limitations laws specifying the length of time permitted to lapse between the commission of a crime and the initiation of prosecution.

stipulate agree not to contest.

straight plea a guilty plea without negotiation.

true bill the record of the number of grand jurors voting for indictment.

venue the place where a trial is held.

voir dire the examination of prospective jurors.

Notes

1. *United States v. Udziela*, 671 F.2d 995, 1001 (7th Cir. 1982).

2. Bureau of Justice Statistics, *Report to the Nation on Crime and Justice*, 2d ed. (Washington, DC: Bureau of Justice Statistics, 1988).

3. *Federal Rules of Criminal Procedure*, 5(c) (1987).

4. *Lem Woon v. Oregon*, 229 U.S. 586, 33 S.Ct. 783, 57 L.Ed. 1340 (1913); *Gerstein v. Pugh*, 420 U.S. 103, 95 S.Ct. 854, 43 L.Ed.2d 54 (1975).

5. *Coleman v. Alabama*, 399 U.S. 1, 90 S.Ct. 1999, 26 L.Ed.2d 387 (1970).

6. Rule 5(c).

7. Wayne R. LaFave and Jerold H. Israel, *Criminal Procedure* (St. Paul: West, 1984), 2: 247–48.

8. *United States v. Quinn*, 357 F.Supp. 1348 (N.D.Ga. 1973).

9. LaFave and Israel, *Criminal Procedure*, 249.

10. Ibid., 250–51.

11. *Hawkins v. Superior Court*, 22 Cal.3d 584, 150 Cal.Rptr. 435, 586 P.2d 916 (1978).

12. LaFave and Israel, *Criminal Procedure*, 263–64.

13. *Myers v. Commonwealth*, 363 Mass. 843, 298 N.E.2d 819, 824 (1973).

14. Thomas Y. Davies, "Affirmed: A Study of Criminal Appeals and Decision-Making Norms in a California Court of Appeal," *American Bar Foundation Research Journal* (1982): 548–52.

15. *McDonald v. District Court*, 195 Colo. 159, 576 P.2d 169 (1978).

16. LaFave and Israel, *Criminal Procedure*, 265.

17. Ibid., 266.

18. *Federal Rules of Criminal Procedure*, 21 (1987).

19. *Goldsby v. United States*, 160 U.S. 70, 16 S.Ct. 216, 40 L.Ed. 343 (1895).

20. 107 Ariz. 93, 482 P.2d 460 (1971).

21. 66 Cal.2d 867, 59 Cal.Rptr. 440, 428 P.2d 304 (1967).

22. LaFave and Israel, *Criminal Procedure*, 434, 239–40.

23. Ibid., 240–41.

24. Anthony Amsterdam, *Trial Manual for the Defense of Criminal Cases*, 4th ed. (Philadelphia: American Law Institute, 1984), 1: 152–53.

25. *Hearings on Federal Magistrates Act Before Subcommittee on Improvements in Judicial Machinery of Senate Committee on Judiciary*, 89th Cong., 2d Sess., 90th Cong., 1st Sess. (1966–67), 133.

26. 399 U.S. 1, 9, 90 S.Ct. 1999, 2003, 26 L.Ed.2d 387 (1970).

27. LaFave and Israel, *Criminal Procedure*, 241–42.

28. *Coleman v. Alabama*, 399 U.S. 1, 90 S.Ct. 1999, 26 L.Ed.2d 387 (1970).

29. *California v. Green*, 399 U.S. 149, 90 S.Ct. 1930, 26 L.Ed.2d 489 (1970).

30. *Mechler v. Procunier*, 754 F.2d 1294 (5th Cir. 1985).

31. *Hurtado v. California*, 110 U.S. 516, 4 S.Ct. 111, 28 L.Ed. 232 (1884).

32. LaFave and Israel, *Criminal Procedure*, 280–81.

33. This description is based on *Federal Rules of Criminal Procedure*, 6 (1987), and Marvin E. Frankel and

Gary F. Naftalis, *The Grand Jury: An Institution on Trial* (New York: Hill and Wang, 1977), Chap. 4.

34. *Hobby v. United States*, 468 U.S. 339, 344–45, 104 S.Ct. 3093, 3096–97, 82 L.Ed.2d 260 (1984).

35. Conyers Read, ed., *William Lambarde and Local Government* (Ithaca, NY: Cornell University Press, 1962).

36. Conclusions about the early years of the twentieth century rest on Joel Samaha's research in early twentieth-century criminal justice, not yet published. Support for these conclusions is abundant. For a few references, see Maurice Parmelee, *Anthropology and Sociology in Relation to Criminal Procedure* (New York: Macmillan, 1911); National Commission on Law Observance and Law Enforcement (Wickersham Commission), *Report on Prosecution* (Washington, DC: Government Printing Office, 1931); National Advisory Commission on Criminal Justice Standards and Goals, *Courts* (Washington, DC: Government Printing Office, 1973); Note, *Southern Illinois Law Review* (1981): 281, 284.

37. LaFave and Israel, *Criminal Procedure*, 282–83.

38. National Advisory Commission on Criminal Justice Standards and Goals, *Courts*, 75.

39. New York Temporary Commission on the Constitutional Convention, *Individual Liberties* (1967), 117–42; Robert Younger, *The People's Panel* (1967).

40. Kenneth Graham and Leon Letwin, "The Preliminary Hearing in Los Angeles: Some Field Findings and Legal-Policy Questions," *U.C.L.A. Law Review* 18 (1971): 636, 681.

41. *United States v. Vetere*, 663 F.Supp. 381, 386 (S.D.N.Y.1987); *United States v. Udziela*, 671 F.2d 995, 1001 (7th Cir. 1982).

42. *United States v. Griffith*, 756 F.2d 1244, 1249 (6th Cir. 1985).

43. 302 U.S. 319, 58 S.Ct. 149, 82 L.Ed. 288 (1937).

44. *Crist v. Bretz*, 437 U.S. 28, 98 S.Ct. 2156, 57 L.Ed.2d 24 (1978).

45. *United States v. Perez*, 22 U.S. (9 Wheat.) 579, 6 L.Ed. 165 (1824).

46. *Illinois v. Somerville*, 410 U.S. 458, 93 S.Ct. 1066, 35 L.Ed.2d 425 (1973); *Wade v. Hunter*, 336 U.S. 684, 69 S.Ct. 834, 93 L.Ed. 974 (1949).

47. 474 U.S. 82, 106 S.Ct. 433, 88 L.Ed.2d 387 (1985).

48. Ibid.

49. *Ciucci v. Illinois*, 356 U.S. 571, 78 S.Ct. 839, 2 L.Ed.2d 983 (1958).

50. *Klopfer v. North Carolina*, 386 U.S. 213, 87 S.Ct. 988, 18 L.Ed.2d 1 (1967) (speedy trial clause applies to states).

51. *Report to the Nation on Crime and Justice*, 2d ed. (Washington, DC: Bureau of Justice Statistics, 1988), 123.

52. *United States v. Marion*, 404 U.S. 307, 92 S.Ct. 455, 30 L.Ed.2d 468 (1971) (federal speedy trial right attaches at arrest); *Dixon v. State*, 605 P.2d 882 (Alaska 1980) (Alaska speedy trial provision extends to period prior to charge).

53. *Strunk v. United States*, 412 U.S. 434, 93 S.Ct. 2260, 37 L.Ed.2d 56 (1973); Anthony Amsterdam, "Speedy Criminal Trial: Rights and Remedies," *Stanford Law Review* 27 (1975): 525.

54. *Federal Criminal Code and Rules*, 21(a) (1997).

55. 384 U.S. 333, 363, 86 S.Ct. 1507, 1552, 16 L.Ed.2d 600 (1966).

56. 267 Ark. 418, 592 S.W.2d 91 (1979).

57. *Sheppard v. Maxwell*, 384 U.S. 333, 86 S.Ct. 1507, 16 L.Ed.2d 600 (1966); *Nebraska Press Association v. Stuart*, 96 S.Ct. 2791; *Schenck v. United States*, 249 U.S. 47, 39 S.Ct. 247, 63 L.Ed. 470 (1919) (clear and present danger).

58. *Gannett Co. v. DePasquale*, 443 U.S. 368, 99 S.Ct. 2898, 61 L.Ed.2d 608 (1979) (defendant's personal right to a public trial); *Richmond Newspapers v. Virginia*, 448 U.S. 555, 100 S.Ct. 2814, 65 L.Ed.2d 973 (1980) (public's right of access to a criminal trial).

59. *Globe Newspaper Co. v. Superior Court*, 457 U.S. 596, 102 S.Ct. 2613, 73 L.Ed.2d 248 (1982).

60. *Tumey v. Ohio*, 273 U.S. 510, 47 S.Ct. 437, 71 L.Ed. 749 (1927).

61. *Mayberry v. Pennsylvania*, 400 U.S. 455, 91 S.Ct. 499, 27 L.Ed.2d 532 (1971) (defendant repeatedly insulted and vilified trial judge and at conclusion of trial was pronounced guilty of eleven contempts and sentenced to eleven to twenty-two years, judgment of contempt vacated).

62. 404 U.S. 477, 92 S.Ct. 619, 30 L.Ed.2d 618 (1972).

63. 49 N.J. 373, 230 A.2d 489 (1967).

64. James B. Haddad, et al., *Criminal Procedure*, 3d ed. (St. Paul: West, 1987), 970.

65. *Duncan v. Louisiana*, 391 U.S. 145, 88 S.Ct. 1444, 20 L.Ed.2d 491 (1968).

66. Ibid.

67. Ibid.

68. *Baldwin v. New York*, 399 U.S. 66, 90 S.Ct. 1886, 26 L.Ed.2d 437 (1970) (offenses punishable by less than six months' imprisonment are petty offenses); *United States v. Sanchez-Meza*, 547 F.2d 461 (9th Cir. 1976) (conspiring to deceive immigration officials); *United States v. Craner*, 652 F.2d 23 (9th Cir. 1981) (driving while intoxicated); *State v. Superior Court*, 121 Ariz. 174, 589 P.2d 48 (1978) (shoplifting).

69. *Thompson v. Utah*, 170 U.S. 343, 18 S.Ct. 620, 42 L.Ed. 1061 (1898) (requiring twelve-member jury); *Williams v. Florida*, 399 U.S. 78, 90 S.Ct. 1893, 26 L.Ed.2d 446 (1970) (upholding Florida's six-member jury in criminal trials).

70. *Williams v. Florida*, 399 U.S. 78, 90 S.Ct. 1893, 26 L.Ed.2d 446 (1970).

71. For references to several social science studies that support the twelve-member jury, see LaFave and Israel, *Criminal Procedure*, 2: 695, n. 97; 696, n. 57 (Zeisel quotation).

72. *Maxwell v. Dow*, 176 U.S. 581, 20 S.Ct. 448, 44 L.Ed. 597 (1900) (unanimous verdict required); *Apodaca v. Oregon*, 406 U.S. 404, 92 S.Ct. 1628, 32 L.Ed.2d 184 (1972) (unanimous verdict not constitutionally required—the quotation is from that opinion).

73. 406 U.S. 356, 92 S.Ct. 1620, 32 L.Ed.2d 152 (1972).

74. LaFave and Israel, *Criminal Procedure*, 698.

75. *Burch v. Louisiana*, 441 U.S. 130, 99 S.Ct. 1623, 60 L.Ed.2d 96 (1979).

76. Quoted in LaFave and Israel, *Criminal Procedure*, 700. *Sparf & Hansen v. United States*, 156 U.S. 51, 15 S.Ct. 273, 39 L.Ed. 343 (1895).

77. *United States v. Dougherty*, 473 F.2d 1113 (D.C.Cir. 1972).

78. 28 U.S.C.A. §§ 1861, 1862.

79. LaFave and Israel, *Criminal Procedure*, 708.

80. Ibid., 708–09.

81. J. Van Dyke, *Jury Selection Procedures* (1977), 140.

82. 409 U.S. 524, 93 S.Ct. 848, 35 L.Ed.2d 46 (1973).

83. 536 F.2d 469 (1st Cir. 1976), cert. denied 429 U.S. 932, 97 S.Ct. 340, 50 L.Ed.2d 302 (1976); *Turner v. Murray*, 476 U.S. 28, 106 S.Ct. 1683, 90 L.Ed.2d 27 (1986) (questioning about racial bias in capital cases involving black defendants and white victims).

84. *United States v. Dennis*, 183 F.2d 201 (2d Cir. 1950), affirmed 341 U.S. 494, 71 S.Ct. 857, 95 L.Ed. 1137 (1951).

85. *United States ex rel. Latimore v. Sielaff*, 561 F.2d 691 (7th Cir. 1977), cert. denied 434 U.S. 1076, 98 S.Ct. 1266, 55 L.Ed.2d 782 (1978).

86. *Illinois v. Allen*, 397 U.S. 337, 90 S.Ct. 1057, 25 L.Ed.2d 353 (1970).

87. *Holbrook v. Flynn*, 475 U.S. 560, 106 S.Ct. 1340, 89 L.Ed.2d 525 (1986) (defendant is brought to trial under guard); *Estelle v. Williams*, 425 U.S. 501, 96 S.Ct. 1691, 48 L.Ed.2d 126 (1976) (appearing in prison garb prejudiced defendant).

88. 397 U.S. 358, 90 S.Ct. 1068, 25 L.Ed.2d 368 (1970).

89. *United States v. Jones*, 663 F.2d 567 (5th Cir. 1981) (definition 1); *United States v. DeVincent*, 632 F.2d 147 (1st Cir. 1980) (definition 2); *Tsoumas v. New Hampshire*, 611 F.2d 412 (1st Cir. 1980) (definition 3); *State v. Butler*, 277 S.C. 452, 290 S.E.2d 1 (1982) (definition 4); *Commonwealth v. Conceicao*, 388 Mass. 255, 446 N.E.2d 383 (1983) (definition 5); *State v. Moss*, 189 Conn. 364, 456 A.2d 274 (1983) (definition-by-reversal 1); *United States v. Regilio*, 669 F.2d 1169 (7th Cir. 1981) (definition-by-reversal 2).

90. *United States v. Werbrouck*, 589 F.2d 273 (7th Cir. 1978).

91. LaFave and Israel, *Criminal Procedure*, 3: 12.

92. *People v. McClellan*, 71 Cal.2d 793, 80 Cal.Rptr. 31, 457 P.2d 871 (1969).

93. *Bowles v. United States*, 439 F.2d 536 (D.C. Cir. 1970).

94. 390 U.S. 129, 88 S.Ct. 748, 19 L.Ed.2d 956 (1968).

95. LaFave and Israel, *Criminal Procedure*, 3: 15.

96. 448 U.S. 56, 100 S.Ct. 2531, 65 L.Ed.2d 597 (1980).

97. American Bar Association, *Standards for Criminal Justice*, 2d ed. (1980), § 3.5.

98. *Dunlop v. United States*, 165 U.S. 486, 17 S.Ct. 375, 41 L.Ed. 799 (1897).

99. LaFave and Israel, *Criminal Procedure*, 35.

100. Ibid., 3: 36.

101. Citation not available.

102. LaFave and Israel, *Criminal Procedure*, 39–40.

103. 397 U.S. 742, 90 S.Ct. 1463, 25 L.Ed.2d 747 (1970).

104. *Blackledge v. Allison*, 431 U.S. 63, 71, 97 S.Ct. 1621, 1627, 52 L.Ed.2d 136 (1977).

105. The guilty plea literature is vast. Nothing produced in the last twenty years surpasses the selections in *Law and Society Review* 13 (1979, no. 2), a special issue devoted entirely to some of the plea bargaining

issues that contains some of the best social science research and public policy debate surrounding it.

106. *Brady v. United States,* 397 U.S. 742, 748, 90 S.Ct. 1463, 1469, 25 L.Ed.2d 747 (1970).

107. *Brady v. United States,* 397 U.S. 742, 90 S.Ct. 1463, 25 L.Ed.2d 747 (1970).

108. *Boykin v. Alabama,* 395 U.S. 238, 89 S.Ct. 1709, 23 L.Ed.2d 274 (1969).

109. *North Carolina v. Alford,* 400 U.S. 25, 91 S.Ct. 160, 27 L.Ed.2d 162 (1970); *Federal Criminal Code and Rules, 1988* (St. Paul: West, 1988), Rule 11(f) and Commentary, 45.

110. *Santobello v. New York,* 404 U.S. 257, 92 S.Ct. 495, 30 L.Ed.2d 427 (1971).

111. *Ricketts v. Adamson,* 483 U.S. 1, 107 S.Ct. 2680, 97 L.Ed.2d 1 (1987) (defendant's broken promise).

CHAPTER THIRTEEN

After Conviction

CHAPTER OUTLINE

CHAPTER MAIN POINTS

1. A firm distinction exists between the trial stage and the sentencing stage of the criminal process.

2. Defendants enjoy fewer procedural rights at the sentencing stage than during trial.

3. Sentencing reform a century ago meant shifting from fixed prison sentences to indeterminate sentences.

4. Increasingly, sentencing today is fixed according to either sentencing guidelines or mandatory minimum sentence statutes.

5. Defendants have a right to a lawyer at the sentencing stage.

6. The cruel-and-unusual-punishment clause limits legislatures in prescribing sentences and judges in imposing them.

7. Death penalty cases require closer scrutiny both in the crimes to which the death penalty applies and in the procedures for and review of its imposition.

8. The Supreme Court has held that it is not always cruel and unusual punishment to impose the death penalty for murder.

9. No constitutional right to appeal exists, but both federal and state statutes have created the right to appeal.

10. Most states and the federal government allow automatic appeals to intermediate courts and then discretionary appeals to the state supreme court and to the United States Supreme Court.

11. The principles of mootness, raise or waive, and plain error govern the scope of appellate review.

12. Appeals are direct attacks on convictions; *habeas corpus* attacks convictions indirectly or collaterally.

13. *Habeas corpus* challenges the lawfulness of detention, not the merits of guilt or innocence.

14. The Supreme Court has increasingly limited *habeas corpus* proceedings of state prisoners in federal courts.

Should Her Sentence Be Reduced?

Ms. Rivera transported about one pound of cocaine from New York to Providence with intent to distribute it, in violation of 21 U.S.C. § 841(a)(1), (b)(1)(B). The Sentencing Guidelines provide a sentence of 33 to 41 months' imprisonment for a first-time offender who has engaged in this conduct. Ms. Rivera argued to the district court that it should depart downward from this Guidelines sentence for the following reasons: she has three small children, ages three, five, and six, who need a mother's care. She lives solely on welfare, receiving no financial aid from her former husband. She has virtually no contact with any other family member (except for a sister, with five children, also on welfare). She has never before engaged in any criminal activity. She committed this single offense because of an unwise wish to obtain money for Christmas presents for her children.

AFTER CONVICTION

The trial represents the high point of formal criminal procedure. At the trial, criminal defendants have the most procedural rights. The Fifth, Sixth, and Fourteenth Amendments all apply in the criminal trial to their fullest extent. After conviction, procedural rights diminish considerably, although they do not disappear entirely. Defendants have some procedural rights at sentencing. The Constitution does not require states to provide appeals, but once they are granted, the state must follow minimal constitutional standards in the appeal process. The Constitution does require both the federal and state governments to justify in court the detention and incarceration of prisoners. *Habeas corpus* proceedings provide the vehicle for testing the lawfulness of detention and imprisonment.

SENTENCING

For more than a thousand years, policy makers have debated whether to fit sentences to the crime or to tailor sentences to suit the criminal. *Determinate* or fixed sentencing (fitting sentences to the crime) places most of the sentencing authority in the hands of legislatures. *Indeterminate* sentencing (tailoring punishment to suit the criminal) relies heavily on the discretion of judges and parole boards in exercising the sentencing authority. As early as 700 A.D., the Roman Catholic Church's penitential books reveal a tension between prescribing penance strictly according to the sin and tailoring it to suit individual sinners. The concern over judicial discretion in sentencing also has an ancient heritage. Arguments abound in the history of sentencing not only over what sentences to impose, but also over who should impose them. These early arguments regarding sinners and penance and judges and punishment strikingly resemble current thought about the proper authority, aims, and types of criminal sentencing.[1]

Fixed sentencing tailored to fit the crime prevailed from the seventeenth century until the latter part of the nineteenth century. Then a shift toward indeterminate sentences tailored to fit individual criminals began. However, neither fixed nor indeterminate sentences have ever totally dominated criminal sentencing. The tension between the need for certainty and flexibility has always required both a measure of predictability in punishment and a degree of flexibility toward individual needs in sentencing. Shifting ideological commitments, as well as other informed influences on sentencing, ensure that neither fixed nor indeterminate sentences will ever exclusively prevail in sentencing policies and practices.

Following the American Revolution, fixed but relatively moderate penalties became the rule. States abolished the death penalty for many offenses. Rarity of use in practice rendered corporal punishment (whipping), mutilation (cutting off ears and slitting tongues), and shaming (the ducking stool) virtually obsolete. Imprisonment, up to that time used mainly to detain accused persons before trial, became the dominant form of criminal punishment by 1850. Statutes fixed prison terms for most felonies. In practice, liberal use of pardons, early release for "good time," and other devices permitted judges to use informal discretionary judgment in altering formally fixed sentences.[2]

The modern history of sentencing begins around 1870. Ironically, demands for reform at that time were the opposite of those today; they grew out of deep dissatisfaction with legislatively fixed harsh prison sentences. Reformers complained that prisons were nothing more than warehouses for the poor and the undesirable and that harsh prison punishment did not work. Proof of that, the reformers maintained, was the crime rates that continued to grow at unacceptable rates despite harsh, fixed prison sentences. Furthermore, the reformers documented that the prisons were full of recent immigrants and others on the lower rungs of society. Many public officials and concerned citizens agreed. Particularly instrumental in demanding reform were prison administrators and other criminal justice officials. By 1922, all but four states had adopted some form of indeterminate sentencing law.

When the indeterminate sentence became the prevailing practice, administrative sentencing by parole boards and prison officials took precedence over legislative and judicial sentence fixing. At its extreme, judges set no time on sentencing, leaving it wholly to parole boards and correctional officers to determine informally the length of a prisoner's incarceration. More commonly, judges were free to grant probation, suspend sentences in favor of alternatives to incarceration such as community service, or pick confinement times within minimums and maximums prescribed by statutes. Parole boards and corrections officers determined the exact release time.

Indeterminate sentencing remained dominant until the 1970s, when several forces coalesced to oppose it. Prison uprisings, especially at Attica and the Tombs in New York in the late 1960s, dramatically portrayed rehabilitation as little more than rhetoric and prisoners as deeply and dangerously discontented. Individual rights advocates challenged the widespread and unreviewable informal discretionary powers exercised by criminal justice officials in general and judges in particular. Demands for increased formal accountability spread throughout the criminal justice system. Courts required public officials to justify their decisions in writing and empowered defendants to dispute allegations against them at sentencing. The courts required even prisons to publish their rules and grant prisoners the right to challenge rules that they were accused of breaking.

Furthermore, widespread disillusionment with rehabilitation arose during the late 1960s, after it had dominated the rhetoric of penal policy for more than a half century. Several statistical and experimental studies showed a pernicious discrimination in sentencing. In particular, some research strongly suggested that the poor and blacks were sentenced more harshly than whites and middle- and upper-class Americans. Finally, official reports showed steeply rising street-crime rates. The National Research Council created a distinguished panel to review sentencing. It concluded that by the early 1970s, a "remarkable consensus emerged along left and right, law enforcement officials and prisoners groups, reformers and bureaucrats that the indeterminate sentencing era was at its end."[3]

By the late 1970s, the emphasis in crime policy shifted from fairness to crime prevention. Crime prevention was based on incarceration, general deterrence, and retribution. Prevention by rehabilitation was definitely losing ground. Civil libertarians and "law and order" supporters alike called for sentencing practices that would advance swift and certain punishment. They differed only on the length of sentences. To civil libertarians, determinate sentencing meant *short*, fixed sentences; to conservatives, it meant *long*, fixed sentences. Three ideas came to dominate thinking about sentencing:

1. Many offenders deserve severe punishment because they have committed serious crimes.

2. Repeat career offenders require severe punishment to incapacitate them.

3. All crimes deserve some punishment in order to retain the deterrent potency of the criminal law.

According to the National Council on Crime and Delinquency,

> by 1990, the shift in goals of sentencing reform was complete. Virtually all new sentencing law was designed to increase the certainty and length of prison sentences to incapacitate the active criminal and deter the rest.[4]

Harsher penalties accompanied the shift in the philosophy of punishment. Public support for the death penalty grew, the U.S. Supreme Court ruled that the death penalty was not cruel and unusual punishment, courts sentenced more people to death, and the states began to execute criminals. Judges sentenced more people to prison and sentenced them to longer prison terms; by 1990, the United States sentenced more people to prison for longer terms than any other country in the world.

Sentencing Authority

Throughout American history, three institutions have exercised sentencing power—legislatures, courts, and administrative agencies—in varying degrees of formality. In the **legislative sentencing model,** legislatures prescribe specific penalties that judges and parole boards cannot alter. The legislatively fixed model restricts discretion to alter penalties determined in advance of the crime and without regard to the person who committed it. In other words, the punishment fits the crime, not the criminal. Removing discretion from judges and parole boards does not eliminate evils arising from prejudicial laws that criminalize conduct peculiar to certain groups in society, but it does limit the making of criminal law to legislatures.

In the **judicial sentencing model,** judges prescribe sentences within broad formal contours set by legislative acts. Typically, a statute prescribes a range, such as one to ten years, zero to five years, or twenty years to life. Judges then fix the exact time that convicted criminals serve.

In the **administrative sentencing model,** both the legislature and the judge prescribe a wide range of allowable prison times for particular crimes. Administrative agencies, typically parole boards and prison administrators, determine the exact release date. Under this model, administrative agencies have broad discretion to determine how long prisoners serve and under what conditions they can be released.

As models, these sentencing schemes never operate in pure form. At all times in American history, all three sentencing institutions have overlapped considerably; all have exercised wide discretion. For example, plea bargaining has prevented fixing sentencing authority in any of these three. Charge bargaining circumvents legislatively fixed sentences, sentence bargaining avoids judicially fixed sentencing, and both provide means to alter administratively fixed sentences. In general, however, until recent sentencing reforms began to change policy and practice, legislatures set the general range of penalties, judges picked a specific penalty within that range, and parole boards released imprisoned offenders after a time in prison. According to this practice, judges, parole boards, and prison authorities possess considerable discretion in sentencing criminal defendants.

Guidelines and Mandatory Minimum Sentencing

The indeterminate sentence, parole boards, and good time remain a part of the sentencing structure of most states, at least for offenders sentenced before sentencing reforms. However, fixed sentences of some sort are the most rapidly growing type of sentencing in the United States today. Fixed sentencing has taken two primary forms—sentencing guidelines and mandatory minimum prison sentences. The federal government and most states have adopted both types of reforms. Both types of sentences are, at least in theory, based on limiting or even eliminating discretion in sentencing. Both respond to three demands from experts and the public:

1. *Uniformity.* Similar offenses should receive similar punishment.

2. *Certainty and Truth in Sentencing.* Convicted offenders, victims, and the public should know that the sentence imposed is similar to the sentence actually served.

3. *Retribution, Deterrence, Incapacitation.* The rehabilitation of individual offenders is not the primary aim of punishment.

In **sentencing guidelines,** a commission establishes a relatively narrow range of penalties from within which judges are supposed to choose a specific sentence. The seriousness of the crime and the offender's criminal history are the major determinants of the guideline sentence. Sentences are ordinarily either presumptively incarceration or presumptively probation. Judges can depart from the range set in the guidelines, but in typical guidelines jurisdictions they must provide reasons for their departure. Permitting judges to choose within a range without departing from the guidelines builds flexibility into the system, a flexibility that allows for differences in individual cases. Characteristics such as the amount of money stolen, the extent of personal injury inflicted, and the criminal history of the offender can affect the sentence that judges impose without undermining the basic goals of uniformity and equity. The First Circuit U.S. Court of Appeals applied the U.S. Sentencing Guidelines to departures from the permissible range of sentences in two cases consolidated for appeal. Chief Judge Breyer, now an associate U.S. Supreme Court justice, discussed the philosophy of the Guidelines and how that philosophy affects departures from the Guidelines in *United States v. Rivera.*

C A S E

Were Departures Justified?

United States v. Rivera
994 F.2d 942 (1st Cir. 1993)

Rivera, a single mother of three children, was convicted of carrying a pound of cocaine from New York to Providence, Rhode Island, and sentenced to thirty-three months in prison by the United States District Court for the District of Rhode Island. Adamo, a union official, was convicted of embezzlement from the union's health and welfare fund and was sentenced by the district court to a term of probation without confinement so that he could continue to work and make restitution to the fund. In a consolidated appeal, the Court of Appeals vacated the sentences and remanded the cases, before Chief Judge Breyer and Senior Circuit Judges Campbell and Bownes. Judge Breyer wrote the opinion for the court.

FACTS

Each of these two appeals concerns the district court's power to impose a sentence that departs from the Sentencing Guidelines. The first case involves Mirna Rivera, a single mother of three small children. Ms. Rivera was convicted of carrying about a pound of co-

caine from New York to Providence. She appeals her thirty-three month sentence of imprisonment. She argues that the district court would have departed downward from the minimum thirty-three month Guidelines prison term but for the court's view that it lacked the legal "authority" to depart. She says that this view is legally "incorrect" and she asks us to set aside her sentence.

The second case involves a union official, Robert Adamo, who embezzled about $100,000 from his union's Health and Welfare Fund. The district court departed downward from the fifteen to twenty-one month prison term that the Guidelines themselves would have required. Instead, the court imposed a term of probation without confinement. The court said that it was departing downward so that Mr. Adamo could continue to work and to make restitution to the Fund. The Government appeals. It argues that Adamo's circumstances are insufficiently unusual to warrant the departure.

We agree with the appellants in both cases. In our view, the district court sentencing Ms. Rivera held an unduly narrow view of its departure powers. The district court sentencing Mr. Adamo failed to analyze the need for departure in the way that the law requires. We consider both cases in this single opinion because doing so may help to illustrate an appropriate legal analysis for "departures." We shall first set forth our view of the portion of the law here applicable; and we shall then apply that law to the two appeals.

OPINION

I. Departures

The basic theory of the Sentencing Guidelines is a simple one. In order to lessen the degree to which different judges imposed different sentences in comparable cases, an expert Sentencing Commission would write Guidelines, applicable to most ordinary sentencing situations. In an ordinary situation, the statutes, and the Guidelines themselves, would require the judge to apply the appropriate guideline — a guideline that would normally cabin, within fairly narrow limits, the judge's power to choose the length of a prison term. Should the judge face a situation that was not ordinary, the judge could depart from the Guidelines sentence, provided that the judge then sets forth the reasons for departure. A court of appeals would review the departure for "reasonableness." And, the Commission itself would collect and study both the district courts' departure determinations and the courts of appeals' decisions, thereby learning about the Guidelines' actual workings and using that knowledge to help revise or clarify the Guidelines for the future.

This basic theory is embodied in statutory provisions and in the Guidelines themselves. We believe it important to refer to this theory in explaining our own view of the legal provisions concerning departures, and of how both district courts and courts of appeals are to apply them.

A

The Statute

The Sentencing Statute itself sets forth the basic law governing departures. It tells the sentencing court that it shall impose a sentence of the kind, and within the range . . . established for the applicable category of offense committed by the applicable category of defendant as set forth in the Guidelines. . . . The statute goes on immediately to create an exception for departures by adding that the sentencing court shall "im-

pose" this Guidelines sentence unless the court finds that there exists an aggravating or mitigating circumstance of a kind, or to a degree, not adequately taken into consideration by the Sentencing Commission in formulating the Guidelines that should result in a sentence different from that described. . . . If the sentencing court makes this finding and sentences "outside the [Guidelines'] range," it must state in open court . . . the specific reason for the imposition of a sentence different from that described [in the Guidelines]. The defendant may then appeal an upward departure, and the Government may appeal a downward departure. On appeal, if the court of appeals determines that the sentence . . . is unreasonable, . . . it shall state specific reasons for its conclusions and . . . set aside the sentence and remand the case for further sentencing proceedings with such instructions as the court considers appropriate.

. . .

B

The Guidelines

The Guidelines deal with departures in four basic ways.

1. Cases Outside the "Heartland." The Introduction to the Guidelines (which the Commission calls a "Policy Statement") makes an important distinction between a "heartland case" and an "unusual case." The Introduction says that the Commission intends the sentencing courts to treat each guideline as carving out a "heartland," a set of typical cases embodying the conduct that each guideline describes. The Introduction goes on to say that when a court finds an atypical case, one to which a particular guideline linguistically applies, but where conduct significantly differs from the norm, the court may consider whether a departure is warranted. The Introduction further adds that, with a few stated exceptions, the Commission does not intend to limit the kinds of factors, whether or not mentioned anywhere else in the guidelines, that could constitute grounds for departure in an unusual case.

The Introduction thus makes clear that (with a few exceptions) a case that falls outside the linguistically applicable guideline's "heartland" is a candidate for departure. It is, by definition, an "unusual case." And, the sentencing court may then go on to consider, in light of the sentencing system's purposes, whether or not the "unusual" features of the case justify departure.... Thus, (with a few exceptions) the law tells the judge, considering departure, to ask basically, "Does this case fall within the 'heartland,' or is it an 'unusual case?'"

2. Encouraged Departures. In certain circumstances, the Guidelines offer the district court, which is considering whether to depart, special assistance, by specifically encouraging departures. Part 5K lists a host of considerations that may take a particular case outside the "heartland" of any individual guideline and, in doing so, may warrant a departure. The individual guidelines do not take account, for example, of an offender's "diminished capacity," which circumstance, in the Commission's view would normally warrant a downward departure. Nor do certain guidelines (say, immigration offense guidelines) take account of, say, use of a gun, which circumstance would remove the situation (the immigration offense) from that guideline's "heartland" and would normally warrant an upward departure....

3. Discouraged Departures. The Guidelines sometimes discourage departures. Part 5H, for example, lists various "specific offender" characteristics, such as age, education, employment record, family ties and responsibilities, mental and physical conditions, and various good works. The Guidelines say that these features are "not ordinarily relevant" in determining departures....

At the same time, the Commission recognizes that such circumstances could remove a case from the heartland, but only if they are present in a manner that is unusual or special, rather than "ordinary." It may not be unusual, for example, to find that a convicted drug offender is a single mother with family responsibilities, but, at some point, the nature and magnitude of family responsibilities (many children? with handicaps? no money? no place for children to go?) may transform the "ordinary" case of such circumstances into a case that is not at all ordinary. Thus, a sentencing court, considering whether or not the presence of these "discouraged" factors warrants departure, must ask whether the factors themselves are present in unusual kind or degree. The Commission, in stating that those factors do not "ordinarily"

take a case outside the heartland, discourages, but does not absolutely forbid, their use.

4. Forbidden Departures. The Commission has made several explicit exceptions to the basic principle that a sentencing court can consider any "unusual case" (any case outside the heartland) as a candidate for departure. The Guidelines state that a sentencing court "cannot take into account as grounds for departure" race, sex, national origin, creed, religion, and socio-economic status. The Guidelines also state that "lack of guidance as a youth" cannot justify departure, that drug or alcohol abuse is not a reason for imposing a sentence below the Guidelines range, and that personal financial difficulties and economic pressure upon a trade or business do not warrant a decrease in sentence. Thus, even if these factors make a case "unusual," taking it outside an individual guideline's heartland, the sentencing court is not free to consider departing. But, with these ... exceptions, the sentencing court is free to consider, in an "unusual case," whether or not the factors that make it unusual (which remove it from the heartland) are present in sufficient kind or degree to warrant a departure. The court retains this freedom to depart whether such departure is encouraged, discouraged, or unconsidered by the Guidelines.

C
The Sentencing Court's Departure Decision

Given the statutory provisions, and the relevant Guidelines statements, we suggest (but we do not require) that, as an initial matter, a sentencing court considering departure analyze the case along the following lines:

1. What features of this case, potentially, take it outside the Guidelines' "heartland" and make of it a special, or unusual, case?

2. Has the Commission forbidden departures based on those features?

3. If not, has the Commission encouraged departures based on those features?

4. If not, has the Commission discouraged departures based on those features? If no special features are present, or if special features are also "forbidden" features, then the sentencing court,

in all likelihood, simply would apply the relevant guidelines. If the special features are "encouraged" features, the court would likely depart, sentencing in accordance with the Guidelines' suggestions. If the special features are "discouraged" features, the court would go on to decide whether the case is nonetheless not "ordinary," i.e., whether the case differs from the ordinary case in which those features are present. If the case is ordinary, the court would not depart. If it is not ordinary, the court would go on to consider departure. . . .

D

Review on Appeal

If the district court decides to depart, the defendant may appeal (an upward departure) or the Government may appeal (a downward departure). The statute then provides the appellate court with two important instructions. First, the court of appeals must decide if the resulting sentence is "unreasonable, having regard for" the sentencing court's reasons and the statute's general sentencing factors. Second, the court of appeals must (as it ordinarily does) give "specific reasons" for its decision. . . .

II. Applying the Analysis

We now apply our "departure" analysis to the circumstances of the two cases before us, the appeal of Ms. Mirna Rivera, and that of Mr. Robert Adamo.

A

Mirna Rivera

For purposes of this appeal, we take Ms. Rivera to have transported about one pound of cocaine, from New York to Providence, with intent to distribute it, in violation of 21 U.S.C. § 841(a)(1), (b)(1)(B). The Guidelines provide a sentence of 33 to 41 months' imprisonment for a first time offender who has engaged in this conduct. See U.S.S.G. § 2D1.1(a)(3), (c)(10) (base offense level of 24); U.S.S.G. § 3B1.2(a) (reduction of 4 points for minimal participation); U.S.S.G. Ch. 5, Pt. A (sentencing table). Ms. Rivera argued to the district court that it should depart downward from this Guidelines sentence for the following reasons:

1. She has three small children, ages three, five, and six, who need a mother's care.

2. She lives solely on welfare, receiving no financial aid from her former husband.

3. She has virtually no contact with any other family member (except for a sister, with five children, also on welfare).

4. She has never before engaged in any criminal activity.

5. She committed this single offense because of an unwise wish to obtain money for Christmas presents for her children.

The district court decided not to depart. Rivera claims that this decision reflects the court's incorrect belief that it lacked the legal authority to depart. And, she asks us to order a new proceeding.

After reviewing the record of the sentencing proceeding, we conclude that Rivera is correct. The district court's analysis of the nature of its power to depart is not consistent with the view of departures that we set forth in this opinion. We recognize a difference between "forbidden departures," and "discouraged departures." And, we believe that the district court did not realize that it had the legal power to consider departure, where departure is discouraged (but not forbidden), if it finds features of the case that show it is not ordinary.

At the sentencing hearing, the district court said:

With respect to Defendant's argument that the Defendant's family situation, economic situation, warrants a departure, I must say that the guidelines are drawn to apply to everyone in exactly the same way, that it is clear from the guidelines that the economic situation and the family situation of the Defendant is not a consideration. There are those who certainly would disagree with that, but that is the principle that is embodied in the guidelines. They are age blind, they are sex blind, they are blind to family circumstances, and can result in their application in a certain amount of cruelty. But, that isn't a basis for making a departure. It's a situation where somebody tries to draw a straight line that applies to every situation that can possibly arise and this Court is without discretion to take what might well be thought by most people, at least, legitimate concerns into consideration. Simply put, I can't do that because the guidelines do not permit me to do that. So that Defendant's objection or request to make a downward departure is denied. . . . Your Counsel says that a court somewhere observed that these guidelines are not a straightjacket for a District Court. Well, I don't agree with that. Here is a circumstance where I'm satisfied that the reason you did this was to buy toys for your children at Christmas. It was a serious mistake. The pre-sentence report says this: There is no information suggesting that Ms. Rivera had any previous participation in a similar type criminal activity. The Defendant's lifestyle is not indicative of that of a drug dealer who has profited from ongoing criminal activity. Rather she appears destitute, relying on public assistance to support herself and her children. . . . If I had the authority to do it, I would not impose the sentence that I am about to impose. I would impose a lesser sentence because I think that these guidelines simply are unrealistic when applied to real life situations like this. They may work in many circumstances, but they certainly don't work here.

In these statements, the court repeatedly said that it lacked the legal power to depart; it characterized the case before it as different from the "many circumstances" where the Guidelines might work; it added that it would depart if it could; it set forth several circumstances that might make the case a special one; and it described as identical ("sex blind" and "blind to family circumstances") guidelines that, in fact, differ significantly, the former involving a "forbidden" departure, and the latter a "discouraged" departure. Taken together, these features of the case warrant a new sentencing proceeding, conducted with the district court fully aware of its power to depart in "unusual cases" and where family circumstances are out of the "ordinary." . . .

. . . The upshot is a difficult departure decision. On the one hand lie a host of quite special circumstances (though many are of the "discouraged" sort),

and on the other hand lies the simple fact that Ms. Mirna Rivera did transport a pound of cocaine from New York to Providence. This is the kind of case in which, if the district court departs, its informed views as to why the case is special would seem especially useful and would warrant appellate court "respect."

We remand the case for further proceedings.

B

Robert Adamo

Mr. Adamo was convicted of embezzling about $100,000 belonging to the union Health and Welfare Fund of which he was a fiduciary, in violation of 18 U.S.C. § 664. He accepted responsibility for the crime, U.S.S.G. § 3E1.1. It was his first offense. The Guidelines provided a minimum prison term of fifteen months. See U.S.S.G. §§ 2E5.2, 2B1.1, 3B1.3 (base offense level of 4; increase of 8 points for amount of loss; 2 level enhancement for more than minimal planning; 2 level enhancement for fiduciary); U.S.S.G. Ch. 5, Pt. A (sentencing table). The district court, departing downward from the Guidelines, sentenced Mr. Adamo to probation alone, without any imprisonment.

The court gave the following reasons for its downward departure:

When I look at these cases of sentencing, the first thing I ask myself is, "What sentence would I impose if there were no guidelines?" That's what I did for more than 20 years. And then I ask myself, "What's a just sentence in these circumstances? Am I going to be limited by these artificial guidelines made by people who have no idea of what kind of a case I'm going to have to decide?" No two cases are the same. . . . So that's where justice is in this case, having restitution made to this Health & Welfare Fund. If I send this defendant to prison I think it's foreordained that restitution will not be made. It may be made in some respect, but I'm sure the defendant would lose both his jobs and would find it very difficult to have employment which would allow him to make restitution. And a time in prison would serve no useful purpose in this case. The only factor in sentencing which would be accomplished is punishment, but the defendant has been punished just by being here — just being here and what's he's gone through in the last 6 months, and the notoriety of this. So, imprisonment serves no useful purpose in this case. It certainly isn't a matter of deterrence. I'm sure the defendant will never do anything like this again. Here is a man who has lived an exemplary life, he's worked two jobs to take care of his family. His wife has worked, and although they were making in the range of $70,000 a year, the problem of educating two children came up. It's a problem that everyone faces. This is where the error of judgment comes in. He took this money, not out of greed, not out of desire to own a fancy car or a palatial home and a boat, but to educate his children. He didn't think about the other alternatives. His daughter wanted to go to an expensive private school, instead of going to a local state school of some sort, and he thought that's what she should have. He didn't consider loans and other types of programs. This money was available, he took it — a terrible mistake. But that's the only mistake that he seems to have made, and I just don't think he should spend time in prison because of this one mistake. I want restitution made, so I'm going to exercise my best judgment in these circumstances. My best judgment is to have as long a term of probation as possible so that restitution can be made with the guidance of the probation office. So, I'm going to depart downward and impose a term of probation of 5 years. That's the maximum that I can impose. And one of the conditions of probation will be, and is, that the defendant shall pay restitution in the amount of $91,125.62 to the Health & Welfare Fund of the Building Service Employees International Union, AFL-CIO Local 334.

The court's explication of its reasons is useful, for it produces understanding and permits evaluation, both by appellate courts and by the Commission. We nonetheless believe the analysis does not permit the departure before us.

First, we believe . . . that the embezzlement guidelines encompass, within their "heartland," embezzlement accompanied by normal restitution needs and practicalities (i.e., the simple facts that restitution is desirable and that a prison term will make restitution harder to achieve). It would seem obvious, and no one denies, that the embezzlement guidelines are written for ordinary cases of embezzlement, that restitution is called for in many such cases, and that prison terms often make restitution somewhat more difficult to achieve. Moreover, the embezzlement guideline reflects the Commission's intent to equalize punishments for "white collar" and "blue collar" crime. Yet, as the Sixth Circuit has pointed out, a rule permitting greater leniency in sentencing in those cases in which restitution is at issue and is a meaningful possibility (i.e., generally white collar crimes) would . . . nurture the unfortunate practice of disparate sentencing based on socio-economic status, which the guidelines were intended to supplant. Further, the district court itself, stating that it did not wish "to be limited by these artificial guidelines," and that "no two cases are alike," seemed to disregard, rather than to deny, the scope of the embezzlement guideline. For these reasons, we join the Fourth and Sixth Circuits, in holding that ordinary restitution circumstances of this sort do not fall outside the embezzlement guideline's "heartland," and therefore do not warrant a downward departure.

Second, we recognize that a special need of a victim for restitution, and the surrounding practicalities, might, in an unusual case, justify a departure. But, we cannot review a district court determination to that effect here, for the district court made no such determination. . . . We mention this fact because the defendant has pointed to one unusual feature of the case. The record before us contains a suggestion that Mr. Adamo could keep his job (and therefore remain able to make restitution) were his prison term only one year, but he could not keep his job (and thus would lose his ability to make restitution) were he sentenced to the Guidelines prison term of one year and three months. We can imagine an argument for departure resting upon a strong need for restitution, an important practical advantage to the lesser sentence, and a departure limited to three months.

We are not arguing such a departure or saying that we would eventually find it lawful. We mention the special circumstance to underscore the need for reasoned departure analysis, sensitive to the way in which the Guidelines seek to structure departure decisions and to the role that such departures, and their accompanying reasons, can play in the continued development of the Sentencing Guidelines. . . . The district court, in Mr. Adamo's case, may wish to conduct such an analysis in light of the special features of the case to which the defendant has pointed. We therefore remand this case for new sentencing proceedings.

The sentences in both cases are vacated and the cases are remanded to the district court for resentencing.

So ordered.

CASE DISCUSSION

What is the basic philosophy of the federal sentencing guidelines, according to Chief Judge Breyer? Explain the difference between "heartland" cases and "unusual" cases and this difference's effect on sentencing under the Guidelines. What specific facts justify the departure in the case of Ms. Rivera? Would you allow the departure? Argue the case for and against the departure, and then give your reasons for departing or not departing. What facts do not justify the departure in the case of Mr. Adamo? Would you disallow the departure? Give reasons why or why not.

———————————— ◼◻ ————————————

The other type of fixed sentence, **mandatory minimum sentences,** prescribe a nondiscretionary amount of prison time that all offenders convicted of the offense must serve. Judges can sentence offenders to more than the minimum but not less. Mandatory minimum sentence laws, at least in theory, promise that "if you do the crime, you will do the time." Mandatory penalties are very old. The "eye for an eye" and "tooth for a tooth" in the Old Testament were mandatory penalties. So, too, did King Alfred, the Anglo-Saxon king, prescribe a detailed mandatory penal code, including such provisions as "If one knocks out another's eye, he shall pay 66 shillings, 6 1/3 pence. If the eye is still in the head, but the injured man can see nothing with it, one-third of the payment shall be withheld." And, as early as 1790 in the United States, most states had established mandatory penalties for capital crimes. Throughout the nineteenth century, Congress enacted mandatory penalties — usually short prison sentences — for a long list of crimes, including refusal to testify before Congress, failure to report seaboard saloon purchases, or causing a ship to run aground by use of a false light.[5]

From 1900 to the 1950s, the use of mandatory minimum penalties fell into relative disuse. Fear of crime and drugs in the 1950s, brought on in part, it was believed, by a Communist plot to get Americans "hooked" on especially potent "pure Communist heroin" from China, led Congress to enact the Narcotic Control Act of 1956. The Boggs Act, as it was called after its sponsor, signaled a shift to a heavier reliance on mandatory minimum sentences. The Senate Judiciary explained why Congress needed a mandatory minimum sentence drug law:

> [T]here is a need for the continuation of the policy of punishment of a severe character as a deterrent to narcotic law violations. [The Committee] therefore recommends an increase in maximum sentences for first as well as subsequent offenses. With respect to the mandatory minimum features of such penalties, and prohibition of suspended sentences or probation, the Committee recognizes objections in principle. It feels, however, that, in order to define the gravity of this class of crime and the assured penalty to follow, these features of the law must be regarded as es-

sential elements of the desired deterrents, although some differences of opinion still exist regarding their application to first offenses of certain types.[6]

The statute imposed stiff mandatory minimum sentences for narcotics offenses, requiring judges to pick within a range of penalties. Judges could not suspend sentences or put convicted offenders on probation. Offenders were not eligible for parole if they were convicted under the act. For example, the act punished the first conviction for selling heroin by a term of from five to ten years of imprisonment. Judges had to sentence offenders to at least five years in prison, judges could not suspend the sentence or put offenders on probation, and offenders were not eligible for parole for at least the minimum period of the sentence. For second offenders, the mandatory minimum was raised to ten years. The penalty for the sale of narcotics to persons under eighteen years of age ranged from a mandatory minimum of ten years to a maximum of life imprisonment or death.[7]

In 1970, Congress retreated from the mandatory minimum sentence approach. In the Comprehensive Drug Abuse Prevention and Control Act of 1970, Congress repealed virtually all of the mandatory minimum provisions adopted in the 1956 act because the increased sentence lengths "had not shown the expected overall reduction in drug law violations." Among the reasons for the repeal of mandatory minimum penalties for drug law offenses were that they

- Alienated youth from the general society
- Hampered the rehabilitation of drug offenders
- Infringed on judicial authority by drastically reducing discretion in sentencing
- Reduced the deterrent effect of drug laws because even prosecutors thought the laws were too severe

According to the House committee that considered the repeal of the bill,

> The severity of existing penalties, involving in many instances minimum sentences, have led in many instances to reluctance on the part of prosecutors to prosecute some violations, where the penalties seem to be out of line with the seriousness of the offenses. In addition, severe penalties, which do not take into account individual circumstances, and which treat casual violators as severely as they treat hardened criminals, tend to make conviction more difficult to obtain.[8]

The retreat from mandatory minimum sentences was short-lived. Public concern about violence and drugs rose to the top of the national agenda. The public and legislatures blamed rising crime rates, in part at least, on the uncertainty and the "leniency" of indeterminate sentences. Beginning in the early 1970s, the states and the federal government enacted more and longer mandatory minimum prison sentences. By 1991, forty-six states and the federal government had enacted mandatory minimum sentencing laws. Although the list of mandatory minimum laws is long (the United States Criminal Code contains at least one hundred), the main targets of mandatory minimum sentences are drug offenses, violent crimes, and crimes committed with a weapon.[9]

Mandatory minimum sentences aim to satisfy three basic aims of criminal punishment: retribution, incapacitation, and deterrence. According to the supporters of mandatory minimum sentence laws, serious crimes will receive severe punishment. Furthermore, violent criminals, criminals who use weapons, and drug offenders cannot harm the public if they are in prison. And the knowledge that committing mandatory minimum crimes will bring certain, severe punishment should deter potential drug offenders, violent criminals, and criminals who use weapons. The United States Supreme Court discussed the constitutionality of the United States mandatory minimum sentence statute for selling LSD in *Chapman v. United States.*

C A S E

Is the Paper Part of the "Amount" of LSD?

Chapman v. United States
500 U.S. 453, 111 S.Ct. 1919,
114 L.Ed.2d 524 (1991)

Chapman and others were convicted in the United States District Court, Central District of Illinois, and the United States District Court, Western District of Wisconsin, of distributing and selling lysergic acid diethylamide (LSD). On consolidated appeals, the United States Court of Appeals for the Seventh Circuit affirmed. On writ of certiorari, the United States Supreme Court affirmed. Chief Justice Rehnquist wrote the opinion of the Court, which Justices White, Blackmun, O'Connor, Scalia, Kennedy, and Souter joined. Justice Stevens filed a dissenting opinion, which Justice Marshall joined.

FACTS

Petitioners Richard L. Chapman, John M. Schoenecker, and Patrick Brumm were convicted of selling 10 sheets (1000 doses) of blotter paper containing LSD, in violation of 21 U.S.C. § 841(a). The District Court included the total weight of the paper and LSD in determining the weight of the drug to be used in calculating petitioners' sentences. Accordingly, although the weight of the LSD alone was approximately 50 milligrams, the 5.7 grams combined weight of LSD and blotter paper resulted in the imposition of mandatory minimum sentence of five years required by 21 U.S.C. § 841(b)(1)(B)(v) for distributing more than one gram of a mixture or substance containing a detectable amount of LSD. The entire 5.7 grams was also used to determine the base offense level under

the United States Sentencing Commission Guidelines Manual (1990) (Sentencing Guidelines).

[COURT NOTE: Chapman was sentenced to 96 months; Schoenecker was sentenced to 63 months; and Brumm was sentenced to 60 months' imprisonment.] Petitioners appealed, claiming that the blotter paper is only a carrier medium, and that its weight should not be included in the weight of the drug for sentencing purposes. Alternatively, they argued that if the statute and Sentencing Guidelines were construed so as to require inclusion of the blotter paper or other carrier medium when calculating the weight of the drug, this would violate the right to equal protection incorporated in the Due Process Clause of the Fifth Amendment.

The Court of Appeals for the Seventh Circuit en banc held that the weight of the blotter paper or other carrier should be included in the weight of the "mixture or substance containing a detectable amount" of LSD when computing the sentence for a defendant convicted of distributing LSD. The Court of Appeals also found that Congress had a rational basis for including the carrier along with the weight of the drug, and therefore the statute and the Sentencing Guidelines did not violate the Constitution. We granted certiorari, and now affirm.

OPINION

Section 841(b)(1)(B)(v) of Title 21 of the United States Code calls for a mandatory minimum sentence of five years for the offense of distributing more than one gram of a "mixture or substance containing a detectable amount of lysergic acid diethylamide

(LSD)." . . . 21 U.S.C. § 841(b)(1)(B) provides that "any person who violates subsection (a) of this section [making it unlawful to knowingly or intentionally manufacture, distribute, dispense, or possess with intent to manufacture, distribute, or dispense, a controlled substance], shall be sentenced as follows: "(1)(B) In the case of a violation of subsection (a) of this section involving— . . . (v) 1 gram or more of a mixture or substance containing a detectable amount of lysergic acid diethylamide (LSD); . . . such person shall be sentenced to a term of imprisonment which may not be less than 5 years. . . ." Section 841(b)(1)(A)(v) provides for a mandatory minimum of 10 years imprisonment for a violation of subsection (a) involving "10 grams or more of a mixture or substance containing a detectable amount of [LSD]." Section 2D1.1(c) of the Sentencing Guidelines parallels the statutory language and requires the base offense level to be determined based upon the weight of a "mixture of substance containing a detectable amount of" LSD.

According to the Sentencing Commission, the LSD in an average dose weighs 0.05 milligrams; there are therefore 20,000 pure doses in a gram. The pure dose is such an infinitesimal amount that it must be sold to retail customers in a "carrier." Pure LSD is dissolved in a solvent such as alcohol, and either the solution is sprayed on paper or gelatin, or paper is dipped in the solution. The solvent evaporates, leaving minute amounts of LSD trapped in the paper or gel. Then the paper or gel is cut into "one-dose" squares and sold by the dose. Users either swallow the squares, lick them until the drug is released, or drop them into a beverage, thereby releasing the drug. Although gelatin and paper are light, they weigh much more than the LSD. The ten sheets of blotter paper carrying the 1,000 doses sold by petitioners weighed 5.7 grams; the LSD by itself weighed only about 50 milligrams, not even close to the one gram necessary to trigger the 5-year mandatory minimum of § 841(b)(1)(B)(v).

Petitioners argue that § 841(b) should not require that the weight of the carrier be included when computing the appropriate sentence for LSD distribution, for the words "mixture or substance" are ambiguous, and should not be construed to reach an illogical result. Because LSD is sold by dose, rather than by

weight, the weight of the LSD carrier should not be included when determining a defendant's sentence because it is irrelevant to culpability. They argue that including the weight of the carrier leads to anomalous results, viz: a major wholesaler caught with 19,999 doses of pure LSD would not be subject to the 5-year mandatory minimum sentence, while a minor pusher with 200 doses on blotter paper, or even one dose on a sugar cube, would be subject to the mandatory minimum sentence. Thus, they contend, the weight of the carrier should be excluded, the weight of the pure LSD should be determined, and that weight should be used to set the appropriate sentence.

Even among dealers using blotter paper, the sentences can vary because the weight of the blotter paper varies from dealer to dealer. Petitioners' blotter paper, containing 1,000 doses of LSD, weighed 5.7 grams, or 5.7 milligrams per dose. . . .

We think that petitioner's reading of the statute — a reading that makes the penalty turn on the net weight of the drug rather than the gross weight of the carrier and drug together — is not a plausible one. The statute refers to a "mixture or substance containing a detectable amount." So long as it contains a detectable amount, the entire mixture or substance is to be weighed when calculating the sentence. . . .

Chapman maintains that Congress could not have intended to include the weight of an LSD carrier for sentencing purposes because the carrier will constitute nearly all of the weight of the entire unit, and the sentence will, therefore, be based on the weight of the carrier, rather than the drug. The same point can be made about drugs like heroin and cocaine, however, and Congress clearly intended the dilutant, cutting agent, or carrier medium to be included in the weight of those drugs for sentencing purposes. Inactive ingredients are combined with pure heroin or cocaine, and the mixture is then sold to consumers as a heavily diluted form of the drug. In some cases, the concentration of the drug in the mixture is very low. E.g., *United States v. Buggs*, 904 F.2d 1070 (CA7 1990) (1.2% heroin); *United States v. Dorsey*, 192 U.S.App.D.C. 313, 591 F.2d 922 (DC 1978) (2% heroin); *United States v. Smith*, 601 F.2d 972 (CA8) (2.7% and 8.5% heroin), cert. denied, 444 U.S. 879, 100 S.Ct. 166, 62 L.Ed.2d 108 (1979). But, if the carrier is a "mixture or substance containing a detectable amount of the drug," then under the language of the statute the weight of the mixture or substance, and not the weight of the pure drug, is controlling. . . .

The current penalties for LSD distribution originated in the Anti-Drug Abuse Act of 1986, Pub.L. 99–570, 100 Stat. 3207 (1986). Congress adopted a "market-oriented" approach to punishing drug trafficking, under which the total quantity of what is distributed, rather than the amount of pure drug involved, is used to determine the length of the sentence. To implement that principle, Congress set mandatory minimum sentences corresponding to the weight of a "mixture or substance containing a detectable amount of" the various controlled substances, including LSD. 21 U.S.C. §§ 841(b)(1)(A)(i)–(viii) and (B)(i)–(viii). It intended the penalties for drug trafficking to be graduated according to the weight of the drugs in whatever form they were found — cut or uncut, pure or impure, ready for wholesale or ready for distribution at the retail level. Congress did not want to punish retail traffickers less severely, even though they deal in smaller quantities of the pure drug, because such traffickers keep the street markets going.

We think that the blotter paper used in this case, and blotter paper customarily used to distribute LSD, is a "mixture or substance containing a detectable amount" of LSD. In so holding, we confirm the unanimous conclusion of the Courts of Appeals that have addressed the issue. Neither the statute nor the Sentencing Guidelines define the terms "mixture" and "substance," nor do they have any established common law meaning. Those terms, therefore, must be given their ordinary meaning. A "mixture" is defined to include "a portion of matter consisting of two or more components that do not bear a fixed proportion to one another and that however thoroughly commingled are regarded as retaining a separate existence." *Webster's Third New International Dictionary* 1449 (1986). A "mixture" may also consist of two substances blended together so that the particles of one are diffused among the particles of the other. 9 *Oxford English Dictionary* 921 (2d ed. 1989). LSD is applied to blotter paper in a solvent, which is absorbed into the paper and ultimately evaporates. After the solvent evaporates, the LSD is left behind in a form that can

be said to "mix" with the paper. The LSD crystals are inside of the paper, so that they are commingled with it, but the LSD does not chemically combine with the paper. Thus, it retains a separate existence and can be released by dropping the paper into a liquid, or by swallowing the paper itself. The LSD is diffused among the fibers of the paper. Like heroin or cocaine mixed with cutting agents, the LSD cannot be distinguished from the blotter paper, nor easily separated from it. Like cutting agents used with other drugs that are ingested, the blotter paper, gel, or sugar cube carrying LSD can be and often is ingested with the drug.

Petitioners argue that the terms "mixture" or "substance" cannot be given their dictionary meaning because then the clause could be interpreted to include carriers like a glass vial or an automobile in which the drugs are being transported, thus making the phrase nonsensical. But such nonsense is not the necessary result of giving the term "mixture" its dictionary meaning. The term does not include LSD in a bottle, or LSD in a car, because the drug is easily distinguished from, and separated from, such a "container." The drug is clearly not mixed with a glass vial or automobile; nor has the drug chemically bonded with the vial or car. It may be true that the weights of containers and packaging materials generally are not included in determining a sentence for drug distribution, but that is because those items are also clearly not mixed or otherwise combined with the drug. . . .

Petitioners argue that the due process of law guaranteed them by the Fifth Amendment is violated by determining the lengths of their sentences in accordance with the weight of the LSD "carrier," a factor which they insist is arbitrary. They argue preliminarily that the right to be free from deprivations of liberty as a result of arbitrary sentences is fundamental, and therefore the statutory provision at issue may be upheld only if the government has a compelling interest in the classification in question. But we have never subjected the criminal process to this sort of truncated analysis, and we decline to do so now. Every person has a fundamental right to liberty in the sense that the Government may not punish him unless and until it proves his guilt beyond a reasonable doubt at a criminal trial conducted in accordance with the relevant constitutional guarantees. But a person who has been so convicted is eligible for, and the court may impose, whatever punishment is authorized by statute for his offense, so long as that penalty is not cruel and unusual, and so long as the penalty is not based on an arbitrary distinction that would violate the Due Process Clause of the Fifth Amendment. In this context, an argument based on equal protection essentially duplicates an argument based on due process.

We find that Congress had a rational basis for its choice of penalties for LSD distribution. The penalty scheme set out in the Anti-Drug Abuse Act of 1986 is intended to punish severely large-volume drug traffickers at any level. It assigns more severe penalties to the distribution of larger quantities of drugs. By measuring the quantity of the drugs according to the "street weight" of the drugs in the diluted form in which they are sold, rather than according to the net weight of the active component, the statute and the Sentencing Guidelines increase the penalty for persons who possess large quantities of drugs, regardless of their purity. That is a rational sentencing scheme.

This is as true with respect to LSD as it is with respect to other drugs. Although LSD is not sold by weight, but by dose, and a carrier medium is not, strictly speaking, used to "dilute" the drug, that medium is used to facilitate the distribution of the drug. Blotter paper makes LSD easier to transport, store, conceal, and sell. It is a tool of the trade for those who traffic in the drug, and therefore it was rational for Congress to set penalties based on this chosen tool. Congress was also justified in seeking to avoid arguments about the accurate weight of pure drugs which might have been extracted from blotter paper had it chosen to calibrate sentences according to that weight.

Petitioners do not claim that the sentencing scheme at issue here has actually produced an arbitrary array of sentences, nor did their motions in district court contain any proof of actual disparities in sentencing. Rather, they challenge the Act on its face on the ground that it will inevitably lead to arbitrary punishments. While hypothetical cases can be imagined involving very heavy carriers and very little LSD, those cases are of no import in considering a claim by persons such as petitioners, who used a standard LSD carrier. Blotter paper seems to be the carrier of choice, and the vast majority of cases will therefore do

exactly what the sentencing scheme was designed to do — punish more heavily those who deal in larger amounts of drugs.

Petitioners argue that those selling different numbers of doses, and, therefore, with different degrees of culpability, will be subject to the same minimum sentence because of choosing different carriers. [COURT NOTE: We note that distributors of LSD make their own choice of carrier, and could act to minimize their potential sentences. As it is, almost all distributors choose blotter paper, rather than the heavier and bulkier sugar cubes.] . . .

We hold that the statute requires the weight of the carrier medium to be included when determining the appropriate sentence for trafficking in LSD, and this construction is neither a violation of due process, nor unconstitutionally vague. Accordingly, the judgment of the Court of Appeals is affirmed.

DISSENT

Justice Stevens, whom Justice Marshall joins, dissenting.

The consequences of the majority's construction of 21 U.S.C. § 841 are so bizarre that I cannot believe they were intended by Congress. Neither the ambiguous language of the statute, nor its sparse legislative history, supports the interpretation reached by the majority today. Indeed, the majority's construction of the statute will necessarily produce sentences that are so anomalous that they will undermine the very uniformity that Congress sought to achieve when it adopted the Sentencing Guidelines.

This was the conclusion reached by five Circuit judges in their two opinions dissenting from the holding of the majority of the Court of Appeals for the Seventh Circuit sitting en banc in this case. . . . As Judge Posner noted in . . . [a] dissenting opinion, the severity of the sentences in LSD cases would be comparable to those in other drug cases only if the weight of the LSD carrier were disregarded.

If we begin with the language of the statute, . . . it becomes immediately apparent that the phrase "mixture or substance" is far from clear. . . . Although it is true that ink which is absorbed by a blotter "can be said to 'mix' with the paper," I would not describe a used blotter as a "mixture" of ink and paper. So here, I do not believe the word "mixture" comfortably describes the relatively large blotter which carries the grains of LSD that adhere to its surface.

Because I do not believe that the term "mixture" encompasses the LSD and carrier at issue here . . . I turn to the legislative history to see if it provides any guidance as to congressional intent or purpose. . . . In a letter to Senator Joseph R. Biden, Jr., dated April 26, 1989, the Chairman of the Sentencing Commission, William W. Wilkens, Jr., commented on the ambiguity of the statute:

> With respect to LSD, it is unclear whether Congress intended the carrier to be considered as a packaging material, or, since it is commonly consumed along with the illicit drug, as a dilutant ingredient in the drug mixture. . . . The Commission suggests that Congress may wish to further consider the LSD carrier issue in order to clarify legislative intent as to whether the weight of the carrier should or should not be considered in determining the quantity of LSD mixture for punishment purposes.

Presumably in response, Senator Biden offered a technical amendment, the purpose of which was to correct an inequity that had become apparent from several recent court decisions. According to Senator Biden, "[t]he amendment remedies this inequity by removing the weight of the carrier from the calculation of the weight of the mixture or substance."

[COURT NOTE: Senator Biden offered the following example to highlight the inequities that resulted if the carrier weight were included in determining the weight of the "mixture or substance" of LSD: "The inequity in these decisions is apparent in the following example. A single dose of LSD weighs approximately .05 mg. The sugar cube on which the dose may be dropped for purposes of ingestion and transportation, however, weighs approximately 2 grams. Under 21 U.S.C. § 841(b) a person distributing more than one gram of a 'mixture or substance' containing LSD is punishable by a minimum sentence of 5 years and a maximum sentence of 40 years. A person distributing less than a gram of LSD, however, is subject only to a maximum sentence of 20 years. Thus a person distributing 1,000 doses of LSD in liquid form is subject to no minimum penalty, while a person handing another person a single dose

on a sugar cube is subject to the mandatory five year penalty." 135 Cong.Rec. S12748 (Oct. 5, 1989).] Although Senator Biden's amendment was adopted as part of Amendment No. 976 to S. 1711, the bill never passed the House of Representatives. . . .

In light of the ambiguity of the phrase "mixture or substance" and the lack of legislative history to guide us, it is necessary to examine the congressional purpose behind the statute and to determine whether the majority's reading of the statute leads to results that Congress clearly could not have intended. . . . [O]ne of the central purposes of the Sentencing Guidelines . . . was to eliminate disparity in sentencing. . . . As the majority . . . makes clear, widely divergent sentences may be imposed for the sale of identical amounts of a controlled substance simply because of the nature of the carrier. If 100 doses of LSD were sold on sugar cubes, the sentence would range from 188–235 months, whereas if the same dosage were sold in its pure liquid form, the sentence would range only from 10–16 months. The absurdity and inequity of this result is emphasized in Judge Posner's dissent:

> A person who sells LSD on blotter paper is not a worse criminal than one who sells the same number of doses on gelatin cubes, but he is subject to a heavier punishment. A person who sells five doses of LSD on sugar cubes is not a worse person than a manufacturer of LSD who is caught with 19,999 doses in pure form, but the former is subject to ten-year mandatory minimum no-parole sentence while the latter is not even subject to the five-year minimum. If defendant Chapman, who received five years for selling a thousand doses of LSD on blotter paper, had sold the same number of doses in pure form, his Guidelines sentence would have been fourteen months. And defendant Marshall's sentence for selling almost 12,000 doses would have been four years rather than twenty. The defendant in *United States v. Rose*, 881 F.2d 386, 387 (7th Cir. 1989), must have bought an unusually heavy blotter paper, for he sold only 472 doses, yet his blotter paper weighed 7.3 grams—more than Chapman's, although Chapman sold more than twice as many doses. Depending on the weight of the carrier medium

(zero when the stuff is sold in pure form), and excluding the orange juice case, the Guidelines range for selling 198 doses (the amount in *Dean*) or 472 doses (the amount in *Rose*) stretches from ten months to 365 months; for selling a thousand doses (Chapman), from fifteen to 365 months; and for selling 11,751 doses (Marshall), from 33 months to life. In none of these computations, by the way, does the weight of the LSD itself make a difference—so slight is its weight relative to that of the carrier—except of course when it is sold in pure form. Congress might as well have said: if there is a carrier, weigh the carrier and forget the LSD. "This is a quilt the pattern whereof no one has been able to discern. The legislative history is silent, and since even the Justice Department cannot explain the why of the punishment scheme that it is defending, the most plausible inference is that Congress simply did not realize how LSD is sold." 908 F.2d, at 1333.

[DISSENT NOTE: His (Judge Posner's) comparison between the treatment of LSD and other more harmful drugs is also illuminating: "That irrationality is magnified when we compare the sentences for people who sell other drugs prohibited by 21 U.S.C. § 841. Marshall, remember, sold fewer than 12,000 doses and was sentenced to twenty years. Twelve thousand doses sounds like a lot, but to receive a comparable sentence for selling heroin Marshall would have had to sell ten kilograms, which would yield between one and two million doses. To receive a comparable sentence for selling cocaine he would have had to sell fifty kilograms, which would yield anywhere from 325,000 to five million doses. While the corresponding weight is lower for crack—half a kilogram—this still translates into 50,000 doses."]

Sentencing disparities that have been described as "crazy," and "loony," could well be avoided if the majority did not insist upon stretching the definition of "mixture" to include the carrier along with the LSD. It does not make sense to include a carrier in calculating the weight of the LSD because LSD, unlike drugs such as cocaine or marijuana, is sold by dosage rather than by weight. Thus, whether one dose of LSD is added to

a glass of orange juice or to a pitcher of orange juice, it is still only one dose that has been added. But if the weight of the orange juice is to be added to the calculation, then the person who sells the single dose of LSD in a pitcher rather than in a glass will receive a substantially higher sentence. If the weight of the carrier is included in the calculation not only does it lead to huge disparities in sentencing among LSD offenders, but also it leads to disparities when LSD sentences are compared to sentences for other drugs. . . .

There is nothing in our jurisprudence that compels us to interpret an ambiguous statute to reach such an absurd result. . . .

Undoubtedly, Congress intended to punish drug traffickers severely, and in particular, Congress intended to punish those who sell large quantities of drugs more severely than those who sell small quantities. But it did not express any intention to treat those who sell LSD differently from those who sell other dangerous drugs. The majority's construction of the statute fails to embody these legitimate goals of Congress. Instead of punishing more severely those who sell large quantities of LSD, the Court would punish more severely those who sell small quantities of LSD in weighty carriers, and instead of sentencing in comparable ways those who sell different types of drugs, the Court would sentence those who sell LSD to longer terms than those who sell proportionately equivalent quantities of other equally dangerous drugs. The Court today shows little respect for Congress' handiwork when it construes a statute to undermine the very goals that Congress sought to achieve.

I respectfully dissent.

CASE DISCUSSION

According to the Court, what is the "rational basis" for including the carrier in determining the amount of LSD? What are the main arguments that Chapman makes against including the weight of the carrier in determining the amount of LSD that he possessed? What are Justice Stevens's major reasons for dissenting? Who has made the better arguments? Do you think it is fair to punish Chapman according to the paper and the LSD contained in it, or is it fairer to punish him solely for the amount of LSD? Defend your answer.

Several evaluations suggest that mandatory minimum penalties in practice do not always achieve the goals that their proponents hoped they would. In 1990, Congress ordered the United States Sentencing Commission to evaluate the rapidly increasing number of mandatory minimum sentencing provisions in the federal system. The results of the Sentencing Commission's study provided little empirical support for the success of mandatory sentencing laws:

- Only a few of the mandatory minimum sentencing provisions are ever used. Nearly all those used relate to drug and weapons offenses.

- Only 41 percent of defendants whose characteristics and behavior qualify them for mandatory minimum sentences actually receive them.

- Mandatory minimum sentences actually introduce disparity in sentencing. For example, the Commission found that race influences disparity in a number of ways. Whites are less likely than blacks and Hispanics to be indicted or convicted at the mandatory minimum. Whites are also more likely than blacks and Hispanics to receive reductions for "substantial assistance" in aiding in the prosecution of other offenders. The mandatory minimum sentence laws allow an exception for offenders who provide "substantial assistance" in investigating other offenders. Only on the motion of the prosecutors can judges reduce the minimum for substantial assistance. Substantial assistance also leads to disparities quite apart from race. It tends to favor the very people the law was intended to reach — those higher up in the chain of drug dealing — because underlings can offer less assistance to the government. In one case, for example, Stanley Marshall, who sold less than one gram of LSD, got a twenty-year mandatory prison sentence. Jose Cabrera, on the other hand, who the government estimated made more than $40 million from importing cocaine and who would have qualified for life plus 200 years, received a prison term of eight years for providing "substantial assistance" in the case of Manuel Noriega. According to Judge Terry J. Hatter, Jr., "The people at the very bottom who can't provide substantial assistance end up getting [punished] more severely than those at the top."[10]

- Mandatory minimum sentences do not eliminate discretion; they merely shift it from judges to prosecutors. Prosecutors can use their discretion in a number of ways, including the manipulation of the "substantial assistance" exception and the decision to not charge defendants with crimes carrying mandatory minimum sentences, or to charge them with mandatory minimum crimes of lesser degree. New York prosecutors gave three reasons why they avoided mandatory minimum sentence laws: first, because of limited resources, charging every drug courier with a mandatory minimum crime would overwhelm the courts. Second, most couriers have limited culpability; therefore, they do not deserve mandatory prison sentences. Third, judges do not like sentencing low-level couriers to prison.[11]

The Commission recommended further study before making any final conclusions about the effectiveness of mandatory penalties. But the findings of the Commission, along with other research on federal and state mandatory minimum sentences, suggest that mandatory minimum penalties are not the easy answer to the crime problem that politicians promise and that the public hopes.[12]

Objections to mandatory minimum sentences come not only from the findings of empirical research but also from the experiences of judges who administer them. In

United States v. Brigham, Judge Easterbrook of the Seventh Circuit United States Court of Appeals revealed why some judges, including conservative judges, object to the mandatory minimum sentences.

C A S E

Was the Mandatory Minimum Sentence Appropriate?

United States v. Brigham
977 F.2d 317 (7th Cir. 1992)

Brigham was convicted in the United States District Court for the Northern District of Illinois of conspiracy to sell cocaine. The defendant appealed. The court of appeals affirmed before Bauer, Chief Judge, and Posner and Easterbrook, Circuit Judges. Judge Easterbrook wrote the opinion of the court.

FACTS

Steep penalties await those who deal in drugs. Buying or selling 10 kilograms of cocaine—even agreeing to do so, without carrying through—means a minimum penalty of 10 years' imprisonment, without possibility of parole. 21 U.S.C. §§ 841(b)(1)(A), 846. The "mandatory" minimum is mandatory only from the perspective of judges. To the parties, the sentence is negotiable. Did a marginal participant in a conspiracy really understand that a 10-kilo deal lay in store? A prosecutor may charge a lesser crime, if he offers something in return. Let's make a deal. Does the participant have valuable information; can he offer other assistance? Congress authorized prosecutors to pay for aid with sentences below the "floor." Let's make a deal.

Bold dealers may turn on their former comrades, setting up phony sales and testifying at the ensuing trials. Timorous dealers may provide information about their sources and customers. Drones of the organization—the runners, mules, drivers, and lookouts—have nothing comparable to offer. They lack the contacts and trust necessary to set up big deals, and they know little information of value. Whatever tales they have to tell, their bosses will have related. Defendants unlucky enough to be innocent have no information

at all and are more likely to want vindication at trial, losing not only the opportunity to make a deal but also the 2-level reduction the sentencing guidelines provide for accepting responsibility.

Mandatory minimum penalties, combined with a power to grant exceptions, create a prospect of inverted sentencing. The more serious the defendant's crimes, the lower the sentence—because the greater his wrongs, the more information and assistance he has to offer to a prosecutor. Discounts for the top dogs have the virtue of necessity, because rewards for assistance are essential to the business of detecting and punishing crime. But what makes the post-discount sentencing structure topsy-turvy is the mandatory minimum, binding only for the hangers on. What is to be said for such terms, which can visit draconian penalties on the small fry without increasing prosecutors' ability to wring information from their bosses?

Our case illustrates a sentencing inversion. Such an outcome is neither illegal nor unconstitutional, because offenders have no right to be sentenced in proportion to their wrongs. *Chapman v. United States,* — U.S. —, ———, 111 S.Ct. 1919, 1928–29, 114 L.Ed.2d 524 (1991). Still, meting out the harshest penalties to those least culpable is troubling, because it accords with no one's theory of appropriate punishments.

Agents of the Drug Enforcement Agency learned from an informant that Craig Thompson was in the market to buy 10 kilograms of cocaine. The DEA's undercover agents feigned willingness to supply him. During negotiations, Thompson said that he had just sold 17 kilograms and needed 10 more that very day to tide his organization over until the arrival of a shipment that he was expecting. Thompson and the agents did not trust one another. Jeffrey Carter, one of Thompson's goons, searched an agent; the agent's gun, normal in the business, did not trouble Carter, but a transmitter or recorder would mean big trouble. Carter was not very good at his job; he didn't find the concealed recorder. Thompson ultimately agreed to pay $30,000 per kilogram, a premium price for quick service. After the agents let on that they didn't trust Thompson any more than Thompson trusted them, Thompson agreed to let the agents hold his Rolls Royce as collateral until payment. In the agents' presence, Thompson called Tyrone Amos and told him to pick up "ten of those things today" at a suburban motel. Thompson and Carter would hand over the Rolls in a different suburb.

At the appointed time, less than five hours after the agents first met Thompson, one team descended on a restaurant to receive the Rolls Royce and another decamped to the motel to "deliver" the cocaine. Amos arrived at the motel in a car driven by Anthony Brigham. Amos and the agents at the motel had a conversation; Brigham stayed in the car. Carter had not appeared at the restaurant with the Rolls Royce, so everyone settled down to wait. Brigham looked around the parking lot but scrunched down in his seat when the agents' Corvette drove slowly by. At the restaurant Thompson and the agents discussed future deals of 50–100 kilograms per month. At the motel Brigham paced nervously in the lobby. After touring the parking lot again, lingering over the Corvette, Brigham joined Amos at a nearby gas station, where Amos placed a phone call. The two had a conversation and returned to the motel, where Amos told the agents that Carter and the Rolls were still missing. While Amos and one agent were dining together some distance from the motel, Thompson paged Amos with news that the Rolls had arrived.

Back at the motel, the agents went through the motions of delivering cocaine. As Amos headed for the agents' car to retrieve the drug from the trunk, Brigham moved his car to a location from which he could keep the delivery in sight. But there was no cocaine. Before Amos could open the trunk other agents moved in, arresting Amos and Brigham, just as they pinched Thompson and Carter at the restaurant.

All but Brigham pleaded guilty and provided valuable assistance to prosecutors. All but Brigham were sentenced to less than the "mandatory" minimums.

Thompson received 84 months' imprisonment and Amos 75 months, after the prosecutor made motions under § 3553(e). Carter, who was allowed to plead to a charge that did not carry a minimum term, received 4 years' probation, 4 months of which were to be in a work-release program run by the Salvation Army. That left Brigham, who went to trial, was convicted, and received the "mandatory" term of 120 months' imprisonment.

OPINION

Was the evidence sufficient? Appellate judges do not serve as additional jurors. After a jury convicts, the question becomes whether any sensible person could find, beyond a reasonable doubt, that the defendant committed the crime. That is a steep burden, for 12 persons, presumably sensible and having a more direct appreciation of the evidence than the written record affords to appellate judges, have unanimously found exactly that.

Brigham emphasizes that "mere" presence at a crime does not implicate the bystander in that offense. Conspiracy is agreement, and what proof of agreement did the prosecutor present? Brigham arrived with Amos, conferred with Amos, and was in position to watch an exchange occur. No one testified that Brigham had any role in the exchange or Thompson's organization. Although the prosecutor portrayed Brigham as a lookout, he asks: What kind of lookout would be unarmed, without radio, pager, cellular phone, or any other way to give or receive alerts? What counter surveillance operative would hunker down in the car rather than keep a hawk-eyed watch? Thompson, Carter, and Amos, who reaped rewards for their assistance, were conspicuously absent at Brigham's trial. Had they no evidence to offer against him?

No one questions the rule that "mere presence" at the scene of a crime does not prove conspiracy. "Mere" presence differs from, say, "revealing" presence. Like many a weasel word, "mere" summarizes a conclusion rather than assisting in analysis. When the evidence does not permit an inference that the defendant was part of the criminal organization, the court applies the label "mere presence." So we must examine the evidence, taking inferences in the light most favorable to the jury's verdict, rather than resting content with slogans.

Brigham shows up on short notice with Amos, who the jury could conclude was there to receive 10 kilograms of cocaine from strangers whom Thompson and Amos do not trust. Is Amos likely to come alone? Is a companion apt to be ignorant of the nature and risks of the transaction? For almost three hours Brigham remains at the motel, generally observant and generally nervous; he follows Amos to a pay phone where a telephone call and conversation ensue. Amos reveals the contents of this conversation to the agents; the jury could conclude that he revealed it to Brigham too. While Amos and an agent go to dinner, Brigham keeps watch. After Amos returns, eye contact and a nod from Amos lead Brigham to take up position where he can watch the trunk of the agents' car. Just what was Brigham doing for three hours in the lobby and parking lot of the motel, if not assisting Amos? He was not exactly passing through while a drug deal went down around him. Brigham did not testify, and his lawyer offered no hypothesis at trial. At oral argument of this appeal the best his counsel could do was to suggest that Brigham might have believed that Amos was picking up counterfeit money rather than drugs. Tell us another! The jury was entitled to conclude that Brigham knew about, and joined, a conspiracy to distribute cocaine.

Thin the evidence was, but it was also sufficient. Evidence at sentencing shows that the jury drew the right inference. Amos related that he brought Brigham as a lookout. Brigham told the prosecutor that he was part of the organization and had been involved in some big-stakes transactions. But he was unable to provide enough information to induce the prosecutor to make the motion under § 3553(e) that unlocks the trap door in the sentencing "floor." Pleading guilty would have produced the 10-year minimum term, so Brigham went to trial; he had nothing to lose and some chance of being acquitted. The evidence at sentencing showed that Brigham knew that Thompson's organization dealt in multi-kilogram quantities, which supports the judge's conclusion that Brigham qualifies for the 10-year minimum.

All that remains is Brigham's argument that the judge should have invoked U.S.S.G. § 5K2.0 to give him a break. Section 5K2.0 describes appropriate departures from the guidelines, but Brigham needed a departure from a minimum sentence prescribed by statute. That was available only on motion of the prosecutor under § 3553(e). Brigham does not contend that in declining to make the motion the prosecutor violated the Constitution. . . .

Wise exercise of prosecutorial discretion can prevent egregious sentencing inversions. How that discretion is to be exercised is a subject for the political branches. Brigham joined the conspiracy and received a sentence authorized by Congress. His judicial remedies are at a close.

Affirmed.

DISSENT

Bauer, Chief Judge, dissenting.

I respectfully dissent. Taking all the evidence as described in the majority opinion as absolutely true, and viewing it in the light most favorable to the government, I still do not find that any sensible juror could find Brigham guilty of the crime of conspiracy beyond a reasonable doubt. At oral argument, counsel for Brigham could only suggest, in answer to a question from the bench as to what explanation he could give for Brigham's actions on the day in question, "that Brigham might have believed that Amos was picking up counterfeit money rather than drugs." An unbelievable scenario. The fact is, no one testified as to what exactly Brigham was doing or why he was doing it; no one, in spite of the marvelous totally cooperating witnesses who, if the government's theory is correct, could have nailed Brigham's hide to the jailhouse wall. But they didn't. And it is not Brigham's missing explanation that is fatal; it is the government's inability to explain that creates the problem.

Tell us another, indeed, but only if it is the government tale; the accused has absolutely no burden to explain anything. The government accuses, the defendant says "prove it," and the government says the suspicious activity is enough to convince and convict.

And so it proved.

I would have directed a verdict of "not guilty" had I been the trial judge and I construe my role in review to be the same. I do not believe the evidence sufficient

to convince a sensible juror of proof beyond a reasonable doubt. The existence of cooperating witnesses
who knew all and told nothing virtually implies the
missing witness analysis: you had the control, you did-
n't produce, I infer the testimony would have been adverse to you.

I would reverse.

CASE DISCUSSION

What are Judge Easterbrook's exact objections to the
mandatory minimum sentence that he was obliged to
impose in this case? Do you agree? Defend your
answer.

Offenders' Rights at Sentencing

The U.S. Supreme Court has repeatedly held that convicted offenders enjoy considerably fewer procedural safeguards than do defendants during trial. The Court has established a firm distinction between the trial stage and the sentencing stage of the criminal
process. In part, this separation depends on history. Most of the procedural safeguards
written into the Constitution were originally intended to protect the trial itself from
abuse. Also, the distinction rests on the objective of sentencing. Determining the proper
punishment for the individual and the crime demands the flexibility that rigid rules of
procedure inhibit.

The Sixth Amendment right of convicted offenders to confront their accusers is considerably reduced at sentencing. Trial judges can consider information supplied outside
court, such as the reports of probation officers or of others who know about an offender's personal life and the circumstances of the crime but who do not appear in
court. Subject only to the trustworthiness of the information, judges can draw upon it.
Offenders have no right either to confront or to cross-examine persons who have supplied adverse information about them.[13]

The due process rights of convicted offenders are also reduced during the sentencing stage. Trial judges can consider numerous issues outside the record of the trial, and
they may also consider the conduct of defendants during the trial. For example, the
Supreme Court held that it did not violate the due process rights of a convicted offender for a trial judge to consider, as an issue in sentencing, the refusal of the defendant to assist officers in their investigation of a conspiracy in which the defendant
admittedly participated.

Defendants have a right to counsel at sentencing. Furthermore, the equal protection
clause restricts the type of sentence that judges can impose. Usually, the claim of denial
of equal protection arises in cases of sentences combining imprisonment and a fine or
probation conditioned on the payment of money. For example, it violates equal protection to limit payment of fines to those who can afford to pay them but to convert the
fines to imprisonment for those who cannot pay them. Furthermore, a court cannot re-
voke offenders' probation and imprison them because they fail to pay a fine and restitution, except in cases when an offender is either able to pay and refuses or no available
alternatives satisfy the state's interest in punishment and deterrence.[14]

The cruel-and-unusual-punishment clause of the Eighth Amendment limits both
legislatures in prescribing some sentences and judges in imposing sentences. According
to a plurality of the Supreme Court, this clause does not apply to the length of a sen-

tence. According to a majority of the same court, it is not cruel and unusual punishment for the legislature to prescribe a mandatory life sentence without parole for the intent to possess 600 grams of cocaine, even through the only other crime punishable by a sentence that severe is first-degree murder.[15]

A majority of the Court adheres to the view that "death is different," so the cruel-and-unusual-punishment clause applies both to death penalty statutes and to the imposition of the death sentence in the courts. Although the clause "appl[ies] to capital punishment," this does not mean that capital punishment violates the clause in all cases. The Court addressed the question of the application of the cruel-and-unusual-punishment clause to a sentence of death for rape in *Coker v. Georgia.*

C A S E

Was the Death Sentence Cruel and Unusual Punishment?

Coker v. Georgia
433 U.S. 584, 97 S.Ct. 2861, 53 L.Ed.2d 982 (1977)

Coker was convicted of rape and sentenced to death. Both the conviction and the sentence were affirmed by the Georgia Supreme Court. Coker was granted a writ of certiorari, *limited to the single claim, rejected by the Georgia court, that the punishment of death for rape violates the Eighth Amendment, which proscribes "cruel and unusual punishments" and which must be observed by the states as well as the federal government. Justice White announced the judgment of the Court and filed an opinion in which Justice Stewart, Justice Blackmun, and Justice Stevens joined. Chief Justice Burger, whom Justice Rehnquist joined, dissented.*

FACTS

While serving various sentences for murder, rape, kidnapping, and aggravated assault, petitioner escaped from the Ware Correctional Institute near Waycross, Ga., on September 2, 1974. At approximately 11 o'clock that night, petitioner entered the home of Allen and Elnita Carver through an unlocked kitchen door. Threatening the couple with a "board," he tied up Mr. Carver in the bathroom, obtained a knife from the kitchen, and took Mr. Carver's money and the keys to the family car. Brandishing the knife and saying "you know

what's going to happen to you if you try anything, don't you," Coker then raped Mrs. Carver. Soon thereafter, petitioner drove away in the Carver car, taking Mrs. Carver with him. Mr. Carver, freeing himself, notified the police; and not long thereafter petitioner was apprehended. Mrs. Carver was unharmed.

Petitioner was charged with escape, armed robbery, vehicle theft, kidnapping, and rape. Counsel was appointed to represent him. Having been found competent to stand trial, he was tried. The jury returned a verdict of guilty, rejecting his general plea of insanity. A sentencing hearing was then conducted in accordance with the procedures dealt with at length in *Gregg v. Georgia* (1976), where this Court sustained the death penalty for murder when imposed pursuant to the statutory procedures. The jury was instructed that it could consider as aggravating circumstances whether the rape had been committed by a person with a prior record of conviction for a capital felony and whether the rape had been committed in the course of committing another capital felony, namely, the armed robbery of Allen Carver. The court also instructed, pursuant to statute, that even if aggravating circumstances were present, the death penalty need not be imposed if the jury found they were out-weighed by mitigating circumstances, that is, circumstances not constituting justification or excuse for the offense in question, "but which, in fairness and mercy, may be considered as extenuating or reducing the degree" of moral culpability or punishment. The jury's verdict on the rape count was death by electro-cution. Both aggravating circumstances on which the court instructed were found to be present by the jury.

OPINION

Furman v. Georgia (1972), and the Court's decisions last Term in *Gregg v. Georgia* (1976); *Proffitt v. Florida* (1976); *Jurek v. Texas* (1976); *Woodson v. North Carolina* (1976); and *Roberts v. Louisiana*, make unnecessary the recanvassing of certain critical aspects of the controversy about the constitutionality of capital punishment. It is now settled that the death penalty is not invariably cruel and unusual punish-ment within the meaning of the Eighth Amendment; it is not inherently barbaric or an unacceptable mode of punishment for crime; neither is it always dispro-portionate to the crime for which it is imposed. It is also established that imposing capital punishment, at least for murder, in accordance with the procedures provided under the Georgia statutes saves the sen-tence from the infirmities which led the Court to in-validate the prior Georgia capital punishment statute in *Furman v. Georgia.*

In sustaining the imposition of the death penalty in *Gregg,* however, the Court firmly embraced the holdings and dicta from prior cases to the effect that the Eighth Amendment bars not only those punish-ments that are "barbaric" but also those that are "ex-cessive" in relation to the crime committed. Under *Gregg,* a punishment is "excessive" and unconstitu-tional if it

1. makes no measurable contribution to acceptable goals of punishment and hence is nothing more than the purposeless and needless imposition of pain and suffering; or

2. is grossly out of proportion to the severity of the crime.

A punishment might fail the test on either ground.

Furthermore, these Eighth Amendment judgments should not be, or appear to be, merely the subjective views of individual Justices; judgment should be in-formed by objective factors to the maximum possible extent. To this end, attention must be given to the pub-lic attitudes concerning a particular sentence history and precedent, legislative attitudes, and the response of

juries reflected in their sentencing decisions are to be consulted. In *Gregg,* after giving due regard to such sources, the Court's judgment was that the death penalty for deliberate murder was neither the purpose-less imposition of severe punishment nor a punishment grossly disproportionate to the crime. But the Court re-served the question of the constitutionality of the death penalty when imposed for other crimes.

That question, with respect to rape of an adult woman, is now before us. We have concluded that a sentence of death is grossly disproportionate and ex-cessive punishment for the crime of rape and is there-fore forbidden by the Eighth Amendment as cruel and unusual punishment.

Because the death sentence is a disproportionate punishment for rape, it is cruel and unusual punish-ment within the meaning of the Eighth Amendment even though it may measurably serve the legitimate ends of punishment and therefore is not invalid for its failure to do so. We observe that in the light of the leg-islative decisions in almost all of the States and in most of the countries around the world, it would be difficult to support a claim that the death penalty for rape is an indispensable part of the States' criminal justice system. . . .

We do not discount the seriousness of rape as a crime. It is highly reprehensible, both in a moral sense and in its almost total contempt for the personal integrity and autonomy of the female victim and for the latter's privilege of choosing those with whom in-timate relationships are to be established. Short of homicide, it is the "ultimate violation of self." It is also a violent crime because it normally involves force, or the threat of force or intimidation, to overcome the will and the capacity of the victim to resist. Rape is very often accompanied by physical injury to the fe-male and can also inflict mental and psychological damage. Because it undermines the community's sense of security, there is public injury as well.

Rape is without doubt deserving of serious punish-ment; but in terms of moral depravity and of the in-jury to the person and to the public, it does not compare with murder, which does involve the unjus-tified taking of human life. Although it may be ac-companied by another crime, rape by definition does not include the death of or even the serious injury to another person. The murderer kills; the rapist, if no more than that, does not. Life is over for the victim of the murderer; for the rape victim, life may not be nearly so happy as it was, but it is not over and normally is not beyond repair. We have the abiding conviction that the death penalty, which "is unique in its severity and irrevocability," is an excessive penalty for the rapist who, as such, does not take human life. . . .

The judgment of the Georgia Supreme Court upholding the death sentence is reversed, and the case is remanded to that court for further proceedings not inconsistent with this opinion.

So ordered.

[NOTE: Concurring opinions holding that the death penalty in all cases is unconstitutional are omitted here.]

DISSENT

Chief Justice Burger, whom Justice Rehnquist joins, dissenting.

In a case such as this, confusion often arises as to the Court's proper role in reaching a decision. Our task is not to give effect to our individual views on capital punishment; rather, we must determine what the Constitution permits a State to do under its reserved powers. In striking down the death penalty imposed upon the petitioner in this case, the Court has overstepped the bounds of proper constitutional adjudication by substituting its policy judgment for that of the state legislature. I accept that the Eighth Amendment's concept of disproportionality bars the death penalty for minor crimes. But rape is not a minor crime; hence the Cruel and Unusual Punishments Clause does not give the Members of this Court license to engraft their conceptions of proper public policy onto the considered legislative judgments of the States. Since I cannot agree that Georgia lacked the constitutional power to impose the penalty of death for rape, I dissent from the Court's judgment. . . .

In sum, once the Court has held that "the punishment of death does not invariably violate the Constitution," it seriously impinges upon the State's legislative judgment to hold that it may not impose such sentence upon an individual who has shown total and repeated disregard for the welfare, safety, personal integrity, and human worth of others, and who seemingly cannot be deterred from continuing such conduct. I therefore

would hold that the death sentence here imposed is within the power reserved to the State and leave for another day the question of whether such sanction would be proper under other circumstances. The dangers which inhere whenever the Court casts its constitutional decisions in terms sweeping beyond the facts of the case presented, are magnified in the context of the Eighth Amendment. . . .

Victims may recover from the physical damage of knife or bullet wounds, or a beating with fists or a club, but recovery from such a gross assault on the human personality is not healed by medicine or surgery. . . . Despite its strong condemnation of rape, the Court reaches the inexplicable conclusion that "the death penalty . . . is an excessive penalty" for the perpetrator of this heinous offense. This, the Court holds, is true even though in Georgia the death penalty may be imposed only where the rape is coupled with one or more aggravating circumstances. . . .

Only one year ago the Court held it constitutionally permissible to impose the death penalty for the crime of murder, provided that certain procedural safeguards are followed. Today, the plurality readily admits that "(s)hort of homicide, (rape) is the 'ultimate violation of self.'" Moreover, as stated by Mr. Justice Powell: "The threat of serious injury is implicit in the definition of rape; the victim is either forced into submission by physical violence or by the threat of violence."

Rape thus is not a crime "light years" removed from murder in the degree of its heinousness; it certainly poses a serious potential danger to the life and safety of innocent victims apart from the devastating psychic consequences. It would seem to follow therefore that, affording the States proper leeway under the broad standard of the Eighth Amendment, [if] murder is properly punishable by death, rape should be also, if that is the considered judgment of the legislators.

The Court's conclusion to the contrary is very disturbing indeed. The clear implication of today's holding appears to be that the death penalty may be properly imposed only as to crimes resulting in death of the victim. This casts serious doubts upon the constitutional validity of statutes imposing the death penalty for a variety of conduct which, though dangerous, may not necessarily result in any immediate death, e.g., treason, airplane hijacking, and kidnap-ping. In that respect, today's holding does even more than is initially apparent. We cannot avoid taking judicial notice that crimes such as airplane hijacking, kidnapping, and mass terrorist activity constitute a serious and increasing danger to the safety of the public. It would be unfortunate indeed if the effect of today's holding were to inhibit States and the Federal Government from experimenting with various remedies including possibly imposition of the penalty of death to prevent and deter such crimes. . . .

Whatever our individual views as to the wisdom of capital punishment, I cannot agree that it is constitutionally impermissible for a state legislature to make the "solemn judgment" to impose such penalty for the crime of rape. Accordingly, I would leave to the States the task of legislating in this area of the law.

CASE DISCUSSION

How did the majority arrive at the conclusion that the death penalty for rape is cruel and unusual punishment? Was it, as the dissent argues, a subjective judgment, or did the majority apply objective criteria? Should the states be allowed to determine for themselves what punishments to apply to specific crimes? What, in your opinion, does *cruel and unusual* mean? How would you apply it to this case?

The Court has held that capital punishment for murder is not cruel and unusual punishment as long as the sentencing process allows the judge or jury to consider — and offers adequate guidance in weighing — mitigating and aggravating circumstances (see Table 13.1) and provides for a review procedure to ensure against discriminatory application of the death penalty.[16] According to the Supreme Court, the rationale for the requirements of weighing mitigating and aggravating circumstances according to a procedure of adequate guidance to juries and judges and of reviewing the death sentence is that "[i]t is of vital importance to the defendant and to the community that any decision to impose the death sentence be, and appear to be, based on reason rather than caprice or emotion."[17]

Statistics indicate that there is a pronounced racial disparity in death sentences. African Americans who kill whites are more likely to receive the death sentence than either African Americans who kill African Americans or whites who kill African Americans. This has led to an argument that death sentences discriminate against blacks and undermine the confidence of the public in the fairness and impartiality of capital punishment. The Supreme Court has held that such statistical evidence does not establish cruel and unusual punishment in the administration of the death penalty. Defendants must prove that the sentence of death in their particular case was racially motivated; it is not enough to produce general statistical evidence of disparity.[18]

APPEALS

Convicted offenders do not have a constitutional right to appeal their convictions. According to the Supreme Court, "[I]t is clear that the State need not provide any appeal at all." In a case upholding the denial of an indigent defendant of the right to a lawyer on a discretionary appeal to a state supreme court, the Court explained the differences between trial and appeal:

TABLE 13.1 AGGRAVATING AND MITIGATING CIRCUMSTANCES IN DEATH PENALTY CASES

Aggravating Circumstances	Mitigating Circumstances
Prior record of violent felony	No significant prior criminal record
Felony murder	Extreme mental or emotional disturbance
Murder of more than one person	Minor participant in the murder
Murder of police officer or other public official	Youth at the time of the murder
Torture or other heinous killing	
Killing to avoid arrest	
Killing during escape from lawful custody	

. . . [T]here are significant differences between the trial and appellate stages of a criminal proceeding. The purpose of the trial stage from the State's point of view is to convert a criminal defendant from a person presumed innocent to one found guilty beyond a reasonable doubt. To accomplish this purpose, the State employs a prosecuting attorney who presents evidence to the court, challenges any witnesses offered by the defendant, argues rulings of the court, and makes direct arguments to the court and jury seeking to persuade them of the defendant's guilt. Under these circumstances "reason and reflection require us to recognize that in our adversary system of criminal justice, any person haled into court, who is too poor to hire a lawyer, cannot be assured a fair trial unless counsel is provided for him."

By contrast, it is ordinarily the defendant, rather than the state, who initiates the appellate process, seeking not to fend off the efforts of the state's prosecutor but rather to overturn a finding of guilty made by a judge or a jury below. The defendant needs an attorney on appeal not as a shield to protect him against being "haled into court" by the state and stripped of his presumption of innocence, but rather as a sword to upset the prior determination of guilt. This difference is significant for, while no one would agree that the state may simply dispense with the trial stage of proceedings without a criminal defendant's consent, it is clear that the state need not provide any appeal at all.[19]

Even though the United States Constitution does not require it, every jurisdiction has created a statutory right to appeal. The federal government and most states have a two-tiered appellate structure. Appeal to the intermediate appellate court is a right; appeal to the state supreme court from the intermediate appellate court is discretionary. Most of the cases in this book, the United States Supreme Court opinions, are discretionary appeal cases. The writ of *certiorari* is a discretionary writ, allowing appeals only in cases that the Court believes are of significance beyond the interests of the particular defendants appealing them.

The Court accepts cases in which lower courts and criminal justice personnel throughout the country require the Court's guidance. Many of the cases you have read refer to the Court's granting *certiorari* to settle a conflict among the circuits — that is, circuits have disagreed about the interpretation or application of constitutional requirements. In other cases, the Court refers to the importance of the case in guiding law enforcement officers in searches, stops and frisks, arrests, interrogation, and identification procedures involving confusion or uncertainty about what the Constitution allows or requires. The Court began in the late 1980s to reduce the number of cases it accepts by means of *certiorari*. By this reduction, the Court has reaffirmed the principle that final appeal is not a right, but lies within the discretion of the appellate court.

Three principal doctrines define the scope of appellate review of criminal cases:

1. Mootness
2. Raise or waive
3. Plain error

The **mootness doctrine** traditionally excluded from appeal cases in which the sentence was satisfied. Defendants who had served their time in prison or who had paid their fines could not appeal. Some jurisdictions have retained the traditional rule of mootness. Several others have gone to the other extreme, holding that criminal cases are never moot because defendants always have an interest in removing the "stigma of guilt" even after serving a full sentence. However, most jurisdictions have taken a middle ground, retaining the mootness doctrine but carving exceptions to it.

The **collateral consequences exception** is the doctrine that if defendants might suffer legal consequences from a criminal conviction, then even if the sentence is served, the case is not moot. These consequences include such impediments as the possibility of loss of professional license, rejection for admission to a professional school, or loss of employment because of criminal conviction. Some jurisdictions require appellants to demonstrate specific legal consequences that might arise out of the conviction after sentence is served in order to qualify for the collateral consequences exception.

The **raise-or-waive doctrine** requires defendants to raise their objections at trial and preserve them in the record of proceedings, or else they waive their right to appeal trial court rulings. The most common limit on the scope of appellate review of criminal cases, this doctrine rests principally on the rationale of judicial economy. If the loser at trial can obtain reversal because of an error not objected to, the parties and the public spend time and money on second trials and appeals that they could have avoided by objecting during the trial. The Oregon Court of Appeals dealt with the raise-or-waive doctrine and the rationales for it in *State v. Applegate*.

C A S E

Did He Waive the Objection By Not Raising It?

State v. Applegate
39 Or.App. 17, 591 P.2d 371 (1979)

The Circuit Court, Multnomah County, found Applegate guilty of third-degree robbery, unauthorized use of an automobile, and first-degree theft. Applegate appealed. The court of appeals affirmed before Chief Judge Schwab and Judges Tanzer, Richardson, and

Roberts. Chief Judge Schwab wrote the opinion of the court.

FACTS

The evidence established that Mr. Rowe owned the Roaring West Tavern and Mr. Dixon was the manager. The evening of July 22, 1977, Dixon was tending bar and defendant was a customer. When the tavern closed, Dixon and defendant left together to socialize elsewhere. Dixon placed over $500 in tavern receipts in the trunk of his car, presumably to deposit in the bank the next day. Dixon and defendant then went tavern-hopping for several hours, traveling in Dixon's 1970 Cadillac. Later, by which time it was the early morning hours of July 23, defendant struck Dixon in the face and head and demanded and took the money in his wallet[:] the basis of the robbery charge. Defendant then drove off in Dixon's car[:] the basis of the unauthorized-use charge. When the car was recovered a couple of days later, the tavern receipts were gone from the trunk[:] the basis of the charge of theft of Rowe's property.

Defendant was represented at trial by an experienced criminal defense attorney from the office of Metropolitan Public Defender. At no point in the proceedings did his counsel in any way suggest that the merger doctrine was applicable or that defendant could not be separately convicted and sentenced on the three counts. When the trial court did, in fact, enter separate convictions and sentences on the three counts, there was not a single syllable of objection.

OPINION

Whether and to what extent merger questions have to be first raised in the trial court as a condition precedent to appellate consideration has long been a problem in this court. . . . [A]s various facets of the merger doctrine have become firmly established by our decisions, we have stated that we will not consider those particular facets unless the merger issue was first raised in the trial court. Such pronouncements were not intended to, and have not, barred us from considering new and different facets of the merger problem on our own initiative. Thus, a synthesis of our decisions would be: generally, merger questions must be raised in the trial court, especially those merger questions that are relatively settled; but in exceptional circumstances this court reverses the right to consider a merger question not raised in the trial court, especially when it presents a novel problem.

This synthesis was recently challenged in *State v. Harris* (1978) (specially concurring opinion). There it was argued that merger "ought not to be the kind of

error that is waived if not raised in the trial court." Because of this challenge, we here reconsider and attempt to finally resolve the question of whether merger issues must be presented to and preserved in the trial courts. The presentment-and-preservation or raise-or-waive rule has a partially statutory basis, ORS 17.505 to 17.515 and is embodied in Rule 7.19, Rules of Procedure of the Supreme Court and Court of Appeals. And aside from the statute and court rule, a general common-law raise-or-waive rule has been applied in all types of cases, including criminal. There are definitely dozens, possibly hundreds, of Oregon appellate decisions that have declined to reach a tendered issue on the ground that it was not raised in the trial court.

There are many rationales for the raise-or-waive rule: that it is a necessary corollary of our adversary system in which issues are framed by the litigants and presented to a court; that fairness to all parties requires a litigant to advance his contentions at a time when there is an opportunity to respond to them factually, if his opponent chooses to; that the rule promotes efficient trial proceedings; that reversing for error not preserved permits the losing side to second-guess its tactical decisions after they do not produce the desired result; and that there is something unseemly about telling a lower court it was wrong when it never was presented with the opportunity to be right. The principal rationale, however, is judicial economy. There are two components to judicial economy: (1) if the losing side can obtain an appellate reversal because of error not objected to, the parties and public are put to the expense that could have been avoided had an objection been made; and (2) if an issue had been raised in the trial court, it could have been resolved there, and the parties and public would be spared the expense of an appeal.

Admittedly, not all of the rationales for requiring preservation of claimed error are fully applicable to merger issues. However, the needless appeal rationale is fully applicable. Thus, to illustrate, suppose a person were separately charged with transporting and with possessing the same illegal drug at the same time and place, and the jury returned guilty verdicts on both counts. If the defendant then raised the merger question in the trial court, it is settled that the counts should be merged and only one conviction entered and one sentence imposed. If, instead, the defendant were permitted to ignore merger in the trial court and to appeal on the sole ground that the trial court erred in not merging, he would be correct, but the parties and public would assume the expense of an appeal that could have been avoided. In this era when the number of appeals and the cost of appeals are both increasing, the needless appeal rationale is sufficient reason standing alone to justify general application of a raise-or-waive rule to merger issues. . . .

    Affirmed.

CASE DISCUSSION

What objection did Applegate fail to raise at trial? What reasons did the court give for applying the raise-or-waive rule to the facts of this case? Are these reasons in the interests of correct result, finality, efficiency, individual rights, control of government, crime control, or some other interest? Which interest ought to take precedence? Do you think that Applegate should forfeit his appeal because his lawyer did not raise the objection of merger at trial? Defend your answer.

    Defendants do not always waive their right to appeal by failing to object at trial. When procedural requirements do not provide adequate time for a defendant to object to a trial court error, the defendant does not waive the right to appeal the error. Sometimes, the rule of timely objection may be fair, but circumstances can make it impossible for a defendant to comply with it. For example, a defendant represented by incompetent counsel does not waive the right to appeal on the grounds of ineffective counsel by failing to raise the objection during the trial. Obviously, incompetent counsel do not routinely object to their own ineffectiveness. Furthermore, appellate courts sometimes accept appeals despite the raise-or-waive doctrine. If an appeal serves the interest of **judicial economy,** appellate courts might accept it. For example, accepting appeals in cases that raise a "strong possibility of reoccurrence" saves time and expense by settling the issues in the present appeals.[20]

    Courts in most jurisdictions reverse trial court rulings in cases of plain error even if an objection was not raised at trial. The **plain error doctrine** applies when "plain errors affecting substantial rights" cause "manifest injustice or miscarriage of justice." However, most courts apply the doctrine "sparingly." Plain error does not require or justify a review "of every alleged trial error that has not been properly preserved for appellate review." Furthermore, in most jurisdictions, the "defendant bears the burden of proving that an alleged error is of such magnitude that it constitutes plain error." According to one commentator, " '[P]lain error' is a concept appellate courts find it impossible to define, save that they know it when they see it." Professors Wayne R. LaFave and Jerold Israel find some guidelines from the cases:

1. The closer the evidence is balanced, the more likely courts are to apply the doctrine.

2. Constitutional errors are more likely to call the doctrine into play than statutory or rule errors.

3. Where error could easily have been corrected during trial, the appellate courts are less likely to apply the doctrine.[21]

    The Missouri Court of Appeals applied the plain error doctrine in *State v. Vanzandt.*

C A S E

Did the Trial Court Commit Plain Error?

State v. Vanzandt
809 S.W.2d 881 (Mo.App. 1991)

Kenneth Vanzandt (defendant) appeals from judgments of the Circuit Court of Lawrence County. He appeals a judgment of conviction, following a jury trial, of assault in the first degree in which he was charged with and found guilty of inflicting serious injury on the victim in the course of committing that offense. § 565.050. He was tried and sentenced as a persistent offender. § 558.016.3. The defendant filed a post-conviction motion pursuant to Rule 29.15 that was overruled following an evidentiary hearing. He also appeals the judgment that overruled that motion. The defendant's appeals were consolidated as required by Rule 29.15(1). Both judgments are affirmed. Parrish, Presiding Judge.

FACTS

Defendant left the home of Kenneth Cooper. He was accompanied by Cooper and a fifteen-year old girl Cooper was dating, Hazel Cross. Defendant and Cooper had been drinking beer. Defendant had also taken small, football-shaped pills. The three were in an automobile that was traveling in a southerly direction on Highway 37 in Barry County. Defendant was driving. Hazel Cross and Kenneth Cooper were sitting in the front seat with defendant—Hazel sat in the middle. Defendant's automobile overtook, but did not pass, a truck, a tractor-trailer unit, that was going the same direction as defendant. The truck was driven by Virgil Eckhardt.

Eckhardt saw defendant's car approaching. He thought the car struck the back of his truck. He attempted to pull the truck onto the shoulder of the highway, but stopped short of doing so. He thought he saw the headlights from defendant's car at a location that would interfere with his effort to pull onto that shoulder. Eckhardt stopped his truck partially on the highway and partially on his right-hand shoulder. He

got out of the truck, taking a device used to strike tires to determine whether they were flat, a "tire buddy." The tire buddy had a wooden handle. Eckhardt put it in his right, rear pocket "for protection." He walked toward the back of the truck where defendant's car had stopped.

Defendant had gotten out of his car after first removing a knife that he was carrying in his boot. Defendant approached Eckhardt, knife in hand. Defendant told Eckhardt, with the use of some profanity, that he had stopped the wrong car. Eckhardt backed away. Defendant continued to move forward and stabbed Eckhardt in the stomach. Eckhardt hit defendant's hand with the tire buddy in an attempt to dislodge the knife. Defendant stabbed Eckhardt four more times. Sometime during the skirmish, defendant had taken the tire buddy from Eckhardt and hit Eckhardt with it above the right eye.

Hazel remained in the car. Cooper had gotten out of the passenger side. As the altercation moved toward the front of Eckhardt's truck, Cooper got back inside the car. Hazel moved to the driver's side of the car and drove it alongside defendant and Eckhardt. Defendant got into the car on the driver's side and drove it away. After entering the car, defendant asked Hazel and Cooper how many times they had seen him stab Eckhardt. Cooper told him, "About three times."

When defendant got back inside the car, he placed the knife on the visor. Blood was visible on the knife. He later moved the knife to the rear view mirror. Defendant had part of the tire buddy—it had been broken. He gave that part of the tire buddy to Cooper and told Cooper to throw it out the window. Cooper did as told.

Defendant drove to his mother's house where his car became stuck in the ditch. A deputy sheriff observed defendant and his passengers trying to move the car. The deputy sheriff approached the car and told defendant to get out of the car. After some delay in responding to the deputy sheriff's request, defendant complied. He was then arrested.

OPINION

Defendant's first point on appeal seeks plain error review of the trial court's failure to *sua sponte* disqualify the attorney who represented defendant at trial as a result of remarks made during voir dire. Defendant complains that his attorney in the criminal case "stated, during voir dire, that he and his partners served 'intermittently between us' as the city attorney for Monett, Missouri"; that this constituted a "conflict of interest due to counsel's prosecutorial responsibilities."

Having reviewed the transcript of the criminal trial, this court declines to invoke plain error review as to defendant's first point on appeal. However, it is appropriate to note, as aptly raised in respondent's brief, "[t]he mere existence of a possible conflict of interest does not preclude effective representation." A claim of conflict of interest is not cognizable on the basis of speculation. Defendant's first point is denied.

Defendant's second point on appeal contends that plain error occurred by the trial court's "allowing the state to present evidence that [defendant] had taken 'some little football-shaped pills' and in allowing the prosecuting attorney, during closing argument, to argue that on the day of and prior to the commission of the charged offense, [defendant] had been 'piling it up.'" Defendant argues that this resulted in an improper assertion that defendant had "a bad character and propensity to commit crimes."

The request that this court grant plain error review of defendant's second point is denied. Defendant's guilt was established, as demonstrated by the facts stated, by overwhelming evidence. There is no showing of manifest injustice or miscarriage of justice.

Defendant's third point on appeal is directed to the trial court's ruling on an objection made to a question the prosecuting attorney posed to defense witness Dr. Jerald Johnson. Defendant argues that the overruling of the objection was plain error. The trial transcript reflects the following:

Redirect examination by Mr. Woods [defendant's attorney]:

Q: Do you recall the date of the last time before this date that you treated him, Doctor?

A: No sir, I didn't bring those records with me. It was some time —

Q: Was it over a year, or six months?

A: I would think 1982, but I'd have to check my records.

Mr. Woods: No further questions.

Recross-examination by Mr. Lewright [prosecuting attorney]:

Q: Do you recall where?

Mr. Woods: If the Court please, I'll object to where.

Mr. Lewright: Your Honor, he asked for the date, and he opened it up.

The Court: I'll overrule the objection. You may answer, if you can, Doctor. Where?

The Witness: It was at the Barry County jail.

Defendant argues that the doctor's response inferred "that [defendant] had been previously incarcerated for a prior, uncharged crime."

Considering the entire record on appeal and the fact that defendant's guilt was established by overwhelming evidence, no manifest injustice or miscarriage of justice appears. Defendant's third point is denied.

Defendant's fourth point on appeal is directed to the judgment by which the motion court overruled defendant's Rule 29.15 motion. Defendant alleges that the motion court erred in not granting relief because he received ineffective assistance of trial counsel. Defendant asserts that his trial counsel was ineffective, "when defense counsel knew that [defendant] was taking Xanax under the supervision of a physician and did not introduce such evidence to rebut the prejudicial effect of the state's evidence that [defendant] was taking football-shaped pills on the day of the offense and 'piling it up.'"

Defendant raises this issue for the first time on appeal. "Appellate court review of a motion under Rule 29.15 is limited to a determination of whether the findings and conclusions of the trial court are clearly erroneous. Rule 29.15(j)." *Hayes v. State* (Mo.App. 1989). Since defendant's complaint was not presented to the motion court, that allegation is not cognizable on appeal. Defendant's fourth point is denied. The judgment of conviction of the trial court and the judgment of the motion court overruling defendant's Rule 29.15 motion are affirmed.

Flanigan, C. J., and Shrum, J., concur.

CASE DISCUSSION

What were the errors to which Kenneth Vanzandt objected? How did the court define the plain error doctrine? When does the doctrine apply, according to the court? Why does it not apply to the facts of this case, according to the court? Do you agree? Explain. What is the difference between plain error and prejudicial error, according to the court?

———————————◼◻——————————

HABEAS CORPUS

In appeals, defendants take their cases from the state or federal trial courts to intermediate state and federal appellate courts, and then to the state supreme courts and to the United States Supreme Court. If all appeals fail, defendants can wage an indirect attack, or **collateral attack,** on their convictions. The principal collateral attack is *habeas corpus.* Most states have *habeas corpus*-like proceedings. The following discussion concentrates on the more widely used federal ***habeas corpus* proceeding,** which begins in the federal district court and proceeds through the court of appeals to the Supreme Court. It is a civil action, not a criminal proceeding. It challenges the lawfulness of the defendant's imprisonment, either in jails prior to conviction or in state or federal prisons following conviction. It is not a trial of the guilt of the defendant.

Jurisdiction in *habeas corpus* arises from the United States Constitution, Article I: " . . . [T]he privilege of the Writ of Habeas Corpus shall not be suspended, unless when in Cases of Rebellion or Invasion the public Safety may require it." Two federal statutes have empowered the federal courts to grant petitions of *habeas corpus,* conduct *habeas corpus* proceedings, and issue writs of *habeas corpus.* The Judiciary Act of 1789 authorized federal courts to proceed with the petitions of *federal* prisoners. The Habeas Corpus Act of 1867 provides the basis of federal jurisdiction over *state* prisoners. According to the Habeas Corpus Act,

> the several courts of the United States . . . within their respective jurisdictions, in addition to the authority already conferred by law, shall have power to grant writs of habeas corpus in all cases where any person may be restrained of his or her liberty in violation of the Constitution, or of any treaty or law of the United States.[22]

The language of the act of 1867 lends itself both to a narrow interpretation and a broad interpretation of the power of the federal courts to review the imprisonment of state prisoners. According to the narrow view, the act authorizes the courts only to review the **jurisdiction of the court**—that is, its authority over the person and subject matter of the case. In other words, the review asks only whether the court has the power to hear criminal cases and whether it can decide criminal cases involving the prisoner. According to the broader view, the act empowers the federal courts to review the whole state proceeding to determine possible violations of federal law and constitutional provisions.[23]

During the years of the Warren Court, when federal rights were expanding through the incorporation doctrine (see Chapter 2), the Court opted for the broad interpretation. Justice William Brennan, especially, argued that the broader view fulfilled the historical purpose of *habeas corpus,* "providing relief against the detention of persons in violation of their fundamental liberties." As to objections that such expansive review of lower court proceedings threatened the interest in finality, he argued that "conventional notions of finality of litigation" should "have no place where life or liberty is at stake and infringement of constitutional rights is alleged." In addition to preserving fundamental liberties, the broader view, according to its supporters, furthers the interest in correct results. The more chances to review, the greater the accuracy of the final decision, they maintain. According to one judge,

> We would not send two astronauts to the moon without providing them with at least three or four back-up systems. Should we send literally thousands of men to prison with even less reserves? . . . [W]ith knowledge of our fallibility and a realization of past errors, we can hardly insure our confidence by creating an irrevocable end to the guil[t] determining process.[24]

Justice Brennan and the Warren Court majority's view has received strong criticism from judges and commentators. Most focus on the threat to finality and the costs of "endless" reviews of legal issues, sometimes extending over years. However, some doubt the effectiveness of the review in protecting prisoners from violations of their fundamental rights. According to Justice Robert H. Jackson, we have no reason to expect more accuracy in a second review than in the initial decision:

> [R]eversal by a higher court is not proof that justice is thereby better done. There is no doubt that if there were a super-Supreme Court, a substantial proportion of our reversals of state courts would also be reversed. We are not final because we are infallible, but we are infallible only because we are final.[25]

Justice Jackson attributed the controversy over *habeas corpus* to three causes:

1. The Supreme Court's use of the due process clause of the Fourteenth Amendment to "subject state courts to increasing federal control"
2. The determination of what due process means by "personal notions of justice instead of by known rules of law"
3. The "breakdown of procedural safeguards against abuse of the writ"[26]

The Burger and Rehnquist Courts have adopted the narrower view of *habeas corpus,* at least in determining what the Congress meant when it enacted the statute in 1867. Warren Court precedents up to the early 1990s stood in the way of a total adoption of the narrow view that would limit *habeas corpus* review to the jurisdiction of the court over the person and the subject matter of the case. But the activist members of the Rehnquist Court have, nevertheless, restricted *habeas corpus* as a means to overturn convictions.

The Rehnquist Court emphasizes the balance of interests that *habeas corpus* proceedings require. On one side of the balance are the constitutional rights of individuals and the need to control government misconduct. On the other side, and in many *habeas corpus* cases outweighing individual rights in specific cases and the need to control government misconduct, are the interests in the following:

- Finality of decisions
- Reliability, or obtaining the correct result
- Certainty in decisions, or promoting reliance on decisions
- Stability of decisions, or promoting the permanence of decisions

- Federalism, or respect for state criminal court decisions
- Burden on federal judicial resources in hearing repeated challenges
- Contempt for the system from repeated and long-drawn-out proceedings
- Impediment that many frivolous claims are to the success of meritorious claims

The main problem in *habeas corpus* arises out of what the Court calls an "endless succession of writs." Historically, an English subject could take a petition to every judge in England. The rule of **res judicata**—that once a matter is decided it cannot be reopened—did not apply to *habeas corpus*. The remnants of that rule linger in the rule that denial of a first petition for *habeas corpus* does not prohibit filing a second petition. Although the rule of *res judicata* does not apply, neither does the modern law allow unlimited petitions. Courts have discretion to deny successive petitions if petitioners try to raise issues that they failed to raise in the first petition.[27]

The **abuse-of-the-writ rule** requires petitioners to prove that they neither deliberately nor negligently failed to raise an issue in the first petition. Tactical decisions by attorneys and the inadvertent failure of competent counsel to raise claims are not cause to grant a petition under the abuse-of-the-writ rule. However, failure to raise a claim because counsel is ineffective *is* cause under the rule (see Chapter 11). In addition to cause, petitioners must also show that the failure to raise the issue prejudiced their case. Although the Court has not specifically defined what *prejudice* means, it probably means that the failure to raise the claim affected the outcome of the case. Placing this burden of proof on *habeas* petitioners discourages baseless petitions and keeps the system open for valid claims for relief, according to the Supreme Court.[28]

The requirement that petitioners demonstrate that they did not abuse the writ—the **cause-and-prejudice rule**—is not hard and fast. It permits, but does not require, courts to deny petitions if defendants fail to satisfy its requirements. For example, **cases of manifest injustice,** those in which the petitioner is likely innocent, are an exception to the rule. The word *innocent* here refers to *factual innocence*—that is, a case in which the petitioner did not in fact commit the crime. It does not refer to cases where the petitioner may be entitled to an acquittal owing either to procedural irregularities or to the government's inability to prove legal guilt beyond a reasonable doubt.[29]

Limits in addition to the cause-and-prejudice rule fall upon state prisoners who seek federal *habeas corpus* relief. State prisoners must exhaust all available state remedies before they seek federal *habeas corpus* relief. When a state prisoner files a petition containing any claim for which a state remedy remains available, the court must dismiss the petition in its entirety. In such a case, the state prisoner may either strike the unexhausted state claim and file again in federal court or exhaust the claim by filing in state court. Furthermore, the claim must violate a *federal* right. Errors in state procedures that do not violate a federal right must be pursued in state courts. Also, federal courts must respect state findings of fact. For example, federal courts, in reviewing petitions of state court convictions, cannot review the credibility of witnesses.[30]

The Supreme Court placed perhaps the most significant limit on federal review of state *habeas corpus* petitions in *Stone v. Powell.* In *Stone*, the Court held that a state prisoner cannot raise a Fourth Amendment illegal-search-and-seizure claim in a federal *habeas corpus* proceeding if the state has already provided an opportunity for the petitioner to raise the issue in state court. The Court held that the interests in finality and economy outweighed the costs of the exclusionary rule.

SUMMARY

After conviction, the procedural rights of defendants diminish. Formal rule gives way to an increase in judicial discretion. Judges have wide discretion in sentencing defendants, subject only to the cruel-and-unusual-punishment standard and the due process clause, which prohibits arbitrary and discriminatory sentences. Judges can consider information outside the trial record in determining a sentence without consulting defendants and without giving defendants the opportunity to confront or cross-examine the source of the information. Defendants do have the right to counsel at sentencing because it is considered a critical stage of the criminal process.

Appellate courts rarely review sentences unless sentencing judges abuse their discretion. Death sentences are an exception. Courts regularly review death sentences to make sure that judges and juries have followed established procedures for assessing mitigating and aggravating circumstances in the decision to impose the ultimate sentence.

Defendants do not have a constitutional right to appeal, but every jurisdiction provides an automatic statutory right to appeal to an intermediate appellate court and a discretionary right to appeal to the state or federal supreme court. To appeal, defendants must preserve claims of error at trial; that is, they have to object at the time of the alleged error and make sure that the objection gets into the record. If they fail to object, they ordinarily waive their right to appeal the error except in cases of plain error. Furthermore, defendants usually cannot appeal in a case where the defendant has already satisfied the sentence unless the conviction has collateral legal consequences, such as loss of employment or disqualification from admission to or continuing in a profession.

Prisoners can bring *habeas corpus* proceedings to challenge the lawfulness of their confinement. *Habeas corpus* proceedings are not appeals of criminal convictions; they are in fact not criminal proceedings, but civil actions. As such, they involve no right to counsel, no presumption of innocence, or other rights provided for criminal defendants. *Habeas corpus* petitioners have the burden of proof in showing the unlawfulness of their imprisonment. Furthermore, if they bring successive petitions, they must show cause and prejudice for their failure to raise issues in their first petition unless they have evidence of a fundamental miscarriage of justice. *Habeas corpus* balances the interest of the individual's right against unlawful imprisonment; the legal interests in the correct result and in the finality, predictability, and stability of and respect for the judicial process; and the organizational interests in economy, efficiency, and the preservation of scarce resources.

REVIEW QUESTIONS

1. Contrast the rights of defendants before and after conviction.

2. What circumstances may judges consider in sentencing?

3. Define *sentencing guidelines* and *mandatory minimum sentence laws*.

4. Briefly explain the history of mandatory minimum sentences and of sentencing guidelines.

5. Why have sentencing guidelines and mandatory minimum sentences come into prominence?

6. What are the arguments for and against sentencing guidelines and mandatory minimum sentences?

7. What are the results of empirical research regarding the mandatory minimum sentencing laws?

8. How do the procedures for death sentences differ from those for other sentences?

9. What is the basis for the right to appeal?

10. Identify and define the major principles governing the scope of appellate review.

11. How do appeals differ from *habeas corpus* proceedings?

12. What are the main elements of *habeas corpus*?

13. What interests does the law of *habeas corpus* balance?

14. Describe the narrow interpretation and the broad interpretation of the Habeas Corpus Act.

15. How does the cause-and-prejudice rule and the exhaustion-of-state-remedies rule promote the interests in finality and federalism?

KEY TERMS

abuse-of-the-writ rule the rule that *habeas corpus* petitioners must demonstrate that they neither deliberately nor negligently failed to raise an issue in a prior *habeas* petition.

administrative sentencing model a sentencing structure in which parole boards and prison administrators determine the exact release date within sentences prescribed by legislatures and judges.

cases of manifest injustice cases in which *habeas corpus* petitioners are likely factually innocent.

cause-and-prejudice rule the rule that permits but does not require courts to deny *habeas* petitions if defendants fail to show cause and prejudice.

collateral attack an indirect challenge to criminal proceedings.

collateral consequences exception the principle that cases are not moot if conviction can still cause legal consequences despite completion of sentence.

factual guilt a case in which the petitioner actually committed the crime but the state has not proved or could not prove legal guilt.

habeas corpus proceeding a civil action challenging the lawfulness of detention or imprisonment.

judicial economy the rationale of saving judicial resources by limiting appeals.

judicial sentencing model a structure in which judges prescribe sentences within broad contours set by legislative acts.

jurisdiction of the court the authority of a court over the person and subject matter of a case.

legislative sentencing model a structure in which legislatures exercise sentencing authority.

mandatory minimum sentences the legislatively prescribed, nondiscretionary amount of prison time that all offenders convicted of the offense must serve.

mootness doctrine the rule that excludes from appeal cases in which the sentence is satisfied.

plain error doctrine the rule that applies when plain errors affecting substantial rights cause manifest injustice or miscarriage of justice.

raise-or-waive doctrine the rule that defendants must raise and preserve objections to errors at trial or waive their right to appeal the errors.

res judicata a matter already decided by judicial proceeding.

sentencing guidelines a narrow range of penalties established by a commission within which judges are supposed to choose a specific sentence.

Notes

1. Joel Samaha, "Discretion and Law in the Early Penitential Books," in *Social Psychology and Discretionary Law*, ed. Richard Abt (New York: Norton, 1978).

2. David Rothman, *The Discovery of the Asylum* (Boston: Little, Brown, 1971).

3. Alfred Blumstein et al., eds., *Research on Sentencing: The Search for Reform* (Washington, DC: National Academy Press, 1983), 48–52.

4. National Council on Crime and Delinquency, *Criminal Justice Sentencing Policy Statement* (San Francisco: NCCD, 1992), 6.

5. Henry Scott Wallace, "Mandatory Minimums and the Betrayal of Sentencing Reform: A Legislative Dr. Jekyll and Mr. Hyde," *Federal Probation*, September 1993, 9.

6. United States Sentencing Commission, *Mandatory Minimum Penalties in the Federal Criminal Justice System* (Washington, DC: United States Sentencing Commission, August 1991), 5–7. For a discussion of the Communist role in the perceived increased use of illicit drugs, see United States Congress, Senate, Committee on the Judiciary, *Hearing Before the Subcommittee to Investigate Juvenile Delinquency*, Miami, Florida, 83d Cong., 2d sess., 1954, 7.

7. Ibid., 6.

8. H. Rep. No. 1444, 91st Cong., 2d Sess. 11 (1970).

9. Judith A. Lachman, "Daring the Courts: Trial and Bargaining Consequences of Minimum Penalties," *Yale Law Journal* 90 (1981): 597–631.

10. Wallace, "Mandatory Minimums . . . ," 11.

11. Ibid.; *Criminal Justice Newsletter*, November 15, 1993, 5.

12. Stephen J. Schulhofer, "Rethinking Mandatory Minimums," *Wake Forest Law Review* 28 (1993): 199; Campaign for an Effective Crime Policy, "Evaluating Mandatory Minimum Sentences" (Washington, DC: Campaign for an Effective Crime Policy, unpublished manuscript, October 1993).

13. *Williams v. Oklahoma*, 358 U.S. 576, 79 S.Ct. 421, 3 L.Ed.2d 516 (1959) (requirement of trustworthiness); *Williams v. New York*, 337 U.S. 241, 69 S.Ct. 1079, 93 L.Ed. 1337 (1949) (no right to confront or cross-examine).

14. *Mempa v. Rhay*, 389 U.S. 128, 88 S.Ct. 254, 19 L.Ed.2d 336 (1967) (sentencing); *Gagnon v. Scarpelli*, 411 U.S. 778, 93 S.Ct. 1756, 36 L.Ed.2d 656 (1973)

(probation and parole revocation hearing); *Tate v. Short*, 401 U.S. 395, 91 S.Ct. 668, 28 L.Ed.2d 130 (1971) (fine converted to imprisonment); *Bearden v. Georgia*, 461 U.S. 660, 103 S.Ct. 2064, 76 L.Ed.2d 221 (1983) (probation revocation).

15. *Harmelin v. Michigan*, 501 U.S. 957, 111 S.Ct. 2680, 115 L.Ed.2d 836 (1991).

16. *Gregg v. Georgia*, 428 U.S. 153, 96 S.Ct. 2909, 49 L.Ed.2d 859 (1976); *Lockett v. Ohio*, 438 U.S. 586, 98 S.Ct. 2954, 57 L.Ed.2d 973 (1978).

17. *Gardner v. Florida*, 430 U.S. 349, 97 S.Ct. 1197, 51 L.Ed.2d 393 (1977).

18. *McCleskey v. Kemp*, 481 U.S. 279, 107 S.Ct. 1756, 95 L.Ed.2d 262 (1987).

19. *Ross v. Moffitt*, 417 U.S. 600, 609, 94 S.Ct. 2437, 2443, 41 L.Ed.2d 341 (1974).

20. Wayne R. LaFave and Jerold Israel, *Criminal Procedure* (St. Paul: West, 1984), 3: 252–54.

21. Ibid., 256.

22. 14 Stat. 385 (1867).

23. LaFave and Israel, *Criminal Procedure*, 292–94.

24. Quoted in Ibid., 298–99.

25. *Brown v. Allen*, 344 U.S. 443, 73 S.Ct. 397, 97 L.Ed. 469 (1953).

26. Ibid.

27. *McCleskey v. Zant*, 499 U.S. 467, 111 S.Ct. 1454, 113 L.Ed.2d 517 (1991).

28. Ibid.

29. Ibid.

30. *Rose v. Lundy*, 455 U.S. 509, 102 S.Ct. 1198, 71 L.Ed.2d 379 (1982); *Marshall v. Lonberger*, 459 U.S. 422, 103 S.Ct. 843, 74 L.Ed.2d 646 (1983).

Constitution of the United States

Preamble

We the People of the United States, in Order to form a more perfect Union, establish Justice, insure domestic Tranquility, provide for the common defence, promote the general Welfare, and secure the Blessings of Liberty to ourselves and our Posterity, do ordain and establish this Constitution for the United States of America.

Article I

Section 1 All legislative Powers herein granted shall be vested in a Congress of the United States, which shall consist of a Senate and House of Representatives.

Section 2 The House of Representatives shall be composed of Members chosen every second Year by the People of the several States, and the Electors in each State shall have the Qualifications requisite for Electors of the most numerous Branch of the State Legislature.

No Person shall be a Representative who shall not have attained to the Age of twenty five Years, and been seven Years a Citizen of the United States, and who shall not, when elected, be an Inhabitant of that State in which he shall be chosen.

Representatives and direct Taxes shall be apportioned among the several States which may be included within this Union, according to their respective Numbers, which shall be determined by adding to the whole Number of free Persons, including those bound to Service for a Term of Years, and excluding Indians not taxed, three fifths of all other Persons. The actual Enumeration shall be made within three Years after the first Meeting of the Congress of the United States, and within every subsequent Term of ten Years, in such Manner as they shall by Law direct. The Number of Representatives shall not exceed one for every thirty Thousand, but each State shall have at Least one Representative; and until such enumeration shall be made, the State of New

Hampshire shall be entitled to choose three, Massachusetts eight, Rhode Island and Providence Plantations one, Connecticut five, New York six, New Jersey four, Pennsylvania eight, Delaware one, Maryland six, Virginia ten, North Carolina five, South Carolina five, and Georgia three.

When vacancies happen in the Representation from any State, the Executive Authority thereof shall issue Writs of Election to fill such Vacancies.

The House of Representatives shall choose their Speaker and other Officers; and shall have the sole Power of Impeachment.

Section 3 The Senate of the United States shall be composed of two Senators from each State, chosen by the Legislature thereof, for six Years; and each Senator shall have one Vote.

Immediately after they shall be assembled in Consequence of the first Election, they shall be divided as equally as may be into three Classes. The Seats of the Senators of the first Class shall be vacated at the Expiration of the second Year, of the second Class at the Expiration of the fourth Year, and of the third Class at the Expiration of the sixth Year, so that one third may be chosen every second Year; and if Vacancies happen by Resignation, or otherwise, during the Recess of the Legislature of any State, the Executive thereof may make temporary Appointments until the next Meeting of the Legislature, which shall then fill such Vacancies.

No Person shall be a Senator who shall not have attained to the Age of thirty Years, and been nine Years a Citizen of the United States, and who shall not, when elected, be an Inhabitant of that State for which he shall be chosen.

The Vice President of the United States shall be President of the Senate, but shall have no Vote, unless they be equally divided.

The Senate shall choose their other Officers, and also a President pro tempore, in the Absence of the Vice President, or when he shall exercise the Office of President of the United States.

The Senate shall have the sole Power to try all Impeachments. When sitting for that Purpose, they shall be on Oath or Affirmation. When the President of the United States is tried, the Chief Justice shall preside: And no Person shall be convicted without the Concurrence of two thirds of the Members present.

Judgment in Cases of Impeachment shall not extend further than to removal from Office, and disqualification to hold and enjoy any Office of honor, Trust, or Profit under the United States: but the Party convicted shall nevertheless be liable and subject to Indictment, Trial, Judgment, and Punishment, according to Law.

Section 4 The Times, Places and Manner of holding Elections for Senators and Representatives, shall be prescribed in each State by the Legislature thereof; but the Congress may at any time by Law make or alter such Regulations, except as to the Places of choosing Senators.

The Congress shall assemble at least once in every Year, and such Meeting shall be on the first Monday in December, unless they shall by Law appoint a different Day.

Section 5 Each House shall be the Judge of the Elections, Returns, and Qualifications of its own Members, and a Majority of each shall constitute a Quorum to do Business;

but a smaller Number may adjourn from day to day, and may be authorized to compel the Attendance of absent Members, in such Manner, and under such Penalties as each House may provide.

Each House may determine the Rules of its Proceedings, punish its Members for disorderly Behavior, and, with the Concurrence of two thirds, expel a Member.

Each House shall keep a Journal of its Proceedings, and from time to time publish the same, excepting such Parts as may in their Judgment require Secrecy; and the Yeas and Nays of the Members of either House on any question shall, at the Desire of one fifth of those Present, be entered on the Journal.

Neither House, during the Session of Congress, shall, without the Consent of the other, adjourn for more than three days, nor to any other Place than that in which the two Houses shall be sitting.

Section 6 The Senators and Representatives shall receive a Compensation for their Services, to be ascertained by Law, and paid out of the Treasury of the United States. They shall in all Cases, except Treason, Felony and Breach of the Peace, be privileged from Arrest during their Attendance at the Session of their respective Houses, and in going to and returning from the same; and for any Speech or Debate in either House, they shall not be questioned in any other Place.

No Senator or Representative shall, during the Time for which he was elected, be appointed to any civil Office under the Authority of the United States, which shall have been created, or the Emoluments whereof shall have been increased during such time; and no Person holding any Office under the United States, shall be a Member of either House during his Continuance in Office.

Section 7 All Bills for raising Revenue shall originate in the House of Representatives; but the Senate may propose or concur with Amendments as on other Bills.

Every Bill which shall have passed the House of Representatives and the Senate, shall, before it become a Law, be presented to the President of the United States; If he approve he shall sign it, but if not he shall return it, with his Objections to the House in which it shall have originated, who shall enter the Objections at large on their Journal, and proceed to reconsider it. If after such Reconsideration two thirds of that House shall agree to pass the Bill, it shall be sent together with the Objections, to the other House, by which it shall likewise be reconsidered, and if approved by two thirds of that House, it shall become a Law. But in all such Cases the Votes of both Houses shall be determined by Yeas and Nays, and the Names of the Persons voting for and against the Bill shall be entered on the Journal of each House respectively. If any Bill shall not be returned by the President within ten Days (Sundays excepted) after it shall have been presented to him, the Same shall be a Law, in like Manner as if he had signed it, unless the Congress by their Adjournment prevent its Return in which Case it shall not be a Law.

Every Order, Resolution, or Vote, to which the Concurrence of the Senate and House of Representatives may be necessary (except on a question of Adjournment) shall be presented to the President of the United States; and before the Same shall take Effect, shall be approved by him, or being disapproved by him, shall be repassed by two thirds of the Senate and House of Representatives, according to the Rules and Limitations prescribed in the Case of a Bill.

Section 8 The Congress shall have Power To lay and collect Taxes, Duties, Imposts and Excises, to pay the Debts and provide for the common Defence and general Welfare of the United States; but all Duties, Imposts and Excises shall be uniform throughout the United States;

To borrow Money on the credit of the United States;

To regulate Commerce with foreign Nations, and among the several States, and with the Indian Tribes;

To establish an uniform Rule of Naturalization, and uniform Laws on the subject of Bankruptcies throughout the United States;

To coin Money, regulate the Value thereof, and of foreign Coin, and fix the Standard of Weights and Measures;

To provide for the Punishment of counterfeiting the Securities and current Coin of the United States;

To establish Post Offices and post Roads;

To promote the Progress of Science and useful Arts, by securing for limited Times to Authors and Inventors the exclusive Right to their respective Writings and Discoveries;

To constitute Tribunals inferior to the supreme Court;

To define and punish Piracies and Felonies committed on the high Seas, and Offenses against the Law of Nations;

To declare War, grant Letters of Marque and Reprisal, and make Rules concerning Captures on Land and Water;

To raise and support Armies, but no Appropriation of Money to that Use shall be for a longer Term than two Years;

To provide and maintain a Navy;

To make Rules for the Government and Regulation of the land and naval Forces;

To provide for calling forth the Militia to execute the Laws of the Union, suppress Insurrections and repel Invasions;

To provide for organizing, arming, and disciplining, the Militia, and for governing such Part of Them as may be employed in the Service of the United States, reserving to the States respectively, the Appointment of the Officers, and the Authority of training the Militia according to the discipline prescribed by Congress;

To exercise exclusive Legislation in all Cases whatsoever, over such District (not exceeding ten Miles square) as may, by Cession of particular States, and the Acceptance of Congress, become the Seat of the Government of the United States, and to exercise like Authority over all Places purchased by the Consent of the Legislature of the State in which the Same shall be, for the Erection of Forts, Magazines, Arsenals, dock-Yards, and other needful Buildings;—And

To make all Laws which shall be necessary and proper for carrying into Execution the foregoing Powers, and all other Powers vested by this Constitution in the Government of the United States, or in any Department or Officer thereof.

Section 9 The Migration or Importation of such Persons as any of the States now existing shall think proper to admit, shall not be prohibited by the Congress prior to the Year one thousand eight hundred and eight, but a Tax or duty may be imposed on such Importation, not exceeding ten dollars for each Person.

The privilege of the Writ of Habeas Corpus shall not be suspended, unless when in Cases of Rebellion or Invasion the public Safety may require it.

No Bill of Attainder or ex post facto Law shall be passed.

No Capitation, or other direct, Tax shall be laid, unless in Proportion to the Census or Enumeration herein before directed to be taken.

No Tax or Duty shall be laid on Articles exported from any State.

No Preference shall be given by any Regulation of Commerce or Revenue to the Ports of one State over those of another: nor shall Vessels bound to, or from, one State be obliged to enter, clear, or pay Duties in another.

No Money shall be drawn from the Treasury, but in Consequence of Appropriations made by Law; and a regular Statement and Account of the Receipts and Expenditures of all public Money shall be published from time to time.

No Title of Nobility shall be granted by the United States: And no Person holding any Office of Profit or Trust under them, shall, without the Consent of the Congress, accept of any present, Emolument, Office, or Title, of any kind whatever, from any King, Prince, or foreign State.

Section 10 No State shall enter into any Treaty, Alliance, or Confederation; grant Letters of Marque and Reprisal; coin Money; emit Bills of Credit; make any Thing but gold and silver Coin a Tender in Payment of Debts; pass any Bill of Attainder, ex post facto Law, or Law impairing the Obligation of Contracts, or grant any Title of Nobility.

No State shall, without the Consent of the Congress, lay any Imposts or Duties on Imports or Exports, except what may be absolutely necessary for executing it's inspection Laws: and the net Produce of all Duties and Imposts, laid by any State on Imports or Exports, shall be for the Use of the Treasury of the United States; and all such Laws shall be subject to the Revision and Control of the Congress.

No State shall, without the Consent of Congress, lay any Duty of Tonnage, keep Troops, or Ships of War in time of Peace, enter into any Agreement or Compact with another State, or with a foreign Power, or engage in War, unless actually invaded, or in such imminent Danger as will not admit of delay.

Article II

Section 1 The executive Power shall be vested in a President of the United States of America. He shall hold his Office during the Term of four Years, and, together with the Vice President, chosen for the same Term, be elected, as follows:

Each State shall appoint, in such Manner as the Legislature thereof may direct, a Number of Electors, equal to the whole Number of Senators and Representatives to which the State may be entitled in the Congress; but no Senator or Representative, or Person holding an Office of Trust or Profit under the United States, shall be appointed an Elector.

The Electors shall meet in their respective States, and vote by Ballot for two Persons, of whom one at least shall not be an Inhabitant of the same State with themselves. And they shall make a List of all the Persons voted for, and of the Number of Votes for each; which List they shall sign and certify, and transmit sealed to the Seat of the Government of the United States, directed to the President of the Senate. The President of the Senate shall, in the Presence of the Senate and House of Representatives, open all the Certificates, and the Votes shall then be counted. The Person having the greatest Number of Votes shall be the President, if such Number be a Majority of the whole Number of

Electors appointed; and if there be more than one who have such Majority, and have an equal Number of Votes, then the House of Representatives shall immediately choose by Ballot one of them for President; and if no Person have a Majority, then from the five highest on the List the said House shall in like Manner choose the President. But in choosing the President, the Votes shall be taken by States, the Representation from each State having one Vote; A quorum for this Purpose shall consist of a Member or Members from two thirds of the States, and a Majority of all the States shall be necessary to a Choice. In every Case, after the Choice of the President, the Person having the greater Number of Votes of the Electors shall be the Vice President. But if there should remain two or more who have equal Votes, the Senate shall choose from them by Ballot the Vice President.

The Congress may determine the Time of choosing the Electors, and the Day on which they shall give their Votes; which Day shall be the same throughout the United States.

No person except a natural born Citizen, or a Citizen of the United States, at the time of the Adoption of this Constitution, shall be eligible to the Office of President; neither shall any Person be eligible to that Office who shall not have attained to the Age of thirty five Years, and been fourteen Years a Resident within the United States.

In Case of the Removal of the President from Office, or of his Death, Resignation or Inability to discharge the Powers and Duties of the said Office, the same shall devolve on the Vice President, and the Congress may by Law provide for the Case of Removal, Death, Resignation or Inability, both of the President and Vice President, declaring what Officer shall then act as President, and such Officer shall act accordingly, until the Disability be removed, or a President shall be elected.

The President shall, at stated Times, receive for his Services, a Compensation, which shall neither be increased nor diminished during the Period for which he shall have been elected, and he shall not receive within that Period any other Emolument from the United States, or any of them.

Before he enter on the Execution of his Office, he shall take the following Oath or Affirmation: "I do solemnly swear (or affirm) that I will faithfully execute the Office of President of the United States, and will to the best of my Ability, preserve, protect and defend the Constitution of the United States."

Section 2 The President shall be Commander in Chief of the Army and Navy of the United States, and of the Militia of the several States, when called into the actual Service of the United States: he may require the Opinion, in writing, of the principal Officer in each of the executive Departments, upon any Subject relating to the Duties of their respective Offices, and he shall have Power to grant Reprieves and Pardons for Offenses against the United States, except in Cases of Impeachment.

He shall have Power, by and with the Advice and Consent of the Senate to make Treaties, provided two thirds of the Senators present concur; and he shall nominate, and by and with the Advice and Consent of the Senate, shall appoint Ambassadors, other public Ministers and Consuls, Judges of the supreme Court, and all other Officers of the United States, whose Appointments are not herein otherwise provided for, and which shall be established by Law; but the Congress may by Law vest the Appointment of such inferior Officers, as they think proper, in the President alone, in the Courts of Law, or in the Heads of Departments.

The President shall have Power to fill up all Vacancies that may happen during the Recess of the Senate, by granting Commissions which shall expire at the End of their next Session.

Section 3 He shall from time to time give to the Congress Information of the State of the Union, and recommend to their Consideration such Measures as he shall judge necessary and expedient; he may, on extraordinary Occasions, convene both Houses, or either of them, and in Case of Disagreement between them, with Respect to the Time of Adjournment, he may adjourn them to such Time as he shall think proper; he shall receive Ambassadors and other public Ministers; he shall take Care that the Laws be faithfully executed, and shall Commission all the Officers of the United States.

Section 4 The President, Vice President and all civil Officers of the United States, shall be removed from Office on Impeachment for, and Conviction of, Treason, Bribery, or other high Crimes and Misdemeanors.

Article III

Section 1 The judicial Power of the United States, shall be vested in one supreme Court, and in such inferior Courts as the Congress may from time to time ordain and establish. The Judges, both of the supreme and inferior Courts, shall hold their Offices during good Behavior, and shall, at stated Times, receive for their Services a Compensation, which shall not be diminished during their Continuance in Office.

Section 2 The judicial Power shall extend to all Cases, in Law and Equity, arising under this Constitution, the Laws of the United States, and Treaties made, or which shall be made, under their Authority; — to all Cases affecting Ambassadors, other public Ministers and Consuls; — to all Cases of admiralty and maritime Jurisdiction; — to Controversies to which the United States shall be a Party; — to Controversies between two or more States; — between a State and Citizens of another State; — between Citizens of different States; — between Citizens of the same State claiming Lands under Grants of different States, and between a State, or the Citizens thereof, and foreign States, Citizens or Subjects.

In all Cases affecting Ambassadors, other public Ministers and Consuls, and those in which a State shall be a Party, the supreme Court shall have original Jurisdiction. In all the other Cases before mentioned, the supreme Court shall have appellate Jurisdiction, both as to Law and Fact, with such Exceptions, and under such Regulations as the Congress shall make.

The Trial of all Crimes, except in Cases of Impeachment, shall be by Jury; and such Trial shall be held in the State where the said Crimes shall have been committed; but when not committed within any State, the Trial shall be at such Place or Places as the Congress may by Law have directed.

Section 3 Treason against the United States, shall consist only in levying War against them, or, in adhering to their Enemies, giving them Aid and Comfort. No Person shall be convicted of Treason unless on the Testimony of two Witnesses to the same overt Act, or on Confession in open Court.

The Congress shall have Power to declare the Punishment of Treason, but no Attainder of Treason shall work Corruption of Blood, or Forfeiture except during the Life of the Person attainted.

Article IV

Section 1 Full Faith and Credit shall be given in each State to the public Acts, Records, and judicial Proceedings of every other State. And the Congress may by general Laws prescribe the Manner in which such Acts, Records and Proceedings shall be proved, and the Effect thereof.

Section 2 The Citizens of each State shall be entitled to all Privileges and Immunities of Citizens in the several States.

A Person charged in any State with Treason, Felony, or other Crime, who shall flee from Justice, and be found in another State, shall on Demand of the executive Authority of the State from which he fled, be delivered up, to be removed to the State having Jurisdiction of the Crime.

No Person held to Service or Labour in one State, under the Laws thereof, escaping into another, shall, in Consequence of any Law or Regulation therein, be discharged from such Service or Labor, but shall be delivered up on Claim of the Party to whom such Service or Labor may be due.

Section 3 New States may be admitted by the Congress into this Union; but no new State shall be formed or erected within the Jurisdiction of any other State; nor any State be formed by the Junction of two or more States, or Parts of States, without the Consent of the Legislatures of the States concerned as well as of the Congress.

The Congress shall have Power to dispose of and make all needful Rules and Regulations respecting the Territory or other Property belonging to the United States; and nothing in this Constitution shall be so construed as to Prejudice any Claims of the United States, or of any particular State.

Section 4 The United States shall guarantee to every State in this Union a Republican Form of Government, and shall protect each of them against Invasion; and on Application of the Legislature, or of the Executive (when the Legislature cannot be convened) against domestic Violence.

Article V

The Congress, whenever two thirds of both Houses shall deem it necessary, shall propose Amendments to this Constitution, or, on the Application of the Legislatures of two thirds of the several States, shall call a Convention for proposing Amendments, which, in either Case, shall be valid to all Intents and Purposes, as part of this Constitution, when ratified by the Legislatures of three fourths of the several States, or by Conventions in three fourths thereof, as the one or the other Mode of Ratification may be proposed by the Congress; Provided that no Amendment which may be made prior to the Year One thousand eight hundred and eight shall in any Manner affect the first and fourth Clauses in the Ninth Section of the first Article; and that no State, without its Consent, shall be deprived of its equal Suffrage in the Senate.

Article VI

All Debts contracted and Engagements entered into, before the Adoption of this Constitution shall be as valid against the United States under this Constitution, as under the Confederation.

This Constitution, and the Laws of the United States which shall be made in Pursuance thereof; and all Treaties made, or which shall be made, under the Authority of the United States, shall be the supreme Law of the Land; and the Judges in every State shall be bound thereby, any Thing in the Constitution or Laws of any State to the Contrary notwithstanding.

The Senators and Representatives before mentioned, and the Members of the several State Legislatures, and all executive and judicial Officers, both of the United States and of the several States, shall be bound by Oath or Affirmation, to support this Constitution; but no religious Test shall ever be required as a Qualification to any Office or public Trust under the United States.

Article VII

The Ratification of the Conventions of nine States shall be sufficient for the Establishment of this Constitution between the States so ratifying the Same.

Amendment I [1791]

Congress shall make no law respecting an establishment of religion, or prohibiting the free exercise thereof; or abridging the freedom of speech, or of the press; or the right of the people peaceably to assemble, and to petition the Government for a redress of grievances.

Amendment II [1791]

A well regulated Militia, being necessary to the security of a free State, the right of the people to keep and bear Arms, shall not be infringed.

Amendment III [1791]

No Soldier shall, in time of peace be quartered in any house, without the consent of the Owner, nor in time of war, but in a manner to be prescribed by law.

Amendment IV [1791]

The right of the people to be secure in their persons, houses, papers, and effects, against unreasonable searches and seizures, shall not be violated, and no Warrants shall issue, but upon probable cause, supported by Oath or affirmation, and particularly describing the place to be searched, and the persons or things to be seized.

Amendment V [1791]

No person shall be held to answer for a capital, or otherwise infamous crime, unless on a presentment or indictment of a Grand Jury, except in cases arising in the land or naval forces, or in the Militia, when in actual service in time of War or public danger; nor shall any person be subject for the same offence to be twice put in jeopardy of life or limb; nor shall be compelled in any criminal case to be a witness against himself, nor be deprived of life, liberty, or property, without due process of law; nor shall private property be taken for public use, without just compensation.

Amendment VI [1791]

In all criminal prosecutions, the accused shall enjoy the right to a speedy and public trial, by an impartial jury of the State and district wherein the crime shall have been committed, which district shall have been previously ascertained by law, and to be informed of the nature and cause of the accusation; to be confronted with the witnesses against him; to have compulsory process for obtaining witnesses in his favor, and to have the Assistance of Counsel for his defence.

Amendment VII [1791]

In Suits at common law, where the value in controversy shall exceed twenty dollars, the right of trial by jury shall be preserved, and no fact tried by jury, shall be otherwise re-examined in any Court of the United States, than according to the rules of the common law.

Amendment VIII [1791]

Excessive bail shall not be required, nor excessive fines imposed, nor cruel and unusual punishments inflicted.

Amendment IX [1791]

The enumeration in the Constitution, of certain rights, shall not be construed to deny or disparage others retained by the people.

Amendment X [1791]

The powers not delegated to the United States by the Constitution, nor prohibited by it to the States, are reserved to the States respectively, or to the people.

Amendment XI [1798]

The Judicial power of the United States shall not be construed to extend to any suit in law or equity, commenced or prosecuted against one of the United States by Citizens of another State, or by Citizens or Subjects of any Foreign State.

Amendment XII [1804]

The Electors shall meet in their respective states, and vote by ballot for President and Vice-President, one of whom, at least, shall not be an inhabitant of the same state with themselves; they shall name in their ballots the person voted for as President, and in distinct ballots the person voted for as Vice-President, and they shall make distinct lists of all persons voted for as President, and of all persons voted for as Vice-President, and of the number of votes for each, which lists they shall sign and certify, and transmit sealed to the seat of the government of the United States, directed to the President of the Senate;—The President of the Senate shall, in the presence of the Senate and House of Representatives, open all the certificates and the votes shall then be counted;—The person having the greatest number of votes for President, shall be the President, if such number be a majority of the whole number of Electors appointed; and if no person have such majority, then from the persons having the highest numbers not exceeding three on the list of those voted for as President, the House of Representatives shall choose immediately, by ballot, the President. But in choosing the President, the votes shall be taken by states, the representation from each state having one vote; a quorum for this purpose shall consist of a member or members from two thirds of the states, and a majority of all states shall be necessary to a choice. And if the House of Representatives shall not choose a President whenever the right of choice shall devolve upon them, before the fourth day of March next following, then the Vice-President shall act as President, as in the case of the death or other constitutional disability of the President.—The person having the greatest number of votes as Vice-President, shall be the Vice-President, if such number be a majority of the whole number of Electors appointed, and if no person have a majority, then from the two highest numbers on the list, the Senate shall choose the Vice-President; a quorum for the purpose shall consist of two thirds of the whole number of Senators, and a majority of the whole number shall be necessary to a choice. But no person constitutionally ineligible to the office of President shall be eligible to that of Vice-President of the United States.

Amendment XIII [1865]

Section 1 Neither slavery nor involuntary servitude, except as a punishment for crime whereof the party shall have been duly convicted, shall exist within the United States, or any place subject to their jurisdiction.

Section 2 Congress shall have power to enforce this article by appropriate legislation.

Amendment XIV [1868]

Section 1 All persons born or naturalized in the United States, and subject to the jurisdiction thereof, are citizens of the United States and of the State wherein they reside. No State shall make or enforce any law which shall abridge the privileges or immunities of citizens of the United States; nor shall any State deprive any person of life, liberty, or property, without due process of law; nor deny to any person within its jurisdiction the equal protection of the laws.

Section 2 Representatives shall be apportioned among the several States according to their respective numbers, counting the whole number of persons in each State, excluding Indians not taxed. But when the right to vote at any election for the choice of electors for President and Vice President of the United States, Representatives in Congress, the Executive and Judicial officers of a State, or the members of the Legislature thereof, is denied to any of the male inhabitants of such State, being twenty-one years of age, and citizens of the United States, or in any way abridged, except for participation in rebellion, or other crime, the basis of representation therein shall be reduced in the proportion which the number of such male citizens shall bear to the whole number of male citizens twenty-one years of age in such State.

Section 3 No person shall be a Senator or Representative in Congress, or elector of President and Vice-President, or hold any office, civil or military, under the United States, or under any State, who having previously taken an oath, as a member of Congress, or as an officer of the United States, or as a member of any State legislature, or as an executive or judicial officer of any State, to support the Constitution of the United States, shall have engaged in insurrection or rebellion against the same, or given aid or comfort to the enemies thereof. But Congress may by a vote of two thirds of each House, remove such disability.

Section 4 The validity of the public debt of the United States, authorized by law, including debts incurred for payment of pensions and bounties for services in suppressing insurrection or rebellion, shall not be questioned. But neither the United States nor any State shall assume or pay any debt or obligation incurred in aid of insurrection or rebellion against the United States, or any claim for the loss or emancipation of any slave; but all such debts, obligations and claims shall be held illegal and void.

Section 5 The Congress shall have power to enforce, by appropriate legislation, the provisions of this article.

Amendment XV [1870]

Section 1 The right of citizens of the United States to vote shall not be denied or abridged by the United States or by any State on account of race, color, or previous condition of servitude.

Section 2 The Congress shall have power to enforce this article by appropriate legislation.

Amendment XVI [1913]

The Congress shall have power to lay and collect taxes on incomes, from whatever source derived, without apportionment among the several States, and without regard to any census or enumeration.

Amendment XVII [1913]

Section 1 The Senate of the United States shall be composed of two Senators from each State, elected by the people thereof, for six years; and each Senator shall have one vote. The electors in each State shall have the qualifications requisite for electors of the most numerous branch of the State legislatures.

Section 2 When vacancies happen in the representation of any State in the Senate, the executive authority of such State shall issue writs of election to fill such vacancies: Provided, That the legislature of any State may empower the executive thereof to make temporary appointments until the people fill the vacancies by election as the legislature may direct.

Section 3 This amendment shall not be so construed as to affect the election or term of any Senator chosen before it becomes valid as part of the Constitution.

Amendment XVIII [1919]

Section 1 After one year from the ratification of this article the manufacture, sale, or transportation of intoxicating liquors within, the importation thereof into, or the exportation thereof from the United States and all territory subject to the jurisdiction thereof for beverage purposes is hereby prohibited.

Section 2 The Congress and the several States shall have concurrent power to enforce this article by appropriate legislation.

Section 3 This article shall be inoperative unless it shall have been ratified as an amendment to the Constitution by the legislatures of the several States, as provided in the Constitution, within seven years from the date of the submission hereof to the States by the Congress.

Amendment XIX [1920]

Section 1 The right of citizens of the United States to vote shall not be denied or abridged by the United States or by any State on account of sex.

Section 2 Congress shall have power to enforce this article by appropriate legislation.

Amendment XX [1933]

Section 1 The terms of the President and Vice President shall end at noon on the 20th day of January, and the terms of Senators and Representatives at noon on the 3d day of January, of the years in which such terms would have ended if this article had not been ratified; and the terms of their successors shall then begin.

Section 2 The Congress shall assemble at least once in every year, and such meeting shall begin at noon on the 3d day of January, unless they shall by law appoint a different day.

Section 3 If, at the time fixed for the beginning of the term of the President, the President elect shall have died, the Vice President elect shall become President. If the President shall not have been chosen before the time fixed for the beginning of his term, or if the President elect shall have failed to qualify, then the Vice President elect shall act as President until a President shall have qualified; and the Congress may by law provide for the case wherein neither a President elect nor a Vice President elect shall have qualified, declaring who shall then act as President, or the manner in which one who is to act shall be selected, and such person shall act accordingly until a President or Vice-President shall have qualified.

Section 4 The Congress may by law provide for the case of the death of any of the persons from whom the House of Representatives may choose a President whenever the right of choice shall have devolved upon them, and for the case of the death of any of the persons from whom the Senate may choose a Vice-President whenever the right of choice shall have devolved upon them.

Section 5 Sections 1 and 2 shall take effect on the 15th day of October following the ratification of this article.

Section 6 This article shall be inoperative unless it shall have been ratified as an amendment to the Constitution by the legislatures of three-fourths of the several States within seven years from the date of its submission.

Amendment XXI [1933]

Section 1 The eighteenth article of amendment to the Constitution of the United States is hereby repealed.

Section 2 The transportation or importation into any State, Territory, or possession of the United States for delivery or use therein of intoxicating liquors, in violation of the laws thereof, is hereby prohibited.

Section 3 This article shall be inoperative unless it shall have been ratified as an amendment to the Constitution by conventions in the several States, as provided in the Constitution, within seven years from the date of the submission hereof to the States by the Congress.

Amendment XXII [1951]

Section 1 No person shall be elected to the office of the President more than twice, and no person who has held the office of President, or acted as President, for more than two years of a term to which some other person was elected President shall be elected to the office of President more than once. But this Article shall not apply to any person holding the office of President when this Article was proposed by the Congress, and shall not prevent any person who may be holding the office of President, or acting as President, during the term within which this Article becomes operative from holding the office of President or acting as President during the remainder of such term.

Section 2 This article shall be inoperative unless it shall have been ratified as an amendment to the Constitution by the legislatures of three-fourths of the several States within seven years from the date of its submission to the States by the Congress.

Amendment XXIII [1961]

Section 1 The District constituting the seat of Government of the United States shall appoint in such manner as the Congress may direct:

A number of electors of President and Vice President equal to the whole number of Senators and Representatives in Congress to which the District would be entitled if it were a State, but in no event more than the least populous state; they shall be in addition to those appointed by the states, but they shall be considered, for the purposes of the election of President and Vice President, to be electors appointed by a state; and they shall meet in the District and perform such duties as provided by the twelfth article of amendment.

Section 2 The Congress shall have power to enforce this article by appropriate legislation.

Amendment XXIV [1964]

Section 1 The right of citizens of the United States to vote in any primary or other election for President or Vice President, for electors for President or Vice-President, or for Senator or Representative in Congress, shall not be denied or abridged by the United States, or any State by reason of failure to pay any poll tax or other tax.

Section 2 The Congress shall have power to enforce this article by appropriate legislation.

Amendment XXV [1967]

Section 1 In case of the removal of the President from office or of his death or resignation, the Vice President shall become President.

Section 2 Whenever there is a vacancy in the office of the Vice President, the President shall nominate a Vice President who shall take office upon confirmation by a majority vote of both Houses of Congress.

Section 3 Whenever the President transmits to the President pro tempore of the Senate and the Speaker of the House of Representatives his written declaration that he is unable to discharge the powers and duties of his office, and until he transmits to them a written declaration to the contrary, such powers and duties shall be discharged by the Vice President as Acting President.

Section 4 Whenever the Vice President and a majority of either the principal officers of the executive departments or of such other body as Congress may by law provide, transmit to the President pro tempore of the Senate and the Speaker of the House of Representatives their written declaration that the President is unable to discharge the powers and duties of his office, the Vice President shall immediately assume the powers and duties of the office as Acting President.

Thereafter, when the President transmits to the President pro tempore of the Senate and the Speaker of the House of Representatives his written declaration that no inability exists, he shall resume the powers and duties of his office unless the Vice President and a majority of either the principal officers of the executive department or of such other body as Congress may by law provide, transmit within four days to the President pro tempore of the Senate and the Speaker of the House of Representatives their written declaration and the President is unable to discharge the powers and duties of his office. Thereupon Congress shall decide the issue, assembling within forty-eight hours for that purpose if not in session. If the Congress, within twenty-one days after receipt of the latter written declaration, or, if Congress is not in session, within twenty-one days after Congress is required to assemble, determines by two thirds vote of both Houses that the President is unable to discharge the powers and duties of his office, the Vice President shall continue to discharge the same as Acting President; otherwise, the President shall resume the powers and duties of his office.

Amendment XXVI [1971]

Section 1 The right of citizens of the United States, who are eighteen years of age or older, to vote shall not be denied or abridged by the United States or by any State on account of age.

Section 2 The Congress shall have power to enforce this article by appropriate legislation.

Amendment XXVII
[Proposed 1789; Ratified 1992]

No law, varying the compensation for the services of Senators and Representatives, shall take effect until an election of Representatives have intervened.

Glossary

abandonment The intentional throwing away of property that removes it from the protection of the Fourth Amendment.

absolute immunity The absence of liability for actions within the scope of duties.

abuse-of-the-writ rule The rule that *habeas corpus* petitioners must demonstrate they neither deliberately nor negligently failed to raise an issue in a prior *habeas* petition.

accusatorial system rationale The justification for reviewing state confession cases based on the idea that confessions are typical of inquisitorial not adversarial systems of justice.

accusatory stage The period when investigation focuses on a particular suspect or suspects.

accusatory system A system in which the government bears the burden of proof.

actual prejudice test Proof that a defendant cannot get a fair trial.

actual seizure stops The physical grabbing of a suspect.

adjudication Decisions made in court.

administrative sentencing model A sentencing structure in which parole boards and prison administrators determine the exact release date within sentences prescribed by legislatures and judges.

adversary system A system in which the defense and the government are opponents, with an impartial judge to monitor proceedings.

affidavits Written statements sworn to before a person who is officially authorized to administer oaths.

affirmative defense A defense, such as self-defense or insanity, that requires defendants to present facts in addition to denying the charge.

affirmed An appellate court upholding the decision of a lower court.

***Allen* charge** A charge in which judges encourage deadlocked juries to reach a verdict.

***amicus curiae* brief** An argument submitted by a party that has a strong interest in a case but is not a party to it.

appeals Reviewing the proceedings of a lower court.

appellant A party appealing a lower court ruling or decision to a higher court.

appellate case A case appealed from a trial or other lower court.

arraignment The process of bringing a defendant to court to hear and plead to charges.

articulable facts The specific, identifiable facts that provide the objective basis for a stop.

attenuation doctrine The principle that evidence remote from illegal conduct is admissible.

bail schedules Lists of amounts of bail required for specific offenses.

balancing approach to the Fourth Amendment The element of reasonableness that balances government interest in law enforcement against individual interests in privacy and liberty.

balancing test of local government liability The test that balances the need for effective law enforcement against avoiding putting members of the public at risk.

basis-of-knowledge prong The part of the two-pronged test of reliability that considers the source of an informant's information.

bench trial A trial without a jury.

bind over To send a criminal case on for trial.

border searches Searches of persons and property at or near the borders of the United States in order to protect the integrity of international borders.

bright line approach The determination of reasonableness according to a specific rule that applies to all cases.

bright line rule The rule prescribing specific behavior.

case-by-case method The determination of reasonableness by considering the totality of circumstances in each individual case.

cases of manifest injustice Cases in which *habeas corpus* petitioners are likely factually innocent.

cause-and-prejudice rule The rule that permits but does not require courts to deny *habeas* petitions if defendants fail to show cause and prejudice.

certiorari A discretionary order of the Supreme Court to review a lower court decision.

challenges for cause Removals of prospective jurors upon showing impartiality.

charge the grand jury The address of the judge to the grand jury.

citation release A summons to appear in court in lieu of being detained.

collateral attack An indirect challenge to criminal proceedings.

collateral consequences exception The principle that cases are not moot if conviction can still cause legal consequences despite completion of sentence.

collateral estoppel The doctrine that an issue of fact determined in favor of the defendant prohibits the government from retrying the same issue in a later prosecution.

common law The ancient judge-made English law brought to America by the English colonists.

complaint A formal charging document to initiate a criminal proceeding.

concurring opinion Statements in which justices agree with the decision, not the reasoning of a court's opinion.

confrontation A lineup or show-up where the witness and the suspect are physically present in the same place.

confrontation requirement The Sixth Amendment right of defendants to confront the accusers and witnesses against them.

constitutional rationale The idea that the exclusionary rule is an essential part of constitutional rights.

constitutional torts Civil actions for violating federal constitutional rights.

conventional Fourth Amendment approach The warrant and reasonableness clauses are firmly connected.

criminal complaint The formal charging document.

curtilage The area immediately surrounding a house that is not part of the open fields doctrine.

custodial interrogation The questioning that occurs after the police have taken suspects into custody.

damages A remedy in private lawsuits in the form of money for injuries.

defendant The person formally charged with a crime.

demand-waiver rule A delay in trial is measured from the point a defendant demands a speedy trial.

deterrence rationale The justification that excluding evidence obtained in violation of the Constitution prevents illegal law enforcement.

direct information Information officers know firsthand.

discovery One party's providing evidence in its possession to the other party.

discretion Informal, unwritten decision making in criminal procedure.

dismissal with prejudice The termination of a case with the provision that it cannot be prosecuted again.

dismissal without prejudice The termination of a case with the provision that it can be prosecuted again.

dissenting opinion Part of an appellate court case in which justices write opinions disagreeing with the decision and reasoning of a court.

distinguishing cases Recognizing that the rule in a prior decision does not apply to current facts.

divert To transfer a case from the criminal justice system to a community service, restitution, or treatment program.

DNA fingerprinting or DNA profiling Measuring and comparing the lengths of selected strands of DNA in chromosomes.

doctrine of official immunity The rule that limits the liability of individual criminal justice personnel to willful or malicious wrongdoing.

drug courier profile A list of general characteristics that the government associates with illicit drug dealing.

dual sovereignty doctrine A crime arising out of the same facts in one state is not the same crime in another state.

due process clause The Fifth and Fourteenth Amendment provisions prohibiting the federal government and the states, respectively, from depriving citizens of life, liberty, or property without due process of law.

entrapment A defense to crime based on a law enforcement officer's illegal inducement to commit the crime.

***ex parte* proceedings** Proceedings in which the defendant is not present or represented.

exclusionary rule The rule that illegally seized evidence cannot be admitted in criminal trials.

exculpatory evidence Evidence that shows the defendant did not commit the crime.

exigent circumstances Circumstances requiring prompt action that eliminates the warrant requirement.

expungement The removal of criminal records from official files.

factual innocence A case in which the petitioner did not commit the crime.

factually innocent The cases in which defendants did not commit the crime.

Federal Rules of Evidence standard The test of admissibility of DNA testing is whether the relevancy of the evidence outweighs the tendency of the evidence to unfairly prejudice the defendant.

federal constitutional tort The legal action based on the violation of constitutional rights by federal officers.

felony A crime punishable by more than one year in prison.

first appearance The appearance of a defendant in court for determination of probable cause, determination of bail, assignment of attorney, and notification of rights.

frisks Pat-downs of the outer clothing for weapons.

fruit of the poisonous tree doctrine The principle that evidence derived from illegally obtained sources is not admissible.

***Frye* plus standard** The test of admissibility that requires showing not only general acceptance of DNA theory but also that "the testing laboratory in the particular case performed the accepted scientific techniques in analyzing forensic samples."

***Frye* standard** The rule that DNA evidence is admissible if the technique is "sufficiently established to have gained general acceptance in the particular field in which it belongs."

functional equivalent standard The test for determining Fifth Amendment interrogation.

fundamental fairness doctrine The principle that state procedures cannot violate basic standards of ordered liberty.

fundamental fairness rationale The justification for reviewing state confessions cases based on the idea that coerced confessions violate due process of law even if they are true.

good faith exception The principle that evidence is not excluded when police reasonably rely on a defective search warrant.

grand jury review A secret proceeding to test a government case.

grand jury targets Grand jury witnesses who are themselves under investigation.

***habeas corpus* proceeding** A civil action challenging the lawfulness of detention or imprisonment.

hand up the indictment To deliver an indictment to the judge.

harmless error An irregularity in proceedings that does not affect the outcome of the case.

harmless error rule A mistake in lower court proceedings that does not affect the outcome of the case and does not require reversal.

hearsay Information derived from third persons, not known firsthand by the person providing it.

hearsay rule The ban on introducing into evidence out-of-court statements to prove the truth of the matter stated.

hearsay testimony Testimony introduced as truth by a witness not present in court.

hot pursuit The exigent circumstance constituting the need to apprehend a fleeing suspect.

hung jury A jury that is unable to reach a verdict after protracted deliberations.

hybrid test of entrapment The test of entrapment that considers both subjective and objective elements.

impeach To show that a witness's testimony is not credible.

in loco parentis **doctrine** The principle by which the government stands in place of parents.

incorporation doctrine The principle that the Fourteenth Amendment due process clause incorporates the provisions of the Bill of Rights and applies them to state criminal procedure.

independent source doctrine The principle of admitting evidence obtained independently of illegal conduct.

indictment A formal criminal charge issued by a grand jury.

indigent defendants Defendants who are too poor to afford a lawyer.

individualized suspicion Facts that point to suspecting a particular individual of illegal activity.

inevitable discovery rule The principle of admitting illegally seized evidence that would eventually come to light by alternative legal means.

information A formal charging instrument drawn up by the prosecutor.

injunctions Court orders to act or to refrain from acting.

interlocutory appeals Provisional appeals taken before judgment.

interrogation The questioning of suspects by the police.

inventory searches Searches conducted without probable cause or warrants in order to protect property and the safety of police and to prevent claims against police.

judgment The final outcome of a case.

judicial bias The favoring of a particular legal principle.

judicial economy The rationale of saving judicial resources by limiting appeals.

judicial integrity rationale The idea that the honor and honesty of the courts justifies the exclusionary rule.

judicial review The power of courts to review legislation.

judicial sentencing model A structure in which judges prescribe sentences within broad contours set by legislative penalties.

jurisdiction The authority of a court to hear and decide cases.

jurisdiction of the court The authority of a court over the person and subject matter of the case.

jury challenges Removals of prospective jurors.

jury instructions A judge's explanation of law to a jury.

jury nullification The jury's authority to reach a not guilty verdict despite proof of guilt.

legally guilty The cases in which the government has proved beyond a reasonable doubt the guilt of defendants.

legislative sentencing model A structure in which legislatures exercise sentencing authority.

lesser included offenses Crimes composed of some of, but not all, the elements of a more serious crime.

liberty The right of locomotion, that is, the right of citizens to come and go as they please, without government interference.

lineups Identification procedures in which the suspect stands in a line with other individuals.

lower criminal courts Courts conducting pretrial felony proceedings and misdemeanor trials.

majority opinion The law of a case in an appellate court.

mandatory minimum sentences The legislatively prescribed, nondiscretionary amount of prison time that all offenders convicted of the offense must serve.

manifest necessity A circumstance that requires the termination of proceedings.

mere evidence rule The precept that the seizure of evidence that is not stolen property or contraband does not violate the Fourth Amendment.

misdemeanor An offense punishable by a fine or jail term of less than a year or both.

missing witness instruction The instruction that jurors can draw a negative inference from prosecution witnesses' failure to testify.

mockery of justice standard The standard under which counsel is deemed ineffective only if circumstances reduced the trial to a farce.

mootness doctrine The rule that excludes from appeal cases in which the sentence is satisfied.

moral seriousness standard The principle that the Sixth Amendment right to a jury trial extends to morally serious misdemeanors.

more-probable-than-not test The test under which an activity is not considered probable cause if it is as susceptible to an innocent as a guilty interpretation.

negotiated pleas Guilty pleas entered in return for concessions from the state.

no-bills Grand jury finding of insufficient evidence.

nolo contendere A plea not to contest the indictment.

objective basis The quantity of facts required to justify government invasions in individual liberty, privacy, and property.

objective test of entrapment The test of entrapment that focuses on the actions of government agents to induce defendants to commit crimes.

one-step rule Defendants have standing to object to searches only if their expectation of privacy is violated.

open fields doctrine The rule that the Fourth Amendment does not prevent government officials from gathering and using information they see, hear, smell, or touch in open fields.

O.R. (own recognizance) A type of pretrial release made on the promise of the defendant to appear in court.

orthodox rule The principle that courts decide the admissibility of evidence.

particularity requirement The requirement that a warrant must identify the person or place to be searched and the items or persons to be seized.

pattern instructions Published, standard jury instructions.

per se **rules** Specific rules that apply with little or no discretion.

peremptory challenges Removals of jurors without showing cause.

petitioner A party whose case has come to court by judicial writ.

photo identification A procedure in which the witness observes pictures or "mug shots" in order to identify the suspect.

plain error doctrine The rule that applies when plain errors affecting substantial rights cause manifest injustice or miscarriage of justice.

plain view doctrine The rule that detection by means of the ordinary senses is not a Fourth Amendment search.

plaintiff in error Another term for appellant.

plaintiffs Parties who bring a civil action.

plea A defendant's answer to the government's criminal charge.

plurality opinion A statement in which the greatest number, but not a majority, of the justices favor a court's decision.

precedent A prior decision that is binding on a similar present case.

preliminary hearing The adversary proceeding that tests the government's case.

presumption of innocence The principle that defendants are presumed innocent until the government proves guilt beyond a reasonable doubt.

pretext search A search that is made subsequent to an arrest for one crime but is motivated by the desire to search for another.

preventive detention Pretrial detention based on the need to preserve community safety.

prima facie **case** A case with enough facts to convict unless they are contradicted.

prior testimony exception The rule that testimony given under oath prior to trial is admissible at trial.

privacy The value that is sometimes called the right to be let alone from government invasions.

privacy doctrine The doctrine that holds that the Fourth Amendment protects *persons*, not *places*, when persons have an expectation of privacy that society is prepared to recognize.

pro bono **(for the good of doing so)** Lawyers provide their services to defendants without a fee.

probable cause to arrest Facts that would lead a reasonable person to believe that a crime has been, is being, or is about to be committed and that the person arrested is the perpetrator.

proof beyond a reasonable doubt The quantum of proof required for conviction.

property The right to acquire, own, possess, use, and dispose of property.

prophylactic rules Mechanisms to guarantee rights, not themselves constitutional rights.

public safety exception The rule that *Miranda* warnings need not be administered if doing so endangers the public.

purging the grand jury Eliminating prospective grand jurors who have compelling reasons not to serve.

qualified immunity Immunity from tort action that is granted if a party was acting reasonably within the scope of duties.

raise-or-waive doctrine The rule that defendants must raise and preserve objections to errors at trial or waive their right to appeal the errors.

reasonable doubt standard Doubt based on facts that would cause a reasonable person to hesitate before making a decision of importance to himself or herself.

reasonable-likelihood-of-prejudice test The determination that circumstances may prevent a fair trial.

reasonable stop standard The rule under which a show-of-authority stop is determined by whether a reasonable person would believe he or she was not free to leave or otherwise terminate an encounter with a police officer.

reasonable suspicion Facts, apparent facts, or circumstances that would lead a reasonable person to suspect that a crime may have been, may be about to be, or may be in the process of being committed.

reasonableness clause The "unreasonable searches and seizures" section of the Fourth Amendment.

reasonableness Fourth Amendment approach The warrant and reasonableness clauses are distinct.

reasonableness test The reasonableness of searches and seizures depends on balancing government and individual interests and the objective basis of the searches and seizures.

reasonably competent attorney standard Performance measured by customary skills and diligence.

recoupment programs States can recover from indigent defendants expenses for their defense.

relevancy plus standard The test of the admissibility evidence that adds the *Frye* standard and other requirements to the Federal Rules of Evidence standard.

reliability rationale The justification for reviewing state confessions based on their untrustworthiness.

remanded Sent back to a lower court for further proceedings.

res gestae **witnesses** Eyewitnesses.

res judicata A matter already decided by judicial proceeding.

respondeat superior A superior who is liable for a subordinate's torts within the scope of employment.

return of warrant The act of filing a search warrant with the court that issued it.

reversed Overturned by an appellate court.

reversible errors Errors that affect the outcome of a case.

rule of four The requirement that four Supreme Court justices must vote to review a case for its appeal to be heard by the Supreme Court.

search incident to arrest A search made of a lawfully arrested suspect without probable cause or warrant.

Section 1983 action An action brought under the Civil Rights Act, U.S. Code §1983, for violation of federal civil rights under color of state law.

selective incorporation The concept that only some federal rights are incorporated by the due process clause.

sentencing guidelines A narrow range of penalties established by a commission within which judges are supposed to choose a specific sentence.

sequesters the jury Puts the jury in a room to deliberate without outside interference.

show-of-authority stops Submissions to the display of official force.

show-up A procedure in which the witness identifies the suspect without other possible suspects present.

"special needs" searches Government inspections and other regulatory measures not conducted to gather criminal evidence.

standing The right to challenge a government's constitutional violations.

stare decisis The doctrine in which a prior decision binds a present case with similar facts.

statutes of limitations Laws specifying the length of time permitted to lapse between the commission of a crime and the initiation of prosecution.

stipulates Does not contest.

stops Brief, on-the-spot detentions that freeze suspicious situations so that law enforcement officers can determine whether to arrest, investigate further, or terminate further action.

straight plea A guilty plea without negotiation.

subjective test of entrapment The test of entrapment that focuses on the predisposition of defendants to commit crimes.

supervised release Pretrial release conditioned on the defendant's reporting to an agency or a third person.

supervisory power The ability of the United States Supreme Court to oversee lower federal court and state court proceedings.

supremacy clause The principle that the United States Constitution and laws are supreme over state law.

torts Civil lawsuits for damages.

total incorporation The principle that all federal rights are incorporated by the due process clause.

totality of circumstances All of the facts surrounding a government invasion of privacy, liberty, or property.

totality-of-circumstances test The test that considers all relevant issues to measure the trustworthiness of informants' information.

trespass doctrine The Fourth Amendment doctrine that requires physical intrusions into a "constitutionally protected area" to qualify as a search.

trial courts Courts that conduct trials.

true bill A bill of indictment stating that a grand jury finds sufficient evidence to prosecute.

two-pronged test of reliability (*Spinelli Aguilar* test) The test used to establish the veracity and basis of knowledge of an informant.

venue The place where a trial is held.

veracity prong The part of the two-pronged test of reliability that considers the honesty and reliability of an informant.

vicarious official immunity The rule that allows government units to benefit from the official immunity of their employees.

voir dire The examination of prospective jurors.

voluntariness test (for confessions) The test that relies on the totality of circumstances to determine both whether waivers and confessions are voluntary.

voluntariness test (for consent searches) A test in which the totality of circumstances is used to determine whether a consent to search was obtained without coercion, deception, or promises.

waiver The giving up or relinquishing of rights.

waiver test A test in which consent is based only on a knowing, specific, and intelligent waiver of a specific right.

warrant clause The Fourth Amendment section relating to requirements of warrants.

writs of assistance or general warrants The official documents, good for the life of the monarch, that granted blanket authority to search and seize.

Index